Professional XML Databases

Kevin Williams

Michael Brundage
Patrick Dengler
Jeff Gabriel
Andy Hoskinson
Michael Kay
Thomas Maxwell
Marcelo Ochoa
Johnny Papa
Mohan Vanmane

Wrox Press Ltd.

Professional XML Databases

Published by Wrox Press Ltd,
Arden House, 1102 Warwick Road, Acocks Green,
Birmingham, B27 6BH, UK
Printed in Canada
ISBN 1861003587

Trademark Acknowledgements

Credits

Authors
Kevin Williams

Michael Brundage,
Patrick Dengler
Jeff Gabriel,
Andy Hoskinson,
Michael Kay
Thomas Maxwell,
Marcelo Ochoa
Johnny Papa,
Mohan Vanmane

Technical Reviewers
Danny Ayers
David Baliles
Cary Beuershausen
Matt Birbeck
Maxime Bombadier
Bob Cherinka
Michael Corning
Jeremy Crosbie
Dino Esposito
Nazir Faisal
Sam Ferguson
Constantinos Hadjisotiriou
Scott Haley
Alex Homer
Michael Kay
Jim Macintosh
Craig McQueen
Thomas B. Passin
David Schult
Marc H. Simkin
Dave Sussman
Dorai Thodla
Beverley Treadwell
Warren Wiltsie

Technical Architect
Jon Duckett

Technical Editors
Chris Mills
Andrew Polshaw
Lisa Stephenson

Category Manager
Dave Galloway

Author Agent
Tony Berry

Project Manager
Avril Corbin

Production Manager
Simon Hardware

Production Project Coordinator
Mark Burdett

Indexing
Alessandro Ansa

Figures
Shabnam Hussain

Cover
Shelley Frazier

Proof Readers
Diana Skeldon
Agnes Wiggers

About the Authors

Kevin Williams

Kevin's first experience with computers was at the age of 10 (in 1980) when he took a BASIC class at a local community college on their PDP-9, and by the time he was 12, he stayed up for four days straight hand-assembling 6502 code on his Atari 400. His professional career has been focussed on Windows development – first client-server, then onto Internet work. He's done a little bit of everything, from VB to Powerbuilder to Delphi to C/C++ to MASM to ISAPI, CGI, ASP, HTML, XML, and any other acronym you might care to name; but these days, he's focusing on XML work. Kevin is currently working with the Mortgage Bankers' Association of America to help them put together an XML standard for the mortgage industry.

Michael Brundage

Michael Brundage works as a software developer on Microsoft's WebData Internet team, where he develops XML features for SQL Server 2000. Michael participates actively in the design of the XML Query Language, producing Microsoft's prototype for the W3C Working Group. Before Microsoft, Michael was the Senior Software Engineer for NASA's Interferometry Science Center at Caltech, where he developed networked collaborative environments and a simulation of radiative transfer.

Michael would like to thank his wife Yvonne for her patience; Dave Van Buren, friend and mentor, for starting it all; Microsoft for allowing him to write; Chris Suver and Paul Cotton for reviewing early drafts; and everyone at Wrox Press for their help, humor, and flexibility.

Patrick Dengler

Patrick is busily growing Internet startups throughout the "Silicon Forest" area. His interests include building companies by creating frameworks for Internet architectures. He has received several patents in stateless Internet database architectures.

I want to thank my lovely, graceful and beautiful wife Kelly for simply putting up with me. Without her and my family, Devin, Casey, and Dexter, I wouldn't be whole.

Jeff Gabriel

Jeff Gabriel currently works as a developer for eNationwide, the e-commerce arm of Nationwide Insurance Systems. Jeff is an MCSE, and was formerly a Webmaster before finding the call to be true geek too strong. He enjoys spending time with his wife Meredith and two children; Max and Lily. He also likes to read books about technology and computers when not working on same."

Thanks to my family for understanding the long hours it took to write for this book, and my great desire to do it. I also thank God, who has answered my prayers with many great opportunities.

Finally, thanks to the guys at ATGI Inc. Thanks to Matt for your excellent direction and support over the years, and to Jason, an incomparable source for all things Java.

Andy Hoskinson

Andy Hoskinson is a senior technical director for a leading Internet professional services firm. He develops enterprise-class Internet solutions using a variety of technologies, including Java and XML. Andy is a co-author of Professional Java Server Programming, J2EE Edition (Wrox Press, Sept. 2000). He is also a co-author of Microsoft Commerce Solutions (Microsoft Press, April 1999), and has contributed to several different technical publications, including Active Server Developer's Journal and Visual J++ Developer's Journal.

Andy is a Sun Certified Java Programmer and Microsoft Certified Solution Developer, and lives in Northern Virginia with his wife Angie. Andy can be reached at andy@hoskinson.net.

Michael Kay

Michael Kay has spent most of his career as a software designer and systems architect with ICL, the IT services supplier. As an ICL Fellow, he divides his time between external activities and mainstream projects for clients, mainly in the area of electronic commerce and publishing. His background is in database technology: he has worked on the design of network, relational, and object-oriented database software products – as well as a text search engine. In the XML world he is known as the developer of the open source Saxon product, the first fully-conformant implementation of the XSLT standard.

Michael lives in Reading, Berkshire with his wife and daughter. His hobbies include genealogy and choral singing.

Thomas Maxwell

Thomas Maxwell has worked the last few years for eNationwide, the Internet arm of one of the world's largest insurance companies, developing advanced internet/intranet applications – Many of which utilized XML databases. He also continues to work with his wife Rene to develop cutting edge Internet applications, such as the XML based Squirrel Tech Engine, for Creative Squirrel Solutions – a technical project implementation firm. Tom's technical repertoire includes such tools as Visual Basic, ASP, COM+, Windows DNA and of course XML. Tom can be reached at tmaxwell@creativesquirrel.com

During the writing of this book I became the proud father of my wife's and my first child. So I would like to thank, firstly my wife for being understanding of my desire to meet the book's deadlines. And secondly to the staff of Wrox for understanding that a new baby sometimes makes it difficult to meet deadlines. I would also like to thank the understanding people who helped with the non-book things that allowed me the time to contribute to this book, including Tom Holquist, who understands why one may be a little late to the office once in a while and my family including Marlene and Sharon for helping with Gabrielle in the first few weeks.

Marcelo Ochoa

Marcelo Ochoa works at the System Laboratory of Facultad de Ciencias Exactas, of the Universidad Nacional del Centro de la Provincia de Buenos Aires and as an external consultant and trainer for Oracle Argentina. He divides his time between University jobs and external projects related to Oracle web technologies. He has worked in several Oracle related projects like translation of Oracle manuals and multimedia CBTs. His background is in database, network, Web and Java technologies. In the XML world he is known as the developer of the DB Producer for the Apache Cocoon project, the framework that permits generate XML in the database side.

Marcelo Ochoa lives in Tandil, Argentina with his wife Claudia and their dog Terkoz. His hobbies are HiFi electronics systems and making open fired barbecues with his friends (known as "asado al asador" in Argentina). Tandil is a medium sized city located in the center of the Pampa Humeda. The hills that surround Tandil are part of the oldest mountain range of the world.

I wish to thank Claudia and Marisa for your revision on the English on the case study. I would also like to offer my thanks to the contributors of the DB Prism project.

Johnny Papa

Johnny develops eCommerce, Internet, Intranet and LAN based business solutions for Lancelot Web Solutions, in Raleigh, NC. He can regularly be found speaking at high-tech events such as VSlive and WinDev. Johnny is certified in the critical technological areas of Microsoft solutions and is merited with the MCP, MCSD and MCT. He has also published several technical books on how to implement leading edge technologies in a business solution such as *Professional ADO RDS 2.5 with ASP 3.0* and *SQL Server 7.0 Programming Unleashed* and is regularly published in such trade journals as *MSDN* magazine and *Visual Basic Programmers Journal* (VBPJ). You can reach Johnny at pub@lancelotweb.com.

Foremost, I would like to thank my family. To my wife, Colleen, thank you for supporting me through long nights and early mornings of preparing this book. You are my rock, which without, I would certainly fall. To my daughter Haley, my little angel, for the big hugs, and for reminding of who it is that I really work for. To my mother, Peggy, thanks for everything you've inspired me to become and especially for the support and the enduring love you've freely given. Although it may seem otherwise at times, I'll always love you. To my father, John, I can only hope to become half of the man you are. You are my best friend and I am very proud to be your son. To my sisters Julie, Sandy, Laurie and Debbie, thank you for staying so close. Our family is the source from which I have always drawn my strength. And to my Kadi girl, for keeping me company on long nights of writing. Without you all, I could never have come so far.

Mohan Vanmane

Mohan Vanmane works at Microsoft in the SQL Server documentation team. He joined Microsoft in 1995 as Senior Database Engineer. After working a couple of years in the Information Technology group, he joined the SQL Server group. Prior to working at Microsoft, he worked as an Instructor at Seattle University from 1986 to 1995. He taught various courses in the Computer Science and Software Engineering program at Seattle University.

While teaching, Mohan also provided consulting services to the industry in designing and developing database applications.

"I would like to thank my wife and my parents who have been constant source of inspiration to me, my mentors, Trichi and Shivpuri Swamy, who guided and supported me. Thanks goes to Roger Wolter, Tim Toyoshima, for their encouragement, and finally to Wrox for their timely help."

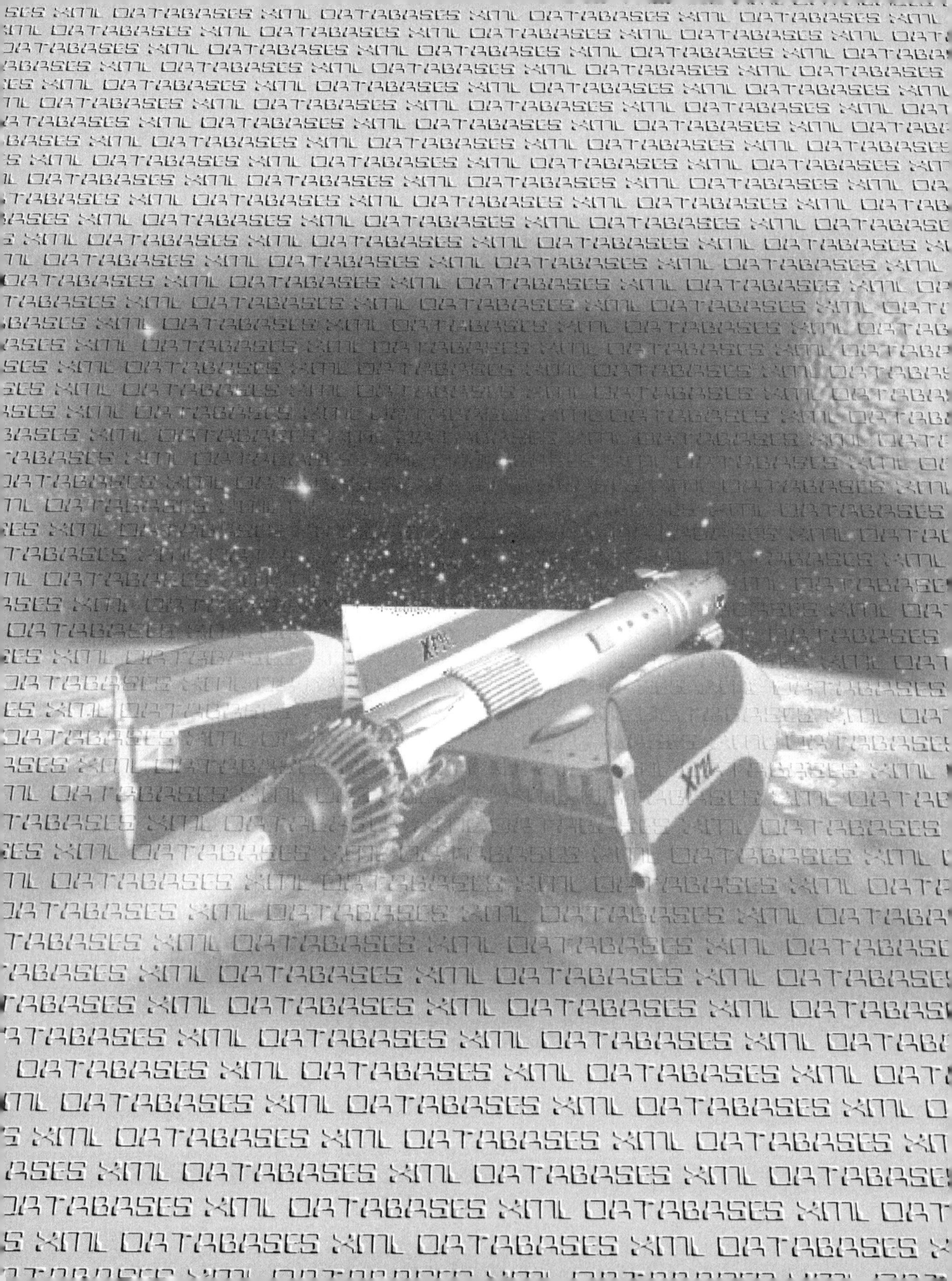
XML DATABASES
XML

Table of Contents

Table of Contents

Table of Contents

Table of Contents

Table of Contents

Table of Contents

Table of Contents

Table of Contents

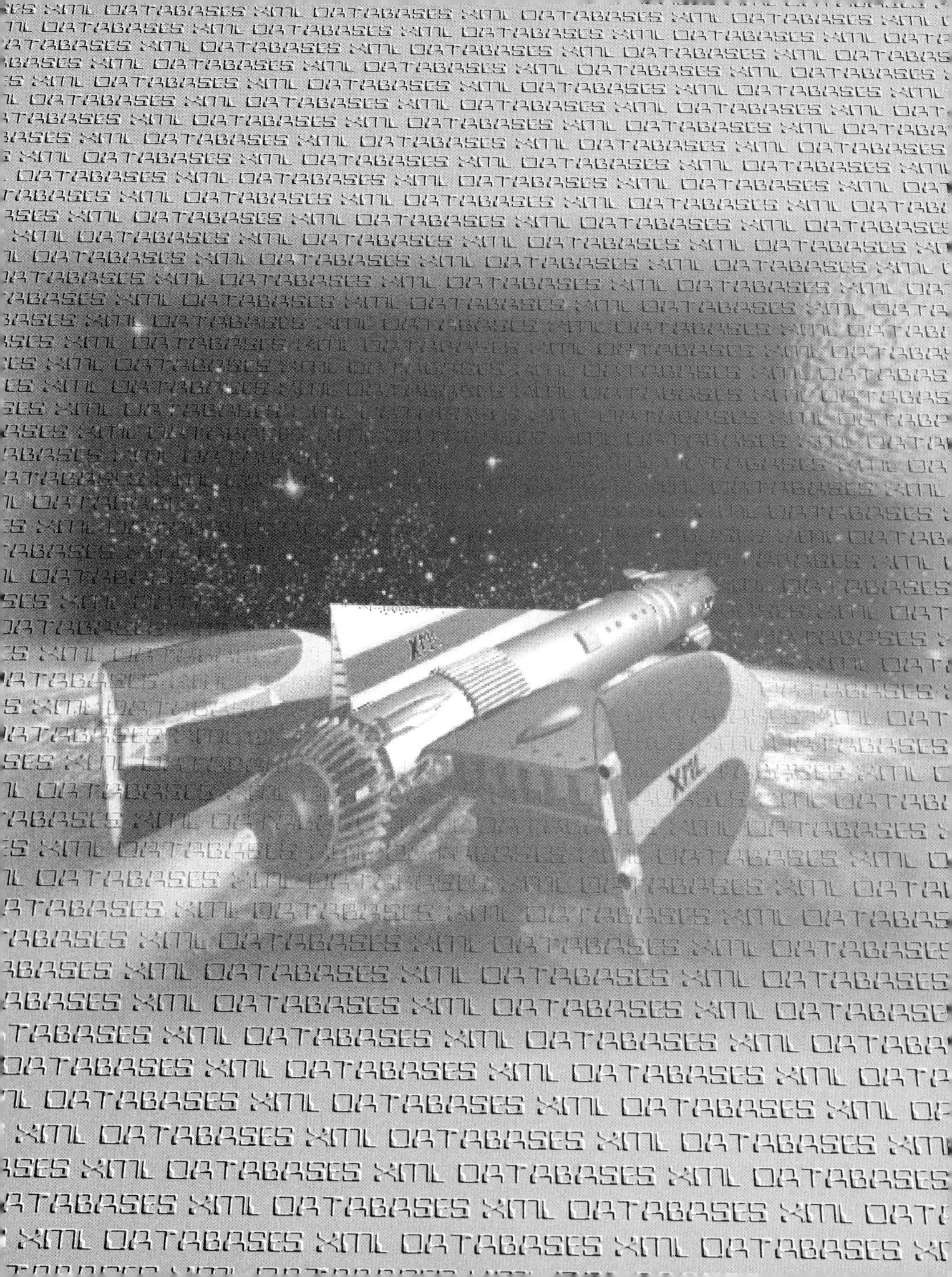
XML DATABASES
XML
XML

Introduction

In a very short space of time, XML has become a hugely popular format for marking up all kinds of data, from web content to data used by applications. It is finding its way across all tiers of development: storage, transport, and display - and it is being used by developers writing programs in many languages.

Meanwhile, relational databases are currently by far the most commonly used type of databases, and can be found in most organizations. While there have been many formats for data storage in the past, because relational databases can provide data for large numbers of users, with quick access, and security mechanisms built in to the database itself, they are set to remain a central tool for programmers for a long while yet.

There are rich and compelling reasons for using both XML and database technologies, however when put side by side they can be seen as complimentary technologies – and like all good partnerships, when working together the sum of what they can achieve is greater than their individual merits. If we think about the strengths of relational databases, they provide strong management and security features. Large numbers of people can connect to the same data source, and the integrity of the source can be ensured through its locking mechanisms. Meanwhile, XML, being plain text, can easily be sent across a network and is cross-platform (you can use XML in any programming language that you can write a parser for). Furthermore, it can easily be transformed from one vocabulary to another.

With the strong hold relational databases have as a datea storage format, and with the flexibility offered by XML as a data exchange mechanism, we have an ideal partnership to store and serve data when creating loosely coupled, networked applications. The partnership easily allows us to securely share data with clients of varying levels of sophistication, making the data more widely accessible.

If you think about the structure of the two, however, there is a lot to learn when using these two technologies side by side. The hierarchical structure of XML can be used to create models that do not easily fit into the relational database paradigm of tables with relationships. There are complex nested structures that cannot be represented in table creation scripts, and we can model constraints in DTDs that cannot be represented between tables and keys. Then, when we provide data as XML, there are a whole set of issues relating to its processing, and the technologies that have been built around XML that we must be aware of in order to make use of the data.

Why XML *and* Databases

There are many reasons why we might wish to expose our database content as XML, or store our XML documents in a database. In this book, we'll see how XML may be used to make our systems perform better and require less coding time.

One obvious advantage to XML is that it provides a way to represent structured data without any additional information. Because this structure is "inherent" in the XML document rather than needing to be driven by an additional document that describes how the structure appears as you do with, say, a flat file, it becomes very easy to send structured information between systems. Since XML documents are simply text files, they may also be produced and consumed by legacy systems allowing these systems to expose their legacy data in a way that can easily be accessed by different consumers.

Another advantage to the use of XML is the ability to leverage tools, either already available, or starting to appear, that use XML to drive more sophisticated behavior. For example, XSLT may be used to style XML documents, producing HTML documents, WML decks, or any other type of text document. XML servers such as Biztalk allow XML to be encapsulated in routing information, which then may be used to drive documents to their appropriate consumers in our workflow.

Data serialized in an XML format provides flexibility with regard to transmission and presentation. With the recent boom in wireless computing, one challenge that many developers are facing is how to easily reuse their data to drive both traditional presentation layers (such as HTML browsers) and new technologies (such as WML-aware cell phones). We'll see how XML provides a great way to decouple the structure of the data from the exact syntactical presentation of that data. Additionally, since XML contains both data and structure, it avoids some of the typical data transmission issues that arise when sending normalized data from one system to another (such as denormalization, record type discovery, and so on).

One caveat to remember is that, at least at this time, relational databases will perform better than XML documents. This means that for many internal uses, if there are no network or usage barriers, relational databases will be a better "home" for our data than XML. This is especially important if we intend to perform queries across our data – in this case a relational database is much better suited to the task than XML documents would be. We'll look at where these approaches make sense later in the book, as well as seeing how a hybrid structure can be created that combines the best of both the relational database world and the XML world.

If we imagine that you are running an e-commerce system and that we take your orders as XML, perhaps some of our information needs to be sent to some internal source (such as our customer service department) as well as to some external partner (an external service department). In this case, we might want to store past customer order details in a relational database but make them available to both parties, and XML would be the ideal format for exposing this data. It could be read no matter what language the application was written in or what platform it was running on. It makes the system more loosely coupled and does not require us to write code that ties us to either part of the application. Clearly, in the case where numerous users (especially external B2B *and* B2C) need different views of the same data, then XML can provide a huge advantage.

What This Book is About

This book teaches us how to integrate XML into our current relational data source strategies. Apart from discussing structural concerns to aid us in designing our XML files, it covers how to store and manage the data we have been working with. It will demonstrate how to store XML in its native format and in a relational database, as well as how to create models that will allow quick and efficient access (such as data-driven web pages). Then, we'll discuss the similarities and differences between relational database design and XML design, and look at some algorithms for moving between the two.

Next, we'll look into the developer's XML toolbox, discussing such technologies as the DOM, SAX, XLink, XPointer, and XML covers. We will also look at the most common data manipulation tasks and discuss some strategies using the technologies we've discussed.

Whether we are using XML for storage, as an interchange format, or for display, this book looks at some of the key issues we should be aware of, such as:

- ❏ Guidelines for how to handle translating an XML structure to a relational database model.
- ❏ Rules for modeling XML based upon a relational database structure.
- ❏ Common techniques for storing, transmitting, and displaying your content.
- ❏ Data access mechanisms that expose relational data as XML.
- ❏ How to use related technologies when processing our XML data.
- ❏ XML support in SQL Server 2000.

For those in need of a refresher in relational databases or XML, primers have been provided on both of these topics in the appendices.

Who Should Use This Book?

While this book will discuss some conceptual issues, its focus is on development and implementation. This is a book for programmers and analysts who are already familiar with both XML and using relational databases. For those who do not have much knowledge of XML, it is advisable that you read a title like **Beginning XML** *Wrox Press (ISBN - 1861003412)*. There are really three groups of readers that may benefit from the information in this book:

Data Analysts

Data analysts, those responsible for taking business data requirements and converting them into data repository strategies, will find a lot of useful information in this book. Compatibility issues between XML data structures and relational data structures are discussed, as are system architecture strategies that leverage the strengths of each technology. Technologies that facilitate the marshalling of relational data through XML to the business logic and/or presentation layer are also discussed.

Relational Database Developers

Developers who have good relational database skills and want to improve their XML skills will also find the book useful. The first group of chapters specifically discusses relational database design and how it corresponds to XML design. There is a chapter devoted to the problem of data transmission, and the ways in which XML can make this easier to overcome. Some alternative strategies for providing data services are also discussed, such as using XSLT to transform an XML document for presentation, rather than processing the data through a custom middle tier.

XML Developers

Developers who are already skilled in the use of XML to represent documents but want to move to more of a data focused approach will find good information in this book as well. The differences between the use of XML for document markup and the use of XML for data representation are clearly defined, and some common pitfalls of XML data design are described (as well as strategies for avoiding them). Algorithms for the persistence of XML documents in relational databases are provided, as well as some indexing strategies using relational databases that may be used to speed access to XML documents while retaining their flexibility and platform independence.

Understanding the Problems We Face

In the relatively short period of time that XML has been around, early adopters have learned some valuable lessons. Two of the most important ones are:

❑ How to model their data for quick and efficient data access.

❑ How to retain flexibilityof data so that it meets ongoing business needs.

When exposing database content as XML, we need to look at issues such as how to create the XML from the table structure, and then how to describe relationships between the XML representations of this data.

When looking at storing XML in a database, we need to see how we reproduce models, which contain hierarchical structures in tables with columns and rows. We need to see how to represent features such as containment with relationships, and how to express complex forms in a structured fashion.

And in both cases we need to make sure that the XML we create is in a format that can be processed and exchanged.

There have also been a number of technologies that have fallen into the toolboxes of developers, such as the DOM, SAX, and XSLT, each of which has a part to play in data handling and manipulation. There are important choices to be made when deciding which of these technologies to use. Some of these technologies are still in development, but it is important to be aware of the features that they will offer in the near future, and how they may help solve problems or influence design in the long run.

Structure of the Book

To help you navigate this book and it has been divided into four sections based on:

❑ Design techniques.

❑ Technologies.

❑ Data Access Technologies.

❑ Common Tasks.

This is rounded off with two case study chapters, which show the application of some of the concepts we have learnt, and two appendices for those less familiar with the core topics of the book: XML and Relational Databases.

Design Techniques

The first section discusses best-practice design techniques that should be used when designing relational databases and XML documents concurrently, and consists of chapters 1 through 4.

- ❏ Chapter 1, **XML Design for Data**, provides some good strategies for the design of XML structures to represent data. It outlines the differences between an XML document to be used for document markup and an XML document to be used for data. It also gives some design strategies based on the audience for the documents and the performance that is required, as well as defining how these designs map onto relational database designs and vice versa.

- ❏ Chapter 2, **XML Structures for Existing Databases**, contains some algorithmic strategies for representing preexisting relational data in the form of XML. Common problems, such as the modeling of complex relationships and the containment versus. pointing approach, are discussed.

- ❏ Chapter 3, **Database Structures for Existing XML**, includes some algorithmic strategies for representing preexisting XML documents in a relational database. Strategies for handling predefined structures (DTDs or schemas) as well as unstructured documents are described. In addition, challenging issues such as the handling of the ANY element content model and MIXED element content model are tackled.

- ❏ Chapter 4, **Standards Design**, discusses the design of *data standards*, common representations of data that may be used by many different consumers and/or producers. It covers common problems encountered during standards development, including type agreement, enumeration mapping, levels of summarization, and collaboration techniques.

Technologies

The second section mainly introduces the various XML technologies (either existing or emergent) that developers will use to create XML data solutions. We also discuss flat file formats at the end of this section. It is made up of Chapters 5 through 12.

- ❏ Chapter 5, **XML Schemas**, covers the new document definition language currently being created by the W3C. It discusses the status of XML Schemas and provides a list of processors that perform validation of documents against XML schemas. It also covers the (extensive) list of advantages to using XML schemas for data documents as opposed to DTDs. It then provides a reference to XML schema syntax, ending up with some sample schemas to demonstrate their strengths.

- ❏ Chapter 6, **DOM**, discusses the XML Document Object Model. It includes a list of DOM-compliant parsers, and discusses the syntax and usage of the DOM. The DOM's strengths are summarized, and some sample applications of the DOM are demonstrated.

- ❏ Chapter 7, **SAX**, describes the Simple API for XML. It also includes a list of SAX-compliant parsers, and discusses the syntax and usage of SAX. It then compares the strengths and weaknesses of SAX, compared with the DOM to help us decide which API should be used in different situations. Finally, there are some sample applications that use SAX.

- ❏ Chapter 8, **XSLT andXPath**, discusses the XML transformation technologies created by the W3C. Itdiscusses the sytax ofboth XSLT and Xpath. Examples of the use of XSLT/XPath for data manipulation and data presentation are also provided.

- ❏ Chapter 9, **XLink**, introduces information about the XML resource linking mechanism defined by the W3C. The chapter covers the XLink specification (both simple and extended links), and discusses some ways that XLink may be used to describe relationships between data, with examples.

❏ Chapter 10, **Other technologies**, covers some other XML technologies related to linking, retrieving, and describing relationships between data. It discusses how these technologies might be applied to data design and development. Technologies covered include XBase, XPointer, XInclude, and XForms.

❏ Chapter 11, XML Query, introduces the new query language in development by the W3C. It discusses the status of the XML Query specification(s), and describes how XML Query can be used to facilitate access to XML documents. It then goes on to look at other ways of querying XML documents, and compares the abilities of each.

❏ Chapter 12, **Flat File formats**, discusses flat files, and some of the issues encountered when moving data between flat files and XML (for example, using the DOM). We'll also learn some strategies for mapping XML to flat files (using XSLT) and some of the issues we may encounter when doing so.

Data Access

In this third section we will start with a look at two specific data access technologies: JDBC and ADO (we also provide a preview to ADO+). We will then look at the XML support offered in SQL Server 2000..

❏ Chapter 13, **ADO and ADO+**, shows how we can use ADO to make data available as XML and provide updates as XML. It builds upon the new functionality provided with SQL Server 2000, showing how to exploit it from the ADO object model. To finish with, ADO+ makes a cameo appearance as we provide a preview of the capabilities of this new technology.

❏ Chapter 14, **XML Support in SQL Server 2000**, discusses the XML Support added to SQL Server 2000. It shows us how you can write SQL queries that will return XML from SQL Server, and how we can send SQL Server XML documents for it to store. It finishes off with describing how to handle bulk loads from XML to SQL Server.

❏ Chapter 15, **XML Views in SQL Server 2000**, builds on what we saw in the last chapter, looking at how we can use schemas to create views of the data held in SQL Server, and map this to XML, so that we can run queries, as well as add, delete and update records. These make use of two new features called templates and updategrams.

❏ Chapter 16, **JDBC**, looks at how XML (and associated technologies) can be used to enhance the use of JDBC (and vice versa), to produce scalable and extensible architectures with the minimum of coding. The two sections of this chapter specifically look at generation of XML from a JDBC data source, and using XML to update a JDBC data source.

Common Tasks

The fourth section of the book discusses some common applications of XML to data implementations, and provides some strategies for tackling each type of problem discussed. It is made up of Chapters 17 through 19.

❏ Chapter 17, **Data Warehousing**, covers strategies for near-line archival and retrieval of XML documents. It describes strategies for indexing XML documents using a relational database, and includes some samples of archival and near-line storage.

❏ Chapter 18, **Data Transmission**, discusses the ubiquitous problem of data transmission between dissimilar data repositories and the use of XML to facilitate that transmission. Import and export techniques are discussed, as well as ways to bypass corporate firewalls when transmitting XML documents (using technologies such as XML-RPC or SOAP).

❑ Chapter 19, **Marshalling and Presentation**, describes the use of XML as a driver, for the marshalling of a more useful form of data from our relational databases, and for the presentation layer. SQL script and VBScript examples are provided that drive these processes, as well as the use of XForm's to move data in the other direction (from client to server).

Case Studies

We round off this book with two very different chapters as case studies:

❑ Chapter 20, **SQL Server 2000 XML sample applications**, is designed to introduce us to, and show us how to get results from, some of the more advanced XML features in SQL Server 2000; and how to program them. We will do this by building up two separate projects, each of which is designed to show us how to get the most out of specific features. The first one deals with SQL Server 2000 data access over HTTP, and the second one looks at building a sample e-commerce site - the eLemerade site.

❑ Chapter 21, **DB Prism**, looks at DB Prism, an open source tool for generating dynamic XML from a database, either running as a stand-alone servlet, or by acting as an adapter to connect any database with a publishing framework such as Cocoon (the particular framework used in this chapter). This study shows how to implement and use this technology.

Appendices

We have also provided two primers in the appendices for those that are unfamiliar with, or need to brush up on, XML, or relational databases.

❑ Appendix A, **XML Basics Primer**, contains a quick refresher on XML for those who aren't familiar with basic XML concepts, or just needs to get back up to speed. It discusses the origins of XML, the various pieces that go together to make up an XML document, elements, attributes, text nodes, CDATA nodes, and so on, and discusses the use of DTDs (document type definitions).

❑ Appendix B, **Relational Database Primer**, provides a similar refresher on relational databases. It covers the building blocks of relational databases, tables, columns, relationships, and so forth. It also discusses normalization (which will be important when we talk about structuring XML documents later in the book) and the relationship between RDBMS constructs and XML constructs.

These are followed by appendices on Schema datatypes, SAX, and Setting up virtual directories in SQL Server

Technologies Used in the Book

This book demonstrates data access and manipulation in a number of languages. There are examples in ECMAScript, Java, Visual Basic, and ASP. While some of us may not be familiar with the languages used in all of the chapters, we have endeavoured to make the descriptions adequate enough us you to transfer what you have learnt in the chapter to our language of choice. Also, in many cases, algorithms are presented in a conceptual or pseudocoded way so that they may be applied to the any target platform of choice.

We have intentionally focused most of our examples on the use of document type definitions (or DTDs), rather than the technically superior XML Schemas. The reason for this should be obvious - until the W3C reaches full recommendation status with the XML Schemas standard documents, there will be a lack of processors that can actually validate against XML Schemas. This book is intended to get us up and running fast - in other words, to provide us with real examples of code that we can adopt to our own business solutions. All of the examples provided in this book (with the obvious exception of the examples in the emergent technology chapters such as the XLink chapter and the XML Schemas chapter) will work out-of-the-box with commonly used, widely available processors.

Conventions

We have used a number of different styles of text and layout in this book to help differentiate between the different kinds of information. Here are examples of the styles we used and an explanation of what they mean:

Code has several fonts. If it's a word that we're talking about in the text – for example, when discussing a For...Next loop, it's in this font. If it's a block of code that can be typed as a program and run, then it's also in a gray box:

```
<?xml version 1.0?>
```

Sometimes we'll see code in a mixture of styles, like this:

```
<?xml version 1.0?>
<Invoice>
    <part>
        <name>Widget</name>
        <price>$10.00</price>
    </part>
</invoice>
```

In cases like this, the code with a white background is code we are already familiar with; the line highlighted in grey is a new addition to the code since we last looked at it.

Advice, hints, and background information comes in this type of font.

Important pieces of information come in boxes like this.

Bullets appear indented, with each new bullet marked as follows:

❑ **Important Words** are in a bold type font.

❑ Words that appear on the screen, in menus like the File or Window, are in a similar font to that which we would see on a Windows desktop.

❑ Keys that we press on the keyboard like *Ctrl* and *Enter*, are in italics.

Customer Support

We've tried to make this book as accurate and enjoyable as possible, but what really matters is what the book actually does for you. Please let us know your views, either by returning the reply card in the back of the book, or by contacting us via email at feedback@wrox.com.

Source Code and Updates

As we work through the examples in this book, we may decide that we prefer to type in all the code by hand. Many readers prefer this because it's a good way to get familiar with the coding techniques that are being used.

Whether you want to type the code in or not, we have made all the source code for this book is available at our web site at the following address:

http://www.wrox.com/

If you're one of those readers who likes to type in the code, you can use our files to check the results you should be getting - they should be your first stop if you think you might have typed in an error. If you're one of those readers who doesn't like typing, then downloading the source code from our web site is a must!

Either way, it'll help you with updates and debugging.

Errata

We've made every effort to make sure that there are no errors in the text or the code. However, to err is human, and as such, we recognize the need to keep you informed of any mistakes as they're spotted and corrected. Errata sheets are available for all our books at http://www.wrox.com. If you find an error that hasn't already been reported, please let us know.

Our web site acts as a focus for other information and support, including the code from all Wrox books, sample chapters, previews of forthcoming titles, and articles and opinions on related topics.

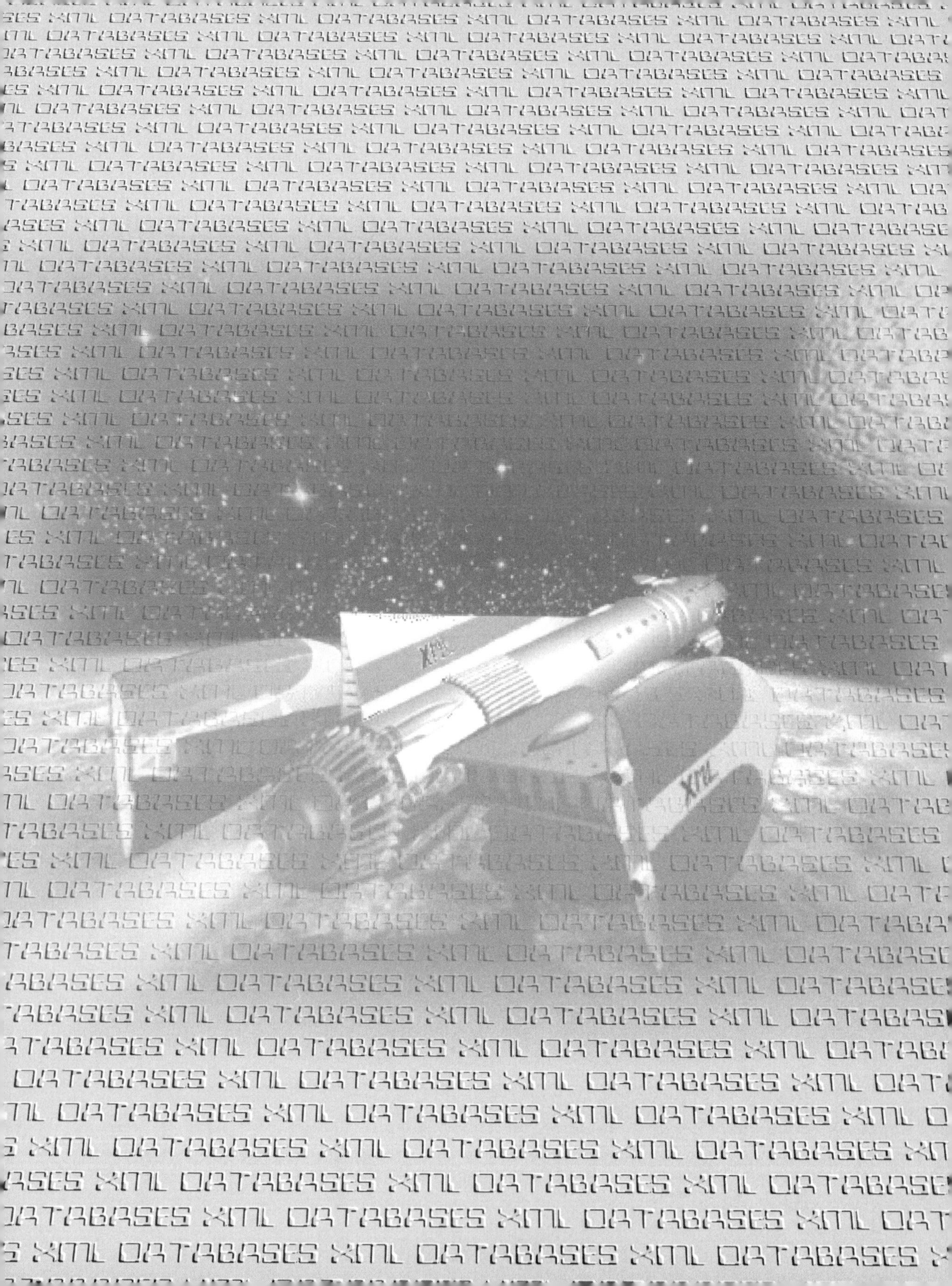
XML DATABASES
XML

XML Design for Data

In this chapter, we will look at some of the issues and strategies that we need to think about when designing the structure of our XML documents. The modeling approach we take in our XML documents will have a direct and significant impact on performance, document size, readability, and code size. We'll see some of the ramifications of certain design decisions, and recommend some best practice techniques.

One of the key factors to understand when creating models for storing data in XML, is that there are important differences between XML documents that represent marked up text, and XML documents that represent data with a mixed content model. We'll start this chapter with an outline of these differences, and see how the data we're modeling impacts our approach.

This chapter makes reference to relational database concepts to explain some of the issues likely to be encountered when working with XML for data. If relational database concepts are unfamiliar, it is advisable to look at Appendix B before tackling this chapter.

Finally, in this chapter, table creation scripts are written to run with SQL Server – if you are using a relational database platform other than SQL Server, you may need to tweak the scripts to get them to work properly.

In this chapter we will see:

- ❑ How the types of data we are marking up will affect the way we model the information.
- ❑ How to model data structures.
- ❑ How to model data points.
- ❑ How to model the relationships between the structures.
- ❑ A sample application illustrating some best practices.

First, though, we need to understand the difference between using XML to mark up text, and XML for data.

XML for Text Versus XML for Data

As I indicated, before we can start modeling our data, it is important that we understand just what it is that we're trying to model. Let's take a look at two different uses of XML:

- ❑   for marking up text documents
- ❑   for the representation of raw data

and see how they differ.

XML for Text

XML grew from SGML, which was used for marking up documents in electronic format. That's why much of the early literature on XML – and the work developers did with it – was concerned with the use of XML for annotating blocks of text with additional semantic information about that text. For example, if we were marking up a chapter of a book, we might do something like the following:

```
<paragraph>
   <quote speaker="Eustace">"I don't believe I've seen that orange pie
   plate before,"</quote>Eustace said. He examined it closely, noting
   that <plotpoint>there was a purple stain about halfway around one
   edge.</plotpoint><quote speaker="Eustace">"Peculiar,"</quote> he
   declared.
</paragraph>
```

There are two important points to note in this example. Because we are marking up text:

- ❑   If the markup were removed, the text of the paragraph itself would still have the same meaning outside the XML document.
- ❑   The order of the information is of critical importance to understanding its meaning – we cannot start reordering the text we mark up and still expect it to have the same meaning.

This is typical of how XML has been used to mark up text; we can think of this as marking up content.

There is, however, a sharp contrast between marking up this sort of text and using XML to hold raw data, as we will see next.

XML for Data

As this book's focus is XML and databases, the second type of information that we mark up is of greater interest to us. Our databases hold all kinds of business information. For the rest of the chapter, we will focus on how we should be looking at marking up this kind of information. As we will see, there are a number of ways in which we could mark up this data without changing its meaning.

One of the key differences between marking up text and data is that text must usually stay in the order in which it's presented, and the markup adds meaning to the text. However, data can be represented in a number of different ways and still have the same functionality. Having seen an example of text that we have marked up, let's look at an example of data to make this distinction clearer.

Here's an example of a document that is designed to hold data:

```
<Invoice
    orderDate="7/23/2000"
    shipDate="7/28/2000">
    <Customer
        name="Homer Simpson"
        address="742 Evergreen Terrace"
        city="Springfield"
        state="KY"
        postalCode="12345" />
    <LineItem
        productDescription="Widgets (0.5 inch)"
        quantity="17"
        unitPrice="0.10" />
    <LineItem
        productDescription="Grommets (2 inch)"
        quantity="22"
        unitPrice="0.05" />
</Invoice>
```

As you can see, this is an example of an invoice marked up in XML.

Now, if we were to show this data outside of the document, we could present it in a number of different ways. For example, we might represent the data this way:

```
Invoice

Homer Simpson
742 Evergreen Terrace
Springfield, KY 12345

Ordered on: 7/23/2000
Shipped on: 7/28/2000

Product                 Quantity            Price
Widgets (0.5 inch)         17               0.10
Grommets (2 inch)          22               0.05
```

Alternatively, it would be equally valid to represent the data this way:

```
Homer Simpson|742 Evergreen Terrace|Springfield|KY|12345
07232000|07282000
Widgets (0.5 inch)|17|0.10
Grommets (2 inch)|22|0.05
```

When we're looking at this type of data, the order in which it is stored does not matter as much to the meaning of the document as it did to the previous section, where we were marking up the book.

For example, it does not change the meaning of the document if the order date is stored before or after the ship date in the XML document – as long as they can be identified, and as long as they are associated with the invoice to which they belong. Similarly, the order in which the line items are stored is not meaningful – as long as they are associated with the appropriate invoice.

So, we have already seen a clear distinction here between the different types of data that we are marking up. When we are using XML to mark up data that does not have to follow a strict order we can be more flexible in the way we store it, which in turn can impact upon how easy it is to retrieve or process the data.

Representing Data in XML

Because XML allows us to be so flexible in the way that we can mark up our data, let's take a look at some ways in which we should restrict our XML structure designs for data.

Element Content Models

We will start our discussion about how we can structure our XML vocabularies by looking at how to model **element content**. When using a DTD to define the structure of an XML vocabulary, there are five possible content models for elements:

❑   Element-only content.

❑   Mixed content.

❑   Text-only content (a special case of mixed content).

❑   The EMPTY model.

❑   The ANY model.

Let's take a look at each of these in turn and see how they might be used to represent data.

Element-only Content

Element-only content is used when elements may only contain other elements. For example, the following content model is element-only:

```
<!ELEMENT Invoice (Customer, LineItem+)>
```

Here we have an Invoice element, as the root element, which can contain a Customer element, followed by one or more LineItem elements. An example of a document that conforms to this would be:

```
<Invoice>
    <Customer />
    <LineItem />
    <LineItem />
</Invoice>
```

This structure provides the cleanest way to contain one structure inside another. This will be our representation of choice for the nesting of elements.

Mixed Content

In the mixed content model, elements may contain zero or more instances of a list of elements, in any order, along with any amount of text in any position. An example of the mixed content model might be:

```
<!ELEMENT Invoice (#PCDATA | LineItem | Customer)*>
```

A couple of example documents might be:

```
<Invoice>
    This is the invoice for <Customer>Kevin Williams</Customer>
</Invoice>
```

or:

```
<Invoice>
    <LineItem />
    <Customer>Kevin Williams</Customer>
    <LineItem />
</Invoice>
```

This model isn't good for modeling data because the allowable subelements might appear at any point within the element, and any number of times. This makes it very difficult to map to data elements, and makes writing code to handle the document (and move it to a data repository, such as a relational database) a nightmare. We should avoid the use of the mixed content model for data.

Text-only Content

In the text-only content model, elements may only contain text strings. An example of the text-only content model might be:

```
<!ELEMENT Customer (#PCDATA)>
```

and a sample document might be:

```
<Customer>Kevin Williams</Customer>
```

Using text-only elements is one way to include **data points** in our document.

> **When we refer to data points in this context, we mean single values, analogous to columns in a relational database or fields in a flat file.**

However, we could also use **attributes**, which can have advantages over this method – as we'll see a little later in the chapter.

EMPTY Content

In the EMPTY content model, an element cannot contain anything at all; it must be expressed either as the empty-element-tag, or as a start-tag followed immediately by an end-tag (the preferred notation being an empty-element-tag). The following is an example of the empty content model:

```
<!ELEMENT Customer EMPTY>
```

A sample document might be:

```
<Customer />
```

This content model will come in useful when we have a situation where the only additional information associated with an element is at the data point level. For example, let's say we had a `Customer` element that only had a `FirstName` and `LastName` associated with it. Since these pieces of information are data points – that is, single values – we could use the empty content model for the `Customer` element and represent the data points as attributes. We will see how that's done shortly.

ANY Content

The last content model we could use is the `ANY` content model. In this model, any element or text may appear inside the element when defined this way, in any order. So, for this example:

```
<!ELEMENT Customer ANY>
```

we might have the following document:

```
<Customer>Kevin Williams</Customer>
```

or:

```
<Customer>
    <Customer>
        <Customer>Kevin Williams</Customer>
    </Customer>
</Customer>
```

Like the mixed content model, this content model is too permissive for data. Without some idea of what structures might appear, and in what order, leveraging and operating upon the data will be extremely difficult. For this reason, we will avoid using the `ANY` content model in the structures we design.

Using Attributes

The other way to represent data points, and the recommended method for doing so in data documents, is by using **attributes**. For example, in the following sample structure:

```
<!ELEMENT Customer EMPTY>
<!ATTLIST Customer
    FirstName CDATA #REQUIRED
    LastName CDATA #REQUIRED>
```

we would have a document that looks like the following:

```
<Customer
    FirstName="Kevin"
    LastName="Williams"/>
```

This approach has several inherent advantages over using text-only elements to represent data points. We'll take a look at some of these later in the chapter.

Other Considerations

So far, we have looked at some of the obvious considerations to take into account when creating our data model, but we should always be asking ourselves if all of the relevant data for the document is being represented in as efficient and accessible a manner as possible. So, let's take a look at some of the other considerations that we need to take into account when designing XML structures, namely:

- ❑ Audience.
- ❑ Performance.
- ❑ Data modeling versus representation modeling.

Audience

When designing XML structures, we should take into account the universe of producers and consumers that might be manipulating documents based on those structures.

We need to ask ourselves the following questions:

- ❑ **Does the document need to be human-readable?**
  Depending on the planned usage of our documents, they might only be read by automatic processes, or they might need to be read by humans. If a document is not intended to be human-readable, abbreviations and other modifications may be made to reduce document size.

- ❑ **Is the document intended primarily for display or for processing?**
  If our documents will most commonly be styled to flattened structures – for example, flat file exports – we may want to flatten the structures in our XML so that the XSLT engine's workload will be reduced.

- ❑ **How many consumers will be processing the document?**
  If we want our data to be made available to as many consumers as possible – as we would with an industrywide standard – we might try to keep the structure as flexible as possible. If it is only to be read by one type of application, we can tune it specifically to the requirements of that application.

- ❑ **Is the document intended to operate under a standard that constrains the allowable structure?**
  If our structures are being designed to run under the BizTalk Framework (or another e-commerce initiative), we may want to represent data points as text-only elements rather than attributes – as that's the recommended structure for BizTalk messages.

Performance

Often, performance is the other side of the audience coin; the narrower the audience, the more finely tuned the document structures may be for performance. For example, say we have an XML document, stored in a file or streamed across the Web, that looks like the following:

```
<Invoice
    customerName="Kevin Williams">
    <LineItem
        productName="Grommets (2 inch)"
        quantity="17"
        price="0.10" />
</Invoice>
```

This document is mostly human-readable – the customer and product names are spelled out, and the document has white space added to make it easy to comprehend. Now, let's suppose that human-readability is not a factor, and instead the document has to perform as well as possible. The following might be an alternative design:

```
<I c="c17"><L p="p22" q="17" pr=".1" /></I>
```

In this case:

❑ We've abbreviated the element and attribute names (because the document is being read by a machine process).

❑ We've removed unnecessary whitespace (again, because readability is not a factor).

❑ We've used customer and product lookup codes rather than spelling out their names.

This document works very well if it is being passed between two known systems that understand the cryptic abbreviations, but it doesn't work as well for documents that might have to be human-readable. Which version we choose all comes down to the planned usage of the document, and the other design factors that have to be taken into consideration.

Data Modeling Versus Representation Modeling

When designing XML structures for data, it's important to focus on the data itself and not the common representation of the data in the real world. For example, say we have an invoice that looks like this:

```
Widgets, Inc.
Invoice

Customer:    Kevin Williams
             742 Evergreen Terrace
             Springfield, KY 12345

Ship to:     Kevin Williams
             742 Evergreen Terrace
             Springfield, KY 12345
Shipper:     FedEx

Item Code   Description        Quantity      Price        Total
1A2A3AB     Widget (3 inch)       17        $0.10        $1.70
2BC3DCB     Grommet (2 inch)      22        $0.05        $1.10

Total                                                    $2.80
```

We might be tempted to construct an XML document that looks like this:

```
<Invoice>
Widgets, Inc.
Invoice

Customer:    <customerName>Kevin Williams</customerName>
             <orderAddress>742 Evergreen Terrace</orderAddress>
             <orderCity>Springfield</orderCity>,
             <orderState>KY</orderState>
             <orderPostalCode>12345</orderPostalCode>
```

```
Ship to:     <shipName>Kevin Williams</shipName>
             <shipAddress>742 Evergreen Terrace</shipAddress>
             <shipCity>Springfield</shipCity>,
             <shipState>KY</shipState>
             <shipPostalCode>12345</shipPostalCode>
Shipper:     <shippingCompany>FedEx</shippingCompany>

Item Code    Description          Quantity        Price        Total
   <LineItem>
       <itemCode>1A2A3AB</itemCode>
       <itemDescription>Widget (3 inch)</itemDescription>
       <quantity>17</quantity>
       <price>$0.10</price>
       <linePrice>$1.70</linePrice>
   </LineItem>
   <LineItem>
       <itemCode>2BC3DCB</itemCode>
       <itemDescription>Grommet (0.5 inch)</itemDescription>
       <quantity>22</quantity>
       <price>$0.05</price>
       <linePrice>$1.10</linePrice>
   </LineItem>

Total
   <totalPrice>$2.80</totalPrice>
</Invoice>
```

However, this is an example of modeling to the representation, not the data itself. Here are some of the problems with this approach:

❑ **Formatting information is retained in the XML document.**
Information about the location of data in a particular representation, or text that always appears in the representation of XML documents of this type, should not be retained in XML. If we need to reconstruct the appearance of the representation later, we should use XSLT or some other formatting mechanism to recreate it.

❑ **Summary information is retained in the XML document.**
Information such as the line item totals and grand total for the invoice should not be retained in the XML document, unless there's a compelling reason to do so. This follows the same argument as to why summary information shouldn't be retained in a relational database unless there's a compelling reason to do so. Summary information may always be extrapolated from the detail information provided, so it isn't strictly necessary in the XML document. If a value included in an XML document cannot be brought into a nonXML representation for manipulation, then the document has virtually no worth as a data medium. An exception could be, for example, when the information needs to be accessible directly from the document at a summary level, perhaps via XSLT.

❑ **Field formatting information is retained.**
The dollar symbol for the price element, for example, does not belong in the `price` field – it is part of the formatting of the information for a particular representation, not part of the actual information content.

A much better structure would be:

```
<Invoice
   customerName="Kevin Williams">
   <Address
     addressType="billing"
     street="742 Evergreen Terrace"
     city="Springfield"
     state="KY"
     postalCode="12345" />
   <Address
     addressType="shipping"
     street="742 Evergreen Terrace"
     city="Springfield"
     state="KY"
     postalCode="12345" />
   <LineItem
      itemCode="1A2A3AB"
      itemDescription="Widget (3 inch)"
      quantity="17"
      price="0.10"
      currency="USD" />
   <LineItem
      itemCode="2BC3DCB"
      itemDescription="Grommet (0.5 inch)"
      quantity="22"
      price="0.05"
      currency="USD" />
</Invoice>
```

In this sample, all formatting information has been discarded, and the XML document represents the pure data representation of the document content.

XML Data Structures – A Summary

In this section, we've looked at some of the issues that should be taken into consideration when developing our XML structures for data. We've learned that the mixed content and ANY content elements should be avoided under most circumstances, and that the structures that we define should be designed to carry the data, not any specific representation of the data. Beyond that, we should take into account the audience for documents, and any performance constraints that producers or consumers may impose.

Next, we'll take a look at the various structures in RDBMS systems and XML, and how they map to one another.

Mapping Between RDBMS and XML Structures

In this section, we'll see how relational data may be moved into XML structures. We'll see how structures, data points, and relationships are modeled in XML, and see some common pitfalls and how to avoid them. We'll follow that discussion with an example modeling exercise, to see how the techniques we have learned can be put into action.

Structure

Let's see how we can map information between tables in databases and elements in XML. We'll start with a look at how we might model some sample data for a customer in a relational database. We'll then look at two possible ways in which we might store the same data in XML.

In relational databases, groups of data points that together describe a larger concept are represented by tables that are made up of columns. Here we can create a table to hold all the details about an address:

```
CREATE TABLE Customer (
    firstName varchar(50),
    lastName varchar(50),
    mailingAddress varchar(50),
    mailingCity varchar(60),
    mailingState char(2),
    mailingPostalCode varchar(10))
```

and the table would look like this:

firstName	lastName	mailingAddress	mailingCity	mailingState	mailingPostalCode
Kevin	Williams	742 Springfield Road	Springfield	KY	12345

In XML, groups of data points can be grouped together to describe a larger concept represented by an element. Going back to our customer details, we might use a `<Customer>` element to represent the same information as we had in our Customer table.

> **When moving data between XML form and a relational database, a table should always become an element with element-only content, and an element with element-only content should always become a table – unless we are performing additional normalization or denormalization when we are moving the information.**

Within our `<Customer>` element, the details about the customer can be represented in one of two ways:

- ❑ Using text-only elements.
- ❑ Using attributes.

Elements

The first way data points are represented in XML documents is by using elements. For text-only elements, we might define our `<Customer>` element like this:

```
<!ELEMENT Customer (firstName, lastName, mailingAddress, mailingCity,
                    mailingState, mailingPostalCode)>
<!ELEMENT firstName (#PCDATA)>
<!ELEMENT lastName (#PCDATA)>
<!ELEMENT mailingAddress (#PCDATA)>
<!ELEMENT mailingCity (#PCDATA)>
<!ELEMENT mailingState (#PCDATA)>
<!ELEMENT mailingPostalCode (#PCDATA)>
```

which would result in details being nested in separate elements under the `<Customer>` element like this:

```
<Customer>
    <firstName>Kevin<firstName>
    <lastName>Williams<lastName>
    <mailingAddress>742 Evergreen Terrace <mailingAddress>
    <mailingCity>Springfield<mailingCity>
    <mailingState>KY<mailingState>
    <mailingPostalCode>12345<mailingPostalCode>
</Customer>
```

> **When representing data in an XML document, any element that is defined as having text-only content using the #PCDATA keyword will correspond to a column in a relational database.**

Attributes

Another way of representing data points in XML documents is with attributes. In this approach, elements that represent tables have attributes associated with them that represent columns:

```
<!ELEMENT Customer EMPTY>
<!ATTLIST Customer
    firstName CDATA #REQUIRED
    lastName CDATA #REQUIRED
    mailingAddress CDATA #REQUIRED
    mailingCity CDATA #REQUIRED
    mailingState CDATA #REQUIRED
    mailingPostalCode CDATA #REQUIRED>
```

Here we are storing the details of the customer as attributes on the `<Customer>` element:

```
<Customer
    firstName="Kevin"
    lastName="Williams"
    mailingAddress="742 Evergreen Terrace"
    mailingCity "Springfield"
    mailingState="KY"
    mailingPostalCode="12345" />
```

Let's look in more detail at the two alternatives for the representation of data points.

Data Points

As we have just seen, there are two primary design strategies that may be used to represent columns as XML structures:

❑ Elements, which are nested as children of the element that represents the grouping of information.

❑ Attributes, which are added to the element that represents the grouping of information.

Each approach has its proponents, and they tend to be quite vocal about their opinions. So what are the advantages and disadvantages of each of these two different approaches?

In order to compare the different ways we can represent data, let's use the invoice for a widget manufacturing plant that we saw earlier. Here, again, is how the invoice looks:

```
Widgets, Inc.
Invoice

Customer:    Kevin Williams
             742 Evergreen Terrace
             Springfield, KY 12345

Ship to:     Kevin Williams
             742 Evergreen Terrace
             Springfield, KY 12345
Shipper:     FedEx

Item Code   Description          Quantity    Price       Total
1A2A3AB     Widget (3 inch)         17       $0.10       $1.70
2BC3DCB     Grommet (0.5 inch)      22       $0.05       $1.10

Total                                                    $2.80
```

For this invoice, we're interested in the following data points:

- ❑ Customer name.
- ❑ Billing address.
- ❑ Billing city.
- ❑ Billing state.
- ❑ Billing postal code.
- ❑ Shipping address.
- ❑ Shipping city.
- ❑ Shipping state.
- ❑ Shipping postal code.
- ❑ Shipping company.
- ❑ Item code.
- ❑ Item description.
- ❑ Quantity purchased.
- ❑ Price per unit.

We'll assume that the consumer of our XML document will recalculate the line totals and invoice total, if it requires them. As we saw earlier, our consumer should be able to calculate these kinds of values from our XML data, otherwise our XML isn't worth a great deal!

The invoice has the following data point groupings:

❑ Invoice.

❑ Line Item.

Notice that we're discussing structure internal to the invoice, and not as it relates to some external system. For example, it's likely that this customer will order from us again (assuming we get him his widgets and grommets in a timely manner), so in our invoice database we will probably keep a Customer table that retains information about each of our customers. However, since each of our documents represents one invoice, we will pass the customer information as part of the invoice information, as there is a one-to-one relationship.

There are circumstances where we should break up a one-to-one relationship, but generally it's not a good idea, as it will increase the document size and slow down processing. We will go into XML design in much more detail in Chapter 4.

Our Invoice Using Elements

Now, back to the comparison. Using elements, our structure would look something like this (ch02_ex1.dtd):

```
<!ELEMENT Invoice (customerName, billingAddress, billingCity, billingState,
                   billingPostalCode, shippingAddress, shippingCity,
                   shippingState, shippingPostalCode, shippingCompany,
                   LineItem+)>
<!ELEMENT customerName (#PCDATA)>
<!ELEMENT billingAddress (#PCDATA)>
<!ELEMENT billingCity (#PCDATA)>
<!ELEMENT billingState (#PCDATA)>
<!ELEMENT billingPostalCode (#PCDATA)>
<!ELEMENT shippingAddress (#PCDATA)>
<!ELEMENT shippingCity (#PCDATA)>
<!ELEMENT shippingState (#PCDATA)>
<!ELEMENT shippingPostalCode (#PCDATA)>
<!ELEMENT shippingCompany (#PCDATA)>
<!ELEMENT LineItem (itemCode, itemDescription, quantity, price)>
<!ELEMENT itemCode (#PCDATA)>
<!ELEMENT itemDescription (#PCDATA)>
<!ELEMENT quantity (#PCDATA)>
<!ELEMENT price (#PCDATA)>
```

and here's an example of data marked up using this model (ch02_ex1.xml):

```
<?xml version="1.0" ?>
<!DOCTYPE Invoice SYSTEM "http://myserver/xmldb/ch02_ex1_elements.dtd">

<Invoice>
    <customerName>Kevin Williams</customerName>
    <billingAddress>742 Evergreen Terrace</billingAddress>
    <billingCity>Springfield</billingCity>
    <billingState>KY</billingState>
```

```
        <billingPostalCode>12345</billingPostalCode>
        <shippingAddress>742 Evergreen Terrace</shippingAddress>
        <shippingCity>Springfield</shippingCity>
        <shippingState>KY</shippingState>
        <shippingPostalCode>12345</shippingPostalCode>
        <shippingCompany>FedEx</shippingCompany>
        <LineItem>
            <itemCode>1A2A3AB</itemCode>
            <itemDescription>Widget (3 inch)</itemDescription>
            <quantity>17</quantity>
            <price>0.10</price>
        </LineItem>
        <LineItem>
            <itemCode>2BC3DCB</itemCode>
            <itemDescription>Grommet (0.5 inch)</itemDescription>
            <quantity>22</quantity>
            <price>0.05</price>
        </LineItem>
    </Invoice>
```

Our Invoice Using Attributes

Using attributes, rather than elements, the DTD would look like this (ch02_ex1_attributes.dtd):

```
<!ELEMENT Invoice (LineItem+)>
<!ATTLIST Invoice
    customerName CDATA #REQUIRED
    billingAddress CDATA #REQUIRED
    billingCity CDATA #REQUIRED
    billingState CDATA #REQUIRED
    billingPostalCode CDATA #REQUIRED
    shippingAddress CDATA #REQUIRED
    shippingCity CDATA #REQUIRED
    shippingState CDATA #REQUIRED
    shippingPostalCode CDATA #REQUIRED
    shippingCompany (FedEx | USPS | UPS) #REQUIRED>

<!ELEMENT LineItem EMPTY>
<!ATTLIST LineItem
    itemCode CDATA #REQUIRED
    itemDescription CDATA #REQUIRED
    quantity CDATA #REQUIRED
    price CDATA #REQUIRED>
```

and the corresponding XML would look like this (ch02_ex1_attributes.xml):

```
<?xml version="1.0" ?>
<!DOCTYPE Invoice SYSTEM "http://myserver/xmldb/ch02_ex1_elements.dtd">

<Invoice
    customerName="Kevin Williams"
    billingAddress="742 Evergreen Terrace"
    billingCity="Springfield"
```

```
        billingState="KY"
        billingPostalCode="12345"
        shippingAddress="742 Evergreen Terrace"
        shippingCity="Springfield"
        shippingState="KY"
        shippingPostalCode="12345"
        shippingCompany="FedEx">
        <LineItem
           itemCode="1A2A3AB"
           itemDescription="Widget (3 inch)"
           quantity="17"
           price="0.10" />
        <LineItem
           itemCode="2BC3DCB"
           itemDescription="Grommet (0.5 inch)"
           quantity="22"
           price="0.05" />
</Invoice>
```

Having created two examples of the invoice – one that uses element content, and another that uses attributes to store the information – let's take a look at how the two examples stack up based upon some basic document metrics.

Comparing the Two Approaches

The things we will look at are:

- ❑ Readability.
- ❑ Compatibility with databases.
- ❑ Strong data typing.
- ❑ Programming complexity.
- ❑ Document size.

Readability

In both sample documents above, the documents are equally readable. All data points for a given structural element are grouped together, and structures are clearly delineated.

Compatibility with Databases

In relational databases, content (data points), and structure are clearly disambiguated. Structure is represented with tables and relationships, and data points are represented with columns. Since we're probably going to be spending a lot of our time moving data in and out of relational databases, we would like our XML documents to disambiguate content and structure as well.

Unfortunately, if we use text-only elements to represent data points, we lose this clear distinction – sometimes elements represent structure, and other times they represent content. Any code that is parsing these structures must be aware which element represents data and which represents structure, and must handle it appropriately (or check to see whether text is contained in the element or not, before deciding how to handle that element).

However, if we use attributes for data points, structure and content are separate and distinct – structure is represented by the elements and the way they are nested, while content is represented in attributes. This is possibly the strongest argument for using attributes.

In addition, attributes are unordered. Look at the following two documents:

```
<?xml version="1.0"?>
<Book Author="Ron Obvious" CreateDate="7/23/2000">
  This is a simple XML document.
</Book>
```

and:

```
<?xml version="1.0"?>
<Book CreateDate="7/23/2000" Author="Ron Obvious">
  This is a simple XML document.
</Book>
```

They are identical from the perspective of an XML parser – the parser doesn't attach any particular importance to the order in which attributes are encountered in the original document. This is similar to the way a relational database works, where the meaning of a data point is simply indicated by its name, and not a combination of its name and location.

While element order has meaning for documents (for example, it's important to understand that the second paragraph comes after the first one), it loses importance when representing data. Thus, the ordering of elements just adds unnecessary complexity.

Strong Data Typing

When using DTDs to govern the content of XML structures, there is little scope for strong datatyping. The one exception would be the ability to constrain attributes to a particular list of allowable values. For example, the shippingCompany data point in our example might take one of the three values FedEx, USPS, or UPS. If we describe the data point with an attribute, we can constrain the value of the attribute to this list of three values (and in fact did so in the second DTD example). However, we have no similar way to limit these allowable values for the data point if it is expressed as an element.

Programming Complexity

One of the most important concerns when designing XML documents, has to be the programming complexity and parser speed for solutions implemented around the XML structures. To illustrate this, let's look at retrieving some information from the two invoice examples we developed, using the element and attribute models.

Parsing technologies – the DOM and SAX – are discussed in Chapters 6 and 7 respectively. Without going into too much depth here, let's make some comparisons between the number of steps it take to retrieve the quantity of the first lineItem for each of the data models. We will first compare the element and attribute approaches when parsed by the DOM, and then look at the same two models under SAX.

The DOM

When an XML document is parsed using the **Document Object Model**, it is pulled into memory and decomposed into a tree that may then be walked by code. In order to access the quantity of the first line item ordered on an invoice, the following steps would be required for the element approach:

1. Get the root element (the `Invoice` element).

2. Go to the first `LineItem` child of the `Invoice` element.

3. Go to the `quantity` child of the `LineItem` element.

4. Go to the text node child of the `quantity` element and return its value.

On the other hand, the following steps would be required to access the document if the attribute approach was used:

1. Get the root element (the `Invoice` element).

2. Get the first `LineItem` child of the `Invoice` element.

3. Iterate through the `LineItem` element for the attribute name-value pair list of the `quantity` attribute, and return its value.

In other words, fewer steps are required to obtain the value of an attribute when using the DOM than to retrieve the value of a text-only element. Since the DOM pulls everything into memory, the odds are that we will see little to no performance difference between the two strategies, but the code will be simpler when using attributes.

SAX

SAX is the **Simple API for XML**, and it is intended to be an event-driven alternative to the memory-hungry DOM. SAX is covered in much more detail in Chapter 7, but suffice to say it has a much smaller memory footprint than the DOM. However, when using SAX to handle documents, things get more complicated. Because SAX is event driven, there are a few additional steps required when obtaining the text value of an element as opposed to retrieving the value of an attribute.

Using the same example with elements, the steps for SAX for elements would be:

1. Before starting, set the Booleans bInInvoice, bInLineItem, and bInQuantity to false, and also, set the value of the counter iLineItem to zero and the string sQuantity to a blank string.

2. In the startElement event, when the Invoice start tag is encountered, set the value of the Boolean variable bInInvoice to true.

3. In the startElement event, when the LineItem start tag is encountered, set the value of the Boolean variable bInLineItem to true if bInInvoice is true, indicating that the processor window is inside a LineItem tag. Also increment the iLineItem counter to indicate which LineItem is being read.

4. In the `startElement` event, when the `quantity` start tag is encountered, if the Boolean `bInLineItem` is `true` and the `iLineItem` counter is 1, set the value of the `bInQuantity` Boolean variable to `true`.

5. In the `characters` event, if `bInQuantity` is `true`, append the received text to the `sQuantity` string.

6. In the `endElement` event, if the `quantity` end tag is encountered, set the `bInQuantity` Boolean to `false`. The value for the quantity is now available for use.

7. In the `endElement` event, if the `LineItem` end tag is encountered, set the `bInLineItem` Boolean to `false`. In addition, if the `Invoice` end tag is encountered, set the `bInInvoice` Boolean to `false`.

Whereas if we were using attributes, these would be the steps:

1. Before starting, set the Boolean `bInInvoice` to `false`, and also set the value of the counter `iLineItem` to zero.

2. In the `startElement` event, when the `Invoice` start tag is encountered, set the value of the Boolean variable `bInInvoice` to `true`.

3. In the `startElement` event, when the `LineItem` start tag is encountered, if `bInInvoice` is `true`, increment the value of the `iLineItem` counter. If this value is 1, pull the value of the `quantity` attribute from the attribute name-value pair set provided as a parameter to the `startElement` event. The value for the quantity is now available for use.

4. In the `endElement` event, if the `LineItem` end tag is encountered, set the `bInLineItem` Boolean to `false`.

5. In the `endElement` event, if the `Invoice` end tag is encountered, set the `bInInvoice` Boolean to `false`.

As you can see, fewer event handlers are required when using attributes to represent data points, and this results in simpler code. The code size improvement will be significant for handlers that are more complex. From a performance perspective, there will probably be virtually no difference – the additional event handlers are not particularly complex.

Document Size

When an element is used to describe a data point, three strings appear in the serialized XML document: the start tag, the value of the data point, and the end tag:

```
<shippingAddress>742 Evergreen Terrace</shippingAddress>
```

However, when an attribute is used to describe a data point, the attribute name, the equals sign, the quotes, and the attribute value are required:

```
shippingAddress="742 Evergreen Terrace"
```

It should be obvious that repeating the name of the data point in the end element tag increases the size of the document, compared with the size of the document when an attribute is used to represent the data point. As a result, more network bandwidth will be consumed when transmitting files using elements than when using attributes; more disk space will be consumed by the documents if they are persisted to files, and so on. If these things are important to us, we should think about using attributes to minimize our document size.

Elements or Attributes – The Conclusion

In the author's opinion, attributes are better suited to the representation of data points than text-only elements are. In other words, attributes are best suited when only one value is to be expected (data points) whereas elements are a necessity when multiple values are needed (like our lineItem in the example above). When using attributes:

❑   Accessing the information is easier.

❑   Documents are smaller.

❑   The disambiguation of structure and data closely mirrors the way structure and data are disambiguated in a relational database.

For the remainder of this book, we will be using attributes to represent data points in our sample structures.

Relationships

When we need to associate groups of data points with other groups of data points in a relational database, we do so by adding a **relationship** between the two tables in question. In order to see how we can do this in XML, let's look at two sample tables Invoice and LineItem and the relationships between them. Here is the SQL script to create the tables (ch02_ex3.sql):

```
CREATE TABLE Invoice (
    invoiceID integer PRIMARY KEY,
    customerID integer,
    orderDate datetime,
    shipDate datetime)
CREATE TABLE LineItem (
    lineItemID integer,
    invoiceID integer,
    productDescription varchar(255),
    quantity integer,
    unitPrice float,
    CONSTRAINT fk_LineItemInvoice
        FOREIGN KEY (invoiceID)
        REFERENCES Invoice (invoiceID))
```

Remember, the scripts in this chapter are for SQL Server – if you want to run them in a different database you may have to modify them. For example, here you'll need to change float to number to run the script in Oracle.

Here are the tables that this script will create, and their relationships:

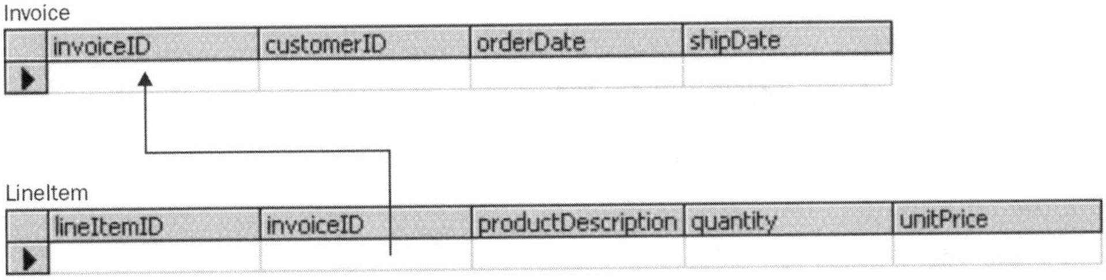

Note that the arrow is used to show the relationship between the tables - how they are linked, by means of keys. The arrow points from the foreign key on the LineItem table to the primary key on the Invoice table. We could say that the LineItem table "refers back to" the Invoice table. We will encounter these diagrams at numerous times as we progress through the book.

In the above table definitions, we have added a foreign key in the LineItem table , invoiceID , that points back to the primary key in the Invoice table. This indicates that the invoiceID value in the LineItem table must always correspond to an invoiceID value for a customer record.

Containment

In XML, one-to-one and one-to-many relationships (such as the one above between Invoice and LineItem) are best represented by **containment**, as shown here (ch02_ex2.dtd):

```
<!ELEMENT Invoice (LineItem+)>
<!ATTLIST Invoice
    orderDate CDATA #REQUIRED
    shipDate CDATA #REQUIRED>
<!ELEMENT LineItem EMPTY>
<!ATTLIST LineItem
    productDescription CDATA #REQUIRED
    quantity CDATA #REQUIRED
    unitPrice CDATA #REQUIRED>
```

An example of a document with this structure looks like this (ch02_ex2.xml):

```
<?xml version="1.0" ?>
<!DOCTYPE Invoice SYSTEM "http://myserver/xmldb/ch02_ex2.dtd">

<Invoice
    orderDate="7/23/2000"
    shipDate="7/28/2000">
    <LineItem
        productDescription="Widgets (3 inch)"
        quantity="17"
        unitPrice="0.10" />
    <LineItem
        productDescription="Grommets (0.5 inch)"
        quantity="22"
        unitPrice="0.05" />
</Invoice>
```

Here, it is clear that the `LineItem` information is part of the `Invoice`. One-to-one and one-to-many relationships (such as the relationship between `Invoice` and `LineItem`) are best represented by containment. However, it is possible to have more complex relationships in relational databases than can be represented with containment alone.

More Complex Relationships – Pointers

Let's extend our previous example by adding a `Product` table (`ch02_ex3.sql`):

```
CREATE TABLE Invoice (
    invoiceID integer PRIMARY KEY,
    customerID integer,
    orderDate datetime,
    shipDate datetime)
CREATE TABLE Product (
    productID integer PRIMARY KEY,
    productShortName varchar (50),
    productDescription varchar(255))
CREATE TABLE LineItem (
    lineItemID integer PRIMARY KEY,
    invoiceID integer
    CONSTRAINT fk_LineItemInvoice
       FOREIGN KEY (invoiceID)
       REFERENCES Invoice (invoiceID),
    productID integer
    CONSTRAINT fk_LineItemProduct
       FOREIGN KEY (productID)
       REFERENCES Product (productID),
    quantity integer,
    unitPrice float)
```

and here are the tables with their relationships:

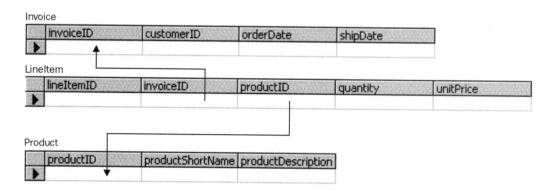

In this case, there is a many-to-many relationship being expressed between `Invoice` and `Product`. Many products may appear on one invoice, and one product may appear on many invoices. In a relational database, this is expressed through the relating table `LineItem`. An invoice may have many line items, and a product may appear on many line items.

Let's see how we could show this more complex relationship in XML. Here is another version of the data model (ch02_ex3.dtd):

```
<!ELEMENT OrderData (Invoice+, Product+)>
<!ELEMENT Invoice (LineItem+)>
<!ATTLIST Invoice
    orderDate CDATA #REQUIRED
    shipDate CDATA #REQUIRED>
<!ELEMENT LineItem EMPTY>
<!ATTLIST LineItem
    productIDREF IDREF #REQUIRED
    quantity CDATA #REQUIRED
    unitPrice CDATA #REQUIRED>
<!ELEMENT Product EMPTY>
<!ATTLIST Product
    productID ID #REQUIRED
    productShortName CDATA #REQUIRED
    productDescription CDATA #REQUIRED>
```

In this case, we are using an ID/IDREF pair to indicate which product is indicated by which line item. We do it this way because we're trying to avoid the repetition of information. If we nested Product inside LineItem, we'd have to repeat the product information for every invoice where it appears.

An example document might look like this (ch02_ex3.xml):

```
<?xml version="1.0" ?>
<!DOCTYPE OrderData SYSTEM "http://myserver/xmldb/ch02_ex3.dtd">

<OrderData>
  <Invoice
      orderDate="7/23/2000"
      shipDate="7/28/2000">
      <LineItem
          productIDREF="prod1"
          quantity="17"
          unitPrice="0.10" />
      <LineItem
          productIDREF="prod2"
          quantity="22"
          unitPrice="0.05" />
  </Invoice>
  <Invoice
      orderDate="7/23/2000"
      shipDate="7/28/2000">
      <LineItem
          productIDREF="prod2"
          quantity="30"
          unitPrice="0.05" />
      <LineItem
          productIDREF="prod3"
          quantity="19"
          unitPrice="0.15" />
  </Invoice>
  <Product
      productID="prod1"
      productShortName="Widgets (3 inch)"
      productDescription="Rubberized Brown Widgets (3 inch)" />
```

```
    <Product
       productID="prod2"
       productShortName="Grommets (0.5 inch)"
       productDescription="Vulcanized Orange Grommets (0.5 inch)" />
    <Product
       productID="prod3"
       productShortName="Sprockets (1 inch)"
       productDescription="Anodized Silver Sprockets (one inch)" />
 </OrderData>
```

In this case, the first invoice is for widgets and grommets, while the second invoice is for grommets and sprockets. However, we've only included the specific product information once for grommets; it's pointed to by the two line items that use it.

Disadvantages of Pointers

While this layout seems better from a relational perspective, there are some problems with it:

❑ **It can slow processing down**. This is because neither the DOM nor SAX provide a way to easily navigate ID/IDREF relationships. (Some implementations of the DOM, such as Microsoft's MSXML parser, provide a way to look up an element by its ID value – but such functions are extensions to the base DOM level 1 architecture as defined by the W3C. The DOM level 2 has just been released, however, and may make this less of a problem once compliant parsers start appearing).

❑ **We might have to parse the document more than once**. If our document is laid out in such a way that the element with a particular ID may appear before the element with an IDREF pointing to that ID, using SAX will be even more of a headache. We'll either need to make multiple passes through the document to get the element to pass through the parse window again, or we'll need to cache the element when it passes through the parse window the first time.

❑ **ID/IDREF (or ID/IDREFS) relationships are unidirectional**. That is, it's easy to navigate from an IDREF to the associated ID, but not as easy to navigate from an ID to any IDREFs that point to that ID. The problem is compounded if the relationship is ID-IDREFS – in that case, all the IDREFS need to be tokenized and each token compared against the ID currently being examined.

More Complex Relationships – Containment

So let's look at an alternative structure for the same database tables, where the product data is contained inside the LineItem element (ch02_ex4.dtd):

```
<!ELEMENT OrderData (Invoice+)>
<!ELEMENT Invoice (LineItem+)>
<!ATTLIST Invoice
    orderDate CDATA #REQUIRED
    shipDate CDATA #REQUIRED>
<!ELEMENT LineItem (Product)>
<!ATTLIST LineItem
    quantity CDATA #REQUIRED
    unitPrice CDATA #REQUIRED>
<!ELEMENT Product EMPTY>
<!ATTLIST Product
    productShortName CDATA #REQUIRED
    productDescription CDATA #REQUIRED>
```

and here is the new sample document (ch02_ex4.xml):

```xml
<?xml version="1.0" ?>
<!DOCTYPE OrderData SYSTEM "http://myserver/xmldb/ch02_ex4.dtd">

<OrderData>
   <Invoice
      orderDate="7/23/2000"
      shipDate="7/30/2000">
      <LineItem
         quantity="17"
         unitPrice="0.10">
         <Product
            productShortName="Widgets (3 inch)"
            productDescription="Rubberized Brown Widgets (3 inch)" />
      </LineItem>
      <LineItem
         quantity="22"
         unitPrice="0.05">
         <Product
            productShortName="Grommets (0.5 inch)"
            productDescription="Vulcanized Orange Grommets (half inch)" />
      </LineItem>
   </Invoice>
   <Invoice
      orderDate="7/23/2000"
      shipDate="7/30/2000">
      <LineItem
         quantity="30"
         unitPrice="0.05">
         <Product
            productShortName="Grommets (2 inch)"
            productDescription="Vulcanized Orange Grommets (two inch)" />
      </LineItem>
      <LineItem
         quantity="19"
         unitPrice="0.15">
         <Product
            productShortName="Sprockets (1 inch)"
            productDescription="Anodized Silver Sprockets (one inch)" />
      </LineItem>
   </Invoice>
</OrderData>
```

While this document does repeat information (the product info for the grommets), it is a superior document to the first one for most applications. Only containment is used, so there are no issues with the DOM or SAX. The document is slightly larger, but since XML is a fairly verbose language anyway, this doesn't present that much of a problem (especially since SAX becomes a viable out of the box solution again if this approach is adopted).

If the consuming system needs to know that the grommets referenced in the first invoice and the grommets referenced in the second invoice are actually the same grommets, we can add a field to the Product structure to make this clear:

```
<OrderData>
    <Invoice
        orderDate="7/23/2000"
        shipDate="7/30/2000">
        <LineItem
            quantity="17"
            unitPrice="0.10">
            <Product
                productNumber="wid-b-1"
                productShortName="Widgets (3 inch)"
                productDescription="Rubberized Brown Widgets (3 inch)" />
        </LineItem>
        <LineItem
            quantity="22"
            unitPrice="0.05">
            <Product
                productNumber="gro-c-2"
                productShortName="Grommets (0.5 inch)"
                productDescription="Vulcanized Orange Grommets (half inch)" />
        </LineItem>
    </Invoice>
    <Invoice
        orderDate="7/23/2000"
        shipDate="7/30/2000">
        <LineItem
            quantity="30"
            unitPrice="0.05">
            <Product
                productNumber="gro-c-2"
                productShortName="Grommets (0.5 inch)"
                productDescription="Vulcanized Orange Grommets (half inch)" />
        </LineItem>
        <LineItem
            quantity="19"
            unitPrice="0.15">
            <Product
                productNumber="spr-d-3"
                productShortName="Sprockets (1 inch)"
                productDescription="Anodized Silver Sprockets (one inch)" />
        </LineItem>
    </Invoice>
</OrderData>
```

The consumer could then match the productNumber attributes between products to identify which referenced products were exactly the same, allowing an RDBMS consumer, for example, to normalize the product data out of the rest of the structure. This approach is better than leaving it to the consumer to reconcile the products based on the product name and description (as the consumer would need to if there was no productNumber attribute provided in the second scenario).

Relationships – Conclusion

When designing XML data structures we should exercise caution when setting up the relationships between the elements in their DTDs. In particular, the use of pointers – IDREF(S)-ID attributes – can have a profound impact on processing performance, especially when the processing engine is SAX.

In addition, the over use of pointing relationships can create difficulties for developers from a structure comprehension and code complexity perspective. However, pointing relationships may be called for in some cases, especially when document size is an issue. We should bear all of this in mind to ensure that the structure we create is well tuned to its purpose.

Sample Modeling Exercise

Having seen several of the issues involved in creating a model for our XML, let's take a look at a working example of a data structure we might want to model in XML.

To illustrate some of the points that we have learnt, we will take two invoices from a fictional widget factory and move them to an XML model:

```
Widgets, Inc.
Invoice
Order Date: 7/23/2000
Ship Date:  7/28/2000

Customer:   Kevin Williams
            744 Evergreen Terrace
            Springfield, KY 12345
Shipper:    FedEx

Item Code   Description        Quantity     Price       Total
1A2A3AB     Widget (3 inch)       17         $0.10       $1.70
2BC3DCB     Grommet (0.5 inch)    22         $0.05       $1.10

Total                                                    $2.80

Widgets, Inc.
Invoice
Order Date: 7/23/2000
Ship Date:  7/28/2000

Customer:   Homer J. Simpson
            742 Evergreen Terrace
            Springfield, KY 12345
Shipper:    UPS

Item Code   Description        Quantity     Price       Total
1A2A3AB     Widget (0.5 inch)     17         $0.10       $1.10
3D1F2GX     Sprocket (2 inch)     22         $0.20       $1.80

Total                                                    $2.90
```

Before We Begin

When looking at the best way to model this information as XML, there are some questions that we need to ask first:

❑   What is the scope of the document?

❑   Which structures are we modeling?

❑   What are the relationships between entities?

❑   Which data points need to be associated with each structure?

So, we shall start by addressing each of these in turn, and see what this leaves us in terms of a relational database model. Then we can turn this into an XML DTD.

What is the Scope of the Document?

The first thing we need to do is to decide what the scope of our XML document will be. This is important because, based on the granularity of the XML documents, an XML repository could be very flexible or very inflexible. So far, we have two invoices that we need to model, so the question here is whether each XML document should represent just one invoice, or potentially more than one. Let's look at the advantages and disadvantages of each:

Using One XML Document Per Invoice

❏   Advantages:

❏   Better control of the documents, locking and unlocking them, as necessary, and atomic access to a single invoice will be reasonably fast.

❏   Disadvantages:

❏   Aggregating information from many different invoices will be time-consuming, as many different documents will need to be accessed, parsed, and processed.

❏   If there is information that could be shared across many invoices (such as product descriptions), it must instead be repeated in each document to maintain atomicity.

Using One XML Document to Represent Many Invoices

❏   Advantages:

❏   Aggregation and information sharing will be much better.

❏   Disadvantages:

❏   The load on the processor will be greater, as the size of the documents will be greater.

❏   Processors attempting to access single invoices will be likely to contend for access to the same XML documents.

To make the decision, we need to think about the anticipated use of the documents. For our purposes, let's assume that each XML document may contain many invoices.

Which Structures Are We Modeling?

Next, we need to identify the structures that are being modeled. These will correspond to the elements we use in our XML structures. In our example, there are five different entities that need to be modeled:

❏   OrderData. This will be the root element we use for the document. Even though it may or may not have semantic information associated with it, (we might pass the date range for which the document applies, for example), we need to add this element because every XML document needs a root element.

❏   Invoice. Each Invoice element will correspond to one physical invoice in our system.

❏   Customer. Each Customer element will correspond to one customer.

❏   Part. Each Part element will correspond to a part that may appear on an invoice.

❏   LineItem. This is important because it gives us a way to relate parts to an invoice while adding additional information about the part's role in that invoice.

What Are the Relationships Between Entities?

Now let's take a look at the relationships between the various entities that we have identified. Looking at the sample invoices, it becomes clear that the following relationships exist:

- ❑ OrderData consists of many Invoices. Each Invoice may be associated with only one OrderData entity.
  - ❑ Each Invoice entity has one Customer entity associated with it. Each Customer entity may be associated with more than one Invoice.
  - ❑ Each Invoice has one or more LineItem entities associated with it. Each LineItem entity appears on exactly one Invoice.
- ❑ Each LineItem entity has one Part entity associated with it. Each Part entity may be associated with more than one LineItem.

Which Data Points Need to be Associated with Each Structure?

Finally, we need to decide which data points are associated with each structure. Here is how the data points map to the structures that we just defined, these will be elements:

- ❑ OrderData:
  - ❑ startDate – the earliest invoice date found in this particular document.
  - ❑ endDate – the latest invoice date found in this particular document.

- ❑ Invoice:
  - ❑ orderDate – the date the invoice was submitted.
  - ❑ shipDate – the date the order placed on the invoice was shipped to the customer.
  - ❑ shipper – the firm used to ship the order.

- ❑ Customer:
  - ❑ name – the customer's name.
  - ❑ address – the customer's street address.
  - ❑ city – the customer's city.
  - ❑ state – the customer's state.
  - ❑ postalCode – the customer's postal code.

- ❑ Part:
  - ❑ itemCode – the alphanumeric code identifying the part to internal systems.
  - ❑ description – the description of the part.

- ❑ lineItem:
  - ❑ quantity – quantity of the part associated with the line item being ordered.
  - ❑ price – price per unit of the part associated with this line item.

Note that we chose not to include the line item total prices, or the grand total price. This is a conscious choice that needs to depend on the performance and compactness requirements of the producer and consumer of this document. We decided that it was better to have the documents more compact than to add redundant information for the totals. However, if we decide we need the totals later, we'll need to calculate them.

So, let's have a look at a diagram of the structure this would leave us with if we were still in the relational database paradigm:

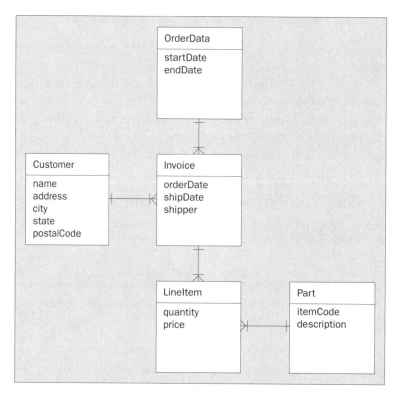

For more explanation of the notation used in this diagram see Appendix B.

Note that in our database, the relationship between Customer and Invoice (and LineItem and Part) might be one-to-zero-or-more rather than one-to-one-or-more; we could have a customer or part that isn't part of an invoice. However, for the purposes of our document, we'll assume that only the customers and parts needed to describe the invoices in the document will be included.

Having answered some questions that help us define a model for this data, let's now translate this into an XML DTD.

Creating the XML DTD

We will approach the writing of the DTD in a manner that reflects the choices we had to make. By approaching the writing of the DTD methodically, it is easier to see our model build up. Here is the order in which we will create the DTD:

- ❑ Add the defined entities.
- ❑ Add the elements to the entities.
- ❑ Create the relationships.

Start With the Structures

First, we defined five structures within the invoices. All of the structures we have identified become elements in our XML DTD, so we start by adding those:

```
<!ELEMENT OrderData EMPTY>
<!ELEMENT Invoice EMPTY>
<!ELEMENT Customer EMPTY>
<!ELEMENT Part EMPTY>
<!ELEMENT LineItem EMPTY>
```

Add the Data Points to the Elements

Next, all of the data points we have defined become attributes of the elements with which they are associated. We'll use the general type of CDATA for all our data points except shipper – we know all the permissible values for this data point, so we'll use an enumeration. We also know that all the information will be required, so all attributes will have the #REQUIRED specifier:

```
<!ELEMENT OrderData EMPTY>
<!ATTLIST OrderData
    startDate CDATA #REQUIRED
    endDate CDATA #REQUIRED>

<!ELEMENT Invoice EMPTY>
<!ATTLIST Invoice
    orderDate CDATA #REQUIRED
    shipDate CDATA #REQUIRED
    shipper (FedEx | UPS | USPS) #REQUIRED>

<!ELEMENT Customer EMPTY>
<!ATTLIST Customer
    name CDATA #REQUIRED
    address CDATA #REQUIRED
    city CDATA #REQUIRED
    state CDATA #REQUIRED
    postalCode CDATA #REQUIRED>

<!ELEMENT Part EMPTY>
<!ATTLIST Part
    itemCode CDATA #REQUIRED
    description CDATA #REQUIRED>

<!ELEMENT LineItem EMPTY>
<!ATTLIST LineItem
    quantity CDATA #REQUIRED
    price CDATA #REQUIRED>
```

Incorporate the Relationships

The final thing we need to do is to model the relationships we defined in our structure. This step requires a certain amount of delicacy, as it's easy to handle this modeling incorrectly. The most important thing to remember is to always use containment whenever possible, and only resort to pointing when it is mandated by our business rules or performance requirements. For the purposes of this exercise, let's assume that we want to keep our documents as small as possible – so we'll use pointing relationships to avoid the repetition of data.

You'll recall that we identified four relationships that needed to be modeled:

❑ OrderData consists of many Invoices. Each Invoice may be associated with only one OrderData entity.

    ❑ Each Invoice entity has one Customer entity associated with it. Each Customer entity may be associated with more than one Invoice.

    ❑ Each Invoice has one or more LineItem entities associated with it. Each LineItem entity appears on exactly one Invoice.

❑ Each LineItem entity has one Part entity associated with it. Each Part entity may be associated with more than one LineItem.

The OrderData to Invoice relationship is pretty straightforward; we'll add a child element to the OrderData element, allowing it to contain one or more Invoices. Similarly, the relationship between Invoices and LineItems is handled the same way. This gives us the following structure:

```
<!ELEMENT OrderData (Invoice+)>
<!ATTLIST OrderData
    startDate CDATA #REQUIRED
    endDate CDATA #REQUIRED>

<!ELEMENT Invoice (LineItem+)>
<!ATTLIST Invoice
    orderDate CDATA #REQUIRED
    shipDate CDATA #REQUIRED
    shipper (FedEx | UPS | USPS) #REQUIRED>

<!ELEMENT Customer EMPTY>
<!ATTLIST Customer
    name CDATA #REQUIRED
    address CDATA #REQUIRED
    city CDATA #REQUIRED
    state CDATA #REQUIRED
    postalCode CDATA #REQUIRED>

<!ELEMENT Part EMPTY>
<!ATTLIST Part
    itemCode CDATA #REQUIRED
    description CDATA #REQUIRED>

<!ELEMENT LineItem EMPTY>
<!ATTLIST LineItem
    quantity CDATA #REQUIRED
    price CDATA #REQUIRED>
```

For the Customer/Invoice one-to-many relationship, we could include a required Customer element for each Invoice – but then if two invoices had the same customer we would have to repeat the data. Instead, we'll create an IDREF attribute on the Invoice element, which points back to the Customer element. Note that when we do this, we still need to have a place to contain the Customer element.

Typically, elements that are only pointed to should be promoted to children of the element for which they will be in scope. This promotes the reusability of fragments of the master document. For example, if the Customer element would only be pointed to from one particular Invoice element, it would appear as a child of that Invoice element, and then the pointing relationship would be redundant. In our case, it may be pointed to by any of the Invoice elements in the document, and thus should be a child of the OrderData element.

Similarly, the `Part`/`LineItem` relationship should be modeled with an `IDREF` attribute, and the `Part` element should appear as a child of the `OrderData` element.

Naturally, for each element that is pointed to, we need to add an `ID` attribute to be the target of the pointer. (Remember, one of our design constraints was that the document needed to be kept as small as possible, which is why we're using this approach instead of using repeated structures.)

So, we are left with the following final structure for our data model (`ch03_ex5.dtd`):

```
<!ELEMENT OrderData (Invoice+, Customer+, Part+)>
<!ATTLIST OrderData
    startDate CDATA #REQUIRED
    endDate CDATA #REQUIRED>

<!ELEMENT Invoice (LineItem+)>
<!ATTLIST Invoice
    orderDate CDATA #REQUIRED
    shipDate CDATA #REQUIRED
    shipper (FedEx | UPS | USPS) #REQUIRED
    customerIDREF IDREF #REQUIRED>

<!ELEMENT Customer EMPTY>
<!ATTLIST Customer
    customerID ID #REQUIRED
    name CDATA #REQUIRED
    address CDATA #REQUIRED
    city CDATA #REQUIRED
    state CDATA #REQUIRED
    postalCode CDATA #REQUIRED>

<!ELEMENT Part EMPTY>
<!ATTLIST Part
    partID ID #REQUIRED
    itemCode CDATA #REQUIRED
    description CDATA #REQUIRED>

<!ELEMENT LineItem EMPTY>
<!ATTLIST LineItem
    quantity CDATA #REQUIRED
    price CDATA #REQUIRED
    partIDREF IDREF #REQUIRED>
```

and that's all there is to it.

Sample XML Documents

We've covered our entities, our attributes, and our relationships, and built a structure suitable for our needs. Let's see how those two sample invoices would be represented in an XML document based on the structures we've defined (`ch02_ex5.xml`):

```
<?xml version="1.0" ?>
<!DOCTYPE OrderData SYSTEM "http://myserver/xmldb/ch02_ex5.dtd">

<OrderData
    startDate="9/12/2000"
    endDate="9/13/2000">
    <Invoice
        orderDate="9/12/2000"
```

```
            shipDate="9/13/2000"
            shipper="FedEx"
            customerIDREF="customer1">
            <LineItem
                quantity="17"
                price="0.10"
                partIDREF="part1" />
            <LineItem
                quantity="22"
                price="0.05"
                partIDREF="part2" />
        </Invoice>
        <Invoice
            orderDate="9/12/2000"
            shipDate="9/13/2000"
            shipper="UPS"
            customerIDREF="customer2">
            <LineItem
                quantity="11"
                price="0.10"
                partIDREF="part1" />
            <LineItem
                quantity="9"
                price="0.20"
                partIDREF="part3" />
        </Invoice>
        <Customer
            customerID="customer1"
            name="Kevin Williams"
            address="742 Evergreen Terrace"
            city="Springfield"
            state="KY"
            postalCode="12345" />
        <Customer
            customerID="customer2"
            name="Homer J. Simpson"
            address="742 Evergreen Terrace"
            city="Springfield"
            state="KY"
            postalCode="12345" />
        <Part
            partID="part1"
            itemCode="1A2A3AB"
            description="Widget (3 inch)" />
        <Part
            partID="part2"
            itemCode="2B3CDCB"
            description="Grommet (0.5 inch)" />
        <Part
            partID="part3"
            itemCode="3D1F2GX"
            description="Sprocket (2 inch)" />
    </OrderData>
```

As you can see, the structure is human-readable and straightforward. The use of human-readable IDs makes it easy for someone to understand what part or customer each IDREF is pointing to. We have captured the structure, the data points, and the relationships we identified in the first part of the development process, and minimized the repetition of data through the use of the pointing relationships.

Summary

In this chapter, we've taken a look at some good strategies for the design of XML structures to support data. We've seen how audience and performance considerations can influence our designs, and taken a look at some ways in which we can standardize our XML structures for consistency and best behavior.

To begin with, we discussed the differences between XML used for marking up text documents, and that used for the representation of raw data. In this book, we'll be concentrating on the latter. The main difference is that the order in which content is presented is less important in the case of data, so we have more flexibility when it comes to designing the structure.

We then moved on to look at XML representations of data in more detail, and saw how we can map data between relational databases and XML:

❑ We've seen that the mixed content and ANY content models for elements are not suited to the representation of data.

❑ The element-only model is useful for nesting elements (structures) – in general, relational database tables become elements with element-only content.

❑ The text-only and EMPTY models can be used to include data points (single values) in our documents. However, we can also use attributes when representing individual data points, and we argue that there are good reasons to why (most of the time) using attributes is the best method.

❑ One-to-one and one-to-many relationships between two elements are generally best represented by containment.

❑ Relationships can also be represented by pointers (an ID/IDREF pair). This can be especially useful in complex many-to-many relationships, and where document size is an issue. However, caution should be exercised when using pointers, as they can have a profound impact on processing performance and complexity.

Using the information presented in this chapter, we should be able to design an XML structure to model any set of structured data we
might encounter. We'll look at designing XML structures for existing databases in the next chapter.

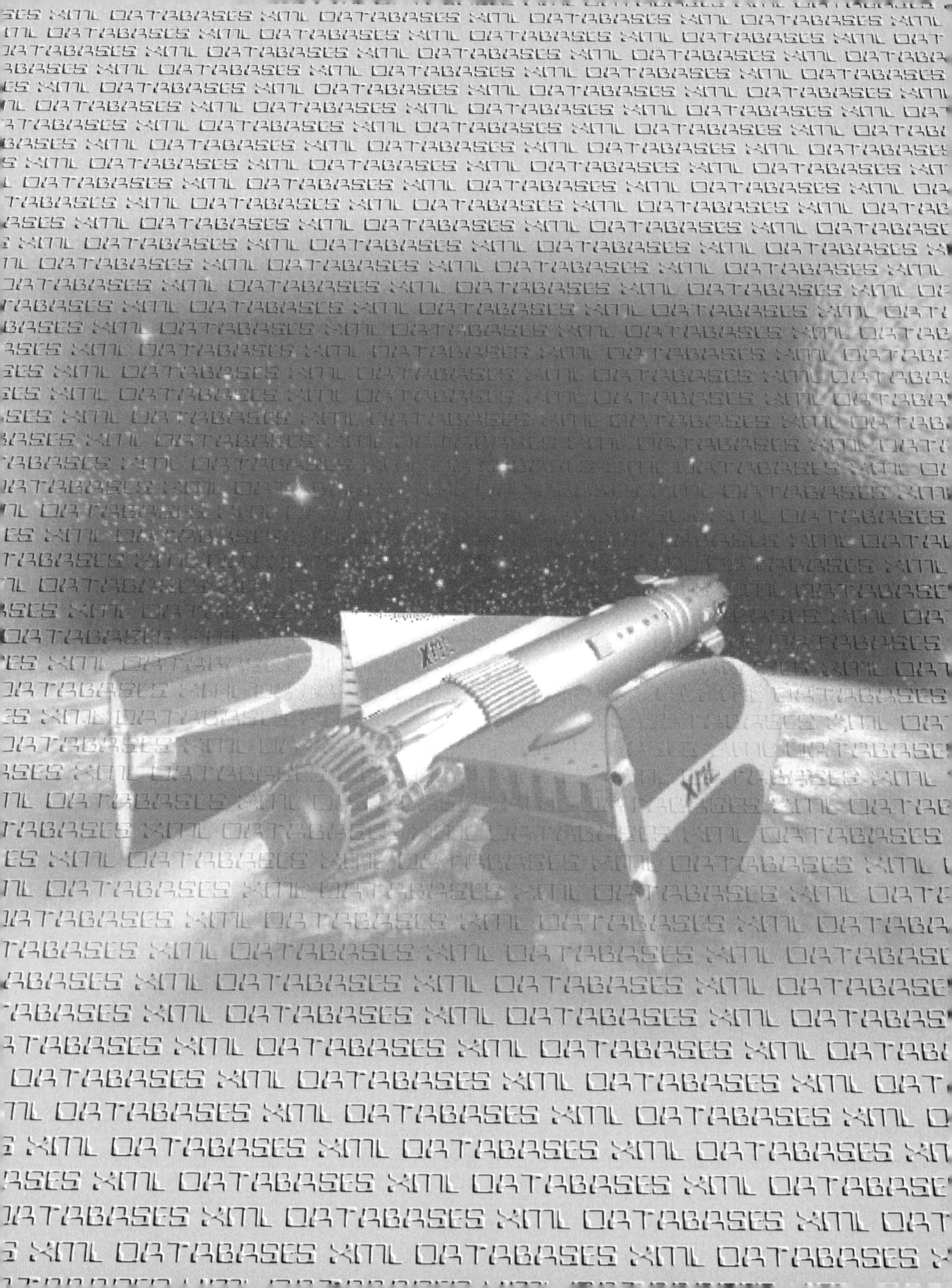
XML DATABASES

2

XML Structures for Existing Databases

In this chapter, we will examine some approaches for taking an existing relational database and moving it to XML.

With much of our business data stored in relational databases, there are going to be a number of reasons why we might want to expose that data as XML:

- ❑ Sharing business data with other systems.
- ❑ Interoperability with incompatible systems.
- ❑ Exposing legacy data to applications that use XML.
- ❑ Business-to-business transactions.
- ❑ Object persistence using XML.
- ❑ Content syndication.

Relational databases are a mature technology, which, as they have evolved, have enabled users to model complex relationships between data that they need to store. In this chapter, we will see how to model some of the complex data structures that are stored in relational databases in XML documents.

To do this, we will be looking at some database structures, and then creating content models using XML DTDs. We will also show some sample content for the data in XML to illustrate this. In the process, we will come up with a set of guidelines that will prove helpful when creating XML models for relational data.

Note that there are some mechanisms out there already that provide a "default" way to derive XML from existing relational database structures. ADO 2.5 will return a "flattened" recordset in an XML representation, while SQL Server 2000 provides direct extraction of joined structures as XML. However, these technologies are still maturing, and can't handle more complex situations, like many-to-many relationships, that must be represented by IDREF-ID pointers. In this chapter, we'll see how structures can be handcrafted to properly represent these types of relationships. We will tune our structures to maximize performance, and minimize document size.

Migrating a Database to XML

In this chapter, we'll be using an example to see how the rules we are creating would be applied in a real-world situation. The structure we'll be migrating to XML is an invoice tracking and reporting system, and looks like this:

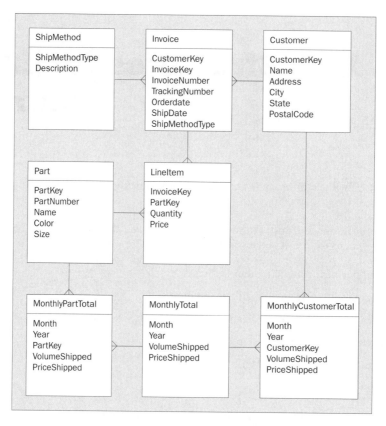

Our invoice database maintains information about invoices submitted by customers, and the parts ordered on those invoices, as well as some summary information about those parts. We'll create our XML structure to hold this information.

Please note that as we're building up our structure over the course of the chapter, some processors may balk at the resultant DTDs created – specifically those that detect orphan element declarations – but the final product should be handled properly by any processor.

Scoping the XML Document

The first rule when designing an XML structure to hold relational information is to decide what the **scope** of the document is. The scope refers to the data and relationships that we want to reproduce when creating our XML document – after all, when exposing the database content, we may not need all of the data that the database stores.

If we think about executing a query against a database, we may only require a subset of the information that it holds. For example, an e-commerce site stores data with relationships that model everything the customer has bought in the past, as well as current orders being processed. If we were writing a CRM application, we would not necessarily need to retrieve all of their past purchases – only those that had recently been placed.

In short, the scope of the document that we are creating is driven by **business requirements** – what the data is going to be used for, and how it is going to be used – and these business requirements may vary widely.

For example, our business requirement could be to transmit information to our accounting office about summarizing the monthly invoice totals, as well as a customer-by-customer breakdown so that billing may be performed. In this case, we may want to send only a certain subset of the information to our accounting office (the shaded tables):

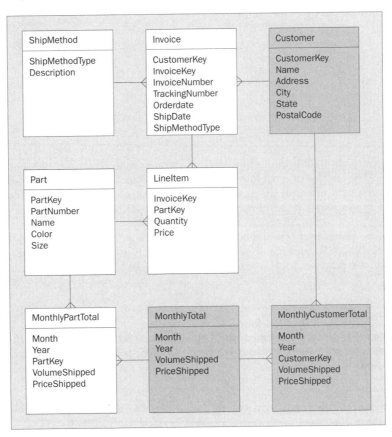

An alternative business requirement might be to transmit an XML copy of an invoice to a customer each time a new invoice is submitted, in which case the subset of the information we would be transmitting might look like this:

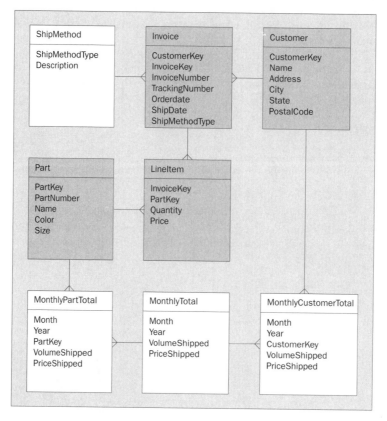

Additionally, we might want to control the specific columns that are transmitted. For example, say our customer wanted to query a product they had ordered; they have their invoice number to identify their purchase, but they aren't necessarily going to care about the invoice tracking number that our application uses internally. The extra number may in fact confuse them more.

By identifying the specific set of tables and columns that are going to be transmitted, we can start to get a feel for how the XML document needs to be laid out. If we happen to have access to a logical data diagram of the database, such as an ErWIN model, it can also be very helpful when constructing our XML.

> **Rule 1: Choose the Data to Include.**
> Based on the business requirement the XML document will be fulfilling, decide which tables and columns from our relational database will need to be included in our documents.

For the purposes of our example, we'll assume that all the information in our structure is relevant to the process (with the exception of the system-generated keys, which we can discard).

Creating the Root Element

Once we've clarified the scope of the document that we need to create, which may be driven by business needs, we need to create the **root element** within which our XML representation of the data is nested.

For our example, we'll create a root element called `<SalesData>` to hold the other elements we will create:

```
<SalesData>
...other elements go here
</SalesData>
```

It's also possible that we may want to add some information to our XML document that isn't part of our relational database. This information might be used to indicate transmittal, routing, or behavioral information. For example, we might want to add a source attribute, so that the consuming process can decide which custom handler needs to be run to parse the document being passed. If we choose to add information about the document like this, it makes the most sense to add it as attributes of the root element we create. As we'll see in Chapter 18, many of the emergent XML servers (such as BizTalk) provide just such a mechanism, known as the **envelope**.

For our example, we'll add an attribute to our root element, to govern what the consuming processor should do with the document when it is received. Specifically, we'll add a `Status` attribute. This attribute will let the processor know whether the information in the document is new, an update to existing data, or a courtesy copy.

So far then, we have the following structure:

```
<!ELEMENT SalesData EMPTY>
<!ATTLIST SalesData
   Status (NewVersion | UpdatedVersion | CourtesyCopy) #REQUIRED>
```

> **Rule 2: Create a Root Element.**
> Create a root element for the document. Add the root element to our DTD, and declare any attributes of that element that are required to hold additional semantic information (such as routing information). Root element's names should describe their content.

Model the Tables

Having defined our root element, the next step is to model the tables that we've chosen to include in our XML document. As we saw in the last chapter, tables map directly to elements in XML.

Loosely speaking, these tables should either be:

❑ **Content tables**, which, for our purposes, simply contain a set of records (for example, all the customer addresses for a certain company).

❑ **Lookup tables**, which contain a list of ID-description pairs, that are used to further classify information, in a particular row of a table, by storing a description for each ID encountered in a content table. Tables such as `ShipMethod` in our example are lookup tables.

*There is another type of table – a **relating** table – whose sole purpose is to express a many-to-many relationship between two other tables. For our purposes, we shall model a table like this as a content table.*

At this stage we will only be modeling content tables. Lookup tables will actually be modeled as enumerated attributes later in the process.

For each content table that we've chosen to include from our relational database, we will need to create an element in our DTD. Applying this rule to our example, we'll add the `<Invoice>`, `<Customer>`, `<Part>`, `<MonthlyTotal>`, and other elements to our DTD:

```
<!ELEMENT SalesData EMPTY>
<!ATTLIST SalesData
  Status (NewVersion | UpdatedVersion | CourtesyCopy) #REQUIRED>
<!ELEMENT Invoice EMPTY>
<!ELEMENT Customer EMPTY>
<!ELEMENT Part EMPTY>
<!ELEMENT MonthlyTotal EMPTY>
<!ELEMENT MonthlyCustomerTotal EMPTY>
<!ELEMENT MonthlyPartTotal EMPTY>
<!ELEMENT LineItem EMPTY>
```

For the moment, we will just add the element definitions to the DTD. We'll come back to ensure that they are reflected in the necessary element content models, (including those of the root element), when we model the relationships between the tables.

Note that we didn't model the `ShipMethod` table, because it's a lookup table. We'll handle this table in Rule 6.

Rule 3: Model the Content Tables.
Create an element in the DTD for each content table we have chosen to model. Declare these elements as EMPTY for now.

Model the Nonforeign Key Columns

Using this rule, we'll create attributes on the elements we have already defined to hold the column values from our database. In a DTD, these attributes should appear in the `!ATTLIST` declaration of the element corresponding to the table in which the column appears.

If a column is a foreign key joining to another table, don't include it in this rule – we'll handle foreign key columns later in the process, when we model the relationships between the elements we have created.

Declare each attribute created this way as having the type CDATA. If the column is defined in your database as not allowing NULL values, then make the corresponding attribute #REQUIRED; otherwise, make the corresponding attribute #IMPLIED.

We have four choices here. #FIXED means the DTD provides the value. #REQUIRED means it must appear in the document. #IMPLIED means that it may or may not appear in the document. Finally, a value with these means that the processor must substitute that value for the attribute if it is not provided in the document. #IMPLIED is the only way to legitimately leave off an attribute value.

If we choose to store table column values as the content of elements, rather than attributes, we can take the same approach – create an element for each data point, and add it to the content list of the element for the table in which the column appears. Use no suffix if the column does not allow nulls; or the optional suffix (?) if the column allows nulls. Be aware that if we take this approach, we'll need to be on the look out for possible name collisions between columns in different tables with the same name. This is not an issue when using attributes.

To summarise:

Does the column allow NULLS?	Elements	Attributes
Allows NULLS	Use the ? suffix	Declare as #IMPLIED
Doesn't allow NULLS	Use no suffix	Declare as #REQUIRED

For our example, remember that we want to keep all the nonforeign key columns, with the exception of the system-generated primary keys:

```
<!ELEMENT SalesData EMPTY>
<!ATTLIST SalesData
  Status (NewVersion | UpdatedVersion | CourtesyCopy) #REQUIRED>
<!ELEMENT Invoice EMPTY>
<!ATTLIST Invoice
    InvoiceNumber CDATA #REQUIRED
    TrackingNumber CDATA #REQUIRED
    OrderDate CDATA #REQUIRED
    ShipDate CDATA #REQUIRED>
<!ELEMENT Customer EMPTY>
<!ATTLIST Customer
    Name CDATA #REQUIRED
    Address CDATA #REQUIRED
    City CDATA #REQUIRED
    State CDATA #REQUIRED
    PostalCode CDATA #REQUIRED>
<!ELEMENT Part EMPTY>
<!ATTLIST Part
    PartNumber CDATA #REQUIRED
    Name CDATA #REQUIRED
    Color CDATA #REQUIRED
    Size CDATA #REQUIRED>
<!ELEMENT MonthlyTotal EMPTY>
<!ATTLIST MonthlyTotal
    Month CDATA #REQUIRED
    Year CDATA #REQUIRED
    VolumeShipped CDATA #REQUIRED
    PriceShipped CDATA #REQUIRED>
<!ELEMENT MonthlyCustomerTotal EMPTY>
<!ATTLIST MonthlyCustomerTotal
    VolumeShipped CDATA #REQUIRED
    PriceShipped CDATA #REQUIRED>
<!ELEMENT MonthlyPartTotal EMPTY>
<!ATTLIST MonthlyPartTotal
    VolumeShipped CDATA #REQUIRED
    PriceShipped CDATA #REQUIRED>
<!ELEMENT LineItem EMPTY>
<!ATTLIST LineItem
    Quantity CDATA #REQUIRED
    Price CDATA #REQUIRED>
```

Note that we left off Month and Year on the <MonthlyPartTotal> and <MonthlySummaryTotal> structures, since these will be dictated by the <MonthlyTotal> element associated with these elements.

> **Rule 4: Modeling Nonforeign Key Columns.**
> Create an attribute for each column we have chosen to include in our XML document (except foreign key columns). These attributes should appear in the `!ATTLIST` declaration of the element corresponding to the table in which they appear. Declare each of these attributes as `CDATA`, and declare it as `#IMPLIED` or `#REQUIRED` depending on whether the original column allowed nulls or not.

Adding ID Attributes

The next step is to create an `ID` attribute for each of the structural (nondata point) elements we have defined so far in our XML database (with the exception of the root element). This is to uniquely identify elements that need to be referred to by other elements.

For the name of the attribute, we use the element name followed by `ID`. This might cause name collisions with other attributes that have already been added to the XML, in which case we need to change the names of these as appropriate. These should be defined as being of type `ID`, and must be declared as `#REQUIRED`. If we add these `ID` attributes to each element for now, we can optionally remove some from the created XML structures when we come to model all of the relationships.

When populating these structures, a unique ID will need to be created for each instance of an element that is generated. We need to ensure that these IDs are unique not only across all elements of a specific type, but across all elements in our document. One way to do this programmatically (assuming that we're using automatically incremented integers for the primary keys in our database) is to use the primary key for the row being created, prefixed by the name of the table in which it appears.

For example, for the customer in our database with the ID number 17, we might use the string `Customer17` for the value of the `CustomerID` attribute on the `Customer` element. If we have nonnumeric keys in our database, or similar table names with numeric suffixes (like `Customer` and `Customer1`), this may cause name collisions – as always, be on the look out for these.

In our example, then, we have:

```
<!ELEMENT SalesData EMPTY>
<!ATTLIST SalesData
   Status (NewVersion | UpdatedVersion | CourtesyCopy) #REQUIRED>
<!ELEMENT Invoice EMPTY>
<!ATTLIST Invoice
   InvoiceID ID #REQUIRED
   InvoiceNumber CDATA #REQUIRED
   TrackingNumber CDATA #REQUIRED
   OrderDate CDATA #REQUIRED
   ShipDate CDATA #REQUIRED>
<!ELEMENT Customer EMPTY>
<!ATTLIST Customer
   CustomerID ID #REQUIRED
   Name CDATA #REQUIRED
   Address CDATA #REQUIRED
   City CDATA #REQUIRED
   State CDATA #REQUIRED
   PostalCode CDATA #REQUIRED>
<!ELEMENT Part EMPTY>
<!ATTLIST Part
   PartID ID #REQUIRED
   PartNumber CDATA #REQUIRED
   Name CDATA #REQUIRED
   Color CDATA #REQUIRED
   Size CDATA #REQUIRED>
```

```
<!ELEMENT MonthlyTotal EMPTY>
<!ATTLIST MonthlyTotal
    MonthlyTotalID ID #REQUIRED
    Month CDATA #REQUIRED
    Year CDATA #REQUIRED
    VolumeShipped CDATA #REQUIRED
    PriceShipped CDATA #REQUIRED>
<!ELEMENT MonthlyCustomerTotal EMPTY>
<!ATTLIST MonthlyCustomerTotal
    MonthlyCustomerTotalID ID #REQUIRED
    VolumeShipped CDATA #REQUIRED
    PriceShipped CDATA #REQUIRED>
<!ELEMENT MonthlyPartTotal EMPTY>
<!ATTLIST MonthlyPartTotal
    MonthlyPartTotalID ID #REQUIRED
    VolumeShipped CDATA #REQUIRED
    PriceShipped CDATA #REQUIRED>
<!ELEMENT LineItem EMPTY>
<!ATTLIST LineItem
    LineItemID ID #REQUIRED
    Quantity CDATA #REQUIRED
    Price CDATA #REQUIRED>
```

> **Rule 5: Add ID Attributes to the Elements.**
> **Add an ID attribute to each of the elements we have created in our XML structure (with the exception of the root element). Use the element name followed by `ID` for the name of the new attribute, watching as always for name collisions. Declare the attribute as type `ID`, and `#REQUIRED`.**

Handling Foreign Keys

In relational database structures, the only way to show a relationship between data kept in different tables is via a foreign key. As we saw in the previous chapter, there are two ways to show this relationship in XML. We can create hierarchical structures, which allow us to use **containment** to show relationships between data (where related information is nested inside a parent element). Alternatively, if we want to keep the XML structures separate – like the tables of a database – we can use an `ID` to **point** to a corresponding structure that has an `IDREF` attribute.

Each way has its benefits and drawbacks. Pointing is more flexible than containment, but pointing relationships may only typically be navigated in one direction by the processor, and tend to be slower than navigating parent-child relationships.

The next thing we need to decide is whether to use containment or pointing to represent the relationships between our tables. In addition, we need to add the enumerated attributes that correspond to the lookup tables we are using. Let's see how to do that first.

Add Enumerated Attributes for Lookup Tables

If we have a foreign key in a table that points to a lookup table, we need to add an enumerated attribute to the element representing the table in which that foreign key appears.

Before we can do so with our example transformation, we need to identify the nature of the relationships between the tables we have selected to include in our XML structures. For each relationship, we need to identify:

- ❑ Whether it's a lookup or content relationship

- ❑ Whether it is a content relationship, and if so the direction in which it will be navigated

This is important in larger structures because some relationships can be navigated in more than one direction, depending on how the relationships are arrived at. As a general rule, relationships should be navigated in the same direction that a program would most often navigate them. For example, in our case we're much more likely to navigate from `Invoice` to `LineItem` than we are to navigate from `LineItem` to `Invoice`.

We need to determine the direction we'll be navigating between our elements because it determines where our `ID-IDREF` relationships should be. Remember that these are effectively unidirectional – it's relatively easy to traverse a structure from an `IDREF` value to an `ID` value, but not the other way around. Deciding how we will normally be traversing our structures helps us to determine how we should structure them. If we need to navigate between two elements in either direction, we may need to add an `IDREF` in each element pointing back to the other element in the relationship. However, this will increase document creation time and size.

Since we want our document to support invoices and monthly summary information, we conclude that we want our relationships to provide a way to navigate from invoices to associated information. For example, we want to be able to go from an invoice, to its line items, to the part associated with each line item; or from an invoice, to the customer who ordered it. Under other circumstances, we might order our relationships differently – for example, if we wanted a customer-centric XML document.

After assessing all the relationships in our structure, we can conclude that the navigation between the tables looks something like this:

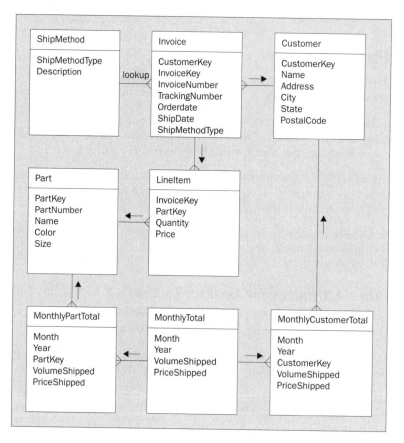

We have a foreign key called `ShipMethodType` pointing to a table called `ShipMethod`, therefore we need to add an enumerated value for `ShipMethod` to the `<Invoice>` element. Let's assume that in our database, the `ShipMethod` table contains the following values:

ShipMethod	Description
1	US Postal Service
2	Federal Express
3	UPS

The enumerated attribute should take the name of the lookup table, and should be declared as `#REQUIRED` if the foreign key does not allow `NULLS`, or `#IMPLIED` otherwise. The determination of the allowable values for the enumeration is a subjective process, and will depend on other design constraints (such as size). The values allowed should typically be human-readable versions of the description for each record.

So, creating an attribute with allowable enumerated values for the three possible lookup values, and adding the attribute to the `<Invoice>` element, gives us this:

```
...
<!ELEMENT Invoice EMPTY>
<!ATTLIST Invoice
    InvoiceID ID #REQUIRED
    InvoiceNumber CDATA #REQUIRED
    TrackingNumber CDATA #REQUIRED
    OrderDate CDATA #REQUIRED
    ShipDate CDATA #REQUIRED>
    ShipMethod (USPS | FedEx | UPS) #REQUIRED>
<!ELEMENT Customer EMPTY>
...
```

> **Rule 6: Representing Lookup Tables.**
> For each foreign key that we have chosen to include in our XML structures that references a lookup table:
> 1. Create an attribute on the element representing the table in which the foreign key is found.
> 2. Give the attribute the same name as the table referenced by the foreign key, and make it **#REQUIRED** if the foreign key does not allow **NULLS** or **#IMPLIED** otherwise.
> 3. Make the attribute of the enumerated list type. The allowable values should be some human-readable form of the description column for all rows in the lookup table.

Add Element Content to the Root Element

When we created the root element for the DTD, and added child elements for tables, we did not define the content models for the elements in the DTD – we said we would cover that when looking at relationships, and here we are.

The next rule, therefore, is to add the content model for the root element to the DTD. We should add element content that is appropriate for the type of information we are trying to communicate in our documents.

For our example, we decided that the primary concepts we want to convey are related to the `Invoice` and `MonthlyTotal`. When we add the elements representing those contents as allowable element content for the root element, we get the following:

```
<!ELEMENT SalesData (Invoice*, MonthlyTotal*)>
<!ATTLIST SalesData
  Status (NewVersion | UpdatedVersion | CourtesyCopy) #REQUIRED>
<!ELEMENT Invoice EMPTY>
...
```

> **Rule 7: Adding Element Content to Root elements.**
> **Add a child element or elements to the allowable content of the root element for each table that models the type of information we want to represent in our document.**

Walk the Relationships

The next rule is a little tricky. We need to walk the relationships between the table (or tables) to add element content or `ID-IDREF(S)` pairs as appropriate. This process is similar to the process we would use when walking a tree data structure – we navigate each of the relationships, then each of the relationships from the children of the previous relationships, and so on, until all the relationships contained in the subset of tables we have chosen to include in our XML document have been traversed. Relationships that lead outside of the subset of tables we're representing do not need to be traversed.

Again, when we have a choice of directions in which a relationship may be followed, we do so in the direction that makes the most business sense – for example, we'll probably need to go from `Invoice` to `LineItem` pretty frequently, but much less often from `LineItem` to `Invoice`. On the other hand, a relationship such as the one between `Customer` and `Invoice` may need to be walked in either direction as frequently, making it necessary to define the relationship in both directions. We need to determine the direction in which the relationships will be walked, in order to determine whether pointing or containment should be used to represent the relationships.

One-to-One or One-to-Many Relationships

First consider the case where a relationship is one-to-one or one-to-many in the direction we selected for the relationship traversal, and the relationship is the only one in the selected subset of tables where this table is the destination of a relationship traversal. Then we should represent the relationship by adding the child element as element content of the parent content.

Assign the multiplicity of the element according to the following table:

If the relationship is	Set the multiplicity to
One-to-one	?
One-to-many	*

For our example DTD, adding the containment relationships gives us the following:

```
<!ELEMENT SalesData (Invoice*, MonthlyTotal*)>
<!ATTLIST SalesData
  Status (NewVersion | UpdatedVersion | CourtesyCopy) #REQUIRED>
<!ELEMENT Invoice (LineItem*)>
```

```
<!ATTLIST Invoice
    InvoiceID ID #REQUIRED
    InvoiceNumber CDATA #REQUIRED
    TrackingNumber CDATA #REQUIRED
    OrderDate CDATA #REQUIRED
    ShipDate CDATA #REQUIRED>
    ShipMethod (USPS | FedEx | UPS) #REQUIRED>

...

<!ELEMENT MonthlyTotal (MonthlyCustomerTotal*, MonthlyPartTotal*)>
<!ATTLIST MonthlyTotal
    MonthlyTotalID ID #REQUIRED
    Month CDATA #REQUIRED
    Year CDATA #REQUIRED
    VolumeShipped CDATA #REQUIRED
    PriceShipped CDATA #REQUIRED>
...
```

> **Rule 8: Adding Relationships through Containment.**
> For each relationship we have defined, if the relationship is one-to-one or one-to-many
> in the direction it is being navigated, and no other relationship leads to the child
> within the selected subset, then add the child element as element content of the parent
> element with the appropriate cardinality.

Many-to-One or Multiple Parent Relationships

If the relationship is many-to-one, or the child has more than one parent, then we need to use pointing to describe the relationship. This is done by adding an IDREF or IDREFS attribute to the element on the parent side of the relationship. The IDREF should point to the ID of the child element. If the relationship is one-to-many, and the child has more than one parent, we should use an IDREFS attribute instead.

> *Note that if we have defined a relationship to be navigable in either direction, for the purposes of this analysis it really counts as two different relationships.*

Note that these rules emphasize the use of containment over pointing whenever it is possible. Because of the inherent performance penalties when using the DOM and SAX with pointing relationships, containment is almost always the preferred solution. If we have a situation that requires pointing, however, and its presence in our structures is causing too much slowdown in our processing, we may want to consider changing the relationship to a containment relationship, and repeating the information pointed to wherever it would have appeared before.

Applying this rule to our example and adding IDREF/IDREFS attributes, we arrive at the following:

```
<!ELEMENT SalesData (Invoice*, MonthlyTotal*)>
<!ATTLIST SalesData
    Status (NewVersion | UpdatedVersion | CourtesyCopy) #REQUIRED>
<!ELEMENT Invoice (LineItem*)>
<!ATTLIST Invoice
    InvoiceID ID #REQUIRED
    InvoiceNumber CDATA #REQUIRED
    TrackingNumber CDATA #REQUIRED
```

```
        OrderDate CDATA #REQUIRED
        ShipDate CDATA #REQUIRED
        ShipMethod (USPS | FedEx | UPS) #REQUIRED
        CustomerIDREF IDREF #REQUIRED>
<!ELEMENT Customer EMPTY>

...

<!ELEMENT MonthlyCustomerTotal EMPTY>
<!ATTLIST MonthlyCustomerTotal
        MonthlyCustomerTotalID ID #REQUIRED
        VolumeShipped CDATA #REQUIRED
        PriceShipped CDATA #REQUIRED
        CustomerIDREF IDREF #REQUIRED>
<!ELEMENT MonthlyPartTotal EMPTY>
<!ATTLIST MonthlyPartTotal
        MonthlyPartTotalID ID #REQUIRED
        VolumeShipped CDATA #REQUIRED
        PriceShipped CDATA #REQUIRED
        PartIDREF IDREF #REQUIRED>
<!ELEMENT LineItem EMPTY>
<!ATTLIST LineItem
        LineItemID ID #REQUIRED
        Quantity CDATA #REQUIRED
        Price CDATA #REQUIRED
        PartIDREF IDREF #REQUIRED>
```

> **Rule 9: Adding Relationships using `IDREF/IDREFS`.**
> Identify each relationship that is many-to-one in the direction we have defined it, or whose child is the child in more than one relationship we have defined. For each of these relationships, add an `IDREF` or `IDREFS` attribute to the element on the parent side of the relationship, which points to the `ID` of the element on the child side of the relationship.

We're getting close to our final result, but there are still a couple of things we need to do to finalize the structure. We'll see how this is done in the next couple of sections.

Add Missing Elements to the Root Element

A significant flaw may have been noticed in the final structure we arrived at in the last section – when building documents using this DTD, there's no place to add a `<Customer>` element. It's not the root element of the document, and it doesn't appear in any of the element content models of any of the other elements in the structure. This is because it is only pointed to, not contained.

Elements that turn out to only be referenced by `IDREF(S)` need to be added as allowable element content to the root element of the DTD. Then, when creating the document, the **orphaned** elements are created within the root element and then pointed to, where appropriate.

Applying this rule to our example, we see that we are missing the `<Customer>` and `<Part>` elements. Adding these as allowable structural content to our root element gives us:

```
<!ELEMENT SalesData (Invoice*, Customer*, Part*, MonthlyTotal*)>
<!ATTLIST SalesData
  Status (NewVersion | UpdatedVersion | CourtesyCopy) #REQUIRED>
<!ELEMENT Invoice (LineItem*)>
...
```

> **Rule 10: Add Missing Elements.**
> **For any element that is only pointed to in the structure created so far, add that element as allowable element content of the root element. Set the cardinality suffix of the element being added to *.**

Discard Unreferenced ID attributes

Finally, we need to discard those ID attributes that we created in Rule 5 that do not have IDREF(S) pointing to them. Since we created these attributes in the process of building the XML structures, discarding them if they are not used does not sacrifice information, and saves developers the trouble of generating unique values for the attributes.

> **Rule 11: Remove Unwanted ID Attributes.**
> **Remove ID attributes that are not referenced by IDREF or IDREFS attributes elsewhere in the XML structures.**

Applying Rule 11 to our example gives us our final structure. On review, the InvoiceID, LineItemID, MonthlyPartTotalID, MonthlyTotalID, and MonthlyCustomerTotalID attributes are not referenced by any IDREF or IDREFS attributes. Removing them, we arrive at our final structure, ch03_ex01.dtd:

```
<!ELEMENT SalesData (Invoice*, Customer*, Part*, MonthlyTotal*)>
<!ATTLIST SalesData
  Status (NewVersion | UpdatedVersion | CourtesyCopy) #REQUIRED>
<!ELEMENT Invoice (LineItem*)>
<!ATTLIST Invoice
  InvoiceNumber CDATA #REQUIRED
  TrackingNumber CDATA #REQUIRED
  OrderDate CDATA #REQUIRED
  ShipDate CDATA #REQUIRED
  ShipMethod (USPS | FedEx | UPS) #REQUIRED
  CustomerIDREF IDREF #REQUIRED>
<!ELEMENT Customer EMPTY>
<!ATTLIST Customer
  CustomerID ID #REQUIRED
  Name CDATA #REQUIRED
  Address CDATA #REQUIRED
  City CDATA #REQUIRED
  State CDATA #REQUIRED
  PostalCode CDATA #REQUIRED>
<!ELEMENT Part EMPTY>
<!ATTLIST Part
  PartID ID #REQUIRED
  PartNumber CDATA #REQUIRED
  Name CDATA #REQUIRED
```

```
   Color CDATA #REQUIRED
   Size CDATA #REQUIRED>
<!ELEMENT MonthlyTotal (MonthlyCustomerTotal*, MonthlyPartTotal*)>
<!ATTLIST MonthlyTotal
   Month CDATA #REQUIRED
   Year CDATA #REQUIRED
   VolumeShipped CDATA #REQUIRED
   PriceShipped CDATA #REQUIRED>
<!ELEMENT MonthlyCustomerTotal EMPTY>
<!ATTLIST MonthlyCustomerTotal
   VolumeShipped CDATA #REQUIRED
   PriceShipped CDATA #REQUIRED
   CustomerIDREF IDREF #REQUIRED>
<!ELEMENT MonthlyPartTotal EMPTY>
<!ATTLIST MonthlyPartTotal
   VolumeShipped CDATA #REQUIRED
   PriceShipped CDATA #REQUIRED
   PartIDREF IDREF #REQUIRED>
<!ELEMENT LineItem EMPTY>
<!ATTLIST LineItem
   Quantity CDATA #REQUIRED
   Price CDATA #REQUIRED
   PartIDREF IDREF #REQUIRED>
```

An Example XML Document

Finally, here's an example of an XML document (ch03_ex01.xml) that would be valid for this DTD:

```
<?xml version="1.0"?>
<!DOCTYPE SalesData SYSTEM "http://myserver/xmldb/ch03_ex01.dtd" >
<SalesData Status="NewVersion">
   <Invoice InvoiceNumber="1"
            TrackingNumber="1"
            OrderDate="01012000"
            ShipDate="07012000"
            ShipMethod="FedEx"
            CustomerIDREF="Customer2">
      <LineItem Quantity="2"
                Price="5"
                PartIDREF="Part2" />
   </Invoice>
   <Customer CustomerID="Customer2"
            Name="BobSmith"
            Address="2AnyStreet"
            City="Anytown"
            State="AS"
            PostalCode="ANYCODE" />
   <Part PartID="Part2"
        PartNumber="13"
        Name="Winkle"
        Color="Red"
        Size="10" />
   <MonthlyTotal Month="January"
                 Year="2000"
                 VolumeShipped="2"
                 PriceShipped="10">
```

```
          <MonthlyCustomerTotal VolumeShipped="5"
                                PriceShipped="25"
                                CustomerIDREF="Customer2" />
          <MonthlyPartTotal VolumeShipped="8"
                            PriceShipped="40"
                            PartIDREF="Part2" />
      </MonthlyTotal>
  </SalesData>
```

Summary

In this chapter, we've seen some guidelines for the creation of XML structures to hold data from existing relational databases. We've seen that this isn't an exact science, and that many of the decisions we will make while creating XML structures will entirely depend on the kinds of information we wish to represent in our documents.

If there's one point in particular we should come away with from this chapter, it's that we need to try to represent relationships in our XML documents with containment as much as possible. XML is designed around the concept of containment – the DOM and XSLT treat XML documents as trees, while SAX and SAX-based parsers treat them as a sequence of branch begin and end events and leaf events. The more pointing relationships we use, the more complicated the navigation of your document will be, and the more of a performance hit our processor will take – especially if we are using SAX or a SAX-based parser.

We must bear in mind as we create these structures that there are usually many XML structures that may be used to represent the same relational database data. The techniques described in this chapter should allow us to optimize our documents for rapid processing and minimum document size. Using the techniques discussed in this chapter, and the next, we should be able to easily move information between our relational database and XML documents.

Here are the eleven rules we have defined for the development of XML structures from relational database structures:

❑ **Rule 1: Choose the Data to Include.**
Based on the business requirement the XML document will be fulfilling, we decide which tables and columns from your relational database will need to be included in our documents.

❑ **Rule 2: Create a Root Element.**
Create a root element for the document. We add the root element to our DTD, and declare any attributes of that element that are required to hold additional semantic information (such as routing information). Root element's names should describe their content.

❑ **Rule 3: Model the Content Tables.**
Create an element in the DTD for each content table we have chosen to model. Declare these elements as EMPTY for now.

❑ **Rule 4: Modeling Non-Foreign Key Columns.**
Create an attribute for each column we have chosen to include in our XML document (except foreign key columns). These attributes should appear in the !ATTLIST declaration of the element corresponding to the table in which they appear. Declare each of these attributes as CDATA, and declare it as #IMPLIED or #REQUIRED depending on whether the original column allows NULLS or not.

❏ **Rule 5: Add ID Attributes to the Elements.**
Add an ID attribute to each of the elements you have created in our XML structure (with the exception of the root element). Use the element name followed by ID for the name of the new attribute, watching as always for name collisions. Declare the attribute as type ID, and #REQUIRED.

❏ **Rule 6: Representing Lookup Tables.**
For each foreign key that we have chosen to include in our XML structures that references a lookup table:
1. Create an attribute on the element representing the table in which the foreign key is found.
2. Give the attribute the same name as the table referenced by the foreign key, and make it #REQUIRED if the foreign key does not allow NULLS or #IMPLIED otherwise.
3. Make the attribute of the enumerated list type. The allowable values should be some human-readable form of the description column for all rows in the lookup table.

❏ **Rule 7: Adding Element Content to Root elements.**
Add a child element or elements to the allowable content of the root element for each table that models the type of information we want to represent in our document.

❏ **Rule 8: Adding Relationships through Containment.**
For each relationship we have defined, if the relationship is one-to-one or one-to-many in the direction it is being navigated, and no other relationship leads to the child within the selected subset, then add the child element as element content of the parent element with the appropriate cardinality.

❏ **Rule 9: Adding Relationships using IDREF/IDREFS.**
Identify each relationship that is many-to-one in the direction we have defined it, or whose child is the child in more than one relationship we have defined. For each of these relationships, add an IDREF or IDREFS attribute to the element on the parent side of the relationship, which points to the ID of the element on the child side of the relationship.

❏ **Rule 10: Add Missing Elements.**
For any element that is only pointed to in the structure created so far, add that element as allowable element content of the root element. Set the cardinality suffix of the element being added to *.

❏ **Rule 11: Remove Unwanted ID Attributes.**
Remove ID attributes that are not referenced by IDREF or IDREFS attributes elsewhere in the XML structures.

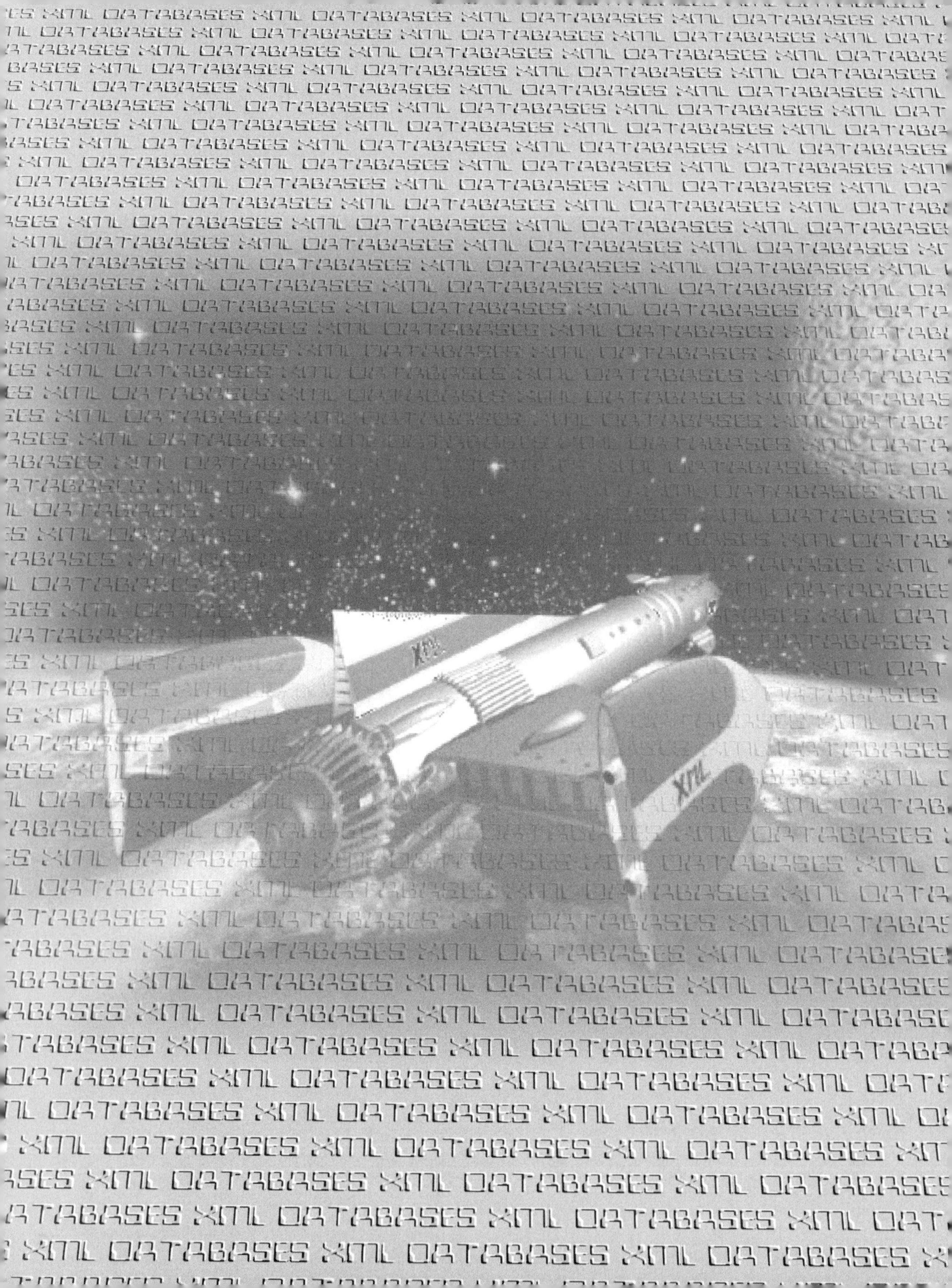
XML DATABASES

Database Structures for Existing XML

So far, we have seen some general points on designing XML structures, and how best to design XML documents to represent existing database structures. In this chapter, we'll take a look at how database structures can be designed to store the information contained in an already existing XML structure.

There are a number of reasons why we might need to move data from an XML repository to a relational database. For example, we might have a large amount of data stored in XML that needs to be queried against. XML (at least with the tools currently available) is not very good at performing queries, especially queries that require more than one document to be examined. In this case, we might want to extract the data content (or some portion of it) from the XML repository and move it to a relational database. Remember that XML's strengths are cross-platform transparency and presentation, while relational databases are vastly better at searching and summarization. Another good reason why we might want to move data into relational structures, would be to take advantage of the relational database's built-in locking and transactional features. Finally, our documents might contain huge amounts of data - more than we need to access when performing queries and/or summarizing data - and moving the data to a relational database will allow us to obtain just the data that is of interest to us.

In this chapter, we will see how the various types of element and attribute content that can occur in XML are modeled in a relational database. In the process of doing this, we will go on to develop a set of rules that can be used to generically transform XML DTDs into SQL table creation scripts.

How to Handle the Various DTD Declarations

As we are looking at creating database structures from existing XML structures, we will approach this chapter by looking at the four types of declarations that may appear in DTDs:

❑ **element** declarations.

❑ **attribute list** declarations.

❑ **entity** declarations.

❑ **notation** declarations.

We can then see how each of these types of declaration can best be modeled in relational database structures. To help us demonstrate this we will create examples that persist XML documents to a SQL database and show the SQL create scripts. So, let's start with element declarations.

Element Declarations

As we have seen, in DTDs there are five types of element declaration:

❑ element-only.

❑ text-only.

❑ EMPTY.

❑ MIXED.

❑ ANY.

So, let's look at each of these in turn, and see how each element content model would be modeled in a relational database.

The Element-only (Structured Content) Model

In this content model, the element may only contain other elements. Let's start with a simple example.

Simple Element Content

In the following DTD (ch03_ex01.dtd) we have a simple content model for an Invoice element:

```
<!ELEMENT Invoice (Customer, LineItem*)>
<!ELEMENT Customer (#PCDATA)>
<!ELEMENT LineItem (#PCDATA)>
```

The Invoice element can have two child elements, a Customer, and zero or more LineItem elements. So, let's see some sample XML that this DTD describes (ch03_ex01.xml):

```
<?xml version="1.0"?>
<!DOCTYPE listing SYSTEM "ch03_ex01.dtd" >

<Invoice>
    <Customer> </Customer>
    <LineItem> </LineItem>
    <LineItem> </LineItem>
</Invoice>
```

This type of element is naturally represented in a relational database by a set of tables.

We can model the relationships between the element and its child element(s) by including a reference from the subelement table back to the element table, in ch03_ex01.sql, as follows:

```
CREATE TABLE Customer (
    CustomerKey integer PRIMARY KEY
    )

CREATE TABLE Invoice (
    InvoiceKey integer PRIMARY KEY,
    CustomerKey integer
    CONSTRAINT FK_Invoice_Customer FOREIGN KEY (CustomerKey)
      REFERENCES Customer (CustomerKey)
    )

CREATE TABLE LineItem (
    LineItemKey integer,
    InvoiceKey integer
    CONSTRAINT FK_LineItem_Invoice FOREIGN KEY (InvoiceKey)
      REFERENCES Invoice (InvoiceKey)
    )
```

When the above script is run, it creates the following set of tables:

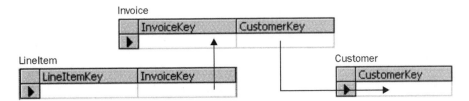

Note that we've added key columns to each table; the relationship between the foreign keys in the Customer and LineItem tables, and the primary key in the Invoice table, as indicated by the arrows.

It's good practice when developing relational databases to keep a "data-clear" ID (a value that does not contain application data, but that uniquely identifies each record) on each table. Since XML doesn't provide an ID *per se* (ID attributes are handled a little differently, as we'll see later), it makes sense to generate one whenever a row is added to one of our relational database tables.

> **Rule 1: Always Create a Primary Key.**
> **Whenever creating a table in the relational database:**
> **1. Add a column to it that holds an automatically incremented integer.**
> **2. Name the column after the element with Key appended.**
> **3. Set this column to be the primary key on the created table.**

Note that there isn't any way in the table creation script to specify that each invoice must have exactly one customer, or each invoice may have zero or more line items. This means that it is technically possible to populate the relational structures with data that could not be used to create a valid XML document:

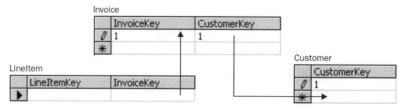

So, while this data set is perfectly acceptable given the table structures we have defined, it is not valid given the XML constraints we have defined - there are no line items associated with invoice 1. If we want to enforce more strict rules such as this in our relational database, we'll need to add triggers or other mechanisms to do so.

So, we have seen how we can transfer a simple content model to a relational structure, but that it is not possible to enforce the rules of the DTD unless we use a trigger or some other code mechanism to enforce those rules. Next, let's look at what happens with a more complex content model.

Elements That Contain One Element OR Another

We can have greater problems when defining more complex relationships in XML that cannot be represented in table creation scripts. For example, say we had this hypothetical data model:

```
<!ELEMENT A (B | (C, D))>
<!ELEMENT B (...)>
<!ELEMENT C (...)>
<!ELEMENT D (...)>
```

Here element A can contain either element B or element C followed by element D. The best we can do with this sample structure is something like this:

```
CREATE TABLE A (
    AKey integer,
    )

CREATE TABLE B (
    BKey integer,
    AKey integer,
    )

CREATE TABLE C (
    CKey integer,
    AKey integer,
    )

CREATE TABLE D (
    DKey integer,
    AKey integer,
    )
```

The table structure produced by the above script looks like this:

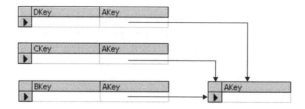

Because there's no way we can enforce the "choice" mechanism in our relational database, there's no way to specify that for an A row we might have a B row, or that we may have a C row and a D row, but that we are not going to get both a B row, and a C and D row.

If we want to enforce more complex relationships like this in our database, we'll need to add triggers or other logic that prevents nonvalidating cases from occurring. For example, we might add a trigger on an insertion to the B table that removes the C and D rows for the A row referenced in the B row, and vice versa.

Rule 2: Basic Table Creation.
For every structural element found in the DTD:
1. Create a table in the relational database.
2. If the structural element has exactly one allowable parent element (or is the root element of the DTD), add a column to the table. This column will be a foreign key that references the parent element.
3. Make the foreign key required.

Subelements That Can Be Contained By More Than One Element

An other problem we may run into is where a particular subelement may be contained in more than one element. Let's take a look at an example (ch03_ex02.dtd) to see how to work around the problem.

```
<!ELEMENT Invoice (Customer, LineItem*)>
<!ELEMENT Customer (Address)>
<!ELEMENT LineItem (Product)>
<!ELEMENT Product (Manufacturer)>
<!ELEMENT Manufacturer (Address)>
<!ELEMENT Address (#PCDATA)>
```

The interesting point to note here, is that the Address element can be a child of Customer or of Manufacturer. Here is some sample XML that represents the structure in this DTD, ch03_ex02.xml:

```
<?xml version="1.0"?>
<!DOCTYPE listing SYSTEM "ch03_ex02.dtd" >

<Invoice>

    <Customer>
        <Address> </Address>
    </Customer>

    <LineItem>
        <Product>
            <Manufacturer>
                <Address> </Address>
            </Manufacturer>
        </Product>
    </LineItem>

    <LineItem>
...
    </LineItem>

</Invoice>
```

In this case, how do we represent the `Address` element? We can't simply add an `Address` table that has both a `ManufacturerKey` and a `CustomerKey` (as we did in the first example when `Customer` and `LineItem` were both foreign keys to `Invoice`). If we did this we would associate the manufacturer with the same address as the customer – by enforcing the foreign keys, we would always have to associate both records with a particular address.

To overcome this problem, we have to adopt a slightly different approach. There is more than one solution to this problem, so let's start off by looking at what happens if we do not add a foreign key.

Don't Add the Foreign Key

The first way to get around this problem would be to create a structure where the `Address` table would contain both the `ManufacturerKey` and `CustomerKey` fields, but the foreign key wouldn't be added, as shown here, in `ch03_ex02.sql`:

```
CREATE TABLE Customer (
    CustomerKey integer,
    )

CREATE TABLE Manufacturer (
    ManufacturerKey integer,
    )

CREATE TABLE Address (
    CustomerKey integer NULL,
    ManufacturerKey integer NULL,
    )
```

Here are the tables that this script would generate:

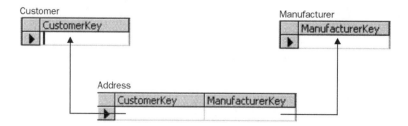

This would work, but could lead to performance degradation on most relational database platforms (depending on the way joins are handled internally), and is not typically a good idea. So, let's look at some other options.

Use an AddressKey Field in Customer and Manufacturer Instead

As another option, we could move the `AddressKey` into the `Customer` and `Manufacturer` tables, as shown in the following script (`ch03_ex03.sql`):

```
CREATE TABLE Address (
    AddressKey integer, PRIMARY KEY (AddressKey)
    )
```

```
CREATE TABLE Customer (
    CustomerKey integer,
    AddressKey integer,

    CONSTRAINT FK_Customer_Address FOREIGN KEY (AddressKey)
        REFERENCES Address (AddressKey))

CREATE TABLE Manufacturer (
    ManufacturerKey integer,
    AddressKey integer,

    CONSTRAINT FK_Manufacturer_Address FOREIGN KEY (AddressKey)
        REFERENCES Address (AddressKey))
```

This script serves to create the following table structure:

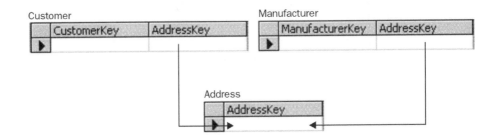

This works very well when the `Address` subelement appears only once in each element. However, what would happen if the `Address` subelement could appear more than once in a particular element, for example maybe we have a separate invoice address and delivery address (in the DTD this could be represented by the + or * modifier)? Here, one `AddressKey` would not then be sufficient, and the design would not work.

Promote Data Points

If all of the relationships that the subelement participates in are one-to-one, promoting the data points to the next higher structure is a good solution, as seen in the following, `ch03_ex04.sql`:

```
CREATE TABLE Customer (
    CustomerKey integer,
    CustomerAddress varchar(30),
    CustomerCity varchar(30),
    CustomerState char(2),
    CustomerPostalCode varchar(10))

CREATE TABLE Manufacturer (
    ManufacturerKey integer,
    ManufacturerAddress varchar(30),
    ManufacturerCity varchar(30),
    ManufacturerState char(2),
    ManufacturerPostalCode varchar(10))
```

This script creates the following tables:

Manufacturer

	ManufacturerKey	ManufacturerAddress	ManufacturerCity	ManufacturerState	ManufacturerPostalCode
▶					

Customer

	CustomerKey	CustomerAddress	CustomerCity	CustomerState	CustomerPostalCode
▶					

This solution works just as well as moving the foreign key to the parent elements. It may also make more sense from a relational database perspective (improving query speed) as well. How many databases have you worked on that stored general address information separate from the other information about the addressee?

Add Intermediate Tables

This is the most general case, and will handle the situation where multiple addresses may appear for the same customer or manufacturer - see ch03_ex05.sql, below:

```
CREATE TABLE Customer (
    CustomerKey,
    ...)

CREATE TABLE Manufacturer (
    ManufacturerKey,
    ...)

CREATE TABLE Address (
    AddressKey,
    ...)

CREATE TABLE CustomerAddress (
    CustomerKey,
    AddressKey)
CONSTRAINT FK_CustomerAddress_Customer FOREIGN KEY (CustomerKey)
    REFERENCES Customer (CustomerKey)
CONSTRAINT FK_CustomerAddress_Address FOREIGN KEY (AddressKey)
    REFERENCES Address (AddressKey)

CREATE TABLE ManufacturerAddress (
    ManufacturerKey,
    AddressKey)
CONSTRAINT FK_ManufacturerAddress_Manufacturer FOREIGN KEY (ManufacturerKey)
    REFERENCES Manufacturer (ManufacturerKey)
CONSTRAINT FK_ManufacturerAddress_Address FOREIGN KEY (AddressKey)
    REFERENCES Address (AddressKey)
```

This creates the table structure shown below:

It is worth noting, however, that this will cause significant performance degradation when retrieving an address associated with a particular customer or manufacturer, because the query engine will need to locate the record in the intermediate table before it can retrieve the final result. However, this solution is also the most flexible in terms of how items of data may be related to one another. Our approach will vary depending on the needs of our particular solution.

Conclusion

We have seen several solutions for representing different element content models. When dealing with element-only content, we have seen that we should create a table in our database for each element. However, because of the constraints that a DTD can impose upon the XML it is describing, it can be difficult to model these in the database.

Hopefully we should not have to encounter the last situation we looked at – where an element can be a child of more than one element and that it can have different content – too often. But if we do have to deal with it, when possible we should try to move the foreign key into the parent elements (the second solution we presented) or promote the data points in the subelement (the third solution). If not, then we should go with the intermediate table solution and be aware of the inherent performance consequences.

> **Rule 3: Handling Multiple Parent Elements.**
> If a particular element may have more than one parent element, and the element may occur in the parent element zero times or one time:
> 1. Add a foreign key to the table representing the parent element that points to the corresponding record in the child table, making it optional or required as makes sense.
> 2. If the element may occur zero-or-more or one-or-more times, add an intermediate table to the database that expresses the relationship between the parent element and this element.

So, we've seen how to create tables that represent structural content for elements, and how to link them to other structural content. But that only works for subelements that do not have the text-only content model. Let's see how to handle text only next.

The Text-only Content Model

If we have an element that has text-only content, it should be represented by a column in our database added to the table corresponding to the element in which it appears. Let's look at an example DTD (ch03_ex06.dtd):

```
<!ELEMENT Customer (Name, Address, City?, State?, PostalCode)>
<!ELEMENT Name (#PCDATA)>
<!ELEMENT Address (#PCDATA)>
<!ELEMENT City (#PCDATA)>
<!ELEMENT State (#PCDATA)>
<!ELEMENT PostalCode (#PCDATA)>
```

Here we are trying to store the customer details. For example, here is some sample XML (ch03_ex06.xml):

```
<?xml version="1.0"?>
<!DOCTYPE listing SYSTEM "ch03_ex06.dtd" >
```

```
<Customer>
    <Name> </Name>
    <Address> </Address>
    <City> </City>
    <State> </State>
    <PostalCode> </PostalCode>
</Customer>
```

The corresponding table creation script (`ch03_ex06.sql`) might look like this:

```
CREATE TABLE Customer (
    CustomerKey integer,
    Name varchar(50),
    Address varchar(100),
    City varchar(50) NULL,
    State char(2) NULL,
    PostalCode varchar(10))
```

which would create the following table:

CustomerKey	Name	Address	City	State	PostalCode

Note that we have arbitrarily assigned sizes to the various columns. Remember that DTDs are extremely weakly typed - all we know is that each of these elements may contain a string of unknown size. If we want to impose constraints like these on our database, we need to make sure that any XML documents we store in these structures meet the constraints we have imposed. If we choose to use XML Schemas (once they become available), this problem will disappear.

Since `City` and `State` are optional fields in our `Customer` structure, we've allowed them to be NULL in our table – if the elements have no value in the XML document, set the appropriate columns to NULL in the table.

Rule 4: Representing Text-Only Elements.
If an element is text-only, and may appear in a particular parent element once at most:
1. Add a column to the table representing the parent element to hold the content of this element.
2. Make sure that the size of the column created is large enough to hold the anticipated content of the element.
3. If the element is optional, make the column nullable.

This covers elements that are specified with either no modifier or the `?` modifier, but there will be cases where we will have something more complex.

Multiple Text-Only Elements

There may be times when we have to deal with more than one text-only element. Let's look at an example where we can have more than one customer name (`ch4_ex07.dtd`):

```
<!ELEMENT Customer (Name+, Address, City?, State?, PostalCode)>
<!ELEMENT Name (#PCDATA)>
<!ELEMENT Address (#PCDATA)>
<!ELEMENT City (#PCDATA)>
<!ELEMENT State (#PCDATA)>
<!ELEMENT PostalCode (#PCDATA)>
```

Here, we actually need to add another table to represent the customer name:

```
CREATE TABLE Customer (
    CustomerKey integer,
    Address varchar(100),
    City varchar(50) NULL,
    State char(2) NULL,
    PostalCode varchar(10),
    PRIMARY KEY (CustomerKey))

CREATE TABLE CustomerName (
    CustomerKey integer,
    Name varchar(50)
    CONSTRAINT FK_CustomerName_Customer FOREIGN KEY (CustomerKey)
        REFERENCES Customer (CustomerKey))
```

This script gives us the following table structure:

For each instance of the child `Name` element under the `Customer` element, a new record is added to the `CustomerName` table with a `CustomerKey` linking back to that `Customer` element.

Note that if this text-only element may appear in more than one parent element, we need to add an intermediate table (similar to the one we used in Rule 3) to show the relationship between the parent element and the child element.

Rule 5: Representing Multiple Text Only Elements
If an element is text-only, and it may appear in a parent element more than once:
1. Create a table to hold the text values of the element and a foreign key that relates them back to their parent element.
2. And if the element may appear in more than one parent element more than once, create intermediate tables to express the relationship between each parent element and this element.

Note that the three preceding rules will often need to be used at the same time. For example, in an XML structure that uses text-only elements to represent data we might have the following:

```
<!ELEMENT Invoice (InvoiceDate, InvoiceNumber, Customer, LineItem*)>
<!ELEMENT Customer (...)>
<!ELEMENT LineItem (...)>
<!ELEMENT InvoiceDate (#PCDATA)>
<!ELEMENT InvoiceNumber (#PCDATA)>
```

In this case, applying both parts of rule 5 simultaneously yields the following structure, (ch03_ex08.sql):

```
CREATE TABLE Invoice (
    InvoiceKey integer,
    InvoiceDate datetime,
    InvoiceNumber integer,
    PRIMARY KEY (InvoiceKey))

CREATE TABLE Customer (
    CustomerKey integer,
    InvoiceKey integer,

    CONSTRAINT FK_Customer_Invoice FOREIGN KEY (InvoiceKey)
      REFERENCES Invoice (InvoiceKey))

CREATE TABLE LineItem (
    LineItemKey integer,
    InvoiceKey integer,

    CONSTRAINT FK_LineItem_Invoice FOREIGN KEY (InvoiceKey)
      REFERENCES Invoice (InvoiceKey))
```

This script would generate the following tables:

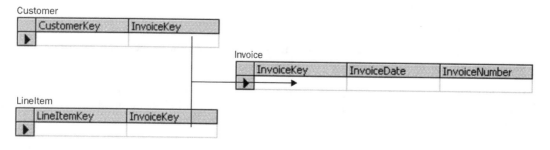

Designing our structures with these intermediate tables, will allow us to express the multiple occurrences of a text element, within a parent element, in our relational database.

The EMPTY Content Model

In a system where attributes are used to contain data points, the EMPTY content model will often be encountered. An element with the EMPTY content model should be modeled as a table - columns in that table will come either from this element's relationships with its parents (foreign keys) or any attributes associated with this element (which we'll discuss a little later). For example, we might see the following structure (ch03_ex09.dtd):

```
<!ELEMENT Customer EMPTY>
<!ATTLIST Customer
    Name CDATA #REQUIRED
    Address CDATA #REQUIRED
    City CDATA #IMPLIED
    State CDATA #IMPLIED
    PostalCode CDATA #IMPLIED>
```

The following XML (ch03_ex09.xml) can be represented by such a DTD:

```
<?xml version="1.0"?>
<!DOCTYPE listing SYSTEM "ch03_ex09.dtd" >

<Customer Name="Bob"
          Address="Somewhere"
          City="Sometown"
          State="Someplace"
          PostalCode="SC" />
```

This would translate to the following script in a relational database (ch03_ex09.sql):

```
CREATE TABLE Customer (
    CustomerKey integer,
    Name varchar(50),
    Address varchar(100),
    City varchar(50) NULL,
    State char(2) NULL,
    PostalCode varchar(10))
```

which would produce the following table:

CustomerKey	Name	Address	City	State	PostalCode

We'll see more examples of the EMPTY content model when we talk about the proper handling of attributes.

> **Rule 6: Handling Empty Elements**
> **For every EMPTY element found in the DTD:**
> **1. Create a table in the relational database.**
> **2. If the structural element has exactly one allowable parent element, add a column to the table - this column will be a foreign key that references the parent element.**
> **3. Make the foreign key required.**

These three content models should be the ones we encounter the most often - especially in structures that were designed to hold data. However, we might be unlucky enough to have to contend with the mixed or ANY content models - so let's take a look at them next.

The Mixed Content Model

We will remember that an element having the mixed content model provides a list of possible child elements that may appear, along with text content, in any order and with any frequency. So, for example, let's look at the model for the paragraph element in XHTML 1.0 (ch03_ex10.dtd):

```
<!ELEMENT p (#PCDATA | a | br | span | bdo | object | img | map | tt | i | b |
            big | small | em | strong | dfn | code | q | sub | sup | samp |
            kbd | var | cite | abbr | acronym | input | select | textarea |
            label | button | ins | del | script | noscript)*>
```

Whew! What this means is that a <p> element, in XHTML 1.0, may contain any of the other elements listed, or text data (#PCDATA), in any combination, in any order. This would not be fun to store in a relational database, but it is not impossible either. Let's look at one possible solution (ch03_ex10.sql).

```
CREATE TABLE p (
   pKey integer,
   PRIMARY KEY (pKey))

CREATE TABLE TableLookup (
   TableLookupKey integer,
   TableName varchar(255),
   PRIMARY KEY (TableLookupKey))

CREATE TABLE TextContent (
   TextContentKey integer,
   ElementName varchar(255) NULL,
   TextContent varchar(255))

CREATE TABLE pSubelements (
   pKey integer
   CONSTRAINT FK_pSubelements_p FOREIGN KEY (pKey)
      REFERENCES p (pKey),
   TableLookupKey integer
   CONSTRAINT FK_pSubelements_TableLookup FOREIGN KEY (TableLookupKey)
      REFERENCES TableLookup (TableLookupKey),
   TableKey integer,
   Sequence integer

   )
```

This gives us the following table structure:

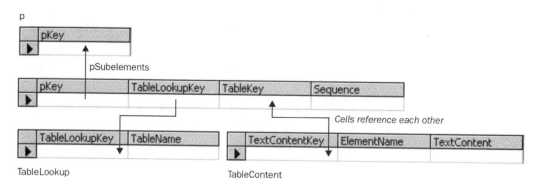

How does this work? Well, the **p** table corresponds to the \<p> element - each \<p> element will correspond to one row in the **p** table. Beyond that, it gets interesting. Let's see an example before we dig deeper. Say we use our definition from before:

```
<!ELEMENT p (#PCDATA | a | br | span | bdo | object | img | map | tt | i | b |
          big | small | em | strong | dfn | code | q | sub | sup | samp |
          kbd | var | cite | abbr | acronym | input | select | textarea |
          label | button | ins | del | script | noscript)*>
```

For the sake of argument, let's pretend that all the other elements have other structures embedded in them. We'll discuss how to handle embedded text-only content in a mixed-content model a little later in the chapter. So, take the following document fragment:

```
<p>This is some text. Here's something in <b>bold</b>, and something in
<i>italics</i>. And finally, here's the last of the text.</p>
```

How do we represent this? Well, we'll have a column in the **p** table, of course:

	pKey
𝟘	1
✱	

We will pre-populate the `TableLookup` table with one row for each element that corresponds to a table in our database. We will also add a record with a key of 0 that corresponds to our generic text table, called `TextContent`:

	TableLookupKey	TableName
	0	Textcontent
	1	p
	2	a
	3	br
	4	span
	5	bdo
	6	object
	7	img
	8	map
	9	tt
	10	i
	11	b
	12	big
	13	small
	14	em
▶	15	strong
	16	dfn
	17	code
	18	q
	19	sub
	20	sup
	21	samp
	22	kbd
	23	var
	24	cite
	25	abbr
	26	acronym
	27	input
	28	select
	29	textarea
	30	label
	31	button
	32	ins
	33	del
	34	script
	35	noscript
✱		

Now, let's take a look at the `pSubelements` table. For each node contained in a particular <p> element, we'll create a record in this table linking it to the particular bit of information associated with it. If we decompose the <p> element in our example, we will see that it has the following children:

- ❑ Text node: `"This is some text. Here's something in "`
- ❑ A <b> element
- ❑ Text node: `", and something in "`
- ❑ An <i> element
- ❑ Text node: `". And finally, here's the last of the text."`

We represent this in our tables like this:

pSubelements

pKey	TableLookupKey	TableKey	Sequence
1	0	1	1
1	11	1	2
1	0	2	3
1	10	1	4
1	0	3	5

Text Content

TextContentKey	ElementName	TextContent
1	NULL	This is some text. Here's something in
2	NULL	, and something in
3	NULL	here's the last of the text.

The `pSubelements` table tells us that there are five pieces of information in the p element. The first, third, and fifth ones are text - that's why the table lookup ID is 0. To discover the value of these text strings, we take the `TableKey` and use it to look up the appropriate text string in the `TextContent` table. For the second and fourth pieces of information, we use the value of the `TableLookupKeys` to find out what kind of element was found in these positions - a <b> element and an <i> element, respectively. We can then go to the tables representing those elements to discover what further content they hold.

Note that there's another column in `TextContent` that we haven't used yet - the `ElementName` column. This column should be used if the subelement has a text-only content model. This keeps us from needing to add another table that simply holds a text value, and is similar to the way we deal with text-only content for subelements of structural elements.

So, if we take our previous example and assume that all of the possible subelements may only contain text, we will represent the content in our data tables in this way:

pSubelements

pKey	TableLookupKey	TableKey	Sequence
1	0	1	1
1	11	1	2
1	0	2	3
1	10	1	4
1	0	3	5

TextContent

	TextContentKey	ElementName	TextContent
	1	NULL	This is some text. Here's something in
	2	"b"	bold
	3	NULL	, and something in
	4	"i"	italics
	5	NULL	. And finally, here's the last of the text
▶			

The content definition for the element will tell us what the allowable values for ElementName and/or TableLookupKey are. If we want to constrain this in the database, we'll need to add a trigger or some other mechanism to prevent unacceptable values from appearing in these columns for p elements or their text subelements.

> **Rule 7: Representing Mixed Content Elements.**
> **If an element has the mixed content model:**
> **1. Create a table called TableLookup (if it doesn't already exist) and add rows for each table in the database. Also add a row zero that points to a table called TextContent.**
> **2. Create this table with a key, a string representing the element name for text only elements, and a text value.**
> **3. Next, create two tables - one for the element, and one to link to the various content of that element - called the element name, and the element name followed by subelement, respectively.**
> **4. In the subelement table, add a foreign key that points back to the main element table, a table lookup key that points to the element table for subelement content, a table key that points to the specific row within that table, and a sequence counter that indicates that subelement or text element's position within this element.**

By now, it is probably becoming understandable jus why we should avoid this content model for the representation of data - the resulting relational structures are difficult to navigate and search, and the parse and store process is relatively complex. But before we steer back to calmer waters, we need to briefly discuss the ANY content model.

The ANY Content Model

Fortunately (or unfortunately), the ANY content model is simply a more general case of the specific mixed content case defined above. The same strategy may be employed to store an element with the ANY content model - the only difference being that there is no constraint on the allowable values of the ElementName and TableLookupKey. The ANY content model, by definition, allows any element defined in the DTD to appear here. We won't bother with another example here, as the technique for storing an element with the ANY content model is exactly the same as the technique for storing a mixed-content element.

> **Rule 8: Handling the "ANY" Content Elements.**
> **If an element has the ANY content model:**
> **1. Create a table called TableLookup (if it doesn't already exist) and add rows for each table in the database.**
> **2. Add a row zero that points to a table called TextContent.**
> **3. Create this table with a key, a string representing the element name for text-only elements, and a text value.**
> **4. Create two tables - one for the element and one to link to the various content of that element - name these after the element name and the element name followed by subelement, respectively.**
> **5. In the subelement table, add a foreign key that points back to the main element table, a table lookup key that points to the element table for subelement content, a table key that points to the specific row within that table, and a sequence counter that indicates that subelement or text element's position within this element.**

Next, let's take a look at attributes and how they are represented in a relational database.

Attribute List Declarations

There are six types of attribute that we will need to develop a handling strategy for if we are to store them in our relational database. These types are:

❑   CDATA

❑   Enumerated lists

❑   ID

❑   IDREF/IDREFS

❑   NMTOKEN/NMTOKENS

❑   ENTITY/ENTITIES

We'll tackle each one in turn, as we did with the element content models, and see how we can build structures to persist them.

CDATA

Attributes that are of type CDATA are the ones most commonly encountered. We'll recall, that these attributes may take any string value. This makes them ideal candidates for columns associated with the table that was created by the element to which they belong. For example, take this DTD (ch03_ex11.dtd):

```
<!ELEMENT Customer EMPTY>
<!ATTLIST Customer
    Name CDATA #REQUIRED
    Address CDATA #REQUIRED
    City CDATA #REQUIRED
    State CDATA #REQUIRED
    PostalCode CDATA #REQUIRED>
```

This would correspond to the following table script (ch03_ex11.sql):

```
CREATE TABLE Customer (
    CustomerKey integer,
    Name varchar(50),
    Address varchar(100),
    City varchar(50) NULL,
    State char(2) NULL,
    PostalCode varchar(10))
```

which looks like this when run:

CustomerKey	Name	Address	City	State	PostalCode

Remember that the CDATA attribute can be specified as #REQUIRED, #IMPLIED, or #FIXED. As in the example above, if a CDATA attribute is specified as #REQUIRED, then its value should be required in the relational database. However, if it is specified as #IMPLIED, then its value should be allowed to be NULL. Attributes that carry the #FIXED specification should probably be discarded, unless your relational database needs that information for some other purpose (such as documents coming from various sources, tagged with information on their routing that needs to be tracked).

> **Rule 9: CDATA Attributes.**
> **For each attribute with a CDATA type:**
> **1. Add a column to the table corresponding to the element that carries that attribute, and give the table the name of the element.**
> **2. Set the column to be a variable length string, and set its maximum size large enough to handle expected values of the attribute without exceeding that size.**

> **Rule 10: REQUIRED/IMPLIED/FIXED Attributes.**
> **1. If an attribute is specified as #REQUIRED, then it should be required in the database.**
> **2. If the attribute is specified as #IMPLIED, then allow nulls in any column that is created as a result.**
> **3. If the attribute is specified as #FIXED, it should be stored as it might be needed by the database, for example, as a constant in a calculation - treat it the same as #REQUIRED attributes.**

Enumerated Lists

When an attribute provides an enumerated list of possible values it may take, we can model that in our relational database with a lookup table. Take this example where we are specifying the type of customer:

```
<!ELEMENT Customer EMPTY>
<!ATTLIST Customer
    CustomerType (Commercial | Consumer | Government) #REQUIRED>
```

Here, the CustomerType attribute must be one of three values: Commercial, Consumer, or Government. The following example (ch03_ex12.sql) details the lookup table needed to add these constraints to this attribute in our database:

```
CREATE TABLE CustomerTypeLookup (
    CustomerType smallint,
    CustomerTypeDesc varchar(100)
    PRIMARY KEY (CustomerType))

CREATE TABLE Customer (
    CustomerKey integer,
    CustomerType smallint
    CONSTRAINT FK_Customer_CustomerTypeLookup FOREIGN KEY (CustomerType)
        REFERENCES CustomerTypeLookup (CustomerType))

INSERT CustomerTypeLookup (CustomerType, CustomerTypeDesc)
    VALUES (1, 'Commercial')

INSERT CustomerTypeLookup (CustomerType, CustomerTypeDesc)
    VALUES (2, 'Consumer')

INSERT CustomerTypeLookup (CustomerType, CustomerTypeDesc)
    VALUES (3, 'Government')
```

This script produces the following set of tables:

Customer

	CustomerKey	CustomerType
▶		

	CustomerType	CustomerTypeDesc
▶	1	Commercial
	2	Consumer
	3	Government
✳		

CustomerTypeLookup

Now, any records that are added to the Customer table must map to CustomerType values found in the CustomerTypeLookup table.

The only caveat when using this technique is to watch out for multiple attributes with the same name but different allowable values. Take for example this DTD fragment:

```
<!ELEMENT Customer EMPTY>
<!ATTLIST Customer
    CustomerType (Commercial | Consumer | Government) #REQUIRED>

<!ELEMENT Invoice EMPTY>
<!ATTLIST Invoice
    CustomerType (FirstTime | Regular | Preferred) #REQUIRED>
```

Here, there are two attributes called CustomerType that have different meanings based on the context of the element to which they are attached. For the Customer element, CustomerType represents the type of business for the customer; for the Invoice element, CustomerType represents the type of customer for pricing purposes. Obviously we can't just create one table called CustomerTypeLookup that contains both lists; instead, two different lookup tables need to be created. One approach when this happens is to prefix the attribute name with the element name for the purposes of the lookup table - so CustomerTypeLookup would become CustomerCustomerTypeLookup and InvoiceCustomerTypeLookup.

> **Rule 11: ENUMERATED Attribute Values.**
> **For attributes with enumerated values:**
> **1. Create a two byte integer field that will contain the enumerated value translated to an integer.**
> **2. Create a lookup table with the same name as the attribute and the word Lookup appended.**
> **3. Insert a row in this table corresponding to each possible value for the enumerated attribute.**
> **4. When inserting rows into the element table in which the attribute is found, translate the value of the attribute to the integer value corresponding to it.**

ID and IDREF

Attributes that are declared as having type ID are used to uniquely identify elements within an XML document. Attributes declared with the IDREF type are used to point back to other elements with ID attributes that match the token in the attribute. There are a couple of approaches we can take to store ID information, based on the circumstances - here are some examples:

Example 1

In the first example, perhaps the CustomerID actually represents a key in the consumer's relational database.

```
<!ELEMENT Customer EMPTY>
<!ATTLIST Customer
    CustomerID ID #REQUIRED>


<Customer CustomerID="Cust3917" />
```

The information being passed as part of the XML document might be used to insert or update rows into a relational database, based on whether a row matching the provided key (with CustomerID = "Cust3917") is available. In this case, we should persist the ID value to the CustomerID column, inserting or updating as necessary.

In the next case, the IDs (for whatever reason) have meaning outside the context of the XML document - they indicate whether a particular customer was the billing or shipping customer for this invoice.

```
<!ELEMENT Customer EMPTY>
<!ATTLIST Customer
  CustomerID ID #REQUIRED>


<Customer CustomerID="BillingCustomer" />
<Customer CustomerID="ShippingCustomer" />
```

In this case, the information should be persisted to a non key field as if it were of type CDATA, since the value itself has meaning (in addition to anything it might point to).

Example 2

In the next example, the CustomerID may be intended only to allow ID-IDREF(S) relationships to be expressed - the value CustomerOne has no intrinsic meaning outside of the context of the particular XML document in which it appears:

```
<!ELEMENT Customer EMPTY>
<!ATTLIST Customer
    CustomerID ID #REQUIRED>


<Customer CustomerID="CustomerOne" />
```

In this case, we should store the ID in a lookup table to allow other data to be related back to this record when IDREF(S) appear that reference it.

Let's expand this example, with the following DTD (ch03_ex12.dtd):

```
<!ELEMENT Order (Customer, Invoice)>

<!ELEMENT Customer EMPTY>
<!ATTLIST Customer
    CustomerID ID #REQUIRED>

<!ELEMENT Invoice EMPTY>
<!ATTLIST Invoice
    InvoiceID ID #REQUIRED
    CustomerIDREF IDREF #REQUIRED>
```

and here is some corresponding XML (ch03_ex12.xml):

```
<?xml version="1.0"?>
<!DOCTYPE listing SYSTEM "ch03_ex12.dtd" >

<Order>
    <Customer CustomerID="Cust3917" />
    <Invoice InvoiceID="Inv19283" CustomerIDREF="Cust3917" />
</Order>
```

Here we can see how the ID corresponds to the IDREF within the document instance. The customer ID corresponds with the invoice number. In a database, the IDREF attribute should be represented as a foreign key pointing back to the row corresponding to the element that contained the ID value.

Let's see how this works in the database. In the following script, ch03_ex12.sql, we create a Customer table and an Invoice table. The Invoice table contains the foreign key, which points back to the Primary key in the Customer table:

```
CREATE TABLE Customer (
    CustomerKey integer,
    PRIMARY KEY (CustomerKey))

CREATE TABLE Invoice (
    InvoiceKey integer,
    CustomerKey integer
    CONSTRAINT FK_Invoice_Customer FOREIGN KEY (CustomerKey)
        REFERENCES Customer (CustomerKey))
```

and here is the table structure we have created:

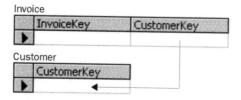

When the `Invoice` element is parsed, we see that there's a reference to a `Customer` element; we then set the `CustomerKey` of the newly created `Invoice` row to match the `CustomerKey` of the customer whose `ID` matches the `IDREF` found in the `Invoice` element.

Again, we note that the `Invoice` element might appear in the document before the `Customer` element it points to, so we must be careful when linking up the foreign keys - we may need to "remember" the IDs we encounter (and the rows created as a result) while parsing the document so that we can set foreign keys accordingly.

If we didn't design the XML structures, we should also be on the lookout for `IDREF` attributes that don't make it clear what type of element they point back to. For example, the following structure is perfectly acceptable in XML:

```
<!ELEMENT Customer EMPTY>
<!ATTLIST Customer
   CustomerID ID #REQUIRED>

<!ELEMENT Invoice EMPTY>
<!ATTLIST Invoice
   InvoiceID ID #REQUIRED
   ClientIDREF IDREF #REQUIRED>


<Customer CustomerID="Cust3917" />
<Invoice InvoiceID="Inv19283" ClientIDREF="Cust3917" />
```

In this case, the `ClientIDREF` actually points back to a `Customer` element - but this would only be revealed through some analysis.

Finally, it could be that the XML structure is designed so that an `IDREF` attribute actually points to some unknown element type. Take this example (`ch03_ex13.dtd`):

```
<!ELEMENT Order (Business, Consumer, Invoice)>

<!ELEMENT Business EMPTY>
<!ATTLIST Business
   BusinessID ID #REQUIRED>

<!ELEMENT Consumer EMPTY>
<!ATTLIST Consumer
   ConsumerID ID #REQUIRED>

<!ELEMENT Invoice EMPTY>
<!ATTLIST Invoice
   InvoiceID ID #REQUIRED
   ClientIDREF IDREF #REQUIRED>
```

and here is some sample XML (`ch03_ex13.xml`):

```
<?xml version="1.0"?>
<!DOCTYPE listing SYSTEM "ch03_ex13.dtd" >

<Order>
   <Business BusinessID="Bus281" />
   <Consumer ConsumerID="Cons27615" />
   <Invoice InvoiceID="Inv19283" ClientIDREF="Bus281" />
   <Invoice InvoiceID="Inv19284" ClientIDREF="Cons27615" />
</Order>
```

In this case, we need to add some sort of discriminator to indicate what element is being pointed to. This is similar to the way mixed content elements are handled. First, we need to create a lookup table that contains all the tables in the SQL structures. We then add a `TableLookupKey` to the `Invoice` structure, making it clear which element is being pointed to by the foreign key. This gives us table creation script (`ch03_ex13.sql`), as seen below:

```
CREATE TABLE TableLookup (
    TableLookupKey integer,
    TableName varchar(255),
    PRIMARY KEY(TableLookupKey))

CREATE TABLE Business (
    BusinessKey integer)

CREATE TABLE Consumer (
    ConsumerKey integer)

CREATE TABLE Invoice (
    InvoiceKey integer,
    ClientKeyTableLookupKey integer,
    ClientKey integer
    CONSTRAINT FK_Invoice_TableLookup FOREIGN KEY (ClientKeyTableLookupKey)
        REFERENCES TableLookup (TableLookupKey))
```

The resulting tables, when populated with some example values, would then look like this:

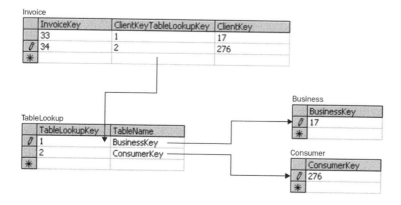

The `Invoice` table references the `TableLookup` table through the `ClientKeyTableLookupKey` column to find the table name that holds the `ClientKey` it needs. The `TableLookup` table then references the `Business` and `Consumer` tables, and returns the correct `ClientKey` value.

> **Rule 12: Handling ID Attributes.**
> **1. If an attribute with type ID has meaning outside the context of the XML document, store it in the database.**
> **2. If it's a representation of the primary key value, we can use it to insert or update records in the database as necessary.**
> **3. Otherwise, we just hang on to it so that we can link up any IDREF or IDREFS that point to it elsewhere in the document.**

> **Rule 13: Handling IDREF Attributes.**
> **1. If an IDREF attribute is present for an element and is known to always point to a specific element type, add a foreign key to the element that references the primary key of the element to which the attribute points.**
> **2. If the IDREF attribute may point to more than one element type, add a table lookup key that indicates to which table the key corresponds.**

IDREFS

Attributes with the `IDREFS` type have to be handled a little differently, as they allow the expression of many-to-many relationships. Let's look at an example (`ch03_ex14.dtd`):

```
<!ELEMENT Order (Invoice, Item)>

<!ELEMENT Invoice EMPTY>
<!ATTLIST Invoice
    InvoiceID ID #REQUIRED>

<!ELEMENT Item EMPTY>
<!ATTLIST Item
    ItemID ID #REQUIRED
    InvoiceIDREFS IDREFS #REQUIRED>
```

We can use this to write some sample XML that illustrates a many-to-many relationship. The `Item` with the `ID` `Item1` is found on two different invoices, the invoice may contain many different items, and one item may appear on many different invoices (`ch03_ex14.dtd`).

```
<?xml version="1.0"?>
<!DOCTYPE listing SYSTEM "ch03_ex14.dtd" >

<Order>
    <Invoice InvoiceID="Inv1" />
    <Invoice InvoiceID="Inv2" />
    <Item ItemID="Item1" InvoiceIDREFS="Inv1 Inv2" />
    <Item ItemID="Item2" InvoiceIDREFS="Inv1" />
</Order>
```

In order to represent this in a relational database, we need to create a join table to support the relationship. Let's see how that would be done (`ch03_ex14.sql`):

```
CREATE TABLE Invoice (
    InvoiceKey integer,
    PRIMARY KEY (InvoiceKey))

CREATE TABLE Item (
    ItemKey integer,
    PRIMARY KEY (ItemKey))

CREATE TABLE InvoiceItem (
    InvoiceKey integer
CONSTRAINT FK_InvoiceItem_Invoice FOREIGN KEY (InvoiceKey)
        REFERENCES Invoice (InvoiceKey),
    ItemKey integer
    CONSTRAINT FK_InvoiceItem_Item FOREIGN KEY (ItemKey)
        REFERENCES Item (ItemKey))
```

Here, we've created a join table called InvoiceItem that contains foreign keys referencing the Invoice and Item tables. This allows us to express the many-to-many relationship between the two tables, as shown below:

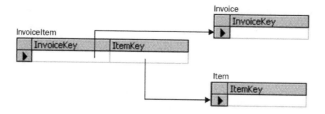

Again, this strategy only works properly if the IDREFS attribute is known to point only to elements of a specific type.

If the IDREFS attribute points to elements of more than one type, we need to add a table lookup key to the join table to indicate which type of element is being referenced. For example, when modeling the case shown below (ch03_ex15.dtd and ch03_ex15.xml):

```
<!ELEMENT Order (Invoice, POS, Item)>

<!ELEMENT Invoice EMPTY>
<!ATTLIST Invoice
    InvoiceID ID #REQUIRED>

<!ELEMENT POS EMPTY>
<!ATTLIST POS
    POSID ID #REQUIRED>

<!ELEMENT Item EMPTY>
<!ATTLIST Item
    ItemID ID #REQUIRED
    DeliveryIDREFS IDREFS #REQUIRED>
```

```
<?xml version="1.0"?>
<!DOCTYPE listing SYSTEM "ch03_ex15.dtd" >

<Order>
    <Invoice InvoiceID="Inv1" />
    <POS POSID="POS1" />
    <Item ItemID="Item1" DeliveryIDREFS="Inv1 POS1" />
    <Item ItemID="Item2" DeliveryIDREFS="Inv1" />
</Order>
```

The SQL table creation script to handle this case, (ch03_ex15.sql), looks like this:

```
CREATE TABLE TableLookup (
    TableLookupKey integer,
    TableName varchar(255),
    PRIMARY KEY (TableLookupKey))

CREATE TABLE Invoice (
    InvoiceKey integer)
```

```
CREATE TABLE POS (
   POSKey integer)

CREATE TABLE Item (
   ItemKey integer,
   PRIMARY KEY (ItemKey))

CREATE TABLE InvoiceDelivery (
   TableLookupKey integer
CONSTRAINT FK_DeliveryItem_TableLookup FOREIGN KEY (TableLookupKey)
      REFERENCES TableLookup (TableLookupKey),
   DeliveryKey integer,
   ItemKey integer
   CONSTRAINT FK_DeliveryItem_Item FOREIGN KEY (ItemKey)
      REFERENCES Item (ItemKey))
```

The table lookup key column would then be populated (much as it was in the case where an IDREF could point to more than one element type) as shown in the diagram below:

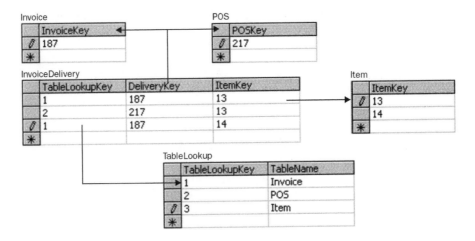

NMTOKEN and NMTOKENS

An attribute defined to have the type NMTOKEN must contain a value consisting of letters, digits, periods, dashes, underscores, and colons. We can think of this as being similar to an attribute with the type CDATA, but with greater restrictions on the possible values for the attribute. As a result, we can store an attribute of this type in the same way that we would store an attribute of type CDATA, as shown in the following DTD and XML fragments:

```
<!ELEMENT Customer EMPTY>
<!ATTLIST Customer
    ReferenceNumber NMTOKEN #REQUIRED>
```

```
<Customer ReferenceNumber="H127X9Y57" />
```

This would correspond to the following table:

```
CREATE TABLE Customer (
    ReferenceNumber varchar(50))
```

If the attribute takes the type NMTOKENS on the other hand, it must contain a sequence of whitespace delimited tokens obeying the same rules as NMTOKEN attributes. For example, we might have this definition, ch03_ex16.dtd and ch03_ex16.xml:

```
<!ELEMENT Customer EMPTY>
<!ATTLIST Customer
    ReferenceNumber NMTOKENS #REQUIRED>
```

```
<?xml version="1.0"?>
<!DOCTYPE listing SYSTEM "ch03_ex16.dtd" >
```

```
<Customer ReferenceNumber="H127X9Y57 B235Z2X99" />
```

In this case, we need to create an additional table to hold the reference numbers, as many of them may occur for the same Customer element. This is shown below, in ch03_ex16.sql:

```
CREATE TABLE Customer (
    CustomerKey integer)

CREATE TABLE ReferenceNumber (
    ReferenceNumberKey integer,
    CustomerKey integer,
    ReferenceNumber varchar(50))
```

This creates the following tables:

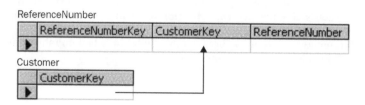

For the previous XML example, we'd create one `Customer` row and two `ReferenceNumber` rows - one for each token in the NMTOKENS attribute.

> **Rule 15: NMTOKEN Attributes.**
> For each attribute with the NMTOKEN type, create a column in the table corresponding to that element to hold the value for that attribute.

> **Rule 16: NMTOKENS Attributes.**
> 1. For each attribute with the NMTOKENS type, create a table with an automatically incremented primary key, a foreign key referencing the row in the table that corresponds to the element in which the attribute is found, and a string that will contain the value of each token found in the attribute.
> 2. Add a row to this table for each token found in the attribute for the element.

ENTITY and ENTITIES

Attributes declared with the ENTITY or ENTITIES type are used to specify unparsed entities associated with an element. The attribute contains a token (or tokens, in the case of attributes declared as ENTITIES) that match the name of an entity declared in the document's DTD. Let's see how we would store this information.

```
<!NOTATION gif PUBLIC "GIF">
<!ENTITY BlueLine SYSTEM "blueline.gif" NDATA gif>
<!ELEMENT Separator EMPTY>
<!ATTLIST Separator
    img ENTITY #REQUIRED>


<Separator img="BlueLine" />
```

We'll look at how we store the actual entity information later, when we talk about entity and notation declarations. For now, what's important is that we should be able to identify which entity is being referenced by the ENTITY attribute on the Separator element. For the purposes of this discussion, we'll assume that the goal of the XML persistence is to store the information in the XML document, as opposed to the definitions of entities in the DTD associated with it. To that end, we should simply store the value of the attribute as if it were declared as NMTOKEN or NMTOKENS; Details about the unparsed entity, and the notation associated with it, are found in the document's DTD and are outside the scope of this process.

> **Rule 17: ENTITY and ENTITIES Attributes.**
> Attributes declared with the **ENTITY** or **ENTITIES** type should be handled as if they were declared with the **NMTOKEN** or **NMTOKENS** types, respectively (see rules 15 and 16).

Entity Declarations

Entity declarations appear in DTDs, and are called by references that appear in the XML document. There are three ways a parser may handle a reference to an entity in an XML document. Let's look at these:

1. If the entity is an internal parsed entity, or an external parsed entity, that the parser chooses to expand, the reference to the entity will not be returned by the parser; instead, the expanded content will be returned as if it were stated in-line in the document. In this case, no special steps need to be taken to store the entity information - instead, the content will be stored according to the content model expressed in the DTD.

2. If the entity is an unparsed entity, it will appear as an attribute of an element, as seen in the above example.

3. If the entity is an external parsed entity, and the parser is nonvalidating, the parser may choose not to expand the reference into the corresponding node set when returning information about the document. However, we have intentionally limited our discussion here to validating parsers, so external entities should always be parsed.

Because all of these possibilities result in either the entity disappearing (from the parser's perspective), or being referenced from an attribute, entity declarations do not need to be modeled in our SQL database.

Notation Declarations

Notation declarations are used to describe the way unparsed entities should be handled by the parser. As such, they are aspects of the DTD, and not of the document itself; therefore, notation declarations do not need to be modeled in our SQL database either.

Avoid Name Collisions!

With the aforementioned set of rules, it's fairly easy to anticipate a situation where a name collision might occur. That is, a situation where two tables or columns dictated by the XML DTD have the same name. For example, let's say we had the following DTD:

```
<!ELEMENT Customer (CustomerKey)>
<!ELEMENT CustomerKey (#PCDATA)>
```

According to the rules we've set out, this would translate to the following table definition:

```
CREATE TABLE Customer (
    CustomerKey integer,
    CustomerKey varchar(10))
```

Clearly, this is invalid. In a case like this, one of the column names must be changed to avoid colliding with the other. It makes more sense to change the nonkey field name, as it will not be referenced in other tables. So we might change the table definition to this:

```
CREATE TABLE Customer (
    CustomerKey integer,
    XMLCustomerKey varchar(10))
```

> **Rule 18: Check for Name Collisions.**
> After applying all the preceding rules, check the results of the process for name collisions. If name collisions exist, change the names of columns or tables as necessary to resolve the name collision.

Summary

In the preceding pages, we've devised 18 rules that may be used to create a relational database schema from an XML DTD. Using these rules, we should be able to take any document type definition for any document we have and build a relational database that can hold the contents of the document. Using these rules will also abstract the data away from the structure as much as possible, making the data that was found in the XML document available for querying or other processing by the relational database. We have collated all the rules at the end of the chapter - now let's go through an example to see how to use many of the rules together.

Example

Here's an example that uses many of the rules we have defined. This example corresponds to a simple order data document containing multiple invoices, much like we will see used in other chapters throughout the book. Let's see how we would apply these rules to transform this XML DTD (ch03_ex17.dtd) into a relational database creation script.

```
<!ELEMENT OrderData (Invoice+, Customer+, Part+)>

<!ELEMENT Invoice (Address,
                   LineItem+)>
<!ATTLIST Invoice
   invoiceDate CDATA #REQUIRED
   shipDate CDATA #IMPLIED
   shipMethod (FedEx | USPS | UPS) #REQUIRED
   CustomerIDREF IDREF #REQUIRED>

<!ELEMENT Address EMPTY>
<!ATTLIST Address
   Street CDATA #REQUIRED
   City CDATA #IMPLIED
   State CDATA #IMPLIED
   PostalCode CDATA #REQUIRED>

<!ELEMENT LineItem EMPTY>
<!ATTLIST LineItem
   PartIDREF IDREF #REQUIRED
   Quantity CDATA #REQUIRED
   Price CDATA #REQUIRED>

<!ELEMENT Customer (Address,
                    ShipMethod+)>
<!ATTLIST Customer
   firstName CDATA #REQUIRED
   lastName CDATA #REQUIRED
   emailAddress CDATA #IMPLIED>

<!ELEMENT ShipMethod (#PCDATA)>
```

```
<!ELEMENT Part EMPTY>
<!ATTLIST Part
   name CDATA #REQUIRED
   size CDATA #IMPLIED
   color CDATA #IMPLIED>
```

This DTD is for a more detailed invoice than those examples we have seen so far. Let's look at a sample XML document, `ch03_ex17.xml`:

```
<?xml version="1.0"?>
<!DOCTYPE listing SYSTEM "ch03_ex17.dtd" >

<OrderData>

   <Invoice invoiceDate="05052000"
           shipDate="05122000"
           shipMethod="FedEx">
      <Address Street="AnyStreet"
              City="AnyTown"
              State="AS"
              PostCode="Any Code" />
      <LineItem PartIDREF="2015"
               Quantity="2"
               Price="20.99" />
   </Invoice>

   <Customer>
      <Address Street="AnyStreet"
              City="AnyTown"
              State="AS"
              PostCode="Any Code" />
      <ShipMethod> FedEx </ShipMethod>
   </Customer>

   <Part name="Winkle"
        size="10.5"
        color="Blue" />

</OrderData>
```

First, let's look at which tables we need to create in our database to represent these elements.

Applying Rule 2, we see that we need to create tables called `OrderData`, `Invoice`, `LineItem`, `Customer`, and `Part`. `OrderData` is the root element, and each of the others only has one element type that may be its parent. Rule 2 also tells us to create a foreign key back to each of these element's parent element tables. This gives us `ch03_ex17a.sql`:

```
CREATE TABLE OrderData (
   OrderDataKey integer,
   PRIMARY KEY (OrderDataKey))

CREATE TABLE Invoice (
   InvoiceKey integer,
   PRIMARY KEY (InvoiceKey),
   OrderDataKey integer
CONSTRAINT FK_Invoice_OrderData FOREIGN KEY (OrderDataKey)
   REFERENCES OrderData (OrderDataKey))
```

```
CREATE TABLE LineItem (
    LineItemKey integer,
    InvoiceKey integer
CONSTRAINT FK_LineItem_Invoice FOREIGN KEY (InvoiceKey)
    REFERENCES Invoice (InvoiceKey))

CREATE TABLE Customer (
    CustomerKey integer,
    OrderDataKey integer
CONSTRAINT FK_Customer_OrderData FOREIGN KEY (OrderDataKey)
    REFERENCES OrderData (OrderDataKey))

CREATE TABLE Part (
    PartKey integer,
    OrderDataKey integer
CONSTRAINT FK_Part_OrderData FOREIGN KEY (OrderDataKey)
    REFERENCES OrderData (OrderDataKey))
```

This gives us the following table structure:

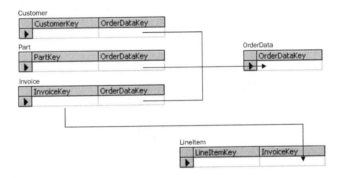

But what do we do about the Address element? Well, since it may have more than one parent (Customer or Invoice), we apply rule 3. Since the Address element may appear exactly once in each of these parent elements, we can simply add a foreign key pointing to the Address element from each of its parents. This gives us ch03_ex17b.sql:

```
CREATE TABLE OrderData (
    OrderDataKey integer,
    PRIMARY KEY (OrderDataKey))

CREATE TABLE Address (
AddressKey integer,
    PRIMARY KEY (AddressKey))

CREATE TABLE Invoice (
    InvoiceKey integer,
    PRIMARY KEY (InvoiceKey),
    OrderDataKey integer
CONSTRAINT FK_Invoice_OrderData FOREIGN KEY (OrderDataKey)
    REFERENCES OrderData (OrderDataKey),
    AddressKey integer
CONSTRAINT FK_Invoice_Address FOREIGN KEY (AddressKey)
    REFERENCES Address (AddressKey))
```

```
CREATE TABLE LineItem (
    LineItemKey integer,
    InvoiceKey integer,
CONSTRAINT FK_LineItem_Invoice FOREIGN KEY (InvoiceKey)
    REFERENCES Invoice (InvoiceKey))

CREATE TABLE Customer (
    CustomerKey integer,
    OrderDataKey integer
CONSTRAINT FK_Customer_OrderData FOREIGN KEY (OrderDataKey)
    REFERENCES OrderData (OrderDataKey),
    AddressKey integer
CONSTRAINT FK_Customer_Address FOREIGN KEY (AddressKey)
    REFERENCES Address (AddressKey))

CREATE TABLE Part (
    PartKey integer,
    OrderDataKey integer,
CONSTRAINT FK_Part_OrderData FOREIGN KEY (OrderDataKey)
    REFERENCES OrderData (OrderDataKey))
```

The updated version of our creation script gives us this set of tables:

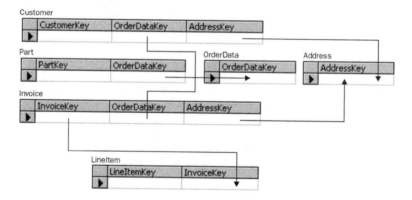

Looking at our original DTD, this covers all the elements except for ShipMethod. In our example, we're going to use ShipMethod to hold all the various shipping methods that a customer can accept. We can see that it's defined as #PCDATA, so we need to apply either rule 4 or rule 5. Since ShipMethod may appear more than once in its only parent (Customer), we need to apply rule 5. It states that we need to add a table for ShipMethod and a foreign key pointing back to the Customer with which the ShipMethod is associated. Now, we have this script, ch03_ex17c.sql:

```
CREATE TABLE OrderData (
    OrderDataKey integer,
    PRIMARY KEY (OrderDataKey))

CREATE TABLE Address (
    AddressKey integer,
    PRIMARY KEY (AddressKey))
```

```
CREATE TABLE Invoice (
    InvoiceKey integer,
    PRIMARY KEY (InvoiceKey),
    OrderDataKey integer
CONSTRAINT FK_Invoice_OrderData FOREIGN KEY (OrderDataKey)
    REFERENCES OrderData (OrderDataKey),
    AddressKey integer
CONSTRAINT FK_Invoice_Address FOREIGN KEY (AddressKey)
    REFERENCES Address (AddressKey))

CREATE TABLE LineItem (
    LineItemKey integer,
    InvoiceKey integer,
CONSTRAINT FK_LineItem_Invoice FOREIGN KEY (InvoiceKey)
    REFERENCES Invoice (InvoiceKey))

CREATE TABLE Customer (
    CustomerKey integer,
    PRIMARY KEY (CustomerKey),
    OrderDataKey integer
CONSTRAINT FK_Customer_OrderData FOREIGN KEY (OrderDataKey)
    REFERENCES OrderData (OrderDataKey),
    AddressKey integer
CONSTRAINT FK_Customer_Address FOREIGN KEY (AddressKey)
    REFERENCES Address (AddressKey))

CREATE TABLE ShipMethod (
    ShipMethodKey integer,
    CustomerKey integer,
    ShipMethod varchar(10),
CONSTRAINT FK_ShipMethod_Customer FOREIGN KEY (CustomerKey)
    REFERENCES Customer (CustomerKey))

CREATE TABLE Part (
    PartKey integer,
    OrderDataKey integer,
CONSTRAINT FK_Part_OrderData FOREIGN KEY (OrderDataKey)
    REFERENCES OrderData (OrderDataKey))
```

The database table structure now looks like this:

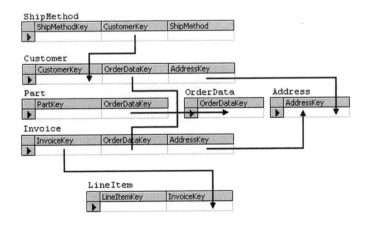

Note that we arbitrarily assigned ShipMethod to have a length of ten bytes.

Modeling the Attributes

Now, let's start looking at the attributes on each of the elements. We can skip the `OrderData` element, since it doesn't have any attributes declared. Next, we have the `Invoice` element:

```
<!ATTLIST Invoice
    invoiceDate CDATA #REQUIRED,
    shipDate CDATA #IMPLIED,
    shipMethod (FedEx | USPS | UPS) #REQUIRED,
    CustomerIDREF IDREF #REQUIRED>
```

We need to use three different rules to handle the attributes listed here. Applying Rule 9 to the `invoiceDate` and `shipDate` attributes, we see that we need to add two columns to the `Invoice` table. Rule 11 tells us that we need to add a lookup value column to the `Invoice` table and create a `shipMethod` table, and Rule 13 tells us that we need to add a foreign key pointing back to the `Customer` table. We now have:

```
CREATE TABLE Invoice (
    InvoiceKey integer,
    OrderDataKey integer
CONSTRAINT FK_Invoice_OrderData FOREIGN KEY (OrderDataKey)
    REFERENCES OrderData (OrderDataKey),
    AddressKey integer,
    invoiceDate datetime,
    shipDate datetime,
    shipMethodKey integer,
    CustomerKey integer)

CREATE TABLE shipMethod (
    shipMethodKey integer,
    shipMethod varchar(5))

INSERT shipMethod (shipMethodKey, shipMethod) VALUES (1, "FedEx")
INSERT shipMethod (shipMethodKey, shipMethod) VALUES (2, "USPS")
INSERT shipMethod (shipMethodKey, shipMethod) VALUES (3, "UPS")
```

Again, we've added stronger typing that may need to be verified when storing valid documents in our database.

Next, let's tackle `Address`:

```
<!ATTLIST Address
    Street CDATA #REQUIRED,
    City CDATA #IMPLIED,
    State CDATA #IMPLIED,
    PostalCode CDATA #REQUIRED>
```

Rule 9 works for all four of these:

```
CREATE TABLE Address (
    AddressKey integer,
    Street varchar(50),
    City varchar(40) NULL,
    State varchar(2) NULL,
    PostalCode varchar(10))
```

Then, for `LineItem`:

```
<!ATTLIST LineItem
    PartIDREF IDREF #REQUIRED,
    Quantity CDATA #REQUIRED,
    Price CDATA #REQUIRED>
```

One application of Rule 13 and two applications of Rule 9 yields this:

```
CREATE TABLE LineItem (
    LineItemKey integer,
    InvoiceKey integer
CONSTRAINT FK_LineItem_Invoice FOREIGN KEY (InvoiceKey)
    REFERENCES Invoice (InvoiceKey),
    PartKey integer
CONSTRAINT FK_LineItem_Part FOREIGN KEY (PartKey)
    REFERENCES Part (PartKey),
    Quantity integer,
    Price float)
```

For this alteration to be complete of course, we must also add a `PRIMARY KEY (PartKey)` line to the `Part` table creation script. Next, we look at `Customer`:

```
<!ATTLIST Customer
    firstName CDATA #REQUIRED,
    lastName CDATA #REQUIRED,
    emailAddress CDATA #IMPLIED>
```

This requires, three applications of Rule 9 for handling `CDATA` attributes, giving us:

```
CREATE TABLE Customer (
    CustomerKey integer,
    OrderDataKey integer
CONSTRAINT FK_Customer_OrderData FOREIGN KEY (OrderDataKey)
    REFERENCES OrderData (OrderDataKey),
    AddressKey integer,
    firstName varchar(30),
    lastName varchar(30),
    emailAddress varchar(100) NULL)
```

Finally we have `Part`, which looks like this:

```
<!ATTLIST Part
    name CDATA #REQUIRED,
    size CDATA #IMPLIED,
    color CDATA #IMPLIED>
```

This, along with three applications of rule 9 gives:

```
CREATE TABLE Part (
    PartKey integer,
    OrderDataKey integer
CONSTRAINT FK_Part_OrderData FOREIGN KEY (OrderDataKey)
    REFERENCES OrderData (OrderDataKey),
    name varchar(20),
    size varchar(10) NULL,
    color varchar(10) NULL)
```

Now that we've tackled all the elements and attributes, we have the following structure - (ch03_ex17d.sql):

```sql
CREATE TABLE OrderData (
    OrderDataKey integer,
    PRIMARY KEY (OrderDataKey))

CREATE TABLE Address (
    AddressKey integer,
    PRIMARY KEY (AddressKey),
    Street varchar(50),
    City varchar(40) NULL,
    State varchar(2) NULL,
    PostalCode varchar(10))

CREATE TABLE Invoice (
    InvoiceKey integer,
    PRIMARY KEY (InvoiceKey),
    OrderDataKey integer
CONSTRAINT FK_Invoice_OrderData FOREIGN KEY (OrderDataKey)
    REFERENCES OrderData (OrderDataKey),
    AddressKey integer
CONSTRAINT FK_Invoice_Address FOREIGN KEY (AddressKey)
    REFERENCES Address (AddressKey),
    invoiceDate datetime,
    shipDate datetime,
    shipMethodKey integer,
    CustomerKey integer)

CREATE TABLE Part (
    PartKey integer,
    PRIMARY KEY (PartKey),
    OrderDataKey integer,
CONSTRAINT FK_Part_OrderData FOREIGN KEY (OrderDataKey)
    REFERENCES OrderData (OrderDataKey))

CREATE TABLE LineItem (
    LineItemKey integer,
    InvoiceKey integer,
CONSTRAINT FK_LineItem_Invoice FOREIGN KEY (InvoiceKey)
    REFERENCES Invoice (InvoiceKey),
    PartKey integer,
CONSTRAINT FK_LineItem_Part FOREIGN KEY (PartKey)
    REFERENCES Part (PartKey),
    Quantity integer,
    Price float)

CREATE TABLE Customer (
    CustomerKey integer,
    PRIMARY KEY (CustomerKey),
    OrderDataKey integer
CONSTRAINT FK_Customer_OrderData FOREIGN KEY (OrderDataKey)
    REFERENCES OrderData (OrderDataKey),
    AddressKey integer
CONSTRAINT FK_Customer_Address FOREIGN KEY (AddressKey)
    REFERENCES Address (AddressKey),
    firstName varchar(30),
    lastName varchar(30),
    emailAddress varchar(100) NULL)
```

```
CREATE TABLE ShipMethod  (
    ShipMethodKey integer,
    CustomerKey integer,
    ShipMethod varchar(10),
CONSTRAINT FK_ShipMethod_Customer FOREIGN KEY (CustomerKey)
    REFERENCES Customer (CustomerKey))

INSERT shipMethod (shipMethodKey, shipMethod) VALUES (1, 'FedEx')
INSERT shipMethod (shipMethodKey, shipMethod) VALUES (2, 'USPS')
INSERT shipMethod (shipMethodKey, shipMethod) VALUES (3, 'USPS')
```

But we have one more problem - we've got a name collision on ShipMethod. Admittedly one of the ShipMethod tables is upper camel case and the other is lower, but this will cause a problem if you're running your relational database in case-insensitive mode. At any rate, having tables with extremely similar names will cause no end of confusion when developers attempt to write code that accesses the database. With that in mind, let's apply Rule 18 and change the second ShipMethod table (the one that comes from the ShipMethod element) to be CustomerShipMethod. This gives us the following, ch03_ex17final.sql:

```
CREATE TABLE OrderData (
    OrderDataKey integer,
    PRIMARY KEY (OrderDataKey))

CREATE TABLE Address (
    AddressKey integer,
    PRIMARY KEY (AddressKey),
    Street varchar(50),
    City varchar(40) NULL,
    State varchar(2) NULL,
    PostalCode varchar(10))

CREATE TABLE Invoice (
    InvoiceKey integer,
    PRIMARY KEY (InvoiceKey),
    OrderDataKey integer
CONSTRAINT FK_Invoice_OrderData FOREIGN KEY (OrderDataKey)
    REFERENCES OrderData (OrderDataKey),
    AddressKey integer
CONSTRAINT FK_Invoice_Address FOREIGN KEY (AddressKey)
    REFERENCES Address (AddressKey),
    invoiceDate datetime,
    shipDate datetime,
    shipMethodKey integer,
    CustomerKey integer)

CREATE TABLE Part (
    PartKey integer,
    PRIMARY KEY (PartKey),
    OrderDataKey integer,
CONSTRAINT FK_Part_OrderData FOREIGN KEY (OrderDataKey)
    REFERENCES OrderData (OrderDataKey))

CREATE TABLE LineItem (
    LineItemKey integer,
    InvoiceKey integer,
CONSTRAINT FK_LineItem_Invoice FOREIGN KEY (InvoiceKey)
    REFERENCES Invoice (InvoiceKey),
    PartKey integer,
CONSTRAINT FK_LineItem_Part FOREIGN KEY (PartKey)
    REFERENCES Part (PartKey),
    Quantity integer,
    Price float)
```

```
CREATE TABLE Customer (
    CustomerKey integer,
    PRIMARY KEY (CustomerKey),
    OrderDataKey integer
CONSTRAINT FK_Customer_OrderData FOREIGN KEY (OrderDataKey)
    REFERENCES OrderData (OrderDataKey),
    AddressKey integer
CONSTRAINT FK_Customer_Address FOREIGN KEY (AddressKey)
    REFERENCES Address (AddressKey),
    firstName varchar(30),
    lastName varchar(30),
    emailAddress varchar(100) NULL)

CREATE TABLE ShipMethod  (
    ShipMethodKey integer,
    CustomerKey integer,
    ShipMethod varchar(10),
CONSTRAINT FK_ShipMethod_Customer FOREIGN KEY (CustomerKey)
    REFERENCES Customer (CustomerKey))

INSERT shipMethod (shipMethodKey, shipMethod) VALUES (1,
'FedEx')
INSERT shipMethod (shipMethodKey, shipMethod) VALUES (2,
'USPS')
INSERT shipMethod (shipMethodKey, shipMethod) VALUES (3,
'USPS')

CREATE TABLE CustomerShipMethod (
    CustomerShipMethodKey integer,
    CustomerKey integer,
    CustomerShipMethod varchar(10))
```

Our final table structure looks like this:

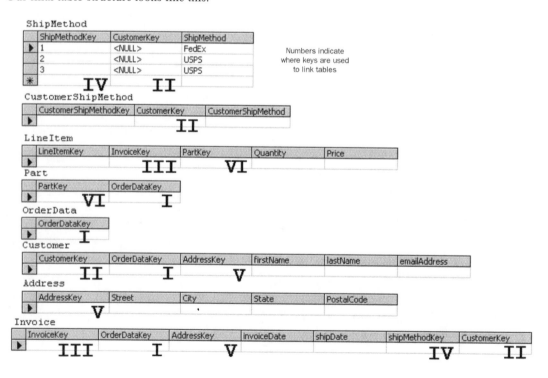

Summary

In this chapter, we've seen how to build relational structures to store XML content that conforms to a known document type definition. We should be able to take any existing DTD and create a table structure for it using the 18 rules we have defined. Remember that these rules are intended to allow us to do two things: using them, the data is abstracted from the structure as much as possible to allow us to perform queries and summarization against it; and we should be able to recreate our original XML document from the information stored in the database. If our particular business problem has other constraints (such as needing to have the XML document available without necessarily querying against it), then we may need to take some other approach - such as persisting the serialized XML document string to our database in a text field, rather than breaking it apart. Nevertheless, for most querying and summarization problems, these rules present a good solution.

The Rules

❏ **Rule 1: Always Create a Primary Key**
Whenever creating a table in the relational database:
1. Add a column to it that holds an automatically incremented integer.
2. Name the column after the element with Key appended.
3. Set this column to be the primary key on the created table.

❏ **Rule 2: Basic Table Creation**
For every structural element found in the DTD:
1. Create a table in the relational database.
2. If the structural element has exactly one allowable parent element (or is the root element of the DTD), add a column to the table. This column will be a foreign key that references the parent element.
3. Make the foreign key required.

❏ **Rule 3: Handling Multiple Parent Elements**
If a particular element may have more than one parent element, and the element may occur in the parent element zero or one times:
1. Add a foreign key to the table representing the parent element that points to the corresponding record in the child element, making it optional or required as makes sense.
2. If the element may occur zero-or-more or one-or-more times, add an intermediate table to the database that expresses the relationship between the parent element and this element.

❏ **Rule 4: Representing Text Only Elements**
If an element is text only, and may appear in a particular parent element once at most:
1. Add a column to the table representing the parent element to hold the content of this element.
2. Make sure that the size of the column created is large enough to hold the anticipated content of the element.
3. If the element is optional, make the column nullable.

❏ **Rule 5: Representing Multiple Text-Only Elements**
If an element is text-only, and it may appear in a parent element more than once:
1. Create a table to hold the text values of the element and a foreign key that relates them back to their parent element.
2. If the element may appear in more than one parent element more than once, create intermediate tables to express the relationship between each parent element and this element.

❑ **Rule 6: Handling Empty Elements**
For every EMPTY element found in the DTD:
1. Create a table in the relational database.
2. If the structural element has exactly one allowable parent element, add a column to the table - this column will be a foreign key that references the parent element.
3. Make the foreign key required.

❑ **Rule 7: Representing Mixed Content Elements**
If an element has the mixed content model:
1. Create a table called TableLookup (if it doesn't already exist) and add rows for each table in the database. Also add a row zero that points to a table called TextContent.
2. Create this table with a key, a string representing the element name for text-only elements, and a text value.
3. Next, create two tables - one for the element and one to link to the various content of that element - called the element name and the element name followed by subelement, respectively.
4. In the subelement table, add a foreign key that points back to the main element table, a table lookup key that points to the element table for subelement content, a table key that points to the specific row within that table, and a sequence counter that indicates that subelement or text element's position within this element.

❑ **Rule 8: Handling the "ANY" Content Elements**
If an element has the ANY content model:
1. Create a table called TableLookup (if it doesn't already exist) and add rows for each table in the database.
2. Add a row zero that points to a table called TextContent.
3. Create this table with a key, a string representing the element name for text-only elements, and a text value.
4. Create two tables - one for the element and one to link to the various content of that element - called the element name and the element name followed by Subelement, respectively.
5. In the subelement table, add a foreign key that points back to the main element table, a table lookup key that points to the element table for subelement content, a table key that points to the specific row within that table, and a sequence counter that indicates that subelement or text element's position within this element.

❑ **Rule 9: CDATA Attributes**
For each attribute with a CDATA type:
1. Add a column to the table corresponding to the element that carries that attribute, and give the table the name of the element.
2. Set the column to be a variable-length string, and set its maximum size large enough that expected values of the attribute won't exceed that size.

❑ **Rule 10: REQUIRED/IMPLIED/FIXED Attributes**
If an attribute is specified as #REQUIRED, then it should be required in the database.
1. If an attribute is specified as #REQUIRED, then it should be required in the database.
2. If the attribute is specified as #IMPLIED, then allow nulls in any column that is created as a result.
3. If the attribute is specified as #FIXED, it should be stored as is it might be needed by the database, e.g. as a constant in a calculation - treat it the same as #REQUIRED attributes.

❑ **Rule 11: ENUMERATED Attribute Values**
For attributes with enumerated values:
1. Create a two byte integer field that will contain the enumerated value translated to an integer.
2. Create a lookup table with the same name as the attribute and the word Lookup appended.
3. Insert a row in this table corresponding to each possible value for the enumerated attribute.
4. When inserting rows into the element table in which the attribute is found, translate the value of the attribute to the integer value corresponding to it.

❑ **Rule 12: Handling ID Attributes**
1. If an attribute with type ID has meaning outside the context of the XML document, store it in the database.
2. If it's a representation of the primary key value, we can use it to insert or update records in the database as necessary.
3. Otherwise, we just hang on to it so that we can link up any IDREF or IDREFS that point to it elsewhere in the document.

❑ **Rule 13: Handling IDREF Attributes**
1. If an IDREF attribute is present for an element and is known to always point to a specific element type, add a foreign key to the element that references the primary key of the element to which the attribute points.
2. If the IDREF attribute may point to more than one element type, add a table lookup key as well that indicates which table the key corresponds to.

❑ **Rule 14: Handling IDREFS Attributes**
1. If an IDREFS attribute is present for an element, add a join table (with the names of both the element containing the attribute and the element being pointed to concatenated) that contains a foreign key referencing both the element containing the attribute and the element being pointed to.
2. If the IDREFS attribute may point to elements of different types, remove the foreign key referencing the element being pointed to and add a table lookup key that indicates the type of element pointed to.
3. Add a foreign key relationship between this table and a lookup table containing the names of all the tables in the SQL database.

❑ **Rule 15: NMTOKEN Attributes**
For each attribute with the NMTOKEN type, create a column in the table corresponding to that element to hold the value for that attribute.

❑ **Rule 16: NMTOKENS Attributes**
1. For each attribute with the NMTOKENS type, create a table with an automatically incremented primary key, a foreign key referencing the row in the table that corresponds to the element in which the attribute is found, and a string that will contain the value of each token found in the attribute.
2. Add a row to this table for each token found in the attribute for the element.

❑ **Rule 17: ENTITY and ENTITIES Attributes**
Attributes declared with the ENTITY or ENTITIES type should be handled as if they were declared with the NMTOKEN or NMTOKENS types, respectively (see rules 15 and 16).

❑ **Rule 18: Check for Name Collisions**
After applying all the preceding rules, check the results of the process for name collisions. If name collisions exist, change the names of columns or tables as necessary to resolve the name collision.

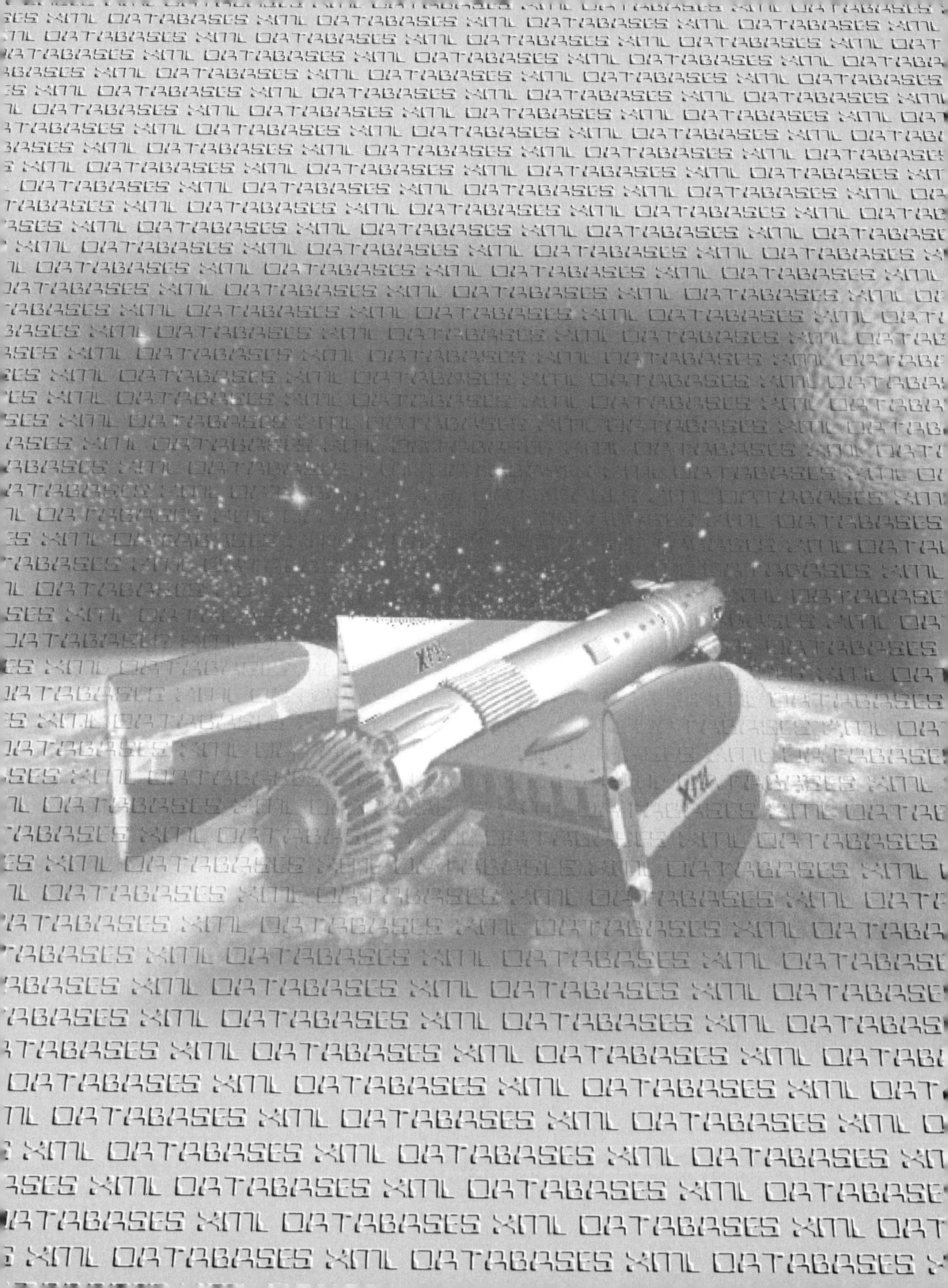
XML DATABASES
XML

4

Standards Design

One of the biggest challenges facing the XML designer in today's market is standards design. Whether it's two machines sitting in a room next to one another, or a thousand enterprise-level solutions located all around the planet, they need to have a way to communicate clearly and unambiguously with one another. XML provides a grammar for this conversation, but we also need to have a vocabulary – and that vocabulary is an XML standard.

In this chapter, we'll look at some of the issues that may arise when developing XML standards, including:

❑ Approaches that you can use to streamline the standards design process

❑ How to make sure everyone involved in the standards design process is comfortable with the outcome

❑ How to facilitate adoption and implementation once the standard has been created

Scoping the Solution

When the need for an XML standard is identified, the first step is to understand the purpose and usage of the document structure(s) that are part of the standard. Who is the anticipated producer (or producers) of the document? Who is the anticipated consumer (or consumers)? How will the document be used? To convey information? To archive information? To drive a presentation layer? The answers to all of these questions will help govern the approach you take to designing and implementing your solution.

Types of Standards

There are three types of standards that we'll be discussing here.

System Internal Standards

The easiest type of standard to design is one that is used internally for a particular system. For example, we might decide that we want to maintain records of all invoices processed by our system as XML documents, so that we can more easily present them (via HTML, WAP, or some other presentation mechanism) and archive them (by storing atomic documents to some near-line medium such as DVD-RAM).

In a standard with this scope, one person (or a very small group of people) will be tasked with creating the document structure. All the people on the team will share the same goals for the structure, and will probably be able to reach a consensus on its layout pretty quickly. Additionally, since systems often have a relational database back-end, the database can be used to directly drive the XML structures to be created (using some of the techniques we learned in Chapter 3).

Cross-system Standards

A more complex type of standard is one that is shared by more than one system. To continue our example, perhaps the team responsible for the inventory system and the team responsible for the accounting system decide that they want to create an XML standard that allows them to transmit information from one system to another.

In this case, the systems that are communicating with one another may have very different internal architectures – one might be a legacy system using an ISAM database, while the other is a Sparc running Solaris with Oracle 8i as the database. In addition, the various platforms may have different requirements with regards to performance, parser compatibility, and so on, that need to be taken into account. The data teams responsible for each system participating in the standards development will have to meet, share information about production and consumption requirements, haggle over data formats and enumerated values, and reach some sort of common ground that all the participating members can be happy with.

We'll see how a standards team leader can help to facilitate that process later in this chapter. We'll also see more about data transmission in Chapter 28.

Industry-level Standards

The most complex type of standard development effort you are likely to encounter is an industry-level standards effort. In this type of effort, the structures being developed are intended to be used by many different participants in a particular type of business, or brokers in a particular type of information. Examples of these structures include MISMO (www.mismo.org) for mortgage data, SMBXML (www.smbxml.org) for small- to medium-sized application service providers, and the HR-XML consortium that aims to provide a standard for job postings and resumes (see www.hr-xml.org/channels/home.htm for more details).

Designing these structures is often a protracted and cumbersome process, involving dozens of participants who all have very specific requirements for the structures being created. More often than not, these requirements will be in conflict with one another, requiring some sort of mediation process to continue moving forward. In efforts with this scope, defining ground rules and restrictions at the beginning of the standards process is critical to ensuring that the effort proceeds smoothly and results in a good compromise for all involved.

Many times when developing a standard of this scope, the adoption of the standard over competing standards or legacy standards is an issue. Therefore, the simpler and more comprehensible the new standard is, the more likely it is that it will be accepted by the industry at large. This can lead to some counterintuitive design decisions, such as repeating information as children of different parent elements, rather than creating the element containing the information once and pointing to it with IDREF attributes.

An additional concern when designing an industry standard is that (in theory) many of the IT groups that will ultimately be using the standard may not be directly involved with its creation. It is then incumbent upon the developers who are creating the standard to try to think ahead and take the needs of all the possible participants into account.

> *It may, however, be useful to look for existing standards before embarking on your own – for example, a list can be obtained from http://www.xml.com.*

Once we've decided who the target audience for the standard is, we need to take a look at how the structures we are designing are intended to be used.

Document Usage

The role a particular type of document will be playing in the system, enterprise, or industry is also very important when designing XML structures. If the document is being used to archive information, it should have a different set of design goals to a document that is being used to drive a presentation layer, or convey information from one system to another. Let's discuss how we would deal with each of these situations.

Archival Documents

When designing documents that will be used for archiving data, the documents should be designed to be as self-contained as possible. That is, the document should not rely on the use of system identifiers or any other information that would make the document impossible to interpret without knowing the context in which the document was created.

For example, let's say we wanted to create a document structure to hold invoices from our inventory system, and we had the following structured data to store in our XML documents:

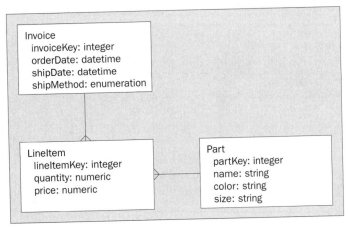

Our initial impulse might be to design the structures to reference the `Part` identifier – after all, if we need to access the information in the archive, we could always refer it back to our relational database to discover the details of the part being referenced. This would give us a structure such as the following (`ch05_ex01.dtd`):

```
<!ELEMENT Invoice (Customer, LineItem+)>
<!ATTLIST Invoice
   orderDate CDATA #REQUIRED
   shipDate CDATA #REQUIRED
   shipMethod CDATA #REQUIRED>
<!ELEMENT Customer EMPTY>
<!ATTLIST Customer
   name CDATA #REQUIRED
   address CDATA #REQUIRED
   city CDATA #REQUIRED
   state CDATA #REQUIRED
   zip CDATA #REQUIRED>
<!ELEMENT LineItem EMPTY>
<!ATTLIST LineItem
    partKey CDATA #REQUIRED
    quantity CDATA #REQUIRED
    price CDATA #REQUIRED>
```

However, what if the system were to be phased out five years later, and then a customer called demanding to know detailed information about an invoice from the old system? With only an identifier that was previously internal to the old system to track down the part, the person tasked with figuring out just what parts were on the invoice is in for a long night. There are also other problems involved – details can change over time, so customer and part numbers can disappear and/or be reissued.

The better representation would be to include all the part detail information you can, so that the document will make sense independent of any other representation, as shown here in `ch05_ex02.dtd`:

```
<!ELEMENT Invoice (Customer, LineItem+)>
<!ATTLIST Invoice
   orderDate CDATA #REQUIRED
   shipDate CDATA #REQUIRED
   shipMethod CDATA #REQUIRED>
<!ELEMENT Customer EMPTY>
<!ATTLIST Customer
   name CDATA #REQUIRED
   address CDATA #REQUIRED
   city CDATA #REQUIRED
   state CDATA #REQUIRED
   zip CDATA #REQUIRED>
<!ELEMENT LineItem EMPTY>
<!ATTLIST LineItem
    partNumber CDATA #REQUIRED
    name CDATA #REQUIRED
    color CDATA #REQUIRED
    size CDATA #REQUIRED
    quantity CDATA #REQUIRED
    price CDATA #REQUIRED>
```

This way, the actual information (and not simply handles to the representation in some other context) may be retrieved directly from the document, and hours of aggravation may be avoided when trying to recover the meaning of the document later in its lifecycle.

However, as we said earlier the representation you choose depends on the purpose of the document. If the purpose of the document is to send data to a target system that will never understand the system keys (like `partKey` in the previous example), then the `partKey` is just unnecessary information. On the other hand, if a document is created for the sole purpose of transferring information between two systems that comprehend the same system identifiers, then it's OK to use those identifiers. Let's look at this latter situation in more detail.

Transactional Data Documents

Documents designed to be used to transmit information between two processes require a very different approach. These documents are usually discarded – the consumer tears the document apart, picks out the bits of information it needs to handle the transaction, and discards the document itself – so the documents don't need to be as atomic. If the scope of the standard permits it, the documents may reference internal system identifiers or other information that has no meaning without context.

If we need to support a number of different transactions, we might also want to implement an enveloping mechanism that describes the behavior we're expecting from the system receiving the XML document. Let's see an example of this. Say we wanted to be able to use the same document to update a part or request a current price on a part. We might design a structure that looks like the following (`ch05_ex03.dtd`):

```
<!ELEMENT PartRequest (Part)>
<!ATTLIST PartRequest
    requestType (UpdatePart | GetCurrentPrice) #REQUIRED
    requestKey CDATA #REQUIRED>
<!ELEMENT Part EMPTY>
<!ATTLIST Part
    partKey CDATA #REQUIRED
    partNumber CDATA #IMPLIED
    name CDATA #IMPLIED
    color CDATA #IMPLIED
    size CDATA #IMPLIED>
```

The response structure might look like this (`ch05_ex04.dtd`):

```
<!ELEMENT PartResponse EMPTY>
<!ATTLIST PartResponse
    requestKey CDATA #REQUIRED
    status (Success | Failure) #REQUIRED
    price CDATA #IMPLIED>
```

The `requestKey` attribute is used so that we can perform an asynchronous request and response. Passing the `requestKey` back in the response allows the requesting program to match it up with information about the original request.

So to update the information on the part with the key 17, you would send this document (`ch05_ex03a.xml`):

```
<?xml version="1.0"?>
<!DOCTYPE listing SYSTEM "ch05_ex03.dtd" >


<PartRequest
    requestType="UpdatePart"
    requestKey="1028">
    <Part
        partKey="17"
```

```
        partNumber="1A2A3AB"
        name="Sprocket"
        color="Blue"
        size="2 in." />
</PartRequest>
```

In response, you might receive:

```
<PartResponse
    requestKey="1028"
    status="Failure" />
```

or:

```
<PartResponse
    requestKey = "1028"
    status="Success" />
```

The `price` attribute is omitted here because `price` is not part of the `updatePart` request-response pair.

To request the price on the part with the key 17, you would send this document (ch05_ex03b.xml):

```
<?xml version="1.0"?>
<!DOCTYPE listing SYSTEM "ch05_ex03.dtd" >

<PartRequest
    requestType="GetCurrentPrice"
    requestKey="1028">
    <Part
        partKey="17" />
</PartRequest>
```

and you might receive:

```
<PartResponse
    requestKey="1028"
    status="Failure" />
```

or:

```
<PartResponse
    requestKey = "1028"
    status="Success"
    price="0.10" />
```

There are two schools of thought on this strategy. One says that having fewer structures to maintain makes extending the structures simpler. If you add an attribute called `material` to the `Part` element, it will probably need to be added to each structure that contains the `Part` element. On the other hand, a more flexible structure tends to be more difficult to use – witness the number of attributes that are present or absent in the above examples depending on how the structures are being used. You should use whichever method best suits your needs.

The other thing to keep in mind with transmitted documents is that they are usually intended for machine eyes only, so they can be tuned for minimum document size at the expense of readability. For example, take the `PartRequest` structure we were examining before (ch05_ex03.dtd):

```
<!ELEMENT PartRequest (Part)>
<!ATTLIST PartRequest
    requestType (UpdatePart | GetCurrentPrice) #REQUIRED
    requestKey CDATA #REQUIRED>
<!ELEMENT Part EMPTY>
<!ATTLIST Part
    partKey CDATA #REQUIRED
    partNumber CDATA #IMPLIED
    name CDATA #IMPLIED
    color CDATA #IMPLIED
    size CDATA #IMPLIED>
```

If we tune this document for minimum document size, we could use the following structure instead (ch05_ex05.dtd):

```
<!ELEMENT Q (P)>
<!ATTLIST Q
    t (U | G) #REQUIRED
    k CDATA #REQUIRED>
<!ELEMENT P EMPTY>
<!ATTLIST P
    k CDATA #REQUIRED
    n CDATA #IMPLIED
    m CDATA #IMPLIED
    c CDATA #IMPLIED
    s CDATA #IMPLIED>
```

A sample request using this minimal DTD would look like this (ch05_ex05.xml):

```
<?xml version="1.0"?>
<!DOCTYPE listing SYSTEM "ch05_ex05.dtd" >

<Q t="U" k="1028"><P k="17" n="1A2A3AB" m="Sprocket" c="Blue" s="2 in." /></Q>
```

This document is 151 bytes as opposed to the original request sample which was 279 bytes – a significantly smaller document (the difference will be greater, of course, the larger the document is). If your systems are moving millions of these transaction documents back and forth, minimizing your documents in this way can ease any network bandwidth concerns you might have. It's an especially good idea if you are utilizing the DOM in your application, due to the DOM's memory hungry nature

However, there are additional ramp-up issues for developers (due to the obscure nature of the element and attribute names) and code maintainability issues (documentation is a must) when working with documents like these. As with pretty much anything else in programming, this decision involves a tradeoff.

Presentation Layer Documents

Often, your systems may need to be able to easily render content in different contexts. The obvious example in the emerging wireless age is handheld devices and cellular phones, which all have their own markup languages for the representation of content. One good way to provide this functionality (and to disambiguate content and presentation in the same step) is to first render information to XML, and then style the XML with XSLT to produce the representation appropriate for the target platform.

When designing structures that are only intended to support a specific presentation of content, the XML should be designed to match the planned presentation layout as closely as possible to avoid slow XSLT transformation of that data. For example, say you wanted to see the following general output layout for a document containing multiple invoices for a particular customer from our sample data set:

Invoice
Order date: 12/1/2000
Ship date: 12/4/2000
Ship method: UPS

Part	Quantity	Unit Price	Price
2 in. blue grommet	17	0.10	1.70
3 in. silver widget	22	0.20	4.40
Total			6.10

Invoice
Order date: 12/2/2000
Ship date: 12/5/2000
Ship method: USPS

Part	Quantity	Unit Price	Price
1 in. red sprocket	13	0.30	3.90
2 in. blue grommet	11	0.10	1.10
Total			5.00

You might be tempted to design your structure to minimize the repetition of data, and to leverage the way data is stored natively in your system, as is shown in the following examples (ch05_ex06.dtd and ch05_ex06.xml):

```
<!ELEMENT InvoiceData (Invoice+, Part+)>
<!ELEMENT Invoice (LineItem+)>
<!ATTLIST Invoice
    orderDate CDATA #REQUIRED
    shipDate CDATA #REQUIRED
    shipMethod (UPS | USPS | FedEx) #REQUIRED>
<!ELEMENT LineItem EMPTY>
<!ATTLIST LineItem
    partIDREF IDREF #REQUIRED
    quantity CDATA #REQUIRED
    price CDATA #REQUIRED>
<!ELEMENT Part EMPTY>
<!ATTLIST Part
    partID ID #REQUIRED
    name CDATA #REQUIRED
    size CDATA #REQUIRED
    color CDATA #REQUIRED>
```

```
<?xml version="1.0"?>
<!DOCTYPE listing SYSTEM "ch05_ex06.dtd" >
```

```
<InvoiceData>
    <Invoice
        orderDate="12/1/2000"
        shipDate="12/4/2000"
        shipMethod="UPS">
        <LineItem
            partIDREF="p1"
            quantity="17"
            price="0.10" />
        <LineItem
            partIDREF="p2"
            quantity="22"
            price="0.20" />
    </Invoice>
    <Invoice
        orderDate="12/2/2000"
        shipDate="12/5/2000"
        shipMethod="USPS">
        <LineItem
            partIDREF="p3"
            quantity="13"
            price="0.30" />
        <LineItem
            partIDREF="p1"
            quantity="11"
            price="0.10" />
    </Invoice>
    <Part
        partID="p1"
        name="grommet"
        size="2 in."
        color="blue" />
    <Part
        partID="p2"
        name="widget"
        size="3 in."
        color="silver" />
    <Part
        partID="p3"
        name="sprocket"
        size="1 in."
        color="red" />
</InvoiceData>
```

However, you'd be better off designing the structure to be similar to the output structure, like this (ch05_ex07.dtd and ch05_ex07.xml):

```
<!ELEMENT InvoiceData (Invoice+)>
<!ELEMENT Invoice (LineItem+)>
<!ATTLIST Invoice
    orderDate CDATA #REQUIRED
    shipDate CDATA #REQUIRED
    shipMethod (UPS | USPS | FedEx) #REQUIRED
    total CDATA #REQUIRED>
<!ELEMENT LineItem EMPTY>
<!ATTLIST LineItem
    partDescription CDATA #REQUIRED
    quantity CDATA #REQUIRED
    price CDATA #REQUIRED
    linePrice CDATA #REQUIRED>
```

```
<?xml version="1.0"?>
<!DOCTYPE listing SYSTEM "ch05_ex07.dtd" >

<InvoiceData>
    <Invoice
        orderDate="12/1/2000"
        shipDate="12/4/2000"
        shipMethod="UPS"
        total="6.10">
        <LineItem
            partDescription="2 in. blue grommet"
            quantity="17"
            price="0.10"
            linePrice="1.70" />
        <LineItem
            partDescription="3 in. silver widget"
            quantity="22"
            price="0.20"
            linePrice="2.20" />
    </Invoice>
    <Invoice
        orderDate="12/2/2000"
        shipDate="12/5/2000"
        shipMethod="USPS"
        total="5.00">
        <LineItem
            partDescription="1 in. red sprocket"
            quantity="13"
            price="0.30"
            linePrice="3.90" />
        <LineItem
            partDescription="2 in. blue grommet"
            quantity="11"
            price="0.10"
            linePrice="1.10" />
    </Invoice>
</InvoiceData>
```

The reason is simple: the first example requires the navigation of pointing relationships, the calculation of values, and generally requires processing that XSLT is not adept at performing. Actually, base implementations of XSLT cannot even calculate the final total for each invoice from the first structure! However, XSLT can transform the second example to the planned output format(s) quickly and easily.

Once you've established the audience and usage intent of the designed XML structures, you should make that information available to all the participants in the standard process. This will allow the designers to constrain the structures they create to make sure that these desired end results are achieved.

Next, let's take a look at other preparatory work you can do to facilitate the standards design process.

Before Diving In: Ground Rules

Before starting on a standards design effort, it's important to agree on some ground rules about the structures being designed. This is especially important on standards with larger scopes, as there tend to be more people (both geographically and functionally diverse) working on the effort simultaneously. XML is a quite flexible grammar, and there are myriad different ways of expressing the same semantic content in an XML structure.

Let's take a look at some ways you can constrain the design direction and help to ensure a coherent final outcome.

Implementation Assumptions

Before proceeding with the design of your structures, you first need to determine which platforms and software are likely to be used to access the structures. Using this information, you can set limitations on the way your structures are created, so that they work as harmoniously as possible with the software used by the document producers and consumers.

Again, scope is a major factor here – if you are simply designing a structure to be used internally by one system, it should be pretty easy to pin down the technologies used to create and consume documents for that structure. If you're designing for the industry, however, you need to anticipate users accessing your documents with any sort of hardware and software imaginable – and thus need to keep the complexity of the structure as minimal as possible.

If you have any doubt what software and hardware will be used to access the documents, the worst-case assumption should be that the documents are being accessed using baseline implementations of the DOM, XSLT, and SAX as defined by the W3C and David Megginson (the lead developer of the SAX toolset – visit his website for more on him and SAX at http://www.megginson.com).

A perfect example of this is the MSXML `nodeFromID()` extension function. This function is an extension of the W3C DOM that allows a node to be quickly identified in the document tree based on a given ID value. If you know that producers and consumers will be using the MSXML library to access the documents, then the navigation of pointing relationships (`IDREF(S)` to `ID`) will be relatively easy. However, if a process is accessing the document using an implementation of the DOM that does not provide a helper function like this, the navigation of pointing relationships is a little more tricky (it requires manual iteration of the elements in the tree looking for one that has an attribute of type `ID` that matches the `IDREF` you're trying to locate).

Of course, this has a big impact on design. Design, performance, and code complexity are all inextricably intertwined. If you have to take a huge performance hit for pointers, you need to avoid them at all costs – but if there are helper functions on your anticipated platform(s), then you don't have to worry quite so much

Elements vs. Attributes

This is the one issue that will probably cause the most heated debate among the participants in your standards process. Everyone has an opinion on whether elements or attributes should be used for data content, and in most cases those opinions are strongly held. There are other factors that may influence your decision as well, such as code reuse or compliance with XML servers such as BizTalk.

Whether you choose to use elements or attributes for text content, you should decide before starting to create the structures – and you should stick to one or the other throughout the structures you create. Otherwise, element definitions like these will begin to appear (`ch05_ex08.dtd` and `ch04_ex08.xml`):

```
<!ELEMENT Invoice (orderDate, shipDate, shipMethod, LineItem+)>
<!ELEMENT orderDate (#PCDATA)>
<!ELEMENT shipDate (#PCDATA)>
<!ELEMENT shipMethod (#PCDATA)>
<!ELEMENT LineItem EMPTY>
<!ATTLIST LineItem
    partID ID #REQUIRED
    quantity CDATA #REQUIRED
    price CDATA #REQUIRED>
```

```
<?xml version="1.0"?>
<!DOCTYPE listing SYSTEM "ch05_ex08.dtd" >

<Invoice>
    <orderDate>12/1/2000</orderDate>
    <shipDate>12/4/2000</shipDate>
    <shipMethod>UPS</shipMethod>
    <LineItem
        partID="p17"
        quantity="11"
        price="0.10" />
</Invoice>
```

Structures like this are difficult to learn and code for, making the time to implement them greater, and increasing the amount of code necessary to support them. If you choose to use only elements or only attributes to represent your data points, and enforce that decision, the resulting structures will be more readily accessible and implementable.

We discussed the subject of elements versus attributes for data points more thoroughly in Chapter 3.

Restricting Element Content

Because XML has its origins in SGML, it allows many different types of structures. Some of the allowable structures in XML are better suited to text markup purposes than data structures, and as such should be avoided whenever possible. If you set the ground rule up front that these text-centric structures should be avoided, it will make your generated structures more usable.

Let's see some recommended guidelines for restricting element content.

Don't Allow the ANY Element Type

As we've seen in the preceding chapters, the ANY element type allows a great deal of flexibility in what the element may contain. Say we have the following DTD:

```
<!ELEMENT a ANY>
<!ELEMENT b (#PCDATA)>
<!ELEMENT c (#PCDATA)>
```

Then the following structures would all be perfectly legitimate:

```
<a>
<a><b>some string</b><c>some other string</c></a>
<a>This element has some <b>text</b> content</a>
<a><b /><c>foo</c>foo<b>foo</b>foo<c>foo</c></a>
<a><a><a><a /></a></a></a>
```

As you can see, the freedom to mix text content and element content makes the processing of these elements a nightmare. If you forbid the developers working on the standard to use this content type, you can avoid the headaches documents like these can cause.

Don't Allow the Mixed-content Element Type

Structures of this type have the same sort of issues as structures of the ANY type. Text and elements may be freely mixed in any combination allowed by the content specification. You should also specify that this type of element content may not be used in your structures. The obvious exception is the element that is only text (really a special case of the mixed-content element type): this type of element is used when data points are being represented as elements.

Constrain Elements that have Structured Content

XML allows designers to specify complex structural content for elements using the grouping, choice, and cardinality operators. While these complex structures allow fine control over the order and frequency of elements appearing as children of the element being defined, they can be somewhat problematic to code for.

In general, you should restrict structured content to sequential elements only, using commas to separate the elements that may appear. The one situation where that doesn't strictly apply is when a true "either-or" relationship is being modeled.

For example, let's say we had the following structure (ch05_ex09.dtd):

```
<!ELEMENT User (Supplier | Customer)>
<!ATTLIST User
    login CDATA #REQUIRED
    hashedPassword CDATA #REQUIRED>
<!ELEMENT Supplier EMPTY>
<!ATTLIST Supplier
    name CDATA #REQUIRED
    supplyFrequency CDATA #REQUIRED
    partIDREFS IDREFS #REQUIRED>
<!ELEMENT Customer EMPTY>
<!ATTLIST Customer
    name CDATA #REQUIRED
    address CDATA #REQUIRED
    city CDATA #REQUIRED
    state CDATA #REQUIRED
    postalCode CDATA #REQUIRED>
```

If the User could be a Supplier, a Customer, or both, then the correct content model for the user element should be:

```
<!ELEMENT User (Supplier?, Customer?)>
```

The argument could then be made that the actual correct structure would be:

```
<!ELEMENT User ((Supplier, Customer) | Supplier | Customer)>
```

However, as you can imagine, the structures would become quite complex quickly if this sort of structure were used often. Instead, it's better to ensure that at least one of Supplier or Customer is provided in your code.

Capturing Strong Typing Information

When gathering data points for the standard, it's important to capture strong typing information for that data. Even though DTDs cannot enforce the strong typing, having it available in some form will help implementers understand the exact format and purpose of each of the data points included in the standard. Additionally, when XML Schemas become available, and it becomes possible to strongly type the data points, the migration will be less painful, since you won't have to go through the additional step of recapturing the typing for each of the data points.

Say you had the following structure:

```
<!ELEMENT Invoice EMPTY>
<!ATTLIST Invoice
    orderDate CDATA #REQUIRED
    shipDate CDATA #REQUIRED
    shipMethod (USPS | UPS | FedEx) #REQUIRED>
```

It's important to specify the format of the date, especially if the company does business internationally; some countries represent dates as MM/DD/YYYY and some as DD/MM/YYYY. In the United States, for example, 07/04/2000 means July 4, 2000, while in Germany and England the same string would indicate April 7, 2000. The best way to add this sort of information to your DTD is in the form of a comment block:

```
<!-- Element: Invoice                                                    -->
<!-- Attributes:                                                         -->
<!--    orderDate                                                        -->
<!--       Data type:   datetime                                        -->
<!--       Format:      YYYY-MM-DD                                      -->
<!--       Description: This field contains the date the invoice was    -->
<!--                    submitted.                                       -->
<!--    shipDate                                                         -->
<!--       Data type:   datetime                                        -->
<!--       Format:      YYYY-MM-DD                                      -->
<!--       Description: This field contains the date the parts ordered  -->
<!--                    on the invoice were shipped to the customer.     -->
<!--    shipMethod                                                       -->
<!--       Data type:   enumerated attribute                            -->
<!--       Format:      USPS:  United States Postal Service             -->
<!--                    UPS:   United Parcel Service                     -->
<!--                    FedEx: Federal Express                           -->
<!--       Description: This field indicates what shipper was used to    -->
<!--                    ship the parts to the customer.                  -->
<!ELEMENT Invoice EMPTY>
<!ATTLIST Invoice
    orderDate CDATA #REQUIRED
    shipDate CDATA #REQUIRED
    shipMethod (USPS | UPS | FedEx) #REQUIRED>
```

While this will drastically increase the size of your DTD, many processors parse and cache DTDs, making the extra comments irrelevant. If you find that your processor's performance is degraded when using heavily commented DTDs, you might want to store the comments in some other medium (such as the implementation guide, which we'll cover later).

Naming Conventions

In order for your standard to be internally coherent and comprehensible, a naming convention should be used for all elements and attributes. The naming convention should be detailed enough that someone who is implementing the standard may determine, at a glance, what a particular element or attribute represents. For example, here's one possible naming convention you might use:

- ❏ Element names should be upper-camel-case (words concatenated, with the first letter of each word capitalized).

- ❏ Attribute names should be lower-camel-case (words concatenated, with the first letter of each word capitalized except for the first word in the attribute name).

- ❏ Attribute names should not repeat the element name in which they appear (for example, in the `Invoice` element use the attribute name `orderDate`, not `invoiceOrderDate`).

- ❏ Attribute names should consist of (optionally) one or more prefixes describing the role of the data point in the overall structure, followed by a main name describing the data point, followed by a suffix describing the type of data that the data value may hold (including scaling information, if any).

- ❏ Attributes that represent Boolean values take the prefix `is`.

So the following structure would agree with the above naming convention list:

```
<!ELEMENT SalesTax EMPTY>
<!ATTLIST SalesTax
   stateText CDATA #REQUIRED
   valuePercent CDATA #REQUIRED
   isExempt (Y | N) #REQUIRED>
```

but this structure would not:

```
<!ELEMENT salestax EMPTY>            (does not follow naming convention for
                                      elements)
<!ATTLIST salestax
   state CDATA #REQUIRED             (does not indicate the type of
                                      information)
   percentValue CDATA #REQUIRED      (does not have the type of data as a
                                      suffix)
   TaxExempt (Y | N) #REQUIRED       (repeats the prefix, and does not begin
                                      with "is")
```

The exact details of the naming convention aren't as important as the existence of the convention itself. As long as the convention makes it easy to understand the role and meaning of each element and attribute simply by looking at its name, you can choose the syntactical style that suits the standards group best.

Of course, the decisions you make regarding these ground rules will affect the entire future project, so it's important to get it right. Therefore, the next thing we need to assess is exactly what bearing these decisions will have.

Understanding the Impact of Design Decisions

There is a great temptation when designing XML structures to try to design the most elegant solution, regardless of the implications for development of using the structures created. However, it's important to take the development and production implications of your design decisions into account from the outset. Let's look at some common metrics that can be adversely affected by design decisions.

Performance

The most obvious production metric is performance. With any XML implementation, careful attention has to be paid to the way the documents are constructed, their size, and the way they are parsed to avoid memory and network bottlenecks. Let's look at some common design decisions that can adversely impact performance.

Document Size

If a developer is using the DOM, or some toolset or library that is based on the DOM, the entire XML document is read into memory and parsed into the node tree before actions are taken on the document. This creates an obvious memory bottleneck if the documents are too large, or if too many concurrent sessions of the DOM (or DOM-dependent) parser are instantiated on a single machine.

If you are concerned about memory consumption, there are several approaches you can take to mitigate the problem:

❑ **Reduce the Tag Sizes.**

As we saw earlier in the document, reducing the tag sizes on your elements can significantly reduce the size of documents. This translates directly to a reduced footprint for each instance of the DOM processor loaded and reading documents. This is probably the best approach to the problem, but it has the significant downside of making the documents less human-readable.

❑ **Add more Memory/Hardware.**

As with any production system bottleneck, you can improve the system performance if you distribute the load across additional systems, or add more memory to the system that is experiencing the memory bottleneck. Unfortunately, this has the obvious drawback of requiring new hardware or memory to be purchased and installed.

❑ **Reduce the Scope of the Structures.**

If the XML documents cover a wide range of information, one way to reduce the memory footprint is to remove information from your structures that is not accessed by your consumers. Perhaps you elected to add some information to support theoretical future consumers who might need it, or you tried to create a structure that was "one-size-fits-all." In this case, consider breaking the structure into smaller structures, which may be used to satisfy particular consumer requirements separately to control the system load.

□　**Use SAX Technology Instead.**

SAX parsers, or processors that are based on SAX, have a significantly smaller footprint than DOM parsers, since they stream the document through a parse window rather than loading the entire document into memory. However, SAX parsers can be notoriously difficult to work with, especially if your document has pointing relationships (ID-IDREF connections) that need to be navigated. If a pointing relationship is a backward reference (i.e., the ID pointed to by the IDREF appears earlier in the document), then either multiple passes or some sort of memory caching mechanism will be required to navigate the relationship – which defeats the whole purpose of the small memory footprint.

Overnormalization

Another factor that can affect performance is how normalized your structure is – in other words, how many nodes deep the created tree is. Depending on the specific processor implementation, a deeper tree can take longer to navigate. If you think that your structures might be overnormalized, look for one-to-one relationships between elements and their element content. These can typically be denormalized easily, and the attributes of the child element brought into the parent.

Too Many Pointing Relationships

An overabundance of pointing relationships in your structures can have serious performance implications for processors. As we mentioned earlier in the chapter, most implementations of the DOM don't have a built-in way to navigate ID-IDREF relationships. Those that do still have to iterate through the entire element node list looking for the element whose ID matches the IDREF you have.

The problem is only compounded if you are using the SAX processor. The more pointing relationships that are in your structures, the more likely it is that one of the relationships will point backwards in the document, forcing implementers to write caching schemes or perform multiple parse passes on documents.

If you find that the number of pointing relationships is having performance implications for you, you might try transforming some of the pointers to containment relationships. This may cause your document to be slightly larger, but it will in fact be processed faster than one containing the pointing relationships. Let's see an example of this.

Recall the sample invoice DTD we used to show how XML might be used to drive a presentation layer (ch05_ex06.dtd and ch05_ex06.xml):

```
<!ELEMENT InvoiceData (Invoice+, Part+)>
<!ELEMENT Invoice (LineItem+)>
<!ATTLIST Invoice
    orderDate CDATA #REQUIRED
    shipDate CDATA #REQUIRED
    shipMethod (UPS | USPS | FedEx) #REQUIRED>
<!ELEMENT LineItem EMPTY>
<!ATTLIST LineItem
    partIDREF IDREF #REQUIRED
    quantity CDATA #REQUIRED
    price CDATA #REQUIRED>
<!ELEMENT Part EMPTY>
<!ATTLIST Part
    partID ID #REQUIRED
    name CDATA #REQUIRED
    size CDATA #REQUIRED
    color CDATA #REQUIRED>
```

```
<InvoiceData>
    <Invoice
        orderDate="12/1/2000"
        shipDate="12/4/2000"
        shipMethod="UPS">
        <LineItem
            partIDREF="p1"
            quantity="17"
            price="0.10" />
        <LineItem
            partIDREF="p2"
            quantity="22"
            price="0.20" />
    </Invoice>
    <Invoice
        orderDate="12/2/2000"
        shipDate="12/5/2000"
        shipMethod="USPS">
        <LineItem
            partIDREF="p3"
            quantity="13"
            price="0.30" />
        <LineItem
            partIDREF="p1"
            quantity="11"
            price="0.10" />
    </Invoice>
    <Part
        PartID="p1"
        name="grommet"
        size="2 in."
        color="blue" />
    <Part
        PartID="p2"
        name="widget"
        size="3 in."
        color="silver" />
    <Part
        PartID="p3"
        name="sprocket"
        size="1 in."
        color="red" />
</InvoiceData>
```

In this example, an ID-IDREF navigation is required – taking the PartIDREF value and navigating to the appropriate information about the part. We can improve the performance of the document by changing this relationship to a containment relationship, denormalizing it into the LineItem structure, and repeating the part data where necessary (ch05_ex10.dtd and ch05_ex10.xml):

```
<!ELEMENT InvoiceData (Invoice+)>
<!ELEMENT Invoice (LineItem+)>
<!ATTLIST Invoice
    orderDate CDATA #REQUIRED
    shipDate CDATA #REQUIRED
    shipMethod (UPS | USPS | FedEx) #REQUIRED>
<!ELEMENT LineItem EMPTY>
<!ATTLIST LineItem
    name CDATA #REQUIRED
    size CDATA #REQUIRED
    color CDATA #REQUIRED
    quantity CDATA #REQUIRED
    price CDATA #REQUIRED>
```

```
<?xml version="1.0"?>
<!DOCTYPE listing SYSTEM "ch05_ex10.dtd" >

<InvoiceData>
    <Invoice
        orderDate="12/1/2000"
        shipDate="12/4/2000"
        shipMethod="UPS">
        <LineItem
            name="grommet"
            size="2 in."
            color="blue"
            quantity="17"
            price="0.10" />
        <LineItem
            name="widget"
            size="3 in."
            color="silver"
            quantity="22"
            price="0.20" />
    </Invoice>
    <Invoice
        orderDate="12/2/2000"
        shipDate="12/5/2000"
        shipMethod="USPS">
        <LineItem
            name="sprocket"
            size="1 in."
            color="red"
            quantity="13"
            price="0.30" />
        <LineItem
            name="grommet"
            size="2 in."
            color="blue"
            quantity="11"
            price="0.10" />
    </Invoice>
</InvoiceData>
```

If the consuming system needs to know that the grommet referenced in the first invoice is the same as the grommet referenced in the second invoice, it will need to reconcile that information by comparing the name, size, and so on. The ch05_ex06 version will be smaller, while the ch05_ex10 version parses more quickly – it all depends on your specific performance requirements.

Coding Time

Another important factor to take into consideration when developing XML structures is the time it will take for code processors to produce and consume them. There are several ways that your structure design can influence the time it takes to write code against it.

Document Complexity

One pretty obvious way that your structure can influence the coding time required to build against it is its complexity. The more complex a document structure, the more lines of code will need to be written to produce or consume it.

While there's no way around a certain level of complexity – after all, the XML document needs to contain all the information relevant to the task at hand – you can avoid document complexity by avoiding overnormalization. If an element has a one-to-one relationship with another element, and there's no compelling reason to keep the two separate, pulling the attributes of the child into the parent and discarding the child will make the document tighter and easier to parse.

Pointing Relationships

The more pointing relationships your document uses, the more difficult it will be to write code that produces or consumes it. Producers will need to generate identifiers and make sure all the references properly link back to the identifiers, while consumers will need to hop around the tree pursuing pointing relationships to extract the information they need. Removing pointing relationships where possible will help to shorten the coding cycle.

Levels of Abstraction

When designing data structures, the developer can choose the level of abstraction to which the structures will be taken. While additional abstraction can produce real benefits in a relational model, it only introduces unnecessary processing for a producer or consumer of an XML document, as the level of abstraction has to be rectified before the information can be accessed.

Let's see an example. Say we have this structure for the `Invoice` element:

```
<!ELEMENT Invoice (Date+)>
<!ELEMENT Date EMPTY>
<!ATTLIST Date
    dateType (orderDate | shipDate) #REQUIRED
    dateValue CDATA #REQUIRED>
```

```
<Invoice>
    <Date dateType="orderDate" dateValue="12/1/2000" />
    <Date dateType="shipDate" dateValue="12/4/2000" />
</Invoice>
```

Many developers are drawn to this type of implementation, as it seems more backward-compatible: if you want to add a different kind of date for the invoice, just add a possible value to the enumerated value and you're done. However, there are some issues with this type of structure in XML.

First, there's no way to state that only one `orderDate` and one `shipDate` date may appear. Thus, the following document would be perfectly legal:

```
<Invoice>
    <Date dateType="orderDate" dateValue="12/1/2000" />
    <Date dateType="orderDate" dateValue="12/4/2000" />
</Invoice>
```

Additionally, a consumer now has to retrieve all the child `Date` elements of the `Invoice` element, look at the `dateType` to figure out what type of `Date` each is, and then act accordingly. A much better structure, and one that is much easier to code to, is one that explicitly states each date type:

```
<!ELEMENT Invoice EMPTY>
<!ATTLIST Invoice
    orderDate CDATA #REQUIRED
    shipDate CDATA #REQUIRED>
```

```
<Invoice
    orderDate="12/1/2000"
    shipDate="12/4/2000" />
```

Developer Ramp-up Time

Another issue to consider when designing your structures is the developer ramp-up time; in other words, how long it will take the developer to understand the representation of the data found in the XML structure you have created. This concern is similar to the concern over coding time, and naturally may be addressed in similar ways. The main issues that will extend developer ramp-up time are the document complexity, the number of pointing relationships used in the document, and the abstractness of the document.

Extensibility

One thing to keep in mind when developing your XML structures is that they are likely to change over time. While true backward compatibility is a difficult goal to attain with XML, you can at least design your structures so that old documents may be migrated upward with a minimum of effort.

Again, one major thing you can do to make this easier is to avoid too many pointing relationships – these will make understanding the impact of any changes you choose to make difficult at best. You should also think about whether elements and attributes should be required or optional. If you are striving for backward compatibility, any elements and attributes you add should be optional. However, be aware that you lose a certain level of ability to perform business rule enforcement if you choose to do so.

During the Development

Next, we need to look at some issues that are likely to arise during the development of your documents.

Subdividing the Workload

Since standards design efforts are typically collaborative efforts, there need to be some clearly-defined ways to control who is working on what portion of the document. Typically, the best approach is to subdivide the work and allow the domain experts to concentrate their efforts (initially, at least) on the areas of the document that pertain to their skills.

For example, say you were developing the invoice system we have been using as an example. You might assign the design of the parts structures to your inventory control data developer, the invoice structures to your point-of-sale data developer, and the summary tables to your accounting developer. A good rule of thumb is to assign each part of the workload to the person or team that has the greatest vested interest in the way that part of the structure is designed.

One good approach to subdividing the effort is to first meet as a team to map out the overall structure of the document. For example, you might all agree that a document contains invoices, each of which reference parts, and are summarized in a monthly element. Once consensus has been reached on this, then each individual element (or group of elements) should be doled out to the developer who will be working on it (or them). Once everyone has finished their own designs, you should meet again to bring the structures together (and we'll see how this is done later in the chapter).

Data issues

While developing the structures, there are some common data issues you are likely to encounter. These issues may stem from a disagreement among participants, or from issues associated with the resultant structures. We'll look at the following issues, and how they may be addressed:

❑ General vs. specific

❑ Required vs. optional

❑ "Tag soup"

❑ Keeping the Structure "Representation Independent"

General vs. Specific

This problem is the one that tends to crop up more often than any other, especially in standards with wider scope. Let's say that we are designing an invoice and summary document to be passed back and forth between the point-of-sale system and the accounting system. From the point-of-sale perspective, the natural way to reference prices is going to be at the line item level – the customer paid a certain price for each unit of a certain part, and a certain quantity of parts were ordered. However, from the accounting perspective, the natural way to reference prices is at the invoice level – that way, accounting can ensure that all customers are billed properly without having to recalculate totals for every invoice. Which representation is correct in the structures we're creating?

One way to resolve this issue is to state that both the general and the specific representations are correct, but that they should be declared as optional. This allows all producers of the document to simply store whatever information is available. However, this introduces a problem: what if the accounting system produces a document, and the point-of-sale system tries to consume it? It will not have the information necessary (the line item information), and so the point-of-sale system cannot recreate the line items for the invoice. Typically, a producer that includes the specific information can create a document that can be consumed by a consumer looking for the general information, but not vice-versa.

Another place where this crops up is in the discussion of enumerated values. For example, say the point-of-sale designers propose the following structure for shipMethod:

```
<!ATTLIST Invoice
    shipMethod (USPS | UPS | FedEx) #REQUIRED>
```

However, the fulfillment designer proposes this structure:

```
<!ATTLIST Invoice
    shipMethod (USPSGround |
                USPSPriority |
                UPSGround |
                UPSOvernight |
                FedExGround |
                FedExOvernight) #REQUIRED>
```

Again, we have the case of one designer proposing the general values, and one designer proposing more specific values. Similar techniques must be used to determine what the representation used in the standard should be. In this case, the ideal structure probably looks something like this:

```
<!ATTLIST Invoice
    shipper (USPS |
             UPS |
             FedEx) #REQUIRED
    shipMethod (Ground |
                Overnight) #OPTIONAL>
```

Required vs. Optional

Another issue that often arises is debate over whether a particular element or attribute should be required or optional. For example, the point-of-sale designer might insist that the LineItem child element of the Invoice element is required – after all, you can't have an invoice without line items, right? On the other hand, the accounting designer insists that the LineItem child element should be optional – by the time the invoice reaches the accounting system, all they care about is the customer and the amount due.

This decision is usually a toss-up – either you make the element optional, losing some of your ability to control the content of the XML document (because a point-of-sale system could now leave off the LineItem elements in the Invoice element), or you make the element required (meaning that the Accounting system now has to remember the line items for every invoice). Typically, the wider scope an XML standards effort has, the more likely that items will be optional rather than required.

"Tag soup"

Developers familiar with relational database design, but unfamiliar with XML design, often tend to overuse pointing relationships, as pointing relationships are highly reminiscent of foreign key relationships in relational databases. However, using too many pointing relationships causes the document to degenerate into "tag soup" in other words, rather than being a tree structure, the document is simply a large pile of leaves with pointers connecting back and forth between them.

We've already seen some of the perils of a document that has too many pointing relationships. It's important that issues of incipient tag soup are addressed and resolved during the peer reviews (which we'll discuss later).

Keeping the Structure Representation-Independent

A common mistake that new XML developers often make is to tie their structures too closely to a specific representation of the data contained in those structures. The greatest benefit of XML is its ability to abstract the data away from the specific representation of that data.

Here's an example. Say we had the following printed invoice document, which has been our standard document for the past twenty years:

Invoice
Order date: 12/1/2000
Ship date: 12/4/2000
Ship method: UPS

Part	Quantity	Unit Price	Price
2 in. blue grommet	17	0.10	1.70
3 in. silver widget	22	0.20	4.40
Total			6.10

A developer might be tempted to design a structure that looked like this (ch05_ex11.dtd):

```
<!ELEMENT Invoice (orderDate, shipDate, shipMethod, Line1, Line2, Line3)>
<!ELEMENT orderDate (#PCDATA)>
<!ELEMENT shipDate (#PCDATA)>
<!ELEMENT shipMethod (#PCDATA)>
<!ELEMENT Line1 EMPTY>
<!ATTLIST Line1
    partDescription CDATA #REQUIRED
    quantity CDATA #REQUIRED
    price CDATA #REQUIRED>
<!ELEMENT Line2 EMPTY>
<!ATTLIST Line2
    partDescription CDATA #REQUIRED
    quantity CDATA #REQUIRED
    price CDATA #REQUIRED>
<!ELEMENT Line3 EMPTY>
<!ATTLIST Line3
    partDescription CDATA #REQUIRED
    quantity CDATA #REQUIRED
    price CDATA #REQUIRED>
```

The problem is that now the tag names in the XML refer back to a specific representation of the data – the printed invoice – not the data itself. This problem tends to crop up more frequently when discussing commonly used forms across an industry, such as a mortgage application form or an income tax form. You should avoid making reference to specific aspects of a single representation of data, such as line numbers, whenever possible. The only exception to this rule would be if your XML was intended only to drive a presentation layer, and all planned representations of the data followed the same general layout

Obviously, the better structure to use here would be this (ch05_ex11a.dtd):

```
<!ELEMENT Invoice (orderDate, shipDate, shipMethod, Line+)>
<!ELEMENT orderDate (#PCDATA)>
<!ELEMENT shipDate (#PCDATA)>
<!ELEMENT shipMethod (#PCDATA)>
<!ELEMENT Line EMPTY>
<!ATTLIST Line
    partDescription CDATA #REQUIRED
    quantity CDATA #REQUIRED
    price CDATA #REQUIRED>
```

Pulling it all Together

Once the developers have all produced their portions of the XML structures, it's time to pull it all together into one coherent standard. However, as you might imagine, problems often arise when attempting to do so. Let's see some of the ways you can deal with these problems and prepare associated information to make the adoption of the standard as painless as possible.

Peer Review

It's important that the entire structure be subject to peer review. This helps ensure that the work done by each team member is accurate and consistent with work done by the others on the team. In this step, issues such as too many pointing relationships and too implementation-specific designs can be identified and resolved.

In addition to the structure being reviewed by the team who developed it, it should be reviewed by developers who did not work on the structure. These don't necessarily need to be XML designers, but they should have a good working understanding of the data that drives the structures. As issues are identified by the peer review, they should be addressed and resolved, either by the developer responsible or the team as a whole.

Resolving Disputes

When everyone meets to discuss the structures, inevitably some disputes will arise that cannot be resolved through a simple discussion. Most data developers have strongly-held opinions about the way data should be represented (all interest rates should be shown as ratios, for example, or all data points with similar types should be grouped together). No amount of debate is likely to create a consensus on these types of issues. When arbitration fails, the way to resolve a dispute is to put it to a vote. If the team consists of an even number of participants, the lead developer can decide ties. This way, the resultant structures will be satisfactory to the majority of the participants in the process.

The Implementation Guide

When you deliver the XML structures you have created to the developers who will be using them, you should also provide an **implementation guide**. This document should include:

- ❏   A brief statement of the purpose of the structure
- ❏   A dictionary describing the elements and attributes in the structure
- ❏   A diagram of the structure
- ❏   A few sample documents that exercise the various permutations of the structure that are allowed

Let's see how each part of the guide should be created.

Statement of Purpose

The first part of the document should talk about the purpose of the document. It should describe:

- ❏   The scope of the structure (who will be using it)
- ❏   The type of data described in the structure
- ❏   The purpose to which documents using the structure will be put
- ❏   Any other considerations you took into account when designing the structure

This should help identify the role of the document, and deter developers from using the document for a purpose for which it was not originally intended (although you can pretty much guarantee that someone will do this anyway – and then complain about the fact that it doesn't suit their needs perfectly).

Dictionary

Next, you should describe the various elements and attributes in the document in a human-readable way. In this dictionary, you should provide detailed definitions, as well as describing the structure in terms of "this-points-to-that" or "this-contains-one-or-more-of-those".

Let's see a sample dictionary for a structure we've been working with in this chapter (ch05_ex06.dtd):

```
<!ELEMENT InvoiceData (Invoice+, Part+)>
<!ELEMENT Invoice (LineItem+)>
<!ATTLIST Invoice
    orderDate CDATA #REQUIRED
    shipDate CDATA #REQUIRED
    shipMethod (UPS | USPS | FedEx) #REQUIRED>
<!ELEMENT LineItem EMPTY>
<!ATTLIST LineItem
    partIDREF IDREF #REQUIRED
    quantity CDATA #REQUIRED
    price CDATA #REQUIRED>
<!ELEMENT Part EMPTY>
<!ATTLIST Part
    partID ID #REQUIRED
    name CDATA #REQUIRED
    size CDATA #REQUIRED
    color CDATA #REQUIRED>
```

Our dictionary might look like this:

Element	Details
InvoiceData	**Contains**: Invoice (one or more), followed by Part (one or more)
	Is contained by: None
	Is pointed to by: None
	Description: This element is the root element of the document
	Attributes: None
Invoice	**Contains**: LineItem (one or more)
	Is contained by: InvoiceData
	Is pointed to by: None
	Description: This element represents one physical invoice
	Attributes:
	orderDate Data type: Datetime Format: MM/DD/YYYY

Element	Details
Invoice (continued)	Description: This is the date the invoice was submitted (the date the order was placed)
	shipDate Data type: Datetime Format: MM/DD/YYYY Description: This is the date the parts on this invoice shipped, or are anticipated to ship
	shipMethod Data type: Enumerated Format: USPS: United States Postal Service UPS: United Parcel Service FedEx: Federal Express Description: This is the method used to ship the parts on this invoice, or the anticipated shipping method for the parts on this invoice
LineItem	**Contains**: None
	Is contained by: Invoice
	Is pointed to by: None
	Description: This element represents one detail line on an invoice
	Attributes:
	partIDREF Data type: IDREF (points to a Part element) Format: N/A Description: This attribute points to the Part element that describes the part ordered on this line of the invoice
	quantity Data type: Numeric Format: ##### Description: This attribute indicates how many of the specific parts were ordered on this line of the invoice
	price Data type: Numeric Format: #####.## Description: This attribute indicates the unit price paid by the customer for the part ordered on this line of the invoice
Part	**Contains**: None
	Is contained by: InvoiceData
	Is pointed to by: LineItem
	Description: This element describes a particular part referenced on one or more of the invoices in this document

Table continued on following page

Element	Details
Part (continued)	**Attributes**:
	partID Data type: ID (uniquely identifies this element within the document) Format: N/A Description: This attribute identifies this element within the document, so that it may be pointed to from the LineItem element
	name Data type: String Format: Maximum length 50 characters Description: This attribute contains the name of the part being described in this Part element
	color Data type: String Format: Maximum length 10 characters Description: This attribute describes the color of the part being described in this Part element
	size Data type: String Format: Maximum length 20 characters Description: This attribute describes the size of the part being described in this Part element

Document Structure Diagram

It's important to create a diagram of the XML structures you create. You can either do this as an aid to development during the design process, or at the end of the process to identify problems such as orphaned mislinked elements. In addition, this model should be distributed along with the structures to the developers that must use them – this will help the developers ramp up on the structures and improve their time-to-delivery.

The W3C provides an example of "Elm tree" diagramming for XML structures (http://www.w3.org/XML/1998/06/xmlspec-report-v21.htm). However, it does not go far enough in addressing pointing relationships. We recommend that you use a modified form of the W3C diagramming proposal, with an additional connector type to indicate pointing relationships. We also recommend that you list the data points associated with an element, whether they are text elements or attributes, inside the box representing that element (much as you might for a relational database diagram).

Let's see an example of a diagram using this method for our example:

```
<!ELEMENT InvoiceData (Invoice+, Part+)>
<!ELEMENT Invoice (LineItem+)>
<!ATTLIST Invoice
    orderDate CDATA #REQUIRED
    shipDate CDATA #REQUIRED
    shipMethod (UPS | USPS | FedEx) #REQUIRED>
<!ELEMENT LineItem EMPTY>
```

```
<!ATTLIST LineItem
    partIDREF IDREF #REQUIRED
    quantity CDATA #REQUIRED
    price CDATA #REQUIRED>
<!ELEMENT Part EMPTY>
<!ATTLIST Part
    partID ID #REQUIRED
    name CDATA #REQUIRED
    size CDATA #REQUIRED
    color CDATA #REQUIRED>
```

For this sample structure, the corresponding diagram would be:

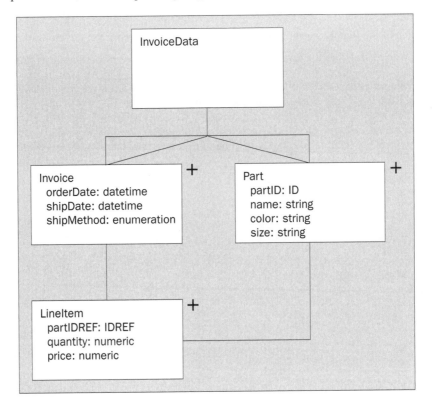

Sample Documents

Finally, you should include some sample documents in your implementation guide. These documents should cover all of the anticipated uses of the structures you have designed, and exercise as many variations of the structures as possible. You should annotate each sample document with a description of what it represents, as well as any comments on less-clear parts of the structure (such as how pointing relationships are used).

Summary

As XML becomes increasingly pervasive, the need for XML standards to be developed will grow. These standards may be as simple as a way for two systems in your enterprise to communicate with one another, or complex enough to support a worldwide industry with thousands of participating companies.

In this chapter, we've taken a look at some things to keep in mind when designing your structures, including:

❑ Understanding how the type of standard and document usage will determine the structure of our designs

❑ Understanding the need to assess the way our design decisions will affect the finished solution

❑ Some of the factors we should take into consideration during the development process

❑ How to ensure that the final standard can be implemented as painlessly as possible

Using the techniques covered in this chapter, you should be able to create standards that will be both easy to understand and well-suited to the tasks at hand.

This chapter brings us to the end of the Design Techniques section of this book. We'll now move on to look at some of the specific technologies we'll need to use in more detail, starting with XML Schemas.

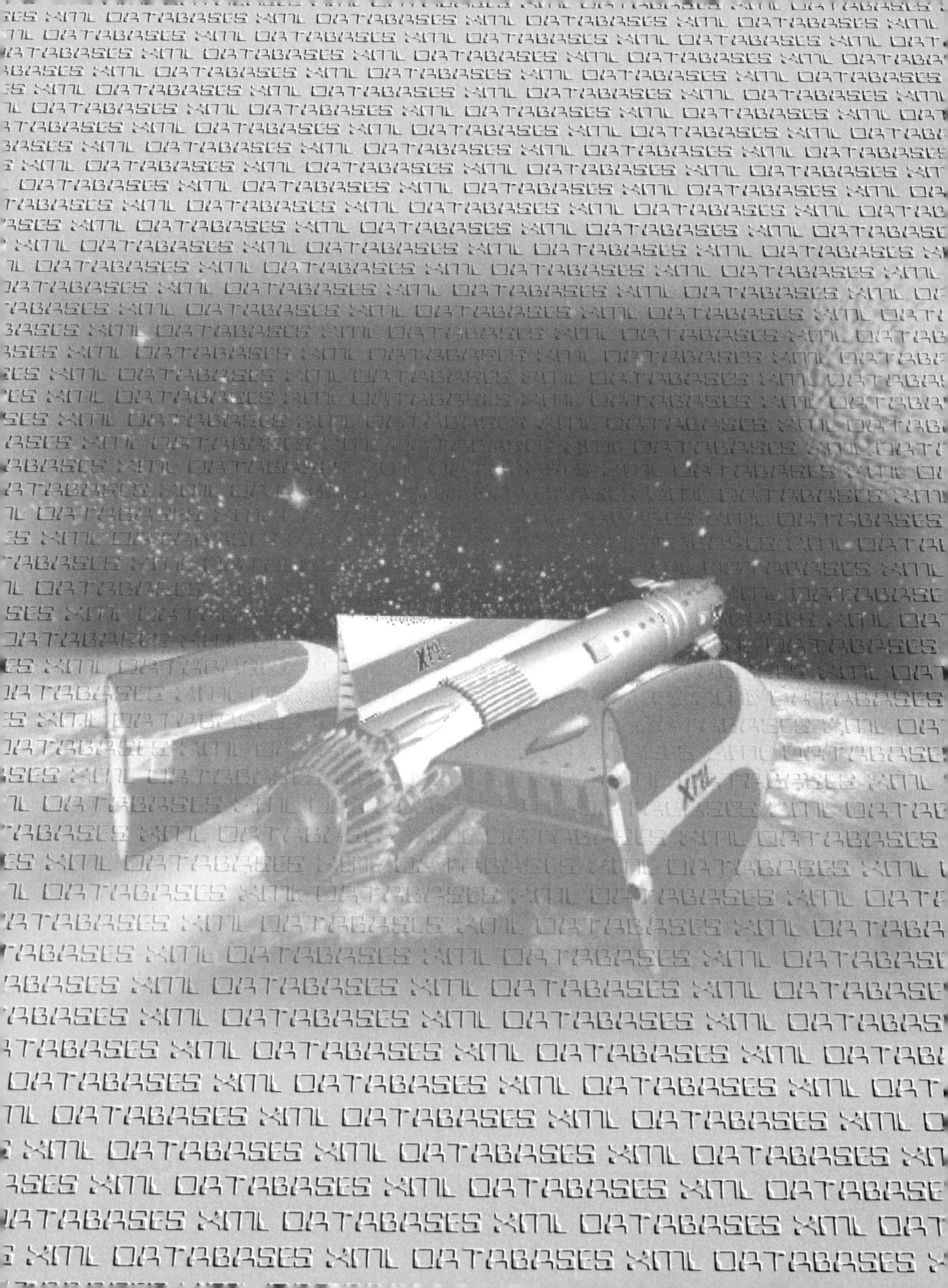
XML DATABASES

5

XML Schemas

Throughout this book, we have been looking at constraining our XML documents using Document Type Definitions. However you may be well aware, however, an alternative form of constraining XML documents has been under development by the W3C, namely **XML Schemas**.

XML technologies and database technologies, by themselves, do not share many of the same characteristics, except for schemas. As we will learn throughout this chapter, there is a much closer relationship between XML schemas and relational database schemas, than there is between DTDs and relational database schemas.

Strictly speaking, a DTD is a form of schema, and so are many of the data dictionaries and schemas used with existing relational database management systems. However, when we are talking about schemas in XML, we are usually talking about the pending W3C proposal for an XML Schema standard. When we use the term schema in this chapter, unless otherwise stated, this is what we shall be referring to.

One of the most interesting things about XML Schemas is that they are actually written in XML, which means they are a vocabulary of XML themselves. In this chapter, we will be looking at:

- ❏ The differences between XML schemas and Document Type Definitions.

- ❏ How to write XML schemas.

- ❏ The reasons why they can be seen as a more powerful alternative, and what they mean to database developers.

- ❏ Why, and when, you should consider using XML Schemas rather than DTDs.

At the time of writing, XML Schemas were a candidate recommendation from the W3C. This means that the technology has received significant review from its immediate technical community, and that the W3C are looking for technical feedback about their early implementations before making it a final recommendation. This means that the syntax is still subject to change; however, this chapter will give you a good idea of what they offer and how to write XML Schemas.

Introducing Schemas

Let's start with a general definition of a database schema: "*the organization or structure of a database, usually derived from data modeling*". This structure is typically described using some sort of controlled vocabulary that names items of data and lists any constraints that may apply (datatype, legal/illegal values, special formatting, etc.). The relationships between data items (the object of data models) are also an important part of any schema.

When the W3C started working on XML schemas, they published a set of requirements for what the schema language should be able to do (this document was published in February 1999, and can be viewed at http://www.w3.org/TR/NOTE-xml-schema-req). Some of the main drivers for the group were to:

❑ Provide a richer set of datatypes than a DTD (for example, string, Boolean, float)

❑ Provide a datatype system that allows built-in and user defined datatypes to be created with various constraining properties, which must be adequate to support import/export from any RDBMS or OODBMS.

❑ Distinguish lexical data representation from an underlying information set (more on this later);

As a result, the W3C XML Schema specification consists of three parts:

❑ **XML Schemas Part 0: Primer.** The first part is a primer, which explains what schemas are, how they differ from DTDs, and how someone builds a schema.

❑ **XML Schemas Part 1: Structures.** The next part proposes methods for describing the structure and constraining the contents of XML documents, and defines the rules governing schemavalidation of documents.

❑ **XML Schemas Part 2: Datatypes.** The third part defines a set of simple data types, which can be associated with XML element types and attributes; this allows XML software to do a better job of managing dates, numbers, and other special forms of information.

In this section, we will start with a small example of an XML schema, to give us an idea of the documents that we will be creating, this is because without an example some of the concepts can be hard to grasp. Then we will go on to see how Schemas differ from DTDs and why we should use them. Then we will go on to look at their syntax and how to write them.

A Note Before We Start – Other Schema Technologies

Because the ability to validate document instances and describe vocabularies is so important to XML, during the wait for schemas to become a W3C standard a number of other proposed schema languages have arisen. Some of these were just proposals, while others have been implemented in software so that people could make use of the functionality that schemas in XML offer.

We may have already seen or used such a schema language in XML. Microsoft's **XML-Data Reduced (XDR)**, for example, which was implemented in MSXML 2 and IE5, and is used in strategies such as BizTalk. It is based on a submission to the W3C called XML-Data, which has greatly influenced the development of XML Schemas. There are definitely strong similarities between the two, but, because Microsoft took the initiative to implement schemas with their XML parser before Schemas become a recommendation, there are definite differences as well. XDR schemas have allowed many people to work on projects that they would have been unable to otherwise had they not implemented them, although Microsoft is also committed to supporting XML Schemas when the W3C release them.

> Throughout this chapter, we will cover to the W3C version of Schemas.

Jumping Right In

Here is a small example to give us a feel for what schemas are and what they can do. Do not worry if it does not all make sense immediately, this will be a helpful reference to work with as we go through the concepts in the chapter.

Schemas are Just XML Files

As we already know, schemas are written in XML. The schema specification lays out an XML vocabulary for describing the contents of our schema documents in XML (and as such there is a DTD for the XML Schema syntax).

Because XML is supposed to be self-describing, and because XML schemas are written in XML, it is hardly surprising that elements are declared using `<element>` and that their names are declared using an attribute called `name`, like so:

```
<element name="Invoice" />
```

Attributes, meanwhile, are declared using an element called `attribute`, again with an attribute called `name` to declare their name:

```
<attribute name="CustomerId" />
```

This illustrates the kind of markup we will be using in our schema files. Elements and attributes are probably the two most important pieces of information we have to declare in an XML document, so let's get on with the example.

Our First Simple Schema

Say we wanted to create a schema for this simple `OrderData`:

```
<OrderData>
<Customer
    firstName="Bob"
    lastName="Warren"
    emailAddress="bob@mymailaddress.com" />
<Invoice type="string" />
</OrderData>
```

`Invoice` just contains character data for now to avoid overcomplicating the example at the start. If we were to write a DTD to constrain this document, it could look like this:

```
<!ELEMENT OrderData (Customer, Invoice)>
<!ELEMENT Customer>
<!ATTLIST Customer
    firstName CDATA #REQUIRED
    lastName CDATA #REQUIRED
    emailAddress CDATA #IMPLIED>
<!ELEMENT Invoice (#PCDATA) >
```

Now, it may seem obvious to point this out, but the `OrderData` element has a child element called `Customer`, and the `Customer` element has three attributes. However, schemas make an important distinction between elements that carry child elements or attributes and those that don't.

- ❑ Elements with child elements, or that carry attributes, are defined using **complex types**.
- ❑ Elements that do not carry attributes or have any child elements are called **simple types**.
- ❑ All attribute values are **simple types** because they are not able to have any child elements or attributes themselves.

Here we will see why this is important (ch05_ex1.xsd):

```
<schema xmlns="http://www.w3.org/2000/10/XMLSchema">
    <element name="OrderData" type="OrderDataType" />

    <complexType name="OrderDataType">
      <sequence>
         <element name="Customer" type="CustomerType" />
           <element name="Invoice" type="string" />
      </sequence>
    </complexType>

    <complexType name="CustomerType">
       <attribute name="firstName" type="string" use="required"/>
       <attribute name="lastName" type="string" use="required"/>
       <attribute name="emailAddress" type="string" use="required"/>
    </complexType>

</schema>
```

> **Schemas have the .xsd file extension.**

Notice that we haven't declared the content model of the OrderData element. Instead, we have declared its **type**. The declaration of an element is the association of the name with a type. There is a separate definition that specifies the nature of that type, within the complexType element.

An element whose content is a simple type can be defined in one element (such as Invoice). While elements with complex types have to be declared first using two attributes called name and type. The name is the name of the element, while the type is used to associate the name with its type definition containing. It is the type definition that defines the content model for that type (which any other element can then also use); needless to say that the complex type is defined in an element called complexType. It is also possible to nest the complexType element in the element declaration if it only applies to that one element (in which case the type attribute is not needed).

So, let's look at the construction of this document. We start with the root element of the schema, which is unsurprisingly – following the self-describing nature – <schema>. This holds the namespace for the schema specification.

```
<schema xmlns="http://www.w3.org/2000/10/XMLSchema">
...schema declarations go here
</schema>
```

Next we declare the root element OrderData:

```
<element name="OrderData" type="OrderDataType" />
```

using the name attribute to define the element's name, we also have a type attribute with the value OrderDataType. This is because the OrderData element contains nontext content that is not a built-in type – it has two child elements, one of which has several attributes. We define the content of this element in the complexType element:

```
<complexType name="OrderDataType">
    <sequence>
        <element name="Customer" type="CustomerType" />
        <element name="Invoice" type="string" />
    </sequence>
</complexType>
```

Here we can see how we define the type `OrderDataType`, which in this case, is the element content model for the `OrderData` element. The `name` attribute of the opening `<complexType>` tag contains the same name as the value of the `type` attribute where the element was declared. These two complimentary structures are how we define element content models.

We can see that there is a `sequence` element. This indicates that the child elements held within it must appear in sequence and that they must occur in the document. If we had a choice over whether they appeared or not, or if they could appear in different orders, they would appear inside a `choice` element instead.

This is followed by another two element declarations, for `Customer` and `Invoice`. We know that `Customer` is a complex type because a simple type, by definition, only applies to values of attributes and to text-only content of an element, and `Customer` carries several attributes. This means that we must add a type definition to match the declared `type` in the `Customer` element, which will specify its content. Here is the content model for the `Customer` element:

```
<complexType name="CustomerType">
    <attribute name="firstName" type="string" use="required"/>
    <attribute name="lastName" type="string" use="required"/>
    <attribute name="emailAddress" type="string" use="required"/>
</complexType>
```

The attributes that are part of the `Customer` element are all of simple type, so we just add them with the attribute declaration, which itself takes two attributes:

- name to declare the name of the attribute.
- type to declare its data type.

Now this may seem a little more complicated than the DTD at first. However, if we are not familiar with EBNF (the language that DTDs are written in) its descriptions are a lot more logical, and are actually a lot more powerful. Having seen a simple example of a schema, we will now be able to explain why they are so powerful.

Why Schemas

So far, we have used DTDs to define and constrain our XML documents, in using them we have already come across some of their limitations. Rather than dwelling in the past, let's see what this new schema language will offer us:

- Description and constraint of documents using XML Syntax.
- Support for data types.
- Description of content models and the re-use of elements via inheritance.
- Extensibility.
- The ability to write dynamic schemas.
- Self documenting capabilities when a style sheet is applied.

Let's look a little closer at each of these advantages.

Use XML Syntax

Probably the most obvious difference between XML Schemas and DTDs, and arguably the most significant advantage of them, is that XML Schemas are actually written in XML. The XML Schemas specification describes a vocabulary that can be used to constrain XML documents.

When first learning XML, many people find the notation used to write DTDs difficult to understand. DTDs are written in Extended Backus Naur Form (EBNF). Because XML Schemas use XML to describe a document, it means that users do not have to learn another syntax. Like many things, they are not too difficult when we get the hang of using them, but often they are a lot more complex than the data they describe.

While there are mature tools for working in EBNF, many of them are expensive and complex. Because XML Schemas are in XML syntax, however, there is a wealth of readily available tools that can be used straightaway with them – standard XML parsers, the DOM, SAX, XSLT, and XML-aware browsers.

It also means that it will be possible to construct schemas or transform them on the fly using standard XML technologies such as the DOM, or XSLT. This is important when we think about how XML will be used programmatically for exchange of information.

Data Typing

As we have already seen, database schemas allow us to constrain the type of data that is held within the database fields. This helps keep down the size of the database, and helps receiving applications know the format of the data that they are going to be receiving; which means that they do not need to convert the data from a string – as they would when DTDs are used to constrain a document.

Unlike DTD's XML schemas offer pretty much all the data types that we are likely to want to see. Applications can now use most of the traditional programming language data types, as well as the conceptual and maintenance benefits of the OO inheritance of data types; and structures. This is incredibly powerful when we think that, if we are creating our own markup, and have a tag called <Number> we could make sure that it holds a number as a value.

The addition of strong data-typing not only means that we can better describe and validate our documents, however. There are strong advantages for programs, which will understand the data type, for example, programs will be able to directly perform calculations on numeric data, without having to work out what data type it is supposed to be and translate it from a string to the appropriate form. We will be able to search more specifically on dates or ranges of dates. In addition, we will be better able to validate the data that we receive into our applications, making sure that it is within an allowable range and of the correct type; removing the need for writing complex validation code.

Content Models

DTDs' content models are weak, only allowing us to constrain the document to a simple sequence or choice list. They cannot be used to validate mixed content models (elements that can contain character data as well as other markup); can only contain zero, one, or many occurrences of an element, and there are no named element or attribute groups (which allow us to re-use content models). Schemas, on the other hand, allow for more detailed and robust content models. They are not mutually exclusive from mixed content, they can be used to specify exact numbers of occurrences, and can be used to name groups of elements. These are all valuable additions whether we are working with representing text or other forms of data.

Applications such as e-commerce, data exchange, and RPC (remote procedure calls), all depend upon the more advanced features of schemas, (including the ability to create complex content models), and benefit greatly from the superior description and validation of mixed content.

Extensible

When we think about the full name of XML, it is somewhat ironic that the description language is not extensible too, which is another drawback of DTDs. With XML schemas, however, this is no longer the case. Features such as user-derived datatypes, and the ability to define complex structures provide open-ended ways to extend schemas. The ability to reference multiple schemas from one document instance (it is possible to use either namespaces in the document or to avoid specifying the schema altogether), and the ability to reuse parts of schemas in other schemas (especially their content types), also allows much greater control of shared and standard vocabularies. Rather than everyone inventing their own vocabularies, people will be able to combine standard schemas that they need to define their documents.

If we think about the use of XML for interchange, and think about some of the examples where XML documents are generated on the fly from several data sources, we can see why the ability to support content models from different schemas is important. As we share more data between departments, and companies, sending the same data between different programs, the ability to support multiple schemas will be useful.

Imagine that we were writing an application that required sets of data both from our supplier and from our accounts department, and that we were getting data from these two sources into our one application. With XML Schemas, we could write a schema that the processing application could use to validate the documents (including mixed content and datatypes), or trigger some part of the system, based upon sharing of the two vocabularies.

Dynamic Schemas

XML Schemas let us use a dynamic subset of standardized schemas, that is, schema portions that are selected in response to some user input, which is a very powerful mechanism indeed. For example, after conducting a bibliographic search that's governed by an appropriate schema, a user could then purchase a book using a completely different schema for the purchase order. Even though this is theoretically possible with DTDs' by using external entities, this is a hideously complicated and error-prone approach. It is even more complicated if a number of organizations are involved. With XML Schemas it is relatively straight forward.

Self Documenting

As we shall see later, XML Schemas allow us to use `annotation` elements to describe the intended purpose. Because the schemas are written in XML, we can simply attach a style sheet to a properly annotated schema and create documentation for it. As with all programming, use of comments is simply good practice and leads to more maintainable code, as such schemas have this added way of annotating documents to describe the intentions of the author, and help those who want to use the same schema.

XML Parsers with Schema Support

At the present time, very few XML parsers and tools support the XML Schema Working Drafts. Microsoft chose to implement its own proprietary schema language (XDR), but has promised to conform to the XML Schema recommendation once it becomes a formal W3C Recommendation. IBM and Oracle have both chosen to support the open standards effort, and typically have updated their parsers soon after each Working Draft is published. Several commercial XML editors have also been developed, including a few that support schemas.

❑ **Xerces** from the Apache XML Project, which is based on technology given from IBMs XML4C and XML4J parsers – http://xml.apache.org. Although IBM still maintains the two XML parsers, **XML4C** (C++) and **XML4J** (Java) saying that they are based on the Xerces code. Information and downloads are available at http://www.alphaworks.ibm.com/. IBM has also begun to provide XML support in their flagship **DB2** product, as well as other applications.

❑ Information about Oracle's **XML Parser for Java v2** can be found on-line at http://technet.oracle.com/tech/xml/. It is integrated into the **Oracle 8i** DBMS, and thus provides XML support on the multitude of systems that can run this popular DBMS.

❑ **XML Spy 3.0** from Icon Informations-System GmbH (Icon Information-Systems) supports several types of schema, including XML 1.0 DTDs, the 7 April 2000 draft of XML Schema, XDR (plus its BizTalk flavor), and even DCD. This product began as a structured XML editor and has grown into a full-blown IDE for XML. Product info can be found at http://new.xmlspy.com/features_intro.html; and the company's general web site is at http://www.icon-is.com.

❑ **XML Authority 1.2** is Extensibility's XML schema design environment that offers support for DTDs, XDR, a subset of XML Schema, Software AG's Tamino Server, and BizTalk. They also offer an editor (**XML Instance**), and a new conversion tool (**XML Console**). The company's web site is at http://www.extensibility.com.

There is likely to be a flood of other parsers that support schemas as soon as they become a W3C recommendation.

Learning the New Vocabulary

Having heard some of the advantages, let's get into looking at the schema specification. As explained earlier, there are three parts to the XML Schemas specification. There is the primer, which introduces the key topics in schemas in a different way to the usual specifications (this is informative, and while it is not a complete reference, it does get us started with the main concepts) and two reference sections: **structures**, and **datatypes**.

❑ Datatypes are the basic building blocks of XML Schemas, which are used as the basis of all the larger components of a schema.

❑ Structures are more like the compounds: these can be constructed from the datatypes, and are used to describe the element, attribute, and validation structure of a document type.

Let's take a quick look at these before studying the syntax of schemas of these specifications.

Datatypes

Like most modern programming languages, XML Schemas provide two basic kinds of datatypes:

❑ **Primitive datatypes** – those that are not defined in terms of other datatypes. They are like the most basic building blocks of XML schemas, rather like atoms, and indeed are the basis for all other types. For example, `string`, `Boolean`, `Float`, `Double`, `ID`, `IDREF`, and `Entity` are examples of primitive datatypes in XML Schemas.

❑ **Derived datatypes** – those that are defined in terms of existing types. New types may be derived from either a primitive type or another derived type. For example, the XML Schema `CDATA` type is derived from the `string` type, which is its base type, represents white space normalized strings of characters and is derived from the primitive type `string`.

We should get the idea that from these **datatypes**, we can then build simple and complex **types**. If we remember the first example, a simple type was the empty element with a declared datatype, and the complex type was the element that had the complex content model. In meeting the schemas specification, we could be reminded of the age-old problem of: *Which came first – the chicken or the egg?* It certainly makes describing schemas interesting because datatypes are required to describe simple and complex types, which make up the structure of the document, but without the structure there would be no need for the datatypes.

Like most programming languages, there are predefined datatypes, known as **built-in types**, which can be used in any instance of a schema that is written according to the XML Schemas specification. By definition, all primitive types are also built-in types – so we cannot add your own primitive types, they could only be added by the W3C if they updated the XML Schema specification.

It is worth noting here that the W3C has also defined a set of built-in *derived* types. Built-in types were believed to be so universal, that they would end up being reinvented by most schema designers anyway, examples include CDATA (which we just met as an example of a derived type), `integer`, `long`, `Short`, `Byte`, and `date`.

There are also user-derived types that are not part of the specification, but are derived from existing datatypes. For example, we may wish to create a derived type to represent our order ID system.

Structures

Having got an idea of datatypes, and simple and complex types, we can briefly look at the other major part of schemas specification – the structure of the document and its **content models**.

Just as with DTDs, content models are the way in which we explicitly define the valid structure of elements and their other components as a **document type**. The schema can be used just like a DTD to validate the instances of documents that are supposed to be written with that structure.

There are two distinct types of markup in XML Schema that loosely correspond to these two parts of the specification:

❑ **Definitions** – which create new types (both simple and complex).

❑ **Declaration** – which describes the content models of elements and attributes.

With one exception (which we will meet later), there are two kinds of **type declarations** that create structures:

❑ **Simple declarations** – which create **simple types**. These are how we can create the derived datatypes we just spoke of, including those that were built in to use the schema specification – remember that we said that these derived datatypes are a form of structure.

❑ **Complex declarations** – which create **complex types**. These are primarily used to describe content models.

XML Schema Preamble – The `<schema>` Element

An XML Schema consists of a **preamble**, followed by zero or more declarations (though an empty schema isn't very useful, of course). The preamble can contain three optional attributes within the opening `<schema>` tag. This need not be the schema's document element – a schema may be embedded within another XML document. In fact, there is no requirement that a schema is a discrete text document – for example, it could be constructed via the DOM.

The following is an example of the <schema> element, with references to some commonly used XML vocabularies:

```
<schema
    xmlns="http://www.w3.org/2000/10/XMLSchema/"
    xmlns:xsd="http://www.w3.org/2000/10/XMLSchema-datatypes"
    xmlns:xsi="http://www.w3.org/2000/10/XMLSchema-instances"
    version="1.42.57" >
    ...
<schema>
```

The <schema> element uses its attributes to identify any external schemas that are to be used by this schema and all of its child elements.

Specifying the Namespaces

The first two attributes use XML namespaces to identify the two W3C schema specifications that are used in almost every XML Schema. The first includes the basic XML Schema elements such as <element>, <attribute>, <group>, <simpleType>, <complexType>, and so on. The latter is used to define the standard XML Schema datatypes, such as string, float, integer, etc.

We don't have to use xsd or xsi as the namespace identifiers (although we do have to bind our namespaces to a prefix, they could just as easily be foo, bar, or anything that didn't conflict with our own namespaces), but xsd and xsi *are* the recommended conventions.

We could also make the most widely-used namespace our default, instead of using a prefix:

```
<schema xmlns="http://www.w3.org/2000/10/XMLSchema" ...
```

This way, we don't need to include the prefix in every XML Schema declaration, and can use unqualified names, which can greatly improve the readability of our schemas.

Specifying the Version

The version attribute is strictly informational, and represents the version number of the schema in which it is located. Our XML application might want to ensure that a specific version number is used to validate our documents. We could also use multiple versions: one for development, another for testing, and yet another for production purposes.

Attribute Declarations

We have already seen that attributes can be declared using <attribute>. When we declare the attribute we use the following syntax:

```
<attribute name="firstName" />
```

Here we use the name attribute to give the name of the attribute. If we want to be available to different content models, we declare it outside of a complex type at the top of a document. Then, when we want it to appear in a complex type definition, we use the ref attribute instead of name.

```
<attribute name="firstName" />

<element name="fullName" type="fullNameType" />
```

```
<complexType name="fullNameType">
     <attribute ref="firstName" />
     <attribute name="lastName" />
</complexType>

<element name="contactDetails" type="contactDetailsType" />
<complexType name="contactDetailsType">
     <attribute ref="firstName" />
</complexType>
```

Here we are using the `firstName` attribute in two different elements, so we have declared it globally, while the `lastName` attribute is only used in the `fullName` element. This means that we can re-use the attribute declaration and set defaults in a central location.

There are some other useful things we can declare as attributes of the `attribute` construct:

- ❑   We can specify a default value for it, using the `value` attribute, which takes a string.

- ❑   We can define a primitive or built-in type with a `type` attribute.

- ❑   We can also specify one of the following values for the `use` attribute (`default`, `fixed`, `optional`, `required` or `prohibited`). If none is specified the default is `optional`. The values represent:
    - ❑   `default` – the attribute being declared has a default value (as specified with the `value` attribute).
    - ❑   `fixed` – the attribute has a constant value (specified with the `value` attribute).
    - ❑   `optional` – the attribute is optional (the default value of the `use` attribute).
    - ❑   `required` – the attribute is required, and must always be used with the parent element.
    - ❑   `prohibited` – no attribute may be present for the parent element.

Here is another example that demonstrates some of these:

```
<attribute name="widgetLength" type="xsd:float" value="0.5" use="required" />
```

Element Definitions

Again, we define elements using the `element` construct (which is itself an element):

```
<element name="BookType" />
```

If we declare the complex type for this element at the top of the document, we will be able to reuse it through the rest of the document using the `ref` attribute.

```
<element name="Book" />
   <complexType>
      <element name="title" />
      <element name="author" />
   </complexType>
</element>

<element name="Catalog">
   <complexType>
       <element ref="Book">
   </complexType>
<element>
```

Here we are declaring a `complexType` (which is used to describe a content model).

We could also specify a simple type, which is how we declare our own derived datatypes:

```
<element name="myelement" type="mySimpleType"/>
```

We will be seeing how to declare our own derived types later in the chapter, for the moment, this example means that `myElement` will be constrained by our derived datatype of `mySimpleType`.

If we do not define a type for the element, it takes the **ur-type** definition (which is unconstrained and the base type of all simple and complex types):

```
<element name="unconstrained" />
```

Default or Fixed Element Content

We can also supply `default` or `fixed` attributes on an element definition. If an element is empty in an instance document and `default` is specified, then the value (which is a `string`) is taken to be the content of that element. If `fixed` is specified, then the element's content must either be empty, in which case `fixed` behaves as default, or it must match the supplied value which is a `string`.

Specifying Null Values in Document Instances

If we wanted to represent an element as having a null value when sending information to or from a database, we can use the `nullable` attribute in the element declaration (which takes a Boolean, whose default is `false`). In this case a null value is not sent as element content, rather it is specified as an attribute. For example:

```
<element name="ackReceived" nullable="true" />
```

In the instance document, we then represent that the `ackRecieved` element has a null value using the null attribute (this is defined in the XML Schema namespace for instances at http://www.w3.org/2000/10/XMLSchema-instance, and must therefore use the `xsi` namespace prefix):

```
<ackReceived xsi:null="true"></ackReceived>
```

> We can also specify an **ID** attribute, which is very important, especially in describing relationships, but we will come back to this point later.

Cardinality – minOccurs and maxOccurs

If we want to specify the occurrences of an element's children, we have two optional attributes that help us, these are `minOccurs` and `maxOccurs`. If both attributes are omitted, there may only be one occurrence of the element and it is required (just like the absence of a cardinality operator in a DTD).

Obviously, we can only use them on element declarations because attributes of the same name can only appear once in a given element. The following table shows the mapping of DTD cardinality operators to the equivalent values of `minOccurs` and `maxOccurs` schema attributes:

Cardinality Operator	minOccurs Value	maxOccurs Value	Number of Child Element(s)
[none]	1	1	One and only one.
?	0	1	Zero or one.
*	0	unbounded	Zero or more.
+	1	unbounded	One or more.

If we do not specify a value for minOccurs, the default value is 1, but there is no single default for maxOccurs *per se*.

If minOccurs is present and maxOccurs is omitted, its value is assumed to be equal to the value of minOccurs.

```
<element ref="emailAddress" minOccurs="1" />
```

would mean that the emailAddress element that we had previously declared must occur at least once.

The special value of unbounded, which is allowed only for maxOccurs, is just the formal way of saying "...or more [without a limit]" in a schema.

For example, if we were limiting the number of orders a customer could make, we might want to constrain the number of lineItem elements an order could take.

Complex Type Definitions

As we saw in the first example, new Complex Type Definitions use the <complexType> element, its attributes, and any valid constraining facet(s). Usually, they will contain a set of element declarations, attribute declarations and element references.

As we have seen, elements are declared using element, and attributes are declared using attribute. Here we can define a complex type for the Customer element to show its content model.

```
<element name="Customer">
   <complexType name="CustomerType">
      <attribute name="firstName" type="string"/>
      <attribute name="lastName" type="string" />
      <attribute name="emailAddress" type="string" />
   </complexType>
</element>
```

So, whenever a Customer element is used, it must have three attributes, each of which have a string as a value. If we had wanted child elements, however, we could have declared them so:

```
<element name="Customer">
   <complexType name="CustomerType">
      <sequence>
         <element name="firstName" type="string"/>
         <element name="lastName" type="string" />
         <element name="emailAddress" type="string" />
      </sequence>
   </complexType>
</element>
```

Here we have added the `sequence` element, which means that the elements must appear in the order they are declared.

Just to reenforce the idea of types, the `firstName`, `lastName` and `emailAddress` attributes and elements in these examples involve the simple type (which is a data type) `string`, while the `Customer` element is a complex type (describing the content model). Both, however, use the same attribute of `type` to identify the type.

Choice Sequence and All Groups – *<choice>, <sequence> and <all>*

These first two elements are, pretty much, self-describing – they correspond to the choice (|) and sequence (,) list operators in a DTD.

Although the schema representation is more verbose than that of the DTD, it is arguably easier to read and understand a schema content model, especially if we use an XML-aware editor or browser (complex DTD content models would feature confusing parentheses, which are very difficult to read). This is another time where XML syntax is a great advantage – the content model can be revealed and manipulated as XML, using a nice GUI tree structure tool that can collapse/expand the content model's element tree structure.

If we want to offer a list of elements that *can* appear, where we are not worried about the order or whether they do appear, we can use the `<all>` element. Each child element is optional, and none of them may appear more than once.

> **This grouping element is limited to the top level of the content model, and none of the children may be any kind of element group.**

For example, imagine that we were dealing with customers who may not have an email address, and that we did not mind whether the first name or the last name was the first child element, we could redefine it as:

```
<element name="PersonName">
  <complexType>
    <all>
      <element name="FirstName" minOccurs="1" />
      <element name="LastName" minOccurs="1" />
      <element ref="emailAddress" minOccurs="0" maxOccurs="1" />
    </all>
  </complexType>
</element>
```

Due to one of the restrictions of the `<all>` declaration, we've had to change our `<emailAddress>` child element to occur once or not at all, instead of allowing multiple email addresses as before.

Examples of documents using this content model are:

```
<Customer>
  <LastName>Rivers</LastName>
  <FirstName>Joan</FirstName>
</Customer>
```

and:

```
<Customer>
  <emailAddress>joan@rivers.org</emailAddress>
  <FirstName>Joan</FirstName>
  <LastName>Rivers</LastName>
</Customer>
```

Whilst there is no need for a name attribute for the `<all>` element (due to its defined limits), it may have a unique identifier (ID attribute) for reference purposes.

Content From Another Schema – `<any>`

This element can be used to provide something similar to a DTD's ANY content model, but only in conjunction with namespaces. This allows inclusion of any wellformed XML, for example if we ran an e-commerce site that acted as a middleman for other suppliers, we could use their catalog schema in our catalog, like so:

For example:

```
<element name="myCatalog">
  <complexType>
    <any
        namespace="http://www.ourSupplier.com/catalog"
        minOccurs="0" maxOccurs="unbounded"
        processContents="skip" />
  </complexType>
</element>
```

This schema fragment allows our `<myCatalog>` element to contain any well-formed XML data that appears in the supplier's specified namespace.

The `processContents` attribute value of `"skip"` tells the XML parser that it doesn't need to validate the supplier's content. If this attribute is set to `"strict"` (the default value), the parser must obtain the schema associated with the namespace and validate the supplier's XML data – and if it can't find the schema, it reports an error. The middle ground is the `"lax"` value – if the parser can find the schema, it will validate the data as much as possible, but if the schema isn't found, no error is reported.

Named Model Groups – `<group>`

If we want to reuse a set of elements in several content type definitions (element content models), we can use a **model group** to define a set of elements that can be repeated. They are very helpful when building up complex type definitions, and act rather like parameter entities in DTDs. Model groups can further be constrained using an `sequence`, `choice`, `all`, or `group` child elements.

> When we are creating a complex type definition for an element, but we do not use the group element, the content model is known as an un-named group.

A model group consists of element declarations, wildcards, and other model groups. In our complex type definitions so far, there's an implicit group of elements, but it's also possible to create **named** model groups that can then be used by reference elsewhere in a schema. Named model groups use the `<group>` element, and must be declared at the top level of the schema.

For example, we can create a model group to allow a limited set of 1-5 `lineItems` to appear:

```
<group name="lineItems">
  <sequence>
    <element name="lineItem" minOccurs="1" maxOccurs="5" />
  </sequence>
</group>
```

Later in the schema, we can simply refer to the group by name, and it will inherit this description, as if it were inline within the choice list below:

```
<element name="Order">
  <complexType>
  ...
    <choice>
      <element name="Customer" minOccurs="1" />
      <group ref="lineItems" minOccurs="0" maxOccurs="1" />
    </choice>
  </complexType>
</element>
```

Notice how, again, the `<group>` element is used for both the definition of a group and any reference to a named group. In the first fragment of this section, the group is defined using `<group name="lineItems"..>`. In the second fragment, it's used by reference within a Complex Type Definition (i.e. `<group ref="lineItems"...>`).

Attribute Groups

In the same way that we can build up groups of elements using the `<group>` element, which help us build complicated complex type declarations by reusing common sets of elements; we can also group together sets of attributes that might be held together. Obviously, we do not need to constrain the order of these, however we can set all the attributes on the attribute elements that we met in the earlier section on declaring attributes.

The syntax is very simple, having seen model groups:

```
<attributeGroup name="fullName">
  <attribute name="firstName" use="required" />
  <attribute name="MI" use="optional" />
  <attribute name="lastName" use="required" />
</attributeGroup>
```

So that now, if we want the group of attributes for a full name on an element, we just have to add a reference to it using the `ref` attribute of the `attributeGroup` element:

```
<element name="Customer">
  <complexType>
    <attributeGroup ref="fullName" />
  </complexType>
</element>
```

Notation declarations

Notation declarations associate a name with an identifier for a notation. While they do not participate in validation, they are referenced when validating strings that are members of NOTATION simple type definitions. For example, if we wanted to include a jpeg file, and associate something that could we view it with, we would use the following declaration:

```
<picture pictype="jpeg">...</picture>
```

The content of this element would be a binary definition of the jpeg. Here is how we would define this element (don't worry about the extension element for the moment, we will meet it in the datatypes section):

```
<notation name="jpeg" public="image/jpeg" system="viewer.exe" />

<element name="picture">
 <complexType>
  <complexContent>
   <extension base="xs:binary">
    <attribute name="pictype" type="NOTATION"/>
   </extension>
  </complexContent>
 </complexType>
</element>
```

The public attribute of the notation element takes a public identifier from the ISO 8879 specification, while the system attribute takes a URI reference.

Annotations

Since an XML schema is just regular well-formed XML, it may include comments using the XML comment syntax:

```
<!-- This is an inline XML comment! -->
```

However, due to the XML 1.0 parser rules, an XML parser doesn't need to pass comments on to the application – any comments that appear in an XML document instance may just be discarded. Whilst this design decision makes sense in view of the widespread (and problematic) practice of embedding scripting languages within HTML comments, we do sometimes need to be able to annotate a schema and have these annotations preserved.

XML Schema has provided three elements for schema meta data, for both applications and human readers:

❑ <annotation> – the parent of the other two, it can appear almost anywhere in a schema, usually as the first child of some other element.

❑ <appInfo> – this element is designated for schema information that's useful to external applications.

❑ <documentation> – this element is the place for "comments" that are intended for people using the schema, such as an abstract, copyright and other legal information.

> It is important to remember that the <appInfo> and <documentation> elements cannot be used alone – they must be children of the <annotation> element.

An interesting example use of the <appInfo> element is within the XML Schema specification itself. The schema that describes the constraining facets of simple datatypes includes this annotation element. An application then used these elements to generate additional text for the Datatypes part of the specification.

By properly using these elements, we can make our schema self-documenting. By attaching a style sheet to the schema, we could create a readable version that explains its usage. This is particularly useful if we want to share our schema with others, or make it an industry standard.

Using Annotation Elements

We can add several of these elements in various places within our ongoing example schema.

Make the following changes to our earlier example:

```
<?xml version="1.0">
<schema xmlns="http://www.w3.org/2000/10/XMLSchema">
  <annotation>
    <appInfo>Wrox Schema - Annotations example</appInfo>
    <documentation>Schema is Copyright 2000 by Wrox Press Ltd.
    </documentation>
  </annotation>

  . . .

  <element name="PersonName">
    <complexType content="elementOnly">
      <annotation>
        <documentation>
          The use of the &lt;SingleName&gt; element solves the 'Cher'
          problem.
        </documentation>
      </annotation>
      <choice>
  . . .
      </choice>
  . . .
    </complexType>
  </element>
</schema>
```

Noticed that we made the XML Schema our default namespace, so we don't need to prefix every element type name with "xsd:".

The <appInfo> element provides a title for this schema that could be used by our XML application for display, or some other purpose. The <documentation> elements all provide information for the author and other readers of this schema.

Using Other Namespaces

We can also reference other schemas using a child of the schema element by using the special include element, which allows us to use content models and derived datatypes from other schemas rather than redefining them in each schema that needs them.

```
<schema xmlns="http://www.w3.org/2000/10/XMLSchema"
        xmlns:xsd="http://www.w3.org/2000/10/XMLSchema-datatypes"
        targetNamespace="http://www.thisSite.com">
  . . .
</schema>

<include xmlns:wrox="http://www.wrox.com/schemas/books/catalog.xsd" />
```

This brings in the definitions and declarations from the `catalog` schema making them available as part of this schema, meaning that, if we are creating a *new* schema we can borrow from existing schemas. Alternatively, if we wanted to merge data from documents marked up according to two schemas, we could create a schema that would validate our new document instances. In the instance of a document marked up according to this schema we only need to declare this schema (not the included schemas).

You can nest multiple schemas as long as they are part of the same `targetNamespace`.

This could be particularly useful if we wanted to create new XML documents based on data coming from disparate sources. Here we have the start of the marketing department schema, which includes content models from the general Wrox `books` schema (where content models for `book` and `author` are defined):

```
<schema xmlns="http://www.w3.org/2000/10/XMLSchema"
        targetNamespace="http://www.wrox.com/schemas/marketing">

<import schemaLocation="http://www.wrox.com/schemas/books.xsd" />

    <element name="catalog" type="catalogType" />
    <complexType name="catalogType">
      <sequence>
        <element name="book" type="marketing:bookType" />
        <element name="author" type="marketing:authorType" />
      </sequence>
      <attribute name="myISBN" type="marketing:ISBN" />
    </complexType>
</schema>
```

Here the first element that we declare, `catalog`, has a complex type definition that we define in this schema. In its complex type definition, we declare two more elements (`book` and `author`), but we are borrowing their content models from the general Wrox books schema (rather than declaring them again here). Note how the types from the general Wrox books schema have really been included here – we are not having to use their original namespace as if they were in another schema. The `catalog` element also has an attribute, which we have given a name of `myISBN`, although its type definition is still set in the Wrox schema.

Summary of Structures

We have already seen plenty of content models that describe the structure of an XML vocabulary and its conformant document instances. A content model can restrict a document to a certain set of element types and attributes, describe and constrain the relationships between these different components, and uniquely identify specific elements. Sharing a content model allows business partners to exchange structured information and bridge the differences between their disparate internal data representations. The declarations which describe a content model in an XML schema are a bit more complex than those in a DTD but they are also much more powerful. However, in order to build the content models, the structures, and compounds, we need to understand the atoms that make them up, so we will look at datatypes.

Datatypes

We have already seen some of the advantages of datatypes, and that XML Schemas provide two basic kinds of datatypes:

❑   **Primitive datatypes** – those that are not defined in terms of other datatypes.

❑   **Derived datatypes** – those that are defined in terms of existing types.

So, let's see how datatypes can help us restrict the content of our XML documents.

Primitive Datatypes

Primitive datatypes are the basis for all other types, and cannot themselves be defined from smaller components. By definition, they can never contain element content or attributes, since they are the **base types** from which all other types are derived.

> **Primitive types can be used for element or attribute values, but cannot contain child element or attributes. Primitive types are always built-in.**

A string of characters is a common primitive type, known as the `string` datatype.

It may seem as though the distinction between primitive and derived types is a little arbitrary, so the schema classifications don't necessarily correspond to those of any particular programming language. Just as the exact definition of a string or a float is different in Java and C++, so too is the definition of these types in XML schemas.

Primitive type	Description
string	Represents any legal character strings in XML.
boolean	Represents true or false.
float	Standard concept of real numbers corresponding to a single precision 32 bit floating point type.
double	Standard concept of real numbers corresponding to a single precision 64 bit floating point type
decimal	Represents arbitrary precision decimal numbers.
timeDuration	Represents a duration of time.
recurringDuration	Represents a specific span of time that recurs with a specific frequency, starting from a specific point in time.
binary	Represents arbitrary binary data.
uriReference	Represents a URI.

Primitive type	Description
ID	Represents the ID attribute type as defined in the XML 1.0 recommendation.
IDREF	Represents the IDREF attribute type as defined in the XML 1.0 recommendation.
ENTITY	Represents the ENTITY attribute type as defined in the XML 1.0 recommendation.
Qname	Represents XML qualified names, as defined in the the XML 1.0 recommendation.

Derived Datatypes

A derived datatype is one that is defined in terms of an existing datatype (known as its **based** type). Derived types may have attributes, and may have element or mixed content.

> **Instances of derived types can contain any well-formed XML that is valid according to their datatype definition. They may be built-in or user-derived.**

New types may be derived from either a primitive type or another derived type. For example, integers are a subset of real numbers. Therefore the XML Schema integer type is derived from the decimal number type, which is its base type. We can in turn derive an even more restricted type of integer. This is an example of an XML Schema structure known as a **Simple Type Definition**. It uses the `<simpleType>` element to describe a derived integer datatype that's limited to negative values.

```
<simpleType name="negativeInteger" >
    <restriction base="xsi:integer">
        <minInclusive value="unbounded" />
        <maxInclusive value="-1" />
    </restriction>
</simpleType>
```

Don't worry about the specifics of the code in this excerpt – we'll look at the `<simpleType>` element and its companion, the `<complexType>` element (the complex type definition) in the Structures section.

As with the primitive types, the W3C has defined a set of built-in derived datatypes. These types are so common, that it was felt that they should be an integral part of the XML Schemas specification.

Built-in Derived Types for XML Schema

Here are some of the derived datatypes that are built into XML schemas:

Derived type	Description	Base type
CDATA	Represents whitespace normalized strings.	string
token	Represents tokenized strings.	CDATA
language	Represents natural language identifiers. For example, the XML language ID of "en".	Token
NMTOKEN	XML 1.0 NMTOKEN.	Token
NMTOKENS	XML 1.0 NMTOKENS.	NMTOKEN
Name	Represents XML Names.	Token
NCName	Represents XML "non-colonized" Names.	Name
integer	An integer number.	Integer
long	Derived from integer by setting the value of maxInclusive to be 9223372036854775807 and minInclusive to be -9223372036854775808.	Integer
short	Derived from int by setting the value of maxInclusive to be 32767 and minInclusive to be -32768.	Int which is derived from long.
byte	Derived from short by setting the value of maxInclusive to be 127 and minInclusive to be -128.	Short
date	Represents a particular day.	TimePeriod, which is generated from recurringDuration.

Atomic, List and Union Datatypes

There is one last split of XML Schema datatypes:

❑ **atomic datatypes** – that have values that are defined to be indivisible.
❑ **list datatypes** – that are defined in terms of an allowable sequence of values of atomic datatypes .
❑ **union datatypes** – that mix atomic and/or list types.

We shall look at each next:

Atomic Datatypes

An atomic datatype is one that has a value that cannot be divided, at least not within the context of XML Schema.

> **Note that atomic is not analogous to primitive.**

Atomic types may either be primitive or derived types. Let's have a look at some examples:

Numbers and strings are atomic types since their values cannot be descibed using any smaller pieces. The former is pretty obvious, but can't a string be defined in terms of a smaller component, such as characters? While it is true in the abstract sense, XML Schema has no concept of a character as a datatype – and thus the string is an atomic primitive type, (of `string`):

```
<atom>This string is as fine as we can slice textual data - there are no character
atoms in XML Schema.</atom>
```

The second example is an atomic derived type. It is a date which could be derived from the `string` primitive type, though in XML Schema it is derived indirectly from three other types, but it cannot be divided:

```
<atom2>1927-01-16</atom2>
```

The third example is also an atomic derived type; an `integer` is derived from the `float` primitive type.

```
<atom3>469557</atom3>
```

List Datatypes

A list type has a value that's comprised of a finite length sequence of atomic values. Unlike most programming languages, an XML Schema list datatype cannot be made from other lists. This type can be considered a special case of the more general aggregate or collection of a datatype.

List types are always derived types, which must be delimited by whitespace character(s), just like the `IDREFS` or `NMTOKENS` attribute types defined in XML 1.0. Thus, a list type must allow the presence of whitespace, but can't use any white space within the individual values of list items.

An important consideration about a list type is its length – this descriptive value is always the number of items in the list, and is not related to the number of characters that represent the items.

For example, we can define a simple user derived list type for generic sizes:

```
<simpleType name="sizes">
   <list itemType="size" />
</simpleType>
```

This new datatype might then be used within a more specific element in a document:

```
<dressSizes type="sizes">small medium large xlarge</dressSizes>
```

On the other hand, using whitespace as a delimiter causes problems when we want to create lists of strings. In this context, the following example is not true – it's is a list of six items:

```
<bad_list>this is a simgle list item<bad_list>
```

List types can be a very useful way to represent collections of numbers, or standard XML 1.0 attribute types, like IDREFs or NMTOKENS. On the other hand, they are all but worthless for manipulation of textual data that involves anything more than words – sentences and larger groupings of text cannot be represented with a list type.

Union Datatypes

Union types allow us to build an element or attribute value from a mixture of atomic and/or list types. Imagine that we had short abbreviations for the sizes of clothes (s, m, l, xl) called shortSize; we could create a type that would either allow us to use the full name of the size or the abbreviation.

Now, we could create a union and define it with the memberTypes attribute:

```
<simpleType name="deliveryUnion>
    <union memberTypes="sizes shortSize" />
<simpleType />
```

Aspects of Datatypes

All XML Schema datatypes are comprised of three parts:

❑   A **value space** – the set of distinct values where each of the values is denoted by one or more literals in the datatype's lexical space.

❑   A **lexical space** – the set of lexical representations, in other words a set of valid literal strings representing values.

❑   A set of **facets** – properties of the value space, its individual values, and/or lexical items.

To illustrate the difference between lexical and value spaces, we'll look at a snippet of a document. We'll assume that the <Item> element is a string datatype, and that the <Quantity> element is defined as an integer type:

```
<Order>
    <Item>Widget</Item>
    <Quantity>465000</Quantity>
</Order>
```

In the <Item> element, the value and lexical spaces are the same thing – the lexical representation of a string is also its value.

The <Quantity> element, however, is represented in XML as a string, but its value is the mathematical concept of "four hundred and sixty five thousand". Any comparison of <Quantity> elements (such as multiplying them by the price to get a total) would mean using their numeric values, not their lexical string representations. This means that there are three different forms of the same value, although they are lexically different: 465000, 465000.00, 4650.00E2.

Let's take a closer look at these concepts.

Value Spaces

Each schema datatype has a range of possible values. These value spaces are implicit in the definition of a primitive datatype. For example, the built-in float datatype has a value space that ranges from negative to positive infinity. The string datatype is comprised of values that correspond to any of the legal XML characters.

> **Derived types inherit their value space from their base type, and may also constrain that value space to an explicit subset of the base type's value space.**

A derived datatype such as `integer` would allow any positive or negative whole number value, but wouldn't allow decimal fractions. Another integer type could be derived from `integer`, but this type might limit the range of acceptable values to only positive numbers, or to only 3 digit numbers. Value spaces may also have a set of explicitly enumerated values, or be derived from the members of a list of types.

Value spaces always have certain facets (or abstract properties), such as **equality**, **order**, **bounds**, **cardinality**, and the age-old **numeric / nonnumeric** dichotomy.

Lexical Spaces

A lexical space is the set of string literals that *represent* the values of a datatype. These literals are always comprised of "text" characters, which may be any of the XML legal subset of the Unicode character set.

For example,

```
<a_string>The name of the sorority was ΑΓΔ, and their motto was "plus ça change,
plus c'est la même chose"</a_string>
```

By definition, string literals only have one lexical representation (see the discussion of the Equality facet in the next section). On the other hand, numeric values may have several equivalent and equally valid lexical representations. For example, the string literals "100", "1.0E2", and "10²" obviously have different lexical values, but they have identical numeric values in the floating-point number value space.

Facets

A facet is one of the defining properties of a datatype which distinguish as that datatype from others. Facets include properties such as a string's length, or the bounds of a numeric datatype.

The abstract properties that define the semantic characteristics of a value space are known as the **fundamental facets** of the datatype. There is another kind of facet: **constraining facets**, which are optional limits on the permissible values of a datatype's value space. We'll discuss both of these here.

Fundamental Facets

There are five fundamental facets:

❑ Equality – different values can be compared and determined to be equal or not.

❑ Order – for some datatypes, defined relationships exist between values (for example, numbers may have ordered values).

❑ Bounds – ordered datatypes may be constrained to a range of values.

❑ Cardinality– the number of values within the value space.

❑ Numeric/non-numeric.

Let's look at some of the details of these fundamental facets. (See Appendix C for more detail.)

Equality

This property applies to all types, whether numeric or not. Given two values **A** and **B**, the following rules apply:

- ❑ It is always true that "**A = A**" (identity).
- ❑ If "**A = B**" then "**A ≠ B**" is never possible.
- ❑ If "**A = B**" then "**B = A**" (value equality is commutative, or independent of order).
- ❑ If "**A = B**" and "**B = C**" then "**A = C**" (value equality is transitive).
- ❑ The operation "**Equal(A,B)**" is true if "**A = B**".

When dealing with nonnumeric types, remember that XML is casesensitive, so the string "YES" is *not* equal to "yes" or "Yes".

Many accented and ideographic characters can have multiple representations. For example, the letter "n" with a tilde accent can be represented in ASCII (or for an input device like a keyboard) as the two letter sequence: "~n". An alternate representation, using the Latin-1 encoding would be a single accented letter: "ñ". By definition, these are equal only if they are of the same form ("~n" is *not* equal to "ñ").

Order

A datatype is ordered if a defined relationship (known as an **order-relation**) exists between values. This property also applies to both numeric and nonnumeric values. An order relation has these rules:

- ❑ For every value "**A**", then "**A < A**" and "**A > A**" are never true.
- ❑ For every two values "**(A, B)**", then one of the following must be true: "**A = B**", "**A < B**", or "**A > B**".
- ❑ For every three values "**(A, B, C)**" then it is true that: if "**A < B**" and "**B < C**", then "**A < C**".

Numeric order is intrinsic to the mathematical definition of numbers. On the other hand, the order of characters, or strings of characters, depends on the *encoded* numeric value (in other words the UCS code point) of the characters: "0" (ASCII zero) is less than "a", "a" is less than "b", "e" is less than "è", and so on.

> *We must be careful not to assume that upper case letters are always less than lower-case letters. Whilst this is true for the ASCII and Latin-1 encodings, the Latin Extended-A and -B encodings mix the two cases together. Also remember that the concept of case doesn't even exist in many non latin alphabets.*

Bounds

Datatype values may have either lower or upper bounds, or both.

- ❑ An upper bound is the unique value **U**, where for all values **v** in the value space, the statement "**v ≤ U**" is true. Such a value space is said to be **bounded above**.
- ❑ A lower bound is the unique value **L**, where it is always true that "**v ≥ L**". In this case, the value space is said to be **bounded below**.

If a value space has both upper and lower bounds, its datatype is simply considered to be **bounded**, with an assumption that the bounding is both "above" and "below".

These may be inclusive or exclusive, as we saw a while back in a Simple Type Definition example:

```
<simpleType name="negativeInteger" base="xsi:integer">
  <minInclusive value="unbounded" />
  <maxExclusive value="0" />
</simpleType>
```

This example shows a value space that is **bounded above** (has a finite maximum value), but is not **bounded below** (there is no minimum).

Cardinality

All value spaces have an associated concept of cardinality – the number of values within the value space. A value space may be:

❑　Finite – such as a list of enumerated values.

❑　Countably infinite.

❑　Uncountably infinite.

The first two of these are the categories of cardinality that are significant (we'll leave the last one to the mathematicians, eh?).

Numeric / Nonnumeric

A datatype and its associated value space is classified as numeric if the values can be considered numeric quantities in some number system. Contrariwise, any datatype with values that aren't represented by numbers is, of course, considered nonnumeric.

Remember that XML isn't limited to ASCII digits – any of the several sets of Unicode "Number" characters can be used to represent numeric values. For example, the familiar so-called Arabic numerals used in the ASCII character set are not actually Arabic. Unicode does have the ten Arabic digits, as well as those of many other languages.

Constraining Facets

Constraining facets are those that limit the value space of a *derived* datatype, which in turn limits that datatype's lexical space. Strictly speaking, *primitive* types don't have constraining facets, but these may be added by creating a derived datatype that's **derived by restriction** (see the section on this later).

There are several types of constraining facet, that apply to three groups of simple types:

Facets that apply only to simple types which are **ordered**:

❑　length, minLength, maxLength

❑　pattern

❑　enumeration

Facets that only apply to simple types that define **Bounds**:

- ❑ minExclusive, maxExclusive, minInclusive, maxInclusive
- ❑ precision, scale
- ❑ encoding

Facets that apply to **temporal** simple types:

- ❑ duration, period

Let's look at the details of these constraining facets.

length, minLength, maxLength

These three facets all deal with the number of units of length of a datatype, the value of which must always be a nonnegative integer. The nature of the units will vary, depending on the base datatype:

- ❑ For those derived from the **string type**, length is the number of Unicode code points ("characters") – and it's important to remember that each Unicode characters may be 8, 16, or 32-bits long, or even variable-length sequences of 8-bit values.

- ❑ Types that are derived from the **binary type** measure length as the number of octets (8-bit bytes) of the binary data.

- ❑ **List types** define length as the number of items in the list.

The minLength and maxLength facets are the minimum and maximum number of units permitted for the datatype respectively. For example, we could use these if we wanted to constrain some datatype (such as an Area Code) to always be a 3-digit number:

```
<simpleType name="AreaCode">
    <restriction base="xsi:string">
        <minLength value="3" />
        <maxLength value="3" />
    </restriction>
</simpleType>
```

Note that the restrictions are held within a restriction element, and the base type we are deriving from is held in a base attribute.

pattern

This facet is a constraint on the datatype's *lexical* space, which indirectly constrains the value space. A pattern is a regular expression (**regex**) that a datatype's lexical representation must match for that latter literal to be considered valid. The regex language used in XML Schema is similar to the one defined for the Perl programming language.

> *For more about the use of regular expressions, see the main web site for Perl at* http://www.perl.com/pub *or **Appendix E** of **XML Schema Part 2: Datatypes** at* http://www.w3.org/TR/xmlschema-2/#regexs.

whitespace

This facet is a constraint on whether whitespace is allowed

Here is a table that shows which constraining facets can be applied to which simple datatypes:

Simple Types	Facets					
	length	minLength	maxLength	pattern	enumeration	whitespace
string	y	y	y	y	y	y
CDATA	y	y	y	y	y	y
token	y	y	y	y	y	y
byte				y	y	
unsignedByte				y	y	
binary	y	y	y		y	
integer				y	y	
positive Integer				y	y	
negative Integer				y	y	
nonNegative Integer				y	y	
nonPositive Integer				y	y	
int				y	y	
unsignedInt				y	y	
long				y	y	
unsignedLong				y	y	
short				y	y	
unsigned Short				y	y	
decimal				y	y	
float				y	y	
double				y	y	
boolean				y		
time				y	y	
timeInstant				y	y	
timePeriod				y	y	
timeDuration				y	y	
date				y	y	
month				y	y	

Simple Types	Facets					
	length	minLength	maxLength	pattern	enumeration	whitespace
year				y	y	
century				y	y	
recurringDay				y	y	
recurring Date				y	y	
recurring Duration				y	y	
Name	y	y	y	y	y	
QName	y	y	y	y	y	
NCName	y	y	y	y	y	
uriReference	y	y	y	y	y	
language	y	y	y	y	y	
ID	y	y	y	y	y	
IDREF	y	y	y	y	y	
IDREFS	y	y	y		y	
ENTITY	y	y	y	y	y	
ENTITIES	y	y	y		y	
NOTATION	y	y	y	y	y	
NMTOKEN	y	y	y	y	y	
NMTOKENS	y	y	y		y	

enumeration

This facet is very much like a DTD's specification of an element type choice list or the enumerated values of an attribute. Enumeration limits a value space to a specific set of values – if the value isn't specified in the schema, it isn't valid.

Using this facet does *not* impose an additional or different order relation on the value space, due to the order of the enumerated values – any ordered property of the derived datatype remains the same as that of its base type.

minExclusive, maxExclusive, minInclusive, maxInclusive

All of these facets can only apply to a datatype that has an order relation (see the earlier description of the Order fundamental facet).

❑ The two "min" facets define the minimum (lower bound) of a value space.

❑ The two "max" facets define its maximum (upper bound).

❑ An exclusive bound means that the bounding value is *not* included in the value space (meaning that for all values **V** in the value space, **minExclusive < V < maxExclusive**).

❑ An inclusive bound is one that *is* included within the value space (**minInclusive   V   maxInclusive**).

Of course, these two types of bounds are not coupled – a lower bound might be *ex*clusive, whilst the upper bound is *in*clusive. Obviously, we must choose between the two types of bounds for each end of the spectrum – it's never possible for a bound to be both *in*clusive and *ex*clusive!

> If the element `minOccurs` equals 0, then make sure that the column representing it in a database is able to contain Null values.

precision, scale

These two facets apply to all datatypes derived from the **decimal type**. `precision` is the maximum number of decimal digits allowed for the entire number (which must always be a positive integer), and `scale` is the maximum number of digits (always a nonnegative integer) in the fractional portion of the number.

encoding

This facet is a constraint on the *lexical* space of datatypes that are derived from the `binary` base type. The value of this facet must either be `hex` or `base64`.

If the value is `hex`, then each binary byte is encoded as a 2-digit hexadecimal number, using the ten ASCII digits and the letters A through F (either upper or lowercase letters are permitted). For example, the hexencoded string `"312D322D33"` is the encoded version of the ASCII string `"1-2-3"` (`"2D"` being the hex encoding of the hyphen character, and `"3x"` the ASCII representation of the digits `"x"`).

If the value is `base64`, then the entire binary stream is encoded using the widely used Internet standard Base64 Content-Transfer-Encoding method.

> *Base64 encoding is defined in* **RFC 2045: Multipurpose Internet Mail Extensions (MIME) Part One: Format of Internet Message Bodies** *(1996) at http://www.ietf.org/rfc/rfc2045.txt.*

Simple Types	Facets						
	max Inclusive	max Exclusive	min Inclusive	min Exclusive	precision	scale	encoding
byte	y	y	y	y	y	y	
unsigned Byte	y	y	y	y	y	y	
binary							y
integer	y	y	y	y	y	y	
positive Integer	y	y	y	y	y	y	
negative Integer	y	y	y	y	y	y	
non Negative Integer	y	y	y	y	y	y	

Table continued on following page

Simple Types	Facets						
	max Inclusive	max Exclusive	min Inclusive	min Exclusive	precision	scale	encoding
non Positive Integer	y	y	y	y	y	y	
int	y	y	y	y	y	y	
unsigned Int	y	y	y	y	y	y	
long	y	y	y	y	y	y	
unsigned Long	y	y	y	y	y	y	
short	y	y	y	y	y	y	
unsigned Short	y	y	y	y	y	y	
decimal	y	y	y	y	y	y	
float	y	y	y	y			
double	y	y	y	y			
time	y	y	y	y			
time Instant	y	y	y	y			
time Period	y	y	y	y			
time Duration	y	y	y	y			
date	y	y	y	y			
month	y	y	y	y			
year	y	y	y	y			
century	y	y	y	y			
recurring Day	y	y	y	y			
recurring Date	y	y	y	y			
recurring Duration	y	y	y	y			

duration, period

These facets only apply to the `recurringDuration` datatype and its derived datatypes. The value must always be a `timeDuration`.

❑ The `duration` facet is the duration of `recurringDuration` values.

❑ The `period` facet is the frequency of recurrence for these values.

See the discussion of `recurringDuration` in Appendix C for more on the meaning of these two facets.

Simple Types	Facets	
	period	duration
time	y	y
timeInstant	y	y
timePeriod	y	y
timeDuration		
date	y	y
month	y	y
year	y	y
century	y	y
recurringDay	y	y
recurringDate	y	y
recurringDuration	y	y

Constraining Facets in a Database

Ideally, when we create a derived datatype, we should also create a user defined datatype for the corresponding field in your database that closely matches the constraints put on the XML datatype.

If we are able to validate documents before they go into the database, because schemas are so much more powerful than DTD's at constraining content of documents, after all this is not as important. Otherwise, if we do need some validation, we could validate the values before we insert it into the database. But, just as in life, there is always an exception to the rule: Enumeration – see the enumeration example later in the chapter.

Simple Type Definitions

> A Simple Type Definition is a set of constraints on the value space *and* the lexical space of a datatype.

These constraints are either a **restriction** on the base type, or the specification of a **list** type that's constrained by some other Simple Type Definition.

By definition, Simple Type Definitions for all the built-in primitive and derived datatypes are present in every schema. All of these are in the XML Schema target namespace (http://www.w3.org/2000/10/XMLSchema).

The <simpleType> Element

A Simple Type Definition uses the <simpleType> element, its attributes, and any valid constraining facet(s). The attribute names, and the attribute value's primitive datatype or enumerated values, are:

- ❏   name – NCName
- ❏   base – QName – OPTIONAL
- ❏   abstract – boolean – OPTIONAL
- ❏   derivedBy – (list | restriction) – OPTIONAL (default is restriction)

The meaning of the name attribute should be fairly obvious – it's the name of the datatype we are describing. Like all names in XML Schema, this must conform to the XML 1.0 name rules, and in this case, the name must be a simple unqualified name.

The base attribute is the name of the base datatype. It must use a qualified name, in other words a name with a namespace identifier. If this is omitted, the ur-type is assumed to be the base type.

If abstract's value is true, then this type cannot appear as the type definition in an element declaration (rather it is used to derive other datatypes), and cannot be referenced as an xsi:type attribute in a document (see the definition of this attribute later in the chapter). This attribute is optional, and its default value is false.

The derivedBy attribute is used to declare whether the new <simpleType> is an atomic type (derived from another type, and restricting some facet of that base type), or a list type.

Simple types are identified by name and target namespace, and must be unique within a schema. No Simple Type Definition can have the same name as any other Simple or Complex Type Definition – the scope of type names includes both simple and complex types. However, datatype names can be the same as the name of an element or attribute.

The content of <simpleType> is comprised of one or more constraining facets (which were just described), represented as empty child elements. We can also include an annotation element with the content. As we've seen, the list of legal constraining facets depends on the base datatype.

Derivation by Restriction

The built-in derived type negativeInteger is one example of a type derived by restriction:

```
<simpleType name="negativeInteger" base="xsi:integer">
  <maxInclusive value="-1" />
</simpleType>
```

In this definition, we've named the new simple datatype negativeInteger, and defined it as being derived from the built-in integer type. Remember that restriction is the default of the derivedBy attribute, so it can be omitted here.

Since integers are infinite, we wouldn't want to define a lower bound, but the upper bound is the very essence of this definition. This one constraining facet could just as easily have been expressed as:

```
  <maxExclusive value="0" />
```

Let's look at a more complicated simple datatype, which uses the pattern facet. All telephone numbersn North America are 10-digit numbers comprise of a 3-digit Area Code, a 3-digit local exchange, and a 4-digit local number. The area code and exchange have some additional restrictions. The first digit of these can never be 0 or 1, since these numbers are used to signal operator and direct-dial long distance dialling.

At one time, area codes also required the second digit of the area code to be limited to only 0 and 1, as a way of distinguishing between calls that were local (7 digits) and long distance (10 digits). This original style of area code could be specified as follows:

```
<simpleType name="AreaCode" base="xsi:string">
  <minLength value="3" />
  <maxLength value="3" />
  <pattern value="[2-9][0-1][0-9]" />
</simpleType>
```

An example of this derived datatype in a document instance might be:

```
<TelephoneNumber>
  <AreaCode>312</AreaCode>
  <Exchange>555</Exchange>
  <Number>1212</Number>
</TelephoneNumber>
```

Since hardwired relay switching matrices have been replaced with solid-state electronics, this restriction is no longer needed. Therefore, we could define this less restricted area code more simply as any integer in the range from 200 to 999, inclusive:

```
<simpleType name="AreaCode" base="xsi:integer">
  <minInclusive value="200" />
  <maxInclusive value="999" />
</simpleType>
```

This newer style would allow an area code that was formerly invalid, such as:

```
<AreaCode>925</AreaCode>
```

Because new style area codes are *less* restrictive than the original ones, we cannot derive the new type from the old – derivation by extension is limited to complex datatypes. Another reason why we can't derive the new from the old is that we've changed the base type from string to integer.

Derivation by List

Datatypes derived by list contain a whitespace delimited list of values that conform to the base type. A list datatype *must* be derived from an atomic datatype: it cannot be derived from another list type. The atomic type must also be suitable for inclusion in a list – remember that unconstrained strings containing whitespace cause problems when we attempt to make a list of strings.

For example, we might create a simple unbounded list of floating-point numbers:

```
<simpleType name="ListOfFloats" base="xsi:float" derivedBy="list" />
```

An example of this list datatype in a document instance might be:

```
<ListOfFloats>-INF -1.02E01 -0.42e1 0</ListOfFloats>
```

This example has a length of 4 (remember that the units of length depend on the datatype, and list types count the number of items in the list). If we wanted to further constrain our datatype to require a length of 4, we can do so using the length facet. The new type definition would look something like this:

```
<simpleType name="ListOfFloats" base="xsi:float" derivedBy="list">
  <length value="4" />
</simpleType>
```

This limits our type to being a list of exactly 4 items. If we wanted the list to be of variable-length, but restricted to a specific finite length, we could specify a range instead:

```
<simpleType name="ListOfFloats" base="xsi:float" derivedBy="list">
  <minLength value="1" />
  <maxLength value="100" />
</simpleType>
```

This redefinition allows any list of 1 to 100 floating-point numbers.

As with `<simpleType>`, the content of `<complexType>` is comprised of one or more constraining facets, which are represented as empty child elements. There are also a number of additional children, such as `<element>` and `<attribute>`, that are used to describe the content model of the complex datatype. As before, annotation elements may also be included in the content.

Scope of Simple Type Definitions

As with element and attribute definitions, we can add scope to Simple Type Definitions, by either declaring them in line or globally.

Global Scope of Simple Type Definitions

If we define a simple type at the top of a document, we can use simple type definitions to constrain attribute and element content anywhere within a document. For example if we declare a type for chart positions:

```
<simpleType name="chartPosition"  base="positiveInteger">
  <minInclusive value="1" />
  <maxInclusive value="50" />
</simpleType>
```

we can use the type throughout the documents, for example in an element:

```
<element name="bestseller" type="chartPosition" />
```

or we can use it in an attribute:

```
<attribute name="bestseller" type="chartPosition" />
```

Here the value will be constrained to a positive integer in the range 1 to 50 (inclusive).

Local Scope of Simple Type Definitions

An alternate way to declare the type of an attribute is in-line, using a `<simpleType>` child element within the `<attribute>`. This introduces scope to the type definition restricted to the element or attribute in question, although it does allow us to add extra information. If this alternative is used, the `type` attribute may not appear:

```
<attribute name="chartPosition" use="default" value="50" >
  <simpleType base="positiveInteger">
    <minInclusive value="1" />
    <maxInclusive value="50" />
  </simpleType>
</attribute>
```

This example shows the same form of declaration, where the `type` of the attribute is explicitly defined within the declaration. However, we have been able to add a default value.

ID, IDREF and IDREFS

In Chapter 2 we saw how it is possible to use ID, IDREF, and IDREFS to express relationships between XML elements that represented tables (which helped in the normalization of the data). In that chapter we saw, for each relationship we have defined, if the relationship is one-to-one or one-to-many in the direction it is being navigated, and no other relationship leads to the child within the selected subset, then we suggested that you use containment to represent the relationship. This worked by adding the child element as element content of the parent element with the appropriate cardinality. This was suggested largely because of the processing overhead required to traverse between ID and IDREF attributes. However, if the relationship is many-to-one, or the child has more than one parent, then we said you would need to use pointing to describe the relationship, and that this could be done using ID and IDREF attributes.

The idea was that we could declare relationships between tables using an XML ID to represent a SQL primary key, scoped to one document. Then an IDREF could be used like a foreign key, because an IDREF refers to an ID value in the document (while IDREFS are a space separated list of IDREF values).

When using IDs in DTDs. the value of the ID has to be unique within the document. However, because ID, IDREF, and IDREFS are simple types in schemas, we can derive a new simple type from them, introducing scope within which the uniqueness applies. We can do this by applying the type to our own attributes as well as elements (so we can create our own attributes that act as IDs and IDREFs).

Using ID as a Primary Key and IDREF for Foreign Keys

In Chapter 2, we were using ID to uniquely identify an element – namely a table that would be referred to by an IDREF. We declared these as required in the DTD. The direction was important because it should be the same as we are likely to travel in the program – for example if we are writing a call center application we are more likely to go from an invoice to a customer to check their details once we have been given an invoice number. If the relationship is one-to-many, and the child has more than one parent, we would use an IDREFS attribute instead.

> Note that if we have defined a relationship to be navigable in either direction, it really counted as two different relationships.

For example, if we wanted to find a customer from an invoice number we could add an IDREF attribute to the Invoice element, and an ID on the Customer element. Because they are simple types, we can use any name to represent the ID and IDREFs. So, we could declare the following attribute on the Invoice elements:

```
<attributeType name="customerIDREF" type="IDREF" use="required" />
```

which would refer to the Customer element that had this attribute in its definition:

```
<attributeType name="customer" type="ID" use="required" />
```

This helps greatly with normalization. However, there are still concerns over the processing power needed to traverse these relationships. XML schemas however, allow us to express a *new* kind of constraint, called an **Identity-Constraint** that offers a lot more power and flexibility than using ID and IDREF attributes.

Identity-Constraints

In addition to being able to use ID, IDREF, and IDREFS to define relationships between data, XML Schemas introduce new unique, key and keyref elements, which allow us to specify uniqueness and points of reference when there are multiple elements and attributes in a document.

Furthermore, they utilize XPath syntax to help in the traversal between elements, which can greatly reduce the processing power required to traverse relationships or guarantee uniqueness.

Unsurprisingly, it is the unique element which allows us to specify that an element or attribute value must be unique within a document, while the key and keyref elements act as keys within our documents.

Unique Values

There are times when we need to ensure that there are unique values for elements and attributes. For example if we are using a value as unique identifier. Furthermore, if we are using an element or attribute to represent a primary key, we want to ensure that this is unique within that table, but not necessarily unique to the document. The unique element allows we to do this in XML Schemas (and it would be the job of a validating processor to ensure that the values were unique as intended).

In order to facilitate the uniqueness of values both across the document and within a range of elements or attributes, a clever use of XPath statements is employed.

For example, if we want to ensure that the CustomerID attribute of the Customer element in our SalesData element is unique, we can use the following syntax:

```
<unique name="userID">
   <selector xpath="Customers/Customer"/>
   <field xpath="@CustID"/>
</unique>
```

There are three key steps going on here:

❑   First, we specify the unique element, and give it a name.

❑   Then we use an XPath expression to select the range of elements that we want to make sure contain some unique value. This is done with the selector element, whose xpath attribute holds the XPath expression that retrieves the range of elements, in this case all Customer elements.

❑   In our case, we want to make sure that the value of the Customer element's CustID attribute is unique (after all we would not want two customers to have the same ID). So we set the another xpath attribute with a second expression that specifies the value that we want to remain unique. In this case the CustID attribute of the given range.

This will ensure that all values of the CustID attribute on Customer are unique. However, it only corresponds to Customer elements; if we had a distinction between elements called tradeCustomer and publicCustomer – each of which had a CustID attribute – the value would only have to be unique to the kind of element specified in the selector element's xpath attribute.

If we wanted to make the uniqueness constraint apply to more than one value in the document, we could just add more field paths:

```
<unique name="telNo">
   <selector xpath="Customers/"/>
   <field xpath="tradeCustomer/@CustID"/>
   <field xpath="publicCustomer/@CustID"/>
</unique>
```

Here we are making sure that when a new customer is added, (whether they are a trade or public customer), they are given an unique customer ID.

Key and KeyRef

When looking at ID, IDREF, and IDREFS as a method of describing relationships, and of normalizing data, we saw that the traversal of these relationships was resources intensive. Also, there were constraints because the ID had to have a value that was unique to the document – hence we used the customer name followed by the primary key number of a table to make up the value of an ID in Chapter 2.

The new key and keyref attributes in schemas, however, offer us a lot more flexibility. Rather than repeating values in XML documents, and representing the functionality of link tables in relational databases, we can use the key element to make sure that an item of information only needs to appear once, and that other items are related to it. The unique values that they take only have to be unique to a specified range of elements. Therefore, it is possible to create a key that is only unique to a chosen table, if the table is represented as an element.

For example, if (like in the ID, IDREF example) we have several invoices for the same customer, we do not need to store their personal details several times; rather we can use a key element to associate the customers with their invoices, which are declared with a keyref. Here key acts like the primary key, while keyref acts as a foreign key. Let's have a look at an example:

```
<key name="customerID">
 <selector xpath="SalesData/" />
 <field xpath="Customer/@CustID" />
</key>

<keyref name="item" refer="customerID">
 <selector xpath="SalesData/" />
 <field xpath="/Invoice/@invoiceID" />
</keyref>
```

Notice that the syntax is similar to that of the unique element, where we use selector and field elements as children of the key and keyref elements to describe where we want the key relationship to be placed, and in what range it must be unique. The refer attribute on the keyref is the name of the key we want to refer back to.

The constraints can be specified independently of the types of attributes and elements involved, so an integer may also serve as a key, and this would mean that 3.0 and 3 would be conflicting keys.

Furthermore, because this is actually a constraining mechanism, we cannot create an Invoice element unless it contains an invoiceID attribute whose value corresponds to an existing CustID attribute on a given Customer element.

That just about brings us to the end of looking at the syntax of using XML Schemas. Now we can take a look at how we can actually use them with the help of some examples.

Example Schemas

In this final section, we will look at some examples to make sure that we have the idea of using schemas. We will start by converting an existing DTD into a schema, then we will look at three particular types of content that we may have to represent (groups of attributes that may appear on several elements, mixed content models, and enumeration).

Example 1 – Name Details

In this first example, we want to be able to define a content model for a `<PersonName>` element that holds the details of their name. We want to be able to represent their name in two ways:

```
<PersonName honorific="Mr." suffix="Jr.">
   <FirstName>Matthew</FirstName>
   <MiddleName>Warren</MiddleName>
   <LastName>Jones</LastName>
</PersonName>
```

where the presence of a `MiddleName` element is optional, or in a short form:

```
<PersonName honorific="Mr." suffix="Jr.">
   <singleName>Matthew Jones</singleName>
</PersonName>
```

Here is an example of how we could describe an element type of `<PersonName>` using a DTD:

```
<!ELEMENT   FirstName   (#PCDATA) >
<!ELEMENT   MiddleName  (#PCDATA) >
<!ELEMENT   LastName    (#PCDATA) >
<!ELEMENT   SingleName  (#PCDATA) >

<!ELEMENT   PersonName (SingleName | (FirstName, MiddleName*, LastName)) >
<!ATTLIST   PersonName
   honorific (Mr. | Ms. | Dr. | Rev.) #IMPLIED
   suffix    (Jr. | Sr. | I | II | III | IV | V | VI | VII | VIII) #IMPLIED
>
```

This involves five element types: `<PersonName>` and its four children; and two optional attributes, each of which uses an enumerated attribute type. The content model of `<PersonName>` is fairly simple: a sequence list (for a full name) nested within a choice list that allows for the `<SingleName>` alternate name form.

All of the children of `<PersonName>` are restricted to be simple `#PCDATA` (character data only), and all except one are required to be present and singular. The exception, `<MiddleName>`, is optional, with zero or more occurrences allowed (as indicated by the * cardinality operator).

The following is an XML Schema representation of these element types and attribute definitions:

```
<?xml version="1.0" ?>

<schema xmlns="http://www.w3.org/2000/10/XMLSchema">

 <simpleType name="PersonTitle">
   <restriction base="string">
      <enumeration value="Mr." />
      <enumeration value="Ms." />
      <enumeration value="Dr." />
      <enumeration value="Rev." />
   </restriction>
 </simpleType>
```

```
<complexType name="Text" content="textOnly" >
  <restriction base="string" />
</complexType>

<element name="PersonName">
 <complexType content="element">
 <choice>
   <element name="SingleName" type="Text" minOccurs="1" maxOccurs="1" />
   <sequence>
    <element name="FirstName" type="Text" minOccurs="1" maxOccurs="1" />
    <element name="MiddleName" type="Text" minOccurs="0"
             maxOccurs="unbounded" />
    <element name="LastName" type="Text" minOccurs="1" maxOccurs="1" />
   </sequence>
  </choice>

  <attribute name="honorific" ref="PersonTitle" />

  <attribute name="suffix">
   <simpleType>
     <restriction base="string">
        <enumeration value="Jr." />
        <enumeration value="Sr." />
        <enumeration value="I" />
        <enumeration value="II" />
        <enumeration value="III" />
        <!-- ..and so on... -->
     </restriction>
    </simpleType>
   </attribute>

  </complexType>
</element>

</schema>
```

Most of these names and values are common to both the DTD and the schema, but let's look a little closer at the new type of declarations.

The first line is the XML declaration which *should* begin all XML files; schema or otherwise:

```
<?xml version="1.0" ?>
```

We've omitted the `encoding` attribute since we're using the default value (UTF-8). However, this can be any valid XML encoding.

The second line probably looks familiar since we saw one just like it earlier in the chapter:

```
<schema xmlns="http://www.w3.org/2000/10/XMLSchema">
```

The next definition uses a `<simpleType>` definition:

```
<simpleType name="PersonTitle">
    <restriction base="string">
       <enumeration value="Mr." />
       <enumeration value="Ms." />
       <enumeration value="Dr." />
       <enumeration value="Rev." />
    </restriction>
</simpleType>
```

183

We've used the <enumeration> constraining facet to limit this datatype to a small list of legal string values, just like we did with an enumerated attribute type in the DTD.

Our first <complexType> definition illustrates a simple form of this schema component:

```
<complexType name="Text" content="textOnly">
   <restriction base="string" />
</complexType>
```

This will be useful shorthand when we use it later in some <element> declarations. The key issue here is the content attribute – any element that's declared to be of the Text type may only contain character data, no child elements are permitted. This is the equivalent of the #PCDATA attribute type in the DTD.

We can now declare the <PersonName> element type, with element only content:

```
<element name="PersonName">
  <complexType content="element">

  <choice>
    <element name="SingleName" type="Text" minOccurs="1" maxOccurs="1" />
   <sequence>
    <element name="FirstName" type="Text" minOccurs="1" maxOccurs="1" />
    <element name="MiddleName" type="Text" minOccurs="0"
            maxOccurs="unbounded" />
    <element name="LastName" type="Text" minOccurs="1" maxOccurs="1" />
   </sequence>
  </choice>
```

The <element> element is analogous to a part of the <!ELEMENT..> declaration in a DTD.

The <choice> element is analogous to the | operator in a DTD. So this allows a choice between a single <SingleName> element and a sequence list (like the comma separated list in a DTD) that gives a person's full name.

Like all such datatypes and declarations in XML Schema, <PersonName> will inherit its properties from other components of the schema (such as our Text user derived datatype, which in turn inherits properties from the string built-in primitive datatype).

The <complexType> without any name attribute shows the use of an **anonymous type**. This intermediary is necessary because an <element> cannot use the content attribute to specify the element-only content model. In XML Schema, <element> is used for naming the element type, but content models need to be described with a <complexType>, either named or anonymous.

We've declared the <PersonName> element at the **global** level (it's a direct child of <schema>), so this element definition can be used anywhere within the schema, and can be shared with another external schema. On the other hand, the children of <PersonName> are declared within an anonymous <complexType> and therefore only have a **local** scope.

We also declare two attributes of <PersonName> here. The first uses the named <simpleType> that we defined earlier in this example:

```
<attribute name="honorific" ref="PersonTitle" />
```

The second uses an anonymous type to connect a series of enumerated values to the enclosing <attribute> declaration. This declaration is similar to the <!ATTLIST..> declaration in a DTD.

```
<attribute name="suffix">
 <simpleType>
   <restriction base="string">
      <enumeration value="Jr." />
      <enumeration value="Sr." />
      <enumeration value="I" />
      <enumeration value="II" />
      <enumeration value="III" />
      <!-- ..and so on... -->
   </restriction>
 </simpleType>
</attribute>
```

Lastly, we need to close the <schema> element to indicate the end of the schema. Although in this example, <schema> is the document element, it could instead have been contained within some other element. This allows us to include a schema within another XML document – which can of course be another schema, or perhaps a text document that describes the schema embedded within.

Example 2 – Using an Attribute Group to Represent Rows

If there are groups of elements that share a common set of attributes, rather than declare them for each element, we can use an attribute group which can be passed by reference to each element. Also, if we are to use attributes to model column values, we can use attribute groups to neatly model the columns of a table.

The following example shows an alternative way to model name details, using attributes to hold all of the details about a customer. We define an <attributeGroup> and use it later by reference on the <Customer> content model:

```
<attributeGroup name="CustomerDetails">
    <attribute name="honorific" type="string" />
    <attribute name="firstName" type="string" />
    <attribute name="MI" type="string" />
    <attribute name="lastName" type="string" />
</attributeGroup>

<element name="Customer">
  <complexType>
    <attributeGroup ref="CustomerDetails" />
  </complexType>
</element>
```

The empty <attributeGroup> element within the <Customer> element declaration is functionally equivalent to including all the <attribute> declarations individually, because it declares the attribute group that contains that information.

Example 3 – Mixed Content Models

With a DTD, when we specify mixed content (in other words the first item in the content model is #PCDATA), we lose the ability to dictate the sequence of child elements within their parent. So, despite the *appearance* of a sequence list that could be validated using the DTD, the children may actually appear in any order in the document instance. In a schema, the sequence of the children within an <element> declaration is respected, and thus the order of the children in a document instance *can* be validated against the schema.

XML Schemas provide for the construction of schemas where character data can appear alongside child elements, and character data is not confined to the deepest subelements. Let's look at another example, this time we are using character data that could explain details about an order alongside child elements that contain data. Here is an example of an `Invoice` using mixed content, where the main information is also held in element values (rather than attributes):

```
<orderInvoice>
    <Shipto>
        <Customer>
            <firstName>Lenny</firstName>
            <lastName>Bruce</lastName>
            <custID>1b10023w</custID>
        </Customer>
        <Address>
            <addressID>212</addressID>
            <street>101 South Blvd.</street>
            <city>Columbus</city>
            <state>OH</state>
        </Address>
    </Shipto>
    <Order>Your order
        <orderID>bm123</orderID> of
        <quantity>1</quantity>
        <productName>Baby Monitor</productName>
        shipped from our warehouse on
        <shipDate>2000-05-21</shipDate>.
    </Order>
</orderInvoice>
```

Now, let's develop a schema for this document, which will allow us to validate its content. Note how the `Order` element has an attribute called `content`, which takes a value of `mixed`:

```
<schema
    xmlns="http://www.w3.org/2000/10/XMLSchema"
    version="1.42.57" >

  <key name="customer">
    <selector xpath="orderInvoice" />
    <field xpath="/customerID" />
  </key>

  <keyref name="item" refer="customer">
    <selector xpath="orderInvoice/Address" />
    <field xpath="/AddressID" />
  </keyref>
  <keyref name="item" refer="customer">
    <selector xpath="orderInvoice/Invoice" />
    <field xpath="/invoiceID" />
  </keyref>

<element name="Customer" type="customerType">
<complexType name="customerType">
    <sequence>
        <element name="firstName" type="string" />
        <element name="lastName" type="string" />
        <element name="custID" type="ID" />
    </sequence>
</complexType>
```

```
<element name="Address" type=addressType" />
<complexType name="addressType">
    <sequence>
        <element name="addressID" type="IDREF" />
        <element name="street" type="string" />
        <element name="city" type="string" nullable="true" />
        <element name="state" type="string" />
    </sequence>
</complexType>

<element name=" orderInvoice">
    <complexType>
        <sequence>
            <element name="Shipto">
                <complexType>
                    <sequence>
                        <element ref="Customer" />
                        <element ref="Address" />
                    </sequence>
                </complexType>
            </element>
            <element name="Order" content="mixed">
                <complexType>
                    <sequence>
                        <element name="orderID" type="string" />
                        <element name="quantity" type="positiveInteger"/>
                        <element name="productName" type="string"/>
                        <element name="shipDate" type="date" minOccurs="0"/>
                    </sequence>
                </complexType>
            </element>
        </sequence>
    </complexType>
</element>
</schema>
```

The elements appearing in the order invoice are declared, and their types are defined using the element and `complexType` element constructions we have seen before. To enable character data to appear between the child elements of `order`, the `content` attribute on the element definition is set to `mixed`. When this is added to the element, the order and number of child elements appearing in an instance must agree with the order and number of child elements specified in the model.

We have made use of the `nullable` attribute on the `city` element. We have also set the `key` attribute to the `CustomerID` attribute with a `keyref` reference to `OrderID` and `AddressID` (in a database, such a relationship could be modeled with a foreign key).

To finish this example, let's look at what our database for this mixed content model might look like.

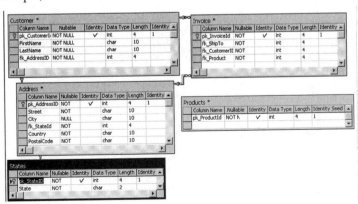

Example 4 – Enumeration

Most modern databases allow users to create their own data types, and as we saw earlier, we should try to constrain our database with a user defined type as close to that we have defined in our XML schema. However, there is one exception – that of enumeration. Imagine that we had to enumerate the states of the USA, we could this in our database as shown here:

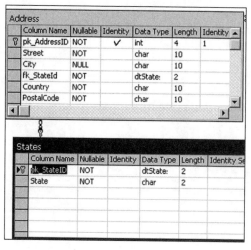

It might make more sense to maintain a separate state table, and have the Address table refer to it via the state's primaryKey.

usStateId	stateAbbreviation	stateName	stateNumber
1	AL	ALABAMA	01
2	AZ	ARIZONA	02
3	AR	ARKANSAS	03
4	CA	CALIFORNIA	04
5	CO	COLORADO	05
6	CT	CONNECTICUT	06
7	DE	DELAWARE	07
8	DC	DISTRICT OF COLL	08
9	FL	FLORIDA	09
10	GA	GEORGIA	10
11	ID	IDAHO	11
12	IL	ILLINOIS	12
13	IN	INDIANA	13
14	IA	IOWA	14
15	KS	KANSAS	15
16	KY	KENTUCKY	16
17	LA	LOUISIANA	17
18	ME	MAINE	18
19	MD	MARYLAND	19
20	MA	MASSACHUSETTS	20
21	MI	MICHIGAN	21
22	MN	MINNESOTA	22
23	MS	MISSISSIPPI	23
24	MO	MISSOURI	24
25	MT	MONTANA	25
26	NE	NEBRASKA	26
27	NV	NEVADA	27
28	NH	NEW HAMPSHIRE	28
29	NJ	NEW JERSEY	29
30	NM	NEW MEXICO	30
31	NY	NEW YORK	31
32	NC	NORTH CAROLINA	32
33	ND	NORTH DAKOTA	33

This would allow us to enumerate through our states in our schema:

```
<element name="States">
    <attribute name="StateID" type="ID">
        <simpleType>
            <restriction base=" string">
                <enumeration value="AL" />
                <enumeration value="AZ" />
                <enumeration value="AR" />
                <enumeration value="CA" />
                <enumeration value="CO" />
                <enumeration value="CT" />
                <enumeration value="DE" />
                <!-- And so on -->
            </restriction>
        </simpleType>
    </attribute>
</element>
```

If we were thinking of this point of view for every element that has a type of enumeration, we should create a table in the relational database. So we add a column to the table representing the enumeration value. Add an auto incrementing primary key to the table as well.

Summary

We have learned that there are stronger similarities between XML schemas and a typical database schema than between DTDs and database schemas. We discovered that XML schemas allow us more robustness to define and constrain our document and database. In particular, we can define use defined datatypes to constrain element and attribute content, and we can even create our own derived datatypes to make sure that the values are what we want. This extra ability to validate documents will be able to save us programming validation code because the constraints are a lot more powerful. In addition, there are some extra features which ensure uniqueness and help us to model relationships.

We have seen how we can:

- ❑ write XML Schemas.

- ❑ constrain our documents with a lot more precision than with DTDs.

- ❑ create our own datatypes.

- ❑ build up complex content models from complex types.

- ❑ validate mixed content models.

- ❑ model key relationships using key and keyref attributes.

- ❑ ensure unique values in documents.

We have seen that XML Schemas offer a far more powerful and descriptive alternative to schemas. We can now look forward to their implementation in more widely available products as soon as they have been standardized by the W3C.

6

DOM

Having seen how to model our XML data, we now need to know how to work with that data. In the next two chapters, we are going to learn how to manipulate, add, update, and delete that data while it is still in its XML document, and make it available to processing applications.

The **Document Object Model (DOM)** provides a means for working with XML documents (and other types of documents) through the use of code, and a way to interface with that code in the programs we write. In a sentence, the Document Object Model provides standardized access to parts of an XML document. For example, the DOM enables us to:

❑   Create documents and parts of documents.

❑   Navigate through the document.

❑   Move, copy, and remove parts of the document.

❑   Add or modify attributes.

In this chapter, we'll discuss how to work with the DOM to achieve such tasks, as well as seeing:

❑   What the DOM is.

❑   What interfaces are, and how they differ from objects.

❑   What XML related interfaces exist in the DOM, and what we can do with them.

❑   How to use exceptions.

The DOM specification is being built level-by-level. That is, when the W3C produced the first DOM Recommendation, it was **DOM Level 1**. Level 1 was then added to, to produce **Level 2**. At the time of writing, DOM Level 3 was in its development stages, so in this chapter, we'll be discussing the DOM Level 2.

You can find the DOM Level 2 specification at:
http://www.w3.org/TR/DOM-Level-2/, and there's more information at:
http://www.w3.org/TR/1999/CR-DOM-Level-2-19991210/core.html.

What is the DOM?

As we are able to create our own XML vocabularies, and document instances that conform to these vocabularies, we need a standard way to interact with this data. The DOM provides us with an object model that can model any XML document – regardless of how it is structured – giving us access to its content. So, as long as we create our documents according to the rules laid down in the XML 1.0 specification, the DOM will be able to represent them and give us interfaces to work with them programmatically.

While the DOM is an object model, the model is abstract – the DOM is not a program itself, and the specification does not tell us how to implement the interfaces it exposes. In actual fact, the DOM specification just declares a set of **Application Programming Interface**s, or **API**s, that define how a DOM compliant piece of software would allow us to access a document and manipulate its contents.

When we looked at how we use XML in association with databases, we saw that it is a powerful device in any developer's toolkit. It provides methods for our XML documents to be updated, and created, records added, elements removed, attributes changed, etc.

How Does the DOM Work?

As we said, the DOM specification defines interfaces that a program can implement to be DOM compliant. It does so in a programming language independent manner, so implementations of the DOM can be written in our language of choice. Rather than writing the implementations of the interfaces specified by the DOM, however, there are many pieces of software that implement it for us.

The DOM is usually added as a layer between the XML parser and the application that needs the information in the document, meaning that the parser reads the data from the XML document and then feeds that data into a DOM. The DOM is then used by a higher-level application. The application can do whatever it wants with this information, including putting it into another proprietary object model, if so desired.

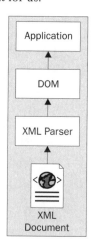

So, in order to write an application that will be accessing an XML document through the DOM, we need to have an XML parser and a DOM implementation installed on our machine. Some DOM implementations, such as MSXML (http://msdn.microsoft.com/downloads/default.asp), have the parser built right in, while others can be configured to sit on top of one of many parsers.

Most of the time, when working with the DOM, the developer will never even have to know that an XML parser is involved, because the parser is at a lower level than the DOM, and will be hidden away. Here are some other implementations that we may be interested in:

Xerces	Part of the Apache Project, Xerces provides fully-validating parsers available for Java and C++, implementing the W3C XML and DOM (Level 1 and 2) standards. See http://xml.apache.org.
4DOM	4DOM was designed to provide Python developers with a tool that could help them rapidly design applications for reading, writing, or otherwise manipulating HTML and XML documents.
ActiveDOM	ActiveDOM is an Active-X control that enables XML files to be loaded and created based upon the W3C DOM 1.0 specification.
Docuverse DOM SDK	Docuverse DOM SDK is a full implementation of the W3C DOM (Document Object Model) API in Java.
PullDOM and MiniDOM	PullDOM is simple Application Programming Interface (API) for working with Document Object Model (DOM) objects in a streaming manner with Python.
TclDOM	TclDOM is a language binding for the DOM to the Tcl scripting language.
XDBM	XDBM is an XML Database Manager provided as an embedded database for use within other software applications through the use of a DOM-based API.

DOMString

In order to ensure that all DOM implementations work in the same way, the DOM specifies a data type called DOMString. This is a sequence of 16-bit units (characters) which is used anywhere that a string is expected.

In other words, the DOM specifies that all strings must be UTF-16. Although the DOM specification uses this DOMString type anywhere it's talking about strings, this is just for the sake of convenience; a DOM implementation doesn't actually need to make any type of DOMString object available.

Many programming languages, such as Java, JavaScript, and Visual Basic, work with strings in 16-bit units natively, so anywhere a DOMString is specified, these programming languages could use their native string types. On the other hand, C and C++ can work with strings in 8-bit units or in 16-bit units, so care must be taken to ensure that we are always using the 16-bit units in these languages.

DOM Implementations

Because there are different types of DOM implementations, the DOM provides the **DOM Core** – a core set of interfaces for working with basic documents – and a number of optional modules for working with other documents. For example, the DOM can also be used for working with HTML documents cascading style sheets (CSS). These modules are sets of additional interfaces that can be implemented as required.

The DOM Level 2 specification defines the following optional modules:

DOM Views	Allows programs and scripts to dynamically access and update the content of a representation of a document (http://www.w3.org/TR/DOM-Level-2-Views)
DOM Events	Gives programs and scripts a generic event system (http://www.w3.org/TR/DOM-Level-2-Events)
DOM HTML	Allows programs and scripts to dynamically access and update the content and structure of HTML documents (http://www.w3.org/TR/DOM-Level-2-HTML)
DOM Style Sheets and Cascading Style Sheets (CSS)	Allows programs and scripts to dynamically access and update the content and structure of style sheet documents (http://www.w3.org/TR/DOM-Level-2-Style)
DOM Traversal and Range	Allows programs and scripts to dynamically traverse and identify a range of content in a document. (http://www.w3.org/TR/DOM-Level-2-Traversal-Range)

For the rest of this chapter, we're going to be concentrating on the DOM Core.

DOM Interfaces

The name "Document Object Model" clearly has the word "object" in it. This is because the implementation of the DOM creates an in-memory tree that represents the document as objects. These objects are just the internal representation, which we refer to as **Nodes**. So when thinking about the DOM's representation of a document, we talk in terms of nodes.

These objects, or nodes, expose a set of **interfaces**, and the DOM specification tells us what these interfaces are, and what we can expect in return when calling a method or property on them. So, when we are programming, we manipulate the objects through the interfaces. For example, using the interfaces supplied, we can say *"go get the Customer object [of the document that is loaded] and tell me its properties"*. Then we can manipulate the properties for that object.

Since that's the case, we'd better take a look at what these interfaces are, and what they're good for. To get an idea of what interfaces are involved in the DOM, let's take a very simple XML document, such as this one:

```
<parent>
  <child id="123">text goes here</child>
</parent>
```

When loaded into an implementation of the DOM, it would create the following set of nodes:

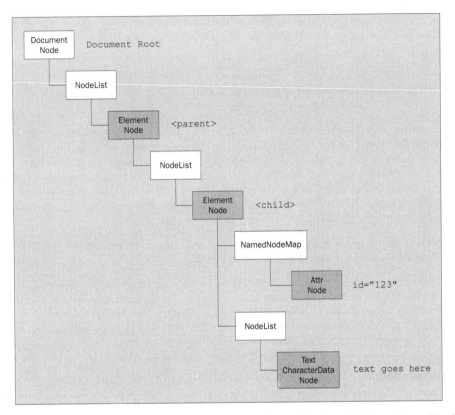

As we can see from this diagram, the in-memory representation that is created is a hierarchical structure (that reflects the document), and each of the boxes represents a **Node object** that will be created. Some of these nodes have child nodes, others are **leaf** nodes, which means that they do not have any children.

The names in the boxes are the interfaces that will be implemented by each object. For example, we have nodes to represent the whole document, and nodes to represent each of the elements. Each object implements a number of appropriate interfaces, such as Text, CharacterData, and Node for the object that represents the "text goes here" character data. Let's look at what these interfaces signify in more detail.

The Structure Model

When the document is loaded into the DOM, it creates the representation of the document in memory so that we can alter and work with it. While it is held in memory, it is the interfaces that the DOM exposes that allow us to manipulate the document's content.

In our previous example there are four key items of information that we may want to work with, which have to be represented:

- ❑ The <parent> element.
- ❑ The <child> element.
- ❑ The id attribute on the child and its value.
- ❑ The text content of the <child> element.

However, in the diagram there are clearly more than the four nodes that represent each piece of information from the document – the grayed out nodes. The other nodes do have a purpose, as we shall see.

> **Each Node object created implements the Node interface.**

Firstly, there is a node to represent the whole document, known as the **Document** node. We can see this at the root of this tree. This is required because it is the **conceptual** root of the tree. It has to be there in order to create the rest of the object model that represents the document, because elements, text nodes, comments, etc. cannot appear outside the context of a document. The Document node implements the methods to create these objects, and it will create nodes for all of the types of content we have in the document. Because the first node in this example is the document element, this Node object also supports the Document interface.

There are two other types of important interface that we can see in this hierarchy – NodeList and NamedNodeMap – which are also shown in the white boxes:

❑ **NodeList**: this Node object implements the NodeList interface. The NodeList is created to handle lists of Nodes. This is necessary, even though we have only one child element here, because we may want to use the DOM to add another element at this level. Although the NodeList handles Nodes it does not actually support the Node interface itself – we can think of it as being more like a handler. These are automatically inserted before elements and other markup, and would be used to handle other nodes at the same level.

❑ **NamedNodeMap**: this is required to handle unordered sets of nodes referenced by their name attribute, such as the attributes of an element. Again, these are automatically inserted.

Both NodeLists and NamedNodeMaps change dynamically as the document changes. For example, if another child element is added to a NodeList, it is immediately reflected in the NodeList.

Because XML documents need to have a unique root tag, the Document node can only have one element as a child. In this case we have the <parent> element. It could, however, also have other legal XML markup (a processing instruction, comment, document type declaration), which is why we need the NodeList object in there.

The root element of this document is <Parent>. As we can see from the diagram, this node supports the Element interface as well as the Node interface, because it represents an element.

Next we have another NodeList node, followed by the <child> element. Again we need the NodeList object to handle other types of markup that could be at the same level, and to give us the ability to handle other elements that we may want to add at this level.

The <child> element – like the <parent> element – is represented as an element node object, and implements the Node and Element interfaces.

Next we have NamedNodeMap and NodeList node objects. In this example, the NamedNodeMap handles the id attribute and its value, while the NodeList handles the element content.

Then, the id attribute is represented as a child of the NamedNodeMap, and implements the Node and Attribute interfaces. The element content is represented as a child of NodeList and implements the Text, CharacterData, and Node interfaces.

As we have seen, each node implements the Node interface. As we head down the tree, we see more specialized interfaces that are **inherited** from the Node interface.

Inheritance and Flattened Views

When we come to look at the Node interface in a moment, we will see that it is, in fact, quite powerful. We could do a lot with each object if it just implemented the Node interface. However, as we have seen, nodes can implement other more specific interfaces that inherit from parent interfaces. The DOM does, in fact, allow two different sets of interfaces to a document:

❑   A "**simplified**" view that allows all manipulation to be done via the Node interface.

❑   An "**object oriented**" approach with a hierarchy of inheritance.

The DOM allows for these two approaches because the object oriented approach requires casts in Java and other C-like languages, or query interface calls in COM environments, and both of these techniques are resource intensive. To allow us to work with documents without having this memory overhead, it is possible to use a document with the Node interface alone, which is the simplified or **flattened** view. However, because the inheritance approach is easier to understand than thinking of everything as a node, the higher level interfaces were added to give more object orientation.

This means that there may appear to be a lot of redundancy in the API. For example, as we shall see, the Node interface allows things such as a nodeName attribute, whereas the Element interface will be more specific and use a tagName attribute. While the value of both may be the same, it was considered a worthwhile addition.

In this chapter, we will look at the Node interface, so we will get a feel for the simplified or flattened view, although we will cover the full DOM Core interfaces that are available to us.

The DOM Core

In all, the DOM Core provides the following interfaces:

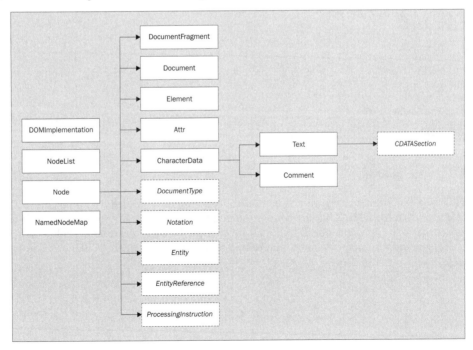

These core interfaces are further broken down into **Fundamental Interfaces** and **Extended Interfaces**.

- ❑ The Fundamental Interfaces must be implemented by all DOM implementations, even ones that will only be working with non XML documents (such as HTML documents and CSS style sheets).

- ❑ The Extended Interfaces only need to be implemented by DOM implementations that will be working with XML – they are not needed to work with HTML.

We might wonder why the Extended Interfaces were included in the DOM Core, instead of being in an optional XML module. That may be to do with the move of HTML syntax towards XHTML.

Remember, there are several optional modules that build on the core implementation of the DOM, for working with other types of documents – DOM HTML, DOM CSS, etc. Since this is a book on XML, we will only study the DOM Core interfaces here. However, many of the concepts we learn will be useful if we ever need to learn one of the optional modules.

Fundamental interfaces

The fundamental interfaces are so named because they are considered fundamental to all applications that wish to be DOM compliant, so all such applications must implement these interfaces. In this section we will quickly review each of the fundamental:

- ❑ Node
- ❑ Document
- ❑ DOMImplementation
- ❑ DocumentFragment
- ❑ NodeList
- ❑ Element
- ❑ NamedNodeMap
- ❑ Attr
- ❑ CharacterData
- ❑ Text
- ❑ Comments
- ❑ DOMException

To get us started, in this section we will demonstrate examples of how to use the DOM in IE5.x with MSXML (we used MSXML 3 but the code presented here will generally work just as well with earlier versions)– that is, using client-side HTML and JavaScript. To keep it simple, we'll look at some template code here, and then use some snippets that can be added to this template to demonstrate some of the features.

In order to work with this template we need to save the following document in the same folder as the template (ch06_ex1.xml):

```
<root>
  <DemoElement DemoAttribute="stuff">This is the PCDATA</DemoElement>
</root>
```

Here is the template that we will be using (ch06_ex1.html):

```
<HTML>
<HEAD><TITLE>DOM Demo</TITLE>

<SCRIPT language="JavaScript">

  var objDOM;
  objDOM = new ActiveXObject("MSXML3.DOMDocument");
  objDOM.async = false;
  objDOM.load("ch06_ex1.xml");

  //our code will go here...

</SCRIPT>

</HEAD>
<BODY>
  <P>This page demos some of the DOM capabilities.</P>
</BODY>
</HTML>
```

If we're using an old version of MSXML, we may need to change MSXML2.DOMDocument to MSXML.DOMDocument.

The HTML page itself doesn't actually do anything, except display the text, This page demos some of the DOM capabilities. All of the work is actually done in that <SCRIPT> block, and any results we want to see are displayed in message boxes.

Note that the DOM specification does not supply instructions on how a document should be loaded. In this example, we load the XML document into Microsoft's DOM implementation, MSXML, using two of the extensions Microsoft added to the DOM: the async property, and the load method. The load method takes in a URL to an XML file, and loads it. The async property tells the parser whether it should load the file **synchronously** or **asynchronously**.

If we load the file synchronously, load won't return until the file has finished loading. Loading the file asynchronously would allow our code to do other things while the document is loading, which isn't necessary in this case.

So let's start with the Node interface.

Node

`Node` is the most fundamental interface in the DOM. Almost all of the objects we will be dealing with will extend this interface, which makes sense, since any part of an XML document is a node.

Although `Node` is implemented in all DOM objects, some of its properties and methods may not be appropriate for certain node types. These methods and properties are just included for the sake of convenience, so that if we're working with a variable of type `Node`, we will have access to some of the functionality of the other interfaces, without having to cast to one of those types.

There are three key things that the `Node` object allows us to do:

❑ **Traverse the Tree**. In order to interrogate the tree, or make any adjustments to it, we need to be in the correct place on the tree.

❑ **Get information about the Node**. By interrogating the `Node` object using the available methods on this interface, we can get information such as the type of node, attributes of the node, it's name, and its value.

❑ **Add, remove, and update nodes**. If we want to alter the structure of a document, we need to be able to add, remove, or replace nodes – for example, we might want to add another line item to an invoice.

Here are the properties that are available on the `Node` object. As we can see, some of the attributes – such as `nodeName` and `nodeValue` – allow us to get information about a node without casting down to the specific derived interface:

Property	Description
nodeName	The name of the node. Will return different values depending on the nodeType, as listed in Appendix C.
nodeValue	The value of the node. Will return different values depending on the nodeType, as listed in Appendix C.
nodeType	The type of node. Will be one of the values from the table in Appendix C.
parentNode	The node that is this node's parent.
childNodes	A NodeList containing all of this node's children. If there are no children, an empty NodeList will be returned – not NULL.
firstChild	The first child of this node. If there are no children, this returns NULL.
lastChild	The last child of this node. If there are no children, this returns NULL.
previousSibling	The node immediately preceding this node. If there is no preceding node, this returns NULL.
nextSibling	The node immediately following this node. If there is no following node, this returns NULL.
attributes	A NamedNodeMap containing the attributes of this node. If the node is not an element, this returns NULL.
ownerDocument	The document to which this node belongs.
namespaceURI	The namespace URI of this node. Returns NULL if a namespace is not specified.
prefix	The namespace prefix of this node. Returns NULL if a namespace is not specified.
localName	Returns the local part of this node's QName.

The value of the `nodeName` and `nodeValue` properties depends on the value of the `nodeType` property, which can return a constant.

Here are the methods that are exposed by the `node` object:

Method	Description
insertBefore(*newChild*, *refChild*)	Inserts the *newChild* node before the existing *refChild*. If *refChild* is NULL, it inserts the node at the end of the list. Returns the inserted node.
replaceChild(*newChild*, *oldChild*)	Replaces *oldChild* with *newChild*. Used to update existing records. Returns *oldChild*.
removeChild(*oldChild*)	Removes *oldChild* from the list, and returns it.
appendChild(*newChild*)	Adds *newChild* to the end of the list, and returns it.
hasChildNodes()	Returns a Boolean; true if the node has any children, false otherwise.
cloneNode(*deep*)	Returns a duplicate of this node. If the Boolean *deep* parameter is true, this will recursively clone the subtree under the node, otherwise it will only clone the node itself.
normalize()	If there are multiple adjacent Text child nodes (from a previous call to Text.splitText – which we'll see more of later) this method will combine them again. It doesn't return a value.
supports(*feature*, *version*)	Indicates whether this implementation of the DOM supports the *feature* passed. Returns a Boolean, true if it supports the feature, false otherwise.

Getting Node Information

As we can see, the Node interface has several properties that let us get information about the node in question. To demonstrate showing information on a node, we have to navigate to that node in the tree. We'll see how to do this next. To navigate in these examples we use a simple dot notation.

The nodeType Property

If we're ever not sure what type of node we're dealing with, the `nodeType` property can tell you (all of the possible values for `nodeType` are listed in Appendix C). For example, we could check to see if we're working with an Element like so:

```
if(objNode.nodeType == 1)
```

Luckily for us, most DOM implementations will include predefined constants for these node types. For example, a constant might be defined called NODE_ELEMENT, with the value of 1, meaning that we could write code like this:

```
if(objNode.nodeType == NODE_ELEMENT)
```

This makes it easier to tell what it is we are checking for, without having to remember that `nodeType` returns 1 for an element.

The attributes Property

A good example of a property of Node that doesn't apply to every node type is the attributes property, which is *only* applicable if the node is an element with attributes. The attributes property returns a NamedNodeMap containing any attributes of the node. If the node is not an element, or is an element with no attributes, the attributes property returns null.

The nodeName and nodeValue Properties

Two pieces if information that we will probably want from any type of node are its name and its value, and Node provides the nodeName and nodeValue attributes to retrieve this information. nodeName is **read-only**, meaning that we can get the value from the property but not change it, and nodeValue is **read-write**, meaning that we can change the value of a node if desired.

The values returned from these properties differ from nodetype to nodetype. For example, for an element, nodeName will return the name of the element, but for a text node, nodeName will return the string "#text", since PCDATA nodes don't really have a name.

If we have a variable named objNode referencing an element like <name>John</name>, then we can write code like this:

```
alert(objNode.nodeName);
//pops up a message box saying "name"

objNode.nodeName = "FirstName";
//will raise an exception!  nodeName is read-only

alert(objNode.nodeValue);
//pops up a message box saying "null"
```

The result of that second alert may surprise us; why does it return "null", instead of "John"? The answer is that the text inside an element is not part of the element itself; it actually belongs to a text node, which is a child of the element node.

If we have a variable named objText, which points to the text node child of this element, we can write code like this:

```
alert(objText.nodeName);
//pops up a message box saying "#text"

alert(objText.nodeValue);
//pops up a message box saying "John"

objText.nodeValue = "Bill";
//this is allowed, the element is now <name>Bill</name>
```

Accessing Element Information with Node

We can navigate down the nodes in the tree, in this case using the documentElement and firstChild, and display the nodeName and nodeValue in an alert box.

To show how this works, we open the template HTML file that we created, and enter the following code after the comment //our code will go here.

To display the nodeName we use the following code (ch06_ex2.html):

```
//our code will go here...
var objMainNode;
objMainNode = objDOM.documentElement.firstChild;
alert(objMainNode.nodeName);
```

Here is the result:

If we want to display its value, we change it to this:

```
var objMainNode;
objMainNode = objDOM.documentElement.firstChild;
alert(objMainNode.nodeValue);
```

and again, here is the result:

Remember that this is an element we're talking about. The text in that element is contained not in the element itself, but in a Text child. Therefore, an element doesn't have any values of its own, only children.

Traversing the Tree

XML documents can be represented as trees of information because of their hierarchical nature. We tend to express relationships between these nodes like those in a family tree, in terms such as parent/child, ancestor/descendent etc. The DOM exposes properties that allow us to navigate through the tree using this kind of terminology. These properties are parentNode, firstChild, lastChild, previousSibling, and nextSibling properties, all of which return a Node, or the childNodes property, which returns a NodeList.

Being able to traverse the tree is vital so that we can get to the node that we want to operate on, whether we just want to retrieve some value, update its content, add something in at that position in the document/structure, or indeed delete it.

Not all nodes can have children (attributes, for example), and even if a node can have children, it might not. When that happens, any properties that are supposed to return children will just return NULL. Or, in the case of childNodes, will return a NodeList with no nodes.

The following diagram shows a node (in the grayed out box), and the relationships of the other nodes in the tree to this node. It indicates the node that would be returned from each of these properties:

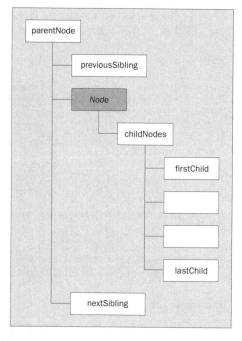

This diagram shows the relationships using the DOM terminology. If we want to get at the children of the node with the gray background, we access the childNodes property. Or, if we want the first or the last child, there are properties which directly return these nodes. That's easier than having to navigate through the childNodes property. (If a node has only one child, firstChild and lastChild will both return that node.)

The parentNode property returns the node to which this node belongs in the tree, and previousSibling and nextSibling return the two nodes that are children of that parent node, and are on either side of the node we're working with.

The hasChildNodes Method

If we just want to check if the node has any children, there is a method named hasChildNodes, which returns a Boolean value indicating whether or not it does. (Note that this includes text nodes, so even if an element contains only text, hasChildNodes will return true.)

For example, we could write code like the following, so that if a node has any children, a message box will pop up with the name of the first one:

```
if(objNode.hasChildNodes())
{
  alert(objNode.firstChild.nodeName);
}
```

The ownerDocument Property

Since every node must belong to a document, there's also a property called `ownerDocument`, which returns an object implementing the `Document` interface to which this node belongs. Almost all of the objects in the DOM implement the `Node` interface, so this allows us to find the owner document from any object in the DOM.

Navigating the Tree with Node

Let's show an example of this working. Open up our template file and add the following code beneath the comment:

```
//our code will go here...
var objMainNode;
objMainNode = objDOM.selectSingleNode("/root/DemoElement");
alert(objMainNode.firstChild.nodeName);
alert(objMainNode.firstChild.nodeValue);
```

This navigates to the `DemoElement` of the `root`, and generates two alert boxes with the `nodeName` and `nodeValue`. As mentioned before, `Text` nodes always return **#text** from `nodeName`, since PCDATA nodes don't have names. `nodeValue` returns the value of the PCDATA in the element.

Adding, Updating, and Removing Nodes

All of the above properties for traversing the tree are read-only, meaning that we can get at the existing children, but can't add new ones or remove old ones. To do that, there are a number of methods exposed from the `Node` interface.

The appendChild Method

The simplest is the `appendChild` method, which takes an object implementing `Node` as a parameter, and just appends it to the end of the list of children. We might append one node to another like this:

```
objParentNode.appendChild(objChildNode);
```

The `objChildNode` node is now the last child node of `objParentNode`, regardless of what type of node it is.

The insertBefore Method

To have more control over where the node is inserted, we can call `insertBefore`. This takes two parameters: the node to insert and the "reference node", which is the one before which we want the new child inserted. (If the reference value is NULL, this produces a result like `appendChild`.)

The following will add the same objChildNode to the same objParentNode as the previous example, but the child will be added as the second from last child:

```
objParentNode.insertBefore(objChildNode, objParentNode.lastChild);
```

If we try an insertBefore and it finds the same node already exists, it will just update it (mimicking replaceChild which we'll see shortly) rather than adding a new node.

The removeChild Method

To remove a child, we would call the removeChild method, which takes a reference to the child we want to remove, and returns that object back to us in case we want to use it somewhere else. Even though the node is removed from the tree, it still belongs to the document. However, if we were to remove the child and then save the document, it would be lost.

So we could remove the last child of any node, and keep it in a variable, like this:

```
objOldChild = objParent.removeChild(objParent.lastChild);
```

The replaceChild Method

There is also a timesaving method, replaceChild, which can remove one node, and replace it with another. This is quicker than calling removeChild, and then appendChild or insertBefore. (Although if we just call insertBefore and the node already exists, we get the same result as calling replaceChild). Again, the child that's removed is returned from the method, in case we want to use it somewhere else.

To replace the first child of a node with another node, we would do this:

```
objOldChild = objParent.replaceChild(objNewChild, objParent.firstChild);
```

The cloneNode Method

Finally, there is a method to create a copy of the node as a new separate node: cloneNode. cloneNode takes a Boolean parameter that indicates whether this should be a **deep clone** (true) or a **shallow clone** (false). If it's a deep clone, the method will recursively clone the subtree under the node (in other words all of the children will also be cloned), otherwise only the node itself will be copied.

If the node is an element, a shallow clone will not copy the PCDATA content of the node, since the PCDATA is a child. However, attributes and their values will be copied. So if we have a node object, called objNode, which contains an element like <name id="1">John</name>", we could do this:

```
objNewNode = objNode.cloneNode(false);
//objNewNode is now <name id="1"/>

objNewNode = objNode.cloneNode(true);
//objNewNode is now <name id="1">John</name>
```

Again, notice that the attribute is copied, even when we do a shallow clone.

Nodes that are created using cloneNode can only be used in the same document as the original node; we can't clone a node from one document, and insert it into another one.

Modifying the Tree with Node

Let's go back to our simple HTML file and see how we can modify the tree structure (ch06_ex4.xml):

```
var objMainNode;
objMainNode = objDOM.documentElement.firstChild;

var objNewNode;
objNewNode = objMainNode.cloneNode(false);
objMainNode.appendChild(objNewNode);

alert(objDOM.xml);
```

In this example, we copy our node, and then append it back into the XML tree. We're performing a shallow clone, meaning that none of the children of the node is copied.

Note that the xml property we call in that last line is a Microsoft-specific extension to the DOM, which displays the XML that is held in a node. Here we've used it to return the entire XML document as a string and display it easily. This property is very useful when debugging applications, and when we want to retrieve the content of a fragment. We just add the xml property to the node that we have in memory.

Here is the result:

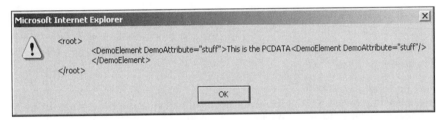

Notice that although not one of the child elements of <DemoElement> gets cloned, the attribute and its value does.

We can also attach that element before our text, by modifying our code as shown here:

```
//our code will go here...
var objMainNode;
objMainNode = objDOM.selectSingleNode("/root/DemoElement");

var objNewNode;
objNewNode = objMainNode.cloneNode(false);
objMainNode.insertBefore(objNewNode, objMainNode.firstChild);

alert(objDOM.xml);
```

For the reference node, we just use the firstChild property. The XML now looks like this:

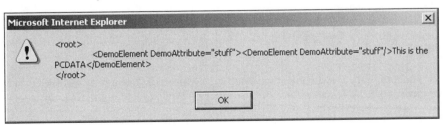

By simply changing the parameter of `cloneNode` to `true`, we can copy all of the node's children:

```
var objNewNode;
objNewNode = objMainNode.cloneNode(true);
objMainNode.insertBefore(objNewNode, objMainNode.firstChild);

alert(objDOM.xml);
```

In this case, that's just the one `Text` node. Our XML now looks like this:

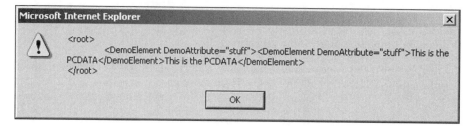

Document

The `Document` interface represents an entire XML document. It extends the `Node` interface, so any `Node` properties and methods will also be available from a `Document` object. For `Document`, the node will be the document root – not the root element. All nodes must belong to one, and only one, document.

> **Remember that for an XML document, the document root is a conceptual node which contains everything else in the document, including the root element.**

In addition to the properties and methods provided by `Node` for navigating the tree, the `Document` interface provides some additional navigational functionality. This is especially useful in finding elements in a document and creating XML documents.

One of the most commonly used properties is `documentElement`, which returns an `Element` object corresponding to the root element. Two other very helpful functions of note are:

❑   `getElementsByTagName` to find elements in the document based on their name. It takes the name of the element we are looking for as a string, and returns a `NodeList` containing all of the matching elements. (We'll be studying the `NodeList` interface in a later section.)

❑   `getElementsByID` which allows us to find elements by their ID attributes. This again returns a `NodeList` containing all of the matching elements. This is useful if we have used `ID`s to model relationships.

The `Document` object is also important when we want to create an XML document from scratch.

> **We cannot create a `Node` object without first creating the `Document` object. Once the `Document` has been created, we can use other methods to add nodes to it.**

The Document interface provides **factory methods** that can be used to create other objects. These methods are named createNodeType, where NodeType is the type of node you want to create, for example, createElement or createAttribute. When creating an element or attribute, however, because we are creating them from the Document node, we also need to append them to the tree where we want them to appear:

❑   First, create the node using one of the Document factory methods.

❑   Second, append the child in the appropriate spot (using the appendxxxx methods inherited from the Node interface).

The alternative is to navigate to that part of the tree, and then use one of the Node interfaces methods.

An interesting point to note here is that, until we append the node to the tree, it will belong to the document that created it, although it will not be part of the tree-structure until it has been appended.

Let's see how we would create an XML document from scratch. Open the template file again, and delete the lines:

```
objDOM.async = false;
  objDOM.load("ch06_ex1.xml");
```

First, we need to create a Document object called objDom. Once that has been created, we can use the document object to create an element and a text node. Here is the code for doing this:

```
//our code will go here...
var objNode, objText;
objNode = objDOM.createElement("root");
objText = objDOM.createTextNode("root PCDATA");
```

The createElement method takes the name of the element to be created as its parameter, and createTextNode takes as its parameter, the text we want to go into the node.

With these objects created, we can now perform the second required step of adding the element to our document. We will make it the root element, and add the text node to that element. Add the following code right after the code we've already entered:

```
objDOM.appendChild(objNode);
objNode.appendChild(objText);
alert(objDOM.xml);
```

The first command adds the tags, and the second the PCDATA.

If we save the HTML as ch06_ex5.html, and view it with IE5, the following message box will appear:

If we then want to add an attribute to that node, it is as simple as this (ch06_ex6.html):

```
objNode.appendChild(objText);
```

```
var objAttr;
objAttr = objDOM.createAttribute("id");

//set the attribute's value
objAttr.nodeValue = "123";

//append the attribute to the element
objNode.attributes.setNamedItem(objAttr);
```

```
alert(objDOM.xml)
```

The createAttribute method takes the name of the attribute as its parameter, so we've created an attribute named id, given it the value 123, and then added that attribute to the node. (In the examples at the end of the chapter we'll see an easier way of doing this, using the setAttribute method.

Our XML now looks like this:

and thus, we have created an entire XML document, all from code.

DOMImplementation

The DOMImplementation interface provides methods that apply to any document from this DOM implementation. Just like most of the other types of DOM objects, we can't directly create a DOMImplementation object. Instead, we retrieve it from the implementation property of the Document interface.

The first method we'll look at is createDocument, which works just like the create*NodeType* methods of the Document interface. We probably won't use createDocument very often, though, since we can't directly create a DOMImplementation object. We would first have to create a Document, and access its implementation property to get a DOMImplementation object, before we could even use this method. However, if we're creating multiple documents, meaning that we already have one or more Document objects in existence, it might come in handy.

A more important method is the hasFeature method, which we can use to find out if the current DOM implementation supports a certain feature (for example, for MSXML 3 the candidates are XML, DOM, and MS-DOM). The method takes two parameters: a string representing the feature we're looking for, and a string representing the version of the feature we need. If we don't pass the second parameter, then hasFeature will indicate whether this DOM supports *any* version of the feature. This can be useful for finding out whether a particular browser supports certain features – so we can run different code for different browsers, for example.

Say we want to know if a DOM implementation implements the Extended Interfaces, and is based on version 2.0 or later of the DOM specification:

❑ `hasFeature("XML", "2.0")` would then return `true` if it did. (Note that this would refer to the DOM specification rather than a second version of the XML specification.)

❑ `hasFeature("XML")` would return true if this DOM implementation implements the Extended Interfaces from *any* version of the DOM specification.

Most of the time we won't need to create a separate `DOMImplementation` object, but will instead just call its methods directly from the `Document` interface's `implementation` property, like this:

```
objDoc.implementation.hasFeature("XML", "2.0")
```

DocumentFragment

As we all know by now, an XML document can have only one root element. However, when working with XML information, it might be handy sometimes to have a few not-so-well-formed fragments of XML gathered together, in a temporary holding place.

For example, if we think back to the invoice that we used in earlier chapters this is particularly useful when dealing with line items. Maybe we want to create a number of nodes, and then insert them into the document tree in one bunch. Alternatively we might want to remove a number of nodes from the document and keep them around to be inserted back later, like a cut and paste type of operation. This is what the `DocumentFragment` interface provides.

As far as the interface itself, there are no added properties or methods to those provided by the `Node` interface.

For its children, a `DocumentFragment` has zero or more nodes. These are usually element nodes, but a `DocumentFragment` could even contain just a text node. `DocumentFragment` objects can be passed to methods which are used to insert nodes into a tree; for example, the `appendChild` method of `Node`. In this case, all of the children of the `DocumentFragment` are copied to the destination `Node`, but the `DocumentFragment` itself is not.

To demonstrate the `DocumentFragment` interface in action, we'll write some quick code, which will use one as a temporary holding place.

First off, we'll create our root element, as usual. Modify the HTML template as follows:

```
<HTML>
<HEAD><TITLE>DOM Demo</TITLE>

<SCRIPT language="JavaScript">
  var objDOM;
  objDOM = new ActiveXObject("MSXML2.DOMDocument");

  var objNode;
  objNode = objDOM.createElement("root");
  objDOM.appendChild(objNode);

</SCRIPT>
```

```
</HEAD>
<BODY>
  <P>This page demos some of the DOM capabilities.</P>
</BODY>
</HTML>
```

We'll then create a `DocumentFragment`, and store a couple of elements in it:

```
var objFrag;
objFrag = objDOM.createDocumentFragment();

objNode = objDOM.createElement("child1");
objFrag.appendChild(objNode);
objNode = objDOM.createElement("child2");
objFrag.appendChild(objNode);
```

Notice that we are reusing our `objNode` variable numerous times, instead of creating various node variables for all of the nodes we're dealing with. This just makes it easier to code, rather than declaring a number of variables for all of the nodes. Note that the nodes in this fragment have no root element – this isn't a well-formed XML document, it's just a number of nodes that we want to keep together for the moment.

Since our elements aren't much fun without any text in them, let's add a text child node to each one:

```
objFrag.firstChild.appendChild(objDOM.createTextNode("First child node"));
objFrag.lastChild.appendChild(objDOM.createTextNode("Second child node"));
```

In this case, we don't bother to create a variable to hold the `Text` node, we just create it and immediately append it to the element.

Finally, we'll add the elements in our `DocumentFragment` to the root element of our document:

```
objDOM.documentElement.appendChild(objFrag);
alert(objDOM.xml);
```

As mentioned earlier, this appends the *children* of the `DocumentFragment`, not the `DocumentFragment` itself. If we save the file as `ch06_ex7.html`, our final XML looks like this:

NodeList

We've already touched on it a couple of times, so let's talk about the `NodeList` interface. Many of the properties and methods in the DOM will return an ordered collection of `Nodes` instead of just one, which is why the `NodeList` interface was created.

It's actually a very simple interface. There is only one property and one method:

- ❑ The length property returns the number of items in the NodeList.
- ❑ The item method returns a particular item from the list. As a parameter, it takes the **index** of the Node we want.

Items in a NodeList are numbered starting at 0, not at 1. That means that if there are five items in a NodeList, the length property will return 5, but to get at the first item we would call item(0), and to get the fifth item we would call item(4). So the last Node in the NodeList is always at position (length - 1). If we call item with a number that's out of the range of this NodeList, it will return null.

A node list is always "live"; that means that if we add some nodes to, and remove nodes from the document, a node list will always reflect those changes. For example, if we got a node list of all elements in the document with a name of first, then appended an element named first, the node list would automatically contain this new element, without us having to ask it to recalculate itself.

Element

When we're not just referring to every item in an XML document as a "node", one of the pieces we're going to be accessing most will be elements, so of course the DOM provides an Element interface. As we saw in the earlier chapters, we will often be selecting an element to represent a table or a row of information from a database.

In addition to the properties and methods available from the Node interface, Element also provides a tagName property and a getElementsByTagName method. The tagName property returns exactly the same results as the nodeName property of Node, and getElementsByTagName works exactly the same as the method of the same name on the Document interface.

However, note that getElementsByTagName on the Element interface will only return elements that are children of the one from which the method is called. Of course, that applies to the getElementsByTagName on the Document interface as well, but the Document happens to include all of the elements in the document anyway. This means that we can use these methods on a specific table if we have two elements by the same name in the document as a whole.

All of the rest of the methods on the Element interface are concerned with attributes. Firstly, there are getAttribute and getAttributeNode methods. Both methods take the name of the attribute we want as a parameter, but getAttribute returns the value of that attribute in a string, whereas getAttributeNode returns an object implementing the Attr interface. We might use these to retrieve data points for processing.

If we want to alter values of data points or other attributes, there is also a setAttribute method and a setAttributeNode method. setAttribute takes two string parameters: the name of the attribute we want to set, and the value we want to give it. If an attribute of that name doesn't exist, it is created, but if the attribute already exists, it is replaced. setAttributeNode takes one parameter, an object implementing the Attr interface. Again, if an attribute with the same name already exists, it is replaced by the new attribute, but in this case, the old attribute is returned from the method, in case we need it for something else.

Finally, there's a removeAttribute method and a removeAttributeNode method. removeAttribute takes a string parameter, specifying the name of the attribute we wish to remove, and removeAttributeNode takes as a parameter an Attr object, which is the attribute we want to remove. removeAttributeNode returns the Attr object that was removed.

Since most of the functionality of the `Element` interface revolves around attributes, all we'll really need to use to demonstrate it is a small XML document.

We will save the following to our hard drive as `ch06_ex8.xml`:

```
<?xml version="1.0"?>
<root first='John' last='Doe'/>
```

then use the following modification to our template HTML file to load the document into MSXML, and create an `Element` variable to point to the `documentElement` (`ch06_ex8.html`):

```
<HTML>
<HEAD><TITLE>DOM Demo</TITLE>

<SCRIPT language="JavaScript">

  var objDOM;
  objDOM = new ActiveXObject("MSXML2.DOMDocument");
  objDOM.async = false;
  objDOM.load("ch06_ex8.xml");

  //our code will go here...
  var objElement;
  objElement = objDOM.documentElement;
  alert(objElement.getAttribute("first"));

</SCRIPT>

</HEAD>
</HTML>
```

Getting the value of an attribute is easy – we just need the following:

```
alert(objElement.getAttribute("first"));
```

This gets the value of the `first` attribute. We will save the page as `domelement.htm` and view it: the resulting message box contains the word John:

We can change the value of the first attribute by adding the following line of code:

```
var objElement;
objElement = objDOM.documentElement;

objElement.setAttribute("first", "Bill");

alert(objElement.getAttribute("first"));
```

Our message box will then read:

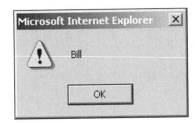

But, as we learned earlier, we can also do this using an `Attr` object. Let's try replacing the previous line of code with the following:

```
objElement = objDOM.documentElement;

var objAttr;
objAttr = objElement.getAttributeNode("first");
objAttr.nodeValue = "Bill";

alert(objElement.getAttribute("first"));var objAttr;
```

Alternatively, we can use the `Element` object like this:

```
objElement.getAttributeNode("first").nodeValue = "Bill";
```

Both of these methods will return the same result: a message box containing the name Bill.

Finally, we have two ways to add a `middle` attribute to our element. We can add the following code to append an `Attr` object (ch06_ex9.html):

```
objElement.getAttributeNode("first").nodeValue = "Bill";

alert(objElement.getAttribute("first"));

var objAttr;
objAttr = objDOM.createAttribute("middle");
objAttr.nodeValue = "Fitzgerald Johansen";
objElement.setAttributeNode(objAttr);

alert(objDOM.xml);
```

The resulting XML looks like this:

We can get exactly the same result by just using the `setAttribute` method, like this:

```
objElement.getAttributeNode("first").nodeValue = "Bill";

alert(objElement.getAttribute("first"));

objElement.setAttribute("middle", "Fitzgerald Johansen");

alert(objDOM.xml);
```

There isn't any way to arrange the `middle` attribute between the `first` and `last` attributes, but we don't really mind, since the order of attributes on an XML element is insignificant. This is because attributes are usually accessed by name.

NamedNodeMap

In addition to the `NodeList` interface, there's also a `NamedNodeMap` interface, which is used to represent an unordered collection of nodes. Items in a `NamedNodeMap` are usually retrieved by name.

Like NodeList objects, objects contained in a `NamedNodeMap` are live, which means that the contents dynamically reflect changes.

It is possible to access objects implementing `NamedNodeMap` using an ordinal index, but since the collection is unordered (and particularly because attributes are unordered in XML documents) it is not wise to use this method for retrieving or setting values of objects in a `NamedNodeMap`, it is more for the enumeration of the contents.

It should come as no surprise to us, then, that there is a `getNamedItem` method, which takes a string parameter specifying the name of the node, and returns a `Node` object. This is particularly useful if we wish to perform some operation on a particular attribute of the XML document, and because it is specific to an element, we can think of this as finding the data point in a particular row.

There is also a `removeNamedItem` method, which takes a string parameter specifying the name of the item we wish to remove, and returns the `Node` that was removed; and, to round out the functionality, there's a `setNamedItem` method, which takes a parameter for the `Node` we want to insert into the `NamedNodeMap`.

Even though the items in a `NamedNodeMap` are not ordered, we still might want to iterate through them one by one. For this reason, `NamedNodeMap` provides a `length` property and an `item` method, which work the same as `length` and `item` on the `NodeList` interface. The `item` can refer to the node at any position in the range 0 to `length-1` inclusive; but the DOM specification is clear that this "does not imply that the DOM specifies an order to these Nodes". (We can see this for ourselves at http://www.w3.org/TR/1999/CR-DOM-Level-2-19991210/core.html#ID-1780488922).

Attr

Although most of the interfaces in the DOM are spelled out in full, for some reason, the interface for attributes was abbreviated to `Attr`.

The `Attr` interface extends the `Node` interface, but it is good to keep in mind the differences between attributes and other items in the XML document. For one thing, attributes are not directly part of the tree structure in a document; that is, attributes are not children of elements, they are just properties of the elements to which they are attached. That means that the `parentNode`, `previousSibling`, and `nextSibling` properties for an attribute will always return `null`: but, since `parentNode` returns `null`, `Attr` provides instead an `ownerElement` property, which returns the `Element` to which this attribute belongs.

`Attr` also supplies `name` and `value` attributes, which return the name and value of the attribute. These properties have the same values as the `nodeName` and `nodeValue` properties of `Node`.

The final property supplied by the `Attr` interface is the `specified` property. The `specified` property indicates whether this attribute is really a physical attribute on the element, with a real value, or whether it is just an *implied* attribute, with the default value supplied.

CharacterData and Text

As we're well aware, working with XML documents involves a lot of work with text: sometimes in PCDATA in the XML document, and sometimes in other places, like attribute values, or comments. The DOM defines two interfaces for this purpose:

❑   A `CharacterData` interface, which has a number of properties and methods for working with text.

❑   A `Text` interface, which extends `CharacterData`, and is used specifically for PCDATA in the XML document.

Because `CharacterData` extends `Node`, both `CharacterData` objects and `Text` objects are also `Node` objects. `CharacterData` nodes, like `Attr` nodes, can't have children, so the same rules for `Attr`'s handling of child properties also apply to `CharacterData` objects.

Handling Complete Strings

The simplest way to get or set the PCDATA in a `CharacterData` object is to simply get it from the `data` property. This sets or returns the whole string, in one chunk.

There is also a `length` property, which returns the number of Unicode characters in the string.

> When we are dealing with strings in `CharacterData` objects, we should note that the characters in the string are numbered starting at 0, not 1. So in the string "Hi ", "H" would be letter 0, and "i " would be letter 1.

So, if we have a `Text` node object named `objText` containing the string "John", then:

```
alert(objText.length);
```

pops-up a message box saying 4, and :

```
alert(objText.data);
```

pops-up a message box saying John.

Handling Substrings

If we only want a part of the string, there is a `substringData` method, which takes two parameters:

- ❑ The offset at which to start taking characters.
- ❑ The number of characters to take.

If we specify more characters than are available in the string, `substringData` just returns the number of characters up until the end, and stops.

For example, if we have a `CharacterData` object named `objText`, and the contents of that object are `This is the main string`, then:

```
alert(objText.substring(12, 4));
```

would pop-up a message box saying main, and:

```
alert(objText.substringData(12, 2000));
```

would pop-up a message box saying main string.

Modifying Strings

Adding text to the end of a string is done with the `appendData` function, which takes a single string parameter containing the text to add to the end of the existing text.

If we used the same `objText` node as above, then:

```
objText.appendData(".");
```

would change the contents to "`This is the main string.`" with the period added.

Since we sometimes need to add data to the middle of a string, there is also the `insertData` method, which takes two parameters:

- ❑ The offset at which to start inserting characters (like the other parameters for this method, the numbering starts at 0).
- ❑ The string we wish to insert.

The following code would change the data to "`This is the groovy main string.`":

```
objText.insertData(12, "groovy ");
```

Deleting characters from the string is done via the `deleteData` method, which we use exactly the same as the `substringData` method. So calling:

```
objText.deleteData(12, 7);
```

on the `CharacterData` node we've been working with, would change the string back to "This is the main string." removing the text "groovy".

Finally, if we want to replace characters in a string with other characters, instead of calling `deleteData` and then `insertData`, we can simply use `replaceData`. This method takes three arguments:

- ❏ The offset position at which to start replacing.
- ❏ The number of characters to replace.
- ❏ The string to replace them with.

Note that the number of characters we're inserting doesn't have to be the same as the number of characters we're replacing.

If we still have the same `objText` node containing "This is the main string.", we can do the following:

```
objText.replaceData(8, 8, "a");
```

which will replace "the main" with "a", thus changing the string to "This is a string.".

Splitting Text

The `Text` interface only adds one method to the ones inherited from `CharacterData`, which is the `splitText` method. This takes one `Text` object and splits it up into two, which are siblings of each other. The method takes one parameter, which is the offset at which to make the split.

The result is that the first `Text` node will contain the text from the old node up until (but not including) the offset point, and the second `Text` node will contain the rest of the text from the old node. If the offset is equal to the length of the string, the first `Text` node will contain the old string as it was, and the new node will be empty; and if the offset is greater than the string's length, a `DOMException` will be raised.

We could, therefore, write code like this:

```
objText.splitText(11);
```

and the result would look something like this:

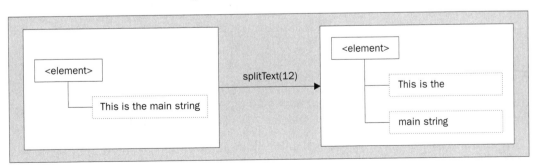

Of course, if we were to save this XML document like that, our change would be lost, since the PCDATA would then just become one string again. splitText() comes in most handy when we are going to be inserting other elements in the middle of the text.

Comments

The Comment interface is one of the easiest interfaces we'll be studying in this chapter. Comment extends the CharacterData interface, but it does not add any properties or methods! Working with a comment in the DOM is just like working with any other text.

In fact, the only benefit we get from working with this interface is that when we create a Comment object and append it to the document, the DOM automatically adds the "<!-- -->" markup.

DOMException

DOM operations raise an exception when a requested operation cannot be performed, either because the data is lost or because the implementation has become unstable. DOM methods tend to return a specific error value in ordinary situations, such as out-of-bound errors when using NodeList.

Some languages and object systems (such as Java) require that exceptions be caught for a program to continue functioning, while others (such as VB or C) do not support the concept of exceptions. If a language does not support error handling, it can be indicated using native error reporting mechanisms (a method may return the error code for example).

Beyond this, an implementation may raise other errors if they are needed for the implementation, such as if a null argument is passed.

Here are some examples of the exceptions that can be raised (you'll find more in Appendix C):

NOT_FOUND_ERR	If an attempt is made to reference a node in a context where it does not exist.
DOMSTRING_SIZE_ERR	If the specified range of text does not fit into a DOMString.
HIERARCHY_REQUEST_ERR	If any node is inserted somewhere it doesn't belong.
INDEX_SIZE_ERR	If index or size is negative, or greater than the allowed value.
NOT_SUPPORTED_ERR	If the implementation does not support the type of object requested.

Extended Interfaces

The Extended Interfaces form part of the DOM Core specification, but the objects that expose these interfaces will only be encountered in a DOM implementation of an XML document.

To work out whether a DOM application implements these interfaces, we can use the hasFeature method of the DOMImplementation interface. The feature string for all the interfaces listed in this section is "XML" and the version is "2.0".

The Extended Interfaces are:

- CDATA Section.
- DocumentType.
- Notation.
- Entity.
- EntityReference.
- ProcessingInstruction.

We will cover these a lot more quickly than the previous ones, because we should now have more of an idea of the interfaces supported by the DOM.

CData Sections

The CDATASection interface is just as simple as the Comment interface we met earlier. CDATASection extends Text, but does not add any properties or methods. Working with a CDATA section in the DOM is just like working with any other text.

In fact, the only benefit we get from working with this interface is that when we create a CDATASection and append it, the DOM automatically adds the "<![CDATA[ ]]>" markup.

DocumentType

The DocumentType interface only provides a list of entities that are defined for the document, which are not editable.

Notation

The Notation interface represents a notation declared in the DTD. This could either be the format of an unparsed entity by name, or the formal declaration of processing instruction targets. The nodeName attribute inherited from Node is set to the declared name of the notation. They are read-only values and do not have a parent.

EntityReference

EntityReference objects may only be inserted into the structure model when an entity reference is in the source document, or when the user wishes to insert an entity reference. EntityReference nodes and all their descendants are read-only.

Note, however, that the XML processor may completely expand references to entities while building the structure model, instead of providing EntityReference objects. Even if it does provide such objects, then for a given EntityReference node, it may be that there is no Entity node representing the referenced entity.

Entity

This interface represents an entity, either parsed or unparsed, in an XML document (though not its declaration). The `nodeName` attribute contains the name of the entity.

> Note that if the DOM is implemented on top of an XML processor that expands entities before passing the structure model to the DOM, there will be no `EntityReference` nodes in the document tree.

`Entity` nodes and all their descendants are read-only. This means that if we want to change the contents of the `Entity`, we will have to clone each `EntityReference`, and replace the old ones with the new one.

Processing Instructions

Finally, no DOM would be complete without a method for adding processing instructions. The `ProcessingInstruction` interface extends `Node`, and adds two properties of its own: `target` and `data`.

The `target` property is the name of the target to which we want to pass the PI, and the `data` is the instruction itself. The `data` property can be changed, but `target` is read-only.

Working With Our Data

Let's go back now and look at the invoice record that we have been working with throughout the book, and see what the DOM allows us to do with it.

Accessing the DOM from JavaScript

In this section we will use some simple client-side pages to show how we can manipulate an XML document in the DOM. These will generate simple alerts, like those earlier in the chapter, but will show us:

❑ How to access values in the DOM.

❑ How to update documents in the DOM.

Here is the document that we will be accessing (`salesData.html`):

```xml
<?xml version="1.0"?>
<SalesData Status="NewVersion">
   <Invoice InvoiceNumber="1"
            TrackingNumber="1"
            OrderDate="01012000"
            ShipDate="07012000"
            ShipMethod="FedEx"
            CustomerIDREF="Customer2">
      <LineItem Quantity="2"
                Price="5"
                PartIDREF="Part2" />
```

```
    </Invoice>
    <Customer ID="Customer2"
              firstName="Bob"
              lastName="Smith"
              Address="2AnyStreet"
              City="Anytown"
              State="AS"
              PostalCode="ANYCODE" />
    <Part PartID="Part2"
          PartNumber="13"
          Name="Winkle"
          Color="Red"
          Size="10" />
</SalesData>
```

We have a root element, SalesData, with children of Invoice, Customer, and Part. We will mainly be working with the Customer element. The customer element has the following attributes:

- ❑ Customer ID.
- ❑ firstName.
- ❑ lastName.
- ❑ Address.
- ❑ City.
- ❑ State.
- ❑ PostalCode.

Let's start by looking at how we retrieve data from the document.

Retrieving the Data from an XML Document using the DOM

In this example, we will retrieve values from a document loaded into memory. It will demonstrate a number of the methods that we can use to retrieve different values, and will write them to a browser. We'll be retrieving:

- ❑ An element.
- ❑ An attribute.
- ❑ An attribute value.
- ❑ The tag name of an element.

With this information, we will be creating a page that displays the customer's first and last names and their customer ID.

Here is the page that we will be using (ch06_ex11.html):

```
<HTML>
<HEAD>
<TITLE>DOM Demo</TITLE>

<SCRIPT language="JavaScript">
```

```
var objDOM;
objDOM = new ActiveXObject("MSXML2.DOMDocument");
objDOM.async = false;
objDOM.load("salesData.xml");

//Get to the root element
document.write("<B>We have found the root element: </B>");

varSalesData = objDOM.documentElement;
alert(varSalesData.tagName);
document.write(varSalesData.tagName);

//Find the Customer elements and select the first one
document.write
    ("<B><P>We have found the first Customer Element, its name is: </B>");

varElemCust1 = varSalesData.getElementsByTagName("Customer").item(0);
alert(varElemCust1.xml);
document.write(varElemCust1.tagName);

//Find the Customer ID Attribute
document.write
        ("<B><P>Now we can retrieve the Customer ID attribute, it is: </B>");

varAttrCustID = varElemCust1.getAttribute("ID");
alert(varAttrCustID);
document.write(varAttrCustID);

//Find the next attribute of Name
document.write("<B><P>The customer's name is: </B>");

varAttrFirstName = varElemCust1.getAttribute("firstName");
alert(varAttrFirstName);
document.write(varAttrFirstName);

varAttrLastName = varElemCust1.getAttribute("lastName");
alert(varAttrLastName);
document.write(varAttrLastName);

//Now let's write out the address
document.write("<B><P>Their address is: </B>");
varAttrAddr = varElemCust1.getAttribute("Address");
alert(varAttrAddr);
document.write(varAttrAddr);

//Find the next attribute of City
varAttrCity = varElemCust1.getAttribute("City");
alert(varAttrCity);
document.write(varAttrCity);

</SCRIPT>

</HEAD>
<BODY>
<P>We have retrieved a lot<P>
</BODY>
</HTML>
```

Let's see what this is doing. We start with a simple HTML page. All of the real work for this page is done in the <script>:

```
<HTML>
<HEAD>
<TITLE>DOM Demo</TITLE>

<SCRIPT language="JavaScript">
```

We start by creating an instance of the Microsoft MSXML parser. Because the DOM does not specify how a document should be loaded into an instance of a parser, we use the load method of MSXML. The document is then held in a variable called objDOM, so that we can work with it:

```
var objDOM;
objDOM = new ActiveXObject("MSXML2.DOMDocument");
objDOM.async = false;
objDOM.load("salesData.xml");
```

We can now retrieve the document element (or root element of the document instance) using the documentElement attribute, and write it out using the tagName attribute. We show this in an alert dialog – as we do with the other values that we retrieve – so that we can see what is happening. We'll also write it to the page using the write method of the browser object model:

```
//Get to the root element
document.write("<B>We have found the root element: </B>");

varSalesData = objDOM.documentElement;
alert(varSalesData.tagName);
document.write(varSalesData.tagName);
```

We saved the document element in a variable so that we can use this same reference later. Here is the alert that it displays:

Remember that the document had three children. We want to find the middle one: Customer. If we have a mixed content model, or we're not sure of how many child elements there are before Customer, we can make use of the getElementByTagName method. This is how we'll retrieve Customer, to illustrate the point:

```
//Find the Customer elements and select the first one
  document.write
    ("<B><P>We have found the first Customer Element, its name is: </B>");

varElemCust1 = varSalesData.getElementsByTagName("Customer").item(0);
alert(varElemCust1.xml);
document.write(varElemCust1.tagName);
```

We again hold a reference to this child element in a new variable – `varElemCust1` – which will allow us to use it again later in the document. This time, we have written the value of the `Customer` element to the alert box.

We can also see this in the following screenshot. Here, we have also written out the document element we just met, and we're prepared to write the name of the tag we are currently on:

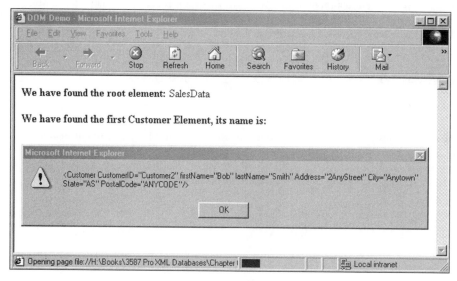

Next we want to find the `ID` attribute of the `Customer`. To do this, we will be using the `getAttribute` method:

```
//Find the Customer ID Attribute
  document.write
       ("<B><P>Now we can retrieve the Customer ID attribute, it is: </B>");

    varAttrCustID = varElemCust1.getAttribute("ID");
    alert(varAttrCustID);
    document.write(varAttrCustID);
```

Again, we create a new variable to hold this, and we write it to an alert box, as well as illustrating it on the screen.

The remaining tasks involve getting the remaining attribute values out of their nodes. We do this using the same method we just met:

```
//Find the next attribute of Name
  document.write("<B><P>The customer's name is: </B>");

  varAttrFirstName = varElemCust1.getAttribute("firstName");
  alert(varAttrFirstName);
  document.write(varAttrFirstName);

  varAttrLastName = varElemCust1.getAttribute("lastName");
  alert(varAttrLastName);
  document.write(varAttrLastName);
```

```
//Now let's write out the address
  document.write("<B><P>Their address is: </B>");
  varAttrAddr = varElemCust1.getAttribute("Address");
  alert(varAttrAddr);
  document.write(varAttrAddr);

  //Find the next attribute of City
  varAttrCity = varElemCust1.getAttribute("City");
  alert(varAttrCity);
  document.write(varAttrCity);

</SCRIPT>

</HEAD>
<BODY>
<P>We have retrieved a lot<P>
</BODY>
</HTML>
```

Having finished off the page, we can see that we have retrieved all of the information from the attributes of the Customer element, as well as retrieving the document element and one of its children:

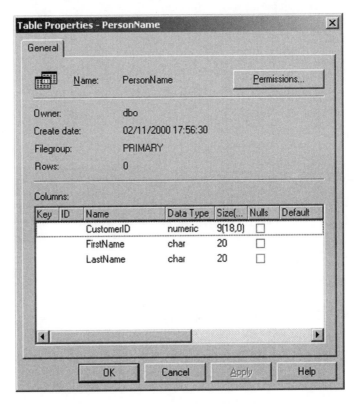

This may not be the most visually enticing presentation that we could come up with, but it illustrates getting values out of the DOM. Next, let's go on to looking at updating the contents of the DOM.

Adding to the Contents of the Document Using the DOM

In this section, will be demonstrated the following useful techniques:

❑ Adding elements to a document.

❑ Adding text to the new element.

❑ Adding attributes to a document.

❑ Setting the value of the new attribute.

Here is the code we'll use to do this (ch06_ex11.htm):

```
<HTML>
<HEAD>
<TITLE>DOM Demo</TITLE>

<SCRIPT language="JavaScript">

  var objDOM;
  objDOM = new ActiveXObject("MSXML2.DOMDocument");
  objDOM.async = false;
  objDOM.load("salesData.xml");

//Get to the root element
  varSalesData = objDOM.documentElement;

//show the original XML document
  alert(varSalesData.xml);

//Find the Customer elements and select the first one
  varElemCust1 = varSalesData.getElementsByTagName("Customer").item(0);

<!-- adding an element -->
  document.write("<HR><H1>Updates appear in alert boxes:</H1>");

//create a new element
  varNewElem = objDOM.createElement("MonthlySalesData");

//append the element
  varNewElem = varSalesData.insertBefore(varNewElem, varElemCust1);

//create a new text-type node and append it
  newText = objDOM.createTextNode
                  ("Can you see that we have created a new element?");
  varNewElem.appendChild(newText);

  alert(objDOM.xml);


<!-- adding an attribute -->

//create a new attribute and give it a value
  varElemCust1.setAttribute("telephoneNo", "3591765524");

  alert(objDOM.xml);

</SCRIPT>

</HEAD>
<BODY>
<HR>
</BODY>
</HTML>
```

In this example we will be writing all of the results to alert boxes. The first part of the example simply loads the XML document into the DOM, just as we did before, and displays the original XML document. We then retrieve a couple of useful values using the techniques we saw in the last example. After that, we get onto the interesting part.

We will start by adding a new element to the document. Remember that this is a two-stage process:

❑ First we need to create this node off the document element.

❑ Then we append it to the tree in the place that we want.

The new element will be called `MonthlySalesData`. We have chosen to append this to the tree in front of the `Customer` element:

```
//create a new element
  varNewElem = objDOM.createElement("MonthlySalesData");

//append the element
  varNewElem = varSalesData.insertBefore(varNewElem, varElemCust1);
```

Now we need to put some content into this element. To do this, we again create a new node and append it to the tree in two separate stages. This requires a `Text` node, whose value is written as a parameter to the method. We then append this to the new element:

```
//create a new text-type node and append it
  newText = objDOM.createTextNode
                    ("Can you see that we have created a new element?");
  varNewElem.appendChild(newText);
```

Finally, we will write the content of the file to an alert box:

```
  alert(objDOM.xml);
```

Here we can see the result. We have created the new `MonthlySalesData` element with a value in front of the `Customer` element:

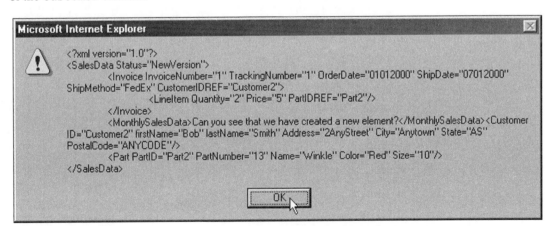

Next let's see how we add an attribute. We will be adding a `telephoneNo` attribute to the `Customer` element. We use `setAttribute` to do this, giving it the name (`telephoneNo`) and value of the attribute we want to include:

```
//create a new attribute and give it a value
  varElemCust1.setAttribute("telephoneNo", "3591765524");

  alert(objDOM.xml);
```

and here is the resulting attribute shown in the XML document:

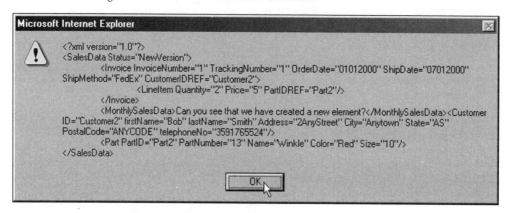

Adding Information from Another DOM Tree

Next, we're going to try merging information from two different XML sources. This time, we will be pulling in customer data from a second file called `salesData2.xml`:

```
<?xml version="1.0"?>
<SalesData Status="NewVersion">
    <Invoice InvoiceNumber="1"
             TrackingNumber="1"
             OrderDate="01012000"
             ShipDate="07012000"
             ShipMethod="FedEx"
             CustomerIDREF="Customer2">
        <LineItem Quantity="2"
                  Price="5"
                  PartIDREF="Part2" />
    </Invoice>
    <Customer ID="Customer1"
              firstName="Tom"
              lastName="Boswell"
              Address="39BrownhillCrescent"
              City="Anothertown"
              State="IN"
              PostalCode="OTHERCODE" />
    <Part PartID="Part2"
          PartNumber="13"
          Name="Winkle"
          Color="Red"
          Size="10" />
</SalesData>
```

The page that does this is called ch06_ex12.html:

```
<HTML>
<HEAD>
<TITLE>DOM Demo</TITLE>

<SCRIPT language="JavaScript">

  var objDOM;
  objDOM = new ActiveXObject("MSXML2.DOMDocument");
  objDOM.async = true;
  objDOM.load("salesData.xml");

//Get to the root element
  varSalesData = objDOM.documentElement;

//second instance of the DOM
  var objSecondDOM;
  objSecondDOM = new ActiveXObject("MSXML2.DOMDocument");
  objSecondDOM.async = true;
  objSecondDOM.load("salesData2.xml");

//Get to the root element
  varSalesDataB = objSecondDOM.documentElement;

  varImportCust1 = varSalesDataB.getElementsByTagName("Customer").item(0);


<!-- adding an element -->
  document.write("<HR><H1>Updates appear in alert boxes:</H1>");

//clone the node from the second DOM
   varClone = varImportCust1.cloneNode(true);

//append node to the first DOM
varSalesData.appendChild(varClone);

alert(objDOM.xml);

</SCRIPT>

</HEAD>
<BODY>
<HR>
</BODY>
</HTML>
```

We start as we did in the other two examples: loading up the XML document into the parser. This time, however, we add a second instance of the DOM to hold the document that we want to retrieve more information from. We need to collect the element that we want to insert into the first tree from this second DOM tree, so we do this now, and store it in varImportCust1:

```
//second instance of the DOM
  var objSecondDOM;
  objSecondDOM = new ActiveXObject("MSXML2.DOMDocument");
  objSecondDOM.async = true;
  objSecondDOM.load("salesData2.xml");

//Get to the root element
  varSalesDataB = objSecondDOM.documentElement;

  varImportCust1 = varSalesDataB.getElementsByTagName("Customer").item(0);
```

In order to add the `Customer` element from the second document into the first document, we clone it. This is why we just stored it. We do this using the `cloneNode` method. We use a shallow clone, which will still collect the attributes of this element:

```
//clone the node from the second DOM
   varClone = varImportCust1.cloneNode(true);
```

If `Customer` had child attributes, we could make sure that the clone cloned these as well by setting the parameter of the `cloneNode` method to `true`, creating a deep (rather than shallow) clone.

Having cloned the node, we simply append it to the tree representing the first document, and write the new document to an alert box:

```
//append node to the first DOM
varSalesData.appendChild(varClone);

alert(objDOM.xml);
```

and here is the result:

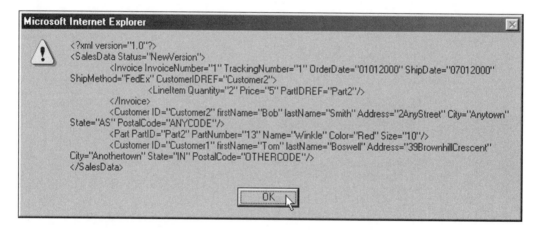

When To Use or Not Use the DOM

As we have seen, the Document Object Model presents a standardized interpretation of an XML document that makes the contents of the document available for processing, along with a set of interfaces that expose properties and methods that will be useful when integrating XML into our programs and data strategies. Because DOM implementations have been written for most major programming and scripting languages, the programming language we wish to use in creating our applications is not a major consideration.

Rather the two major considerations are:

❑   The size of the document with which we are working.

❑   What type of processing we want to do with the document that we load.

We shall look at each of these in turn, although we should think about the issues surrounding both when deciding how to process our documents. Once we have looked at some of the major issues in deciding whether the DOM is an appropriate technology, we will look at some of the alternative technologies that we may wish to consider.

Size of Document

When deciding whether the DOM is an appropriate technology for our programming endeavors, we should consider the size of the documents that we are likely to be dealing with. This is because of the way in which DOM implementations expose the contents of XML documents.

Remember that the DOM creates an in-memory representation of the XML Document in order to work with it. A DOM representation can need 5-10 times as much memory as the corresponding XML file itself. This means that we can end up with some pretty memory intensive situations when dealing with large amounts of data. In order to make a large document available, the DOM implementation must load it into memory so that we can work with it.

It can also take more time to load a large file into memory, which is important if performance is a major concern; and as well as the sheer size of the file, the number of nodes can have an effect performance.

On the other side of the coin, if we are creating documents using the DOM, we must consider the size of documents that we want to create.

Because the DOM is so memory intensive there are some strategies that we can consider employing to help reduce system load:

Will it Prevent Others From Using Other Information?

If we are loading the whole document into memory so that we can only change one record, we will need to lock other users out, so that they cannot change the same records and risk the integrity of our documents. The longer it takes to load a whole document into memory and work with it, the longer it locks other users out. If we do not have a locking mechanism in place, then other users who may want the same information may get incorrect records or may try to update the same data – and if we perform our persistence after them, their changes will be lost.

Using Document Fragments to Reduce Bandwidth Demands

Can we afford to keep passing the whole document over the network? Can we just open a fragment, or set of, what would be the whole document, so that we can work with a smaller subsection rather than the whole document? For example, if we are only editing one record, then there is no point in retrieving the whole document and loading it into memory. Rather we could just select the fragment that we want.

Luckily, as we have seen, we can just work with fragments of a document using the DOM. It is always worth trying to limit the granularity of the document to the information that we want to actually work with. If we just want to work with one invoice, we just collect that one invoice rather than opening a file of invoices for a whole month.

Of course, we still need the whole document in memory before we can access a fragment. We'll have to collect that fragment ahead separately, before we start working with it from the DOM.

How the DOM Processes a Document

We have already seen that the DOM implementation sits on top of a parser (or is built in). The XML document is read into the parser: this either exposes the XML document as a DOM tree, or an implementation of the DOM implementation can sit on top of the parser. For the duration of the time that the application wants to work with this document, the DOM representation remains in memory. Once we have finished with the document it can then be persisted in some form.

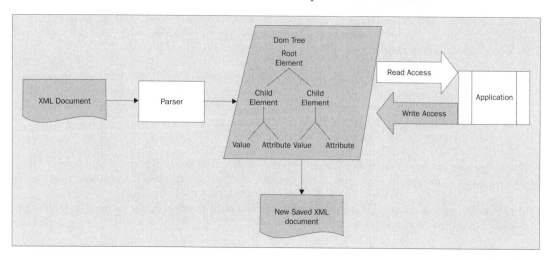

For large documents this means that the resources required to hold a document as a DOM tree can be very intensive.

Alternatives to the DOM

An alternative to this approach would be to allow the document to be passed through as a stream, rather than holding it in memory. This stream could then be used to raise events to the processing applications. This is, in fact, the model that the **Simple API for XML** (**SAX**) uses, as we shall see in the next chapter.

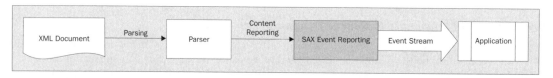

Using this approach we do not need to hold the document in memory, meaning that it takes up fewer resources. However, it makes it far more difficult to do much more than read the document as it is streamed through. If we want to add, update, modify, or create documents, we may require that the document be streamed through the parser several times. We will learn more about how SAX processes a document, and what tasks it is suited to, in the next chapter.

This shows how the size can affect the choice of how we process our documents. Of course, if we are only dealing with small XML documents, then we do not need to worry too much about the memory that will be taken up by the in memory tree that allows the DOM to process documents. When the documents get larger, however, we need to think about the number and size of the files that we want to process, and whether we could build our solution based on SAX instead, or whether there are other strategies we could use.

The Task in Hand

Having seen that the size of the document will affect our choice of which processor to use, let's look at how the task that we wish to achieve can affect the choice we make as well. Keep in mind that size is still a consideration here.

When integrating XML into our database strategies, there are a range of tasks that we may want to perform on the XML data. If we think about our XML invoice example, that we have been looking at in the book so far, we may want to:

- Read values from the invoice into a processing application.

- Edit the values in the document, such as a customer address.

- Add or remove records, such as line items.

- Generate new documents programmatically:

    - From scratch, such as new invoices.

    - From existing documents, creating a summary of invoices that represent customer records.

- Display the invoice in a browser.

- Display the invoice in a program using a custom front-end, say in Visual Basic.

- Transform the invoice from the XML vocabulary we use to another vocabulary, perhaps for an order fulfillment house.

When working with the XML, the tool we use to make it available to other applications depends upon the task in hand. We can split these sorts of tasks into four general groups:

- Add, update, modify.

- Transformations of structure.

- Reading and filtering.

- Creating documents.

We shall look at each of these in turn.

Reading and Filtering

Imagine that we only want to read values from an XML document into a processing application, and then let it get on with what it has found, rather than making any changes to the document. In that case, creating an in-memory representation of the document just to read values out of it, may not be as efficient as catching events as the document is streamed through a processor.

Furthermore, if we wanted a subsection of the document, then we could also use a stream based approach. We could take the items that we want, and write them to a new file or destination, rather than loading the entire document into memory just to retrieve a subset of it.

Both of these are especially true if we want to read values from, or filter, large documents. If the documents are only small and there is not a large load on the system, then it may not be such a problem – it depends on the granularity of information that we are dealing with. For reading and filtering large documents, the DOM is not always the best choice.

Add, Update, Delete

What if we want to do more with the document than just read it into an application? Having got our information in XML format, we might want to keep it up-to-date, meaning that we could need to add records, update existing entries, or delete entries. As we have seen, the DOM provides a rich set of interfaces for manipulating and updating the content of an XML document, so it is a natural candidate. The DOM approach allows developers to take advantage of the logic built into a DOM implementation for managing XML content, rather than having to create their own.

One of the key advantages to the DOM when modifying records is exactly that it holds the document representation in memory. Remember when we were talking about creating new nodes and appending them to the tree, we saw that we can do all of this while the DOM is in memory. However, when working with a stream based approach to processing, we would need to have the content that we wanted to add/change in memory in the processing application, so that we could make our modifications as the document is streamed through.

Of course, we could just delete records as they are passed through a stream, by passing everything that was not to be deleted to a new output. However, applications that perform these kinds of operations usually perform more than just deletion. If we think about a customer call center, we will want to allow operators to update records as well as delete them or add them.

Therefore the DOM is the better choice for modifying an XML document and holding the changed document in memory, because it allows us to update the source, or if we need to browse to the records we want to update.

Transformations of Structure

As far as transformation of documents goes, the main purposes are:

- ❑ To transform the XML for presentation to a web client (say using HTML).
- ❑ To transform the data into another XML vocabulary for a trading partner's application to make use of, or for insertion into a database.
- ❑ To assemble data from selected bits and pieces of the overall data repository held in separate smaller XML files.

The DOM may not always be the most appropriate solution for these transformations. If we think about how the DOM would approach transformation, we would have to tell the DOM which nodes to remove and append elsewhere – perhaps we might need to tell it to change the element and attribute names. In fact, there are a lot of things that we would have to tell it to do in such a program. A popular alternative would be to consider using XSLT instead of the DOM. We will meet XSLT in Chapter 8.

It is worth noting that most XSLT processors do actually use a DOM representation to perform their transformation, so the concerns over document size still apply here. In fact, they are amplified, because an XSLT processor generates three representations of the document to work with:

- ❑ The source tree.
- ❑ The result tree.
- ❑ The style sheet tree.

So, the memory footprint can be very high when transforming large documents. This has been a criticism levelled at using XSLT to process transformations since its inception, and some suggest that it is not suitable for transforming large documents. However, its adoption in the developer community seems to suggest that XSLT will be around for a while, and the language is still sometimes used in other implementations of transformation engines.

The advantages of XSLT, however, lie in the fact that it is a **declarative** language. This means that we tell an XSLT processor how we want the resulting document to appear, and let the XSLT processor implement the transformation for us. We do not need to tell it which nodes to remove and then append elsewhere, we can just specify the format that we want the tree to appear in and let it get on with the job. While there is a learning curve to getting used to the new language and way of working, it can be more useful in the long run. Especially when we consider that we can use one style sheet to transform multiple documents that may not have exactly the same structure, although they conform to the same DTD or schema.

Creating Documents

Another task that we may wish to achieve is the programmatic creation of a new XML document. For example:

- ❑ If we wanted to create a totally new invoice.
- ❑ To create a monthly summary of invoices from all the invoices of one month.

Rather like when we were considering whether to use DOM for adding, updating and deleting records, this would depend on how we built the document. If we want to build a document whose structure we don't yet know, then we need to take the in-memory approach.

Maintaining the document in memory is a lot more helpful here, as we are able to traverse through it. We can use the structure as it is in memory, as well as dealing with incoming data. We could even hold different representations of documents in memory and append them to a new document.

We might want to merge several documents – say we wanted to create one document that contained a month's invoices. To do so, we could create a new document in the DOM, then add a new root node with any necessary summary information, and then append the other instances of invoice documents.

Alternatively, if we wanted to merge invoice data and other customer information, we could load the invoice document, then append the second document, and perform the necessary operations to create the merged document (such as moving or reordering of nodes).

Again, this feeds back to the question of the size of the document that we are creating, but there are few easier ways to create a document programmatically. If we were to look to a stream based approach for creating new documents, we would have to hold the parts of the document that we wanted to append in memory so that they could be added as the document streams through, and these would have to be persisted to a different location.

Summary

In this chapter, we have explored the Document Object Model, which gives us an API to work with our XML documents. We've seen how an implementation of the DOM works with a parser, which loads an XML document into memory, allowing us to access and change values of the XML document.

We have seen how to:

- ❑ Use the interfaces that the DOM API exposes.
- ❑ Change values from a DOM representation of an XML document.
- ❑ Use the methods of the DOM's interfaces to add, remove, clone, and update elements.
- ❑ Set different attributes.
- ❑ ·Tell when it is appropriate to use the DOM.
- ❑ Create some simple examples of using the DOM with JavaScript.

The examples we have seen, illustrated how we can load a document into memory and access it programmatically. Because the DOM is an API reference, and because there are implementations of the DOM in many programming languages, we will now be able to work with it to integrate it into our applications – whatever language they may be written in.

In addition, although we have been focusing on the Level 2 Core, we should now be able to work with future versions, and other extensions the DOM provides.

We also looked at some of the times when the DOM isn't the best answer to our problems. In conclusion we decided that:

- ❑ Developers who need to build applications for specific purposes may find it more efficient to use SAX to read the document, and then manage the information in their internal data structures.
- ❑ Developers who need to transform the structure of a document, either into another vocabulary or for the purposes of presentation, may be better off using XSLT.

We'll cover XSLT in Chapter 8. Before that, though, we'll take a look at SAX.

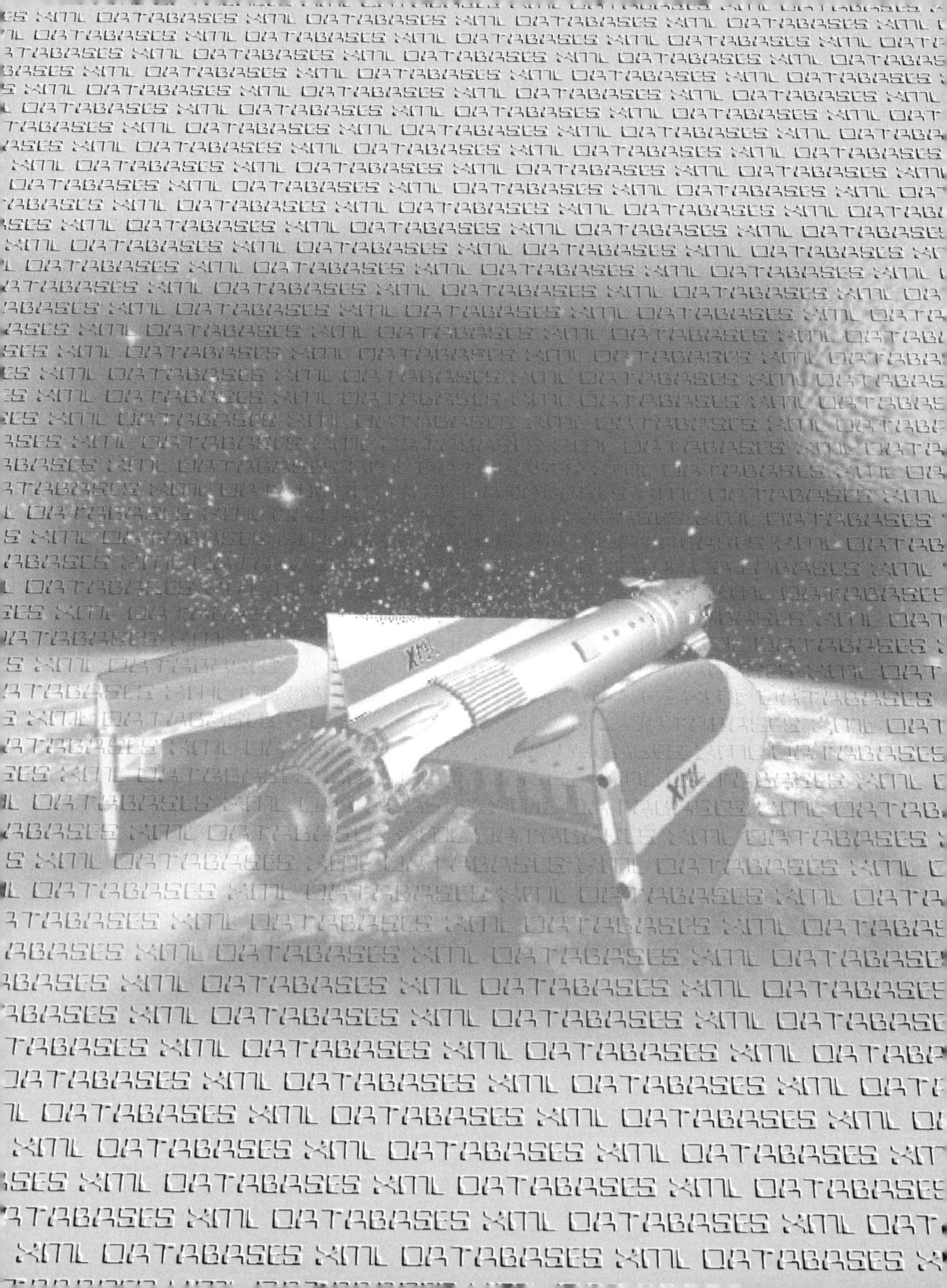
XML DATABASES

SAX – The Simple API for XML

SAX, the **Simple API for XML**, is slightly different from many of the other technologies in the XML programmer's toolkit. Rather than being a specification developed by a standards body, it was created by members of a mailing list called XML-Dev (under the guidance of David Megginson). If you are interested, you can find out more about its history at http://www.megginson.com/SAX/index.html.

In addition to its name's claim to be simple, what else is there about SAX that makes it worth taking a good look at? In a sentence, SAX is an alternative to the DOM as a method of accessing XML documents – or at least, a complement to the DOM. As we will see later in the chapter, there are advantages to using the two different approaches provided by the DOM and SAX to access and manipulate data in XML, depending on what sort of document we are working with, and what sort of things we want to do with it.

This chapter assumes familiarity with the DOM.

When we say that SAX is an alternative to the DOM, it's best not to think in terms of one or the other. Rather, you will find SAX to be another weapon in your arsenal for attacking XML-related problems. A complete SAX reference is beyond the scope of this book, but we will be looking at:

❑   What SAX is

❑   What it allows us to do

❑   How we can use it, with examples in Java and Visual Basic

❑   Guidelines of when it is better to use SAX rather than the DOM

If you need to learn more about using SAX, there are some references at the end of the chapter.

SAX Parsers

It is helpful to understand that SAX is an API, just like the DOM, and can be implemented in a parser. This means that SAX itself does nothing more than provide interfaces and classes to be implemented by a parser or application. It also means that when we talk about a "SAX parser", we are talking about a particular implementation of a SAX-compliant parser, not the standard itself.

There are several freely available SAX parsers around for you to use (so you do not need to write an implementation yourself). The following table provides a list of parsers, and where to get them.

Parser Name	Creator	SAX Version Supported	Location	Language(s) Supported
Aelfred	David Megginson (this version by David Brownell)	2.0	http://home.pacbell.net/ david-b/xml/#utilities	Java
Saxon	Michael Kay	2.0	http://users.iclway.co.uk/ mhkay/saxon/index.html (Saxon uses an implementation of Aelfred, and is not itself strictly a parser.)	Java
MSXML3	Microsoft	2.0	http://msdn.microsoft.com/ downloads/default.asp	C++, VB and any COM-compliant language
Xerces C++ Parser	Apache XML Project	2.0	http://xml.apache.org/ xerces-c/index.html	C++
Xerces Java	Apache	2.0	http://xml.apache.org/ xerces-j/index.html	Java
JAXP	Sun	2.0	http://java.sun.com/ xml/download.html	Java
XP	James Clark	1.0	http://www.jclark.com/ xml/xp/index.html	Java

SAX is currently in version 2, and all the examples in this chapter will implement this version. We'll be using Saxon's implementation of Aelfred and MSXML3.

Understanding SAX

The biggest difference between SAX and the DOM is that SAX is an **event driven interface** that requires certain methods to be declared that can "catch" events from the parser.

When a DOM-based parser parses an XML document, it stores a tree-based representation of the document in memory. SAX, on the other hand, streams the document through from start to finish, looking at the different items it encounters as the document passes. For each structural item in the document, SAX calls a method you have made available.

For example, when the parser encounters an element's start tag, it can say, "Hey, I have a start tag named 'X'", but it then leaves you to do what you like with that information. From there, it moves on and will not concern itself with this element again. What this means to you is that you must maintain **state**, or **context**, while working with a SAX parser.

So, if we had this XML fragment parsed by a content handler:

```
<Start>
<here>This is some text</here>
</Start>
```

We would have the following events:

Event	Returns	Value
startElement	localName	"Start"
startElement	localName	"here"
characters	text	"This is some text"
endElement	localName	"here"
endElement	localName	"Start"

Each of the events raised requires an implementation of the SAX interface to work with the information provided by the parser. The beginning of an element is "caught" by the startElement method, the end by the endElement method, and so on, as we'll explain below. These methods are usually grouped together in a class that implements the ContentHandler class.

One implication of the event-based approach is that the application you build will have to keep track of the element names and other data caught by the content handler. For instance, imagine that we need to connect the character data "This is some text" with its element <here>. Then, the startElement method will need to set a variable of some kind that can be checked in the characters method, as in this pseudo-code:

```
declare variable - boolean bInElement
//Start receiving events
startElement → localName = "Start"
startElement → localName = "here"
if localName = "here" then bInElement = True

characters → text = "This is some text"
if bInElement then this character data belongs to the "here" element
```

We'll introduce the issue of **context** in the second example that we'll look at in this chapter, and work with it in detail in the final example.

If we consider a few implications of this approach, we can start to build an idea of where we can use SAX. We've been given a way to parse a document without the overhead of building an in-memory tree. We can also avoid processing the entire document, because any one of the event-catching methods can return control to the application before the whole document is read. These features mean that SAX is going to be a very practical way to parse large XML documents. We can also ignore, change, or pass along any item that the parser tells us about at runtime. This gives us an excellent opportunity to keep only the parts of a document we want.

SAX will not be great for everything. As we mentioned above, it does not allow us to traverse the tree, and it's not adept at moving backwards and forwards through a document – we only get one shot as it goes through the parser – so it is best understood as an additional tool. We'll start with a look at a basic approach for working with SAX.

Example 1 – A Simple SAX Application

If SAX is simple, let's see if we can't get an example up and running quickly just to demonstrate it. This simple example will be written in Java, and will utilize a SAX2 compliant parser.

This application is called SaxApp, *and you can download the* saxapp.jar *file, or each of the separate application files, from the Wrox web site at* http://www.wrox.com

In this example, we will look at how to implement three interfaces:

❑   XMLReader – the interface for reading an XML document using callbacks

❑   ContentHandler – the interface to receive notification of the logical content of a document

❑   ErrorHandler – the basic interface for SAX error handlers

All SAX parsers should implement these, as they are three of the standard interfaces in the org.xml.sax package. (There is only one other package: org.xml.sax.helpers.)

Our application is going to locate a small XML document from a command line argument, and pass it to the SAX parser specified in the XMLReader class. As the document is parsed, the XMLReader will alert the ContentHandler of the events it has been registered to receive. The event handlers are simply going to write the name of the event they have handled, and the name of the element (or type of character data) they have received. The output will be written to the console.

When you have completed this example, you should be able to understand:

❑   How to implement a basic XMLReader and ContentHandler

❑   What the role of the XMLReader is in relation to the ContentHandler

❑   How you can use the different methods in the ContentHandler class to respond to specific events from the parser

We're going to work out the first example in Java, using the Aelfred parser as provided by Michael Kay's Saxon. That way, we'll see how SAX was originally implemented, and the basics of working with SAX in the Java language. However, the rest of the examples in this chapter will be written with Visual Basic and MSXML3 (the September 2000 release of MSXML from Microsoft).

> **In order to run this example, you will need to have SAX2 and SAX2-ext, both of which are available from http://www.megginson.com/SAX/, as well as Saxon, which is available from http://users.iclway.co.uk/mhkay/saxon/index.html.**

We need to create an application class that will contain the XMLReader, and allow us to set the document content and error handlers. It is possible to do all of this in one class, but we will use different classes for the XMLReader, the ContentHandler, and ErrorHandler implementations. We'll also use DefaultHandler, the default base class for SAX2 event handlers, which is in the org.xml.sax.helpers package.

Preparing the XMLReader Class

The XMLReader class (SAXApp.java) begins as follows:

```
import com.icl.saxon.*;  // The classpath for the SAXON implementation of
                         // Aelfred, the SAX parser chosen for this example.
                         // Our table above contained several possible
                         // choices for this.
import java.io.*;
import org.xml.sax.InputSource;
import org.xml.sax.XMLReader;
import org.xml.sax.SAXException;

public class SAXApp
{
```

SAX is an API, and in order to work with it we need a parser that implements SAX. In this example we are using the Aelfred parser, as provided by Saxon. So, we require a new instance of our chosen parser within the main class to create our parser. We need to set XMLReader to use this parser when our simple application loads the document, so that the parser can raise events to the application.

```
public static void main (String args[]) throws SAXException
{
    XMLReader xr = new com.icl.saxon.aelfred.SAXDriver();
```

Because the parser is going to send messages about what it finds in the XML document it's parsing, we have to tell the parser where it can find the event handlers. We will use the content handler to receive notification of events the parser raises while working through the document, and the error handler will catch exceptions thrown by the parser when something has gone wrong.

```
SaxHandler handler = new SaxHandler();
SAXErrors errHandler = new SAXErrors();
xr.setContentHandler(handler);
xr.setErrorHandler(errHandler);
```

All that's left for this class is to figure out what to parse, and call the parse method of the XMLReader. Here is the whole SAXApp class, with the parse method included:

```
import com.icl.saxon.*;
import java.io.*;
import org.xml.sax.InputSource;
import org.xml.sax.XMLReader;
import org.xml.sax.SAXException;

public class SAXApp
{
    public static void main (String args[]) throws SAXException
    {
        XMLReader xr = new com.icl.saxon.aelfred.SAXDriver();
        SaxHandler handler = new SaxHandler();
        SAXErrors errHandler = new SAXErrors();
        xr.setContentHandler(handler);
        xr.setErrorHandler(errHandler);
```

```
        // Parse each file provided on the command line.
        for (int i = 0; i < args.length; i++) {
            try {
                FileReader r = new FileReader(args[i]);
                xr.parse(new InputSource(r));
            } catch (SAXException se) {
                System.err.println("Error parsing file: " + se);
            } catch(FileNotFoundException fnfe) {
                System.err.println("Error, file not found: " +
                                        args[i] + ": " + fnfe);
            } catch(IOException ioe) {
                System.out.println("Error reading file: " +
                                        args[i] + ": " + ioe);
            }
        }
    }
}
```

The `InputSource` wrapper is a SAX class that resolves the type of XML input being received by the parser. We will take each document provided on the command line in turn, and parse it. There are also some very simple error handlers in order to catch exceptions from the file reader and the parser. The application will simply write some information to the screen as it receives events from the parser.

Of course, this application will not work yet, because it will alert non-existent classes about SAX events. So, let's create the classes to take the messages from the parser.

> Complete API documentation is available at http://www.megginson.com/ SAX/Java/javadoc/index.html

Catching Events from the XMLReader

There are several events that can be caught as a document runs through SAX, but for now we will see the `startDocument`, `endDocument`, `startElement`, `endElement`, and `characters` methods. These are the methods we will deal with most often.

Notice the pairs of "`startElement`" and "`endElement`" methods. As we said above, SAX is going to report on events in document order, so the opening and closing of elements will occur as separate events.

In our example, the events will be passed to `SAXHandler`, which extends the methods of the `DefaultHandler` class. This class will only implement the methods for events we want our application to be aware of. If we were not interested in the `endDocument` event, we could simply drop that method from the class.

> *By the way, this should tip you off to another difference from the DOM. If you refer to a nonexistent node on the tree created by a DOM parser, you will get an error. With a SAX parser, nodes you don't want are simply ignored, and you won't get any messages about nodes that don't exist.*

Each method that is declared must take certain arguments, as defined by the API.

Information on `DefaultHandler` *from the API is instructive on its use. This class is available as a convenience base class for SAX2 applications. It provides default implementations for all of the callbacks in the four core SAX2 handler classes:* `EntityResolver`, `DTDHandler`, `ContentHandler`, *and* `ErrorHandler`. *Application writers can extend this class when they need to implement only part of an interface. Parser writers can instantiate this class to provide default handlers when the application has not supplied its own.*

As application writers, then, our objective is to override the methods provided by the `ContentHandler` interface through the `DefaultHandler` class. By default, these methods do nothing, so if we don't override them, no harm is done. The `SaxHandler` class begins as follows:

```java
import org.xml.sax.helpers.DefaultHandler;
import org.xml.sax.Attributes;

//////////////////////////////////////////////////////////////////////////////
// Event handlers.
//////////////////////////////////////////////////////////////////////////////

public class SaxHandler extends DefaultHandler
{
    public void startDocument()
    {
        System.out.println("Start document");
    }

    public void endDocument()
    {
        System.out.println("End document");
    }
```

Notice the all-important `extends DefaultHandler` modifier on the class declaration. This lets our compiler know we that are overriding the methods of the imported class of that name.

Additionally, because we have implemented the `startDocument` and `endDocument` methods from the `ContentHandler` interface, we will be notified by our parser of these events. What we do with that information is entirely up to us. While this method could be as complicated as we like, our current example is just going to alert the user by writing a message to the console using `System.out.println`.

The rest of the class's methods are similar:

```java
    public void startElement(String uri, String name,
                             String qName, Attributes atts)
    {
        System.out.println("Start element: {" + qName + "}" + name);
    }

    public void endElement(String uri, String name, String qName)
    {
        System.out.println("End element:   {" + uri + "}" + qName);
    }
```

```
    public void characters(char ch[], int start, int length)
    {
        System.out.print("Characters:      \"");
        for(int i = start; i < start + length; i++) {

            switch (ch[i]) {
                case '\\':
                    System.out.print("\\\\");
                    break;
                case '"':
                    System.out.print("\\\"");
                    break;
                case '\n':
                    System.out.print("\\n");
                    break;
                case '\r':
                    System.out.print("\\r");
                    break;
                case '\t':
                    System.out.print("\\t");
                    break;
                default:
                    System.out.print(ch[i]);
                    break;
            }
        }
        System.out.print("\"\n");
    }
}
```

We see a bit more action in the `characters` method due to the way whitespace has been handled. Any whitespace characters occurring within elements are going to be reported to the `characters` method. Because the goal of this application is to write all events to the console, it is more useful to print the escape characters for whitespace, rather than the whitespace itself.

The Error Handler

Finally, we have a SAXErrors class to deal with the three kinds of errors we might come across: fatal errors, parse errors, and parse warnings:

```
import org.xml.sax.SAXParseException ;

public class SAXErrors implements org.xml.sax.ErrorHandler
{
    public void fatalError(SAXParseException spe){
        system.err.println ("Fatal error has occurred: " + spe);
    }

    public void error(SAXParseException spe){
        system.err.println ("A parse error has occurred: " + spe);
    }

    public void warning(SAXParseException spe){
        system.err.println ("Parse warning were issued: " + spe);
    }
}
```

The Result

In order to run this simple application, open a command console and enter the location of the compiled application, with any XML document as an argument. If you are using a Microsoft OS, be sure to include quotation marks around the application location:

```
C:\>"c:\compiled_directory_location\saxapp" sample.xml
```

If we use the simple XML document we met earlier:

```
<?xml version="1.0"?>

<Start>
<Here>
This is some text
</Here>
</Start>
```

and call it example.xml, we should see the following result:

Admittedly, this is not very useful, but it shows us that the parser is indeed reading the document we specified. Once you have this application running, you can try playing with the methods to see what you can do in response to the events firing from the parser.

A Moment with DOM

Just to drive the point home, consider what would have happened if we had used the DOM instead of SAX. First, using Microsoft's MSXML parser and Visual Basic, the XML document would be loaded into memory, so the entire document would be available for inspection.

```
Dim xmlDoc As MSXML2.DOMDocument30
Set xmlDoc = New MSXML2.DOMDocument30

Dim nodes As MSXML2.IXMLDOMNodeList
Dim node As MSXML2.IXMLDOMNode
Dim sXML As String
Dim i As Integer

'Load the text as an XML document
xmlDoc.loadXML ("<Start> <Here> This is some text </Here> </Start>")
```

Once loaded into memory, if we wanted to write the name of all elements to the screen, we would manipulate the document held in memory using:

```
Set nodes = xmlDoc.selectNodes("//")

For i = 0 To (nodes.length - 1)
  Set node = nodes.Item(i)
    If node.nodeType = NODE_TEXT Then
      sXML = sXML & "Node" & node.parentNode.nodeName & _
                    " value = " & node.Text & vbCrLf
    Else
      sXML = sXML & "Node" & i & " name = " & node.nodeName & vbCrLf
    End If
Next

MsgBox "XML: " & vbCrLf & sXML, vbOKOnly, "XML through DOM"
```

Giving us the message box:

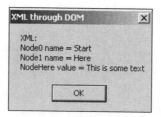

When we use the MSXML `selectNodes` method, we get an entire node list, as specified by the XPath expression. We can then step through that list one at a time and get the names or values of the elements within the result set. Again, this can be done because the entire document is loaded and available to the parser. We can step through the document, rather than collect parts of the document as they are announced.

If we wanted to, and without reloading the document, we could select one node of an element whose name we already knew using this syntax:

```
xmlDoc.selectSingleNode("Start").text
```

The point is that you think about the document in entirely different ways when using the different APIs.

> With the DOM, we consider what we have, and how we can get hold of the values.
>
> With SAX, we have to consider what we might receive, and how we want to handle those events.

Choosing Between SAX and DOM

Before we get to some less trivial examples, let's point out a few of the ways SAX might be more helpful than the DOM. We'll pay special attention to each of these issues during the examples:

❑ **Handling large XML documents.** There can be no doubt that the SAX method of parsing a document shines over DOM when it comes to large documents. "Large" is a relative term, but consider that a DOM-parsed document may take up to ten times its own size in RAM. If you're dealing with a 2-3MB file, that might not be so important. However, if you're dealing with large data sources of 100MB or more, the performance gains with SAX will be staggering.

❑ **Creating your own document as subset of the whole.** SAX can be helpful in preparing a document for the DOM or for another parser, by creating a new smaller document that contains only the pieces we want. Because you're responding to events, you can keep what you want, and let the rest fall to the cutting room floor.

❑ **Filtering documents in an event stream.** SAX provides the XMLFilter interface for defining classes that intercept parsing events as they pass from the XMLReader to a ContentHandler. Setting up a string of filters, with different processing functions, could allow document transformations to occur at several levels.

❑ **Aborting processing.** Again, this is related to large document savings: you can escape from SAX processing during any event handler. When you have what you want from the data source, you get out.

> It is important to note that SAX parsers are only going to reap the memory reward if they are pure, SAX-only implementations. Some parsers may build the tree in memory anyway, eliminating this benefit of the SAX event-driven model, so look carefully into the SAX parser you choose.

Next, it's only fair to consider some of the areas where the DOM is more adept:

❑ **Modifying and saving the original document.** SAX cannot really modify an XML document – it is considered to be read-only. You can make SAX *appear* to modify the original by creating a new document, and even write one by sending your own events to the event handlers, but this is not nearly as simple as actually writing to the in-memory document with the DOM.

❑ **Changing document structure.** Here again, you change document structure in SAX by writing a new document. The DOM allows you to make such changes explicitly.

❑ **Random access; the problem of context.** If you are going to be rooting around the XML document, moving back and forth and working with different nodes at different times, SAX could be very difficult to use. Because SAX doesn't bother with the details of the entire document it is processing, or how the elements relate to one another (apart from document order), you must maintain context programmatically. While you will be working to maintain some context no matter how you use SAX, you will want to use the DOM for complicated document handling. In order to simulate going back and forth in a document, you have several challenges with SAX. You would have to know what you were looking for on the first pass, get it, and then parse the document again in a second pass, getting some other value, and so on.

In short, you can do anything with either API, but you should regard the two APIs as complementary. Each has strengths and weaknesses that you can use to your best advantage depending upon the task in hand. Let's consider a few ways we may want to use each approach.

Best Uses of the DOM

❑   Use the DOM to modify an XML document based on user input to an application, and save the XML in memory before moving to another part of the application.

❑   The DOM is a better fit for retaining complex structures, as the structure is held in memory for you by the tree representation of the document.

Best Uses of SAX

❑   When handling a very large document with only a small amount of relevant data, SAX is a better choice, as you don't have to deal with the elements you don't need.

❑   SAX is the better method in situations where you will make only one pass through the document retaining values.

❑   When you can get out of the document after a certain node or value has been retrieved, SAX is an excellent choice. Any event handler method can be used to end parsing if you have identified the item you need.

❑   You should consider SAX when you have limited resources on the server parsing your document. A very large document could easily overwhelm a computer's memory resources when using the DOM.

The Stateless World of SAX

Although context is important, we do not have any context in SAX. While we may, for example, want to know the current document context (such as which element we are at), in order to determine which element a certain block of PCDATA belongs to, SAX parsers will only raise events in the order it finds them in the document as it is streamed through.

Recall that if we have the XML fragment from the beginning of the chapter:

```
<Start>
<here>This is some text</here>
</Start>
```

we get the opportunity to respond to the following events:

Event	Returns	Value
startElement	localName	"Start"
startElement	localName	"here"
characters	text	"This is some text"
endElement	localName	"here"
endElement	localName	"Start"

In order to do anything intelligent with this information, we'll need to know that the here element is in scope when we encounter the character data. Otherwise, the text will be reported without any qualifiers. Let's look at an example in which we'll turn the elements of an element-centric XML document into an attribute-centric document. This could be useful in a situation where we are receiving a document of the one type, and need to feed it to an application that only understands the other.

In this example, we will maintain context with flags and counters that are declared at a global level and referenced in the methods of the ContentHandler class. Each flag is a Boolean value that can be turned "on" or "off" during execution by setting the variable to True or False. This is valuable when some rule or value has been evaluated in one method that we want to know about in another. While we don't need to know the specific outcome, we do need to know that it has occurred. The counters, we will be using to find the depth of the current element within the document.

We'll be using Microsoft Visual Basic 6 for all of the remaining examples in this chapter. Each project, with all of its supporting code and XML documents, is available from the Wrox web site. The only additional item you will need is a version of MSXML, version 3.0 or higher. The code in this chapter is designed to work with the October 2000 release, which you can download from http://msdn.microsoft.com/downloads/default.asp.

Example 2 – Creating Attribute Centric Content from Element Centric Content

In this example we will be looking at how to create a document that uses an attribute-centric content model from a document that uses an element-centric one. This will demonstrate how SAX can be used to make some transformations to the original document as it writes a new document on the fly. We will also see one technique of maintaining context within the ContentHandler class, using flags and counters.

To do this:

❑ Start a new Visual Basic Standard EXE project called saxSample. Add a reference to the most recent version of the MSXML parser by selecting Project | References... from the toolbar, and checking Microsoft XML, v3.0. If msxml.dll has not been registered on your system, there is a Browse... feature that will allow you to point to the file itself.

❑ Create a Visual Basic form named frmAttsCentric that houses the application. This form needs:

　❑ A textbox, txtInputDoc, with Text property c:\groceries.xml. This contains the name of the XML document that we want to convert.

　❑ A command button, cmdParse, with Caption property Parse. When this button is clicked, the specified XML document will be loaded.

　❑ A command button, cmdExitSub, with Caption property Exit. This button will close the application.

　❑ A textbox, txtResults, with blank Text. This is where the result will be displayed.

The simple form will look something like this:

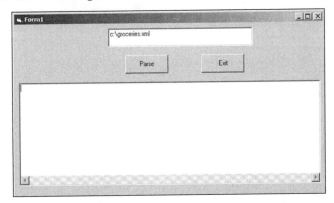

Make sure that the Multiline property of the text box is set to True, otherwise you will see marks inbetween the record.

Now for the code. We need to:

- ❑ Set up the `XMLReader` instance within the `cmdParse_Click()` method.

- ❑ Call the `setContentHandler()` and `setErrorHandler()` methods of the `XMLReader` to assign the `saxElemstoAtts` and `saxErrorHandler` classes respectively.

- ❑ Create the `saxElemstoAtts` class implementing the `IVBSAXContentHandler` interface, and the `saxErrorHandler` class implementing the `IVBSAXErrorHandler` interface.

- ❑ Create code within handler methods to generate the desired result document.

The frmAttsCentric Form

First, we need to instantiate the `XMLReader`, tell it where to send its parsing events, and where to send error messages. Add the following code to the form:

```
Option Explicit

Private Sub cmdParse_Click()

    Dim reader As SAXXMLReader
    Dim contentHandler As saxElemstoAtts
    Dim errorHandler As saxErrorHandler

    txtResults.Text = ""
    Set reader = New SAXXMLReader

    Set contentHandler = New saxElemstoAtts
    Set errorHandler = New saxErrorHandler

    ' Equivalent to setContentHandler() and setErrorHandler() methods in
    ' Java API. Tells the reader which classes will receive the events,
    ' and which will receive error messages.
    Set reader.contentHandler = contentHandler
    Set reader.errorHandler = errorHandler
```

Setting the `XMLReader`'s `contentHandler` and `errorHandler` properties points the reader at the correct classes for this particular application. The reader must have these properties set before the `parseURL()` method can be called. Otherwise, nothing will happen, because the reader has nothing to report events to.

Having done this, we are ready to have the reader parse the document:

```
    On Error GoTo HandleError

    reader.parseURL(txtInputDoc.Text)

    Exit Sub

HandleError:
    txtResults.Text = txtResults.Text & "*** Error *** " & Err.Number & _
                                 " : " & Err.Description

End Sub
```

The `parseURL()` method of the `SAXXMLReader` object is a straightforward way of specifying a document's location. This application will take the location from the form's `txtInputDoc` text box.

Notice that the Java API defined class names are present throughout, but with the addition of prefixes to the classes and interfaces.

Now that we have an XML reader available to raise events, we define the event handlers. When we look at the `contentHandler` class, we'll pay attention to the context in order to transform the structure of the XML document.

Before we look more closely at what each event is going to do, though, we should look at the document that will be parsed by the application.

The XML Document

This application assumes a well-formed document that has a document level element, and then a recurring top-level element that contains all other element types. This would have the generic format:

```
<DocumentElement>
    <TopLevelElement1>
        <QualifierA/>
            ...
        <QualifierN/>
    </TopLevelElement1>
    ...
    <TopLevelElementN>
        ...
    </TopLevelElementN>
</DocumentElement>
```

For example, this could be a document from an inventory database that has repetitive nodes for each item in stock, like the `groceries.xml` document that we'll be using in this example:

```
<?xml version="1.0"?>
<Groceries>
    <Item>
        <ItemKey>1</ItemKey>
        <Name type="dairy" calories="200">Milk</Name>
        <Cost>$2.0000</Cost>
        <PercentVitaminA>75%</PercentVitaminA>
        <IntakeRecommendation>16oz.</IntakeRecommendation>
    </Item>

    <Item>
        <ItemKey>2</ItemKey>
        <Name type="dairy" calories="150">Cheese</Name>
        <Cost>$1.5000</Cost>
        <Origin>Wisconsin</Origin>
        <PercentVitaminA>75%</PercentVitaminA>
        <IntakeRecommendation>5oz.</IntakeRecommendation>
    </Item>
```

```
        <Item>
            <ItemKey>3</ItemKey>
            <Name type="grains" calories="50">Bread</Name>
            <Cost>$2.1500</Cost>
            <Origin>Iowa</Origin>
            <PercentVitaminA>15%</PercentVitaminA>
            <IntakeRecommendation>2 slices</IntakeRecommendation>
        </Item>

        <Item>
            <ItemKey>4</ItemKey>
            <Name type="junkfood" calories="350">Pastries</Name>
            <Cost>$4.2500</Cost>
            <PercentVitaminA>Less than 1%</PercentVitaminA>
            <IntakeRecommendation>none</IntakeRecommendation>
        </Item>
    </Groceries>
```

The ContentHandler Class

We will look first at the `ContentHandler` class. Add a class module called `saxElemstoAtts` to the application, and add the following code to it:

```
Option Explicit

Implements IVBSAXContentHandler

' Set some module-level variables for maintaining context
' from one parse event to the next
Private bContext As Boolean
Private iCounter As Integer
Private sCurrentName, sTopName, sTopChar As String

' Initialize module-level variables
Private Sub class_Initialize()
    bContext = False
    iCounter = 0
    sCurrentName = ""
    sTopName = ""
    sTopChar = ""
End Sub
```

We get started with some variable declarations that can be set on initialization. These variables will help the application maintain context as parse events fire one method after another. The Boolean flag `bContext` will be the primary context variable for this application, and tells the application whether or not a child element that should become an attribute is in scope at any given time. This flag is set to `False` initially, to indicate that no such element is in scope.

The `iCounter` variable will be used to indicate that the document element is in scope, and when top-level elements, are in scope. The remaining string variables will hold the values of particular elements during the course of the application. This enables the application to write values to the result document, even after the next event has fired. Without such variables, we must either write information to the result document during a particular event, or lose the value forever.

Flags, counters, and value-holders are a good jumping off point for the discussion of imlpementing context. We'll look at a more complex state mechanism for larger applications in a later example.

> The **ContentHandler** class must include a method for each of the events the parser might send. In Java, methods that the application will not respond to can be left out of the content handler. In Visual Basic, however, the **Implements** keyword forces the class to implement each method defined in the interface specified.

The startElement Method

Next, we'll add some code for the startElement() method:

```
Private Sub IVBSAXContentHandler_startElement( _
                        sNamespaceURI As String, _
                        sLocalName As String, _
                        sQName As String, _
                        ByVal attributes As MSXML2.IVBSAXAttributes)
```

Notice the use of the SAX attributes class within the startElement() method. Attributes of each element are actually sent as a separate object containing the type, URI, qualified name, local name, and value of each attribute. Each of these values can be accessed from the attributes object while within the startElement() method.

Now we'll start to parse our groceries.xml document. This application will output a document fragment that focuses on the Item element as the top-level element, and treats each of its children as qualifying attributes. Each child element will be added to the Item element as an attribute:

```
Dim i As Integer
Dim sVal
iCounter = iCounter + 1
If iCounter > 2 And sLocalName <> sTopName Then
    sCurrentName = sLocalName
    bContext = True
    frmAttsCentric.txtResults.Text = frmAttsCentric.txtResults.Text & _
                                " " & sCurrentName & "="""
```

Right away, we check the iCounter and the sLocalName because we want to isolate the Item element during subsequent calls, but we also need to skip the root. The iCounter is simply incremented each time we enter the startElement method, so we can ignore the first element and catch the second. Again, this application is dealing with a certain type of XML document structure. If we wanted to capture the fifth element, we could check the iCounter differently. Alternatively, we could change the application to check by element name.

We also set the context to True inside the If statement, so that when we look at character data later, we can generically decide if it should be written as an attribute.

The next order of business is to check the counter again, to see if the current node is now the second:

```
ElseIf iCounter = 2 Then
    ' This is the main element node (the second one encountered by the
    '  parser). There is an assumption that there is a top level element
    '   to be ignored, and the next element will be our 'main' element.
    sTopName = sLocalName
End If
```

When the `iCounter` is 2, we have the name of our repetitive top element, and so we store this in the `sTopName` variable as a way to change our processing for this special element on subsequent parser events:

```
If sLocalName = sTopName Then
    ' Every time we come to this element, we will start the process over
    frmAttsCentric.txtResults.Text = frmAttsCentric.txtResults.Text & _
                            vbCrLf & "<" & sLocalName
```

Now, if our top-level element already has attributes, we want to preserve them, so we roll through the `attributes` collection:

```
If attributes.length > 0 Then
    For i = 0 To (attributes.length - 1)
        frmAttsCentric.txtResults.Text = _
                    frmAttsCentric.txtResults.Text & " " & _
                    attributes.getLocalName(i) & "="
        frmAttsCentric.txtResults.Text = _
                    frmAttsCentric.txtResults.Text & """" & _
                    attributes.getValue(i) & """"
    Next
    End If
    End If
End Sub
```

Attribute values can be referenced either by name or index number. Here we are getting the values by sequential index number. We don't write out the end parenthesis for the top element here, because we want to write future `startElement` events inside this same element. After closing up the logical structures, we are ready to move on to the `characters()` method.

The characters Method

With character data, this application should seek to retain everything except for text that occurs outside of `<Item>` elements. All character data inside the top level `<Item>` element must be stored for later use, as it will have to be printed to the result document only after all other elements inside `<Item>` have been written.

If the text currently being parsed is for an element that should now be an attribute (as noted by `bContext`), it is written directly to the results:

```
Private Sub IVBSAXContentHandler_characters(sText As String)
    sText = strip(sText)
    If bContext Then
        ' If this is the root then any character data will be ignored
        frmAttsCentric.txtResults.Text = _
            frmAttsCentric.txtResults.Text & sText
    ElseIf sTopName <> "" Then
        sTopChar = sTopChar & sText & " "
    End If
End Sub
```

As the text is passed in, we send it to the `strip()` function, which simply removes any newline whitespace characters for the sake of readability in the `txtResults` window:

```
Private Function strip(sText As String)
    Select Case sText
        Case vbCrLf
            sText = Replace(sText, vbCrLf, "")
        Case vbCr
            sText = Replace(sText, vbCr, "")
        Case vbLf
            sText = Replace(sText, vbLf, "")
    End Select
    strip = sText
End Function
```

When using MSXML, all of the text inside a particular element will be returned in one call to the `characters()` method. In general, however, each parser implementation is free to return the characters in any grouping it chooses.

The endElement Method

Next, we will work with the element end tags. Add the following code to the class:

```
Private Sub IVBSAXContentHandler_endElement(sNamespaceURI As String, _
                                            sLocalName As String, _
                                            sQName As String)
    If sLocalName = sTopName Then
        frmAttsCentric.txtResults.Text = frmAttsCentric.txtResults.Text & _
            ">" & vbCrLf & Trim(sTopChar) & "</" & sLocalName & ">" & vbCrLf
        sTopChar = ""
    ElseIf bContext Then
        ' Close the attribute value quotes
        frmAttsCentric.txtResults.Text = _
            frmAttsCentric.txtResults.Text & """" ' Ends the element value

        ' Reset for processing next element
        bContext = False
    End If
End Sub
```

The actions we need to take inside the `endElement()` method can be somewhat less intuitive than the others we have seen so far. Basically, it is at the end of an element that the application should clean up the output to the result document, and prepare the variables for the next run of parser events. In this case, we have two possible end element events that are important.

First, if this is the top-level element, the start element tag itself should be closed with the "greater than" angled bracket, and the characters we have been holding on to in the sTopChar variable can finally be written to the result. At this time, it is also appropriate to write the end element tag as well, and clear out the sTopChar variable ready for the next <Item> element:

```
If sLocalName = sTopName Then
    frmAttsCentric.txtResults.Text = frmAttsCentric.txtResults.Text & _
        ">" & vbCrLf & Trim(sTopChar) & "</" & sLocalName & ">" & vbCrLf
    sTopChar = ""
```

The second case we are interested in is for the ending of those elements that have now been written as attributes of <Item>. The handy bContext variable is ready to help us determine if the current end element belongs to such an element. After checking if bContext is true, we can simply write the ending quotes for the new attribute value:

```
ElseIf bContext Then
    frmAttsCentric.txtResults.Text = _
        frmAttsCentric.txtResults.Text & """"
    bContext = False
```

It is also important to reset bContext, as the next element that is parsed may be a top-level element. If the bContext flag is not reset here, character events sent between elements will not be able to tell whether the text should be written as attribute text, or as top-level element text.

Remember, you'll also need to implement empty procedures for the remaining IVBSAXContentHandler methods in order to be able to compile the project. These are: documentLocator, endDocument, endPrefixMapping, ignorableWhitespace, skippedEntity, startDocument, and startPrefixMapping.

The Error Handler Class

This project also includes the following error handling code. MSXML treats all errors as fatal, so we only need to deal with the fatalError() method:

```
Option Explicit

Implements IVBSAXErrorHandler

Private Sub IVBSAXErrorHandler_fatalError(ByVal lctr As IVBSAXLocator, _
                                    msg As String, _
                                    ByVal errCode As Long)
    frmAttsCentric.txtResults.Text = frmAttsCentric.txtResults.Text & _
                                    "*** error *** " & msg
End Sub
```

```
'Nothing for error() and warning(), MSXML treats all errors as fatal.
Private Sub IVBSAXErrorHandler_error(ByVal lctr As IVBSAXLocator, _
                                msg As String, _
                                ByVal errCode As Long)

End Sub

Private Sub IVBSAXErrorHandler_ignorablewarning( _
                                ByVal lctr As IVBSAXLocator, _
                                msg As String, ByVal errCode As Long)

End Sub
```

The Result

Now compile the application, and point it at the inventory example groceries.xml. You should see this result:

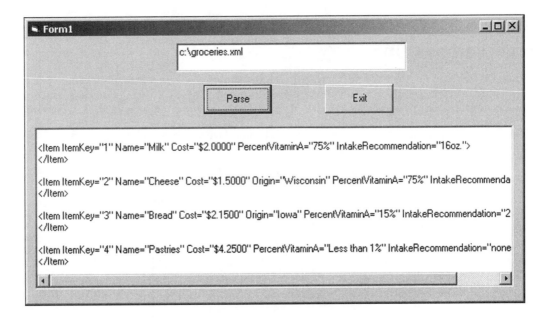

Context Summary

In order to make intelligent decisions about what to do with the data from the XMLReader, we have to maintain document context within our application. The general idea is that we need values outside of the event methods to use within each event. We can maintain context with the name of a particular element, an index number, or a counter, or we can use a Boolean to turn a more generalized context on or off at will. This type of document scanning is well suited to the SAX methodology, as we can move easily in a linear fashion, and don't need to change values within the original document. If the example inventory document included hundreds of thousands of items, the resource savings would be immense.

Handling Large Documents

It is often the case that an XML file may contain irrelevant data for a particular use or need. In a database, all the columns of a data set are not relevant in all situations. We could selectively choose columns in the SELECT statement of a SQL query. In XML, the equivalent of SQL has been said to be XSLT.

XSLT takes an input document, and transforms it into a result document. SAX can be used in a similar fashion by virtue of its nature of passing every item in an XML document through a function before writing the result document. SAX can be ruthless, taking only what it needs from an XML document, and dropping the rest without another thought. Fortunately, in the world of data, ruthless can also mean efficient.

In this section we'll consider the ability of SAX to work with a very large document that may contain only a small amount of relevant data. We will look at a simple transformation example first, utilizing much of the implementation we've already seen, and then introduce SAX filters.

Example 3 – Creating an Efficient XML Document from a Large Verbose One

In this example, we'll use a simple interface to tell the application which document will be our source document, and specify a location for the resulting document. There are two options available: one that produces another XML document, and one that produces a new document with HTML markup added.

This project is called saxTransformExample. The interface is a form called frmTransform, which looks like this:

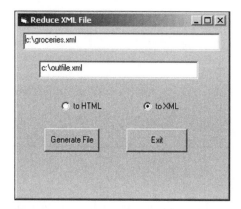

The code behind this form is quite straightforward:

```
Private Sub Frame1_DragDrop(Source As Control, X As Single, Y As Single)

End Sub
```

```
Private Sub cmdCreateFile_Click()

  Dim retval
  If optXML.Item(0) Then
    Dim xOutput As New saxTransformXML
    Call xOutput.StartitUp(txtInputFile.Text, txtOutputFile.Text)
  Else
    Dim hOutput As New saxXMLtoHTML
    Call hOutput.StartitUp(txtInputFile.Text, txtOutputFile.Text)
  End If

End Sub
```

```
Private Sub cmdExit_Click()
  End
End Sub
```

The buttons simply call user-defined functions, StartitUp, to set the document input and output variables with the XMLReader.

> We won't cover the option for HTML output here, but it is implemented in the downloadable support files. It simply demonstrates another way to filter an XML document. Expanded slightly, it could serve as a way to produce XHTML. And the same methodology could be used to produce a document of any type, including a simple CSV file.

For this example, the input document will be the groceries.xml file we saw in Example 2. The goal of this application will be to retain only the <Name>, <Cost>, and <IntakeRecommendation> elements, and wrap them in a new generic document level element called <MYXML>. Additionally, the type attribute of the <Name> element will be converted to a child element, with its value being displayed as the text value of the <Name> element.

The original XML as displayed by the Microsoft XMLReader has the following form:

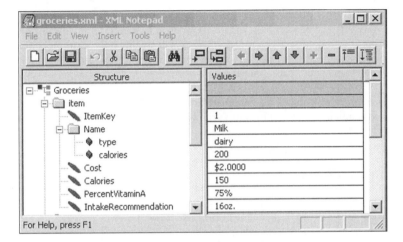

Once the application has been run, the resultant outfile.xml document will have this form:

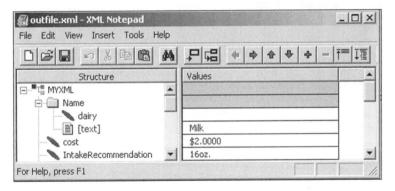

When you have completed this example you should be able to:

❏ Understand how SAX can be used as an alternative method of transforming XML documents from XSLT

❏ Write functions inside the ContentHandler class for additional functionality

❏ Change document types from XML to any other

Prepare the XMLReader Class

Our content handler class is called saxTransformXML, and begins with the usual variable declarations for maintaining context:

```
Option Explicit
Implements IVBSAXContentHandler

Private ts As TextStream
Private fso As FileSystemObject
Private iElementCounter As Integer
Private sFfirstelement As String
Private bContext As Boolean
```

The `TextStream` and `FileSystemObject` will be used to generate our output file. Notice also the `bContext` variable of Example 2 has returned. This will be our only state mechanism, because again our goal is to run through this document, and write to the result document as quickly as possible. We are not really interested in collecting anything.

This particular handler class has a user-defined function called `StartitUp` that will be called by the form to set the document input and output variables with the `XMLReader`:

```
Public Sub StartitUp(infile As String, outfile As String)

    Set fso = New FileSystemObject

    On Error Resume Next
    fso.DeleteFile (outfile) 'clear out the file.

    Set ts = fso.OpenTextFile(outfile, ForWriting, True)

    Dim reader As SAXXMLReader30
    Dim errorhandler As saxErrorHandler

    Set reader = New SAXXMLReader30
    Set errorhandler = New saxErrorHandler

    Set reader.contentHandler = Me
    Set reader.errorhandler = errorhandler

    reader.parseURL (infile)          ' Parse it

End Sub
```

For this example, we have written our reader right into the handler class, and set the `reader` property using Me. This is the reserved word used by VB to indicate the current class:

```
Set reader.contentHandler = Me
```

There is nothing about SAX that requires different classes for any of the class implementations – separation of duties is simply a code practice choice. In this case, we want to open a `TextStream` object with variables from our form, and have the object available throughout the class. We don't want to start parsing until we know our output file, so it is convenient to instantiate the reader at this time.

Begin Parsing Events

The goal of this particular transformation is to produce a smaller XML document that fits our particular data needs, not to change the document type. Therefore, we want to make sure the XML document fragment that comes out of the other end can be used as well-formed XML by the next consumer. We use the startDocument and endDocument methods to insert the proper tags for the beginning and ending of the new result document:

```
Private Sub IVBSAXContentHandler_startDocument()
  ts.Write ("<?xml version='1.0'?><MYXML>")
  bContext = False
End Sub

Private Sub IVBSAXContentHandler_endDocument()
  ts.Write ("</MYXML>")
End Sub
```

The content handler is being used to save only certain elements we have chosen: <Name>, <Cost>, and <IntakeRecommendation>. The process of eliminating the other elements begins in the startElement method. The desired elements are selected by name to be written to the stream. Elements that are not named are simply ignored, and do not really have to be "handled" at all:

```
Private Sub IVBSAXContentHandler_startElement(sNamespaceURI As String, _
                                    sLocalName As String, _
                                    sQName As String, _
                  ByVal Attributes As MSXML2.IVBSAXAttributes)

  Select Case sLocalName
    Case "Name"
      ts.Write ("<" & caseChange(sLocalName, 1) & ">")
      If Attributes.length <> 0 Then
        ts.Write ("<" & Attributes.getValueFromName(sNamespaceURI, "type") _
                  & "/>")
        bContext = True
      End If
    Case "Cost"
      ts.Write ("<" & caseChange(sLocalName, 2) & ">")
      bContext = True
    Case "IntakeRecommendation"
      ts.Write ("<" & sLocalName & ">")
      bContext = True
    End Select

End Sub
```

In order to demonstrate some simple on the fly transformations, we are changing the case of different elements with the caseChange function, which changes either to proper or lower case based on an integer input identifier, iChangeType:

```
Private Function caseChange(sText As String, iChangeType As Integer) _
                    As String

  Select Case iChangeType
    Case 1
      caseChange = StrConv(sText, vbProperCase)
    Case 2
      caseChange = StrConv(sText, vbLowerCase)
    End Select

End Function
```

Of course, the functions you implement to filter the values sent by the SAX parser can be as elaborate as you like.

If we have run into an element we want, we not only write the element name, we also need to set our simple state mechanism:

```
bContext = True
```

This state of True for bContext lets the application know that, for the time being, the parser is throwing events related to an element we are interested in. Now, when we come to the characters method, we can discard the characters of unwanted elements by simply checking the current bContext value:

```
Private Sub IVBSAXContentHandler_characters(sChars As String)

    If bContext Then
      ts.Write (sChars)
    End If

End Sub
```

Ending the elements is very similar to the start. We have to run the element names through caseChange again, so our resulting XML will be well-formed, and reset our state mechanism:

```
Private Sub IVBSAXContentHandler_endElement(sNamespaceURI As String, _
                                  sLocalName As String,
                                  sQName As String)

    Select Case sLocalName
      Case "Name"
        ts.Write ("</" & caseChange(sLocalName, 1) & ">" & vbCrLf)
        bContext = False
      Case "Cost"
        ts.Write ("</" & caseChange(sLocalName, 2) & ">" & vbCrLf)
        bContext = False
      Case "IntakeRecommendation"
        ts.Write ("</" & sLocalName & ">" & vbCrLf)
        bContext = False
    End Select

End Sub
```

That's it: we have a new document that is still well formed, is less than half the size, and meets the specifications of our input or retrieval mechanism.

In the downloadable project, we've also included an extra class – saxXMLtoHTML – to deal with the HTML output, as well as an error handler class similar to the one we saw in the previous example.

The Results

If you use groceries.xml, the output file should now look like this:

```
<?xml version='1.0'?><MYXML><Name><dairy/>Milk</Name>
<cost>$2.0000</cost>
<IntakeRecommendation>16oz.</IntakeRecommendation>
<Name><dairy/>Cheese</Name>
<cost>$1.5000</cost>
<IntakeRecommendation>5oz.</IntakeRecommendation>
<Name><grains/>Bread</Name>
<cost>$2.1500</cost>
<IntakeRecommendation>2 slices</IntakeRecommendation>
<Name><junkfood/>Pastries</Name>
<cost>$4.2500</cost>
<IntakeRecommendation>none</IntakeRecommendation>
</MYXML>
```

You should be able to see how this would be useful when dealing with documents that are either more verbose than necessary, or more importantly, those that do not meet the guidelines of your DTD or Schema. SAX offers a great way to force data into a format you want, and it can do it on the fly.

SAX Filters

It is actually quite common to use a ContentHandler class as an interceptor between the XMLReader and the ContentHandler which will write the document. The contributors to the SAX API advanced this usage as an extension to the XMLReader called **XMLFilter**.

The XMLFilter class takes a reference to a parent XMLReader class. The parent property is set to another instance of an XMLReader, whether it is a base XMLReader, or an implementation of an XMLFilter. In this way, the events of the parsing XMLReader are sent first to the highest level parent, which will (at least) respond to each event by sending another SAX event to the child XMLReader. This may sound a bit confusing, but we'll at look some code in just a moment.

In order to use a filter, we actually want to implement the methods and properties of an XMLFilter in a new class.

> The SAX API provides a helper class called **XMLFilterImpl** that was not provided with MSXML. A VB translation of this helper class has been provided with the downloadable files for this example. It is called **VBXMLFilterImpl.cls**, and contains only the default methods that will pass the XML document on to the next reader unchanged.

Example 4 – Using an Implementation of the XMLFilter Class

For this example, we will build an application that implements a rather trivial XMLFilter. A user interface will collect the location of an input document, and the name of two elements which should be removed from the XML document before it is finally passed to the ContentHandler.

What is implemented in the filters, or whether or not they are separate classes in this example, is not really important. Having the XMLFilterImpl, and seeing how the filters are chained, will make it possible to create any filter based application. The content handler class – saxConentHandler – will simply write the XML document to the txtResults text box on the application's user interface. The application allows you to choose whether the result document should be shown with the filter or without for easy comparison of the output. The interface looks like this:

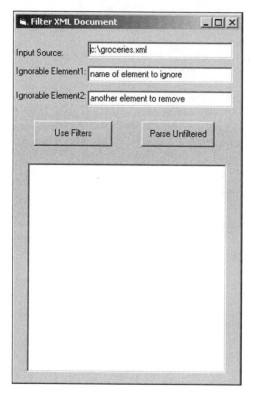

When you have completed this example you should be able to:

❑ Implement the XMLFilter interface in a class that can be used to filter SAX events before passing them on to a ContentHandler

❑ Instantiate a reader that is used as a parent for an XMLFilter implementation

❑ Understand how a chain of filters could be used together in one application

The way that the filters are called is the most important lesson in this example, as we've seen how to actually respond to events in the filters, and the ContentHandler, in previous examples.

Preparing to Use a Chain of XMLFilters

The XMLReader and XMLFilter implementations will be set up in the code for the form (frmReadtoFilter). The XMLFilterImpl is created in one class called saxXMLFilterImpl, and the content handler is created as another class called saxContentHandler.

Our form gives us two options. The one we're really interested in here is where we filter our XML:

```
Private Sub cmdUseFilter_Click()
  Dim reader As SAXXMLReader
  Dim filterImpl1 As saxXMLFilterImpl
  Dim filterImpl2 As saxXMLFilterImpl
  Dim xmlFilter1 As IVBSAXXMLFilter
  Dim xmlFilter2 As IVBSAXXMLFilter
```

Right away, we see a new interface declaration being used for the filter interface definitions: `IVBSAXXMLFilter`. The `IVBSAXXMLFilter` type is the XMLFilter interface, *not* the implementation of that interface. `xmlFilter1` and `2` will be set to the filter class created based on the `saxXMLFilterImpl` template. `filterImpl1` and `2` are instantiated as objects of the type `saxXMLFilterImpl`, which will actually do the work. Notice that the first filter sets an actual instance of an `XMLReader` as its parent. This must be done for the top-level filter to end the chain:

```
  Set reader = New SAXXMLReader

  Set filterImpl1 = New saxXMLFilterImpl
  filterImpl1.setIgnorableElement (txtIgnore.Text)

  Set xmlFilter1 = filterImpl1
  Set xmlFilter1.parent = reader

  Set filterImpl2 = New saxXMLFilterImpl
  filterImpl2.setIgnorableElement (txtIgnoreMore.Text)

  Set xmlFilter2 = filterImpl2
  Set xmlFilter2.parent = filterImpl1
```

The values of the two text boxes are passed to the filter implementations in turn to identify which element name should be ignored for that particular run of the filter. The `setIgnorableElement` procedure contained in the `saxXMLFilterImpl` class (more of that shortly) sets a variable value that can be referenced during processing:

```
Public Sub setIgnorableElement(sElementLocalName)
  sIgnoreElement = sElementLocalName
End Sub
```

After each filter has been set in the `frmReadtoFilter`'s `cmdUseFilter_Click` method, the `reader` variable is reset to the name of the last filter in the chain, in this case `filterImpl2`. Finally, the ContentHandler class – `saxContentHandler` – is declared and instantiated as `xmlHandler`. The next bit should be familiar by now – the `reader` property for `contentHandler` is set to the instance of `saxContentHandler`. And the `parseURL` method is called to set the application in motion:

```
  Set reader = filterImpl2
  Dim xmlHandler As saxContentHandler
  Set xmlHandler = New saxContentHandler
  Set reader.contentHandler = xmlHandler

  ' parse and display output
  reader.parseURL txtFileLoc.Text

End Sub
```

In calling the `parseURL` method on the `contentHandler`, we are actually calling the `parseURL` method of the second instance of the filter implementation. In `saxXMLFilterImpl`, that method looks like this:

```
Private Sub IVBSAXXMLReader_parseURL(ByVal sURL As String)
  setupParse
  saxFilterParent.parseURL sURL
End Sub
```

`saxFilterParent` was declared as of type `XMLReader` in the declarations section of the class. The `setupParse` method is going to set this reader instance to the parent of the filter, which in our case is another filter, `filterImpl1`. Therefore, when the `parseURL` method of `saxFilterParent` is called, the parse event is going to be handed up the chain to the first filter instance.

The other button on our form is much simpler. This just parses the document unfiltered:

```
Private Sub cmdParse_Click()

  Dim reader As SAXXMLReader

  Set reader = New SAXXMLReader
  Dim xmlHandler As saxContentHandler
  Set xmlHandler = New saxContentHandler
  Set reader.contentHandler = xmlHandler

  reader.parseURL txtFileLoc.Text         ' Parse it

End Sub
```

Before we go further, we should look at the implementation class.

Using the XMLFilter Implementation Class

The actual filter implementation has a rather long introduction in the declarations section of `saxXMLFilterImpl`, because it must account for each type of interface the `XMLReader` may implement:

```
Option Explicit

'Visual Basic implementation of the helper class XMLFilterImpl
'class released as part of the SAX2 API.

Implements IVBSAXXMLFilter 'Special helper interface definition
Implements IVBSAXXMLReader
Implements IVBSAXContentHandler
Implements IVBSAXErrorHandler
Implements IVBSAXDTDHandler
Implements IVBSAXEntityResolver

Private saxFilterParent As IVBSAXXMLReader
Private saxErrorHandler As IVBSAXErrorHandler
Private saxContentHandler As IVBSAXContentHandler
Private saxDTDHandler As IVBSAXDTDHandler
Private saxEntityResolver As IVBSAXEntityResolver
```

```
Private sBaseURL As String
Private sSecureBaseURL As String
Private saxLocator As IVBSAXLocator

'Allow filter caller to set the name of an element to be removed from XML
'results passed to next content handler. Use boolean value for context to
'also ignore chars for ignorable element
Private bIgnore As Boolean
Private bNextElem As Boolean
Private sIgnoreElement As String
```

With these declarations the filter will be able to receive any of the property, feature, and event calls that could be sent to the XMLReader, allowing it to effectively sit between the reader and content handler and listen in on all the messages bound for the other side.

So, the setupParse method has been called on the lowest level filter, filterImpl2. This method will set the familiar XMLReader properties for the current filter class, but sets them on the parent of this particular filter. Therefore, the contentHandler property set on the instance of filterImpl2, passes a reference to itself to the instance of filterImpl1 and sets its contentHandler property:

```
Public Sub setupParse()

    Set saxFilterParent.contentHandler = Me
    Set saxFilterParent.errorHandler = Me
    Set saxFilterParent.dtdHandler = Me
    'EntityResolver not yet implemented in MSXML
    '(September 2000 beta release)
    'Set saxFilterParent.entityResolver = Me

End Sub
```

The same routine is used to set filterImpl2 as the errorHandler, dtdHandler, and entityResolver for filterImpl1. Now, when the parseURL method of saxFilterParent is called, it passes that URL up the chain to filterImpl1.

```
Private Sub IVBSAXXMLReader_parseURL(ByVal sURL As String)
    setupParse
    saxFilterParent.parseURL sURL
End Sub
```

Of course, filterImpl1 has the identical parseURL method as filterImpl2, and will also call setupParse. However, this time, the saxFilterParent instance will be an actual XMLReader implementation, and the chain will stop with that reader sending its events to the ContentHandler of record for filterImpl1, which is filterImpl2. Thus, SAX parse events are passed back down the chain until the ContentHandler of the last filter in the chain is reached, which is an actual implementation of the ContentHandler, saxContentHandler in our case.

Confused? Well, in short, the application sets properties and calls parse up the chain, and the XMLReader instance on the other end passes parse events back down the chain to the instance of the content handler.

Parse Events

The parse event handlers in the filters can behave just like the event handlers we have already seen in the `ContentHandler` implementations themselves. However, each must pass the information it receives along as a SAX parse event, just as it received it. Thus, the methods that do the work in this example make the necessary changes, or judgment calls, and then pass the event down the chain to the next `ContentHandler`:

```
Private Sub IVBSAXContentHandler_startDocument()

    bIgnore = False 'initialize ignorable element context flag to false
    bNextElem = True 'init element content context flag to true
    saxContentHandler.startDocument

End Sub

Private Sub IVBSAXContentHandler_startElement(sNamespaceURI As String, _
                                    sLocalName As String, _
                                    sQName As String, _
                        ByVal oAttributes As MSXML2.IVBSAXAttributes)

    'Pass the xmlReader events along except for the element name specified
    'as ignorable
    If sLocalName <> sIgnoreElement Then
      bNextElem = True
      'set/reset context flag to true for non-ignored elements.
      saxContentHandler.startElement sNamespaceURI, sLocalName, _
                            sQName, oAttributes
    Else
      bIgnore = True 'context flag for characters method to
                    'ignore chars from ignorable element
    End If

End Sub

Private Sub IVBSAXContentHandler_characters(sChars As String)

    If Not bIgnore And bNextElem Then
      saxContentHandler.characters sChars
    Else
      bNextElem = False
      'continue to ignore chars until next element starts to strip whitespace
      bIgnore = False 'reset context flag for ignorable element
    End If

End Sub

Private Sub IVBSAXContentHandler_endElement(sNamespaceURI As String,_
                                    sLocalName As String, _
                                    sQName As String)

    If sLocalName <> sIgnoreElement Then
      saxContentHandler.endElement sNamespaceURI, sLocalName, sQName
    End If

End Sub


Private Sub IVBSAXContentHandler_endDocument()
    saxContentHandler.endDocument
End Sub
```

Each method's interface is in fact an implementation of the `ContentHandler` interface methods – there is really nothing new for you to notice here. The only change is the method call at the end of each method. For instance, the `endElement` call:

```
saxContentHandler.endElement sNamespaceURI, sLocalName, sQName
```

Recall that in the declarations section, the `saxContentHandler` variable was set to be of the type `IVBSAXContentHandler`. This variable is set in the `Property Set` statement of the filter:

```
Private Property Set IVBSAXXMLReader_contentHandler_
                       (ByVal handler As MSXML2.IVBSAXContentHandler)
  Set saxContentHandler = handler
End Property
```

Again, this property was set for the first filter when we set everything up in `frmReadtoFilter`:

```
Set reader.contentHandler = xmlHandler
```

This property was sent up the chain for each filter in turn by the `setupParse` method inside the filter implementation.

> You'll find the complete code for this example in the download available from the Wrox web site.

The saxContentHandler Class

The final ContentHandler in this example, will simply write what it receives from the `filterImpl2` just as it comes in, but will add the angle brackets back to the start and end elements.

The code for this class is then trivial:

```
Option Explicit

Implements IVBSAXContentHandler

Dim sResult As String

Private Sub IVBSAXContentHandler_startElement(sNamespaceURI As String, _
                                    sLocalName As String, _
                                    sQName As String, _
                          ByVal attributes As MSXML2.IVBSAXAttributes)

  sResult = sResult & "<" & sLocalName & ">"

End Sub

Private Sub IVBSAXContentHandler_endElement(sNamespaceURI As String, _
                                    sLocalName As String, _
                                    sQName As String)

  sResult = sResult & "</" & sLocalName & ">"
```

```
    End Sub

    Private Sub IVBSAXContentHandler_characters(sText As String)
        sResult = sResult & sText
    End Sub

    Private Sub IVBSAXContentHandler_endDocument()
        frmReadtoFilter.txtResults.Text = sResult
    End Sub
```

The Result

When the `groceries.xml` document is parsed, with the `<ItemKey>` and `<Cost>` elements set as the two ignorable elements, we see this result:

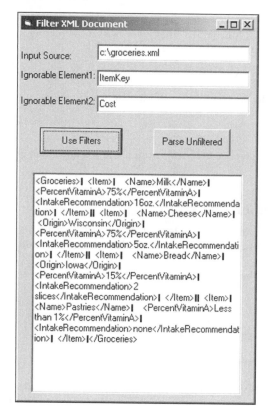

Filters Summary

In this section we have seen that large documents that contain data or nodes that are not needed for the current situation can be transformed by the SAX `ContentHandler` to become more efficient and more useful for our purpose. In addition to using a `ContentHandler` directly, we saw the implementation of a SAX `XMLFilter`, which sits between the `XMLReader` and `ContentHandler` classes. The filter is an ideal way to create XML transformations in separate logical blocks.

Transforming XML documents is an excellent way to prepare the result document for your application to meet the needs of your situation. In the next section, we'll look at retrieving data out of the result documents, and storing those values.

Take What You Need – Storing Result Data

In the previous section, we worked the document we were given into a new file or structure that could be used instead of the original. In the next example, we do not stop with an end document, but will pass the transformed data directly to a database.

We will work with a fanciful stock quote reporting stream that contains numerous nodes for describing each company. However, we are only interested in writing the company name, the current stock price, opening price, and current rating along with minor analysis.

Example 5 – Complex State

Our final application will take the same basic shape as Example 2: in fact the UI is borrowed directly. This time, though, we are going to be more explicit about what we expect to find, and we are going to parse the XML string to get only pieces of data to write to our stock analysis database. The UI form has a small application added inside it that will display the summarized information we wanted to see. Of course, while we are going to use one form to hit both processes, in the real worlds, the saxDeserialize class would be run behind the scenes.

When you have completed this example you should be able to:

❑ Create a complex state mechanism for tracking the value of several elements during the execution of the parser

❑ List yourself among the known masters of SAX parsing

> This example uses Microsoft SQL Server 7.0 (or 2000). The SQL command file used to set up the database, and an Excel spreadsheet of the data, are both available with the code download for this book. You'll also find the stored procedures you need defined in the code package, and the VB project that contains everything else.

In order to try this yourself, you will need a database named Ticker with the following setup:

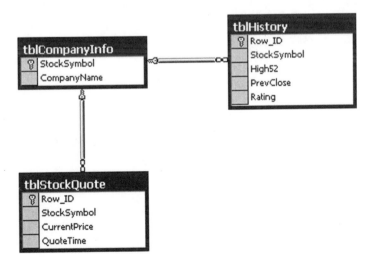

The XML

The XML document we are looking at – `ticker.xml` – at is a series of stock elements, arbitrarily contained within a `TickerTape` element. This represents a stream of stock information. Each stock element has the following format:

```
<TickerTape>
  <Stock symbol="LKSQW">
    <Name>Some Company</Name>
    <Price>112.1224</Price>
    <PE>2.4</PE>
    <R>0.7</R>
    <History>
      <PrevClose>111</PrevClose>
      <High52>154</High52>
      <Low52>98</Low52>
      <Range52>56</Range52>
      <SharesTraded>12,421,753</SharesTraded>
      <SharesActive>981,420,932</SharesActive>
      <Rating>HOLD</Rating>
    </History>
    <TradedOn>NYSE</TradedOn>
    <QuoteTime>14:12:33</QuoteTime>
  </Stock>

  <Stock>
    ...
  </Stock>

</TickerTape>
```

Our goal is to cut out several of the unwanted elements, and hold only the information we find useful. If we had a result document, it would have the form of the following XML fragment:

```
<Name>Some Company</Name>
<Price>112.1224</Price>
<History>
    <PrevClose>111</PrevClose>
    <High52>154</High52>
    <Rating>HOLD</Rating>
</History>
<QuoteTime>14:12:33</QuoteTime>
```

The ContentHandler

We start out with the declarations section of the `ContentHandler` class, this time called `saxDeserialize`:

```
Option Explicit

'The next line is important - it says what is implemented
Implements IVBSAXContentHandler
Dim iCounter As Integer
```

```
'Collection for context(state) variables
Dim colContext As valCollect
Dim quotes As New streamToDb

'Storage variables for element values
Dim curr_Symbol As String
Dim curr_Price As Currency
Dim curr_Prev As Currency
Dim curr_High As Currency
Dim curr_Rating As String

'Set Globals for element state
'enumerations number consecutively if no value is given
Private Enum TickerState
    stateTicker = 1
    stateStock = 2
    statePrice = 3
    stateHistory = 4
    statePrev = 5
    stateHigh = 6
    stateRate = 7
End Enum

Private Sub class_initialize()
  iCounter = 0
  Set colContext = New valCollect
End Sub
```

We promised earlier that we would get into a more complex way of handling state. In this example, we've set up a an enumeration of constants, in addition to some other global variables that hold values, much like in Example 2. We are going to use this enumeration in concert with the context collection colContext, declared above it. The enumeration values will be passed to the collection, and the collection read during the execution of other methods. We will refer to this collection and enumeration setup as a **state machine**.

We set up our state machine in the startElement method, by adding the value of the enumeration variables to the collection for the current element, if it matches an element we are looking for:

```
Private Sub IVBSAXContentHandler_startElement(sNamespaceURI As String, _
                                    sLocalName As String, _
                                    sQName As String, _
                            ByVal oAttributes As MSXML2.IVBSAXAttributes)


    Select Case sLocalName
      Case "TickerTape"
        colContext.Collect (stateTicker)
      Case "Stock"
        colContext.Collect (stateStock)
      Case "Price"
        colContext.Collect (statePrice)
      Case "History"
        colContext.Collect (stateHistory)
      Case "PrevClose"
        colContext.Collect (statePrev)
```

```
      Case "High52"
        colContext.Collect (stateHigh)
      Case "Rating"
        colContext.Collect (stateRate)
      Case Else
    End Select

    If sLocalName = "Stock" Then
      If oAttributes.length > 0 Then
        curr_Symbol = oAttributes.getValue(0)
      End If

    End If

  End Sub
```

Not every element passed into the `ContentHandler` will be useful to us. This is where we can drop whatever we don't want. It's really a matter of being proactive about the elements we do want to keep track of, and just letting the others fall away silently. Each time we find the local name of an element we want, we add the enumerated value to the collection, `colContext`. The collection object has been very simply wrapped in its own class, `valCollect`.

The valCollect Class

Here is this class in its entirety:

```
Dim valCol As Collection

Public Sub Collect(ByVal var As Variant)
  valCol.Add var
End Sub

Public Function Delete() As Variant
  Delete = Peek()
  If valCol.Count > 1 Then
    valCol.Remove valCol.Count
  End If
End Function

Public Function Peek() As Variant
  Peek = valCol.Item(valCol.Count)
End Function

Public Sub Clear()
  Set valCol = Nothing
  Set valCol = New Collection
End Sub

Private Sub class_initialize()
  Set valCol = New Collection
End Sub
```

The `startElement` method of the `saxDeserialize` class calls the `Collect` method of this stack implementation, which adds the value of the variable to the top of the `valCol` collection. This value will then be available to the other methods of the `ContentHandler`.

We have tracked the root element <TickerTape> in order to prime the pump on the state machine. If we don't add an initial value, we won't be able to peek at the top-level value. That initial value is then protected within the Delete method in order to keep our calls to Peek valid.

The Character Handler

The real workhorse for this example is in the character handler. Because we are interested in the values of the elements we have flagged above, we need to know here if we are looking at meaningful characters or not. This is when we call to our state machine for its current value with the Peek method:

```
Private Sub IVBSAXContentHandler_characters(sText As String)

  Select Case colContext.Peek()
    Case statePrice
      curr_Price = sText
    Case statePrev
      curr_Prev = sText
    Case stateHigh
      curr_High = sText
    Case stateRate
      curr_Rating = sText
    End Select

End Sub
```

When we "peek" we get the value of the last member of the enumeration that was added to the collection. The enumerated value we set in the startElement method flags our current state as belonging to that element.

You can see how this "state machine" methodology is going to allow for a much more robust document handler. Imagine how messy our original logic would have become if we internally set a variable to handle every element. We wouldn't be able to perform our simple Select Case statements. Instead, we'd be forced to have an If... Then for every element we wanted to check.

Once we have identified character data from an element we are interested in, our global variables come into play, being assigned their current value in the character method:

```
    Case stateRate
      curr_Rating = sText
```

Setting our variables with only the content of elements we are interested in, neatly cuts out the whitespace associated with formatting a document. You can rid yourself of strings made up entirely of whitespace if you place the following in the characters method:

```
sWhiteSpace = " " & Chr(9) & Chr(10) & Chr(13)
Dim i As Integer

For i = 1 To Len(sChars)
  If (InStr(sWhiteSpace, Mid(sChars, i, 1)) = 0) Then
    WriteIt(sChars)
  End If
Next

Exit Sub

WriteIt(sChars)
textStream.Write sChars
'written here to a text stream, but do whatever with the content
```

Of course, you can add other logical structures to work only on certain elements, or to leave whitespace inside elements, or whatever you need to do in your implementation.

Having set the values for this run through the stock element, we can act on our data. We know we are done with this group of <Stock> values because we have come to the endElement method:

```
Private Sub IVBSAXContentHandler_endElement(sNamespaceURI As String, _
                                            sLocalName As String, _
                                            sQName As String)

  Select Case sLocalName
    Case "Stock" 'If stock has ended, it is safe to update the price
      quotes.addQuote curr_Symbol, curr_Price
      curr_Symbol = ""
      curr_Price = 0
    Case "History" 'if history has ended, update in db.
      quotes.updateHistory curr_Symbol, curr_Prev, curr_High, curr_Rating
      curr_Prev = 0
      curr_High = 0
      curr_Rating = ""
  End Select

  colContext.Delete

End Sub
```

Note that here we have two child elements we can act on. Because the history for a stock is stored separately in the database, we can go ahead and call the updateHistory method as soon as we have the history element completed. While in this application there is really very little between the end of the <History> element and the end of the <Stock> element, our interest is speed, so we write to the database as soon as we are able. When we do come to the end of the particular stock we are evaluating, we write it, and clean up our context variables.

> Don't leave out the delete call on the colContext class, as this refreshes our state machine for the next element.

Writing to the Database

To finish up with this application, we will write the values we have gathered to our database. We do this in the streamToDB class:

```
Option Explicit

Dim oCmnd As ADODB.Command
Dim oConn As ADODB.Connection

Private Sub class_initialize()

  Dim sConnectme As String
  Set oConn = New ADODB.Connection
  sConnectme = "Provider=SQLOLEDB;User ID=sa;Password=;" & _
               "Initial Catalog=Ticker;Data Source=(local)"
  oConn.ConnectionString = sConnectme
```

```
End Sub

Public Sub addQuote(ByVal sSymbol As String, ByVal cPrice As Currency)

    Set oCmnd = New ADODB.Command
    oConn.Open

    With oCmnd
        oCmnd.ActiveConnection = oConn
        'populate the command object's parameters collection
        .Parameters.Append .CreateParameter("@Symbol", adVarChar, _
                                            adParamInput, 8, sSymbol)
        .Parameters.Append .CreateParameter("@Price", adCurrency, _
                                adParamInput, , cPrice)
        'Run stored procedure on specified oConnection
        .CommandText = "addQuote"
        .CommandType = adCmdStoredProc
        .Execute
    End With

    oConn.Close

End Sub
```

We do something similar with the history along the way:

```
Public Sub updateHistory(ByVal sSymbol As String, ByVal cPrev As Currency, _
                    ByVal cHigh As Currency, ByVal sRating As String)

    Set oCmnd = New ADODB.Command
    oConn.Open

    With oCmnd
        .ActiveConnection = oConn
        'populate the command object's parameters collection
        .Parameters.Append .CreateParameter("@Symbol", adVarChar, _
                                        adParamInput, 8, sSymbol)
        .Parameters.Append .CreateParameter("@PrevClose", adCurrency, _
                                    adParamInput, , cPrev)
        .Parameters.Append .CreateParameter("@High52", adCurrency, _
                                    adParamInput, , cHigh)
        .Parameters.Append .CreateParameter("@Rating", adVarChar, _
                                    adParamInput, 20, sRating)
        'Run stored procedure on specified oConnection
        .CommandText = "updateHistory"
        .CommandType = adCmdStoredProc
        .Execute
    End With

    oConn.Close

End Sub
```

Then clean up:

```
Private Sub class_Terminate()
   Set oCmnd = Nothing
   Set oConn = Nothing
End Sub
```

The Result

When we query the database at any given point we can produce the following output:

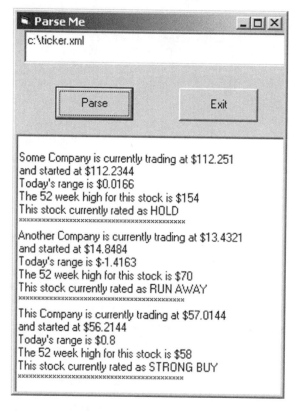

This example is helpful in giving an idea of what is required of a large SAX application. In order to handle the XML document as a series of parts, we have to build the packages of information that relate to one another. Each time we get a package together, we can do something with it. In this case, we have a number of variables that work together in a function call. As soon as we have all of the related items, we call a separate class that can use those values intelligently, writing them to the database in a particular stored procedure.

Summary

In this chapter, we've seen how SAX can be used to:

- ❑ Cut data down to size
- ❑ Reformat data on the fly
- ❑ Pick out values from a large stream of data

The recurrent theme with SAX is its efficient nature, as it does not require an entire document to be stored, but can run through the values, and let you decide what is important.

We should not look to SAX to solve every XML issue – the DOM still plays a major role. However, as you gain more experience with SAX, you will find it to be an effective tool in your toolbox. If you want to know more, try the following resources:

- ❑ Microsoft's XML SDK for the preview release of MSXML v3.0 contains a complete reference to the VB implementation of the SAX API interfaces and classes. Download it at http://msdn.microsoft.com/xml/general/msxmlprev.asp.

- ❑ Chapter 6 of *Professional XML, ISBN 1-861003-11-0*, and Chapter 7 of *Beginning XML, ISBN 1-861003-41-2*, both from Wrox, provide introductions to SAX.

- ❑ XML.COM – An excellent and in-depth site hosted by the O'Reilly publishing group. Thankfully it bears no strong marketing allegiance to its owner, and is packed with white-papers, reviews, and tutorials on everything XML.

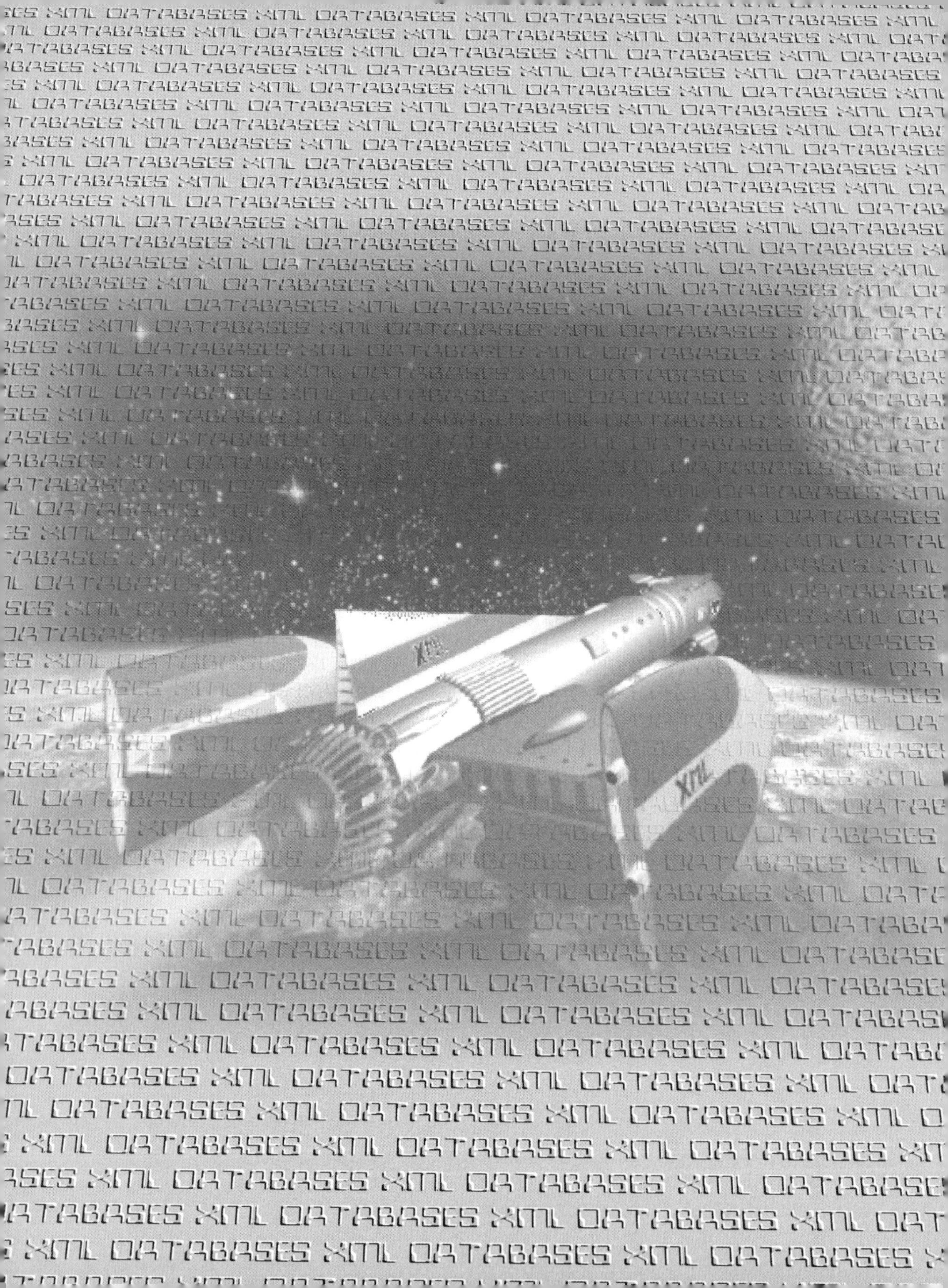
XML DATABASES XML DATABASES XML DATABASES
XML
XML

8

XSLT and XPath

This chapter is designed to give you enough information about XSLT, the XML transformation language, to enable you to write useful stylesheets; and about XPath, the query language used by XSLT stylesheets to access XML data.

We haven't got room here for a complete description of these languages or a detailed guide showing how to take advantage of them: for that see the Wrox Press book *XSLT Programmer's Reference*, written by Michael Kay (ISBN 1861003129). The aim is, instead, to cover enough to give a useful working knowledge.

In this chapter, we'll go through the following:

- ❑ We'll start with an overview of the XSLT language: what it's for, and how it works
- ❑ Then we'll take a detailed look at the XPath query language, which is used in XSLT stylesheets to access data in the source document
- ❑ Having done that, we'll look at the role of template rules and match patterns in an XSLT stylesheet, and review all the instructions you can use within a template
- ❑ Finally, we'll look at the top-level elements you can use in a stylesheet to define processing options

That's a lot of technical detail, so at the end we'll relax with some soccer; using XSLT to display soccer scores from an XML file.

What is XSLT?

XSLT is a high-level language for defining XML transformations. In general, a transformation takes one XML document as input, and produces another XML (or indeed, HTML, WML, plain text, etc.) document as output.

In this sense it's a bit like SQL, which transforms source tables into result tables, and it uses similar declarative queries to express the processing required. The obvious difference is that the data (both the input and the output) is arranged as a hierarchy or tree, rather than as tables.

XML transformations have many possible roles in the architecture of a system. For example:

❏ The most familiar application of XSLT is to format information for display. Here, the transformation is from "pure data" (whatever that means) to data with formatting information: usually the target will be HTML or XHTML, though it might be other formats such as SVG, PDF, or Microsoft's RTF. Of course these aren't all XML-based formats, but that doesn't matter, because as we'll see they can be modeled as XML trees, and that's all that is needed.

❏ XSLT is also very useful when managing data interchange between different computer systems. This might be as part of an eCommerce exchange with customers or suppliers, or simply application integration within the enterprise. The increasing use of XML doesn't mean that data conversion will be outdated. What it does mean is that in future, data conversions will often be translating one XML message format into another XML message format.

❏ XSLT can perform some of the roles traditionally carried out by report writers and 4GLs. As well as pure formatting, this can include tasks such as information selection, aggregation, and exception highlighting. For example, if your web-shopping site generates a transaction log in XML format, it is quite possible to use XSLT to produce a report highlighting which areas of the site were most profitable and which category of customers visited that area.

A program written in XSLT is referred to as a stylesheet. This reflects the original role of the language as a way of defining rules for presenting XML on screen. XSLT grew out of a bigger project called XSL (eXtensible Stylesheet Language), which aimed to provide this support, not only for on-screen display but for every kind of output device including high-quality print publication. XSLT was separated out into a sub-project of its own, because it was recognized that transformation of the input was an essential part of the rendering process, and that the language for transformation was usable in many other contexts. The other part of XSL, which handles the formatting specifications, is currently still under development.

XSLT transformations can be carried out on the server or on the client. They can be done just before the user sees the data, or early on while it is being authored. They can be applied to tiny XML files a few bytes long, or to large datasets. There are no rights and wrongs here: like SQL, the XSLT language is a versatile tool that can be applied in many different ways.

XSLT processors are available from a number of vendors, and in this chapter, we'll stick to describing the language, as defined by W3C, rather than any specific product. There are open source products available (Saxon and Xalan are popular choices), as well as closed source free products from Microsoft and Oracle, and some development tools available commercially. Many of these are written in Java, so they will run on any platform, but processors are also available written in C++ and Python. Here are some pointers to the web sites:

❑   Microsoft (MSXML3): http://msdn.microsoft.com/xml

❑   Oracle (Oracle XML parser): http://technet.oracle.com/

❑   Saxon: http://users.iclway.co.uk/mhkay/saxon/

❑   Xalan: http://xml.apache.org/xalan/overview.html

A good place to look for information about XSLT, including pointers to other products available, is http://www.xslinfo.com/.

One word of warning: when Microsoft shipped Internet Explorer 5, back in 1998, they included a processor that handled a language based on an early draft of XSLT, with many omissions and Microsoft extensions. Microsoft refers to this language as XSL, but it is a distant cousin of XSLT as eventually standardized by W3C. The language is now dated, and Microsoft themselves have a conformant XSLT processor, but millions of copies have shipped and are still being shipped with every copy of IE5 and IE5.5, so it won't go away in a hurry. This chapter is about XSLT, not about Microsoft's 1998 XSL dialect: don't get confused between the two.

Many readers will probably find it simplest to start with the Microsoft XSLT processor (MSXML3). At the time of writing, this is available for download from the MSDN web site, but it is expected to become part of Internet Explorer 6 in due course. In the meantime, do read the installation instructions very carefully, because it is easy to find yourself trying to run XSLT stylesheets through the old 1998 XSL processor, and wondering why nothing happens. Note that MSXML3 also includes a conversion utility for old stylesheets: it's only 90% of the job, but that's still easier than doing it all yourself.

The Transformation Process

We described XSLT as a way of transforming one XML document into another, but that's a simplification. The diagram below illustrates what is really going on:

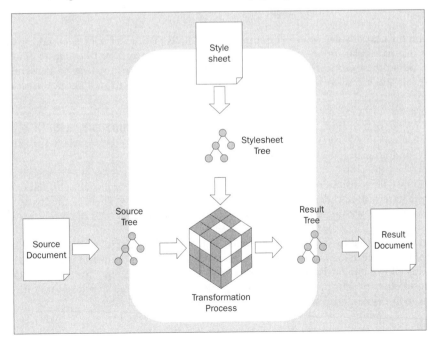

There are three separate stages of processing here:

❑ An XML Parser takes the source XML document and turns it into a tree representation

❑ The XSLT Processor, following the rules expressed in a stylesheet, transforms this tree into another tree

❑ A Serializer takes the result tree and turns it into a XML document

Very often these three bits of software will be bundled together into a single product, so the joins may not be obvious, but it's useful to understand these three stages because it affects what a transformation can and can't do.

On the input side, this means the stylesheet isn't in control of the XML parsing process, and it can't do processing based on distinctions that are present in the source document but not in the tree produced by the parser. For example, you can't write logic in the stylesheet that depends on whether an attribute in the XML was written in single quotes or double quotes. Perhaps less obviously, and on occasions more frustratingly:

❑ You can't tell what order the attributes in a start tag were written in.

❑ You can't discover if the source document contained entities or character references: these will all have been expanded by the time the XSLT processor sees them. Whether the user originally wrote © or © makes no difference; by the time the XSLT processor sees it, the distinction has disappeared.

❑ You can't tell whether the user wrote an empty element as <a></a> or as <a/>.

In all these cases the distinctions are simply different ways of expressing the same information, so you shouldn't need to know which way the input was written. The only frustration is that if you want the output to be physically the same as the input, there is no way of achieving this, which can be irritating if the output XML is to be further edited.

Equally, on the output side, you can't control these details. You can't tell the serializer to write the attributes in a particular order, or to use © in preference to ©, or to generate empty elements as <a></a> rather than <a/>. These constructs are supposed to be equivalent, so you aren't supposed to care. XSLT is about transforming the information held in documents, not about transforming their lexical representation.

Actually, on the output side, the designers of the language were a little pragmatic, and provided a few language features that let you give hints to the serializer. However, they made it very clear that these are hints only, and no processor is obliged to take notice of them.

The fact that stylesheets are reading and writing trees has another important consequence: you read and write elements as a unit, rather than processing each tag separately. There is simply no way of writing a start tag without a matching end tag, because writing an element node to the tree is an atomic operation.

The tree structure used by XSLT is very similar to the DOM model (described in Chapter 6) but it has some important differences, which we'll see later. Many products do in fact use a DOM representation, because this allows standard parsers and serializers to be used, but there are inefficiencies in this approach, so other products have chosen to represent the XSLT tree structure more directly. It's important to understand this structure so we'll describe it in detail later.

XSLT as a Programming Language

You can teach a simple subset of XSLT to HTML authors with no programming knowledge, by pretending that it's just a way of writing the HTML you want to generate with some simple extra tags to insert variable data from an input file. But XSLT is actually much more powerful than this, and as this book is written for programming professionals, it makes more sense to treat XSLT as a programming language and to compare and contrast it with other languages you may have used in the past. In this section, we'll draw out a few of its more striking features.

XML Syntax

Firstly, an XSLT stylesheet is an XML document. Instead of the braces and semicolons of most programming languages, it uses the angle brackets and tags of XML. Therefore, you can write things like this:

```
<xsl:if test="title='Introduction'">
    <b>SUMMARY</b>
</xsl:if>
```

In a conventional language, you might write something like this:

```
if (title='Introduction')
{
    write('<b>Introduction</b>');
}
```

There are a number of reasons for this. One is that you can write the output XML that you want to generate as part of the stylesheet, as with the SUMMARY in the example above. In fact, some stylesheets consist mainly of fixed output text with a few XSLT instructions mixed in. Another reason is that you can easily write stylesheets that transform other stylesheets, which sounds like a strange thing to do but can actually be extremely useful. Pragmatically, it also means that stylesheets are very consistent with XML in things such as handling of character encodings, name syntax, white space, and the like.

The downside is that it's verbose! Typing out hundreds of angle brackets is no-one's idea of fun. Some people like to use specialized editors to make the job easier; but when it comes down to it, typing effort has very little to do with the true ease of use of a language.

Rule-based

There's a strong tradition in text processing languages, like Perl and awk, of expressing the processing you want to do as a set of rules: when the input matches a particular pattern, the rule defines the processing to be performed. XSLT follows this tradition, but extends it to the processing of a hierarchy rather than a sequential text file.

In XSLT the rules are called template rules, and are written in the form of <xsl:template> elements in the stylesheet. Each rule has a match pattern that defines what kind of nodes in the tree it applies to, and a template body that defines what to do when the rule is fired. The template body can consist of a mixture of result nodes to be copied directly to the output tree, and XSLT instructions that can do things such as reading data from the current position in the source tree, or writing calculated results to the output tree. So a simple template rule might say:

```
<xsl:template match="price">
   <b>$<xsl:value-of select="format-number(., '#0.00')" /></b>
</xsl:template>
```

The pattern here is "price", which matches any <price> element; the action is to output the value of the <price> element, formatted as a number with two decimal digits, preceded by a $ sign and enclosed in a <b> element.

One particularly important XSLT instruction is <xsl:apply-templates>, which tells the processor where to go next; whereas in a text processing language, each line can be processed in sequence, with a hierarchy it is possible to process nodes in any order. Normally, however, the template rule for an element will contain an <xsl:apply-templates> instruction to process its children. When it does this, each of the children will be processed by finding the template rule in the stylesheet that matches that node.

Here is an example of a collection of template rules that process <item> elements within <record> elements. The rule for <record> elements outputs a <tr> element, and within it outputs the results of finding and applying the appropriate rule for each of its child elements. There are two template rules for <item> elements depending on whether the element has any text content or not. If it has, it outputs a <td> element containing the string value of the element; otherwise, it outputs a <td> element containing a non-breaking space character (which is familiar to HTML authors as the value of the   entity reference, but is written here as a numeric Unicode character reference).

```
<xsl:template match="record">
   <tr><xsl:apply-templates /></tr>
</xsl:template>

<xsl:template match="item[.!='']">
   <td><xsl:value-of select="." /></td>
</xsl:template>

<xsl:template match="item[.='']">
   <td> </td>
</xsl:template>
```

XPath Queries

When you write an XSLT stylesheet you are actually using two different languages. You use XSLT itself to describe the logic of the transformation process, and within it, you use embedded XPath expressions or queries to fetch the data you need from the source document. It's comparable to using Visual Basic with SQL.

Although its role is similar, the syntax of XPath is not at all like SQL. This is because it's designed to process hierarchic data (trees) rather than tables. A lot of the syntax in SQL is there to handle relationships or joins between different tables. In a hierarchic XML document or tree, most of the relationships are implicit in the hierarchy, so the syntax of XPath has been designed to make it easy to reference data by its position in the hierarchy. In fact, the most obvious resemblance is the way filenames are written to access files in a hierarchic filestore.

It's easiest to show this by some example XPath expressions:

Expression	Meaning
/invoice/billing-address/postcode	Starting at the root of the document, get the invoice element, then within that the billing-address element, then within that the postcode element.
../@title	Starting at the current node, get the title attribute of this node's parent element.
/book/chapter[3]/section[2]/para[1]	Get the first \<para> element, that is a child of the second \<section> element, that is a child of the third \<chapter> element, which is itself, a child of the root of the tree.

Functional Programming

Most programming languages are sequential in nature: the program carries out a sequence of instructions, modified by testing conditions and looping. They can create variables to hold values, and later in their execution, they can access the variables to retrieve results that were calculated earlier.

At one level XSLT looks quite similar. It has constructs like \<xsl:if> to test conditions and \<xsl:for-each> to do looping, and you can write a sequence of instructions, and the stylesheet then looks very much like a conventional sequential program. However, below the surface, it's not like that at all. XSLT is carefully designed so that the instructions can be executed in any order. The innocuous \<xsl:for-each> instruction, for example, may look like a loop that processes a list of nodes, one at a time, in a particular order, but it's carefully designed so that the processing of each node doesn't depend at all on how the previous node was handled, which means it's actually possible to do them in any order or even in parallel.

To achieve this, the theory underlying XSLT is that of functional programming, more often found in rather academic languages such as Lisp and Scheme. The idea is that each piece of the output is defined as a function of a particular piece of the input. These functions are all independent of each other, so they can be done in any order: in theory at least this means that if only a small piece of the input changes, you can work out how to change the output without executing the whole stylesheet again from scratch. Another benefit of this approach is that it's much easier to stop a stylesheet being stuck in an infinite loop.

What this means in practice is that, although a stylesheet may look superficially like a sequential program, it has no working storage. As we'll see, XSLT does have variables, but they aren't like the variables in sequential programming languages, because they are effectively "write-once". You can't update variables, so you can't use them to accumulate a running total and read them later, or count how many times you've been round a loop, because that would only work if things were done in a particular order. For simple stylesheets you probably won't notice the difference, but for more complex transformations you'll find you need to get used to a rather different style of programming. It may be frustrating at first, but it's worth persevering, because once you have learnt to think in functional programming terms, you'll find that it's a very elegant and concise way of expressing solutions to transformation problems.

Data Types

Many of the different properties of different programming languages are determined by their type system. In XSLT, the type system is defined largely by the query language, XPath.

The characteristic data type of XPath is the node-set. Just as SQL queries return a set of table rows, XPath queries like those shown in the previous section return a set of nodes from the input tree. Even if a query returns only a single node, it is always treated as a node-set that just happens to have only one member. A node-set behaves like a mathematical set: there's no intrinsic order to the nodes in the set, and there can't be any duplicates (the same node can't appear more than once).

Many instructions that process node-sets actually handle the nodes in **document order**. This is, essentially, the order in which the nodes appeared in the original XML document. For example, an element appears in document order before its children, and its children appear before the next sibling of their parent element. Document order in some cases isn't fully defined, for example there is no guarantee what the order of the attributes for a particular element will be. The fact that there is a natural ordering to nodes doesn't prevent node-sets being unordered sets, any more than the natural ordering of numbers prevents {1,2,3,5,11} being a pure set.

XPath queries aren't the only data type that node-sets can return; they can also return character strings, numbers, or Boolean values. For example, you can ask for the name of a node (a character string), the number of children it has (a number), or whether it has any attributes (a Boolean):

❑ Character strings in XPath follow the same rules as character strings in XML. They can be of any length (from zero upwards), and the characters they may contain are the Unicode characters that you can use in an XML document.

❑ Numbers in XPath are in general floating point numbers: of course, this includes integers. Integers will usually behave the way you expect, with the possible exception of rounding errors; for example, percentages may not add up to exactly 100. The floating-point arithmetic follows the same rules as Java and JavaScript (specifically, the rules defined in IEEE 754). You don't need to understand these rules in detail, except to know that there is a special value NaN (not a number), which you will get when you try to convert a non-numeric character string (such as "Unknown") to a number. NaN behaves very much like Null in SQL. If you do almost any operation on NaN, the result is NaN. For example, totaling a set of values in which one is the character string "Unknown" will return a total of NaN.

❑ Booleans are just the two values true and false. XPath doesn't have three-valued logic as in SQL – absent values in the source data are represented not by a special Null value, but by an empty node-set. Like SQL Nulls, empty node-sets sometimes give counter-intuitive results, for example an empty node-set is not equal to itself.

An XSLT stylesheet can declare variables. These variables can hold the result of any XPath query, that is, a node-set, a string, a number, or a Boolean. A variable can also hold a temporary tree constructed by the stylesheet itself: for most purposes, this variable is equivalent to a node-set containing a single node, namely the root of this tree. These trees are referred to as **result tree fragments**.

As we mentioned earlier, XSLT variables are "write-once" variables; they are just names for values. Some people have suggested they should really be called constants, but that wouldn't be accurate, since variables can hold different values on different occasions. For example, within a template rule that is processing a <chapter> element, you might set a variable to hold the number of paragraphs in the chapter. The variable will have a different value for each chapter that you process, but for a given chapter, its value will not change during the course of processing.

Here are some examples of variables of each kind:

Variable Declaration	Explanation
`<xsl:variable name="x"` `select="//item" />`	The value is a node-set containing all the `<item>` elements in the source document
`<xsl:variable name="y"` `select="count(@*)" />`	The value is a number containing the number of attributes of the current node. «@*» is an XPath expression that selects all the attributes.
`<xsl:variable name="z"` `select="@type='T'" />`	The value is true if the current node has a type attribute whose value is 'T', false if it does not.

`<xsl:variable name="tree">`
`   <table>`
`   <tr>`
`   <td>`
`      <img src="button1.gif"/>`
`   </td>`
`   <td>`
`      <img src="button2.gif"/>`
`   </td>`
`   </tr>`
`   </table>`
`</xsl:variable>`
	The value is a tree (or result tree fragment) whose root contains the table structure as written.

Although values have different data types, the data types don't have to be declared in variable declarations. XSLT is therefore a dynamically typed language, like JavaScript.

In general, type conversions happen automatically when required, for example if you write `<xsl:value-of select="@name" />` then the node-set returned by the expression @name (it will contain zero or one attribute nodes) is converted automatically to a string. There are some situations where explicit conversions are useful, and these are provided by the XPath functions `boolean()`, `number()`, and `string()`, described later in this chapter.

The XPath Data Model

Understanding the XPath tree model is crucial to stylesheet programming.

The tree structure used in XSLT and XPath is similar in many ways to the DOM, but there are some important differences. For example, in the DOM, every node has a `nodeValue` property, while in XPath every node has a `string-value` property. But the `nodeValue` of an element node in the DOM is null, while in XSLT and XPath, the `string-value` property of an element is the concatenation of all its descendant text nodes.

The properties available for every type of node in an XSLT tree are the same. Each node has a name and a string-value. You can also ask for the node's children, its parent, its attributes, and its namespaces. Where the property is inapplicable (for example comments don't have names) you can still ask for the information, you'll just get an empty result.

There are seven types of node in an XSLT tree:

Node Type	Usage
Root	Represents the root of the tree, corresponding to the Document node in the DOM. This is not the same as the "document element" (the outermost element in the tree). In fact, an XSLT tree does not always represent a well-formed document, so the root may contain several element nodes as well as text nodes. In a well-formed document, the outermost element is represented by an element node, which will be a child of the root node. The root node's properties are as follows: ❏ Its name is an empty string ❏ Its string-value is the concatenation of all the text nodes in the document ❏ Its parent is always null ❏ Its children may be any collection of elements, text nodes, processing instructions, and comments ❏ It has no namespaces or attributes
Element	Each element node corresponds to an element in the source document: that is, either to a matching start tag and end tag, or to an empty element tag such as `<A/>`. An element node's properties are as follows: ❏ Its name is derived from the tag used in the source document, expanded using the namespace declarations in force for the element ❏ Its string-value is the concatenation of all the text between the start and end tags ❏ Its parent is either another element, or if it is the outermost element, it parent is the root node ❏ Its children may be any collection of elements, text nodes, processing instructions, and comments ❏ Its attributes are the attributes written in the element's start tag, plus any attributes given default values in the DTD, but excluding any `xmlns` attributes that serve as namespace declarations ❏ Its namespaces are all the namespace declarations in force for the element, whether they are defined on this element itself or on an outer element

Node Type	Usage
Attribute	There will be an attribute node for each attribute explicitly present in an element tag in the source document, or derived from a default value in the DTD. However, the `xmlns` attributes used as namespace declarations are not represented as attribute nodes in the tree. An attribute will always have a name, and its string-value will be the value given to the attribute in the source XML. An attribute node's properties are as follows: ❏ Its name is derived from the attribute name used in the source document, expanded using the namespace declarations in force for the containing element ❏ Its string-value is the attribute value ❏ Its parent is the containing element (even though the attribute is not considered to be a child of this parent) ❏ An attribute node has no children, attributes, or namespaces
Text	Text nodes are used to represent the textual (PCDATA) content of the document. Adjacent text nodes are always merged, so the tree can never contain two text nodes next to each other. It is possible, however, for two text nodes to be separated only by a comment. The properties of a text node are as follows: ❏ Its name is Null ❏ Its string-value is the text content, after expanding all character references, entity references, and CDATA sections ❏ Its parent is the containing element (or in the case of a result tree fragment, a text node can also be a child of the root node) ❏ A text node has no children, attributes, or namespaces Any entity references, character references, and CDATA sections occurring within the source XML document are expanded by the XML parser, and the XSLT tree contains no trace of them. All that is present on the tree is the string of characters that these constructs represent. Text nodes that consist only of whitespace can be treated specially: the XSLT stylesheet can indicate that such nodes should be removed from the tree. By default, however, whitespace that appears between elements in the source document, will be present as text nodes on the tree and may affect operations such as numbering of nodes.

Table continued on following page

Node Type	Usage
Processing Instruction	Processing instruction nodes on the tree represent processing instructions in the XML source document. Processing instructions in XML are written as `<?target data?>`, where the target is a simple name and the data is everything that follows. The properties of a processing-instruction node are: ❑ Its name is the target part of the source instruction ❑ Its string-value is the data part ❑ Its parent is the containing node, always either an element node or the root ❑ It has no children, attributes, or namespaces Note that the XML declaration at the start of a document, for example `<?xml version="1.0"?>`, looks like a processing instruction, but technically it isn't one, so it doesn't appear on the XPath tree.
Comment	Comment nodes on the tree represent comments in the source XML. The properties of a comment node are: ❑ Its name is Null ❑ Its string-value is the text of the comment ❑ Its parent is the containing node, always either an element node or the root ❑ It has no children, attributes, or namespaces
Namespace	Namespace declarations are increasingly used in XML processing, however you will very rarely need to make explicit reference to namespace nodes in the XPath tree, because the namespace URI that applies to a particular element or attribute is automatically incorporated in the name of that node. Namespace nodes are included in the model for completeness: for example, they allow you to find out about namespace declarations that are never referred to in an element or attribute name. An element has one namespace node for every namespace that is in scope for that element, whether it was declared on the element itself or on some containing element. The properties of a namespace node are: ❑ Its name is the namespace prefix ❑ Its string-value is the namespace URI ❑ Its parent is the containing element ❑ It has no children, attributes, or namespaces

Names and Namespaces

Namespaces play an important role in XPath and XSLT processing, so it's worth understanding how they work. Unlike the base XML standards and DOM, where namespaces were bolted on as an afterthought, they are integral to XPath and XSLT.

In the source XML, an element or attribute name is written with two components: the namespace prefix and the local name. Together these constitute the qualified name or QName. For example in the QName `fo:block`, the prefix is `fo` and the local name is `block`. If the name is written without a prefix, the prefix is taken as an empty string.

When a prefix is used, the XML document must contain a namespace declaration for that prefix. The namespace declaration defines a namespace URI corresponding to the prefix. For example, if the document contains a `<fo:block>` element, then either on that element, or on some containing element, it will contain a namespace declaration in the form `xmlns:fo="http://www.w3.org/XSL/"`. The value `"http://www.w3.org/XSL/"` is the namespace URI, and it is intended to uniquely distinguish `<block>` elements defined in one document type or schema from `<block>` elements defined in any other.

The namespace URI is derived by finding the appropriate namespace declaration for any prefix used in the QName. In comparing two names, it is the local name and the namespace URI that must match; the prefix is irrelevant. The combination of local name and namespace URI is known as the expanded name of the node. In the XPath tree model, the name of a node is its expanded name (namespace URI plus local name). Namespace prefixes will usually be retained intact, but the system is allowed to change them if it wants, so long as the namespace URIs are preserved.

Where a qualified name includes no namespace prefix, the XML rules for forming the expanded name are slightly different for element names and for attribute names. For elements, the namespace URI will be the default namespace URI, obtained by looking for a namespace declaration of the form «xmlns="..."». For attributes, the namespace URI will be the empty string. Consider the example shown below:

```
<template match="para" xmlns="http://www.w3.org/1999/XSL/Transform"/>
```

Here the expanded name of the element has local name `"template"` and namespace URI `"http://www.w3.org/1999/XSL/Transform"`. However, the expanded name of the attribute has local name `"match"` and a null namespace URI. The default namespace URI affects the element name, but not the attribute name.

XPath expressions frequently need to select nodes in the source document by name. The name as written in the XPath expression will also be a qualified name, which needs to be turned into an expanded name so that it can be compared with names in the source document. This is done using the namespace declarations in the stylesheet, specifically those that are in scope where the relevant XPath expression is written.

If a name in an XPath expression uses no namespace prefix, the expanded name is formed using the same rule as for attribute names: the namespace URI will be Null.

In the example above, which might be found in an XSLT stylesheet, "para" is the name of an element type that this template rule is designed to match. Because "para" is written without a namespace prefix, it will only match elements whose expanded name has a local name of "para", and a null namespace URI. The default namespace URI does not affect the name written within the match pattern. If you wanted to match elements with a local name of "para" and a namespace URI of "urn:some-namespace" you would have to assign an explicit prefix to this namespace in the stylesheet, for example:

```
<template match="my:para"
    xmlns="http://www.w3.org/1999/XSL/Transform"
    xmlns:my="urn:some-namespace" />
```

XSLT uses many names to identify things other than XML elements and attributes; for example, it uses names for templates, variables, modes, keys, decimal formats, attribute sets, and system properties. All these names follow the same conventions as XML attribute names. They are written as qualified names; any namespace prefix they use must be declared in a namespace declaration; the equivalence of two names depends on the namespace URI, not the prefix; and if there is no prefix, the namespace URI is null (the default namespace declaration is not used).

Controlling namespace declarations in the output document can sometimes prove troublesome. In general, a namespace declaration will automatically be added to the output document whenever it is needed, because the output document uses a prefixed element or attribute name. Sometimes it may contain namespace declarations that are surplus to requirements. These don't usually cause a problem, although they might do so if you want the result document to be valid against a DTD. In such cases you can sometimes get rid of them by using the attribute exclude-result-prefixes on the <xsl:stylesheet> element.

In very rare cases, you may want to find out what namespace declarations are present in the source document (even if they aren't used). This is the only situation in which you need to explicitly find the namespace nodes in the tree, which you can do using an XPath query that follows the namespace axis.

XPath Expressions

To write an XSLT stylesheet you'll need to write XPath expressions. At the risk of finding you impatient to see a stylesheet in action, we'll talk about XPath expressions first, and then describe the way they are used by XSLT in a stylesheet. Although XPath was designed primarily for use within an XSLT context, it was separated into its own specification because it was seen as being useful in its own right, and in fact, it's increasingly common to see XPath being used as a freestanding query language independently of XSLT.

In this section, we will summarize the rules for writing XPath expressions. We can't hope to give the full syntax, let alone all the rules for how the expressions are evaluated, because of the limited scope of the book, but we'll try to cover all the common cases and also warn you of some of the pitfalls.

Context

The result of an XPath expression may depend on the context in which it is used. The main aspects of this context are the context node, the context size, and the context position. The context node is the node on the source tree for which the expression is being evaluated. The context position is the position of that node in the list of nodes currently being processed, and the context size is the number of nodes in that list. The context node can be accessed directly using the expression, "." (period), while the context position and context size are accessible using the functions position() and last().

Other aspects of the context of an XPath expression, obtained from the containing XSLT stylesheet, include the values of variables, the definitions of keys and decimal formats, the current node being processed by the stylesheet (usually the same as the context node, but different within an XPath predicate), the Base URI of the stylesheet, and the namespace declarations in force.

Primaries

The basic building blocks of an XPath expression are called primaries. There are five of them, listed in the table below:

Construct	Meaning	Examples
String literal	A string constant, written between single or double quotes (these must be different from the quotes used around the containing XML attribute).	`'London'` `"Paris"`

Number	A numeric constant, written in decimal notation. Although XPath numbers are floating point, you can't use scientific notation.	`12`
		`0.0001`
		`5000000`

Variable Reference	A reference to a variable defined elsewhere in the stylesheet. This is always written with a preceding $ sign.	`$x` `$my:variable-name`

Function call	A call on either a system-supplied function, or an extension function provided by the vendor or the user, together with its arguments if any. Each argument is an XPath expression in its own right.	`position()`
		
		`contains($x, ';')`
		`ms:extension('Bill', 'Gates')`

Parenthesized expression	An XPath expression contained in parentheses. Brackets may be used to control operator precedence as in other languages	`3 * ($x + 1)` `(//item)[1]`

Operators

Many of the operators used in XPath will be familiar, but some are more unusual. The table below lists the operators in order of precedence: those that come first in the table are evaluated before those that come lower down.

Operator	Meaning
A [B]	A filter expression. The first operand (A) must be a node-set. The second operand (B), known as the predicate, is an expression that is evaluated once for each node in the node-set, with that node as the context node. The result of the expression is a node-set containing those nodes from A where the predicate succeeds. If the predicate is a number, it succeeds if it equals the position of the node in the node-set, counting from one. So $para[1] selects the first node in the $para node-set. If it is not a number, then it succeeds if the value, after converting to a Boolean using the rules of the boolean() function, is true. So $para[@name] selects all nodes in the $para node-set that have a name attribute.
A / B A // B	A location path. Location paths are discussed in detail below. The first operand, A, defines a starting node or node-set; the second, B, describes a step or navigation route from the starting node to other nodes in the tree.
A | B	A union expression. Both operands must be node-sets. The result contains all nodes that are present in either A or B, with duplicates eliminated.
- A	Unary minus. The value of A is converted if necessary to a number (using the number() function) and the sign is changed.
A * B A div B A mod B	Multiply, divide, and modulus (remainder after division). Both arguments are converted to numbers using the number() function, and the result is a floating-point number. These operators are often useful in formatting tables: for example <xsl:if test="position() mod 2 = 1"> will be true for the odd-numbered rows in a table, and false for the others.
A + B A - B	Addition and subtraction. Both arguments are converted to numbers using the number() function. Because hyphens can be included in names, there must be a space or other punctuation before a minus sign.
A > B A >= B A < B A <= B	Tests whether one operand is numerically greater or smaller than the other one. When the XPath expression is written in a stylesheet, remember to use XML entities: < for <, > for >. Special rules apply when either or both operands are node-sets: see the section on Comparing Node-sets below. If the operands are strings or Booleans, they are converted to numbers using the rules of the number() function. If either operand cannot be converted to a number, the result will always be false.
A = B A != B	Tests whether the two operands are equal or not equal. Special rules apply when either or both operands are node-sets: see the section on Comparing Node-sets below. In other cases, if one operand is a Boolean, the other is converted to a Boolean; otherwise if one is a number, the other is converted to a number; otherwise they are compared as strings. Comparison of strings is case-sensitive: 'Paris' is not equal to 'PARIS'.
A and B	Boolean AND. Converts both arguments to Booleans, and returns true if both are true.
A or B	Boolean OR. Converts both arguments to Booleans, and returns true if either is true.

Comparing Node-sets

When you use the comparison operators =, !=, <, >, <=, or >=, then if either or both of the operands is a node-set, the comparison is made with every member of the node-set, and returns true if any of them succeeds. For example, the expression //@secure='yes' will return true if there is an attribute anywhere in the document with the name secure and the value "yes". Similarly, //@secure!='yes' will return true if there is an attribute anywhere in the document with the name secure and a value other than "yes".

If you compare two node-sets, then every possible pair of nodes is compared. For example, //author=//artist returns true if there is at least one <author> element in the document that has the same string-value as some <artist> element in the document. In relational terms, it returns true if the join of the two sets is not empty. (Depending how clever the processor is at optimizing, this could of course be a very expensive query to run on a large document).

This rule has consequences that may not be intuitive:

❑ Comparing anything with an empty node-set (even another empty node-set) always returns false, regardless of the comparison operators you use. The only exception is when you compare an empty node-set with the Boolean value false: this returns true.

❑ When either A or B is a node-set, testing A!=B doesn't give the same result as testing not(A=B). Usually you want the latter.

❑ The expression: .=/, doesn't test whether the context node is the root, it tests whether the string-value of the context node is the same as the string-value of the root node. This is likely to be true, for example, if the context node is the outermost element in the document. To compare nodes for identity, use the generate-id() function.

Location Paths

Location paths are the cornerstones of the XPath expression language, the construct that gave the language its name.

Because location paths are frequently used, the language provides many shorthand abbreviations for common cases. It's useful to know when you're using a shorthand form, so I'll present the full verbose syntax first, then show the abbreviations.

I'll start with some examples, and then describe the rules.

Example Location Paths

Some examples are given in the table below:

Location Path	Meaning
para	Select the <para> elements that are children of the context node. Short for ./child::para.
@title	Select the title attribute of the current node (if it has one). Short for ./attribute::title.

Table continued on following page

Location Path	Meaning
`../heading`	Select the `<heading>` elements that are children of the parent of the context node. Short for `./parent::node()/child::heading`.
`//item`	Select all the `<item>` elements in the document. Short for `/descendant-or-self::node()/item`.
`section[1]/clause[2]`	Select the second `<clause>` child element of the first `<section>` child element of the context node.
`heading [starts-with(title,'A')]`	Select all the `<heading>` child elements of the context node that have a `<title>` child element whose string-value starts with the character 'A'.

Syntax Rules for Location Paths

A full location path takes one of the following forms:

Format	Meaning
`/`	Selects the root node.
`/ step`	Selects nodes that can be reached from the root by taking the specified step. Steps are defined in the next section.
	For example, `/comment()` selects any top-level comment nodes, that is, comments that are not contained in any element.
`E / step`	Selects nodes that can be reached from nodes in `E` by taking the specified step. `E` can be any expression that returns a node-set; it can be another location path, for example (but not the root expression `/`), or a variable reference, or a call on a function such as `document()`, `id()`, or `key()`, or a union expression `(A|B)` in parentheses.
	For example, `../@title` selects the `title` attribute of the parent node.
`step`	Selects nodes that can be reached from the context node by taking the specified step. For example, `descendant::figure` selects all `<figure>` elements that are descendants of the context node.

Steps

In these constructs, a step defines a route through the tree representation of the source document. A step has three components:

❑ An axis, which defines the relationship of the required nodes to the starting nodes; for example, whether child nodes, following sibling nodes, or ancestor nodes are required. If no axis is specified explicitly, the child axis is assumed.

❑ A node test, which defines two things: the type of nodes that are to be selected, for example elements, text nodes, or comments, and the names of the nodes to be selected. It is also possible to select nodes regardless of their type. There are three kinds of name test: a full name test, which selects only nodes with that name; a namespace test, which selects all nodes in a particular namespace, and an any-name test, which selects nodes regardless of their name. The node-test is always present in some form.

❑ Zero or more predicates, expressions that further restrict the set of nodes selected by the step. If no predicates are specified, all nodes on the axis that satisfy the node test will be selected.

The full syntax for a step is:

```
axis-name «::» node-test ( «[» predicate «]» )*
```

We'll look separately at the axis-name, the node-test, and the predicates, and then describe the various ways in which the full syntax can be abbreviated.

Axis Names

XPath defines the following axes that you can use to navigate the tree structure.

Axis Name	Contents
ancestor	Contains the parent of the starting node, its grandparent, and so on up to the root
ancestor-or-self	Contains the node itself plus all its ancestors
attribute	For any node except an element, this axis is empty. For an element, it contains the attributes of the element, including any that were given default values in the DTD. Namespace declarations are not treated as attributes.
child	Contains the children of the starting node. The only nodes that have children are the root and element nodes; in all other cases, this axis is empty. The children of an element include all the nodes directly contained within the element: they don't include attributes or namespaces.
descendant	Contains the children of the starting node, their children, and so on, recursively.
descendant-or-self	Contains the starting node itself, plus all its descendants.
following	Contains all nodes in the document that follow the starting node in document order, other than its own descendants. In source XML terms, this means all nodes that begin after the end tag of the starting element.
following-sibling	Contains all the nodes that are children of the same parent as the starting node, and follow it in document order.
namespace	Contains nodes representing all the namespace declarations that are in scope for an element. Nodes other than elements have no namespace nodes.

Table continued on following page

Axis Name	Contents
parent	Contains the parent of the starting element. This axis is empty if the starting element is the root.
preceding	Contains all nodes in the document that precede the starting node in document order, other than its own ancestors. In source XML terms, this means all nodes that end before the start tag of the starting element.
preceding-sibling	Contains all nodes that are children of the same parent as the starting node, and that precede it in document order.
self	Contains the starting node itself.

Node-tests

The node-test within a step appears after the «::», and is used to select the type of nodes you are interested in, and to place restrictions on their names. It must be one of the following:

QName	A name optionally qualified with a namespace prefix, for example "para" or "fo:block". Selects nodes with this name that are of the principal node type for the axis. For the attribute axis, the principal nodes are attributes; for the namespace axis, they are namespace nodes; and in all other cases, they are elements.
prefix:*	Selects nodes of the principal node type for the axis, which belong to the namespace defined by the given prefix.
*	Selects all nodes of the principal node type for the axis.
node()	Selects all nodes, regardless of their name and type.
text()	Selects all text nodes.
comment()	Selects all comment nodes.
processing-instruction()	Selects all processing instruction nodes.
processing-instruction('name')	Selects all processing instructions with the given name. Note that the name must be in quotes.

Predicates

A step can optionally include a list of predicates, which define further conditions that the nodes must satisfy if they are to be selected. Each predicate is an XPath expression in its own right, written in square brackets. Each predicate acts as a filter on the node-set, the node-set is passed through each filter in turn, and only those nodes that satisfy all the predicates are selected.

For example the predicate [@title='Introduction'] selects a node only if it has a title attribute whose value is Introduction; the predicate [position() != 1] selects a node only if it is not the first node in the node-set passed through from any previous filter.

The predicate is evaluated for each node in turn. The context for evaluating the predicate is different from the context of the containing expression: specifically, the context node is the node being tested, the context size is the number of nodes left over from the previous filtering operation, and the context position is the position of the context node in this list of remaining nodes. So the predicate [position()=last()] will be true only if the node being tested is the last one in the list.

If the axis is a forward axis, then position() gives the position of each node within the node-set considered in document order; if it is a reverse axis, then the nodes are taken in reverse document order. The only reverse axes are ancestor, ancestor-or-self, preceding, and preceding-sibling.

A predicate can be either numeric or Boolean. If the value is a number N, this is interpreted as a shorthand for the expression position() = N. So following-sibling::*[1] selects the immediately following sibling element (because this is a forward axis) while preceding-sibling::*[1] selects the immediately preceding sibling element (this is a reverse axis, so [1] means the last element in document order).

The syntaxes for predicates within a step, and predicates within a filter expression are extremely similar, and the two can easily be confused. In the following examples, the predicate is part of a step:

```
item[1]
preceding-sibling::*[@type='D'][1]
```

In the following example, the predicate is part of a filter expression:

```
$item[1]
(preceding-sibling::*)[@type='D'][1]
```

The only real difference is that in a filter expression, the nodes are always considered in forward document order, while in a step, they are taken in axis order. This means that in the second example above, the last sibling having @type='D' is taken, whereas in the fourth example, the first sibling with this attribute is used. It only makes a difference if the predicate is numeric, or uses the position() function.

Abbreviations

We've already been using some shortcut notations for location paths, but it's time to describe them more formally.

- ❏ The symbol . (period) is an abbreviation for the step self::node(). It refers to the context node itself. You can't follow it with any predicates; if you want to test whether the context node is a <para> element, write <xsl:if test="self::para">.

- ❏ The symbol .. is short for the step parent::node(). The same considerations apply.

- ❏ The child axis is the default axis, so you can always omit child:: from a step. For example, /section/item is short for /child::section/child::item.

- ❏ The symbol @ can be used to indicate the attribute axis, it is short for attribute::. So @title means the same as attribute::title.

- ❏ The operator // is short for /descendant-or-self::node()/, and is a useful short-cut when searching for all the descendants of a node. For example //item retrieves all the <item> elements in the document. Take care when using positional predicates: //item[1] does not select the first <item> in the document (for that, use (//item)[1], but rather it selects every <item> element that is the first child of its parent element. This is because the predicate only applies to the final step in the expanded location path, which implicitly uses the child axis.

XPath Functions

We've used a number of XPath functions in examples: it's time now to give a complete list. Most of these functions are defined in the XPath specification itself. A few of them are added in the XSLT specification, which means that these functions are only available when you use XPath in the context of an XSLT stylesheet.

Vendors are allowed to add more functions of their own, or to provide mechanisms for users to implement their own functions, typically in an external language such as Java or JavaScript. These external functions will always use a namespace prefix to distinguish them from the built-in functions. For details of these extensions, see the vendor's documentation.

In the descriptions of the functions, I often say that a particular argument should be a string, or a number, or a Boolean. In nearly all cases this means that you can supply a value of any type, and it will be automatically converted to the type required: the conversion rules are those described under the functions `boolean()`, `number()`, and `string()`, which can be called directly if you want to make the conversion explicit.

Because of space limitations, these descriptions of the functions are very brief. If you want a full explanation of the behavior, or more examples of how to make use of each function, you'll find it in the Wrox Press book *XSLT Programmer's Reference*.

boolean(arg1)

The `boolean()` function converts its argument to a Boolean value.

The argument may be of any data type. The rules for conversion are as follows:

Argument Data Type	Conversion Rules
Boolean	No conversion
Number	0 is false, anything else is true
String	A zero length string is false, anything else is true
Node-set	An empty node-set is false, anything else is true
Tree	Always true

ceiling(arg1)

The argument arg1 is a number. The `ceiling()` function returns the smallest integer that is greater than or equal to the numeric value of arg1. For example, `ceiling(1.2)` returns 2.

concat(arg1, arg2, ...)

The `concat()` function takes two or more arguments. Each of the arguments is converted to a string, and the resulting strings are concatenated.

contains(arg1, arg2)

The `contains()` function tests whether arg1 contains arg2 as a substring (in which case true is returned, otherwise false). Both arguments are strings. Like all other string comparisons in XPath, this is case-sensitive: `contains('Paris', 'A')` is false.

count(arg1)

The count() function takes a node-set as its argument, and returns the number of nodes present in the node-set. The argument must be a node-set. (Avoid using count() to test if a node-set is empty: you can do this more efficiently by converting the node-set to a Boolean, either explicitly using the boolean() function, or implicitly by using the node-set in a context where a Boolean is expected, such as a predicate.)

current()

The current() function has no arguments, and it returns a node-set containing a single node, the current node. This is the node currently being processed by the most recent <xsl:for-each> or <xsl:apply-templates> instruction. Usually this will be the same as the context node, which is referenced simply as .: but within a predicate the two are generally different. This allows you to write, for example:

```
//item[@code=current()/@code]
```

to find all <item> elements with the same code as the current element.

This is an XSLT function: it can only be used in XPath expressions contained in an XSLT stylesheet.

document(arg1 [, arg2])

The document() function finds an external XML document by resolving a URI reference, and returns its root node.

In the most common usage, arg1 is a string and arg2 is omitted. For example document("lookup.xml") finds the file called lookup.xml in the same directory as the stylesheet, parses it, and returns a node-set containing a single node, the root of the resulting tree. When arg1 is a string, relative URIs are resolved relative to the location of the stylesheet. As a special case, document("") retrieves the stylesheet itself.

It is also possible for arg1 to be a node-set. For example document(@href) finds an external XML file using the URI contained in the href attribute of the context node. Because the URI is now obtained from the source document, any relative URI is resolved relative to the source document rather than the stylesheet. If the node-set supplied as an argument contains more than one node, the document() function will load all the referenced documents and return a node-set containing the root node of each one.

The second argument is optional, and is rarely used. It can be used to provide a base URI other than the source document or the stylesheet URI for resolving relative URIs contained in the first argument.

A document loaded using the document() function can be processed by the stylesheet in just the same way as the original source document.

document() is an XSLT function: it can only be used in XPath expressions contained in an XSLT stylesheet.

element-available(arg1)

This function is used to test whether a particular XSLT instruction or extension element is available for use. Vendors are allowed to provide proprietary extensions to the XSLT language, provided they use their own namespace. Some vendors also allow users to implement their own extensions. This function allows the stylesheet author to test whether a particular vendor extension is available before using it.

The argument is a string containing the name of an element, and the result is true if the processor recognizes this as the name of an XSLT instruction or extension element.

This is an XSLT function: it can only be used in XPath expressions contained in an XSLT stylesheet.

false()

This function returns the Boolean value false. There are no arguments. This function is needed because XPath provides no literal constant for the value false.

floor(arg1)

The argument arg1 is a number. The floor() function returns the largest integer that is less than or equal to the value of arg1. For example, floor(3.6) is 3.

format-number(arg1, arg2 [, arg3])

The format-number() function is used to convert numbers into formatted strings, usually for display to a human user, but also to meet the formatting requirements of legacy data standards, such as a need for a fixed number of leading zeroes. The format of the result is controlled using the <xsl:decimal-format> element. The first argument arg1 is the number to be converted. The second argument is a string containing format pattern that indicates the required output format.

The third argument arg3 is optional, and if present it is a string containing the name of an <xsl:decimal-format> element in the stylesheet which defines the formatting rules. A summary of <xsl:decimal-format> is given on later in the section on top-level elements, but the details are outside the scope of this chapter. It allows you, for example, to change the characters that are used to represent a decimal point and the thousands separator. If arg3 is omitted, the system looks for an unnamed <xsl:decimal-format> element in the stylesheet, or uses a built-in default otherwise.

The most commonly used characters in the format pattern are:

Character	Meaning
0	Always include a digit at this position, even if it isn't significant
#	Include a digit at this position if it is significant
. (period)	Marks the position of the decimal point
, (comma)	Marks the position of a thousands separator
%	Show the number as a percentage

For example, the following table shows how the number 1234.56 will be displayed using some different format patterns.

Format Pattern	Output
#	1235
#.#	1234.6
#.#####	1234.56
#,###.000	1,234.560
0,000,000.###	0,001,234.56

`format-number()` is an XSLT function: it can only be used in XPath expressions contained in an XSLT stylesheet

function-available(arg1)

This function is used to test whether a particular function is available for use. Vendors are allowed to add their own functions to those defined in the standard, provided they use their own namespace, and many vendors also allow users to define extension functions of their own. `function-available()` can be used to test the availability both of standard system functions and of extension functions. The argument is a string containing the function name. For an extension function this will always have a namespace prefix.

The result is the Boolean value true if the named function is available to be called, or false otherwise.

This is an XSLT function: it can only be used in XPath expressions contained in an XSLT stylesheet.

generate-id([arg1])

The `generate-id()` function generates a string, in the form of an XML name, that uniquely identifies a node. The argument is optional; if supplied, it must be a node-set. The `id` returned is that of the node that comes first in the node-set, in document order. If the node-set is empty, `generate-id()` returns the empty string. If the argument is omitted, the context node is assumed.

Each XSLT processor will have its own way of generating unique identifiers for nodes. Different processors will return different answers. If you call the function twice for the same node during a particular transformation, you will get the same answer, but the next time you run the same stylesheet the answers may be different. The result is a made-up identifier; it bears no relationship to any ID values that might be present in the source document. The only constraints on the value are that the identifier must be syntactically a valid XML Name, and that it must be different for every node: this allows it to be used as the value of an ID attribute in the output document. This can be useful if you are generating an HTML document and want to generate internal cross references of the form `<a href="#n1234">`.

Testing `generate-id($A) = generate-id($B)` is a good way of testing whether $A and $B are the same node, assuming both node-sets contain singleton nodes. Don't use $A=$B to do this: that compares the string-values of the nodes, which might be the same even if $A and $B are different nodes.

`generate-id()` is an XSLT function: it can only be used in XPath expressions contained in an XSLT stylesheet.

id(arg1)

The `id()` function returns a node-set containing the node or nodes from the source document that have a given ID attribute. This relies on there being a DTD that identifies particular attributes as being of type ID. If the document contains such attributes, they must be unique (assuming the document is valid).

The argument may be a string, in which case it is treated as a whitespace-separated list of ID values. Alternatively, it may be a node-set, in which case the string-value of each node in the node-set is considered as a whitespace-separated list of ID values. All these ID values are assembled, and the result of the function is the set of elements having ID values that are present in this list. Of course, the most common case is that arg1 is a single ID value, and the result will then contain exactly one node, if the ID value is present in the document or none if it is absent.

key(arg1, arg2)

The key() function is used to find the nodes with a given value for a named key. The first argument is a string containing the name of a key: this must match the name of an <xsl:key> element in the stylesheet, as described in the later section on top-level elements. The second argument supplies the key value or values you are looking for. It may be a string, containing a single key value, or a node-set, containing a set of key values, one in each node. The result of the function is a node-set containing all the nodes in the source document that have a key which is present in this list.

This is an XSLT function: it can only be used in XPath expressions contained in an XSLT stylesheet.

lang(arg1)

The lang() function tests whether the language of the context node, as defined by the xml:lang attribute, corresponds to the language supplied as an argument. xml:lang is one of the few attributes whose meaning is defined in the XML specification itself.

The argument is a string that identifies the required language, for example "en" for English, "de" for German, or "cy" for Welsh. The result is true if the context node is in a section of the source document that has an xml:lang attribute identifying the text as being in this language, and is false otherwise. The actual rules for testing the language code are quite complex (to cater for complexities such as US English versus British English) and are outside the scope of this chapter: you will find them in the Wrox Press book *XSLT Programmer's Reference*.

last()

The last() function returns the value of the context size. When processing a list of nodes, if the nodes are numbered from one, last() gives the number assigned to the last node in the list.

The test position()=last() is often used to test whether the context node is the last one in the list.

local-name([arg1])

The local-name() function returns the local part of the name of a node, that is, the part of the QName after the colon if there is one, or the full QName otherwise. For example, if the element name was written as <para> the local name will be para; if it was written as <fo:block> it will be "block". If the argument is omitted, the function returns the local name of the context node. If the argument is supplied, it must be a node-set, and the result is the local name of the first node in this node-set, taking them in document order. If the node-set is empty, the result is an empty string.

name([arg1])

The name() function returns a string containing the qualified name of a node, that is, the name as written in the XML source document, including any namespace prefix. If the argument is omitted, the function returns the name of the context node; if the argument is supplied, it must be a node-set, and the result is the name of the first node in this node-set, taking them in document order. If the node-set is empty, the result is an empty string.

The name() function is useful to display the name of a node. Try to avoid using it in a context such as [name()='my:element'] to test the name of a node, because this won't work if a different namespace prefix has been used. Instead, test [self::my:element], which actually tests the namespace URI corresponding to the prefix "my", rather than the prefix itself.

namespace-uri([arg1])

The `namespace-uri()` function returns a string that represents the URI of the namespace in the expanded name of a node. This will be a URI used in a namespace declaration, that is, the value of an `xmlns` or `xmlns:*` attribute.

If the argument is omitted, the function returns the namespace URI of the context node; if the argument is supplied, it must be a node-set, and the result is the namespace URI of the first node in this node-set, taking them in document order. If the node-set is empty, the result is an empty string.

normalize-space([arg1])

The argument `arg1` is a string; if it omitted, the string-value of the context node is used. The `normalize-space()` function removes leading and trailing whitespace from the argument, and replaces internal sequences of whitespace with a single space character. The result is a string.

not(arg1)

The argument `arg1` is a Boolean. If the argument is true, the `not()` function returns false, and vice versa.

number([arg1])

The `number()` function converts its argument to a number. If the argument is omitted, it converts the string-value of the context node to a number.

The conversion rules are as follows:

Source Data Type	Conversion Rules
Boolean	False converts to zero, true to one.
String	The string is parsed as a decimal number. Leading and trailing whitespace is allowed, as is a leading minus (or plus) sign. If the string cannot be parsed as a number, the result is NaN (Not a Number). The rules for converting a string to a number are essentially the same as the rules for writing a number in an XPath expression: conversion will fail, for example, if the number uses scientific notation or contains a leading "$" sign.
Node-set	Takes the string-value of the first node in the node-set, in document order, and converts this to a string using the rules for string-to-number conversion. If the node-set is empty, the result will be NaN.
Tree	Treats the tree as a node-set containing the root node of the tree, and converts this node-set to a number.

position()

The `position()` function returns the value of the context position. When processing a list of nodes, if the nodes are numbered from one, `position()` gives the number assigned to the current node in the list. There are no arguments.

round(arg1)

The argument `arg1` is a number. The `round()` function returns the closest integer to the numeric value of `arg1`. For example, `round(1.8)` returns 2 and `round(3.1)` returns 3. A value midway between two integers will be rounded up.

starts-with(arg1, arg2)

The `starts-with()` function tests whether the string `arg1` starts with another string `arg2`. Both arguments are strings, and the result is a Boolean. Like all other string comparisons in XPath, this is case-sensitive: `starts-with('Paris', 'p')` is false.

string([arg1])

The `string()` function converts its argument to a string value. If the argument is omitted, it returns the string-value of the context node. This depends on the type of node: see the table in the earlier section on The XPath Data Model for more details.

The conversion rules are as follows:

Source Data Type	Conversion Rules
Boolean	Returns the string "true" or "false".
Number	Returns a string representation of the number, to as many decimal places as are needed to capture its precision.
Node-set	If the node-set is empty, returns the empty string "". Otherwise, the function takes the first node in document order, and returns its string-value. Any other nodes in the node-set are ignored. The string-value of a node is defined for each type of node in the table under *The XPath Data Model* earlier in this chapter.
Tree	Returns the concatenation of all the text nodes in the tree.

string-length(arg1)

The argument `arg1` is a string. The `string-length()` function returns the number of characters in `arg1`.

substring(arg1, arg2 [, arg3])

The `substring()` function returns part of the string supplied as `arg1`, determined by character positions within the string.

`arg2` is a number giving the start position of the required sub-string. Character positions are counted from one. The supplied value is rounded, using the rules of the `round()` function. The function doesn't fail if the value is out of range, it will adjust the start position to either the beginning or end of the string.

`arg3` gives the number of characters to be included in the result string. The value is rounded in the same way as `arg2`. If `arg3` is omitted, you get all the characters up to the end of the string. If the value is outside the range, it is adjusted so you get either no characters, or all the characters up to the end of the string.

substring-after(arg1, arg2)

The arguments `arg1` and `arg2` are strings. The `substring-after()` function returns a string containing the characters from `arg1` that occur after the first occurrence of `arg2`. If `arg2` is not a substring of `arg1`, the function returns the empty string.

substring-before(arg1, arg2)

The arguments `arg1` and `arg2` are strings. The `substring-before()` function returns a string containing the characters from `arg1` that occur before the first occurrence of `arg2`. If `arg2` is not a substring of `arg1`, the function returns the empty string.

sum(arg1)

The argument, `arg1`, must be a node-set. The `sum()` function calculates the total of a set of numeric values contained in the nodes of this node-set. The function takes the string-value of each node in the node-set, converts this to a number using the rules of the `number()` function, and adds this value to the total. If any of the values cannot be converted to a number, the result of the `sum()` function will be NaN (Not a Number).

system-property(arg1)

The `system-property()` function returns information about the processing environment. The argument `arg1` is a string containing a QName; a qualified name that identifies the system property required. Three system properties are defined in the XSLT standard, but others may be provided by individual vendors. The three standard properties are:

`xsl:version`	The version of the XSLT specification implemented by this processor, for example 1.0 or 1.1.
`xsl:vendor`	Identifies the vendor of this XSLT processor
`xsl:vendor-url`	The URL of the vendor's web site

If you supply a property name that the processor doesn't recognize, the function returns an empty string.

This is an XSLT function: it can only be used in XPath expressions contained in an XSLT stylesheet.

translate(arg1, arg2, arg3)

The `translate()` function substitutes characters in a supplied string with nominated replacement characters. It can also be used to remove nominated characters from a string.

All three arguments are strings: `arg1` is the string to be translated. `arg2` gives a list of characters to be replaced, and `arg3` gives the replacement characters.

For each character in `arg1` the following processing is applied:

❑ If the character appears at position n in the list of characters in `arg2`, then if there is a character at position n in `arg3`, it is replaced with that character, otherwise it is removed from the string.

❑ If the character doesn't appear in `arg2`, then it is copied unchanged to the result string.

For example, `translate("ABC-123", "0123456789-", "9999999999")` returns `"ABC999"`, because the effect is to translate all digits to a `"9"`, remove all hyphens, and leave other characters unchanged.

true()

This function returns the Boolean true value. It takes no arguments. The function is needed because XPath provides no constant representing the value true.

unparsed-entity-uri(arg1)

The `unparsed-entity-uri()` function gives access to declarations of unparsed entities in the DTD of the source document. The argument is evaluated as a string containing the name of the unparsed entity required. The function returns a string containing the URI (the system identifier) of the unparsed entity with the given name, if there is one. Otherwise, an empty string.

This is an XSLT function: it can only be used in XPath expressions contained in an XSLT stylesheet.

Stylesheets, Templates, and Patterns

We've now finished our tour of XPath expressions. Let's return now to XSLT and look at the structure of a stylesheet and the templates it defines. We'll be using examples of XPath expressions throughout this section.

The <xsl:stylesheet> Element

A stylesheet is usually an XML document in its own right, and its outermost element will be an `<xsl:stylesheet>` element (you can also use `<xsl:transform>` as a synonym). The `<xsl:stylesheet>` element will usually look something like this:

```
<xsl:stylesheet
    xmlns:xsl="http://www.w3.org/1999/XSL/Transform"
    version="1.0">
</xsl:stylesheet>
```

The namespace URI must be exactly as written, or the processor won't recognize it as an XSLT stylesheet. You can use a different prefix if you like (some people prefer to use "xslt") but you must then use it consistently. The version attribute is mandatory, and indicates that this stylesheet is using facilities only from XSLT version 1.0.

If you see a stylesheet that uses the namespace `http://www.w3.org/TR/WD-xsl`, then it is not an XSLT stylesheet, but one that uses the old Microsoft dialect of the language shipped with IE5 and IE5.5. There are so many differences between these dialects that they are best regarded as separate languages: in this chapter, we are only describing XSLT. As part of the Microsoft XSLT processor, MSXML3 (currently available at http://msdn.Microsoft.com/xml), there is a tool to convert stylesheets from the old Microsoft dialect to XSLT.

The `<xsl:stylesheet>` element will often carry a number of other namespace declarations; for example, to define the namespaces for any extension functions you are using, or the namespaces of elements in your source document that you want to match. There are several other attributes you can have on this element:

Attribute Name	Usage
`id`	An identifying name for the stylesheet. Not used by XSLT itself.
`extension-element-prefixes`	A list of namespace prefixes (separated by whitespace) that are being used for vendor-defined or user-defined stylesheet instructions (so-called extension elements).
`exclude-result-prefixes`	A list of namespace prefixes (separated by whitespace) that are not to be included in the result document unless they are actually referenced.

In a typical stylesheet, most of the elements immediately within the `<xsl:stylesheet>` element (which are known, rather inaccurately, as top-level elements) are likely to be `<xsl:template>` elements. We'll discuss these now, and return to the other kinds of top-level element in a later section.

The `<xsl:template>` Element

Templates are the building blocks of an XSLT stylesheet, like the procedures and functions in a conventional program. When a template is triggered (or "instantiated", in the jargon of the standard), it generally causes things to be written to the result tree. The contents of a template in the stylesheet consist of two kinds of node: instructions and data. When the template is triggered, any instructions are executed, and any data nodes (referred to as literal result elements and text nodes) are copied directly to the output.

For example, when the following template is triggered, it writes a `<para>` element to the result tree, containing the text of the current node in the source document:

```
<xsl:template match="author">
    <para>By: <xsl:value-of select="."/></para>
</xsl:template>
```

This little template contains a literal result element (the `<para>` element), literal result text «By: », and an instruction (the `<xsl:value-of>` element).

There are two ways of triggering a template: it can be invoked explicitly, using the `<xsl:call-template>` instruction, or implicitly, using `<xsl:apply-templates>`.

The `<xsl:call-template>` instruction is very like a conventional subroutine call. It has a name attribute, which must match the name attribute of an `<xsl:template>` element somewhere in the stylesheet. When the instruction `<xsl:call-template name="table-of-contents"/>` is executed, the template declared as `<xsl:template name="table-of-contents">` springs into life.

The other mechanism, using `<xsl:apply-templates>`, is more subtle. This instruction has a select attribute whose value is an XPath expression that selects the set of nodes to be processed. The default is `select="child::node()"` which selects all the children of the current node. For each of these nodes, the system searches all the templates in the stylesheet to find one that best matches that node. This search is based on the match attribute of the `<xsl:template>` element, which defines a pattern that the node must match in order to qualify.

We'll look in a moment at the detail of how match patterns work. First let's look at a complete stylesheet that uses template rules to define its processing.

Our example will be a very simple kind of transformation: subsetting of a file of records to include only those that satisfy certain criteria. The input will be a product file such as:

```
<?xml version="1.0"?>
<products>
    <product code="Z123-888" category="tools">
        <description>Large claw hammer</description>
        <weight units="gms">850</weight>
        <price>12.99</price>
    </product>
    <product code="X853-122" category="books">
        <title>Plumbing for beginners</title>
        <ISBN>0-123-456-9876</ISBN>
        <price>10.95</price>
    </product>
    <product code="S14-8532" category="tools">
        <description>Adjustable spanner</description>
        <weight units="gms">330</weight>
        <price>5.25</price>
    </product>
</products>
```

The requirement is to produce another product file, with the same structure, but selecting only those products whose price exceeds ten dollars, and omitting the price from the output.

The following stylesheet achieves this:

```
<?xml version="1.0"?>
<xsl:stylesheet xmlns:xsl="http://www.w3.org/1999/XSL/Transform" version="1.0">
    <xsl:template match="*">
        <xsl:copy>
            <xsl:copy-of select="@*" />
            <xsl:apply-templates />
        </xsl:copy>
    </xsl:template>
    <xsl:template match="product[price &lt; 10.00]" />
    <xsl:template match="price" />
</xsl:stylesheet>
```

How does it work?

There are three template rules. The first one matches all elements (match="*"). This template rule uses the <xsl:copy> instruction to copy the element node from the source tree to the result tree. It also copies the attributes of the element using <xsl:copy-of>: the expression select="@*" selects all the attribute nodes of the current element. It then calls <xsl:apply-templates/> to process the children of the current element, each one using the appropriate rule for that element.

The next two template rules are empty: they match an input element and produce no output, thus effectively removing that element and its contents from the file. The first of these two matches <product> elements that have a child <price> element, whose value is less than 10.00; the second matches <price> elements. Because these two rules have match patterns that are more specific than the first template rule, they take priority over it when the relevant conditions are satisfied.

The other nodes in the tree (for example the root node and text nodes) are handled by the built-in template rules used when no explicit rule is provided. For the root, this built-in template rule just calls `<xsl:apply-templates />` to process the children of the root node. For a text node, it copies the text to the result tree.

The output of the stylesheet looks like this (whitespace added for clarity).

```xml
<?xml version="1.0" encoding="utf-8"?>
<products>
    <product code="Z123-888" category="tools">
        <description>Large claw hammer</description>
        <weight units="gms">850</weight>
    </product>
    <product code="X853-122" category="books">
        <title>Plumbing for beginners</title>
        <ISBN>0-123-456-9876</ISBN>
    </product>
</products>
```

If you want to try this example out for yourself, follow the steps below:

❑ Download the sample files for this book from http://www.wrox.com

❑ Download Instant Saxon from http://users.iclway.co.uk/mhkay/saxon/

❑ Extract the executable `saxon.exe` into a suitable directory, say `c:\saxon`

❑ Open an MS-DOS console

❑ Change directory to the folder containing the Wrox examples, and then run the processor, as follows:

```
cd path-of-wrox-download
c:\saxon\saxon.exe products.xml products.xsl
```

Of course, if you already have another XSLT processor installed, such as Xalan or Oracle XSL, you can equally well run the example with that, changing the command line as required.

Patterns

The patterns that you can write in the match attribute of `<xsl:template>` are very similar to XPath expressions. In fact, they are a subset of XPath expressions and every pattern is a valid XPath expression. The converse is not true however.

By far the most common kind of pattern is a simple element name, for example author in the example above. This will match all `<author>` elements (but remember to include a namespace prefix if the element has a namespace URI).

Instead of a name, you can use any node test. The different kinds of node test were listed in an earlier section. For example, you can write `text()` to match all text nodes, or `svg:*` to match all elements in the svg namespace.

You can also add one or more predicates after the name. The predicate can be any XPath expression so long as it doesn't use variables or the `current()` function (which would be meaningless). For example, you could write `section[@title='Introduction']` to match a `<section>` element having a title attribute with the value Introduction. Or you could use `para[1]` to match any `<para>` element that is the first `<para>` child of its parent element.

You can also qualify the pattern by specifying the names of parent or ancestor elements, using the same syntax as a location path in an XPath expression. For example, scene/title matches any <title> element whose parent is a <scene> element, and chap//note matches any <note> element provided it is a descendant of a <chap> element.

If you want to define a single template that matches several different patterns, you can use the union operator | to separate them. For example, the pattern scene | prologue | epilogue, matches <scene>, <prologue>, and <epilogue> elements.

The full rules for patterns are a bit more complex than this, but it's good practice to keep patterns reasonably simple, so the examples described here should be more than adequate for most stylesheets.

Selecting a Template Rule

When <xsl:apply-templates> is used to process a set of nodes, it won't necessarily happen that there's exactly one template rule that matches each node. There may be none, and there may be several.

It's possible to steer the process by using modes. If the <xsl:apply-templates> instruction has a mode attribute, the selected <xsl:template> element must have a matching mode attribute. If there's no mode attribute on the <xsl:apply-templates> element, it will only match <xsl:template> elements with no mode attribute. Modes are useful when there are several different ways of processing the same input nodes, for example you may want to process them one way while generating the body of the document, and another way when generating an index.

Here's an example that outputs all the sections in a chapter, preceded by a table of contents. The entries in the table of contents are hyperlinks to the relevant sections, with the identifiers for the links constructed using the XPath generate-id() function:

```
<xsl:template match="chapter">
    <h2>Table of Contents</h2>
    <xsl:apply-templates select="section" mode="toc"/>
    <xsl:apply-templates select="section" mode="body"/>
</xsl:template>
<xsl:template match="section" mode="toc">
    <p><a href="#{generate-id()}">
    <xsl:value-of select="title"/>
    </a></p>
</xsl:template>
<xsl:template match="section" mode="body">
    <h2><a name="{generate-id()}">
    <xsl:value-of select="title"/>
    </a></h2>
    <xsl:apply-templates select="para"/>
</xsl:template>
```

If there's no matching template rule for a node, a default rule is invoked. The default processing depends on the node type, as follows:

❑   For the root node and element nodes, it invokes <xsl:apply-templates /> to process the children of this node. This may find explicit rules for these children, or it may again invoke the default rule.

❑   For text nodes and attribute nodes, it copies the string-value of the node to the result tree.

❑   For other nodes, it does nothing.

If there's more than one rule, a priority scheme comes into play. This works as follows:

- ❏ The processor must first see if the matching rules have different import precedence, and if so, reject any that have lower precedence than others. This will only happen if one template is in a separate stylesheet imported using <xsl:import>, which we'll describe in the later section on top-level elements within templates.

- ❏ Then the processor must look at the priorities of the rules. You can set a priority explicitly on a rule by using its priority attribute, for example a rule with priority="2" will be chosen in preference to one with priority="1". If there's no explicit priority, the system allocates a default priority based on the syntax you use in the match pattern. This tries to ensure that highly selective patterns like section[@title='Introduction'] get a higher priority than catch-all patterns like node(), but it's a hit-and-miss process, and it's safer to allocate priorities explicitly.

- ❏ If, after all this, there are still several possible candidates, the specification says it's an error. However, it gives the processor a choice of what to do about this. A strict processor is allowed to report the error and terminate processing. A more lenient processor is allowed to choose whichever rule comes last in the stylesheet, and use that. Some processors actually adopt a middle course, of continuing after a warning message.

Parameters

Whether a template rule is called using <xsl:call-template> or <xsl:apply-templates>, it's possible to supply parameters with the call. The calling instruction uses <xsl:with-param> to set a value for a parameter; the called template uses <xsl:param> to receive the value. If the caller sets a parameter that the called template isn't expecting, it is simply ignored; if the caller fails to set a parameter that's expected, it will take a default value, which can be specified in the <xsl:param> element.

The <xsl:param> and <xsl:with-param> elements have identical syntax: a name attribute to give the name of the parameter, and a select attribute containing an XPath expression to give its value. (In the case of <xsl:param>, this is the default value.) They can also have content, to express the value as a tree, in the same way as <xsl:variable> which we'll describe later in this Chapter.

Here's an example of a template that copies a node and its descendants, down to a specified depth. The template calls itself recursively: this is very much part of the programming style when you want to do anything complex with XSLT. Each time the template calls itself, it reduces the depth by one, until it reaches zero and the template does nothing, and returns immediately.

```
<xsl:template match="/ | * | text()" mode="shallow-copy">
    <xsl:param name="depth"/>
    <xsl:if test="$depth &gt; 0">
        <xsl:copy>
            <!-- copy all the attributes -->
            <xsl:copy-of select="@*"/>
            <!-- process all the children -->
            <xsl:apply-templates mode="shallow-copy">
                <xsl:with-param name="depth" select="$depth - 1"/>
            </xsl:apply-templates>
        </xsl:copy>
    </xsl:if>
</xsl:template>
```

You can call this to copy the root node to a depth of three with a call such as:

```
<xsl:apply-templates select="/" mode="shallow-copy">
   <xsl:with-param name="depth" select="3"/>
</xsl:apply-templates>
```

The match pattern on the template uses a union pattern to specify that the template will match the root node /, any element *, or any text node text(). If comments or processing instructions are encountered, the built-in template kicks in, which for these types of node causes them to be ignored.

The Contents of a Template

The contents of an <xsl:template> element (after any <xsl:param> elements, which must come first) form a template body.

A template body consists of a sequence of element and text nodes. The stylesheet may also contain comments and processing instructions, but these are ignored completely, so we won't consider them. Any text nodes that consist entirely of whitespace will also have been removed.

The element nodes in a template body can be further categorized:

❏ Elements in the XSLT namespace are instructions. These are conventionally prefixed "xsl:" but you can use any prefix you like.

❏ Elements in a namespace designated as an extension element namespace are instructions. The meaning of these instructions is vendor-dependent.

❏ Any other elements are literal result elements. These are copied to the result tree.

Text nodes appearing within a template body are also copied to the result tree.

Extension elements are outside the scope of this chapter: see the vendor's documentation if you want to use them. In this section, we'll review the XSLT-defined instructions, and then look more closely at literal result elements.

We've introduced the template body as the contents of an <xsl:template> element, but in fact many other elements, such as <xsl:if> and <xsl:element>, have content that follows the same rules and is handled the same way as a template body contained directly in an <xsl:template> element. So, the term template body is used generally to describe the content of all these elements.

Attribute Value Templates

Some attributes in an XSLT stylesheet are designated as attribute value templates. Examples are the name attribute of the <xsl:attribute> and <xsl:element> instructions. In these attributes, instead of writing a fixed value, such as «name="description"», you can parameterize the value by writing XPath expressions within curly brackets, for example name="{$prefix}:{$localname}". When the instruction is executed, these XPath expressions will be evaluated, and the resulting attribute value will be substituted into the attribute value in place of the expression.

If the XML source document uses curly braces within the attribute value and you don't want it to trigger this mechanism, write it twice, for example value="{{not an AVT}}".

The most common mistake with attribute value templates is to assume you can use them anywhere. You can't; they are allowed in only a few specific places. These are indicated in the descriptions of each XSLT element below. Don't attempt, for example, to write `<xsl:call-template name="{$tname}" />`: it won't work.

One particular point is that you never use curly brackets **inside** an XPath expression, only to surround an XPath expression within an attribute that would otherwise be interpreted as a text value.

XSLT Instructions

XSLT instructions are a subset of XSLT elements: essentially, those that can be used directly as part of a template body.

The instructions defined in XSLT 1.0 are as follows:

```
<xsl:apply-imports>           <xsl:fallback>
<xsl:apply-templates>         <xsl:for-each>
<xsl:attribute>               <xsl:if>
<xsl:call-template>           <xsl:message>
<xsl:choose>                  <xsl:number>
<xsl:comment>                 <xsl:processing-instruction>
<xsl:copy>                    <xsl:text>
<xsl:copy-of>                 <xsl:value-of>
<xsl:element>                 <xsl:variable>
```

In the following sections, we'll look briefly at each one.

<xsl:apply-imports>

This is a very rarely used instruction. It has no attributes and is always empty. It is used while processing a particular node to invoke template rules from an imported stylesheet, overriding the normal rules for template selection based on import precedence.

<xsl:apply-templates>

We have already described this instruction earlier in the chapter. It causes a selected set of nodes to be processed, each one using the appropriate template rule based on match patterns and priorities.

The instruction takes two attributes, both optional. The `select` attribute is an XPath expression that defines the set of nodes to be processed: by default, the children of the current node are processed. The `mode` attribute gives the name of a processing mode: only those `<xsl:template>` elements with the same mode name are candidates for matching.

Within the invoked templates, any XPath expressions are evaluated with the context set by the `<xsl:apply-templates>` instruction. Specifically, the context node will be the node currently being processed, the context position (the result of the `position()` function) will be 1 for the first node processed, 2 for the second, and so on, and the context size (the result of the `last()` function) will be the total number of nodes to be processed.

The `<xsl:apply-templates>` instruction is often written as an empty element, but there are two other elements it may optionally contain: `<xsl:with-param>`, to define any parameters to be passed to the called template, and `<xsl:sort>`, which defines the sort order of the nodes to be processed. In the absence of `<xsl:sort>`, the nodes are processed in document order. `<xsl:sort>` is described later in the section titled *Sorting*.

<xsl:attribute>

The effect of `<xsl:attribute>` is to write an attribute node to the result tree. This is only possible if the last thing written was an element or another attribute. The `<xsl:attribute>` instruction has two attributes, `name` and `namespace`. The `name` attribute gives the name of the new attribute (this is mandatory), and the `namespace` attribute gives the namespace URI. If no `namespace` is specified, the namespace is taken from the prefix of the `name`, if this has one.

Both the `name` and `namespace` attributes are interpreted as Attribute Value Templates. The value of the new attribute is constructed from the content of the `<xsl:attribute>` element. This is another template body, but it should generate only text nodes. For example:

```
<xsl:attribute name="color">
    <xsl:value-of select="concat('#', $bgcolor)"/>
</xsl:attribute>
```

<xsl:call-template>

This instruction has already been discussed, in the earlier section on the `<xsl:template>` element. It takes a mandatory `name` attribute, which names the template to be called. There must be a template with this name in the stylesheet.

The only elements permitted in the content of `<xsl:call-template>` are `<xsl:with-param>` elements. These set the values of any parameters to be passed to the called template. The names used in the `<xsl:with-param>` elements should match the names used in the `<xsl:param>` elements of the called template.

<xsl:choose>

In a similar manner to If-else in Visual Basic, this instruction is used to perform conditional processing. The `<xsl:choose>` element itself has no attributes. It contains a sequence of one or more `<xsl:when>` elements, optionally followed by an `<xsl:otherwise>` element. Each `<xsl:when>` element specifies a condition, and the first one whose condition is satisfied is executed. If none of the conditions is satisfied, the `<xsl:otherwise>` element is used. For example:

```
<xsl:choose>
    <xsl:when test="lang('en')">Welcome</xsl:when>
    <xsl:when test="lang('de')">Willkommen</xsl:when>
    <xsl:when test="lang('fr')">Bienvenue</xsl:when>
    <xsl:otherwise>System error!</xsl:otherwise>
</xsl:choose>
```

The `test` attribute of `<xsl:when>` is an XPath expression, whose result is converted to a Boolean. The content of the `<xsl:when>` and `<xsl:otherwise>` elements need not be simple text as in this example, it can be any template body.

<xsl:comment>

This instruction is used to output a comment node to the result tree. It takes no attributes. The content of the `<xsl:comment>` element is a template body, but this should generate nothing other than text nodes. For example:

```
<xsl:comment>
    Generated with param1=<xsl:value-of select="$param1"/>
</xsl:comment>
```

<xsl:copy>

This instruction performs a shallow copy of the current node: that is, it copies the current node, but not its children. When the current node is a root or element node, the content of the `<xsl:copy>` instruction is taken as a template body, which is instantiated to create the content of the copied output node. When the current node is an attribute node, text node, comment, or processing instruction, the content of the `<xsl:copy>` element is ignored.

The `<xsl:copy>` instruction has an optional attribute `use-attribute-sets`. This is relevant only when copying an element. It has the same effect as the `use-attribute-sets` attribute of `<xsl:element>`, which is described later.

<xsl:copy-of>

This instruction performs a deep copy of all the nodes selected by the XPath expression in its `select` attribute. That is, it copies those nodes and all their descendants, as well as their attributes and namespaces, to the result tree.

If the result of evaluating the expression in the `select` attribute is a simple string, number, or Boolean, the `<xsl:copy-of>` instruction has the same effect as `<xsl:value-of>`: it converts the value to a string and writes it to the result tree as a text node. For example:

```
<xsl:copy-of select="@*" />
```

This copies all the attributes of the current node to the result tree.

The following instruction (which might be the only thing a stylesheet does) copies all the news items with a status of "current" to the result tree, together with all their content:

```
<xsl:copy-of select="/news/item[@status='current']" />
```

The `<xsl:copy-of>` instruction is always empty.

<xsl:element>

The `<xsl:element>` instruction writes an element node to the result tree. The content of the `<xsl:element>` instruction is a template body, which is instantiated to construct the content of the generated element.

The `<xsl:element>` instruction has attributes `name` and `namespace`. The `name` attribute gives the name of the new element (this is mandatory), and the `namespace` attribute gives the namespace URI. If no `namespace` is specified, it is taken from the prefix of the supplied element name, if this has one.

Both the `name` and `namespace` attributes are interpreted as Attribute Value Templates. The following example creates an `<html>` element using a namespace URI that is passed in as a parameter:

```
<xsl:element name="html" namespace="{$html-namespace}">
   <head>
      <title><xsl:value-of select="title"/></title>
   </head>
   <body>
      <xsl:call-template name="generate-body"/>
   </body>
</xsl:element>
```

The `<xsl:element>` instruction may also have an attribute `use-attribute-sets`. If present, this is a whitespace-separated list of names, each of which must be the name of an `<xsl:attribute-set>` element at the top level of the stylesheet. The effect is that the new element will be given all the attributes defined in these attribute sets.

<xsl:fallback>

This is a rarely encountered instruction. It is used within the content of a vendor extension element to define the processing that should take place if the extension element is not available. It can also be used if your stylesheet specifies `version="2.0"`, say, (because it uses features defined in XSLT version 2.0), to define what should happen if the stylesheet is run using an XSLT processor that does not support version 2.0 features.

<xsl:for-each>

The `<xsl:for-each>` instruction is used to define processing that should be carried out for each member of a node-set. The node-set to be processed is defined by an XPath expression in the `select` attribute, which is mandatory. The processing itself is defined by the template body contained within the `<xsl:for-each>` element.

The following example creates one attribute node in the result tree corresponding to each child element of the current node in the source tree:

```
<xsl:for-each select="*">
   <xsl:attribute name="{name()}">
      <xsl:value-of select="."/>
   </xsl:attribute>
</xsl:for-each>
```

The node-set is normally processed in document order. To process the nodes in a different order, include one or more `<xsl:sort>` elements immediately within the `<xsl:for-each>` instruction. For more details, see the section on *Sorting*.

The `<xsl:for-each>` instruction changes the current node: each node in the node-set becomes the current node in turn, for as long as the template body is active. Sometimes `<xsl:for-each>` is used solely for this purpose, to set the current node for an instruction such as `<xsl:number>` or `<xsl:copy>` that only works on the current node. For example:

```
<xsl:for-each select="..">
   <xsl:number/>
</xsl:for-each>
```

This outputs the sequence number of the parent node. There is no iteration here: there is only one parent node, so the template body is only instantiated once.

While the `<xsl:for-each>` instruction is active, any XPath expressions are evaluated with the context set by the `<xsl:for-each>`. Specifically, the context node will be the node currently being processed, the context position will be 1 for the first node processed, 2 for the second, and so on, and the context size will be the total number of nodes to be processed. A common error is to write:

```
<xsl:for-each select="item">
   <xsl:value-of select="item" />
</xsl:for-each>
```

This fails (or rather, it produces no output) because the XPath expression in the <xsl:value-of> instruction is evaluated with an <item> as its context node, and the expression item is short for child::item, but the context <item> has no <item> elements as its children. Use <xsl:value-of select="."/> instead.

The two instructions <xsl:apply-templates> and <xsl:for-each> are the only instructions that change the current node in the source tree. They represent two different styles of processing, sometimes called **push** and **pull** respectively. Push processing (using <xsl:apply-templates>) relies on pattern matching, and it works best when the structure of the input is highly variable, for example where <b> elements may be found in many different contexts. Pull processing (using <xsl:for-each>) works better where the structure of the source is very rigid and predictable. It's a good idea to become familiar with both.

<xsl:if>

The <xsl:if> instruction performs an action if a condition is true. There is no else branch: if you need one, use <xsl:choose> instead. <xsl:if> has a mandatory test attribute which defines the condition to be tested, as an XPath expression whose result is automatically converted to a Boolean. The <xsl:if> element contains a template body which is instantiated if and only if the condition is true.

This example outputs a message containing the word "errors" unless there was only one, when it uses the singular "error". It also uses an <xsl:choose> to :

```
There <xsl:choose><xsl:when test="count($errors)=1">was
</xsl:when><xsl:otherwise>were </xsl:otherwise></xsl:choose>
</ <xsl:value-of select="count($errors)" />
error<xsl:if test="count($errors)!=1">s</xsl:if>
```

<xsl:message>

The <xsl:message> instruction is used to output a message. The specification isn't very precise about what happens to the message; this depends on the implementation. The <xsl:message> element contains a template body which is instantiated to construct the message. This may contain any kind of XML markup, though text messages are likely to behave more predictably.

There is an optional attribute terminate="yes" which causes execution of the stylesheet to terminate at once. For example:

```
<xsl:if test="not(/invoice)">
   <xsl:message terminate="yes">
      This stylesheet is only designed to handle invoice documents
   </xsl:message>
</xsl:if>
```

<xsl:number>

The <xsl:number> instruction is designed to perform sequential numbering of nodes. It calculates a number for the current node based on its position in the source tree, formats this number as required, and writes the result to the output tree as a text node.

This is a complex instruction with many attributes to control how the number is calculated and formatted. A detailed treatment is beyond the scope of this chapter: you can find full information in the Wrox book *XSLT Programmers Reference*. (ISBN 1861003129)

When used with no attributes, for example `<xsl:number />`, the result is obtained by counting the number of preceding siblings of the current node that have the same node type and name, adding one for the node itself, and formatting the result using the same rules as the `string()` function. Therefore, if the current node is the fifth `<para>` element within a `<section>`, the output will be 5.

The way nodes are counted may be modified using a number of attributes:

Attribute	Meaning
level	The default value is "single", which counts preceding siblings of the current node. The value "any" counts preceding nodes anywhere in the document, which is useful for example to number figures or equations. The value "multiple" produces a multi-level number such as "10.1.3" or "17a(iv)".
count	This pattern defines which nodes are to be counted. For example count="*" causes all elements to be counted, not only those with the same name as the current node. For multi-level numbering, specify all the levels you want counted, for example count="chapter | section | clause".
from	This is a pattern which indicates where counting is to start. For example, count="p" from="h2" counts the number of `<p>` elements since the last `<h2>` element.

The formatting of the result may also be modified using a number of attributes. The main one is format, which defines a format pattern (this is an attribute value template, so it can be constructed dynamically if you want). The following examples show how the number 4 might be formatted with various format patterns:

Format Pattern	Output
1	4
(a)	(d)
-- i --	-- iv --

For multi-level numbering, you can use a format pattern such as "1.1(a)" to request an output sequence such as 1.1(a), 1.1(b), 1.1(c), 1.2(a), 1.2(b), 2.1(a).

The `<xsl:number>` instruction also has a value attribute. This can be used to supply the value directly, as a way of using the formatting capabilities of `<xsl:number>` without the node-counting features. It is often used in the form:

```
<xsl:number value="position()" format="(a)" />
```

The position() function gives the position of the current node in the sequence that the nodes are being processed, rather than its position in the source tree. This option is particularly useful when producing output in sorted order.

<xsl:processing-instruction>

This instruction is used to output a processing instruction node to the result tree. It takes a mandatory name attribute to define the name of the generated processing instruction. The data part of the processing instruction is obtained by instantiating the template body that the `<xsl:processing-instruction>` element contains.

<xsl:text>

The `<xsl:text>` instruction is used to output a text node to the result tree. This instruction may contain a text node but it must not contain any child elements.

Text contained directly in the stylesheet is written to the result tree automatically, whether or not it is contained in an `<xsl:text>` element. The reason for providing `<xsl:text>` is to give more control over whitespace handling. Text contained within an `<xsl:text>` element will be output exactly as written, even if it is all whitespace, whereas in other contexts whitespace that appears on its own between element tags will be removed from the stylesheet before processing.

For example, to output two names with a space between them, write:

```
<xsl:value-of select="given-name"/>
    <xsl:text> </xsl:text>
<xsl:value-of select="last-name"/>
```

The `<xsl:text>` element also has an optional attribute, `disable-output-escaping="yes"`, which suppresses the normal action of the serializer to convert special characters such as < and > into < and >. This is a dirty feature that should be avoided, but it is sometimes useful if you want to generate not-quite-XML formats, such as ASP, PHP, or JSP pages.

<xsl:value-of>

The `<xsl:value-of>` instruction is used to write computed text to the result tree. It takes a select attribute whose value is an XPath expression. This expression is evaluated, the result is converted to a string (using the rules of the `string()` function), and written as a text node to the result tree. The most common usage is:

```
<xsl:value-of select="." />
```

This simply writes the string-value of the current node.

There is an optional attribute, `disable-output-escaping="yes"`, which has the same effect as with `<xsl:text>`.

<xsl:variable>

The `<xsl:variable>` element, when used as an instruction within a template body, declares a local variable. (It can also be used as a top-level element in the stylesheet, to declare a global variable.)

The name of the variable is given by its name attribute. This must be different from any other local variable that is in scope at that point in the stylesheet, although it can override a global variable of the same name.

The scope of a local variable (that is, the part of the stylesheet where XPath expressions can refer to the variable) comprises those elements in the stylesheet that are following-siblings of the `<xsl:variable>` element, or descendants of those following-sibling elements. Using XPath notation, if the `<xsl:variable>` element is the context node, the scope of the variable is the node-set defined by:

```
following-sibling::*/descendant-or-self::*
```

This means, for example, that if you declare a local variable within an `<xsl:when>` branch of an `<xsl:choose>` instruction, you won't be able to access the variable outside the `<xsl:when>`.

The value of the variable can be determined in three ways:

❑ If the `<xsl:variable>` element has a `select` attribute, this attribute is an XPath expression, which is evaluated to give the variable's value.

❑ If the `<xsl:variable>` element has content, the content is a template body. This is instantiated to create a new tree (called a result tree fragment) and the value of the variable is the node-set containing the root of this tree.

❑ If the `<xsl:variable>` element has no `select` attribute and is empty, its value is the empty string.

Here's an example using the `select` attribute:

```
<xsl:variable name="number-of-items" select="count(//item)" />
```

Here's one that creates a result tree fragment:

```
<xsl:variable name="result-table">
<table>
   <xsl:for-each select="item">
   <tr>
      <td><xsl:value-of select="@description"/></td>
      <td><xsl:value-of select="@price"/></td>
   </tr>
   </xsl:for-each>
</table>
</xsl:variable>
```

With XSLT 1.0, there are restrictions on the way a result tree fragment can be used; in effect, the only things you can do with it are to convert it to a string, or to copy it (by using `<xsl:copy-of>`) to the final result tree. You can't actually process it using XPath queries. Many vendors have relaxed this restriction by providing facilities to convert the result tree fragment to a node-set, and a standard way of doing this is expected to come in the next version of the specification.

As we've already mentioned, variables can't be used in quite the same way as in ordinary programming languages, because they are "write-once" – they can't be updated, because there is no assignment statement. In effect, this means a variable is just a shorthand name for an expression that saves you from using the same expression repeatedly. Variables can also be useful to avoid problems with changing context. For example, if you write:

```
<xsl:variable name="this" select="."/>
```

Then as the first thing within an `<xsl:for-each>` loop, you will always be able to refer to the current node of this loop even from within nested loops.

Literal Result Elements

Any element found within a template body that is not recognized as an instruction is treated as a literal result element. The element is copied to the result tree, together with its attributes and namespaces. If the element is not empty, its content is a template body, and this is instantiated to create the content of the generated element in the result tree. For example:

```
<td valign="top"><xsl:value-of select="." /></td>
```

This is a literal `<td>` result element, whose template body causes the string value of the current node in the source document to be inserted into the `<td>` element generated on the result tree.

The attributes of the literal result element are interpreted as attribute value templates, so they can be generated using XPath expressions. For example:

```
<td valign="{$align}"><xsl:value-of select="." /></td>
```

There are two other ways of generating attributes for the result element:

- ❑ Use the `<xsl:attribute>` instruction within the template body.

- ❑ Use an `xsl:use-attribute-sets` attribute within the start tag of the literal result element. This has the same effect as the `use-attribute-sets` attribute of `<xsl:element>`. It is prefixed with "xsl" to distinguish it from attributes that you want to copy to the result.

A literal result element can also have attributes `xsl:version`, `xsl:extension-element-prefixes`, and `xsl:exclude-result-prefixes`. These override the similarly-named attributes on the `<xsl:stylesheet>` element for the region of the stylesheet enclosed by the literal result element. Again, the prefix "xsl" is used to distinguish them from attributes intended for the result tree.

Sorting

There are two instructions for processing a set of nodes, `<xsl:apply-templates>` and `<xsl:for-each>`, and they both allow the nodes to be sorted by specifying one or more `<xsl:sort>` elements. If you don't specify a sort order, the nodes will be processed in document order, that is, in the order they appear in the source document.

Each `<xsl:sort>` element specifies a sort key. If there is more than one `<xsl:sort>` element, they specify the sort keys in major-to-minor order: for example if the first sort key is last-name, and the second is given-name, you will process the data in the order of ascending given-name within ascending last-name.

The `<xsl:sort>` element has a number of attributes to control sorting:

Attribute	Meaning
select	An XPath expression whose value represents the sort key. If omitted, the nodes are sorted by their string-value.
order	This can be "ascending" or "descending". Specifying descending reverses the sort order. The default is ascending.
data-type	This can be "text" or "number". Specifying number means that the sort keys are converted to numbers and sorted numerically. The default is text.
lang	A language code, for example "en" or "de". Allows the sort to use national collating conventions. The default is implementation-defined.
case-order	This can be "upper-first" or "lower-first". Indicates whether upper-case letters should precede their lower-case equivalents, or vice versa. The default is implementation-defined.

The expression giving the sort key is evaluated with the node being sorted as the context node. For example, to sort a set of <book> elements according to their author attribute, write:

```
<xsl:for-each select="book">
    <xsl:sort select="@author"/>
</xsl:for-each>
```

Or:

```
<xsl:apply-templates select="book">
    <xsl:sort select="@author"/>
</xsl:apply-templates>
```

Top-level Elements

We've looked at all the XSLT elements that can be used inside a template body. Let's now return to the top-level of the stylesheet and look at those elements that can be used as children of the `<xsl:stylesheet>` or `<xsl:transform>` element. Here is a list of them:

<xsl:attribute-set>	<xsl:output>
<xsl:decimal-format>	<xsl:param>
<xsl:import>	<xsl:preserve-space>
<xsl:include>	<xsl:strip-space>
<xsl:key>	<xsl:template>
<xsl:namespace-alias>	<xsl:variable>

We'll look at each one in turn, in alphabetical order. Within the stylesheet itself, the general principle is that top-level elements can appear in any order, except that `<xsl:import>` elements have to come before any others.

A stylesheet can also contain user-defined elements at the top level, provided they are in their own namespace. These will be ignored by the XSLT processor, but they can be useful for look-up tables and other constant data. Within an XPath expression you can access the stylesheet contents by writing `document("")` to refer to the root of the stylesheet tree.

`<xsl:attribute-set>`

This element defines a named set of attributes. This is useful where you want to create many result elements using the same attribute values, which sometimes happens when rendering documents for display.

The `<xsl:attribute-set>` element has a `name` attribute, which provides a unique name for this attribute set. Its content is a set of `<xsl:attribute>` instructions to generate the attribute values. To include this set of attributes in a result element, use the `use-attribute-sets` attribute on `<xsl:copy>` or `<xsl:element>`, or use the `xsl:use-attribute-sets` attribute on a literal result element.

`<xsl:decimal-format>`

This element defines a set of rules for formatting decimal numbers. These rules can be referenced from the `format-number()` function used in an XPath expression with the `format-number()` function elsewhere in the stylesheet. An `<xsl:decimal-format>` element may have a `name` attribute, in which case it is used when the third argument of `format-number()` uses this name, or it may be unnamed, in which case it is used when the `format-number()` function has no third attribute.

The `<xsl:decimal-format>` element allows characters and strings to be nominated for use in formatted numbers, and also in the format pattern used by the `format-number()` function. The ones that are most likely to be used are `decimal-separator`, which defines the character to be used as a decimal point, and `grouping-separator`, which defines the character used as a thousands separator. For example, if you want `format-number()` to use the continental European convention of using . as a thousands separator and , as a decimal point, write:

```
<xsl:decimal-format decimal-point="," grouping-separator="." />
```

The other attributes are outside the scope of this chapter, and are fully described in the Wrox book *XSLT Programmers Reference* (ISBN 1861003129).

`<xsl:import>`

The `<xsl:import>` element allows your stylesheet to incorporate definitions from another stylesheet. The element has an `href` attribute which contains the URI of the stylesheet to be imported. All the top-level definitions from the imported stylesheet are incorporated into the importing stylesheet, except that they have a lower precedence; which means that given a choice, the definitions in the importing stylesheet are preferred.

In many ways this is like sub-classing: the importing stylesheet inherits the definitions from the imported stylesheet, overriding them where necessary; this reflects the way the facility should be used. The imported stylesheet should contain general-purpose definitions for use in a wide range of circumstances, and the importing stylesheet should override these with definitions that are applicable in a narrower sphere.

The imported stylesheet may contain any top-level elements, but there are slight differences in the way the precedence mechanism works for different elements. In most cases, an object in the imported stylesheet is used only when there is no applicable object in the importing stylesheet. In some cases (`<xsl:key>` definitions, `<xsl:output>` definitions), the definitions in the two stylesheets are merged.

The imported stylesheet may contain further `<xsl:import>` elements, so there is a hierarchy just like a class hierarchy in object-oriented programming.

<xsl:include>

The `<xsl:include>` element is similar to `<xsl:import>`, except that it incorporates definitions from the included stylesheet with the same precedence as those in the including stylesheet. Again, the `href` attribute contains the URI of the stylesheet to be included. Whereas `<xsl:import>` allows the importing stylesheet to override definitions in the imported stylesheet, `<xsl:include>` is useful if the definitions are not to be overridden.

The effect is, for all practical purposes, to copy the top-level elements from the included stylesheet into the including stylesheet at the point where the `<xsl:include>` statement occurs. This must, of course, be at the top level, as an immediate child of the `<xsl:stylesheet>` element.

Note, however, that the attributes on the `<xsl:stylesheet>` element (such as `exclude-result-prefixes`) apply only to elements that are physically within that stylesheet, not to elements brought in using `<xsl:include>`.

<xsl:key>

The `<xsl:key>` element is used to create a named key definition, which is referenced when the `key()` function is used in an XPath expression.

The element has three attributes:

Attribute Name	Meaning
Name	Defines the name of the key, corresponding to the first argument of the `key()` function
match	Defines a pattern that determines which nodes in the source document participate in this key
use	Defines an XPath expression which establishes the value that will be used to find these nodes, corresponding to the second argument of the `key()` function

It would be appropriate to explain keys in SQL terms. Effectively the system maintains a table, KEYTABLE, with four columns, DOC, KEY, NODE, and VALUE.

The effect of an `<xsl:key>` definition is that for each source document (that is, the original input document plus any document loaded using the `document()` function), entries are created in this table for each node that matches the `match` pattern in the `<xsl:key>` definition. These entries will have DOC set to the identifier of the document, KEY set to the name of the key, and NODE set to the identifier of the matching node. For each of these matching nodes, the `use` expression is evaluated. If the result is a string, this string is entered in the VALUE column. If the result is a node-set, one row is added to the table for each node in the node-set, with the VALUE column set to the string-value of that node.

The effect of the `key()` function is then to query this table as follows:

```
SELECT distinct NODE FROM KEYTABLE WHERE DOC = current_document AND
    KEY = argument1 AND VALUE = argument2
```

Here `current_document` is the document containing the context node.

The resulting set of NODE identifiers forms the node-set returned by the `key()` function. Note that there can be more than one `<xsl:key>` definition with the same name (they are additive); that there can be several nodes with the same value for a key; and one node can have several values for the same key.

A simple example: to index books by author, write:

```
<xsl:key name="author-key" match="book" use="author" />
```

To retrieve all the books whose author is Milton, use this XPath expression:

```
key('author-key', 'Milton')
```

Note that this works even if a book has multiple authors.

<xsl:namespace-alias>

This is a rarely used element; its main purpose is to enable you to write a stylesheet that generates another stylesheet as output.

There are two attributes, `stylesheet-prefix` and `result-prefix`. In both cases, the value is a namespace prefix, which must correspond to a namespace declaration that is in scope.

The effect of this is that any literal result element that appears in the stylesheet using the namespace URI corresponding to the `stylesheet-prefix`, will be written to the output document under the namespace URI corresponding to the `result-prefix`.

<xsl:output>

This element is used to influence the way that the result tree is serialized. As we saw earlier in the chapter, serialization is not really part of the job of an XSLT processor, and for this reason processors are allowed to ignore this element entirely. However, in practice most processors do include a serializer and have done their best to honor the `<xsl:output>` element: it will be ignored only if you choose to handle the serialization yourself.

The main attribute is method, which may be set to xml, html, or text, or to a vendor-defined method distinguished by a namespace prefix. The value xml indicates that the output should be in XML 1.0 format, html that it should be an HTML document, and text that it should be a plain text file.

The meaning of the other attributes depends on which method is chosen, as shown in the following table:

Attribute	Applies to	Meaning
cdata-section-elements	xml	A whitespace separated list of elements whose content is to be encoded using CDATA sections.
doctype-public	xml, html	The public identifier to be used in the DOCTYPE declaration.
doctype-system	xml, html	The system identifier to be used in the DOCTYPE declaration.
encoding	xml, html, text	The character encoding to be used, e.g. ISO-8859-1. The default is the Unicode UTF-8 encoding.
indent	xml, html	Set to "yes" or "no" to indicate whether the output is to be indented for readability.
media-type	xml, html, text	The media (or MIME) type of the output.
omit-xml-declaration	xml	If set to "yes", indicates that the XML declaration at the start of the file should be omitted.
standalone	xml	Indicates the value for "standalone" in the XML declaration.
version	xml, html	The version of XML or HTML to be used (default for XML is 1.0, for HTML is 4.0).

There are many aspects of the final serialization over which you have no control; for example you can't choose in HTML output whether accented letters will be output directly as themselves, or using numeric character references, or using standard entity names such as ä. Different processors will do this differently. It shouldn't matter, because it will look the same in the browser.

<xsl:param>

We have already met <xsl:param> as an element that can be used inside <xsl:template>, to indicate the parameters to a template that may be supplied when it is called. It is also possible to use <xsl:param> as a top-level element to define parameters that may be supplied when the stylesheet as a whole is invoked: the syntax is the same. The way parameters are supplied is not standardized: each vendor has their own API or command line syntax, but within the stylesheet, parameters can be accessed by means of a variable reference in an XPath expression, just like global variables.

If the <xsl:param> element specifies a value, this is used as a default when no explicit value is supplied when the stylesheet is invoked.

`<xsl:preserve-space>` and `<xsl:strip-space>`

These two top-level elements are used to control how whitespace in the source document is handled. In most data-oriented XML documents, whitespace between element tags is there for layout purposes only, and it is best to eliminate it before processing starts, by specifying `<xsl:strip-space elements="*" />`. For markup-oriented XML documents, spaces between tags may well be significant, and it is best to keep it in the document (which is the default).

Both `<xsl:preserve-space>` and `<xsl:strip-space>` have an `elements` attribute, which is a space-separated list of **NameTests**. A `NameTest` is either `*`, meaning all elements, or `prefix:*`, meaning all elements in a particular namespace, or an element name indicating a specific element. If you want spaces stripped from only a few elements, list these in `<xsl:strip-space>`. If you want spaces stripped from most elements, specify `<xsl:strip-space="*" />`, and list any exceptions using `<xsl:preserve-space>`.

Whitespace is only stripped from the source document when an entire text node consists of whitespace (that is, of the four characters space, tab, carriage return, and line feed). Whitespace that is adjacent to "real" text is never removed. So if you have a source file like this:

```
<president>
    <name>
     Bill Clinton
    </name>
    <address>
     The White House Washington DC
    </address>
</president>
```

The newline characters immediately before the `<name>` element, between the `<name>` and `<address>` elements, and after the `<address>` element will be eligible for removal by whitespace stripping. But the newline characters immediately before "Bill", immediately after "Clinton", and at the start and end of the address, will always be retained because they form part of text nodes that are not whitespace-only. If you want to remove these newline characters, you will have to do it during the course of the transformation, using the `normalize-space()` function.

> **Note for Microsoft users:** when you invoke XSLT transformations using the MSXML3 processor, the normal procedure is first to construct a DOM representation of the input document using the `Document.Load()` method, and then to transform the DOM using the `transformNode()` method. By default, when you create the DOM, it is created without whitespace nodes. This process is carried out without regard to anything the stylesheet says about whitespace. If you want to preserve whitespace, set the `preserveWhitespace` property of the Document object to true.

`<xsl:template>`

We've already seen the `<xsl:template>` element in action earlier in the chapter. Just to recap (because it is about the most important element in XSLT), the `<xsl:template>` element can have either a name attribute (to allow it to be called using `<xsl:call-template>`, or a match attribute (to allow it to be called using `<xsl:apply-templates>`, or both (in which case it can be called either way). In addition, it may have a mode attribute and a priority attribute.

It's an error to have two templates in the stylesheet with the same name and the same import precedence.

<xsl:variable>

We've seen `<xsl:variable>` used within a template body to define a local variable; it can also be used as a top-level element to define a global variable. A global variable can be referenced from anywhere in the stylesheet: unlike local variables, there is no ban on forward references. Global variables can even refer to each other, so long as the definitions aren't circular.

Apart from this, global variable definitions look the same as local variables. They are always evaluated with the root node of the source document as the context node, and with the context position and size both set to 1.

It's an error to have two global variables with the same name and import precedence. If you have two with the same name and different precedence, the one with higher precedence (that is, the one in the importing stylesheet, or the one that was imported last) always wins.

Some Working Examples

This brings us to the end of the technical specifications in this chapter. To get a reasonably complete description of XSLT and XPath into limited space, we've included a lot of definitions and relatively few examples. So to compensate, here are a couple of examples of complete and (almost) realistic stylesheets.

Example: Displaying Soccer Results

We'll use an XML data file containing results of soccer fixtures, such as might be held in a database for a World Cup web site, and we'll show two stylesheets that format this data in different ways.

Source

The source file is `soccer.xml`. If you're interested, it contains the results of the matches played in Group A of the 1998 World Cup:

```xml
<?xml version="1.0"?>
<?xml-stylesheet type="text/xsl" href="soccer1.xsl" ?>

<results group="A">
<match>
   <date>1998-06-10</date>
   <team score="2">Brazil</team>
   <team score="1">Scotland</team>
</match>
<match>
   <date>1998-06-16</date>
   <team score="3">Brazil</team>
   <team score="0">Morocco</team>
</match>
<match>
   <date>1998-06-23</date>
   <team score="1">Brazil</team>
   <team score="2">Norway</team>
</match>
```

```
<match>
   <date>1998-06-10</date>
   <team score="2">Morocco</team>
   <team score="2">Norway</team>
</match>
<match>
   <date>1998-06-16</date>
   <team score="1">Scotland</team>
   <team score="1">Norway</team>
</match>
<match>
   <date>1998-06-23</date>
   <team score="0">Scotland</team>
   <team score="3">Morocco</team>
</match>
</results>
```

The First Stylesheet

The first stylesheet, `soccer1.xsl`, displays the results of the matches in a straightforward way.

First we'll give the standard stylesheet heading, and define a variable to hold the table heading that we'll use to display each result:

```
<xsl:stylesheet version="1.0"
    xmlns:xsl="http://www.w3.org/1999/XSL/Transform">

    <xsl:variable name="table-heading">
       <tr>
           <td><b>Date</b></td>
           <td><b>Home Team</b></td>
           <td><b>Away Team</b></td>
           <td><b>Result</b></td>
       </tr>
    </xsl:variable>
```

Now we'll define a named template to format dates. This takes an ISO-8601 date as a parameter (for example "2000-10-11") and formats it for display as "11 Oct 2000". This involves some simple use of the XPath string functions.

```
<xsl:template name="format-date">
   <xsl:param name="iso-date"/>
   <xsl:variable name="months"
       select="'JanFebMarAprMayJunJulAugSepOctNovDec'" />
   <xsl:value-of select="substring($iso-date, 9, 2)" />
   <xsl:text> </xsl:text>
   <xsl:variable name="month" select="substring($iso-date, 6, 2)" />
   <xsl:value-of select="substring($months, ($month - 1)*3 + 1, 3)" />
   <xsl:text> </xsl:text>
   <xsl:value-of select="substring($iso-date, 1, 4)" />
</xsl:template>
```

For the main part of the processing, we define a template rule for the root node, which calls `<xsl:apply-templates>` to process all the `<match>` elements, sorting them by date, and within the same date, by the name of the first team listed.

```
<xsl:template match="/">
<html><body>
   <h1>Matches in Group <xsl:value-of select="/*/@group"/></h1>
   <xsl:apply-templates select="/results/match">
      <xsl:sort select="date" />
      <xsl:sort select="team[1]" />
   </xsl:apply-templates>
</body></html>
</xsl:template>
```

Finally, we need to cover the logic to display details of a single soccer match. This first calls the named template to format the date into a variable; then it constructs an HTML table, copying data into the table either from the source documents or from variables, as required. (The `match="match"` attribute may be confusing; it's a pure coincidence that one of the elements in our source document has the same name as an XSLT-defined attribute).

```
<xsl:template match="match">
   <xsl:variable name="date-out">
      <xsl:call-template name="format-date">
         <xsl:with-param name="iso-date" select="date" />
      </xsl:call-template>
   </xsl:variable>

   <h2><xsl:value-of select="concat(team[1], ' versus ', team[2])"/></h2>

   <table bgcolor="#cccccc" border="1" cellpadding="5">
      <xsl:copy-of select="$table-heading"/>
      <tr>
         <td><xsl:value-of select="$date-out"/></td>
         <td><xsl:value-of select="team[1]"/></td>
         <td><xsl:value-of select="team[2]"/></td>
         <td><xsl:value-of select="concat(team[1]/@score, '-',
            team[2]/@score)"/></td>
      </tr>
   </table>

</xsl:template>
</xsl:stylesheet>
```

Running the Example

You can run this example using a processor such as Instant Saxon, as with the previous example, but the simplest way to do it is directly in the browser.

Assuming you are using Internet Explorer 5 or 5.5, you can download and install MSXML3 from the Microsoft web site at http://msdn.microsoft.com/xml. Be sure to download and run the utility xmlinst.exe which makes MSXML3 the default parser on your system. Don't try to run this example with the old MSXML parser that came with IE5 or IE5.5: it won't work.

Once you have installed this software, just double-click on the file soccer.xml from Windows Explorer: it's as simple as that. This loads the XML file into Internet Explorer, and because it starts with an <?xml-stylesheet?> processing instruction, it invokes this stylesheet to convert the document to HTML for display.

Output

Here's what the output of the first stylesheet looks like in the browser (and yes, I do know that all the matches were actually played in France):

Stylesheet 2

Now let's write another stylesheet to display the same data in a completely different way. One of the motivations behind XSLT, after all, was to make information reusable by separating the information from the logic for displaying it.

This stylesheet, `soccer2.xsl`, does some calculation to create a league table. We'll start it with `<xsl:transform>` this time, just to show that this works too, and we'll start by creating two global variables, one for the set of all teams, and the other for the set of all matches. If we select all the `<team>` elements in the document, we'll get duplicates: to eliminate these, we have to select only those `<team>` elements that are not the same as a previous team.

```
<xsl:transform
    xmlns:xsl="http://www.w3.org/1999/XSL/Transform"
    version="1.0">

<xsl:variable name="teams" select="//team[not(.=preceding::team)]" />
<xsl:variable name="matches" select="//match" />
```

The actual logic of the stylesheet will go in a single template rule, which we'll set up to be triggered when the `<results>` element is processed. This starts by outputting a standard header:

```
<xsl:template match="results">
<html><body>
    <h1>Results of Group <xsl:value-of select="@group"/></h1>
    <table cellpadding="5">
        <tr>
            <td>Team</td>
            <td>Played</td>
            <td>Won</td>
            <td>Drawn</td>
            <td>Lost</td>
            <td>For</td>
            <td>Against</td>
        </tr>
```

Now the template processes each team in turn. We're only interested in getting totals for the number of matches won and lost and the number of goals scored, so it doesn't matter what order we process them in.

We'll start, for convenience, by setting up a variable called this to refer to the current team.

```
<xsl:for-each select="$teams">
    <xsl:variable name="this" select="." />
```

The number of matches played is easy to work out: it's the number of nodes in the $matches node-set that have a team equal to this team:

```
<xsl:variable name="played"
    select="count($matches[team=$this])"/>
```

The number of matches won is a bit more difficult. It's the number of matches for which the score of this team is greater than the score of the other team, which we can write as:

```
<xsl:variable name="won"
    select="count($matches[team[.=$this]/@score &gt;
    team[.!=$this]/@score])"/>
```

The number of matches lost and drawn follows the same logic, just changing the test from greater-than to less-than in the first case, and equals in the second:

```
<xsl:variable name="lost"
    select="count($matches[team[.=$this]/@score &lt;
    team[.!=$this]/@score])"/>
<xsl:variable name="drawn"
    select="count($matches[team[.=$this]/@score =
    team[.!=$this]/@score])"/>
```

The number of goals scored by this team can be obtained using the sum() function, applied to the node-set consisting of all scores for this team in any match:

```
<xsl:variable name="for"
    select="sum($matches/team[.=$this]/@score)"/>
```

And the simplest way of finding the number of goals scored against this team is to total the scores of all teams in matches that this team participated in, and then subtract the previous total:

```
<xsl:variable name="against"
    select="sum($matches[team=$this]/team/@score) - $for" />
```

Having done the calculations, we can output the results:

```
<tr>
    <td><xsl:value-of select="."/></td>
    <td><xsl:value-of select="$played"/></td>
    <td><xsl:value-of select="$won"/></td>
    <td><xsl:value-of select="$drawn"/></td>
    <td><xsl:value-of select="$lost"/></td>
    <td><xsl:value-of select="$for"/></td>
    <td><xsl:value-of select="$against"/></td>
</tr>
</xsl:for-each>
</table>
</body></html>
</xsl:template>

</xsl:transform>
```

Running the Example

You can run this stylesheet the same way as the previous one. Edit the `<?xml-stylesheet?>` processing instruction in `soccer.xml` to refer to `soccer2.xsl` instead of `soccer1.xsl`, and load `soccer.xml` into the browser again. (Or just click **Refresh** if IE5 is still open).

Of course, this isn't the way you would actually do things in practice. The `<?xml-stylesheet?>` approach, which defines a default stylesheet for a particular XML document, only really works where you always process an XML document using the same stylesheet. If you want to select different stylesheets on different occasions, you'll have to create an HTML page that loads the source document and stylesheet explicitly. We'll explain how to do that next.

Output

This is what the result looks like in the browser:

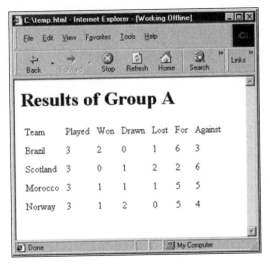

Selecting a Stylesheet Dynamically

You can do XSLT transformations either on the server or in the browser: in fact, you might be using XSLT as part of a batch application that is nothing to do with the Web at all. Therefore, the way in which you invoke the transformation will vary depending on the circumstances, as well as on your choice of XSLT processor.

However, converting XML to HTML in the browser is perhaps one of the most striking ways of using XSLT, so we'll concentrate on that in our next example. Here we will include some simple logic on an HTML page to invoke a transformation based on the user's selection.

The HTML page soccer.html reads like this:

```
<html>
<head>
   <title>Results of Group A</title>
   <script>
      var source = null;
      var style = null;
      var transformer = null;

      function init()
      {
         source = new ActiveXObject("MSXML2.FreeThreadedDOMDocument");
         source.async = false;
         source.load('soccer.xml');
      }

      function apply(stylesheet)
      {
         style = new ActiveXObject("MSXML2.FreeThreadedDOMDocument");
         style.async = false;
         style.load(stylesheet);

         transformer = new ActiveXObject("MSXML2.XSLTemplate");
         transformer.stylesheet = style.documentElement;

         var xslproc = transformer.createProcessor();
         xslproc.input = source;
         xslproc.transform();
         displayarea.innerHTML = xslproc.output;
      }
   </script>
   <script for="window" event="onload">
      init();
   </script>
</head>
<body>
   <button onclick="apply('soccer1.xsl')">Results</button>
   <button onclick="apply('soccer2.xsl')">League table</button>
   <div id="displayarea"></div>
</body>
</html>
```

What this does is to display two buttons on the screen, as shown below:

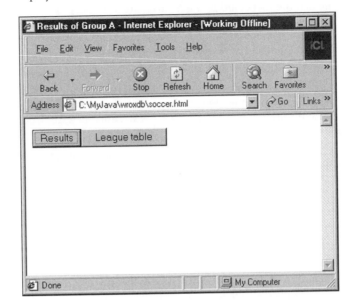

When you click on **Results**, the XML file is shown using stylesheet `soccer1.xsl`; when you click on **League table**, it is shown using `soccer2.xsl`.

For more details about the APIs used in this example, see the Microsoft product documentation, or the Wrox book *XSLT Programmers Reference* (ISBN1861003129).

XSLT and Databases

This is a chapter about XSLT and XPath, in a book about using XML with databases. Therefore, it might seem odd that we've said very little about databases in this chapter. However, there's a good reason for that; there's very little direct connection. Typically, your application gets XML out of the database, and then puts that XML through an XSLT stylesheet for display. The application ties the database and the stylesheet together, and neither the database nor the stylesheet knows about each other.

Therefore, at the coding level, there's a clean separation of concerns. At the design level, however, you have plenty of choices:

❑ How much work should you do in the SQL logic to select exactly the data that's needed, and how much should you do in the stylesheet?

❑ Should you grab a large amount of data from the database in one go, or keep going back for more if the user asks for it?

❑ Should you do the XSLT processing on the client or the server?

There is no single right answer to these questions. Be aware that you have choices, and don't automatically assume that the first solution that comes into your head is the best one. Some points to bear in mind are:

❑ Transforming a large data file (anything over a megabyte) can be very expensive. Use the SQL logic to restrict the amount of data you need to process.

❑ XSLT works well when the structure of the data is explicit, for example when sets of related items are grouped within an element rather than being implicit through common values. Use the SQL and application logic to generate an XML document in which the structure is as explicit as possible.

❑ Remember that by processing data in the browser, you can take a lot of the processing load off the server. In fact, you can sometimes dramatically reduce the number of visits the user makes to the server by allowing them to navigate within a data set locally. However, be prepared to explain the fall in your web site's hit rate to your management!

Summary

In this chapter, we've looked at the role of XSLT as a transformation language for XML documents, and the role that XPath queries play within an XSLT stylesheet. We've given a lightning tour of XPath syntax, noting in particular the important role played by location paths as the way of navigating around the hierarchic structure of the source document.

Then we looked at how an XSLT stylesheet uses template rules and match patterns to define how each part of the source document should be processed. We looked at all the different instructions you can use inside a template body, and then came back to review the top-level elements you can use in a stylesheet to control processing options.

Then we relaxed to watch some soccer; and finally we looked briefly at how XSLT technology and SQL databases can work together.

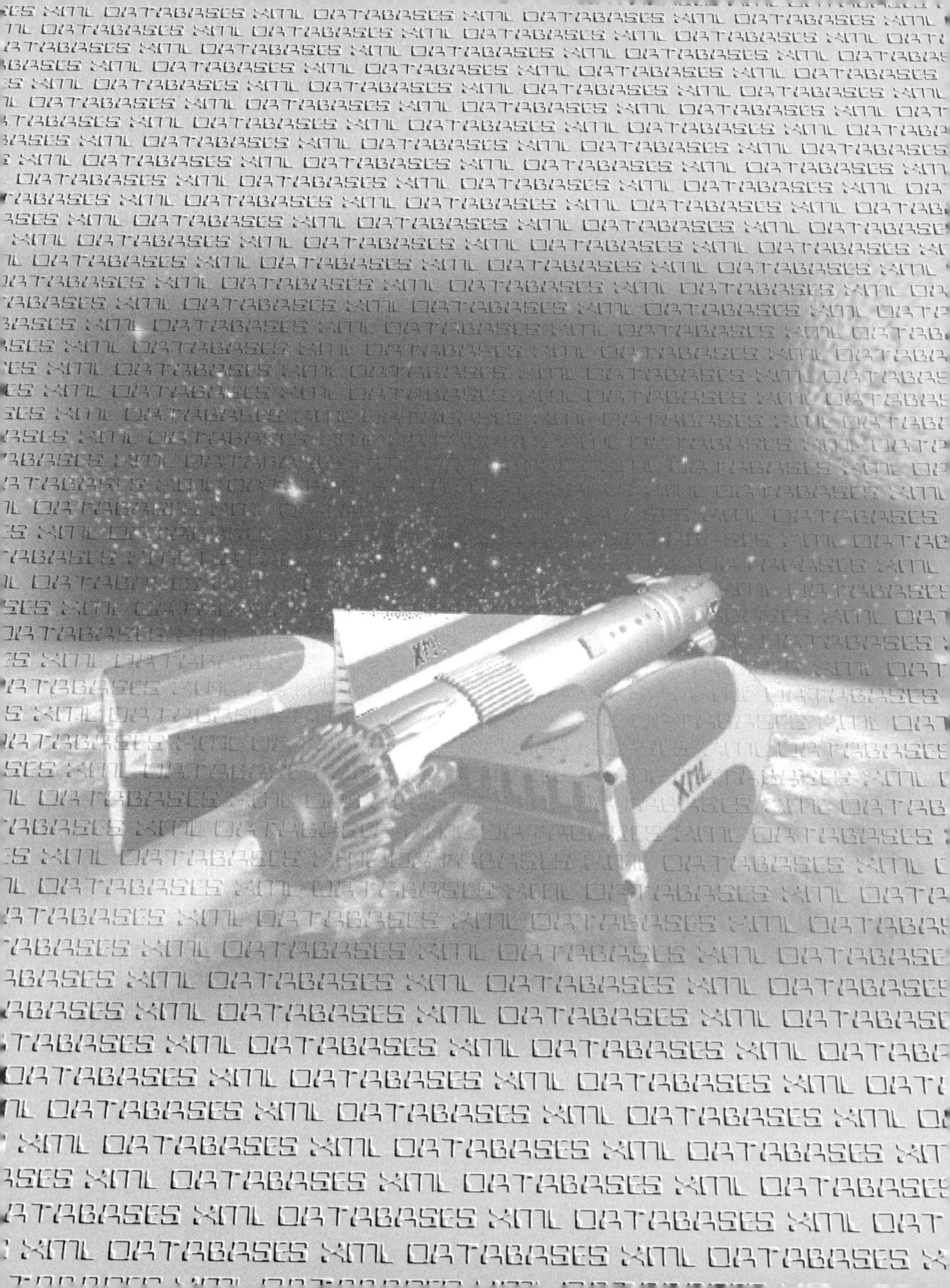
XML DATABASES

Relational References with XLink

The XML Linking Language (XLink) is a specification, which according to the W3C "allows elements to be inserted into XML documents in order to create and describe links between resources". Xlink provides six element types that can be used to create and describe characteristics of links. Only two element types create XLink links:

❑ There are **simple** XLinks, which reproduce the functionality of HTML links

❑ Also **extended** elements, which are far more powerful links, although their syntax is more complex

These two types of XLink links may take several attributes or child XLink elements to further describe the behavior and characteristics of the links. Before we proceed any further, there are a few things that you should be aware of that illustrate the power of XLink:

❑ You can use your own element names as links; you are not limited to using one tag like the <a> tag in HTML, so any element can become a linking element.

❑ With extended links, your linking element does not have to reside in the document you are linking from; imagine being able to add a link to a document that you do not own, or to link from a read-only or non-XML resource.

❑ Extended links allow you to provide **LinkBases**, which provide a convenient database of extended links that can be related to any other resource. It will be possible for example, to store all of your favorite links to articles on XML in a linkbase, and in any document reference all of those links with an extended link reference. You could then update or change the links in all documents at once by updating the linkbase.

❑ XLinks can be used to describe relationships between several documents (rather like keys used in a relational database).

Shortly, we will look at the simple XLink syntax, gaining an understanding of the XLink namespace, some common link attributes, and the difference between local and remote resources. We will then spend the rest of the chapter understanding how to use the power of the Extended link. It is the Extended link that allows us to create relationships outside the scope of anything possible with HTML anchors, or other unidirectional links. We will see that with the multi-directional extended link it is possible to create relational links that can associate different data sets.

One of the difficulties in looking at XLink is that the standard had not been completed at the time of writing, which means that there are few implementations of XLink in programs to illustrate the concepts. It is, nevertheless, well worth learning about because XLink will be used in the very near future and the possibilities of this language are too rich to be ignored. Also, if you are reading this book, you are trying to use XML with databases, and XLink provides a way for us to describe database style relationships in an XML context. As an encore, XLink also provides a way to describe these relationships between non-XML resources! As we will see in the next chapter, it can also work with XPointer to allow you to create links between parts of a document.

> The XLink specification as it stands today is in what the W3C calls a **Candidate Recommendation**. This is considered to be a stable recommendation stage with 2 stages left before it is a Full Recommendation. This is significant because most software developers are hesitant to write to a specification before it is stable, and most will not consider serious efforts until a full recommendation has been made. Check out the intro page to the specification at www.w3.org/XML/Linking for an updated list of applications that implement the standard.

In this chapter we will look at:

❑ Understanding the XLink specification as it is today

❑ How simple XLinks allow us to reproduce the linking capabilities of HTML on any element

❑ How extended XLinks allow us to offer far more complex relationships and links between resources

❑ Introduce the use of extended links for defining relationships that map to relational databases

The current W3C XLink work can be found at http://www.w3.org/TR/2000/CR-xlink-20000703/.

In the next chapter, we will look at other technologies that expand upon XLink including XPointer, and XInclude.

Resource Linking

The idea of **linking resources** in a document is a rather well covered topic. The primary virtue of the Web is the ability to get from one resource to another via hyperlinks. As you will be aware, hyperlinks are defined in an HTML document with the anchor tag <a>. When this is given an href resource attribute with a URI value, it becomes a link.

```
<A HREF="http://www.mydomain.com/resource.html">DISPLAYED TEXT</A>
```

This is good, and has provided many an 18 year old with a way to skip college and make millions of dollars. However, let's say you have the following tables in an order fulfillment database (as described in Chapter 3):

Invoice

InvoiceKey
187
188

Item

ItemKey
13
14

InvoiceItem

InvoiceKey	ItemKey
187	13
188	13
187	14

The `Invoice` and `Item` keys being the primary keys for their respective tables, and the `InvoiceItem` table exercising foreign keys to each key shown, such that `InvoiceItem` allows us to find each invoice containing each of the various items.

If we only had HTML anchor tags to work with, could we describe the relationship of these resources (the data in each table) to one another? In practical terms, could we display links to the order details of each order? No, at best, we are able to point from the current document to one of the resources in order to show that item, but no relationship is defined. Therefore, in current practice, we can only have a "show order detail" link that sends data to a server application that retrieves the desired output. As we progress with this chapter, we'll see how XLink can be used to describe relationships like those in a relational database. But for the moment, let's just look at how XLink implements simple links.

Simple XLink Elements

A simple XLink element is like the HTML anchor in that it describes a unidirectional link relationship; we can add a linking element to our documents that will point to another resource.

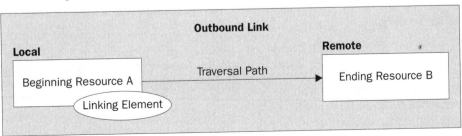

349

In this diagram we have:

❑ The **Local resource** – The child of a linking element, or the actual linking element itself. In a unidirectional HTML anchor, the local resource is the anchor tag (or the visible text which provides a link to the user).

❑ The **Remote resource** – The document, or document portion that is addressed by the linking element. Any resource that is the target of a URI reference is considered remote. Again in HTML, the bookmark style reference which points to a named anchor elsewhere in the same document is still said to be pointing to a remote resource.

❑ A **Traversal Path** between the local and remote resources, which simply means you can get from resource A to resource B by following the defined link.

With simple links, you can only link from a local resource to a remote resource, and the link can be followed from the point it has been added into the document. This local to remote behavior is known as an **outbound link**.

In order to get a feel for this, if we wanted to express the HTML link example from above in XLink syntax, we would write it like this:

```
<myLink
    xmlns:xlink="http://www.w3.org/1999/xlink"
    xlink:type="simple"
    xlink:href="http://www.mydomain.com/resource.html">
    DISPLAYED TEXT
</myLink>
```

Using this syntax, our XLink application would exhibit the same behavior as the HTML anchor. Though the simple XLink cannot really accomplish what we want to do with database relationships, we can still use it as a way to introduce some common XLink concepts we'll develop more fully with extended links later in the chapter.

The first thing to be aware of is the need for the required namespace declaration:

```
xmlns:xlink="http://www.w3.org/1999/xlink"
```

This is the proper namespace to use for the XLink specification. Namespaces are used to declare to a parser or application which XML vocabulary or specification a particular element or attribute is implementing.

The first XLink attribute used is type:

```
xlink:type="simple"
```

As we said earlier there are simple links and extended links, and because we are looking at simple links we will give it the value of simple.

The type attribute from the XLink namespace has a very special meaning in XLink, in that it defines what an element's role in creating and describing a link will be. The type attribute is a required attribute in all XLink elements. This typing of all elements is what denotes them as belonging to an XLink link. Each element in an XML document that is XLink typed will be evaluated against the W3 recommendation by an XLink application.

The locator attribute href is used in exactly the same manner as in HTML, where it includes as its value a URI for some resource:

```
xlink:href="http://my.domain/resouce.html"
```

In XLink, the href attribute is not required for a simple link. A simple link without an href attribute is acting as a resource only, which may contain properties about the document in which it resides. Consider again the anchor tag in HTML that also has an optional href attribute. The <a> tag using an attribute of name provides a destination within a document, but does not itself provide an outbound link. A simple link with no href is simply non traversable, but may still contain any of the following attributes to provide properties for the local resource:

role

The role attribute is an optional URI reference that describes how the link relates to the remote resource. For example, a link referring to a list of authors may contain the role attribute

```
xlink:role="http://my.domain/linkproperties/authors"
```

The resource identified by the URI will contain information describing the author list as it relates to the document in which the link is defined. How an XLink application will use such information is yet to be seen, but the intended use is to allow for greater detail about a resource than would be displayed via the content of the link, or the title attribute. This attribute would be used by an application, rather than by the user. The reference could be used as a categorical identifier, to let an application know a particular link is, for instance, about authors rather than titles. One such use may be for an application to categorize links in a search of resources. Another use would be to display links of different types according to rules defined in the role resource. The W3C recommendation does not specify the nature of the contents to be found in the specified role-describing resource.

arcrole

Arcs are used in XLink link structures to determine traversal rules, such as whether a link traverses from resource A to resource B, or vice-versa. However, a simple link does not actually allow for the specification of an arc, as it is explicitly a one to one outbound link. Yet, because the simple link does have an implied arc, the arcrole attribute is carried over. The definition and use is the same as that of the role attribute, but presumably would apply to the nature of the traversal, rather than the resources involved. The W3C recommendation does not specify the nature of the contents to be found in the specified role-describing resource.

title

A single title attribute may be optionally defined to provide a human readable description of the link on which it is given. A title attribute would be defined as follows

```
xlink:title="Go To Another Resource"
```

Such a title could either be used to display an available link if the linking element had no content, or to provide information to a user when they initiated traversal of the given link.

show

This is an optional behavioral attribute which must take new, replace, embed, other, or none as its value in order to describe for the XLink application how the link will be traversed by the user. If no value is specified, no XLink specified default it given.

❑ Use new to open a new display window with the contents of the remote resource. This is similar to the behavior of an HTML link with an unrecognizable, or "_blank" target attribute value.

351

❏ Use `replace` to replace the contents of the current resource in the display window. This is similar to the default linking behavior of web browsers.

❏ Use `embed` to put the remote resource into the current resource at the location of the linking element. This could be used to place non-XML content into a document, such as an image, or an application.

❏ Use `other` for user or application defined behaviors. In this case, the XLink application would look for other related markup in the link definition to provide the behavior of this link.

  ❏ Use `none` as a placeholder that may tell the application to behave differently than if the attribute is simply empty. For instance, `none` may be used to override a default behavior when you don't want the link to be traversable, and yet the `href` attribute is available for other reasons. Perhaps locator references in the document will be read by another application, but the user interface should not provide a way to use the links. However, no behavior is explicitly defined for this attribute value, so an individual application may handle it differently.

actuate

This optional behavioral attribute describes when the link should be traversed, and must take either `onLoad`, `onRequest`, `other`, or `none` as its value. If no value is supplied, no XLink specified default is given.

❏ `onLoad` would actuate the `show` link behavior as the page is loaded, effectively working as a redirect with `xlink:show="replace"` or as an include with `xlink:show="embed"`.

❏ `onRequest` would actuate the link on the users' action; acting as a standard hyperlink with `new` or `replace`, or a dynamic text area (or other yet unknown possibility) with `embed`.

❏ Again, `other` would provide a way to offer customizable actuation behaviors.

❏ Override an application default, by explicitly declaring there is no way to actuate the link.

We will see most of these again when we discuss the extended element.

Simplify the Simple Link with a DTD

Compared to the HTML `<A>` tag, the simple links we have just seen may seem incredibly complicated, but we can make our lives much easier. Because we are dealing with XML, we can make use of a DTD to generically describe the recurring attributes. Consider the following DTD fragment we could use with simple links:

```
<!ELEMENT myLink ANY>
<!ATTLIST myLink
    xmlns:xlink      CDATA        #FIXED "http://www.w3.org/1999/xlink"
    xlink:type       (simple)     #FIXED "simple"
    xlink:href       CDATA        #IMPLIED
    xlink:role       NMTOKEN      #FIXED "http://www.mydomain.com/simplelink.html"
    xlink:arcrole    CDATA        #IMPLIED
    xlink:title      CDATA        #IMPLIED
    xlink:show       (new
                     |replace
                     |embed
                     |other
```

```
                         |none)        #FIXED "replace"
       xlink:actuate     (onLoad
                         |onRequest
                         |other
                         |none)        #FIXED "onRequest">
```

If our earlier document was validated with a DTD containing this definition for the element `myLink` we could then write our simple element:

```
<myLink xlink:href="http://www.mydomain.com/resource.html">DISPLAY TEXT</myLink>
```

We are using the DTD to supply default, or fixed values for commonly recurring attributes. This means we don't have to write them in every time, and could write all of our links in a document using the `<myLink>` element the same way you would use `<a>` in an HTML document.

> Only browsers that offer some level of XLink conformance will be able to even display the examples shown here. At the time of this writing, Microsoft Explorer 5.5 and Netscape Communicator 4.6 cannot load an XML document with XLink namespaces defined; Netscape 6 beta 2 can load the document but cannot display the link.

We then have something more familiar to our HTML experience. Again, keep this lesson in mind as it also applies to extended links.

It is helpful to understand that with XLink we are not constrained by the names of elements as we are in HTML. The whole idea that we can define and extend links on our own, with a flexible format, is one of the goals of the XLink editors. We have seen that we can name an element `<myLink>`, and then by assigning a namespace to the element along with a few prescribed attributes, give it linking behaviors. In so doing we are not necessarily confining our `<myLink>` element to be a linking element only. Any other content or attributes of the link element will merely be ignored by the XLink application while retaining their meaning for other parsers or applications.

Extended XLink Elements

When I introduced the idea of linking with an HTML anchor tag, I asked if we could define any relationships between the data with our links. The answer was no, and the same is true of the simple XLink element. But we wouldn't have much to say in this chapter if it couldn't be done, so without further ado, here are extended links.

The last look at resources A and B showed A as the resource that contained a link, and was by definition local. It pointed in a uni-directional way to a single remote resource, B. With extended links, the resources that participate in the link may be expanded both in number (a link can point to several resources) and in traversal behavior (the links can indicate two-way traversal without expressly pointing this out in all resources – remember I said earlier that it was possible to provide an inbound link from a resource you do not own and/or is read-only on your local server).

In contrast to the simple link, the extended link provides for the linking direction to be set with the **arc-type** element in conjunction with any number of **resource** and **locator** type elements. Whereas the simple link is one element with several attributes, the extended link is a parent element with several child attributes and elements.

Let's start off with an example where we want to create links between our homes and local shops that describe a relationship. We will see in this example that we define remote resources with the `locator` element, and local resources with the `resource-type` element. These resources are then given their link direction, or **traversal rules**, by the `arc` element. This may look quite complicated at first, but it will become clear shortly:

```
<ROUTE xmlns:xlink="http://www.w3.org/1999/xlink"
    xlink:type="extended"
    xlink:title="A sample extended link">
    <HOME xlink:type="resource"
        xlink:href="home.xml"
        xlink:label="myhouse"
        xlink:title="Directions to my house" />
    <STORE xlink:type="locator"
        xlink:href="store.xml"
        xlink:label="thestore" />
    <GETMILK xlink:type="arc"
        xlink:from="thestore"
        xlink:to="myhouse" />
</ROUTE>
```

You might be surprised that it takes so much code to write one link, but it is quite powerful compared with HTML linking.

Here ROUTE is the extended linking element. There are three child elements of the linking element: HOME, STORE and GETMILK:

❑ HOME represents details of directions to our house, stored in the `home.xml` file, and is the local resource defined in a `resource-type` element

❑ STORE represents a store that we want to get milk from, and is the remote resource defined in a `locator-type` element

❑ GETMILK, the `arc-type element`, defines a relationship from the STORE to our HOME, so that the store can know how to deliver the milk we want from the store. If you look at the `to` and `from` attributes on this element you might be able to see that we will be creating a link from the STORE to our HOME.

Let's look at the syntax again. We have defined ROUTE as an **extended-type** linking element (using the `type` attribute with the value of `extended`).

```
<ROUTE xmlns:xlink="http://www.w3.org/1999/xlink"
    xlink:type="extended"
    xlink:title="A sample extended link">
```

If you were looking closely, you may have noticed that the child elements have different values for their `type` attributes, and that these child elements inherit the namespace of the ROUTE element, so we do not need to declare it again.

Here we can see how extended XLinks use both elements and attributes to describe the intended relationship between the data; here, their child elements within the link element and their attributes on these child elements.

The child elements of the extended linking element (which remember is ROUTE) have different values for their type attributes:

- The value of the HOME element's type attribute is resource

- The value of the STORE element's type attribute is locator

- And we have declared a traversal behavior for our resources in GETMILK, by defining the value of type as arc

The arc is the key here, as it is describing a link from the HOME to the STORE. Arcs tell the application what should be done with each of the locator and resource-type elements found in the extended link. In the simple link, the arc is implied, but some of its attributes were present. In an extended link, it is inside the arc that you will not only set the direction, but also declare the show and actuate behaviors as well. The arc uses the labels that have been defined on each participating resource.

```
<STORE xlink:type="locator"
    xlink:href="store.xml"
    xlink:label="thestore" />
```

The label attribute is optional for the locator and resource elements, but must be provided if the element is going to participate in a link.

```
<GETMILK xlink:type="arc"
    xlink:from="thestore"
    xlink:to="myhouse"/>
```

We'll see later that labels can be reused on several resources in order to define several linking structures with one arc.

If we go to a diagram of resources A and B again, we will see that we have created an inbound link because we have defined our local resource, "myhouse" as the ending resource from "thestore", our remote starting resource. It is the addition of the traversal element GETMILK, of type arc, which makes this possible.

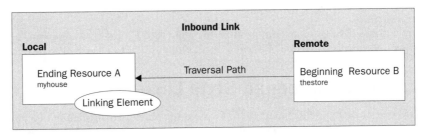

This is a neat trick if you think about it, because we don't need to own the thestore resource in order to suggest that it links to myhouse – meaning that the store could own the store.xml file, but we can still link from it.

If an XLink aware application were to parse an XML document with our example link, it would pre-load the remote resource upon recognition of the `locator` element in the extended link element on our local resource. So, prior to displaying anything, the `store.xml` resource is read into memory and a temporary file is created. Such a file may be created on the fly by a browser, or cached in a database before being made available; the actual implementation would depend on the application. Either way, you end up with a copy of the remote resource that now belongs to your application, and may have new information written to it.

If the application were written to create links to the local resource at the end of the page under the heading "Helpful Resources", you would get:

The remote resource, `store.xml` contained a simple sentence about the store. Our local resource provides directions to our house, and the store document has now been enhanced with the ability to provide those directions. Because the `arc` can be set with the `show` and actuate behavioral attributes, the directions to my house could be embedded in the document instead of just having a link to the `home.xml` document.

The linking element is still maintained in our document, but now is not implicitly set to be only a one way traversal. If you look at the structure of the extended link, and realize that there is no limit to the `resource`, `locator`, and `arc` elements you can define, you start to see the power of this linking structure.

I imagine you may still have some confusion at this point, but I wanted to whet your appetite a bit before getting into details. Now, let's hit some detail and apply it to what you have read already.

The Elements of Extended Style Links

As I noted above, the extended element is made up of the attributes the element contains, along with the child elements that appear within it. Each element then has elements that define its own role within the extended link, and its particular behavior. I think we will benefit from first looking at a diagram and then explaining it.

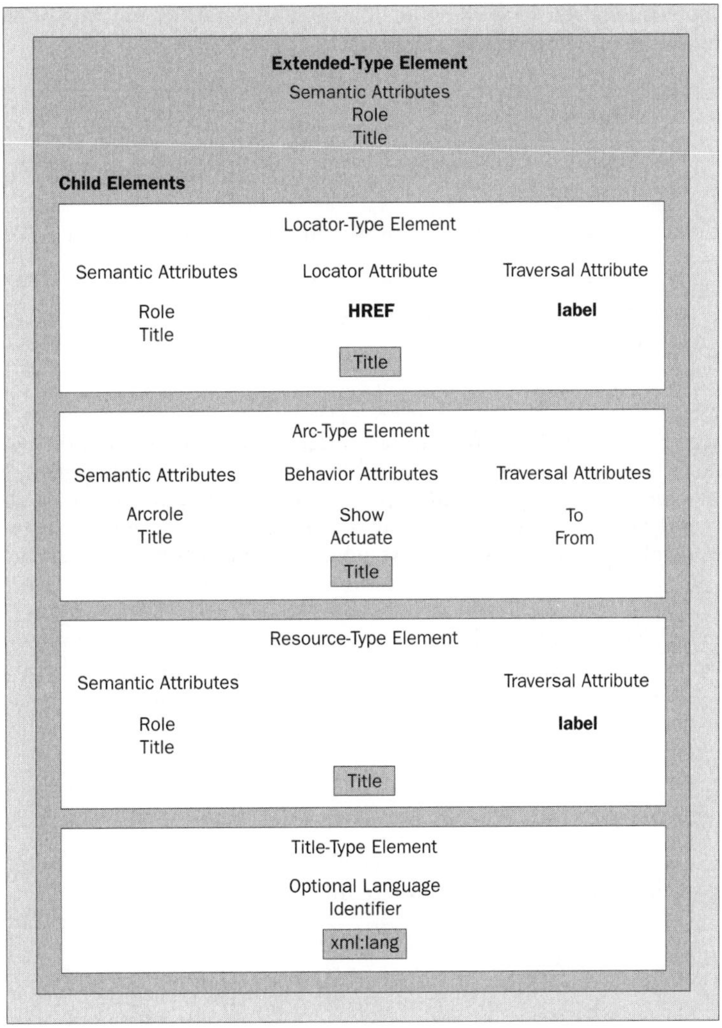

The entire box represents the extended linking element, with its child elements. As we saw in the last example, the child elements can take different values for the `type` attribute than the parent linking element. Each internal box represents one of the values for the type attribute that may appear within it:

❑   `locator`

❑   `arc`

❑   `resource`

❑   `title`

We shall look at each of these in turn shortly. Within each box, the available attributes are listed in a column that corresponds with its attribute type.

The `type` attribute is required on each child element, and describes the type of element. We have put the other attributes in the following classifications:

Classification	Meaning
Semantic	Describes the meaning of resource in the context of the link (`role`, `arcrole`, and `title`)
Traversal	These are used to write traversal rules (`label`, `to`, and `from`)
Behavior	Describe what happens upon traversal of an `arc` (show and `actuate`)
Locator	The familiar `href` attribute you recognize from HTML that takes a URI as its value

> **Title can be both an attribute and an element, and both may be contained within an XLink extended element and each of its children. This is a confusing point and the W3C recommendation doesn't really help to clarify what applications should do when they encounter different title values. One possible use for `title` elements would be to declare several types of titles for one extended link, ideally one per language.**

The `title` element has an additional attribute, `xml:lang`. The W3C recommendation states that this may be included to identify the current language choice in an application. The implementation of this addition to the `title` element will be entirely up to the writer of an XLink application.

So, let's take a look at each of the types of element:

The arc-type Element

The element with a value of `arc` for the `type` attribute describes the linking behavior in an extended link. In our last example, the `arc` defined where the link was between:

```
<GETMILK xlink:type="arc"
    xlink:from="thestore"
    xlink:to="myhouse" />
```

As we have just seen, an element whose `type` attribute has a value of `arc` can take the following attributes:

Semantic attributes:

- ❑   arcrole
- ❑   title

Behavior attributes:

- ❑   show
- ❑   actuate

Traversal attributes:

- ❑   to
- ❑   from

We discussed the `title` and the behavioral attributes when we talked about simple links. The new ones are `arcrole` (which we come back to later) and the traversal attributes.

The `to` and `from` attributes are used within the arc itself to show directionality. As a value, these attributes take the value of the `label` attribute of the resource or element type elements. In our last example, we defined the resource that represented our home with a label of `myhouse`:

```
<HOME xlink:type="resource"
    xlink:href="home.xml"
    xlink:label="myhouse"/>
```

Now, let's modify our earlier extended link so that we have to go to two different stores on our ROUTE: the GROCERY store and another resource called BOOKSTORE. Because arcs are describing generic behavior, if you use the same `label` on different resources, the `arc` will define a relationship between all the elements with the same label. If we make the label for both stores a generic "store" we can see how the `arc` is extended. The changes have been highlighted here:

```
<ROUTE xmlns:xlink="http://www.w3.org/1999/xlink"
    xlink:type="extended"
    xlink:title="A sample extended link">
    <HOME xlink:type="resource"
        xlink:label="myhouse" address="123 Main St.">
        I live in my home
    </HOME>
    <GROCERY xlink:type="locator"
        xlink:href="food.xml"
        xlink:label="store"/>
    <BOOKSTORE xlink:type="locator"
        xlink:href="books.xml"
        xlink:label="store"/>
    <GETSTUFF xlink:type="arc"
        xlink:from="store"
        xlink:to="myhouse"/>
</ROUTE>
```

The traversal of links now defined allows both the bookstore and the grocery store to be linked into "myhouse". We can see this in the following diagram:

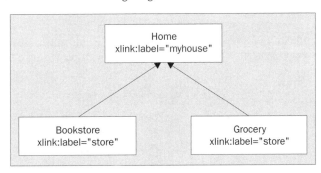

When we define an arc with the `to` and `from` attributes, this creates a traversal rule. Each traversal rule will explicitly set the behavior for a set of resources. Thus, it is significant to note that each `arc` element within an extended link must define a unique traversal rule. This makes sense, because once it is possible to traverse a certain direction from one resource to another, there is no need to define that traversal path again.

> **If you need to set a rule that you can get from resource A to resource B, then you can only set that rule once.**

Remember though that directionality is explicit, so that if we switch the `to` and the `from` attribute values:

```
<RETURNSTUFF
...
    xlink:from="myhouse"
    xlink"to="store" />
```

we have a different unique traversal rule, even though the same resources are in play.

> **If we need to set a rule that you can go from Resource B to Resource A, this is different from before, and we would require a new rule.**

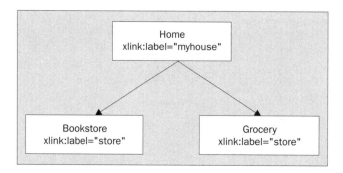

However, if the `from` or `to` attributes are absent from the `arc` element, then all resources in the extended link are assumed to be in play. In other words:

```
<STUFF xlink:type="arc">
```

This would be a legitimate `arc` for our example above that would accomplish the same thing as the `<GETSTUFF/>` and `<RETURNSTUFF/>` arc elements, along with providing a traversal between the store elements themselves.

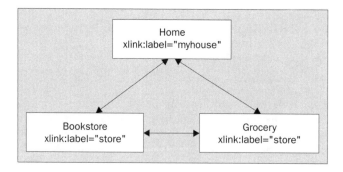

It would be illegal according to the XLink rules to define <STUFF/> in the same extended link as the other two, because <STUFF/> makes the other two repetitive.

> **If we have defined rules for getting from Resource A to Resource B, and for getting from Resource B to Resource A, we cannot also define a rule which allows us to move in both directions.**

The resource-type Element

The resource-type element is used for local resources in the extended link.

Note here that there is a distinction between local and remote resources. Remembering back to the last example, the type of our HOME element was resource, while the stores' type was locator.

```
<ROUTE xmlns:xlink="http://www.w3.org/1999/xlink"
...
        <HOME xlink:type="resource" ...></HOME>
        <GROCERY xlink:type="locator" .../>
...
</ROUTE>
```

HOME represented a local resource, while the stores represented remote resources.

In the resource element the link itself, along with any content of the link, is considered to be a local resource. It takes the following attributes:

Semantic:

- ❑ role
- ❑ title

Traversal:

- ❑ label

The local resource can be both a starting resource, and an ending resource in the same extended link. I hinted before at the possibilities for inbound links, and their magic starts here. If we put some meaningful content into our resource element:

```
<HOME xlink:type="resource"
    xlink:label="myhouse" address="123 Main St.">
    Go west on 5th until you come to Main St. Go east on Main St. to 123.
    I live on the 5th floor.
</HOME>
```

We can give our arc some behavior:

```
<GETSTUFF xlink:type="arc"
    xlink:from="store"
    xlink:to="myhouse"
    xlink:show="embed"
    xlink:actuate="onRequest" />
```

We have now done something neat. We have told our XLink application to display the directions to my house embedded in the current document when a person viewing a store resource clicks on the route.

Consider an application that is set to load an XML document called `orders.xml`. The `orders` document contains a `route` element for every location contained in a database of customers. Furthermore, the `route` elements have been written with the same arcs, to reference the order information documents for each type of store. If a user were to request the `orders.xml` document, our application would load each `store` resource document into a temporary file either on disk, or in memory. This would be based on the XLink aware application recognizing that `food.xml` and `books.xml` are remote resources as defined by the `locator-type` elements.

After each remote file has been loaded, its contents could be scanned for placeholders we have set. In this case, we might be working with a document we own, and can structure any way we like, but it will be read-only when parsed by our application. If we take one of the remote resources, `food.xml`, and give it the following structure:

```
<Food>
<Store type="Grocery">
   <Order id="383232" location="myhouse">
      <Item id="232" name="milk" />
      <Item id="565" name="cheese" />
   </Order>
</Store>
</Food>
```

then we could build our application to key on the `location` attribute in the `<Order>` element of each remote resource. The application can then insert the defined link at each place in each `store` resource document where a match for the label `myhouse` occurred, effectively attaching directions to each store order. Then, a final document containing all the information of the remote resources could be displayed to the user.

This may be hard to visualize since we don't have such an application, but consider this possible interpretation:

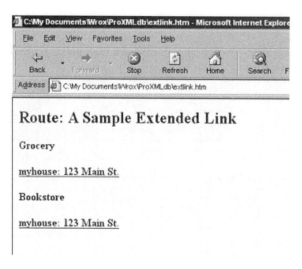

This display would be possible if an application were to display the extended link element names and attributes. As you can see, myhouse can be linked to from both store elements. If the user were to click on the myhouse element with the arc defined above they would get:

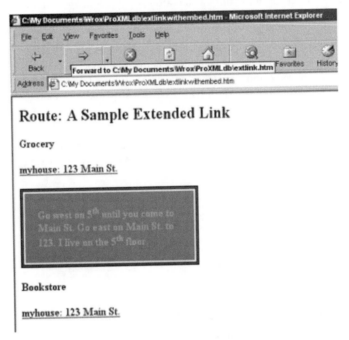

The document loaded for the user is not any one of the resources we have been working with. The user has asked to view the orders.xml document, which is nothing more than a placeholder for customer information. This customer information has been made useful via inbound links from documents containing order information. The orders.xml document as displayed appears to contain all of this information in one place. In actuality, it has loaded two read-only resources in the background, and enhanced their display with the local customer information.

The locator-type Element

As we have seen, the locator-type element is the remote resource being defined by the extended link element. It can take four attributes:

Semantic:

- ❑ role
- ❑ title

Locator:

- ❑ href

Traversal:

- ❑ label

There is only one mandatory attribute, href, which must have a URI value specified. However, the mere presence of an href attribute value does not give the locator element linking behavior.

Remember that it is the `arc` element that provides the linking behavior, and that the `arc` element uses the value of the `label` attribute to define the link. If a locator is missing from the `label` attribute, it simply cannot be identified in an `arc`, although it may still be useful to an XLink application as a descriptive element. However, it cannot participate in any XLink specified link..

It is the locator element that gives the extended link a lot of its power because it is able to identify resources that may be outside the control, or scope, of the document defining the link.

If an `arc` identifies a traversal rule between two locator elements, it is creating a **third-party** link. Third-party links are two or more remote resources being linked by a local document's linking element. The ability to describe links from remote resources provides a special `arc` called a linkbase.

Linkbases

Special collections of remote resources identified with locator elements can be defined with a **locating** `linkbase`. Linkbases are a special type of `arc` definition, which allows for simplified management of remote resources.

You specify this special `arc` with the `arcrole` attribute set to the following:

```
xlink:arcrole="http://www.w3.org/1999/xlink/properties/linkbase"
```

If we have numerous remote resources we would like to relate to one another, it may be simpler to hold each of these links in one document that can be loaded by our local documents.

This could be useful for:

❑   Creating a reference between documents you don't own

❑   Annotating documents written by others

❑   Maintaining a central link repository for easier maintenance

For example, imagine we had a number of stores, and all of them should be able to link to or from a shopping list. Rather than defining all of these stores inside of our particular extended element, we can load a pre-set listing of stores with a traversal rule for getting from stores to `myhouse`. In order for the XLink application to make use of these links, we define a `linkbase` arc that has the listing of links as the ending resource.

> A linkbase must be written as a well-formed XML document according to the W3C candidate recommendation. This makes sense because the `linkbase` document will be processed in order to retrieve the extended link information contained within.

In this way, if I have several remote resources that may all traverse to or from stores, not just my shopping list, then I can re-use the `store` resources again and again without putting all the stores in each extended linking element.

```
<ROUTE xmlns:xlink="http://www.w3.org/1999/xlink" xlink:type="extended">
    <HOME address="123 Main St."
        xlink:type="locator"
        xlink:label="myhouse"
        xlink:href="house.xml">
        All Stores
    </HOME>
```

```
    <STORES xlink:type="locator"
        xlink:href="storelinks.xml"
        xlink:label="allstores"/>
    <GROUPOLINKS xlink:type="arc"
        xlink:arcrole="http://www.w3.org/1999/xlink/properties/linkbase"
        xlink:from="myhouse"
        xlink:to="allstores"
        xlink:actuate="onRequest"/>
    </ROUTE>
```

Here, within our ROUTE, we have:

❑   HOME – which refers to a document that contains the directions to my house

❑   STORES – the locator, which specifies list of stores that I might wish to shop from, which points to the linkbase document. This is **not** a participating link resource. The document that it specifies will provide the link participants.

❑   GROUPOLINKS – which specifies the special arcrole attribute. The arc with this special arcrole will load the extended links in the document specified by the labeled locator listed as the ending resource in the arc.

Consider the following diagram:

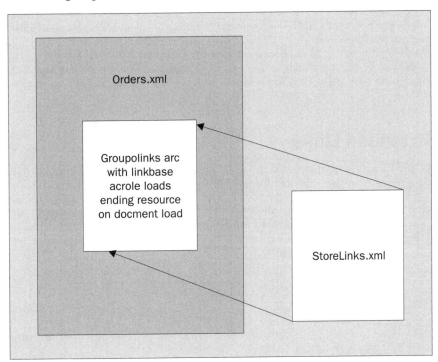

Whatever the contents of the storelinks.xml file, the extended links contained within will be pre-loaded when the orders.xml document is loaded. The links defined there are then available for the orders.xml document to use. This is a convenient way to locate each resource required for processing the orders.xml document before anything is displayed for the user. It also provides a way to keep the stores listing separated from the orders.xml document.

The `storelinks.xml` document, which is the `linkbase` document, may look like this:

```
<?xml version="1.0"?>
<LINKS xmlns:xlink="http://www.w3.org/1999/xlink" xlink:type="extended">
   <GROCERY xlink:type="locator" xlink:href="groceries.xml"
      xlink:label="store"/>
   <BOOKSTORE xlink:type="locator" xlink:href="books.xml" xlink:label="store"/>
   <CLOTHING xlink:type="locator" xlink:href="clothes.xml" xlink:label="store"/>
   <UTILITY xlink:type="locator" xlink:href="electricity.xml"
      xlink:label="store"/>
   <PLACESTOSHOP xlink:type="arc" xlink:from="store"  xlink:show="new"
      xlink:actuate="onRequest"/>
</LINKS>
```

in this case, a single extended link allowing all stores to traverse to the `house.xml` document. Notice that in this case, the `to` attribute has been left blank in order to relate all of these `store` locators to all resources in the `orders` document. However, the links within a linkbase can specify any traversal rule, even if this requires re-processing the originating document (`orders.xml`) to handle the links. When `orders.xml` is loaded, the only item to show for the user may be a link that says "All Stores". It would be upon selection of that link, that the stores information would become available. This would differ from the earlier example, which would have loaded all of the `store` resources along with directions right at load time.

> **Note that linkbases are not to be traversed. That is, they provide a document a list of links that may be traversed, but when linkbases themselves are loaded, they are only providing information to the document about the location of remote resources. This means that the show attribute is irrelevant in a linkbase. The actuate attribute is still relevant because we may not want all the links to show up until the user has asked for them.**

Using Extended Links

Before we move on, let's be sure we have a good picture of extended links by looking at a full example. We will look at the example of an invoice in XML.

The invoice document contains some standard elements such as `item`, `invoiceid`, `customers`, and `directions` to a particular customer's location. The attributes from the XLink namespace have been added to the various elements such that we now have the following XLink types:

Invoices.xml Element Name	XLink Type	Link Location
Invoice	Extended Link	
Description	Title	
invoiceid	local Resource resource	local – in document
item	remote Locator resource	/inventory/items.xml
customer	remote Locator resource	/contacts/customers.xml
directions	local Resource resource	local – in document
getdetail	Arc	

Here is the DTD for the XML invoice, so that we can work with a validated XML document, and get the benefit of writing the actual elements in a more simplified manner as well (ch09_ex1.dtd):

```
<!ELEMENT invoice ((description|invoiceid|item|customer|directions|getdetail)*)>
<!ATTLIST invoice
    xlink:type        (extended)    #FIXED "extended"
    xlink:role        CDATA         #IMPLIED
    xlink:title       CDATA         #IMPLIED>

<!ELEMENT description ANY>
<!ATTLIST description
    xlink:type        (title)       #FIXED "title">

<!ELEMENT invoiceid ANY>
<!ATTLIST invoiceid
    xlink:type        (resource)    #FIXED "resource"
    xlink:role        CDATA         #IMPLIED
    xlink:title       CDATA         #IMPLIED
    xlink:label       CDATA         #FIXED "invoiceid">

<!ELEMENT item EMPTY>
<!ATTLIST item
    itemid            CDATA         #REQUIRED
    qty               CDATA         #REQUIRED
    xlink:type        (locator)     #FIXED "locator"
    xlink:href        CDATA         #REQUIRED
    xlink:role        CDATA         #IMPLIED
    xlink:title       CDATA         #IMPLIED
    xlink:label       NMTOKEN       #FIXED "item">

<!ELEMENT customer EMPTY>
<!ATTLIST customer
    customerid        CDATA         #REQUIRED
    xlink:type        (locator)     #FIXED "locator"
    xlink:href        CDATA         #REQUIRED
    xlink:role        CDATA         #IMPLIED
    xlink:title       CDATA         #IMPLIED
    xlink:label       NMTOKEN       #FIXED "customer">

<!ELEMENT directions ANY>
<!ATTLIST directions
    xlink:type        (resource)    #FIXED "resource"
    xlink:role        CDATA         #IMPLIED
    xlink:title       CDATA         #IMPLIED
    xlink:label       NMTOKEN       #FIXED "directions">
<!ELEMENT getdetail EMPTY>
<!ATTLIST getdetail
    xlink:type        (arc)                         #FIXED "arc"
    xlink:arcrole     CDATA                         #IMPLIED
    xlink:title       CDATA                         #IMPLIED
    xlink:show (new|replace|embed|other|none)       #IMPLIED
    xlink:actuate (onLoad|onRequest|other|none)     #IMPLIED
    xlink:from        NMTOKEN                       #IMPLIED
    xlink:to          NMTOKEN                       #IMPLIED>
```

Remember, you can type this in if you want the practice, or you can go and download it from the web site for this book along with all of the other sample code: http://www.wrox.com.

The DTD provides the necessary structure, and gets some of the mundane details down in one place. This will be more important as you go to implement this in the real world, because unlike our example you would likely be generating numerous instances of the same element type. That being said, here is the XML document (ch11_ex1.xml):

```
<?xml version="1.0"?>
<!DOCTYPE invoice SYSTEM " ch11_ex1.dtd">

    <invoice xmlns:xlink="http://www.w3.org/1999/xlink"
        xlink:title="Invoice Detail for Order number 123456">

        <description xlink:type="title">
        Customer Details for Invoices</description>

        <invoiceid>123456</invoiceid>

        <item itemid="9876" qty="500"
              xlink:href="/inventory/items.xml"
              xlink:title="items on customer invoice"/>

        <item itemid="4321" qty="25"
              xlink:href="/inventory/items.xml"/>

        <customer customerid="765423"
              xlink:href="/contacts/customers.xml"
              xlink:role="http://sample.bigwarehouse.ex/customer/invoiceref"/>

        <directions>Turn left from warehouse, drive 5mi. on route 3 to Johnson.
                Turn left onto Johnson and continue to Main St.
        </directions>

        <getdetail arcrole="http://sample.bigwarehouse.ex/invoice/details"
              xlink:show="replace"
              xlink:actuate="onRequest"
              xlink:from="invoiceid"/>
    </invoice>
```

While this XML document is well formed and valid, it is not likely that such a document would stand-alone in the real world. Rather, this would be a single invoice in a list of invoices in a document. As we'll see in the next section, a document like this could easily represent the data in a table from a relational database. Before we move on I would like to note a few features of this example.

Notice the use of the title attribute as well as the title element.

```
<invoice xmlns:xlink="http://www.w3.org/1999/xlink"
    xlink:title="Invoice Detail for Order number 123456">

    <description xlink:type="title">
        Customer Details for Invoices</description>
```

The proliferation of titles throughout XLink may seem like overkill, but consider that the attribute may be rendered as something like a tool tip for the invoice link, while the title-type element may be used for the entire resulting document.

I would also like to draw attention to the addition of non-XLink attributes in the locator elements. XLink is not a set of element names that only describe links; it is a set of element types declared through the use of namespace-prefixed attributes. Other non-XLink attributes, child elements and content of the elements used to create a link are not a hindrance for XLink to do its job.

Extended Link Summary

We have seen how to use the XLink language to create both simple and extended linking elements. In looking at extended links, the usefulness of arcs was introduced to show the added feature of multi-directional linking. Of particular importance was the notion of the in-bound link, which had a remote link as a starting resource. In the next section we will look at how an extended link can be used in conjunction with XPointer to create structures that describe relational data.

Extended Links and Relational Data

Okay, we have given a good coverage of the basics on writing extended links and they look cool and seem useful, but why are they in a book about XML databases? Well, the reason is that they provide a great way to describe relational data within an XML document. Let's see our simple database tables from the beginning of this chapter written as XML. We'll call the database Orders:

```
<Orders>
    <Invoice InvoiceKey="187">
        <invoiceitem ItemKey="13"/>
        <invoiceitem ItemKey="14"/>
    </Invoice>
    <Invoice InvoiceKey="188">
        <invoiceitem ItemKey="13"/>
    </Invoice>
</Orders>
```

Tables are expressed as elements, with one for each row. I am showing each value from the table rows as an attribute value, but each could be the text content value of the element if you like. In the hierarchical way of XML we express the joining table, InvoiceItem, by the appropriate nesting of elements.

> *This particular view is invoice-centric. If we wanted to look at invoices by item, the nesting would be reversed, and sorted by the item key. If you need to understand the XML to relational table transfer more fully, see Chapter 2.*

As we will see in Chapter 14, we could produce this output from SQL server 2000 using the new XML aware processing features. If you want to produce this output with SQL Server 2000 you would use the following query:

```
SELECT 1 AS Tag, Null AS Parent, invoice.invoicekey AS [Invoice!1!InvoiceKey],
    Null AS [invoiceitem!2!ItemKey] FROM invoice
UNION
SELECT 2,1,invoice.invoicekey,invoiceitem.itemkey FROM invoice,invoiceitem
    WHERE invoice.invoicekey = invoiceitem.invoicekey
ORDER BY [invoice!1!invoicekey],[invoiceitem!2!itemkey] FOR xml EXPLICIT
```

Making the Relationship with XLink

Now that we have the data-set defined in XML, we can take a look at the power of XLink to make it a more useful document. First, we have to have a business case that makes sense. Let's consider the following scenario:

❑ We have built an XML application for a warehouse that receives order documents from a data entry application. The order documents contain invoice information, tying customers to invoices, and displaying items that will be needed to complete the order.

❑ Our application then presents the information to a stock handler for processing; the stock handler will need to know where in the warehouse to retrieve each item requested on the invoice.

❑ The document we have received is read-only, and the item location information is located in a different document. In other words, we need some way to mark up the invoice with location information to help the stock handlers, but we cannot edit the invoices directly.

In this example, we will relate the `orders` documents with the proper locations from the locations documents in order to mark up the invoice in such a way that stock handlers can look at just one document for all the information they need.

If our item key is an SKU or other ID recognized by the order taker and our warehouse, we can mark up our location document like this:

```
<?xml version="1.0"?>
<ItemLocations
    xmlns:xlink="http://www.w3.org/1999/xlink"
    xlink:type="extended">

    <itemlocation
        xlink:type="resource"
        xlink:label="location"
        itemkey="13">
        R15L5
    </itemlocation>

    <Item
        xlink:type="locator"
        xlink:href="acme.mfg.com/invoice.xml#itemkey(13)"
        xlink:label="item" />
    <itemlocation
        xlink:type="resource"
        xlink:label="location"
        itemkey="14">
        R3L1
    </itemlocation>

    <Item
        xlink:type="locator"
        xlink:href="acme.mfg.com/invoice.xml#itemkey(14)"
        xlink:label="item" />
```

```
  <itemlocation
    xlink:type="resource"
    xlink:label="location"
    itemkey="15">
    R5L6
</itemlocation>

<Item
    xlink:type="locator"
    xlink:href="acme.mfg.com/invoice.xml#itemkey(15)"
    xlink:label="item" />

<itemlocation
    xlink:type="resource"
    xlink:label="location"
    itemkey="16">
    R13L3
</itemlocation>

<Item
    xlink:type="locator"
    xlink:href="acme.mfg.com/invoice.xml#itemkey(16)"
    xlink:label="item" />

<itemlocation
    xlink:type="resource"
    xlink:label="location"
    itemkey="17">
    R11L3
</itemlocation>

<Item
    xlink:type="locator"
    xlink:href="acme.mfg.com/invoice.xml#itemkey(17)"
    xlink:label="item" />

<getdetail
    xlink:type="arc"
    xlink:show="embed"
    xlink:actuate="onRequest"
    xlink:to="location"
    xlink:from="item" />

</ItemLocations>
```

The item location document has been declared an extended link, so each child element that has XLink attributes can be understood to display some XLink behavior. This document is generic and presents only two pieces of information, the bin location, and the name of the XML document we expect to receive from the order application. As the warehouse, we control this document and can change the information within. However, we do not want the stock handlers to view this document, but rather the orders which have come in. The locator declaration:

```
<Item
    xlink:type="locator"
    xlink:href="acme.mfg.com/invoice.xml#itemkey(14)"
    xlink:label="item" />
```

points to the main document. This locator includes the very simple XPointer reference

```
xlink:href="acme.mfg.com/invoice.xml#itemkey(14)"
```

which states: get a result set from `invoice.xml` where the `itemkey` is 14. This will return a portion of the invoice document, rather than the entire contents. This will allow us to retrieve only the location information for our particular item to display at this point, rather than displaying all item locations. You can read about XPointer in the next chapter on other XML technologies, or in the book *Professional XML*, also by Wrox Press (ISBN18610031110).

We know that `ch09_ex1.xml` should be the starting document resource from the `arc` declaration:

```
<getdetail
   xlink:type="arc"
   xlink:show="embed"
   xlink:actuate="onRequest"
   xlink:to="location" xlink:from="item" />
```

This shows the item-labeled element to be the `xlink:from` resource. In this way, our XLink aware application is able to show the user the `invoice.xml` document, but provide the location information as embedded in the document when the user requests the information (presumably by selecting a link). It is also difficult to say how an application will handle the specific references to items. The application may choose to aggregate all the links on the screen at one time because all are declared within the same document, or it may choose to strictly display one at a time. If the latter is true, some mechanism will be required to alert the application that the user is finished with one link, and prepare for the next.

> Application developers will have to carefully consider how to handle a circumstance where a local resource contains more than one remote resource as the starting resource for links contained within the document. One possible solution would be to only display the first such link. Therefore, you should be careful not to depend on a second inbound link, and really should avoid this situation altogether.

What has happened here? We owned a data source that was particular to our own warehouse, and made a relationship with data coming from a third party. Because we only have control over our document, it would not have been possible to create such links in HTML. Furthermore, we would have required either an RDBMS to query for locations, or would have to process the XML document before display to achieve similar results.

Summary

In this chapter we have seen that XLink is a powerful new standard offering linking mechanisms beyond HTML's one-way links. The multi-directional extended XLink element provides the greatest opportunity to define meaningful relationships between documents. As XLink moves toward the end of the W3C recommendation stage, we can be sure browser developers will move quickly to include this powerful linking mechanism. Simple additions to existing documents, or new linking documents can be created to take advantage of XLink in a relatively short time period. By the time you are reading this, some applications may already be available. Experiment and enjoy!

Additional Resources

Check out the early Xlink application efforts of Fujitsu at:
http://www.fujitsu.co.jp/hypertext/free/xlp/en/sample.html

This application uses linkbases on a special server to create links in read-only documents. There is also an extended link server implementation from Empolis UK called X2X at:
http://www.empolis.co.uk/products/prod_X2X.asp

This demo application gives an idea of what your links would do, but actually won't do much of anything. It also does not support the use of DTDs. Neither application is a complete XLink implementation, but are the best available examples, and will almost certainly be improved over time.

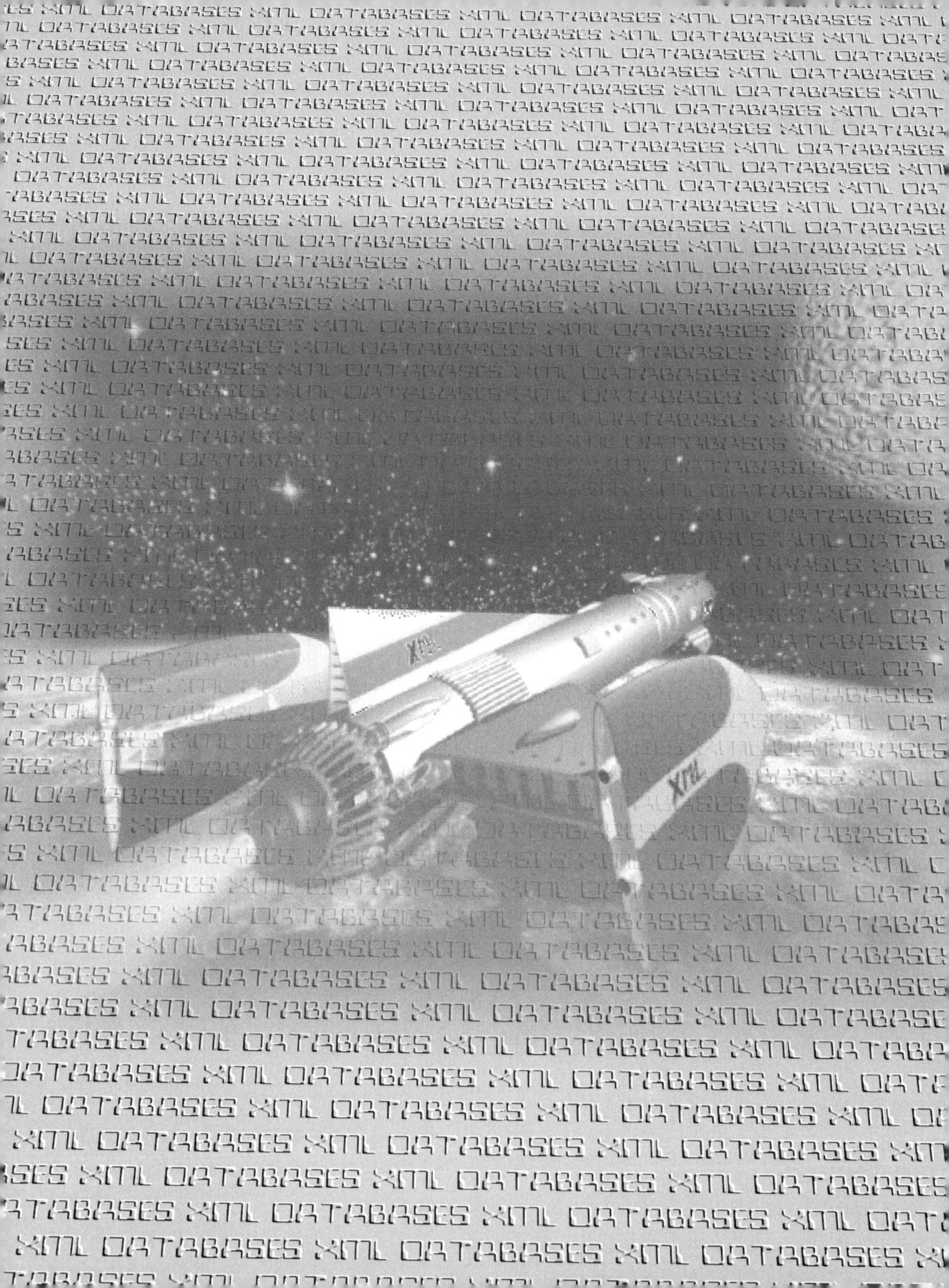
XML DATABASES XML DATABASES XML DATABASES

10

Other Technologies (XBase, XPointer, XInclude, XHTML, XForms)

In the first section of this book, many of the topics dealt directly with XML 1.0 and its use with databases. In the second section, we have been looking at related specifications and how they have been extended into their own technologies. As we saw in the last chapter, XLink is an example of such a specification, although we are still waiting to see implementations of it. In this chapter we are going to learn more about some other related technologies. Many of these technologies do not directly manipulate data within a database, but they do provide different methods to present data:

❑ **XBase** – underpins linking technologies providing a base URL for relative URLs to feed off so that you only need change the base URL

❑ **XPointer** – The XML pointing language, used with XLink, allowing you to point to a certain part of an XML document

❑ **XInclude** – The powerful inclusion method, to save replication of common data in several places

❑ **XHTML** – an existing standard that enforces XML syntax when writing HTML – ensuring that it is well-formed and can be read by an XML processor

❑ **XForms** – The next generation of XML based forms

We will not go into great depth with XBase, XPointer, and XInclude since they are still likely to evolve. However, just like XLink, they are still important to understand so that you will be able to make use of the power that they will offer. At first, because they are complementary technologies, and some extend features offered by others, it can be difficult to see the exact difference or intended use of each, this chapter will help clear up questions like this.

XHTML is the latest reformulation of HTML. We'll be looking at how it differs from HTML, and why HTML needed to be improved in the first place.

XForms are the next generation of web forms, and are aimed at enabling the creation of form structures that are independent of the end user interface. XForms achieve this by separating the user interface from the data model and logic layer. That means XForms are split into three different layers, which allow a means to exchange data between a client and database.

We'll start by exploring the possibilities of XBase.

XBase

XLink, as we learned in the previous chapter, is the XML linking language that provides a way to describe links between resources. These resources can be XML documents, data objects, a list of HTML links, or any data source to be exposed to other technologies. One of the stated requirements set by the W3C XLink Working Group (who create the XLink standard), is to support HTML linking constructs. This has its pros and cons, but it does allow us to utilize a Base type construct like that of the <BASE> element in HTML. This XML version is called XBase.

> *At the time of writing XBase is a candidate recommendation, so now is the time to give your input to this technology via the W3C web site (http://www.w3.org/XML/Linking). Because there is still a good chance that XBase will change, it is not widely supported at present.*

In HTML the <HEAD> element appears inside the <HEAD> element, and defines the base URL, or original location of the document. If <BASE> is included, the URL it specifies is used to create absolute addresses for any relative ones. This means that when a document is moved, we only need to update the URL in the <BASE> element, and all of the relative links still work (links that do not include the entire server and directory path). This is because the base URL is defined as the new, current URL for the document.

In HTML, we declare the <BASE> element like so:

```
<BASE HREF="http://myserver.org/inthisdir/filename.html">
```

So, when we use a link like this in our HTML document:

```
<A HREF="#section2">
```

it would resolve to http://myserver.org/inthisdir/filename.html#section2.

XBase offers similar functionality in a single attribute xml:base. With this simplicity comes flexibility. It can be used in conjunction with XLink, to specify the base URI as something other than that of the document. For example, if we wanted to resolve a link to several different resources, including images, data objects, and XML documents, we can specify the relative URI while using xml:base to define the resource base URI.

Let's see just how simple this is. Look at this list of XLinks:

```
<?xml version="1.0"?>

<ItemLocations xml:base="http://acme.mfg.com/invoice.xml/"
    xmlns:xlink="http://www.w3.org/1999/xlink"
    xlink:type="extended">

    <itemlocation xlink:type="resource"
       xlink:label="location"
       itemkey="13">
       R15L5
    </itemlocation>

    <Item xlink:type="locator"
       xlink:href="#itemkey(13)"
       xlink:label="item" />

    <itemlocation xlink:type="resource"
       xlink:label="location"
       itemkey="14">
       R3L1
    </itemlocation>

    <Item xlink:type="locator"
       xlink:href="#itemkey(14)"
       xlink:label="item" />

    <itemlocation xlink:type="resource"
       xlink:label="location"
       itemkey="15">
       R5L6
    </itemlocation>

    <Item xlink:type="locator"
       xlink:href="#itemkey(15)"
       xlink:label="item"/>

    <itemlocation xlink:type="resource"
       xlink:label="location"
       itemkey="16">R13L3</itemlocation>

     <Item xlink:type="locator"
       xlink:href="#itemkey(16)"
        xlink:label="item"/>

    <itemlocation xlink:type="resource"
       xlink:label="location"
       itemkey="17">
       R11L3
    </itemlocation>

    <Item xlink:type="locator"
       xlink:href="#itemkey(17)"
       xlink:label="item"/>

    <getdetail xlink:type="arc"
       xlink:show="embed"
       xlink:actuate="onRequest"
       xlink:to="location"
       xlink:from="item"/>

</ItemLocations>
```

This is almost the same as one of our examples from the previous chapter, but we've made a few changes. We are no longer explicitly stating the full URI as a resource. Originally we stated the XLink with this form:

```
<Item
    xlink:type="locator"
    xlink:href="acme.mfg.com/invoice.xml#itemkey(17)"
    xlink:label="item" />
```

In our new example, we have used the XML attribute `xml:base` to identify the base or root URI:

```
xml:base="http://acme.mfg.com/invoice.xml/"
```

Note the trailing / at the end. This is essential with XLink, but not with HTML. This allows our new XLink:

```
xlink:href="#itemkey(17)"
```

to resolve to http://acme.mfg.com/invoice.xml#itemkey(17). This is the core of XBase.

"Advanced" XBase

We have seen the principle behind XBase, and it doesn't get much more advanced than this. One thing we can do is define several base URIs.

In the last example, we made all URIs resolve to the same file, `invoice.xml`, which was in http://acme.mfg.com. However, if we wanted to supply links to other documents as well, we can use containment to do this.

For example, say the path to our XML document for the ACME manufacturing division is http://acme.mfg.com/manufacturing, and we also want to add links that resolve to http://acme.mfg.com/supply, where our hypothetical XML document for the ACME supply division is located. We could do something like this:

```
<?xml version="1.0"?>

<ItemLocations xml:base="http://acme.mfg.com"
    xmlns:xlink="http://www.w3.org/1999/xlink"
    xlink:type="extended">

    <itemlocation xlink:type="resource"
        xlink:label="location"
        itemkey="13">R15L5</itemlocation>

<companyinvoice companyid="1"
    xml:base="/manufacturing/">

    <Item xlink:type="locator"
        xlink:href=" invoice.xml#itemkey(13)"
        xlink:label="item"/>
    ...
```

```
    <getdetail xlink:type="arc"
       xlink:show="embed"
       xlink:actuate="onRequest"
       xlink:to="location"
       xlink:from="item"/>
</companyinvoice>

<companyinvoice companyid="2" xml:base="/supply/">

    <itemlocation xlink:type="resource"
       xlink:label="location"
       itemkey="16">R13L3</itemlocation>

    <Item xlink:type="locator"
       xlink:href="invoice.xml#itemkey(16)"
       xlink:label="item"/>

    <itemlocation xlink:type="resource"
       xlink:label="location"
       itemkey="17">R11L3</itemlocation>

    <Item xlink:type="locator"
       xlink:href=" invoice.xml#itemkey(17)"
       xlink:label="item"/>

    <getdetail xlink:type="arc"
       xlink:show="embed"
       xlink:actuate="onRequest"
       xlink:to="location"
       xlink:from="item"/>

</companyinvoice>

</ItemLocations>
```

We have made a few changes to the example, so let's break down what is happening.

The document base refers to http://acme.mfg.com, which is the parent base embedded in the parent element of the document's content:

```
<ItemLocations xml:base="http://acme.mfg.com"
    xmlns:xlink="http://www.w3.org/1999/xlink"
    xlink:type="extended">
```

All other child elements referring to XBase then resolve to an extension of the parent base. We have added child bases in the <companyinvoice> elements. In the first <companyinvoice> element we point to the manufacturing section:

```
<companyinvoice companyid="1" xml:base="/manufacturing/">

    <Item xlink:type="locator"
       xlink:href="invoice.xml#itemkey(13)"
       xlink:label="item"/>
```

This address resolves to http://acme.mfg.com/manufacturing/invoice.xml#itemkey(13).

In the second <companyinvoice> element, however, we are resolving to http://acme.mfg.com/supply/invoice.xml#itemkey(16):

```
<companyinvoice companyid="2" xml:base="/supply/">

    <itemlocation xlink:type="resource"
        xlink:label="location"
        itemkey="16">R13L3</itemlocation>
```

There are some simple rules that you should follow when using XBase.

Determining the Base URI and Relative URIs

In an XML document, the value of a relative URI is determined relative to either an element or the document – the granularity doesn't get any finer than the element level.

The W3C recommendation specifies the following rules governing how the base URI of an element is determined:

1. If the xml:base attribute is specified on the element, this is taken as the base URI of the element

2. If no xml:base attribute is specified on the element itself, but the element has a parent element for which an xml:base attribute is specified, the element takes the base URI of its ancestor

3. If the xml:base attribute is not specified, the base URI is the URI used to retrieve the XML document (or in the case of XLINK or XPointer, which we'll learn about later, the URI that the data is retrieved from)

For example, in our first example, there is no xml:base attribute specified for the Item element:

```
<Item xlink:type="locator"
    xlink:href="#itemkey(13)"
    xlink:label="item" />
```

Following rule 2, this takes the base URI of its parent ItemLocations:

```
<ItemLocations xml:base="http://acme.mfg.com/invoice.xml/"
```

Relative URIs are then related to their corresponding base URI as follows:

1. If the relative URI reference appears in text content, the base URI is that of the element containing the text.

2. If the relative URI reference appears in the xml:base attribute of an element, the base URI is that of the parent of that element. If no base URI is specified for the parent, the base URI is that of the document containing the element.

3. If the relative URI reference appears in any other attribute value (including default attribute values), the base URI is that of the element bearing the attribute.

4. If the relative URI reference appears in a processing instruction, the base URI is that of the parent element of the processing instruction. If there isn't one, the base URI of the document containing the processing instruction is taken.

So in our second example, where a relative URI is specified in the xml:base attribute of the companyinvoice element:

```
<companyinvoice companyid="2" xml:base="/supply/">
```

the base URI is that of the element's parent, ItemLocations:

```
<ItemLocations xml:base="http://acme.mfg.com"
```

XBase Summary

As we have seen, XBase is really quite simple. It is there to support the requirement from the W3C that XML Linking should support the functionality offered by HTML 4.0 linking constructs, and it can be very useful despite its simplicity. We have also seen how we can specify several base documents, and how containment can give us flexibility in where our links point to.

At the time of writing, XBase is a recommendation, and may be subject to change. The details on its implementation are necessarily still sketchy, but keep an eye on the W3C site for the latest updates (http://www.w3.org/XML/Linking and http://www.w3.org/TR/xmlbase).

XBase is best used in conjunction with XPointer and XLink. We've seen XLink in the previous chapter, but what does this XPointer thing do?

XPointer

XPointer extends XPath and can be used in conjunction with XLink. It allows you to identify specific data within a resource described in an XLink.

Imagine we have a set of large XML documents, perhaps a year's worth of invoices, with each document holding the invoices for a calendar month. If we wanted to process individual invoices from the month's records, we might not want to have to pull up the whole document. XLink allows us to specify the document that holds a certain month's records. XPath goes a step further by allowing us to point to the specific instance of the invoice (or any other part of the document) we want within that document, so that an application can retrieve that section.

XPointer works by extending the XPath syntax. The power of XPointer lies in the fact that we can use it to retrieve data on any scale from within documents: whole documents, elements, sections of character data, or any valid part of an XML entity. We don't even have to retrieve whole nodes: we can, for example, just select the first few characters in a text node, or the last few characters of the text node in one element and the first few characters of the text node from the next element.

XPath was created for use in both linking and XSLT.

Note that XPointer only works with resources that have a media type of text/xml or application/xml.

The XPointer specification will also allow documents to identify themselves, and allow alternative addressing of such languages such as SVG or SMIL. Remember XPointer simply points to or exposes a target.

Technology Status

At the time of writing, XPointer is a candidate recommendation. For the full specification, and latest details as to the progress of the technology, check out http://www.w3.org/XML/Linking and http://www.w3.org/TR/xptr.

The W3C currently list the following implementations of XPointer:

❑ Fujitsu XLink Processor: an implementation of XLink and XPointer, developed by Fujitsu Laboratories Ltd (http://www.fujitsu.co.jp/hypertext/free/xlp/en/index.html)

❑ libxml: the Gnome XML library has a beta implementation of XPointer, which supports the full syntax although not all aspects are covered (http://xmlsoft.org/)

❑ 4XPointer: an XPointer processor written in Python by Fourthought, Inc (http://fourthought.com/4Suite/4XPointer/)

Locations and Targets

XPointer allows us to examine the internal structure of XML data, and it calls these internal workings **location sets**. More specifically, it defines how to expose an XML document to obtain **targets** – elements, character strings, and other parts of an XML document – irrespective of whether or not they bear an explicit ID attribute.

While using ID attributes within XML is desirable, it's not required. Yes, the desired targets could be obtained using the DOM or SAX: but what if the desired target was a bit of data, such as that specific invoice item located within our XML document? It would be overkill to link to the XML document, load the document, and walk the DOM to the specific node or target we were looking to expose.

Putting it in traditional RDBMS speak, imagine using an API to open a database system, then programmatically opening the database, then selecting all of the fields, before finally arriving at the data element you were after. In reality you would simply write one query. For example if we wanted to query the database used in the previous chapter we would do something like this:

```
SELECT invoiceitem FROM invoice WHERE invoicekey = 187
```

With the help of XPath, we can accomplish this type of request with XPointer.

Keep in mind that XPointer does not query a document, it only points within the document

Identifiers Using XPointer and XLink

The W3C specification defines how identifiers, called **fragment identifiers**, can be used to point to targets within XML documents, or any valid XML entity. The specification is complex, but does allow the kind of flexibility that should really generate creativity in the use of XPointer in the future.

As we will see, there are three types of fragment identifier:

- ❑ Full form
- ❑ Bare names
- ❑ Child sequences

Let's expand on an example from the previous chapter, using the `Orders.xml` document located at http://www.orders.com/orders/:

```
<ORDERS>
 ...
  <Invoice InvoiceKey="187">
      <invoiceitem ItemKey="13"/>
      <invoiceitem ItemKey="14"/>
  </Invoice>

  <Invoice InvoiceKey="188">
      <invoiceitem ItemKey="13"/>
  </Invoice>
 ...
  </ORDERS>
```

We'll see how we can point to a section of it using the different types of fragment identifier.

Full Form

In this document we have several invoices. If our desired target is the invoice information with the `Invoicekey` of 187, we can point to this information, along with its child elements, and disregard the rest of the document.

In this first example, we will use a **full form** fragment identifier to target the part of the document we want. To point to the invoice with a key of 187, we would add something like this to our referring XML document:

```
xlink:href =
      "http://www.orders.com/orders/orders.xml#xpointer(InvoiceKey("187"))"
```

This form of addressing starts with the schema name `xpointer`, followed by an expression identifying the target. In this case the target is `InvoiceKey("187")`. We can use this in our XML in pretty much the same way as we use normal `xlink:href` attributes: it's just that in this case we're pointing to a specific section of `orders.xml` document.

Bare Names

We can also point to the invoice with an `Invoicekey` of 187 using a **bare name** fragment identifier. To do so, we can simply state:

```
xlink:href = "http://www.orders.com/orders/orders.xml#187"
```

This just uses the id (187). It has shed its XPointer clothing for a shorter form. The idea behind bare names is that they encourage the use of explicit, unique IDs (so in our example, the `InvoiceKey` would have to be declared as a datatype of ID in our schema).

However, using bare names instead of the full form leads to much less readable code – so for reasons of code legibility, you might prefer to avoid them.

Child Sequences

The **child sequence** fragment identifier is often referred to as the **tumbler identifier**. These identifiers allow us to tumble through a target tree, a little bit like walking the DOM. Let's look at the sample data again:

```
<ORDERS>

<Invoice InvoiceKey="187">
    <invoiceitem ItemKey="13"/>
    <invoiceitem ItemKey="14"/>
</Invoice>
<Invoice InvoiceKey="188">
    <invoiceitem ItemKey="13"/>
</Invoice>
<Invoice InvoiceKey="189">
    <invoiceitem ItemKey="11"/>
</Invoice>

</ORDERS>
```

If the desired target is a single point, called a **singleton**, we could point to it with the following child sequence fragment identifier. Let's see how we would point to a single invoiceitem from the invoice with an invoicekey of 189:

```
xlink:href = "http://www.orders.com/orders/orders.xml#1/3/1"
```

This is not as foreign as it would appear, as it is indicating the positional number of the element. Let's look at what is going on step by step:

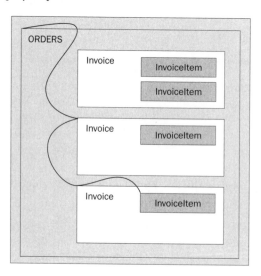

#1/3/1 is used as the fragment identifier because we need to:

1. Go to the first element <ORDERS> (hence the 1 in #1/3/1)

2. Then go to the third child element of ORDERS, <Invoice InvoiceKey="189"> (hence the 3)

3. Then go to the first child element of the current element, <invoiceitem ItemKey="11"/> (hence the 1)

Extensions to XPath

In the last example, we exposed a single target or **point**. These points can be any valid part of an XML entity. This is very useful for pointing to a specific item of data, but we may also need to define a range of content, which is not neatly nested within a particular element. For example, we may want a selection of elements from a group that are at the same level from a parent element. In these cases, we can use a pair of points to define a **range.**

Points

> A point **is simply a spot in the XML document. It is defined using the usual XPointer expressions.**

There are two pieces of information needed to define a point: a **container node** and an **index**. Points are located between bits of XML; that is between two elements or between two characters in a CDATA section. Whether the point refers to characters or elements depends on the nature of the container node. An index of zero indicates the point before any child nodes, and a non-zero index n indicates the point immediately after the nth child node. (So an index of 5 indicates the point right after the 5th child node.)

When the container node is an element (or the document root), the index becomes an index of the child elements, and the point is called a **node-point**. In the following diagram, the container node is the <name> element, and the index is 2. This means the point indicates a spot right after the second child element of <name>, which is the <middle> element:

The XPointer expression for this would be:

```
#xpointer(/name[2])
```

If the container is any other node-type, the index refers to the characters of the string value of that node, and the point is called a **character-point.**

In the following diagram, the container node is the PCDATA child of `<middle>`, and the index is 2, indicating a point right after the i and right before the t of Fitzgerald:

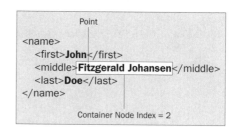

The XPointer expression for this would be:

```
#xpointer(/name/middle/text()[2])
```

Ranges

A range **is defined by two points – a** start point **and an** end point **– and consists of all of the XML structure and content between those two points.**

The start point and end point must both be in the same document. If the start point and the end point are equal, the range is a **collapsed range**. However, a range can't have a start point that is *later* in the document than the end point.

If the container node of either point is anything other than an element node, text node, or document root node, then the container node of the other point must be the same. For example, the following range is valid, because both the start point and the end point are in the same PI:

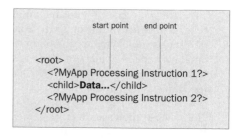

whereas this one is not, because the start point and end point are in different PIs:

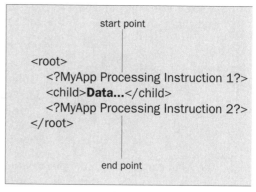

The concept of a range is the reason that the XPath usage of nodes and node-sets weren't good enough for XPointer; the information contained in a range might include only parts of nodes, which XPath can't handle.

How Do We Select Ranges?

XPointer adds the keyword `to`, which we can insert in our XPointer expressions to specify a range. It's used as follows:

```
xpointer(/order/name to /order/item)
```

This selects a range where the start point is just before the `<name>` element, and the end point is just after the `<item>` element:

```
                        <?xml version="1.0" ?>
                        <order>
Start point  ──────▶    <name>
                           <first>John</first>
                           <middle />
                           <last>Doe</last>
                        </name>
                        <item>Production-Class Widget</item>
End point  ──────▶      <quantity>16</quantity>
                        <date>
                           <m>1</m>
                           <d>1</d>
                           <y>2000</y>
                        </date>
                        <customer>Sally Finkelstein</customer>
                        </order>
```

In other words, the `<name>` and `<item>` elements would both be part of this range, which would be the only member in the location set.

Going back to our previous invoice example, we could point to the data within the range where our `itemkey` element values are between 11 and 14. If you think about a SQL query like:

```
SELECT * FROM Invoiceitems WHERE itemkey between 11 AND 14
```

The XPointer equivalent using the full form identifier would be:

```
#xpointer(itemkey(11 to 14))
```

This allows us to just point to the data within our document from `<itemkey="11">` to `<itemkey="14">`.

Ranges with Multiple Locations

This is pretty easy when the expressions on either side of the `to` keyword return a single location, but what about when the expressions return multiple locations in their location sets? Well then things get a bit more complicated. Let's create an example, and work our way through it.

Consider the following XML:

```
<people>
  <person name="John">
    <phone>(555)555-1212</phone>
    <phone>(555)555-1213</phone>
  </person>
  <person name="David">
    <phone>(555)555-1214</phone>
  </person>
  <person name="Andrea">
    <phone>(555)555-1215</phone>
    <phone>(555)555-1216</phone>
    <phone>(555)555-1217</phone>
  </person>
  <person name="Ify">
    <phone>(555)555-1218</phone>
    <phone>(555)555-1219</phone>
  </person>
  <!--more people could follow-->
</people>
```

We have a list of people, and each person can have one or more phone numbers. Now consider the following XPointer:

```
xpointer(//person to phone[1])
```

As you can see, the first expression will return a number of `<person>` elements, and the second expression will return the first `<phone>` element. XPointer tackles this as follows:

1. It evaluates the expression on the left side of the `to` keyword, and saves the returned location set. In this case, it will be a location set of all of the `<person>` elements.

```
<person name="John"/>
<person name="David"/>
<person name="Andrea"/>
<person name="Ify"/>
```

2. Using the first location in that set as the context location, XPath then evaluates the expression on the right side of the `to` keyword. In this case, it will select the first `<phone>` child of the first `<person>` element in the location set on the left.

```
<person name="John"/> ———— <phone>(555)555-1212</phone>
<person name="David"/>
<person name="Andrea"/>
<person name="Ify"/>
```

3. For each location in this second location set, XPointer adds a range to the result, with the start point at the beginning of the location in the first location set, and the end point at the end of the location in the second location set. In this case, only one range will be created, since the second expression only returned one location.

4. Steps 2 and 3 are then repeated for each location in the first location set, with all of the additional ranges being added to the result. So, as a result of the XPointer above, we would end up with the following pieces of XML selected in our document:

```
<person name="John">
    <phone>(555)555-1212</phone>
  <person name="David">
    <phone>(555)555-1214</phone>
  <person name="Andrea">
    <phone>(555)555-1215</phone>
  <person name="Ify">
    <phone>(555)555-1218</phone>
```

Querying with XPointer

Throughout this section we have been explicitly stating our desired target and using a fragment identifier to expose the target. However, the flexibility of the specification allows us to use other means of stating our target.

For example we could dynamically identify our data set with the help of XLink and then query that dataset using XML Query to expose our target. Let's look at an example from the previous chapter again:

```
<?xml version="1.0"?>

<ItemLocations xmlns:xlink="http://www.w3.org/1999/xlink"
    xlink:type="extended">

    <itemlocation xlink:type="resource"
        xlink:label="location"
        itemkey="13">
        R15L5
    </itemlocation>

    <Item xlink:type="locator"
        xlink:href="acme.mfg.com/invoice.xml#itemkey(13)"
        xlink:label="item"/>

    <itemlocation xlink:type="resource"
        xlink:label="location"
        itemkey="14">
        R3L1
    </itemlocation>
```

```
    <Item xlink:type="locator"
       xlink:href="acme.mfg.com/invoice.xml#itemkey(14)"
       xlink:label="item"/>

    <itemlocation xlink:type="resource"
       xlink:label="location"
       itemkey="15">
       R5L6
    </itemlocation>

    <Item xlink:type="locator"
       xlink:href="acme.mfg.com/invoice.xml#itemkey(15)"
       xlink:label="item"/>

    <itemlocation xlink:type="resource"
       xlink:label="location"
       itemkey="16">
       R13L3
    </itemlocation>

    <Item xlink:type="locator"
       xlink:href="acme.mfg.com/invoice.xml#itemkey(16)"
       xlink:label="item"/>

    <itemlocation xlink:type="resource"
       xlink:label="location"
       itemkey="17">
       R11L3
    </itemlocation>

    <Item xlink:type="locator"
       xlink:href="acme.mfg.com/invoice.xml#itemkey(17)"
       xlink:label="item"/>

    <getdetail xlink:type="arc"
       xlink:show="embed"
       xlink:actuate="onRequest"
       xlink:to="location"
       xlink:from="item"/>

</ItemLocations>
```

The location set could look something like our earlier XML sample:

```
<ORDERS>

  <Invoice InvoiceKey="187">
    <invoiceitem ItemKey="13"/>
    <invoiceitem ItemKey="14"/>
  </Invoice>

  <Invoice InvoiceKey="188">
    <invoiceitem ItemKey="13"/>
  </Invoice>

  <Invoice InvoiceKey="189">
    <invoiceitem ItemKey="11"/>
  </Invoice>

</ORDERS>
```

We are explicitly identifying the targets within our link, very much like an HTML pointer. Let's look at our first XLink:

```
<Item xlink:type="locator"
    xlink:href="acme.mfg.com/invoice.xml#itemkey(14)"
    xlink:label="item"/>
```

We are using the link `acme.mfg.com/invoice.xml` to get our location set. By adding the XPointer (`#itemkey(14)`) to the XLink we are exposing our target `Invoiceitem`.

What about if we cannot explicitly state the identifier? With a creative twist and the flexibility of the specification, we could combine technologies and use XML Query to identify our target:

```
xlink:type="locator"
xlink:href="acme.mfg.com/invoice.xml#xpointer(//invoice.invoicekey="187")
```

to point to data with an `InvoiceKey` of 187. This is just one example of the many uses of XPointer that are sure to come.

Other Points

As I mentioned before the W3C specification for XPointer is very complex and long – maybe overly so on both counts – but it does present some useful uses for the technology. Let's explorer some of these:

XPointer Function Extensions to XPath

Of course, to deal with these new concepts, XPointer adds a few functions to the ones supplied by XPath. We won't go into their details here, but the following is a brief description of the new functions.

Range Related Functions

As we discovered, ranges can be very powerful and the technology recognizes that with several functions.

Function	Description
location-set range-to (*expression*)	Returns a range for each location in the *location-set*. The start point of the range is the start of the context location, and the end point of the range is the end of the location found by evaluating the *expression* argument with respect to that context location. For example: `xpointer(itemkey("11")/range-to(itemkey("14")))`
location-set string-range (*location-set*, *string*, *position*, *number*)	A more formal version of `range-to`, returning a set of sub-strings matching the string argument. So: `string-range(/,"!",1,2)[5]` selects the fifth exclamation mark in any text node in the document, and the character immediately following it.

Table continued on following page

Function	Description
	The *position* is the position of the first character to be in the resulting range, relative to the start of the match. The default value of 1 makes the range start immediately before the first character of the matched string. *number* is the number of characters in the range; the default is that the range extends to the end of the matched string.
location-set range(*location-set*)	The result returns ranges covering the locations in the argument location set.
location-set range-inside (*location-set*)	This function returns ranges covering the contents of the locations in the argument. This differs from range in that the range it creates for each location is only for the *contents* of the location, not the entire thing.

Other Functions

Function	Description
start-point() & end-point()	These functions add a location of type point to the result location set. For example, the start-point function takes a location set as a parameter, and returns a location set containing the start points of all of the locations in the location set. So: `start-point(//child[1])` would return the start point of the first <child> element in the document, and: `start-point(//child)` would return a set containing the start points of all of the <child> elements in the document. The end-point() function works exactly the same, but returns end points.
here()	The here function returns the element which contains the XPointer. That is, if we define an XPointer which points to a specific piece of an XML document, here returns the element which contains that piece, as a location set with a single member.
origin()	This function allows us to enable addresses relative to out-of-line links, as we learned about in the previous chapter about XLink. The origin function returns the element from which a user or program initiated traversal of a link.

Function	Description
unique()	Returns true if and only if the location size is equal to 1.This is very much like the Unique key word in SQL Server except that it returns a true if the context size of the target is equal to 1.

Rules and Errors

We can't get away from them – XML and validity rules seem like synonyms. So as you would imagine, a technology such as XPointer has both its own set of validity rules and errors. The best way to describe both is to explain the errors. The understanding is that if you break a rule, then you get an error.

Errors

Errors	Description
Syntax Error	Simply stated, the syntax does not match that of the document.
Resource Error	This is bubbled when an identifier is valid but points to an improper resource.
Sub-Resource Error	This occurs when both the identifier and the resource are valid but the result set is empty. Remember, XPointer is not a query language, but is used to point within a document.

XPointer Summary

XPointer provides a way to point within a document as an extension of XPath, and is used with other technologies like XLink. The flexibility of XPointer should allow creative uses of this straightforward technology once the specification becomes a standard sometime in the next year. Again, keep an eye on the W3C web site for up the minute information on XPointer status.

XInclude

Several of the technologies covered in this chapter are related to, extend, or overlap with XLink. The relationship between XLink and XInclude could not be much closer.

At the time of writing, the October 2000 working draft of XInclude had just been published. As this is likely to undergo some changes, you might like to investigate this fully at http://www.w3.org/TR/2000/WD-xinclude-20001026/.

Modular Development

One of the core foundations of XML, and for that matter modern development, is the process of developing in specific components, or **modularity**. As we'll learn later in this chapter, XHTML is modular HTML. Many languages provide an inclusion method to support this modularity. This development practice is the principal behind XInclude. At its simplest, XInclude allows a way to merge XML documents by utilizing XML constructs – attributes and URI references.

> XInclude (or XInclusions) simply defines a processing model for merging information sets.

So why do we need XInclude? Can't we do that with XLink combined with XPointer? Well, they each have their own unique differences. XInclude does for XML what Server side includes do for ASP.

In the previous chapter, we learned that XLink simply facilitates the detection of links, it doesn't define any particular processing model. XInclude is much more explicit, in that it does define a specific processing model for merging information sets.

OK, so what does that mean in practice? Let's clarify things with an example.

An XInclude Example

Imagine that the information from our invoice example was contained in two separate XML documents, and we needed to merge specific nodes into our primary document.

First let's look at a loosely formatted hypothetical primary document:

```xml
<?xml version="1.0"?>

<ItemLocations xmlns:xinclude="http://www.w3.org/1999/XML/xinclude"
               xmlns:xlink="http://www.w3.org/1999/xlink"
               xlink:type="extended">

<Title>XInclude Invoice Items</Title>
<BODY>

    <P>
       <font color="red"><I>invoice from file invoiceA.xml</I></font>
    </P>

    <ORDERS ID="A">
       <xinclude:include
          href="http://acme.mfg.com/invoices.xml#InvoiceKey(187)" />
    </ORDERS>

    <ORDERS ID="B">
       <xinclude:include
          href="http://www.acme.com/supply/invoices.xml#InvoiceKey(200)" />
    </ORDERS>

</BODY>
</ItemLocations>
```

This is the input for our inclusion transformation, known as a **source infoset**.

> *An XML Information Set (**infoset**) is a description of the information available in a well-formed XML document. For the full specification see http://www.w3.org/TR/xml-infoset.*

The first document we reference is http://acme.mfg.com/invoices.xml. This contains the following data:

```
<ORDERS>

    <Invoice InvoiceKey="187">
       <invoiceitem ItemKey="13"/>
       <invoiceitem ItemKey="14"/>
    </Invoice>

    <Invoice InvoiceKey="188">
       <invoiceitem ItemKey="13"/>
    </Invoice>

</ORDERS>
```

And our second document, http://www.acme.com/supply/invoices.xml, contains:

```
<ORDERS>

    <Invoice InvoiceKey="10">
       <invoiceitem ItemKey="1"/>
    </Invoice>

    <Invoice InvoiceKey="200">
       <invoiceitem ItemKey="18"/>
       <invoiceitem ItemKey="69"/>
    </Invoice>

</ORDERS>
```

Once our primary page is loaded, our two invoice documents are identified with the URI identified in the XInclude. With the help of XPointer, we are able to expose the specific data we are trying to merge within our primary document.

So what happens next?

Syntax

An XInclude processor identifies the **included items** by the URI following the xinclude:include clause in the href attribute:

```
<ORDERS ID="A">
    <xinclude:include href="http://www.acme.mfg.com/invoices.xml#
                           InvoiceKey(187)" />
</ORDERS>

<ORDERS ID="B">
    <xinclude:include href="http://www.acme.supply.com/invoices.xml#
                           InvoiceKey(200)" />
</ORDERS>
```

If the resource identified by the URI is unavailable, or if they don't contain well-formed XML, we'll get an error.

In the resulting document – or **result infoset** – the include element is replaced by the elements matching the XPointer expression. This produces one XML tree, not two linked trees.

```
<?xml version="1.0"?>

<ItemLocations xmlns:xinclude="http://www.w3.org/1999/XML/xinclude"
               xmlns:xlink="http://www.w3.org/1999/xlink"
               xlink:type="extended">

<Title>XInclude Invoice Items</Title>

<BODY>
  <P>
     <font color="red"><I>invoice from file invoiceA.xml</I></font>
  </P>

    <ORDERS ID="A">
       Invoice InvoiceKey="187">
          <invoiceitem ItemKey="13"/>
          <invoiceitem ItemKey="14"/>
       </Invoice>
    </ORDERS>

    <ORDERS ID="B">
       <Invoice InvoiceKey="200">
          <invoiceitem ItemKey="18"/>
          <invoiceitem ItemKey="69"/>
       </Invoice>
    </ORDERS>

</BODY>
</ItemLocations>
```

Elements of three separate modules, or documents representing a database have been merged to produce a fourth valid document. Our goal of modularization has been accomplished.

It is important to remember that XInclude only deals with infosets. So the primary document created by XInclude is only an infoset within a document. It is also possible to include a complete XML document as an inclusion, but only the elements of the document will replace the XInclude, not the document's definition or schema.

Another point worth noting is that the base URI property of the included items is retained after merging. That means relative URI references in the included infoset resolve to the same URI that would have applied in the original documents, despite being included into a document with a potentially different base URI. Other properties of the original infosets (including namespaces) are also preserved.

The parse Attribute and Other Considerations

As well as the href attribute, which specifies the location of the items we want to include, the include element has an optional parse attribute. This specifies whether or not to include the resource as parsed XML or as text:

❑   A value of xml indicates that the resource must be parsed as XML and the infosets merged

❑   A value of text indicates that the resource must be included as the contents of a text node

If the `parse` attribute is not specified, `xml` is assumed. The value of this attribute can have several effects.

For one thing, when `parse="xml"`, the fragment part of the URI reference is interpreted as an XPointer, indicating that only part of the included item is the target for inclusion. However, there is currently no standard that defines fragment identifiers for plain text, so it's not allowed to specify a fragment identifier when `parse="text"`.

There are also a few points to be aware of when recursively processing an `include` element. Processing an `include` element with an include location that has already been processed is not allowed. That gives us the following rules:

❏ An inclusion with `parse="text"` or `parse="cdata"` may reference itself, although an include element with `parse="xml"` (or no specified parse value) cannot

❏ An inclusion may identify a different part of the same resource

❏ Two non-nested inclusions may identify a resource which itself contains an inclusion

❏ An inclusion of the `xinclude:include`, its elements, or ancestors that have already been parsed is not allowed

XInclude Advantages

Besides the obvious time saving qualities of XInclude, why else would we want to use it? Let's look why XInclude compliments XML so well:

❏ Processing of an XML document occurs at parse time, while XInclude operates on information sets not capable of being parsed by themselves.

❏ Because XInclude deals with information sets, it is also independent of XML validation.

❏ Because XInclude is free from XML validity tests, information sets can be included within a parent document independently on the fly, without having to pre-declare inclusions.

❏ XInclude combined with XPointer can replace certain forms of XML altogether. In other words, the desired data can be combined from several different databases without having to validate any of them to form a XML-like document.

Why have the XInclude parsed by a different processor? Well, the problem is that if you use an XLink, for example, to point towards some data, everything returned has to be parsed and validated as if it was a self-contained XML document. With an XInclude, the document might not be valid until complete, and possibly not even then. The XInclude allows parsing to occur at a low level, validating against any DTDs, if specified, before returning the entire XML to the requestor.

XInclude Summary

XInclude allows the dynamic creation of infosets without the need for validation. This advance form of XML modularity is very powerful, and will allow for rich interaction with XML databases when the draft becomes a recommendation.

XHTML

XHTML is a reformulation of HTML in XML. The main motivation is two-fold:

❑ There have been many new elements introduced within various specialized versions of HTML that have led to cross-platform compatibility problems. XML allows us to introduce new elements or additional element attributes to cope with the increasing need for new markup, without compromising compatibility. XHTML allows extensions through XHTML modules, which let developers combine existing and new feature sets.

❑ There's a growing need to provide a standard that encompasses the whole range of browser platforms (cell phones, televisions, desktops, etc). XHTML is aimed at a broader range of end user agents than HTML.

XHTML inherits some of the stricter rules of XML, including validity. XHTML will also allow simple HTML type documents to use the technologies listed in this chapter.

XHTML 1.0 was the first reformulation of HTML 4.0 in XML (http://www.w3.org/TR/xhtml1/). One of our stated aims is also to modularize the elements and attributes into collections, so that they can be used in documents that combine HTML with other tag sets. These modules are defined in **HTML Modularization** (http://www.w3.org/TR/xhtml-modularization/)

One of the cores to XHTML is this modular format, making it easy to use with other XML technologies. This modularization is also extended to the other technologies mentioned in this chapter.

How XHTML differs from HTML

In this section, we'll look at the differences between XHTML and HTML 4. Bear these differences in mind – there aren't that many of them, and to anyone who knows XML, they are all quite obvious. However, if you're familiar with any HTML, they may catch you out if you've already slipped into any 'bad' coding habits with HTML.

Since XHTML is a reformulation of HTML in XML, everything we know about well-formed documents in XML applies in XHTML. That means that, unlike in HTML, XHTML requires that:

❑ We must provide a DTD declaration at the top of the file:

```
PUBLIC "-//W3C//DTD XHTML 1.0 Strict//EN"

SYSTEM "http://www.w3.org/TR/xhtml1/DTD/xhtml1-strict.dtd"
```

We didn't need this in HTML because the latest browsers came equipped able to decipher any type of HTML. But now with extensibility there is no way a browser can second guess new additions to XHTML.

❑ We must include a reference to the XML namespace in the `<html>` element:

```
<html xmlns="http://www.w3.org/TR/xhtml1">
```

Note that the above reads ...XHTML1, ending with a number '1' and not two letter 'L's.

❑ XHTML like XML is case sensitive, and tag names and attribute names must be given in lower case. In HTML, case wasn't important.

❑ In HTML, we could get away with not including closing tags, and having elements overlap. In XHTML, we must close tags and indicate empty elements, just like in XML. Tags must also nest properly.

❑ `<head>` and `<body>` elements in HTML were optional. In XHTML, we may not omit `<head>` and `<body>` elements, and the first element in the head *must* be the `<title>` element.

❑ All attribute values must be enclosed in quotation marks, and may not be 'minimized'; we must write, for example:

```
<input checked="checked">
```

whereas in HTML we could get away with:

```
<input checked>
```

❑ To avoid < and & characters within `<style>` and `<script>` elements being interpreted as the beginning of markup, they must contain a CDATA line:

```
<script>
<![CDATA[
... unescaped script content ...
]]>
</script>
```

These rules make it trivially easy for browsers to determine the hierarchical structure described by the tags without knowing the exact tags beforehand. This is unlike HTML, which in practice demands an expert system that embodies knowledge of what elements can include which tags, and knowledge of how to deal with the real-world errors commonly found in HTML documents. XHTML makes it much easier for browsers to support combinations of XHTML and other XML tag sets, like those we might design ourselves. The parser will be able to completely parse the document without any external information.

Let's see how these differences might affect us by comparing a bare-bones HTML page (full of 'bad code') and its corresponding XHTML page.

First, the HTML page (ch11_ex01.html):

```
<TITLE>very lax<HTML>
  <HEAD>
    <TITLE>wrong</TITLE>
    <META name="description"
          content="Working, but really messy code, isn't it.">
    <META name="keywords" content="many, many keywords">
  </HEAD>
  <BODY>
    <CENTER>
    <H1>HTML to XHTML</H1>
    <P>
      It is not that difficult to upgrade one's HTML to XHTML.<BR>
      Just follow a few rules:
    <OL>
      <LI>You need a <EM>DTD</EM> to validate against.
      <LI>refer to <EM>namespaces</EM>.
      <LI>Tags should be <EM>nested</LI>.</EM>
      <LI>Elements should be in <EM>lower case.</LI></EM>
```

```
      <LI><EM>Quote</EM> all attributes.
      <LI><EM>Unminimize</EM> attributes.
      <LI>Correctly tag <EM>empty elements</EM>.
      <LI><EM>White space</EM> handling.
      <LI>Escape or externalize
        <EM>script</EM> and <EM>style elements</EM>.
      <LI><EM>id</EM> instead of name.
      <LI>Tags should be <EM>closed</EM> properly.
      <LI>Handle <EM>layout</EM> with styles.
    <HR width=60% size=1>
```

This is what the messy HTML looks like on IE 5:

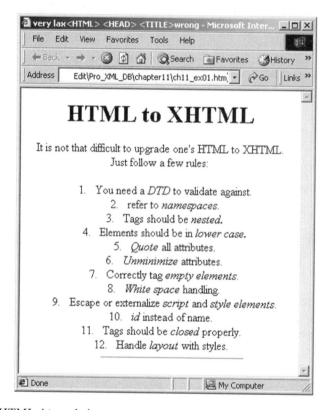

When recast into XHTML this code becomes:

```
<?xml version="1.0" encoding="UTF-8"?>
<!DOCTYPE html
    PUBLIC "-//W3C//DTD XHTML 1.0 Transitional//EN"
    "http://www.w3.org/TR/xhtml1/DTD/xhtml1-transitional.dtd">
<html xmlns="http://www.w3.org/1999/xhtml" xml:lang="en" lang="en">
<head>
    <title>Proper XHTML</title>
    <meta name="description"
        content="Working, but really messy code, isn't it." />
    <meta name="keywords" content="many, many keywords" />
```

```
    </head>
    <body>
      <div style="text-align:center">
        <h1>HTML to XHTML</h1>
        <p>
          It is not that difficult to upgrade one's HTML to XHTML.<br />
          Just follow a few rules:
        </p>
        <ol>
          <li>You need a <em>DTD</em> to validate against.</li>
          <li>refer to <em>namespaces</em>.</li>
          <li>Tags should be <em>nested</em>.</li>
          <li>Elements should be in <em>lower case</em>.</li>
          <li><em>Quote</em> all attributes.</li>
          <li><em>Unminimize</em> attributes.</li>
          <li>Correctly tag <em>empty elements</em>.</li>
          <li><em>White space</em> handling.</li>
          <li>Escape or externalize
              <em>script</em> and <em>style elements</em>.</li>
          <li><em>id</em> instead of name.</li>
          <li>Tags should be <em>closed</em> properly.</li>
          <li>Handle <em>layout</em> with styles.</li>
        </ol>
        <hr width="60%" size="1" />
      </div>
    </body>
  </html>
```

If you run both of these examples through an IE 5 browser the displayed results will look exactly the same. Why is this? To decipher the example of bad code, IE 5 already contains the DTDs for all the old versions of HTML. This is one of the reasons why your browser program needs so much space on your hard drive and so many megabytes of RAM to run. Your browser does not, however, contain the DTD for XHTML, so this is why you need to include it in the above example of valid XHTML code. The tags used in both examples are the same, but the example of good code presents them according to the rules.

XHTML Flavors

XHTML currently has three flavors, making it a little looser than a true XML document. This will allow for easier conversion between legacy HTML documents and XHTML. If you build client-independent XML database applications in the future, it is most likely that your device front end will be one of the flavors of XHTML.

We specify which flavor we're using in the DTD declaration at the top of the file. Let's briefly look at each flavor.

Transitional

This flavor allows the advantage of many of the features mentioned within this chapter while making only small changes to existing HTML practices. It ensures the bad practices we saw above can no longer be used, but still lets you use formatting tags.

We need to specify the following in our DTD declaration:

```
PUBLIC "-//W3C//DTD XHTML 1.0 Transitional//EN"
    SYSTEM "http://www.w3.org/TR/xhtml1/DTD/xhtml1-transitional.dtd"
```

Strict

This flavor forces the strict validation of XML upon the document. This type of XHTML is free of any tags associated with layout, transferring the layout format to (CSS) style sheets.

```
PUBLIC "-//W3C//DTD XHTML 1.0 Strict//EN"
    SYSTEM "http://www.w3.org/TR/xhtml1/DTD/xhtml1-strict.dtd"
```

Frameset

This allows the partition of a browser into frames. We would suggest you stay away from this flavor.

```
PUBLIC "-//W3C//DTD XHTML 1.0 Frameset//EN"
    SYSTEM "http://www.w3.org/TR/xhtml1/DTD/xhtml1-frameset.dtd"
```

XHTML Summary

XHTML is the chosen vehicle to bring about change to HTML. The combination of the rigor of XML with the flexibility to allow richer web pages on a range of devices – including pagers, cell phones, televisions, and cars – is the next generation of modularized HTML.

XHTML is a currently a recommendation; while browser support is not widespread we do suggest you gear up on it.

If you would like more of an introduction to XHTML, Wrox's Beginning XHTML, ISBN 1-861003-43-9, *is a great book for more information.*

XForms

XForms are the next generation of web forms. The idea behind XForms is to separate the user interface from the data model and logic layer. This will enable the same form to be used irrespective of the user interface, be it a sheet of paper or a handheld device.

XForms should also reduce the need for scripting (although scripts can be used if necessary) – validations, dependencies, and basic calculations will be possible without the use of a scripting language. They will work by transferring form data as XML. So, as XForms are an application of XML, you'll be able to combine them with other XML based languages, like XHTML.

How Do XForms Differ from HTML Forms?

We are all familiar with the most useful way to allow browsers to exchange data – HTML forms. A typical HTML form might look something like this:

```
<FORM ACTION="process.asp" METHOD="GET" NAME="userform">
    <P>What is your name?
    <INPUT TYPE="text" NAME="namequery">
    <P>What is your sex?    
    Male <INPUT TYPE="radio" NAME="optsex" VALUE="male">  
    Female <INPUT TYPE="radio" NAME="optsex" VALUE="female">
    <P>Click if you don't want junk mail 
    <INPUT TYPE="checkbox" NAME="chkjunk" VALUE="no">
</FORM>
```

As you can see from the code, this very basic HTML form has three different types of input encased by FORM tags. The ACTION attribute of the FORM tag tells us that this form will be processed by an ASP page called process.asp. The process.asp file would mostly likely provide some form validation, and insert this information into a database.

Most HTML forms take on this basic idea in one way or another. This is great for desktop browsers, but what about the other thin devices?

For example, if we sent this form to a pager via WML, it would be impossible for the pager to answer the first question without a text interface. Some modern pagers do have a text interface, but we would be limiting our device types. By splitting the presentation layer away from the backend, we could easily adjust the way this question is presented depending on the type of user device being used.

That's the essence of XForms. We can just define the one data model, and this can be used via any interface to interact with the user – handheld devices, television, accessibility devices, printers, and scanners. And don't forget paper as well. Yes, I said paper. The aim is that XForms should allow a user to print a form, fill it in by hand, and scan it back. Wow!

The Model

So how are XForms going to achieve all of this? Take a look at the following diagram:

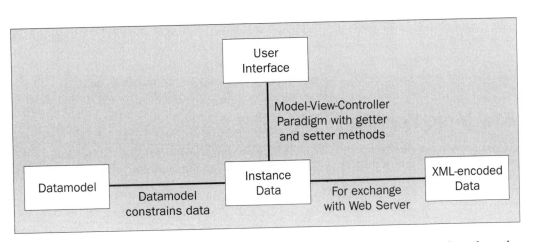

XForms comprise three layers, which allows us to clearly separate the purpose of the form from the presentation.

Let's briefly look at each layer.

The Data Model

The purpose of the XForms data layer is to define the data model for the form. You can use built-in data types or roll your own. Currently the data types are being built on top of XML Schema, although the syntax is a light-weight version, simpler than XML Schema proper.

The Logic Layer

This layer is where we specify dependencies between our fields (or data values), and define whatever constraints are required. Although one of the aims of XForms is to reduce the need for scripting, you will still be able to use other scripting languages such as JavaScript, if that's the way you want to go. However, the XForms syntax itself will build on the familiar technologies of spread sheets and existing forms packages. This is all part of the aim to make XForms easy for current HTML programmers to understand.

The Presentation Layer

The presentation layer is where the data model is translated into the media-specific end product. This layer basically consists of markup for form controls. The presentation is tailored to meet a particular user's needs, while keeping the intended business logic of the form. We'll see the functions that allow us to do this shortly.

Each form control is bound to a field in the data model, where this field can have more than one presentation control bound to it. Two or more form controls will be able to be bound to the same data value, so that if the data value is updated, then the related form controls indicate that value.

Current Status

At the time of writing, the W3C were preparing a new working draft of XForms. The data model is likely to allow either XML Schema or the light-weight syntax to be used to define the data model. The light-weight syntax for the data model and logic is largely designed to allow HTML users with no knowledge of the complexities of XML Schema to take full advantage of XForms.

For news on the latest working draft, see http://www.w3.org/TR/xforms-datamodel.

A Few More Features

As you can see, XForms promises to be incredibly powerful, and an excellent progression from the old inefficient HTML forms. Considering their current status, and the fact that the specification is likely to undergo some change, we won't continue our discussion on them beyond a basic introduction. Like so much else in this chapter, you would be advised to make regular visits to W3C web site if you want to keep abreast of the latest situation.

However, there are a few more features we felt as though were important enough to mention here.

DataTypes

The data types of the form elements are where a lot of the strength of XForms is developed. They are not limited to this small subset of built-in types, but this is a good starting point. Each datatype supports several *facets,* which you can use to constrain data items:

Type	Description	Facet
String	The most basic of types, similar to that of a string or variant	Min (number of characters), max (number of characters), mask (i.e. ddddd), pattern (a regular expression)
Boolean	True or false	
Number	A data type where numeric calculation could be performed in the data layer	Min (minimum value), Max (maximum value, integer (if true only integer values are permitted), decimals (digits after the decimal points)
Money	A monetary value	Min, Max, currency (currency codes)
Date	Specified in Years, Months, and days	Min, Max, Precision
Time	Used for such things as an appointment time	Min, Max, Precision
Duration	a duration represented in years, months, hours, minutes, days or seconds	Precision
URI	Representation of a URI	Schema
Binary	Used for specific media types	Type (mime types)

Common Facets

We can further constrain data types using the following facets:

Type	Description	Example
Default	An explicit default value to a form field.	`<string name="city" default="New York City"/>`

Read-only	A datatype that cannot be edited. Specified with the use of the `range` or `fixed` attribute.	`<string name="customerid" range="closed"><value>CHOPS</value>`
		
		or
		
		`<string name="customerid" fixed="CHOPS"/>`

Required	Requirement of a value to be filled in.	`<string name="city" required="true"/>`
Calculated	Computed values.	`<string name="billamount" calc="sum(item, orderamount * price)"/>`
Validation	To verify that a file has a valid value.	`<string name="zipcode" validate="validzipcode(this.value)"/>`

Data Models

The latest working draft specifies the following data model structures:

Type	Description	Example

enumeration	Specifies a set of values.	```<string name="billingmethod" range="closed">```
		``` <value>Account</value>```
		``` <value>Credit Card```
		``` </value>```
		``` <value>Cash</value```
		``` <value>Check</value```
		```</string>```

Unions	Similar to enumeration but as a collection of data types.	```<union name="days">```
		``` <string name="Monday">```
		``` <string name="Tuesday">```
		``` ...```
		```</union>```

Groups	Made up of several datatypes. Groups are different from unions as they can be nested.	```<group name="customer">```
		``` <string```
		``` name="fullname"/>```
		``` <string name="street"/>```
		``` <string name="city"/>```
		``` <string name="state"/>```
		```</group>```

Variant	Usually used in conjunction with group to specify a unique users grouping.	```<variant name="address">```
		``` <case locale="us">```
		``` <string```
		``` name="street"/>```
		``` <string name="city"/>```
		``` <string name="state"/>```
		``` <string name="zip"/>```
		``` </case>```
		``` <case locale="uk">```
		``` <string```
		``` name="street"/>```
		``` <string name="town"/>```
		``` <string```
		``` name="county"/>```
		``` <string```
		``` name="postcode"/>```
		``` </case>```
		```</variant>```

Arrays	A sequence of data types. Used with <group> or <union> while specifying minOccurs or maxOccurs.	```<group name="shoppingbasket" minOccurs="1">```
		``` <integer```
		``` name="quantity">```
		``` <string name="product">```
		```</group>```

XForms Summary

At the time of writing the latest XForms working draft is due for publication, and will probably under go some changes before becoming a recommendation. However, XForms looks set to be a new and exciting attribute for the future. Finally developers will be able to use XSL and style sheets to modify and manipulate the presentation of forms for different clients. Developers will no longer be totally dependent on outside scripting languages to catch input errors and validate user input while asking different device types for input.

Summary

In this chapter we touched on several important technologies that are extensions of XML. Some of these technologies don't necessarily manipulate data to and from a database, but rather present the data or point to location-sets of data.

We have also discovered that these technologies can and do work best with each other, and as part of XML. Some of the points we learned were how:

❏ XBase builds on the HTML 4.0 BASE element to allow us to specify a base URI for an XML document

❏ XPointer provides a way to point within a document as an extension of XPath, and how it can be used with other technologies like XLink

❏ XInclude allows the dynamic creation of infosets without the need for validation

❏ XHTML is the chosen leader to bring about change to HTML. It brings the rigor of XML, while allowing richer web pages on a wide range of devices

❏ XForms are set to become the next generation of forms, extending and simplifying the provision of user-interface independent forms

As we've said throughout the chapter, at the time of writing many of these technologies are a way from being implemented, and will undergo changes from their current state. There's little doubt though that all of these will have an impact on the future of how we develop XML applications. Make sure you stay tuned to http://www.w3.org so you don't miss anything.

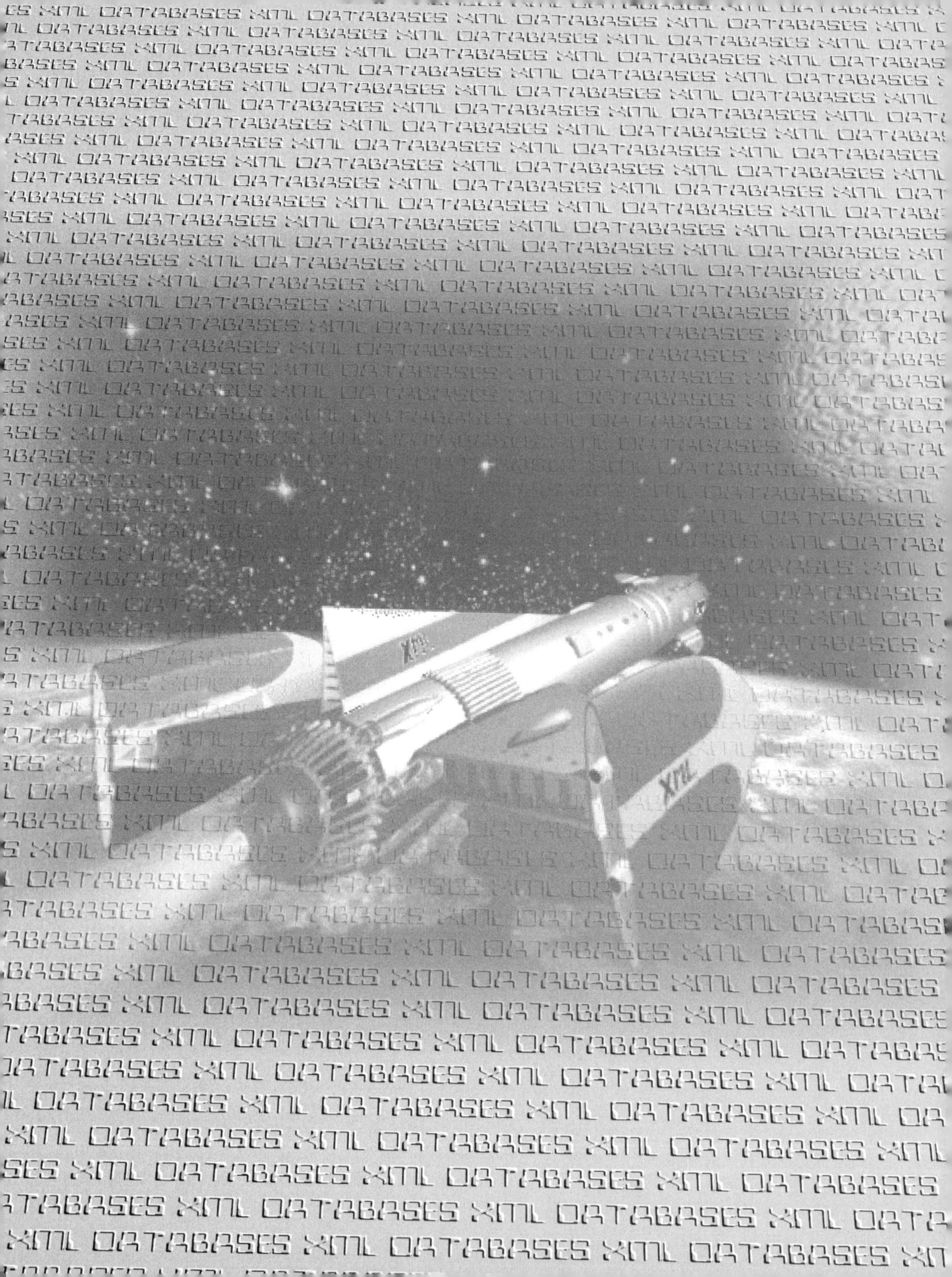
XML DATABASES
XML

11

The XML Query Language

The XML Query Language may be the most important XML standard the W3C produces, outside of XML itself. It is to XML what SQL is to relational data, and all the major vendors are expected to support it. We encourage every developer who uses XML and databases to follow its development closely. The web address where you can find more information is http://www.w3.org/XML/Query.

Except for the language syntax, the W3C XML Query Language specification is focused more on theoretical models than implementation details. The specification is divided into four parts, each building on the one before it: requirements, data model, algebra, and syntax. The **requirements** describe a set of use cases that the XML Query Language must support. The **data model** lays the foundation for the query language by formally describing the set of information available to a query. These queries have an abstract representation in the **algebra**, which describes the core operations of the XML Query Language. Of course, the most visible aspect of the XML Query Language is its **syntax** (of which there will be more than one).

The W3C XML Query Language Working Group is designing the XML Query Language. At the time of this writing, the working group has published draft versions of the requirements and data model, and is developing the algebra and syntax. Consequently, all the information in this chapter is subject to change. It is too early to speculate what forms the components of the XML Query Language will ultimately take, but we can already review the existing draft documentation and some proposals that we expect will strongly influence the design of the XML Query Language.

In addition to the W3C, other standards bodies such as the ANSI SQL 99 committee are likely to propose XML query languages. Also, we expect that XSLT and XPath will continue to be used widely and separately from the XML Query Language. Because the XML Query Language will undoubtedly influence all of these XML query languages, we will also highlight them in the context of the W3C XML Query Language.

Requirements and Use Cases

In every design, user scenarios are paramount. These scenarios, or **use cases**, set out the core requirements that the design must fulfill, and also focus the design in a particular direction.

In the case of the XML Query Language, the primary use cases involve **document-centric** and **data-centric** views of XML. The document-centric view includes scenarios such as generating indices and other summary information about a document and searching a document for information. In contrast, the data-centric view treats XML as a data representation layer (in which the XML may not really exist as documents, but instead may be surfaced through an XML interface as virtual documents). Data-centric scenarios include data mining and updating.

We will highlight some of the use cases that the XML Query Language must support. The description given here purposely distills the formal document into its key points. For complete details on the formal requirements of the XML Query Language, please read the XML Query Requirements Working Draft at http://www.w3.org/TR/xmlquery-req. Our explanations are based on the 16 August, 2000 draft.

Selection

First, the XML Query Language must support selecting portions of a document based on certain criteria, such as the values of elements and attributes. This requirement improves on the selection capabilities of XPath in at least two noteworthy respects:

- ❏ a query can use any XSD data type, including date
- ❏ a query can follow inter- and intra-document links, including XLinks and `ID/IDREF/IDREFS`-typed values

An XML `ID` is analogous to a SQL primary key, scoped to one document. Within the document, all the `ID` values must be unique. Each `IDREF` is then like a foreign key; an `IDREF` refers to an `ID` value in the document. (`IDREFS` are a space-separated list of `IDREF` values). For example, consider this XML document, which describes employees grouped by job function but with an ID-typed attribute (`ID`) and an `IDREF`-typed attribute (`Manager`) to indicate the organization reporting structure:

```
<Team>
    <Developer>
        <Employee ID="D1" Manager="M1"/>
        <Employee ID="D2" Manager="D1"/>
    </Developer>
    <Tester>
        <Employee ID="T1" Manager="T2"/>
        <Employee ID="T2" Manager="M2"/>
        <Employee ID="T3" Manager="T2"/>
    </Tester>
    <Manager>
        <Employee ID="M1" Manager="M3"/>
        <Employee ID="M2" Manager="M3"/>
        <Employee ID="M3"/>
    </Manager>
</Team>
```

Given an <Employee> element, an XPath that selects its <Manager> is id(./@Manager). Selecting an Employee's direct reports (those <Employee> elements for which this <Employee> is their <Manager>) using XPath is more awkward, but can be done with a query like //Employee[@Manager=$this/@ID]. Given an Employee (stored in the parameter $this), this XPath searches from the top of the document for all employee elements (//Employee) and then selects only those whose Manager attribute equals the ID attribute of this <Employee> element.

The XML Query Language will be able to follow these relationships and others more easily. Technically, this makes the XML Query Language a graph query language; however, we expect that most implementations will optimize the XML Query Language for tree-like navigation. It is not clear at this time how the XML Query Language will handle ID values in document fragments or in intermediate XML data formed during the course of a query.

Other than better data type support, improved link chasing, and possibly some subtle differences in the handling of sets and document ordering, the selection capabilities of the XML Query Language should be functionally equivalent to those of XPath.

Transformation

A large number of the use cases amount to being able to rearrange XML into different shapes. Queries will be able to flatten XML, promote children in the hierarchy, and create new XML content. Also, queries will be able to select portions of XML while preserving the structure and order of the original. This is useful if, for example, you have the text of a screen play in XML form, and you want to create a list of all the actors in their order of appearance in the play.

An especially important scenario is projection. **Projection**, or pruning sub-trees, selects only part of an element instead of all of the element's content (including all of its descendants). For example, examine the following XML:

```
<Food>
    <Fruits>
        <Kiwi/>
        <Lime/>
        <Plum/>
    </Fruits>
</Food>
```

There is no XPath that produces:

```
<Fruits>
    <Kiwi/>
    <Lime/>
</Fruits>
```

Nor any XML that produces <Plum/> as its result.

An XPath such as Food/Fruits or Food/Fruits[Kiwi or Lime] selects all of the <Fruits> elements:

```
<Fruits>
    <Kiwi/>
    <Lime/>
    <Plum/>
</Fruits>
```

Also, an XPath such as (Food/Fruits/Kiwi | Food/Fruits/Lime) selects only the children, and not the enclosing <Fruits> element:

```
<Kiwi/>
<Lime/>
```

To select the <Fruits> element and only some of its children requires some kind of projection, which we will detail shortly. In general, the transformational capabilities of the XML Query Language will probably correspond to many features of XSLT, which can already rearrange existing XML data and inject new XML content into the results of a transformation. However, XSLT is like using SQL over a single table, without the ability to join to other tables!

When completed, the XML Query Language will go a step beyond XSLT in allowing content from multiple XML documents to be incorporated into a single result. Inter-document transformation is a powerful feature that opens the door to many new applications of XML. For example, a web developer might use a single XML query to easily produce tables of contents or localize the content of an entire web site.

Data Centricity

In fact, the XML Query Language will be capable of operating not only on multiple documents, but also on document fragments. A document fragment is to a document what a tree is to a forest. Unlike a document, which always has one top-level element, a fragment need not have an enclosing root element. This capability is especially useful for data-centric scenarios, in which an enclosing element is often superfluous.

The XML Query Language also includes explicit support for relational data exposed as XML through an XML View. (For a practical example of such views in a commercial product, see Chapter 19 *XML Views in SQL Server 2000*). This capability will be especially intriguing to see in released products, as relational database vendors find ways to optimize the XML Query Language for relational data, and not for XML.

Types and Operators

The XML Query Language will support all of the XML Schema data types (**XSD**), and therefore includes user-derived data types. See http://www.w3.org/TR/xmlschema-2 for complete details on the XML Schema Data Types. We'll just remark here that at the time of this writing, XSD has 45 built-in types (for more detail see Chapter 5). In addition, the XML Query Language will probably define a generic type that is the ancestor of all other types, and some collection types to be used by intermediate query expressions.

Additional requirements stipulate that the XML Query Language support the usual collection of arithmetic, logic, and string operations – including various kinds of sorting and indexing. Many operations, such as sorting, will probably be expressed syntactically in a query as functions (like sort()).

Data Model

The XML Query Data Model provides a foundation for the XML Query Language. The current draft recommendation is at http://www.w3.org/TR/query-datamodel (dated 11 May, 2000 at the time of writing). Please note that the draft recommendation is a work in progress and not an official specification.

The data model describes the set of information available to a query, as well as basic operations for constructing this information from new (**constructors**) and accessing this information (**accessors**). The syntax used to describe the data model is irrelevant; it is an abstract model, not an API. In this section, we will give an overview of the data model and some of the implementation issues that arise.

Collections

The data model defines three collection types: ordered **lists** (allowing duplicates), unordered **sets** (without duplicates), and unordered **bags** (allowing duplicates).The fourth kind of collection (ordered, without duplicates) is currently not defined in the data model. All three collection types are heterogeneous (meaning their members may have arbitrary types, including collection types).

It is interesting to note that the data model does not treat a tree hierarchy as a collection (like most programming languages would), but rather as a separate Node type. Before exploring the node types, however, we should explain node references.

References

The data model includes the concept of **node identity**. Every instantiation of a node has its own unique identity. Copying a node creates a new node with a different identity. The query language uses **node references** to point to the original node. Operations on node references change the original, rather than a copy of the node.

The reference to a node N is denoted by Ref(N). The data model provides two functions, ref and deref, to map from a node instance to its reference, and vice-versa. The special reference value NaR (Not a Reference) is used to handle the case when a value does not represent a valid node reference (for example, an IDREF value that names an ID not in the document).

Nodes

The data model defines eight node types. One of these, ValueNode, includes a separate type definition, so we will consider it separately in the next section. Another, InfoItemNode corresponds to information in the infoset, so we also describe it in a separate section.

The other six node types are DocNode, ElemNode, AttrNode, NSNode, PINode, and CommentNode. As the names suggest, ElemNode corresponds to an element, AttrNode to an attribute, NSNode to a namespace declaration, PINode to a processing-instruction, and CommentNode to a comment. These are the usual XML document parts with which you are already familiar. The DocNode type is used to represent document nodes; however, because the data model supports fragments a DocNode is not required.

In fact, a **data model instance** is a list, bag, or set of zero or more document, element, value, processing-instruction, and comment node instances. Because of node identity, this means that a node cannot belong to more than one data model instance.

Each of these node types has a constructor and zero or more accessors. The accessors return information that was stored with the constructor. Together, the constructors and accessors suggest an obvious, literal implementation of the data model; however, in practice other methods (such as relational backing stores or edge tables) will likely prove to be more efficient representations.

We will describe the constructors and accessors of the node types after first explaining the scalar types on which they depend.

Scalars and ValueNodes

In the XML Query Data Model, scalar values are exposed through the ValueNode type. Each value node represents one of fourteen simple-type values (or a derivation of one of these simple-types). These are binary, Boolean, decimal, double, ENTITY, float, ID, IDREF, QName, NOTATION, recurringDuration, string, timeDuration, and uriReference.

As the names suggest, some of these are numeric types (double, decimal, float), some are date/time types (timeDuration and recurringDuration are abstract types from which date, time, and other traditional time types derive), and others are XML-related (ENTITY, ID, etc.). For a complete description of these types, see the XML Schema Data Types specification at http://www.w3.org/TR/xmlschema-2. Note that at the time of this writing, the Data Model and XML Schema specifications are slightly out of sync (NOTATION has become a derived type in XML Schema).

The parameters to the constructors of these types, are the value and a reference to the node that defines the type. In this way, ValueNode seamlessly supports sub-typing, because the reference can be to the node defining the sub-type. The ValueNode type itself is a kind of abstract type; it defines no constructor. The QName constructor (which constructs a **qualified name**, that is a local name possibly with a namespace prefix) is unique among the value constructors in that it takes two values as parameters: an optional namespace URI, and a local part. Its namespace prefix is not used, and is not considered part of the data model.

Every ValueNode has two accessors, one to get the type reference node, and another to get a string representation of the value. Every ValueNode also has fifteen Boolean-valued accessors to test its type: isStringValue, isBoolValue, and more as detailed in the Schema Data Type specification.

In addition, specific sub-types of ValueNode may have their own accessors. String values have an infoItems accessor that returns a (possibly empty) list of references to any associated InfoItemNodes (see description of InfoItemNode later in this section). A QName value has the accessors uriPart and localPart to retrieve the namespace-uri and local-name of the qualified name. Finally, IDREF and uriReference both have a referent accessor that returns a reference to the ElemNode referred to, or else NaR if no such element exists.

The various types of value nodes (or references to them) are used as parameters to the constructors for the other node types.

Node Constructors and Accessors

We will now describe the other six node constructors and accessors:

The DocNode constructor takes as parameters a location and a non-empty list of child nodes. The location is a uriReference value node, and the children are references to elements, processing-instructions, or comments; or in other words, the usual contents of an XML document. The DocNode provides accessors for both its location and its child list.

The ElemNode constructor takes the following parameters: a reference to a QName value node that is its name; a set of namespace node references corresponding to namespace declarations on the element; a set of attribute node references; a list of child node references; and a reference to a node defining the (schema) type of the element. When there is no schema, then the type of the element is the XSD ur-type. The children are references to element, value, processing-instruction, comment, or information item nodes. The accessors of ElemNode correspond to these items (name, namespaces, attributes, children, and type), plus an accessor returning a reference to the parent element of the ElemNode.

The AttrNode constructor has two parameters; one is the attribute name (a reference to a QName), and the other is its value (a reference to a ValueNode). Like ElemNode, AttrNode provides accessors for both of these and its parent element.

The NSNode constructor has two parameters, one a reference to the string value node that is the namespace prefix (if any) the other a reference to a uriReference value node that is the namespace URI (if any). Like AttrNode, NSNode provides accessors for both of these and its parent element.

The PINode constructor also takes two arguments, both references to string value nodes. The first argument is the processing-instruction target, and the other is its string value. PINode defines accessors for both of these and the parent node of the PINode. Unlike NSNode and AttrNode, however, PINode can have a parent, which is a DocNode; or no parent at all if the PINode is directly part of the data model instance.

Finally, the CommentNode constructor takes a single argument, a reference to a string value, which contains the contents of the comment. This value reference is accessible through an accessor, and so is a reference to the comment's parent, which, like PINode, may be a DocNode or NaR.

Information Items

The InfoItemNode type is a special, opaque node type corresponding to one of the ten **infoItems** in the infoset. Because it is opaque, it cannot be queried; therefore, implementations are free to disregard it (provided of course that they do not need to implement the infoset). For more details on InfoItemNode, please see the infoset specification at http://www.w3.org/TR/xml-infoset, or Appendix A of the data model specification.

Types

The data model working draft identifies a number of open issues. One in particular is the handling of types.

For example, the data model defines the schema type of a node at the time of the node's construction. This restriction can be unnecessarily limiting. Not only might one want to view a node as a different type during a query (for instance, a float value as an integer), but also transformational queries will want to alter a node's shape (and therefore its type) without altering its identity.

Also, the data model currently does not yet handle the XSD simple types `list` and `union`. We expect the type issues of the data model, and the XML Query Language, more generally to change before the final specification.

Implementation Issues

From an implementer's point of view, the data model specification is primarily useful as a requirements document. Any implementation that includes all the functionality of the data model will be able to implement the XML Query Language on top of it. Thus the XML Query Language achieves theoretical closure.

An implementation must provide all the functionality of the data model to support the algebra. However, in practice, many algebraic operations will be implemented differently than suggested by the formal data model. For example, the current data model specification requires one to have constructed all of a node's children first (for example, a DOM-like implementation) in order to construct the node. In practice, implementations either will not have this information (for example, SAX-like implementation) or else will find this construction method inefficient, and will therefore not use the formal node constructors of the data model.

Although the data model is described in a **node-centric** way (in which the data model is represented as nodes in a tree, like the DOM), this does not prevent an **edge-centric** implementation (in which the data model is represented as nodes in a graph). In fact, some algebraic operations may be more conveniently expressed over an edge-centric model than a node-centric one.

Algebra

The XML Query Algebra describes the core set of operations that make up the XML Query Language. The query algebra does not describe an implementation, but rather the abstract capabilities of the XML Query Language. In some cases, the implementation falls out naturally from the algebra, and in other cases there is plenty of room for experimentation.

The algebra has not yet crystallized into even a draft recommendation, so we are not permitted to describe the algebra in any detail at this time. The query working group is expected to produce a working draft of the algebra soon after I write this, so keep an eye on the W3C XML Query web site.

Additional background material for the interested reader is provided in the proposed algebra by Fernández, Siméon, Suciu, and Wadler (see http://cm.bell-labs.com/cm/cs/who/wadler/xml/index.html#algebra). From public remarks and presentations made by working group members over the past months, we expect this paper will strongly influence the design of the XML Query Algebra. In their paper, the authors propose a strongly-typed query algebra (in which every expression has a known compile-time type). This algebra supports structural recursion, simple `for` loops, local variables, function definitions, and all the usual features of an XML query language: arithmetic, node construction, and an equivalent of XPath predicates or SQL `WHERE` clauses.

Whatever form and function the algebra finally presents, most users will interact with it through a higher-level query language. Although the algebra constitutes the formal basis for the XML Query Language, the most visible facet of the XML Query Language will be its syntax. In the next section, we explore the syntax of several popular XML Query Languages, many of which have implementations available already today.

Syntax

It is interesting to note that one XML Query Language requirement is that at least one syntax be expressed using XML. We expect that the XML version(s) will be essentially XML representations of the abstract syntax tree for the usual version(s). For instance, to represent the sum: 2+2=4, something along the lines of the following may be used:

```
<equal>
   <add>
      <number>2</number>
      <number>2</number>
   </add>
   <number>4</number>
</equal>
```

The primary benefit of an XML syntax, is that it can be operated on and transformed using XML tools, such as the XML Query Language itself.

Although some people will claim that there should be only one method of performing a task, we tend to agree with the Perl community and say that there's more than one way to do it. We fully expect that there will be multiple languages supporting queries over XML, even if only one is chosen as the standard. Some of these languages will share common technical foundations with the official XML Query Language (such as its data model or algebra), and others will diverge completely. One can also reasonably predict there will be small, special-purpose XML query languages, designed for particular needs.

There are numerous languages that can query XML. A great deal of research has also gone into graph query languages. In this section, we will review four examples the XML community has produced in recent years, all of which will influence the design of the XML Query Language:

❑ **XPath** already a first-version standard

❑ **XSLT** already a first-version standard

❑ **Quilt** still under development

❑ **XSQL** still under development

All are subject to changes and improvements as the XML community gains greater experience with them.

For each language, we give a brief overview, followed by a critical evaluation of its merits and shortcomings as a query language. For comparison purposes, in each language we will express four sample queries over the same original XML data. We base these sample queries on use case "R", as described in the XML Query Requirements document.

The XML fragment we use for the sample queries is called ch10_ex1.xml and is as follows:

```
<users>
   <user_tuple>
      <userid>U01</userid><name>Tom Jones</name><rating>B</rating>
   </user_tuple>
   <user_tuple>
      <userid>U02</userid><name>Mary Doe</name><rating>A</rating>
   </user_tuple>
```

```xml
    <user_tuple>
        <userid>U03</userid><name>Dee Linquent</name><rating>D</rating>
    </user_tuple>
    <user_tuple>
        <userid>U04</userid><name>Roger Smith</name><rating>C</rating>
    </user_tuple>
    <user_tuple>
        <userid>U05</userid><name>Jack Sprat</name><rating>B</rating>
    </user_tuple>
    <user_tuple>
        <userid>U06</userid><name>Rip Van Winkle</name><rating>B</rating>
    </user_tuple>
</users>
<items>
    <item_tuple>
        <item>1001</item><desc>Red Bicycle</desc>
        <offered_by>U01</offered_by><reserve_price>40</reserve_price>
        <start>1999-01-05</start><end>1999-01-20</end>
    </item_tuple>
    <item_tuple>
        <item>1002</item><desc>Motorcycle</desc>
        <start>1999-02-11</start><end>1999-03-15</end>
        <offered_by>U02</offered_by><reserve_price>500</reserve_price>
    </item_tuple>
    <item_tuple>
        <item>1003</item><desc>Old Bicycle</desc>
        <start>1999-01-10</start><end>1999-02-20</end>
        <offered_by>U02</offered_by><reserve_price>25</reserve_price>
    </item_tuple>
    <item_tuple>
        <item>1004</item><desc>Tricycle</desc>
        <start>1999-02-25</start><end>1999-03-08</end>
        <offered_by>U01</offered_by><reserve_price>15</reserve_price>
    </item_tuple>
    <item_tuple>
        <item>1005</item><desc>Tennis Racket</desc>
        <start>1999-03-19</start><end>1999-04-30</end>
        <offered_by>U03</offered_by><reserve_price>20</reserve_price>
    </item_tuple>
    <item_tuple>
        <item>1006</item><desc>Helicopter</desc>
        <start>1999-05-05</start><end>1999-05-25</end>
        <offered_by>U03</offered_by><reserve_price>50000</reserve_price>
    </item_tuple>
    <item_tuple>
        <item>1007</item><desc>Racing Bike</desc>
        <start>1999-01-20</start><end>1999-02-20</end>
        <offered_by>U04</offered_by><reserve_price>200</reserve_price>
    </item_tuple>
    <item_tuple>
        <item>1008</item><desc>Broken Bike</desc>
        <start>1999-02-05</start><end>1999-03-06</end>
        <offered_by>U01</offered_by><reserve_price>25</reserve_price>
    </item_tuple>
</items>
<bids>
<bid_tuple>
    <userid>U02</userid><item>1001</item><bid>35</bid><date>1999-01-07</date>
</bid_tuple>
```

```
<bid_tuple>
    <userid>U04</userid><item>1001</item><bid>40</bid><date>1999-01-08</date>
</bid_tuple>
<bid_tuple>
    <userid>U02</userid><item>1001</item><bid>45</bid><date>1999-01-11</date>
</bid_tuple>
<bid_tuple>
    <userid>U04</userid><item>1001</item><bid>50</bid><date>1999-01-13</date>
</bid_tuple>
<bid_tuple>
    <userid>U02</userid><item>1001</item><bid>55</bid><date>1999-01-15</date>
</bid_tuple>
<bid_tuple>
    <userid>U01</userid><item>1002</item><bid>400</bid><date>1999-02-14</date>
</bid_tuple>
<bid_tuple>
    <userid>U02</userid><item>1002</item><bid>600</bid><date>1999-02-16</date>
</bid_tuple>
<bid_tuple>
    <userid>U03</userid><item>1002</item><bid>800</bid><date>1999-02-17</date>
</bid_tuple>
<bid_tuple>
    <userid>U04</userid><item>1002</item><bid>1000</bid><date>1999-02-25</date>
</bid_tuple>
<bid_tuple>
    <userid>U02</userid><item>1002</item><bid>1200</bid><date>1999-03-02</date>
</bid_tuple>
<bid_tuple>
    <userid>U04</userid><item>1003</item><bid>15</bid><date>1999-01-22</date>
</bid_tuple>
<bid_tuple>
    <userid>U05</userid><item>1003</item><bid>20</bid><date>1999-02-03</date>
</bid_tuple>
<bid_tuple>
    <userid>U01</userid><item>1004</item><bid>40</bid><date>1999-03-05</date>
</bid_tuple>
<bid_tuple>
    <userid>U03</userid><item>1007</item><bid>175</bid><date>1999-01-25</date>
</bid_tuple>
<bid_tuple>
    <userid>U05</userid><item>1007</item><bid>200</bid><date>1999-02-08</date>
</bid_tuple>
<bid_tuple>
    <userid>U04</userid><item>1007</item><bid>225</bid><date>1999-02-12</date>
</bid_tuple>
</bids>
```

Note this is an XML fragment, not a well-formed XML document.

The four sample queries we will demonstrate for this data are:

1. List the item number and description of all bicycles whose auction was in progress on 1 February, 1999, ordered by item number. For this query, the expected result is:

```
<item_tuple><item>1003</item><desc>Old Bicycle</desc></item_tuple>
<item_tuple><item>1007</item><desc>Racing Bike</desc></item_tuple>
```

2. Create a warning for all users with rating worse than "C" offering an item with reserve price exceeding 1000. For this query, the expected result is:

```
<warning>
    <name>Dee Linquent</name><rating>D</rating>
    <desc>Helicopter</desc><reserve_price>50000</reserve_price>
</warning>
```

3. Find all items having no bids; for each one, list its item number and description. For this query, the expected result is:

```
<item_tuple><itemno>1005</itemno><desc>Tennis Racket</desc></item_tuple>
<item_tuple><itemno>1006</itemno><desc>Helicopter</desc></item_tuple>
<item_tuple><itemno>1008</itemno><desc>Broken Bike</desc></item_tuple>
```

4. List each user alphabetically by name, with a list of the items (if any) for which the user has placed bids (in alphabetical order of description). For this query, the expected result is:

```
<user>
    <name>Dee Linquent</name>
    <item>Motorcycle</item>
    <item>Racing Bike</item>
</user>
<user>
    <name>Jack Sprat</name>
    <item>Old Bicycle</item>
    <item>Racing Bike</item>
</user>
<user>
    <name>Mary Doe</name>
    <item>Motorcycle</item>
    <item>Red Bicycle</item>
</user>
<user>
    <name>Rip Van Winkle</name>
</user>
<user>
    <name>Roger Smith</name>
    <item>Motorcycle</item>
    <item>Old Bicycle</item>
    <item>Racing Bike</item>
    <item>Red Bicycle</item>
</user>
<user>
    <name>Tom Jones</name>
    <item>Motorcycle</item>
    <item>Tricycle</item>
</user>
```

Now let's consider some query languages, and their abilities to execute these queries.

XPath

The XML Path Language, more commonly known as XPath, is a prototypical special-purpose XML query language. Originally designed as a helper language for XSL (for some history, see http://www.w3.org/TandS/QL/QL98/pp/xql.html), XPath has enjoyed wider acceptance in part because of its compact syntax and ease-of-use. XPath provides ways to select nodes in an XML document based on simple criteria such as structure, position, or content. XPath is fully described in the W3C Recommendation at http://www.w3.org/TR/xpath (dated 16 November, 1999 at the time of this writing) and is also covered in Chapter 8 of this book.

XPath Overview

Each XPath query is built from two basic components: navigation (using location steps) and predication (using filter expressions). The components can be combined in a variety of ways to provide a rich expression language from only a few syntactic elements.

Navigation involves walking from one part of the XML document to another. For example, the XPath `/Customer/child::Order` consists of two location steps: one absolute step `/Customer` which selects all top-level elements named `<Customer>`, followed by a relative step `child::Order` that then selects the child elements named `<Order>` of the current selection. Similarly, the XPath `/Customer/attribute::Name` selects the set of all attributes named `Name` from the top-level elements named `<Customer>`. Because these are common operations, XPath provides shorthand versions `/Customer/Order` and `/Customer/@Name` for these two queries, respectively. There are other forms to navigate to namespaces, comments, text nodes, parents, ancestors, descendents, and so on.

Predication can be performed either by selecting one node based on its position in the current selection, or (more commonly) by removing nodes from the current selection if they do not meet a Boolean condition. For example, `Customer[@Name='Penelope']` selects only those `Customer` elements having an attribute `Name` whose string value is `Penelope`. We often read this as "select Customers where Name equals Penelope." `Customer[2]` selects the second `Customer` element. XPath provides the usual kinds of arithmetic and string operations, as well as functions for getting the current node's position or finding a node by XML ID.

Evaluating XPath as a Query Language

Despite these features, XPath leaves a lot to be desired as a query language. Although XPath provides a very compact syntax, that syntax is definitely strange. For example, there is no character escaping mechanism for strings, and predicates cannot be applied to the shorthand forms for the `parent` (`..`) and `self` (`.`) axes.

Aside from these arbitrary syntactic limitations, XPath also has strange semantics. Perhaps the greatest inconsistency is in its handling of expressions involving node sets. Sometimes XPath uses "any" semantics; for example, relational and equality comparisons operate on any member of the set. The rest of the time, XPath operates only on the first node in the set; for example, conversions to string or number – which occur implicitly in many expressions – operate on only the first member of the set. Consequently, the XPath `Customer[Order/@Number > 10]` may produce different results than the XPath `Customer[0+Order/@Number > 10]`, in spite of their deceptive similarity.

Once you learn to avoid hazards like these, XPath becomes a very convenient way to select parts of an XML document. XPath is so compact and its syntax so familiar, since it closely resembles the syntax of file paths and URLs, that most of the XML query languages today incorporate at least part of its syntax.

Beyond selection, however, XPath is very limited. XPath has only three simple data types (Boolean, string, and number), with no provision for any others. XPath has numerous string manipulation functions, but no convenient (or efficient) way to work with case-insensitive strings or to perform regular expressions, which many programmers are keen on using. Also, XPath queries select entire nodes; they cannot select part of a node, or produce results combined from disparate node sources.

Finally, XPath is not a general-purpose language; it cannot construct data that was not in the original XML, and cannot modify the original XML. Consequently, XPath cannot perform any of the sample queries listed previously in their entirety; however, as we shall see, it comes very close.

XPath Examples

1. List the item number and description of all bicycles whose auction was in progress on 1 February, 1999, ordered by item number.

XPath cannot selectively choose only the item number and description, and it cannot sort by item number (although it will get this sorting because that was the original document order). Unfortunately, XPath also is incapable of performing string or date relational comparisons, so it cannot compare the start and end dates to Feb. 1 to obtain the desired result.

Many implementations of XPath incorrectly allow an expression such as @Name > 'M' to select all attributes Name that are greater than 'M' in the usual string order. However, the XPath specification actually says that in such comparisons, both sides must be converted to number, and then the numbers compared.

If XPath supported string comparisons, then this XPath:

```
/items/item_tuple[ ( contains(desc, 'Bike') or contains(desc, 'Bicycle') ) and
    start<='1999-02-01' and end >= '1999-02-01' ]
```

would select the entire item_tuple for the two items matching the query criteria:

```
<item_tuple>
    <item>1003</item><desc>Old Bicycle</desc>
    <start>1999-01-10</start><end>1999-02-20</end>
    <offered_by>U02</offered_by><reserve_price>25</reserve_price>
</item_tuple>
<item_tuple>
    <item>1007</item><desc>Racing Bike</desc>
    <start>1999-01-20</start><end>1999-02-20</end>
    <offered_by>U04</offered_by><reserve_price>200</reserve_price>
</item_tuple>
```

2. Create a warning for all users with rating worse than "C" offering an item with reserve price exceeding 1000.

Again, XPath cannot create elements that were not in the original document, and cannot merge portions of two different elements into a single result. However, XPath can select the user_tuple elements matching the query:

```
/users/user_tuple[rating > 'C' and
    userid = /items/item_tuple[reserve_price > 1000]/offered_by ]
```

This produces the result:

```
<user_tuple>
    <userid>U03</userid><name>Dee Linquent</name><rating>D</rating>
</user_tuple>
```

3. Find all items having no bids; for each, list its item number and description.

The following XPath:

```
/items/item_tuple[ not(item = /bids/bid_tuple/item) ]
```

selects all items having no bids:

```
<item_tuple>
    <item>1005</item><desc>Tennis Racket</desc>
    <start>1999-03-19</start><end>1999-04-30</end>
    <offered_by>U03</offered_by><reserve_price>20</reserve_price>
</item_tuple>
<item_tuple>
    <item>1006</item><desc>Helicopter</desc>
    <start>1999-05-05</start><end>1999-05-25</end>
    <offered_by>U03</offered_by><reserve_price>50000</reserve_price>
</item_tuple>
<item_tuple>
    <item>1007</item><desc>Racing Bike</desc>
    <start>1999-01-20</start><end>1999-02-20</end>
    <offered_by>U04</offered_by><reserve_price>200</reserve_price>
</item_tuple>
<item_tuple>
    <item>1008</item><desc>Broken Bike</desc>
    <start>1999-02-05</start><end>1999-03-06</end>
    <offered_by>U01</offered_by><reserve_price>25</reserve_price>
</item_tuple>
```

4. List each user alphabetically by name, with a list of the items (if any) for which the user has placed bids (in alphabetical order of description).

Unable to sort alphabetically and unable to combine items with users; XPath cannot perform any meaningful likeness of this query.

XSLT

XSLT, the eXtensible Stylesheet Language: Transformations is a language for transforming existing XML documents into new shapes. To achieve this goal, XSLT provides a way (XPath) to easily select parts of an XML document, and then ways to reformat or otherwise operate on that selection. For more information about XSLT, please see the W3C specification at http://www.w3.org/TR/xslt or *XSLT Programmer's Reference, from Wrox Press ISBN 1861003129.*

XSLT Overview

XSLT uses an XML-based syntax that is declarative and inherently recursive. XSLT expresses transformations using rules, or **templates**, having no side effects (meaning each template affects no global variables or other state outside of itself). Instead of using explicitly described operations to be carried out in a particular order, XSLT executes rules by matching them with data content. In this way, XSLT is a data-driven query language.

XSLT provides a wide variety of transformational capabilities. By design, XSLT has no mechanism for modifying the original XML; instead, an XSLT query results in a copy of the data (often transformed into another representation, such as HTML). A style sheet can also create a new XML document from fresh (by embedding it in the style sheet) and delete an XML document (by producing no output), although these are interesting only as theoretical exercises.

A typical XSLT style sheet contains one or more templates that match elements by name. When a template is matched by the input data, the template's rules are executed. All XPath selections are made relative to the current context, which is that matching element.

Ordinary XML in the template is output directly, but more importantly, elements in the XSLT namespace describe operations on the input data. These operations include copying the input data directly to the output, or using some portion of the input data in the output. We will see examples of these operations later in this section. Finally, a default rule is applied to input data that is not matched by any rule; the default rule copies the values of attribute and text nodes to the output.

XSLT as a Query Language

Overall, XSLT is a very flexible language, capable of performing all four of our example queries. Using include, XSLT can even operate on multiple documents. However, XSLT does suffer from a few drawbacks. One is that it is not currently XSD-aware, and has the same limited data type support as XPath. A few features are noticeably absent in XSLT; for example, there is no (standard) method for getting the current date or time.

Also, XSLT is not prepared to operate on XML fragments, but instead requires well-formed XML documents. Finally, XSLT is very hard to optimize; in fact, every XSLT implementation at the time of this writing requires the entire document to be loaded into memory before the XSLT can be executed. Obviously, this limitation must be solved before XSLT can be applied effectively to large XML datasets (with many millions of nodes).

XSLT Examples

All of these examples require that we wrap the instance data with an enclosing top-level element, say `<root>`. Otherwise, XSLT is capable of performing all four queries; in fact, we will use the XPath partial solutions previously described in constructing these XSLT queries.

1. List the item number and description of all bicycles whose auction was in progress on 1 February, 1999, ordered by item number.

XSLT solves this query very effectively:

```
<xsl:transform version="1.0" xmlns:xsl="http://www.w3.org/1999/XSL/Transform">
  <xsl:template match="root">
    <xsl:apply-templates select="items/item_tuple[ ( contains(desc, 'Bike') or
        contains(desc, 'Bicycle') ) and start &lt;= '1999-02-01' and end &gt;=
        '1999-02-01' ]">
```

```
                <xsl:sort select="item"/>
            </xsl:apply-templates>
        </xsl:template>
        <xsl:template match="item_tuple">
            <item_tuple>
                <item><xsl:value-of select="item"/></item>
                <desc><xsl:value-of select="desc"/></desc>
            </item_tuple>
        </xsl:template>
    </xsl:transform>
```

2. Create a warning for all users with rating worse than "C" offering an item with reserve price exceeding 1000.

Joins are somewhat more difficult in XSLT (just like in XPath), but they can be done. In this example, we cannot reuse the XPath query used previously without modification, because the results must contain data from several parts of the XPath. Also, we must use variables or some other workaround that allows us to select values from both side of the join.

```
<xsl:transform version="1.0" xmlns:xsl="http://www.w3.org/1999/XSL/Transform">
    <xsl:template match="root">
        <xsl:apply-templates select="items/item_tuple[reserve_price &gt; 1000]"/>
    </xsl:template>
    <xsl:template match="item_tuple">
        <xsl:variable name="desc" select="desc"/>
        <xsl:variable name="price" select="reserve_price"/>
        <xsl:variable name="by" select="offered_by"/>
        <xsl:for-each select="/root/users/user_tuple[rating &gt; 'C' and userid =
            $by]">
            <warning>
                <name><xsl:value-of select="name"/></name>
                <rating><xsl:value-of select="rating"/></rating>
                <desc><xsl:value-of select="$desc"/></desc>
                <reserve_price><xsl:value-of select="$price"/></reserve_price>
            </warning>
        </xsl:for-each>
    </xsl:template>
</xsl:transform>
```

3. Find all items having no bids; for each, list its item number and description.

```
<xsl:transform version="1.0" xmlns:xsl="http://www.w3.org/1999/XSL/Transform">
    <xsl:template match="root">
        <xsl:apply-templates select="items/item_tuple[ not(item =
            /root/bids/bid_tuple/item) ]"/>
    </xsl:template>
    <xsl:template match="item_tuple">
        <item_tuple>
            <itemno><xsl:value-of select="item"/></itemno>
            <desc><xsl:value-of select="desc"/></desc>
        </item_tuple>
    </xsl:template>
</xsl:transform>
```

4. List each user alphabetically by name, with a list of the items (if any) for which the user has placed bids (in alphabetical order of description).

```
<xsl:transform version="1.0" xmlns:xsl="http://www.w3.org/1999/XSL/Transform">
   <xsl:template match="root">
      <xsl:apply-templates select="users/user_tuple">
         <xsl:sort select="name"/>
      </xsl:apply-templates>
   </xsl:template>
   <xsl:template match="user_tuple">
      <user>
         <name><xsl:value-of select="name"/></name>
         <xsl:variable name="id" select="userid"/>
         <xsl:apply-templates select="/root/bids/bid_tuple[userid=$id]" />
      </user>
   </xsl:template>
   <xsl:template match="bid_tuple">
      <xsl:variable name="item" select="item"/>
      <xsl:apply-templates select="//item_tuple[item = $item]">
         <xsl:sort select="desc"/>
      </xsl:apply-templates>
   </xsl:template>
   <xsl:template match="item_tuple">
      <item><xsl:value-of select="desc"/></item>
   </xsl:template>
</xsl:transform>
```

Quilt

Created by Don Chamberlain, Dana Florescu, and Jonathan Robie, Quilt is one of many proposed XML Query Languages. See http://www.almaden.ibm.com/cs/people/chamberlin/quilt.html for more details and prototype implementations. In this section, we describe the version of Quilt outlined in the document "Quilt: An XML Query Language for Heterogeneous Data Sources" which can be found on the Web at the site above.

Quilt Overview

Named for its patchwork heritage, Quilt includes concepts from many other languages. Like XSLT, Quilt uses path expressions based on XPath to refer to parts of the document. Quilt adds to this a function document() to load XML from a URL, and a dereference operator -> similar to the id() function in XPath to follow ID references.

A typical Quilt query consists of a so-called "flower" expression, named after the initials FLWR that stand for the individual parts of the query: FOR, LET, WHERE, RETURN. The FOR clause binds variables to the members of a nodeset-valued expression, similar to iterators in other languages. The LET clause binds variables to expressions, possibly formed from the variables bound in the FOR clause. The WHERE clause filters the variable expressions like an SQL WHERE clause, or XPath predicate. Finally, the RETURN clause generates the output of the query.

Every query contains one or more FOR clauses, zero or more LET clauses, an optional WHERE clause, and one RETURN clause. Quilt also supports NAMESPACE clauses for binding namespace prefixes to URIs and FUNCTION clauses for user-defined functions.

Quilt as a Query Language

As a proposed syntax, Quilt is intended to satisfy every requirement of the XML Query Language except one: an XML-based syntax. However, this last requirement is not an onerous one. Overall, Quilt provides solid capabilities for selecting and creating XML, and appears to be one of the most "mature" XML query languages after XSLT.

Quilt queries are also very compact. As you'll see in the examples later, Quilt can express the same functionality as XSLT, in about half the space. This is partly because Quilt makes good use of variables, and partly because Quilt is a human-readable syntax instead of an XML one.

At the time of this writing, Quilt is deficient in two respects: It has essentially no typing rules, and it does not provide means for accessing the XML schema information associated with an XML instance. Consequently, the computational capabilities of Quilt are less well defined than its navigation and transformation capabilities.

Quilt Examples

It should come as no surprise that Quilt is capable or executing all four of the example queries. In fact, there are several possible answers for each; we chose solutions to demonstrate features of Quilt, not necessarily optimally. In each query, we refer to the original XML data as `ch10_ex1.xml`.

1. List the item number and description of all bicycles whose auction was in progress on 1 February, 1999, ordered by item number.

```
FOR $i IN document("ch10_ex1.xml")//item_tuple
WHERE (contains($i/desc, "Bike") OR contains($i/desc, "Bicycle"))
    AND $i/start <= "1999-02-01" AND $i/end >= "1999-02-01"
RETURN <item_tuple>$i/item, $i/desc</item_tuple> SORTBY(item)
```

2. Create a warning for all users with rating worse than "C" offering an item with reserve price exceeding 1000.

```
FOR $u IN document("ch10_ex1.xml")//user_tuple[rating > "C"],
    $i IN document("ch10_ex1.xml")//item_tuple[reserve_price > 1000]
WHERE $u/userid = $i/offered_by
RETURN <warning>$u/name, $u/rating, $i/desc, $i/reserve_price</warning>
```

3. Find all items having no bids; for each, list its item number and description.

```
FOR $bid_items IN distinct(document("ch10_ex1.xml")/bids/bid_tuple/item)
LET $i := document("ch10_ex1.xml")//item_tuple[not(item = $bid_items/item)]
RETURN <item_tuple><itemno>$i/item/text()</itemno>,$i/desc</item_tuple>
```

4. List each user alphabetically by name, with a list of the items (if any) for which the user has placed bids (in alphabetical order of description).

```
FOR $u IN document("ch10_ex1.xml")//user_tuple
RETURN
<user>$u/name,
    FOR $b IN document("ch10_ex1.xml")//bid_tuple[userid = $u/userid]
    LET $i := document("ch10_ex1.xml")//item_tuple[item = $b/item]
    RETURN <item>$i/desc/text()</item> SORTBY(.)
</user> SORTBY(name)
```

XSQL

Created by David Beech at Oracle, the XML Structured Query Language (XSQL) takes a different tack. Designed to be fully compatible with SQL-99 and SQL/MM Full-Text, XSQL has as much or more in common with SQL than with other XML query languages.

XSQL Overview

XSQL extends SQL with two important syntactic expressions. A FOR clause replaces the standard FROM clause with iteration over a collection; this is similar in function to Quilt's FOR clause, but with a different syntax. An AS clause names a collection. In practical terms, this wraps the results of a SELECT (which would otherwise be an unnamed collection) with a tag element (AS tag SELECT ...).

XSQL also makes use of existing features of SQL-99, such as the dereference operator -> to follow intra-document links and WITH RECURSIVE to define recursive queries. XSQL also uses a path syntax that is a combination of XPath and SQL-99, using . instead of / to separate steps.

XSQL as a Query Language

XSQL has the mixed blessing of building on the well-defined relational algebra and SQL syntax. It inherits all of the benefits of SQL-99, with only small modifications to the SQL syntax and semantics. This means XSQL is likely to see rapid adoption among SQL-99 vendors, whether or not it is chosen as the W3C XML Query Language syntax. Developers familiar with SQL-99 will be able to transfer much of their knowledge to XSQL.

However, this also means that XSQL carries with it all of the baggage of SQL, including many features that are not necessary for an XML query language. By requiring implementers to support most of SQL-99 and SQL/MM Full-text, XSQL raises the barrier to entry for new implementations from scratch. Also, developers unfamiliar with SQL-99 may find the XSQL syntax more difficult to learn than that of other XML query languages.

XSQL works very well for XML that is somewhat relational in structure (such as the examples we are using to demonstrate each query language), but requires more contortions for less relational XML and for complicated transformations. There are also places where the SQL and XML data models differ greatly. In particular, it is not clear how XSQL will address the XSD type system.

XSQL Examples

1. List the item number and description of all bicycles whose auction was in progress on 1 February, 1999, ordered by item number.

```
SELECT (i.item, i.description) AS item_tuple
FOR i IN "example.xml".items
WHERE i.start <= '1999-02-01' AND i.end >= '1999-02-01'
  AND (Contains(i.desc, "Bicycle" OR Contains(i.desc, "Bike"))
ORDER BY i.item
```

2. Create a warning for all users with rating worse than "C" offering an item with reserve price exceeding 1000.

```
SELECT (u.name, u.rating, i.desc, i.reserve_price) AS warning
FOR i IN "example.xml".items, u IN "example.xml".users
WHERE u.rating > 'C' AND i.reserve_price > 1000 AND u.userid = i.offered_by
```

3. Find all items having no bids; for each, list its item number and reserve price.

```
SELECT (i.item AS itemno, i.desc) AS item_tuple
FOR i IN "example.xml"
WHERE NOT EXISTS
(
    SELECT b
    FOR b IN "example.xml".bids
    WHERE b.item = i.item
)
```

4. List each user alphabetically by name, with a list of the items (if any) for which the user has placed bids (in alphabetical order of description).

```
SELECT (u.name, (
    SELECT i.desc AS item
    FOR i IN "example.xml".items, b IN "example.xml".bids
    WHERE b.userid = u.userid AND b.item = i.item
    ORDER BY i.desc
    )
) AS user
FOR u IN "example.xml".users
ORDER BY u.name
```

Summary

The XML Query Language consists of a data model, formal algebra, and one or more syntaxes. The data model describes the information available to a query, including all XML node types, scalar types, and ID/IDREF links. The algebra describes the operations that are supported over the data model, such as navigating XML hierarchies, computing values, joining multiple XML sources, and constructing XML results. The syntaxes are user-visible representations of the algebra; at least one will be expressed using XML itself.

The XML Query Language should reach "candidate recommendation" status in late 2001. Many of the technical underpinnings are already in place, and the rest of the details are being sorted out even as this book goes to press. We expect the XML Query Language to significantly enhance the developer's toolkit with great new ways to query XML.

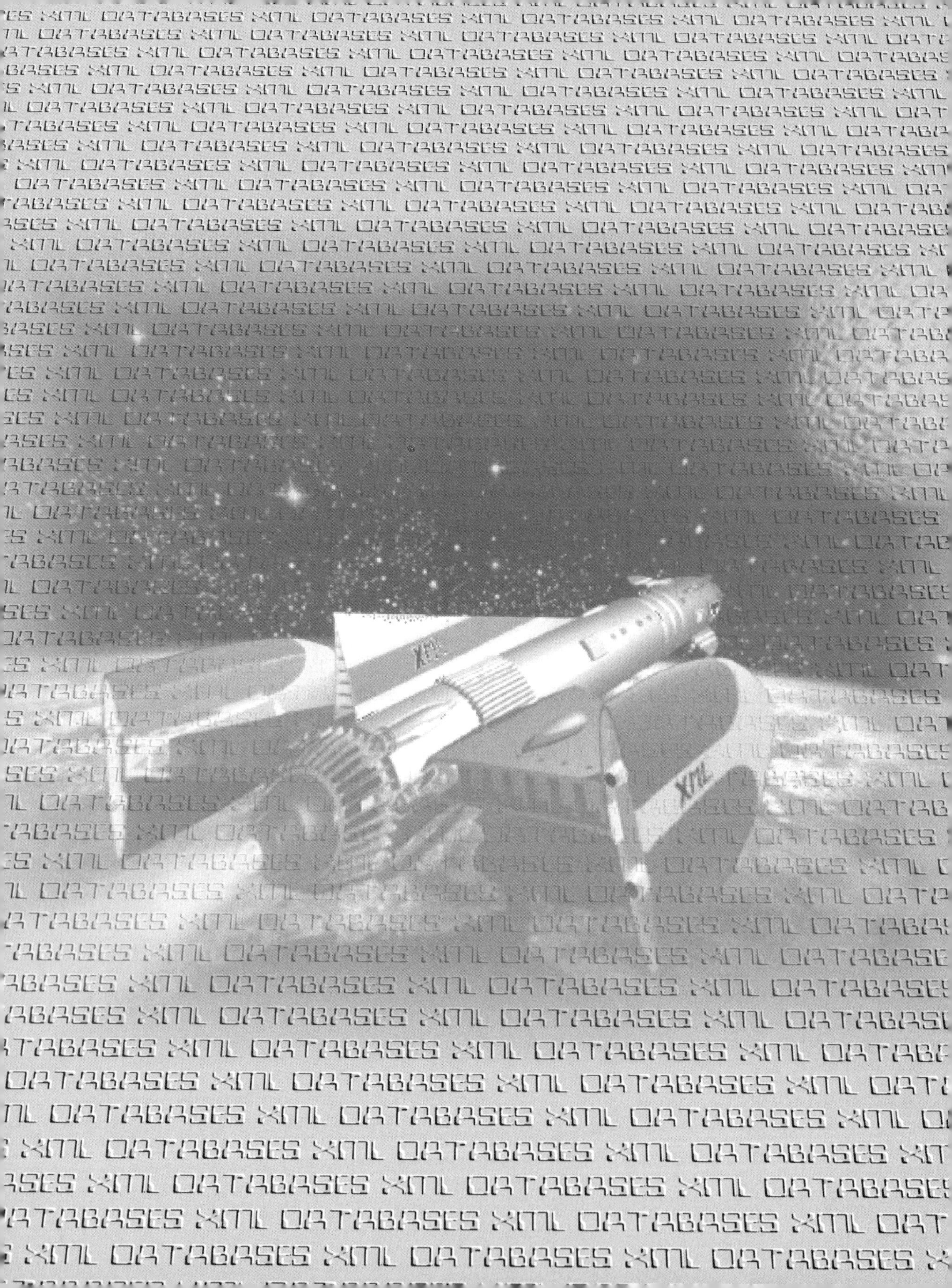
XML DATABASES
XML

12

Flat Files

In this chapter, we are going to look at flat files and some of the issues encountered when moving data between flat files and XML. We'll also learn some strategies for mapping XML to flat files and some of the issues you may encounter when doing so; we'll also take a look at the technologies for actually performing the mapping and see which ones best fit the bill.

Flat files store data in a way that is generally specific to the application using them and are commonly encountered when working with legacy systems. Configuration files can often be flat files. On MS Windows, system.ini and win.ini are examples of flat files; on UNIX, just about any configuration file you will find is a flat file, as are the system mailboxes. Legacy systems store their data natively in a flat-file format, or they already have mechanisms in place to import and export data in that form. One advantage behind a flat file compared to a hash file, for instance, is that a developer can tweak settings, or otherwise read and process data that would otherwise be in a proprietary file format. Learning to accept data in this form and how to transform it to a more useful form in your new system can save you from costly legacy code updates.

In this chapter, we will learn how to:

- ❏ Break flat files down into name-value pairs (to aid mapping)
- ❏ Transform delimited files to XML files
- ❏ Transform fixed-width files to XML files
- ❏ Transform tagged-record files to XML files
- ❏ Transform XML files to delimited files
- ❏ Transform XML files to fixed-width files
- ❏ Transform XML files to tagged-record files

Types of flat files

There are three general types of flat files that are commonly used for data. If you learn how to manipulate, create, and consume files in these three forms, you should be able to process just about any flat file you receive, or create any flat file required by a client system.

Delimited

In a **delimited** file, data fields appear just as you might imagine – they are separated, or delimited, by some predefined character (one that is not expected to appear in any of the data fields). Common delimiters are commas, colons, tab characters, and pipe characters. Each record is typically terminated by a hard return (a line feed-carriage return pair). If a hard return is the terminating character used, then this causes problems when converting between UNIX and DOS/Windows, for instance. Below is an example of a delimited file, using commas for the delimiting character. If a field is empty, there are just two delimiting characters together, like on the second line of this example:

```
Kevin Williams,744 Evergreen
Terrace,Springfield,KY,12345,12/01/2000,12/04/2000
Homer Simpson,742 Evergreen Terrace,Springfield,KY,,12/02/2000,12/05/2000
```

Fixed-width

In a **fixed-width** file, each data field is allocated a particular number of bytes. This is the type of file you are most likely to encounter if you work with COBOL legacy systems. There is often (but not always) a hard return stored at the end of every record. Here is an example of a fixed-width file. This is a contrived example. Typically, the length of each field will demand that the line is longer than the width of a screen, but as long as there isn't a hard return, there is no problem.

```
Kevin Williams 744 Evergreen Terrace   Springfield   KY12345
12/01/200012/04/2000
Homer Simpson  742 Evergreen Terrace   Springfield   KY12345
12/02/200012/05/2000
```

Tagged record

Tagged-record files introduce a rudimentary form of structure into flat files. Tags may be used for delimited or fixed width files, and serve to indicate what the rest of the record in which they appear represents. They are typically the first field in a record. For example, we might have the first character of our record be a tag indicating whether that record is an invoice (I), a customer (C), or an invoice line item (L); the rest of the record's meaning would then depend on the type of record. Here is an example of a tagged record file:

```
I,12/01/2000,12/04/2000
C,Kevin Williams,744 Evergreen Terrace,Springfield,KY,12345
L,blue,2 in. grommet,0001700000.10
L,silver,3 in. widget,0002200000.20
I,12/02/2000,12/05/2000
C,Homer Simpson,742 Evergreen Terrace,Springfield,KY,12345
L,red,1 in. sprocket,0001300000.30
L,blue,2 in. grommet,0001100000.10
```

Issues

There are a couple of common issues you will encounter when moving data from XML to flat files and vice-versa. Let's look at those issues, and what you'll need to do to resolve them appropriately when writing your code.

Level of Normalization

The most obvious difference between XML documents and flat files is the level of normalization – flat files (with the exception of tagged record files) are usually completely de-normalized. Since a well-designed XML structure will be fairly normalized, your code will have to de-normalize or normalize data when moving to or from flat file structures. When we talk about the plan of attack for these sorts of transformations later in the chapter, we'll see how you can perform this normalization or denormalization with a minimum of effort.

To learn more about normalization and de-normalization, please look at Appendix B, which covers relational databases.

Data Formatting

Another issue commonly encountered when working with flat files is the format of data. Many legacy systems, due to size constraints or other concerns, use arcane formatting schemes that may not be readily comprehensible to today's programmer. For example, say that a numeric field in a flat file contains the following data:

```
D5417
```

To decipher this value, we look in the flat file description. It says that the field has two implied decimal places, and that the first digit is replaced by the corresponding letter in the alphabet (A is 0, J is 9) if the number represented is negative. Applying those rules to our data, we see that the human-readable value of the field is -554.17.

If you are going to be doing a lot of work with legacy systems, you should build up a library of routines that handle common transformations like this one.

Plan of Attack

Flat files can vary widely – there are just about as many ways to create a flat file, as there are programmers to create them. In this section, we'll look at a process that almost always may be used to map data from one form to another, making programming that much easier.

Transform the XML Document to name-value Pairs

The first thing you should do when attempting to transform between an XML document and a flat file is to flatten the XML document into a list of name-value pairs. This helps to ensure that you understand where each piece of information may appear in an XML document. Let's look at this flattening process to see what's involved.

Say we have the following XML structure:

```
<!ELEMENT InvoiceData (Invoice+, Part+, Customer+)>
<!ELEMENT Invoice (LineItem+)>
<!ATTLIST Invoice
   customerIDREF IDREF #REQUIRED
   orderDate CDATA #REQUIRED
   shipDate CDATA #REQUIRED
   shipMethod (USPS | UPS | FedEx) #REQUIRED>
<!ELEMENT LineItem EMPTY>
<!ATTLIST LineItem
   partIDREF IDREF #REQUIRED
   quantity CDATA #REQUIRED
   price CDATA #REQUIRED>
<!ELEMENT Part EMPTY>
<!ATTLIST Part
   partID ID #REQUIRED
   name CDATA #REQUIRED
   size CDATA #REQUIRED
   color CDATA #REQUIRED>
<!ELEMENT Customer EMPTY>
<!ATTLIST Customer
   customerID ID #REQUIRED
   name CDATA #REQUIRED
   address CDATA #REQUIRED
   city CDATA #REQUIRED
   state CDATA #REQUIRED
   zip CDATA #REQUIRED>
```

In order to understand the information that may appear in this document, first we need to decompose it into name-value pairs. To do this, we need to look at each data-level point in our XML document and describe it in a name-value table. For each data element, we should describe what that point represents and the format it takes. We should also describe where each data element might appear in the XML document, using shorthand to indicate where more than one record may appear. In this notation, an upper-case letter by itself indicates the instance of a particular element in our structure. For the example DTD above, our name-value pair table looks like this:

Attribute	Details
`InvoiceData.Invoice[N].customerIDREF`	**Data type**: IDREF
	Description: A pointer to the customer associated with invoice N
`InvoiceData.Invoice[N].orderDate`	**Data type**: Datetime
	Format: MM/DD/YYYY
	Description: The date invoice N was submitted
`InvoiceData.Invoice[N].shipDate`	**Data type**: Datetime
	Format: MM/DD/YYYY
	Description: The date invoice N was or will be fulfilled

Attribute	Details
`InvoiceData.Invoice[N].shipMethod`	**Data type**: Enumerated list
	Values: `USPS`: United States Postal Service; `UPS`: United Parcel Service; `FedEx`: Federal Express
	Description: The method used to ship the parts ordered on invoice N
`InvoiceData.Invoice[N].LineItem[M].partIDREF`	**Data type**: IDREF
	Description: A pointer to the part ordered on line M of invoice N
`InvoiceData.Invoice[N].LineItem[M].quantity`	**Data type**: Numeric
	Format: #####
	Description: The quantity of the specified part ordered on line M of invoice N
`InvoiceData.Invoice[N].LineItem[M].price`	**Data type**: Numeric
	Format: #####.##
	Description: The price paid by the customer for each part ordered on line M of invoice N
`InvoiceData.Part[N].partID`	**Data type**: ID
	Description: The identifier of part N
`InvoiceData.Part[N].name`	**Data type**: String
	Format: No more than 20 characters
	Description: The name of part N
`InvoiceData.Part[N].size`	**Data type**: String
	Format: No more than 10 characters
	Description: The size of part N
`InvoiceData.Part[N].color`	**Data type**: String
	Format: No more than 10 characters
	Description: The color of part N
`InvoiceData.Customer[N].name`	**Data type**: String
	Format: No more than 20 characters
	Description: The name of customer N

Table continued on following page

Attribute	Details
`InvoiceData.Customer[N].address`	**Data type**: String
	Format: No more than 30 characters
	Description: The address of customer N
`InvoiceData.Customer[N].city`	**Data type**: String
	Format: No more than 30 characters
	Description: The city of customer N
`InvoiceData.Customer[N].state`	**Data type**: String
	Format: No more than 30 characters
	Description: The state of customer N
`InvoiceData.Customer[N].postalCode`	**Data type**: String
	Format: No more than 30 characters
	Description: The postal code of customer N

Transform the Flat File to name-value Pairs

A similar process needs to be performed on flat files. Often, if the flat file comes with the appropriate documentation, this information will already be available in the form of a field list or some other document. We'll see how to create name-value maps for all our example flat file documents later in the chapter, but for now let's look at the example delimited file. A carriage return is the record delimiter as expected. There aren't any spaces after each line, it is just where it wraps around to the next line.

```
Kevin Williams,744 Evergreen
Terrace,Springfield,KY,12345,12/01/2000,12/04/2000,blue 2 in.
grommet,17,0.10,silver 3 in. widget,22,0.20,,0,0.00,,0,0.00,,0,0.00
Homer Simpson,742 Evergreen
Terrace,Springfield,KY,12345,12/02/2000,12/05/2000,2,red 1 in.
sprocket,13,0.30,blue 2 in. grommet,11,0.10,,0,0.00,,0,0.00,,0,0.00
```

In this case, our name-value pair table would look something like this:

Value	Details
`record[N].field1`	**Data type**: String
	Format: No more than 20 characters
	Description: The name of the customer on invoice N
`record[N].field2`	**Data type**: String
	Format: No more than 30 characters
	Description: The address of the customer on invoice N

Value	Details
record[N].field3	**Data type**: String **Format**: No more than 20 characters **Description**: The city of the customer on invoice N.
record[N].field4	**Data type**: String **Format**: Two characters **Description**: The state of the customer on invoice N
record[N].field5	**Data type**: String **Format**: No more than 10 characters **Description**: The postal code of the customer on invoice N
record[N].field6	**Data type**: Datetime **Format**: MM/DD/YYYY **Description**: The order date for invoice N
record[N].field7	**Data type**: Datetime **Format**: MM/DD/YYYY **Description**: The ship date for invoice N.
record[N].field8	**Data type**: Enumerated value **Values**: 1: United States Postal Service; 2: United Parcel Service; 3: Federal Express **Description**: The shipping method used to ship the parts ordered on invoice N
record[N].field9	**Data type**: String **Format**: No more than 30 characters **Description**: The description of the part ordered in the first line item of invoice N, in the form {color} {size} {name}
record[N].field10	**Data type**: Numeric **Format**: ##### **Description**: The quantity of the part ordered in the first line item of invoice N
record[N].field11	**Data type**: Numeric **Format**: #####.## **Description**: The price of the part ordered in the first line item of invoice N

Table continued on following page

Value	Details
record[N].field12	**Data type:** String
	Format: No more than 30 characters
	Description: The description of the part ordered in the second line item of invoice N, in the form *color size name*
record[N].field13	**Data type:** Numeric
	Format: #####
	Description: The quantity of the part ordered in the second line item of invoice N
record[N].field14	**Data type:** Numeric
	Format: #####.##
	Description: The price of the part ordered in the second line item of invoice N
record[N].field15	**Data type:** String
	Format: No more than 30 characters
	Description: The description of the part ordered in the third line item of invoice N, in the form *color size name*.
record[N].field16	**Data type:** Numeric
	Format: #####
	Description: The quantity of the part ordered in the third line item of invoice N
record[N].field17	**Data type:** Numeric
	Format: #####.##
	Description: The price of the part ordered in the third line item of invoice N
record[N].field18	**Data type:** String
	Format: No more than 30 characters
	Description: The description of the part ordered in the fourth line item of invoice N, in the form *color size name*
record[N].field19	**Data type:** Numeric
	Format: #####
	Description: The quantity of the part ordered in the fourth line item of invoice N

Value	Details
record[N].field20	**Data type**: Numeric
	Format: #####.##
	Description: The price of the part ordered in the fourth line item of invoice N
record[N].field21	**Data type**: String
	Format: No more than 30 characters
	Description: The description of the part ordered in the fifth line item of invoice N, in the form *color size name*
record[N].field22	**Data type**: Numeric
	Format: #####
	Description: The quantity of the part ordered in the fifth line item of invoice N
record[N].field23	**Data type**: Numeric
	Format: #####.##
	Description: The price of the part ordered in the fifth line item of invoice N

Map the Transform

Next, we need to look at the way the data maps from our source format to our destination format. The order in which we do this analysis is important; depending on the data we are working with, we may be able to map the transform in one direction but not the other. Let's see an example. Say we have the following fields in our XML structure:

InvoiceData.Invoice[N].subtotal	**Data type**: Numeric
	Format: ########.##
	Description: The subtotal of the invoice (less any applicable sales tax)
InvoiceData.Invoice[N].salestax	**Data type**: Numeric
	Format: ########.##
	Description: The sales tax applied to this invoice

And this field in the flat file structure:

record[N].field23	**Data type**: Numeric
	Format: ########.##
	Description: The total of the invoice, including applicable sales tax

If we are transforming between these formats, we can take the data points in the XML structure and map them to the field in the flat file structure by simply adding together the two XML data points. However, we cannot take the field in the flat file and transform it to the two data points in the XML structure. There's no way to reconstruct the subtotal and sales tax, given only the total (and assuming we don't know what the sales tax rate for the invoice was, or for the purposes of this example the individual line totals). If you are trying to move data from one format to another and it would involve the generation of information (as in this case), you won't be able to do so without modifying either the input or output structure.

You also need to pay attention to the formats of the data in the input and output structures. Often, you will need to transform the data in some way to get it from the input format to the output format. It can be useful if you derive a notation for referring to XML data points in this mapping. For example, you might use a period (.) to indicate a contained child, and an arrow (->) to indicate a pointed-to element.

For the two samples we have been examining, the map from the delimited flat-file source to the XML target looks something like this:

Source	Target	Comments
record[N].field1	InvoiceData.Invoice[N]->Customer.Name	Create a new customer and link back to it from the Invoice record created
record[N].field2	InvoiceData.Invoice[N]->Customer.Address	
record[N].field3	InvoiceData.Invoice[N]->Customer.City	
record[N].field4	InvoiceData.Invoice[N]->Customer.State	
record[N].field5	InvoiceData.Invoice[N]->Customer.PostalCode	
record[N].field6	InvoiceData.Invoice[N].orderDate	
record[N].field7	InvoiceData.Invoice[N].shipDate	
record[N].field8	InvoiceData.Invoice[N].shipMethod	Enumerated transform: 1 to USPS 2 to UPS 3 to FedEx
record[N].field9	InvoiceData.Invoice[N].LineItem[1]->Part.Name, InvoiceData. Invoice[N].LineItem[1]->Part.Size, InvoiceData. Invoice[N].LineItem[1]->Part.Color	
record[N].field10	InvoiceData.Invoice[N].LineItem[1].quantity	
record[N].field11	InvoiceData.Invoice[N].LineItem[1].price	

Source	Target	Comments

`record[N].field12`	`InvoiceData.Invoice[N].LineItem[2]->Part.Name,`
	
	`InvoiceData. Invoice[N].LineItem[2]->Part.Size,`
	
	`InvoiceData. Invoice[N].LineItem[2]->Part.Color`
		Blank (all spaces) if no line 2 appears on the invoice.

`record[N].field13`	`InvoiceData.Invoice[N].LineItem[2].quantity`	
`record[N].field14`	`InvoiceData.Invoice[N].LineItem[2].price`	

`record[N].field15`	`InvoiceData.Invoice[N].LineItem[3]->Part.Name,`
	
	`InvoiceData. Invoice[N].LineItem[3]->Part.Size,`
	
	`InvoiceData. Invoice[N].LineItem[3]->Part.Color`
		Blank (all spaces) if no line 3 appears on the invoice.

`record[N].field16`	`InvoiceData.Invoice[N].LineItem[3].quantity`	
`record[N].field17`	`InvoiceData.Invoice[N].LineItem[3].price`	

`record[N].field18`	`InvoiceData.Invoice[N].LineItem[4]->Part.Name,`
	
	`InvoiceData. Invoice[N].LineItem[4]->Part.Size,`
	
	`InvoiceData. Invoice[N].LineItem[4]->Part.Color`
		Blank (all spaces) if no line 4 appears on the invoice.

`record[N].field19`	`InvoiceData.Invoice[N].LineItem[4].quantity`	
`record[N].field20`	`InvoiceData.Invoice[N].LineItem[4].price`	

`record[N].field21`	`InvoiceData.Invoice[N].LineItem[5]->Part.Name,`
	
	`InvoiceData. Invoice[N].LineItem[5]->Part.Size,`
	
	`InvoiceData. Invoice[N].LineItem[5]->Part.Color`
		Blank (all spaces) if no line 5 appears on the invoice.

`record[N].field22`	`InvoiceData.Invoice[N].LineItem[5].quantity`	
`record[N].field23`	`InvoiceData.Invoice[N].LineItem[5].price`	

Transforming from Flat Files to XML

First, let's look at how to approach transforming data from flat files into XML. We'll determine which technology makes the most sense for this problem, and then see an example of each of the different file types and code that processes them into XML.

Programming Approaches

When transforming flat files to XML, there are a couple of obvious approaches. To extract the data from the flat file, you'll need to do traditional file parsing – reading the file a line at a time and breaking it apart into its individual components. To produce XML output, either you can serialize the XML structure into a string or file target manually, or you can use the XML DOM to do so. Let's look at the advantages and disadvantages of each approach.

Manual Serialization

In this approach, the XML document, including all of the tags and other text that goes with an XML document, is created on the fly by appending to a string. This approach has a relatively small memory footprint, you don't need to allocate any more memory than is necessary, but tends to be error-prone (if you accidentally write the start tag, but not the end tag, for example). The other problem with this approach is it forces the information to be written to the target in the order prescribed by the target – you can't append objects to the tree at will. This requires some more sophisticated parsing approaches to obtain the desired output, especially if the target document has pointing relationships. Traditional I/O functions can be used to generate the output string or file.

SAX

In this approach, a SAX handler is initialized and a stream of events are sent to it, causing it to generate an XML document. Unfortunately, as you still need to manually generate start and end element events to send to the SAX event handler, this approach is not much better than manual serialization. SAX also requires that the document be serialized in the order mandated by its DTD. While this technique doesn't afford much better control of XML document serialization than creating the document manually, it is often the best choice when creating very large XML documents.

The DOM

Using this approach, a document tree is created using an implementation of the XML DOM. This approach tends to consume more memory than a simple serialization approach, but is much less error prone – there's no risk of accidentally omitting a start or end-tag. The random-access nature of the DOM also allows elements to be added to the result document tree as natural processing obtains them, rather than being required to be cached and written in the order required by the target document. Unless you are expecting to have particular performance or memory requirements, for ease of coding and fewer errors, you should always use the DOM to construct XML documents. We'll be using the DOM in the examples that follow.

Handling Different Flat File Types

Let's see examples of processing for each of the file types we have discussed. For the purpose of these examples, we'll be using VBScript and the Microsoft DOM (the technology preview version). However, this processing approach should port equally well to any platform you choose. We'll see how to handle delimited, fixed-width, and flat file mappings. In our examples, we'll assume that the files have specific local filenames. Of course, you'll need to modify this code to correspond to your particular environment and requirements.

Delimited

First, let's see how to read a delimited file and save the results to an XML document. We've already seen examples of the delimited file and XML document that we'll be transforming. In this example, this file is called ch12_ex1.txt

```
Kevin Williams,744 Evergreen
Terrace,Springfield,KY,12345,12/01/2000,12/04/2000,1,blue 2 in.
grommet,17,0.10,silver 3 in. widget,22,0.20,,0,0.00,,0,0.00
Homer Simpson,742 Evergreen
Terrace,Springfield,KY,12345,12/02/2000,12/05/2000,2,red 1 in.
sprocket,13,0.30,blue 2 in. grommet,11,0.10,,0,0.00,,0,0.00
```

This is mapping into the file ch12_ex1.xml:

```
<InvoiceData>
    <Invoice
        customerIDREF="c1"
        orderDate="12/01/2000"
        shipDate="12/04/2000"
        shipMethod="UPS">
        <LineItem
            partIDREF="p1"
            quantity="17"
            price="0.10" />
        <LineItem
            partIDREF="p2"
            quantity="22"
            price="0.20" />
    </Invoice>
    <Invoice
        customerIDREF="c2"
        orderDate="12/02/2000"
        shipDate="12/05/2000"
        shipMethod="USPS">
        <LineItem
            partIDREF="p3"
            quantity="13"
            price="0.30" />
        <LineItem
            partIDREF="p1"
            quantity="11"
            price="0.10" />
    </Invoice>
    <Part
        partID="p1"
        name="grommet"
        size="2 in."
        color="blue" />
    <Part
        partID="p2"
        name="widget"
        size="3 in."
        color="silver" />
    <Part
        partID="p3"
        name="sprocket"
        size="1 in."
        color="red" />
```

```
        <Customer
          customerID="c1"
          name="Kevin Williams"
          address="744 Evergreen Terrace"
          city="Springfield"
          state="KY"
          postalCode="12345" />
        <Customer
          customerID="c2"
          name="Homer Simpson"
          address="742 Evergreen Terrace"
          city="Springfield"
          state="KY"
          postalCode="12345" />
  </InvoiceData>
```

First, we need to map from the delimited file to the XML document. We've already done this a couple of pages earlier when we were discussing how transform maps are created.

Armed with this information, we can use the following VBScript code to open the flat file, break it apart, and use the DOM to construct the XML equivalent. The entire listing can be found in the file, `ch12_ex1.vbs`, but we'll analyze it here section by section:

```
Dim fso, ts, sLine
Dim el, dom, root

Dim sField(23)
Dim sThisName, sThisSize, sThisColor
Dim sSize, sColor, sName, sAddress
Dim iLineItem
Dim invoiceBucket, partBucket, customerBucket
Dim li, nl, iCust, iPart, cust, part, sDelimit

iCust = 1
iPart = 1
sDelimit = Chr(44) ' This sets the delimiter to be a comma
```

We're using the `iCust` and `iPart` variables to keep track of our customers and parts that we create, so that we can generate a unique ID for each element created.

```
Set fso = CreateObject("Scripting.FileSystemObject")
Set dom = CreateObject("Microsoft.XMLDOM")
Set root = dom.createElement("InvoiceData")
dom.appendChild root
```

We create a `FileSystemObject` for reading the flat file and writing the XML output, and a DOM object for building the XML output. We also go ahead, create the root element for the DOM output, and add it to the document tree.

```
Set invoiceBucket = dom.createDocumentFragment()
Set partBucket = dom.createDocumentFragment()
Set customerBucket = dom.createDocumentFragment()
```

This is a common technique when building up an XML document with ordered elements. As we parse the invoices from the flat file, we'll be generating `Part` and `Customer` elements, as we need them. The above variables are going to act as buckets to hold the invoice, part, and customer information in three different places so that they can be output consecutively as we require. Sorting them into groups as the flat file is being parsed by using `XMLDocumentFragment` objects, allows us to easily build the final output for the file – as our output structure requires us to write every `Invoice` element, then all the `Part` elements, and then all the `Customer` elements to the document, in that order.

```
Set ts = fso.OpenTextFile("invoicedelim.txt")
do while ts.AtEndOfStream <> True
    s = ts.ReadLine
    for iField = 1 to 22
        sField(iField) = left(s, InStr(s, sDelimit) - 1)
        s = mid(s, InStr(s, sDelimit) + 1)
    next
    sField(23) = s
```

We know we have a comma-delimited file, so we break apart each line into fields based on the delimiting character we are expecting. Naturally, if we can't do this (for example, if there aren't enough delimiters in one record – or too many), we would add error handling to report this error to the user. At this point, the `sField()` array contains all of the fields found on one record of the flat file.

```
Set el = dom.createElement ("Invoice")
```

Since each record in our flat file corresponds to one invoice, we can create that `Invoice` element now. We add it to our Invoice document fragment so that we will be able to write all the invoices out as a group to the main document at the end of the process.

```
' check to see if we have this customer yet
el.setAttribute "customerIDREF", "NOTFOUND"
Set nl = customerBucket.childNodes
for iNode = 0 to nl.length - 1
    sName = nl.item(iNode).getAttribute("name")
    sAddress = nl.item(iNode).getAttribute("address")
    if sName = sField(1) and sAddress = sField(2) Then
        ' we presume we have this one already
        el.setAttribute "customerIDREF", _
            nl.item(iNode).getAttribute("customerID")
    end if
next
```

Here, we're examining all the customers in our Customer document fragment to see if we already have the customer referenced in this invoice. Since our XML document normalizes customers together, we want to reuse a customer that matches the customer on this invoice if possible. For the purposes of this analysis, we are assuming that a customer with the same name and address is a match. If we find a match for the customer, we simply set the `customerIDREF` attribute of the invoice to point to it.

```
if el.getAttribute("customerIDREF") = "NOTFOUND" Then
    ' we need to create a new customer
    Set cust = dom.createElement("Customer")
    cust.setAttribute "customerID", "CUST" & iCust
    cust.setAttribute "name", sField(1)
```

```
        cust.setAttribute "address", sField(2)
        cust.setAttribute "city", sField(3)
        cust.setAttribute "state", sField(4)
        cust.setAttribute "postalCode", sField(5)
        customerBucket.appendChild cust
        el.setAttribute "customerIDREF", "CUST" & iCust
        iCust = iCust + 1
    end if
```

If we didn't find the customer, we create one and add it to the Customer document fragment, assigning a new ID to the element. We then reference that ID from the `customerIDREF` attribute of the invoice element we are creating.

```
    el.setAttribute "orderDate", sField(6)
    el.setAttribute "shipDate", sField(7)
    if sField(8) = 1 Then el.setAttribute "shipMethod", "USPS"
    if sField(8) = 2 Then el.setAttribute "shipMethod", "UPS"
    if sField(8) = 3 Then el.setAttribute "shipMethod", "FedEx"
    invoiceBucket.appendChild el
```

We continue to set attributes on the `Invoice` element, translating the values provided in the flat file to their appropriate analogues, elements or attributes, depending on what we're using, in our XML document as necessary. Once we've done this, we append the element to our Invoice document fragment.

```
    for iLineItem = 1 to 5
        if sField(6 + iLineItem * 3) > "" Then
            ' this line item exists
```

Here, we iterate through each of the three-field sets that represent a line item. We know that if the description for the item is present, the line item exists and needs to be represented in our XML target.

```
        Set li = dom.createElement ("LineItem")
        li.setAttribute "quantity", sField(6 + iLineItem * 3 + 1)
        li.setAttribute "price", sField(6 + iLineItem * 3 + 2)
```

We create our line item element and set its attributes based on the contents of the flat file.

```
        ' break apart the description field
        sWork = sField(6 + iLineItem * 3)
        sThisColor = left(sWork, InStr(sWork, " ") - 1)
        sWork = Mid(sWork, InStr(sWork, " ") + 1)
        sThisSize = ""
        While InStr(sWork, " ") > 0
            sThisSize = sThisSize + left(sWork, InStr(sWork, " "))
            sWork = Mid(sWork, InStr(sWork, " ") + 1)
        Wend
        sThisSize = Left(sThisSize, len(sThisSize) - 1)
        sThisName = sWork
```

Here, we've decomposed the description of the part provided in the flat file into the name, size, and color data points our XML document needs.

```
Set nl = partBucket.childNodes
li.setAttribute "partIDREF", "NOTFOUND"
for iNode = 0 to nl.length - 1
    sName = nl.item(iNode).getAttribute("name")
    sSize = nl.item(iNode).getAttribute("size")
    sColor = nl.item(iNode).getAttribute("color")
    If sThisName = sName And sThisSize = sSize And sThisColor = sColor _
    Then
        ' we presume we have this one already
        li.setAttribute "partIDREF", _
            nl.item(iNode).getAttribute("partID")
    end if
next
if li.getAttribute("partIDREF") = "NOTFOUND" Then
    ' we need to create a new part
    Set part = dom.createElement("Part")
    part.setAttribute "partID", "PART" & iPart
    part.setAttribute "name", sThisName
    part.setAttribute "size", sThisSize
    part.setAttribute "color", sThisColor
    partBucket.appendChild part
    li.setAttribute "partIDREF", "PART" & iPart
    iPart = iPart + 1
end if
```

This code is similar to the corresponding code for Customer – we check to see if we have a part in our part list yet, and if not, we add it with a new ID. For the purposes of parts, we assume that if a part shares the same name, size, and color with a part already created, it is the same part.

```
el.appendChild li
```

Finally, we add the line item to the Invoice element we created earlier.

```
        end if
    next
Loop
ts.Close

root.appendChild invoiceBucket
root.appendChild partBucket
root.appendChild customerBucket
```

Once the entire flat file has been processed and we have created all the appropriate elements, we need to add them back to the document we are creating. We can do this by appending the document fragments for each element type, to the root element of the XML document.

```
Set ts = fso.CreateTextFile("ch12_ex1.xml", True)
ts.Write dom.xml
ts.close
Set ts = Nothing
```

Finally, we flush the XML to the output file, and we're done.

The output of the preceding script, when run against the sample delimited file we saw earlier, should be the XML file detailed earlier, with the whitespace absent.

Fixed-width

You'll recall the fixed-width example we looked at earlier. Below is a similar example but with all of the information from the last example included and a more realistic spacing between fields.

```
Kevin Williams              744 Evergreen Terrace       Springfield
KY12345     12/01/200012/04/2000UPS  blue 2 in. grommet
0001700000.10silver 3 in. widget          0002200000.20
0000000000.00                             0000000000.00
0000000000.00
Homer Simpson               742 Evergreen Terrace       Springfield
KY12345     12/02/200012/05/2000USPS red 1 in. sprocket
0001300000.30blue 2 in. grommet           0001100000.10
0000000000.00                             0000000000.00
0000000000.00
```

The first thing we need to do is to map the contents of this file. Here is the map:

Value	Details
record[N].field1	**Data type**: String
	Position: 1-30
	Description: The name of the customer on invoice N
record[N].field2	**Data type**: String
	Position: 31-60
	Description: The address of the customer on invoice N
record[N].field3	**Data type**: String
	Position: 61-80
	Description: The city of the customer on invoice N
record[N].field4	**Data type**: String
	Position: 81-82
	Description: The state of the customer on invoice N
record[N].field5	**Data type**: String
	Position: 83-92
	Description: The postal code of the customer on invoice N.

Value	Details
record[N].field6	**Data type**: Datetime
	Position: 93-102
	Format: MM/DD/YYYY
	Description: The order date for invoice N
record[N].field7	**Data type**: Datetime
	Position: 103-112
	Format: MM/DD/YYYY
	Description: The ship date for invoice N
record[N].field8	**Data type**: Enumerated value
	Position: 113-117
	Values: UPS: United States Postal Service; USPS: United Parcel Service; FedEx: Federal Express
	Description: The shipping method used to ship the parts ordered on invoice N
record[N].field9	**Data type**: String
	Position: 118-147
	Format: No more than 30 characters
	Description: The description of the part ordered in the first line item of invoice N, in the form color size name
record[N].field10	**Data type**: Numeric
	Position: 148-152
	Format: #####
	Description: The quantity of the part ordered in the first line item of invoice N
record[N].field11	**Data type**: Numeric
	Position: 153-160
	Format: #####.##
	Description: The price of the part ordered in the first line item of invoice N

Table continued on following page

Value	Details
record[N].field12	**Data type**: String **Position**: 161-190 **Description**: The description of the part ordered in the second line item of invoice N, in the form color size name
record[N].field13	**Data type**: Numeric **Position**: 191-195 **Format**: ##### **Description**: The quantity of the part ordered in the second line item of invoice N
record[N].field14	**Data type**: Numeric **Position**: 196-203 **Format**: #####.## **Description**: The price of the part ordered in the second line item of invoice N
record[N].field15	**Data type**: String **Position**: 204-233 **Format**: No more than 30 characters **Description**: The description of the part ordered in the third line item of invoice N, in the form color size name
record[N].field16	**Data type**: Numeric **Position**: 234-238 **Format**: ##### **Description**: The quantity of the part ordered in the third line item of invoice N
record[N].field17	**Data type**: Numeric **Position**: 239-246 **Format**: #####.## **Description**: The price of the part ordered in the third line item of invoice N
record[N].field18	**Data type**: String **Position**: 247-276 **Description**: The description of the part ordered in the fourth line item of invoice N, in the form color size name

Value	Details
record[N].field19	**Data type**: Numeric **Position**: 277-281 **Format**: ##### **Description**: The quantity of the part ordered in the fourth line item of invoice N
record[N].field20	**Data type**: Numeric **Position**: 282-289 **Format**: #####.## **Description**: The price of the part ordered in the fourth line item of invoice N
record[N].field21	**Data type**: String **Position**: 290-319 **Description**: The description of the part ordered in the fifth line item of invoice N, in the form color size name
record[N].field22	**Data type**: Numeric **Position**: 320-324 **Format**: ##### **Description**: The quantity of the part ordered in the fifth line item of invoice N
record[N].field23	**Data type**: Numeric **Position**: 325-332 **Format**: #####.## **Description**: The price of the part ordered in the fifth line item of invoice N

Next, we map the fields back to the XML fields:

Source	Target	Comments
record[N].field1	InvoiceData.Invoice[N]->Customer.Name	Create a new customer and link back to it from the Invoice record created
record[N].field2	InvoiceData.Invoice[N]->Customer.Address	
record[N].field3	InvoiceData.Invoice[N]->Customer.City	
record[N].field4	InvoiceData.Invoice[N]->Customer.State	
record[N].field5	InvoiceData.Invoice[N]->Customer.PostalCode	

Table continued on following page

Source	Target	Comments
record[N].field6	InvoiceData.Invoice[N].orderDate	
record[N].field7	InvoiceData.Invoice[N].shipDate	
record[N].field8	InvoiceData.Invoice[N].shipMethod	
record[N].field9	InvoiceData.Invoice[N].LineItem[1]->Part.Name, InvoiceData.Invoice[N].LineItem[1]->Part.Size, InvoiceData.Invoice[N].LineItem[1]->Part.Color	
record[N].field10	InvoiceData.Invoice[N].LineItem[1].quantity	
record[N].field11	InvoiceData.Invoice[N].LineItem[1].price	
record[N].field12	InvoiceData.Invoice[N].LineItem[2]->Part.Name, InvoiceData.Invoice[N].LineItem[2]->Part.Size, InvoiceData.Invoice[N].LineItem[2]->Part.Color	Blank (all spaces) if no line 2 appears on the invoice.
record[N].field13	InvoiceData.Invoice[N].LineItem[2].quantity	
record[N].field14	InvoiceData.Invoice[N].LineItem[2].price	
record[N].field15	InvoiceData.Invoice[N].LineItem[3]->Part.Name, InvoiceData.Invoice[N].LineItem[3]->Part.Size, InvoiceData.Invoice[N].LineItem[3]->Part.Color	Blank (all spaces) if no line 3 appears on the invoice.
record[N].field16	InvoiceData.Invoice[N].LineItem[3].quantity	
record[N].field17	InvoiceData.Invoice[N].LineItem[3].price	
record[N].field18	InvoiceData.Invoice[N].LineItem[4]->Part.Name, InvoiceData.Invoice[N].LineItem[4]->Part.Size, InvoiceData.Invoice[N].LineItem[4]->Part.Color	Blank (all spaces) if no line 4 appears on the invoice.

Source	Target	Comments
record[N].field19	InvoiceData.Invoice[N].LineItem[4].quantity	
record[N].field20	InvoiceData.Invoice[N].LineItem[4].price	
record[N].field21	InvoiceData.Invoice[N].LineItem[5]->Part.Name,	Blank (all spaces) if no line 5 appears on the invoice.
	InvoiceData. Invoice[N].LineItem[5]->Part.Size,	
	InvoiceData. Invoice[N].LineItem[5]->Part.Color	
record[N].field22	InvoiceData.Invoice[N].LineItem[5].quantity	
record[N].field23	InvoiceData.Invoice[N].LineItem[5].price	

We can now write the code to perform the transformation. This code can be found in the file ch12_ex2.vbs:

```vbs
Dim fso, ts, sLine
Dim el, dom, root
Dim sField(23)
Dim sThisName, sThisSize, sThisColor
Dim sSize, sColor, sName, sAddress
Dim iLineItem
Dim invoiceBucket, partBucket, customerBucket
Dim li, nl, iCust, iPart, cust, part

iCust = 1
iPart = 1

Set fso = CreateObject("Scripting.FileSystemObject")
Set dom = CreateObject("Microsoft.XMLDOM")
Set root = dom.createElement("InvoiceData")
dom.appendChild root

Set invoiceBucket = dom.createDocumentFragment()
Set partBucket = dom.createDocumentFragment()
Set customerBucket = dom.createDocumentFragment()

Set ts = fso.OpenTextFile("ch12_ex2.txt")
do while ts.AtEndOfStream <> True
    s = ts.ReadLine
    sField(1) = trim(mid(s, 1, 30))
    sField(2) = trim(mid(s, 31, 30))
    sField(3) = trim(mid(s, 61, 20))
    sField(4) = trim(mid(s, 81, 2))
    sField(5) = trim(mid(s, 83, 10))
    sField(6) = trim(mid(s, 93, 10))
    sField(7) = trim(mid(s, 103, 10))
    sField(8) = trim(mid(s, 113, 5))
    sField(9) = trim(mid(s, 118, 30))
    sField(10) = trim(mid(s, 148, 5))
    sField(11) = trim(mid(s, 153, 8))
```

```
sField(12) = trim(mid(s, 161, 30))
sField(13) = trim(mid(s, 191, 5))
sField(14) = trim(mid(s, 196, 8))
sField(15) = trim(mid(s, 204, 30))
sField(16) = trim(mid(s, 234, 5))
sField(17) = trim(mid(s, 239, 8))
sField(18) = trim(mid(s, 247, 30))
sField(19) = trim(mid(s, 277, 5))
sField(20) = trim(mid(s, 282, 8))
sField(21) = trim(mid(s, 290, 30))
sField(22) = trim(mid(s, 320, 5))
sField(23) = trim(mid(s, 325, 8))
Set el = dom.createElement ("Invoice")
' check to see if we have this customer yet
el.setAttribute "customerIDREF", "NOTFOUND"
Set nl = customerBucket.childNodes
for iNode = 0 to nl.length - 1
   sName = nl.item(iNode).getAttribute("name")
   sAddress = nl.item(iNode).getAttribute("address")
   if sName = sField(1) and sAddress = sField(2) Then
      ' we presume we have this one already
      el.setAttribute "customerIDREF", _
         nl.item(iNode).getAttribute("customerID")
   end if
next
if el.getAttribute("customerIDREF") = "NOTFOUND" Then
   ' we need to create a new customer
   Set cust = dom.createElement("Customer")
   cust.setAttribute "customerID", "CUST" & iCust
   cust.setAttribute "name", sField(1)
   cust.setAttribute "address", sField(2)
   cust.setAttribute "city", sField(3)
   cust.setAttribute "state", sField(4)
   cust.setAttribute "postalCode", sField(5)
   customerBucket.appendChild cust
   el.setAttribute "customerIDREF", "CUST" & iCust
   iCust = iCust + 1
end if
el.setAttribute "orderDate", sField(6)
el.setAttribute "shipDate", sField(7)
el.setAttribute "shipMethod", sField(8)
invoiceBucket.appendChild el
for iLineItem = 1 to 5
   if trim(sField(6 + iLineItem * 3)) > "" Then
      ' this line item exists
      Set li = dom.createElement ("LineItem")
      li.setAttribute "quantity", sField(6 + iLineItem * 3 + 1)
      li.setAttribute "price", sField(6 + iLineItem * 3 + 2)
      ' break apart the description field
      sWork = sField(6 + iLineItem * 3)
      sThisColor = left(sWork, InStr(sWork, " ") - 1)
      sWork = Mid(sWork, InStr(sWork, " ") + 1)
      sThisSize = ""
      While InStr(sWork, " ") > 0
         sThisSize = sThisSize + left(sWork, InStr(sWork, " "))
         sWork = Mid(sWork, InStr(sWork, " ") + 1)
      Wend
      sThisSize = Left(sThisSize, len(sThisSize) - 1)
      sThisName = sWork
      Set nl = partBucket.childNodes
      li.setAttribute "partIDREF", "NOTFOUND"
      for iNode = 0 to nl.length - 1
```

```
                sName = nl.item(iNode).getAttribute("name")
                sSize = nl.item(iNode).getAttribute("size")
                sColor = nl.item(iNode).getAttribute("color")
                If sThisName = sName And sThisSize = sSize And _
                  sThisColor = sColor Then
                  ' we presume we have this one already
                  li.setAttribute "partIDREF", nl.item(iNode).getAttribute("partID")
              end if
            next
            if li.getAttribute("partIDREF") = "NOTFOUND" Then
              ' we need to create a new part
              Set part = dom.createElement("Part")
              part.setAttribute "partID", "PART" & iPart
              part.setAttribute "name", sThisName
              part.setAttribute "size", sThisSize
              part.setAttribute "color", sThisColor
              partBucket.appendChild part
              li.setAttribute "partIDREF", "PART" & iPart
              iPart = iPart + 1
            end if
            el.appendChild li
        end if
    next
Loop
ts.Close

root.appendChild invoiceBucket
root.appendChild partBucket
root.appendChild customerBucket

set ts = fso.CreateTextFile("ch12_ex2.xml", True)
ts.Write dom.xml
ts.close
Set ts = Nothing
```

This code is virtually identical to the code used to create an XML document from a delimited file, so we won't drill into it in too much depth here. One interesting thing to point out is the code used to create the sField() array:

```
    sField(1)  = trim(mid(s, 1, 30))
    sField(2)  = trim(mid(s, 31, 30))
    sField(3)  = trim(mid(s, 61, 20))
    sField(4)  = trim(mid(s, 81, 2))
    sField(5)  = trim(mid(s, 83, 10))
    sField(6)  = trim(mid(s, 93, 10))
    sField(7)  = trim(mid(s, 103, 10))
    sField(8)  = trim(mid(s, 113, 5))
    sField(9)  = trim(mid(s, 118, 30))
    sField(10) = trim(mid(s, 148, 5))
    sField(11) = trim(mid(s, 153, 8))
    sField(12) = trim(mid(s, 161, 30))
    sField(13) = trim(mid(s, 191, 5))
    sField(14) = trim(mid(s, 196, 8))
    sField(15) = trim(mid(s, 204, 30))
    sField(16) = trim(mid(s, 234, 5))
    sField(17) = trim(mid(s, 239, 8))
    sField(18) = trim(mid(s, 247, 30))
    sField(19) = trim(mid(s, 277, 5))
    sField(20) = trim(mid(s, 282, 8))
    sField(21) = trim(mid(s, 290, 30))
    sField(22) = trim(mid(s, 320, 5))
    sField(23) = trim(mid(s, 325, 8))
```

Here, we're simply taking the fields from their appropriate location in the source file line. The extraction code could be separated into a separate subroutine that could be changed for different file formats, while the rest of the code would stay the same for all formats. This increases the possibility of code reuse, as the extraction process could be pulled out into a separate procedure independent of the mapping process.

The output of this transformation, when applied to our sample, is the same as for `ch12_ex1.xml` above.

Tagged Record

This is another example of a tagged record format. This one uses a fixed width as its delimiter:

```
I12/01/200012/04/2000UPS
CKevin Williams              744 Evergreen Terrace        Springfield
KY12345
Lblue 2 in. grommet          0001700000.10
Lsilver 3 in. widget         0002200000.20
I12/02/200012/05/2000USPS
CHomer Simpson               742 Evergreen Terrace        Springfield
KY12345
Lred 1 in. sprocket          0001300000.30
Lblue 2 in. grommet          0001100000.10
```

We need to create a mapping table for this format. For the purposes of showing how code may be reused, we'll assume that no more than five parts may appear on one invoice (to make the tagged format consistent with the other flat file formats we've examined). The mapping looks like this:

Value	Details
Record[N].Customer.field1	**Data Type**: String
	Position: 2-31
	Description: The name of the customer on invoice N
Record[N].Customer.field2	**Data Type**: String
	Position: 32-61
	Description: The address of the customer on invoice N
Record[N].Customer.field3	**Data Type**: String
	Position: 62-81
	Description: The city of the customer on invoice N
Record[N].Customer.field4	**Data Type**: String
	Position: 82-83
	Description: The state of the customer on invoice N

Value	Details
Record[N].Customer.field5	**Data Type**: String
	Position: 84-93
	Description: The postal code of the customer on invoice N
Record[N].Invoice.field1	**Data Type**: Datetime
	Position: 2-11
	Format: MM/DD/YYYY
	Description: The order date for invoice N
Record[N].Invoice.field2	**Data Type**: Datetime
	Position: 12-21
	Format: MM/DD/YYYY
	Description: The ship date for invoice N
Record[N].Invoice.field3	**Data Type**: Enumerated value
	Position: 22-26
	Values: **USPS**: United States Postal Service; **UPS**: United Parcel Service; **FedEx**: Federal Express
	Description: The shipping method used to ship the parts ordered on invoice N
Record[N].LineItem[M].field1	**Data Type**: String
	Position: 2-31
	Format: No more than 30 characters
	Description: The description of the part ordered in the Mth line item of invoice N, in the form color size name
Record[N].LineItem[M].field2	**Data Type**: Numeric
	Position: 32-36
	Format: #####
	Description: The quantity of the part ordered in the Mth line item of invoice N
record[N].LineItem[M].field3	**Data Type**: Numeric
	Position: 37-44
	Format: #####.##
	Description: The price of the part ordered in the Mth line item of invoice N

457

Now, we map the fields back to the XML fields:

Source	Target	Comments
`record[N].Customer.field1`	InvoiceData.Invoice[N]->Customer.Name	Create a new customer and link back to it from the Invoice record created
`record[N].Customer.field2`	InvoiceData.Invoice[N]->Customer.Address	
`record[N].Customer.field3`	InvoiceData.Invoice[N]->Customer.City	
`record[N].Customer.field4`	InvoiceData.Invoice[N]->Customer.State	
`record[N].Customer.field5`	InvoiceData.Invoice[N]->Customer.PostalCode	
`record[N].Invoice.field1`	InvoiceData.Invoice[N].orderDate	
`record[N].Invoice.field2`	InvoiceData.Invoice[N].shipDate	
`record[N].Invoice.field3`	InvoiceData.Invoice[N].shipMethod	
`record[N].LineItem[M].field1`	InvoiceData.Invoice[N].LineItem[M]->Part.Name, InvoiceData.Invoice[N].LineItem[M]->Part.Size, InvoiceData.Invoice[N].LineItem[M]->Part.Color	
`record[N].LineItem[M].field2`	InvoiceData.Invoice[N].LineItem[M].quantity	
`record[N].LineItem[M].field3`	InvoiceData.Invoice[N].LineItem[M].price	

We can now write the code to perform the transformation:

```
Dim fso, ts, sLine
Dim el, dom, root

Dim sField(23)
Dim sThisName, sThisSize, sThisColor
Dim sSize, sColor, sName, sAddress
Dim iLineItem
Dim invoiceBucket, partBucket, customerBucket
Dim li, nl, iCust, iPart, cust, part
Dim bDone

iCust = 1
iPart = 1

Set fso = CreateObject("Scripting.FileSystemObject")
Set dom = CreateObject("Microsoft.XMLDOM")
Set root = dom.createElement("InvoiceData")
dom.appendChild root
Set invoiceBucket = dom.createDocumentFragment()
Set partBucket = dom.createDocumentFragment()
Set customerBucket = dom.createDocumentFragment()
```

```
Set ts = fso.OpenTextFile("ch12_ex3.txt")
bDone = False
If ts.AtEndOfStream Then
    bDone = True ' we had an empty file
Else
    sLine = ts.ReadLine
End If ' This checks to see if we have an empty file so as not to proceed

do while not bDone
    If left(sLine, 1) <> "I" Then
        ' raise an error
    End If
    sField(1) = trim(mid(sLine, 2, 10))
    sField(2) = trim(mid(sLine, 12, 10))
    sField(3) = trim(mid(sLine, 22, 5))
    Set el = dom.createElement ("Invoice")
    el.setAttribute "orderDate", sField(1)
    el.setAttribute "shipDate", sField(2)
    el.setAttribute "shipMethod", sField(3)
    invoiceBucket.appendChild el

    If ts.AtEndOfStream Then
        ' raise an error
    Else
        sLine = ts.ReadLine
    End If
    If Left(sLine, 1) <> "C" Then
        ' raise an error
    End If
    sField(1) = trim(mid(sLine, 2, 30))
    sField(2) = trim(mid(sLine, 32, 30))
    sField(3) = trim(mid(sLine, 62, 20))
    sField(4) = trim(mid(sLine, 82, 2))
    sField(5) = trim(mid(sLine, 84, 10))
    ' check to see if we have this customer yet
    el.setAttribute "customerIDREF", "NOTFOUND"
    Set nl = customerBucket.childNodes
    for iNode = 0 to nl.length - 1
        sName = nl.item(iNode).getAttribute("name")
        sAddress = nl.item(iNode).getAttribute("address")
        if sName = sField(1) and sAddress = sField(2) Then
            ' we presume we have this one already
            el.setAttribute "customerIDREF", _
                nl.item(iNode).getAttribute("customerID")
        end if
    next
    if el.getAttribute("customerIDREF") = "NOTFOUND" Then
        ' we need to create a new customer
        Set cust = dom.createElement("Customer")
        cust.setAttribute "customerID", "CUST" & iCust
        cust.setAttribute "name", sField(1)
        cust.setAttribute "address", sField(2)
        cust.setAttribute "city", sField(3)
        cust.setAttribute "state", sField(4)
        cust.setAttribute "postalCode", sField(5)
        customerBucket.appendChild cust
        el.setAttribute "customerIDREF", "CUST" & iCust
        iCust = iCust + 1
    end if
    If ts.AtEndOfStream Then
        ' raise an error
```

```
      Else
         sLine = ts.ReadLine
      End If
      If Left(sLine, 1) <> "L" Then
         ' raise an error
      End If
      Do While Left(sLine, 1) = "L"
         sField(1) = trim(mid(sLine, 2, 30))
         sField(2) = trim(mid(sLine, 32, 5))
         sField(3) = trim(mid(sLine, 37, 8))
         Set li = dom.createElement ("LineItem")
         li.setAttribute "quantity", sField(2)
         li.setAttribute "price", sField(3)
         ' break apart the description field
         sWork = sField(1)
         sThisColor = left(sWork, InStr(sWork, " ") - 1)
         sWork = Mid(sWork, InStr(sWork, " ") + 1)
         sThisSize = ""
         While InStr(sWork, " ") > 0
            sThisSize = sThisSize + left(sWork, InStr(sWork, " "))
            sWork = Mid(sWork, InStr(sWork, " ") + 1)
         Wend
         sThisSize = Left(sThisSize, len(sThisSize) - 1)
         sThisName = sWork
         Set nl = partBucket.childNodes
         li.setAttribute "partIDREF", "NOTFOUND"
         for iNode = 0 to nl.length - 1
            sName = nl.item(iNode).getAttribute("name")
            sSize = nl.item(iNode).getAttribute("size")
            sColor = nl.item(iNode).getAttribute("color")
            If sThisName = sName And sThisSize = sSize And sThisColor = sColor Then
               ' we presume we have this one already
               li.setAttribute "partIDREF", nl.item(iNode).getAttribute("partID")
            end if
         next
         if li.getAttribute("partIDREF") = "NOTFOUND" Then
            ' we need to create a new part
            Set part = dom.createElement("Part")
            part.setAttribute "partID", "PART" & iPart
            part.setAttribute "name", sThisName
            part.setAttribute "size", sThisSize
            part.setAttribute "color", sThisColor
            partBucket.appendChild part
            li.setAttribute "partIDREF", "PART" & iPart
            iPart = iPart + 1
         end if
         el.appendChild li
         If ts.AtEndOfStream Then
            bDone = True
            sLine = "DONE"
         Else
            sLine = ts.ReadLine
            If left(sLine, 1) <> "I" And left(sLine, 1) <> "L" Then
               ' raise an error
            End If
         End If
      Loop
Loop
ts.Close

root.appendChild invoiceBucket
root.appendChild partBucket
root.appendChild customerBucket

set ts = fso.CreateTextFile("ch12_ex3.xml", True)
ts.Write dom.xml
ts.close
```

This code is very similar to code we have already seen. The major difference is that elements are created as the document is read as necessary – so when an invoice line is read, an `Invoice` element is created; when a customer line is read, a `Customer` element is created, and so on.

The result of this code when applied to our sample is again the same as the previous XML.

Transforming from XML to Flat Files

The other type of transformation, from XML to flat files, calls for a significantly different approach. Let's look at the different programming techniques that may be used to transform an XML document to a flat file, and then see some examples of our strategy in action.

Programming Approaches

Again, there are a couple of different ways you can tackle the conversion of XML to flat files. The most obvious one is to parse the document and serialize it out to a flat file. However, another approach that works a little better is to use XSLT to transform the XML document into the required output format. Let's look at the advantages and disadvantages of each approach.

Parse and Serialize

One strategy would be to parse the XML document, using either SAX or the DOM, and then serialize its contents to a flat file. This approach works perfectly well; however, whenever we add a new type of flat file transformation, we need to write more code and potentially recompile it. It would be nice if we could tweak these transforms without requiring significant code modifications.

XSLT

It's not widely used this way, yet, but XSLT is actually rather good at producing non-tagged results. It can be used to generate tab-delimited files, or fixed-width files, or any other sort of result you might want to produce. The extra benefit is that, to generate a different type of output for an XML document, all you have to do is to add another style sheet. We'll be using XSLT for our examples.

Handling Different File Types

Let's take a look at an example of each of our different file types, and how we would go about producing it from our XML document. These samples have all been tested using James Clark's XT. The MS Windows executable can be downloaded from: ftp://ftp.jclark.com/pub/xml/xt-win32.zip. The homepage can be found at: http://www.jclark.com/xml/xt.html.

Here is the input XML document we have been, and will continue, using:

```
<InvoiceData>
  <Invoice
      customerIDREF="c1"
      orderDate="12/01/2000"
      shipDate="12/04/2000"
      shipMethod="UPS">
    <LineItem
        partIDREF="p1"
        quantity="17"
```

```
                  price="0.10" />
            <LineItem
               partIDREF="p2"
               quantity="22"
               price="0.20" />
      </Invoice>
      <Invoice
         customerIDREF="c2"
         orderDate="12/02/2000"
         shipDate="12/05/2000"
         shipMethod="USPS">
            <LineItem
               partIDREF="p3"
               quantity="13"
               price="0.30" />
            <LineItem
               partIDREF="p1"
               quantity="11"
               price="0.10" />
      </Invoice>
      <Part
         partID="p1"
         name="grommet"
         size="2 in."
         color="blue" />
      <Part
         partID="p2"
         name="widget"
         size="3 in."
         color="silver" />
      <Part
         partID="p3"
         name="sprocket"
         size="1 in."
         color="red" />
      <Customer
         customerID="c1"
         name="Kevin Williams"
         address="744 Evergreen Terrace"
         city="Springfield"
         state="KY"
         postalCode="12345" />
      <Customer
         customerID="c2"
         name="Homer Simpson"
         address="742 Evergreen Terrace"
         city="Springfield"
         state="KY"
         postalCode="12345" />
   </InvoiceData>
```

Delimited

You remember our sample delimited file from earlier in the chapter? We've already performed the mapping analysis on it. This time, however, we are going to use a tab character as the delimiter. Of course, you can't see this character, but if you download the code from the Wrox web site, then you will find this file as ch12_ex4.txt:

Value	Details
Record[N].field1	**Data type**: String
	Format: No more than 20 characters
	Description: The name of the customer on invoice N
Record[N].field2	**Data type**: String
	Format: No more than 30 characters
	Description: The address of the customer on invoice N
record[N].field3	**Data type**: String
	Format: No more than 20 characters
	Description: The city of the customer on invoice N
record[N].field4	**Data type**: String
	Format: Two characters
	Description: The state of the customer on invoice N
record[N].field5	**Data type**: String
	Format: No more than 10 characters
	Description: The postal code of the customer on invoice N
record[N].field6	**Data type**: Datetime
	Format: MM/DD/YYYY
	Description: The order date for invoice N
record[N].field7	**Data type**: Datetime
	Format: MM/DD/YYYY
	Description: The ship date for invoice N
record[N].field8	**Data type**: Enumerated value
	Values: 1: United States Postal Service; 2: United Parcel Service; 3: Federal Express
	Description: The shipping method used to ship the parts ordered on invoice N
record[N].field9	**Data type**: String
	Format: No more than 30 characters
	Description: The description of the part ordered in the first line item of invoice N, in the form color size name
record[N].field10	**Data type**: Numeric
	Format: #####
	Description: The quantity of the part ordered in the first line item of invoice N
record[N].field11	**Data type**: Numeric
	Format: #####.##
	Description: The price of the part ordered in the first line item of invoice N

Table continued on following page

Value	Details
record[N].field12	**Data type**: String
	Format: No more than 30 characters
	Description: The description of the part ordered in the second line item of invoice N, in the form color size name
record[N].field13	**Data type**: Numeric
	Format: #####
	Description: The quantity of the part ordered in the second line item of invoice N
record[N].field14	**Data type**: Numeric
	Format: #####.##
	Description: The price of the part ordered in the second line item of invoice N
record[N].field15	**Data type**: String
	Format: No more than 30 characters
	Description: The description of the part ordered in the third line item of invoice N, in the form color size name
record[N].field16	**Data type**: Numeric
	Format: #####
	Description: The quantity of the part ordered in the third line item of invoice N
record[N].field17	**Data type**: Numeric
	Format: #####.##
	Description: The price of the part ordered in the third line item of invoice N
record[N].field18	**Data type**: String
	Format: No more than 30 characters
	Description: The description of the part ordered in the fourth line item of invoice N, in the form color size name
record[N].field19	**Data type**: Numeric
	Format: #####
	Description: The quantity of the part ordered in the fourth line item of invoice N
record[N].field20	**Data type**: Numeric
	Format: #####.##
	Description: The price of the part ordered in the fourth line item of invoice N

Value	Details
record[N].field21	**Data type**: String
	Format: No more than 30 characters
	Description: The description of the part ordered in the fifth line item of invoice N, in the form color size name
record[N].field22	**Data type**: Numeric
	Format: #####
	Description: The quantity of the part ordered in the fifth line item of invoice N
record[N].field23	**Data type**: Numeric
	Format: #####.##
	Description: The price of the part ordered in the fifth line item of invoice N

We now have to create a map in the opposite direction from the map we created earlier; that is, we need to describe how each element in our XML document would map to the flat file.

Source	Target	Comments
InvoiceData.Invoice[N]->Customer.Name	record[N].field1	
InvoiceData.Invoice[N]->Customer.Address	record[N].field2	
InvoiceData.Invoice[N]->Customer.City	record[N].field3	
InvoiceData.Invoice[N]->Customer.State	record[N].field4	
InvoiceData.Invoice[N]->Customer.PostalCode	record[N].field5	
InvoiceData.Invoice[N].orderDate	record[N].field6	
InvoiceData.Invoice[N].shipDate	record[N].field7	
InvoiceData.Invoice[N].shipMethod	record[N].field8	Enumerated transform: USPS to 1 UPS to 2 FedEx to 3
InvoiceData.Invoice[N].LineItem[1]->Part.Name, InvoiceData.Invoice[N].LineItem[1]->Part.Size, InvoiceData.Invoice[N].LineItem[1]->Part.Color	record[N].field9	
InvoiceData.Invoice[N].LineItem[1].quantity	record[N].field10	
InvoiceData.Invoice[N].LineItem[1].price	record[N].field11	

Table continued on following page

Source	Target	Comments
InvoiceData.Invoice[N].LineItem[2]->Part.Name, InvoiceData. Invoice[N].LineItem[2]->Part.Size, InvoiceData. Invoice[N].LineItem[2]->Part.Color	record[N].field12	Blank (all spaces) if no line 2 appears on the invoice.
InvoiceData.Invoice[N].LineItem[2].quantity	record[N].field13	
InvoiceData.Invoice[N].LineItem[2].price	record[N].field14	
InvoiceData.Invoice[N].LineItem[3]->Part.Name, InvoiceData.Invoice[N].LineItem[3]->Part.Size, InvoiceData.Invoice[N].LineItem[3]->Part.Color	record[N].field15	Blank (all spaces) if no line 3 appears on the invoice.
InvoiceData.Invoice[N].LineItem[3].quantity	record[N].field16	
InvoiceData.Invoice[N].LineItem[3].price	record[N].field17	
InvoiceData.Invoice[N].LineItem[4]->Part.Name, InvoiceData. Invoice[N].LineItem[4]->Part.Size, InvoiceData. Invoice[N].LineItem[4]->Part.Color	record[N].field18	Blank (all spaces) if no line 4 appears on the invoice.
InvoiceData.Invoice[N].LineItem[4].quantity	record[N].field19	
InvoiceData.Invoice[N].LineItem[4].price	record[N].field20	
InvoiceData.Invoice[N].LineItem[5]->Part.Name, InvoiceData. Invoice[N].LineItem[5]->Part.Size, InvoiceData. Invoice[N].LineItem[5]->Part.Color	record[N].field21	Blank (all spaces) if no line 5 appears on the invoice.
InvoiceData.Invoice[N].LineItem[5].quantity	record[N].field22	
InvoiceData.Invoice[N].LineItem[5].price	record[N].field23	

The style sheet that performs this translation follows. We'll include the entire style sheet first, then dissect it afterwards. You can find the stylesheet below if you download the code from the Wrox web site, in ch12_ex4.xsl

```
<?xml version="1.0"?>
<xsl:stylesheet xmlns:xsl="http://www.w3.org/1999/XSL/Transform" version="1.0">
  <xsl:output method="text" />
  <xsl:template match="InvoiceData">
  <xsl:for-each select="Invoice">
    <xsl:variable name="customerID" select="@customerIDREF" />
    <xsl:value-of select="../Customer[@customerID=$customerID]/@name" />
    <xsl:text>&#x09;</xsl:text>
    <xsl:value-of select="../Customer[@customerID=$customerID]/@address" />
    <xsl:text>&#x09;</xsl:text>
    <xsl:value-of select="../Customer[@customerID=$customerID]/@city" />
    <xsl:text>&#x09;</xsl:text>
    <xsl:value-of select="../Customer[@customerID=$customerID]/@state" />
    <xsl:text>&#x09;</xsl:text>
```

```
        <xsl:value-of select="../Customer[@customerID=$customerID]/@postalCode" />
        <xsl:text>&#x09;</xsl:text>
        <xsl:value-of select="@orderDate" />
        <xsl:text>&#x09;</xsl:text>
        <xsl:value-of select="@shipDate" />
        <xsl:text>&#x09;</xsl:text>
        <xsl:choose>
            <xsl:when test="@shipMethod='UPS'">
                <xsl:text>1</xsl:text>
            </xsl:when>
            <xsl:when test="@shipMethod='USPS'">
                <xsl:text>2</xsl:text>
            </xsl:when>
            <xsl:when test="@shipMethod='FedEx'">
                <xsl:text>3</xsl:text>
            </xsl:when>
        </xsl:choose>
        <xsl:text>&#x09;</xsl:text>
        <xsl:for-each select="LineItem[position()&lt;=5]">
            <xsl:variable name="partID" select="@partIDREF" />
            <xsl:variable name="partName"
                select="../../Part[@partID=$partID]/@name" />
            <xsl:variable name="partSize"
                select="../../Part[@partID=$partID]/@size" />
            <xsl:variable name="partColor"
                select="../../Part[@partID=$partID]/@color" />
            <xsl:value-of select="concat($partColor,' ', $partSize,' ',
                $partName)" />
            <xsl:text>&#x09;</xsl:text>
            <xsl:value-of select="format-number(@quantity, '#####')" />
            <xsl:text>&#x09;</xsl:text>
            <xsl:value-of select="format-number(@price, '####0.00')" />
            <xsl:text>&#x09;</xsl:text>
        </xsl:for-each>
        <xsl:if test="count(LineItem)&lt;2">
            <xsl:text>&#x09;0&#x09;0.00&#x09;</xsl:text>
        </xsl:if>
        <xsl:if test="count(LineItem)&lt;3">
            <xsl:text>&#x09;0&#x09;0.00&#x09;</xsl:text>
        </xsl:if>
        <xsl:if test="count(LineItem)&lt;4">
            <xsl:text>&#x09;0&#x09;0.00&#x09;</xsl:text>
        </xsl:if>
        <xsl:if test="count(LineItem)&lt;5">
            <xsl:text>&#x09;0&#x09;0.00&#x09;</xsl:text>
        </xsl:if>
        <xsl:text>&#x0D;&#x0A;</xsl:text>
    </xsl:for-each>
    </xsl:template>
</xsl:stylesheet>
```

Let's take a close look at our stylesheet to see how it works:

```
<?xml version="1.0"?>
<xsl:stylesheet xmlns:xsl="http://www.w3.org/1999/XSL/Transform" version="1.0">
    <xsl:output method="text" />
```

It is important to declare the output method for the style sheet as text. In effect, this prevents XSLT from making any assumptions about how you want the results formatted (specifically, it extracts all the text nodes in the result tree without any escape characters like < and &.).

```
<xsl:template match="InvoiceData">
```

`InvoiceData` is the root element, so the template will be executed once for the entire document.

```
<xsl:for-each select="Invoice">
```

We will process each `Invoice` element in our source document – these correspond to the records in our output format. We'll navigate to the `Customer` and `Part` information as necessary.

```
<xsl:variable name="customerID" select="@customerIDREF" />
<xsl:value-of select="../Customer[@customerID=$customerID]/@name" />
```

This syntax is important, as it shows how the IDREF-ID relationships may be navigated in XSLT. In the previous lines, we stored the `customerIDREF` attribute of the current invoice in the variable called `customerID`; we then connect to the `Customer` element whose `customerID` attribute matches the `customerIDREF` specified for the invoice, and obtain the `name` attribute from that element.

```
<xsl:text>&#x09;</xsl:text>
```

This is how we put in our tab delimiter. Notice that we don't need to disable output-escaping, since we've already declared that the style sheet should output (unescaped) text. &#x09 is the UTF-8 Unicode identifier for a tab character.

```
<xsl:value-of select="../Customer[@customerID=$customerID]/@address" />
<xsl:text>&#x09;</xsl:text>
<xsl:value-of select="../Customer[@customerID=$customerID]/@city" />
<xsl:text>&#x09;</xsl:text>
<xsl:value-of select="../Customer[@customerID=$customerID]/@state" />
<xsl:text>&#x09;</xsl:text>
<xsl:value-of select="../Customer[@customerID=$customerID]/@postalCode" />
<xsl:text>&#x09;</xsl:text>
<xsl:value-of select="@orderDate" />
<xsl:text>&#x09;</xsl:text>
<xsl:value-of select="@shipDate" />
<xsl:text>&#x09;</xsl:text>
```

We continue to put fields into our output, including the rest of the `Customer` fields and the `Invoice` fields.

```
<xsl:choose>
   <xsl:when test="@shipMethod='UPS'">
      <xsl:text>1</xsl:text>
   </xsl:when>
   <xsl:when test="@shipMethod='USPS'">
      <xsl:text>2</xsl:text>
   </xsl:when>
   <xsl:when test="@shipMethod='FedEx'">
      <xsl:text>3</xsl:text>
   </xsl:when>
</xsl:choose>
```

Using `xsl:choose`, we translate the XML enumerated value for the `shipMethod` attribute into the desired format for the output.

```
<xsl:text>&#x09;</xsl:text>
```

Next, we need to process each `LineItem` child for the Invoice element. Note that we restrict this to five elements, as our output format only allows five line items to be written to it.

```
<xsl:for-each select="LineItem[position()&lt;=5]">
    <xsl:variable name="partID" select="@partIDREF" />
    <xsl:variable name="partName"
        select="../../Part[@partID=$partID]/@name" />
```

Again, here we navigate to the appropriate part for the line item based on the `partIDREF` attribute of the `LineItem` element.

```
<xsl:variable name="partSize"
    select="../../Part[@partID=$partID]/@size" />
<xsl:variable name="partColor"
    select="../../Part[@partID=$partID]/@color" />
<xsl:value-of select="concat($partColor,' ', $partSize,' ',
    $partName)" />
```

We create the description field in the output by concatenating the color, size, and name attributes from the source.

```
<xsl:text>&#x09;</xsl:text>
<xsl:value-of select="format-number(@quantity, '#####')" />
```

XSLT provides a number formatting function called `format-number`; we use it here to make sure our number is in the format required by the target file.

```
<xsl:text>&#x09;</xsl:text>
<xsl:value-of select="format-number(@price, '####0.00')" />
<xsl:text>&#x09;</xsl:text>
</xsl:for-each>
```

Next, we have to do some de-normalization cleaning up. Since there are five line item slots, and we may actually have less than five line items in our original document, we need to write blank information to our destination file if less than five line items were found.

```
<xsl:if test="count(LineItem)&lt;2">
    <xsl:text>&#x09;0&#x09;0.00&#x09;</xsl:text>
</xsl:if>
<xsl:if test="count(LineItem)&lt;3">
    <xsl:text>&#x09;0&#x09;0.00&#x09;</xsl:text>
</xsl:if>
<xsl:if test="count(LineItem)&lt;4">
    <xsl:text>&#x09;0&#x09;0.00&#x09;</xsl:text>
</xsl:if>
<xsl:if test="count(LineItem)&lt;5">
    <xsl:text>&#x09;0&#x09;0.00&#x09;</xsl:text>
</xsl:if>
<xsl:text>&#x0D;&#x0A;</xsl:text>
```

Here, we write the characters for a carriage return and a line feed to ensure our target file has the hard return at the end of the record. If the destination delimited file is intended for a UNIX system, you will either have to change the order of the CR/LF pair being entered, or use a tool like dos2unix, or d2u to convert the hard return character.

```
    </xsl:for-each>
      </xsl:template>
  </xsl:stylesheet>
```

That's all there is to it. The output from this style sheet when applied to our example should be as follows:

```
Kevin Williams    744 Evergreen Terrace    Springfield    KY    12345    12/01/2000
12/04/2000    1    blue 2 in. grommet    17    0.10    silver 3 in. widget    22    0.20
0    0.00        0    0.00        0    0.00
Homer Simpson    742 Evergreen Terrace    Springfield    KY    12345    12/02/2000
12/05/2000    2    red 1 in. sprocket    13    0.30    blue 2 in. grommet    11    0.10
0    0.00        0    0.00        0    0.00
```

Note that we could actually take this one step further, and use the mapping tables we have created in another document that could be used to drive the transforming document. This exercise is left to the reader.

Fixed-width

Fixed-width files can be created in a similar fashion using XSLT. There are a couple of new tricks that may be used to ensure that fields are the proper width – we'll see how these are done when we examine the code. Remember that the map for our fixed-width sample file looks like this:

Value	Details
record[N].field1	**Data type**: String
	Position: 1-30
	Description: The name of the customer on invoice N
record[N].field2	**Data type**: String
	Position: 31-60
	Description: The address of the customer on invoice N
record[N].field3	**Data type**: String
	Position: 61-80
	Description: The city of the customer on invoice N
record[N].field4	**Data type**: String
	Position: 81-82
	Description: The state of the customer on invoice N

Value	Details
record[N].field5	**Data type**: String
	Position: 83-92
	Description: The postal code of the customer on invoice N.
record[N].field6	**Data type**: Datetime
	Position: 93-102
	Format: MM/DD/YYYY
	Description: The order date for invoice N
record[N].field7	**Data type**: Datetime
	Position: 103-112
	Format: MM/DD/YYYY
	Description: The ship date for invoice N
record[N].field8	**Data type**: Enumerated value
	Position: 113-117
	Values: UPS: United States Postal Service; USPS: United Parcel Service; FedEx: Federal Express
	Description: The shipping method used to ship the parts ordered on invoice N
record[N].field9	**Data type**: String
	Position: 118-147
	Format: No more than 30 characters
	Description: The description of the part ordered in the first line item of invoice N, in the form color size name
record[N].field10	**Data type**: Numeric
	Position: 148-152
	Format: #####
	Description: The quantity of the part ordered in the first line item of invoice N
record[N].field11	**Data type**: Numeric
	Position: 153-160
	Format: #####.##
	Description: The price of the part ordered in the first line item of invoice N

Table continued on following page

Value	Details
`record[N].field12`	**Data type**: String
	Position: 161-190
	Description: The description of the part ordered in the second line item of invoice N, in the form color size name
`record[N].field13`	**Data type**: Numeric
	Position: 191-195
	Format: #####
	Description: The quantity of the part ordered in the second line item of invoice N
`record[N].field14`	**Data type**: Numeric
	Position: 196-203
	Format: #####.##
	Description: The price of the part ordered in the second line item of invoice N
`record[N].field15`	**Data type**: String
	Position: 204-233
	Format: No more than 30 characters
	Description: The description of the part ordered in the third line item of invoice N, in the form color size name
`record[N].field16`	**Data type**: Numeric
	Position: 234-238
	Format: #####
	Description: The quantity of the part ordered in the third line item of invoice N
`record[N].field17`	**Data type**: Numeric
	Position: 239-246
	Format: #####.##
	Description: The price of the part ordered in the third line item of invoice N
`record[N].field18`	**Data type**: String
	Position: 247-276
	Description: The description of the part ordered in the fourth line item of invoice N, in the form color size name

Value	Details
record[N].field19	**Data type**: Numeric
	Position: 277-281
	Format: #####
	Description: The quantity of the part ordered in the fourth line item of invoice N
record[N].field20	**Data type**: Numeric
	Position: 282-289
	Format: #####.##
	Description: The price of the part ordered in the fourth line item of invoice N
record[N].field21	**Data type**: String
	Position: 290-319
	Description: The description of the part ordered in the fifth line item of invoice N, in the form color size name
record[N].field22	**Data type**: Numeric
	Position: 320-324
	Format: #####
	Description: The quantity of the part ordered in the fifth line item of invoice N
record[N].field23	**Data type**: Numeric
	Position: 325-332
	Format: #####.##
	Description: The price of the part ordered in the fifth line item of invoice N

Next, we need to map from the XML data points to the target fields. The table detailing this mapping is repeated below:

Source	Target	Comments
InvoiceData.Invoice[N]->Customer.Name	record[N].field1	
InvoiceData.Invoice[N]->Customer.Address	record[N].field2	
InvoiceData.Invoice[N]->Customer.City	record[N].field3	
InvoiceData.Invoice[N]->Customer.State	record[N].field4	
InvoiceData.Invoice[N]->Customer.PostalCode	record[N].field5	

Table continued on following page

Source	Target	Comments
InvoiceData.Invoice[N].orderDate	record[N].field6	
InvoiceData.Invoice[N].shipDate	record[N].field7	
InvoiceData.Invoice[N].shipMethod	record[N].field8	
InvoiceData.Invoice[N].LineItem[1]->Part.Name,	record[N].field9	
InvoiceData.Invoice[N].LineItem[1]->Part.Size,		
InvoiceData.Invoice[N].LineItem[1]->Part.Color		
InvoiceData.Invoice[N].LineItem[1].quantity	record[N].field10	
InvoiceData.Invoice[N].LineItem[1].price	record[N].field11	
InvoiceData.Invoice[N].LineItem[2]->Part.Name,	record[N].field12	Blank (all spaces) if no line 2 appears on the invoice.
InvoiceData.Invoice[N].LineItem[2]->Part.Size,		
InvoiceData.Invoice[N].LineItem[2]->Part.Color		
InvoiceData.Invoice[N].LineItem[2].quantity	record[N].field13	
InvoiceData.Invoice[N].LineItem[2].price	record[N].field14	
InvoiceData.Invoice[N].LineItem[3]->Part.Name,	record[N].field15	Blank (all spaces) if no line 3 appears on the invoice.
InvoiceData.Invoice[N].LineItem[3]->Part.Size,		
InvoiceData.Invoice[N].LineItem[3]->Part.Color		
InvoiceData.Invoice[N].LineItem[3].quantity	record[N].field16	
InvoiceData.Invoice[N].LineItem[3].price	record[N].field17	
InvoiceData.Invoice[N].LineItem[4]->Part.Name,	record[N].field18	Blank (all spaces) if no line 4 appears on the invoice.
InvoiceData.Invoice[N].LineItem[4]->Part.Size,		
InvoiceData.Invoice[N].LineItem[4]->Part.Color		
InvoiceData.Invoice[N].LineItem[4].quantity	record[N].field19	
InvoiceData.Invoice[N].LineItem[4].price	record[N].field20	
InvoiceData.Invoice[N].LineItem[5]->Part.Name,	record[N].field21	Blank (all spaces) if no line 5 appears on the invoice.
InvoiceData.Invoice[N].LineItem[5]->Part.Size,		
InvoiceData.Invoice[N].LineItem[5]->Part.Color		
InvoiceData.Invoice[N].LineItem[5].quantity	record[N].field22	
InvoiceData.Invoice[N].LineItem[5].price	record[N].field23	

The style sheet that performs the translation is shown below and can be found in the code zipfile for this book as ch12_ex5.xsl:

```xml
<?xml version="1.0"?>
<xsl:stylesheet xmlns:xsl="http://www.w3.org/1999/XSL/Transform" version="1.0">
   <xsl:output method="text" />
   <xsl:template match="InvoiceData">
   <xsl:for-each select="Invoice">
      <xsl:variable name="customerID" select="@customerIDREF" />
      <xsl:value-of
         select="substring(concat(../Customer[@customerID=$customerID]/@name,
                        '                '), 1, 30)" />
      <xsl:value-of
         select="substring(concat(../Customer[@customerID=$customerID]/@address,
                        '                '), 1, 30)" />
      <xsl:value-of
         select="substring(concat(../Customer[@customerID=$customerID]/@city,
                        '                '), 1, 20)" />
      <xsl:value-of select="../Customer[@customerID=$customerID]/@state" />
      <xsl:value-of
         select="substring(concat
         (../Customer[@customerID=$customerID]/@postalCode, '          '),
         1, 10)" />
      <xsl:value-of select="substring(concat(@orderDate, '          '),
         1, 10)" />
      <xsl:value-of select="substring(concat(@shipDate, '          '),
         1, 10)" />
      <xsl:value-of select="substring(concat(@shipMethod, '      '), 1, 5)" />
      <xsl:for-each select="LineItem[position()&lt;=5]">
         <xsl:variable name="partID" select="@partIDREF" />
         <xsl:variable name="partName"
            select="../../Part[@partID=$partID]/@name" />
         <xsl:variable name="partSize"
            select="../../Part[@partID=$partID]/@size" />
         <xsl:variable name="partColor"
            select="../../Part[@partID=$partID]/@color" />
         <xsl:value-of select="substring(concat(
            $partColor, ' ', $partSize, ' ', $partName,
            '                    '), 1, 30)" />
         <xsl:value-of select="format-number(@quantity, '00000')" />
         <xsl:value-of select="format-number(@price, '00000.00')" />
      </xsl:for-each>
      <xsl:if test="count(LineItem)&lt;2">
         <xsl:text>                              0000000000.00</xsl:text>
      </xsl:if>
      <xsl:if test="count(LineItem)&lt;3">
         <xsl:text>                              0000000000.00</xsl:text>
      </xsl:if>
      <xsl:if test="count(LineItem)&lt;4">
         <xsl:text>                              0000000000.00</xsl:text>
      </xsl:if>
      <xsl:if test="count(LineItem)&lt;5">
         <xsl:text>                              0000000000.00</xsl:text>
      </xsl:if>
      <xsl:text>&#x0D;&#x0A;</xsl:text>
   </xsl:for-each>
   </xsl:template>
</xsl:stylesheet>
```

Since the order in which fields appear in the fixed-width file is almost the same as the order in which they appear in the delimited file, this style sheet is very similar to the previous one. We do introduce one new technique in this style sheet that bears examination though:

```
xsl:value-of select="substring(concat(@orderDate, '          '), 1, 10)" />
```

The `substring-concat` pair is the easiest way to get a string of a particular length in XSLT. The above select string will always return a string that is exactly ten characters long – if the attribute is more than ten characters, only the first ten will be returned; if the attribute is less than ten characters, it will be right-padded with spaces.

The output of the style sheet above, when applied to our sample XML, is this, the file we started with in the earlier section:

```
Kevin Williams             744 Evergreen Terrace        Springfield
KY12345     12/01/200012/04/2000UPS  blue 2 in. grommet
0001700000.10silver 3 in. widget          0002200000.20
0000000000.00                             0000000000.00
0000000000.00
Homer Simpson              742 Evergreen Terrace        Springfield
KY12345     12/02/200012/05/2000USPS red 1 in. sprocket
0001300000.30blue 2 in. grommet           0001100000.10
0000000000.00                             0000000000.00
0000000000.00
```

Tagged Record

Again, creating tagged record output files is no problem with XSLT. First, recall the map we created for the tagged record format:

Value	Details
record[N].Customer.field1	Data Type: String
	Position: 2-31
	Description: The name of the customer on invoice N
record[N].Customer.field2	Data Type: String
	Position: 32-61
	Description: The address of the customer on invoice N
record[N].Customer.field3	Data Type: String
	Position: 62-81
	Description: The city of the customer on invoice N
record[N].Customer.field4	Data Type: String
	Position: 82-83
	Description: The state of the customer on invoice N

Value	Details
record[N].Customer.field5	**Data Type**: String **Position**: 84-93 **Description**: The postal code of the customer on invoice N
record[N].Invoice.field1	**Data Type**: Datetime **Position**: 2-11 **Format**: MM/DD/YYYY **Description**: The order date for invoice N
record[N].Invoice.field2	**Data Type**: Datetime **Position**: 12-21 **Format**: MM/DD/YYYY **Description**: The ship date for invoice N
record[N].Invoice.field3	**Data Type**: Enumerated value **Position**: 22-26 **Values**: **USPS**: United States Postal Service; **UPS**: United Parcel Service; **FedEx**: Federal Express **Description**: The shipping method used to ship the parts ordered on invoice N
record[N].LineItem[M].field1	**Data Type**: String **Position**: 2-31 **Format**: No more than 30 characters **Description**: The description of the part ordered in the Mth line item of invoice N, in the form color size name
record[N].LineItem[M].field2	**Data Type**: Numeric **Position**: 32-36 **Format**: ##### **Description**: The quantity of the part ordered in the Mth line item of invoice N
record[N].LineItem[M].field3	**Data Type**: Numeric **Position**: 37-44 **Format**: #####.## **Description**: The price of the part ordered in the Mth line item of invoice N

We need to map from the XML fields to the target file fields, as shown below:

Target	Source
InvoiceData.Invoice[N]->Customer.Name	record[N].Customer.field1
InvoiceData.Invoice[N]->Customer.Address	record[N].Customer.field2
InvoiceData.Invoice[N]->Customer.City	record[N].Customer.field3
InvoiceData.Invoice[N]->Customer.State	record[N].Customer.field4
InvoiceData.Invoice[N]->Customer.PostalCode	record[N].Customer.field5
InvoiceData.Invoice[N].orderDate	record[N].Invoice.field1
InvoiceData.Invoice[N].shipDate	record[N].Invoice.field2
InvoiceData.Invoice[N].shipMethod	record[N].Invoice.field3
InvoiceData.Invoice[N].LineItem[M]->Part.Name,	record[N].LineItem[M].field1
InvoiceData.Invoice[N].LineItem[M]->Part.Size,	
InvoiceData.Invoice[N].LineItem[M]->Part.Color	
InvoiceData.Invoice[N].LineItem[M].quantity	record[N].LineItem[M].field2
InvoiceData.Invoice[N].LineItem[M].price	record[N].LineItem[M].field3

Now that we have the mapping, we can create the stylesheet, ch12_ex6.xsl:

```
<?xml version="1.0"?>
<xsl:stylesheet xmlns:xsl="http://www.w3.org/1999/XSL/Transform" version="1.0">
   <xsl:output method="text" />
   <xsl:template match="InvoiceData">
   <xsl:for-each select="Invoice">
      <xsl:text>I</xsl:text>
      <xsl:value-of select="substring(concat(@orderDate, '          '),
         1, 10)" />
      <xsl:value-of select="substring(concat(@shipDate, '          '),
         1, 10)" />
      <xsl:value-of select="substring(concat(@shipMethod, '     '), 1, 5)" />
      <xsl:text>&#x0D;&#x0A;C</xsl:text>
      <xsl:variable name="customerID" select="@customerIDREF" />
      <xsl:value-of select="substring(concat(
         ../Customer[@customerID=$customerID]/@name,
         '                              '), 1, 30)" />
      <xsl:value-of select="substring(concat(
         ../Customer[@customerID=$customerID]/@address,
         '                              '), 1, 30)" />
      <xsl:value-of select="substring(concat(
         ../Customer[@customerID=$customerID]/@city,
         '                    '), 1, 20)" />
      <xsl:value-of select="../Customer[@customerID=$customerID]/@state" />
      <xsl:value-of select="substring(concat(
         ../Customer[@customerID=$customerID]/@postalCode,
         '          '), 1, 10)" />
```

```
    <xsl:for-each select="LineItem[position()&lt;=5]">
        <xsl:text>&#x0D;&#x0A;L</xsl:text>
        <xsl:variable name="partID" select="@partIDREF" />
        <xsl:variable name="partName"
            select="../../Part[@partID=$partID]/@name" />
        <xsl:variable name="partSize"
            select="../../Part[@partID=$partID]/@size" />
        <xsl:variable name="partColor"
            select="../../Part[@partID=$partID]/@color" />
        <xsl:value-of select="substring(concat(
            $partColor, ' ', $partSize, ' ', $partName,
                            '), 1, 30)" />
        <xsl:value-of select="format-number(@quantity, '00000')" />
        <xsl:value-of select="format-number(@price, '00000.00')" />
    </xsl:for-each>
    <xsl:text>&#x0D;&#x0A;</xsl:text>
    </xsl:for-each>
    </xsl:template>
</xsl:stylesheet>
```

This style sheet reflects some of the approaches we have taken in our previous examples. Note that we don't have to worry about the number of line items present or absent, as each line item gets its own record in our tagged format. To create the records, we simply insert the appropriate header marker and the hard line feeds where necessary.

The output of the style sheet when applied to the sample XML is this:

```
I12/01/200012/04/2000UPS
CKevin Williams              744 Evergreen Terrace      Springfield
KY12345
Lblue 2 in. grommet          0001700000.10
Lsilver 3 in. widget         0002200000.20
I12/02/200012/05/2000USPS
CHomer Simpson               742 Evergreen Terrace      Springfield
KY12345
Lred 1 in. sprocket          0001300000.30
Lblue 2 in. grommet          0001100000.10
```

Summary

In this chapter, we've learned some techniques for working with flat files and moving data between flat files and XML. We've seen that, to create a translator between the two, you should follow these steps:

- ❑ Map the source format to name-value pairs
- ❑ Map the target format to name-value pairs
- ❑ Correlate the source and target name-value pairs
- ❑ Write DOM code (for XML targets) or an XSLT stylesheet (for flat file targets)

Using this strategy will allow you to connect your systems to legacy systems or other platforms that produce or consume flat files, resulting in less programming overhead.

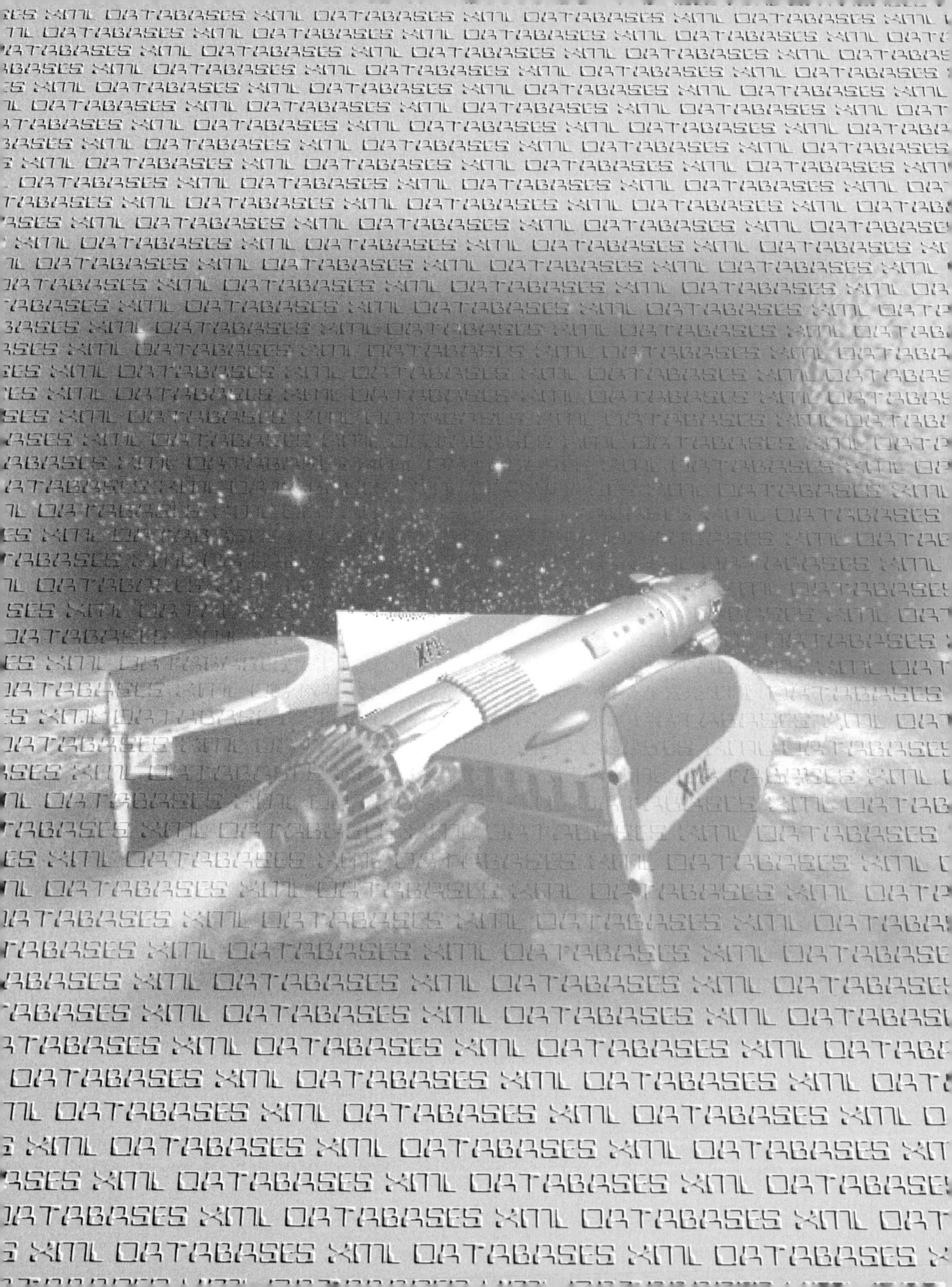
XML DATABASES

13

ADO, ADO+, and XML

Active Data Objects (ADO) first supported XML in version 2.1 with the ability to persist `Recordset` objects to and from XML to the file system. The subsequent release of ADO 2.5 expanded on its XML features by introducing support for loading XML to and from the `Stream` object (a stream of text or binary bytes). Now, with the release of ADO 2.6 and SQL Server 2000, we have a lot more power. ADO 2.6 allows us to retrieve XML results in streams instead of recordsets. This allows us to retrieve XML data from any OLE DB data source that can send XML.

We'll see a lot of the functionality that SQL Server 2000 exposes in Chapters 14 and 15. Essentially, we can use the `FOR XML` extensions to SQL, Open XML, and XML Views via ADO, to offer similar functionality through ADO. This works with any data source that will return XML, not just SQL Server 2000.

ADO can run queries via XML, join XML datasets to relational data, and even stream XML in and out of stored procedures and ASP pages.

> *It's beyond the scope of this chapter to teach you ADO, so if you're not familiar with ADO, or you just want to know more, we'd recommend you get hold of a copy of* ADO 2.6 Programmer's Reference, ISBN 1-861004-63-x, *from Wrox Press.*

In this chapter, we will discuss the following topics:

- ❏ How ADO has progressed to include a more robust XML feature set than in the past. Here we will discuss what's supported in ADO 2.6, and its new XML properties.

- ❏ Different ways in which we can persist XML via ADO, and how the `Stream` makes some of this possible, including a look at the ASP `Response` object.

- ❏ How we can query SQL Server and return XML data, both using extensions to the SQL language, and querying using XPath and mapping schemas.

- ❏ How we can merge XML data sets with SQL data sets to retrieve and even modify SQL data.

We'll also take a sneak preview look at what's coming in the future, by investigating ADO+.

As you can see already, we have a full agenda up ahead. So grab a comfy chair and kick back as we dive right in to explore ADO and XML.

> **The code in this chapter relies on ADO 2.6 and SQL Server 2000. The XML in this chapter is displayed in the Internet Explorer 5 browser. While other browsers may not display the data in the same way, it is important to keep in mind that the same XML can be passed to any client; whether or not that client can display the data depends entirely on the client.**

XML Support in ADO 2.6 and SQL Server 2000

We'll start out by discussing the features of ADO 2.6 that facilitate the integration between ADO and XML:

❑   The Stream object

❑   The ability to persist data as XML

❑   Running queries against data in XML

❑   Annotated schemas that allow us to map an XML vocabulary to SQL Server tables

❑   Merging XML with relational data

The topics in this section will introduce you to the concepts and techniques, while the remaining sections of this chapter will concentrate on showing you how to tackle XML integration with ADO and SQL Server 2000 with plenty of code examples. First, however, we'll tackle what a stream is, and what its role is with respect to ADO and XML. Then we'll discuss, at a high level, the different ways in which we can use the stream and the other XML based features of ADO and SQL Server 2000.

What is a Stream?

The ADO Stream object provides the means to read, write, and manage the binary (or text) stream of bytes that make up a file or message. In particular, we can use a Stream object to read a file, write to a file, or read or write data to or from a binary stream (temporary memory). We can also send the Stream over a network from a business object to a client. So what can the Stream object do for you?

❑   We can use a Stream as a means to save or persist data. For example we can take a Recordset and save it in the XML format to a Stream object. Once the XML is in the Stream, we can then save it to a string variable, or even load it into the XML DOM.

❑   If you remember that the ASP Response object supports an interface for the stream, you will see that we can send XML directly to the Response object, thus writing it to a client's browser.

❑   Last but not least, we can load different types of queries into a Stream object and execute them against a SQL Server database. So, all the types of queries we'll meet in Chapters 14 and 15, whether they are in SQL or in XML, can be stored in the Stream object.

OK, by now you're probably sold on the concept of a Stream object, so the next logical question is, "Where can I get one of these Stream objects?" Well, you can't pick one up at the corner drug store, but there are several ways in which you can get one.

Obtaining a Stream

So how do we get a Stream object and populate it with a stream? Here are a couple of different methods that we can use to obtain a stream intended for use with XML:

Files

We can obtain a Stream from a file that contains text (or binary) data. When we open a Stream on a file, we are opening the contents of that file. We can then directly manipulate those contents for reading and writing. The following lines are examples to show how a Stream is opened:

```
Dim oStm
Set oStm = Server.CreateObject("ADODB.Stream")

oStm.Open "URL=http://localhost/XMLDB/customer.xml"
```

or:

```
Dim oStm
Set oStm = Server.CreateObject("ADODB.Stream")

oStm.Open "d:\customer.xml"
```

Roll Your Own

We can create an instance of the Stream object in code and write XML data to it. We can then add XML data or an XML based query to the Stream. We could use this technique to open an empty Stream and then fill it with any data we want. For example, the following code snippet fills an empty Stream with a string of XML:

```
Dim oStm

sXML = "<customer CustID='123' CustName='XYZ Records'></customer>"
'--- Create the Stream
Set oStm = Server.CreateObject("ADODB.Stream")
'--- Open an empty Stream
oStm.Open
'--- Load the Stream from an XML string
oStm.WriteText sXML
```

We've just looked at some basic examples of how a Stream object can interact with XML. So using ADO's Stream object we can

❑ Get the queries and updates into a Stream.

❑ Save the results of these queries into a Stream, which can then be persisted to:

    ❑ A file;

    ❑ SQL Server 2000;

    ❑ Sent across a network;

    ❑ ASP's Response object.

Persistence of XML

Persisting our XML data can be explained as simply saving the contents of an XML dataset to some storage area. That storage area can take on many forms, as we've discussed thus far. By using ADO's new persistence techniques, we can open new doors to how we interact with our data centers. For example, we can persist XML data to a `Stream` object, to a text file, or even to the ASP `Response` object.

If we save our data to a `Stream` object, we can:

❑ Edit the XML inside of the `Stream` or even load the XML directly into the XML DOM.

❑ Save XML into a text file, so we can save this data permanently in the file and later use it as a data source for a `Recordset`.

❑ Save XML data from a `Recordset` and send the XML via an ASP page directly to a client's browser (or to another machine in a web service scenario). Once the XML is on the client it can be stored in an XML data island, or even be used as the data source of an RDS `DataControl` object.

> *Keep in mind that sending the XML to an XML Data Island or an RDS DataControl is only intended to work in Internet Explorer. However, you can send the XML to a non-browser client, such as a web service.*

So as you can see, there are not only several ways in which we can save our data to XML, there are also a number of ways in which we can take advantage of XML persistence.

Running XML Queries

There are two new ways that we can query SQL Server from ADO, both of which we discuss in Chapters 14 and 15:

❑ Queries using FOR XML

❑ Queries using annotated XML Data schemas – XML Views

Queries Using FOR XML

SQL Server 2000's Transact SQL (T-SQL) language now supports the FOR XML clause. This offers developers a way in which we can write standard SQL queries to a SQL Server database, and instead of an ADO recordset being returned, we can get the data in an XML format. In other words, we can run our queries against a SQL Server 2000 database and return XML directly to our application.

In fact, there are a few different choices we have in returning the data. For example, we can return the data in its raw XML format, or in a hierarchical structure based on the underlying table relations (by the use of the elements option, to specify element-centric XML over the default attribute-centric XML). The bottom line is that the FOR XML clause opens the doors of relational data in SQL Server to XML data. For a more thorough discussion of the FOR XML clause, refer to Chapter 14.

Queries Using Annotated Schema

The concept of annotated schema, as developed by Microsoft, is an extension to the XML Data schema specification. In short, annotated schemas allow applications to retrieve data from a database without having to use SQL. All of this is accomplished using what is called a **mapping schema**, which acts as a View of the data, mapping XML elements and attributes to tables and columns of a relational database.

Once we have created the schema, we can query the data it represents in the database using an XPath statement, which means we can query SQL Server 2000 data without having to write any SQL queries. For more detail see Chapter 15.

> For more information on the XPath syntax for querying XML data and the XPath version 1 W3C recommendation, see http://www.w3.org/TR/xpath.

Merging XML with Relational Data

Included in the new features of SQL Server 2000 is an extension to the T-SQL language: `OpenXML`. The `OpenXML` function allows stored procedures (or any T-SQL batch) to process XML and generate rowsets for use by T-SQL statements.

So where would we use this new feature? Well, for example, we could pass an XML document into a stored procedure, and insert the data from the XML document into a table. The point is that we can now, with the `OpenXML` T-SQL function, take XML data and convert it to a relational rowset. We can then use this rowset as we would any other rowset inside of a T-SQL batch or stored procedure (that is, to join to other data sets, insert, or update a table).

New XML Properties

To support further XML integration, ADO 2.6 features the addition of some new dynamic properties to the mix:

❑   `Mapping Schema`

❑   `Base Path`

❑   `Output Stream`

The `Mapping Schema` and `Base Path` properties are used in conjunction with annotated schemas and XPath as we'll see in Chapter 15 when discussing XML Views. The `Output Stream` property is used to define where a `Command` object should send its data stream. The syntax of each property is shown below.

Mapping Schema

The `Mapping Schema` property indicates a filename that points to the mapping schema used by the provider to translate the XPath command:

```
oCmd.Properties("Mapping Schema") = "Orders.xml"
```

Base Path

The `Base Path` property indicates the URL used for resolving relative paths in a template used to translate an XPath command:

```
oCmd.Properties("Base Path") = "C:\Inetpub\wwwroot\XMLDB\"
```

Output Stream

The `Output Stream` property indicates to the `Stream` object where the `Command.Execute` method will return its results. For example, we can return our results to the ASP `Response` object, which will send the data back to the client. Or, we could send the data to an ADO `Stream` object.

```
oCmd.Properties("Output Stream") = Response
```

Now that we've outlined these features from the conceptual level, let's take a closer look at all of these properties, as well as XML queries and the `FOR XML` clause.

XML Persistence

It's time to see some examples of what we can do to integrate XML into our strategies. As we discussed previously, since ADO 2.1 we have been able to persist XML to a file, and since ADO 2.5 we've been able to save XML to a `Stream` object. In this section we'll show how to persist our XML data in three different formats. On the way, we'll also demonstrate some practical situations where persisting XML data can come in handy, such as:

❑ Persisting to a file

    ❑ And then how to open a `Recordset` from the file

❑ Persisting to a `Stream` object

    ❑ And then how to open a `Recordset` from a stream

❑ Persisting to the ASP `Response` object

    ❑ And writing a stream to a client

    ❑ And persisting a stream to a client

Let's start out by examining how and when to persist to and from an XML file.

Persisting to a File

Persisting to a file is perhaps the most logical of places to begin, since it involves saving our data to a tangible data store: a file on a hard drive. You might want to take this approach when you need to save data between computer boots. For example, say a laptop user on your network is connected to your database application, and you write the data to files (persist them) on the user's laptop. Then, when this same user disconnects from the network and goes on the road, they can still use parts of the application, since you persisted some of the data to their hard drive.

ADO allows us to take a `Recordset` full of data and save it directly to a file in XML format. We can then open that XML file directly into another `Recordset` and edit the data using the file as the data source. This is one alternative to using the XML DOM to edit XML data. The code to save XML data to a file is quite simple. All we have to do is use the `Recordset` object's `Save` method and pass it the file name and the file format.

The ASP code below shows how to save a data set containing all of the customers in the `Northwind` database that comes with SQL Server to a file, using an XML format (`ch13_ex01.asp`):

```
<%@ Language=VBScript %>
<HTML>
<HEAD>
<TITLE>ADO 2.6 persist to File Example: ch13_ex01.asp</TITLE>
<!-- #include file="adovbs.inc" -->
<%
    Dim oCmd
    Dim oCn
    Dim oRs
    Dim sConn
    Dim sProvider

    sConn = "Data Source=(local);Initial Catalog=Northwind;" & _
            "User ID=sa;Password=;"
    sProvider = "SQLOLEDB"

    Set oCn = Server.CreateObject("ADODB.Connection")
    oCn.Provider = sProvider
    oCn.ConnectionString = sConn
    oCn.CursorLocation = adUseClient
    oCn.Open

        Set oCmd = CreateObject("ADODB.Command")
        Set oCmd.ActiveConnection = oCn
        oCmd.CommandText = "SELECT CustomerID, CompanyName FROM Customers"
        oCmd.CommandType = adCmdText
    Set oRs = oCmd.Execute()
    oRs.Save "c:\Customers.xml", adPersistXML
    oRs.Close
%>
</HEAD>
<BODY>
    <H2>ADO 2.6 persist to File Example: ch13_ex01.asp</H2>
    File saved.
</BODY>
</HTML>
```

You may need to change the connection string in this example to point to your SQL Server, and specify the path to `adovbs.inc` on your machine.

In this code example, we create a `Recordset` object and populate it with some data from the `Customers` table – specifically the customer ID and company name. Then we save this data to a file called `Customers.xml`, which looks something like this:

```
<xml xmlns:s='uuid:BDC6E3F0-6DA3-11d1-A2A3-00AA00C14882'
    xmlns:dt='uuid:C2F41010-65B3-11d1-A29F-00AA00C14882'
    xmlns:rs='urn:schemas-microsoft-com:rowset'
    xmlns:z='#RowsetSchema'>
<s:Schema id='RowsetSchema'>
    <s:ElementType name='row' content='eltOnly'>
        <s:AttributeType name='CustomerID' rs:number='1'
                         rs:writeunknown='true'>
        <s:datatype dt:type='string' dt:maxLength='5'
                rs:fixedlength='true' rs:maybenull='false'/>
        </s:AttributeType>
        <s:AttributeType name='CompanyName' rs:number='2'
                         rs:writeunknown='true'>
        <s:datatype dt:type='string' dt:maxLength='40' rs:maybenull='false'/>
        </s:AttributeType>
        <s:extends type='rs:rowbase'/>
    </s:ElementType>
</s:Schema>
<rs:data>
    <z:row CustomerID='ALFKI' CompanyName='Alfreds Futterkiste'/>
    <z:row CustomerID='ANATR'
                CompanyName='Ana Trujillo Emparedados y helados'/>
    <z:row CustomerID='ANTON' CompanyName='Antonio Moreno Taquería'/>
    ...
    <z:row CustomerID='WOLZA' CompanyName='Wolski  Zajazd'/>
</rs:data>
</xml>
```

Note that the `Save` method will not overwrite an existing file unless the recordset was opened from it.

We could follow this sample code up by saving the `Recordset` to a `Stream`, writing it out to the client via the `Response.Write` technique or opening a `Recordset` object from it. Below are some code samples that demonstrate these techniques.

Opening a Recordset from a File

Having saved the XML to the file in the previous example, what if we wanted to then open the file containing this XML into a `Recordset` object? Of course, we can transform ADO into an HTML table using XSLT, but sometimes we might not want to use XSLT: like if we want, say, a pure data stream.

> **The key to opening a recordset from XML is that the XML has to be derived from a recordset. You can't take any old XML as only XML that came from a recordset can be used to open a recordset.**

The code to tackle this is shown below (ch13_ex02.asp).

```
<%@ Language=VBScript %>
<HTML>
<HEAD>
<TITLE>
    ADO 2.6 Open Recordset from Persisted File Example: ch13_ex02.asp
</TITLE>
<!-- #include file="adovbs.inc" -->
<%
    Dim i
    Dim oRs
    Dim sTable
```

We could start by creating a `Recordset` object that has no data source connection. Since we aren't planning to get our data from a database, we'll set the `ActiveConnection` property to `Nothing` in this case:

```
Set oRs = Server.CreateObject("ADODB.Recordset")
Set oRs.ActiveConnection = Nothing
```

Then, we'll establish our `Recordset` as a client-side cursor whose source is an XML file on the local drive:

```
    oRs.CursorLocation = adUseClient
    oRs.CursorType = adOpenStatic
    oRs.LockType = adLockReadOnly
    oRs.Source = "c:\Customers.xml"
    oRs.Open
%>
</HEAD>
```

Finally, to prove that the XML was opened from the file, we will loop through the recordset and write the contents out in a table:

```
<BODY>
    <CENTER>
    <HR>
    <H2>
      ADO 2.6 Open Recordset from Persisted File Example: ch13_02.asp
    </H2>
    <HR>
<%
    sTable = "<table border='1'>"
    sTable = sTable & "<tr>"

    For i = 0 to oRs.Fields.Count - 1
    sTable = sTable & "<td><b>" & oRs.Fields(i).Name & "</b></td>"
    Next

    oRs.MoveNext
    sTable = sTable & "</tr>"
    Do While Not oRs.EOF
        sTable = sTable & "<tr>"
        For i = 0 to oRs.Fields.Count - 1
          sTable = sTable & "<td>" & oRs.Fields(i).Value & "</td>"
        Next
        oRs.MoveNext
        sTable = sTable & "</tr>"
    Loop

    sTable = sTable & "</table>"
    Response.Write sTable
%>
    </center>
</BODY>
</HTML>
<%
    oRs.Close
    Set oRs = Nothing
%>
```

This produces the following result:

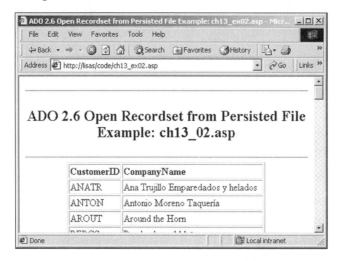

> Keep in mind that in a production enterprise environment you may not want a large
> file containing XML to be passed around, thus jamming your network bandwidth.
> XML solutions should be considered with this in mind. While XML is very flexible, its
> one drawback is that its text data is not suited for large amounts of data.

Persisting to a Stream

Another way to save XML to a file is to use the Stream object. This technique doesn't involve the
Recordset object to save the XML to a file. The Stream object has its own method called
SaveToFile, which does just that. So, assuming you have an XML file or a string variable containing
XML, the code below (ch13_ex03.asp) reads that XML from a file (using the LoadFromFile
method) and saves it directly to a new file (here called test.xml):

```
<%@ Language=VBScript %>
<HTML>
<HEAD>
<TITLE>ADO 2.6 Stream to File Example: ch13_ex03.asp</TITLE>
<!-- #include file="adovbs.inc" -->
<%
   Dim oStm
   Dim sXML


   '--- Create the Stream
   Set oStm = Server.CreateObject("ADODB.Stream")
   '--- Tell the Stream that we are opening standard Windows text
   oStm.Charset = "Windows-1252"
   '--- Open the Stream
   oStm.Open
   oStm.LoadFromFile "c:\customers.xml"
   '--- Read the XML to a variable
   '--- we'll use this to write to the stream later
   sXML = oStm.ReadText(adReadAll)
   '--- Close the Stream
   oStm.Close
```

```
    '--- Create the Stream
    Set oStm = Server.CreateObject("ADODB.Stream")
    '--- Open an empty Stream
    oStm.Open
    '--- Load the Stream from an XML string
    oStm.WriteText sXML
    '--- Save the Stream to a local file
    oStm.SaveToFile "c:\test.xml", adSaveCreateOverWrite
    oStm.Close
    Set oStm = Nothing %>
</HEAD>
<BODY>
    <center>
    <hr>
    <H2>ADO 2.6 Stream to File Example: ch13_03.asp</H2>
    <hr>
    File saved.
    </center>
</BODY>
</HTML>
```

Note that this method isn't specific to XML: it is a generic way to copy data using a stream.

Opening a Recordset from a Stream

We can also open a `Recordset` from a stream of XML. Assuming we had a file containing the XML previously persisted from another `Recordset`, we could use the following code to read the stream and write it out to a table (ch13_ex04.asp):

```
<%@ Language=VBScript %>
<HTML>
<HEAD>
<TITLE>ADO 2.6 Stream to Recordset Example: ch13_04.asp</TITLE>
<!-- #include file="adovbs.inc" -->
<%
    Dim i
    Dim oRs
    Dim oStm
    Dim sTable
    Dim sXML
```

```
    '--- Create the Stream
    Set oStm = Server.CreateObject("ADODB.Stream")
    '--- Tell the Stream that we are opening standard Windows text
    oStm.Charset = "Windows-1252"
    '--- Open the Stream
    oStm.Open
    oStm.LoadFromFile "c:\customers.xml"
    '--- Read the XML to a variable
    sXML = oStm.ReadText(adReadAll)
    oStm.Position = 0

    '--- Open the Recordset from the Stream of XML
    Set oRs = Server.CreateObject("ADODB.Recordset")
    Set oRs.ActiveConnection = nothing
    oRs.CursorLocation = adUseClient
    oRs.CursorType = adOpenStatic
    oRs.LockType = adLockReadOnly
    Set oRs.Source = oStm
    oRs.Open
```

```
    '--- Close the Stream
    oStm.Close
    Set oStm = Nothing
%>
</HEAD>
<BODY>
    <center>
    <hr>
    <H2>ADO 2.6 Stream to Recordset Example: ch13_04.asp</H2>
    <hr>
<%
    sTable = "<table border='1'>"
    sTable = sTable & "<tr>"
    For i = 0 to oRs.Fields.Count - 1
        sTable = sTable & "<td><b>" & oRs.Fields(i).Name & "</b></td>"
    Next
    oRs.MoveNext
    sTable = sTable & "</tr>"
    Do while not oRs.EOF
        sTable = sTable & "<tr>"
        For i = 0 to oRs.Fields.Count - 1
            sTable = sTable & "<td>" & oRs.Fields(i).Value & "</td>"
        Next
        oRs.MoveNext
        sTable = sTable & "</tr>"
    Loop
    sTable = sTable & "</table>"
    Response.Write sTable
%>
    </center>
</BODY>
</HTML>
<%
    oRs.Close
    Set oRs = Nothing
%>
```

Persisting to the Response Object

Up until this point, we've shown several ways to move XML in and out of files. However, often files aren't practical storage devices for our data. Consider a web solution that needs to pass XML to a client. We wouldn't want to store the XML on the server in between calls to a file – we may end up with hundreds or thousands of files, making for an awful mess to have to clean up, not to mention a great burden on precious resources. So, for those times when we want to send our XML to the client, we have a few alternatives to saving to a file, three of which are shown below:

❑ Send the XML data to the client to be embedded within an XML data island

❑ Send the XML data to the client to be used in an RDS application within Internet Explorer

❑ Send the XML data in its raw format (text) to the client application to be consumed as a web service

An XML data island is an XML formatted set of data that resides within XML tags in HTML. This data is not displayed in the browser, but can be used by client side code.

Each of these persistence techniques has its own merits and purposes. By sending the XML to a data island, we can then use that XML data in a client browser (such as IE5.5) through the XML DOM object to interact with the user. Likewise, we could send the XML data to an RDS client, which could read and/or update the data, and send it back to make any modifications to the database.

To create a Web Service, you don't need the .Net framework from Microsoft, but rather, you could create a standard ASP page that accepts parameters and returns a stream of XML back to the client application. It isn't as fancy as the .Net framework techniques, and doesn't involve SOAP, but in its purest sense, you are accepting input and sending back a resultset via HTTP and XML: that's a service you are providing via the web.

OK, so all of these techniques are useful, but now let's examine two different techniques to stream data to a client using the Response object – after all, the whole key of these solutions is to stream the data to the client:

❑ Loading a Stream object with an XML document and writing it to the browser directly

❑ Persisting a Recordset object directly to the Response object

Let's demonstrate both of these streaming techniques by giving a code example for each of them, starting with loading a Stream object and writing it to the browser.

Writing a Stream to a Client

The example below (ch13_ex05.asp) shows how to load a Stream object from an XML file (Territories.xml) and then write the XML to the client inside of a data island.

In case you were wondering what the source XML looks like, here it is, as displayed in IE5.5:

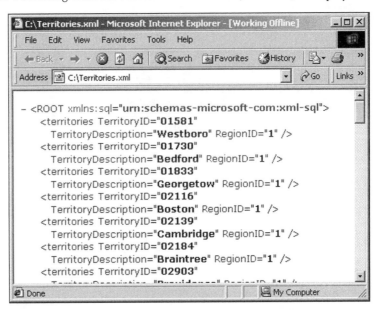

Here, we open a sample XML file containing a list of territories and load them into the Stream object. Then, we read the Stream contents into a string variable sXML. Finally, we write the XML to the client, embedded within an XML data island:

```
<%@ Language=VBScript %>
<HTML>
<HEAD>
<TITLE>ADO 2.6 Stream to Data Island Example: ch13_ex05.asp</TITLE>
<!-- #include file="adovbs.inc" -->
<%
    Dim oStm
    Dim sXML

    '--- Create the Stream
    Set oStm = Server.CreateObject("ADODB.Stream")
    '--- Tell the Stream that we are opening standard Windows text
    oStm.Charset = "Windows-1252"
    '--- Open the Stream
    oStm.Open
    oStm.LoadFromFile "c:\Territories.xml"
    '--- Read the XML to a variable
    sXML = oStm.ReadText(adReadAll)

    oStm.Close
    Set oStm = Nothing
    Response.Write "<XML ID='MyDataIsle'>"
    Response.Write sXML
    Response.Write "</XML>"
%>

<SCRIPT language="VBScript" For="window" Event="onload">
    Dim oXML
    Dim oRoot
    Dim oChild
    Dim sOutputXML

    Set oXML = MyDataIsle.XMLDocument
    oXML.resolveExternals=false
    oXML.async=false

    Set oRoot = oXML.documentElement

    For each oChild in oRoot.childNodes
        sOutputXML = document.all("log").innerHTML
        document.all("log").innerHTML = sOutputXML & "<LI>" & _
            oChild.getAttribute("TerritoryDescription") & "</LI>"
    Next
</SCRIPT>
</HEAD>
<BODY>
    <center>
    <hr>
    <H2>ADO 2.6 Stream to Data Island Example: ch13_ex05.asp</H2>
    <hr>

    <H3>Client-side processing of XML Document MyDataIsle</H3>
    </center>

    <UL id=log>
    </UL>
</BODY>
</HTML>
```

We have streamed XML down to the client browser, displayed it by using client-side VBScript to bind the XML document to an instance of the DOM, and looped through each child node to build a list in HTML:

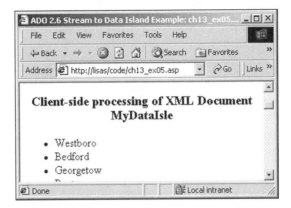

Keep in mind that client-side VBScript code will only work in Internet Explorer browsers. If you want to write client-side code that works in both Netscape and Internet Explorer, you'll need to use JavaScript.

Persisting a Stream to a Client

So we've seen how to stream XML to a data island. Now let's examine how we can stream an XML document, and only an XML document, to a client.

This example could be used as a web service, where applications could navigate to your URL via the web, and get only an XML document in return. Of course, you could always return the data in an XML data island or some other fashion as well, but we've already shown that, so let's look at how we can return all of the territories in the Territories table in Northwind to the client (ch13_ex06.xml):

```
<%@ Language=VBScript %>
<!-- #include file="adovbs.inc" -->
<%
    '--- ch13_ex06.asp
    Dim oCmd
    Dim oCn
    Dim oRs
    Dim sConn
    Dim sProvider

    sConn = "Data Source=(local);Initial Catalog=Northwind;" & _
            "User ID=sa;Password=;"
    sProvider = "SQLOLEDB"

    Set oCn = Server.CreateObject("ADODB.Connection")
    oCn.Provider = sProvider
    oCn.ConnectionString = sConn
    oCn.CursorLocation = adUseClient
    oCn.Open
```

```
        Set oCmd = CreateObject("ADODB.Command")
        Set oCmd.ActiveConnection = oCn
        oCmd.CommandText = "SELECT * FROM Territories"
        oCmd.CommandType = adCmdText

    Set oRs = oCmd.Execute()
    oRs.Save Response, adPersistXML
    oRs.Close
    oCn.Close
    Set oRs = Nothing
    Set oCmd = Nothing
    Set oCn = Nothing
%>
```

Notice that we use the `Recordset` object's `Save` method once again. But this time, instead of saving to a file, we're saving the contents of the `Recordset` to a type of stream: the ASP `Response` object:

```
oRs.Save Response, adPersistXML
```

Since the `Response` object is just another form of a stream, we can basically skip the steps of reading the data into a `Stream` object from the `Recordset` and then into a variable before writing it to the client.

Keep in mind that we could take advantage of the `Command` object's new features to persist XML data to the client. However, let's save that discussion for the next section, when we get into the FOR XML clause of SQL Server 2000.

XML Queries via ADO

The addition of the new FOR XML clause in SQL Server 2000 brings a new weapon to a developer's arsenal. With this new weapon, we now have the ability to return XML data sets from SQL queries simply by appending the FOR XML clause at the end of a SQL command. To better clarify the value of this new feature, let's examine how we used to get XML out of databases prior to SQL Server 2000.

We'd start by sending a SQL query to SQL Server, for example via an ADO `Command`. The `Command` would send the SQL to the database, and a data set would be returned to our application and put into an ADO `Recordset` object. Then, if we wanted the data to be in a specific XML format, we would have to loop through the `Recordset` and build a string of XML manually, either using the XML DOM, or by using a custom built routine. We could have used the XML schema built by ADO's `Save` method, but that restricts the format of the XML to a format that we may not want.

These techniques were not uncommon for those of us trying to integrate XML into our existing ADO and SQL based applications – not too shabby a solution. However, this approach does have some downfalls. For example, we get the data from SQL Server in a standard rowset, we convert it to a `Recordset` then into XML. This process would obviously be better served if we could send the data directly into XML, and skip the `Recordset` step altogether.

By running our queries against the SQL Server 2000 database and returning XML directly to our application, we avoid the overhead of creating a `Recordset` object for the sole purpose of looping through it and building our XML. This means we don't have to create the extra objects such as the `Recordset` object or the XML DOM object. Nor do we have to loop through the returned data, which can be very costly depending on how many rows we retrieve. So as you can clearly see, this new feature of ADO and SQL Server truly opens the doors of our applications to XML.

Now that we've outlined its merits, let's look at how to use the FOR XML clause.

FOR XML Usage

We cover the details of using FOR XML in Chapter 14, but we will briefly summarize it here. The basic syntax can be quite simple, as depicted below:

```
sql_query FOR XML [RAW|AUTO|EXPLICIT]
```

Here, we see that the FOR XML clause can be appended to the end of any data retrieving SQL query. But you do have a choice in how the data is returned. Actually, you have a choice of three **modes**, as shown in the following table:

Mode	Description
FOR XML RAW	Generates generic row elements with column values as attributes.
FOR XML AUTO	Generates a hierarchical tree with element names based on table names.
FOR XML EXPLICIT	Generates a universal table with relationships fully described by meta data.

Let's take a look at how we could return a simple SQL query from the Northwind database using the FOR XML RAW syntax:

```
SELECT * FROM PRODUCTS ORDER BY PRODUCTNAME FOR XML RAW
```

The results of this query return all of the products in an XML fragment:

```
<row ProductID="17" ProductName="Alice Mutton" SupplierID="7"
     CategoryID="6" QuantityPerUnit="20 - 1 kg tins" UnitPrice="39.0000"
     UnitsInStock="0" UnitsOnOrder="0" ReorderLevel="0" Discontinued="1"/>
<row ProductID="3" ProductName="Aniseed Syrup" SupplierID="1"
     CategoryID="2" QuantityPerUnit="12 - 550 ml bottles" UnitPrice="10.0000"
     UnitsInStock="13" UnitsOnOrder="70" ReorderLevel="25" Discontinued="0"/>

   . . .
```

The nodes of the fragment are called row. Each row element contains an attribute that corresponds directly to the name of each column in the SQL query.

If we run this same query using the FOR XML AUTO clause, as shown below:

```
SELECT * FROM PRODUCTS ORDER BY PRODUCTNAME FOR XML AUTO
```

we'll get similar results:

```
<PRODUCTS ProductID="17" ProductName="Alice Mutton" SupplierID="7"
          CategoryID="6" QuantityPerUnit="20 - 1 kg tins"
          UnitPrice="39.0000" UnitsInStock="0" UnitsOnOrder="0"
          ReorderLevel="0" Discontinued="1"/>
<PRODUCTS ProductID="3" ProductName="Aniseed Syrup" SupplierID="1"
          CategoryID="2" QuantityPerUnit="12 - 550 ml bottles"
          UnitPrice="10.0000" UnitsInStock="13" UnitsOnOrder="70"
          ReorderLevel="25" Discontinued="0"/>
   . . .
```

We still get the rows from the resultset represented as XML elements, and each column as an attribute of those elements. However, the row elements are now named to represent the hierarchical structure that they are derived from. In this T-SQL example, the elements are named PRODUCTS.

The EXPLICIT mode is a lot more complex, although it allows a lot greater flexibility. For detailed usage of the EXPLICIT mode see Chapter 14.

FOR XML Template Queries

As long as you set the SQL Server database up as a virtual directory under IIS (see Appendix E), we can also run these same queries from within an XML file. The previous query that retrieved the customer and order data using the hierarchical format, could have been run from an XML file that might look like this (ch13_ex07.xml):

```
<ROOT xmlns:sql="urn:schemas-microsoft-com:xml-sql">
    <sql:query>
    SELECT
        Customers.CustomerID,
        Customers.CompanyName,
        Orders.OrderID,
        Orders.OrderDate
    FROM Customers
        INNER JOIN Orders ON Customers.CustomerID = Orders.CustomerID
    ORDER BY
        Customers.CompanyName
    FOR XML AUTO
    </sql:query>
</ROOT>
```

Notice that the additions to SQL are exactly the same as when using FOR XML in SQL statements. The only difference in the code is that we now wrap the query within an XML document within <ROOT> tags. The namespace indicates that we want the XML to be parsed using the Microsoft namespace for XML SQL. Thus, the SQL query contained within the <sql:query> tags is executed and the results are returned to the browser.

FOR XML URL Queries

We can even run a FOR XML query from a browser's URL. The syntax is pretty straightforward, as is shown below:

```
http://localhost/northwind?sql=select%20'<root>';
select%20*%20from%20customers%20for%20xml%20auto;select%20'</root>';
```

If you run this query from within the URL, the XML results of this query are written to the browser. Notice that that URL specified is the web server name (localhost) and the virtual directory for the SQL Server database (my virtual directory is called northwind). Next, we pass a querystring parameter to the virtual directory called sql. To this argument, we pass the SQL statement wrapped within <root> tags.

> You may notice that there are %20 expressions embedded throughout this XML URL query example. The web doesn't always react to spaces well. Therefore the spaces are converted to their hexadecimal URL representation (%20).

FOR XML via ADO

OK, so we've seen how to retrieve XML via SQL queries on their own, via template queries and via URL queries, but what about running these types of queries via ADO? ADO 2.6 introduced the ability to execute a FOR XML query via a Command object with or without a Stream object.

Running a FOR XML Command

We can run a FOR XML query from a Command object by setting either one of the following two properties:

❑   The CommandText property
❑   The CommandStream property

Regardless of which is used, we need to set the new Dialect property of the Command object, because the Dialect indicates how the Command's query should be parsed. For example, here are some of the different Dialect settings. As you can see, the Dialect settings take on the form of somewhat cryptic GUIDs.

XML Template query dialect:

```
oCmd.Dialect="{5D531CB2-E6Ed-11D2-B252-00C04F681B71}" '--- XML Template
```

SQL query dialect:

```
oCmd.Dialect="{C8B522D7-5CF3-11CE-ADE5-00AA0044773D}" '--- T-SQL query
```

Unknown query dialect:

```
oCmd.Dialect="{C8B521FB-5CF3-11CE-ADE5-00AA0044773D}" '--- UNKNOWN query
```

XPath query dialect:

```
oCmd.Dialect="{EC2A4293-E898-11D2-B1B7-00C04F680C56}" '--- XPath query
```

We'll examine the template query dialect in this section, since it tells the provider to parse the incoming command as a template query (FOR XML query wrapped in XML).

Specifically, the dialect tells the SQL Server OLE DB Provider how to interpret the command text it receives from ADO. The dialect is specified by a GUID, and is set via the Command.Dialect property. Keep in mind that all of the dialect settings are provider specific, as the dialects shown here are specific to SQL Server.

Running FOR XML via CommandText

Let's jump right into an example of how we can run a template query via ADO by using some properties of the Command object. Below you'll see the code to run a FOR XML query by setting the CommandText of the Command to the FOR XML query document (ch13_ex08.asp):

```
<%@ LANGUAGE="VBScript"%>
<%Option Explicit%>
<HTML>
<HEAD>
```

```
<TITLE>ADO 2.6 FOR XML via CommandText Example - ch13_ex08.asp</TITLE>
<!-- #include file="adovbs.inc" -->
<%
    Dim oCmd
    Dim oCn
    Dim sConn
    Dim sProvider
    Dim sQuery

    sProvider = "SQLOLEDB"
    sConn = "Data Source=(local);Initial Catalog=Northwind;User ID=sa"
    Set oCn = Server.CreateObject("ADODB.Connection")
    oCn.Provider = sProvider
    oCn.ConnectionString = sConn
    oCn.CursorLocation = adUseClient
    oCn.Open

    Set oCmd = Server.CreateObject("ADODB.Command")
    Set oCmd.ActiveConnection = oCn
```

We hard code the query into the string `sQuery`:

```
'--- The FOR XML query (hard coded)
sQuery = "<ROOT xmlns:sql='urn:schemas-microsoft-com:xml-sql'>" & _
    "<sql:query>SELECT * FROM PRODUCTS ORDER BY PRODUCTNAME " & _
    " FOR XML AUTO </sql:query></ROOT>"
```

And set the `CommandText` property to the value of the query:

```
oCmd.CommandText = sQuery
oCmd.CommandType = adCmdText
```

Then we set the dialect so that SQL Server will know this is an XML template query:

```
'--- XML Template query dialect
oCmd.Dialect = "{5D531CB2-E6Ed-11D2-B252-00C04F681B71}"
```

We wrap up by telling the `Command` where to stream the resulting dataset. We have to send the data to a stream of some sorts. Our two obvious choices are either a `Stream` object or the `Response` object. That's right, the ASP `Response` object is also a type of stream. By setting the `Output Stream` dynamic property (Output Stream) to the `Response` object, we are telling the `Command` to send the XML directly to the client:

```
'--- Output the XML to the Response object
oCmd.Properties("Output Stream") = Response
Response.Write "<XML ID=MyDataIsle>"
oCmd.Execute , , adExecuteStream
Response.Write "</XML>"
Set oCmd = Nothing
oCn.Close
Set oCn = Nothing
%>
```

We wrap the response in data island tags, and write the response between them. This allows us to loop through them later when we come to the results on the client where we want to display them.

The rest of the code loops through the XML DOM on the client to display the data in a bulleted list:

```
<SCRIPT language="VBScript" For="window" Event="onload">
    Dim oXML
    Dim oRoot
    Dim oChild
    Dim sOutputXML

    Set oXML = MyDataIsle.XMLDocument
    oXML.resolveExternals=false
    oXML.async=false

    Set oRoot = oXML.documentElement

    For each oChild in oRoot.childNodes
        sOutputXML = document.all("log").innerHTML
        document.all("log").innerHTML = sOutputXML & "<LI>" & _
                            oChild.getAttribute("ProductName") & "</LI>"
    Next
    Set oXML = Nothing
    Set oRoot = Nothing
    Set oChild = Nothing
</SCRIPT>
</HEAD>
<BODY>
    <center>
    <hr>
    <h2>ADO 2.6 FOR XML via CommandText Example - ch13_ex08.asp</h2>
    <hr>
    </center>
    <UL id=log>
    </UL>
</BODY>
</HTML>
```

Of course, you could do whatever you want with the data once you stream it out of the Command.

Running FOR XML via CommandStream

OK, so we've seen how to run a template query via CommandText, so now let's look at how to tackle this through the CommandStream property. The CommandStream property is new to ADO 2.6, and specifies the stream from which the query is derived. This enables us to pass a template query from a file, or any other source of the template query, into a Command via the Stream object. The following is an example file that shows how this property is used to achieve this (ch13_ex09.asp):

```
<%@ LANGUAGE = "VBScript"%>
<% Option Explicit %>
<HTML>
<HEAD>
<TITLE>ADO 2.6 FOR XML via CommandStream Example - ch13_ex09.asp</TITLE>
<!-- #include file="adovbs.inc" -->
<%
    Dim oCmd
    Dim oCn
    Dim oStm
    Dim sConn
    Dim sProvider
    Dim sQuery
```

```
sProvider = "SQLOLEDB"
sConn = "Data Source=(local);Initial Catalog=Northwind;User ID=sa"
Set oCn = Server.CreateObject("ADODB.Connection")
oCn.Provider = sProvider
oCn.ConnectionString = sConn
oCn.CursorLocation = adUseClient
oCn.Open

Set oCmd = Server.CreateObject("ADODB.Command")
Set oCmd.ActiveConnection = oCn
'--- The FOR XML query (hard coded)
sQuery = "<ROOT xmlns:sql='urn:schemas-microsoft-com:xml-sql'>" & _
    "<sql:query>SELECT * FROM PRODUCTS ORDER BY PRODUCTNAME " & _
    " FOR XML AUTO </sql:query></ROOT>"
```

We create and open the `Stream` object:

```
Set oStm = Server.CreateObject("ADODB.Stream")
'--- Open the Stream
oStm.Open
```

Write the XML to it:

```
oStm.WriteText sQuery, adWriteChar
oStm.Position = 0
set oCmd.CommandStream = oStm
oCmd.CommandType = adCmdText
```

Specify the dialect to be an XML template query:

```
oCmd.Dialect = "{5D531CB2-E6Ed-11D2-B252-00C04F681B71}"
```

And specify that we want to send the XML to the ASP `Response` object:

```
oCmd.Properties("Output Stream") = Response
Response.Write "<XML ID=MyDataIsle>"
oCmd.Execute , , adExecuteStream
Response.Write "</XML>"
oCn.Close
Set oStm = Nothing
Set oCmd = Nothing
Set oCn = Nothing
%>
```

Then iterate through the data and output it as in the previous example:

```
<SCRIPT language="VBScript" For="window" Event="onload">
    Dim oXML
    Dim oRoot
    Dim oChild
    Dim sOutputXML

    Set oXML = MyDataIsle.XMLDocument
    oXML.resolveExternals=false
    oXML.async=false
```

```
      Set oRoot = oXML.documentElement

      For each oChild in oRoot.childNodes
          sOutputXML = document.all("log").innerHTML
          document.all("log").innerHTML = sOutputXML & "<LI>" & _
                              oChild.getAttribute("ProductName") & "</LI>"
      Next

      Set oXML = Nothing
      Set oRoot = Nothing
      Set oChild = Nothing
  </SCRIPT>
  </HEAD>
  <BODY>
      <center>
      <hr>
      <h2>ADO 2.6 FOR XML via CommandStream Example - ch13_ex09.asp</h2>
      <hr>
      </center>
      <UL id=log>
      </UL>
  </BODY>
  </HTML>
```

Notice here that we read an XML template query into a Stream object, then we set that Stream object to the CommandStream property of the Command object. This is basically the same code we saw earlier, with the exception that we are using a Stream object as the source of the template query command, so why go this route?

It becomes more apparent when you consider that the Stream object can be used to house an XML template query from a file rather easily. Simply load the Stream with the XML template query using the LoadFromFile method, and we're ready to go!

As you can see, running template queries via ADO is not that different from running SQL queries. Besides the template query syntax, we only have to indicate that the Command is a Stream and we need to direct the XML output to a Stream as well.

So, retrieving XML from a SQL Server data source via ADO is well within our grasp. What you do with the XML is another story. As we listed earlier, some possibilities are:

❑ Passing the XML data to the client to be used within an XML data island

❑ Passing the XML to an RDS client to be bound to an HTML table

❑ More intriguingly, passing the XML only to a remote client as some sort of web service that your application provides

Now that we've explored how to write SQL queries against ADO, let's see how we could retrieve XML from a SQL Server database – without writing any SQL!

Non-SQL Queries via ADO

By combining XPath with Microsoft's Mapping Schema feature, we can now query SQL Server 2000 data without having to write any SQL queries. The concept is that we create a mapping schema that translates a relational structure of a database schema to XML elements. Then, we use the XPath language to query the XML elements to retrieve our data. So in a sense we are writing a query, but it is not a SQL query. Rather, we are writing a query using XPath against an XML translation (or map). By using XPath, we can query against any node in the XML document.

> Using these two technologies together (XPath and a Mapping Schema) allows applications to query SQL Server 2000 data without using SQL commands, and without needing to know the underlying relational schema of the database (except to build the mapping schema).

Before we begin, let's go over a few terms that are vital to querying the data via XPath:

- ❑ The Mapping Schema file
- ❑ The Mapping Schema property
- ❑ The Base Path property
- ❑ The XPath query

We'll also go on to look at some code examples.

Mapping Schema File

The concept of Mapping Schema is an extension to the XML data specification. The extensions map XML elements and attributes to tables and columns of a relational database. For example, say we wanted to represent the customer-to-order relationship that is defined in the Northwind database via a mapping schema:

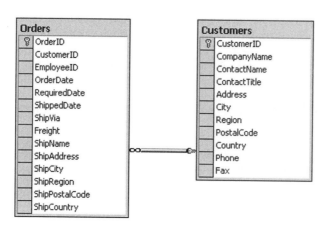

We would have to define the table elements as well as the relationship in our mapping schema.

Let's jump right to the mapping schema file and examine how it is structured (ch13_ex10.xml):

```xml
<?xml version="1.0" ?>
<!-- ch13_ex10.xml-->
<Schema xmlns="urn:schemas-microsoft-com:xml-data"
        xmlns:dt="urn:schemas-microsoft-com:datatypes"
        xmlns:sql="urn:schemas-microsoft-com:xml-sql">

<ElementType name="Order" sql:relation="Orders" >
    <AttributeType name="CustID" />
    <AttributeType name="OrderID" />
    <AttributeType name="OrderDate" />
    <attribute type="CustID" sql:field="CustomerID" />
    <attribute type="OrderID" sql:field="OrderID" />
    <attribute type="OrderDate" sql:field="OrderDate" />
</ElementType>

<ElementType name="Customer" sql:relation="Customers" >
    <AttributeType name="CustID" />
    <AttributeType name="CompanyName" />
    <attribute type="CustID" sql:field="CustomerID" />
    <attribute type="CompanyName" sql:field="CompanyName" />
        <element type="Order" >
        <sql:relationship key-relation="Customers" key="CustomerID"
            foreign-key="CustomerID" foreign-relation="Orders" />
        </element>
</ElementType>
</Schema>
```

Our document begins with the namespace declarations, and then has an ElementType node for each underlying table schema. Our first ElementType node represents that Orders table, as shown by its sql:relation attribute, but it is referred to via XPath using its name, which is Order:

```xml
<ElementType name="Order" sql:relation="Orders" >
```

Then, each ElementType node (table) contains an AttributeType and an Attribute node pair for each column in the underlying table. The sql:field attribute is used to identify the corresponding field in the SQL table:

```xml
    <AttributeType name="CustID" />
...
    <attribute type="CustID" sql:field="CustomerID" />
```

The key aspects of this mapping schema are in the sql:relation and the sql:relationship attributes. The sql:relation attribute is used to identify the table name in the database, while the sql:relationship attribute is used to identify the primary key to foreign key relationships between the two tables:

```xml
<sql:relationship key-relation="Customers" key="CustomerID"
    foreign-key="CustomerID" foreign-relation="Orders" />
```

Notice that the `key-relation` attribute indicates the database's parent table, and the `key` attribute identifies the primary key in the parent table. Likewise the `foreign-relation` attribute indicates the database's child table, and the `foreign-key` attribute identifies the foreign key in the child table. Now that we have the Mapping Schema written and saved to an XML file, we'll focus on how to query against it using ADO and an XPath query.

Mapping Schema & Base Path Properties

The `Mapping Schema` Property is a new property of the `Command` object's `Properties` collection. This property points to the location of the XML Mapping Schema file. The `Base Path` property of the `Command` object's `Properties` collection indicates the file path used for resolving the relative paths of a mapping schema used to translate an XPath command.

The Mapping Schema Property

```
oCmd.Properties("Mapping Schema") = "Orders_MappingSchema.xml"
```

The Base Path Property

```
oCmd.Properties("Base Path") = "C:\Inetpub\wwwroot\XMLDB\"
```

Code Examples

So now that we've taken a look at all of the players in running an XPath query, let's show a complete example of how we might tackle this. For starter's we need a Mapping Schema file. We'll use the one from the previous section (`ch13_ex10.xml`), for consistency's sake. The next step is to create an ASP page that we can run our XPath query against, like so (`ch13_ex10.asp`):

```
<%@LANGUAGE=VBSCRIPT%>
<HTML>
<HEAD>
<TITLE>ADO 2.6 XPath Example - ch13_ex10.asp</TITLE>
<!-- #include file="adovbs.inc" -->
<%
    Dim oCmd
    Dim oCn
    Dim sCompanyName
    Dim sConn
    Dim sProvider

    '--- Get the parameter
    sCompanyName = Request.QueryString("CompanyName")

    '--- Establish the connection to the database
    sProvider = "SQLOLEDB"
    sConn = "Data Source=(local); Initial Catalog=Northwind;" & _
        "User ID=sa;Password=;"
    Set oCn = Server.CreateObject("ADODB.Connection")
    oCn.ConnectionString = sConn
    oCn.Provider = sProvider
    oCn.CursorLocation = adUseClient
    oCn.Open
        Set oCmd = CreateObject("ADODB.Command")
        Set oCmd.ActiveConnection = oCn
```

Once we have a connection to the SQL Server 2000 database, we create a `Command` object to run our query. Then, we set our `Command` object's `CommandText` property to the XPath query:

```
'--- Generate the XPath query
    oCmd.CommandText = "Customer[@CompanyName = '" & sCompanyName & "']"
```

This takes our QueryString argument for the company name and passes it to the XPath query. Then we set the dialect to be the XPath dialect, so SQL Server can parse the query accordingly:

```
'--- Specify the dialect to be an XPath query
oCmd.Dialect = "{ec2a4293-e898-11d2-b1b7-00c04f680c56}"
'--- XPath dialect
```

Next we specify the mapping schema and base path properties to point to the mapping schema file:

```
'--- Indentify the mapping schema
    oCmd.Properties("Mapping Schema") = "ch13_ex10.xml"
        oCmd.Properties("Base Path") = "C:\Inetpub\wwwroot\XMLDB\"
```

Make sure that you specify the correct base path your ch13_ex10.xml file here.

Finally, we wrap up by setting the `Output Stream` to be the `Response` object and writing the XML to the client using the `oCmd.Execute` method:

```
'--- Set the output stream to go to the ASP Response object
    oCmd.Properties("Output Stream") = Response
'--- Write the XML to the client
Response.write "<XML ID='MyDataIsle'><Customers>"
oCmd.Execute , , adExecuteStream
Response.write "</Customers></XML>"
oCn.Close
Set oCmd = Nothing
Set oCn = Nothing
%>
</HEAD>
```

Notice that we set the `oCmd.Execute` method's `adExecuteStream` parameter to tell ADO that results are expected back in the form of a stream instead of the default `Recordset`.

The rest of the code just iterates through the data and creates the output:

```
<BODY>
    <H3>Client-side processing of XML Document MyDataIsle</H3>
    <SCRIPT language="VBScript">

        Dim oXMLDoc
        Dim sOutputOrders
        Dim sOrderList
        Dim oRoot, oChild, oHeader
        Dim sOutputHeader
        Dim iCustomerNumber
        Dim sTotalPage
```

```
      Set oXMLDoc = MyDataIsle.XMLDocument
      oXMLDoc.resolveExternals=false
      oXMLDoc.async=false

      Set oRoot = oXMLDoc.documentElement

      iCustomerNumber = 1
      For each oCurrentCustomer in oRoot.childNodes
          '--- Create the appropriate header for each customer
          document.write "<DIV id=Header" & iCustomerNumber & "></DIV>"
          '--- Create the order lists for each customer
          document.write "<UL id=Orders" & iCustomerNumber & "></UL>"

          sOutputHeader = document.all("header" & _
              iCustomerNumber).innerHTML
          sOutputHeader = sOutputHeader & "CustomerID: " & _
              oCurrentCustomer.getAttribute("CustID")
          document.all("Header" & iCustomerNumber).innerHTML = _
              sOutputHeader

          For each oChild in oCurrentCustomer.childNodes
              sOutputOrders = document.all("Orders" & _
                  iCustomerNumber).innerHTML
              '--- Create the order list items
              sOrderList = "<LI> Order # " & _
                  oChild.getAttribute("OrderID") & _
                  ", Date: " & oChild.getAttribute("OrderDate") & _
                  "</LI>"
              sTotalPage = sOutputOrders & sOrderList
              '--- Set the order list items to the order list
              document.all("Orders" & iCustomerNumber).innerHTML = _
                  sTotalPage
          Next
          '--- Process next customer
          iCustomerNumber = iCustomerNumber + 1
      Next
      Set oXMLDoc = Nothing
      Set oRoot = Nothing
      Set oChild = Nothing
      Set oHeader = Nothing
    </SCRIPT>
  </BODY>
</HTML>
```

To run this query, simply generate a URL with an XPath query containing a company name that you want to see orders for. For example:

```
http://localhost/XMLDB/ch13_ex10.asp?companyname=ernst%20handel
```

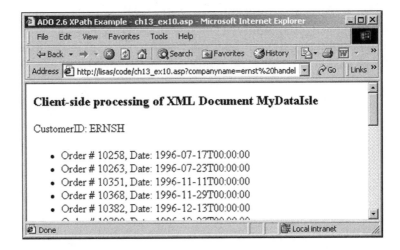

> At the time this chapter was written, there was an outstanding issue according to Microsoft (#223396), that the SQLOLEDB provider does not support using the CommandStream for input of XPath queries. Until this issue is resolved, we'll simply use CommandText to specify the XPath query, as shown in the previous example.

As some of our other examples in this chapter have done, the VBScript, client-side code binds the XML document to an instance of the DOM in order to display the data to the browser in HTML.

Joining XML and SQL Data

One of the top features on the bulleted list of things to do for SQL Server 2000 was to create a mechanism to integrate XML with SQL data. We'll see how we can do this in Chapter 14 using the SQL extensions provided in the OpenXML function. This allows stored procedures to process XML and generate rowsets for use by SQL statements. So now we have the ability to pass XML data into stored procedures, join with SQL data sets, and return XML data, if we so desire.

Since the XML data that we pass in can be translated to a data set that SQL Server 2000 understands, we can use the data set (XML document, in this case) as we would in any SQL operation. For example, we could join on the dataset, insert rows from the dataset into a table or use the dataset to update other SQL data.

This uses two stored procedures:

- ❑ The sp_xml_preparedocument stored procedure translates the XML document to a data set format that SQL Server can comprehend.

- ❑ The sp_xml_removedocument stored procedure removes the XML document from SQL Server's memory when we're done with it.

The code below defines a stored procedure (spOpenXML) that we wrote to join a particular XML document with data from the SQL Server Northwind database. Specifically, we'll pass in an XML document containing customer data, and we'll join that with the orders for those customers in the database. The end result is that we get back a SQL data set containing the orders for the customer that we passed in.

Create this stored procedure in your database:

```
ALTER PROCEDURE spOpenXML
    @sXML VARCHAR(2000)
AS

DECLARE @iDoc INT

-- Prepare the XML document for SQL Server
EXEC sp_xml_preparedocument @iDoc OUTPUT, @sXML

-- Query the XML data set joined to a SQL Server table
SELECT
    c.CustomerID,
    c.ContactName,
    o.OrderID,
    o.OrderDate
FROM OPENXML(@iDoc, '/ROOT/Customers', 1)
    WITH (CustomerID varchar(10), ContactName varchar(20))
    AS c
    INNER JOIN Orders o ON c.CustomerID = o.CustomerID

-- Remove the internal representation of the XML document.
EXEC sp_xml_removedocument @iDoc

GO
```

This code starts out by using the system stored procedure sp_xml_preparedocument to create an in-memory representation of the XML document that we pass in via the @sXML parameter. The first parameter of sp_xml_preparedocument, @iDoc, is an output parameter. It returns a handle to the prepared XML document that resides in SQL Server's memory. The second parameter, @XMLDoc, is an input parameter that accepts the XML document.

Once we have our handle to the XML document within SQL Server's memory, we can use the OpenXML function with our XML document just like we could use a standard SQL data set within SQL. Let's take a closer look at the SELECT statement in the spOpenXML stored procedure.

```
SELECT
    c.CustomerID,
    c.ContactName,
    o.OrderID,
    o.OrderDate
FROM OPENXML(@iDoc, '/ROOT/Customers', 1)
    WITH (CustomerID varchar(10), ContactName varchar(20))
    AS c
    INNER JOIN Orders o ON c.CustomerID = o.CustomerID
```

Here, we passed in the @iDoc handle to the in memory XML document, an XPath query command, and a flag indicating that the XML is attribute-centric. We also tacked on a WITH clause to describe the structure of the rowset that we get back from the OpenXML function.

> To indicate that we want all columns back from the OpenXML function, we would simply use a WITH clause that looks like this: WITH Customers.

The OpenXML function through the WITH clause translates into a data set that we can then use like any other data set in T-SQL. We took this data set of customers and joined it to the orders data from the Northwind database. In fact, any T-SQL statement that operates with a data set can be used with the OpenXML keyword.

We've just shown a very simple example showing a SELECT, but any type of query can be used using this formula. And once we are finished with the in memory XML document, we release it by passing the document handle @iDoc to the sp_xml_removedocument system stored procedure.

The ASP Page

Now, to invoke the stored procedure and return our SQL data set back, we run some ADO code as shown below (ch13_ex11.asp). First we create a standard connection to a SQL Server database:

```
<HTML>
<HEAD>
<TITLE>ADO 2.6 OpenXML Example - ch13_ex11.asp</TITLE>
<!-- #include file="adovbs.inc" -->
<%
    Dim i
    Dim oCmd
    Dim oCn
    Dim oRs
    Dim sConn
    Dim sProvider
    Dim sQuery
    Dim sXMLDoc

    '--- Open the connection to the database
    sProvider = "SQLOLEDB"
    sConn = "Data Source=(local);Initial Catalog=Northwind;User ID=sa"
    Set oCn = Server.CreateObject("ADODB.Connection")
    oCn.Provider = sProvider
    oCn.ConnectionString = sConn
    oCn.CursorLocation = adUseClient
    oCn.Open
```

Then we prepare the XML document that we want to pass into our stored procedure. We could have opened a file to load an XML document, or even be passed the XML from another application:

```
'--- Prepare the XML document to pass in to the stored procedure
sXMLDoc = "<ROOT>"
sXMLDoc = sXMLDoc & "<Customers CustomerID='VINET' " & _
        "ContactName='Paul Henriot'>"
sXMLDoc = sXMLDoc & "<Orders CustomerID='VINET' " & _
        "EmployeeID='5' OrderDate='1996-07-04T00:00:00'>"
sXMLDoc = sXMLDoc & "<OrderDetails OrderID='10248' " & _
        "ProductID='11' Quantity='12'/>"
```

```
sXMLDoc = sXMLDoc & "<OrderDetails OrderID='10248' " & _
        "ProductID='42' Quantity='10'/>"
sXMLDoc = sXMLDoc & "</Orders>"
sXMLDoc = sXMLDoc & "</Customers>"
sXMLDoc = sXMLDoc & "<Customers CustomerID='LILAS' " & _
        "ContactName='Carlos Gonzlez'>"
sXMLDoc = sXMLDoc & "<Orders CustomerID='LILAS' " & _
        "EmployeeID='3' OrderDate='1996-08-16T00:00:00'>"
sXMLDoc = sXMLDoc & "<OrderDetails OrderID='10283' " & _
        "ProductID='72' Quantity='3'/>"
sXMLDoc = sXMLDoc & "</Orders>"
sXMLDoc = sXMLDoc & "</Customers>"
sXMLDoc = sXMLDoc & "</ROOT>"
```

Next we simply invoke the stored procedure from a `Command` object, and return the data to a `Recordset` object:

```
'--- Invoke the stored procedure
sQuery = "spOpenXML"
Set oCmd = Server.CreateObject("ADODB.Command")
Set oCmd.ActiveConnection = oCn
oCmd.CommandText = sQuery
oCmd.CommandType = adCmdStoredProc
oCmd.Parameters.Item("@sXML").Value = sXMLDoc
```

And finally we loop through the `Recordset` object in server-side code to display the data to the browser as HMTL:

```
'--- Write the data set back out to the client via a Recordset
Set oRs = oCmd.Execute()

Response.Write "<ul>"
Do While Not oRs.Eof
   Response.Write "<li>"
   For i = 0 to oRs.Fields.Count - 1
      Response.Write oRs(i) & _
         "        "
   Next
   Response.Write "</li>"
   oRs.MoveNext
Loop
Response.Write "</ul>"

oRs.Close
oCn.Close
Set oRs = Nothing
Set oCmd = Nothing
Set oCn = Nothing
%>
</HEAD>
<BODY>
</BODY>
</HTML>
```

The result is a list of the orders our chosen customers – Paul Henriot and Carlos Gonzlez – have made.

Returning XML

Notice that we returned the data as a SQL data set from this stored procedure. So we could take this data and return it back to an ADO `Recordset` object. However, if we simply add the line `FOR XML AUTO` to the end of the query, we could send back an XML document in return. So as you can see, there are several ways we can mix SQL and XLM data.

```
ALTER PROCEDURE spOpenXML2
    @sXML VARCHAR(2000)
AS

DECLARE @iDoc INT

-- Prepare the XML document for SQL Server
EXEC sp_xml_preparedocument @iDoc OUTPUT, @sXML

-- Query the XML data set joined to a SQL Server table
SELECT    Customer.CustomerID,
    Customer.ContactName,
    Orders.OrderID,
    Orders.OrderDate
FROM OPENXML(@iDoc, '/ROOT/Customers', 1)
    WITH (CustomerID varchar(10), ContactName varchar(20))
    AS Customer
    INNER JOIN Orders ON Customer.CustomerID = Orders.CustomerID
FOR XML AUTO

-- Remove the internal representation of the XML document.
EXEC sp_xml_removedocument @iDoc

GO
```

The ASP code below demonstrates how we could pass XML to this stored procedure (spOpenXML2) and return an XML document back instead of a SQL data set going into a `Recordset` object. The only difference in this ASP/ADO code is that we indicate that the `Output Stream` of the `Command` object should be a stream: the ASP `Response` object. Then we write the data to an XML data island and we display the data using client-side VBScript code (ch13_ex12.asp).

```
<%@LANGUAGE=VBSCRIPT%>
<HTML>
<HEAD>
<TITLE>ADO 2.6 OpenXML Returning XML Example - ch13_ex12.asp</TITLE>
<!-- #include file="adovbs.inc" -->
<%
    Dim oCmd
    Dim oCn
    Dim sConn
    Dim sProvider
    Dim sQuery
    Dim sXMLDoc

    '--- Open the connection to the database
    sProvider = "SQLOLEDB"
    sConn = "Data Source=(local);Initial Catalog=Northwind;User ID=sa"
    Set oCn = Server.CreateObject("ADODB.Connection")
    oCn.Provider = sProvider
    oCn.ConnectionString = sConn
    oCn.CursorLocation = adUseClient
    oCn.Open
```

```
'--- Prepare the XML document to pass in to the stored procedure
sXMLDoc = "<ROOT>"
sXMLDoc = sXMLDoc & "<Customers CustomerID='VINET' " & _
    "ContactName='Paul Henriot'>"
sXMLDoc = sXMLDoc & "<Orders CustomerID='VINET' " & _
    "EmployeeID='5' OrderDate='1996-07-04T00:00:00'>"
sXMLDoc = sXMLDoc & "<OrderDetails OrderID='10248' " & _
    "ProductID='11' Quantity='12'/>"
sXMLDoc = sXMLDoc & "<OrderDetails OrderID='10248' " & _
    "ProductID='42' Quantity='10'/>"
sXMLDoc = sXMLDoc & "</Orders>"
sXMLDoc = sXMLDoc & "</Customers>"
sXMLDoc = sXMLDoc & "<Customers CustomerID='LILAS' " & _
    "ContactName='Carlos Gonzlez'>"
sXMLDoc = sXMLDoc & "<Orders CustomerID='LILAS' " & _
    "EmployeeID='3' OrderDate='1996-08-16T00:00:00'>"
sXMLDoc = sXMLDoc & "<OrderDetails OrderID='10283' " & _
    "ProductID='72' Quantity='3'/>"
sXMLDoc = sXMLDoc & "</Orders>"
sXMLDoc = sXMLDoc & "</Customers>"
sXMLDoc = sXMLDoc & "</ROOT>"

'--- Invoke the stored procedure
sQuery = "spOpenXML2"
Set oCmd = Server.CreateObject("ADODB.Command")
Set oCmd.ActiveConnection = oCn
oCmd.CommandText = sQuery
oCmd.CommandType = adCmdStoredProc
oCmd.Parameters.Item("@sXML").Value = sXMLDoc

'--- Write the XML data set back out to the client
oCmd.Properties("Output Stream") = Response
Response.Write "<XML ID='MyDataIsle'><ROOT>"
oCmd.Execute , , adExecuteStream
Response.Write "</ROOT></XML>"
oCn.Close
Set oCmd = Nothing
Set oCn = Nothing
%>

<SCRIPT language="VBScript" For="window" Event="onload">
    Dim oXML
    Dim oRoot
    Dim oChild
    Dim sOutputXML

    Set oXML = MyDataIsle.XMLDocument
    oXML.resolveExternals=false
    oXML.async=false

    Set oRoot = oXML.documentElement

    For each oChild in oRoot.childNodes
        sOutputXML = document.all("log").innerHTML
        document.all("log").innerHTML = sOutputXML & "<LI>" & _
            oChild.getAttribute("ContactName") & "</LI>"
    Next
    Set oXML = Nothing
    Set oRoot = Nothing
    Set oChild = Nothing
```

```
    </SCRIPT>
    </HEAD>
    <BODY>
        <center>
        <hr>
        <H2>ADO 2.6 OpenXML Returning XML Example - ch13_ex12.asp</H2>
        <hr>

        <H3>Client-side processing of XML Document MyDataIsle</H3>
        </center>

        <UL id=log>
        </UL>
    </BODY>
    </HTML>
```

This just returns us the bulleted list containing the two customers we specified: Paul Henriot and Carlos Gonzlez.

Inserting Data

The examples using the OpenXML function we've shown thus far, have demonstrated how we can query an XML data set inside of a stored procedure and even join it to a standard SQL data set. However, we can also pass an XML data set into a stored procedure that could insert its records into a SQL table. Let's look at the T-SQL in the stored procedure that would handle this for us (spOpenXML_Insert):

```
ALTER PROCEDURE spOpenXML_Insert
    @sXML VARCHAR(2000)
AS

DECLARE @iDoc INT

-- Prepare the XML document for SQL Server
EXEC sp_xml_preparedocument @iDoc OUTPUT, @sXML

INSERT Territories
SELECT    TerritoryID, TerritoryDescription, RegionID
FROM OPENXML(@iDoc, '/ROOT/Territories', 1)
    WITH (TerritoryID nvarchar(20), TerritoryDescription nchar(50), RegionID INT)

-- Remove the internal representation of the XML document.
EXEC sp_xml_removedocument @iDoc

GO
```

Notice that we pass in an XML document and we use the OpenXML ... WITH statement to translate the XML data to a data set that SQL Server can use in the INSERT query. In the end, we are inserting a series of new territories into the Territory table from an XML document. Now, let's look at the ASP/ADO code that call the sp_OpenXML_Insert stored procedure (ch13_ex13.asp):

```
<HTML>
<HEAD>
<TITLE>ADO 2.6 OpenXML Insert Example - ch13_ex13.asp</TITLE>
<!-- #include file="adovbs.inc" -->
<%
    dim i
    Dim oCmd
```

```
        Dim oCn
        Dim sConn
        Dim sProvider
        Dim sQuery
        Dim sXMLDoc

        '--- Open the connection to the database
        sProvider = "SQLOLEDB"
        sConn = "Data Source=(local);Initial Catalog=Northwind;User ID=sa"
        Set oCn = Server.CreateObject("ADODB.Connection")
        oCn.Provider = sProvider
        oCn.ConnectionString = sConn
        oCn.CursorLocation = adUseClient
        oCn.Open

        '--- Prepare the XML document to pass in to the stored procedure
        sXMLDoc = "<ROOT>"
        sXMLDoc = sXMLDoc & "<Territories TerritoryID='77777' " & _
            "TerritoryDescription='Nowhereville' RegionID='1'/>"
        sXMLDoc = sXMLDoc & "<Territories TerritoryID='88888' " & _
            "TerritoryDescription='Somewhere Town' RegionID='2'/>"
        sXMLDoc = sXMLDoc & "<Territories TerritoryID='99999' " & _
            "TerritoryDescription='Anywherebuthere' RegionID='3'/>"
        sXMLDoc = sXMLDoc & "</ROOT>"

        '--- Invoke the stored procedure
        sQuery = "spOpenXML_Insert"
        Set oCmd = Server.CreateObject("ADODB.Command")
        Set oCmd.ActiveConnection = oCn
        oCmd.CommandText = sQuery
        oCmd.CommandType = adCmdStoredProc
        oCmd.Parameters.Item("@sXML").Value = sXMLDoc

        '--- Insert the data
        oCmd.Execute

        oCn.Close
        Set oCmd = Nothing
        Set oCn = Nothing
%>
</HEAD>
<BODY>
    <center>
    <hr>
    <h3>ADO 2.6 OpenXML Insert Example - ch13_ex13.asp</h3>
    <hr>
    </center>
</BODY>
</HTML>
```

Here we are passing in an XML document that contains a list of three territories. We'll then pass these new territories to the stored procedure and execute via the Command.Execute method. In this case, we have no return data to display, but we could have returned data, let's say, to show an updated list containing all of the territories.

To run this, you'll need to execute a command like:

```
http://localhost/XMLDB/ch13_ex13.asp?sql=select%20'<xml>';select%20*%20from%20terr
itories%20where%20territoryid='77777'%20or%20territoryid='88888'%20or%20territoryi
d='99999'%20for%20xml%20auto;select%20'</xml>'
```

That wraps up our look at the currect features available in ADO for working with XML. Around the corner, however, there are exciting new features that will be made available by ADO+. To help you prepare for these, we shall have a brief preview of this new technology.

ADO+

At the time of writing, the Microsoft.NET initiative has been revealed at conferences and on the Internet. There is a tremendous amount of energy surrounding this and for good reason. In any event, the .NET strategy will have significant impact on the development community. I had the privilege of working on this effort in the data and XML area.

This section attempts to give a "cameo" appearance to one of the many new emerging technologies stemming from that effort. A technology that is well related to this book: ADO+.

ADO+ is a piece of a larger framework including but not limited to ASP+. The following will not address the entirety of the new framework (including but not limited to new languages, new compilers and new systems) but rather will focus on the interoperability between classic database access and XML.

Evolution

A quick note should be made regarding the evolution of database access technologies. These will stem from a Microsoft perspective, as the author is most familiar with these (for good or for bad). Aside from proprietary API's (DBLIB, etc), DAO was the first automation library to address database access. Based primarily on a single tier system, DAO was targeted at Access databases. It was later evolved to work with 2-tier systems. However, a solution architected for the client/server world, ADO, soon followed to address the nature of 2-tier data access. Ambiguous as it was, ADO was also soon swept along with the next architecture wave and was also evolved within its domain to address the issues of 3 or n-tier systems. The introduction of the Remote Recordset was an example of dealing with the statelessness of the Web.

To better address the inherent distributed architecture of the Web a ground up approach was to design the next evolution of data access: ADO+. ADO+ was developed to address the tiered, or message based architecture of the Web.

The Idea

The founding of ADO+ relied on specific technologies for specific applications. ADO (classic) provided an automation API for abstracted database access for client server systems. Despite this, some found it difficult to apply the technology specifically. Often, when delivering data, in forms such as XML, the database is much more distant than the data itself. One of the main thrusts behind ADO+ was to be simple and targeted. When interfacing with databases, speak the language of databases; when interfacing with abstract data types, speak the language of abstract data types. ADO+ addresses these by properly fragmenting the technologies and allowing the developer to focus on the "lingo" specific to the job, without mixing metaphors so to say.

First we will introduce the new objects of the ADO+ framework. Next we will use those objects practically to expose the uniqueness of the solution in an isolated environment, only hinting at the actual application of such through sample. Finally, we will expose some of the exciting new tools that allow sleek and novel exposure to the rest of the world through the Internet.

Disclaimer

The content of this chapter was based on early designs of ADO+, and is not necessarily consistent with the beta or final version of the product. Please be advised that the code may change.

The ADO+ Framework

Part of a larger framework, the ADO+ technologies introduce simple, targeted objects to access data, update data, and interoperate with XML. The primary objects are: `DataSet`, `DataSetCommand` (and the `Command`), and `Connection`. The following is a quick overview of the objects, followed by a detailed look at each of them.

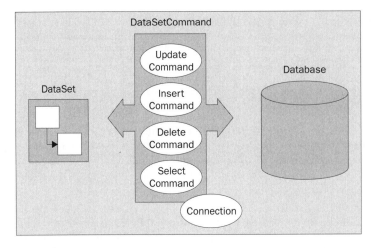

The diagram is intended to illustrate one potential model for the ADO+ objects.

DataSet

A new object in the ADO family is the `DataSet` object. Think of the `DataSet` object as a tiny, in memory database that stores data. A `DataSet` can store many pieces of data. For example, a good example of a `DataSet` is a `PurchaseOrderDataSet`. It stores information about customers, orders, order details, status, etc. All of the data can and is stored in one object. It is like a remote `Recordset` object without any database notions. It is easy to remote (as it remotes in XML) and it is easy to program. The `DataSet` also tracks changes made to its internal data. We will go into more detail on the `DataSet` object later.

Connection

The `Connection` (or `ADOConnection`) is familiar and parallel to the classic `ADO Connection` object. However, it, has a more targeted and simple job: to connect `DataSetCommands` (and commands) to ADO databases. The reason why I refer to these as ADO databases, is because the `ADOConnection` object is compatible with OLEDB. ADO+ allows the developer to circumvent the ADO abstraction, meaning, that there also exists a `SQLConnection` object also. Although you can use the `ADOConnection` object to talk to MS-SQL Server databases, the `SQLConnection` object speaks natively to MS-SQL Server, without going through the many layers of ADO that provide database abstraction at the connection and command level, thus it is more efficient. This is an example of targeted objects that I mentioned before.

DataSetCommand

The `DataSetCommand` is the object that *pushes* data into a `DataSet` from a Database. It also can *pull* changes from a `DataSet` and *push* them into a database. I purposefully use the push word here to indicate a shift in data access architectures. This is a push model (where data is pushed in a chunk into a data structure), not a pull model (where data is pulled from a stream on demand or sometimes without developer control, that is, `MoveNext`). The `DataSetCommand` is made up of four Commands:

- ❑ `SelectCommand`
- ❑ `UpdateCommand`
- ❑ `InsertCommand`
- ❑ `DeleteCommand`

These Commands are similar to the ADO commands, with some of the same themes as the connection object: simple and targeted. The ADO+ Command, like the ADO Command, defines that which is executed against a database, including `CommandText` and `Parameters`, for example. Though you can use a Command standalone to get at a stream of data, the `DataSetCommand` allows the developer to establish `Select`, `Insert`, `Update` and `Delete` Commands for your set of data. And, just like the connection, the `DataSetCommand` is technology specific: both the `ADODataSetCommand`, and the `SQLDataSetCommand` are provided.

DataSet

As mentioned before, the `DataSet` stores the data. It knows *nothing* about where the data is coming from, or where the data is going. A `DataSet` has a collection of tables. Tables have a collection of columns and data. Relationships can also be expressed between tables. It can be compared to a "never connected" recordset in the sense that it never talks to a database, a subtle but important distinction. The importance of not communicating with the databases is that there is no technology specific baggage within the `DataSet` to slow down its function. The `DataSet` is platform neutral and the data it stores is not database type specific. The `DataSet` stores types native to the Microsoft.NET framework. (Note: The default set of types in the `DataSet` is those of the framework and of XML. You can define your own types, like `SQLTinyInt`).

One advantage to the `DataSet` is that it can have both characteristics of, and work well with, a normalized relational database and have characteristics of hierarchical or semi-structure XML documents. You will soon see how the `DataSet` begins to bridge the gap between the XML Web world and traditional corporate databases.

The `DataSet` was not necessarily designed for streaming large amounts of data. Though it can perform well at caching larger amounts of read-only data (and is multi-threaded for read-only scenarios such as cached stock quotes), and there are properties for anticipating the size of the data to improve performance, the standalone `Command` object is best suited for streaming data. The `Command` object provides interfaces for streaming read-only forward only data.

Schema

In order for a `DataSet` to store data, the `DataSet` must have a schema. `DataSet` schemas can be constructed in code, via XML and from `CommandSets`; the `DataSet` can also infer schema from data, so it is not always necessary to construct schema. However, one can simply define a `DataSet` and start adding schemas via the collections.

Note: You will see a lot of syntax that is new to VB.NET including fully qualified library names, constructors, object assignment without using Set, and many others in the samples. This code can and will compile under VB.NET only. The code from this chapter can be found in two files in the download - ch13_ex01plus.aspx and ch13_ex02plus.aspx

```
Dim dsPurchaseOrder as New DataSet()
dsPurchaseOrder.Tables.Add("Customers")
dsPurchaseOrder.Tables.Add("Orders")
```

The code fragment above establishes a data type to store purchase order data. We have added two tables, `Customers` and `Orders`. Next, using the Tables collection on the `DataSet` and the `Columns` collection on `Table` we can add the columns to the tables to describe the data types and column names.

```
dsPurchaseOrder.Tables("Customers").Columns.Add("CustomerId",GetType(System.Int32)
)
dsPurchaseOrder.Tables("Customers").Columns.Add("CustomerName",GetType(System.Stri
ng))

dsPurchaseOrder.Tables("Orders").Columns.Add("OrderId",GetType(System.Int32))
dsPurchaseOrder.Tables("Orders").Columns.Add("CustomerId",GetType(System.Int32))
dsPurchaseOrder.Tables("Orders").Columns.Add("OrderStatus",GetType(System.String))
dsPurchaseOrder.Tables("Orders").Columns.Add("OrderDate",GetType(System.Date))

dsPurchaseOrder.Tables("Customers").Columns("CustomerId").AutoIncrement=True
dsPurchaseOrder.Tables("Orders").Columns("OrderId").AutoIncrement=True
```

Notice that in defining the columns we also define the types. This is because, unlike previous Variant based data access models, the ADO+ has a vertical internal storage model. This means that instead of storing data arrays of rows (where data can differ between columns, thus forcing a Variant model), the `DataSet` stores data in arrays of columns, preserving the type of the data, as well as increasing efficiencies in storage and performance. Also, we set `AutoIncrement` properties on the keys to `True`. This is so they will automatically assign a new ID to each new Customer and to each new Order. Note: the ID assignment (autoincrement) is internal to the `DataSet` only. When, however, using `DataSet` commands, the IDs are synched with the `Dataset`.

Notice that in our purchase order `DataSet` above, we have established the data to store customers and orders. However, wouldn't it be nice to describe a relation between these two tables and implement relational support typically found in databases, like cascading deletes and updates, and other constraints?

In our `Orders` table there exists a column: `CustomerId`. This is to establish the foreign key to the `Customer` table (note: XML typically establishes relations through hierarchies. The `DataSet` supports this functionality and hides the foreign key from the schema). To add the relationship, we can use the following method:

```
dsPurchaseOrder.Relations.Add(dsPurchaseOrder.Tables("Customers").Columns("Custome
rId"),_ dsPurchaseOrder.Tables("Orders").Columns("CustomerId"),True)
```

The last flag in the call, `True`, creates the constraints between the two tables.

Now that we have our `DataSet` with its schema we can start adding data. Data can be added in many ways (as well as through schemas, both to be discussed as the chapter goes on). Data is stored in rows. First you construct a `Row`, and then you add it to the `DataSet` table. A helper function on the `Table` object, `NewRow()` is used to construct and allocate a new `Row` object. The reason why it is on the table, and needs to be done this way, is that the schema for the `Row` needs to match the schema of the other rows in the tables. The `NewRow()` function creates the `Row` with appropriate schema. The following code will add a customer to the `DataSet`.

```
Dim rowCustomer as DataRow
rowCustomer = dsPurchaseOrder.Tables("Customers").NewRow()
rowCustomer.Item("CustomerName") = "Kelly"
dsPurchaseOrder.Tables("Customers").Rows.Add(rowCustomer)
```

So, we created a row, set a data point in the `Row`, and then added it to the tables `Rows` collection. Notice that I did not set the `CustomerId`, as I had originally established this as a column that AutoIncrements. (Later, when we reconcile this with the databases, the database will assign a new key, but all of the data and related data will stay intact.)

When a one-to-many relationship is established as was done here, not only can we keep the data organized in such a manner, but we can also access it relationally. To add orders to the customer record, we use the child row of the `Customer` row. Again we will not set the `PrimaryKey`, and we will not have to set the `ForeignKey` (`CustomerId`) either. The following code adds to order rows to the Customer "Kelly".

```
Dim rowOrder as DataRow
rowOrder = dsPurchaseOrder.Tables("Orders").NewRow()
rowOrder.Item("OrderDate") = "07/26/00"
rowOrder.Item("OrderStatus") = "New"
rowOrder.Item("CustomerId") =
dsPurchaseOrder.Tables("Customers").Rows(0)("CustomerId")
dsPurchaseOrder.Tables("Orders").Rows.Add(rowOrder)
rowOrder = dsPurchaseOrder.Tables("Orders").NewRow()
rowOrder.Item("OrderDate") = "10/21/00"
rowOrder.Item("OrderStatus") = "Deleted"
rowOrder.Item("CustomerId") =
dsPurchaseOrder.Tables("Customers").Rows(0)("CustomerId")
dsPurchaseOrder.Tables("Orders").Rows.Add(rowOrder)
```

By setting the `CustomerId` field in the `Order` record to the same value as the `CustomerId` field in the `Customers` record we created previously, we indicate that it is related to the customer. We can then easily iterate over the orders for every customer using the `For Each` syntax.

```
For Each rowCustomer in dsPurchaseOrder.Tables("Customers").Rows
    Response.Write("<br>" & rowCustomer("CustomerName"))
    Response.Write("<br><blockquote>")
    For Each rowOrder in rowCustomer.GetChildRows("rel1")
        Response.Write("<BR>" & rowOrder("OrderStatus") & " " &
rowOrder("OrderDate"))
    Next
    Response.Write("</blockquote>")
Next
```

The output of the above code is the following:

```
<br>Kelly<br><blockquote><BR>New 7/26/2000<BR>Deleted 10/21/2000</blockquote>
```

or

```
Kelly
   New 7/26/2000
   Deleted 10/21/2000
```

Accessing and changing data is done by simply setting the new value. You can access the particular column through name or ordinal.

```
dsPurchaseOrder.Tables("Customers").Rows(0)("CustomerName") = "Kelly Smith"
```

Realize, though, that when you are programming against a DataSet (as seen above), you are only changing the data in the DataSet, you will need to submit those changes to a database in order to store them. Note that you, the developer, are in control of when and if that happens. Also remember that this is not a variant based model, and that a string is expecting a string, that is, a database or function will not be doing the type-checking later – this is done by the run time.

When changes are made such as the change to the column above, or adding a new row, or deleting a row (DeleteRow not illustrated here), the DataSet is tracking all of these changes. This is so that at some point and time, you can extract these changes and apply them elsewhere. The DataSet has its own internal commit and rollback model also (AcceptChanges, RejectChanges and even GetChanges to see them) As is the case of the web and databases, this usually means that changes are submitted to a queue, another web server, or a component. And since these changes can be formatted in XML, it is easy to go cross platform as well. The format of the XML in the GetChanges() method is compliant with SQL Server 2000 XML "updateGrams".

```
Response.Write(dsPurchaseOrder.GetChanges().XMLData)
```

GetChanges() returns another DataSet that represents the changes made in the dsPurchaseOrder Dataset since the last AcceptChanges was called, or since it was created. Also, the XMLData property can be used as the updategram for the SQL server. Using the XMLData method, we get an XML representation of the DataSet. The output is shown below:

```
<DocumentElement>
   <Customers>
      <CustomerId>0</CustomerId>
      <CustomerName>Kelly Smith</CustomerName>
   </Customers>
   <Orders>
      <OrderId>0</OrderId>
      <CustomerId>0</CustomerId>
      <OrderStatus>New</OrderStatus>
      <OrderDate>2000-07-26T07:00:00</OrderDate>
   </Orders>
   <Orders>
      <OrderId>1</OrderId>
      <CustomerId>0</CustomerId>
      <OrderStatus>Deleted</OrderStatus>
      <OrderDate>2000-10-21T07:00:00</OrderDate>
   </Orders>
</DocumentElement>
```

Note that if a value is NULL, then it will effectively not exist, so would not be returned as an element or attribute in the above method.

Finally, to round out the discussion on the `DataSet`, and to provide some context to the rest of this book, the `DataSet` was intended to interoperate smoothly with XML. The `DataSet` can easily show XML, stream in and out XML, express changes in XML and even compile from XML schema (discussed later).

To create an XML document from a `DataSet` you can use one of three methods: `XMLData`, `XMLSchema` and `XML`

```
'display the XML
Response.write(dsPurchaseOrder.XMLData)

'To write the schema use
Response.Write(dsPurchaseOrder.XMLSchema)

To Write them both use
Response.Write(dsPurchaseOrder.XML)
```

The output of the `XML property` (which is `XMLSchema` and `XMLData` combined) is as follows:

XMLSchema

```
<schema id="" targetNamespace="" xmlns="http://www.w3.org/1999/XMLSchema"
xmlns:msdata="urn:schemas-microsoft-com:xml-msdata">
  <element name="Customers">
    <complexType content="elementOnly">
      <all>
        <element name="CustomerId" msdata:AutoIncrement="True" minOccurs="0"
type="int"/>
        <element name="CustomerName" minOccurs="0" type="string"/>
      </all>
    </complexType>
    <unique name="Constraint1">
      <selector>.</selector>
      <field>CustomerId</field>
    </unique>
  </element>
  <element name="Orders">
    <complexType content="elementOnly">
      <all>
        <element name="OrderId" msdata:AutoIncrement="True" minOccurs="0"
type="int"/>
        <element name="CustomerId" minOccurs="0" type="int"/>
        <element name="OrderStatus" minOccurs="0" type="string"/>
        <element name="OrderDate" minOccurs="0" type="timeInstant"/>
      </all>
    </complexType>
    <keyref name="rel1" refer="Constraint1">
      <selector>.</selector>
      <field>CustomerId</field>
    </keyref>
  </element>
</schema>
```

XMLData

```
<DocumentElement>
  <Customers>
    <CustomerId>0</CustomerId>
    <CustomerName>Kelly Smith</CustomerName>
  <Orders>
    <OrderId>0</OrderId>
    <CustomerId>0</CustomerId>
    <OrderStatus>New</OrderStatus>
    <OrderDate>2000-07-26T07:00:00</OrderDate>
  </Orders>
  <Orders>
    <OrderId>1</OrderId>
    <CustomerId>0</CustomerId>
    <OrderStatus>Deleted</OrderStatus>
    <OrderDate>2000-10-21T07:00:00</OrderDate>
  </Orders>
  </Customers>
</DocumentElement>
```

In order to get the data nested within customers as above, set the Nested property on the DataRelation to True. This will create the Nested XML data (orders nested within customers).

Having XML native to the DataSet is very powerful. Once data is pushed into a dataset, either by code or by DataSetCommands, the data is now interoperable with many technologies including SOAP, the WEB, XSL, and even cross platform. It is the best example of abstracting data away from databases. To fully understand some of these concepts, let's use a DataSetCommand to push data into a DataSet and then display it as an XML Document. First, let's discuss the DataSetCommand (the Connection).

The DataSetCommand and the Connection Objects

As mentioned in the overview, the DataSetCommand uses the Connection object to fill DataSets. It also can reconcile DataSet changes.

Constructing a Connection object is simple and familiar to ADO programmers. The ConnectionString property and the Open method are used to establish the connection. In these examples I will use the SQLConnection object and the SQLDataSetCommand object.

VB

```
Dim sqlConnection as New SQLConnection("server=(local);uid=sa;database=northwind")
sqlConnection.Open()
```

I took the liberty here of leveraging the constructor, instead of setting the ConnectionString. A constructor is a convenient way to set primary properties on an object when creating it. I also opened the connection, which would be done by the DataSetCommand on fillDataSet if the connection were closed, but is done explicitly in the example for clarity. Opening the connection explicitly gives the developer more control over lifetime, and gives access to transactions (different of course, from the DataSets).

The DataSetCommand has four commands: insert, update, delete and select. The DataSet command is intended to handle all operations against a database. Because these objects are typically stateless, it is suggested that, if updates are going to occur, that the DataSetCommands Insert, Update and Delete commands are set up by the developer in code. If they are not set, they will be constructed at run-time if needed, which can be costly for stateless objects.

Additionally, proper architectures call for stored procedures. Setting each of the commands to point to stored procedures can also be done and parameters are established in the same way as in classic ADO Commands.

For this example, I am going simply set the Select statement to an SQL statement.

```
Dim dsCommandSet as New SQLDataSetCommand("select * from customers",sqlConnection)
```

Notice that I set the Select Command's `CommandText` and `ActiveConnection` in the constructor. Constructors are great shortcuts for setting often used properties. Now we can use this `DataSetCommand` to push Data into the `DataSet`. As indicated, this is a push model - in order to remind the developer of its push nature, the APIs reflect the action well: `FillDataSet`.

```
Dim dsCustomers as new DataSet
dsCommandSet.FillDataSet(dsCustomers,"Customers")
```

The `FillDataSet` method is that which makes everything happen. It opens a cursor, reads the data, and pushes into the `DataSet`. Once in the `DataSet` it is completely disconnected from the database. Notice that I didn't establish any schema in the `DataSet`. However, I did tell it the table name to create in the second parameter `Customers`. If there exists no schema, the `DataSetCommand` will create it for you. If schema does exist, you may need to map schema to schema (for example `CustId` -> `CustomerId`) if there are mismatches. See the `MissingSchemaAction` property in the SDK documentation for more details on how and when the `DataSet` creates schema, if at all.

The `FillDataSet` method executed the `SelectCommand` (the command object on the `DataSetCommand`) and pushed Schema and Data into the `Dataset`. We can now look at the schema and the Data.

```
'Look at schema
dim t as DataTable
dim c as DataColumn

For Each t in dsCustomers.Tables
    Response.Write("<br>" & t.TableName)
    Response.Write("<BlockQuote>")
    For Each c in t.columns
        Response.Write("<br>" & c.ColumnName)
    Next
    Response.Write("</blockquote>")
Next

'look at data
response.write("<P><TABLE><TR>")
dim rowTemp as DataRow
For Each rowTemp in dsCustomers.Tables("Customers").Rows
    Response.write("<tr>")
    For Each c in dsCustomers.Tables("Customers").Columns
        response.write("<TD>" & rowTemp(c) & "</td>")
    Next
    Response.write("</tr>")
Next
Response.Write("</table>")
```

Notice that I interleaved HTML throughout the code to get a more uniform output, as seen in the following screenshots:

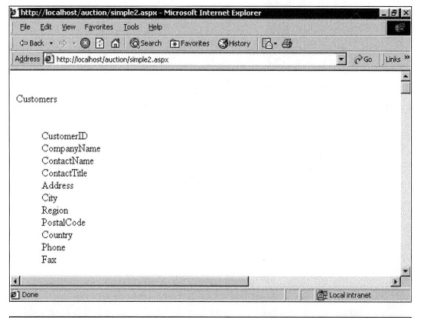

We could further push more data from `DataSetCommands`, or add more data in. We can than move and program against all of the data as one unit. Instead of having a `Customers` recordset, and `Orders` recordset, and one `OrderDetails` recordset, we have one `PurchaseOrder DataSet`

Now, suppose we wanted to write a function to return the set of customers in XML format. There are two ways to do this: `string` and `DataSet`.

When working with the .NET framework you can easily move `DataSets` around because they are inherently disconnected. We can write a function that returns our dataset:

```
Public Function GetCustomersList() as DataSet
Dim sqlConnection as New SQLConnection("server=(local);uid=sa;database=northwind
")
Dim dsCommandSet as New SQLDataSetCommand("select * from customers",sqlConnection)
Dim dsCustomers as new DataSet

    dsCommandSet.FillDataSet(dsCustomers,"Customers")
    GetCustomersList = dsCustomers

End Function
```

Applications can expose `DataSets` in this manner. However, a useful side-effect of `DataSets` is that when used as a Web Service, they expose XML. A Web Service in this context can be summed up as a function that can be called from the Web (from an HTTP request). By attributing the above function as a Web function, a URL is created to route the request from the function.

> *It is not clear at the time of this writing how and what attributes will be required. Attributes are a new concept to VB and decorate a function or code with more meaning without polluting the language.*

When the function is invoked by another .NET component, a `DataSet` is returned. When the function is invoked by a non-.NET component, the data is returned as an XML document.

If you simply want to force the return of XML in a string format, declare the function as `String`, and then return `dsCustomers.XMLData`.

If changes are made to the `DataSet` that is filled by a `DataSetCommand`, that same `DataSetCommand` can reconcile those changes with the Database, using the `Update` method.

```
dsCommandSet.FillDataSet(dsCustomers,"Customers")

dsCustomers.tables("customers").Rows(0)("CompanyName") = "foo"
'...
'Remote the dataset
'send it in mail
'change it in any way
'at some point send it back and then
'...
dsCommandSet.Update(dsCustomers,"Customers")
```

If you have stored procedures or SQL statements associated with the `insert`/`update` and `delete` commands, these will fire appropriately when the `update` method is invoked. You also have the ability to just send the changes (using the `GetChanges` method on the `DataSet`), as the `Update` method simply ignores rows that haven't been changed.

Typeness of DataSet

Not only does the `DataSet` have internal typed storage, but there are also some nice tools to create typed accessors customized to your schema. These typed accessors are further help in obtaining compile time type checking bugs instead of run-time; which overcomes a great source of stress in the current variant-based data access models.

The idea behind a typed accessor for a `DataSet` is, that you can program directly against the tables and columns through the name and type of data structure (that is, `Customer(0).FirstName`). So if, as before, we wanted to access the data in our "generic" `Dataset`, we would use notation such as the following:

Just to get at the data, you can access the objects by tables and column names (there is a default 0 based index property, as well as `PrimaryKey` property).

```
Response.Write(dsPurchaseOrders.Customers(0).FirstName)
'Or
Response.Write(dsPurchaseOrders.Customers.PrimaryKey(10001010).FirstName
```

It is also very clean when you iterate through the relationships. We can now use the following syntax:

```
For each Customer in dsPurchaseOrders.Customers
    For Each Order in Customer.Orders
        Response.Write(Order.OrderDate)
    Next
Next
```

These typed accessors are available essentially through code wrappers only. However, there are some very nice tools, which allow easy and efficient creation of them. The first tool is that of the language. VB.NET introduces some new object oriented programming techniques such as, and most important for this discussion, inheritance. By inheriting from `System.Data.DataSet`, we can easily add accessors to the columns and tables allowing inherited calls to pass through to the parent `Dataset` objects.

Visual Studio 7 introduces a new XML Schema designer used to create XML schema and data. The tool allows for many scenarios, including mapping databases to XML schema, creating XML schema from databases, etc. Once the format is in XML Schema, a code generator (`xsd.exe`) can be invoked to create the classes that inherit from `DataSet` and provide the typed accessors mentioned above. This code generator is part of the framework and can be used to form the command line, as illustrated here.

The executable simply generates a wrapper class that inherits from `DataSet`, and has accessors consistent with the schema of the XML, including relationships (interpreted from hierarchies or schema). This class, when included with your project, will provide the programming model as sampled above. Using the `DataSet` created above against the customers table in the database, I grabbed the `.XMLSchema` property and created a file:

```
C:\>customers.xsd

<schema id="" targetNamespace="" xmlns="http://www.w3.org/1999/XMLSchema"
xmlns:msdata="urn:schemas-microsoft-com:xml-msdata">
<element name="Customers">
   <complexType content="elementOnly">
   <all>
      <element name="CustomerID" type="string"/>
      <element name="CompanyName" type="string"/>
```

```
            <element name="ContactName" minOccurs="0" type="string"/>
            <element name="ContactTitle" minOccurs="0" type="string"/>
            <element name="Address" minOccurs="0" type="string"/>
            <element name="City" minOccurs="0" type="string"/>
            <element name="Region" minOccurs="0" type="string"/>
            <element name="PostalCode" minOccurs="0" type="string"/>
            <element name="Country" minOccurs="0" type="string"/>
            <element name="Phone" minOccurs="0" type="string"/>
            <element name="Fax" minOccurs="0" type="string"/>
        </all>
        </complexType>
    </element>
    </schema>
```

Notice the database schema generated an XML (XSD versioned) schema. The class generator, XSD, can be found in the \bin directory of the FrameworksSDK. This will generate both general classes (using the /c switch) and subsetted Dataset classes (using the /d switch), as seen below.

```
C:\>xsd.exe customers.xsd /d

'NOTE THIS IS NOT ALL OF THE CODE GENERATED, JUST SAMPLE WRAPPERS

Public Class CustomersRow
    Inherits DataRow

    Private tableCustomers As Customers

    …


    Public Overloads Overridable Function AddCustomersRow( _
    ByVal columnCustomerID As String, _
    ByVal columnCompanyName As String, _
    ByVal columnContactName As String, _
    ByVal columnContactTitle As String, _
    ByVal columnAddress As String, _
    ByVal columnCity As String, _
    ByVal columnRegion As String, _
    ByVal columnPostalCode As String, _
    ByVal columnCountry As String, _
    ByVal columnPhone As String, _
    ByVal columnFax As String) As CustomersRow

    Dim rowCustomersRow As CustomersRow
    rowCustomersRow = CType(Me.NewRow,CustomersRow)
    rowCustomersRow.ItemArray = New [Object]() {
    columnCustomerID, _
    columnCompanyName, _
    columnContactName, _
    columnContactTitle, _
    columnAddress, _
    columnCity, _
    columnRegion, _
    columnPostalCode, _
    columnCountry, _
    columnPhone, _
    columnFax}
    Me.Rows.Add(rowCustomersRow)
    Return rowCustomersRow
End Function
```

```
Public Overridable Property Address As String
    Get
        Return CType(Me(Me.tableCustomers.AddressColumn),String)
    End Get
    Set
        Me(Me.tableCustomers.AddressColumn) = value
    End Set
End Property
```

The above code illustrates some of the accessors that are generated. These include:

```
MyDataSet.Customers.CustomersRow
MyDataSet.Customers.AddCustomersRow([ID],[Name],[etc])
MyDataSet.Customers(0).Address
```

I encourage you to use the generator and explore the code, or use the generator and use statement completion in the Visual Studio editor to explore. These classes can help expose the schemas that you export to other developers, easily and quickly.

Summary

Throughout this chapter we've examined a series of topics all revolving around XML support within ADO 2.6 and SQL Server 2000. As we've seen, there are quite a few techniques now at our disposal that we can employ to integrate XML into our applications.

We've discussed:

❑ How to persist data to files and streams of different sorts.

❑ How to query SQL data without writing any SQL, via the XPath and Mapping Schema techniques.

❑ The technique of writing XML template queries against SQL database.

❑ How we can merge XML data sets with SQL data sets to retrieve and even modify SQL data.

We've also been introduced to ADO+. In summary, ADO+ will provide many new ways to communicate with databases and XML, as well as interoperate between them. We barely scratched the surface of ADO+ as well as the new Microsoft.NET framework. Keep up with the latest at http://msdn.microsoft.com.

XML is coming from all angles in today's technology surge. These new features and techniques help to prepare us for the next generation of application development as we move to an XML data-centric world.

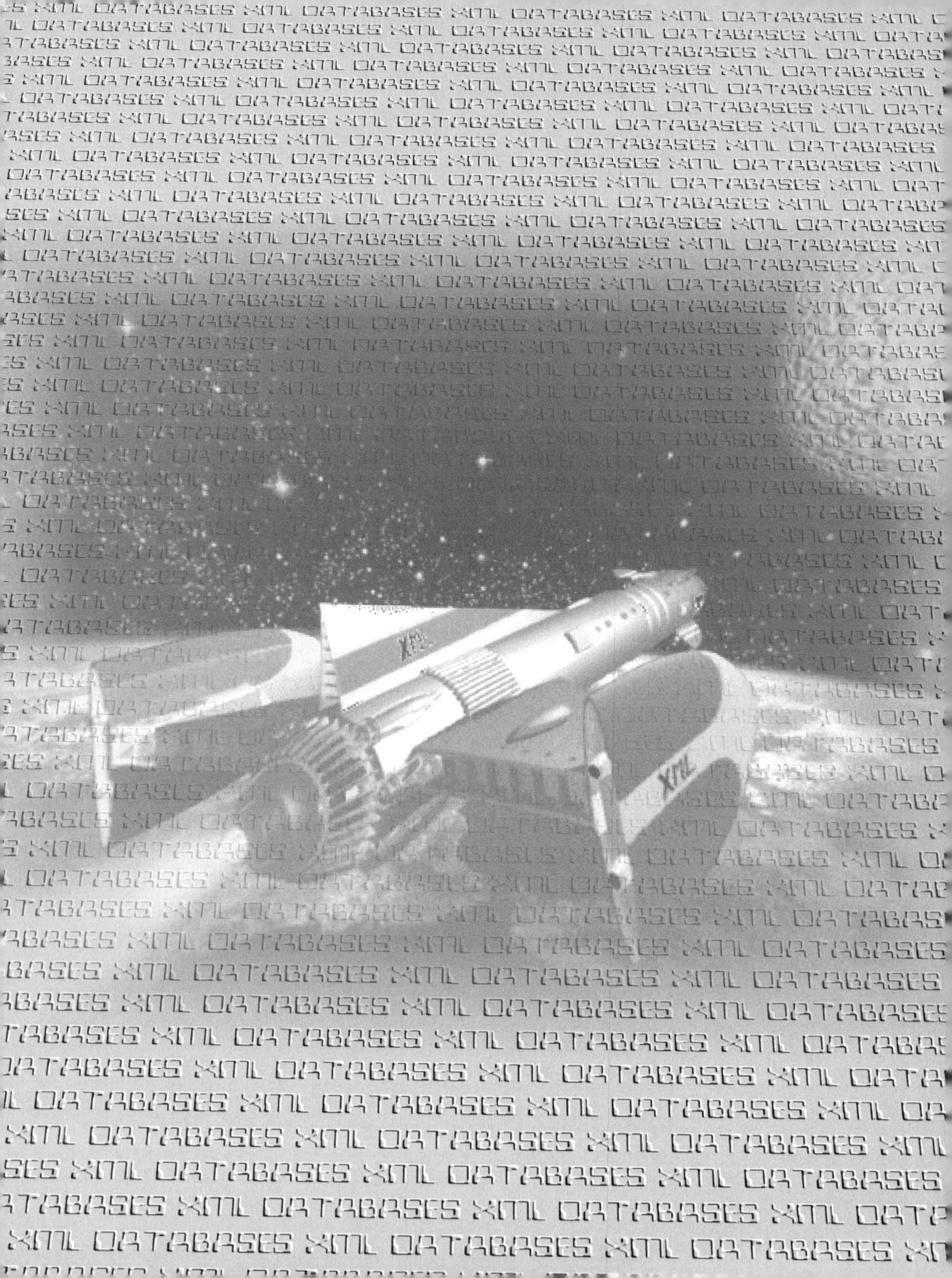
XML DATABASES

14

Storing and Retrieving XML in SQL Server 2000

In this Internet world, many of the applications you'll come across will be Web applications that share a common requirement – having HTML pages with dynamic data. We can write ASP (Active Server Pages) applications that retrieve data from the database and do the necessary conversion to display data in those HTML or XML pages, but this requires a certain amount of development work. SQL Server 2000 now includes XML support, which we can use to get these Internet documents in and out of SQL Server 2000 without having to write complex ASP applications. These new XML features allow us to literally view the entire relational database as XML. Thus we can write end-to-end XML applications.

A number of XML-related technologies have been introduced to support the storage and retrieval of XML into and out of SQL Server. There are a number of new features on the server side, as well as some on the middle tier. The middle tier features are discussed in the next chapter. In this chapter, we'll concentrate on the server side features.

These server side features include:

❑   FOR XML – allows you to retrieve data from SQL Server as an XML

❑   OPENXML – allows you to shred XML documents and store them in relational tables

❑   XML Bulk Load – allows you to bulk load from an XML document into SQL

❑   XML Views – provide an XML view of relational data

❑   XPath query support – allows you to query the XML view

❑   XML Updategrams – allow you to update data in relational tables using the XML views

In SQL Server 2000, we can write SELECT queries that return XML instead of the standard rowsets. The new **FOR XML** clause is used to get the results of a query returned as an XML tree instead of a rowset. These features are built in to the database query processor, which significantly enhances query performance.

If we want to update data in SQL Server 2000 from an XML document source, we can do that as well, using extensions to SQL INSERT, UPDATE, and DELETE statements. The new **OPENXML** functionality generates a rowset view of the XML. This rowset view can then be used in place of a recordset to update database tables.

Finally, when we have a large amount of XML that we want to put into SQL Server 2000, we can use the Bulk Load object to add this data for us.

There are many cases where we may require data to be returned in an XML format. For example, to his is typically the case if our application uses public XML schemas (such as Microsoft's Biz Talk schemas). There are two main ways in which you can retrieve XML:

❑ Writing SQL queries – with special extensions – directly against SQL Server 2000 tables

❑ Defining **XML views** of relational data, and retrieving the data as XML using these XML views

With both of these methods, the transformation of the relational data into XML is all done for you. All of this makes Web application development much simpler, because you avoid writing complex programs to retrieve and display data.

> Note that almost all the examples in this chapter use the Northwind database that comes with SQL Server 2000. We assume that you already have some knowledge of SQL.

Retrieving XML from SQL Server 2000: FOR XML

In relational databases, as you well know, the standard practice employed to query or summarize data is to run queries against that data. In SQL, queries specified against the database return results as a rowset.

For example, the following query, ch14_ex01.sql:

```
SELECT  CustomerID,
        ContactName
FROM    Customers
```

when run against the Northwind database, returns a 2-column rowset of customer IDs and contact names from the Customers table as a result, as shown opposite:

	CustomerID	ContactName
1	ALFKI	Maria Anders
2	ANATR	Ana Trujillo
3	ANTON	Antonio Moreno
4	AROUT	Thomas Hardy
5	BERGS	Christina Berglund
6	BLAUS	Hanna Moos
7	BLONP	Frédérique Citeaux
8	BOLID	Martín Sommer
9	BONAP	Laurence Lebihan
10	BOTTM	Elizabeth Lincoln

New SQL Server Query Support

SQL Server 2000 provides enhanced query support, in which we can request the result of a SELECT statement be returned as an XML document. To retrieve the result of a SELECT statement as XML, we must specify the FOR XML clause in the SELECT statement, along with one of three **modes**: **RAW**, **AUTO**, or **EXPLICIT**.

For example, if we wanted our previous sample query to return XML instead of a results table, we could append to it as follows:

```
SELECT CustomerID,
    ContactName
FROM  Customers
FOR XML AUTO
```

This query uses the AUTO mode (which is specified after the FOR XML clause) and returns a long list of customer information as XML, of which the following is a fragment:

```
<Customers CustomerID="ALFKI" ContactName="Maria Anders" />
<Customers CustomerID="ANATR" ContactName="Ana Trujillo" />
```

> *We've added formatting to the output XML in this chapter to make it more readable – the result you obtain will be a continuous string.*

However, note that while the FOR XML mode can be used in a SELECT statement, it cannot be used in nested SELECTs, such as:

```
SELECT    *
FROM      Table1
WHERE     … = SELECT * FROM Table2 FOR XML AUTO
```

Let's briefly summarize what each of the three FOR XML modes does, before going on to look at each one in more detail:

❑   The RAW mode produces attribute-centric XML with a flat structure. Each row in the table is represented in a generic tag called ROW, with the columns represented as attributes. The RAW mode is the easiest of the three modes to administer, although it does limit you to this structure.

❑   The AUTO mode produces XML where the hierarchy of elements in the resulting XML is determined by the order of columns in the SELECT statements, so you have limited control over the shape of the XML produced. This mode provides a compromise between control and complexity.

❑   The EXPLICIT mode allows the user to have total control over the shape of the resulting XML. However, the downside is that it is more complicated to administer than the other modes.

FOR XML: General Syntax

Here is the syntax for the FOR XML clause that is specified in the SELECT statement:

```
FOR XML xml_mode [,XMLDATA], [,ELEMENTS], [BINARY BASE64]
```

❑   If the optional XMLDATA option is specified, an XML-Data schema for the resulting XML is returned as part of the result. The schema is prepended to the XML.

❑   The ELEMENTS option is specified if an element-centric document is to be returned in which the column values are returned as sub-elements. By default the column values map to the element attributes in XML. The ELEMENTS option only applies in AUTO mode. We can request an element-centric document in EXPLICIT mode, but the ELEMENTS option isn't the way to do it.

❑   If the BINARY Base64 option is specified in the FOR XML clause, any binary data returned (for example, from a SQL Server IMAGE-type field) is represented in base64-encoded format. To retrieve binary data using the RAW and EXPLICIT modes, this option must be specified. It is not required when AUTO mode is specified, but without it, the AUTO mode returns binary data as a URL reference by default.

For example this query retrieves employee ID and photo (an image type column) for employee 1:

```
SELECT  EmployeeID, Photo
FROM    Employees
WHERE   EmployeeID=1
FOR XML AUTO
```

The query returns this result:

```
<Employees EmployeeID="1"
        Photo="dbobject/Employees[@EmployeeID='1']/@Photo"/>
```

Notice the URL reference to the Photo column returned. This URL reference can be used later to retrieve the employee photo. The dbobject is a virtual name of dbobject type. And the Employees[@EmployeeID='1']/@Photo is an XPath expression that is used to retrieve the image. The virtual names are created as part of creating a virtual directory for SQL Server.

Now let's look at each of the modes in detail.

The RAW Mode

If the RAW mode is specified, each row in the rowset returned by the SELECT statement is transformed into an element with a generic tag <row> and the columns as attribute values. The resulting XML does not have any hierarchy. If we take the following query (ch14_ex02.sql):

```
SELECT  C.CustomerID, O.OrderID, O.OrderDate
FROM    Customers C, Orders O
WHERE   C.CustomerID = O.CustomerID
ORDER BY C.CustomerID, O.OrderID
FOR XML RAW
```

the result is as follows:

```
<row CustomerID="ALFKI" OrderID="10643" OrderDate="1997-08-25T00:00:00"/>
<row CustomerID="ALFKI" OrderID="10692" OrderDate="1997-10-03T00:00:00"/>
<row CustomerID="ALFKI" OrderID="10702" OrderDate="1997-10-13T00:00:00"/>
...
```

> *Note that if you execute these queries in Query Analyzer, as we are here, you get a document fragment – the XML this produces is not well-formed, as we're missing a top-level element. When you write applications, you would normally specify these queries in an XML template, in which you can specify a single top-level element. The templates are discussed in Chapter 20.*

This kind of simple XML structure is efficient for parsing, and is useful if there is no requirement to generate XML in a specific format. If you want to transfer data from one source to another, it's easy to generate such a flat XML document, and pass it on to a receiving application.

> *Note that the RAW mode is not the same as the persistence format of ADO, but it can be transformed into it if required.*

We could also request an XDR schema for the resulting XML as follows (ch14_ex03.sql):

```
SELECT C.CustomerID, O.OrderID, O.OrderDate
FROM Customers C, Orders O
WHERE C.CustomerID = O.CustomerID
ORDER BY C.CustomerID, O.OrderID
FOR XML RAW, XMLDATA
```

This is the result:

```
<Schema name="Schema1" xmlns="urn:schemas-microsoft-com:xml-data"
                        xmlns:dt="urn:schemas-microsoft-com:datatypes">
    <ElementType name="row" content="empty" model="closed">
        <AttributeType name="CustomerID" dt:type="string"/>
        <AttributeType name="OrderID" dt:type="i4"/>
        <AttributeType name="OrderDate" dt:type="dateTime"/>
        <attribute type="CustomerID"/>
        <attribute type="OrderID"/>
        <attribute type="OrderDate"/>
```

```
        </ElementType>
    </Schema>
    <row xmlns="x-schema:#Schema1" CustomerID="ALFKI"
        OrderID="10643" OrderDate="1997-08-25T00:00:00"/>
    <row xmlns="x-schema:#Schema1" CustomerID="ALFKI"
        OrderID="10692" OrderDate="1997-10-03T00:00:00"/>
    <row xmlns="x-schema:#Schema1" CustomerID="ALFKI"
        OrderID="10702" OrderDate="1997-10-13T00:00:00"/>
    ...
```

You may need to change your settings in SQL Server to increase the maximum number of characters allowed per column in order to obtain this result (Options | Results).

As you can see, we again get a flat structure without a hierarchy. If you want XML generated with a particular hierarchy – for example a <Customers> element containing <Orders> sub-elements – then you need to specify AUTO or EXPLICIT mode.

The AUTO Mode

Unlike RAW mode, the query specified with AUTO mode does generate hierarchical XML, although you have limited control over the shape of the XML produced. The shape of the XML document generated is mainly governed by the order in which you specify the table columns in the SELECT clause – this is the only control you have.

Let's look at an example (ch14_ex04.sql):

```
SELECT    Customers.CustomerID, ContactName,
          OrderID, OrderDate
FROM      Customers, Orders
WHERE     Customers.CustomerID=Orders.CustomerID
ORDER BY Customers.CustomerID, OrderID
FOR XML AUTO
```

The syntax of each line in the code above is very similar to the equivalent lines in the FOR XML RAW example we saw in the previous section. The main exception is the first line, which works somewhat differently here:

❑ Each table name (from which at least one column is specified in the SELECT clause) maps to an element

❑ Each column name specified in the SELECT clause maps to the attribute name in the XML unless the ELEMENTS option is specified

❑ If the ELEMENTS option is specified, then each column name maps to sub-elements with text only contents

So the result of the previous query is:

```
<Customers CustomerID="ALFKI" ContactName="Maria Anders">
    <Orders OrderID="10643" OrderDate="1997-08-25T00:00:00"/>
    <Orders OrderID="10692" OrderDate="1997-10-03T00:00:00"/>
    <Orders OrderID="10702" OrderDate="1997-10-13T00:00:00"/><Orders
    ...
```

```
</Customers>
<Customers CustomerID="ANATR" ContactName="Ana Trujillo">
   <Orders OrderID="10308" OrderDate="1996-09-18T00:00:00"/>
   <Orders OrderID="10625" OrderDate="1997-08-08T00:00:00"/>
   ...
</Customers>
...
```

The first table identified in our SELECT statement is the Customers table. Therefore the <Customers> element is created first, with the columns that belong to this table (CustomerID and ContactName) as attributes. The next identified table is Orders, so the <Orders> elements are created as child elements of CustomerID, with the column taken from the Orders table as attributes.

However, if the ELEMENTS option is specified, as it is here:

```
SELECT    Customers.CustomerID, ContactName,
          OrderID, OrderDate
FROM      Customers, Orders
WHERE     Customers.CustomerID=Orders.CustomerID
ORDER BY Customers.CustomerID, OrderID
FOR XML AUTO, ELEMENTS
```

then the columns become sub-elements with text only contents:

```
<Customers>
    <CustomerID>ALFKI</CustomerID>
    <ContactName>Maria Anders</ContactName>
    <Orders>
        <OrderID>10643</OrderID>
        <OrderDate>1997-08-25T00:00:00</OrderDate>
    </Orders>
    <Orders>
        <OrderID>10692</OrderID>
        <OrderDate>1997-10-03T00:00:00</OrderDate>
    </Orders>
    ...
</Customers>
<Customers>
    <CustomerID>ANATR</CustomerID>
    <ContactName>Ana Trujillo</ContactName>
    <Orders>
        <OrderID>10308</OrderID>
        <OrderDate>1996-09-18T00:00:00</OrderDate>
    </Orders>
    ...
</Customers>
```

Again, the first table identified in our SELECT statement is the Customers table. The CustomerID and ContactName columns this time map to children of <Customers>, as does the <Orders> element (in the order in which they are specified). The OrderID and OrderDate are then created as child elements of <Orders>.

If you change the column order in the `SELECT` clause like this (`ch14_ex05.sql`):

```
SELECT      OrderID, Customers.CustomerID, ContactName, OrderDate
FROM        Customers, Orders
WHERE       Customers.CustomerID=Orders.CustomerID
ORDER BY    Customers.CustomerID, OrderID
FOR XML AUTO
```

the XML produced has a different hierarchy, in which `<Orders>` elements appear as parent and `<Customers>` as child elements:

```
<Orders OrderID="10643" OrderDate="1997-08-25T00:00:00">
    <Customers CustomerID="ALFKI" ContactName="Maria Anders"/>
</Orders>
<Orders OrderID="10692" OrderDate="1997-10-03T00:00:00">
    <Customers CustomerID="ALFKI" ContactName="Maria Anders"/>
</Orders>
...
```

Here, the `OrderID` appears before the `Customers.CustomerID`. Therefore, an `<Order>` element is created first, and then a `<Customer>` child element is added. The `ContactName` is added to the existing `<Customer>` element, and the `OrderDate` is added to the existing `<Order>` element.

Thus, the `AUTO` mode allows the user limited control over the shape of the XML. If you want greater control and flexibility in determining the shape and contents of the XML produced by the `SELECT` statement, you need to specify `EXPLICIT` mode. We'll discussed this next.

The Explicit Mode

The `EXPLICIT` mode allows you total control over the resulting XML. Using this mode, we can decide the shape of the resulting XML, but this flexibility comes with a price. As well as specifying what data we want, we also need to provide explicit information about the shape of the XML that we want generated. This makes writing `SELECT` queries more difficult than in `AUTO` or `RAW` mode.

There are four components of the `SELECT` statement that we need to be particularly concerned with when using the `EXPLICIT` mode. These are:

❑   **Column aliases**. We need to specify column aliases following a specific syntax for each column we specify in the `SELECT` clause. The information in the column aliases is used to generate the XML hierarchy.

❑   **Metadata columns**. In addition to specifying the columns from which to retrieve the information, the `SELECT` clause must specify two additional columns, with aliases `Tag` and `Parent` (the column aliases are not case sensitive). These columns must be the first columns specified in the `SELECT` clause. The parent-child relationship identified by the values in the `Tag` and `Parent` columns are used along with the column aliases in generating the hierarchy in the resulting XML.

❑   Some optional **directives** (discussed later).

❑   The **ORDER BY clause** specifying the ordering of rows. We must specify an appropriate order in the `ORDER BY` clause to generate the correct document hierarchy. For example, if the resulting XML has `<Customer>` elements with `<Order>` child elements, then you need to specify the `ORDER BY` clause to order records by customers, and within customers, by orders.

Let's look at each of these in more detail.

Specifying Column Aliases

The column aliases in the SELECT clause must be specified in a particular way, because the information in the column aliases, along with the Tag and Parent column values, is used to generate the hierarchy.

For example, the following query returns the customer information (ch14_ex06.sql). To keep this example simple, only CustomerID and ContactName columns are specified:

```
SELECT      1                        as Tag,
            NULL                     as Parent,
            Customers.CustomerID     as [Cust!1!CustID],
            Customers.ContactName    as [Cust!1!Contact]
FROM        Customers
ORDER BY    [Cust!1!CustID]
FOR XML EXPLICIT
```

The query generates the following XML:

```
<Cust CustID="ALFKI" Contact="Maria Anders"/>
<Cust CustID="ANATR" Contact="Ana Trujillo"/>
...
```

Note that we are just starting with a simple example. To generate this flat XML fragment, you don't need to specify EXPLICIT mode: either RAW or AUTO mode will produce this result without pain. We are taking this simple example only to understand the basic mechanics of specifying EXPLICIT mode. The power of EXPLICIT mode will become more clear when we generate complex XML hierarchies.

In this query, the CustomerID column has the alias [Cust!1!CustID], and the ContactName column has the alias [Cust!1!Contact].

The general syntax for column alias is:

```
ElementName!TagNumber!PropertyName!Directive
```

where:

- ❑   *ElementName* is the name of the element that will appear in the resulting XML (in the above example, Cust is the element name).

- ❑   *TagNumber* is the unique tag number of the element. In the above example, *TagNumber* is 1.

- ❑   PropertyName is the name given to this particular attribute in the resulting XML (assuming the default attribute-centric mapping). If you specify element-centric mapping using the optional *Directive*, then it is the name of the sub-element. In this example, the PropertyName CustID, and Contact are the names of the attribute in the resulting XML.

- ❑   Directive modifies the resulting XML in various ways. Directives are discussed in the section after next. No directives are specified in the column aliases in this example.

Specifying the Metadata Columns

Since in the EXPLICIT mode we specify the shape of the XML, one of the things we do is specify two additional columns in the SELECT clause. The alias for these two columns must be Tag and Parent. These two columns provide parent-child relationship information between the elements in the XML that is generated by the query.

These metadata columns must be the first two columns specified in the SELECT clause.

❏ The Tag column provides a numeric tag number of the element. It can be any number you want, as long as the number is unique for each element defined.

❏ The Parent column is used to define which element is the parent of this element. If the current element has no parent, then the value in this column is NULL.

Let us look at the previous query again:

```
SELECT      1                          as Tag,
            NULL                       as Parent,
            Customers.CustomerID   as [Cust!1!CustID],
            Customers.ContactName  as [Cust!1!Contact]
FROM        Customers
ORDER BY    [Cust!1!CustID]
FOR XML EXPLICIT
```

The Tag value 1 is the unique tag value of the <Cust> element. In processing the query result to produce the XML, if the value in the Tag column is 1, then all the columns in the rowset produced by the query with *TagNumber* 1 are identified. These are the columns mapped to the attributes (or sub-elements) in the Cust element. This will be discussed later in more detail.

As you see in the result, the <Cust> element has no parent element, so the Parent metadata column is assigned a NULL value.

The rest of the query is straightforward. Although we specify one, the ORDER BY clause is not required in this example. The ORDER BY clause only becomes important when you are generating XML containing hierarchies.

Before we come back to look at some more complicated examples, let's look at the different directives that can be included in the column alias.

Specifying the Directive in the Column Alias

The EXPLICIT mode allows additional controls in the generation of XML. We can:

❏ Identify certain attributes in the query as being of type id, idref, or idrefs

❏ Request the resulting XML be an element-centric document (by default you get an attribute-centric XML)

❏ Wrap certain data in the XML in a CDATA section

❏ Specify how to deal with characters in the data returned by SQL Server that are special in XML

Specifying the **directive** in the column alias does all this. These are the directives you can specify:

- ❑ id
- ❑ idref
- ❑ idrefs
- ❑ Hide
- ❑ element
- ❑ xml
- ❑ cdata
- ❑ xmltext

Let's familiarize ourselves with these directives.

id, idref, idrefs Directives

The directives id, idref, and idrefs identify the attribute as being of type id, idref, or idrefs. If you specify one of these you will see the effect in the XML-Data schema of the resulting XML. (Remember that you can request the XML-Data schema by specifying the XMLDATA option in the query.)

In this query, the CustID attribute is identified as being of type id by specifying the id directive in the column alias. The query also requests the XML-Data schema for the generated XML. (ch14_ex07.sql):

```
SELECT  1                    as TAG,
        NULL                 as parent,
        Customers.CustomerID as [Cust!1!CustID!id],
        Customers.ContactName as [Cust!1!Contact]
FROM    Customers
ORDER BY [Cust!1!CustID!id]
FOR XML EXPLICIT, XMLDATA
```

The schema is prepended to the result. Also note the dt:type attribute added in the definition of the CustID AttributeType:

```
<Schema name="Schema2" xmlns="urn:schemas-microsoft-com:xml-data"
                       xmlns:dt="urn:schemas-microsoft-com:datatypes">
   <ElementType name="Cust" content="mixed" model="open">
      <AttributeType name="CustID" dt:type="id"/>
      <AttributeType name="Contact" dt:type="string"/>
      <attribute type="CustID"/>
      <attribute type="Contact"/>
   </ElementType>
</Schema>

<Cust xmlns="x-schema:#Schema2" CustID="ALFKI" Contact="Maria Anders"/>
<Cust xmlns="x-schema:#Schema2" CustID="ANATR" Contact="Ana Trujillo"/>
<Cust xmlns="x-schema:#Schema2" CustID="ANTON" Contact="Antonio Moreno"/>
...
```

element and xml Directives

The `element` and `xml` directives produce element-centric XML rather than attribute-centric. For example, our `ch14_ex06.sql` example of the `EXPLICIT` section returned the following attribute-centric XML:

```
<Cust CustID="ALFKI" Contact="Maria Anders"/>
<Cust CustID="ANATR" Contact="Ana Trujillo"/>
...
```

If we add the `element` directive to the column aliases in this example, the query will now look like this (`ch14_ex08.sql`):

```
SELECT    1                       as TAG,
          NULL                    as parent,
          Customers.CustomerID    as [Cust!1!CustID!element],
          Customers.ContactName   as [Cust!1!Contact!element]
FROM      Customers
ORDER BY [Cust!1!CustID!element]
FOR XML EXPLICIT
```

The XML returned by this query looks like this:

```
<Cust>
   <CustID>ALFKI</CustID>
   <Contact>Maria Anders</Contact>
</Cust>
<Cust>
   <CustID>ANATR</CustID>
   <Contact>Ana Trujillo</Contact>
</Cust>
...
```

The only difference between the `xml` and `element` directives is that when `element` is specified, the data is encoded into escape codes. For example, if you have the special XML character '<' in the data, it would be encoded as `&lt;`. When `xml` is used, this encoding does not take place.

You can also generate mixed mode XML by specifying `element` or `xml` on one of the columns only, as seen below (`ch14_ex09.sql`):

```
SELECT    1                       as TAG,
          NULL                    as parent,
          Customers.CustomerID    as [Cust!1!CustID],
          Customers.ContactName   as [Cust!1!Contact!element]
FROM      Customers
ORDER BY [Cust!1!CustID]
FOR XML EXPLICIT
```

This is the result (using `xml` in the above query would give the same result):

```
<Cust CustID="ALFKI">
   <Contact>Maria Anders</Contact>
</Cust>
<Cust CustID="ANATR">
   <Contact>Ana Trujillo</Contact>
</Cust>
...
```

Here, since the `element` directive is specified only for the `ContactName` column, `ContactName` is returned as a sub-element. The `CustomerID` column remains mapped to the corresponding attribute because attribute-centric mapping is the default.

The cdata Directive

The `cdata` directive wraps the data within a CDATA section. To specify this directive, the original data must be a text type (such as the `text`, `ntext`, `varchar`, `nvarchar`, SQL Server data types). It is important to remember that the `PropertyName` of the column alias must not be specified when you specify the `cdata` directive in the alias.

So for the following example (`ch14_ex10.sql`):

```
SELECT  1                      as TAG,
        NULL                   as parent,
        Customers.CustomerID   as [Cust!1!CustID],
        Customers.ContactName  as [Cust!1!!cdata]
FROM    Customers
ORDER BY [Cust!1!CustID]
FOR XML EXPLICIT
```

the resulting XML is in the following format:

```
<Cust CustID="ALFKI"><![CDATA[Maria Anders]]>
</Cust><Cust CustID="ANATR"><![CDATA[Ana Trujillo]]>
...
```

The xmltext Directive

Sometimes when we are inserting information in an XML format into a database, not all of the elements will be inserted directly into the database as standard column entries. In such a case, we may want to put any spare XML (also referred to as **unconsumed XML**) into its own column (referred to as an **overflow column**) for safe keeping, until it is needed again. This can be done as part of the functionality of `OPENXML`, discussed later in the chapter.

The `xmltext` directive is used to identify a database column as an overflow column, pull out all of the XML contained within this column, and put it back into an XML format.

For example, assume we have the following `Employee` table, and have previously stored an XML document using `OPENXML`:

```
EmployeeID   EmployeeName   OverflowColumn
-----------------------------------------------------------------
Emp1         Joe            <Tag HomePhone="data">content</Tag>
Emp2         Bob            <Tag MaritalStatus="data"/>
Emp3         Mary           <Tag HomePhone="data"
                                 MaritalStatus="data"></Tag>
```

We can write a query with `EXPLICIT` mode to return the XML such that the data in the overflow is appropriately added to the elements in the XML document. An example of such a query is seen below (`ch14_ex11.sql`):

```
SELECT  1            as Tag,
        NULL         as parent,
        EmployeeID   as [Emp!1!EmpID],
        EmployeeName as [Emp!1!EmpName],
        OverflowColumn as [Emp!1!!xmltext]
FROM    Employee
FOR XML EXPLICIT
```

For the overflow column (OverflowColumn), PropertyName is not specified in the column alias, but directive is set to xmltext. This identifies the column as containing overflow text. In the resulting XML, all of this content gets appended to the attributes of the enclosing <Emp> parent as further attributes:

```
<Emp EmpID="Emp1" EmpName="Joe" HomePhone="data">content</Emp>
<Emp EmpID="Emp2" EmpName="Bob" MaritalStatus="data"></Emp>
<Emp EmpID="Emp3" EmpName="Mary" HomePhone="data"
                              MaritalStatus="data"></Emp>
```

If you specify a PropertyName in the column alias for OverflowColumn, then the overflow data is inserted into the XML as attributes of a child element of the element defined by the query. This child element takes the name specified in the PropertyName (ch14_ex12.sql).

```
SELECT 1            as Tag,
       NULL         as parent,
       EmployeeID   as [Emp!1!EmpID],
       EmployeeName as [Emp!1!EmpName],
       OverflowColumn as [Emp!1!UnconsumedData!xmltext]
FROM   Employee
FOR XML EXPLICIT
```

This will produce this result:

```
<Emp EmpID="Emp1" EmpName="Joe">
   <UnconsumedData HomePhone="data">content</UnconsumedData>
</Emp>
<Emp EmpID="Emp2" EmpName="Bob">
   <UnconsumedData MaritalStatus="data"/>
</Emp>
<Emp EmpID="Emp3" EmpName="Mary">
   <UnconsumedData HomePhone="data" MaritalStatus="data">
</UnconsumedData>
</Emp>
```

In most of the examples of the EXPLICIT mode that we have seen so far, the resulting XML was rather lacking in hierarchical structure. Most of the queries simply returned one or more of the same element with their property (attribute or sub-element) values. However, with EXPLICIT mode we have full control over the shape of the XML. We can generate hierarchies such as <Customer> elements consisting of <Order> elements, and <Order> elements consisting of <OrderDetail> elements.

Now that we understand the basics of writing EXPLICIT mode queries, let's look at how XML is generated in EXPLICIT mode queries – that is, how the rowset produced by the execution of a SELECT statement is transformed into an XML. We must specify our SELECT query in such a way that the resulting rowset has all the information necessary to generate the XML.

Generating XML from the Rowset (Universal Table)

One thing we haven't explained is the logic behind generating the XML from an EXPLICIT query. Upon the execution of the EXPLICIT query, a rowset is generated (just like from any other SELECT statement), which acts as a kind of intermediate stage between the execution of the query against the database, and the completion of the XML result. This rowset is referred to as the **universal table**, so called because it is not a normalized rowset.

Let's look again at the first simple EXPLICIT query we encountered (ch14_ex06.sql):

```
SELECT          1                       as Tag,
                NULL                    as Parent,
                Customers.CustomerID    as [Cust!1!CustID],
                Customers.ContactName   as [Cust!1!Contact]
FROM            Customers
ORDER BY        [Cust!1!CustID]
FOR XML EXPLICIT
```

The partial rowset (universal table) generated when this query is executed is given below:

```
Tag    Parent    Cust!1!CustID    Cust!1!Contact
--------------------------------------------------
1      NULL      "ALFKI"          "Maria Anders"
1      NULL      "ANATR"          "Ana Trujillo"
1      NULL      "ANTON"          "Antonio Moreno"
    ...
```

To see the universal table rowset generated for a query, execute the query against the Northwind database without the FOR XML clause.

To generate the XML, the rows in this universal table are processed as follows.

As the first row is read, it identifies the Tag as being 1. Therefore, all the columns in the row with a TagNumber of 1 in the column names are identified (here we have Cust!1!CustID and Cust!1!Contact). These column names provide values for the properties of the element identified by Tag 1. These columns names identify Cust as the ElementName, therefore a <Cust> element is created. The column names also identify CustID and Contact as the PropertyNames. Therefore CustID and Contact attributes are added to the <Cust> element.

When the second row is read, it identifies NULL as its Parent. Therefore, the previous tag is closed by adding the end tag (</Cust>). Again, the second row identifies 1 as Tag, so all the columns with *TagNumber* 1 in the column name are identified (again we have Cust!1!CustID and Cust!1Contact). These column names identify Cust as the ElementName, and as a result, another <Cust> element is created and the process continues.

When all three cycles have been completed, the following query result is returned:

```
<Cust CustID="ALFKI" Contact="Maria Anders"/>
<Cust CustID="ANATR" Contact="Ana Trujillo"/>
<Cust CustID="ANTON" Contact="Antonio Moreno"/>
    ...
```

Hierarchy Generation

As we write SELECT queries to generate complex XML, the basic process of writing queries to generate hierarchy is still the same. For example, consider the following two SQL Server table fragments, taken from the Northwind database:

CustomerID	CompanyName	ContactName	ContactTitle	Address
ALFKI	Alfreds Futterkiste	Maria Anders	Sales Representati·	Obere Str. 57
ANATR	Ana Trujillo Empare	Ana Trujillo	Owner	Avda. de la Constit
ANTON	Antonio Moreno Ta	Antonio Moreno	Owner	Mataderos 2312
AROUT	Around the Horn	Thomas Hardy	Sales Representati·	120 Hanover Sq.
BERGS	Berglunds snabbköj	Christina Berglund	Order Administrato	Berguvsvägen 8
BLAUS	Blauer See Delikate	Hanna Moos	Sales Representati·	Forsterstr. 57

OrderID	CustomerID	EmployeeID	OrderDate
10248	VINET	5	04/07/1996
10249	TOMSP	6	05/07/1996
10250	HANAR	4	08/07/1996
10251	VICTE	3	08/07/1996
10252	SUPRD	4	09/07/1996
10253	HANAR	3	10/07/1996

Assume that we want to generate the following XML about customer order information from the data stored in these tables:

```
<Customer CustomerID="ALFKI">
   <Order OrderID=10643>
   <Order OrderID=10692>
   ...
</Customer>
<Customer CustomerID="ANATR" >
   <Order OrderID=10308 >
   <Order OrderID=10625 >
   ...
</Customer>
```

One way to write the query to generate this XML is to specify two SELECT statements and join them with UNION ALL, where the first SELECT statement is written to produce the customer information, and the second SELECT statement is written to produce the order information.

The two SELECT statements must produce rowsets that are union compatible in order to apply UNION ALL. For union compatibility, each rowset produced must have same number of columns and the corresponding columns must be of same data type.

Let's use Tag value 1 for the <Customer> element and Tag value 2 for the <Order> element.

We'll look at this step by step to see how we get from the database data to the final XML output. We will take the following:

❑   The first and second rowsets, that represent the two elements separately

❑   The SELECT query to create to XML

❑   The universal table: the intermediate between the query and the XML

❑   The XML

The First Rowset: Representing the <customer> Element

So we need our first SELECT query to produce a rowset in this format:

```
Tag   Parent   Customer!1!CustomerID   Order!2!OrderID
1     NULL     ALFKI                   NULL
1     NULL     ANATR                   NULL
...   ...      ...                     ...
```

Here, 1 is the Tag number assigned to the <Customer> element. Again, recall that the Tag value can be any number as long as each element produced has a unique tag number. The same value is specified for the *TagNumber* in the column alias – [Customer!1!CustomerID]. The OrderID column is generated only because this rowset needs to have the same number of columns as the second SELECT statement, in order to be union compatible with it.

This is the first SELECT query:

```
SELECT  1                       as Tag,
        NULL                    as Parent,
        Customers.CustomerID    as [Customer!1!CustomerID],
        NULL                    as [Order!2!OrderID]
FROM    Customers
```

The Second Rowset: Representing the <order> Element

We need a second SELECT statement to produce a rowset with this format:

```
Tag   Parent   Customer!1!CustomerID   Order!2!OrderID
2     1        ALFKI                   10643
2     1        ALFKI                   10692
2     1        ANATR                   10308
2     1        ANATR                   10625
...   ...      ...                     ...
```

Here, the unique Tag value assigned to the <Order> element is 2. We want the <Order> element to be the child of the <Customer> element. Therefore, the Parent value for the <Order> element is 1, identifying <Customer> as the parent. In this query, the CustomerID values are produced again for the ORDER BY clause, to produce the necessary ordering of customers and orders.

This is our second SELECT query:

```
SELECT  2,
        1,
        Customers.CustomerID,
        Orders.OrderID
FROM    Customers, Orders
WHERE   Customers.CustomerID = Orders.CustomerID
```

Each of the queries must also provide appropriate column aliases (remember the format, *ElementName*!*TagNumber*!*PropertyName*!*Directive*). For the CustomerID column, we need to specify the alias as Customer!1!CustomerID, where CustomerID is the *ElementName*, and 1 is the *TagNumber*, which is same as the Tag value we decided for the Customer ElementType.

In the same way, we assign `Order!2!OrderID` alias to the `OrderID` column, to define it as a property of the `<order>` element.

The SELECT Query

Finally, we put these two queries together with a UNION ALL. We must also specify the ORDER BY clause so that the `<Order>` elements appear below their `<Customer>` parent. The resulting query is given below (`ch14_ex13.sql`):

```
SELECT    1                       as Tag,
          NULL                    as Parent,
          Customers.CustomerID as [Customer!1!CustomerID],
          NULL                    as [Order!2!OrderID]
FROM      Customers
UNION ALL
SELECT    2,
          1,
          Customers.CustomerID,
          Orders.OrderID
FROM      Customers, Orders
WHERE     Customers.CustomerID = Orders.CustomerID
ORDER BY [Customer!1!CustomerID],
         [Order!2!OrderID]
FOR XML EXPLICIT
```

Note that the column aliases are provided as part of the first SELECT statement. Aliases provided in the subsequent SELECT will be ignored, so we don't need to state them again.

The ORDER BY clause ensures that the records in the rowset are generated in the proper order. This isn't simply stating that the `<Customer>` elements will be sorted by `CustomerID` and the `<Order>` elements by `OrderID`. We're also ensuring that when the rowset is processed, the final XML will have the `<Order>` elements appear as child elements of appropriate the `<Customer>` parent.

Processing the Rowset (Universal Table)

The query produces this rowset (only partial rows are shown) or universal table:

Tag	Parent	Customer!1!CustomerID	Order!2!OrderID
1	NULL	ALFKI	NULL
2	1	ALFKI	10643
2	1	ALFKI	10692
2	1	ALFKI	...
1	NULL	ANATR	NULL
2	1	ANATR	10308
2	1	ANATR	10625
2	1	ANATR	...

This universal table is then processed to produce the desired XML. The rows are processed in order, so let's start with the first row.

The Tag value in this row is 1. All the columns with a Tag number of 1 specified in the column name are identified. In this case, there is only one column, i.e. `Customer!1!CustomerID`.

Now the rest of the information in the alias is used, which identifies `Customer` as the element name, and `CustomerID` as the property value. Therefore, a `<Customer>` element is created, with an attribute `CustomerID` with a value "ALFKI" – the value from the column in the table.

The second row identifies `Tag` value 2. Now, all the columns with `TagNumber` 2 in the column alias are identified. In this example, the `Order!2!OrderID` is the only column. The column name identifies `Order` as the element name, `OrderID` as the property value, and the `<Customer>` element as the parent. So, an `<Order>` element is created, with an attribute `OrderID` that has the value "10643", from the column value in the table. This element is then placed into the XML as a child of the `<Customer>` element.

The process is repeated for the remaining rows of the universal table. One thing to note is that when the `Tag` number encountered at the start of the table row changes from 2 to 1 again, the first customer tag is automatically closed off, and the next one opened.

The ResultingXML

When the rows have all been processed, the XML is produced, as expected. Let's have another look at it, to remind us:

```
<Customer CustomerID="ALFKI">
   <Order OrderID="10643" />
   <Order OrderID="10692" />
   ...
</Customer>
<Customer CustomerID="ANATR">
   <Order OrderID="10308" />
   <Order OrderID="10625" />
   ...
</Customer>
...
```

Further Examples

Now we understand the process of XML creation inside out, lets affirm our knowledge by going through some slightly more complicated examples.

Example 1 – Using idrefs to Create Attributes

Assume we want this `<Customer>` and `<Order>` hierarchy generated:

```
<Customer xmlns="x-schema:#Schema1" CustomerID="ALFKI">
   <Order OrderID="10643" CustomerID="ALFKI"/>
   <Order OrderID="10692" CustomerID="ALFKI"/>
...
</Customer>
<Customer xmlns="x-schema:#Schema1" CustomerID="ANTON">
   <Order OrderID="10365" CustomerID="ANTON"/>
   <Order OrderID="10507" CustomerID="ANTON"/>
   ...
</Customer>
   ...
```

where the `CustomerID` attribute of the `<Customer>` element is an `id` type attribute, and the `CustomerID` attribute of the `<Order>` element is an `idref` type attribute, referring to the `id` type attribute.

This is the query (`ch14_ex14.sql`) that produces the desired XML:

```
SELECT  1                       as Tag,
        NULL                    as Parent,
        Customers.CustomerID as [Customer!1!CustomerID!id],
        NULL                    as [Order!2!OrderID],
        NULL                    as [Order!2!CustomerID!idref]
FROM    Customers
UNION ALL
SELECT  2,
        1,
        Customers.CustomerID,
        Orders.OrderID,
        Orders.CustomerID
FROM    Customers, Orders
WHERE   Customers.CustomerID = Orders.CustomerID
ORDER BY [Customer!1!CustomerID!id], [Order!2!OrderID]
FOR XML EXPLICIT, XMLDATA
```

Here, the `id` and `idref` directives are specified in the first `SELECT` clause. The query also requests an XDR schema by specifying the `XMLDATA` option, so that we can see the changes in the schema due to the `id` and `idref` directives.

This is the partial result.

```
<Schema name="Schema1" xmlns="urn:schemas-microsoft-com:xml-data"
                        xmlns:dt="urn:schemas-microsoft-com:datatypes">
    <ElementType name="Customer" content="mixed" model="open">
        <AttributeType name="CustomerID" dt:type="id"/>
        <attribute type="CustomerID"/>
    </ElementType>
    <ElementType name="Order" content="mixed" model="open">
        <AttributeType name="OrderID" dt:type="i4"/>
        <AttributeType name="CustomerID" dt:type="idref"/>
        <attribute type="OrderID"/>
        <attribute type="CustomerID"/>
    </ElementType></Schema>
<Customer xmlns="x-schema:#Schema1" CustomerID="ALFKI">
    <Order OrderID="10643" CustomerID="ALFKI"/>
    <Order OrderID="10692" CustomerID="ALFKI"/>
...
</Customer>
<Customer xmlns="x-schema:#Schema1" CustomerID="ANTON">
    <Order OrderID="10365" CustomerID="ANTON"/>
    <Order OrderID="10507" CustomerID="ANTON"/>
    ...
</Customer>
```

The schema specifies the `dt:type` as `id` for the `CustomerID` attribute of the `<Customer>` element, and `dt:type` as `idref` for the `CustomerID` attribute of `<Order>` element.

Now you can see how `EXPLICIT` queries can become more of a challenge. Assume we want to generate the following hierarchy with attributes of type `idrefs`:

```
<Customer CustomerID="ALFKI" OrderList="Ord-10643 Ord-10692 ...">
    <Order OrderID="Ord-10643" OrderDate="1997-08-25T00:00:00"/>
    <Order OrderID="Ord-10692" OrderDate="1997-10-03T00:00:00"/>
...
</Customer>
<Customer CustomerID="ANATR" OrderList="Ord-10308 Ord-10625 ... ">
    <Order OrderID="Ord-10308" OrderDate="1996-09-18T00:00:00"/>
    <Order OrderID="Ord-10625" OrderDate="1997-08-08T00:00:00"/>
...
</Customer>
```

This XML contains two elements (`Customer`, `Order`). The `<Customer>` element has an attribute `Orderlist`, which refers to the `OrderID` attributes of the `<Order>` elements for that customer. Thus we need to specify the `OrderID` attribute of the `<Order>` element as of type `id`, and the `OrderList` attribute as an `idrefs` value.

We therefore require three `SELECT` statements: one each for `<Customer>`, `OrderList` as `idrefs`, and `<Order>`. The `OrderList` `idrefs` attribute and `Order` element are both children of the `Customer` element, so their `SELECT` statements will appear after the `Customer` `SELECT`. They must also include a key (such as `CustomerID`) from the `Customer` to get the right ordering/nesting.

This is demonstrated in the query below (`ch14_ex15.sql`):

```
-- Customer element
SELECT  1                       as Tag,
        NULL                    as Parent,
        Customers.CustomerID as [Customer!1!CustomerID],
        NULL                    as [Customer!1!OrderList!idrefs],
        NULL                    as [Order!2!OrderID!id],
        NULL                    as [Order!2!OrderDate]
FROM    Customers
UNION ALL
-- OrderList attribute
SELECT  1,
        NULL,
        Customers.CustomerID,
        'Ord-'+CAST(Orders.OrderID as varchar(5)),
        NULL,
        NULL
FROM    Customers, Orders
WHERE Customers.CustomerID = Orders.CustomerID
UNION ALL
-- Order element
SELECT  2,
        1,
        Customers.CustomerID,
        NULL,
        'Ord-'+CAST(Orders.OrderID as varchar(5)),
        Orders.OrderDate
FROM    Customers, Orders
WHERE Customers.CustomerID = Orders.CustomerID
ORDER BY [Customer!1!CustomerID],
         [Order!2!OrderID!id],
         [Customer!1!OrderList!idrefs]
FOR XML EXPLICIT
```

In general, descendants must inherit keys from their ancestors to get the right ordering. The ordering is best explained by looking at the shape of the universal table this query produces, and considering why this shape is needed (only partial rowset is shown below):

Corresponding XML	TAG	PARENT	[Customer!1! CustomerID]	[Customer!1! OrderList!idrefs]	[Order!2! OrderID]
\<Customer>	1	NULL	ALFKI	NULL	NULL
OrderList	1	NULL	ALFKI	Ord-10692	NULL
\<Order>	2	1	ALFKI	NULL	Ord-10692
\<Order>	2	1	ALFKI	NULL	Ord-11001
\<Customer>	1	NULL	ANATR	NULL	NULL
...					

The first column shows the XML produced, which is not part of the rowset generated by the above query – we have added that column for explanation purposes only.

First, we want to have the top-level Customer elements ordered by CustomerID in the ORDER BY clause. If we did not select the CustomerID in every descendant of Customer (instead selecting NULL in the SELECT clause), then the descendant rows would rise to the top of the table, which is not what we want.

Second, we want to have the OrderList idrefs attribute appear after the Customer element begins, but before the child elements of Customer begin. If we just sorted by the OrderList values next, this would not produce the ordering we want. The NULLs would rise to the top of the Customer!1!OrderList!idrefs column, and the Order children would appear before the OrderList idrefs attribute, as shown in the following universal table:

Corresponding XML	TAG	PARENT	[Customer!1! CustomerID]	[Customer!1! OrderList!idrefs]	[Order!2! OrderID]
\<Customer>	1	NULL	ALFKI	NULL	NULL
\<Order>	2	1	ALFKI	NULL	Ord-10692
\<Order>	2	1	ALFKI	NULL	Ord-11001
OrderList	1	NULL	ALFKI	Ord-10692	NULL
\<Customer>	1	NULL	ANATR	NULL	NULL
...					

So instead, we need to order by the non-idrefs children first, and then by the idrefs children. For this example, that means ordering by Order!2!OrderID first, and then ordering by Customer!1!OrderList!idrefs:

```
ORDER BY [Customer!1!CustomerID],
         [Order!2!OrderID!id],
         [Customer!1!OrderList!idrefs]
```

Also note the casting specified in the query:

```
'Ord-'+CAST(Orders.OrderID as varchar(5)),
```

This is done because all of these queries are against the Northwind database in SQL Server. In this database, the OrderID values are integers. However, in XML the idrefs can't be numbers, so we need to convert them.

In summary, it is very important to specify the appropriate ORDER BY clause. For the OrderList idrefs type attributes, the corresponding <Order> instances must appear immediately after the <Customer> element to which the idrefs attribute belongs.

Example 2 – Producing XML Containing Siblings

The query in this example produces XML containing siblings. Assume we want this XML hierarchy:

```
<Employee ID="1">
    <Order ID="10258">
        <Product ID="2"/>
        <Product ID="5"/>
        <Product ID="32"/>
    </Order>
    <Order ID="10270">
        <Product ID="36"/>
        <Product ID="43"/>
    </Order>
    ...
    <Customer ID="AROUT"/>
    <Customer ID="BSBEV"/>
    <Customer ID="CONSH"/>
    <Customer ID="EASTC"/>
    <Customer ID="NORTS"/>
    <Customer ID="SEVES"/>
</Employee>
```

where the <Employee> element consists of <Order> and <Customer> child elements (siblings). The <Order> child elements are the orders the parent employee has taken, and the <Customer> child elements are the customers who live in the same city as the parent employee. Note that in this example there is no relationship between <Order> and <Customer> elements, except that they are children of the same parent. The <Order> element in turn has <Product> child elements, just to add more complexity.

To generate this, we will use four SELECT statements, one for each of the <Employee>, <Order>, <Product>, and <Customer> elements. It is important to understand that each SELECT clause selects all its ancestor's keys. Again, the ordering is important in the ORDER BY clause.

Here is the query (ch14_ex16.sql):

```
SELECT  1 as TAG, 0 as parent,
        E.EmployeeID as [Employee!1!ID],
        NULL as [Order!2!ID],
        NULL as [Product!3!ID],
        NULL as [Customer!4!ID]
FROM    Employees E
UNION ALL
SELECT  2 as TAG, 1 as parent,
        E.EmployeeID,
        O.OrderID,
        NULL,
        NULL
FROM    Employees E join Orders O on E.EmployeeID=O.EmployeeID
UNION ALL
```

```
SELECT  3 as TAG, 2 as parent,
        E.EmployeeID,
        O.OrderID,
        P.ProductID,
        NULL
FROM    Employees E join Orders O on E.EmployeeID=O.EmployeeID
JOIN    [Order Details] D on O.OrderID=D.OrderID
JOIN    Products P on D.ProductID=P.ProductID
UNION ALL
SELECT  4 as TAG, 1 as parent,
        E.EmployeeID,
        NULL,
        NULL,
        C.CustomerID
FROM    Employees E join Customers C on E.City=C.City
ORDER BY [Employee!1!ID], [Customer!4!ID], [Order!2!ID], [Product!3!ID]
FOR XML EXPLICIT
```

Among siblings, we order by the last child first. So in this example, we order by:

❑   The top-level element (Employee)

❑   Then the last child of employee (Customer)

❑   Then the children of Customer (none)

❑   Then the next child of Employee (Order)

❑   Then the children of Order (Product)

Alternative Ways to Retrieve XML

As we've seen, the EXPLICIT mode queries are a bit complex – writing these queries to produce complex XML documents can be a challenge. However, there is an alternative. We can create **XML Views** of the relational data, and specify XPath queries against these views.

In SQL Server 2000, we can create XML views using **XML-Data reduced** language (a subset of XML-Data schema language). XPath queries generate FOR XML EXPLICIT queries to retrieve data from the database. To get the simplicity of XPath queries against XML views, and the control of explicit queries, we can use the SQL Server profiler to capture the explicit queries that XPath generates.

There's more on XML views and XPath in the next chapter. For now, let's look at another of those new server side features that SQL Server 2000 provides.

Storing XML in SQL Server 2000: OPENXML

In the world of relational databases, when we are updating a table we need to provide the necessary data as a rowset to the INSERT, UPDATE, or DELETE statements. However, if our source data is an XML document, and we want to INSERT this data into the database, UPDATE the existing relational data from the source XML document, or DELETE existing records in the tables based on the data in the XML document, then somehow we need to create a **rowset** from the XML data and pass it to the INSERT, UPDATE, or DELETE statement.

OPENXML provides this functionality. The OPENXML function in SQL Server 2000 is a **rowset provider**, which means it creates a rowset view of an XML document. Since a rowset is like a table, it can be used in place of a table or relational view in SELECT queries. Thus, the OPENXML feature in SQL Server 2000 allows you to store data from XML documents or document fragments in database tables.

> *OPENXML is one way of storing XML in the database using SQL. In addition, you can store XML using XML **updategrams**, which are discussed in the next chapter.*

To do this there are a number of steps that take place, we need to:

❑ Create an in-memory DOM representation of the XML document

❑ Use OPENXML to create a rowset view of this XML. As part of OPENXML, specify an XPath expression to retrieve the desired elements

❑ Pass this rowset to INSERT, UPDATE, and DELETE statements to update the database

❑ Destroy the in-memory DOM representation of the XML document

Using OPENXML in SQL Statements

If we think about a typical SELECT statement for retrieving rows from a table, it is written in the form:

```
SELECT    *
FROM      <TableName>
WHERE     <Some Condition>
```

This statement will retrieve data from the specified table(s). However, our data source is not in a table form, it is an XML document. So, OPENXML is first used to generate a rowset view of this XML document, which is then provided to the SELECT statement.

```
SELECT    *
FROM      OPENXML ...
WHERE     ...
```

Thus, if we want to apply updates to a database table from data that is XML, then OPENXML can be used with INSERT, UPDATE, or DELETE statements to apply necessary updates from the XML data. For example:

```
INSERT INTO Customers
    SELECT    *
    FROM      OPENXML ...
    WHERE     ..
```

Creating the In-Memory Representation of the Document

As we said, we need to create a DOM tree that represents the XML, so that OPENXML can generate a rowset of this data, and then destroy it later so that we do not waste resources. There are two special stored procedures to do this:

❑ sp_xml_preparedocument

❑ sp_xml_removedocument

Before OPENXML can access the XML document, the sp_xml_preparedocument stored procedure must be called to generate an in-memory DOM representation of the XML. The stored procedure returns a document handle of this in-memory DOM tree. This document handle is passed to OPENXML, which then generates the rowset used in the SQL queries. The document handle allows OPENXML to access the data:

```
DECLARE @hdoc int
DECLARE @doc  varchar(1000)
-- Source XML document
SET @doc ='
<root>
   <Customer cid= "Cust1" name="Bob" city="Seattle">
       <Order oid="Ord1" empid="1" orderdate="10/1/2000" />
       <Order oid="Ord2" empid="1" orderdate="10/2/2000" />
   </Customer>
   <Customer cid="C2" name="John" city="NewYork" >
       <Order oid="Ord3" empid="2" orderdate="9/1/2000" />
       <Order oid="Ord4" empid="3" orderdate="9/2/2000" />
   </Customer>
</root>
'--Create an internal representation of the XML document.
EXEC sp_xml_preparedocument @hdoc OUTPUT, @doc
EXEC sp_xml_removedocument @hdoc
```

Note that 8K is the maximum size of XML allowed when the nvarchar *data type is used. If your XML is larger than 8K you may want to specify* ntext *data type.*

The first line here declares an integer variable – @hdoc –to hold the document handle returned by the sp_xml_preparedocument stored procedure. The second variable – @doc – holds the source XML that we are mapping using the following:

```
EXEC sp_xml_preparedocument @hdoc OUTPUT, @doc
```

And again, since the entire XML document is read in memory, it is important that we call the sp_xml_removedocument stored procedure when the XML document is no longer needed. This frees up memory and resources:

```
EXEC sp_xml_removedocument @hdoc
```

We can use this general template for all of our queries in this section:

```
DECLARE @hdoc int
DECLARE @doc  varchar(1000)
-- Source XML document
SET @doc ='Copy XML document here
'--Create an internal representation of the XML document.
EXEC sp_xml_preparedocument @hdoc OUTPUT, @doc
    Your SELECT statement goes here
EXEC sp_xml_removedocument @hdoc
```

Understanding OPENXML

Having seen how we create the DOM representation that lets OPENXML generate a rowset, let's look at the general syntax for an OPENXML query:

```
OPENXML (DocHandle       int,
         XPathPattern    nvarchar,
         [Flags          byte])
    [WITH (RowsetSchema  | TableName)]
```

Only the first two of these parameters of the OPENXML function are required. The parameters are:

❑ DocHandle: This is the XML document handle returned by sp_xml_preparedocument.

❑ XpathPattern: An XPath expression (XPathPattern). This expression identifies the nodes in the XML document that will be mapped to the rowset generated. For example, the XPath pattern /root/Order/OrderDetail identifies the <OrderDetail> child element nodes of the <Order> child element node of the <root> element.

❑ Flags: The Flags parameter specifies how the attributes/sub-elements in the XML document map to the columns of the rowset being generated. Flags can be set to 1 for attribute-centric mapping, 2 for element-centric mapping, 3 for mixed mapping (remember this parameter is of byte type). The value 3 is obtained by combining, using a logical OR, 1 (attribute-centric) and 2 (element-centric).

The Flags value 8 has a special meaning: it is used in connection with the @mp:xmltext metaproperty attribute which we'll discuss later. We can also combine values logically – again, we'll see more of this later.

❑ WITH Clause: This is used to provide the description of the rowset to generate (optional). Here we have 3 options:

  ❑ Don't specify anything, in which case a predefined rowset schema (also referred to as an **edge table** schema) is used.

  ❑ Specify an existing table name, in which case that table schema is used to generate the rowset view.

  ❑ Specify the rowset schema (column names and data types and the necessary mapping) yourself. By default, the rowset columns map to the same name attributes/sub-elements in the XML. If the rowset column names are different or we want to map the columns to meta attributes in XML (as we'll discuss later) we can specify additional mapping information.

Here is an example where an existing table name is provided to OPENXML, which generates the rowset view using this table schema.

Assume you have a CustOrder table with this schema:

```
CustOrder(oid varchar(10), orderdate datetime, requireddate datetime)
```

and an XML document such as the following:

```
<root>
    <Customer cid= "Cust1" name="Bob" city="Seattle">
        <Order oid="Ord1" empid="1" orderdate="10/1/2000"
                requireddate="11/1/2000"
                note="ship 2nd day UPS" />
```

```
            <Order oid="Ord2" empid="1" orderdate="10/2/2000"
                    requireddate="12/1/2000" />
        </Customer>
        <Customer cid="C2" name="John" city="NewYork" >
            <Order oid="Ord3" empid="2" orderdate="9/1/2000"
                    requireddate="10/1/2000" />
            <Order oid="Ord4" empid="3" orderdate="9/2/2000"
                    requireddate="10/2/2000" />
        </Customer>
    </root>
```

The document handle and the table name are passed to OPENXML like this (ch14_17.sql):

```
SELECT *
FROM    OPENXML (@hdoc, '/root/Customer/Order')
            WITH CustOrder
```

The resulting three-column rowset returned by the SELECT statement looks like this:

oid	orderdate	requireddate
Ord1	2000-10-01 00:00:00.000	2000-11-01 00:00:00.000
Ord2	2000-10-02 00:00:00.000	2000-12-01 00:00:00.000
Ord3	2000-09-01 00:00:00.000	2000-10-01 00:00:00.000
Ord4	2000-09-02 00:00:00.000	2000-10-02 00:00:00.000

In the result, there is one row for each <Order> element in the original XML document.

If we want to insert the XML into the CustOrder table, we can specify the INSERT statement as follows (ch14_ex18.sql):

```
INSERT INTO CustOrder
    SELECT *
    FROM    OPENXML (@hdoc, '/root/Customer/Order')
                WITH CustOrder
```

And the following is an UPDATE statement that updates the requireddate of order ord1 (ch14_ex19.sql).

```
UPDATE CustOrder
SET     requireddate =
            (SELECT requireddate
            FROM OPENXML (@hdoc, '/root/Customer/Order')
                    WITH CustOrder
            WHERE oid = 'Ord1')
```

Instead of specifying a table name, we can explicitly specify the rowset schema (column names and the data types) in OPENXML, as seen here (ch14_ex20.sql):

```
SELECT  *
FROM    OPENXML (@hdoc, '/root/Customer/Order')
            WITH (oid          varchar(20),
                  orderdate    datetime,
                  requireddate datetime)
```

which gives the same result as ch14_ex17.sql.

By default, the columns specified in the rowset schema map to the attributes (or sub-elements in case of element-centric mapping) of the same name. Note that attribute-centric mapping is the default – that is, the oid column in the resulting rowset maps to the oid attribute of the <Order> element.

If the column names in the rowset differ from the XML element/attribute names to which they map, or you want to map a column to a meta property attribute (discussed later), then you need to provide additional mapping information as part of the rowset schema.

Before we discuss this additional mapping information, let's first discuss the concepts of attribute-centric and element-centric mapping in the context of OPENXML:

OPENXML: Attribute-centric and Element-centric Mapping

By default, OPENXML assumes that each of the rowset columns maps to the samename attribute in the source XML (i.e. attribute-centric mapping is the default). However, you can set the *Flags* parameter to an appropriate value to specify element-centric (*Flags*=2) or mixed (*Flags*=3).

If *Flags* is set to mixed, then attribute-centric mapping is first applied to the remaining rowset columns, followed by element-centric mapping, as shown in the following example. The <Order> element in the following sample XML document (ch14_ex21.sql) has attributes and sub-elements that map to OPENXML rowset columns. *Flags* is set to 3 to indicate mixed mode mapping:

```
DECLARE @hdoc int
DECLARE @doc varchar(1000)
SET @doc ='
<root>
    <Customer cid= "Cust1" name="Bob" city="Seattle">
    <Order oid="Ord1" empid="1" >
        <orderdate>10/1/2000</orderdate>
        <requireddate>11/1/2000</requireddate>
         note="ship 2nd day UPS" />
    </Order>
    <Order oid="Ord2" empid="1" >
        <orderdate>10/2/2000</orderdate>
        <requireddate>12/1/2000</requireddate>
    </Order>
    </Customer>
    <Customer cid="C2" name="John" city="NewYork" >
    <Order oid="Ord3" empid="2" >
        <orderdate>9/1/2000</orderdate>
        <requireddate>10/1/2000</requireddate>
    </Order>
    <Order oid="Ord4" empid="3" >
        <orderdate>9/2/2000</orderdate>
        <requireddate>10/2/2000</requireddate>
    </Order>
    </Customer>
</root>
'--Create an internal representation of the XML document.
EXEC sp_xml_preparedocument @hdoc OUTPUT, @doc

    SELECT *
    FROM   OPENXML (@hdoc, '/root/Customer/Order', 3)
           WITH (oid            varchar(20),
                 orderdate      datetime,
                 requireddate datetime)

EXEC sp_xml_removedocument @hdoc
```

The result is again the same as for ch14_ex17.sql.

Additional Mapping Information for Specifying the Rowset Schema

As we discussed earlier, we can specify the schema for the rowset (RowsetSchema parameter in
OPENXML syntax). The general syntax in specifying the rowset schema is:

```
ColumnName   datatype   [AdditionalMapping],
ColumnName   datatype   [AdditionalMapping],
ColumnName   datatype   [AdditionalMapping]
```

For example, if we specify a 2-column rowset schema in the WITH clause such as

```
EmployeeID       varchar(5),
LastName         varchar(20)
```

then in the default attribute-centric mapping, the EmployeeID column maps to the EmployeeID
attribute in the XML, and the LastName column maps to the LastName attribute in the XML. If our
column names are different from the attribute names to which they map, then we must provide an
appropriate XPath expression to map the column to its attribute, as shown here:

```
EmployeeID     varchar(5)     @EID
LastName       varchar(20)    @Lname
```

In this rowset schema the EmployeeID column maps to the EID attribute, and the LastName column
maps to the Lname attribute in the XML document (assuming EID and Lname are attributes in the XML
document).

In specifying the rowset schema in the WITH clause, the additional mapping information is provided
using an XPath expression when:

❑   Column names in the rowset being generated are different from those of the attributes/sub-
     elements

❑   We want to map rowset column(s) to meta properties (such as node name, unique ID value,
     name of the previous sibling of the node, and so on)

If the rowset schema specified in the WITH clause has column names different from the attribute/sub-
elements names to which they map, then you need to explicitly identify the attribute/sub-element. The
OPENXML in this example generates a rowset in which the column names are different from the
attribute/sub-element to which they map. The additional mapping is provided in the schema
specification in the WITH clause, seen below (ch14_ex22.sql):

```
DECLARE @hdoc int
DECLARE @doc varchar(1000)
SET @doc ='
<root>
    <Customer cid= "Cust1" name="Bob" city="Seattle">
    <Order oid="Ord1" empid="1" orderdate="10/1/2000"
            requireddate="11/1/2000"
            note="ship 2nd day UPS" />
    <Order oid="Ord2" empid="1" orderdate="10/2/2000"
            requireddate="12/1/2000" />
    </Customer>
```

```
        <Customer cid="C2" name="John" city="NewYork" >
           <Order oid="Ord3" empid="2" orderdate="9/1/2000"
                  requireddate="10/1/2000" />
           <Order oid="Ord4" empid="3" orderdate="9/2/2000"
                  requireddate="10/2/2000" />
        </Customer>
     </root>'
EXEC sp_xml_preparedocument @hdoc OUTPUT, @doc

SELECT *
FROM    OPENXML (@hdoc, '/root/Customer/Order', 1)
              WITH (OrdID       varchar(20) '@oid',
                    OrdDate     datetime    '@orderdate',
                    OrdReqDate  datetime    '@requireddate' )

EXEC sp_xml_removedocument @hdoc
```

So now we have:

```
OrdID    OrdDate                        OrdReqDate
------------------------------------------------------------------
Ord1     2000-10-01 00:00:00.000        2000-11-01 00:00:00.000
Ord2     2000-10-02 00:00:00.000        2000-12-01 00:00:00.000
Ord3     2000-09-01 00:00:00.000        2000-10-01 00:00:00.000
Ord4     2000-09-02 00:00:00.000        2000-10-02 00:00:00.000
```

Notice the XPath patterns (@oid, @orderdate, and @requireddate) specified in the WITH clause. In this example, each of these XPath patterns identifies an attribute node in the XML.

Another reason why we may need to specify additional mapping information in the WITH clause is if we want to map our rowset column to the **metaproperty** attributes.

Metaproperty Attributes

Each node in the XML document has certain metaproperties (node name, unique ID value, name of the previous sibling of the node, and so on). These metaproperties are stored as attributes (hence metaproperty attributes) of the node. We may want to map these metaproperty attributes to the columns in the rowset, thus retrieving the meta information about the nodes.

The meta properties are defined in the namespace (urn:schemas-microsoft-com:xml-metaprop) specific to SQL Server 2000.

The metaproperty attributes supported are:

❑   @mp:id: This metaproperty attribute holds the unique identifier value of the node (@mp:parentid returns id of the parent node).

❑   @mp:localname: Stores the local name of the node (@mp:parentlocalname returns the local name of the parent).

❑   @mp:namespaceuri: Provides the namespace URI of the node. (@mp:parentnamespaceuri returns the namespace URI of the parent node).

❑   @mp:prefix: Provides the namespace prefix of the node (@mp:parentprefix returns the namespace prefix of the parent node).

❑   @mp:prev: Provides the unique id of the previous sibling of the node.

❑   @mp:xmltext: When you map this metaproperty attribute to a column, that column will receive all the unconsumed data (an example is given overleaf).

Note that if you don't specify the rowset schema in the WITH clause, then a predefined rowset schema, also referred to as an edge table, is used. The rowset returned has one column for each of the metaproperties described above.

The OPENXML in this example returns id, localname and prev metaproperty values of each of the <Order> element nodes selected (ch14_ex23.sql):

```
DECLARE @hdoc int
DECLARE @doc varchar(1000)
SET @doc ='
<root>
    <Customer cid= "Cust1" name="Bob" city="Seattle">
       <Order oid="Ord1" empid="1" >
          <orderdate>10/1/2000</orderdate>
          <requireddate>11/1/2000</requireddate>
          note="ship 2nd day UPS" />
       </Order>
       <Order oid="Ord2" empid="1" >
          <orderdate>10/2/2000</orderdate>
          <requireddate>12/1/2000</requireddate>
       </Order>
    </Customer>
    <Customer cid="C2" name="John" city="NewYork" >
       <Order oid="Ord3" empid="2" >
          <orderdate>9/1/2000</orderdate>
          <requireddate>10/1/2000</requireddate>
       </Order>
       <Order oid="Ord4" empid="3" >
          <orderdate>9/2/2000</orderdate>
          <requireddate>10/2/2000</requireddate>
       </Order>
    </Customer>
</root>
'

EXEC sp_xml_preparedocument @hdoc OUTPUT, @doc

SELECT  *
FROM    OPENXML (@hdoc, '/root/Customer/Order', 3)
        WITH ( oid          varchar(20),
               CustName      varchar(10)  '../@name',
               UniqueIDVal   int          '@mp:id',
               NodeName      varchar(10)  '@mp:localname',
               NodeSibling   varchar(10)  '@mp:prev')

EXEC sp_xml_removedocument @hdoc
```

This is the result:

oid	CustName	UniqueIDVal	NodeName	NodeSibling
Ord1	Bob	6	Order	NULL
Ord2	Bob	12	Order	6
Ord3	John	21	Order	NULL
Ord4	John	26	Order	21

The `@mp:xmltext` metaproperty has a special meaning. When this attribute is mapped to a rowset column (and *Flags* is set to 8), that column will contain all the unconsumed XML data. In the following example, *Flags* is set to 11 – logical OR of 3 and 8. The value 3 is for mixed mode mapping, and 8 is to indicate that only unconsumed data should be copied to this column. If the flag is set to 3 (mixed mode mapping), then all the data (consumed and unconsumed) will be copied to the overflow column that is mapped to the `@mp:xmltext` metaproperty attribute (ch14_ex24.sql):

```
DECLARE @hdoc int
DECLARE @doc varchar(1000)
SET @doc ='
<root>
    <Customer cid= "Cust1" name="Bob" city="Seattle">
        <Order oid="Ord1" empid="1" >
            <orderdate>10/1/2000</orderdate>
            <requireddate>11/1/2000</requireddate>
             note="ship 2nd day UPS" />
        </Order>
        <Order oid="Ord2" empid="1" >
            <orderdate>10/2/2000</orderdate>
            <requireddate>12/1/2000</requireddate>
        </Order>
    </Customer>
    <Customer cid="C2" name="John" city="NewYork" >
        <Order oid="Ord3" empid="2" >
            <orderdate>9/1/2000</orderdate>
            <requireddate>10/1/2000</requireddate>
        </Order>
        <Order oid="Ord4" empid="3" >
            <orderdate>9/2/2000</orderdate>
            <requireddate>10/2/2000</requireddate>
        </Order>
    </Customer>
</root>
'
EXEC sp_xml_preparedocument @hdoc OUTPUT, @doc


SELECT *
FROM   OPENXML (@hdoc, '/root/Customer/Order', 11)
          WITH ( oid           varchar(20),
                 CustName       varchar(10)   '../@name',
                 orderdate      datetime,
                 RemainingData  ntext         '@mp:xmltext')

EXEC sp_xml_removedocument @hdoc
```

This is the result. Notice the `RemainingData` column contains only the unconsumed data:

oid	CustName	orderdate	RemainingData
Ord1	Bob	2000-10-01 00:00:00.000	\<Order empid="1"\> \<requireddate\>11/1/2000 \</requireddate\> note="ship 2nd day UPS" /> \</Order\>
Ord2	Bob	2000-10-02 00:00:00.000	\<Order empid="1"\> \<requireddate\>12/1/2000 \</requireddate\>\</Order\>

```
Ord3   John        2000-09-01 00:00:00.000   <Order empid="2">
                                              <requireddate>10/1/2000
                                              </requireddate></Order>
Ord4   John        2000-09-02 00:00:00.000   <Order empid="3">
                                              <requireddate>10/2/2000
                                              </requireddate></Order>
```

We also can retrieve text in the XML nodes identified. The XPath `text` function can be specified as a column pattern, which maps the rowset column to the text in the node identified (`ch14_ex24.sql`):

```
EXEC sp_xml_preparedocument @hdoc OUTPUT, @doc

SELECT  *
FROM    OPENXML (@hdoc, '/root/Customer/Order', 3)
        WITH ( oid          varchar(20),
               CustName      varchar(10)  '../@name',
               comment ntext 'text()')

EXEC sp_xml_removedocument @hdoc
```

This is the result:

```
oid         CustName    comment
Ord1        Bob         note="ship 2nd day UPS" />
Ord2        Bob         NULL
Ord3        John        NULL
Ord4        John        NULL
```

The Edge Table Schema for the Rowset

As mentioned earlier, if we don't provide any schema for the rowset to be generated, then OPENXML generates a rowset using a default schema (edge table). The rowset is called an edge table because the rowset generated has one row for every "edge" in the XML tree (consisting of nodes and edges) generated by the `sp_xml_preparedocument` stored procedure.

The information returned in the rowset includes meta information of the DOM nodes. This meta information includes:

❑ The unique identifier of the node and the parent node

❑ The node type (element, attribute, or text node)

❑ The local name of the node

❑ The namespace prefix in the node name

❑ The namespace URI of the node (NULL if no namespace)

❑ The data type of the node

❑ The unique identifier value of the node's previous sibling

❑ The value of the node

The edge table schema is given below:

```
id              bigint,
parentid        bigint
nodetype        int (1=element; 2=attribute; 3=text node)
localname       nvarchar
prefix          nvarchar
namespaceuri    nvarchar
datatype        nvarchar
prev            bigint
text            ntext
```

As you can see, the edge table returns meta properties of the DOM node. If we specify the rowset schema in the WITH clause, we can obtain these meta property values by mapping the columns to the meta property attributes.

The information in the edge table is useful in analyzing the XML document. For example, we may want to find element/attribute names, namespaces, the datatypes of elements/attributes, the information about the document hierarchy, and so on. This allows the application developer to query the XML document before processing the contents. For instance, we may want to know the number of customers in the document before we process them.

Understanding the Edge Table

The following SELECT statement with OPENXML returns a rowset that has the edge table format (ch14_ex25.sql):

```
DECLARE @hdoc int
DECLARE @doc varchar(1000)
SET @doc ='
<ROOT>
   <Customer CustomerID="VINET" ContactName="Paul Henriot">
      <Order OrderID="10248" CustomerID="VINET" EmployeeID="5" OrderDate=
                "1996-07-04T00:00:00">
         <OrderDetail OrderID="10248" ProductID="11" Quantity="12"/>
         <OrderDetail OrderID="10248" ProductID="42" Quantity="10"/>
      </Order>
   </Customer>
   <Customer CustomerID="LILAS" ContactName="Carlos Gonzlez">
      <Order OrderID="10283" CustomerID="LILAS" EmployeeID="3" OrderDate=
                "1996-08-16T00:00:00">
         <OrderDetail OrderID="10283" ProductID="72" Quantity="3"/>
      </Order>
   </Customer>
</ROOT>'

--Create an internal representation of the XML document.
EXEC sp_xml_preparedocument @hdoc OUTPUT, @doc

-- Execute a SELECT statement using OPENXML rowset provider.
SELECT *
FROM OPENXML (@hdoc,
    '/ROOT/Customer[@CustomerID="VINET"]/Order[@OrderID="10248"]')

EXEC sp_xml_removedocument @hdoc
```

The XPath pattern specified identifies <Order> child element nodes with OrderID 10248, which have a <Customer> parent with CustomerID "VINET".

This is the resulting rowset:

id	parentid	nodetype	localname	prefix	namespaceuri	datatype	prev	text
5	2	1	Order	NULL	NULL	NULL	NULL	NULL
6	5	2	OrderID	NULL	NULL	NULL	NULL	NULL
30	6	3	#text	NULL	NULL	NULL	NULL	10248
7	5	2	CustomerID	NULL	NULL	NULL	NULL	NULL
31	7	3	#text	NULL	NULL	NULL	NULL	VINET
8	5	2	EmployeeID	NULL	NULL	NULL	NULL	NULL
32	8	3	#text	NULL	NULL	NULL	NULL	5
9	5	2	OrderDate	NULL	NULL	NULL	NULL	NULL
33	9	3	#text	NULL	NULL	NULL	NULL	1996-07-04T00:00:00
10	5	1	OrderDetail	NULL	NULL	NULL	NULL	NULL
11	10	2	OrderID	NULL	NULL	NULL	NULL	NULL
34	11	3	#text	NULL	NULL	NULL	NULL	10248
12	10	2	ProductID	NULL	NULL	NULL	NULL	NULL
35	12	3	#text	NULL	NULL	NULL	NULL	11
13	10	2	Quantity	NULL	NULL	NULL	NULL	NULL
36	13	3	#text	NULL	NULL	NULL	NULL	12
14	5	1	OrderDetail	NULL	NULL	NULL	10	NULL
15	14	2	OrderID	NULL	NULL	NULL	NULL	NULL
37	15	3	#text	NULL	NULL	NULL	NULL	10248
16	14	2	ProductID	NULL	NULL	NULL	NULL	NULL
38	16	3	#text	NULL	NULL	NULL	NULL	42
17	14	2	Quantity	NULL	NULL	NULL	NULL	NULL
39	17	3	#text	NULL	NULL	NULL	NULL	10

Let's review the first three rows of this table. Once you understand them, the result in the subsequent rows becomes obvious.

The first row:

id	parentid	nodetype	localname	prefix	namespaceuri	datatype	prev	text
5	2	1	Order	NULL	NULL	NULL	NULL	NULL

identifies the Order node:

```
<Customer CustomerID="VINET" ContactName="Paul Henriot">
    <Order OrderID="10248" CustomerID="VINET" EmployeeID="5" OrderDate=
           "1996-07-04T00:00:00">
```

It is given a unique id value of 5. Its parentid is 2, identifying the Customer node. The result does not show the Customer node because the XPath query does not request the Customer node. The nodetype is 1 because the Order node is an element node. The Order node has no prefix, therefore the value in the prefix column is NULL. The column value NULL indicates that the node has no specific value of the meta property.

The second row:

```
id   parentid nodetype localname  prefix  namespaceuri datatype prev text

6    5        2                  OrderID  NULL    NULL         NULL     NULL NULL
```

identifies the OrderID node with the unique id value of 6. Notice that the parentid column has value 5, identifying the Order node as its parent. The nodetype is 2 because it is an attribute node. The rest of the column values are NULL since they don't apply.

The third row identifies a text node:

```
id   parentid nodetype localname  prefix  namespaceuri datatype prev text

30   6        3                  #text    NULL    NULL         NULL     NULL 10248
```

This is the value of the OrderID attribute in the document. The value 10248 appears in the text column (the last column) in the rowset. Its unique id value is 30, and the parentid is 6, identifying OrderID node as its parent. The nodetype value is 3, indicating this node is a text node.

This should give you some idea of how this information about the document, the hierarchy contained in it, the node names, and their types are returned in the rowset.

Using the Edge Table

The information in the edge table rowset can be quite useful. For example, if you want to find out how many <Customer> elements are in the document, the following query (ch14_ex26.sql) gives you the answer. Replace the SELECT query in the previous example with this:

```
SELECT count(*)
FROM  OPENXML(@hdoc, '/')
WHERE localname = 'Customer'
```

You should get the answer 2.

In addition, the edge table rowsets are useful in dealing with attributes of type idrefs. As we saw in the previous example, OPENXML copies the XML attribute/element values to the columns in the rowset based on the mapping specified in the schema that is declared in the WITH clause.

This works well if the attribute/sub-element has only one value. However, if we have XML attributes of type idrefs that can have multiple values, how do we extract individual values? If we have a document fragment:

```
<Customer CustID="1" OrderList="Ord1 Ord2 Ord3" />
```

then to generate a rowset

```
CustID   OrderID
1        Ord1
1        Ord2
1        Ord3
```

requires additional work. Here is a possible solution using the edge table.

Consider this XML document:

```
<Data>
   <Customer CustomerID = "C1" ContactName = "Joe Smith"
         OrderList = "O1 O2 O3" />
   <Customer CustomerID = "C2" ContactName = "Andrew Fuller"
         OrderList = "O4 O5" />
</Data>'
```

and assume we have these tables:

```
Customer (CustomerID varchar(5) primary key,
      ContactName varchar(30))
CustOrder (CustomerID varchar(5) references Customer (CustomerID),
      OrderID varchar(5) primary key)
```

Say we want to insert values into the `Customer` and `CustOrder` tables from the XML document using OPENXML. Adding records to the `Customer` table is straightforward using OPENXML, but to insert values in the `CustOrder` table is not easy. The solution provided here uses OPENXML to return the rowset in an edge table format. The information in the edge table is then used to retrieve the information.

The solution uses two stored procedures. The `GetIdIDrefsValues` stored procedure returns a result as a two column rowset, such as:

```
CustomerID    OrderList
C1            O1 O2 O3
C2            O4 O5
```

The second stored procedure, `InsertidrefsValues`, then retrieves the individual order id values for each customer, and inserts the `CustomerID OrderID` values in the `CustOrder` table:

The two stored procedures are given below (`ch14_ex27.sql`):

```
DROP PROCEDURE InsertidrefsValues
GO
CREATE PROCEDURE InsertidrefsValues
    @OrderIDList       varchar(500),
    @CustOrder  varchar(50),
    @CustID       varchar(5)
AS
DECLARE @sp int
DECLARE @att varchar(5)
SET @sp = 0
WHILE (LEN(@OrderIDList) > 0)
BEGIN
    SET @sp = CHARINDEX(' ', @OrderIDList+ ' ')
    SET @att = LEFT(@OrderIDList, @sp-1)
    EXEC('INSERT INTO '+@CustOrder+' VALUES ('''+@CustID+''', '''+@att+''')')
    SET @OrderIDList = SUBSTRING(@OrderIDList+ ' ', @sp+1,
                              LEN(@OrderIDList)+1-@sp)

END
Go
```

```
DROP PROCEDURE GetIdIdrefsValues
GO
CREATE PROCEDURE GetIdIdrefsValues
    @xmldoc      int,
    @xpath       varchar(100),
    @from        varchar(50),
    @to          varchar(50),
    @TableName   varchar(100)
AS
DECLARE @OrdIDList varchar(500)
DECLARE @CustID varchar(5)

/* Temporary Edge table */
SELECT *
INTO #TempEdge
FROM OPENXML(@xmldoc, @xpath)

DECLARE fillidrefs_cursor CURSOR FOR
    SELECT CAST(OneSideAttrVal.text AS nvarchar(200)) AS CustID,
           CAST(ManySideAttrVal.text AS nvarchar(4000)) AS OrdIDList
    FROM   #TempEdge Elem, #TempEdge OneSideAttr,
           #TempEdge OneSideAttrVal, #TempEdge ManySideAttr,
           #TempEdge ManySideAttrVal
    WHERE  Elem.id = OneSideAttr.parentid
    AND    UPPER(OneSideAttr.localname) = UPPER(@from)
    AND    OneSideAttr.id = OneSideAttrVal.parentid
    AND    Elem.id = ManySideAttr.parentid
    AND    UPPER(ManySideAttr.localname) = UPPER(@to)
    AND    ManySideAttr.id = ManySideAttrVal.parentid

OPEN fillidrefs_cursor
FETCH NEXT FROM fillidrefs_cursor INTO @CustID, @OrdIDList
WHILE (@@FETCH_STATUS <> -1)
BEGIN
    IF (@@FETCH_STATUS <> -2)
    BEGIN
        execute InsertidrefsValues @OrdIDList, @TableName, @CustID
    END
    FETCH NEXT FROM fillidrefs_cursor INTO @CustID, @OrdIDList
END
CLOSE fillidrefs_cursor
DEALLOCATE fillidrefs_cursor
Go
```

You can test this code using the following (ch14_ex28.sql):

```
DECLARE @h int

EXECUTE sp_xml_preparedocument @h OUTPUT, '
<Data>
  <Customer CustomerID = "C1" ContactName = "Joe Smith"
                OrderList = "O1 O2 O3" />
  <Customer CustomerID = "C2" ContactName = "Roger Wolter"
                OrderList = "O4 O5"  />
</Data>'
```

```
--insert values in the Customer table
INSERT INTO Customer SELECT * FROM OPENXML(@h, '//Customer') WITH Customer
--insert values in the CustOrder table using edge table

EXECUTE GetIdIdrefsValues @h, '//Customer', 'CustomerID', 'OrderList',
                            'CustOrder'

EXECUTE sp_xml_removedocument @h
```

You should find the tables are populated with the required data.

As you can see, the OPENXML feature in SQL Server 2000 is a valuable tool for working with XML documents and databases. OPENXML is a server side implementation that allows us to modify database contents from an XML document source. There are alternative middle-tier features, such as the XML updategrams, that can be used to modify SQL server data. We'll be looking at the middle-tier features in the next chapter.

Bulk Loading XML

SQL Server 2000 allows us to bulk load XML into the database tables. This is an efficient alternative to using OPENXML to shred the document, and then using an INSERT statement to store the data. This is especially useful if we are loading large amounts of XML onto the database.

The XML Bulk Load feature uses XML views, which we'll meet in the next chapter. XML views are schemas written in XDR, with extensions for mapping relational database tables to the elements/attributes in the XML view. However, we'll discuss the XML Bulk Load here because it is a server side feature.

We can use the XML Bulk Load object from code via the Bulk Load object model. We need to pass it two pieces of information:

❑ **The mapping schema**: The mapping XDR schema must be provided to the XML Bulk Load object

❑ **The XML document** that you want to bulk load

The Bulk Load object model has only one object – SQLXMLBulkLoad. It also has several properties that we can set. These properties allow us, among other things, to specify whether we want to execute Bulk Load in a transaction mode or not. In a transaction mode, if some problem occurs, then rollback is guaranteed. The non-transacted Bulk Load is faster because no logging takes place. If your database is empty, then non-transacted Bulk Load is the way to go.

These properties also allow us to specify if we want the tables created before loading the data. We can specify if we want to create a table that doesn't already exist, but not drop the ones already in existence. We can insist on checking any constraint violations, such as primary key or foreign key violations. You can also specify a file in which to log the errors and messages that are generated during execution.

The XML Bulk Load supports the following properties and methods:

Name	Description
Execute	Loads the data using the XML View and the XML data files provided as input.
ConnectionCommand	This property is used to specify the existing connection object that XML Bulk Load should use.
ConnectionString	Instead of a connection command, you can specify a connection string using this property.
KeepNulls	If this Boolean property is set to True, the column value for which the corresponding attribute/sub-element is missing in the XML document is set to NULL (even if the column has a default value, NULL will be assigned). If the property is set to False, then if the column has a default value set, that default value is assigned. The default value for this property is False.
KeepIdentity	SQL Server has identity type columns, where the value of the column is assigned by SQL Server. If this property is set to True, then if the XML document provides a value for the identity type column, that value is stored in the column. If the property is set to False, then any value provided in the XML document for the identity type column is ignored, and the SQL Server assigned value is inserted in the column. The default value for this property is True.
CheckConstraints	If this Boolean property is set to True, then Bulk Load will check each value inserted in a column against the constraints specified on that column (such as primary key/foreign key constraints). The default value for this property is False.
ForceTableLock	If this Boolean property is set to True, the table in which data is inserted is locked for the duration of the Bulk Load. When the property is set to False, a table lock is acquired for each record inserted in the table. The default value for this property is False.
XMLFragment	If this Boolean property is set to True, the source XML document is considered as a fragment (that is, there is no single top-level element in the document). The default value for this property is False.
Transaction	If this Boolean property is set to True, then Bulk Load is performed in transaction mode (which guarantees rollback in case of a failure). By default this property is False.
TempFilePath	This property specifies the file path where XML bulk load creates the temporary files in a transacted Bulk Load. If this property is not set, then the temporary files are stored at location specified in the TEMP environment variable. The temporary files are created only during a transacted Bulk Load.
ErrorLogFile	This property specifies the file name in which errors are logged by XML Bulk Load. If this property is not set, the logging is turned off.

Table continued on following page

Name	Description
SchemaGen	If this Boolean property is set to True, Bulk Load will create the tables necessary to perform the bulk load. If some of the tables already exist, then the SGDroptables property determines whether the existing tables are removed and recreated.
SGDropTables	If this Boolean property is set to True, then the existing tables are dropped and recreated. This property is used along with the SchemaGen property. The default value for this property is False.
SGUseID	In XML Views you can define certain attributes as id type. If the SGUseID property is set to True, then ScheamGen uses the id type attribute as primary key column, and creates necessary constraints on this column when the table is created. The default value for this property is False.

Let's see how all of this works in practice.

How the Database is Generated from XML

Because the XML document can be large, the entire document is not read in memory. Instead, the document is read like a stream, and the data is processed as it is read. Let's take a look at how the records are generated from the data in the source XML document, and when the records are sent to SQL Server.

Say we have a Customer table:

```
Customer(CustomerID, ContactName)
```

and this XML document:

```
<Customer CustomerID="C1" ContactName="Joe" />
<Customer CustomerID="C2" ContactName="Bob" />
...
```

When the start tag of the first <Customer> element is read, a record for the customer table is generated. As the attributes are read, these attribute values are copied to the record already generated. When the end tag is reached, the record is considered complete, and is sent to SQL Server for insertion. Both the <Customer> element and the record, go out of scope at this point. As the next <Customer> element is read, a new record for the Customer table is generated, and the process is repeated.

It is important to understand that the data for the Customer table must be contained between the start and end tag of the <Customer> element. This becomes clear when we have a complex XML document and the associated mapping XDR schema (schema that describes the primary key and foreign key relationships between two elements).

If our document includes hierarchy such as:

```
<Customer CustomerID="C1" ContactName="Joe" >
    <Order OrderID="Ord1" OrderDate="10/10/2000" />
    <Order OrderID="Ord1" OrderDate="10/10/2000" />
</Customer>
...
```

and these tables:

```
Customer(CustomerID, ContactName)
Order (OrderID, OrderDate, CustomerID)
```

then a `customer` record is generated first as the start tag of the `<Customer>` element is read. The `CustomerID` and `ContactName` attribute values are copied to this record. As the start tag of the `<Order>` element is read, a record for the `Order` table is generated, and the `OrderID` and `OrderDate` attribute values are copied to this table. When the end tag is reached, the `Order` record is sent to SQL Server.

The XML Bulk Load uses the primary key foreign key relationship specified in the mapping XDR schema – in this case we'll obtain the `CustomerID` foreign key value from the `<Customer>` element. All the `<Order>` elements are processed in this manner. Finally, when the end tag, `</Customer>`, is reached, the `Customer` record is sent to SQL Server.

The value of the `CustomerID` attribute of the `<Customer>` element must be specified before the `<Order>` child elements. Otherwise, when the end tag of the `<Order>` element is reached, the record will be sent to SQL Server without the foreign key value (and Bulk Load will fail). This is illustrated by the following XML document:

```
<Customer>
    <ContactName>Joe</ContactName>
    <Order OrderID="Ord1" OrderDate="10/10/2000" />
    <Order OrderID="Ord1" OrderDate="10/10/2000" />
    <CustomerID>>C1 </CustomerID>
</Customer>
...
```

In the above document, the key `CustomerID` node appears after the `<Order>` child elements. That's a problem because the `Order` records are sent to SQL Server as soon as the end tag is reached – that is, without the `CustomerID` foreign key value. Therefore, our XML document must have the key attribute appear first.

The only exception to the record generation rule is when you have `idref` or `idrefs` type nodes in the XML document. During Bulk Load, no record is generated if a node of type `idref` or `idrefs` enters the scope (the start tag is read). For example, consider this XML fragment:

```
<Customer CustomerID="C1" OrderList="Ord1 Ord2 Ord3" />
<Customer CustomerID="C2" OrderList="Ord4 Ord5" />
...
```

Assume the mapping schema associates the `<Customer>` element to the `Customer` table, the `CustomerID` attribute to the `CustomerID` column in the `Customer` table, and the `OrderList` attribute to the `OrderID` column of the `CustOrder` table. In this case, when the start tag of the first `<Customer>` element is read, a record for the `Customer` table is generated. The `CustomerID` attribute value is copied to the record, but the `OrderList` attribute does not map to the `Customer` table, so that value is not copied to the record generated for the `Customer` table.

However, if the schema identifies the OrderList as an idrefs type attribute, that attribute is simply ignored. That means we have to make sure that the <Order> element is described somewhere in the document and the schema. If our XML document is revised, like so:

```
<Customer CustomerID="C1" OrderList="Ord1 Ord2 Ord3" />
<Order CustomerID="C1" OrderID="Ord1" />
<Order CustomerID="C1" OrderID="Ord2" />
<Order CustomerID="C1" OrderID="Ord3" />

<Customer CustomerID="C2" OrderList="Ord4 Ord5" />
<Order CustomerID="C2" OrderID="Ord4" />
<Order CustomerID="C2" OrderID="Ord5" />
```

the XML Bulk Load will insert data in the Customer and Order tables. The only problem is that the user is responsible to maintain the referential integrity.

Assume we have this XML View (mapping schema) defined (ch14_ex29.xdr):

```
<?xml version="1.0" ?>
<Schema xmlns="urn:schemas-microsoft-com:xml-data"
    xmlns:dt="urn:schemas-microsoft-com:datatypes"
    xmlns:sql="urn:schemas-microsoft-com:xml-sql" >

  <ElementType name="Customers" sql:relation="Customer" >
   <AttributeType name="CustomerID" />
   <AttributeType name="CompanyName" />
   <AttributeType name="City" />
   <AttributeType name="OrderList" dt:type="idrefs" />

   <attribute type="CustomerID" />
   <attribute type="CompanyName" />
   <attribute type="City" />
   <attribute type="OrderList" sql:relation="CustOrder"
           sql:field="OrderID" >
   <sql:relationship
   key-relation ="Cust"
   key          ="CustomerID"
   foreign-key   ="CustomerID"
   foreign-relation="CustOrder" />
   </attribute>
  </ElementType>

  <ElementType name="Order" sql:relation="CustOrder" >
   <AttributeType name="OrderID" dt:type="id" />
   <AttributeType name="CustomerID" />
   <AttributeType name="OrderDate" />

   <attribute type="OrderID" />
   <attribute type="CustomerID" />
   <attribute type="OrderDate" />
  </ElementType>
 </Schema>
```

and this is our XML data (ch14_ex29.xml):

```
<Customers CustomerID="1111" CompanyName="Sean Chai" City="NY"
    OrderList="Ord1 Ord2" />
<Customers CustomerID="1112" CompanyName="Dont Know" City="LA"
    OrderList="Ord3 Ord4" />
<Order OrderID="Ord1" CustomerID="1111" OrderDate="1999-01-01" />
<Order OrderID="Ord2" CustomerID="1111" OrderDate="1999-02-01" />
<Order OrderID="Ord3" CustomerID="1112" OrderDate="1999-03-01" />
<Order OrderID="Ord4" CustomerID="1112" OrderDate="1999-04-01" />
```

and assume that the XML data is bulk loaded in these tables (ch14_ex29.sql):

```
CREATE TABLE Customer (
        CustomerID    int           primary key,
        CompanyName   varchar(20)   NOT NULL,
        City          varchar(20)   default 'Seattle')
go
CREATE TABLE CustOrder (
        OrderID       varchar(10)   primary key,
        CustomerID    int           foreign key references
                                    Customer (CustomerID),
        OrderDate     datetime default '2000-01-01')
Go
```

we can execute the Bulk Load using the following Visual Basic code (ch14_ex29.vb):

```
Set objBL = CreateObject("SQLXMLBulkLoad.SQLXMLBulkLoad")
objBL.ConnectionString = "provider=SQLOLEDB.1;data " & _
                         "source=server;database=database;uid=sa;pwd="
objBL.ErrorLogFile = "c:\error.log"
objBL.CheckConstraints=True
objBL.XMLFragment = True
objBL.Execute "c:\XMLView.xml", "c:\XMLData.xml"
Set objBL1=Nothing
```

First we create a SQLXMLBulkLoad object (objBL). Then we set various properties on this object. The ConnectionString property is set because we are using a connection string which identifies the server, database, and the necessary login information. The ErrorLogFile property is set so that we can log any errors during Bulk Load.

The CheckConstraint property is set to True. As a result, each time a record is inserted, all the constraints are checked. For example, if we are adding data in the CustOrder table, and specify a CustomerID that doesn't exist in the Customer table, then Bulk Load will fail because of primary key foreign key constraint violation.

The XMLFragment property is set to True, because the source XML document does not have a single top-level element. Finally the Execute method is called. The Execute method takes two parameters: the schema file name and the XML data file name.

In summary, XML Bulk Load feature allows us to bulk load large XML documents into SQL Server tables with great efficiency. The XML Bulk Load requires an XML view of the tables in which we are bulk loading the XML. We'll discuss the XML views in more detail in the next chapter.

Summary

We'll conclude this chapter by summarizing the server side XML features in SQL Server. The two server side features we discussed are FOR XML and OPENXML.

- ❑ FOR XML is an extension to SELECT statement and is used to retrieve data from SQL Server as XML. FOR XML supports three different modes: RAW, AUTO, and EXPLICIT.

- ❑ The RAW mode generates flat XML. It is useful if your application doesn't require specific shape of XML.

- ❑ The AUTO mode generates hierarchy, giving the user limited control over the shape of the XML.

- ❑ The EXPLICIT mode is the most powerful of all, because you have complete control over the shape of the XML.

   Users with good SQL background may find writing these queries easy, but if you find EXPLICIT mode queries complex to write you have another option – create XML views and specify XPath queries against it. We will explore this method in the next chapter.

- ❑ OPENXML does the opposite. It takes an XML document and shreds it to produce a rowset view. This rowset can then be passed to INSERT, UPDATE, and DELETE statements. In this way, XML can be stored in the database or modified using ordinary SQL queries. In the next chapter we'll see how XML updategrams can be used to perform updates based on XML data.

In the next chapter we'll discuss the middle tier features such as XML Views, XML updategrams, and XPath queries.

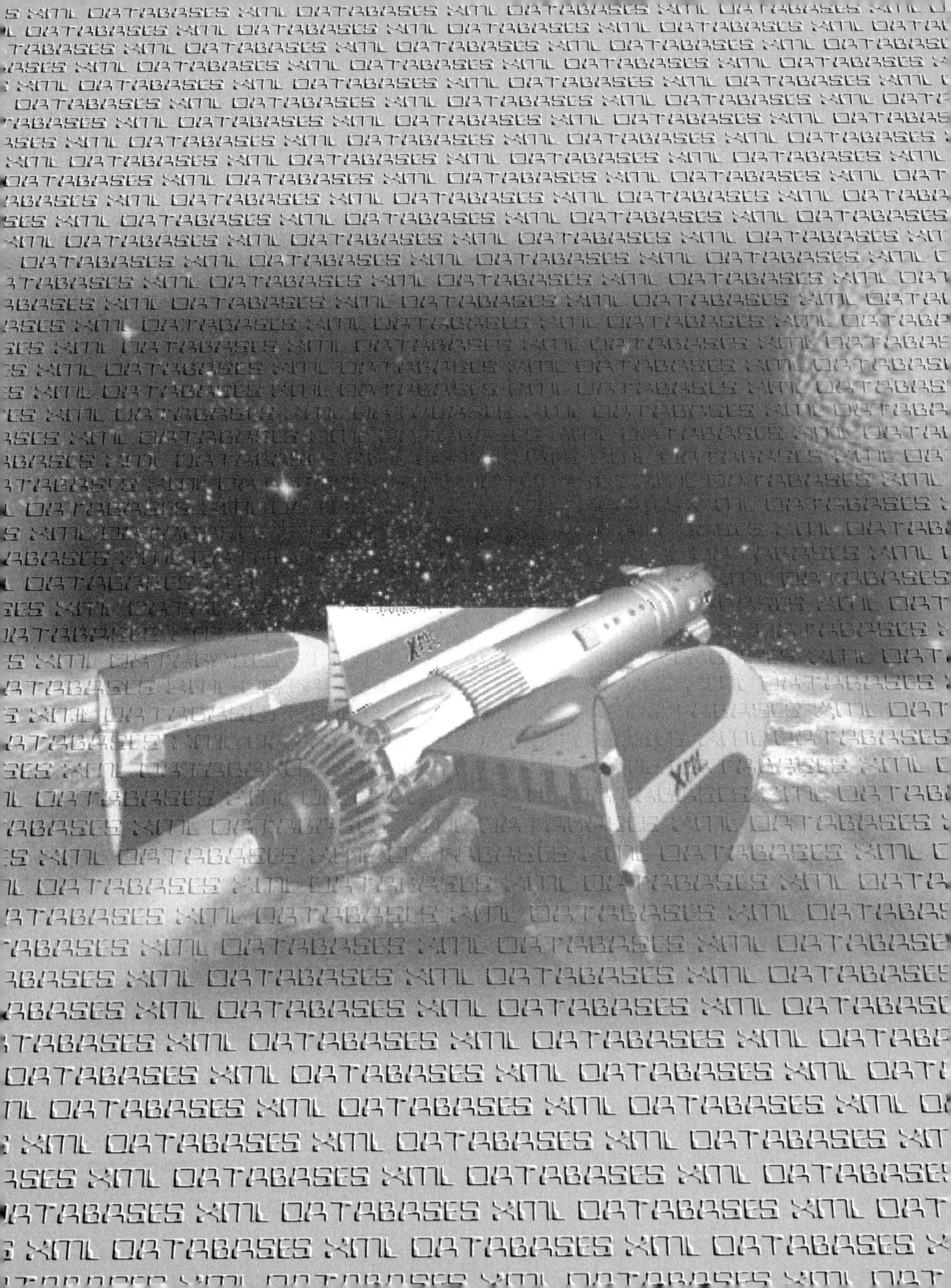
XML DATABASES XML DATABASES XML DATABASES
XML
XML

15

XML Views in SQL Server 2000

In the previous chapter, we learned how to retrieve XML data from a relational database using SQL. Wouldn't it be great if we could also query the database as though it were an XML document (or collection of documents), using XPath and other XML query languages? This is precisely the capability that **XML Views** in SQL Server 2000 provide.

An XML View allows us to query SQL Server 2000 as though it were storing XML. The XML View describes the shape of an XML document, even though the XML does not really exist because it is created on-the-fly from the relational database. Furthermore, it allows us to describe relationships between the XML and the table structure so that we can get XML returned in a format that we want (even if that is different from the table structure and names in the database).

Once we have defined an XML View, which defines the mapping between the XML and the database, we can then query this XML View as though it were a real XML document; the query, together with the view, determines the shape of the resulting XML.

An XML View is created by adding some annotations to an XML schema. The schema describes the shape of an XML document, and the annotations describe the mappings between the XML and the database.

You can then query this XML view (possibly modifying the underlying database) using XML query languages such as **XPath** and **Updategrams**. In this way, the relational database is hidden from the user, and the data appears to be completely XML-based.

At present, XML Views are based on the schema language XDR (see http://www.ltg.ed.ac.uk/~ht/XMLData-Reduced.htm). However, the W3C is defining a standard XML Schema Definition language (XSD) that will be supported in early 2001 (see http://www.w3.org/TR/xmlschema-1/ for details).

Additionally, Microsoft is working closely with the W3C to help design the XML Query Language, which XML Views will eventually support (Watch http://www.w3.org/XML/Query for details on this emerging standard). For more information about the XML Query Language, please read Chapter 11.

XML Views are especially convenient when an XML schema – such as a BizTalk schema (see http://www.biztalk.org/ for a vast collection of schemas) – is already available, but it is also straightforward to construct XML schemas from scratch.

In this chapter we will describe:

- ❑ The basics of XDR schemas, in brief
- ❑ How to annotate an XDR schema into an XML View
- ❑ How to query a database with XPath
- ❑ Updategrams, a novel approach to updating, inserting, and deleting XML data
- ❑ Some advanced uses of XML Views

You will find detailed examples of all of these features in this chapter and the next.

Before reading this chapter, you should be familiar with the basic structure of the Northwind database (which we use for our examples). Also, the section on XPath benefits from – but does not require – an understanding of the FOR XML EXPLICIT mode, as described in the previous chapter.

Fragments and Documents

An XML View actually describes one or more kinds of **XML fragments**. There is a distinction between an XML fragment and an XML **document**.

As you are aware, a well-formed XML document has just one top-level element:

```
<Customer CustomerID="ANATR">
    <Order CustomerID="ANATR" OrderID="10308"/>
    <Order CustomerID="ANATR" OrderID="10625"/>
</Customer>
```

The natural data structure representation of this structure is a **tree**. In contrast, an XML fragment can have many top-level elements. Here we have a fragment of the above document:

```
<Order CustomerID="ANATR" OrderID="10308"/>
<Order CustomerID="ANATR" OrderID="10625"/>
```

The natural representation of a fragment is a **forest** (an ordered collection of trees).

XDR Schemas

As the name **XML Data Reduced** suggests, XDR is a simplified version of XML Data, a schema language for XML (see http://www.w3.org/TR/1998/NOTE-XML-data/ for details.) XDR provides the building blocks to describe complex shapes and data types not possible to describe with DTDs, but lacks the full flexibility (and complexity) of the XML Schema Definition Language (XSD). For a tutorial on schema languages in general and XDR in particular, please see:

http://msdn.microsoft.com/xml/XMLGuide/schema-overview.asp.

Let's quickly review the main points of creating an XDR schema. Consider the following XML fragment, which contains two `Customer` elements, both having a `CustomerID` attribute. One `Customer` element also contains several `Order` elements, all of which have a `CustomerID` attribute and an `OrderID` attribute:

```
<Customer CustomerID="ANATR">
    <Order CustomerID="ANATR" OrderID="10308"/>
    <Order CustomerID="ANATR" OrderID="10625"/>
    <Order CustomerID="ANATR" OrderID="10759"/>
    <Order CustomerID="ANATR" OrderID="10926"/>
</Customer>
<Customer CustomerID="PARIS"/>
```

Now, let's create an XDR schema for this fragment. XDR schemas begin with the top-level element `<Schema>`, which contains declarations of elements and attributes. Elements and attributes are declared by name using `<ElementType>` and `<AttributeType>` tags, respectively. Various attributes on these tags control the content model, data type, and other aspects of the XML data. Here is an XDR schema that describes the above XML fragment:

```
<Schema xmlns="urn:schemas-microsoft-com:xml-data">
    <AttributeType name="CustomerID"/>

    <ElementType name="Order">
       <AttributeType name="OrderID" />
       <attribute type="CustomerID"/>
       <attribute type="OrderID" />
    </ElementType>

    <ElementType name="Customer">
       <attribute type="CustomerID"/>
       <element type="Order" />
    </ElementType>
</Schema>
```

Notice that every component in the schema belongs to the XDR namespace (`urn:schemas-microsoft-com:xml-data`), and that there can be any number of `<ElementType>` or `<AttributeType>` declarations in the schema.

First the schema defines the `CustomerID` attribute, which will appear in both element types:

```
<AttributeType name="CustomerID"/>
```

Next it defines the `Order` element:

```
<ElementType name="Order">
   <AttributeType name="OrderID" />
   <attribute type="CustomerID"/>
   <attribute type="OrderID" />
</ElementType>
```

Remember that the `Order` element contained two attributes: `CustomerID`, which we have already declared, and `OrderID`, which we declare inside the definition of `Order`. These attributes are defined on `Order` using the `<attribute>` tag. It is not enough to declare them using `<AttributeType>`; they must also be defined using `<attribute>`.

These declarations are exactly like local and global variables in a programming language. Because `CustomerID` is declared globally, it can be used in any `<ElementType>`; however, `OrderID` has been declared locally to the `Order` `<ElementType>`, so it can only be used in the `Order` `<ElementType>` (other `ElementType` elements could locally declare their own `OrderID` attributes). XDR allows us to do this so that different elements can contain attributes of the same name but with (potentially) different meaning.

We cannot, however, do the same with `<ElementType>` declarations. `<ElementType>` declarations are always global (they do not have to be declared before they are used). Because `Customer` elements can contain `Order` elements, we must use an `<element>` inside of the `Customer` `<ElementType>`:

```
<ElementType name="Customer">
    <attribute type="CustomerID"/>
    <element type="Order" />
</ElementType>
```

This simple example illustrates the basics of XDR, which will be enough for this chapter, although XDR also provides ways to describe content models, element order, bounds on the minimum or maximum number of occurrences, and much more. For a complete description of XDR, please see http://msdn.microsoft.com/xml/XMLGuide/schema-overview.asp.

The Default Mapping

Now that we've looked at XDR schemas, you may be wondering how much additional work is required to make a schema work with the database. Surprisingly, the answer can be: none! Consider a section of the `Customers` table in the **Northwind** database:

CustomerID	CompanyName	ContactName	ContactTitle
ALFKI	Alfreds Futterkiste	Maria Anders	Sales Representative
ANATR	Ana Trujillo Emparedados y helados	Ana Trujillo	Owner
ANTON	Antonio Moreno Taquería	Antonio Moreno	Owner
AROUT	Around the Horn	Thomas Hardy	Sales Representative
BERGS	Berglunds snabbköp	Christina Berglund	Order Administrator

The following XDR schema (`ch15_ex01.xdr`) can be used without modification as an XML view of this table:

```
<Schema xmlns="urn:schemas-microsoft-com:xml-data">
    <AttributeType name="CustomerID"/>
    <AttributeType name="ContactName"/>
    <ElementType name="Customers">
        <attribute type="CustomerID"/>
        <attribute type="ContactName"/>
    </ElementType>
</Schema>
```

How will values in the database be mapped to the XML? Because there are no annotations describing the mapping between the XML data and SQL Server, a **default mapping** is used. The default mapping takes each `<ElementType>` to the table of the same name (or to a column, if the element's content is `textOnly`), and each `<AttributeType>` to the column of the same name. Attributes and `textOnly` elements inherit the table of their parents.

Thus, in the schema above, each `<Customers>` element selects from one row of the table named `Customers`; because the `<Customers>` element has two attributes named `CustomerID` and `ContactName`, the columns with those names are selected from the `Customers` table. In other words, this XML View describes an XML fragment shaped like this:

```
<Customers CustomerID="ALFKI" ContactName="Maria Anders">
<Customers CustomerID="ANATR" ContactName="Ana Trujillo">
<!-- additional Customers elements ... -->
```

Querying SQL Server

One way to obtain this fragment from SQL Server 2000 is to execute an XPath query using a URL like this:

```
http://localhost/virtualdirectory/schema/ch15_ex01.xdr/Customers
```

All of the examples in this chapter require that you have already created a virtual directory with a virtual name of type `schema` that can execute XPath queries. Appendix E describes how to set up such a virtual directory in detail.

> **Before proceeding, first set up SQL Server to allow XPath queries, as described in Appendix E.**

The XPath query above returns an XML fragment, which is not a well-formed XML document. Most browsers and other XML tools require a well-formed XML document. You can wrap the fragment in a top-level element with any name you desire using the URL `root` parameter, as follows:

```
http://localhost/virtualdirectory/schema/ch15_ex01.xdr/Customers?root=ROOT
```

This second XPath query returns a well-formed XML document corresponding to all the Customers in the database:

```
<?xml version="1.0" encoding="UTF-8" ?>
<ROOT>
  <Customers CustomerID="ALFKI" ContactName="Maria Anders">
  <Customers CustomerID="ANATR" ContactName="Ana Trujillo">
  <!-- more Customers elements ... -->
</ROOT>
```

You can try this out in an XML aware web browser, such as IE5.x, but remember to add the root parameter to the XPath query. The result looks like this:

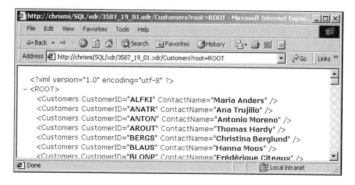

> If you want to try the examples in this chapter using IE5.x or another XML aware
> browser that requires well-formed XML, remember to add a root element to the
> fragment.

We will explain access methods in greater detail in the next chapter.

Names and Other Restrictions

One difficulty in using the default mapping is that XML names are more restrictive than SQL names about the characters they can contain. A special encoding mechanism is provided to map between the two kinds of names. This encoding is described fully in the documentation accompanying SQL Server, but basically amounts to replacing the characters that are not allowed in XML names with _xHHHH_ where H is a hex digit. For example, the SQL name [Order Details] is represented as the XML name _x005B_Order_x0020_Details_0x005D_. (5B and 5D are the hex values of the left and right square brackets, and 20 is the hex value of the space character, none of which are valid XML name characters.)

Also, the default mapping does not allow an <ElementType> to have element children because there is no way to infer the join relationship that should exist between them. Consequently, the default mapping is really only useful when the XML is flat and the XML names are the same as the SQL names. Explicit mappings require annotations, which we will describe next.

Annotated XDR Schemas

The annotations to XDR all belong to the namespace urn:schemas-microsoft-com:xml-sql. For convenience, we use the namespace prefix sql to denote this namespace. We will begin by describing the simplest and most common annotations, and proceed to the more complex, less common annotations. At the end of this section, a table is provided that summarizes all the available annotations and their purposes.

Tables and Columns (sql:relation and sql:field)

Two essential annotations are sql:relation and sql:field. These annotations allow us to explicitly map an element, ElementType, or attribute to a particular table or column in the database. Let's try these annotations on the schema from the previous section to produce a new, annotated schema (ch15_ex02.xdr):

```
<Schema xmlns="urn:schemas-microsoft-com:xml-data"
        xmlns:sql="urn:schemas-microsoft-com:xml-sql">

  <AttributeType name="ID"/>
  <AttributeType name="ContactName"/>
  <ElementType name="Contact" sql:relation="Customers">
      <attribute type="ID" sql:field="CustomerID"/>
      <attribute type="ContactName"/>
  </ElementType>
</Schema>
```

This XML View maps the `<Contact>` element to the `Customers` table, and the `ID` attribute to the `CustomerID` column. It is not necessary to explicitly map the `ID` or `ContactName` attributes to the `Customers` table using `sql:relation`; when an attribute or element mapped to a field does not specify a relation, it inherits its parent's table. The value of `sql:relation` can be a simple table name as it is here, or it can be a three-part SQL name `database.owner.table`. The name can refer to any table or view in the database.

The result of querying this schema is the same as the default mapping from the non-annotated schema, except that the XML names have changed:

```
<Contact ID="ALFKI" ContactName="Maria Anders">
<Contact ID="ANATR" ContactName="Ana Trujillo">
<!-- additional Contact elements ... -->
```

Where previously the attributes had to have the same names as the columns to which they mapped by default, here we map an attribute called `ID` to the `CustomerID` column – illustrating how we can create different XML names than the SQL names.

Here is the URL that you need to try out this XML View in a browser:

```
http://localhost/virtualdirectory/schema/ch15_ex02.xdr/Contact?root=ROOT
```

Another common use of `sql:field` is to create **element-centric** XML, mapping columns to elements instead of to attributes. For example, the schema below (`ch15_ex03.xdr`)

```
<Schema xmlns="urn:schemas-microsoft-com:xml-data"
    xmlns:sql="urn:schemas-microsoft-com:xml-sql">

    <AttributeType name="ID"/>
    <ElementType name="Name" sql:field="ContactName" />
    <ElementType name="Contact" sql:relation="Customers">
        <attribute type="ID" sql:field="CustomerID"/>
        <element type="Name"/>
    </ElementType>
</Schema>
```

maps the `ContactName` column to a sub-element of `<Contact>`, instead of to an attribute:

```
<Contact ID="ALFKI">
    <Name>Maria Anders</Name>
</Contact>
<Contact ID="ALFKI">
    <Name>Ana Trujillo</Name>
</Contact>
```

To display the resulting XML in a web browser, use the URL:

```
http://localhost/virtualdirectory/schema/ch15_ex03.xdr/Contact?root=ROOT
```

Null Values

Although there are many possible interpretations for the SQL NULL value, the one chosen by XML Views is **absence**. When an attribute maps to a NULL value, then that instance of the attribute will not appear in the XML. Similarly, when an element maps to a NULL value, that element instance will not exist in the XML.

If you ever want to fill in these missing values with a default value, XDR allows you to describe the default value to be used when an attribute does not exist. For example:

```
<Schema xmlns="urn:schemas-microsoft-com:xml-data"
    xmlns:sql="urn:schemas-microsoft-com:xml-sql">

    <ElementType name="Customer">
        <AttributeType name="Region" />
        <attribute type="Region" default="WA" />
    </ElementType>
</Schema>
```

The value will still not appear in the XML, but now applications can process the schema and know the appropriate default value to use. This is usually the best solution, as it minimizes the size of the XML (and therefore improves performance). However, when even this solution is not acceptable, one can use SQL default values in the table definition to ensure that the value always appears in the XML data.

Join Relationships (sql:relationship)

The sql:field and sql:relation annotations provide a great deal of flexibility. Now, suppose you want to produce XML data from multiple tables. A new annotation is required to express the join relationship between these tables. Appropriately enough, this annotation is in an element called <sql:relationship>. Don't confuse this with the similar-sounding sql:relation – they are completely different annotations.

The join relationship is placed inside the child element, joining it with its parent. Two attributes on the <sql:relationship> element, key-relation and key, describe the table and column of the parent; two other attributes, foreign-relation and foreign-key, describe the table and column of the child. These need not correspond to actual primary and foreign keys in the database; any columns can be used in the join.

The schema below (ch15_ex04.xdr) demonstrates a join between the elements <Contact> and <Order>:

```
<Schema xmlns="urn:schemas-microsoft-com:xml-data"
    xmlns:sql="urn:schemas-microsoft-com:xml-sql">

    <AttributeType name="ID"/>
    <AttributeType name="Name"/>
    <ElementType name="Order" sql:relation="Orders">
        <attribute type="ID" sql:field="OrderID" />
    </ElementType>
    <ElementType name="Contact" sql:relation="Customers">
        <attribute type="ID" sql:field="CustomerID"/>
        <attribute type="Name" sql:field="ContactName"/>
```

```
        <element type="Order">
                <sql:relationship key-relation="Customers" key="CustomerID"
            foreign-relation="Orders" foreign-key="CustomerID" />
        </element>
    </ElementType>
</Schema>
```

The relationship is equivalent to the SQL join condition `Customers JOIN Orders ON Customers.CustomerID=Orders.CustomerID`, as in the query

```
SELECT Customers.CustomerID, ContactName, OrderID FROM Customers
JOIN Orders ON Customers.CustomerID = Orders.CustomerID
FOR XML AUTO
```

The XML produced by the schema above is as follows:

```
<Contact ID="ALFKI" Name="Maria Anders">
    <Order ID="10643"/>
    <Order ID="10692"/>
    <Order ID="10702"/>
    <Order ID="10835"/>
    <Order ID="11011"/>
</Contact>
<Contact ID="ANATR" Name="Ana Trujillo">
    <Order ID="10308"/>
    <Order ID="10625"/>
    <Order ID="10759"/>
    <Order ID="10926"/>
</Contact>
<!-- ... -->
```

Multi-column Joins

Sometimes, tables are joined along multiple columns. For example, a `Customers` table might be joined with an `Addresses` table along both `FirstName` and `LastName`. In such cases, the column names should be separated by spaces in the key and foreign-key values:

```
<sql:relationship key-relation="Customers" key="FirstName LastName"
    foreign-relation="Addresses" foreign-key="FirstName LastName"/>
```

This is equivalent to the SQL join

```
Customers JOIN Addresses ON
Customers.FirstName=Addresses.FirstName AND Customers.LastName=Addresses.LastName
```

Note that the column order is significant – columns are paired together in the same order in which they appear.

Joins like these pose no problem for column names containing spaces, because such names must already be surrounded by square brackets to be legal SQL names. For example:

```
<sql:relationship key-relation="Customers" key="[First Name] [Last Name]"
    foreign-relation="Addresses" foreign-key="[First Name] [Last Name]"/>
```

Link Tables

Another common join scenario occurs when two tables are joined through one or more intermediate tables (link tables). For example, in the Northwind database, Orders and Products are joined through an Order Details table, like so:

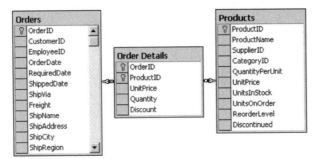

This kind of join can be described using additional sql:relationship elements inside the child. The next example (ch15_ex05.xdr) demonstrates joining Orders and Products using the Order Details table as an intermediate table:

```
<Schema xmlns="urn:schemas-microsoft-com:xml-data"
    xmlns:sql="urn:schemas-microsoft-com:xml-sql">

    <AttributeType name="ID"/>
    <ElementType name="Product" sql:relation="Products">
        <AttributeType name="UnitPrice"/>
        <attribute type="ID" sql:field="ProductID" />
        <attribute type="UnitPrice" />
    </ElementType>
    <ElementType name="Order" sql:relation="Orders">
        <attribute type="ID" sql:field="OrderID" />
        <element type="Product">
                <sql:relationship key-relation="Orders" key="OrderID"
            foreign-relation="[Order Details]" foreign-key="OrderID" />
                <sql:relationship key-relation="[Order Details]" key="ProductID"
            foreign-relation="Products" foreign-key="ProductID" />
        </element>
    </ElementType>
</Schema>
```

The XPath Order with this schema produces the XML shown below:

```
<Order ID="10248">
    <Product ID="11" UnitPrice="21.0000"/>
    <Product ID="42" UnitPrice="14.0000"/>
    <Product ID="72" UnitPrice="34.8000"/>
</Order>
<Order ID="10249">
    <Product ID="14" UnitPrice="23.2500"/>
    <Product ID="51" UnitPrice="53.0000"/>
</Order>
<Order ID="10250">
    <Product ID="41" UnitPrice="9.6500"/>
    <Product ID="51" UnitPrice="53.0000"/>
    <Product ID="65" UnitPrice="21.0500"/>
</Order>
<!-- ... -->
```

As in life, relationships can be challenging. To save yourself from frustration (and possibly a broken heart), follow these three rules:

❑ The last relationship's foreign-relation must be the table of the child.

❑ The first relationship's key-relation must be the table of the parent. (*)

❑ For each relationship beyond the first, its key-relation must be the same table as the previous relationship's foreign-relation.

The second rule is, more specifically: The first relationship's key-relation must be the table of the first mapped ancestor, which is usually – but not always – the parent. We'll explain how this works later, when we describe constant elements.

Qualified Joins (sql:limit-field and sql:limit-value)

Another common database scenario is a **qualified join**. For example, in the Northwind database, the Products table contains both discontinued and current products. The status of a product is indicated using the column named Discontinued in the Products table (the value 1 indicates the product is discontinued, 0 not discontinued). Suppose in our previous example we want only the products that are not discontinued. In SQL, this would be expressed as

```
Orders JOIN [Order Details] ON Orders.OrderID=[Order Details].OrderID
JOIN Products ON [Order Details].ProductID=Products.ProductID
AND Products.Discontinued = 0
```

To express a special join such as this in an annotated schema, a new annotation is required.

The annotations sql:limit-field and sql:limit-value are used to qualify a join. These annotations, when placed on an element or attribute that has a join relationship, select that element or attribute only when the limit-field equals the indicated limit-value (or NULL, if no limit-value was specified).

We demonstrate this by modifying the previous schema to use a qualified join (ch15_ex06.xdr):

```
<Schema xmlns="urn:schemas-microsoft-com:xml-data"
    xmlns:sql="urn:schemas-microsoft-com:xml-sql">

  <AttributeType name="ID"/>
  <ElementType name="Product" sql:relation="Products">
    <AttributeType name="UnitPrice"/>

    <attribute type="ID" sql:field="ProductID" />
    <attribute type="UnitPrice" />
  </ElementType>
  <ElementType name="Order" sql:relation="Orders">
    <attribute type="ID" sql:field="OrderID" />
    <element type="Product"
   sql:limit-field="Discontinued" sql:limit-value="0">
            <sql:relationship key-relation="Orders" key="OrderID"
          foreign-relation="[Order Details]" foreign-key="OrderID" />
            <sql:relationship key-relation="[Order Details]" key="ProductID"
          foreign-relation="Products" foreign-key="ProductID" />
    </element>
  </ElementType>
</Schema>
```

This schema with the XPath `Order` results in XML data that excludes the discontinued products:

```
<Order ID="10248">
    <Product ID="11" UnitPrice="21.0000"/>
    <Product ID="72" UnitPrice="34.8000"/>
</Order>
<Order ID="10249">
    <Product ID="14" UnitPrice="23.2500"/>
    <Product ID="51" UnitPrice="53.0000"/>
</Order>
<!-- ... -->
```

Keys, Nesting and Ordering (sql:key-fields)

XML is ordered, and is therefore hierarchical data. SQL Server uses rowset ordering to produce the XML hierarchy (see the explanation of FOR XML EXPLICIT and the Universal Table in the previous chapter for details). Thus, order is very important to getting the expected XML results from an XPath query. Updategrams also require keys to uniquely identify elements.

Usually, join relationships contain enough information to determine the keys of the tables used. However, sometimes an annotated schema does not contain enough key information. For example, consider the following schema (ch15_ex07.xdr), which uses Order Details and Products:

```
<Schema xmlns="urn:schemas-microsoft-com:xml-data"
    xmlns:sql="urn:schemas-microsoft-com:xml-sql">

    <AttributeType name="ID"/>
    <ElementType name="Product" sql:relation="Products">
        <attribute type="ID" sql:field="ProductID"/>
    </ElementType>
    <ElementType name="Detail" sql:relation="[Order Details]">
        <attribute type="ID" sql:field="OrderID" />
        <element type="Product">
                <sql:relationship key-relation="[Order Details]" key="ProductID"
            foreign-relation="Products" foreign-key="ProductID" />
        </element>
    </ElementType>
</Schema>
```

Rows in the Order Details table are uniquely identified by both OrderID and ProductID; either one alone is not sufficient. However, this schema does not convey that OrderID is a key of the Order Details table.

Consequently, XPath does not have enough information to totally order the XML results. At best, this may result in non-deterministic results (differently ordered XML from one time to the next). At worst, this can cause the resulting XML fragment to nest elements incorrectly. Updategrams will also have problems when using this schema, because it will not be able to uniquely identify the <Detail> elements.

The sql:key-fields annotation provides a solution to this problem by allowing us to list all the key columns used by an element or attribute. Because the errors that can result from missing keys are often cryptic, we recommend always explicitly listing the key-fields on all elements (and on all attributes with join relationships – that is, any attribute that comes from a different table than its parent element).

To see key-fields in action, we correct the schema above to produce the one below (ch15_ex08.xdr):

```
<Schema xmlns="urn:schemas-microsoft-com:xml-data"
    xmlns:sql="urn:schemas-microsoft-com:xml-sql">

    <AttributeType name="ID"/>
    <ElementType name="Product" sql:relation="Products">
        <attribute type="ID" sql:field="ProductID"/>
    </ElementType>
    <ElementType name="Detail" sql:relation="[Order Details]"
                 sql:key-fields="OrderID ProductID">
        <attribute type="ID" sql:field="OrderID" />
        <element type="Product"
            sql:key-fields="ProductID">
                <sql:relationship key-relation="[Order Details]" key="ProductID"
            foreign-relation="Products" foreign-key="ProductID" />
        </element>
    </ElementType>
</Schema>
```

The XML View is the same (the key-fields only appear in the result if they are selected elsewhere in the schema), but the query languages like XPath and updategrams that use the XML View now have the key information they need to function properly.

The columns listed in sql:key-fields can sometimes be used to control sort order. For example, if in the results from an XPath, you want elements ordered not by primary key but by some other column, you can sometimes accomplish this goal by putting the column into the key-fields value. For general-purpose sorting, post-processing (such as XSLT) is required.

Alternative Mappings

So far, all of our XML data has been in one-to-one correspondence with values in the database (and vice-versa). However, there are three annotations that provide other ways to control the mapping between the XML and the database. You can choose to:

❑   ignore some elements or attributes in the schema, and not map them: **unmapped data**

❑   produce elements that map to nothing: **constant elements**

❑   map blocks of XML to a column all at once: **xml-text**

Let's look at each of these and why you would want to do this next.

Unmapped Data (sql:map-field)

Often, there are schema elements or attributes that should not map to anything in the database. This occurs most commonly when working with a pre-existing schema or sharing a schema with other applications, and there is no corresponding information in the database. Such unmapped data is indicated using the sql:map-field annotation. This annotation's value can be either 0 (false) or 1 (true). However, it is not necessary to specify sql:map-field="1", because its default value is true. An example (where it is set to false) is seen below (ch15_ex09.xdr):

```
<Schema xmlns="urn:schemas-microsoft-com:xml-data"
    xmlns:sql="urn:schemas-microsoft-com:xml-sql">
```

```
        <AttributeType name="ID"/>
        <AttributeType name="City"/>
        <AttributeType name="NotMapped" />
        <ElementType name="Contact" sql:relation="Customers" sql:key-
    fields="CustomerID">
            <attribute type="ID" sql:field="CustomerID"/>
            <attribute type="City" />
            <attribute type="NotMapped" sql:map-field="0"/>
        </ElementType>
    </Schema>
```

Unmapped data is completely ignored – it will not appear in the XML results of a query, and will not be processed by an insert or update. Consequently, the schema above produces the same XML as if the NotMapped attribute did not exist at all.

When an element is not mapped, none of its descendants are mapped either.

Constant Elements (sql:is-constant)

At other times, an element does not correspond to any value in the database, but it should still appear in the XML. The most common examples are "wrapper" elements that contribute nothing but structure to the XML data. These elements occur frequently in BizTalk schemas, for example. When the element should appear in the XML results but does not come from the database, use the annotation sql:is-constant. Like sql:map-field, this annotation takes a 0 or 1 value (the default is false).

Here is an example of a superfluous constant element, <OrderList> (ch15_ex10.xdr):

```
<Schema xmlns="urn:schemas-microsoft-com:xml-data"
    xmlns:sql="urn:schemas-microsoft-com:xml-sql">

    <AttributeType name="ID"/>
    <AttributeType name="Name"/>
    <ElementType name="Order" sql:relation="Orders">
        <attribute type="ID" sql:field="OrderID" />
    </ElementType>
    <ElementType name="OrderList" sql:is-constant="1">
        <element type="Order">
                <sql:relationship key-relation="Customers" key="CustomerID"
            foreign-relation="Orders" foreign-key="CustomerID" />
        </element>
    </ElementType>
    <ElementType name="Contact" sql:relation="Customers">
        <attribute type="ID" sql:field="CustomerID"/>
        <attribute type="Name" sql:field="ContactName"/>
        <element type="OrderList"/>
    </ElementType>
</Schema>
```

Note that in this example, <OrderList> actually contributes nothing but wasted space to the XML data. Nevertheless, schemas like this appear quite often in practice. This schema produces XML data like this:

```
<Contact ID="ALFKI" Name="Maria Anders">
   <OrderList>
      <Order ID="10643"/>
      <Order ID="10692"/>
      <Order ID="10702"/>
      <Order ID="10835"/>
      <Order ID="11011"/>
   </OrderList>
</Contact>
<Contact ID="ANATR" Name="Ana Trujillo">
   <OrderList>
      <Order ID="10308"/>
      <Order ID="10625"/>
      <Order ID="10759"/>
      <Order ID="10926"/>
   </OrderList>
</Contact>
<!-- ... -->
```

Constant elements may be nested inside one another and need not have child elements. However, constant elements cannot have mapped attributes, because there is no table from which the attribute can be selected.

For most purposes, constant elements are ignored. As the example above demonstrates, the constant `<OrderList>` element does not factor into the join relationship between `<Contact>` and its `<Order>` descendants. The join relationship between them is exactly the same as if the `<OrderList>` element were not in-between.

XML Text (sql:overflow-field)

There are at least three scenarios in which overflow fields are useful:

1. Perhaps the most common use is to map a chunk of text (usually XML) stored in the database into the XML data without **entitization**. Because XML treats a few characters such as ampersand (&) and less-than (<) specially, these characters normally must be encoded as special entities (& and < respectively). If a column in the database contains data that is already XML, it has already been entitized so you do not want to entitize it a second time (resulting in &amp; instead of &, for example). When you want to preserve the XML structure of the data, or otherwise skip entitization, you can map it using `sql:overflow-field`. (See also the annotation `sql:use-cdata` later in this chapter for a different way to avoid entitization.)

2. Another use is to store chunks of XML inside the database as is, without shredding the XML into individual rows and columns. Such XML data is called 'overflow' because it spills over into the overflow field. In this case, any XML encountered by an Updategram insert or update that was not already mapped to rows and columns will be stuffed into the overflow column and inserted into the database verbatim.

3. A third scenario is to generate mixed content. At the time of this writing, XML Views do not support mixed content directly. Every schema that would generate mixed content (for example, an `<ElementType>` that maps to a field but also has child elements) generates an error. However, the overflow field can be used to generate mixed content, either directly (by containing mixed content itself) or indirectly (in conjunction with other elements). The following example demonstrates both techniques.

First create a table with an overflow column (ch15_ex11.sql):

```
CREATE TABLE MixedContent (cid nchar(5) PRIMARY KEY, xml nvarchar(100))
INSERT INTO MixedContent
VALUES(N'ALFKI', N'<overflow>Overflow combined with child elements can produce
mixed content</overflow>')
INSERT INTO MixedContent
VALUES(N'XXXX', N'<overflow>And overflow by itself can be <mixed/>
content</overflow>')
```

and then a schema that uses it (ch15_ex11.xdr):

```
<Schema xmlns="urn:schemas-microsoft-com:xml-data"
    xmlns:sql="urn:schemas-microsoft-com:xml-sql">

    <AttributeType name="ID"/>
    <ElementType name="Customer" sql:relation="Customers">
       <attribute type="ID" sql:field="CustomerID" />
    </ElementType>
    <ElementType name="MixedContent" sql:overflow-field="xml" content="mixed">
       <element type="Customer">
          <sql:relationship key-relation="MixedContent" key="cid"
                foreign-relation="Customers" foreign-key="CustomerID" />
       </element>
    </ElementType>
</Schema>
```

Together, these produce this XML with mixed content:

```
<MixedContent>
    Overflow combined with child elements can produce mixed content
    <Customer ID="ALFKI"/>
</MixedContent>
<MixedContent>
    And overflow by itself can be <mixed/> content
</MixedContent>
```

> **Note - this example needs web release 2 to function, see MSDN for the updated details.**

Data Types (sql:datatype, dt:type, sql:id-prefix)

Perhaps the trickiest problem in providing an XML view over SQL data is managing the vast differences between their type systems. XDR has a type system; SQL has a different one. XPath has yet another. At the time of this writing, XSD and the XML Query Language are not yet finalized, but both will have their own (different) type systems.

We will not cover the SQL type system in any depth. The sql:datatype annotation exists mainly to allow updategrams to handle certain binary types and to improve performance in XPath (by avoiding unnecessary conversions). In SQL Server 2000, only the BLOB SQL types such as binary and text are allowed in sql:datatype. In the latest SQL XML web release (and in SQL Server 2000 SP1), sql:datatype has been expanded to accept any of the SQL types such as nchar and dateTime. The impact of the sql:datatype annotation is described later with the individual query languages. We also defer a description of XPath types to the XPath section later in this chapter.

The XDR type system is relatively straightforward. The types belong to a different namespace, `urn:schemas-microsoft-com:datatypes`, which we will always assign to the namespace prefix `dt`. Here is an example of a schema with both XDR and SQL types (`ch15_ex12.xdr`):

> **NOTE: The sql:datatype values in this example require the latest SQL XML web release, or SQL Server 2000 SP1 or later. Remove the sql:datatypes to use this schema with any earlier version of SQL XML.**

```
<Schema xmlns="urn:schemas-microsoft-com:xml-data"
    xmlns:sql="urn:schemas-microsoft-com:xml-sql"
    xmlns:dt="urn:schemas-microsoft-com:datatypes">
    <AttributeType name="ProductID" dt:type="id" sql:id-prefix="P"/>
    <AttributeType name="ProductName" dt:type="string"/>
    <AttributeType name="UnitPrice" dt:type="fixed.14.4" sql:datatype="money"/>
    <AttributeType name="SupplierID" dt:type="int" sql:datatype="int"/>
    <AttributeType name="UnitsInStock" dt:type="i4" sql:datatype="smallint"/>
    <AttributeType name="UnitsOnOrder" dt:type="i2" sql:datatype="smallint"/>
    <AttributeType name="Discontinued" dt:type="boolean"/>
    <ElementType name="Product" sql:relation="Products">
        <attribute type="ProductID" />
        <attribute type="ProductName" />
        <attribute type="UnitPrice" />
        <attribute type="SupplierID"/>
        <attribute type="UnitsInStock"/>
        <attribute type="UnitsOnOrder"/>
        <attribute type="Discontinued"/>
    </ElementType>
</Schema>
```

and part of the XML it produces:

```
<Product ProductID="P1" ProductName="Chai" UnitPrice="18.0000"
    SupplierID="1" UnitsInStock="39" UnitsOnOrder="0" Discontinued="0"/>
<Product ProductID="P2" ProductName="Chang" UnitPrice="19.0000"
    SupplierID="1" UnitsInStock="17" UnitsOnOrder="40" Discontinued="0"/>
<Product ProductID="P3" ProductName="Aniseed Syrup" UnitPrice="10.0000"
    SupplierID="1" UnitsInStock="13" UnitsOnOrder="70" Discontinued="0"/>
<Product ProductID="P4" ProductName="Chef Anton&apos;s Cajun Seasoning"
    UnitPrice="22.0000" SupplierID="2" UnitsInStock="53" UnitsOnOrder="0"
    Discontinued="0"/>
<!-- ... -->
```

In all, XDR has thirty-five distinct types.

Booleans and Binaries

We have already seen examples of the XDR `boolean` type, which takes the values 0 (false) and 1 (true). For example, the `sql:map-field` and `sql:is-constant` annotations are both `boolean`-typed. The XDR `boolean` type is thus the same as the SQL `bit` type.

The `bin.base64` and `bin.hex` types are used to indicate that an XML value is really a binary value, but either Base64- or BinHex-encoded in order to be legal XML. There is not really any corresponding SQL value; however, `FOR XML` can Base64-encode binary SQL values. See also the section on the `sql:url-encode` annotation.

Strings

The string type represents any string value, and the char type applies to single-character values. Six other types – entity, entities, enumeration, notation, uri, and uuid – are string values with special meanings in XML, but otherwise are not important as annotations in XML Views. XDR string types are essentially equivalent to SQL Unicode string types such as nvarchar.

Numbers

If you enjoyed maths in school, then you'll love the fourteen number types in XDR. These are fixed.14.4, float, i1, i2, i4, i8, int, number, r4, r8, ui1, ui2, ui4, and ui8. As the name suggests, fixed.14.4 supports up to fourteen digits before the decimal and up to four after it, making fixed.14.4 ideal as a monetary type. The types i1 through i8 are signed integer types, where the number indicates the number of bytes. Similarly, the types ui1 through ui8 are unsigned integer types. The floating-point types r4 and r8 are single-precision and double-precision IEEE 754 floating-point numbers, respectively.

Note that SQL'92 (the version of SQL implemented in SQL Server 2000) does not support unsigned integer types, nor does it support true IEEE 754 floating-point numbers (no infinities, NaNs, etc.). Consequently, it is not always possible to find a perfect match between SQL numbers and XDR numbers. When in doubt, be sure to select a type that is wide enough to hold any value you might store in it.

For convenience, we have enumerated the XDR numeric types – their ranges are summarized in this table:

Type	Range
fixed.14.4	like number, but no more than 14 digits to the left and no more than 4 digits to the right of the decimal point
float	same as r8
i1	-128 to 127
i2	-32768 to 32767
i4	-2147483648 to 2147483647
i8	-9223372036854775808 to 9223372036854775807
int	synonymous with i4
number	same as r8
r4	1.17549435E-38 to 3.40282347E+38
r8	2.2250738585072014E-308 to 1.7976931348623157E+308
ui1	0 to 255
ui2	0 to 65535
ui4	0 to 4294967295
ui8	0 to 18446744073709551615

Identifiers

The id type is a special type in XML. It is a string, but must satisfy the Name rule in the formal XML grammar (See http://www.w3.org/TR/REC-xml#NT-Name). A simplified definition of this rule is that an XML id consists of a letter followed by any number of digit, letter, or underscore characters. More than this, the XML id values in a document must all be unique. In this way, id values act like a primary key in an XML document.

The idref type is a reference to an element with that id. Consequently, idref values must also be valid id values. However, idref values need not be unique (and in general, will not be). The idrefs type is a space-separated list of idref values. The idref and idrefs types can be used with id to produce a graph-like structure within an XML document.

The nmtoken and nmtokens types are similar to idref and idrefs. Although they do not reference other values in the document and need not be unique, values with these types must satisfy the NCName rule.

Because these types must satisfy the NCName rule but the data in the database might not (for example, an integer primary key) or might lack uniqueness within the document (for example, two tables with integer keys whose values happen to overlap), the sql:id-prefix annotation is sometimes necessary. This annotation may be used with any id, idref, idrefs, nmtoken, or nmtokens type. The sql:id-prefix value is prepended to the database value (which is first converted to nvarchar). The user bears the responsibility for ensuring that the id prefix results in unique and properly formatted id values.

Usually, idrefs types contain multiple values. Although the idrefs value might already be stored in a single column in the database as a space-delimited list of id values, it is more common that the idrefs value selects from multiple rows. In this case, the idrefs attribute or element requires a join relationship. The following schema (ch15_ex13.xdr) demonstrates the three identify types:

```
<Schema xmlns="urn:schemas-microsoft-com:xml-data"
    xmlns:sql="urn:schemas-microsoft-com:xml-sql"
    xmlns:dt="urn:schemas-microsoft-com:datatypes">

<ElementType name="Customer" sql:relation="Customers">
    <AttributeType name="ID" dt:type="id"/>
    <AttributeType name="Orders" dt:type="idrefs" sql:id-prefix="O"/>

    <attribute type="ID" sql:field="CustomerID"/>
    <attribute type="Orders" sql:relation="Orders" sql:field="OrderID">
    <sql:relationship key-relation="Customers" key="CustomerID"
        foreign-relation="Orders" foreign-key="CustomerID"/>
</attribute>
<element type="Order">
        <sql:relationship key-relation="Customers" key="CustomerID"
            foreign-relation="Orders" foreign-key="CustomerID"/>
    </element>
</ElementType>
<ElementType name="Order" sql:relation="Orders">
    <AttributeType name="ID" dt:type="id" sql:id-prefix="O"/>
    <AttributeType name="Employee" dt:type="idref" sql:id-prefix="E"/>
```

```
                <attribute type="ID" sql:field="OrderID"/>
                <attribute type="Employee" sql:field="EmployeeID"/>
        <element type="Employee">
                <sql:relationship key-relation="Orders" key="EmployeeID"
                  foreign-relation="Employees" foreign-key="EmployeeID"/>
        </element>
        </ElementType>
        <ElementType name="Employee" sql:relation="Employees">
                <AttributeType name="ID" dt:type="id" sql:id-prefix="E"/>
                <attribute type="ID" sql:field="EmployeeID"/>
        </ElementType>
</Schema>
```

The XML obtained from this schema displays both the `id` prefixes and the concatenated `idrefs` values:

```
<Customer ID="ALFKI" Orders="O10643 O10692 O10702 O10835 O10952 O11011">
    <Order ID="O10835" Employee="E1"/>
    <Order ID="O10952" Employee="E1">
        <Employee ID="E1"/>
        <Employee ID="E1"/>
    </Order>
    <Order ID="O11011" Employee="E3">
        <Employee ID="E3"/>
    </Order>
    <Order ID="O10692" Employee="E4"/>
    <Order ID="O10702" Employee="E4">
        <Employee ID="E4"/>
        <Employee ID="E4"/>
    </Order>
    <Order ID="O10643" Employee="E6">
        <Employee ID="E6"/>
    </Order>
</Customer>
<Customer ID="ANATR" Orders="O10308 O10625 O10759 O10926">
    <Order ID="O10625" Employee="E3"/>
    <Order ID="O10759" Employee="E3">
        <Employee ID="E3"/>
        <Employee ID="E3"/>
    </Order>
    <Order ID="O10926" Employee="E4">
        <Employee ID="E4"/>
    </Order>
    <Order ID="O10308" Employee="E7">
        <Employee ID="E7"/>
    </Order>
</Customer>
<!-- ... -->
```

Dates and Times

There are five date/time types in XDR: `date`, `time`, `dateTime`, `dateTime.tz`, and `time.tz`. These last two are timezone variants of `dateTime` and `time`, respectively. As the names suggest, `date` consists of only the date part, `time` only the time part, and `dateTime` combines the two. The format XDR uses is based on ISO 8601 (see http://www.w3.org/TR/NOTE-datetime). This schema (`ch15_ex14.xdr`) demonstrates all five types:

```
<Schema xmlns="urn:schemas-microsoft-com:xml-data"
    xmlns:sql="urn:schemas-microsoft-com:xml-sql"
    xmlns:dt="urn:schemas-microsoft-com:datatypes">
```

```
        <AttributeType name="date" dt:type="date" />
        <AttributeType name="time" dt:type="time" />
        <AttributeType name="dateTime" dt:type="dateTime"/>
        <AttributeType name="time.tz" dt:type="time.tz"/>
        <AttributeType name="dateTime.tz" dt:type="dateTime.tz"/>
        <ElementType name="Example" sql:relation="Orders">
            <attribute type="date" sql:field="OrderDate"/>
            <attribute type="time" sql:field="OrderDate"/>
            <attribute type="dateTime" sql:field="OrderDate"/>
            <attribute type="time.tz" sql:field="OrderDate"/>
            <attribute type="dateTime.tz" sql:field="OrderDate"/>
        </ElementType>
    </Schema>
```

resulting in the XML:

```
<Example date="1996-07-04" time="00:00:00" dateTime="1996-07-04T00:00:00"
    time.tz="00:00:00" dateTime.tz="1996-07-04T00:00:00"/>
<Example date="1996-07-05" time="00:00:00" dateTime="1996-07-05T00:00:00"
    time.tz="00:00:00" dateTime.tz="1996-07-05T00:00:00"/>
<Example date="1996-07-08" time="00:00:00" dateTime="1996-07-08T00:00:00"
    time.tz="00:00:00" dateTime.tz="1996-07-08T00:00:00"/>
<Example date="1996-07-08" time="00:00:00" dateTime="1996-07-08T00:00:00"
    time.tz="00:00:00" dateTime.tz="1996-07-08T00:00:00"/>
<Example date="1996-07-09" time="00:00:00" dateTime="1996-07-09T00:00:00"
    time.tz="00:00:00" dateTime.tz="1996-07-09T00:00:00"/>
<!-- ... -->
```

SQL has only two date/time types, `datetime` and `smalldatetime`. Neither of these includes a timezone, and both have smaller precision than the XDR date/time types. For example, the XDR `time` type has nanosecond resolution, while the SQL Server `datetime` type has only 1/300 second resolution. If you require greater precision or timezones, store your date/time data in a SQL string type such as `nvarchar`.

Mapping Between XDR Types and SQL Types

In general, it is not possible to force SQL types into XDR types or vice-versa. SQL often does not have any conversion functions that would perform as desired. Some types are automatically converted by `FOR XML EXPLICIT`; others, such as `dateTime`, require an explicit conversion. Also, because SQL Server does not perform implicit type conversions in many cases (such as number to string), some XDR types require an explicit conversion when used in a query language such as XPath or when used as `id` types. Because these type conversions are largely query-dependent, we'll cover them in greater detail in the sections on XPath and updategrams.

CDATA Sections

By default, database values are entitized when mapping to XML. This means that XML special characters such as < are replaced with the corresponding entity `&lt;`. To avoid entitization on an element, indicate that the value should use a CDATA section. This is done with the `sql:use-cdata` annotation (which is boolean-valued like `sql:map-field`, and defaults to false), as seen in action below, in `ch15_ex15.xdr`:

```
<Schema xmlns="urn:schemas-microsoft-com:xml-data"
    xmlns:sql="urn:schemas-microsoft-com:xml-sql">
```

```
        <ElementType name="Name" content="textOnly"/>
        <ElementType name="Customer" sql:relation="Customers">
            <element type="Name" sql:field="CompanyName" sql:use-cdata="1"/>
        </ElementType>
    </Schema>
```

Embedded Binary Values

XML doesn't really have a convenient way to deal with binary data (such as images) embedded in the document. The schema `ch15_ex16.xdr` below

```
<Schema xmlns="urn:schemas-microsoft-com:xml-data"
    xmlns:sql="urn:schemas-microsoft-com:xml-sql">

    <AttributeType name="Name"/>
    <AttributeType name="Photo"/>
    <ElementType name="Employee" sql:relation="Employees"
                 sql:key-fields="EmployeeID">
        <attribute type="Name" sql:field="LastName"/>
        <attribute type="Photo"/>
    </ElementType>
</Schema>
```

will put the Base64-encoded value of each employee's photo into the XML. This wastes both time (to encode on the server, and then unencode to use the data as an image) and space (because the encoded data is much larger than the data itself).

XML Views provide an annotation, `sql:url-encode` (which is boolean-valued and defaults to false, just like `sql:use-cdata`) that instead constructs a relative URL (called a **direct object query**) using an XPath-like syntax to refer to the value in the database. The URL is especially convenient for embedding images into an HTML page, since the `IMG` tag can use the URL as its `SRC` value. Because the query must select a single value from the database, the XML View must contain enough key information (through key fields or join relationships) to uniquely identify each value – `sql:url-encode` is seen below in action (`ch15_ex17.xdr`):

```
<Schema xmlns="urn:schemas-microsoft-com:xml-data"
    xmlns:sql="urn:schemas-microsoft-com:xml-sql">

    <AttributeType name="Name"/>
    <AttributeType name="Photo"/>
    <ElementType name="Employee" sql:relation="Employees"
                 sql:key-fields="EmployeeID">
        <attribute type="Name" sql:field="LastName"/>
        <attribute type="Photo" sql:url-encode="1"/>
    </ElementType>
</Schema>
```

This schema generates XML like

```
<Employee Name="Davolio" Photo="dbobject/Employees[@EmployeeID=1]"/>
```

In the next chapter, we will demonstrate an XSL that transforms these values into `IMG` tags in the HTML.

Table 1. Annotation Summary

Annotation	Context(s)	Purpose
sql:datatype	AttributeType, ElementType	Specifies a column's SQL type. Use with dt:type.
sql:field	attribute, element, ElementType	Maps to a SQL column.
sql:id	Schema	Identifies an inline schema for use in template queries. Use with sql:is-mapping-schema.
sql:id-prefix	AttributeType, ElementType	Prepends a string to the column value. Use with dt:type equal to id, idref, idrefs, nmtoken, or nmtokens.
sql:is-constant	element, ElementType	Indicates that this element appears in the XML but maps to nothing in the database.
sql:is-mapping-schema	Schema	Indicates that an inline schema is an annotated schema. Use with sql:id.
sql:key-fields	attribute, element, ElementType	Specifies a table's key columns.
sql:limit-field	attribute or element with a relationship	Qualifies a join (limit-field specifies the column). Use with sql:limit-value.
sql:limit-value	attribute or element	Qualifies a join (limit-value specifies the value; NULL when absent). Use with sql:limit-field.
sql:map-field	attribute, element, ElementType	Indicates that this maps to nothing in the database.
sql:overflow-field	element, ElementType	Specifies a column for overflow XML data.
sql:relation	attribute, element, ElementType	Maps to a SQL table
sql:relationship	inside an attribute or element	Specifies a join relationship with the parent element (or first mapped ancestor, if the parent is a constant element).
sql:target-namespace	Schema	Places the elements and attribute declared in a schema into a different namespace.
sql:url-encode	attribute, element, ElementType	Generates a dbobject URL to the value instead of the value itself.
sql:use-cdata	element, ElementType	Encloses the content with a CDATA section.

Templates

Before we describe the XPath and Updategram query languages, let us first explain a mechanism, called **templates**, for executing these queries. Each template is just an XML document, but the XML is processed in a special way, at least, in one respect: If a query command node is embedded in the template, then that query is executed and its results replace the command node in the XML. The result is dynamic XML content.

Below is a sample template file (`ch15_ex18.xml`) that contains three kinds of queries. Note that updategrams require the latest SQL XML web release or SQL Server 2000 SP1, and that for various reasons, updategrams reside in a distinct namespace from the rest of the SQL XML components:

> **Updategrams require the latest SQL XML web release or SQL Server 2000 SP1 or later. Remove <u:sync> to use this template with any earlier version of SQL XML.**

```
<AnyXMLContent xmlns:sql="urn:schemas-microsoft-com:xml-sql"
        xmlns:u="urn:schemas-microsoft-com:xml-updategram" >

    <CanBeUsed in="the template" />
    and will be preserved in the output of the template
    <!-- Comments also will be preserved in the output -->

    <!-- This is an SQL query that selects all the Employee elements -->
    <sql:query>
        SELECT * FROM Employees FOR XML AUTO
    </sql:query>

    <!-- This is an updategram query that modifies one Employee -->
    <u:sync mapping-schema="Schema.xdr">
        <u:before>
            <Employee EmployeeID="3">
                <FirstName>Janet</FirstName>
                <LastName>Leverling</LastName>
            </Employee>
        </u:before>
        <u:after>
        <Employee EmployeeID="3">
                <FirstName>Janet</FirstName>
                <LastName>Leverling-Brown</LastName>
            </Employee>
        </u:after>
    </u:sync>

    <!-- This is an XPath query that selects the modified Employee -->
    <sql:xpath-query mapping-schema="Schema.xdr">
        /Employee[@EmployeeID="3"]
    </sql:xpath-query>
</AnyXMLContent>
```

The template can be executed by accessing it through a URL, like this (assuming you have provided a suitable `schema.xdr`, which I have left as another exercise for you to try upon completion of reading this chapter):

```
http://localhost/virtualdirectory/template/yourTemplate.xml
```

or through various other mechanisms such as ADO. The next chapter and the Books Online documentation that accompanies SQL Server 2000 contain more information about these access mechanisms.

A template may contain any number of SQL, updategram, and XPath queries. The queries in a template are executed sequentially. Each query command node corresponds to one SQL transaction; when one fails, the others will still be executed.

Now we will explore how the query languages XPath and updategrams use XML Views.

XPath

In this section, we will describe the subset of XPath supported by SQL XML. For the examples in the first part of this section, we will use this annotated schema (ch15_ex20.xdr):

```
<Schema xmlns="urn:schemas-microsoft-com:xml-data"
    xmlns:sql="urn:schemas-microsoft-com:xml-sql"
    xmlns:dt="urn:schemas-microsoft-com:datatypes">

  <ElementType name="Product" sql:relation="Products">
      <AttributeType name="ProductID" dt:type="id"/>
      <AttributeType name="UnitPrice" dt:type="fixed.14.4"
              sql:datatype="money"/>
      <AttributeType name="Units" />

      <attribute type="ProductID" sql:id-prefix="P"/>
      <attribute type="UnitPrice" />
      <attribute type="Units" sql:field="UnitsInStock"/>
  </ElementType>
  <ElementType name="Order" sql:relation="Orders">
      <AttributeType name="OrderID"/>
      <AttributeType name="OrderDate" dt:type="date"
              sql:datatype="datetime"/>

      <attribute type="OrderID"/>
      <attribute type="OrderDate"/>
      <element type="Product">
              <sql:relationship key-relation="Orders" key="OrderID"
          foreign-relation="[Order Details]" foreign-key="OrderID"/>
              <sql:relationship key-relation="[Order Details]" key="ProductID"
          foreign-relation="Products" foreign-key="ProductID"/>
      </element>
  </ElementType>
  <ElementType name="Customer" sql:relation="Customers">
      <AttributeType name="CustomerID" dt:type="string"
              sql:datatype="nvarchar(5)"/>
      <AttributeType name="ContactName"/>

      <attribute type="CustomerID"/>
      <attribute type="ContactName"/>
      <element type="Order">
         <sql:relationship key-relation="Customers" key="CustomerID"
            foreign-relation="Orders" foreign-key="CustomerID" />
      </element>
  </ElementType>
</Schema>
```

which describes XML shaped like this:

```
<Customer CustomerID="ALFKI" ContactName="Maria Anders">
   <Order OrderID="10643" OrderDate="1997-08-25">
      <Product ProductID="P28" UnitPrice="45.6000" Units="26"/>
      <Product ProductID="P39" UnitPrice="18.0000" Units="69"/>
      <Product ProductID="P46" UnitPrice="12.0000" Units="95"/>
   </Order>
   <Order OrderID="10692" OrderDate="1997-10-03">
      <Product ProductID="P63" UnitPrice="43.9000" Units="24"/>
   </Order>
   <!-- ... -->
</Customer>
<Customer CustomerID="ANATR" ContactName="Ana Trujillo">
   <Order OrderID="10308" OrderDate="1996-09-18">
      <Product ProductID="P69" UnitPrice="36.0000" Units="26"/>
      <Product ProductID="P70" UnitPrice="15.0000" Units="15"/>
   </Order>
   <Order OrderID="10625" OrderDate="1997-08-08">
      <Product ProductID="P14" UnitPrice="23.2500" Units="35"/>
      <Product ProductID="P42" UnitPrice="14.0000" Units="26"/>
      <Product ProductID="P60" UnitPrice="34.0000" Units="19"/>
   </Order>
   <!-- ... -->
</Customer>
<!-- ... -->
```

or this:

```
<Order OrderID="10248" OrderDate="1996-07-04">
   <Product ProductID="P72" UnitPrice="34.8000" Units="14"/>
   <Product ProductID="P11" UnitPrice="21.0000" Units="22"/>
   <Product ProductID="P42" UnitPrice="14.0000" Units="26"/>
</Order>
<Order OrderID="10249" OrderDate="1996-07-05">
   <Product ProductID="P51" UnitPrice="53.0000" Units="20"/>
   <Product ProductID="P14" UnitPrice="23.2500" Units="35"/>
</Order>
<Order OrderID="10250" OrderDate="1996-07-08">
   <Product ProductID="P41" UnitPrice="9.6500" Units="85"/>
   <Product ProductID="P51" UnitPrice="53.0000" Units="20"/>
   <Product ProductID="P65" UnitPrice="21.0500" Units="76"/>
</Order>
<!-- ... -->
```

or even like this:

```
<Product ProductID="P1" UnitPrice="18.0000" Units="39"/>
<Product ProductID="P2" UnitPrice="19.0000" Units="17"/>
<Product ProductID="P3" UnitPrice="10.0000" Units="13"/>
<Product ProductID="P4" UnitPrice="22.0000" Units="53"/>
<!-- ... -->
```

depending on whether the XPath query begins at Customer, Order, or Product, respectively.

Introduction

XPath is an XML query language with an especially compact form. XPath does not provide ways to modify data, but does provide a convenient syntax for selecting XML. For complete details, please see the XPath specification at http://www.w3.org/TR/XPath.

XPath consists of two fundamental operations, **navigation** and **predication**. Navigation selects nodes in the XML. Predication filters that selection according to certain criteria. Although there are many query scenarios that XPath cannot support, these two operations are enough for many common needs. Combined with XML Views, XPath provides a powerful way to interact with relational data as though it were XML.

> *Recall that XPath queries can be executed through either the URL or through a template file. When using an XPath in a URL, be aware of URL encoding, for example, spaces. Similarly, when using an XPath in a template, be aware of XML encoding issues. If the XPath contains special characters like <, you may want to wrap it in a CDATA section.*

Navigation

XPath is especially well designed for navigating the tree-like hierarchy of XML. XPath walks the tree using **steps**. The simplest step walks from one node to one of its children by name. Each XPath step selects some set (possibly empty) of XML nodes. An XPath step may contain not just element nodes, but also attribute nodes, text nodes, processing-instruction nodes, and so on. The syntax is very suggestive of file-system paths.

A very simple XPath is

```
/Customer
```

This XPath is an absolute XPath because of the leading slash; it selects all the top-level elements named Customer. The XML returned includes all the descendants of each Customer. That's the way XPath works – selection always picks a node with all of its content. XPath does not support **projection** (selecting only part of a node); for that, we'll have to wait for the XML Query Language (see chapter 11).

To continue down the XML hierarchy, the XPath

```
/Customer/Order
```

selects all the Order element children of all the top-level Customer elements. This is roughly equivalent to the SQL query

```
SELECT * FROM Orders O
WHERE EXISTS (SELECT * FROM Customers C WHERE C.CustomerID = O.CustomerID)
```

Attributes can be selected by preceding the name with the "at" symbol (@). Before we explore other axes of navigation, however, let's first learn about predicates.

Predication

Predicates are indicated using square brackets, like this:

```
/Customer[@CustomerID='ALFKI']
```

This XPath selects all top-level `Customer` elements whose `CustomerID` is equal to the string `"ALFKI"`, exactly like the SQL query

```
SELECT * from Customers WHERE CustomerID=N'ALFKI'
```

First, the XPath selects the top-level `Customer` elements using `/Customer`. Then a predicate is applied that selects the `CustomerID` attribute of the current selection, and compares that attribute with the string value `"ALFKI"`.

The contents of a predicate are either a boolean-valued expression (like above), or a numeric expression. Numeric predicates are special because they select based on position. The XPath `Customer[3]` selects the third `Customer`. Because document order often has no meaning in an XML View of a relational database, SQL XML does not support numeric predicates.

Predicates can be used multiple times in an XPath, combined sequentially, and nested. The following three examples will clarify the use and subtle nuances of predicates:

1. Single Predicate

```
/Customer[@CustomerID='ALFKI']/Order[@OrderID=10692]
```

selects the `Order` element whose `OrderID` attribute equals `10692` from the `Customer` element whose `CustomerID` attribute equals `"ALFKI"`. An equivalent SQL query is:

```
SELECT * FROM Orders O WHERE OrderID=10692 AND
EXISTS (
    SELECT * FROM Customers C
    WHERE C.CustomerID=O.CustomerID AND C.CustomerID='ALFKI'
)
```

The XML result from this XPath is

```
<Order OrderID="10692" OrderDate="1997-10-03">
    <Product ProductID="P63" UnitPrice="43.9000" Units="24"/>
</Order>
```

Now consider this similar XPath that uses a nested predicate:

2. Nested Predicate

```
/Customer[@CustomerID='ALFKI' and Order[@OrderID=10692]]/Order
```

This selects *all* the `Order` elements from those `Customer` elements with both a `CustomerID` attribute equal to `"ALFKI"` and an `Order` whose `OrderID` attribute equals `10692`.

Note that this XPath selects five `Order` elements from the XML View, while the previous XPath selects only one. The reason is that the `Order` element used inside the predicate is independent of the one used outside of the predicate. The previous XPath filtered its final `Order` selection but this XPath did not.

This is like the SQL query

```
SELECT * FROM Orders O WHERE EXISTS (
    SELECT * FROM Customers C
    WHERE C.CustomerID=O.CustomerID AND C.CustomerID='ALFKI'
    AND EXISTS (
        SELECT * FROM Orders O2
        WHERE C.CustomerID=O2.CustomerID AND O2.OrderID=10692
    )
)
```

Applying non-positional predicates sequentially has the same effect as combining their conditions using `and` in a single predicate:

3. Sequential Predicates

```
/Customer[@CustomerID='ALFKI'][Order/@OrderID=10692]/Order
```

is equivalent to

```
/Customer[@CustomerID='ALFKI' and Order/@OrderID=10692]/Order
```

Note that this XPath is different still – the difference is caused by the `Order/@OrderID=10692` versus `Order[@OrderID=10692]`. We'll explain why in the next two sections, when we explain implicit XPath type conversions. For now, we merely note that this XPath selects nothing at all in an ordinary XML document, but selects five orders (exactly like the previous XPath) in SQL XML.

XPath Types

XPath has a simple type system that includes only four types: `boolean`, `number`, `string`, and `nodeset`. However, the conversions from one type to another can sometimes cause surprising effects, and SQL XML differs from the official specification in a few places. We first describe the XPath types, and then observe a few pitfalls worth avoiding.

An XPath `boolean` is exactly what you would expect – true or false. An XPath `number` is an IEEE 754 double-precision floating-point number – XPath does not have an integer number type. An XPath `string` is a Unicode string. Finally, an XPath `nodeset` is an ordered set of XML nodes (including possibly text nodes).

XPath defines explicit conversion operators `boolean()`, `number()`, and `string()` that convert from any of these types to the corresponding type. A `boolean` is converted to a `number` as one expects (`true` becomes 1, `false` becomes 0). When converted to `string`, the value is `"true"` or `"false"` – note that this is not localized, and differs from the XDR representation of boolean (`"1"` or `"0"`). Also, this means that `string(b)` is different from `string(number(b))`, where b is a `boolean` value.

The `string` and `number` types convert to each other about as you would expect. There are some nuances (for example, the `string` representation of a number uses as many digits as required to uniquely identify it but no more, which is a different representation than what `printf()` produces), but it is unlikely that they will affect you. When in doubt, consult the W3C XPath specification.

A number converted to boolean results in true if and only if the number is non-zero and non-NaN. A string converted to boolean results in true if and only if the string is non-empty. Note that these conversions are not reversible: for example, boolean(string(boolean(x))) does not equal boolean(x) (in fact, it always equals true, because the string value of true or false is always a nonempty string).

The nodeset conversions are unusual. A nodeset converted to boolean becomes an existence test. The result is true if and only if the nodeset is not empty. This means that an XPath like

```
/Customer[Order]
```

converts the nodeset Order to boolean, and therefore selects all Customer elements that have Order children.

A nodeset converted to number first converts the nodeset to string, and then converts that string to number. The conversion of a nodeset to string uses the string value of only the *first* node in the nodeset. This conversion is not implemented for the same reason that numeric predicates are not; however, not supporting it at all would mean being unable to perform almost every useful XPath. SQL XML differs from the XPath specification in a subtle way that we will explain in the next section, when we describe the implicit conversions that occur as part of XPath expressions.

XPath Expressions

XPath supports the usual sort of operations, including arithmetic, string manipulation, equality tests, and relational comparisons.

Of the arithmetic operators, everything but modulus is supported (that is, addition, subtraction, multiplication, and division). Note that SQL Server lacks true IEEE floating-point arithmetic (notably NaNs and infinities), so floating-point arithmetic differs slightly from the XPath specification.

The following XPath demonstrates all the arithmetic operators:

```
/Product[((@Units - 1) * (@UnitPrice + 1)) div 2 > 0]
```

and results in the following XML:

```
<Product ProductID="P1" UnitPrice="18.0000" Units="39"/>
<Product ProductID="P2" UnitPrice="19.0000" Units="17"/>
<Product ProductID="P3" UnitPrice="10.0000" Units="13"/>
<Product ProductID="P4" UnitPrice="22.0000" Units="53"/>
<!-- ... -->
```

There are a few lexical oddities about XPath arithmetic worth noting in this example. Division is represented with div instead of a slash. Because hyphen is a valid XML name character, most subtraction operations require a space between the minus sign and the name in front of it; @Units-1 selects an attribute named Units-1.

Arithmetic operators implicitly cast their operands to number. This has the unexpected side effect that the XPath /Order[0 + Product/@UnitPrice > 10] is different from the XPath /Order[Product/@UnitPrice > 10]. The latter selects all Order elements having any Product with UnitPrice greater than 10. The former selects all Order elements whose *first* Product has UnitPrice greater than 10, because the nodeset Product/@UnitPrice is first converted to number (which has the effect of using the value of only the first node).

XPath oddities like this compel us to recommend against the use of long paths like A/B in predicates. Most likely, the meaning you wanted is actually a nested predicate like /Order[Product[@UnitPrice > 10]] anyway.

Because SQL XML does not support positional predicates, it uses "any" semantics for both of these XPaths. That is, both /Order[0 + Product/@UnitPrice > 10] and /Order[Product/@UnitPrice > 10] produce the same XML result in SQL XML.

This deviation from the W3C standard also applies to relational and equality operators. These operators apply special conversion rules to their operands that we will not explain in detail here. For example, an expression @Date > '1998-10-01' should first convert both the nodeset @Date and the string '1998-10-01' to number (which will result in NaN), and then compare them (which will result in false, since NaN compared with anything is false). SQL XML instead performs a string comparison, with the expected result (true if and only if the value of @Date is a date later than the one indicated in the string).

Here's an XPath that attempts string and date comparisons. These would not work in ordinary XML documents, but do work in SQL XML:

```
/Customer[@CustomerID > 'PARIS']/Order[@OrderDate <= '1999-01-01']
```

which results in the XML

```
<Order OrderID="10322" OrderDate="1996-10-04">
    <Product ProductID="P52" UnitPrice="7.0000" Units="38"/>
</Order>
<Order OrderID="10354" OrderDate="1996-11-14">
    <Product ProductID="P1" UnitPrice="18.0000" Units="39"/>
    <Product ProductID="P29" UnitPrice="123.7900" Units="0"/>
</Order>
<Order OrderID="10474" OrderDate="1997-03-13">
    <Product ProductID="P14" UnitPrice="23.2500" Units="35"/>
    <Product ProductID="P28" UnitPrice="45.6000" Units="26"/>
    <Product ProductID="P40" UnitPrice="18.4000" Units="123"/>
    <Product ProductID="P75" UnitPrice="7.7500" Units="125"/>
</Order>
<!-- ... -->
```

At the time of this writing, none of the XPath string functions (concat(), substring(), etc.) are supported. Microsoft has announced intentions to support these functions in the near future.

XPath and the XML View

XPath works by translating the XPath into an equivalent FOR XML EXPLICIT query. During this translation process, XPath makes use of the many annotations provided in the XML View.

XPath applies join relationships when navigating from one node to another. If the nodes are joined in the schema, then the join relationship will be used in the SQL query. Predicates correspond to existence tests (WHERE EXISTS).

Nodes that have an id-prefix are converted to string, and then the prefix is prepended to the value. Note that this prevents using those values as numbers in the XPath. For example, `/Product[@ProductID=11]` is an error; the correct XPath uses the `id` prefix: `/Product[@ProductID='P11']`.

In many cases, key information is required to correctly order and nest the resulting XML. If an XPath query seems to be returning odd results, or returns a FOR XML EXPLICIT error, the problem may be that the schema is missing `sql:key-fields`. Read the section about this annotation for instructions on its use.

Finally, XPath queries must perform many data conversions. XPath translates first from the SQL type to the XDR type, and then from the XDR type to the XPath type. This means that specifying XDR and SQL types in the schema can help eliminate unnecessary conversions. When the query converts a column used as an index (for example, `/Customer[@CustomerID='ALFKI']`), eliminating the unnecessary conversion can result in a ten-fold performance improvement of the XPath query.

Default Schema

XPath works best with an XML View, but can work without any schema at all – with some restrictions. These restrictions (names, flat hierarchy) are the same restrictions as on the default mapping used by an XML View. (See the earlier section, "*The Default Mapping*," for details.)

In addition, an XPath with no XML View must select the value of a single column from a single row. Because there is no schema to describe how the XML should be shaped, the XPath cannot return XML.

The default schema can be especially convenient for so called "direct object" queries that use an XPath-like syntax to access objects in the database. For example, the XPath

```
/Customers[@CustomerID='ALFKI']/@ContactName
```

is exactly the same as the SQL query

```
SELECT ContactName FROM Customers WHERE CustomerID='ALFKI'
```

XPath Parameters

XPath parameters are prefixed with the dollar-sign symbol (for example, `$param`). SQL XML supports only string-valued parameters, but this presents no great difficulties. Parameters can be shared among other queries in a template. For example, the following template selects the `Customer` element with the `id` parameter value that was passed to the template (which defaults to `"ALFKI"`):

```
<xpath-params xmlns:sql="urn:schemas-microsoft-com:xml-sql">
   <sql:header>
      <sql:param name="id">ALFKI</sql:param>
   </sql:header>
   <sql:xpath-query mapping-schema="xpath.xdr">
      /Customer[@CustomerID=$id]
   </sql:xpath-query>
</xpath-params>
```

Additional XPath Axes

XPath is not limited to top-down navigation (from an element to its children and attributes). XPath has a rich set of navigation axes, including namespaces, descendants, ancestors, and so on. However, at the time of this writing, SQL XML supports only four axes: `child`, `attribute`, `parent`, and `self`. In particular, the popular descendant-or-self shortcut "`//`" is not supported.

All four of these have abbreviated forms that are more commonly used. For the `child` and `attribute` axes, we've seen that the abbreviations have the form `child` or `@attribute`, respectively. For `parent`, the short form is two dots (`..`) and one dot (`.`) is the short form for `self`. Thus, the XPath

```
/Customer/Order[../@CustomerID='ALFKI']
```

is equivalent to the XPath

```
/Customer[@CustomerID='ALFKI']/Order
```

All of these also have longer forms that look like `axisname::nodetest`. So the previous XPath could also be written

```
/child::Customer[attribute::CustomerID='ALFKI']/child::Order
```

In this case, the node test is just the name of the element or attribute. Other node tests include functions like `node()` (selects all nodes) and `text()` (selects all text nodes) and the wildcard * (which is similar to `node()`, but not exactly the same). At the time of this writing, SQL XML supports only names and `node()`.

The abbreviation `..` is short for `parent::node()` and the abbreviation `.` is short for `self::node()`. So the XPath above that uses `..` could also be rewritten as:

```
/child::Customer/child::Order[parent::node()/attribute::CustomerID='ALFKI']
```

Updategrams

At this time, there is no W3C standard for updating XML documents. Updategrams attempt to fill this void by specifying a standard XML-based language for inserting, updating, and deleting XML data.

Updategrams are declarative. You describe what the XML currently is and what you want it to become, and the updategram takes care of all the details necessary to make it so. Updategrams use the namespace URI `urn:schemas-microsoft-com:xml-updategram`, which we will always assign to the prefix `u`.

In SQL Server 2000, updategram queries are executed through templates. Each updategram uses an XML View of the database to determine the SQL query that is required to perform the update.

> **NOTE: Updategrams require the latest SQL XML web release from MSDN, or SQL Server 2000 SP1 or later. The examples in this section are not compatible with the early beta version of updategrams that was released for SQL Server 2000 beta 2.**

Introduction

Every updategram consists of one `<u:sync>` element, corresponding to one database transaction. The transaction is described by a sequence of `<u:before>` and `<u:after>` pairs. Every `<before>` must have a matching `<after>`, and vice-versa; if one is missing, then it is equivalent to one with empty content. The contents of the `<before>` element are compared with the contents of its matching `<after>` element to determine whether an INSERT, UPDATE, or DELETE is required.

To avoid conflicts between multiple, concurrent queries, updategrams employ "optimistic concurrency control". If the current state of the database does not match the XML described in the `<before>` element, then the transaction will not be committed, and no change will be made. Depending on how specific the `<before>` element is, the synchronization will effectively range from none at all ("update always") to total synchronization ("update only if the row has not changed at all").

To demonstrate updategrams, let's create a table:

```
CREATE TABLE FictionalCharacters
    (cid nvarchar(10) PRIMARY KEY, FirstName nvarchar(40), LastName nvarchar(40))
```

We now use the following schema, ch15_ex21.xdr, for mapping the table:

```
<Schema xmlns="urn:schemas-microsoft-com:xml-data"
    xmlns:dt="urn:schemas-microsoft-com:datatypes"
    xmlns:sql="urn:schemas-microsoft-com:xml-sql">

    <ElementType name="First" content="textOnly" />
    <ElementType name="Last" content="textOnly" />
    <ElementType name="Person" sql:relation="FictionalCharacters"
                 sql:key-fields="cid">
      <AttributeType name="ID" dt:type="id"/>
      <attribute type="ID" sql:field="cid"/>
      <element type="First" sql:field="FirstName"/>
      <element type="Last" sql:field="LastName"/>
    </ElementType>
</Schema>
```

This template (ch15_ex22.xml) demonstrates an insert into the FictionalCharacters table:

```
<insert>
    <u:sync mapping-schema="ch15_ex21.xdr"
      xmlns:u="urn:schemas-microsoft-com:xml-updategram">
      <u:before/>
      <u:after>
         <Person ID="HGTTG42">
            <First>Arthur</First>
            <Last>Dent</Last>
         </Person>
      </u:after>
    </u:sync>
    <sql:xpath-query mapping-schema="ch15_ex21.xdr"
            xmlns:sql="urn:schemas-microsoft-com:xml-sql">
    Person
    </sql:xpath-query>
</insert>
```

The result of executing this template, if the updategram succeeds, will be

```
<insert>
   <Person ID="HGTTG42">
      <First>Arthur</First>
      <Last>Dent</Last>
   </Person>
</insert>
```

or

```
<insert>
   <?MSSQLError Some Error Message Here ?>
</insert>
```

if it fails. When successful, the updategram inserts a new row in the FictionalCharacters table with the cid, FirstName, and LastName column values from the XML. Had there been other columns in that row, they would have been set to NULL since their values were not specified.

We can now update this row, using this updategram (ch15_ex22a.xml):

```
<update>
   <u:sync mapping-schema="ch15_ex21.xdr"
      xmlns:u="urn:schemas-microsoft-com:xml-updategram">
      <u:before>
         <Person ID="HGTTG42">
            <First>Arthur</First>
         </Person>
      </u:before>
      <u:after>
         <Person ID="HGTTG42"/>
      </u:after>
   </u:sync>
   <sql:xpath-query mapping-schema="ch15_ex21.xdr"
            xmlns:sql="urn:schemas-microsoft-com:xml-sql">
   Person
   </sql:xpath-query>
</update>
```

The result of this template (when successful) will be:

```
<update>
   <Person ID="HGTTG42">
      <Last>Dent</Last>
   </Person>
</update>
```

because the FirstName value specified in the <before> element is removed (that is, set to NULL) in the <after> element.

In the first template, the <before> element was empty, so the updategram became an INSERT. In the second, the contents of the <before> and <after> elements were matched and the updategram became an UPDATE. However, had the elements matched differently, it could have been a DELETE and an INSERT instead. Before we examine the heuristics used to determine what kind of query an updategram represents, let us first consider how an updategram handles the values given it, especially NULL.

Values, Absence and NULL

Up until now, we've said that absence of XML data is equivalent to a SQL NULL value, and vice-versa. Unfortunately, this equivalence presents a problem for an updategram, because optimistic concurrency control applies only to the values in the before element. If the value was NULL, it would be absent, and thus would not figure into the equation (even though we might not want to perform the update or delete if the value has changed away from NULL). Therefore, updategrams need a way to explicitly differentiate NULL values from absent ones.

Updategrams allow the user to specify a string value that will be used in the XML in place of a SQL NULL. Whenever an XML value is equal to this string, the string is replaced with NULL in the equivalent SQL query. The string is specified with the attribute u:nullvalue on the <u:sync> element or <u:header> element.

A popular value to use for u:nullvalue is the string NULL itself. After having executed the previous templates, let's perform another one that restores the first name of our fictional character (ch15_ex23.xml):

```
<restore>
    <u:sync mapping-schema="ch15_ex21.xdr"
        xmlns:u="urn:schemas-microsoft-com:xml-updategram"
        u:nullvalue="NULL" >
        <u:before>
            <Person ID="HGTTG42">
                <First>NULL</First>
            </Person>
        </u:before>
        <u:after>
            <Person ID="HGTTG42">
                <First>Arthur</First>
            </Person>
        </u:after>
    </u:sync>
</restore>
```

This updategram will commit only if the FirstName is still NULL.

Note that when evaluating the value of an element, updategrams don't use the usual definition of string value. In XPath syntax, string(element) usually takes all the text node descendants of the element and concatenates them together in document order, which is equivalent to the XPath string(element//text()). Updategrams use only the text nodes that are immediate children of the element, equivalent to the XPath string(element/text()). When the string value of the element matches the u:nullvalue, NULL is substituted in its place.

Also, updategrams are aware of XDR default. That is, when an element or attribute value is absent, updategrams use the default value (if given) in the annotated XDR schema. The default is indicated in the schema on an <AttributeType> or <ElementType> using the default attribute. When there is no default value, no value is used for the absent element or attribute.

Insert/Update/Delete Heuristics

Now that you understand how an updategram extracts the XML values out of the `before` and `after` elements and how it handles absence and default values, the only remaining piece of the puzzle is determining which values in the `after` element correspond to which values in the `before` element. Once this matching has been performed, the updategram knows which rows to update, which to delete, and which to insert, and can create the corresponding SQL query to perform that work.

An updategram matches elements based on an element key. This key can be specified in the annotated schema using `sql:key-fields`, or it can be specified in the updategram using the `u:id` annotation. If the `u:id` method is chosen, then it must be used everywhere in the updategram.

As an example, consider the following updategram (`ch15_ex24.xml`):

```
<keys>
    <u:sync xmlns:u="urn:schemas-microsoft-com:xml-updategram"
        mapping-schema="ch15_ex21.xdr">
        <u:before>
            <Person ID="HGTTG42">
                <First>Arthur</First>
                <Last>Dent</Last>
            </Person>
        </u:before>
        <u:after>
            <Person ID="HGTTG42">
                <First>Ford</First>
                <Last>Prefect</Last>
            </Person>
            <Person ID="HGTTG54">
                <First>Arthur</First>
                <Last>Dent</Last>
            </Person>
        </u:after>
    </u:sync>
</keys>
```

Because `EmployeeID` is known from the schema to be a key, and it uniquely identifies the `Employee` elements, this updategram will match the two `Person` elements with ID `HGTTG42`, and find no match for `Person HGTTG54` in the `<before>` image. There are no `default` or `nullvalue` attributes to apply. Therefore, the updategram will perform one `UPDATE` for `HGTTG42`, and one `INSERT` for `HGTTG54`.

As a second example, consider the updategram (`ch15_ex25.xml`)

```
<u:sync xmlns:u="urn:schemas-microsoft-com:xml-updategram"
    mapping-schema="ch15_ex21.xdr">
    <u:before>
        <Person u:id="forty-two" ID="HGTTG42"/>
        <Person u:id="fifty-four" ID="HGTTG54"/>
    </u:before>
    <u:after>
        <Person u:id="fifty-four" ID="54"/>
        <Person u:id="forty-two" ID="42"/>
    </u:after>
</u:sync>
```

This updategram needs to change the value of the key itself. The only way to do this is to identify the elements using u:id. The values used for u:id are arbitrary; they are used only for matching elements in the updategram, and will not be inserted into the database: as a result, this updategram will not work. Of course, u:id is not limited to key changes; it can be used any time.

Parameters

Updategrams use parameters exactly like XPath does, and with a similar syntax. Anywhere an updategram contains the dollar-sign ($) followed by the name of a parameter, the parameter value will be substituted.

As an example, consider the updategram (ch15_ex26.xml)

```
<parameterized-insert xmlns:u="urn:schemas-microsoft-com:xml-updategram">
    <u:header u:nullvalue="NULL">
        <u:param name="first">Bob</u:param>
        <u:param name="last">Doe</u:param>
        <u:param name="id"/>
    </u:header>
    <u:sync mapping-schema="ch15_ex21.xdr" u:nullvalue="NULL">
        <u:before/>
        <u:after>
            <Person ID="$id">
                <First>$first</First>
                <Last>$last</Last>
            </Person>
        </u:after>
    </u:sync>
</parameterized-insert>
```

This updategram will insert a new fictional character using the parameters passed in to the template, or the default values "Bob" and "Doe", if the parameters are not passed to the template (since these are the default parameter values given in the template header).

Default Schema

We previously described the subset of XPath that can be executed without a schema. Updategrams can also use a default mapping, with some restrictions. These restrictions (names, flat hierarchy) are similar to the default mapping used by an XML View (See the earlier section, "*The Default Mapping*," for details).

In addition, updategrams cannot work with any of the SQL types binary, image, ntext, text, or varbinary in the <before> element and binary, image, or varbinary in the <after> element. Values that map to monetary SQL types (money and smallmoney) must be preceded with a currency symbol such as $; conversely, values preceded with a currency symbol cannot be inserted, updated, or deleted from any string type column in the database (char, nvarchar, etc.).

Server-Generated Identities

Automatically-generated column values (such as identity columns) can be indicated in an updategram using the `u:at-identity` attribute. For example:

```
<auto-identity>
    <u:sync xmlns:u="urn:schemas-microsoft-com:xml-updategram">
        <u:after>
            <Employees u:at-identity="x" FirstName="Jack" LastName="Ryan"/>
        </u:after>
    </u:sync>
</auto-identity>
```

will insert a new record into the `Employees` table, which has an auto-identity column (`EmployeeID`). The symbol used to represent the identity (in this example, `x`) can be referred to in sub-elements; wherever the symbol occurs as a value, it will be replaced with the identity that was generated from the insert.

Also, the generated value can be returned as part of the template result by using the `u:returnid` attribute on the `u:after` element. For example, the template

```
<return>
    <u:sync xmlns:u="urn:schemas-microsoft-com:xml-updategram">
        <u:after u:returnid>
            <Employees u:at-identity="x" FirstName="Jack" LastName="Ryan"/>
        </u:after>
    </u:sync>
</return>
```

produces a result like:

```
<return>
    <returnid>
        <x>10</x>
    </returnid>
</return>
```

Multiple auto-generated columns can be returned by specifying them as a space-separated list in the `u:returnid` value.

Unfortunately, auto-generated values are not integrated with parameters, so it is not possible to refer to them in other queries in the same template. However, one could use `u:returnid` to pass the values created in one updategram to another template.

Data Types

All values that map to any of the SQL types `binary`, `image`, `ntext`, `text`, or `varbinary` must be marked in the schema as having that `sql:datatype`. Otherwise, the updategram will not be able to generate a valid SQL query. Similarly, both monetary types (`money`, `smallmoney`) must be marked as having one of the XDR numeric types to be properly used, even though you could still have an attribute type `unitprice`, without either datatype.

The XDR binary types `bin.hex` and `bin.base64` are used when decoding binary values. Binary values cannot be referred to using a **dbobject** URL (as generated by `sql:url-encode`).

If an attribute or element has a `sql:id-prefix` in the schema, then that prefix will be stripped out of the value in the updategram.

Overflow

When an element is marked as having an `sql:overflow-field` in the schema, any data in the `u:after` element that is not otherwise consumed will be placed into the overflow column. (The overflow column must be one of the SQL string types, and should have enough space to store the value.) This includes elements or attributes that were marked as `sql:map-field="0"` but appeared in the updategram.

Advanced Topics

Namespaces and External Schemas

Most uses of XML require namespaces, whether some externally defined namespace or your own custom one. There are two central concepts required when using namespaces in XML Views: namespace declarations and the `sql:target-namespace` annotation.

Recall that namespace declarations come in two forms, `xmlns="uri"` and `xmlns:prefix="uri"`, and are inherited of the descendants of the element where they were declared. Namespace URIs are commonly overloaded for many different purposes – versioning (like the XSL namespaces) and actual URLs (that you can visit on the Web) are just two examples. For XML Views, there are three kinds of namespace URIs worth mentioning.

First, there are the four special namespace URIs corresponding to XDR and SQL XML (all of which begin with `urn:schemas-microsoft-com:`, followed by one of `xml-data`, `datatypes`, `xml-sql`, or `xml-updategram`) that identify schema contents or annotations, respectively. Second, there are **external schema references**, which we will explain next. And finally, everything else – which are treated as ordinary namespace names.

External schema references are distinguished from ordinary namespace URIs by beginning with the string `x-schema:`. Every such namespace URI is treated as a reference to a schema at the file location listed after the colon. The external schema will be loaded, and all its `ElementType` and `AttributeType` declarations made available to the schema that imported it (and in fact, all of the schemas currently being processed).

The following two schemas demonstrate the concept:

```
<!-- ch15_ex27.xdr -->
<Schema xmlns="urn:schemas-microsoft-com:xml-data"
    xmlns:sql="urn:schemas-microsoft-com:xml-sql">
   <ElementType name="Customer" sql:relation="Customers">
      <element type="x:Order" xmlns:x="x-schema:ch15_ex28.xdr">
         <sql:relationship key-relation="Customers" key="CustomerID"
             foreign-relation="Orders" foreign-key="CustomerID" />
      </element>
   </ElementType>
</Schema>
```

```
<!-- ch15_ex28.xdr -->
<Schema xmlns="urn:schemas-microsoft-com:xml-data"
    xmlns:sql="urn:schemas-microsoft-com:xml-sql">
  <ElementType name="Order" sql:relation="Orders">
      <AttributeType name="CustomerID" />
      <AttributeType name="OrderID" />
      <attribute type="CustomerID" />
  </ElementType>
</Schema>
```

Together, these schemas produce XML shaped like this:

```
<Customer>
    <Order CustomerID="ALFKI" OrderID=""/>
    <Order CustomerID="ALFKI" OrderID=""/>
    <Order CustomerID="ALFKI" OrderID=""/>
</Customer>
<Customer>
    <Order CustomerID="ANATR" OrderID=""/>
    <Order CustomerID="ANATR" OrderID=""/>
</Customer>
<!-- ... -->
```

exactly as if there had been only one schema.

The second part of using namespaces in XML Views is the `sql:target-namespace` annotation. The `sql:target-namespace` annotation is used on the Schema element, and declares that all the top-level declarations in the schema will go into that namespace URI. This annotation can be used on a schema by itself; but it is most commonly used in conjunction with external schemas, creating a web of schemas, one for each namespace URI.

If we modify the second schema above to use a target namespace:

```
<!-- ch15_ex28a.xdr -->
<Schema xmlns="urn:schemas-microsoft-com:xml-data"
    xmlns:sql="urn:schemas-microsoft-com:xml-sql"
    sql:target-namespace="your namepsace" >
  <ElementType name="Order" sql:relation="Orders">
      <AttributeType name="CustomerID" />
      <AttributeType name="OrderID" />
      <attribute type="CustomerID" />
  </ElementType>
</Schema>
```

then the resulting XML when you run the first schema (making sure of course, that you change the second schema reference to `ch15_ex28a.xdr`) will look like this:

```
<Customer>
    <y:Order xmlns:y="your namespace" CustomerID="ALFKI" OrderID=""/>
    <y:Order xmlns:y="your namespace" CustomerID="ALFKI" OrderID=""/>
    <y:Order xmlns:y="your namespace" CustomerID="ALFKI" OrderID=""/>
</Customer>
<Customer>
    <y:Order xmlns:y="your namespace" CustomerID="ANATR" OrderID=""/>
    <y:Order xmlns:y="your namespace" CustomerID="ANATR" OrderID=""/>
</Customer>
<!-- ... -->
```

Note that the prefix used in the schema is not necessarily preserved in the XML result. Also note that, although the `Order` element is placed into a namespace, none of its attributes are. This is consistent with the normal interaction between attributes and namespace declarations. If you require an attribute to be placed in the target namespace, declare it at the top-level of the schema.

We should note that the use of namespaces in XPath is currently limited to templates. XPath uses namespace prefixes, so it requires those prefixes to be bound to namespace URIs. Currently SQL Server does not provide a way to perform this binding in a URL, so the binding must occur in XML (using ordinary namespace declarations).

Structural Recursion

Unfortunately, XML Views currently do not directly support recursion. The reason is that creating recursive hierarchies using `FOR XML EXPLICIT` (which XPath uses) requires advance knowledge of the depth of the hierarchy to construct the query. This problem is demonstrated by the SQL query (`ch15_ex30.sql`)

```
SELECT 1 as TAG, 0 as parent,
    E1.EmployeeID as [Employee!1!id],
    NULL as [Employee!2!id],
    NULL as [Employee!3!id]
 FROM Employees E1
 WHERE E1.ReportsTo = NULL
UNION ALL
SELECT 2, 1,
    E1.EmployeeID,
    E2.EmployeeID,
    NULL
 FROM Employees E1 JOIN Employees E2 ON E1.EmployeeID = E2.ReportsTo
 WHERE E1.ReportsTo = NULL
UNION ALL
SELECT 3, 2,
    E1.EmployeeID,
    E2.EmployeeID,
    E3.EmployeeID
 FROM Employees E1 JOIN Employees E2 ON E1.EmployeeID = E2.ReportsTo
                   JOIN Employees E3 ON E2.EmployeeID = E3.ReportsTo
    WHERE E1.ReportsTo = NULL
         ORDER BY 3, 4, 5
FOR XML EXPLICIT
```

This limitation of XML Views prevents the use of recursive schemas like:

```
<Schema xmlns="urn:schemas-microsoft-com:xml-data"
     xmlns:sql="urn:schemas-microsoft-com:xml-sql">
   <ElementType name="Employees">
      <element type="Employees" >
           <sql:relationship key-relation="Employees" key="EmployeeID"
           foreign-relation="Employees" foreign-key="ReportsTo" />
      </element>
   </ElementType>
</Schema>
```

because the EXPLICIT query needed is data-dependent. Until XML Views provides explicit support for recursion, an alternative method is required.

The natural first attempt, an almost-recursive schema like the one below, also does not work. Let's look at this to see why:

```
<!-- This schema will not work! -->
<Schema xmlns="urn:schemas-microsoft-com:xml-data"
        xmlns:sql="urn:schemas-microsoft-com:xml-sql">
  <ElementType name="Employees"/>
  <ElementType name="Manager" sql:relation="Employees">
    <element type="Employees">
      <sql:relationship key-relation="Employees" key="EmployeeID"
        foreign-relation="Employees" foreign-key="ReportsTo" />
    </element>
  </ElementType>
</Schema>
```

The problem with this schema is that the join relationship from the table to itself, a so-called **self-join**, is also not supported by XML Views at the time of this writing.

However, all is not lost! Using a little imagination, it is possible to create recursive hierarchies. One solution is to alias the table using a SQL view, then use that view in the annotated schema. The following example demonstrates this technique using the Employees table in the **Northwind** database.

First, prepare a SQL view that mirrors the Employees table:

```
CREATE VIEW Managers AS SELECT * FROM Employees
```

Then, use the SQL view in the schema (ch15_ex31.xdr):

```
<Schema xmlns="urn:schemas-microsoft-com:xml-data"
        xmlns:sql="urn:schemas-microsoft-com:xml-sql">
  <ElementType name="Employees"/>
  <ElementType name="Managers">
      <element type="Employees">
        <sql:relationship key-relation="Managers" key="EmployeeID"
          foreign-relation="Employees" foreign-key="ReportsTo" />
      </element>
  </ElementType>
</Schema>
```

When true structural recursion is required (in which the element names are equal), the only solution using XML Views at the time of this writing is to post-process the XML. In fact, post-processing to obtain recursive XML avoids the overhead of the SQL unions and joins, possibly performing better than the recursive EXPLICIT query would have performed. Certainly this solution will scale up better, as it off-loads some processing from the database to the middle tier. We provide a complete example of this technique using XSL in the SQL Server case study.

Summary

XML Views permit a flexible, efficient XML representation of relational data. An XML View can select data from disparate tables and join them together into one XML document. Using XPath, you can select an entire XML View or the portions of it. You can also use XPath to refer directly to items (such as images) in the database. Updategrams allow the modification of the underlying relational store through the XML View by inserting, deleting, or updating XML fragments.

Updategrams, XPaths, and ordinary SQL queries can be executed from XML templates, and the results from these queries substituted into the XML template. Combined with other standard XML processing techniques (such as XSL), these query languages provide a powerful way to transport and present XML data on the Web.

XML DATABASES XML DATABASES XML DATABASES XML DATABASES
XML
XML

16

JDBC

If you are an enterprise Java developer who specializes in writing database applications using the JDBC API, you have probably had to confront the thorny issue of extending your applications to today's pervasive computing environment. Nowadays, people expect to be able to access mission-critical data anytime, anywhere, and from any device, regardless of what data access API is being used to manipulate the underlying data source. The challenge of the enterprise Java developer is to create JDBC applications that allow platform-neutral, device-independent access to data. By XML-enabling your JDBC applications, you can accomplish this. Here is the good news; it's easier than you might think.

How XML Enhances JDBC (and vice versa)

When you combine XML with J2EE (Java 2, Enterprise Edition) technologies and standard Internet protocols (such as HTTP), you can write enterprise applications that provide universal data access to JDBC data sources with a minimal amount of coding. With XML, XSLT, and JDBC, you can design scalable and extensible architectures that facilitate device-independent data delivery in J2EE applications. This allows end users to access your data using web browsers, WAP devices, PDAs, or any other current or future device that renders content using an XML-based markup language.

Moreover, combining XML and JDBC facilitates the creation of web services using J2EE. Web services are HTTP applications that provide an *application programming interface* rather than a *user interface*. With web services, your trading partners can integrate your business processes and data with their applications, regardless of which hardware platform and operating system they are built on, or programming language that they are written in.

This chapter will give you some practical, hand-on examples of how to integrate XML with JDBC in your J2EE applications in a manner that facilitates device-and-platform independent universal data access in today's pervasive computing environment. Specifically, it will cover two scenarios:

- **Generating XML from a JDBC data source**: We will walk through the construction of a simple XML gateway architecture for JDBC. This architecture contains software components that allow you to execute SQL statements against arbitrary JDBC data sources, returning the result sets as well-formed XML data structures that can then be consumed by any application with XML parsing capabilities. Next, we will show you how to add server-side XSLT processing capabilities to this architecture to illustrate how easy it is to transform the XML-serialized JDBC result set, to a mark-up language that targets a particular device, such as a web browser.

- **Using XML to update a JDBC data source**: In this scenario, we will show you how to use **WebRowSets**, an emerging Java technology, to create distributed JDBC applications that use XML to marshal disconnected Result sets between remote machines. Please note that, as of this writing, the WebRowSet binaries are still in "early access" status, and could change slightly before becoming part of the core API.

Software Needed for This Chapter

Before getting started, you should make sure that you install and configure the core software needed to work through the examples provided in the chapter. This software includes JDK 1.3, the Xalan XSLT processor for Java, Tomcat 3.1, and a relational database system with a JDBC driver. For the most part, the code samples in this chapter will compile and run on virtually any system for which a reasonable implementation of the Java virtual machine has been ported. Since we developed and tested these samples on Windows NT 4.0, most of the examples in this chapter are NT-centric.

JDK 1.3

The first piece of software needed is JDK 1.3. You can download this free of charge from http://java.sun.com. When you download it, ensure that you select the correct installer for the operating system you are using. If you are using NT, for example, you will download and run the InstallShield self-extracting setup program. I also recommend that you download the JDK documentation, which is available as a separate download. While you can browse this documentation on Sun's Java web site, you will find it infinitely more convenient to have it available on your local file system.

One point of clarification: while we recommend JDK 1.3, we have also tested the code in this chapter on JDK 1.2.2. This is important because JDK 1.3 has not been ported to as many platforms as the ubiquitous JDK 1.2.2. One word of caution: if you do decide to use JDK 1.2.2, make sure you download the JNDI (Java Naming and Directory Interface) reference implementation. The WebRowSet examples covered later require JNDI. While JDK 1.3 includes JNDI, JDK 1.2.2 does not, and you must add this as a separate download. We will discuss this in more detail later in the chapter.

Xalan XSLT Processor for Java

The next piece of software we will use is Xalan for Java version 1.2. Xalan is an open-source XSLT processor that is maintained by the Apache Group. You can download it from http://xml.apache.org. After downloading and unpacking the `xalan-j_1_2_D02.zip` archive, locate the `xalan.jar` and `xerces.jar` (the Xerces XML parser) archives and copy them to the `\jdk1.3\lib` directory.

If you don't want to use Xalan, or you would like to try another XSLT processor, there are several quality XSLT processors implemented in Java. Examples include:

❑ IBM LotusXSL (http://alphaworks.ibm.com/tech/LotusXSL)

❑ James Clark's XT package (http://www.jclark.com/xml/xt.html)

Software Needed to Implement Rowsets

To run the sample distributed JDBC application, you'll need to download the Java packages used to implement the WebRowSet framework. This framework provides a transparent mechanism for serializing the data, metadata, and properties of a JDBC result set to XML for transportation and manipulation by a remote application across the network. We will cover this framework in more detail later. The packages needed to use the WebRowSet framework include the `sun.jdbc.rowset` and `javax.sql` packages, and the JNDI reference implementation. We'll cover the framework in more detail later; for now, just follow the instructions below to download and install the software.

The sun.jdbc.rowset Package

To download this package, point your browser at:
http://developer.java.sun.com/developer/earlyAccess/crs/. This is "early access" technology, so you must create a free account with the Sun Java Developer Connection if you haven't already done so. The samples in this chapter have been tested with the "early access 4" release. Once you have downloaded the `rowset-1_0-ea4.zip` archive, locate the `rowset.jar` file and place it in the `C:\jdk1.3\lib` directory.

> The WebRowSet implementation contained in this package is an experimental, unsupported technology. Therefore, it may change before it becomes an official part of the Java platform. Please do not use this technology in a production application until it is released as a final, stable product.

The javax.sql Package

The JDBC 2.0 API includes two packages: `java.sql`, which contains the JDBC 2.0 core API, and `javax.sql`, which contains the JDBC 2.0 standard extension API. The `java.sql` package is included with the JDK, so it should already be on your system. Since the WebRowSet class uses the JDBC 2.0 standard extension API, we'll need the `javax.sql` package, which is provided as a separate download. To download this package, point your browser at http://java.sun.com/products/jdbc/download.html, and select the JDBC 2.0 Optional Package Binary. Download the `jdbc2_0-stdext.jar` archive, and place it in the `C:\jdk1.3\lib` directory.

The JNDI Reference Implementation

The WebRowSet class uses JNDI (Java Naming and Directory Interface). If you installed JDK version 1.3, you can skip this step. JDK 1.3 ships with JNDI. If you are using JDK 1.2.2, you must download the JNDI reference implementation from Sun's web site. To do so, point your browser at http://java.sun.com/products/jndi/index.html. Download the `jndi1_2_1.zip` archive and unpack it; locate the `jndi.jar` file, and place it in your CLASSPATH.

Tomcat 3.1

Since all of the sample applications covered in this chapter are implemented at least in part using the Java servlet API, you will need to install and configure a servlet container on your system. The examples provided should work in any servlet container that supports the Java servlet API version 2.2 or higher. We recommend Tomcat 3.1, the open-source servlet and JSP reference implementation developed by the Apache Software Foundation. This is a lightweight, high performance servlet container that is easy-to-use, implements the standard religiously (it is, after all, the reference implementation), and includes a lightweight HTTP listener that eliminates the need to install a separate web server. To qualify this comment, the HTTP listener is useful for unit-testing applications. In a production environment, you should use a commercial-quality web server with the appropriate connector. Tomcat provides connectors for Apache, IIS, and Netscape/iPlanet Enterprise Server. Since it is implemented in Java, Tomcat will run on a variety of different platforms. Here are the installation steps for Windows NT 4.0:

❑   Download `jakarta-tomcat.zip` from http://jakarta.apache.org.

❑   Install it by unpacking the zip archive into a directory on your hard drive.

❑   Modify the `jakarta-tomcat\bin\tomcat.bat` file to point the JAVA_HOME variable to the directory in which you installed JDK 1.3. This variable assignment does not exist in the batch file, so you will need to add it. For example, if you installed the JDK on the C drive, add this variable assignment to the file: `set JAVA_HOME=C:\jdk1.3`

❑   You also want to change the `jakarta-tomcat\bin\tomcat.bat` file to add the rowset, JDBC standard extensions, Xerces, and Xalan code base to Tomcat's CLASSPATH. To do so, insert the following code on or about line 35 of `tomcat.bat` (this assumes that you put the JAR files, as recommended, in the `jdk1.3\lib` directory):

```
rem This is an existing line in the batch file.  Look for it to find
rem the right spot to add your additional JARs to the CLASSPATH:

set CLASSPATH=%CLASSPATH%;%JAVA_HOME%\lib\tools.jar

rem Start adding your additional jars here:

set CLASSPATH=%CLASSPATH%;%JAVA_HOME%\lib\rowset.jar
set CLASSPATH=%CLASSPATH%;%JAVA_HOME%\lib\jdbc2_0-stdext.jar
set CLASSPATH=%CLASSPATH%;%JAVA_HOME%\lib\xerces.jar
set CLASSPATH=%CLASSPATH%;%JAVA_HOME%\lib\xalan.jar
```

❑   Run the `jakarta-tomcat\bin\startup.bat` to start Tomcat.

❑   Point your browser to http://127.0.0.1:8080. By default, Tomcat's HTTP server listens on port 8080 to preclude any conflict with a web server that might already be installed on your system and listening on port 80. Of course, you can change the port assignment, if desired, by editing the `server.xml` configuration file (see the Tomcat documentation for more details). When you hit this URL, you will see the Tomcat home page.

If you are using a UNIX variant, the installation and configuration steps are similar, with a few key differences. Instead of downloading the ZIP archive, you want to download and unpack the `tar` archive. In addition, you will need to modify the `tomcat.sh` UNIX shell script instead of the `tomcat.bat` batch file. Refer to the Tomcat documentation for additional information.

At the end of the chapter, we will cover all of the steps required to package our sample applications for deployment to Tomcat or any other J2EE-compliant servlet container. In the meantime, you might want to download the web application archive provided with the sample code for this chapter from our web site; details on how to get all of the code for this book is supplied in the support and errata appendix. This will allow you to test the examples while you are going through the chapter. To do so, follow these steps:

❑ If Tomcat is already running, stop it using the `shutdown.bat` batch file located in the `\jakarta-tomcat\bin` directory.

❑ Locate the `Chapter26\jdbcxml.war` web application archive, and place it in the `\jakarta-tomcat\webapps` directory.

❑ Start Tomcat by running the `startup.bat` (or `startup.sh` for UNIX users) script in the `\jakarta-tomcat\bin` directory.

❑ Point your browser at http://127.0.0.1:8080/jdbcxml/index.html. This file is located in the `jdbcxml.war` archive's file system root. Tomcat will automatically unpack the archive at the first access. You should now see this page:

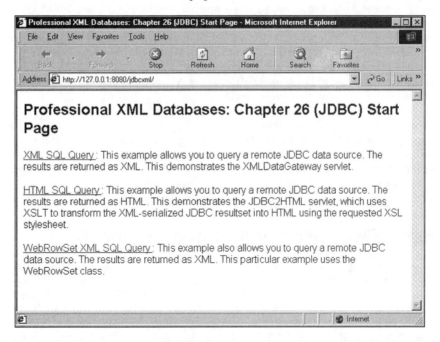

In addition to the HTML and the compiled binaries, this archive also includes all of the source code discussed in this chapter.

A JDBC Data Source and Driver (Oracle, SQL Server, etc.)

Finally, you will need to have access to a database with a JDBC driver. The examples are written generically enough to work with a variety of different relational database products. Most database products on the market today include a JDBC driver. The three that we will use in this chapter are Oracle 8i via the Oracle thin JDBC driver, and Microsoft SQL Server 7.0 and Microsoft Access 97, both via the JDBC-ODBC Bridge.

The Oracle JDBC driver is typically packaged in a file called `classes111.zip`. This file comes with any Oracle installation, so your Oracle database administrator will be able to provide it for you. You can also download it from http://www.oracle.com. The JDBC-ODBC Bridge ships with the JDK.

To preclude any problems from occurring, you want to ensure that the JDBC driver you will use is added to the `CLASSPATH`. If you are using the JDBC-ODBC Bridge, this was taken care of when you installed the JDK, so you don't need to worry about it. If your database does not have a JDBC driver (or you are unsure), you can simply use the JDBC-ODBC Bridge (assuming that the database product provides an ODBC driver, as most do). Please consult your specific database product's documentation for more information.

Generating XML from JDBC

As we touched on earlier, XML and JDBC complement each other very well. Using these two technologies, you can create "universal data access" applications that can run on a variety of different J2EE-compliant application servers and access a variety of different data sources. It gives you the best of all worlds. The use of XML allows you to make your data and metadata available to virtually any application, regardless of how it was written or the type of platform on which it runs. The use of Java and the J2EE APIs gives the application developer platform and vendor freedom of choice; a variety of different vendors have created J2EE-compliant application servers that run on a variety of different hardware and OS combinations. A short list includes ATG, BEA Systems, IBM, and the iPlanet Sun-Netscape Alliance. The use of JDBC as the data access API allows you to leverage decades worth of relational data technology and thought leadership.

The challenge, then, is to create an architecture that allows you to extract data from a JDBC data source, serialize it to XML, and send it to the requesting client, using XSLT as appropriate to create output that targets a particular device. For extensibility purposes, this architecture should be designed in a manner that abstracts the process of accessing the data source via JDBC and serializing the Result set as XML, thereby shielding the application developer from these details, and promoting code reuse. To illustrate this, we will create a simple XML gateway architecture for JDBC.

Our Simple XML Gateway Architecture for JDBC

The heart of our XML gateway architecture for JDBC is the `JDBC2XML` class. This class controls access to the JDBC data source. Briefly, it executes a SQL statement against the specified JDBC data source, serializes the returned JDBC result set as XML, and returns this XML document to the calling client. In our architecture, the `JDBC2XML` class will be reused by two Java servlets: the **XMLDataGateway** servlet and the **JDBC2HTML** servlet. The `XMLDataGateway` servlet provides a generic XML-over-HTTP interface to JDBC data sources for XML-enabled applications. The `JDBC2HTML` servlet returns JDBC result sets as HTML to web browsers using the specified XSL stylesheet. This servlet essentially acts as a filter; when an HTTP user agent submits an HTTP GET or POST request to an XSL stylesheet, the request is delegated to the `JDBC2HTML` servlet for handling. The following figure shows this architecture:

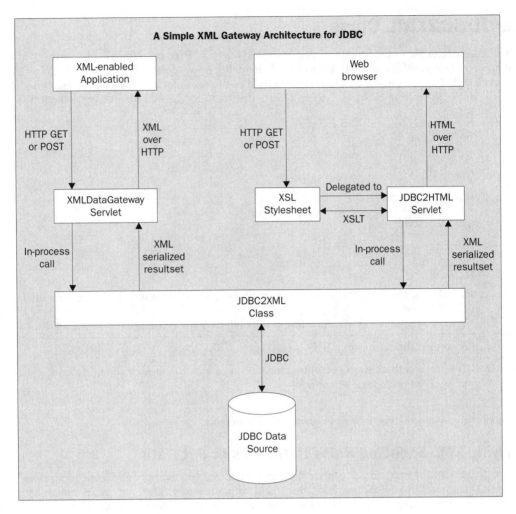

A Simple XML Gateway Architecture for JDBC

This section will walk you through creating and using this architecture. Specifically, it will show you how to do the following:

❑   Develop the JDBC2XML class

❑   Develop the XMLDataGateway servlet

❑   Query a JDBC data source using the XMLDataGateway servlet

❑   Develop the JDBC2HTML servlet

❑   Write an XSL stylesheet that defines HTML presentation logic for our <resultset/> XML schema

❑   Query a JDBC data source using the JDBC2HTML servlet

The JDBC2XML Class

The class encapsulates the functionality required to query a JDBC data source and return the results of that query as a well-formed XML document. Essentially, it executes a SQL statement against the specified JDBC data source, serializes the returned JDBC result set as XML, and returns this XML document to the calling client as a string. Create the `JDBC2XML.java` file and enter the following code:

```
package com.jresources.jdbc;

import java.sql.*;
import java.util.*;

public class JDBC2XML
{
    public JDBC2XML()
    {
        super();
    }
```

To accomplish this, the `JDBC2XML` class implements several different methods. These methods include:

- ❏ Methods that apply XML encoding rules, including the `encodeXML()` method
- ❏ A method that serializes a JDBC result set to XML, the `writeXML()` method
- ❏ The method that brings everything together by executing the search and returning the results as XML (the `execute()` method)

This section will show you how to implement each method.

Applying XML Encoding Rules to the Result Set Data

The `encodeXML()` method is a generic method that allows you to apply XML encoding rules to certain special characters. A well-formed XML document with element or attribute values containing these special characters must be specially encoded to escape them out. Otherwise, an XML parser will not be able to process the document. This table shows those characters and their encoded values:

Character	Encoded value
&	&
<	<
>	>
'	'
"	"

The `encodeXML()` method simply does a search-and-replace operation on the passed-in string, replacing instances of the special characters with their encoded equivalent. This method will be used by the `writeXML()` method to ensure that any data retrieved from the database is encoded properly before being serialized to XML:

```
String encodeXML(String sData)
{
    String[] before = {"&","<",">","\"", "\'"};
    String[] after = {"&amp;","&lt;","&gt;","&quot;", "&apos;"};
    if(sData!=null)
    {
        for(int i=0;i<before.length;i++)
        {
            sData = Replace(sData, before[i], after[i]);
        }
    }
    else {sData="";}
    return sData;
}
```

This code fragment shows the `Replace()` method used by the `encodeXML()` method. As its name implies, the `Replace()` method simply loops through the string represented by the variable `content`, replacing all occurrences of `oldWord` with `newWord`:

```
String Replace(String content, String oldWord, String newWord)
{
    int position = content.indexOf(oldWord);
    while (position > -1)
    {
        content = content.substring(0,position) + newWord +
            content.substring(position + oldWord.length());
        position = content.indexOf(oldWord,position+newWord.length());
    }
    return content;
}
```

Serializing the Result Set's Metadata and Data as XML

The next step is to add code to our `JDBC2XML` class that serializes a JDBC result set to XML. To accomplish this, we need to do two things: design an XML data structure that encapsulates the data and metadata of a result set, and implement the `writeXML()` method that performs the actual serialization.

Designing the `<resultset>` XML Structure

The first step is to define an XML data structure that will represent the serialized state of our JDBC result set. For simplicity, we will create a DTD-less document that can be parsed by non-validating XML parsers. The root element is the `<resultset>` element. This element contains two sub-elements: a `<metadata>` element, and a `<records>` element.

The `<metadata>` element contains a `<field>` element for each database field. This element contains two attributes: a `name` attribute, and a `datatype` attribute. The `<records>` element contains a `<record>` element for each row in the result set. The `<record>` element also contains a `<field>` element for each column. This code fragment shows the structure of our `<resultset>` XML document:

```
<?xml version="1.0" encoding="ISO-8859-1"?>
<resultset>
    <metadata>
        <field name="field name goes here" datatype="field's datatype goes here"/>
    </metadata>
```

```
    <records>
        <record>
            <field name="field name goes here">
                field's value goes here
            </field>
        </record>
    </records>
</resultset>
```

Implementing the writeXML() Method

The writeXML() method serializes the specified JDBC result set as an XML document that conforms to the structure defined above. The first action it performs is to create a StringBuffer that contains the <?xml?> processing instruction and the <resultset> root element. We will use this StringBuffer object to hold our output. Next, it enumerates through the result set's metadata, creating a <field> element for each column. Finally, it enumerates through each record of the result set, creating a <record> element that contains a <field> element for each column. Field values are pre-processed with the encodeXML() method defined above to ensure compliance with XML encoding rules. Once we have looped through the entire result set, we terminate the <resultset> element, and return the XML document:

```java
String writeXML(ResultSet rs)
{
    StringBuffer strResults = new StringBuffer
        ("<?xml version=\"1.0\" encoding=\"ISO-8859-1\"?>\r\n<resultset>\r\n");
    try
    {
        ResultSetMetaData rsMetadata = rs.getMetaData();
        int intFields = rsMetadata.getColumnCount();
        strResults.append("<metadata>\r\n");
        for(int h =1; h <= intFields; h++)
        {
            strResults.append("<field name=\"" + rsMetadata.getColumnName(h) +
                "\" datatype=\"" + rsMetadata.getColumnTypeName(h) + "\"/>\r\n");
        }
        strResults.append("</metadata>\r\n<records>\r\n");
        while(rs.next())
        {
            strResults.append("<record>\r\n");
            for(int i =1; i <= intFields; i++)
            {
                strResults.append("<field name=\"" + rsMetadata.getColumnName(i)
                    + "\">" + encodeXML(rs.getString(i)) + "</field>\r\n");
            }
            strResults.append("</record>\r\n");
        }
    }catch(Exception e) {}
    strResults.append("</records>\r\n</resultset>");
    return strResults.toString();
}
}
```

Executing the Query

The `execute()` method brings it all together by executing a query against a JDBC data source and returning the results as an XML document. It takes five input parameters:

❑ The JDBC driver

❑ The JDBC URL

❑ The user ID

❑ The password

❑ The SQL statement

```
public String execute(String driver, String url, String uid, String pwd,
    String sql)
{
    String output = new String();
```

The first step is to register and instantiate the JDBC driver. Next, we will connect to the database and create a statement object. After that, we will execute the SQL statement using the statement object's `executeQuery()` method. This will return a result set. We will then serialize the result set to XML using the `writeXML()` method we created above:

```
try
{
    Class.forName(driver);
    Connection conn = DriverManager.getConnection(url, uid, pwd);
    Statement s = conn.createStatement();
    ResultSet rs = s.executeQuery(sql);
    output = writeXML(rs);
```

Last, but not least, we will close the result set and the connection and return the XML-serialized result set to the calling client. If an exception occurs, we will return an `<error>` element containing a short description of the exception. The calling client (which is most likely an XML-enabled application) will parse this element to determine the details of the exception that occurred:

```
    rs.close();
    conn.close();
}
catch(Exception e)
{
    output = "<error>" + encodeXML(e.toString()) + "</error>";
}
return output;
}
```

Now our `JDBC2XML` reusable class is complete, and we can start using it in our sample applications.

The XMLDataGateway Servlet

The `XMLDataGateway` servlet uses the `JDBC2XML` class to provide a generic XML-over-HTTP interface to JDBC data sources. In this section, we will show how to implement and use this servlet.

Implementing the Servlet

To implement the XMLDataGateway servlet, we will write a Java class that subclasses the javax.servlet.http.HttpServlet class. We will also override the doGet() and doPost() methods to handle HTTP GET and HTTP POST requests.

```
package com.jresources.jdbc;

import javax.servlet.*;
import javax.servlet.http.*;
import java.io.*;

public class XMLDataGateway extends HttpServlet
{
```

Overriding the doGet() Method

The doGet() method allows the XMLDataGateway servlet to respond to HTTP GET requests. The code in this method is actually simple. First, we will set the MIME type to "text/xml." That way, requesting HTTP user agents will know that the response sent should be handled as an XML document. Next, we will get a reference to the PrintWriter object that enables us to write a response back to the client. Finally, we'll instantiate the JDBC2XML class and call the execute() method. This method will return the XML-serialized result set, which we will pass immediately to the HTTP response stream's PrintWriter. We will obtain the SQL and JDBC connection information needed by the execute() method from the HttpServletRequest object, which encapsulates key-value pairs obtained from the URL's query string. If this seems a little confusing right now, don't worry; it will become much clearer when we run a sample application.

```
public void doGet(HttpServletRequest request, HttpServletResponse response)
    throws IOException, ServletException
{
    response.setContentType("text/xml");
    PrintWriter out = response.getWriter();
    JDBC2XML searchObj = new JDBC2XML();
    out.println(searchObj.execute(request.getParameter("driver"),
        request.getParameter("jdbcurl"), request.getParameter("uid"),
        request.getParameter("pwd"), request.getParameter("sql")));
}
```

Overriding the doPost() Method

The next step is to override the doPost() method. In this particular servlet, we will handle HTTP POSTs the same way we handle HTTP GETs. Therefore, our doPost() implementation will simply make a call to doGet().

```
public void doPost(HttpServletRequest request, HttpServletResponse response)
    throws IOException, ServletException
{
    doGet(request, response);
}
}
```

That's all there is to writing the XMLDataGateway servlet. Now, you would compile the Java source into bytecode and package it for deployment to a J2EE-compliant servlet container. We will cover this process in detail at the end of the chapter once we have completed the entire application. In the meantime, we will walk through a few examples of how to use the XMLDataGateway servlet, using the pre-built jdbcxml.war web application downloaded from the Wrox web site. For more information on how to deploy jdbcxml.war to Tomcat, please refer to the section in this chapter on installing and configuring Tomcat.

Developing an HTML Form Interface

In order to test the XMLDataGateway servlet, we must create a user interface for it. Since the servlet is an HTTP application, we will create a simple HTML form that allows you to test it from a web browser. We will save it in an HTML file, and name that file xmlsqlquery.html.

The XMLDataGateway servlet of course will be the action handler for the HTML form, and the form will use HTTP POST as the request method. The form contains five fields, each corresponding to the associated request parameter expected by the servlet. Here's the source listing for the XMLDataGateway's HTML front end. For brevity purposes, only the HTML form itself is shown, omitting the HTML opening and closing tags and any other tags the file might have:

```html
<form action="/jdbcxml/servlet/XMLDataGateway" method="POST">
    <table border="0">
        <tr>
            <td align="right"><font face="Arial">JDBC Driver: </font></td>
            <td><font face="Arial">
                <input type="text" size="50" name="driver"></td>
        </tr>
        <tr>
            <td align="right"><font face="Arial">JDBC URL: </font></td>
            <td><font face="Arial">
                <input type="text" size="50" name="jdbcurl"></td>
        </tr>
        <tr>
            <td align="right"><font face="Arial">Userid:</font></td>
            <td><font face="Arial"><input type="text" size="50"
                name="uid"></font></td>
        </tr>
        <tr>
            <td align="right"><font face="Arial">password </font></td>
            <td><font face="Arial"><input type="password"
                size="50" name="pwd"></font></td>
        </tr>
        <tr>
            <td align="right"><font face="Arial">SQL Statement:</font></td>
            <td><textarea name="sql" rows="10" cols="50"></textarea></td>
        </tr>
        <tr>
            <td align="right"><input type="submit"></td>
            <td> </td>
        </tr>
    </table>
</form>
```

Using the XMLDataGateway Servlet

As we mentioned earlier, the XMLDataGateway servlet can be used from any HTTP client that knows how to parse and render (or manipulate) well-formed XML. This section will discuss two scenarios for using the XMLDataGateway servlet: from a web browser, and from a Win32 application.

Using XMLDataGateway from a Web Browser

Now we are ready to start using the XMLDataGateway servlet. First, start Tomcat if it isn't already running. Then, point your browser at http://127.0.0.1:8080/jdbcxml/xmlsqlquery.html. Since the results will come back as XML, I recommend you use a browser that knows how to consume and display well-formed XML, such as Microsoft Internet Explorer 5.x or higher. On the HTML form, type in the name of the JDBC driver you want to use, the URL of the JDBC data source, the user ID and password required to log onto the database server, and the SQL statement. Then, click the Submit Query button to execute the query.

To give you a specific example, we will walk through a search of a Microsoft Access database. To facilitate this, we have provided a sample MS-Access database as part of the chapter's sample code download. This database is named contacts.mdb, and is located in the ..\Chapter16\jdbcxml\sql directory.

Prior to running through this example, we need to set up this Access database as a System DSN using the Windows NT Control Panel ODBC applet. After launching this applet, you will see the ODBC Data Source Administrator. Click on the Add button, and you will see this dialog:

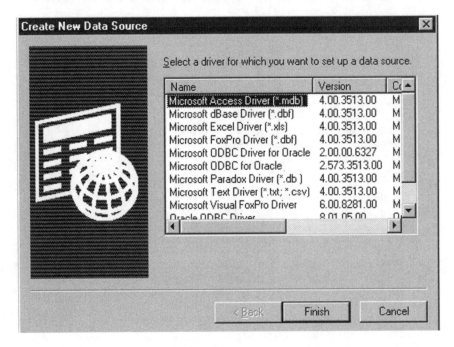

Select the Microsoft Access driver, and click on Finish. You will see this dialog:

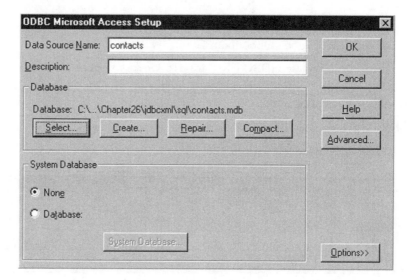

For the data source name, type in `contacts`. Click on the Select button, and browse to the location of the `contacts.mdb` file on your local system. Once you have completed that, click on OK. You should now be back to the ODBC Data Source Administrator, and it should show your new `contacts` System DSN added to the list:

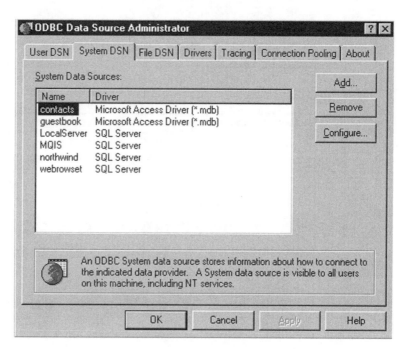

Now we are ready to execute a query. On the `xmlsqlquery.html` form, type in the following information:

❑ The fully qualified class name of the Sun JDBC-ODBC:
driver:(`sun.jdbc.odbc.JdbcOdbcDriver`)

❑ The `Contacts` database's JDBC URL (`jdbc:odbc:contacts`)

❑ Since the `Contacts` database does not implement any security, you can simply leave the user ID and password blank

❑ For the SQL statement, type in `SELECT * FROM contacts`

The completed form should look like this:

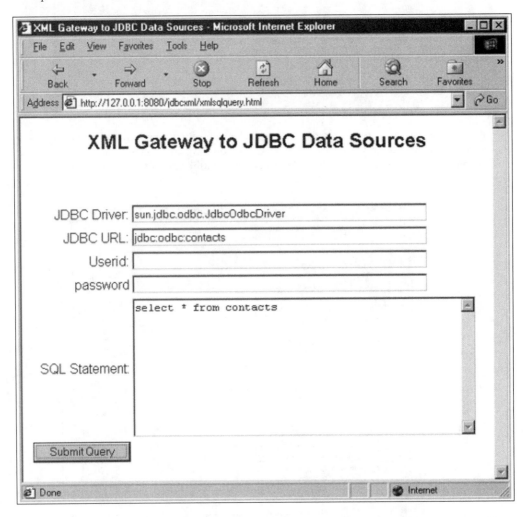

To execute the query, click on the **Submit Query** button. Your results should look like this:

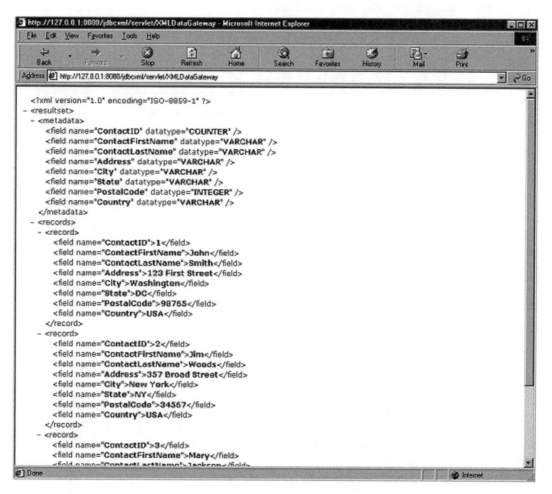

To give you a more advanced example, we will walk through a search of an Oracle 8i database. We will use the Oracle thin driver. This example should work with any Oracle installation, since it merely queries the `user_tables` entity. To make the connection, we'll type in the following information:

- ☐ The fully qualified class name of the Oracle JDBC driver: (`oracle.jdbc.driver.OracleDriver`). You must ensure that the Oracle JDBC driver is in Tomcat's `CLASSPATH`. To add it, please view the Tomcat setup instructions that were covered earlier in this chapter.

- ☐ The Oracle database's JDBC URL, using the following form: `jdbc:oracle:thin:@oraclehostname:port:oracledbname`, where `oraclehostname` is the name of the server on which the Oracle database resides, `port` is the IP port on which to connect to the Oracle database, and `oracledbname` is the name of the particular database to query.

- ☐ The user ID and password with which to log onto the Oracle database server.

Finally, we'll type in the SQL statement. This example is a simple query of the Oracle `user_tables` entity. Here's what the complete query looks like:

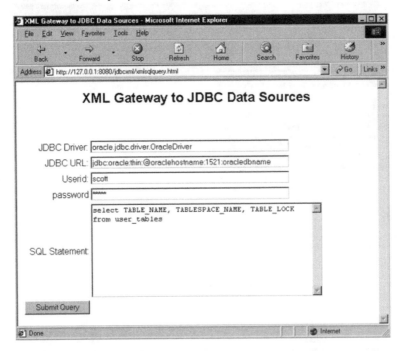

When we execute the query, the servlet sends the XML-serialized result set showing the query results. This is what it looks like in MS Internet Explorer 5.x:

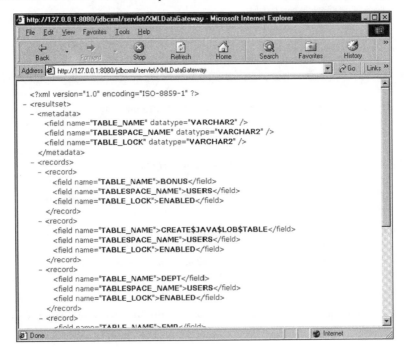

As we have mentioned before, if you don't have access to Oracle, you can use the XMLDataGateway servlet to query any database product for which a JDBC driver has been written. To preclude any problems that might occur when testing it with another database product, please ensure that the JDBC driver for this database is added to Tomcat's CLASSPATH. In addition, if you are using a desktop database product such as Microsoft Access, many of these products allow you to create databases that do not require verification of user credentials. If this is the case, then you simply leave the user ID and password fields blank. You should also note that the JDBC URL format is driver-dependent. Therefore, if you are using a database other than Oracle, please consult the product's documentation for information on how to form a valid JDBC URL.

Using the XMLDataGateway Servlet from Other XML-Enabled Applications

As we mentioned before, one of the great advantages of using the XMLDataGateway servlet is that it allows you to extend the availability of your JDBC data source to non-Java applications. For example, one of your trading partners might use a system that is implemented as a Win32 application written in Visual C++. Your internal systems might be built on the J2EE architecture, using JDBC to access an Oracle database server running on Solaris.

One of the easiest ways to integrate these two systems over the Internet is via XML-over-HTTP, which our XMLDataGateway servlet implements. Your trading partner's Win32 application can be modified to use MSXML to execute SQL statements against your Oracle database via HTTP GET. From there, it can perform any necessary integration steps.

> **Note: If you are planning to make your data available over the Internet via XML-over-HTTP, please ensure that you attend to the security details. For example, ensure that default passwords are changed for database administrator accounts, access control lists are properly set, and SSL encryption is used.**

To show you a simple example of this process, we will use the Microsoft XML Notepad to execute the same Microsoft Access query we covered in the previous section. You can download Microsoft XML Notepad from http://msdn.microsoft.com/xml/notepad/.

After you have installed XML Notepad, launch the application, click on File in the menu bar, and then click on Open. You'll see a dialog box that looks like this:

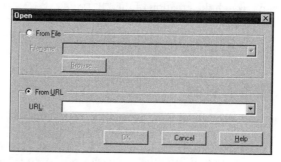

Select the From URL radio button, and then type in the following URL. Yes, it is that long:

http://127.0.0.1:8080/jdbcxml/servlet/XMLDataGateway?driver=sun.jdbc.odbc.JdbcOdbcDriver&jdbcurl=jdbc:odbc:contacts&sql=select+*+from+contacts

In this example, you'll notice that we are using HTTP GET instead of HTTP POST. The input parameters that the servlet takes are placed as ampersand-delimited key-value pairs in the URL's query string. Once the query is executed, XML Notepad will display the results as follows:

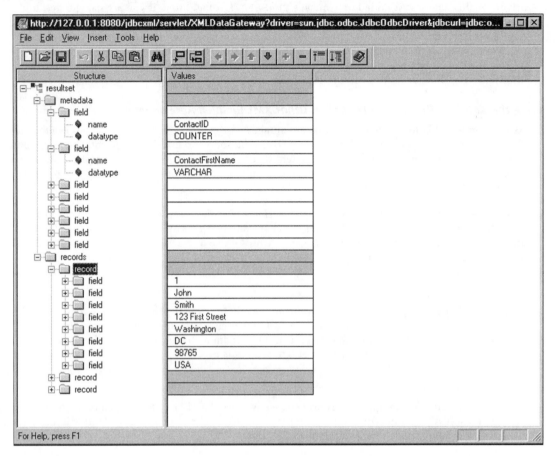

Summary

In this section, we walked through the creation of the XMLDataGateway servlet, a simple example of how you can create an architecture-neutral XML-over-HTTP gateway to your JDBC data sources. In the next section, we will take it a step further by extending this architecture to perform device-specific transformations of JDBC data using XML and XSLT.

The JDBC2HTML Servlet

The JDBC2HTML servlet is an example of how you can use XML and XSLT to target JDBC data to a particular device (in this case, a web browser). This servlet uses the JDBC2XML class we created earlier in the chapter to query a JDBC data source and serialize the returned result set to XML. From there, it uses the Xalan XSLT processor to transform the result set's XML into HTML, using the requested XSL stylesheet.

The JDBC2HTML servlet is designed as a filter; in other words, the servlet is not invoked directly. Instead, the servlet container is configured to dispatch requests for URLs with a particular mapping to this servlet for handling. In the case of the JDBC2HTML servlet, we will configure the servlet container to pass any URL requests for files ending in .xsl to the JDBC2HTML servlet for execution. This is how the servlet will know which XSL stylesheet to use for the XSLT operation. If this sounds confusing, don't worry; we will cover how this process works in detail as the chapter proceeds.

This section will show you how to implement this framework, specifically the following tasks:

❑   Writing the servlet itself

❑   Writing a generic XSL stylesheet that transforms the XML-serialized result set into an HTML table

❑   Using the JDBC2HTML servlet to query a Microsoft SQL Server database

Implementing the JDBC2HTML Servlet

As with the XMLDataGateway servlet, we will implement the JDBC2HTML servlet by writing a Java class that subclasses the `javax.servlet.http.HttpServlet` class. We will also override the `doGet()` and `doPost()` methods to handle HTTP GET and HTTP POST requests respectively. Since we are using the Xalan XSLT processor in the servlet, we will import the `org.apache.xalan.xslt` package. We will also import the `org.xml.sax.SAXException` class, which is thrown by the Xerces SAX parser (the underlying parser used by Xalan) if either the XML document or the XSL stylesheet is not well formed:

```
package com.jresources.jdbc;

import javax.servlet.*;
import javax.servlet.http.*;
import java.io.*;
import org.xml.sax.SAXException;
import org.apache.xalan.xslt.*;

public class JDBC2HTML extends HttpServlet
{
```

Overriding the doGet() Method

The next step is to override the `doGet()` method for HTTP GET request handling. Since the JDBC2HTML servlet is a filter, the first order of business is to determine the physical file location of the requested stylesheet. It first checks the PATH_INFO environment variable. If it is Null, the servlet assumes that it was invoked as a result of a direct URL request for an XSL stylesheet (for example, http://hostname/dir/myStylesheet.xsl), and obtains the stylesheet's real path by passing the SCRIPT_NAME environment variable (obtained via the `getServletPath()` method call) to the servlet context's `getRealPath()` implementation. Otherwise, it uses the PATH_INFO (for example, the PATH_INFO for http://hostname/servlet/JDBC2HTML/dir/myStylesheet.xsl is `/dir/myStylesheet.xsl`), and gets the PATH_INFO 's real path via the Request object's `getPathTranslated()` method.

```
public void doGet(HttpServletRequest request, HttpServletResponse response)
   throws IOException, ServletException
{
   String qryDoc;
```

```
if(request.getPathInfo()==null)
{
    qryDoc = getServletConfig().getServletContext().getRealPath(
        request.getServletPath() );
} else
{
    qryDoc = request.getPathTranslated();
}
```

Next, it sets the MIME type to "text/html", instantiates the JDBC2XML class, and executes the query using the query parameters supplied by the HttpServletRequest object:

```
response.setContentType("text/html");
PrintWriter out = response.getWriter();
JDBC2XML searchObj = new JDBC2XML();
String output = searchObj.execute(request.getParameter("driver"),
    request.getParameter("jdbcurl"), request.getParameter("uid"),
    request.getParameter("pwd"), request.getParameter("sql"));
```

Finally, it will use the Xalan XSLT processor to transform the results of the query to HTML using the requested XSL stylesheet file, and place the output in the HTTP response stream:

```
try
{
    XSLTProcessor processor = XSLTProcessorFactory.getProcessor();
    processor.process(new XSLTInputSource(new
        java.io.StringReader(output)), new XSLTInputSource("file:///" +
        qryDoc), new XSLTResultTarget(out));
}
catch(SAXException se)
{
    throw new ServletException(se);
}
}
```

Overriding the doPost() Method

The next step is to override the doPost() method. As with the XMLDataGateway servlet, the JDBC2HTML servlet will handle HTTP POSTs the same way we handle HTTP GETs. Therefore, our doPost() implementation will simply make a call to doGet().

```
public void doPost(HttpServletRequest request, HttpServletResponse response)
    throws IOException, ServletException
{
    doGet(request, response);
}
}
```

That's all there is to writing the JDBC2HTML servlet. While a bit more complex than the XMLDataGateway servlet, it is still straightforward. Moreover, the same concepts could be easily applied to other device types, such as a WAP phone. The only difference would be in the MIME type (for example, text/vnd.wap.wml vs. text/html), the output syntax (WML vs. HTML), and the display constraints of WAP devices vis-à-vis web browsers.

Now, you would compile the Java source code into bytecode and package it for deployment to a J2EE-compliant servlet container. Part of this packaging process would include creating a mapping that instructs the servlet container to hand off all requests for .xsl files to the JDBC2HTML servlet. We will cover this process in detail at the end of the chapter. In the meantime, we will walk through a few examples of how to use the JDBC2HTML servlet using the jdbcxml.war web application downloaded from our web site, and deployed to Tomcat in an earlier section.

Writing an XSL Stylesheet

To use the JDBC2HTML servlet, you must create XSL stylesheets that transform the <resultset> XML schema to HTML. To show you an example of this, we will create an XSL stylesheet that transforms the XML-serialized result sets returned by the JDBC2XML class into an HTML table. We will call this stylesheet html_table.xsl.

Like any other XSL stylesheet, this stylesheet will contain a variety of templates that contain the presentation logic for elements in the result set XML document. The first template is the template for the document root. This template will simply use the <xsl:apply-templates/> element to instruct the XSLT processor to apply the appropriate template to each element it encounters as it drills down through the hierarchy of the XML document. Please note that the / pattern-matching statement means to match the root element of the document:

```
<?xml version='1.0'?>
<xsl:stylesheet xmlns:xsl="http://www.w3.org/1999/XSL/Transform" version="1.0">
   <xsl:template match="/">
      <xsl:apply-templates/>
   </xsl:template>
```

The Resultset Template

The next template is for the top-level <resultset> element. This template does two things. First, it sets up the basic structure of the HTML document. Second, it uses the <xsl:apply-templates> element at the appropriate spots to apply the templates for the <metadata> element (which will be displayed as the table's heading) and the <records> element (which will be displayed as the table body). In the case of the <records> element, the //resultset/records notation tells the XSLT processor to match any <records> element that is a descendant of the <resultset> element:

```
<xsl:template match="resultset">
   <html>
      <head>
         <title>
            A JDBC Resultset in HTML Table Format
         </title>
      </head>
      <body>
         <h1 align="center">
            A JDBC Resultset in HTML Table Format
         </h1>
         <table border="1" cellspacing="0" cellpadding="5" align="center">
            <xsl:apply-templates select="metadata"/>
            <xsl:apply-templates select="//resultset/records"/>
         </table>
      </body>
   </html>
</xsl:template>
```

The Metadata and Metadata Field Templates

The next two templates set up the table header row from the `<metadata>` element and its `<field>` child elements. The meta-data template creates the table row. The field template creates a table cell for each field:

```
<xsl:template match="metadata">
    <tr bgcolor="#FFD700">
        <xsl:apply-templates/>
    </tr>
</xsl:template>
<xsl:template match="metadata/field">
    <td><b><xsl:value-of select="@name"/></b></td>
    <xsl:apply-templates/>
</xsl:template>
```

The Records and Record Templates

The next two templates create a table row for each record, with a table cell containing the data for each field:

```
<xsl:template match="records">
    <xsl:apply-templates/>
</xsl:template>
<xsl:template match="record">
    <tr>
        <xsl:for-each select="field">
            <td><xsl:value-of select="."/></td>
        </xsl:for-each>
    </tr>
</xsl:template>
```

The Error Template

Finally, we have a template to handle any errors that might occur. As you might recall, the JDBC2XML's `execute()` method returns an `<error>` element containing information from any exception that is thrown within that method. This template ensures that this information is displayed in a user-friendly manner:

```
<xsl:template match="error">
    <html>
        <head>
            <title>
                A JDBC Resultset in HTML Table Format
            </title>
        </head>
        <body>
            Your request caused the following error: <xsl:value-of select="."/>
        </body>
    </html>
</xsl:template>
</xsl:stylesheet>
```

Using the JDBC2HTML Servlet

Now we are ready to start using the JDBC2HTML servlet. First, we'll create an HTML front-end that looks just like the one we created for the XMLGateway servlet. We'll call this file `htmlsqlquery.html`. The only difference between `xmlsqlquery.html` and `htmlsqlquery.html` is that `htmlsqlquery.html` uses the `html_table.xsl` stylesheet that we just created as its HTML form's action handler. In other words, the HTML `<form>` tag looks like this:

```
<form action="html_table.xsl" method="POST">
```

To open it up, point your browser at http://127.0.0.1:8080/jdbcxml/htmlsqlquery.html.

To illustrate how to use this tool, we will execute a query against the `Northwind` sample database that comes with Microsoft SQL Server 7.0. If you don't have SQL Server installed, don't worry; you can use JDBC2HTML with virtually any database for which there is a JDBC driver. We'll use the Sun JDBC-ODBC Bridge that ships with the JDK as the JDBC driver. The JDBC URL is `jdbc:odbc:system_dsn`, where `system_dsn` is the database's System DSN, created using the Windows NT ODBC Control Panel applet. We will write a SQL statement that queries the `products` table. This screenshot shows the complete query:

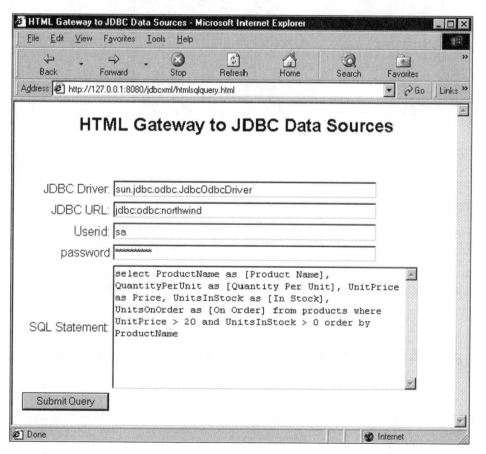

When we execute the query, the result set is returned as an HTML table, as shown in this next screen shot:

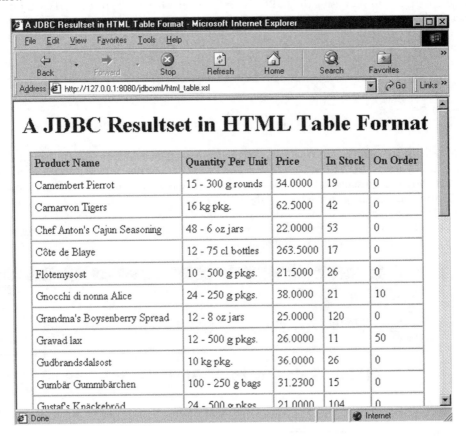

Summary

In this section, we created a simple XML gateway architecture for JDBC. This architecture allows you to access JDBC data as XML over HTTP in an architecture-neutral manner. It also allows you to easily stream JDBC data as HTML to web browsers via XSLT. This simple architecture can be used as a framework to XML-enable your existing JDBC applications. In the next section, we will show you how to create distributed two-way JDBC applications using Sun's emerging XML-based WebRowSet technology.

Using XML for distributed JDBC Applications

The simple XML gateway architecture for JDBC is extremely useful for what it does, namely extract data from a JDBC data source and serialize it to XML. However, suppose you wanted to create a two-way XML-based system that allows you to scroll through an XML-serialized result set, add and modify data, and then submit the modified XML to the application server to update the underlying JDBC data source; how could you do this?

Sun provides a `WebRowSet` class that allows you to do just that. With `WebRowSet`, you can create a disconnected JDBC result set that can be serialized to XML, transported via TCP/IP application-layer protocols to remote clients for data manipulation, and then returned to the original data source for batch updating. This technology is "early access" technology, and is therefore not quite ready for production use; nevertheless, it will be an extremely important technology in the near future, and warrants coverage in this chapter.

> Note: The WebRowSet implementation used in this chapter is Early Access Release 4

The Rowset Interface

To give you a little background, the JDBC 2.0 standard extension API includes a **Rowset** interface. At its simplest level, the `Rowset` interface provides a framework for writing classes that encapsulate a persistent set of rows. The underlying data source for this set of rows can be anything from a comma-delimited ASCII text file to an XML document. What makes the `Rowset` interface particularly interesting, though, is the ability to write implementing classes that encapsulate disconnected JDBC result sets. Once you have done this, you now have a way to make a JDBC result set that is scrollable and updateable, can be passed over a network, and can be used as a JavaBeans component in a GUI application builder. When your implementing class uses XML to persist the state of the JDBC result set (including its connection information to the underlying JDBC data source), you now have a framework for bi-directional access to JDBC data sources via the Internet. Fortunately, Sun is providing a `Rowset` implementation (albeit "early access") that does just that: the `sun.jdbc.rowset.WebRowSet` class.

The `sun.jdbc.rowset.WebRowSet` Class

The `WebRowSet` class is a `Rowset` implementation that can serialize the data, metadata, and properties of a JDBC result set to XML. That way, the result set can be disconnected, transported across the network, and manipulated by a remote application. Later, the `WebRowSet` class can use the information in the XML document to re-establish the connection and update the original data source.

The XML document produced by the `WebRowSet` class is a valid document, and must conform to the DTD defined by the `RowSet.dtd` file provided with the `Rowset` package. Otherwise, a validating parser will not be able to parse it. Underneath the hood, the `WebRowSet` class uses the Sun JAXP parser (this ships with Tomcat, so it should already be on your system) to validate and parse its serialized XML state.

The `WebRowSet` class is, as mentioned before, "early access" (beta) technology, so it should not be used in a production application. You also might find it a little buggy, although we expect that these bugs will be fixed prior to the release of the production version. For example, as of Early Access Release 4, the `WebRowSet` class does not support the SQL Server `nchar` or `nvarchar` data types.

A note about concurrency: In its current implementation, the `WebRowSet` class uses optimistic locking. Therefore, it does not maintain any locks in the underlying database while the `Rowset` is disconnected from the database. This could be problematic, in that another user could modify the underlying database while a `Rowset` is disconnected, and then have his changes overwritten when the `Rowset` is reconnected and the underlying database is updated.

To preclude this from happening, the WebRowSet class maintains a copy of the original value of any row that has been modified. That way, it can compare the Rowset's original value with the database prior to update, and throw an exception if there has been an interim update. Moreover, it provides an extensible architecture to modify this behavior (through the javax.sql.RowSetWriter interface) if a different concurrency model is desired.

Implementing a Distributed JDBC Application Using the WebRowSet Class

In this section, we will implement a distributed JDBC application using the WebRowSet class. In this scenario, a Java application will use WebRowSet to query a remote JDBC data source via HTTP, add a record to the returned Rowset, and then send the updated Rowset back to the application server via HTTP POST to update the original data source. This diagram shows the application's architecture:

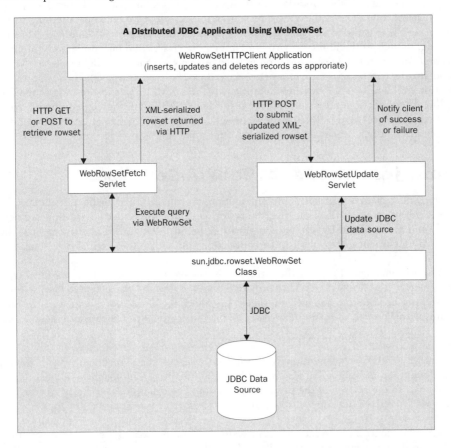

Note: The client application in this sample is implemented in Java. Theoretically, one could also implement it as a Microsoft COM application. To do this would require writing a simple OLEDB provider that transformed the WebRowSet XML schema to a disconnected ADO recordset. While non-trivial to implement, this component would nonetheless go a long way toward facilitating enterprise application integration.

To implement this application, we will cover the following specific tasks:

❑ Writing the WebRowSetFetchServlet class. This servlet provides an interface for fetching a WebRowSet via HTTP GET or POST.

❑ Writing the WebRowsetUpdateServlet class. This servlet provides an HTTP interface for updating the original data source with a modified WebRowSet.

❑ Writing the WebRowSetHTTPClient application. This application uses the WebRowSetFetchServlet to execute a query against a JDBC data source and return the WebRowSet. It then adds a record to the WebRowSet, and uses the WebRowsetUpdateServlet to update the underlying JDBC data source.

Setting up the Sample Database

Please note that this sample application uses a Microsoft SQL Server 7.0 database, however it also works under SQL Server 2000. To set up the database, perform the following tasks:

❑ Open up SQL Server Enterprise Manager and create a new database called WebRowSetTest.

❑ Locate the SQL script named WebRowSet.sql in the sample code distribution for this chapter. You can download this from the Wrox web site under the Code subsection. This script creates the guestbook table.

❑ Execute this script using SQL Server Query Analyzer. Ensure that the database selected is the WebRowSetTest database you just created.

❑ Create a System DSN that points to this database using the Control Panel ODBC applet. Call this DSN webrowset.

If you don't have SQL Server, you can use pretty much any other database for which a JDBC driver exists. The only constraint is that the driver and the underlying database must support batch updates. Just make sure you update the WebRowSetHTTPClient class .properties file to reflect the correct JDBC driver and URL. For your reference, here is the schema of the guestbook table:

Field name	Data Type	Size
ID	varchar	50
Fname	varchar	50
Lname	varchar	50
Comments	varchar	255

Fetching a Rowset Via HTTP: The WebRowSetFetchServlet Class

The WebRowSetFetchServlet essentially duplicates the functionality of the XMLDataGateway servlet we covered earlier in the chapter. In this case, we are using the WebRowSet class to bring back a disconnected JDBC result set, and returning its XML representation to the requesting HTTP client. In this section, we will show how to implement this servlet, and test it using a web browser.

Implementing the Servlet

As with the other servlets we have talked about in this chapter, we will implement the WebRowSetFetchServlet by writing a Java class that subclasses the javax.servlet.http.HttpServlet class. We will also override the doGet() and doPost() methods to handle HTTP GET and HTTP POST requests respectively. Since we are using the WebRowSet class in the servlet, we will import the sun.jdbc.rowset package. We will also import the javax.sql package. This package contains the interfaces that constitute the JDBC 2.0 standard extension API. The sun.jdbc.rowset package (including the WebRowSet class) uses this API:

```
package com.jresources.jdbc;

import javax.servlet.*;
import javax.servlet.http.*;
import java.io.*;
import javax.sql.*;
import sun.jdbc.rowset.*;
import java.sql.*;


public class WebRowSetFetchServlet extends HttpServlet
{
```

The next step is to override the doGet() method for HTTP GET request handling. The doGet() expects five parameters from the request object: the JDBC driver, JDBC URL, user ID, password, and SQL statement. After setting the MIME type and obtaining a reference to the PrintWriter object that encapsulates the HTTP response stream, we will instantiate and register the JDBC driver:

```
public void doGet(HttpServletRequest request, HttpServletResponse response)
    throws IOException, ServletException
{
    response.setContentType("text/xml");
    PrintWriter out = response.getWriter();
    try
    {
        //instantiate and register the JDBC driver
        Class.forName(request.getParameter("driver"));
```

The next step is to create an instance of the WebRowSet class, and set the appropriate properties. These properties include the JDBC URL, the user ID, the password, and the SQL statement. You can also set other properties, such as transaction isolation, as appropriate. Once you have set all of the properties, call the WebRowSet object's execute() method. This will populate the Rowset with the rows returned by your SQL statement, and disconnect from the data source. To write the Rowset's XML state back to the HTTP client, you call the WebRowSet object's writeXml() method, passing in the HTTP response stream's PrintWriter:

```
            WebRowSet wrs;

            wrs = new WebRowSet();
            // set some properties of the rowset
            wrs.setUrl(request.getParameter("jdbcurl"));
            wrs.setUsername(request.getParameter("uid"));
            wrs.setPassword(request.getParameter("pwd"));
            wrs.setCommand(request.getParameter("sql"));
            wrs.setTransactionIsolation
                (java.sql.Connection.TRANSACTION_READ_UNCOMMITTED);
            // populate the rowset.
            wrs.execute();
            wrs.writeXml(out);
        }
        catch(Exception e)
        {
            throw new ServletException(e);
        }
    }
}
```

One word of caution: The `WebRowSet` class contains a static variable called `SYSTEM_ID`. This variable stores the URL for the DTD (Document Type Definition) file that defines the structure of the XML document used by the `WebRowSet` class. The default value is http://java.sun.com/j2ee/dtds/ RowSet.dtd. If you are testing this on a machine that is not connected to the Internet, this could cause you problems, as the calling HTTP user agent (for example, Internet Explorer 5.x) will not be able to locate the DTD with which to validate the document. If this is the case, you might want to change this variable to the location of the DTD on your local machine for testing purposes. For example, add this line of code to the `doGet()` method:

```
WebRowSet.SYSTEM_ID =
    "http://127.0.0.1:8080/jdbcxml/bin/RowSet.dtd";
```

Once again, we will handle HTTP POSTs the same way we handle HTTP GETs. Therefore, our `doPost()` implementation will simply make a call to `doGet()`.

```
public void doPost(HttpServletRequest request, HttpServletResponse response)
    throws IOException, ServletException
{
    doGet(request, response);
}
}
```

Now, you would compile the Java source into bytecode and package it for deployment to a J2EE-compliant servlet container. We will cover this process in detail at the end of the chapter. In the meantime, we will walk through an example of how to use the servlet using the `jdbcxml.war` web application downloaded from our web site, and deployed to Tomcat, as explained in an earlier section.

Testing the Servlet with a Web Browser

Before continuing with the development of the distributed application, we will first unit-test the `WebRowSetFetchServlet` we created. The easiest way to do this is to create an HTML form similar to the one we created for the `XMLDataGateway` servlet. We'll call this HTML file `webrowset.html`. We can unit-test this servlet with virtually any database for which a JDBC driver exists. In this example, we'll use the same Oracle query we did for the `XMLDataGateway` servlet. Here's what it looks like:

When we execute the query, this is what the results look like in Internet Explorer 5.x. Once again, it is similar to the output created by the XMLDataGateway servlet, although the WebRowSet's XML document contains significantly more information. In addition to the Rowset's data and metadata, it also stores other properties, such as connection information required to reconnect back to the underlying data source for future updating:

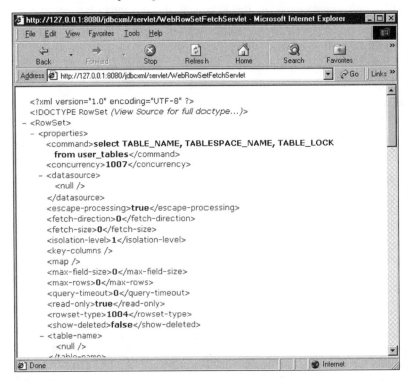

Performing a Batch Update Via HTTP: The WebRowSetUpdateServlet Class

The next step is to write a servlet that allows you to update the underlying data source via HTTP. This servlet will accept a remote WebRowSet's XML representation via HTTP POST and perform a batch update of the underlying data source.

> Note: for this servlet to function properly, the RowSet.dtd file must be in the jakarta-tomcat/bin directory so that the WebRowSet class can find it to validate the uploaded document.

```java
package com.jresources.jdbc;

import javax.servlet.*;
import javax.servlet.http.*;
import java.io.*;
import javax.sql.*;
import sun.jdbc.rowset.*;
import java.sql.*;

public class WebRowSetUpdateServlet extends HttpServlet
{
```

Overriding the doGet() Method

In the previous servlets, we put the bulk of the logic in the doGet() method. In the case of the WebRowSetUpdateServlet, we want to support HTTP POST only, since the uploaded XML documents are likely to be quite large. Therefore, the doGet() method will simply return a 403 (Forbidden) HTTP response code:

```
public void doGet(HttpServletRequest request, HttpServletResponse response)
    throws IOException, ServletException
{
    response.sendError(403);
}
```

Overriding the doPost() Method

The next step is to override the doPost() method to handle the HTTP POST request. The doPost() method expects the HTTP request body's contents to contain WebRowSet's XML document. To update the underlying data source, you simply create an instance of the WebRowSet class and call the readXml() method, passing in the BufferedReader from the Request object. This BufferedReader object encapsulates the contents of the HTTP request body. After that, you call the acceptChanges() method, and the WebRowSet will connect to the underlying data source, perform any inserts, updates, and deletes, and close the connection.

```
public void doPost(HttpServletRequest request, HttpServletResponse response)
    throws IOException, ServletException
{
    response.setContentType("text/plain");
    PrintWriter out = response.getWriter();
    try
    {
        WebRowSet wrs = new WebRowSet();
        wrs.readXml(request.getReader());
        wrs.acceptChanges();
        out.println("The transaction succeeded");
    }
    catch(Exception e)
    {
        out.println("The transaction failed with the following error:  " +
            e.getMessage());
    }
}
```

Inserting, Updating, and Deleting Data at the Client: The WebRowSetHTTPClient Class

Now we are ready to write the client application for our distributed JDBC application. We will call this application WebRowSetHTTPClient. This application is a stand-alone console application written in Java.

Implementing the Application

The WebRowSetHTTPClient class contains three methods:

❑ The executeSearch() method, which encapsulates an HTTP GET request to WebRowSetFetchServlet

❑ The updateDataSource() method, which encapsulates an HTTP POST request to WebRowSetUpdateServlet

❑ The main() method, the application's entry point

```
import java.io.*;
import java.net.*;
import java.util.*;
import javax.sql.*;
import sun.jdbc.rowset.*;

public class WebRowSetHTTPClient
{
    public WebRowSetHTTPClient() {
    super();
    }
}
```

The executeSearch() method encapsulates an HTTP GET request to WebRowSetFetchServlet. It takes six input parameters: the URL of WebRowSetFetchServlet, the JDBC driver, the URL of the JDBC data source, the user ID, the password, and the SQL statement. It returns a populated WebRowSet:

```
public WebRowSet executeSearch(String httpEndpoint, String driver,
    String jdbcurl, String uid, String pwd, String sql) throws Exception
{
    try
    {
```

The first step is to dynamically construct the URL we are requesting. We will do this by concatenating the URL of WebRowSetFetchServlet with a query string dynamically constructed from the parameters passed to the method. After that, we will open up a connection to that URL to initiate the HTTP GET request:

```
        String url = httpEndpoint + "?driver=" + driver + "&jdbcurl=" + jdbcurl
            + "&uid=" + uid + "&pwd=" + pwd + "&sql=" + URLEncoder.encode(sql);
        URL host = new URL(url);
        HttpURLConnection hostConn = (HttpURLConnection)host.openConnection();
        hostConn.connect();
```

The next step is to initialize a new WebRowSet from the response by passing a BufferedReader object derived from the HTTP response stream to the WebRowSet's readXml() method. Once we have populated the WebRowSet, we will return it to the calling client:

```
        BufferedReader xml = new BufferedReader(new
            InputStreamReader(hostConn.getInputStream()));
        WebRowSet wrs = new WebRowSet();
        wrs.readXml(xml);
        hostConn.disconnect();
        return wrs;
    }
    catch(Exception e)
    {
        throw new Exception(e.getMessage());
    }
}
```

Next, we'll implement the updateDataSource() method. This method encapsulates an HTTP POST request to WebRowSetUpdateServlet, thereby allowing you to propagate any changes you made to WebRowSet to the remote data source. It takes two parameters: the updated WebRowSet and the URL of WebRowSetUpdateServlet. It returns the response received from WebRowSetUpdateServlet.

```
public String updateDataSource(WebRowSet wrs, String httpEndPoint)
    throws Exception
{
    try
    {
```

The first step is to post the WebRowSet's XML data structure to WebRowSetUpdateServlet. To accomplish this, we will establish an HTTP connection to the servlet, create a java.io.BufferedWriter object (which writes text to a character output stream) from the OutputStream object that encapsulates the HTTP POST request, and call the WebRowSet's writeXml() method, passing in the BufferedWriter object. Internally, the writeXml() method will write the XML to the BufferedWriter, which will in effect upload the XML to the servlet:

```
URL host = new URL(httpEndPoint);
HttpURLConnection hostConn =  HttpURLConnection)host.openConnection();
hostConn.setRequestMethod("POST");
hostConn.setDoInput(true);
hostConn.setDoOutput(true);
BufferedWriter xml = new BufferedWriter(new
    OutputStreamWriter(hostConn.getOutputStream()));
wrs.writeXml(xml);
xml.close();
```

Next, we will read the response from the servlet, which will either tell us that the operation was a success, or inform us of the specific error that occurred. Once we have read the response, we will return it to the calling client:

```
String line;
StringBuffer results = new StringBuffer();
BufferedReader input = new BufferedReader(new
    InputStreamReader(hostConn.getInputStream()));
while((line = input.readLine()) != null)
{
    results.append(line + "\r\n");
}
input.close();
hostConn.disconnect();
return results.toString();
}
catch(Exception e)
{
    throw new Exception(e.getMessage()+ ", " + e.getClass());
}
}
```

To bring everything together, we will write the application's entry point: the main() method. The main() method executes a query of the guestbook table in our sample webrowset SQL Server database, adds a record to the returned WebRowSet, and posts it back to the server to update the database. It takes three command line arguments, each representing a field in the guestbook table: the first name, last name, and comments for an individual adding a record to the database. The first thing the main() method will do is check to ensure that the proper number of command line arguments was passed in. If not, it will give the user a help message informing him of the proper usage of the application:

```
public static void main(String[] args)
{
    if(args.length < 3)
    {
        System.err.println("Usage: WebRowSetHTTPClient <first name>
            <last name> <comments>");
        return;
    }
```

Next, it will initialize some String variables containing the JDBC connect information required to execute the query. It will also initialize some variables containing the URLs to the fetch and update servlets. The application will read this initialization information from a Properties file called WrsHTTPClient.properties, which is included in the sample code that you can download from the Wrox web site:

```
try
{
    Properties initProps = new Properties();
    initProps.load(new FileInputStream("WrsHTTPClient.properties"));
    //The JDBC connect info:
    String driver = initProps.getProperty("jdbc.driver");
    String jdbcurl = initProps.getProperty("guestbook.url");
    String uid = initProps.getProperty("guestbook.uid");
    String pwd = initProps.getProperty("guestbook.pwd");
    String sql = "select * from guestbook";
    //The fetch and update servlet endpoints
    String httpEndpoint = initProps.getProperty("httpEndpoint");
    String httpUpdateEndpoint = initProps.getProperty("httpUpdateEndpoint");
```

For your reference, here are the contents of the WrsHTTPClient.properties file. You can modify this file, if needed, with an ASCII text editor (such as Notepad) to change any of the initialization data:

```
# WrsHTTPClient initialization properties

jdbc.driver=sun.jdbc.odbc.JdbcOdbcDriver
guestbook.url=jdbc:odbc:webrowset
guestbook.uid=sa
guestbook.pwd=
httpEndpoint=http://127.0.0.1:8080/jdbcxml/servlet/WebRowSetFetchServlet
httpUpdateEndpoint=http://127.0.0.1:8080/jdbcxml/servlet/WebRowSetUpdateServlet
```

Next, it will execute the search using the executeSearch() method we just created. This will return an initialized instance of WebRowSet:

```
WebRowSetHTTPClient me = new WebRowSetHTTPClient();
System.out.println("Fetching remote data...");
WebRowSet data = me.executeSearch(httpEndpoint, driver, jdbcurl, uid,
    pwd, sql);
```

Now it is time to insert our record. First, we must explicitly set the table name to guestbook. The WebRowSet instance on the server needs to know which table to update. Next, we will move the cursor to the insert row to prepare for the insert operation. Then, we will add a record based on command line arguments passed to the main() method. After we're done, we will return the cursor to the previous row. Finally, we will post the batch update back to the server using our updateDataSource() method:

```
            System.out.println("Adding data to the WebRowSet...");
            data.setTableName("guestbook");
            data.moveToInsertRow();
            data.updateString("ID", "ID" + System.currentTimeMillis());
            data.updateString("fname", args[0]);
            data.updateString("lname", args[1]);
            data.updateString("comments", args[2]);
            data.insertRow();
            data.moveToCurrentRow();
            System.out.println("Updating the remote data source with changes...");
            System.out.println(me.updateDataSource(data, httpUpdateEndpoint));
        }
        catch( Exception e)
        {
            System.out.println(e.toString());
        }
    }
}
```

Building the Application

Now it is time to compile our client application. To do this efficiently, we will create a batch file. This batch file, named buildClient.bat, is located in the chapter's sample code distribution. The first thing we need to do is ensure that all of the appropriate code dependencies are added to the CLASSPATH used by the compiler to build the application's bytecode. This code includes the xml.jar archive, which contains the JAXP XML parser; the JDBC 2.0 standard extension API, contained in the jdbc2_0-stdext.jar archive; and the Rowset binaries, contained in the rowset.jar archive:

```
@echo off

REM Change this to reflect the Tomcat and JDK installations on your system
set TOMCAT_HOME=c:\jakarta-tomcat
set JAVA_HOME=c:\jdk1.3

REM add all of the necessary packages to the CLASSPATH
set cp=%CLASSPATH%
set CLASSPATH=.
set CLASSPATH=%CLASSPATH%;%TOMCAT_HOME%\lib\xml.jar
set CLASSPATH=%CLASSPATH%;%JAVA_HOME%\lib\rowset.jar
set CLASSPATH=%CLASSPATH%;%JAVA_HOME%\lib\jdbc2_0-stdext.jar
set CLASSPATH=%CLASSPATH%;%cp%
```

Finally, we will invoke javac to compile our Java source into bytecode:

```
REM This is where javac will place the compiled bytecode
set outputDir=..\WEB-INF\classes

REM This is where javac finds the source code
set basepath=..\src

REM Compile the code...
javac -d %outputDir% -classpath %CLASSPATH% %basepath%\WebRowSetHTTPClient.java
```

Running the Application

Now we can run our application. Once again, we will create a batch file to do this efficiently. This batch file, named `runWrsHTTPClient.bat`, is located in the chapter's sample code, downloadable from our web site. As we did in the build process, we must ensure that the `xml.jar`, `jdbc2_0-stdext.jar`, and `rowset.jar` archives are added to the `CLASSPATH`:

```
@echo off
set cp=%CLASSPATH%
set JAVA_HOME=C:\jdk1.3
set TOMCAT_HOME=C:\jakarta-tomcat
set CLASSPATH=.
set CLASSPATH=%CLASSPATH%;%TOMCAT_HOME%\lib\xml.jar
set CLASSPATH=%CLASSPATH%;%JAVA_HOME%\lib\rowset.jar
set CLASSPATH=%CLASSPATH%;%JAVA_HOME%\lib\jdbc2_0-stdext.jar
set CLASSPATH=%CLASSPATH%;..\WEB-INF\classes;%cp%
java WebRowSetHTTPClient Andy Hoskinson  "Hello world!"
```

> **Note: Prior to running this application, please put the `RowSet.dtd` file in the same directory as the `runWrsHTTPClient.bat` batch file. The `WebRowSet` class needs this file to validate the XML document returned by `WebRowSetFetchServlet`.**

When we run this batch file, the output looks like this:

Packaging the Code for J2EE Deployment

Throughout the chapter, we have promised you that we will tell you how to build and package all of the server-side code discussed in this chapter into a web application archive (WAR) for deployment to a J2EE servlet container. This section will show you how to compile our Java classes, build a JAR archive, and package all of the code that we have written, into a WAR file for easy deployment, distribution, and installation on J2EE servlet containers. Our web application uses the standard directory structure defined in Chapter 9 of the Java Servlet Specification, v2.2. You can download this document from ftp://ftp.java.sun.com/pub/servlet/22final-182874/servlet2_2-spec.pdf.

A key directory in the web application's file system is the `/WEB-INF` directory. This directory contains the application's deployment descriptor, class, and JAR files. Since no file contained in the `WEB-INF` directory is ever served directly to a client, it is a "safe" directory for placing sensitive files for your web application's consumption only. The `WEB-INF` directory generally contains the following files:

- ❑ `/WEB-INF/web.xml`: The web application deployment descriptor
- ❑ `/WEB-INF/classes/*`: Servlet and utility classes.
- ❑ `/WEB-INF/lib/*.jar`: JAR files

The rest of the directories contain web-accessible files. For the purpose of this chapter, these include:

- ❑ `/`: The root directory will contain the HTML files and XSL stylesheets that we created in earlier sections of this chapter.
- ❑ `/src`: The Java source code.
- ❑ `/bin`: Batch files discussed in this chapter.
- ❑ `/sql`: The DDL for our sample SQL Server Guestbook database. This directory also contains our `contacts.mdb` sample MS-Access database.

The Web Application Deployment Descriptor

The first step is to create the web application deployment descriptor. The deployment descriptor is used to configure the web application's container. It includes descriptive meta-data about the web application, as well as application-scope parameters and various servlet registration parameters:

```
<?xml version="1.0" encoding="ISO-8859-1"?>

<!DOCTYPE web-app
    PUBLIC "-//Sun Microsystems, Inc.//DTD Web Application 2.2//EN"
    "http://java.sun.com/j2ee/dtds/web-app_2.2.dtd">

<web-app>
    <display-name>Professional XML Databases:  Chapter 16 (JDBC)</display-name>
    <description>
        This web app contains the sample code for Professional XML Databases:
            Chapter 16 (JDBC)
    </description>
```

Next, we need to register our servlets. First, we'll give each of our servlets an alias. We'll also map the JDBC2HTML servlet to files with an extension of `*.xsl`. This will cause the servlet engine to dispatch all URL requests for XSL files in this web application to the `JDBC2HTML servlet` for handling:

```
<servlet>
    <servlet-name>
        JDBC2HTML
    </servlet-name>
    <servlet-class>
        com.jresources.jdbc.JDBC2HTML
    </servlet-class>
</servlet>
<servlet>
    <servlet-name>
        XMLDataGateway
    </servlet-name>
```

```
        <servlet-class>
            com.jresources.jdbc.XMLDataGateway
        </servlet-class>
    </servlet>
    <servlet>
        <servlet-name>
            WebRowSetFetchServlet
        </servlet-name>
        <servlet-class>
            com.jresources.jdbc.WebRowSetFetchServlet
        </servlet-class>
    </servlet>
    <servlet>
        <servlet-name>
            WebRowSetUpdateServlet
        </servlet-name>
        <servlet-class>
            com.jresources.jdbc.WebRowSetUpdateServlet
        </servlet-class>
    </servlet>
    <servlet-mapping>
        <servlet-name>
            JDBC2HTML
        </servlet-name>
        <url-pattern>
            *.xsl
        </url-pattern>
    </servlet-mapping>
</web-app>
```

Building the Application

The next step is to perform the build process. To accomplish this, we will write an MS Windows batch file. We'll call this file `build.bat`. This batch file is located at `Chapter16\jdbcxml\bin\build.bat`, in this chapter's source code archive downloadable from our web site. This process includes:

❑   Compiling the Java source

❑   Packaging the bytecode into a JAR

❑   Packaging our entire application into a WAR (web application archive), using the `jar` tool. Please note that our directory structure will conform to the standard WAR directory structure as defined by the Servlet 2.2 specification, Chapter 9.

Compile the Java Classes

First, we'll compile our classes using `javac`. Since our classes import classes from the Servlet API packages, we must ensure that Tomcat's `servlet.jar` is in the CLASSPATH. Per the servlet 2.2 specifications, the bytecode goes into the web application's `WEB-INF/classes` directory:

```
@echo off

REM Change this to reflect the Tomcat and JDK installations on your system
set TOMCAT_HOME=c:\jakarta-tomcat
set JAVA_HOME=c:\jdk1.3

REM add all of the necesssary packages to the CLASSPATH
set cp=%CLASSPATH%
set CLASSPATH=.
set CLASSPATH=%CLASSPATH%;%TOMCAT_HOME%\lib\xml.jar
set CLASSPATH=%CLASSPATH%;%TOMCAT_HOME%\lib\servlet.jar
```

```
REM This assumes that these packages are in the JDK's lib directory
set CLASSPATH=%CLASSPATH%;%JAVA_HOME%\lib\rowset.jar
set CLASSPATH=%CLASSPATH%;%JAVA_HOME%\lib\jdbc2_0-stdext.jar
set CLASSPATH=%CLASSPATH%;%JAVA_HOME%\lib\xerces.jar
set CLASSPATH=%CLASSPATH%;%JAVA_HOME%\lib\xalan.jar

set CLASSPATH=%CLASSPATH%;%cp%

REM This is where javac will place the compiled bytecode
set myClasspath=..\WEB-INF\classes

REM This is where javac finds the source code
set basepath=..\src

REM Compile the code...
javac -d %myClasspath% -classpath %CLASSPATH% %basepath%\*.java
```

Package the Bytecode into a JAR

Next, we'll build the JAR archive using the Jar tool that comes with the JDK. This goes into the web application's /WEB-INF/lib/ directory:

```
REM Set the directory where the JAR should be built
set jarpath=..\WEB-INF\lib
REM Build the JAR...
jar cvf %jarpath%\jdbcxml.jar -C %myClasspath%\ .
```

Package the Application into a WAR

Finally, we'll use the jar tool to package the entire application into a WAR file. Once this is built, we can distribute the application to our end users:

```
REM Set the directory where the completed WAR should be built (warpath), and the
directory to be recursively archived (apppath)
set warpath=..\..\
set apppath=..\..\jdbcxml
REM Build the WAR...
jar cvf %warpath%\jdbcxml.war -C %apppath%\ .
```

If you are inexperienced in such Java issues, Wrox Press publishes a number of books on the subject, including *Professional Java Server Programming – J2EE Edition* (ISBN 1861004656), if you want more information on packaging and deployment.

Summary

In this chapter, we showed you how you can use JDBC and XML to create universal data access gateways for your J2EE applications. In the first section, we showed you how to construct a simple XML gateway architecture for JDBC that allows you to execute SQL statements against arbitrary JDBC data sources and return the result sets as well-formed XML data structures for consumption by applications that can parse and consume XML. In the second section, we showed you how to build a distributed JDBC application that allows you to interact with a JDBC data source over the Internet using HTTP. Finally, we showed you how to build and package the application for J2EE deployment.

In the next chapter, we will show you how to use XML to facilitate Data Warehousing.

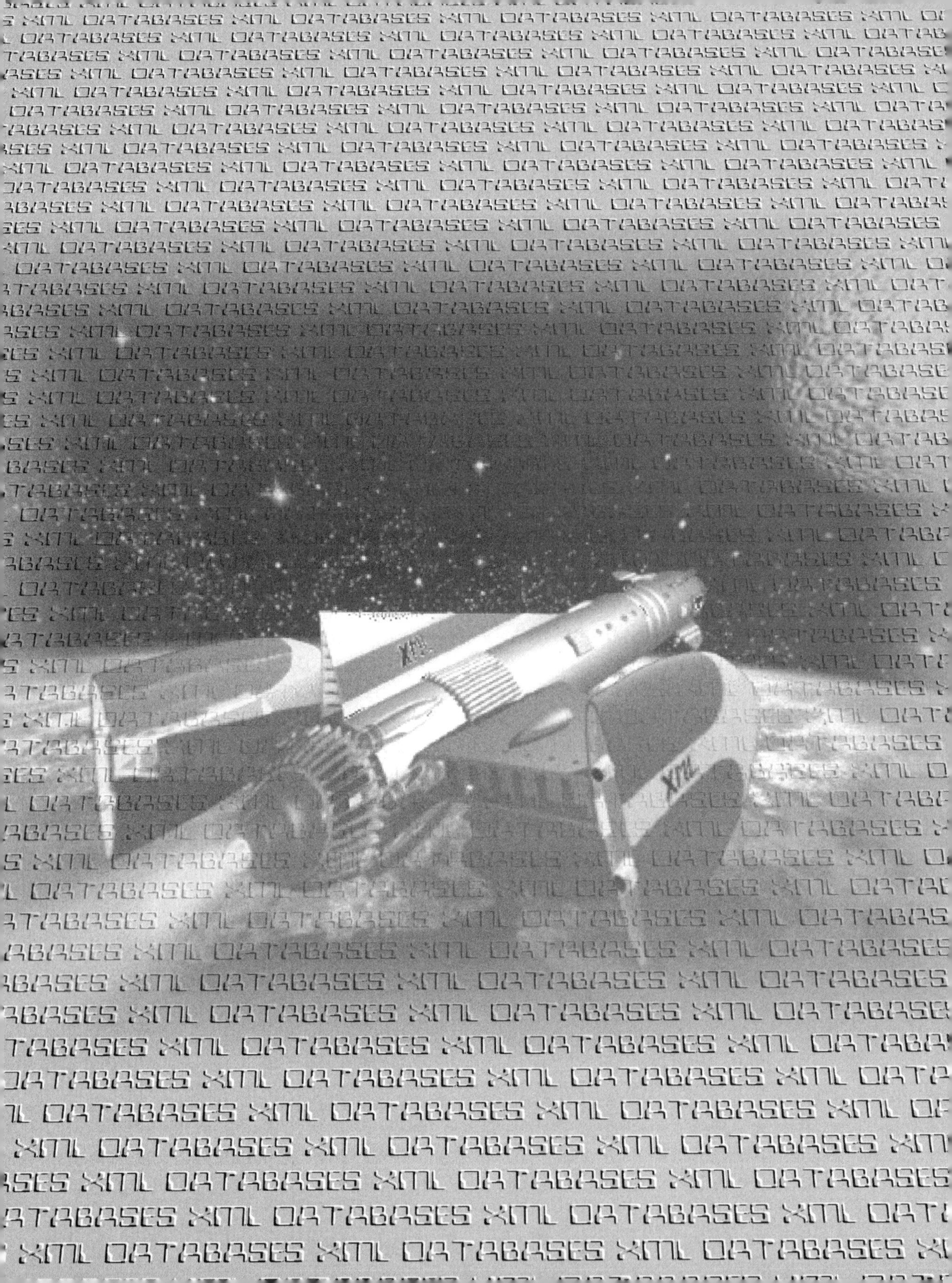
XML DATABASES

Data Warehousing, Archival, and Repositories

In this chapter and the two that follow it, we'll look at some common applications of XML in the enterprise. Whether your system is a large-scale transaction system that's moving millions of detail records a day, or a content management system that has to support multiple presentation formats, the judicious use of XML can improve your ability to reach your goals. This chapter deals specifically with the persistence of information using XML. We'll see some of the traditional strategies for these processes, and then see how adding XML to the mix can benefit the developer.

We'll look at the following topics in this chapter:

❑ **Data warehousing.** In a typical transaction-oriented system, one classic problem faced by developers is how to design a database that supports both the fast creation of transactions and the efficient querying and summarization of those transactions for reporting purposes. One solution that may be considered is creating a data warehouse. We'll look at how data warehouses work and see how XML may be used to streamline the transaction and warehousing process.

❑ **Data archival.** For most systems, data loses its relevance over time and should be moved off the system when some threshold is reached (for example, when the record has been around for a certain period of time). However, we typically want to set this data aside in some form so that, should we need to refer to it later, we can retrieve the data with the minimum of effort. We'll see how XML may be used to make this process easier.

❏ **Data repositories.** In certain circumstances, databases contain information that is only accessed at the detail level – that is, there is no querying or summarization performed against that data. For example, a real estate system might contain information about the minutiae of each property, but that information might only be relevant (in a business sense) when examining that individual property. We'll see how XML may be used to persist detail-only information in a way that makes the relational database perform better, while taking advantage of XML technologies (such as XSLT) to present the detail information when necessary.

All the examples in these three chapters are designed to work with SQL Server 6.x+, ADO 2.5+, and VBScript (the version that comes with Internet Explorer 4.0+); however, the concepts discussed should be applicable to any relational database platform and operating system.

Data Warehousing

One of the problems often faced by data architects is to design a system that facilitates both the quick retrieval of detail information, or transactions, and the ability to easily and efficiently query and summarize that data. As we will see, the two different roles that our information plays have different design requirements. In this section, we'll:

❏ Define data warehousing

❏ Discuss the concepts that drive data warehouse design

❏ Take a look at how XML can facilitate the data warehousing process

❏ Look at examples of XML in use in a data warehouse

The Two Roles of Data

In an enterprise-level data solution, the data in the database plays two roles:

❏ Information gathering

❏ Querying and summarization of data

Let's look at those two roles, and the different constraints they impose on the design of, and access to, our databases.

Detailed Information Gathering

The first use of the database is to gather data from external sources (such as other databases, XML, or simple delimited text files). This could be the insertion of invoice records into an invoice-tracking database as customers submit them, for example, or the periodic update of stock trade information to a stock watch database. Obviously, the specific mechanisms involved will vary from implementation to implementation, but there are some things that remain consistent across all implementations that gather data:

❏ **Detail oriented**. Because this aspect of systems is primarily concerned with getting information into the database from external systems, they typically work with the data at the most granular level supported by your system. For example, an invoice tracking database will be concerned with the details of an invoice, such as items ordered, customer address information etc. A stock watch database, on the other hand, will gather stock level information and supplier details, amongst other things.

❑ **Write-heavy**. Systems designed for information gathering are mostly concerned with writing data to the database. In some systems – such as an invoice tracking system – reads will be performed in the context of performing an update, but this is typically minimal compared to the amount of inserts being performed. In addition, any reads that are performed on the database will be at the single record level – aggregation is typically not performed in this part of the system.

❑ **Transacted**. Because the act of adding information to a database needs to happen seamlessly - either all the information needs to be added, or none of it – writing records to the database usually requires wrapping the inserts in a transaction. Because all the rows, pages, or tables modified during the course of a transaction will be locked until that transaction is committed, our database should be designed so that each transaction may be carried out over as short a time and small a footprint as possible – this is sometimes known as the "get in, get out" approach.

❑ **Space-conscious**. Because many of these systems will be inserting a huge amount of information into the database, they need to be designed with space conservation in mind. A stock watch application, for example, will typically insert millions of trade records into its database every day. If a field is improperly sized – using an `int` where a `smallint` would do, for example – every extra byte that is unused translates to storage space that is lost. In addition, these systems typically rely on being able to insert records quickly, also making smaller records a priority. These systems should be tuned to get away with the smallest possible size for the inserted records.

❑ **Heavily normalized**. Since the space used in the database for the detail information is at a premium, architects will typically design these systems to be as normalized as possible. Look-up tables and other generalization tables will be used wherever possible to minimize the size of the records inserted by the data gathering process. If you're unsure about how normalization works, you can read more about it in the relational database primer in appendix B.

Information Querying and Summarization

The other use of databases is to provide the ability to query the data and summarize it to extrapolate trends, volumes, and other useful information from the details. In an invoice tracking system, for example, you might be interested in the monthly sales of three-inch blue grommets broken down by state; or for a stock watch system, how many shares of a stock were traded on each day of a particular week. Again, the specific mechanisms will vary from implementation to implementation, but there are some constants:

❑ **Summary-oriented**. Code that supports querying and summarization tends to be focused on obtaining summary information from the detail information available. When making a business decision, it's much more useful to see aggregate data reflecting general trends than to browse through detail records looking for the specific information of interest (although it is often useful to have the high detail information available for viewing as well).

❑ **Read-only**. Code that is responsible for the querying and summary of data is always read-only. The information being queried and summarized enters the system during the data gathering part of the database operations.

❑ **Results-conscious**. Since reports and other human-readable information must be produced as the outcome of information querying and summarization, the tables that drive these processes should be concerned with arriving at the result as rapidly as possible. To help this happen, tables may often be designed to hasten the derivation of the queried or summarized information.

❑ **Less normalized**. Since results are typically more important than space consumption for information querying and summarization, systems that support these types of functions tend to be less normalized than systems designed to gather data. This means that you can retrieve meaningful results by looking at a couple of tables and writing a simple query, say, rather than having to write a complicated query involving multiple look-up tables.

As you can see, the two roles that data play in our systems are often at cross-purposes with one another. First, let's look at how databases have traditionally been designed to support these requirements; then, we'll see how data warehousing makes this process easier.

The Traditional Solution

The traditional approach to designing a relational database to support a platform is to design one database to perform both data acquisition functions and querying/summarization functions. For example, the invoice tracking system we've been using as an example throughout the system might be used to support both invoice data entry and summary reporting. You'll recall that the table creation script for the invoice tracking system (first encountered in chapter 3) looks something like this (ch17_ex01.sql):

```
CREATE TABLE Customer (
    CustomerKey integer PRIMARY KEY,
    Name varchar(50),
    Address varchar(50),
    City varchar(30),
    State char(2),
    PostalCode varchar(10))

CREATE TABLE shipMethod (
    shipMethodKey integer PRIMARY KEY,
    shipMethod varchar(5))

INSERT shipMethod (shipMethodKey, shipMethod) VALUES (1, 'FedEx')
INSERT shipMethod (shipMethodKey, shipMethod) VALUES (2, 'USPS')
INSERT shipMethod (shipMethodKey, shipMethod) VALUES (3, 'UPS')

CREATE TABLE Invoice (
    InvoiceKey integer PRIMARY KEY,
    invoiceDate datetime,
    shipDate datetime,
    shipMethodKey integer
        CONSTRAINT FK_Invoice_shipMethodKey FOREIGN KEY (shipMethodKey)
            REFERENCES shipMethod (shipMethodKey),
    CustomerKey integer
        CONSTRAINT FK_Invoice_Customer FOREIGN KEY (CustomerKey)
            REFERENCES Customer (CustomerKey))

CREATE INDEX ix_Invoice_invoiceDate ON Invoice (invoiceDate)
CREATE INDEX ix_Invoice_shipDate ON Invoice (shipDate)
CREATE INDEX ix_Invoice_CustomerKey ON Invoice (CustomerKey)

CREATE TABLE Part (
    PartKey integer PRIMARY KEY,
    name varchar(20),
    size varchar(10) NULL,
    color varchar(10) NULL)
```

```
CREATE TABLE LineItem (
   LineItemKey integer PRIMARY KEY,
   InvoiceKey integer
      CONSTRAINT FK_LineItem_Invoice FOREIGN KEY (InvoiceKey)
         REFERENCES Invoice (InvoiceKey),
   PartKey integer
      CONSTRAINT FK_LineItem_Part FOREIGN KEY (PartKey)
         REFERENCES Part (PartKey),
   Quantity integer,
   Price float)

CREATE INDEX ix_LineItem_PartKey ON LineItem (PartKey)
CREATE INDEX ix_LineItem_InvoiceKey ON LineItem (InvoiceKey)
```

When run, this script creates the following table structure:

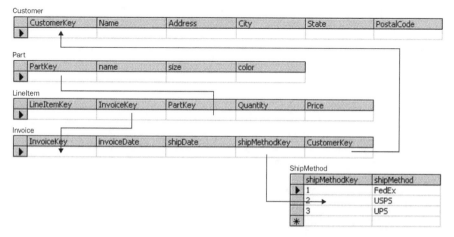

This set of tables supports the addition of invoices (via insertion of records into the Invoice and LineItem tables). Space is conserved for these tables where possible by normalizing out Part and Customer. This normalization also facilitates querying and reporting on Part and Customer. However, there are a couple of issues with using this type of dual-purpose structure.

First, the system is not well tuned to either data entry or reporting. For example, there are indexes on the Invoice and LineItem tables for the orderDate and invoiceDate columns, the customerKey column, and the partKey column. While these indexes are very important for querying and reporting, from a data entry perspective they only serve to slow down inserts into our database – because the index data will also need to be written to the database for each index on the table. If we are only writing data to the table (as we would for a transaction-only database), these indexes do not provide any benefit to the transaction gathering processes. On the other hand, reporting processes will typically need to join to several tables to obtain the information needed to generate reports. Additionally, summarization requires the retrieval of all the detail information before summary information may be returned. We can see that the system as designed is really a compromise between the two roles of data.

In addition, there is a serious danger of wait states for reporting and querying due to the locking being performed by the data entry. If records are being inserted into a table on a regular basis, any report that requires information to be read will have to wait for the write locks to be released on the database. If there are processes in the data entry database that update many records at once (such as marking invoices as shipped, for example), our relational database is likely to escalate the lock to a table lock, making all reporting impossible while the update is taking place.

Many databases try to get around the problem by adding structures that will be used to drive reporting. These tables would be separate from the transaction tables, and have all the appropriate indices to allow data to be queried and summarized from those tables in any way the business rules might call for. For our example, we might add a `MonthlyPartTotal` table, like so (ch17_ex02.sql):

```
CREATE TABLE MonthlyPartTotal (
    summaryMonth tinyint,
    summaryYear smallint,
    PartKey integer
        CONSTRAINT FK_MPT_PartKey FOREIGN KEY (PartKey)
            REFERENCES Part (PartKey),
    Quantity integer)
```

This is a step in the right direction, but then often the database designer shoots himself or herself in the foot by adding a trigger to update this table whenever the `LineItem` table is updated, as could be achieved in our database by the following, ch17_03.sql:

```
CREATE TRIGGER UpdateMPT
ON LineItem
FOR INSERT, UPDATE
AS
BEGIN
   IF (SELECT COUNT(*)
         FROM MonthlyPartTotal, inserted, Invoice
      WHERE summaryMonth = DATEPART(mm, Invoice.invoiceDate)
         AND summaryYear = DATEPART(yyyy, Invoice.invoiceDate)
         AND inserted.InvoiceKey = Invoice.InvoiceKey
         AND MonthlyPartTotal.PartKey = inserted.PartKey) > 0
   UPDATE MonthlyPartTotal
        SET Quantity = MonthlyPartTotal.Quantity + inserted.Quantity
      FROM inserted, Invoice
     WHERE summaryMonth = DATEPART(mm, Invoice.invoiceDate)
        AND summaryYear = DATEPART(yyyy, Invoice.invoiceDate)
        AND inserted.InvoiceKey = Invoice.InvoiceKey
        AND MonthlyPartTotal.PartKey = inserted.PartKey
   ELSE
     INSERT MonthlyPartTotal (summaryMonth, summaryYear, PartKey, Quantity)
        SELECT DATEPART(mm, Invoice.invoiceDate),
               DATEPART(yyyy, Invoice.invoiceDate),
               inserted.PartKey,
               inserted.Quantity
          FROM inserted, Invoice
        WHERE inserted.InvoiceKey = Invoice.InvoiceKey
   IF (SELECT COUNT(*) FROM deleted) > 0
     UPDATE MonthlyPartTotal
        SET Quantity = MonthlyPartTotal.Quantity - deleted.Quantity
      FROM deleted, Invoice
     WHERE summaryMonth = DATEPART(mm, Invoice.invoiceDate)
        AND summaryYear = DATEPART(yyyy, Invoice.invoiceDate)
        AND deleted.InvoiceKey = Invoice.InvoiceKey
        AND MonthlyPartTotal.PartKey = deleted.PartKey
END
```

Now we're right back at square one when querying the `MonthlyPartTotal` table, since it's being updated every time a record gets inserted into the `LineItem` table. Remember that the whole point of segregating the data is to avoid running into write locks on our reporting tables – and this trigger causes an insert or update to the table every time a detail record is added! In order to make both record insertion and querying fast and as lock-free as possible (and to avoid having to perform dirty reads on our database - never a good idea as they may return incomplete or unexpected results), we need to think about taking a different approach. That approach is called data warehousing.

The Data Warehousing Solution

The way that data warehousing works is really very simple – instead of using one database to support all our data access functionality, we actually create two separate databases. Each of the new databases is then designed to support one of our two major data roles, the organization of which is discussed in the following sections:

❑ **On-Line Transaction Processing** (**OLTP**) databases – the information gatherers

❑ **On Line Analytical Processing** (**OLAP**) databases – the query and summarization handlers

❑ Parts that make up an OLAP database

❑ The role of XML in improving the function of OLAP databases.

On-Line Transaction Processing (OLTP)

The gathering of detail information is often referred to as On-Line Transaction Processing, or OLTP. Don't be misled by the term – while the name refers specifically to transaction processing (such as purchases made at a consumer e-commerce site), this part of our design is intended to handle all data gathering processes. In this part of the database, we design our tables to support the acquisition of transactional data – the database is as normalized as possible, with the specific table or tables (in our example, the `Invoice` and `LineItem` tables) being kept as small as possible to reduce insert time and disk consumption. Additionally, we discard indexes on foreign keys and other potentially searchable columns, as they are not needed to gather data. We should also make sure we have data archival strategies in place to make sure our OLTP database does not grow too large.

Here is an example of what our OLTP database structure might look like (`ch17_ex04.sql`):

```
CREATE TABLE Customer (
    CustomerKey integer PRIMARY KEY,
    Name varchar(50),
    Address varchar(50),
    City varchar(30),
    State char(2),
    PostalCode varchar(10))

CREATE TABLE shipMethod (
    shipMethodKey integer PRIMARY KEY,
    shipMethod varchar(5))

INSERT shipMethod (shipMethodKey, shipMethod) VALUES (1, 'FedEx')
INSERT shipMethod (shipMethodKey, shipMethod) VALUES (2, 'USPS')
INSERT shipMethod (shipMethodKey, shipMethod) VALUES (3, 'UPS')
```

```
CREATE TABLE Invoice (
   InvoiceKey integer PRIMARY KEY,
   invoiceDate datetime,
   shipDate datetime,
   shipMethodKey integer
      CONSTRAINT FK_Invoice_shipMethodKey FOREIGN KEY (shipMethodKey)
         REFERENCES shipMethod (shipMethodKey),
   CustomerKey integer
      CONSTRAINT FK_Invoice_Customer FOREIGN KEY (CustomerKey)
         REFERENCES Customer (CustomerKey))

CREATE TABLE Part (
   PartKey integer PRIMARY KEY,
   name varchar(20),
   size varchar(10) NULL,
   color varchar(10) NULL)

CREATE TABLE LineItem (
   LineItemKey integer PRIMARY KEY,
   InvoiceKey integer
      CONSTRAINT FK_LineItem_Invoice FOREIGN KEY (InvoiceKey)
         REFERENCES Invoice (InvoiceKey),
   PartKey integer
      CONSTRAINT FK_LineItem_Part FOREIGN KEY (PartKey)
         REFERENCES Part (PartKey),
   Quantity integer,
   Price float)
```

The SQL script produces the same table structure as before; the only difference is that we have elected not to add the indexes to the tables, making them streamlined for data gathering as we discussed earlier. We are keeping our transaction database consumption to a minimum, making it faster for us to add new transactions.

On-Line Analytical Processing (OLAP)

Databases intended to support querying and summarization are sometimes referred to as On-Line Analytical Processing databases, or OLAP databases. These databases are designed with one goal in mind – the querying and summarization of our detail data by any number of specifics defined in the business rules for our system. For this part of our design, we create our tables to support the querying and retrieval of this information, with the ability to rapidly insert information being a much lower priority. In addition, there are data warehouse indexing technologies that we can leverage, which are designed specifically for OLAP querying to really optimize our ability to query and report on our detail data.

When the term **data warehouse** is used in the industry, normally what is meant is a database tuned for OLAP processing or other processing that requires access to summarized data, such as a billing system for our example invoice database. Another useful term to understand is **data mart** – as you might suspect, a data mart is simply a pared-down data warehouse tuned to a specific business need. For example, in our invoice tracking system there might be a data mart for the accounting department and a data mart for the inventory control department.

Data is transferred from the OLTP database to the OLAP database on a scheduled basis (typically, this should occur when database traffic is low). For example, you might have a process that runs at 3:00 in the morning, every morning, that grabs the previous day's transactions, bundles them up into some transmission format such as BCP files or XML, and sends them to the OLAP system for loading. By transferring this data all at once, in a burst, the availability of the OLTP database for writes (and the OLAP database for reads) is minimally impacted.

Next, let's see how an OLAP database is designed so we can understand how XML can benefit data warehouse developers.

Parts of an OLAP Database

OLAP databases should be constructed in a specific way to leverage the technologies provided by today's relational database platforms. In order to design an OLAP database, first we need to identify some things about the way we plan to query and summarize our data. This section discusses the essential parts of an OLAP database, namely:

❏   **Fact Tables** – where the information we wish to report on is stored.

❏   **Measure Tables** – where you store the measures used to do the reporting.

❏   **Schema** – where the two types of table above interact to give you your reports.

Fact Tables

First, we need to define our fact tables. These tables contain the data that we are planning to report on, at the lowest level of granularity we will need to access. For example, if the consumer of our data warehouse will need to report data at the invoice level, then each record in the fact table should represent one invoice – but if we only need to report data at the customer level, it makes sense to pre-aggregate the data to the customer level before adding it to our fact table. We should also try to keep the fact tables as small as possible, as we will usually have lots of records in those tables – so we should make sure our column datatypes are right (not using a four-byte integer when a one-byte integer would do, for example), and that we don't carry any redundant data in our fact table. Denormalization is usually employed in this step to bring all the facts together into one table. For example, if we were designing a data mart for the inventory control team, we might provide a fact table that contains invoice data and part data, denormalized together, so that a user can easily query how many of part 123 were ordered on invoice 456. Our fact table creation script might look something like this (ch17_ex05.sql):

```
CREATE TABLE factInvoicePart (
    InvoiceKey integer PRIMARY KEY IDENTITY,
    CustomerKey integer,
    ShipDateKey integer,
    ShipMethodKey integer,
    PartKey integer,
    Quantity integer,
    Price float)
```

Don't let the use of an integer for the invoice ship date fool you – we'll see why it's changed to an integer when we discuss measure tables.

On the other hand, if we were designing a data mart for the executive team, we might aggregate the information into daily summaries before creating our fact table, as executives are not going to be interested in specific invoices. A script like the following (ch17_ex06.sql) would serve to create a fact table for executives:

```
CREATE TABLE factDailyTotal (
    DailyTotalKey integer PRIMARY KEY IDENTITY,
    InvoiceDate integer,
    partKey integer,
    partCount integer,
    partUnitPrice float)
```

Measure/Dimension Tables

Next, you need to identify the measures that you will be using. You can think of measures as parameters that you would use in the WHERE clause in your query when accessing the data. We might decide that we want to see invoices broken down by customer, for example, or by ship date. For our example inventory control fact table above, we might have a customer measure table, a ship date measure table, a ship method measure table, and a part measure table. These tables might be created by the following script, ch17_ex07.sql:

```
CREATE TABLE measureCustomer (
    CustomerKey integer PRIMARY KEY,
    Name varchar(50),
    Address varchar(50),
    City varchar(30),
    State char(2),
    PostalCode varchar(10))

CREATE TABLE measureShipDate (
    ShipDateKey integer PRIMARY KEY,
    Month tinyint,
    Day tinyint,
    Year smallint)

CREATE TABLE measureShipMethod (
    shipMethodKey integer PRIMARY KEY,
    shipMethod varchar(5))

CREATE TABLE measurePart (
    PartKey integer PRIMARY KEY,
    name varchar(20),
    size varchar(10) NULL,
    color varchar(10) NULL)
```

Now that we have the fact and measure tables defined, we need to bring them together into a schema.

Schema

Remember that a schema is composed of the tables in our database, joined together by the foreign keys that relate the individual tables together. There are two types of schema that are normally used when designing an OLAP database:

❑   **star** schema

❑   **snowflake** schema

Star Schema

In a star schema, the fact table is in the "center" of the star, and all the measure tables are related to it. All of the columns in the fact table that represent measures should be indexed and related as foreign keys back to the appropriate measure table, as the measures we are tracking for each fact must be represented in our measure tables. For example, the following script (ch17_ex08.sql) would be appropriate for creating the fact and measure tables we have defined for our inventory control OLAP database:

```
CREATE TABLE measureCustomer (
    CustomerKey integer PRIMARY KEY,
    Name varchar(50),
    Address varchar(50),
    City varchar(30),
    State char(2),
    PostalCode varchar(10))

CREATE TABLE measureShipDate (
    ShipDateKey integer PRIMARY KEY,
    ShipMonth tinyint,
    ShipDay tinyint,
    ShipYear smallint)

CREATE TABLE measureShipMethod (
    shipMethodKey integer PRIMARY KEY,
    shipMethod varchar(5))

CREATE TABLE measurePart (
    PartKey integer PRIMARY KEY,
    name varchar(20),
    size varchar(10) NULL,
    color varchar(10) NULL)

CREATE TABLE factInvoicePart (
    InvoiceKey integer PRIMARY KEY IDENTITY,
    CustomerKey integer
        CONSTRAINT fk_fact_Customer FOREIGN KEY (CustomerKey)
            REFERENCES measureCustomer (CustomerKey),
    ShipDateKey integer
        CONSTRAINT fk_fact_ShipDate FOREIGN KEY (ShipDateKey)
            REFERENCES measureShipDate (ShipDateKey),
    ShipMethodKey integer,
        CONSTRAINT fk_fact_ShipMethod FOREIGN KEY (ShipMethodKey)
            REFERENCES measureShipMethod (shipMethodKey),
    PartKey integer,
        CONSTRAINT fk_fact_Part FOREIGN KEY (PartKey)
            REFERENCES measurePart (PartKey),
    Quantity integer,
    Price float)

CREATE INDEX ix_fact_Customer ON factInvoicePart (CustomerKey)
CREATE INDEX ix_fact_ShipDate ON factInvoicePart (ShipDateKey)
CREATE INDEX ix_fact_ShipMethod ON factInvoicePart (shipMethodKey)
CREATE INDEX ix_fact_Part ON factInvoicePart (PartKey)
```

This script creates the structure seen below:

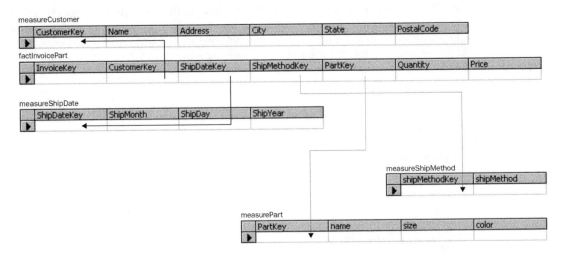

Snowflake Schema

In a snowflake schema, the fact table is in the "center" of the snowflake, and the measure tables that directly correspond to facts are related to it. Again, all of the columns in the fact table that represent measures should be indexed and related as foreign keys back to the appropriate measure table. Each measure may then be broken down into more coarse measures – for example, we might break down a date measure into a month measure, and then into a year measure. For example, the following script (ch17_ex09.sql) would be appropriate for creating the fact and measure tables we have defined for our inventory control OLAP database, assuming that we want to break down the ship date measure:

```
CREATE TABLE measureCustomer (
    CustomerKey integer PRIMARY KEY,
    Name varchar(50),
    Address varchar(50),
    City varchar(30),
    State char(2),
    PostalCode varchar(10))

CREATE TABLE measureShipYear (
    ShipYearKey integer PRIMARY KEY,
    ShipYear smallint)

CREATE TABLE measureShipMonth (
    ShipMonthKey integer PRIMARY KEY,
    ShipMonth tinyint,
    ShipYearKey integer
        CONSTRAINT fk_measure_ShipYear FOREIGN KEY (ShipYearKey)
            REFERENCES measureShipYear (ShipYearKey))

CREATE TABLE measureShipDate (
    ShipDateKey integer PRIMARY KEY,
    ShipDay tinyint,
    ShipMonthKey integer
        CONSTRAINT fk_measure_ShipMonth FOREIGN KEY (ShipMonthKey)
            REFERENCES measureShipMonth (ShipMonthKey))
```

```
CREATE TABLE measureShipMethod (
    shipMethodKey integer PRIMARY KEY,
    shipMethod varchar(5))

CREATE TABLE measurePart (
    PartKey integer PRIMARY KEY,
    name varchar(20),
    size varchar(10) NULL,
    color varchar(10) NULL)

CREATE TABLE factInvoicePart (
    InvoiceKey integer PRIMARY KEY IDENTITY,
    CustomerKey integer
        CONSTRAINT fk_fact_Customer FOREIGN KEY (CustomerKey)
            REFERENCES measureCustomer (CustomerKey),
    ShipDateKey integer
        CONSTRAINT fk_fact_ShipDate FOREIGN KEY (ShipDateKey)
            REFERENCES measureShipDate (ShipDateKey),
    ShipMethodKey integer,
        CONSTRAINT fk_fact_ShipMethod FOREIGN KEY (ShipMethodKey)
            REFERENCES measureShipMethod (shipMethodKey),
    PartKey integer,
        CONSTRAINT fk_fact_Part FOREIGN KEY (PartKey)
            REFERENCES measurePart (PartKey),
    Quantity integer,
    Price float)

CREATE INDEX ix_fact_Customer ON factInvoicePart (CustomerKey)
CREATE INDEX ix_fact_ShipDate ON factInvoicePart (ShipDateKey)
CREATE INDEX ix_fact_ShipMethod ON factInvoicePart (shipMethodKey)
CREATE INDEX ix_fact_Part ON factInvoicePart (PartKey)
CREATE INDEX ix_measure_Month ON measureShipDate (shipMonthKey)
CREATE INDEX ix_measure_Year ON measureShipMonth (shipYearKey)
```

This SQL script creates the following set of tables:

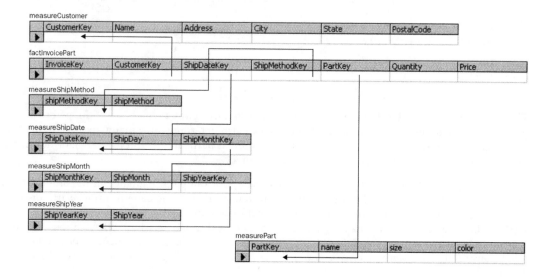

Cubes

To better facilitate the query and retrieval of your OLAP data, each star schema or snowflake schema creates a cube, where the detail information is aggregated along each of the measures. An example will help you understand how this works. Recall our sample structure when we were discussing star schemas earlier:

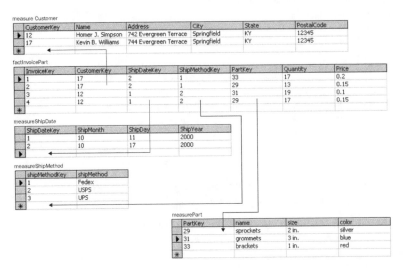

Say that we had 100,000 invoices in our `factInvoicePart` table. We could summarize them by their shipping method:

	FedEx	UPS	USPS
All invoices	72,102	15,209	12,689

If we wanted to know how many invoices were shipped via FedEx, we could simply look at the FedEx number stored in our cube. This is an example of a one-dimensional cube. We can add another dimension by partitioning the data by the customer on the invoice as well:

	FedEx	UPS	USPS
Customer 1	22,615	5,192	3,972
Customer 2	12,541	2,188	918
Customer 3	7,342	3,182	1,212
Customer 4	15,320	716	3,132
Customer 5	14,284	3,931	3,455

This two-dimensional cube allows us to retrieve details of how many invoices were shipped to a particular customer using a particular method. We can also determine how many invoices were shipped to a customer overall (by adding the numbers found on that particular row of the cube), or how many invoices were shipped using a particular shipping method.

You can imagine adding more dimensions to the cube – for example, we might add the order date as a measure, or the shipping state. For each new dimension, the data in the cube is further partitioned – creating a three-dimensional cube, a four-dimensional hypercube, and so on – making it very easy to retrieve the specifics of the fact data for any grouping of measurements. Many OLAP libraries provide mechanisms for accessing the data found in cubes. For more information on OLAP cubes, refer to "*Professional Data Warehousing with SQL Server 7.0 and OLAP Services*", published by Wrox, ISBN 186100281.

As you can see, adopting an OLTP/OLAP structure for your data design promotes quick, low-locking access both from a data acquisition perspective and a querying perspective – data is entered into the OLTP database, which is tuned for data acquisition, and moved to the OLAP database for reporting, which is tuned for querying and summarization. If you have a high-volume database system with extensive querying and summary needs, you should consider moving to a data warehouse model.

Building your Fact Tables

Before we move any further forward, we should discuss the process of moving data from an OLTP database to an OLAP database. As we mentioned before, you typically want to update your OLAP fact tables in the middle of the night (or whenever your transactions are the least frequent). Moving the data obviously consists of two steps – pulling the data out of the OLTP database and updating the OLAP database with that data. In order to perform this update as rapidly as possible, native export forms are often used – for example, data might be extracted from the OLTP database in the form of bulk data files (such as BCP files for SQL Server). This data is then loaded into the OLAP database. However, there are some problems with this approach – the most notable of which is the relative fragility of the export and import code. If the OLTP or OLAP databases change, this code will need to be revisited. Later in the chapter, we'll see how XML may be used to make the process of updating OLAP databases simpler and more efficient.

Now that you have a good understanding of the concepts of data warehousing, let's see how XML may be used to enhance the data warehousing process.

The Role of XML

We can add XML to the mix to help us in the creation and updating of our data warehouse. XML can be used, firstly, to make it easier to update the OLAP database from the OLTP database, and secondly, as an effective way to handle OLTP data. Let's look at both of these.

Using XML for OLAP Update Data

When working with data warehouses on the relational database platform, one of the most important steps is designing a process to move data from the OLTP database to the OLAP database. If the OLTP database and the OLAP database are both on the same platform and reside on the same network, then remote server calls may be used to bring the data from one server to another for processing. However, what happens if the OLTP database is not relational (for example, flat files, Object-oriented database)? A perfect example of this would be a point-of-sale system – if you buy a point-of-sale system off the shelf, the odds are good that the storage and export mechanisms it uses will not be directly compatible with your OLAP database.

The problem is compounded if you have multiple sources of OLTP data. In the stock market data system we suggested earlier, the stock data that is reported will be likely to come from a number of different exchanges, all of which will have their own syntax for the export of data. Rather than building specialized import routines for all the different formats, if you build one XML importer and then leverage the data provider's ability to export in XML (if it has that ability – or you can build an XML server to provide the data from a legacy system in XML format), you can save yourself a lot of aggravation and coding time. Let's see an example.

Say we want to design a common XML format that we can use to load data into our OLAP warehouse. For the purposes of this example, we'll assume that the OLTP provider has awareness of our measures (it translates customers, parts, and so on to the appropriate keys). We could design a structure that looks like this (ch17_ex09.dtd):

```
<!ELEMENT InvoiceBulk (Invoice+)>

<!ELEMENT Invoice (LineItem+)>
<!ATTLIST Invoice
    CustomerKey CDATA #REQUIRED
    ShipDate CDATA #REQUIRED
    ShipMethodKey CDATA #REQUIRED>

<!ELEMENT Part EMPTY>
<!ATTLIST Part
    PartKey CDATA #REQUIRED
    Quantity CDATA #REQUIRED
    Price CDATA #REQUIRED>
```

A sample document for this structure might look like this (ch17_ex09.xml):

```
<?xml version="1.0"?>
<!DOCTYPE listing SYSTEM "ch17_ex09.dtd" >

<InvoiceBulk>
    <Invoice
        CustomerKey="17"
        ShipDate="10/17/2000"
        ShipMethodKey="1">
        <Part
            PartKey="33"
            Quantity="17"
            Price="0.20" />
        <Part
            PartKey="29"
            Quantity="13"
            Price="0.15" />
    </Invoice>
    <Invoice
        CustomerKey="12"
        ShipDate="10/11/2000"
        ShipMethodKey="2">
        <Part
            PartKey="31"
            Quantity="19"
            Price="0.10" />
        <Part
            PartKey="29"
            Quantity="17"
            Price="0.15" />
    </Invoice>
</InvoiceBulk>
```

Note that we've chosen to model these structures as closely as possible to the structures used by the OLTP system. When designing structures for the transmission of data from the OLTP system to the OLAP system, you should always try to minimize the impact on the OLTP system – your motto should be "grab it and go".

Once you have the document extracted from your OLTP system, you'll need to get it loaded into your OLAP database. There are a number of different ways to do this, including using a parsing library like the DOM or SAX to load the data. Emergent platforms such as SQL Server 2000 also offer ways to load XML documents directly into a database. However, let's see a different way you can perform the same function using XSLT.

Consider this stylesheet (ch17_ex10.xsl):

```
<?xml version="1.0"?>
<xsl:stylesheet xmlns:xsl="http://www.w3.org/1999/XSL/Transform" version="1.0">
    <xsl:output method="text" />
    <xsl:template match="/">
        <xsl:for-each select="InvoiceBulk/Invoice/Part">
            <xsl:text>INSERT factInvoicePart (
                CustomerKey,
                ShipDateKey,
                ShipMethodKey,
                PartKey,
                Quantity,
                Price)

SELECT </xsl:text>
                <xsl:value-of select="../@CustomerKey" /><xsl:text>,
                </xsl:text>
                <xsl:text>measureShipDate.ShipDateKey,
                </xsl:text>
                <xsl:value-of select="../@ShipMethodKey" /><xsl:text>,
                </xsl:text>
                <xsl:value-of select="@PartKey" /><xsl:text>,
                </xsl:text>
                <xsl:value-of select="@Quantity" /><xsl:text>,
                </xsl:text>
                <xsl:value-of select="@Price" />
                <xsl:text>
    FROM measureShipDate</xsl:text>
                <xsl:text>
    WHERE DATEPART(mm, '</xsl:text>
                <xsl:value-of select="../@ShipDate" />
                <xsl:text>')=measureShipDate.shipMonth
    AND DATEPART(dd, '</xsl:text>
                <xsl:value-of select="../@ShipDate" />
                <xsl:text>')=measureShipDate.shipDay
    AND DATEPART(yyyy, '</xsl:text>
                <xsl:value-of select="../@ShipDate" />
                <xsl:text>')=measureShipDate.shipYear</xsl:text>
                <xsl:text>&#x0d;&#x0a;GO&#x0d;&#x0a;&#x0d;&#x0a;</xsl:text>

        </xsl:for-each>
    </xsl:template>
</xsl:stylesheet>
```

Bear in mind that if you're running this example, the whitespace is very important! This stylesheet takes the OLAP document we have created and builds a series of INSERT statements that will perform the insertion of the records into our fact tables (the tables created when you run ch17_ex08.sql – the star schema). If you apply the style sheet to the sample OLTP export document we saw earlier (ch17_ex09.xml – it merely needs the inclusion of the association line – see ch17_ex10.xml for a complete version), you get the following output (ch17_ex10a.sql)*:

```
INSERT factInvoicePart (
            CustomerKey,
            ShipDateKey,
            ShipMethodKey,
            PartKey,
            Quantity,
            Price)
```

```
SELECT 17,
          measureShipDate.ShipDateKey,
          1,
          33,
          17,
          0.20
   FROM measureShipDate
   WHERE DATEPART(mm, '10/17/2000')=measureShipDate.shipMonth
   AND DATEPART(dd, '10/17/2000')=measureShipDate.shipDay
   AND DATEPART(yyyy, '10/17/2000')=measureShipDate.shipYear
GO

INSERT factInvoicePart (
             CustomerKey,
             ShipDateKey,
             ShipMethodKey,
             PartKey,
             Quantity,
             Price)

SELECT 17,
          measureShipDate.ShipDateKey,
          1,
          29,
          13,
          0.15
   FROM measureShipDate
   WHERE DATEPART(mm, '10/17/2000')=measureShipDate.shipMonth
   AND DATEPART(dd, '10/17/2000')=measureShipDate.shipDay
   AND DATEPART(yyyy, '10/17/2000')=measureShipDate.shipYear
GO

INSERT factInvoicePart (
             CustomerKey,
             ShipDateKey,
             ShipMethodKey,
             PartKey,
             Quantity,
             Price)

SELECT 12,
          measureShipDate.ShipDateKey,
          2,
          31,
          19,
          0.10
   FROM measureShipDate
   WHERE DATEPART(mm, '10/11/2000')=measureShipDate.shipMonth
   AND DATEPART(dd, '10/11/2000')=measureShipDate.shipDay
   AND DATEPART(yyyy, '10/11/2000')=measureShipDate.shipYear
GO

INSERT factInvoicePart (
             CustomerKey,
             ShipDateKey,
             ShipMethodKey,
             PartKey,
             Quantity,
             Price)
```

```
SELECT 12,
        measureShipDate.ShipDateKey,
        2,
        29,
        17,
        0.15
  FROM measureShipDate
  WHERE DATEPART(mm, '10/11/2000')=measureShipDate.shipMonth
  AND DATEPART(dd, '10/11/2000')=measureShipDate.shipDay
  AND DATEPART(yyyy, '10/11/2000')=measureShipDate.shipYear
GO
```

This output is obtained by using XT to process the stylesheet. If you use IE5.5 with XML support installed (XML for SQL and MSXML3, available from MSDN) instead, you get a working script produced, but without any formatting – you will need to do it yourself. For more on XT, visit http://www.jclark.com/xml/xt.html.

Bear in mind that you need to actually add content into our star schema tables for the above script to work. This can be done easily using the script below (ch17_ex10b.sql):

```
INSERT measureCustomer (
                    CustomerKey,
                    [Name],
                    Address,
                    City,
                    State,
                    PostalCode)

VALUES (
        12,
        'Homer J. Simpson',
        '742 Evergreen Terrace',
        'Springfield',
        'KY',
        '12345')
GO
INSERT measureCustomer (
                    CustomerKey,
                    [Name],
                    Address,
                    City,
                    State,
                    PostalCode)

VALUES (
        17,
        'Kevin B. Williams',
        '744 Evergreen Terrace',
        'Springfield',
        'KY',
        '12345')
GO
INSERT measureShipMethod (
    shipMethodKey,
    shipMethod)

VALUES (
        1,
        'Fedex')
GO
```

```
INSERT measureShipMethod (
                        shipMethodKey,
                        shipMethod)

VALUES (
        2,
        'USPS')
GO

INSERT measureShipMethod (
                        shipMethodKey,
                        shipMethod)

VALUES (
        3,
        'UPS')
GO

INSERT measurePart (
                        PartKey,
                        [name],
                        [size],
                        color)

VALUES (
        31,
        'grommets',
        '3 in.',
        'blue')
GO

INSERT measurePart (
                        PartKey,
                        [name],
                        [size],
                        color)

VALUES (
        29,
        'sprockets',
        '2 in.',
        'silver')
GO

INSERT measurePart (
                        PartKey,
                        [name],
                        [size],
                        color)

VALUES (
        33,
        'brackets',
        '1 in.',
        'red')
GO

INSERT measureShipDate (
        ShipDateKey,
        ShipMonth,
        ShipDay,
        ShipYear)
```

```
        VALUES (
                1,
                10,
                11,
                2000
                )
        GO

        INSERT measureShipDate (
                ShipDateKey,
                ShipMonth,
                ShipDay,
                ShipYear)

        VALUES (
                2,
                10,
                17,
                2000
                )
        GO
```

So, once you have:

❑   Run ch17_ex08.sql against a sample database to create the tables in the first place

❑   Transformed ch17_ex10.xml with ch17_ex10.xsl to produce the output script ch17_ex10a.sql

❑   Run ch17_ex10b.sql to populate tables with initial data

❑   Run ch17_ex10a.sql to add data to populate table factInvoicePart with data

you should finally arrive at the following table structure, PHEW!

measure Customer

CustomerKey	Name	Address	City	State	PostalCode
12	Homer J. Simpson	742 Evergreen Terrace	Springfield	KY	12345
17	Kevin B. Williams	744 Evergreen Terrace	Springfield	KY	12345

factInvoicePart

InvoiceKey	CustomerKey	ShipDateKey	ShipMethodKey	PartKey	Quantity	Price
1	17	2	1	33	17	0.2
2	17	2	1	29	13	0.15
3	12	1	2	31	19	0.1
4	12	1	2	29	17	0.15

measureShipDate

ShipDateKey	ShipMonth	ShipDay	ShipYear
1	10	11	2000
2	10	17	2000

measureShipMethod

shipMethodKey	shipMethod
1	Fedex
2	USPS
3	UPS

measurePart

PartKey	name	size	color
29	sprockets	2 in.	silver
31	grommets	3 in.	blue
33	brackets	1 in.	red

There are a couple of benefits to using stylesheets to create data insertion scripts. The first is maintainability – if an incoming format changes, a new stylesheet may be prepared and deployed without requiring a full build of your system. Additionally, if you are using an implementation of XSLT that performs stylesheet caching (such as MSXML3), your performance will be as good as or better than an implementation using the DOM or SAX. Once the data insertion scripts are created, they may be applied to the OLAP database in an automated way (such as using the command-line version of ISQL to run the script).

Next, let's look at another way that you could use XML to actually replace your OLTP database.

Using XML for OLTP Data

If you consider the way OLTP data is typically organized, you will see that XML could easily be used to support your data gathering functionality.

❑ OLTP systems typically access one discrete transaction at a time. In the example of our invoice system, this might be the invoice record and any line item records associated with it - but they can be treated together as a single unit. Because the information created by OLTP systems is relatively self-contained (you won't typically be accessing several transactions at a time from your OLTP systems), you can store each transaction in a XML document.

❑ Locking can be avoided. Because XML documents are simply text files, they will be locked on a document-by-document basis – so there's no danger of inadvertent lock escalation by a data manager.

❑ XML technology can be easily leveraged. If you store your data as XML documents, it becomes a simple matter to use XSLT to provide many different views of those data – including browser renders, wireless renders, and various data export formats.

Note that you should confine the XML documents to the truly transactional data – all of the other tables you need to validate the transactional data are best left in a relational form so that you can ensure the validity of the transaction data as it arrives. So, in our invoice example, we would keep the following RDBMS structure (ch17_ex11.sql):

```
CREATE TABLE Customer (
   CustomerKey integer PRIMARY KEY,
   Name varchar(50),
   Address varchar(50),
   City varchar(30),
   State char(2),
   PostalCode varchar(10))

CREATE TABLE shipMethod (
   shipMethodKey integer PRIMARY KEY,
   shipMethod varchar(5))

INSERT shipMethod (shipMethodKey, shipMethod) VALUES (1, 'FedEx')
INSERT shipMethod (shipMethodKey, shipMethod) VALUES (2, 'USPS')
INSERT shipMethod (shipMethodKey, shipMethod) VALUES (3, 'UPS')

CREATE TABLE Part (
   PartKey integer PRIMARY KEY,
   name varchar(20),
   size varchar(10) NULL,
   color varchar(10) NULL)
```

A side effect in this case is that all the foreign keys disappear - the tables are relegated to scrubbing individual data points and driving the user interface. Our XML structure would then cover the `Invoice` and `LineItem` tables we pulled out (`ch17_ex12.dtd`):

```
<!ELEMENT Invoice (LineItem+)>
<!ATTLIST Invoice
   CustomerKey CDATA #REQUIRED
   ShipDate CDATA #REQUIRED
   ShipMethodKey CDATA #REQUIRED>

<!ELEMENT LineItem EMPTY>
<!ATTLIST LineItem
   PartKey CDATA #REQUIRED
   Quantity CDATA #REQUIRED
   Price CDATA #REQUIRED>
```

A sample document that could be validated by the above DTD might look like the following (`ch17_ex12.xml`):

```
<?xml version="1.0"?>
<!DOCTYPE listing SYSTEM "ch17_ex12.dtd" >

<InvoiceBulk>
  <Invoice
    CustomerKey="17"
    ShipDate="10/17/2000"
    ShipMethodKey="1">
    <Part
      PartKey="33"
      Quantity="17"
      Price="0.20" />
    <Part
      PartKey="29"
      Quantity="13"
      Price="0.15" />
  </Invoice></InvoiceBulk>
```

We could then use XSLT, the DOM, SAX, or other XML import mechanisms to transfer the OLTP data to the OLAP database as we did in the XML transport example. If you keep the measure tables in your OLAP database and the lookup tables in your OLTP database in sync, the data from your OLTP XML documents may be loaded directly into your OLAP database and all the foreign key relationships will automatically be satisfied.

Summary

If you are designing a system that will involve a large amount of transactional data as well as heavy analytical processing, you may want to consider breaking apart your database and creating a data warehouse. Doing so will help you to reduce locking issues and allow you to tune your databases for their specific purposes.

When you decide to implement a data warehouse, you can leverage XML to make the process less painful. If you have heterogeneous OLTP data sources, you can use XML to make the extraction of data for OLAP processing; and you can even go one step further by converting your OLTP transaction data to XML. Doing so will reduce lock contention and make your OLTP system run more smoothly.

Data Archival

Another fundamental problem that data designers have to contend with on a regular basis is how to properly archive data. As the Information Age swings into full gear, it's going to become increasingly important to maintain archive copies of data, even if it needs to be aged off your primary system for performance and cost reasons. In this section, we'll see how the problem of data archival (and retrieval) has been handled in the past, and how we can use XML to make it easier.

Classical Approaches

In the world of relational databases, the archival of data is a tricky issue. Normally, code is set up to determine when data is archivable (after a certain time period, for example, or once the data reaches a particular workflow state). This code is run at some off-peak time, and any data that is determined to be archivable is removed from the relational database and stored to some other medium. However, there are a couple of problems with this approach. Let's see an example to understand why. Look again at our invoice OLTP system from earlier in the chapter (ch17_ex04.sql).

Our business logic might dictate that once an invoice's ship date is more than a year old, that invoice should be archived from off the system. A typical strategy would be to bulk-copy the records to a flat file, then delete them from the relational database. However, this strategy presents some problems:

❑ What about the LineItem data? LineItem rows are part of invoices, and should be archived off at the same time as the Invoice rows. However, simply bulk-copying the Invoice rows to one flat file and the LineItem rows to another file makes it really difficult to recreate the invoice at some later time (for example, if a customer calls to request a transaction history for the past three years). The only relatively easy way to recreate the invoice is to load the Invoice and LineItem data from the archive and then obtain the data via a join; if the archive files are large, however, this is extremely wasteful.

❑ What about the other tables in the database? In typical circumstances, there are more than one (related) table that will be updated on a regular basis. In our example, the Customer and Part tables are almost certainly going to be changing – new customers and parts will be added, while old parts will be archived off as it becomes possible. As this data becomes archivable (which almost certainly will be driven by a different business rule than the one that drives invoice archival – and therefore will be archived off at a different time), reconstructing an invoice from archive may also require digging through the archive data to locate the customer and part associated with that particular invoice.

❑ What about human readability? Often, a customer will request specific information from an archived source that doesn't necessarily need to be reconstructed. For example, a customer might ask the question, "How many 3-inch blue grommets did I order on April 17 of last year? Because I'm looking at my inventory, and I only see seven of them, and I could have sworn I ordered fifteen, but I've misplaced my copy of the invoice..." In this case, browsing the archive documents by hand would probably be the fastest way to obtain the data. However, if the data is archived in a non-human-readable form, it becomes much more difficult to extract data from the archives simply by searching through them.

If we decide to use XML for our data archival rather than some flat file structure, we can avoid all of these problems and make retrieving archived information much easier.

Using XML for Data Archival

Archiving data to XML is a straightforward process. Each time an archive process is run, each row that is known to be archivable is extracted (or the data that are interesting from an archival perspective are extracted) and expressed in the form of an XML tree; these trees would then be stored together in the archive document for that day. It's important that the XML that is produced this way be self-contained; that is, all keys that have no meaning outside the context of the relational database should be expanded to the information in the related tables. Let's see an example. In our relational OLTP database, we want to archive off all invoices whose ship date is more than a year ago. As you'll recall, the invoice structure looks like this:

```
CREATE TABLE Invoice (
    InvoiceKey integer PRIMARY KEY,
    invoiceDate datetime,
    shipDate datetime,
    shipMethodKey integer
        CONSTRAINT FK_Invoice_shipMethodKey FOREIGN KEY (shipMethodKey)
            REFERENCES shipMethod (shipMethodKey),
    CustomerKey integer
        CONSTRAINT FK_Invoice_Customer FOREIGN KEY (CustomerKey)
            REFERENCES Customer (CustomerKey))
```

When creating an XML structure to hold an archived copy of our invoice, the first thing we do is discard our primary key (as it has no meaning outside the context of the database). Note that we might not always want to discard the primary key data – if the key has some meaning apart from uniquely identifying the record in the database, we may want to hold on to it. We then create data points in our structure for all non-foreign-key columns of the table. This gives us:

```
<!ELEMENT Invoice EMPTY>
<!ATTLIST Invoice
    invoiceDate CDATA #REQUIRED
    shipDate CDATA #REQUIRED>
```

Next, we need to expand the foreign key relationships. In this case, we have two – the ship method key and the customer key. The ship method key is actually a look-up, so we'll express it as an attribute that may take an enumerated value (note that we changed the values to be human-readable):

```
<!ELEMENT Invoice EMPTY>
<!ATTLIST Invoice
    invoiceDate CDATA #REQUIRED
    shipDate CDATA #REQUIRED
    shipMethod (USPS | UPS | FedEx) #REQUIRED>
```

For the customer, however, we'll add a child element that contains all of the data points from the Customer table in lieu of the customer key. We can include the customer key as well, if we like – that will enable us to link back to our relational database later on if we need to – but we definitely have to spell out the customer details as well:

```
<!ELEMENT Invoice (Customer)>
<!ATTLIST Invoice
    invoiceDate CDATA #REQUIRED
    shipDate CDATA #REQUIRED
    shipMethod (USPS | UPS | FedEx) #REQUIRED>
```

```
<!ELEMENT Customer EMPTY>
<!ATTLIST Customer
   Name CDATA #REQUIRED
   Address CDATA #REQUIRED
   City CDATA #REQUIRED
   State CDATA #REQUIRED
   PostalCode CDATA #REQUIRED>
```

However, we also need to store the line items, as they are part of our invoice, so we add a LineItem child element:

```
<!ELEMENT Invoice (Customer, LineItem+)>
<!ATTLIST Invoice
   invoiceDate CDATA #REQUIRED
   shipDate CDATA #REQUIRED
   shipMethod (USPS | UPS | FedEx) #REQUIRED>

<!ELEMENT Customer EMPTY>
<!ATTLIST Customer
   Name CDATA #REQUIRED
   Address CDATA #REQUIRED
   City CDATA #REQUIRED
   State CDATA #REQUIRED
   PostalCode CDATA #REQUIRED>

<!ELEMENT LineItem EMPTY>
<!ATTLIST LineItem
   Quantity CDATA #REQUIRED
   Price CDATA #REQUIRED>
```

Finally, we need to add the part information to the line item as a child element in lieu of the part key. Again, if we want, we can hang onto the part key to associate the part back to our relational database later. The finished structure looks like this (ch17_ex13.dtd):

```
<!ELEMENT Invoice (Customer, LineItem+)>
<!ATTLIST Invoice
   invoiceDate CDATA #REQUIRED
   shipDate CDATA #REQUIRED
   shipMethod (USPS | UPS | FedEx) #REQUIRED>

<!ELEMENT Customer EMPTY>
<!ATTLIST Customer
   Name CDATA #REQUIRED
   Address CDATA #REQUIRED
   City CDATA #REQUIRED
   State CDATA #REQUIRED
   PostalCode CDATA #REQUIRED>

<!ELEMENT LineItem (Part)>
<!ATTLIST LineItem
   Quantity CDATA #REQUIRED
   Price CDATA #REQUIRED>

<!ELEMENT Part EMPTY>
<!ATTLIST Part
   Name CDATA #REQUIRED
   Size CDATA #REQUIRED
   Color CDATA #REQUIRED>
```

An example of a document using this structure is shown below (ch17_ex13.xml):

```xml
<?xml version="1.0"?>
<!DOCTYPE listing SYSTEM "ch17_ex13.dtd" >

<Invoice
  invoiceDate="10/17/2000"
  shipDate="10/20/2000"
  shipMethod="USPS">
  <Customer
    Name="Homer J. Simpson"
    Address="742 Evergreen Terrace"
    City="Springfield"
    State="KY"
    postalCode="12345" />
  <LineItem
    Quantity="12"
    Price="0.10">
    <Part Color="Blue"
      Size="3-inch"
      Name="Grommets" />
  </LineItem>
  <LineItem
    Quantity="12"
    Price="0.10">
    <Part Color="Blue"
      Size="3-inch"
      Name="Grommets" />
  </LineItem>
</Invoice>
```

As you can see, this document handles all of the issues we were encountering with our data archival strategy:

❑   The LineItem data is associated directly with the Invoice. Once the document containing the invoice is opened, all of the line item information is directly accessible.

❑   Because we have designed the document to be self-contained, all of the other information about the invoice – such as the customer and parts for the invoice – is described in place. If the relational database has archived off customer or part information, the full meaning of the archived invoice can be determined by the information contained in the document.

❑   This document is quite easy to read. If a customer has a question about an invoice and this file is identified as the XML document containing information about that particular invoice, it would be a simple matter to glean the information from the document and return it to the customer.

While there is a small price to pay in archive space consumption (as the XML documents contain more information than a traditional bulk-copied file would), the space may be easily recaptured by compressing the XML documents before storing them. At any rate, since archived information is typically stored to a removable medium, space consumption is not as critical an issue as it would be for a live system. If your system has so many transactions that a month's worth would create a file that is too large to be easily handled, you might consider breaking the archive down into smaller files, such as a file per week.

Another great benefit to using XML for a data archive is the ability to apply some of the emergent XML tools to leverage that information. For example, an XML indexer might be used to make your data archive easily searchable, making it almost as efficient for pure reads as the original relational data was.

When you are creating your data archive, you may want to retain some indexing data in your database to help you locate specific information more easily. For example, you might have a table that contains the file name of the archived data, the identifier of the removable medium where it was stored, and the data ranges of the invoices the file contains. That way, when a specific data recovery request is made, you will be able to more easily obtain the data you are looking for.

Summary

In this section, we've seen how XML may be used to improve the data archival process. In a properly designed XML archive, each document will be self-contained and have all the information necessary to reconstruct the original business meaning of the information stored in the document. The documents are human-readable, making manual extraction of data simpler than with traditional data archival methods. Finally, an XML data archive may be manipulated with the emergent XML toolsets to make it a more powerful archival medium than flat bulk-copied files.

Data Repositories

One of the challenges sometimes encountered when designing enterprise solutions is that of building data repositories. Data repositories consist of large amounts of data, much of which is seldom aggregated or queried against. An example where this might occur would be a real estate system – there are literally hundreds of data points associated with a particular property that is for sale, but a buyer is typically only going to run queries against a handful of them. However, the data is interesting once the buyer has drilled down to a particular property and wants to see the detailed information for that property. In this section, we'll see what the traditional approach to creating data repositories has been, and then see how XML can make the process easier.

Classical Approaches

Traditionally, data repositories are built in relational databases. All information, regardless of how often it is queried or summarized, is treated the same – as a column in a normalized structure where it is appropriate. If a column is searched against frequently, it may be indexed to improve performance, but that's about as much as can be done to differentiate it from columns that are only accessed on a single-row basis. Information that is only accessed at a detail level is effectively dead weight in the database from a querying perspective – it clogs up the pages, making more physical reads necessary per row accessed and leading to "cache thrashing". Let's see a simple example. Suppose we had the following table in our database (ch17_ex14a.sql):

```
CREATE TABLE Property (
    PropertyKey integer PRIMARY KEY IDENTITY,
    NumberOfBedrooms tinyint,
    HasSwimmingPool bit,
    Address varchar(50),
    City varchar(30),
    State char(2),
    PostalCode varchar(10),
    SellerName varchar(50),
    SellerAgent varchar(50))
```

Assuming that the character fields are entirely filled, each row in this table would consume about 200 bytes or so. If the database platform where this table resides uses 2K pages, about 20 properties would be able to fit on one page. However, if we want to select all the properties that have three bedrooms and no swimming pool, really we're only interested in six bytes of the record – the key and the two metrics we're querying against. In this case, about 650 properties would fit on one page in our database in this case. Your mileage may vary, depending on the way your platform chooses to store data, fill factors, and other issues, but generally speaking a table with fewer columns will return the results of a query faster than one with more columns (assuming the query isn't covered by an index, in which case that rule of thumb does not apply). We can improve our query speed by taking the columns that are not normally queried and moving them into another table (ch17_ex14b.sql):

```
CREATE TABLE Property (
    PropertyKey integer PRIMARY KEY IDENTITY,
    NumberOfBedrooms tinyint,
    HasSwimmingPool bit)

CREATE TABLE PropertyDetail (
    PropertyKey integer PRIMARY KEY,
    Address varchar(50),
    City varchar(30),
    State char(2),
    PostalCode varchar(10),
    SellerName varchar(50),
    SellerAgent varchar(50))
```

But why stop there? As we've discussed in this chapter, a great way to store detail data that doesn't need to be queried is as XML. In fact, systems with more detail-only data than not can benefit from using XML as their primary data repository. Let's see how we might do this.

Using XML for Data Repositories

Imagine turning the problem around and attacking it from an XML perspective. Information flows into your system in the form of XML. An indexing system picks up the XML document, indexes it into your relational database, and then stores the original XML document in a document repository. To carry on from our previous example, let's say we have XML documents with the following structure coming into our system (ch17_ex15.dtd):

```
<!ELEMENT Property EMPTY>
<!ATTLIST Property
    NumberOfBedrooms CDATA #REQUIRED
    HasSwimmingPool CDATA #REQUIRED
    Address CDATA #REQUIRED
    City CDATA #REQUIRED
    State CDATA #REQUIRED
    PostalCode CDATA #REQUIRED
    SellerName CDATA #REQUIRED
    SellerAgent CDATA #REQUIRED>
```

We need to build a structure in our relational database to hold the index into these documents. We've already decided that the fields we may want to query on or summarize are NumberOfBedrooms and HasSwimmingPool. Therefore, we create the following table in our database (ch17_ex15.sql):

```
CREATE TABLE Property (
    PropertyKey integer PRIMARY KEY IDENTITY,
    NumberOfBedrooms tinyint,
    HasSwimmingPool tinyint,
    DocumentFile varchar(50))
```

We would then store the original XML document to a particular predefined location on our network and use the `DocumentFile` field to point to the document location. If we want to query on the number of bedrooms now, we can do so against the index and return a handful of filenames; these filenames can be used to drill into the original XML documents to provide detail information about the address, the seller, and so on.

There are a number of advantages to using XML for data repositories:

- ❑ **Greater flexibility in providers.** With the tendency towards XML standards, more and more external data providers will have the ability to provide data as XML. If you design your data repository to use XML as its primary storage mechanism, it becomes much easier to get data into and out of your system.

- ❑ **Faster querying and summarization.** If your relational database index is built properly, you can more quickly obtain a set of keys that will allow you to drill down into the specifics of each item in your repository. In addition, querying will be faster due to reduced database size.

- ❑ **More presentation options.** If your data is stored natively as XML, you will have a greater arsenal of tools at your disposal that can be used to leverage that content without additional coding.

- ❑ **Fewer locking concerns.** Like the OLTP database we discussed earlier, keeping most of the information at the file level with only the indexed information in the database will reduce the locking concerns in the database and improve overall performance.

Be aware that if your data archive grows to be a large number of files, and you plan to access those files frequently, you may need to perform file system management to ensure that obtaining the information in those files doesn't become a bottleneck for you.

Summary

If you are designing a system that contains many data points that will never (or rarely) be queried and summarized – but will be reported at the detail level only – then using XML as your data repository platform might be your best bet. Passing the documents in the repository through an indexer – extracting the information needed to query and summarize your detail and storing it in your relational database, providing a way to find specific detail information that matches your search criteria – allows you to create a document index in your database so that you can find the documents you need quickly and easily, while allowing you to leverage existing XML tools to enhance the way you use that data.

Summary

In this chapter, we've seen how XML may be used to improve the way you access and manipulate your data. We've seen:

❑   How XML may be used to help create a data warehouse

❑   The benefits you can realize by using XML as your archival strategy

❑   How XML can improve the functionality of your data repository

As more of your business partners move towards being able to send and receive XML natively, your systems will directly and immediately benefit. In addition, these strategies will help you to decrease lock contention on your systems and improve your data processing speed.

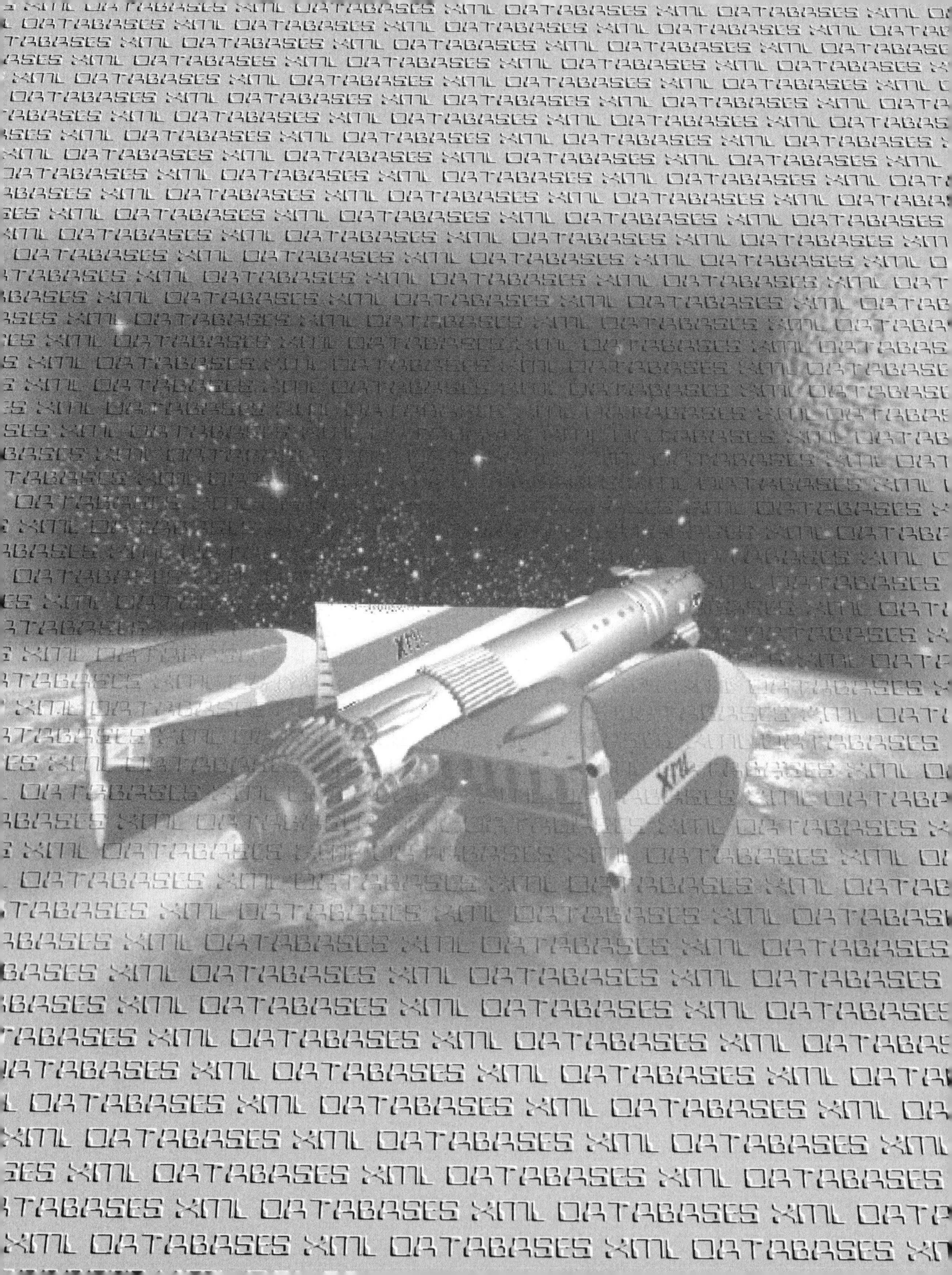
XML DATABASES

18

Data Transmission

One of the most common uses of XML for data in enterprise today, and part of its appeal, is data transmission. Companies need to be able to communicate clearly and unambiguously with one another, and each other's systems, and XML provides a very good medium for doing so. In fact, as we've already seen, XML was created for data transmission between different vendors and systems. XML lets you create your own structure.

In this chapter, we'll take a look at the common goals and engineering tasks involved in data transmission, and see how XML can improve our data transmission strategy. In particular we'll look at:

❑   What data transmission involves

❑   Classic strategies for dealing with data transmission issues, and where their shortcomings lie

❑   How we can overcome some of the problems associated with the classic strategies using XML

❑   SOAP (Simple Object Access Protocol), and the elements that make up SOAP messages

❑   The basics of using SOAP to transmit XML messages over HTTP

Executing a Data Transmission

First, let's take a look at what's involved in transmitting data between two systems. Once we get a feel for the steps involved and the traditional way of handling them, we'll see how XML makes the processing of those steps easier.

Agree on a Format

Before we can send data between two systems, we need to agree what format the data transmission will take. This may or may not involve negotiation between the two teams developing the systems. If one of the systems is larger and has already implemented a data standard, typically the smaller team will write code to handle that standard. If no standard exists, on the other hand, the two development teams will have to collaborate on a standard that suits each team's needs – a process that may be quite time-consuming, as we'll see when we discuss classical strategies later in this chapter.

Transport

Next, the sending party has to have some way of getting the data to the receiving party – will it be e-mail, http, ftp? Again, the sending party and the receiving party will have to agree on the mechanism used to transmit the data, which may involve discussions about firewalls and network security.

Routing

As systems become larger and larger, and begin to exchange data with more and more partners, systems that receive data will need to have some way of routing data to the appropriate system or workflow queue. This decision will be based on the sender and the operation that needs to be performed on that data. There are also security implications here, but we'll discuss that when look at SOAP later in the chapter.

As more and more systems start to interoperate in this scenario, a loosely-coupled information sharing approach becomes more practical. System-to-system transmission requires those systems to build an interface to each other, but as more systems are added, the cost of this interoperability increases exponentially. A loosely coupled approach that uses information brokers could reduce this cost to linear, as systems only require an interface to be built to the broker.

Request-Response Processing

More and more applications are starting to use the Internet as their framework for the processing and transmission of information. It's therefore becoming more important to build a mechanism that allows a specific transmission of data to be responded to in a traceable manner – things like an appraisal verification service, or a credit reporting service. This is especially important for service providers that offer access to their services via the Internet. Microsoft's Biztalk is one application that facilitates this – we'll mention Biztalk again later in the chapter.

Classic Strategies

In this section, we'll see how the issues of data transmission have traditionally been addressed by systems that were not XML-aware. After we've see some of the shortcomings of these strategies, we'll take a look at how XML can improve our ability to control the transmission and routing of data.

Selecting on a Format

When one system transmits data to another, that transmission typically takes the form of a character stream or file. Before two companies can set up a communications channel, they need to agree on the exact format of that channel. Typically, the stream or file is broken up into records, which are further subdivided into fields, as you would expect.

Let's see some of the typical structures we might expect to see in a classic data transmission format.

Delimited Files

This kind of delimited file is quite common, and usually has some character (such as a comma or vertical bar |) to separate the fields, and a carriage return to separate the records. Empty or NULL fields are shown by two delimiting characters immediately following each other. You can read more about these in Chapter 12 – Flat File Formats.

Fixed-width Files

Fixed-width flat files have an advantage in that the systems always know the length and exact format of the data being sent. A carriage return will generally still be used as the record delimiter in this case. Again, you can read more about fixed-width delimited files in Chapter 12.

Proprietary/Tagged Record Formats

As you might imagine, proprietary formats can vary in structure from hybrid delimited/fixed-width formats, to relatively normalized structures. The key to these structures is that typically there are different types of records; each record will have some sort of indicator specifying the type of record (and hence the meaning of the fields found in this record). For each record, however, all of our formatting and other specification rules still apply.

For example, we might have the following specialized format for our invoice example, which we worked on in the first four chapters, where each record is exactly 123 bytes long. The first character of each record is used as the record identifier. Records must always start with the Invoice header record, followed by the Customer record, and then one or more Part records :

1. Invoice header record

2. Customer record

3. One or more Part records

Based on its contents, the fields that make up each record are as follows:

Invoice Header Record

Field	Start Position	Size	Name	Format	Description
1	1	1	Record type	Always H. The letter H means this is an invoice header record	Indicates an invoice header record
2	2	8	Order Date	Datetime YYYYMMDD	The date the order on the invoice was placed
3	10	8	Ship Date	Datetime YYYYMMDD	The date the order on the invoice was shipped
4	18	106	Unused (Filler)	String	Must be filled with all spaces

Customer Record

Field	Start Position	Size	Name	Format	Description
1	1	1	Record type	Always C. The letter C indicates that this is a customer record.	Indicates a customer record
1	2	30	Customer Name	String	The name of the customer for this invoice
2	32	50	Customer Address	String	The street address of the customer
3	82	30	Customer City	String	The city of the customer's address
4	112	2	Customer State	String	The customer's state
5	114	10	Customer Postal Code	String	The customer's postal code

Part Record

Field	Start Position	Size	Name	Format	Description
1	1	1	Record type	Always P	Indicates a part record
2	2	20	Part Description 1	String	The description of the first part ordered
3	22	5	Part Quantity 1	Numeric. Left pad with zeroes.	The quantity of the first part ordered
4	27	7	Part Price 1	Numeric. Two implied decimal places. Left pad with zeroes.	The unit price of the first part ordered
5	34	90	Unused	String	Must be filled with all spaces

A file that follows the above format might look like this (we've had to format this slightly to fit it on the page):

```
H20001017200010223
CHomer J. Simpson            742
Evergreen Terrace                    Springfield
KY12345
P3 inch blue grommets000170000010  P2 inch red sprockets000230000015
H20001017200010223
CKevin B. Williams           744
Evergreen Terrace                    Springfield
KY12345
P1.5 inch silver spro000110000025  P3 inch red grommets 000140000030
P0.5 inch gold widget000090000035
```

Problems with Classic Structures

Let's take a look at some of the shortcomings of classic data transmission structures.

Not Self-Documenting

You'll notice that in all of our examples, there had to be associated documentation with a file format explaining how the records and fields were broken apart, what each field represented, and the specific formatting idiosyncrasies of each field. This is less than ideal, because without the supporting documentation, the files are virtually unusable.

Not Normalized

In most classic structures, records are completely denormalized (although we have seen some custom structures, like tagged-record structures, that allow structure information to be transmitted). In our fixed-width and delimited examples in Chapter 12, there are only a finite number of parts available for use – five in the case of these examples. What if there is a sixth part, however? How can we represent it in our structure?

The example we give of a proprietary format is a little better, but still not ideal. It allows a theoretically unlimited number of parts for each invoice, but there is the added overhead for the parser of determining what type of record each record is, and handling it appropriately.

Fragile

You may or may not remember a little problem that had all of the world's COBOL programmers gainfully employed for the last few years of the twentieth century – the so-called "Y2K" problem. At its heart, this problem boiled down to a data description problem, affecting (among other things) data transmission formats.

If a fixed-width file, for example, had defined a field holding a date as six characters in the form YYMMDD, then this presented a Y2K problem. Changing the file to hold a proper eight-character date in the form YYYYMMDD not only necessitated changing the code that created the file, but changing the code of all of the other programs that consumed that file! Obviously, this is sub-optimal.

While the Y2K problem has passed, we can still see similar issues cropping up for classic data transmission formats on a regular basis. What if we want to pass additional information with our parts in our file? What if we are going international and need to add a country field for our customers? Classic data structures handle these types of changes ungracefully.

Routing and Requesting

When transmitting data, there are really two questions that need to be answered:

❑ What is the data?

❑ What should be done with it?

Take our sample invoice files, for instance. These files do a good job of describing what the data is, but not a very good job of what should be done with it. As the recipient of one of these data transmissions, what do I do? Is this a new copy of an invoice I've never seen, meaning I should insert it into my tracking database? Is this an updated copy, meaning I should find an invoice that matches it and update the information?

Obviously, we can add more fields and/or record types to our formats to help answer the routing questions – for example, in our proprietary format we might add a record type that describes how the contents of the file are to be used. But what if we decide that there's a new way to use data that we didn't think about when we designed the file? What if sometimes we don't have a specific purpose in mind for the data, and are simply transmitting it in a "for-your-records" fashion? It would be useful if there were some way we could specify the purpose of the data, separate and distinct from the data itself, that could be transmitted at the same time in a universally understood way.

Transport

Once we have created our file or character stream, we need to somehow get it from the producer to the consumer. There are many different ways this can happen, depending on how compatible (or incompatible) the sending and receiving systems are. Let's look at a few of them.

Physical Media

The most widely used transmission mechanism for data, in some cases up until just a few years ago, was physical media. The producer cuts a tape, saves to floppy, or prints the data. On receipt, the consumer would then have to load the tape, copy the file, or (believe it or not) re-key the data to make it available to processes at their site.

There are a number of problems with using physical media to transmit data. The most obvious one is the manual intervention issue. There are costs and processing time associated with having an operator load a tape or disk on the producer's side, and ship the results to the consumer. At the consumer, another operator has to load the tape or disk, or re-key the data. Human error is also a big concern when manually generating and loading data.

One important problem is that of speed. Unless the data is traveling a really short distance, it is quite likely that there will be both a delay in transportation, and a delay in getting the data on to the other system. This delay could be days long.

Another major problem with physical media is the fragility issue. Tapes, disks, and printouts are susceptible to damage during the preparation and shipping steps. An incautious delivery person throwing a package a little too hard can render the entire file unusable.

Finally, there's the hardware issue to consider. If a consumer needs to be able to accept data transmissions from a variety of producers, the consumer will need to have hardware available that can read the physical media provided by the producers.

E-mail

Data transmissions may also be performed as e-mail attachments. The file is prepared by the producer, optionally compressed, and then sent as an attachment to the consumer. The consumer can extract the attachment manually and provide it to the systems on their end. Even better, savvy programmers can always write a mail daemon that picks up mail addressed to a particular location, extract the attachments automatically, and provide them to the processing system with no additional human intervention.

The major problem with using e-mail to handle these types of data transmissions is one of message volume and file size. If you are sending many small data transmissions – one file per invoice received for example – then an e-mail system will expend a lot of time and resources managing all of the messages as they arrive at the consumer. On the other hand, if you tend to send fewer transmissions but larger files – one file with all of the invoices received on a particular day, for example – then your e-mail may be blocked by the receiving system because of excessive attachment size. While e-mail is OK as an alternative for transmitting data, it is not strongly recommended.

FTP

About two or three years ago, FTP was being used heavily for data transmission. A consumer machine would have an FTP server installed on it, and files would be dropped into a particular directory. Automated processes could then watch that directory for files and process them as they came in.

Recently, however, there has been a certain amount of concern with leaving FTP access open through a firewall. With the current spate of denial-of-service attacks, many network administrators are closing off access to everything but port 80 (and/or port 443, for HTTPS) on their systems to try to avoid these attacks. Of course, if the FTP port is not available through the firewall, FTP may not be used to transmit data. *One way round this is to have several layers of firewalls with different permissions. The idea is to put a FTP server in between the firewalls, therefore not opening up your internal network.*

Socket Code

With the advent of the Internet, many developers built custom TCP applications to accept data over a particular TCP port. A random port number would be picked, and the producer and consumer would write code to stream data to and accept data from that port. For a while, this seemed an ideal solution – while there was additional developer effort required to get the service up and running, any level of security could be imposed on the packets transmitted to that port, and the software would not interfere with any traditional servers such as HTTP or FTP running on the same machine.

Unfortunately, specialized socket code suffers from the same problem as FTP – firewalls. Denial-of-service attacks don't rely on their packets being accepted to accomplish their goal, so many network administrators simply disallow traffic on custom ports.

Virtual Private Network (VPN)

Another, more secure way of transferring information over the Internet is through the use of a Virtual Private Network. This is a tunneling mechanism that may be used to make two machines on the Internet appear as if they were on the same LAN. Files may be moved across this network as if they were being transferred between nodes on a LAN.

While this is more secure than other transmission mechanisms, it is still vulnerable to vandals – spurious packets, even denial-of-service attacks, may still be launched against a VPN. Each system also has to have the appropriate VPN software in place and running.

Leased-Line

The best possible, and cleanest, classic mechanism for the transmission of data is via a leased-line. Essentially, the producer and/or consumer pay to have a frame-relay, T1, or other physical line installed directly between the two physical locations. Data may then be freely transmitted along that line without bandwidth difficulties, Internet traffic concerns, or security worries.

The obvious downside to leased-line transmission is cost. High-bandwidth leased-lines such as T1 lines can cost thousands of US dollars to install and maintain. If a producer is attempting to transmit data to many consumers, each producer-consumer pair will need to have a leased-line installed to do so. While the transmission of data over leased-lines is as safe as possible, it will probably not be cost-effective for most applications.

How Can XML Help?

We've seen the various problems encountered when attempting to transfer data using traditional means. Now, let's take a look at how using XML to transfer data helps us eliminate many of these challenges.

XML Documents are Self-Documenting

One of the best things about XML is that properly designed XML documents are self-documenting, in the sense that the tags describe the data with which they are associated. Whether we are using elements or attributes, the name of a specific element or attribute should clearly describe the content of that specific element or attribute, assuming the author has designed the XML file well.

Take for example the following XML structure (ch18_ex01.xml):

```xml
<?xml version="1.0"?>
<!DOCTYPE OrderData [
  <!ELEMENT OrderData (Invoice+)>
  <!ELEMENT Invoice (Customer, Part+)>
  <!ATTLIST Invoice
     orderDate CDATA #REQUIRED
     shipDate CDATA #REQUIRED>
  <!ELEMENT Customer EMPTY>
  <!ATTLIST Customer
     name CDATA #REQUIRED
     address CDATA #REQUIRED
     city CDATA #REQUIRED
     state CDATA #REQUIRED
     postalCode CDATA #REQUIRED>
  <!ELEMENT Part EMPTY>
  <!ATTLIST Part
     description CDATA #REQUIRED
     quantity CDATA #REQUIRED
     price CDATA #REQUIRED>
]
>
<OrderData>
   <Invoice
      orderDate="10/17/2000"
      shipDate="10/20/2000">
      <Customer
         name="Homer J. Simpson"
         address="742 Evergreen Terrace"
         city="Springfield"
         state="KY"
         postalCode="12345" />
      <Part
         description="2 inch blue grommets"
         quantity="17"
         price="0.10" />
      <Part
         description="3 inch red sprockets"
         quantity="11"
         price="0.15" />
   </Invoice>
   <Invoice
      orderDate="10/21/2000"
      shipDate="10/25/2000">
```

```
        <Customer
           name="Kevin B. Williams"
           address="744 Evergreen Terrace"
           city="Springfield"
           state="KY"
           postalCode="12345" />
        <Part
           description="1.5 inch silver sprockets"
           quantity="9"
           price="0.25" />
        <Part
           description="0.5 inch gold widgets"
           quantity="3"
           price="0.35" />
     </Invoice>
  </OrderData>
```

Even without any other supporting documentation, it's pretty clear what all of the parts of this document represent. A programmer could conceivably write a program to accept this type of document given a sample like the one shown above. The only thing not provided in this example that would be useful is strong data typing. However, once XML Schemas enter widespread use, we will be able to specify the exact format and size of each data field in our structure.

XML Documents are Flexible

Because of the nature of XML structures, it becomes very easy to add information to them as necessary without breaking existing code. For example, we might decide that we want to add an additional field to the Invoice element, called shipMethod, which describes the type of shipping method to be used to fulfill the order. We can do so by modifying our previous document type definition as follows (ch18_ex02.xml):

```
<!ELEMENT OrderData (Invoice+)>
<!ELEMENT Invoice (Customer, Part+)>
<!ATTLIST Invoice
   orderDate CDATA #REQUIRED
   shipDate CDATA #REQUIRED
   shipMethod (USPS | UPS | FedEx) #IMPLIED>
<!ELEMENT Customer EMPTY>
<!ATTLIST Customer
   name CDATA #REQUIRED
   address CDATA #REQUIRED
   city CDATA #REQUIRED
   state CDATA #REQUIRED
   postalCode CDATA #REQUIRED>
<!ELEMENT Part EMPTY>
<!ATTLIST Part
   description CDATA #REQUIRED
   quantity CDATA #REQUIRED
   price CDATA #REQUIRED>
```

Because we've defined our new attribute as implied (not necessary), any existing documents that were valid against the previous version of our DTD will also validate against this one. This allows us to make modifications to our XML structures as it is necessitated by business requirements without requiring all the consumers receiving the structure to be modified.

XML Documents are Normalized

XML documents, by their nature, are structured. This is more natural when working with data – for most applications, data is best represented by a tree structure. Unlike classic file formats that require a consuming program to extrapolate the normalization, it is available right away when processing an XML document.

XML Documents can Utilize Off-The-Shelf XML Tools

There are many off-the-shelf tools that are well suited to the creation, manipulation, and processing of XML documents. As XML becomes more and more prevalent in the business environment, you can bet that more and more toolsets will be developed that allow programmers to make use of content in an XML form. Significantly, many of the tools that are available are open-source, freely distributed, or made available as standard on a platform – for example MSXML with MS Windows 2000 – making them ideal tools for the programmer on a budget.

Routing and Requesting

Because XML documents are by their nature in tree form, it becomes very easy to wrap an existing XML document in an additional parent element that describes how that document is to be processed and routed. The best way to think of this is as an **envelope**. Like an envelope, the wrapping element might describe whom the document is from, who the intended recipient is, and what the contents are to be used for.

For example, let's say we had our structure from earlier:

```
<!ELEMENT OrderData (Invoice+)>
<!ELEMENT Invoice (Customer, Part+)>
<!ATTLIST Invoice
    orderDate CDATA #REQUIRED
    shipDate CDATA #REQUIRED>
<!ELEMENT Customer EMPTY>
<!ATTLIST Customer
    name CDATA #REQUIRED
    address CDATA #REQUIRED
    city CDATA #REQUIRED
    state CDATA #REQUIRED
    postalCode CDATA #REQUIRED>
<!ELEMENT Part EMPTY>
<!ATTLIST Part
    description CDATA #REQUIRED
    quantity CDATA #REQUIRED
    price CDATA #REQUIRED>
```

The element `<OrderData>` is really acting as an envelope already. It is being used to hold a number of invoices, in much the same way that an envelope may contain many pieces of paper. It makes sense for us to add some routing information to that element.

Let's say we want to add a user name. This will be the user with which the processing system associates the invoices in the document. We'll also add a workflow state that indicates the way the user should handle the data:

```
<!ELEMENT OrderData (Invoice+)>
<!ATTLIST OrderData
  userName CDATA #IMPLIED
  status (PleaseCall | FYI | PleaseFulfill | Fulfilled) #IMPLIED>
<!ELEMENT Invoice (Customer, Part+)>
<!ATTLIST Invoice
  orderDate CDATA #REQUIRED
  shipDate CDATA #REQUIRED>
...
```

Note that our additional workflow attributes have been declared as IMPLIED. This allows us to still transmit the data in the document without specifying any particular behavior on the part of the processor. So here's a sample document using our new structure (ch18_ex03.xml):

```
<OrderData
  userName="Ned Flanders"
  status="FYI">
  <Invoice
    orderDate="10/17/2000"
    shipDate="10/20/2000">
    <Customer
      name="Homer J. Simpson"
      address="742 Evergreen Terrace"
      city="Springfield"
      state="KY"
      postalCode="12345" />
    <Part
      description="2 inch blue grommets"
      quantity="17"
      price="0.10" />
...
```

The processing system would first examine the envelope – the <OrderData> element – to determine whether any routing or workflow information was provided. It would then know that the contents were to be associated with Ned Flanders, and that they should be placed in an FYI workflow state. Then, the processor would open the envelope, start examining the children, and handle each one according to its internal rules for associating invoices with workflow queues and users.

This type of structure also makes it easier to create request-response pairs. We can associate a transaction key with our request, so that when the consumer responds to our request we can identify which request is being responded to. Let's see an example. We'll add an attribute to our structure:

```
<!ELEMENT OrderData (Invoice+)>
<!ATTLIST OrderData
  userName CDATA #IMPLIED
  status (PleaseCall | FYI | PleaseFulfill | Fulfilled) #IMPLIED
  transactionID CDATA #IMPLIED>
<!ELEMENT Invoice (Customer, Part+)>
<!ATTLIST Invoice
  orderDate CDATA #REQUIRED
...
```

Then, each time our code creates a document, it should create an identifier for that document, add it to the XML document, and log it. It then transmits the request to the consumer:

```
<OrderData
    userName="Ned Flanders"
    status="FYI"
    transactionID="101700A1B12">
    <Invoice
        orderDate="10/17/2000"
        shipDate="10/20/2000">
        <Customer
            name="Homer J. Simpson"
    . . .
```

The consumer processes the request for workflow storage, and then responds to the original system that the data has been received and all is well:

```
<!ELEMENT OrderDataResponse EMPTY>
<!ATTLIST OrderDataResponse
    status (Accepted | Errors | TooBusy) #REQUIRED
    stateDetail CDATA #IMPLIED
    transactionID CDATA #REQUIRED>
```

```
<OrderDataResponse
    status="Accepted"
    transactionID="101700A1B12" />
```

or that the request had some problem, and perhaps a description of the problem encountered:

```
<OrderDataResponse
    status="Errors"
    stateDetail="Unknown customer."
    transactionID="101700A1B12" />
```

The next stage in this argument involves SOAP – but that's such a big topic it deserves a section in itself.

SOAP

If you're familiar with SOAP (Simple Object Access Protocol), a lot of what we just described with the enveloping mechanism probably sounds familiar to you. A consortium of technology companies, including Microsoft and IBM, designed SOAP, intending it to address several different challenges:

❏ **Platform-independent component instantiation and remote procedure calls**. SOAP-aware servers can interpret SOAP messages as remote procedure calls where appropriate. This allows, for example, a program running on the Windows 2000 platform to request a process to be run on a legacy system, without requiring specialized code to be written on either side (as long as each has a SOAP-aware server running).

❏ **Providing meta-information about a document in the form of an envelope**. SOAP defines two namespaces – one for the SOAP envelope and another for the body of the document – that provide much of the same functionality we created earlier in the chapter.

❑ **Delivering XML documents over existing HTTP channels**. SOAP provides a well-defined way to transmit XML documents over HTTP. (This is important for firewalls, since most port 80 requests are open.) SOAP-aware servers can interpret the MIME-type and route the XML document being transferred accordingly.

Let's take a look at the way SOAP envelopes are created. We'll do this by building up an example bit by bit, looking at the meaning of each element and attribute as we go.

Before we start, we should mention a couple of peculiarities about SOAP messages. First, SOAP messages cannot contain document type definitions. They need to conform to the informal rules set out below, but these rules are not enforced by a document type definition. Second, SOAP messages may not contain processing instructions. If your documents require processing instructions or DTDs, you may not be able to use SOAP to pass them over HTTP.

If you want to know more about SOAP, see http://www.w3.org/TR/SOAP/ for the latest specification. There's also a detailed introduction to implementing SOAP solutions in Professional XML, ISBN 1-861003-11-0, from Wrox Press.

The SOAP Envelope

To transmit an XML document over HTTP using SOAP, the first thing we need to do is to encapsulate that document in a SOAP envelope structure. The elements and attributes that are used in this structure are in the namespace `http://schemas.xmlsoap.org/soap/envelope`.

In a SOAP message, the topmost element is always an `Envelope`. It then has as its children a `Header` element and a `Body` element. The `Header` element is optional, while the `Body` element is mandatory. All these elements fall in the SOAP envelope namespace.

So for our example, we have:

```
<SOAP-ENV:Envelope
   xmlns:SOAP-ENV="http://schemas.xmlsoap.org/soap/envelope/">
   <SOAP-ENV:Header>
   </SOAP-ENV:Header>
   <SOAP-ENV:Body>
   </SOAP-ENV:Body>
</SOAP-ENV:Envelope>
```

You can attach additional information to the SOAP envelope in the form of attributes or subelements, if you want. However, they must be namespace-qualified, and if they are subelements, they must appear after the Body subelement. Because SOAP allows you to put information about the anticipated usage of the XML payload in the Header element, additional elements or attributes are typically placed there rather than as part of the envelope proper.

The SOAP Header

We can optionally pass a `Header` element in our SOAP message as well. If we choose to do so, the element must be the first child element of the `Envelope` element. The `Header` element is used to pass additional processing information that the client might need to properly handle the message – in effect, giving us the ability to extend the SOAP protocol to suit our needs.

For example, we might specify that our SOAP messages will have a Header element that indicates whether the body of the message is a retransmission of a message already sent, or if it contains new information. We could add an element to our document called MessageStatus that indicates whether the message is a retransmission or not. When we choose to add elements to the Header element in a SOAP message, we need to assign a namespace for that element and make sure all the elements and attributes under it are attributed to that namespace.

So we might have a document that looks like this:

```
<SOAP-ENV:Envelope
    xmlns:SOAP-ENV="http://schemas.xmlsoap.org/soap/envelope/">
  <SOAP-ENV:Header>
    <invoice:MessageStatus
        xmlns:invoice="http://www.invoicesystem.com/soap">
      <invoice:status>Resend</invoice:status>
    </invoice:MessageStatus>
  </SOAP-ENV:Header>
  <SOAP-ENV:Body>
  </SOAP-ENV:Body>
</SOAP-ENV:Envelope>
```

Here, we're saying that there is a MessageStatus associated with the XML payload that's in the body of the SOAP message. If the consuming engine understands the MessageStatus element, it can take an appropriate action – for example, it might attempt to match the information up to information it has already stored in a relational database, rather than inserting a new record. However, the consumer doesn't have to understand how to handle the MessageStatus element – if it doesn't, it can process the message as if the MessageStatus header element were not present.

If we want to make comprehension of the MessageStatus element compulsory – in other words, make it so that a processor must return an error if it does not understand that element – we can do so by adding an attribute defined in SOAP called mustUnderstand. If this attribute is set to the value 1, then processors that do not know how to handle the MessageStatus element must return an error to the sender. We'll see how SOAP errors are returned a little later in the chapter.

Our modified SOAP message now looks like this:

```
<SOAP-ENV:Envelope
    xmlns:SOAP-ENV="http://schemas.xmlsoap.org/soap/envelope/">
  <SOAP-ENV:Header>
    <invoice:MessageStatus
        xmlns:invoice="http://www.invoicesystem.com/soap"
        SOAP-ENV:mustUnderstand="1">
      <invoice:status>Resend</invoice:status>
    </invoice:MessageStatus>
  </SOAP-ENV:Header>
  <SOAP-ENV:Body>
  </SOAP-ENV:Body>
</SOAP-ENV:Envelope>
```

The SOAP Body

Finally, the Body element in a SOAP message contains the actual message that is intended for the recipient. This message will typically be the payload you are attempting to transmit over HTTP. The Body element must appear in all SOAP messages, and must either immediately follow the Header element (if the Header element is present in the message), or be the first child element of the Envelope element (if no Header element exists). Elements and attributes that appear in the XML payload **may** be assigned to a namespace, but are not obliged to be.

Let's say that what we're retransmitting is a copy of an invoice. We might have a SOAP message that looks like this:

```
<SOAP-ENV:Envelope
    xmlns:SOAP-ENV="http://schemas.xmlsoap.org/soap/envelope/">
    <SOAP-ENV:Header>
      <invoice:MessageStatus
          xmlns:invoice="http://www.invoicesystem.com/soap"
          SOAP-ENV:mustUnderstand="1">
        <invoice:status>Resend</invoice:status>
      </invoice:MessageStatus>
    </SOAP-ENV:Header>
    <SOAP-ENV:Body>
      <Invoice
        customerIDREF="c1"
        orderDate="10/17/2000"
        shipDate="10/20/2000">
        <LineItem
          partIDREF="p1"
          quantity="17"
          price="0.15" />
        <LineItem
          partIDREF="p2"
          quantity="13"
          price="0.25" />
      </Invoice>
      <Customer
        CustomerID="c1"
        name="Homer J. Simpson"
        address="742 Evergreen Terrace"
        city="Springfield"
        state="KY"
        postalCode="12345" />
      <Part
        PartID="p1"
        name="grommets"
        size="3 in."
        color="blue" />
      <Part
        PartID="p2"
        name="sprockets"
        size="2 in."
        color="red" />
    </SOAP-ENV:Body>
  </SOAP-ENV:Envelope>
```

A SOAP-aware processor would read this message and determine whether it could correctly process all the Header elements with the mustUnderstand attribute set to true. If it could, it would then "rip open the envelope", extract the XML payload, and act on it according to any instructions provided in the Header elements.

As we mentioned earlier, a SOAP processor must return an error to the caller if a SOAP message cannot be correctly processed. This is done by returning a Fault element in the body of the response – let's see how this would be done.

The SOAP Fault Element

If a SOAP processor encounters difficulty in handling a SOAP message, it must return a `Fault` element as part of its response. The `Fault` element (which is in the SOAP envelope namespace) must appear as a child element of the `Body` element (but it does not have to appear first, or be the only child element of the `Body` element). This allows us to return an error, but still respond to the sent message – as we'll see in a few pages. The `Fault` element contains some subelements that are used to describe the problem encountered by the SOAP-aware processor. Let's see how they work.

The faultcode Element

The `faultcode` element is used to indicate the type of error that occurred when attempting to parse the SOAP message. Its value is intended to be algorithmically processed, and as such takes the form:

```
general_fault.more_specific_fault.more_specific_fault
```

with each further entry in the list, separated by periods, providing more specific information about the type of error that occurred. The values should be (but do not have to be) qualified by the namespace defined for the SOAP envelope. In the SOAP 1.0 Specification, the following values for `faultcode` are defined:

Name	Meaning
`VersionMismatch`	The processing party found an invalid namespace for the SOAP `Envelope` element.
`MustUnderstand`	An immediate child element of the SOAP `Header` element that was either not understood or not obeyed by the processing party contained a SOAP `mustUnderstand` attribute with a value of 1.
`Client`	The message was incorrectly formed or did not contain the appropriate information in order to succeed. For example, the message could lack the proper authentication or payment information. This is generally an indication that the message should not be resent without change.
`Server`	The message could not be processed for reasons not directly attributable to the contents of the message itself, but rather to the processing of the message. For example, processing could include communicating with an upstream processor, which didn't respond. The message may succeed at a later point in time..

So, for example, if the processor ran out of memory, it would be acceptable to pass back a `faultcode` containing the value `Server`:

```
<SOAP-ENV:Fault>
  <SOAP-ENV:faultcode>SOAP-ENV:Server</SOAP-ENV:faultcode>
</SOAP-ENV:Fault>
```

However, it might be more useful for the original sender of the SOAP message to know why there was a server error. In that case, a qualified `faultcode` could be passed:

```
<SOAP-ENV:Fault>
  <SOAP-ENV:faultcode>SOAP-ENV:Server.OutOfMemory</SOAP-ENV:faultcode>
</SOAP-ENV:Fault>
```

The faultstring Element

The `faultstring` subelement is intended to provide a human-readable description of the error that occurred. It must be present in the `Fault` element, and should provide some sort of message about what happened. For our out-of-memory example, then, our fault message might look something like this:

```
<SOAP-ENV:Fault>
  <SOAP-ENV:faultcode>SOAP-ENV:Server.OutOfMemory</SOAP-ENV:faultcode>
  <SOAP-ENV:faultstring>Out of memory.</SOAP-ENV:faultstring>
</SOAP-ENV:Fault>
```

The detail Element

The `detail` subelement is used to describe specific errors related to the processing of the XML payload itself (as opposed to the processing of the SOAP message, server errors, or errors related to the SOAP headers). If the XML payload was incomplete, in an unexpected format, or violated business logic applied to it by the system receiving the SOAP message, these problems would be reported in the `detail` subelement.

The `detail` subelement is not required in a `Fault` element; it should only be present if there was some problem processing the body of the message. Each of the child elements of the `detail` subelement should be qualified with a namespace.

Let's say that one of the business rules applied by the SOAP message consumer is that when it receives an invoice with a status of `Resend`, it must match the resent data to the data in its database. If it does not, it must report this to the SOAP message sender in its fault response. The message might look like this:

```
<SOAP-ENV:Fault>
  <SOAP-ENV:faultcode>SOAP-ENV:Client.BusinessRule.NotFound
  </SOAP-ENV:faultcode>
  <SOAP-ENV:faultstring>The resent record was not found.
  </SOAP-ENV:faultstring>
  <SOAP-ENV:detail>
    <error:BusinessRule xmlns:error="http://www.invoicesystem.com/soap">
      <BusinessRule>ResendNotMatched</BusinessRule>
      <ErrorCode>1007</ErrorCode>
    </error:BusinessRule>
  </SOAP-ENV:detail>
</SOAP-ENV:Fault>
```

Transmission Over HTTP

One of the problems we were facing with our classic data transmission strategies was that of firewalls and restricted network access. Because HTTP is a widely accepted protocol, and because most firewalls will allow traffic to port 80 (and to port 443 for HTTPS access), it is useful to be able to transmit XML over HTTP.

As we've already seen, the SOAP protocol defines a way to transmit XML messages over HTTP, and there are other mechanisms that exist (such as XML-RPC) that are also designed to piggyback on port 80. While there's some dissent among the theorists as to how good a solution this is – one doesn't have to look too hard to find a white paper on the dilution of the http:// URL prefix and why using HTTP for SOAP is a bad idea – HTTP (or HTTPS) nevertheless provides a perfectly acceptable transport mechanism for XML documents.

When transmitting SOAP over HTTP, a request-response mechanism is used. Much as an HTML web page is requested and then sent in response to the HTTP request, a SOAP message will be sent in response to an HTTP SOAP request. Let's see how these requests and responses look.

HTTP SOAP Request

When transmitting a SOAP packet over HTTP, the normal semantics of HTTP should be followed – that is, the HTTP headers appear, followed by a double carriage return, followed by the body of the HTTP request (which in our case will be the SOAP message itself).

There is an additional header field defined for SOAP requests that must be used, called SOAPAction. The value of this header field must be a URI, but the SOAP specification doesn't define what that URI has to mean. Typically, it should represent the procedure or process run by the server on receipt of the SOAP message. If the SOAPAction field takes a blank string ("") as a value, then the intent of the SOAP message is assumed to be provided in the standard HTTP request URI. If there is no value provided, then the sender is not indicating any intent for the message.

Here are some examples of SOAPAction headers:

```
SOAPAction: "http://www.invoiceserver.com/soap/handler.exe#Invoice"
SOAPAction: ""
SOAPAction:
```

Other HTTP headers should appear in the request as normal. We'll see an example of an HTTP SOAP request a little later. First, let's look at the way the HTTP SOAP response is transmitted.

HTTP SOAP Response

SOAP responses over HTTP use the same status codes as you would expect to see when transmitting HTML over HTTP. For example, a status code of 2xx means that the request was handled successfully. If an error is encountered during the processing of the SOAP message itself, the response must contain the status code 500 (internal server error) and report the exact problem encountered in the body of the SOAP response.

An HTTP Transmission Example

Let's revisit our previous example. For our sample transaction, we are resending an invoice that has already been submitted to the receiving party. We will assume that the receiving system will decide how to process the request based on the HTTP request URL. To issue the HTTP request for this transmission, we preface the body of the request with the appropriate HTTP headers, including the SOAPAction header. Note that we specify the content type as text/xml – this should always be the case for SOAP messages:

```
POST /soap/Handler HTTP/1.1
Content-Type: text/xml; charset="utf-8"
Content-Length: nnnn
SOAPAction: ""

<SOAP-ENV:Envelope
    xmlns:SOAP-ENV="http://schemas.xmlsoap.org/soap/envelope/">
    <SOAP-ENV:Header>
      <invoice:MessageStatus
          xmlns:invoice="http://www.invoicesystem.com/soap"
          SOAP-ENV:mustUnderstand="1">
        <invoice:status>Resend</invoice:status>
      </invoice:MessageStatus>
      ...
```

On receipt of this HTTP POST, a SOAP-aware server would forward the packet to the Handler resource for processing. If all is well and the invoice is found on the system, the Handler resource would respond to the client with a HTTP SOAP response message that looks something like this:

```
HTTP/1.1 200 OK
Content-Type: text/xml; charset="utf-8"
Content-Length: nnnn

<SOAP-ENV:Envelope
   <SOAP-ENV:Body />
</SOAP-ENV:Envelope>
```

Note that we have transmitted an empty body element. Since the request doesn't require any information in return (other than confirmation that the request was handled properly), we don't need to pass anything in the body of the SOAP response message.

If the Handler resource doesn't know how to handle the MessageStatus header element, it must respond to the client with a SOAP message containing a Fault element describing the problem:

```
HTTP/1.1 500 Internal Server Error
Content-Type: text/xml; charset="utf-8"
Content-Length: nnnn

<SOAP-ENV:Envelope
  xmlns:SOAP-ENV="http://schemas.xmlsoap.org/soap/envelope/">
   <SOAP-ENV:Body>
      <SOAP-ENV:Fault>
         <faultcode>SOAP-ENV:MustUnderstand</faultcode>
         <faultstring>MessageStatus header not recognized</faultstring>
      </SOAP-ENV:Fault>
   </SOAP-ENV:Body>
</SOAP-ENV:Envelope>
```

If the Handler resource comprehends the MessageStatus header element, but for some reason can't process the body of the message (as in our previous example where the invoice couldn't be matched), it must respond accordingly:

```
HTTP/1.1 500 Internal Server Error
Content-Type: text/xml; charset="utf-8"
Content-Length: nnnn

<SOAP-ENV:Envelope
  xmlns:SOAP-ENV="http://schemas.xmlsoap.org/soap/envelope/">
   <SOAP-ENV:Body>
     <SOAP-ENV:Fault>
       <SOAP-ENV:faultcode>
         SOAP-ENV:Client.BusinessRule.NotFound
       </SOAP-ENV:faultcode>
       <SOAP-ENV:faultstring>
         The resent record was not found.
```

```
          </SOAP-ENV:faultstring>
          <SOAP-ENV:detail>
            <error:BusinessRule xmlns:error="http://www.invoicesystem.com/soap">
              <BusinessRule>ResendNotMatched</BusinessRule>
              <ErrorCode>1007</ErrorCode>
            </error:BusinessRule>
          </SOAP-ENV:detail>
        </SOAP-ENV:Fault>
      </SOAP-ENV:Body>
    </SOAP-ENV:Envelope>
```

Biztalk

Microsoft is developing a SOAP-aware server called Biztalk. This server will be able to process SOAP-based HTTP requests and respond accordingly. A full discussion of Biztalk is outside the scope of this chapter – it's a fairly deep product, with enterprise-class support for schemas, built-in EDI support, a graphical XSLT generator, and much more. If you want to learn more about Biztalk, you can do so at http://www.microsoft.com/biztalk.

Compressing XML

One of the major concerns with XML is the large files that often result when data is represented in an XML document. A system that is attempting to transmit or receive a large number of documents at once, may have to be concerned about the bandwidth consumption of those documents. However, since XML documents are text (and typically repetitive text at that), one approach we can take to minimize the bandwidth consumption when our documents are transmitted is to compress them.

There are any number of third-party compression algorithms that handle the compression of XML documents very well. By compressing the XML document before transmitting it, and uncompressing it upon receipt, bandwidth consumption can often be slashed by two-thirds or more.

The down side is that both the producer and the consumer will need to be able to correctly process the documents, so an XML document transmitted this way will only be receivable by systems that have the decompression software in place. As XML becomes more frequently used for data transmission, standard libraries are likely to become available that handle this compression and decompression behind the scenes.

Summary

In this chapter, we've seen how data transmission may be streamlined by using XML. We've seen some of the shortcomings of classic data transmission strategies, and taken a look at how XML helps us avoid some of the common pitfalls there. Namely, this is because XML documents are:

- ❑ Self-documenting
- ❑ Flexible
- ❑ Normalized
- ❑ Able to utilize off-the-shelf XML tools
- ❑ Able to cope with routing and requesting

Finally, we took a quick look at some of the ways we can augment our XML documents with enveloping information to create a more robust document handling and data processing environment. Specifically, we discussed SOAP – the Simple Object Access Protocol. We saw how SOAP messages are structured, and introduced the concept of the SOAP request-response mechanism used for transmission over HTTP.

In summary, moving your data transmission to XML will help ensure the longevity, maintainability, and adaptability of your systems.

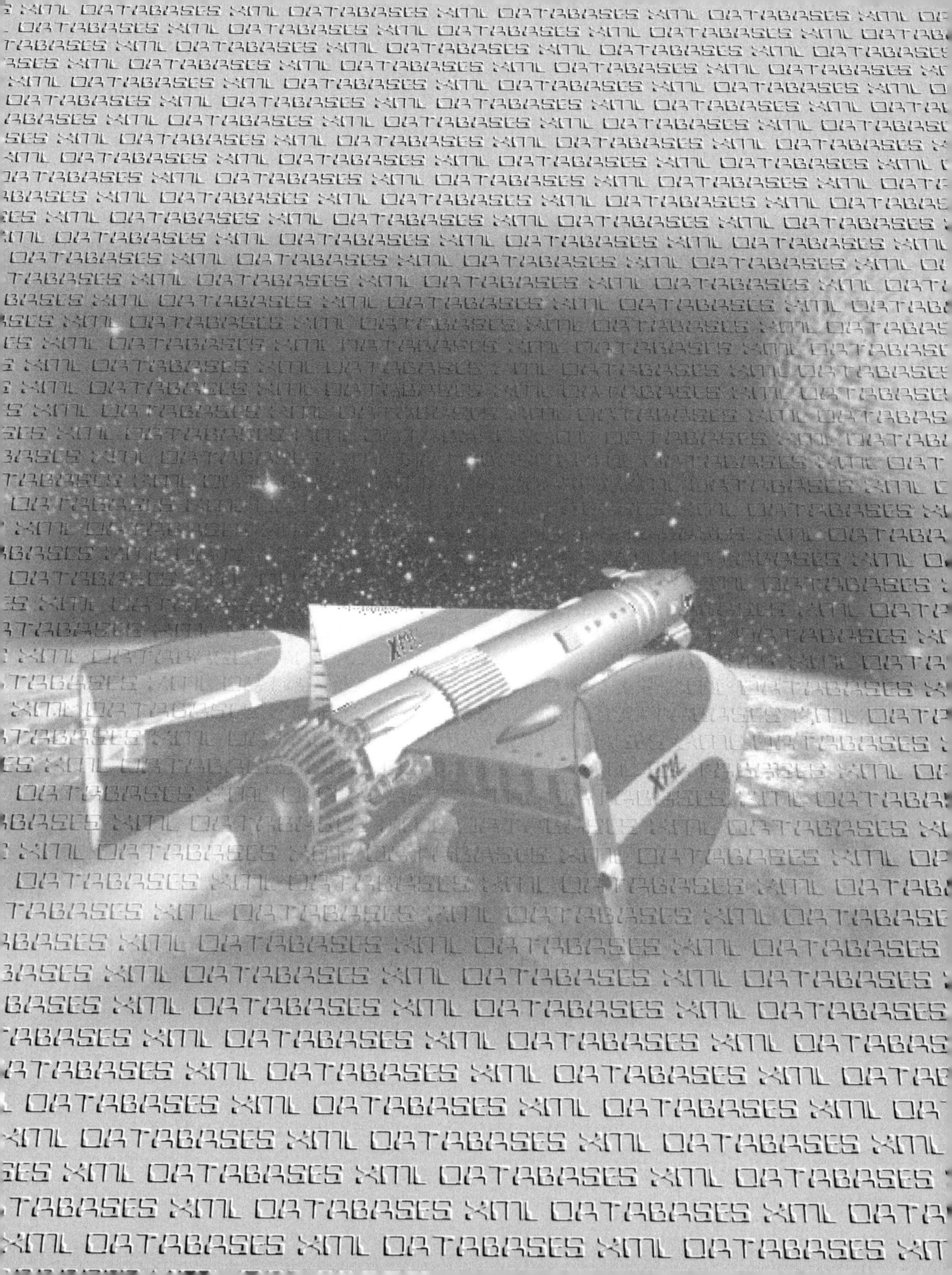
XML DATABASES XML DATABASES XML DATABASES
XML
XML

19

Marshalling and Presentation

In this chapter, we'll look at some ways XML can be used to streamline the data marshalling and presentation process. The chapter is divided into three sections. In the first, we'll see how XML can be used to marshal a more useful form of data from our relational databases; in the second, we'll see how information gathered over the Web can be transformed to XML; and in the last section, we'll see how XML streamlines our presentation pipeline and makes it easy to support multiple platforms, including handheld devices.

The examples in this chapter are all written in VBScript, and are intended for use with SQL Server 7.0+ databases. In addition, if you want to run the examples you should have installed Microsoft's MSXML3 parser, available from Microsoft at http://msdn.microsoft.com/xml/general/xmlparser.asp.

If you are not running in this environment, you can still adopt the strategies outlined to suit your programming language and database platform.

Marshalling

When retrieving data from a relational database in a tiered, enterprise-level solution, the first thing that needs to happen is **marshalling** – the data needs to be extracted from the relational database and provided to the business logic or presentation tier, perhaps by a COM component, in a usable format. In this section, we'll take a look at the likely long-term strategy for extracting data in XML, and then see how we can perform this extraction by hand in the short term.

XML is a great medium for marshalling because it allows structured information to be exposed from the database without requiring custom, inflexible structures to be built to support that information. Using XML as the marshalling medium will make your solution more adaptable as your data requirements change, because it is an open standard available on many different platforms. Let's take a look at some quick examples of other standard marshalling techniques and see why XML is the best choice.

Custom Structures

The traditional way to marshal data from the database layer is via custom structures. Let's say, for example, that you wanted to convey information from the following tables in your marshalled data. The following code can be accessed in the file `tables.sql`:

```sql
CREATE TABLE Customer (
    CustomerKey integer PRIMARY KEY IDENTITY,
    customerName varchar(30),
    customerAddress varchar(30),
    customerCity varchar(30),
    customerState char(2),
    customerPostalCode varchar(10))

CREATE TABLE Invoice (
    InvoiceKey integer PRIMARY KEY IDENTITY,
    CustomerKey integer
        CONSTRAINT fk_Customer FOREIGN KEY (CustomerKey)
            REFERENCES Customer (CustomerKey),
    orderDate datetime,
    shipDate datetime)

CREATE TABLE Part (
    PartKey integer PRIMARY KEY IDENTITY,
    partName varchar(20),
    partColor varchar(10),
    partSize varchar(10))

CREATE TABLE LineItem (
    LineItemKey integer PRIMARY KEY IDENTITY,
    InvoiceKey integer
        CONSTRAINT fk_Invoice FOREIGN KEY (InvoiceKey)
            REFERENCES Invoice (InvoiceKey),
    PartKey integer
        CONSTRAINT fk_Part FOREIGN KEY (PartKey)
            REFERENCES Part (PartKey),
    quantity integer,
    price float)
```

This script produces the following table structure:

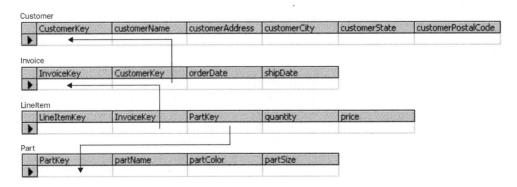

If you wanted to work in a more complicated language, you might define a structure that looks like this (the example below is written in C, and is for illustrative purposes only):

```c
struct partData
{
   struct
   {
      char partName[20];
      char partColor[30];
      char partSize[30];
   } part;
   int quantity;
   float price;
}
struct invoiceData
{
   char orderDate[10];
   char shipDate[10];
   struct
   {
      char customerName[30];
      char customerAddress[30];
      char customerCity[30];
      char customerState[2];
      char customerPostalCode[10];
   } customer;
   struct partData part[10];
}
```

Then, if you populate and marshal this structure back to a caller, the caller has all the information about an invoice in a structured form. It may reference that information using the structure nomenclature for that language. However, what happens if we add a column, say, shipMethod, to the Invoice table? If we want that information to be available through marshalling, now we need to modify our source code to marshal the data and modify any business or presentation layer code that serves to create this structure.

Recordsets

Another common way to marshal data from a database is in the form of recordsets. Recordsets have the benefit of being relatively dynamic, and they include metadata that describes the information that they contain. However, the major disadvantage to recordsets is that they are flattened (unless you are using hierarchical recordsets, which are difficult to use and don't perform well), so data returned by them often contains repeating information. For example, if our query returned one invoice with five line items, the five records returned would each contain the invoice information. This would require software that was trying to use the data in a structured way (to create a report, for example) to examine the keys on each row to determine where the structures began and ended. Let's look at a simplistic example. Say we wanted to return the ship dates for all invoices with a specific order date, and the name, size, color, and quantity from each of the line items ordered. We would write a SELECT statement that looked like this:

```sql
SELECT Invoice.InvoiceKey, shipDate, quantity, partName, partColor, partSize
   FROM Invoice, LineItem, Part
WHERE Invoice.orderDate = "10/21/2000"
   AND LineItem.InvoiceKey = Invoice.InvoiceKey
   AND LineItem.PartKey = Part.PartKey
ORDER BY Invoice.InvoiceKey
```

This query might return a recordset that looks something like this:

InvoiceKey	shipDate	quantity	partName	partColor	partSize
17	10/24/2000	17	grommets	blue	2 inch
17	10/24/2000	13	sprockets	red	1 inch
18	10/25/2000	9	widgets	silver	0.5 inch
18	10/25/2000	11	sprockets	blue	1.5 inch
18	10/25/2000	5	brackets	orange	3 inch

When we try to do something with the recordset in our business layer or presentation layer (such as create an HTML page to return to a browser), our code needs to iterate through the records, watching the `InvoiceKey` for a change – this will indicate to the code that a new invoice page needs to be created. Each piece of code in the business layer or presentation layer will need to handle the data this way. If we could marshal the data in a hierarchical form immediately, this extra code could be avoided.

XML

If we marshal data out of the database in XML, we have the best of both worlds. We have good structural information available without extra code, while we can make modifications to the marshalling code without necessarily breaking the consumer code on the front end.

We can also leverage the constantly growing toolset for the manipulation and processing of XML documents if we marshal our data in XML. XSLT (as we'll see) is especially suited to the transformation of marshalled XML into some client-capable format (such as HTML or WML).

Now that we know that we want to marshal our data into an XML format, let's see how we can accomplish this with the current technology available.

The Long-Term Solution: Built-In Methods

Both SQL Server and Oracle have introduced mechanisms for the automatic marshalling of XML data from the respective relational databases in their latest releases. However, these technologies are still in the development stages, and don't provide the ability to model sophisticated relationships like pointing relationships. Additionally, you don't have a lot of control over the format of the XML created – SQL Server and Oracle simply create an XML string based on the structure of the joined result set created. While these technologies will almost certainly be the way we marshal XML from our relational databases in the long term, for now we will need to take a different approach.

The Manual Approach

To marshal our data into an XML document, there are a few approaches we could take. If we are using ADO, we can return the data as an ADO XML recordset and then use XSLT to transform that data into the target XML. We could also generate a set of SAX events and send them to a SAX handler to create the document in a serial way. However, the most flexible approach (for smaller files – remember that the DOM has a large memory footprint) is to use the DOM to build our XML document based on data returned from the database. Let's take a look at some code we can use to accomplish this.

Example

Let's say we want to create an XML document that includes all the invoices for a particular month. We've decided that we should use the following structure, `ch19_ex1.dtd` to return the data:

```
<!ELEMENT OrderData (Invoice+, Customer+, Part+)>
<!ELEMENT Invoice (LineItem+)>
<!ATTLIST Invoice
   CustomerID IDREF #REQUIRED
   orderDate CDATA #REQUIRED
   shipDate CDATA #REQUIRED>
<!ELEMENT Customer EMPTY>
<!ATTLIST Customer
   CustomerID ID #REQUIRED
   customerName CDATA #REQUIRED
   customerAddress CDATA #REQUIRED
   customerCity CDATA #REQUIRED
   customerState CDATA #REQUIRED
   customerPostalCode CDATA #REQUIRED>
<!ELEMENT LineItem EMPTY>
<!ATTLIST LineItem
   PartID IDREF #REQUIRED
   quantity CDATA #REQUIRED
   price CDATA #REQUIRED>
<!ELEMENT Part EMPTY>
<!ATTLIST Part
   PartID ID #REQUIRED
   partName CDATA #REQUIRED
   partSize CDATA #REQUIRED
   partColor CDATA #REQUIRED>
```

An example of a document using this structure would look like this:

```
<?xml version='1.0'?>
<!DOCTYPE OrderData SYSTEM 'OrderData.dtd'>
<OrderData>
   <Invoice
       orderDate="10/22/00"
       shipDate="10/25/00"
       customerIDREF="CUST1">
       <LineItem
          PartIDREF="PART1"
          quantity="12"
          price="0.15"/>
       <LineItem
          PartIDREF="PART2"
          quantity="17"
          price="0.2"/>
       <LineItem
          PartIDREF="PART4"
          quantity="5"
          price="0.3"/>
   </Invoice>
   <Invoice
       orderDate="10/22/00"
       shipDate="10/22/00"
       customerIDREF="CUST2">
       <LineItem
          PartIDREF="PART2"
          quantity="11"
```

```
                     price="0.15"/>
           <LineItem
             PartIDREF="PART3"
             quantity="3"
             price="0.2"/>
       </Invoice>
       <Invoice
           orderDate="10/25/00"
           shipDate="10/28/00"
           customerIDREF="CUST1">
           <LineItem
               PartIDREF="PART3"
               quantity="11"
               price="0.25"/>
       </Invoice>
       <Customer
           CustomerID="CUST1"
           customerName="Homer J. Simpson"
           customerAddress="742 Evergreen Terrace"
           customerCity="Springfield"
           customerState="KY"
           customerPostalCode="12345"/>
       <Customer
           CustomerID="CUST2"
           customerName="Kevin B. Williams"
           customerAddress="744 Evergreen Terrace"
           customerCity="Springfield"
           customerState="KY"
           customerPostalCode="12345"/>
       <Part
           PartID="PART1"
           partName="grommets"
           partSize="2 inch"
           partColor="blue"/>
       <Part
           PartID="PART2"
           partName="widgets"
           partSize="3 inch"
           partColor="silver"/>
       <Part
           PartID="PART3"
           partName="brackets"
           partSize="1.5 inch"
           partColor="orange"/>
       <Part
           PartID="PART4"
           partName="sprockets"
           partSize="4 inch"
           partColor="green"/>
   </OrderData>
```

To marshal the data out of the database and into this document structure, we need to extract the information for invoices, parts, customers, and line items. Let's see how we would build code to accomplish this task.

The first thing we can note is that invoices, customers, and parts are only related by ID-IDREF relationships in our XML document – they do not participate in any containment relationships. A diagram of the structure would look like this:

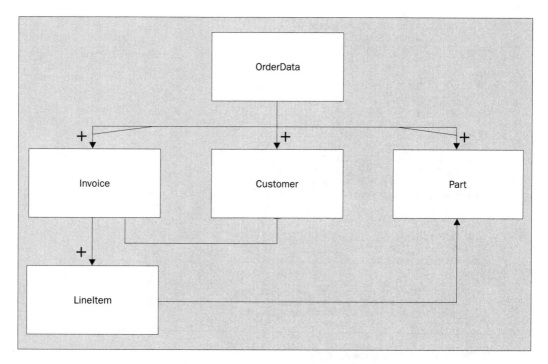

The other important thing to note about our data tables is that each table has an integer, unique across all records in that table that identifies that record. We can take advantage of this to build our ID-IDREF relationships without needing to join the tables when we extract the data from our database.

First, we'll build some stored procedures to return our data. We'll need three stored procedures – one for the invoice and line item data, one for the customer data, and one for the part data. Each one will only return the data that is relevant to a particular month's invoices – for example, the part stored procedure should only return those parts that appeared on invoices during that particular month. The following procedures are saved as GetInvoicesForDateRange.sql, GetPartsForDateRange.sql, and GetCustomersForDateRange.sql respectively:

```
CREATE PROC GetInvoicesForDateRange (
    @startDate AS DATETIME,
    @endDate AS DATETIME)
AS
BEGIN
    SELECT I.InvoiceKey AS InvoiceKey,
        I.orderDate AS orderDate,
        I.shipDate AS shipDate,
        I.CustomerKey AS customerKey,
        LI.PartKey AS partKey,
        LI.quantity AS quantity,
        LI.price AS price
    FROM Invoice I, LineItem LI
    WHERE I.orderDate >= @startDate
        AND I.orderDate < DATEADD(d, 1, @endDate)
        AND I.InvoiceKey = LI.InvoiceKey
    ORDER BY I.InvoiceKey
END
```

```
CREATE PROC GetPartsForDateRange (
    @startDate AS DATETIME,
    @endDate AS DATETIME)
AS
BEGIN
    SELECT DISTINCT P.PartKey AS PartKey,
        P.partColor AS partColor,
        P.partSize AS partSize,
        P.partName AS partName
    FROM Invoice I, LineItem LI, Part P
    WHERE I.orderDate >= @startDate
        AND I.orderDate < DATEADD(d, 1, @endDate)
        AND I.InvoiceKey = LI.InvoiceKey
        AND LI.PartKey = P.PartKey
    ORDER BY partName, partSize, partColor
END
```

```
CREATE PROC GetCustomersForDateRange (
    @startDate AS DATETIME,
    @endDate AS DATETIME)
AS
BEGIN
    SELECT DISTINCT C.CustomerKey AS CustomerKey,
        C.customerName AS customerName,
        C.customerAddress AS customerAddress,
        C.customerCity AS customerCity,
        C.customerState AS customerState,
        C.customerPostalCode AS customerPostalCode
    FROM Invoice I, Customer C
    WHERE I.orderDate >= @startDate
        AND I.orderDate < DATEADD(d, 1, @endDate)
        AND I.CustomerKey = C.CustomerKey
    ORDER BY customerName
END
```

Each of these stored procedures will return data for one of the three main branches of our XML document tree. By using a consistent ID-IDREF generation technique, we can link up the pointing relationships without requiring an explicit JOIN in our SQL – so instead of pulling back a massive four-table-join result set, we can simply pull back the contents of each of the four tables and rely on the generated IDs to link the tables together.

For the purposes of this sample, we'll populate our database this way:

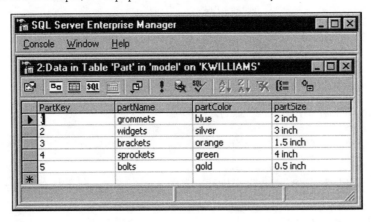

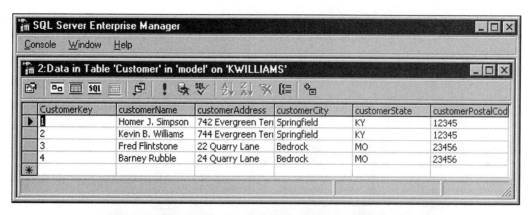

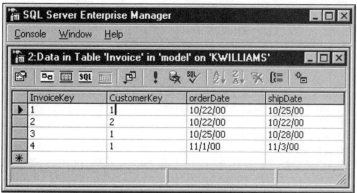

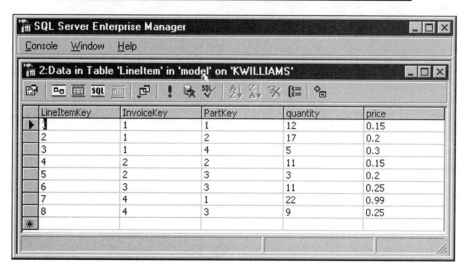

Here's the VBScript that generates the XML document (ch19_ex1.vbs) – note that you may need to change the ADO connection string depending on the name of the database where you created the tables:

```
Dim Conn, rs
Dim Doc, elOrderData, elInvoice, elLineItem, elCustomer, elPart
Dim sSQL
Dim sInvoiceKey

Set Conn = CreateObject("ADODB.Connection")
Set rs = CreateObject("ADODB.Recordset")
Set Doc = CreateObject("Microsoft.XMLDOM")
Set elOrderData = Doc.createElement("OrderData")
Doc.appendChild elOrderData

Conn.Open "Driver={SQL Server};Server=SQL1;Uid=sa;Pwd=;Database=myXML"
sSQL = "GetInvoicesForDateRange '10/1/2000', '10/31/2000'"
rs.Open sSQL, Conn

sInvoiceKey = ""
While Not rs.EOF
    If rs("InvoiceKey") <> sInvoiceKey Then
        ' we need to add this invoice element
        Set elInvoice = Doc.createElement("Invoice")
        elInvoice.setAttribute "orderDate", FormatDateTime(rs("orderDate"), 2)
        elInvoice.setAttribute "shipDate", FormatDateTime(rs("shipDate"), 2)
        elInvoice.setAttribute "CustomerIDREF", "CUST" & rs("customerKey")
        elOrderData.appendChild elInvoice
        sInvoiceKey = rs("InvoiceKey")
    End If
    Set elLineItem = Doc.createElement("LineItem")
    elLineItem.setAttribute "PartIDREF", "PART" & rs("partKey")
    elLineItem.setAttribute "quantity", rs("quantity")
    elLineItem.setAttribute "price", rs("price")
    elInvoice.appendChild elLineItem
    rs.MoveNext
Wend
Set elInvoice = Nothing
Set elLineItem = Nothing
rs.Close

sSQL = "GetCustomersForDateRange '10/1/2000', '10/31/2000'"
rs.Open sSQL, Conn
While Not rs.EOF
    Set elCustomer = Doc.createElement("Customer")
    elCustomer.setAttribute "CustomerID", "CUST" & rs("CustomerKey")
    elCustomer.setAttribute "customerName", rs("customerName")
    elCustomer.setAttribute "customerAddress", rs("customerAddress")
    elCustomer.setAttribute "customerCity", rs("customerCity")
    elCustomer.setAttribute "customerState", rs("customerState")
    elCustomer.setAttribute "customerPostalCode", rs("customerPostalCode")
    elOrderData.appendChild elCustomer
    rs.MoveNext
Wend
Set elCustomer = Nothing
rs.Close
```

```
    sSQL = "GetPartsForDateRange '10/1/2000', '10/31/2000'"
    rs.Open sSQL, Conn
    While Not rs.EOF
        Set elPart = Doc.createElement("Part")
        elPart.setAttribute "PartID", "PART" & rs("PartKey")
        elPart.setAttribute "partName", rs("partName")
        elPart.setAttribute "partSize", rs("partSize")
        elPart.setAttribute "partColor", rs("partColor")
        elOrderData.appendChild elPart
        rs.MoveNext
    Wend
    Set elPart = Nothing
    rs.Close

    Conn.Close

    WScript.Echo "<?xml version='1.0'?>"
    WScript.Echo "<!DOCTYPE OrderData SYSTEM 'ch19_ex1.dtd'>"
    WScript.Echo Doc.xml
    Set Doc = Nothing
    Set rs = Nothing
    Set Conn = Nothing
```

Let's break the code down and see how it works.

```
    Dim Conn, rs
    Dim Doc, elOrderData, elInvoice, elLineItem, elCustomer, elPart
    Dim sSQL
    Dim sInvoiceKey

    Set Conn = CreateObject("ADODB.Connection")
    Set rs = CreateObject("ADODB.Recordset")
    Set Doc = CreateObject("Microsoft.XMLDOM")
```

First, we set up our variable and create the objects we'll need – ADO `Connection` and `Recordset` objects, and a Microsoft DOM object.

```
    Set elOrderData = Doc.createElement("OrderData")
    Doc.appendChild elOrderData
```

Next, we create the `OrderData` root element for our new document and append it to the document child list.

```
    Conn.Open "Chapter19", "sa", ""
    sSQL = "GetInvoicesForDateRange '10/1/2000', '10/31/2000'"
    rs.Open sSQL, Conn
```

As we mentioned before, we're going to return three sets of data from the database. The first will be the `Invoice` and `LineItem` data. We call our stored procedure to obtain all the invoices for October.

```
    sInvoiceKey = ""
```

Because we're retrieving both invoices and line items in one call, we'll watch `InvoiceKey` as we move through the records. Anytime `InvoiceKey` changes, we'll know we've transitioned to a new invoice and we need to create a new `Invoice` element.

```
While Not rs.EOF
    If rs("InvoiceKey") <> sInvoiceKey Then
        ' we need to add this invoice element
        Set elInvoice = Doc.createElement("Invoice")
        elInvoice.setAttribute "orderDate", FormatDateTime(rs("orderDate"), 2)
        elInvoice.setAttribute "shipDate", FormatDateTime(rs("shipDate"), 2)
        elInvoice.setAttribute "CustomerIDREF", "CUST" & rs("customerKey")
        elOrderData.appendChild elInvoice
        sInvoiceKey = rs("InvoiceKey")
```

Here, we create the `Invoice` element and add it to the `OrderData` element we created earlier. Note that we create the `customerIDREF` attribute by prefixing the database key (which we know to be a unique integer across the entire table) with a string uniquely identifying the element – in this case, the letters `CUST`. Later, when we follow the same rule to generate the ID for the customer record, the ID-IDREF relationship will automatically be created.

```
    End If
    Set elLineItem = Doc.createElement("LineItem")
    elLineItem.setAttribute "PartIDREF", "PART" & rs("partKey")
    elLineItem.setAttribute "quantity", rs("quantity")
    elLineItem.setAttribute "price", rs("price")
    elInvoice.appendChild elLineItem
```

For every record in our ADO recordset, we'll create a `LineItem` element under whatever `Invoice` element we currently happen to be in. Note that we use the same technique to generate the `PartIDREF` attribute as we did for the `CustomerIDREF` attribute earlier in the code.

```
    rs.MoveNext
Wend
Set elInvoice = Nothing
Set elLineItem = Nothing
rs.Close

sSQL = "GetCustomersForDateRange '10/1/2000', '10/31/2000'"
rs.Open sSQL, Conn
```

Now, we iterate through all the customers that had invoices for the specified date range, after closing the previous loop and freeing the objects.

```
While Not rs.EOF
    Set elCustomer = Doc.createElement("Customer")
    elCustomer.setAttribute "CustomerID", "CUST" & rs("CustomerKey")
    elCustomer.setAttribute "customerName", rs("customerName")
    elCustomer.setAttribute "customerAddress", rs("customerAddress")
    elCustomer.setAttribute "customerCity", rs("customerCity")
    elCustomer.setAttribute "customerState", rs("customerState")
    elCustomer.setAttribute "customerPostalCode", rs("customerPostalCode")
    elOrderData.appendChild elCustomer
```

For each record in the recordset, we create a Customer element as a child of the orderData element. Again, because we are using the same rule to generate the CustomerID attribute as we did to generate the CustomerIDREF attribute earlier, the pointing relationship is created.

```
        rs.MoveNext
    Wend
    Set elCustomer = Nothing
    rs.Close

    sSQL = "GetPartsForDateRange '10/1/2000', '10/31/2000'"
    rs.Open sSQL, Conn
```

Finally, we go through all the parts that appeared on invoices in the specified date range.

```
    While Not rs.EOF
        Set elPart = Doc.createElement("Part")
        elPart.setAttribute "PartID", "PART" & rs("PartKey")
        elPart.setAttribute "partName", rs("partName")
        elPart.setAttribute "partSize", rs("partSize")
        elPart.setAttribute "partColor", rs("partColor")
        elOrderData.appendChild elPart
```

Again, we create a Part for each record in the recordset as a child of the orderData element.

```
        rs.MoveNext
    Wend
    Set elPart = Nothing
    rs.Close

    Conn.Close
```

Finally, we insert the XML header and the document type header to the Windows Scripting Host output, followed by the XML we have created. Note that, since the DOM level 1 does not provide a way to associate a particular document type with a document created from scratch, this is the way to associate the document with a particular DTD.

```
    WScript.Echo "<?xml version='1.0'?>"
    WScript.Echo "<!DOCTYPE OrderData SYSTEM 'OrderData.dtd'>"
    WScript.Echo Doc.xml
    Set Doc = Nothing
    Set rs = Nothing
    Set Conn = Nothing
```

For our sample data, this script (when run through the Windows Scripting Host) produces the following output (whitespace added for readability):

```
<?xml version='1.0'?>
<!DOCTYPE OrderData SYSTEM 'OrderData.dtd'>
<OrderData>
    <Invoice
        orderDate="10/22/00"
        shipDate="10/25/00"
```

```
               customerIDREF="CUST1">
               <LineItem
                  PartIDREF="PART1"
                  quantity="12"
                  price="0.15"/>
               <LineItem
                  PartIDREF="PART2"
                  quantity="17"
                  price="0.2"/>
               <LineItem
                  PartIDREF="PART4"
                  quantity="5"
                  price="0.3"/>
         </Invoice>
         <Invoice
               orderDate="10/22/00"
               shipDate="10/22/00"
               customerIDREF="CUST2">
               <LineItem
                  PartIDREF="PART2"
                  quantity="11"
                  price="0.15"/>
               <LineItem
                  PartIDREF="PART3"
                  quantity="3"
                  price="0.2"/>
         </Invoice>
         <Invoice
               orderDate="10/25/00"
               shipDate="10/28/00"
               customerIDREF="CUST1">
               <LineItem
                  PartIDREF="PART3"
                  quantity="11"
                  price="0.25"/>
         </Invoice>
         <Customer
               CustomerID="CUST1"
               customerName="Homer J. Simpson"
               customerAddress="742 Evergreen Terrace"
               customerCity="Springfield"
               customerState="KY"
               customerPostalCode="12345"/>
         <Customer
               CustomerID="CUST2"
               customerName="Kevin B. Williams"
               customerAddress="744 Evergreen Terrace"
               customerCity="Springfield"
               customerState="KY"
               customerPostalCode="12345"/>
         <Part
               PartID="PART1"
               partName="grommets"
               partSize="2 inch"
               partColor="blue"/>
```

```
    <Part
       PartID="PART2"
       partName="widgets"
       partSize="3 inch"
       partColor="silver"/>
    <Part
       PartID="PART3"
       partName="brackets"
       partSize="1.5 inch"
       partColor="orange"/>
    <Part
       PartID="PART4"
       partName="sprockets"
       partSize="4 inch"
       partColor="green"/>
  </OrderData>
```

Conclusion

In this section, we have seen that XML provides a good way to marshal structured data out of a relational database. Changes to the data being extracted by the marshaller can be made while minimally impacting business-layer or presentation-layer code, while rich structures can be returned without the flattening that is typical of database recordsets. Marshalling data to XML can also be useful when you want to leverage other XML technologies, such as XSLT, to provide flexible data presentation – as we'll see later in the chapter.

Next, we'll take a look at gathering information from the outside world – specifically, the context of the browser and building XML structures from it.

Information Gathering

There are a number of reasons why you might want to be able to gather data from a web browser directly to XML. For example, you might be using an XML repository as your intermediate data platform of choice – in this case, you'll need to actually get to XML from forms that get submitted using the HTTP POST method. Another reason might be that the back-end systems that are the ultimate consumers of the data are designed to accept a particular XML standard; in that case, it would be more efficient to gather the data directly as XML rather than needing to pass it through an intermediate process. In this section, we'll take a look at some of the technology on the horizon to enable the simple gathering of data structured as XML across the Web, and then see how we can generate XML documents on the fly from CGI forms today.

The long-term solution: XForms

The W3C has a working group dedicated to the next generation of Internet forms, called XForms, as we described in Chapter 10. These forms will use XML as both their format description language and their output platform. While the XForms working group is far too early in their process to provide specifics, you should expect XForms to supersede traditional HTML forms as the preferred means of gathering information over the Internet within the next couple of years. Until support for XForms starts to appear in the leading browsers, we need to come up with an alternative way of gathering information and producing XML documents from HTML forms. Let's see how this would be done.

Manual Approach

When transforming data from HTML forms to XML, arguably the best technology to use is the DOM. In addition, we should perform the transformation to XML on the client, rather than the server, to reduce server load if possible. Unfortunately, many of the current client platforms do not provide DOM implementations, so we may be forced to do our transformations on the server. Let's look at examples of each, then we'll see how to build forms on the fly from XML content.

Example 1: Transforming Form Data to XML on the Client

Let's say we have the following form for entering an invoice:

The code for this form, ch19_ex3.htm, looks like this:

```
<HTML>
    <BODY>
        <H1>Invoice</H1>
        <P>
        <FORM name="frmSubmitInvoice" method="POST" action="submitInvoice.asp">
            <TABLE>
                <TR>
                    <TD>Customer Name:</TD>
                    <TD><INPUT name="customerName" size=30 maxlen=30></TD>
                </TR>
```

```
            <TR>
               <TD>Customer Address:</TD>
               <TD><INPUT name="customerAddress" size=50 maxlen=50></TD>
            </TR>
            <TR>
               <TD>Customer City:</TD>
               <TD><INPUT name="customerCity" size=30 maxlen=30></TD>
            </TR>
            <TR>
               <TD>Customer State:</TD>
               <TD><INPUT name="customerState" size=2 maxlen=2></TD>
            </TR>
            <TR>
               <TD>Customer Postal Code:</TD>
               <TD><INPUT name="customerPostalCode" size=10 maxlen=10></TD>
            </TR>
            <TR>
               <TD>Order Date:</TD>
               <TD><INPUT name="orderDate" size=10 maxlen=10></TD>
            </TR>
            <TR>
               <TD>Ship Date:</TD>
               <TD><INPUT name="shipDate" size=10 maxlen=10></TD>
            </TR>
         </TABLE>
         <P>
         <TABLE>
            <TR>
               <TD><B>Part</B></TD>
               <TD><B>Quantity</B></TD>
               <TD><B>Price</B></TD>
            </TR>
            <TR>
               <TD>
                  <SELECT name="part1">
                     <OPTION VALUE="0"></OPTION>
                     <OPTION VALUE="1">2 inch blue grommets</OPTION>
                     <OPTION VALUE="2">3 inch silver widgets</OPTION>
                     <OPTION VALUE="3">1.5 inch orange brackets</OPTION>
                     <OPTION VALUE="4">4 inch green sprockets</OPTION>
                     <OPTION VALUE="5">0.5 inch gold bolts</OPTION>
                  </SELECT></TD>
               <TD><INPUT name="quantity1" size=5 maxlen=5></TD>
               <TD><INPUT name="price1" size=8 maxlen=8></TD>
            </TR>
            <TR>
               <TD>
                  <SELECT name="part2">
                     <OPTION VALUE="0"></OPTION>
                     <OPTION VALUE="1">2 inch blue grommets</OPTION>
                     <OPTION VALUE="2">3 inch silver widgets</OPTION>
                     <OPTION VALUE="3">1.5 inch orange brackets</OPTION>
                     <OPTION VALUE="4">4 inch green sprockets</OPTION>
                     <OPTION VALUE="5">0.5 inch gold bolts</OPTION>
                  </SELECT>
```

```
                              </TD>
                          <TD><INPUT name="quantity2" size=5 maxlen=5></TD>
                          <TD><INPUT name="price2" size=8 maxlen=8></TD>
                      </TR>
                      <TR>
                          <TD>
                              <SELECT name="part3">
                                  <OPTION VALUE="0"></OPTION>
                                  <OPTION VALUE="1">2 inch blue grommets</OPTION>
                                  <OPTION VALUE="2">3 inch silver widgets</OPTION>
                                  <OPTION VALUE="3">1.5 inch orange brackets</OPTION>
                                  <OPTION VALUE="4">4 inch green sprockets</OPTION>
                                  <OPTION VALUE="5">0.5 inch gold bolts</OPTION>
                              </SELECT>
                          </TD>
                          <TD><INPUT name="quantity3" size=5 maxlen=5></TD>
                          <TD><INPUT name="price3" size=8 maxlen=8></TD>
                      </TR>
                      <TR>
                          <TD>
                              <SELECT name="part4">
                                  <OPTION VALUE="0"></OPTION>
                                  <OPTION VALUE="1">2 inch blue grommets</OPTION>
                                  <OPTION VALUE="2">3 inch silver widgets</OPTION>
                                  <OPTION VALUE="3">1.5 inch orange brackets</OPTION>
                                  <OPTION VALUE="4">4 inch green sprockets</OPTION>
                                  <OPTION VALUE="5">0.5 inch gold bolts</OPTION>
                              </SELECT>
                          </TD>
                          <TD><INPUT name="quantity4" size=5 maxlen=5></TD>
                          <TD><INPUT name="price4" size=8 maxlen=8></TD>
                      </TR>
                      <TR>
                          <TD>
                              <SELECT name="part5">
                                  <OPTION VALUE="0"></OPTION>
                                  <OPTION VALUE="1">2 inch blue grommets</OPTION>
                                  <OPTION VALUE="2">3 inch silver widgets</OPTION>
                                  <OPTION VALUE="3">1.5 inch orange brackets</OPTION>
                                  <OPTION VALUE="4">4 inch green sprockets</OPTION>
                                  <OPTION VALUE="5">0.5 inch gold bolts</OPTION>
                              </SELECT>
                          </TD>
                          <TD><INPUT name="quantity5" size=5 maxlen=5></TD>
                          <TD><INPUT name="price5" size=8 maxlen=8></TD>
                      </TR>
                  </TABLE>
                  <P><INPUT type="submit" name="cmdGo" value="Add invoice">
              </FORM>
          </BODY>
      </HTML>
```

When the user submits this form (by clicking the **Add invoice** button), each of the input fields is returned to the target of the form – in this case, the ASP document `submitInvoice.asp`. However, we have chosen to use XML documents on our server to store the information submitted in these forms, instead of storing that data in a database. We need to come up with a way to get this information into XML as painlessly as possible. Rather than processing the individual fields on the server side, let's use a DOM document on the client side to create the XML document and submit it as a string field to the server. The first thing we need to do is add a hidden field that will act as our XML buffer:

```
<INPUT type="hidden" name="formXML">
```

At the end of the form, we'll modify the Add invoice button, previously a submit button, to be a button that calls a Javascript function instead:

```
<INPUT type="button" name="cmdGo" value="Add invoice"
    onClick="createXML ();">
```

Finally, we have to write the Javascript function. The way the script builds the document is very similar to the previous example – it builds up the tree node by node so we won't go through the entire code. The interesting bit is at the end, where it takes the XML generated by the DOM object and stores it in the hidden field we added earlier. This makes it available to the server that is receiving the form submission. Rather than building up the document on the server, the server can simply take the generated XML and perform whatever actions are appropriate on it.

The entire code, for ch19_ex2.htm is now as follows (we have not repeated the content of the table as it is the same as the last example):

```
<HTML>
    <BODY>
        <H1>Invoice</H1>
        <P>
        <FORM name="frmSubmitInvoice" method="POST" action="submitInvoice.asp">
            <INPUT type="hidden" name="formXML">
            <TABLE>
            </TABLE>
            <P>
            <INPUT type="button" name="cmdGo" value="Add invoice"
                onClick="createXML();">
        </FORM>
    </BODY>
<SCRIPT LANGUAGE="JScript">
<!--
    function createXML()
    {
        var DOM;
        var elInvoice;
        var elLineItem;
        var iLoop;


        DOM = new ActiveXObject("Microsoft.XMLDOM");
        elInvoice = DOM.createElement("Invoice");
        DOM.appendChild(elInvoice);
```

```
elInvoice.setAttribute("customerName",
   frmSubmitInvoice.customerName.value);
elInvoice.setAttribute("customerAddress",
   frmSubmitInvoice.customerAddress.value);
elInvoice.setAttribute("customerCity",
   frmSubmitInvoice.customerCity.value);
elInvoice.setAttribute("customerState",
   frmSubmitInvoice.customerState.value);
elInvoice.setAttribute("customerPostalCode",
   frmSubmitInvoice.customerPostalCode.value);
elInvoice.setAttribute("orderDate", frmSubmitInvoice.orderDate.value);
elInvoice.setAttribute("shipDate", frmSubmitInvoice.shipDate.value);
if (frmSubmitInvoice.part1.value > "0")
{
   elLineItem = DOM.createElement("LineItem");
   elLineItem.setAttribute("partID", frmSubmitInvoice.part1.value);
   elLineItem.setAttribute("quantity",
      frmSubmitInvoice.quantity1.value);
   elLineItem.setAttribute("price", frmSubmitInvoice.price1.value);
   elInvoice.appendChild(elLineItem);
}
if (frmSubmitInvoice.part2.value > "0")
{
   elLineItem = DOM.createElement("LineItem");
   elLineItem.setAttribute("partID", frmSubmitInvoice.part2.value);
   elLineItem.setAttribute("quantity",
      frmSubmitInvoice.quantity2.value);
   elLineItem.setAttribute("price", frmSubmitInvoice.price2.value);
   elInvoice.appendChild(elLineItem);
}
if (frmSubmitInvoice.part3.value > "0")
{
   elLineItem = DOM.createElement("LineItem");
   elLineItem.setAttribute("partID", frmSubmitInvoice.part3.value);
   elLineItem.setAttribute("quantity",
      frmSubmitInvoice.quantity3.value);
   elLineItem.setAttribute("price", frmSubmitInvoice.price3.value);
   elInvoice.appendChild(elLineItem);
}
if (frmSubmitInvoice.part4.value > "0")
{
   elLineItem = DOM.createElement("LineItem");
   elLineItem.setAttribute("partID", frmSubmitInvoice.part4.value);
   elLineItem.setAttribute("quantity",
      frmSubmitInvoice.quantity4.value);
   elLineItem.setAttribute("price", frmSubmitInvoice.price4.value);
   elInvoice.appendChild(elLineItem);
}
if (frmSubmitInvoice.part5.value > "0")
{
```

```
                elLineItem = DOM.createElement("LineItem");
                elLineItem.setAttribute("partID", frmSubmitInvoice.part5.value);
                elLineItem.setAttribute("quantity",
                    frmSubmitInvoice.quantity5.value);
                elLineItem.setAttribute("price", frmSubmitInvoice.price5.value);
                elInvoice.appendChild(elLineItem);
            }
        frmSubmitInvoice.formXML.value = DOM.xml;
        frmSubmitInvoice.submit();
        }
    //-->
    </SCRIPT>
</HTML>
```

If we are able to create the XML documents on the client side, it makes sense - we can do preliminary validation of the content and avoid unnecessary round-trips back to the server where possible. Unfortunately, to use this example the client must be running IE 5.0 or later. If you want to write XML-aware code that runs on any browser, you'll need to create the XML on the server side. Let's see how this would be done.

Example 2: Transforming Form Submissions to XML on the Server

First, let's revert our HTML form code back to our non-Javascript version. Next, we need to write a version of submitInvoice.asp that will take the submitted form and create the appropriate XML from it. The code to handle this is, again, very similar to the code in the first example in the chapter – creating an instance of a DOM document and then building it up; except in this example we're using the information submitted to the ASP page.

```
<%@ Language=VBScript %>
<%
    Dim docInvoice
    Dim elInvoice
    Dim elLineItem
    Dim i

    Set docInvoice = CreateObject("Microsoft.XMLDOM")
    Set elInvoice = docInvoice.createElement("Invoice")
    docInvoice.appendChild elInvoice
    elInvoice.setAttribute "customerName", Request("customerName")
    elInvoice.setAttribute "customerAddress", Request("customerAddress")
    elInvoice.setAttribute "customerCity", Request("customerCity")
    elInvoice.setAttribute "customerState", Request("customerState")
    elInvoice.setAttribute "customerPostalCode", Request("customerPostalCode")
    elInvoice.setAttribute "orderDate", Request("orderDate")
    elInvoice.setAttribute "shipDate", Request("shipDate")
    For i = 1 to 5
        If Request("part" & i) > "0"Then
            Set elLineItem = docInvoice.createElement("LineItem")
            elInvoice.appendChild elLineItem
            elLineItem.setAttribute "partID", Request("part" & i)
            elLineItem.setAttribute "quantity", Request("quantity" & i)
            elLineItem.setAttribute "price", Request("price" & i)
        End If
    Next
    Response.Write "<?xml version='1.0'?>"

    Response.Write docInvoice.xml
%>
```

This example sends the data back to the browser, but it is likely that your code would take the XML and store it, pass it along for storage into a relational database, or take whatever other action is appropriate. However, for demonstration purposes, it is useful to return the XML to the client. The document created by the preceding code should look something like this (depending on the values entered into the form):

```
<?xml version='1.0'?>
<Invoice
    customerName="Homer J. Simpson"
    customerAddress="742 Evergreen Terrace"
    customerCity="Springfield"
    customerState="KY"
    customerPostalCode="12345"
    orderDate="12/20/2000"
    shipDate="12/25/2000">
    <LineItem
        partID="4"
        quantity="21"
        price="1.90"/>
    <LineItem
        partID="1"
        quantity="12"
        price="0.12"/>
</Invoice>
```

Next, let's look at how we can drive our forms with XML – in our example, we'll generate our same HTML form populated with data from the XML document we just created.

Example 3: Creating HMTL Forms with XSLT for Updates

In this example, we'll create an HTML form by styling our XML document. We could use this to drive our forms engine if our native data repository happened to be in XML, or we could use it to drive several different presentation layers (as we'll see later in the chapter when we talk about presentation). We will use the XML file that was returned to the browser above, and we'll call it ch19_ex4.xml. If it makes more sense for your situation, you can programmatically perform the transform using XT or some other tool – visit http://www.jclark.com/xml/xt.html for instructions on obtaining XT.

```
<?xml version='1.0'?>
<?xml-stylesheet type="text/xsl" href="ch19_ex4.xsl"?>
<Invoice
    customerName="Homer J. Simpson"
    customerAddress="742 Evergreen Terrace"
    customerCity="Springfield"
    customerState="KY"
    customerPostalCode="12345"
    orderDate="12/20/2000"
    shipDate="12/25/2000">
    <LineItem
        partID="4"
        quantity="21"
        price="1.90"/>
    <LineItem
        partID="1"
        quantity="12"
        price="0.12"/>
</Invoice>
```

Let's see an XSLT style sheet we could use to go from this XML document to an appropriate HTML form, and then discuss the pros and cons of using XSLT for this purpose. We'll also see some tips on how you can use the document() function to make your style sheets more flexible. The following style sheet is called ch19_ex4.xsl:

```xml
<?xml version="1.0"?>
<xsl:stylesheet xmlns:xsl="http://www.w3.org/1999/XSL/Transform" version="1.0">
    <xsl:output method="html" />
    <xsl:template match="Invoice">
        <HTML>
            <BODY>
                <H1>Invoice</H1>
                <P/>
                <FORM name="frmSubmitInvoice" method="POST"
                    action="submitInvoice.asp">
                    <TABLE>
                        <TR>
                            <TD>Customer Name:</TD>
                            <TD>
                                <INPUT name="customerName" size="30" maxlen="30">
                                    <xsl:attribute name="value">
                                        <xsl:value-of select="@customerName" />
                                    </xsl:attribute>
                                </INPUT>
                            </TD>
                        </TR>
                        <TR>
                            <TD>Customer Address:</TD>
                            <TD>
                                <INPUT name="customerAddress" size="50" maxlen="50">
                                    <xsl:attribute name="value">
                                        <xsl:value-of select="@customerAddress" />
                                    </xsl:attribute>
                                </INPUT>
                            </TD>
                        </TR>
                        <TR>
                            <TD>Customer City:</TD>
                            <TD>
                                <INPUT name="customerCity" size="30" maxlen="30">
                                    <xsl:attribute name="value">
                                        <xsl:value-of select="@customerCity" />
                                    </xsl:attribute>
                                </INPUT>
                            </TD>
                        </TR>
                        <TR>
                            <TD>Customer State:</TD>
                            <TD>
                                <INPUT name="customerState" size="2" maxlen="2">
                                    <xsl:attribute name="value">
                                        <xsl:value-of select="@customerState" />
                                    </xsl:attribute>
                                </INPUT>
                            </TD>
                        </TR>
                        <TR>
                            <TD>Customer Postal Code:</TD>
                            <TD>
                                <INPUT name="customerPostalCode" size="10" maxlen="10">
                                    <xsl:attribute name="value">
```

```
                    <xsl:value-of select="@customerPostalCode" />
                </xsl:attribute>
            </INPUT>
        </TD>
    </TR>
    <TR>
        <TD>Order Date:</TD>
        <TD>
            <INPUT name="orderDate" size="30" maxlen="30">
                <xsl:attribute name="value">
                    <xsl:value-of select="@orderDate" />
                </xsl:attribute>
            </INPUT>
        </TD>
    </TR>
    <TR>
        <TD>Ship Date:</TD>
        <TD>
            <INPUT name="shipDate" size="30" maxlen="30">
                <xsl:attribute name="value">
                    <xsl:value-of select="@shipDate" />
                </xsl:attribute>
            </INPUT>
        </TD>
    </TR>
</TABLE>
<P />
<TABLE>
    <TR>
        <TD><B>Part</B></TD>
        <TD><B>Quantity</B></TD>
        <TD><B>Price</B></TD>
    </TR>
    <xsl:for-each select="LineItem">
        <TR>
            <TD>
                <SELECT>
                    <xsl:attribute name="name">part<xsl:value-of
                        select="position()" />
                    </xsl:attribute>
                    <xsl:variable name="partID" select="@partID" />
                    <xsl:for-each
                        select="document('parts.xml')/Parts/Part">
                        <OPTION>
                            <xsl:attribute name="VALUE">
                                <xsl:value-of select="@partID"
                                    />
                            </xsl:attribute>
                            <xsl:if test="$partID=@partID">
                                <xsl:attribute name="SELECTED">
                                    SELECTED
                                </xsl:attribute>
                            </xsl:if>
                            <xsl:value-of select="@partName" />
                        </OPTION>
                    </xsl:for-each>
                </SELECT>
            </TD>
            <TD>
                <INPUT size="5" maxlen="5">
                    <xsl:attribute name="name">
                        quantity
```

```
                                        <xsl:value-of select="position()" />
                                    </xsl:attribute>
                                    <xsl:attribute name="value">
                                        <xsl:value-of select="@quantity" />
                                    </xsl:attribute>
                                </INPUT>
                            </TD>
                            <TD>
                                <INPUT size="8" maxlen="8">
                                    <xsl:attribute name="name">
                                        price
                                        <xsl:value-of select="position()" />
                                    </xsl:attribute>
                                    <xsl:attribute name="value">
                                        <xsl:value-of select="@price" />
                                    </xsl:attribute>
                                </INPUT>
                            </TD>
                        </TR>
                    </xsl:for-each>
                    <xsl:variable name="LIC" select="count(LineItem)" />
                    <xsl:for-each
                        select="document('forloop.xml')/ForLoop/*[position()>$LIC]">
                        <TR>
                            <TD>
                                <SELECT>
                                    <xsl:attribute name="name">
                                        part
                                        <xsl:value-of select="." />
                                    </xsl:attribute>
                                    <xsl:for-each
                                        select="document('parts.xml')/Parts/Part">
                                        <OPTION>
                                            <xsl:attribute name="VALUE">
                                                <xsl:value-of select="@partID" />
                                            </xsl:attribute>
                                            <xsl:value-of select="@partName" />
                                        </OPTION>
                                    </xsl:for-each>
                                </SELECT>
                            </TD>
                            <TD>
                                <INPUT size="5" maxlen="5">
                                    <xsl:attribute name="name">
                                        quantity<xsl:value-of select="." />
                                    </xsl:attribute>
                                </INPUT>
                            </TD>
                            <TD>
                                <INPUT size="8" maxlen="8">
                                    <xsl:attribute name="name">
                                        price<xsl:value-of select="." />
                                    </xsl:attribute>
                                </INPUT>
                            </TD>
                        </TR>
                    </xsl:for-each>
                </TABLE>
                <P />
                <INPUT type="submit" name="cmdGo" value="Add invoice" />
            </FORM>
        </BODY>
    </HTML>
    </xsl:template>
</xsl:stylesheet>
```

Let's look at some specific techniques we used in this stylesheet to create the form we wanted.

```
<INPUT name="customerName" size="30" maxlen="30">
    <xsl:attribute name="value">
        <xsl:value-of select="@customerName" />
    </xsl:attribute>
</INPUT>
```

Here, we use `xsl:value-of` to add the customer name value as an attribute to the `INPUT` element we have created. Note that we can add the attribute to the `INPUT` element, even though we didn't use `xsl:element` to create that element.

```
<xsl:for-each select="LineItem">
    <TR>
        <TD>
            <SELECT>
                <xsl:attribute name="name">part<xsl:value-of
                    select="position()" /></xsl:attribute>
```

Here we see how `xsl:attribute` can be used on a set of items – in this case, all of the `LineItem` children of the `Invoice` element, to declare HTML input elements with unique names. The `position()` function returns the position of the `LineItem` child within the `Invoice` child list, so if our invoice has two line items (as it does in this example), we will create attributes called `part1` and `part2`. The same technique is used to create the `quantityX` and `priceX` HTML input elements as well.

```
<xsl:variable name="LIC" select="count(LineItem)" />
<xsl:for-each
    select="document('forloop.xml')/ForLoop/*[position()>$LIC]">
    <TR>
        <TD>
            <SELECT>
                <xsl:attribute name="name">
                    part
                    <xsl:value-of select="." />
                </xsl:attribute>
                <xsl:for-each
                    select="document('parts.xml')/Parts/Part">
                    <OPTION>
                        <xsl:attribute name="VALUE">
                            <xsl:value-of select="@partID" />
                        </xsl:attribute>
                        <xsl:value-of select="@partName" />
                    </OPTION>
                </xsl:for-each>
            </SELECT>
        </TD>
        <TD>
            <INPUT size="5" maxlen="5">
                <xsl:attribute name="name">
                    quantity
                    <xsl:value-of select="." />
                </xsl:attribute>
            </INPUT>
        </TD>
        <TD>
            <INPUT size="8" maxlen="8">
                <xsl:attribute name="name">
                    price
```

```
                           <xsl:value-of select="." />
                         </xsl:attribute>
                       </INPUT>
                    </TD>
                 </TR>
              </xsl:for-each>
```

This is an unavoidable part of this stylesheet, and has to do with the fact that we provide five lines on which part data may be entered. XSLT doesn't provide iterative processing *per se*, so there's no way to say "count up the line items, then for any more that are needed up to five, create blank ones." We've used a relatively clever way of getting around the problem here, but your mileage may vary as far as performance goes. There's an external document called forloop.xml that contains an artificial for loop:

```
<ForLoop>
   <X>1</X>
   <X>2</X>
   <X>3</X>
   <X>4</X>
   <X>5</X>
</ForLoop>
```

Here's the code we use to access this document in our XSLT:

```
<xsl:variable name="LIC" select="count(LineItem)" />
<xsl:for-each
   select="document('forloop.xml')/ForLoop/*[position()>$LIC]">
```

What this boils down to is: first, set the variable called LIC to the number of line items present in the invoice (which is 2 here). Then, iterate through the ForLoop child elements where the position is greater than that value. This is the same as saying for i = 3 to 5. For each of these values, we create empty table rows in the same way we created them for the line items that were actually present.

We also use this technique to dynamically generate the drop-down list for the parts. This is driven by our parts.xml document, which looks like the following

```
<Parts>
   <Part
      partID="0"
      partName="" />
   <Part
      partID="1"
      partName="2 inch blue grommets" />
   <Part
      partID="2"
      partName="3 inch silver widgets" />
   <Part
      partID="3"
      partName="1.5 inch orange brackets" />
   <Part
      partID="4"
      partName="4 inch green sprockets" />
   <Part
      partID="5"
      partName="0.5 inch gold bolts" />
</Parts>
```

749

The XSLT that styles up this document and creates the `OPTION` elements inside each `SELECT` element looks like this:

```
<xsl:for-each
    select="document('parts.xml')/Parts/Part">
    <OPTION>
        <xsl:attribute name="VALUE">
            <xsl:value-of select="@partID" />
        </xsl:attribute>
        <xsl:if test="$partID=@partID">
            <xsl:attribute name="SELECTED">
                SELECTED
            </xsl:attribute>
        </xsl:if>
        <xsl:value-of select="@partName" />
    </OPTION>
</xsl:for-each>
```

Depending on the particular XSLT engine and processing engine you are using, this processing should still be fast – and it allows you to change your available parts on the fly by simply modifying the `parts.xml` document.

The output of this style sheet when run against our source invoice (with white space for readability) looks like this:

```
<HTML>
    <BODY>
        <H1>Invoice</H1>
        <P></P>
        <FORM name="frmSubmitInvoice" method="POST" action="submitInvoice.asp">
            <TABLE>
                <TR>
                    <TD>Customer Name:</TD>
                    <TD><INPUT name="customerName"
                        size="30"
                        maxlen="30"
                        value="Homer J. Simpson">
                    </TD>
                </TR>
                <TR>
                    <TD>Customer Address:</TD>
                    <TD><INPUT name="customerAddress"
                        size="50"
                        maxlen="50"
                        value="742 Evergreen Terrace">
                    </TD>
                </TR>
                <TR>
                    <TD>Customer City:</TD>
                    <TD><INPUT name="customerCity"
                        size="30"
                        maxlen="30"
                        value="Springfield">
                    </TD>
                </TR>
```

```
    <TR>
        <TD>Customer State:</TD>
        <TD><INPUT name="customerState"
            size="2"
            maxlen="2"
            value="VA">
        </TD>
    </TR>
    <TR>
        <TD>Customer Postal Code:</TD>
        <TD><INPUT name="customerPostalCode"
            size="10"
            maxlen="10"
            value="12345">
        </TD>
    </TR>
    <TR>
        <TD>Order Date:</TD>
        <TD><INPUT name="orderDate"
            size="30"
            maxlen="30"
            value="12/20/2000">
        </TD>
    </TR>
    <TR>
        <TD>Ship Date:</TD>
        <TD><INPUT name="shipDate"
            size="30"
            maxlen="30"
            value="12/25/2000">
        </TD>
    </TR>
</TABLE>
<P></P>
<TABLE>
    <TR>
        <TD><B>Part</B></TD>
        <TD><B>Quantity</B></TD>
        <TD><B>Price</B></TD>
    </TR>
    <TR>
        <TD>
            <SELECT name="part1">
                <OPTION VALUE="0"></OPTION>
                <OPTION VALUE="1">2 inch blue grommets</OPTION>
                <OPTION VALUE="2">3 inch silver widgets</OPTION>
                <OPTION VALUE="3">1.5 inch orange brackets</OPTION>
                <OPTION VALUE="4" SELECTED>4 inch green sprockets</OPTION>
                <OPTION VALUE="5">0.5 inch gold bolts</OPTION>
            </SELECT>
        </TD>
        <TD><INPUT size="5"
            maxlen="5"
            name="quantity1"
            value="21">
        </TD>
```

```
            <TD><INPUT size="8"
                maxlen="8"
                name="price1"
                value="1.90">
            </TD>
      </TR>
      <TR>
         <TD>
            <SELECT name="part2">
               <OPTION VALUE="0"></OPTION>
               <OPTION VALUE="1" SELECTED>2 inch blue grommets</OPTION>
               <OPTION VALUE="2">3 inch silver widgets</OPTION>
               <OPTION VALUE="3">1.5 inch orange brackets</OPTION>
               <OPTION VALUE="4">4 inch green sprockets</OPTION>
               <OPTION VALUE="5">0.5 inch gold bolts</OPTION>
            </SELECT>
         </TD>
         <TD><INPUT size="5"
             maxlen="5"
             name="quantity2"
             value="12">
         </TD>
         <TD><INPUT size="8"
             maxlen="8"
             name="price2"
             value="0.12">
         </TD>
      </TR>
      <TR>
         <TD>
            <SELECT name="part3">
               <OPTION VALUE="0"></OPTION>
               <OPTION VALUE="1">2 inch blue grommets</OPTION>
               <OPTION VALUE="2">3 inch silver widgets</OPTION>
               <OPTION VALUE="3">1.5 inch orange brackets</OPTION>
               <OPTION VALUE="4">4 inch green sprockets</OPTION>
               <OPTION VALUE="5">0.5 inch gold bolts</OPTION>
            </SELECT>
         </TD>
         <TD><INPUT size="5"
             maxlen="5"
             name="quantity3">
         </TD>
         <TD><INPUT size="8"
             maxlen="8"
             name="price3">
         </TD>
      </TR>
      <TR>
         <TD>
            <SELECT name="part4">
               <OPTION VALUE="0"></OPTION>
               <OPTION VALUE="1">2 inch blue grommets</OPTION>
               <OPTION VALUE="2">3 inch silver widgets</OPTION>
               <OPTION VALUE="3">1.5 inch orange brackets</OPTION>
```

```
                    <OPTION VALUE="4">4 inch green sprockets</OPTION>
                    <OPTION VALUE="5">0.5 inch gold bolts</OPTION>
                </SELECT>
            </TD>
            <TD>INPUT size="5"
                maxlen="5"
                name="quantity4">
            </TD>
            <TD><INPUT size="8"
                maxlen="8"
                name="price4">
            </TD>
        </TR>
        <TR>
            <TD>
                <SELECT name="part5">
                    <OPTION VALUE="0"></OPTION>
                    <OPTION VALUE="1">2 inch blue grommets</OPTION>
                    <OPTION VALUE="2">3 inch silver widgets</OPTION>
                    <OPTION VALUE="3">1.5 inch orange brackets</OPTION>
                    <OPTION VALUE="4">4 inch green sprockets</OPTION>
                    <OPTION VALUE="5">0.5 inch gold bolts</OPTION>
                </SELECT>
            </TD>
            <TD><INPUT size="5"
                maxlen="5"
                name="quantity5">
            </TD>
            <TD><INPUT size="8"
                maxlen="8"
                name="price5">
            </TD>
        </TR>
    </TABLE>
    <P></P>
    <INPUT type="submit" name="cmdGo" value="Add invoice">
  </FORM>
 </BODY>
</HTML>
```

In this example, we've seen how well written XSLT can be used to dynamically generate HTML forms. We've also seen how the document() function may be used to pull in content from other documents, making the content easy to maintain.

Conclusion

In this section of the chapter, we have looked at some techniques for gathering information from Internet browsers and persisting it to XML. We've seen how look-up documents may be used to create pseudo-procedural behavior in W3C-standard XSLT, and how we can generate XML documents either on the server or the client. Until XForms become available, the approaches presented here may be used to gather XML data from standard HTML forms.

Next, let's see how XML may be used to effectively drive our presentation layer.

Presentation

Virtually every Internet-enabled application you write will have some presentation component. Data will need to be marshalled out of a data repository and converted to a target-device-readable-format. In the past, the target device for the presentation layer has almost always been a browser running on a desktop or laptop; however, with the current wireless revolution, your presentation layer will more and more often need to target handheld devices such as PDAs and cell phones. In this section, we'll see some techniques that we can use to make our presentation to multiple target devices more painless.

Why Use XML?

XML helps us to abstract our data-marshalling layer away from our presentation layer. Because XML's structure is similar to that of device-specific markup languages such as HTML and WML (for mobile devices), an XML document with the proper layout can easily be used to drive various permutations, or styles, of output device markup. Let's look at an example. Let's say we have the following XML document for an invoice:

```
<?xml version='1.0'?>
<Invoice
    customerName="Homer J. Simpson"
    customerAddress="742 Evergreen Terrace"
    customerCity="Springfield"
    customerState="KY"
    customerPostalCode="12345"
    orderDate="12/20/2000"
    shipDate="12/25/2000">
    <LineItem
        partID="4"
        quantity="21"
        price="1.90"/>
    <LineItem
        partID="1"
        quantity="12"
        price="0.12"/>
</Invoice>
```

Let's see how we can use XSLT to style this for various output platforms.

Example: XML Detail – HTML Detail

In this first example, we'll use XSLT to style our sample XML document into an HTML document. The approach taken here is straightforward; we style the `Invoice` element first, then each `LineItem` child of the `Invoice` element.

```
<?xml version="1.0"?>
<xsl:stylesheet xmlns:xsl="http://www.w3.org/1999/XSL/Transform" version="1.0">
    <xsl:output method="html" />
    <xsl:template match="Invoice">
        <HTML>
            <BODY>
                <H1>Invoice</H1>
```

```
                <P />
            <TABLE>
                <TR>
                    <TD><B>Customer Name:</B></TD>
                    <TD><xsl:value-of select="@customerName" /></TD>
                </TR>
                <TR>
                    <TD><B>Customer Address:</B></TD>
                    <TD><xsl:value-of select="@customerAddress" /></TD>
                </TR>
                <TR>
                    <TD><B>Customer City:</B></TD>
                    <TD><xsl:value-of select="@customerCity" /></TD>
                </TR>
                <TR>
                    <TD><B>Customer State:</B></TD>
                    <TD><xsl:value-of select="@customerState" /></TD>
                </TR>
                <TR>
                    <TD><B>Customer Postal Code:</B></TD>
                    <TD><xsl:value-of select="@customerPostalCode" /></TD>
                </TR>
                <TR>
                    <TD><B>Order Date:</B></TD>
                    <TD><xsl:value-of select="@orderDate" /></TD>
                </TR>
                <TR>
                    <TD><B>Ship Date:</B></TD>
                    <TD><xsl:value-of select="@shipDate" /></TD>
                </TR>
            </TABLE>
            <P />
            <TABLE BORDER="1">
                <TR>
                    <TD><B>Part</B></TD>
                    <TD><B>Quantity</B></TD>
                    <TD><B>Price</B></TD>
                </TR>
                <xsl:for-each select="LineItem">
                    <TR>
                        <TD>
                            <xsl:variable name="partID" select="@partID" />
                            <xsl:value-of
select="document('parts.xml')/Parts/Part[@partID=$partID]/@partName" />
                        </TD>
                        <TD><xsl:value-of select="@quantity" /></TD>
                        <TD><xsl:value-of select="@price" /></TD>
                    </TR>
                </xsl:for-each>
            </TABLE>
            <P />
        </BODY>
    </HTML>
  </xsl:template>
</xsl:stylesheet>
```

Note that because the XML was already arranged in a similar way to the way we wanted our HTML to look, we didn't have to do a lot of fancy processing in our stylesheet. As a rule, you should always feed XML that is as close as possible to the target layout into the XSLT – this tends to ensure that your styling time is kept to a minimum and your throughput is maximized.

Next, let's see how the same XML document could be styled to WML.

Example: XML Detail – WML Detail

In this example we'll assume that you have knowledge of WML already. If not, *Professional WAP* (1-861004-04-4 for details) can provide all you need to know. We'll style the same XML document into a single-card WML deck. Note that much of the code is exactly the same, and that we haven't introduced any data logic; we've only changed the styling of the structure.

```xml
<?xml version="1.0"?>
<xsl:stylesheet xmlns:xsl="http://www.w3.org/1999/XSL/Transform" version="1.0">
    <xsl:template match="Invoice">
        <wml>
            <card id="invoicetop" title="Invoice" newcontext="true">
                <p>
                <table columns="2">
                    <tr>
                        <td>Customer Name:</td>
                        <td><xsl:value-of select="@customerName" /></td>
                    </tr>
                    <tr>
                        <td>Customer Address:</td>
                        <td><xsl:value-of select="@customerAddress" /></td>
                    </tr>
                    <tr>
                        <td>Customer City:</td>
                        <td><xsl:value-of select="@customerCity" /></td>
                    </tr>
                    <tr>
                        <td>Customer State:</td>
                        <td><xsl:value-of select="@customerState" /></td>
                    </tr>
                    <tr>
                        <td>Customer Postal Code:</td>
                        <td><xsl:value-of select="@customerPostalCode" /></td>
                    </tr>
                    <tr>
                        <td>Order Date:</td>
                        <td><xsl:value-of select="@orderDate" /></td>
                    </tr>
                    <tr>
                        <td>Ship Date:</td>
                        <td><xsl:value-of select="@shipDate" /></td>
                    </tr>
                </table>
                <table columns="3">
                    <tr>
                        <td>Part</td>
                        <td>Quantity</td>
```

```
                <td>Price</td>
            </tr>
            <xsl:for-each select="LineItem">
                <tr>
                    <td>
                        <xsl:variable name="partID" select="@partID" />
                        <xsl:value-of select="document('parts.xml')/Parts/Part
                                      [@partID=$partID]/@partName" />
                    </td>
                    <td><xsl:value-of select="@quantity" /></td>
                    <td><xsl:value-of select="@price" /></td>
                </tr>
            </xsl:for-each>
        </table>
        </p>
    </card>
  </wml>
 </xsl:template>
</xsl:stylesheet>
```

This brings up an important point. On the WML platform, we might only want to present a summary of the invoice, not the details. If our data is stored natively in XML, it might make sense to style the native XML into our summary – taking the extra time to move it into summarized XML before styling it would cause a performance drop. On the other hand, if we are marshalling the XML out of a relational database anyway, we'd be much better off to marshal the data in a summarized form and then style that. Remember, when working with data a good rule of thumb is to perform data manipulations in the lowest tier possible (preferably directly on the relational database platform using stored procedures or some other mechanism); this will reduce network traffic and take advantage of the database's caching mechanisms.

Example: XML Detail – WML Summary

In this example, we'll use XSLT to style our XML detail invoice document into a WML summary. In our summary, the only things we are interested in are the customer name and the total invoice amount. However, this presents a problem, as XSLT doesn't provide a way to calculate the sum of a product in one pass so we'll have to use two style transforms to get at what we want. Remember that our initial invoice document looks like this:

```
<?xml version='1.0'?>
<Invoice
    customerName="Homer J. Simpson"
    customerAddress="742 Evergreen Terrace"
    customerCity="Springfield"
    customerState="KY"
    customerPostalCode="12345"
    orderDate="12/20/2000"
    shipDate="12/25/2000">
    <LineItem
        partID="4"
        quantity="21"
        price="1.90"/>
    <LineItem
        partID="1"
        quantity="12"
        price="0.12"/>
</Invoice>
```

The first thing we do is style it so that we have the line price for each line item (by multiplying the quantity and the price together). The stylesheet we use to do that looks like this:

```xml
<?xml version="1.0"?>
<xsl:stylesheet xmlns:xsl="http://www.w3.org/1999/XSL/Transform" version="1.0">
   <xsl:template match="Invoice">
      <xsl:element name="Invoice">
         <xsl:attribute name="customerName">
            <xsl:value-of select="@customerName" />
         </xsl:attribute>
         <xsl:attribute name="customerAddress">
            <xsl:value-of select="@customerAddress" />
         </xsl:attribute>
         <xsl:attribute name="customerCity">
            <xsl:value-of select="@customerCity" />
         </xsl:attribute>
         <xsl:attribute name="customerState">
            <xsl:value-of select="@customerState" />
         </xsl:attribute>
         <xsl:attribute name="customerPostalCode">
            <xsl:value-of select="@customerPostalCode" />
         </xsl:attribute>
         <xsl:attribute name="orderDate">
            <xsl:value-of select="@orderDate" />
         </xsl:attribute>
         <xsl:attribute name="shipDate">
            <xsl:value-of select="@shipDate" />
         </xsl:attribute>
         <xsl:for-each select="LineItem">
            <xsl:element name="LineItem">
               <xsl:attribute name="linePrice">
                  <xsl:value-of select="@quantity*@price" />
               </xsl:attribute>
            </xsl:element>
         </xsl:for-each>
      </xsl:element>
   </xsl:template>
</xsl:stylesheet>
```

The intermediate result returned after styling the detail invoice with the above stylesheet is below:

```xml
<?xml version="1.0" encoding="utf-8"?>
<Invoice
   customerName="Homer J. Simpson"
   customerAddress="742 Evergreen Terrace"
   customerCity="Springfield"
   customerState="VA"
   customerPostalCode="12345"
   orderDate="12/20/2000"
   shipDate="12/25/2000">
   <LineItem linePrice="39.9"/>
   <LineItem partID="1" linePrice="1.44"/>
</Invoice>
```

Now, we use the sum function to add together the various line prices to get the total for the invoice and style the contents the rest of the way to WML. Note that we round the sum to the nearest two digits – some XSLT processors introduce slight rounding errors when performing calculations, so this code is written to help us get around the problem.

```xml
<?xml version="1.0"?>
<xsl:stylesheet xmlns:xsl="http://www.w3.org/1999/XSL/Transform" version="1.0">
    <xsl:template match="Invoice">
        <wml>
            <card id="invoicetop" title="Invoice" newcontext="true">
                <p>
                <table columns="2">
                    <tr>
                        <td>Customer Name:</td>
                        <td><xsl:value-of select="@customerName" /></td>
                    </tr>
                    <tr>
                        <td>Total invoice:</td>
                        <td>
                            <xsl:value-of select="round(sum(LineItem/@linePrice) * 100
                                + 0.49999) div 100" />
                        </td>
                    </tr>
                </table>
                </p>
            </card>
        </wml>
    </xsl:template>
</xsl:stylesheet>
```

The final result, after we style the intermediate result with this stylesheet, is this:

```xml
<?xml version="1.0" encoding="utf-8"?>
<wml>
    <card
        id="invoicetop"
        title="Invoice"
        newcontext="true">
        <p>
            <table columns="2">
                <tr>
                    <td>Customer Name:</td>
                    <td>Homer J. Simpson</td>
                </tr>
                <tr>
                    <td>Total invoice:</td>
                    <td>41.34</td>
                </tr>
            </table>
        </p>
    </card>
</wml>
```

Summary

In this section, we've seen how XSLT may be used to format XML data for presentation. We've seen why this is a good thing – using XML and XSLT abstracts the data away from the presentation, allowing us to easily superimpose different presentation logic for different target consumers (such as Web browsers or handheld devices). We've also seen some of the limitations of XSLT, and some things we need to watch out for.

You can learn more about XSLT in Chapter 8 – *XSLT/XPath.* For more information about WML, we recommend taking a look at **Professional WAP**, *published by Wrox Press (ISBN 1861004044)*

Conclusion

In this chapter, we've seen how XML may be used for the marshalling, gathering, and presentation of data. XML may be used to provide formatted information to a Web server in a platform-independent way; that information may then easily either be loaded into a relational database or persisted to a document archive for later use. In addition, XML provides a good way to handle multiple target consumers in the presentation layer, as it allows the abstraction of presentation away from data. As you integrate XML into your enterprise solution, you should consider taking advantage of XML for these processes.

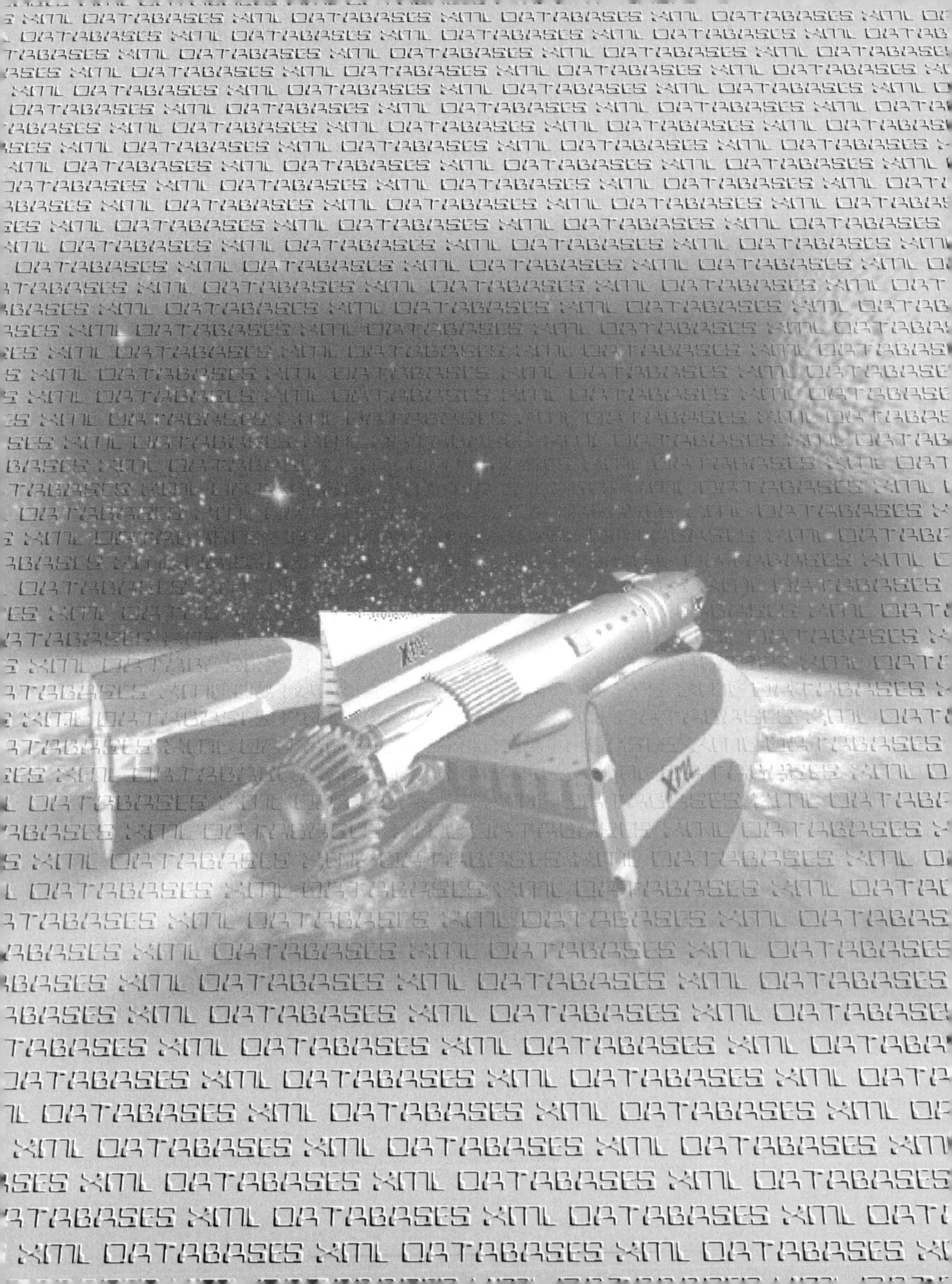
XML DATABASES
XML

20

SQL Server 2000 XML Sample Applications

This chapter is designed to introduce you to, and show you how to get results from, some of the more advanced XML features in SQL Server 2000, and how to program them. We will do this with by building up two separate sets of projects, each of which is designed to show you how to get the most out of specific features.

To test these applications you need SQL Server 2000 installed, and the updategram and bulk load functionality that you can download from the MSDN web site as part of the XML for SQL web release 1 Beta 1. This can be freely downloaded from http://msdn.microsoft.com/downloads/default.asp. This web release both enhances the features that were shipped with SQL Server 2000 and provides you with some totally new SQL Server XML functionality. You can obtain an evaluation copy of SQL Server 2000 from http://www.microsoft.com/sql/productinfo/default.htm.

You also need to have a virtual directory (virtual root) set up to run a lot of the examples. This set up is discussed in Appendix E.

The projects discussed in this chapter are as follows:

Project 1 - Accessing SQL Server 2000 Directly Over HTTP

In this project, we explore different ways to access SQL Server 2000 over HTTP, including:

❑   How to POST an XML template using an HTML form

❑   A simple Visual Basic application using ADO that executes an XML template

❑   An ASP application that executes an XML updategram

All the samples execute a simple XML template (consisting of SQL queries and/or XPath queries). We also show how parameters are passed in each of the applications.

Project 2 - Building an Empire: An eLemonade Company

In this project, we use a fictional e-commerce site to contrast two XML approaches to the same problem. One approach uses FOR XML and OpenXML, and then other uses XML Views, XPath, and Updategrams. We start with business requirements of selling lemonade over the Internet. Based on these requirements, we design a database and then finally write an application that explores these XML features in SQL Server 2000.

Project 1 – Accessing SQL Server 2000 Directly Over HTTP

In this first project, we will be showing you how you can access and even update information directly from your SQL Server 2000 database, using HTTP. This enables you to get results passed to a client (either a web browser, or later on a Visual Basic application) either across a corporate network or across the Internet. We will see two different techniques that allow you execute queries in SQL Server:

❑ Posting XML templates using HTML form

❑ A VB application using ADO to execute an XML template

❑ An ASP application to execute an XML template (consisting an updategram that modifies data)

Templates can include SQL queries that can be simple SELECT statements, which update nothing. But updategrams, which are templates, are used for updating data (INSERT, UPDATE, DELETE). In case of a VB application, the client must install the application and its required components such as an updated version of Microsoft Data Access Components (MDAC). The VB application distributes the load for such things processing the results of a query. In case of an ASP application, the load on the server is heavier but the client platform is less of an issue. As SQL Server 2000 allows data access over HTTP, data retrieval/manipulation can be accomplished through firewalls and across platforms.

Note that the examples in Project 1 are designed to be run against the Northwind database; if you are executing a template in a URL, then you need a virtual root to access Northwind, and a virtual name of type template.

XML Templates – Getting XML from SQL Server Across the Web

We briefly met XML Templates in Chapter 15. The first part of this project is designed to provide you with a quick introduction to the concept of XML templates, and how they can be used to retrieve data from SQL Server 2000 across HTTP.

A template is simply an XML document that uses a specific syntax, which can be interpreted/processed by SQL Server 2000 components. They are called templates because they act like a placeholder for SQL queries, updategrams, and XPath queries, and are processed in a special way. Each template can hold a number of these queries, which are executed sequentially, and if one fails the others will still be executed.

As you may remember from our discussion on XML Views in Chapter 15, when we run XPath queries we need to provide a mapping schema in annotated XDR form. These schemas allow the query to map the information in the database to the format of XML that you want returned. You can also use these schemas with SQL queries (or use the mapping described in Chapter 14 which discussed the FOR XML clause).

We will look at templates containing XPath queries later, but for the moment we will concentrate on more simple templates. The general syntax for an XML template that executes a SQL query is as follows:

```
<ROOT xmlns:sql="urn:schemas-microsoft-com:xml-sql" >
   <sql:header>
      <sql:param ParameterName> Default Value </sql:param>
      <sql:param ParameterName> Default Value </sql:param>...n
   </sql:header>
   <sql:query>
      SQL statement(s)
   </sql:query>
</ROOT>
```

The two main parts of the template are as follows:

❑ The <ROOT> element provides a single top-level element for the resulting XML.

❑ The keywords, header, param, and query, which are defined in the urn:schemas-microsoft-com:xml-sql namespace.

The keyword elements, nested inside the <ROOT> element, allow you to pass parameters to the template:

❑ The <query> element is used to contain the actual SQL statements that make up the query to be run by the template.

❑ The <header> element acts as a container element in which you can specify multiple parameters using the <param> element.

❑ The <param> element is used to define the parameter name and its optional value.

The following XML template (ch20_ex01.xml) executes a simple SELECT query:

```
<ROOT xmlns:sql="urn:schemas-microsoft-com:xml-sql">
   <sql:query>
      SELECT FirstName, LastName
      FROM Employees
      WHERE EmployeeID = 6
      FOR XML AUTO
   </sql:query>
</ROOT>
```

The only parameter that we are passing here is the actual SQL query we want to run. The query is on the Employees table, and asks for the first and last names of the employee whose EmployeeID is 6. The templates are stored in the directory associated with the virtual name of type template (which is Template in the example below, to make things easier to understand) – you can test this template by specifying this URL:

```
http://localhost/Virtualdirectory/Template/ch20_ex01.xml
```

765

Remember to fill in the name of your `Virtualdirectory`. Because we are executing this template via a URL, which is sent over an IIS Server via HTTP, the result will also be returned via HTTP. The file returned will be the template with the result in place of the SQL query, as follows:

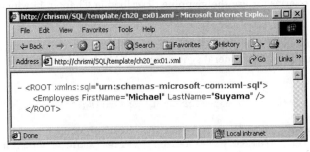

Now let's expand this template (`ch20_ex02.xml`), this time we will add a parameter to the SQL query. Here the parameter that the query takes is `EmpID`:

```
<ROOT xmlns:sql="urn:schemas-microsoft-com:xml-sql">
    <sql:header>
        <sql:param name='EmpID'>1</sql:param>
    </sql:header>
    <sql:query>
        SELECT FirstName, LastName
        FROM Employees
        WHERE EmployeeID = @EmpID
        FOR XML AUTO
    </sql:query>
</ROOT>
```

This example demonstrates how the parameters are used. They allow us to pass values into the template (we will see how to do this programmatically later in the chapter once we have demonstrated their syntax). As you can see, this template has a parameter `EmpID`, as the value of the `name` attribute on the `<param>` element:

```
<sql:param name='EmpID'>1</sql:param>
```

This is then referred to in the SQL query:

```
WHERE EmployeeID = @EmpID
```

In executing this template, if parameter value is not provided, then the default value `1` is used (the default is specified as the content of the element). You can test it by specifying the following URL:

```
http://localhost/Virtualdirectory/Template/ch20_ex02.xml?EmpID=5
```

And here is the result:

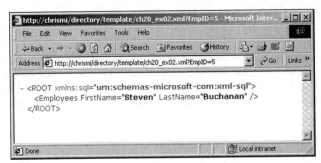

Templates Featuring XPath Queries

In Chapter 15, when we looked at XML Views, we saw that you had to provide a schema with your XPath queries to map the XML structure you want returned to the tables and columns in the database. You can either specify the schema to be used or provide it directly in the template (in the latter case it is known as an **inline schema**). The schema syntax used is XDR, and we must add the annotations we met in Chapter 15 to provide the mapping.

The XPath query is specified in the `<xpath-query>` tag, and the schema file name is provided as a value of the `mapping-schema` attribute (this is the schema against which the XPath query is executed). The following example shows how an XPath query can be specified in a template (`ch20_ex03.xml`):

```
<ROOT xmlns:sql="urn:schemas-microsoft-com:xml-sql">
    <sql:header>
        <sql:param name='EmpID'>1</sql:param>
    </sql:header>
    <sql:xpath-query mapping-schema="ch20_ex04.xml">
        /Employees[@EmployeeID=$EmpID]
    </sql:xpath-query>
</ROOT>
```

Here is the mapping schema to run the query against (`ch20_ex04.xml`), so to test this example the schema must be placed in the directory associated with virtual name of type **template** (or one of its subdirectories in which case path relative to the template directory must be specified):

```
<?xml version="1.0" ?>
<Schema xmlns="urn:schemas-microsoft-com:xml-data"
    xmlns:dt="urn:schemas-microsoft-com:datatypes"
    xmlns:sql="urn:schemas-microsoft-com:xml-sql">

<ElementType name="Employees" >
    <AttributeType name="EmployeeID" />
    <AttributeType name="FirstName" />
    <AttributeType name="LastName" />

    <attribute type="EmployeeID" />
    <attribute type="FirstName" />
    <attribute type="LastName" />
</ElementType>
</Schema>
```

The following URL can be used to test this example:

```
http://localhost/Virtualname/template/ch20_ex03.xml?EmpID=7
```

The `EmpID` in the URL is the parameter with value 7. The isapi extension (`sqlisapi.dll`) inserts the parameter value into the template. When the template is run, using the above URL, the resulting XML looks like this:

```
<ROOT xmlns:sql="urn:schemas-microsoft-com:xml-sql">
    <Employees EmployeeID="7" FirstName="Robert" LastName="King" />
</ROOT>
```

Applying XSLT to a Template

You can even apply an XSL transformation to the resulting XML by specifying an XSL file in the template using the `xsl` attribute, as shown below, in the template, `ch20_ex05.xml`:

```
<root
    xmlns:sql='urn:schemas-microsoft-com:xml-sql'
    sql:xsl='ch20_ex05.xsl'>
<sql:query>
    SELECT CustomerID, ContactName, City
    FROM Customers
    FOR XML AUTO
</sql:query>
</root>
```

The stylesheet below (`ch20_ex05.xsl`) is then applied at the server after the template is successfully executed and prior to the result being sent to the client.

```
<?xml version='1.0' encoding='UTF-8'?>
    <xsl:stylesheet xmlns:xsl="http://www.w3.org/1999/XSL/Transform"
version="1.0">

    <xsl:template match = '*'>
        <xsl:apply-templates />
    </xsl:template>
    <xsl:template match = 'Customers'>
        <TR>
            <TD><xsl:value-of select = '@CustomerID' /></TD>
            <TD><xsl:value-of select = '@ContactName' /></TD>
            <TD><xsl:value-of select = '@City' /></TD>
        </TR>
    </xsl:template>
    <xsl:template match = '/'>
    <HTML>
        <HEAD>
            <STYLE>th { background-color: #CCCCCC }</STYLE>
        </HEAD>
        <BODY>
            <TABLE border='1' style='width:300;'>
                <TR><TH colspan='2'>Customer List</TH></TR>
                <TR><TH >Customer ID</TH><TH>Contact Name</TH><TH>City</TH></TR>
                <xsl:apply-templates select = 'root' />
            </TABLE>
        </BODY>
    </HTML>
    </xsl:template>
</xsl:stylesheet>
```

To test this example, save the template and the stylesheet in the directory associated with virtual name of type template. This URL then executes the template:

```
http://localhost/Virtualroot/Template/ch20_ex05.xml?contenttype=text/html
```

The screenshot below shows part of the resulting output:

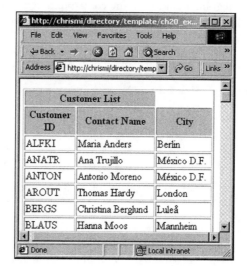

Updategrams

As we said earlier, we can also use an updategram in the XML template, with a SQL query. We met updategrams in Chpater 15, where we used them to update the contents of SQL Server 2000. Updategrams consist of `<sync>`, `<before>` and `<after>` tags.

The following template (ch20_ex06.xml) uses an updategram to insert a record in the Employees table.

```
<ROOT xmlns:updg="urn:schemas-microsoft-com:xml-updategram"
    xmlns:sql="urn:schemas-microsoft-com:xml-sql" >

    <updg:sync >
        <updg:before>
        </updg:before>
        <updg:after>
        <Employees FirstName="Joe" LastName="Smith" />
        </updg:after>
    </updg:sync>
    <sql:query>
        SELECT EmployeeID, FirstName, LastName
        FROM Employees
        FOR XML AUTO
    </sql:query>
</ROOT>
```

This example can be run by using the following URL

```
http://localhost/Virtualroot/Template/ch20_ex06.xml
```

As you may remember updategrams can be used with a mapping schema – if one is provided. In this examples, we have not provided one, so default mapping takes place, which means that element names map to the table name and the attribute names map to columns in the table.

In the following updategram, a mapping schema is specified because the element and attribute names specified in the updategram don't match the corresponding table and column names. This is the updategram (ch20_ex07.xml). Save this file in the directory associated with virtual name of type template.

```
<ROOT xmlns:updg="urn:schemas-microsoft-com:xml-updategram"
    xmlns:sql="urn:schemas-microsoft-com:xml-sql" >
    <updg:sync mapping-schema="ch20_ex07.xdr" >
        <updg:before>
        </updg:before>
        <updg:after>
        <Emp FName="Joeeeee" LName="Smitheeee" />
        </updg:after>
    </updg:sync>
    <sql:query>
        SELECT EmployeeID, FirstName, LastName
        FROM Employees
        FOR XML AUTO
    </sql:query>
</ROOT>
```

This is the mapping schema (ch20_ex07.xdr). Save it in the same directory where template file is stored.

```
<?xml version="1.0" ?>
<Schema xmlns="urn:schemas-microsoft-com:xml-data"
    xmlns:dt="urn:schemas-microsoft-com:datatypes"
    xmlns:sql="urn:schemas-microsoft-com:xml-sql">

<AttributeType name="Contact" />

<ElementType name="Emp" sql:relation="Employees" >
    <AttributeType name="FName" />
    <AttributeType name="LName" />

    <attribute type="FName" sql:field="FirstName" />
    <attribute type="LName" sql:field="LastName" />
</ElementType>
</Schema>
```

This example can be run by using the following URL (same as the previous example):

```
http://localhost/Virtualroot/Template/ch20_ex07.xml
```

Note again that we specified the schema in this case because the element/attribute names are not the same as the table and column names to which they map. For example, the element name <Emp> is different from the table Employees to which it maps. The mapping schema provides the necessary mapping.

Posting a Template Using an HTML Form

So far, we have seen the potential power of using templates, although they have been run from files sitting on the server executed using a URL. We can really take advantage of this functionality, however, by calling it from an HTML form. In this section, we will show you how to call a template from a form. We will start by just triggering them from a button, but will then move on to see how they can be associated with form fields so that the user's input is passed into the template as a parameter.

Posting a Template to the Server

In the first example, we use a simple HTML form to send the template to the server. Here is the code for the form (`ch20_ex08.html`). Save this file anywhere (say on the C:\ drive) and open it in the browser:

```
<html>
   <head>
      <title>Sample Form </title>
   </head>
   <body>
      <form action="http://localhost/northwind" method="POST">
<input type="hidden" name="contenttype" value=text/xml >
<input type="hidden" name="template" value="
   <root xmlns:sql='urn:schemas-microsoft-com:xml-sql' >
   <sql:query>
   SELECT top 5 CustomerID, ContactName, City
   FROM Customers
   FOR XML AUTO
   </sql:query>
   </root>
">
<p><input type="submit" value="Show customers" >
</form>
   </body>
</html>
```

Remember to create a virtual root using IIS Virtual Directory Management for SQL Server utility and specify that virtual root in the HTML form's action. This applies to all following examples of this type.

The form it produces is very simple, with just one button:

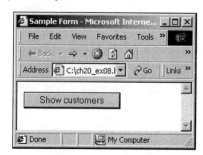

What is actually happening, is that we have the template code in a hidden form field called `template`:

```
<input type="hidden" name="template" value="
   <root xmlns:sql='urn:schemas-microsoft-com:xml-sql' >
   <sql:query>
   SELECT top 5 CustomerID, ContactName, City
   FROM Customers
   FOR XML AUTO
   </sql:query>
   </root>
">
```

For this to work, the form requires one additional hidden field `contenttype`, which sets the content type of the request to XML:

```
<input type="hidden" name="contenttype" value=text/xml >
```

The `action` of the form is set to the URL (that is, the form is posted to the URL) of our virtual directory.

```
<input type="submit" value="Show customers" >
```

For the POST operation to succeed, the virtual directory must allow the POST method. This should provide you with no problems if you have set up the virtual directory as explained in appendix E.

Here is the result that is returned:

```
<root xmlns:sql="urn:schemas-microsoft-com:xml-sql">
<Customers CustomerID="ALFKI" ContactName="Maria Anders" City="Berlin" />
<Customers CustomerID="ANATR" ContactName="Ana Trujillo" City="México D.F." />
<Customers CustomerID="ANTON" ContactName="Antonio Moreno" City="México D.F." />
<Customers CustomerID="AROUT" ContactName="Thomas Hardy" City="London" />
<Customers CustomerID="BERGS" ContactName="Christina Berglund" City="Luleå" />
</root>
```

You can apply XML transformation to the query result. Here is the revised HTML form in which we execute the same query but this time we specify an XSL file. As a result you get the customer information displayed in a table form. Save this file (ch20_ex09.html) anywhere on your machine (say C:\) and open it in the browser:

```
<html>
    <head>
        <title>Sample Form </title>
    </head>
    <body>
        <form action="http://localhost/Virtualroot" method="POST">
        <input type="hidden" name="contenttype" value=text/html >

        <input type="hidden" name="template" value="
        <root xmlns:sql='urn:schemas-microsoft-com:xml-sql' >
        <sql:query>
        SELECT top 5 CustomerID, ContactName, City
        FROM Customers
        FOR XML AUTO
        </sql:query>
        </root>
        ">

    <input type="hidden" name="xsl" value="ch20_ex09.xsl" >
        <p><input type="submit" value=" Show all Customers" >
        </form>
    </body>
</html>
```

Note that the contenttype is specified as text/html because the XSL transforms the result into an HTML format. Therefore, to display it in the browser as a table, the content type is set as text/html.

This is the XSL file (ch20_ex09.xsl) to be placed in your virtual root directory.

```
<?xml version='1.0' encoding='UTF-8'?>
    <xsl:stylesheet xmlns:xsl="http://www.w3.org/1999/XSL/Transform"
version="1.0">

    <xsl:template match = '*'>
       <xsl:apply-templates />
    </xsl:template>
    <xsl:template match = 'Customers'>
       <TR>
          <TD><xsl:value-of select = '@CustomerID' /></TD>
          <TD><xsl:value-of select = '@ContactName' /></TD>
          <TD><xsl:value-of select = '@City' /></TD>
       </TR>
    </xsl:template>
    <xsl:template match = '/'>
    <HTML>
       <HEAD>
          <STYLE>th { background-color: #CCCCCC }</STYLE>
       </HEAD>
       <BODY>
          <TABLE border='1' style='width:300;'>
             <TR><TH colspan='3'>Customer List</TH></TR>
            <TR><TH >Customer ID</TH><TH>Contact Name</TH><TH>City</TH></TR>
             <xsl:apply-templates select = 'root' />
          </TABLE>
       </BODY>
    </HTML>
    </xsl:template>
</xsl:stylesheet>
```

The result of this XSL transformation is a 3-column table (CustomerID, ContactName, City) displayed in the browser, similar to the one produced by ch20_ex05.xml and its associated stylesheet.

Of course, this has the query hard coded into the page – to make this truly useful we would need to be able to pass in parameters to the template – this is what we will look at next.

Passing Parameters to the Query

Remember from our earlier examples, that we can pass parameters to the query if they are identified in the <sql:header> tag in the template. We can modify our HTML code to pass the parameter value. This application is similar to the previous application with the following exceptions:

❑ The XML template takes one parameter which limits the scope of the SELECT statement specified in it.

❑ The client provides the value of this parameter as one of the values in the form (CustomerID).

Save the following file (ch20_ex10.html) anywhere (say, the root of your C:\ drive) and open it in the browser. When the form is submitted, the template and the parameter value are sent as two separate items in the POST header:

```
<html>
    <head>
        <title>Sample Form </title>
    </head>
    <body>
    For a given customer ID, contact name and city information retrieved.
    <form action="http://localhost/Virtualroot" method="POST">
        <b>Customer ID:</b>
        <input type="text" name="CustomerID" value="ALFKI">
        <input type="hidden" name="contenttype" value="text/xml" >
        <input type="hidden" name="template" value="
        <root xmlns:sql='urn:schemas-microsoft-com:xml-sql' >
        <sql:header>
            <sql:param name='CustomerID'>ALFKI</sql:param>
        </sql:header>
        <sql:query>
            SELECT CustomerID, ContactName, City
            FROM Customers
            WHERE CustomerID=@CustomerID
            FOR XML AUTO
        </sql:query>
        </root>
        ">
    <p><input type="submit">
    </form>
    </body>
</head>
```

There are security implications with executing templates in this manner. As the template is contained in the HTML form, the client has complete access to its contents and can therefore change the query. For this reason, it is best to store the XML template on the IIS server and have the client POST to a virtual name of template type that has been configured using the SQL Server virtual directory administration tool. We will discuss this later.

Executing Template Files

Rather than passing the template to the server from a hidden form field, you can have the form execute the XML template on the server when you click a button on the HTML file. In this example, instead of specifying the XML template in the HTML form, the XML template file is stored (ch20_ex11.xml) on the IIS server in the directory associated with the virtual name of template type. To do this, we just set the form's action to the URL of the template file. Here is the template:

```
<ROOT xmlns:sql="urn:schemas-microsoft-com:xml-sql" >
<sql:query>
    SELECT top 5 CustomerID, ContactName, City
    FROM Customers
    FOR XML AUTO
</sql:query>
</ROOT>
```

Since this template file is stored in the virtual directory, all the requests for the file are handled by the ISAPI extension (sqlisapi.dll). Therefore, users do not have access to the contents of the template file and cannot change the query inside the template. Here is the revised HTML (ch20_ex11.html). Save this file anywhere (say your C:\ drive root).

```
<html>
   <head>
      <title>Sample Form </title>
   </head>
   <body>
      Display first 5 customers.
      <form action="http://localhost/Virtualroot/template/ch20_ex11.xml"
      method="POST">
      <input type="hidden" name="contenttype" value="text/xml" >
      <p><input type="submit" value="Find customers" >
      </form>
   </body>
</html>
```

Passing Parameters to Template Files

We promised earlier that we would show you how to pass parameters to the XML templates from form fields. This can be done quite simply, by adding a form field whose names match the parameters accepted by the template.

Let's start with a simple example, where the template takes just one parameter (EmployeeID). This will allow us to enter the ID of the employee and retrieve their first and last names.

Here is the revised template (you should be familiar with the syntax by now). Save this template file (ch20_ex12.xml) on the IIS server in the directory associated with the virtual name of template type.

```
<ROOT xmlns:sql="urn:schemas-microsoft-com:xml-sql" >
   <sql:header>
      <sql:param name="CustomerID">ALFKI</sql:param>
   </sql:header>
   <sql:query>
      SELECT CustomerID, ContactName, City
      FROM Customers
      WHERE CustomerID=@CustomerID
      FOR XML AUTO
   </sql:query>
</ROOT>
```

And here is the revised HTML form (ch20_ex12.html). Note that we have the action of the form pointing to the URL of the template. The addition of the input element where we type the number of the employee we wish to retrieve, allows us to pass the value added by the user to the template:

```
<html>
   <head>
      <title>Sample Form </title>
   </head>
   <body>
      For a given employee ID, employee first and last name is retrieved.
      <form action="http://localhost/Virtualroot/template/ch20_ex12.xml"
         method="POST">
         <input type="text" name="CustomerID" value="ALFKI" >
         <input type="hidden" name="contenttype" value="text/xml" >
         <p><input type="submit" value="Find Customer" >
      </form>
   </body>
</html>
```

The simple form looks like this:

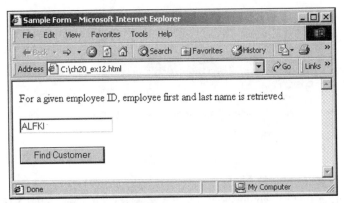

And here is the result that is returned to us when we execute this query:

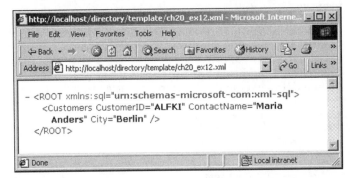

Sample ASP Application

Now we come to a more interesting application that makes use of Active Server Pages (ASP), which allows the user to update the records in the database.

We will create a single ASP page which will generate a form for the user to enter the employee ID in a form when it is first accessed, and which will then return the employee name details when the user clicks on the button to submit the ID. This is done using the methods that we have already demonstrated. (If no ID is presented when the user clicks on the button, the blank form is returned for them to fill in.) When the result is displayed, the user then gets the option to edit the record using an XML updategram.

Here is the form that the ASP generates if no ID is specified:

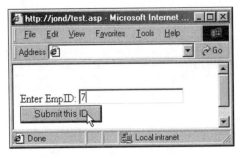

When a value is entered into the form, the ASP page uses this value to execute the following XML template to retrieve the specified employee's record.

```
<root xmlns:sql="urn:schemas-microsoft-com:xml-sql">
   <sql:header>
      <sql:param name="eid"></sql:param>
   </sql:header>
   <sql:query>
      SELECT eid, fname, lname
      FROM Employee
      WHERE eid=@eid
      FOR XML AUTO
   </sql:query>
</root>
```

The template is executed using the server-side HTTP functionality provided in MSXML 3.0. The resulting employee record is in the form of an XML document. The server then uses MSXML to parse this document and retrieve the fname and lname attribute values. These values are then passed to the client as values of fields in a dynamically generated HTML form. Here are the returned details for the user to update:

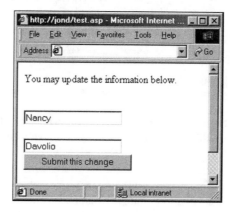

The client can then modify these values and submit this new form whose action is set to execute another template, which contains an XML updategram:

```
<ROOT xmlns:updg="urn:schemas-microsoft-com:xml-updategram">
<updg:header>
   <updg:param name="eid"/>
   <updg:param name="fname" />
   <updg:param name="lname" />
</updg:header>
<updg:sync >
   <updg:before>
      <Employee eid="$eid" />
   </updg:before>
   <updg:after>
      <Employee eid="$eid" fname="$fname" lname="$lname" />
   </updg:after>
</updg:sync>
</ROOT>
```

Note that the field names in the dynamically generated HTML form match the parameter names specified in the template.

Creating the Application

Now let's build this application. There are a number of things we need to do here:

- ❏ Create a new database
- ❏ Write the two templates
- ❏ Compose the ASP page that houses the functionality

Let's look at each of these in turn:

Creating the Table

In this example, first use the following SQL script (`ch20_ex15.sql`) to create a new table called `EditEmployees` in **Northwind** database, so that we can edit the entries.

> *We are not using the **Northwind** `Employees` table here because the sample modifies data in the table. Therefore we create our own table and change data as we want*

```
CREATE TABLE EditEmployees (eid int, fname varchar(20), lname varchar(20))

INSERT INTO EditEmployees VALUES (1, 'Nancy', 'Davolio')
INSERT INTO EditEmployees VALUES (2, 'Andrew', 'Fuller')
```

This simply creates a table for us called `EditEmployees`, with the columns `eid`, `fname`, and `lname`. We populate this table using `INSERT` statements so that we have some values to work with.

Creating the Templates

There are two templates in this application, the first to retrieve the employee details based on the ID supplied in the form, and the second to update the database content.

The code for the first template is as follows (`ch20_ex16.xml`):

```
<root xmlns:sql="urn:schemas-microsoft-com:xml-sql">
   <sql:header>
      <sql:param name="eid"></sql:param>
   </sql:header>
   <sql:query>
      SELECT eid, fname, lname
      FROM EditEmployees
      WHERE eid=@eid
      FOR XML AUTO
   </sql:query>
</root>
```

This template needs to be saved in the directory associated with the virtual name of `template` type.

The second template is a little more complicated, as it uses the updategram to allow the user to edit the record. We explored using updategrams in Chapter 15. This template is called `ch20_ex17.xml`.

```xml
<ROOT xmlns:updg="urn:schemas-microsoft-com:xml-updategram">
<updg:header>
   <updg:param name="eid"/>
   <updg:param name="fname" />
   <updg:param name="lname" />
</updg:header>
<updg:sync >
   <updg:before>
      <EditEmployees eid="$eid" />
   </updg:before>
   <updg:after>
      <EditEmployees eid="$eid" fname="$fname" lname="$lname" />
   </updg:after>
</updg:sync>
</ROOT>
```

The template will take the employee id, and use this to select the appropriate record, because we do not allow the user to re-write the id for the user (only the names) we write this back in to make sure that it overwrites the correct record. Save this in the same place as the first template.

Writing the ASP Page

Now we come on to the main ASP page. Since the page we will be creating is an ASP application, it must be placed in a virtual root, which must be created using the Internet Services Manager tool. You cannot use the virtual root that was created using the IIS Virtual Directory Management for SQL Server utility, because that virtual root is only configured for use with SQL Server and cannot handle ASP requests.

To create a new virtual root for the ASP application, start the Internet Services Manager tool. To create a new virtual directory, highlight the Default Web Site, go to the Action menu, and select New. Provide the virtual directory name, and then path to the physical directory in which the following ASP application will be saved (`ch20_ex17.asp`).

Let's step through the code for the ASP Page and see what it is doing here. We start by declaring our scripting language, VBScript, and the `EmpID` variable to hold the `EmpID`. :

```asp
<% LANGUAGE=VBSCRIPT %>
<%
   Dim EmpID
```

Remember that, if the user is loading the page for the first time, we want to show them the form to collect user data, so we need to check if the id has been specified. So, we set `EmpID` to the value of the input box that would contain the employee id if the user had already seen the form. We then write out the start of the HTML code for the page to be displayed, and start an `if... then` statement to display the first form if the `id` has not been specified.

```asp
   EmpID=Request.Form("eid")
%>

<html>
<body>

<%
   'if employee id value is not yet provided, display this form
   if EmpID="" then
%>
```

If `EmpID` is empty, we start the `<FORM>` element and write that back to the client. When the user submits the id, it will be posted back to the same ASP page.

```
<!-- the EmpID has not been specified so we display the form that allows users to
enter an id -->

<form action="ch20_ex16.asp" method="POST">

<br>

Enter EmpID: <input type=text name="eid"><br>
<input type=submit value="Submit this ID" ><br><br>
```

Once the user has specified an `id`, we get passed onto this section, which creates retrieves the record.

```
<-- Otherwise, we have already entered an employee ID, so display the second part
of the form where the user can change fname and lname -->

<%
  else
%>

<form name="Employee" action="http://localhost/VirtualRoot/Template/Ch20_ex17.xml"
method="POST">

You may update the first name and last name information below.<br><br>

<!-- comment goes here to separate the parts of the application or page -->
<br>
<%
  ' Let us load the document in the parser and extract the values to populate the
form.
  Set objXML=Server.CreateObject("MSXML2.DomDocument")

  objXML.async=False
  objXML.Load("http://localhost/northwind/Template/Ch20_ex16.xml?eid=" & EmpID)
  set objEmployee=objXML.documentElement.childNodes.Item(0)


  ' In retrieving data form the database, if a value in the column is NULL,
  ' we don't get any attribute for the corresponding element. In this
  ' case we want to skip the error generation and go to the next attribute
  On Error Resume Next

  ' get the eid attribute value
  Response.Write "Emp ID: <input type=text readonly=true style='background-
color:silver' name=eid value="""
  Response.Write objEmployee.attributes(0).value
  Response.Write """><br><br>"

  ' get the fname attribute value
  Response.Write "First Name: <input type=text name=fname value="""
  Response.Write objEmployee.attributes(1).value
  Response.Write """><br><br>"
```

```
' the "lname" attribute
  Response.Write "Last Name: <input type=text name=lname value="""
  Response.Write objEmployee.attributes(2).value
  Response.Write """><br>"

  set objEmployee=Nothing
  Set objXML=Nothing
%>
<input type="submit" value="Submit this change" ><br><br>
<input type=hidden name="contenttype" value="text/xml">
<input type=hidden name="eeid" value="<%=EmpID%>"><br><br>

<% end if %>
</form>
</body>
</html>
```

This example illustrates how easy it is to write ASP applications to retrieve and process XML with SQL Server XML functionality. The size of the code is much smaller and the application is more secure as all the business logic is controlled by the server and not present in the HTML transmitted to the client.

Sample ADO Applications

Having seen how to pass the records as XML across HTTP using URLs to call templates, we will now look at how we can use ADO from a Visual Basic form. ADO is a client dependent method of accessing and manipulating SQL Server data using XML. The clients must have Microsoft Data Access Components 2.6 or higher for this functionality. One immediate advantage of this method is a distributed load. Whereas in ASP applications the server handles all the processing of data, client-side ADO applications use the processing power of the client to manage data. One of the more likely usages of ADO is the custom client applications that may require high speed batch editing of data sets where an HTML interface may not be appropriate. For a more complete discussion of the XML capabilities of ADO and ADO+, refer to chapter 13.

In this Visual Basic application a command is executed using ADO. The command executes a simple SELECT query against the Northwind database. The query specifies the FOR XML clause. Therefore, instead of getting a record set, XML is returned upon the execution of the command, and since the result itself is XML, it must be returned as a stream. It is important to note here that the structure of the returned XML document is entirely controlled by the query executed. This method is more flexible than using other ADO features which transform record sets into XML documents.

Executing a Command

To get us going with using VB and ADO, we'll start by simply executing a SELECT statement that is hard coded into the VB form. The SELECT statement uses the FOR XML clause to return XML as a string that is displayed to the user.

Start up Visual Basic and create a new Visual Basic Project. A Standard EXE project is sufficient. Add a reference to ADO 2.6. We need at least this version because earlier versions of ADO where not designed to work with SQL Server XML features. This code can be found in the download, saved as ch20_ex18:

```
Private Sub Form_Load()

Dim cmd As New ADODB.Command
Dim conn As New ADODB.Connection
Dim strmOut As New ADODB.Stream

' Open a connection to the SQL Server.
conn.Provider = "SQLOLEDB"
conn.Open "server=(local); database=Northwind; uid=sa; "

Set cmd.ActiveConnection = conn
cmd.CommandText = "SELECT FirstName, LastName FROM Employees FOR XML AUTO"

' Execute the command, open the return stream, and read the result.
strmOut.Open
strmOut.LineSeparator = adCRLF
cmd.Properties("Output Stream").Value = strmOut

cmd.Execute , , adExecuteStream
strmOut.Position = 0
Debug.Print strmOut.ReadText

End Sub
```

When we run this application it will retrieve the records from Northwind specified in the query, and displays them in the immediate window:

Executing an XML Template

Now let's look at an example that makes use of an XML template. This time, we will be using ADO to execute the template. There are three key parts to this example:

❑ We use the FileSystemObject to open a text stream over a text file, which contains the XML template. This method returns TextStream object.

❑ The data in this stream is passed to an ADO stream. To do this we convert the TextStream object into ADOStream object which is understood by the ADO command object (cmd). We need to do this because the ADO command object doesn't understand TextStream, but does understand ADOStream.

❑ The ADO stream is then executed using the connection to SQL Server.

In testing this application, you must include the Microsoft Scripting Runtime project reference. It contains the FileSystemObject, which is needed to perform the file operations. You also need a reference to ADO 2.6.

Let's step through this code (ch20_ex20): The application first opens a standard connection to SQL Server 2000 using the ADO connection object (ADODB.Connection).

```
Private Sub Form_Load()
Dim cmd As New ADODB.Command
Dim conn As New ADODB.Connection
Dim strmIn As New ADODB.Stream
Dim txtStream As TextStream
Dim strmOut As New ADODB.Stream
Dim objFSO As New FileSystemObject

' Open a connection to the SQL Server.
conn.Provider = "SQLOLEDB"
conn.Open "server=(local); database=Northwind; uid=sa; "

Set cmd.ActiveConnection = conn
```

Next we set the dialect for the ADO command object (ADODB.Command). Since you are executing an XML template, we must set the ADO commands dialect to MSSQLXML. This setting instructs ADO to specifically interact with SQL Server XML features.

```
' Set the command dialect to XML (DBGUID_MSSQLXML).
cmd.Dialect = "{5d531cb2-e6ed-11d2-b252-00c04f681b71}"
```

Then a stream is opened over the XML template file using the OpenTextFile method of the FileSystemObject (objFSO). Using the ReadALL method on the TextStream object (txtStream), the contents of the template file are written into an ADO stream (strmIn). The position of each stream is reset to 0 prior to executing the command and prior to reading the result. We use the TextStream.ReadALL command to return a string and then later used this string to create the ADOStream object.

```
' Open the command stream and write our template to it.
strmIn.Open

Set txtStream =
objFSO.OpenTextFile("C:\inetpub\wwwroot\Northwind\template\ch20_ex20.xml",_
                   ForReading)
strmIn.WriteText txtStream.ReadAll
strmIn.Position = 0
```

The ADO stream (strmIn) is then assigned to the CommandStream property of the ADO command object (cmd).

```
Set cmd.CommandStream = strmIn
```

To execute the template we first open the output stream (strmOut.Open) and set the command's Output Stream property to this stream.

```
' Execute the command, open the return stream, and read the result.
strmOut.Open
strmOut.LineSeparator = adCRLF
cmd.Properties("Output Stream").Value = strmOut
```

Finally the command's execute method (cmd.Execute) is called specifying adExecuteStream as the third parameter (the options parameter). The data in the output stream (strmOut) is accessed using the ReadText method of the ADO stream object (ADODB.Stream).

```
cmd.Execute , , adExecuteStream
strmOut.Position = 0
Debug.Print strmOut.ReadText


End Sub
```

Here is the sample XML template that is executed in our Visual Basic application. Save this template (ch20_ex20.xml) in the directory associated with virtual name of template type (it doesn't have to be in this directory for ADO application. But we will use the same template in another application later):

```
<ROOT xmlns:sql="urn:schemas-microsoft-com:xml-sql" >
<sql:query>
    SELECT FirstName, LastName
    FROM Employees
    where EmployeeID=1
    FOR XML AUTO
</sql:query>
</ROOT>
```

As before the results are passed to the immediate window.

Passing Parameters

The next application is similar to the previous one, except for the following:

❑   The XML template executes an XPath query against XML View

❑   This template accepts one parameter which must be passed through ADO

The Visual Basic application is given below. It is similar to the previous example except now parameter information is added in the code. Here is the code again; we have highlighted the differences in the two versions:

```
Private Sub Form_Load ()

Dim cmd As New ADODB.Command
Dim conn As New ADODB.Connection
Dim strmIn As New ADODB.Stream
Dim txtStream As TextStream
Dim strmOut As New ADODB.Stream
Dim objFSO As New FileSystemObject
```

Prior to executing the command, an ADO parameter (ADODB.Parameter) is added to the command object's parameters collection. This parameter stores The employeeID, which is required by the XPath query in the template.

```
Dim objParam As ADODB.Parameter

' Open a connection to the SQL Server.
conn.Provider = "SQLOLEDB"
conn.Open "server=(local); database=Northwind; uid=sa; "

Set cmd.ActiveConnection = conn
```

```
' Set the command dialect to XML (DBGUID_MSSQLXML).
cmd.Dialect = "{5d531cb2-e6ed-11d2-b252-00c04f681b71}"

' Open the command stream and write our template to it.
strmIn.Open

Set txtStream =
objFSO.OpenTextFile("C:\inetpub\wwwroot\Northwind\template\ch20_ex21.xml",_
        ForReading)
strmIn.WriteText txtStream.ReadAll
strmIn.Position = 0

Set cmd.CommandStream = strmIn
' Execute the command, open the return stream, and read the result.
strmOut.Open
strmOut.LineSeparator = adCRLF
cmd.Properties("Output Stream").Value = strmOut
```

The parameter name must be prefixed with the @ in the parameter's definition. The parameter is marked as an input parameter by specifying adParamInput as the value of the Direction property. The value of the Size property determines the maximum number of characters that will be passed to the template. In this example 25 is sufficient. In passing parameters to templates that execute an XPath query, note that XPath can use only string-valued parameters.

```
Set objParam = cmd.CreateParameter

objParam.Name = "@EmployeeID"
objParam.Direction = adParamInput
objParam.Type = adWChar
objParam.Size = 25
objParam.Value = "6"
cmd.Parameters.Append objParam
cmd.NamedParameters = True

cmd.Execute , , adExecuteStream
strmOut.Position = 0
Debug.Print strmOut.ReadText

End Sub
```

In testing this application (ch20_ex21), you must include the Microsoft Scripting Runtime project reference. It contains the FileSystemObject, which is needed to perform the file operations, as well as a reference to the ADO 2.6 library.

Now let's look at the revised template. Notice that the XML template specifies XML view using an inline XDR schema. Since the schema is inline, the value of mapping-schema attribute has the '#' character in the beginning indicating the schema is inline (in the same template file).

In the XPath query:

```
Employees[@EmployeeID=$EmployeeID]
```

785

the $EmployeeID is the parameter passed to the template. The query retrieves Employees elements with specific value for its EmployeeID attribute. The template parameter is defined in the <sql:header> tag in the template.

Save this template (ch20_ex21.xml) in the directory associated with the virtual name of template type (it can be anywhere for this application but we will use this template in later examples, executed in the URL).

```
<ROOT xmlns:sql="urn:schemas-microsoft-com:xml-sql">
    <Schema xmlns="urn:schemas-microsoft-com:xml-data"
    sql:id="MyMappingSchema"
    sql:is-mapping-schema="1">

    <ElementType name="Employees" >
        <AttributeType name="EmployeeID" />
        <AttributeType name="FirstName" />
        <AttributeType name="LastName" />

        <attribute type="EmployeeID" />
        <attribute type="FirstName" />
        <attribute type="LastName" />
    </ElementType>
    </Schema>

    <sql:header>
        <sql:param name='EmployeeID'>1</sql:param>
    </sql:header>
    <sql:xpath-query mapping-schema="#MyMappingSchema">
        Employees[@EmployeeID=$EmployeeID]
    </sql:xpath-query>
</ROOT>
```

Again the results are printed out to the immediate window.

Having seen some examples of accessing SQL server's XML capabilities over HTTP, let's look at a more integrated case study that brings together some of the ideas that we have seen so far.

Building an Empire: an eLemonade Company

For the rest of this chapter, we will use a prototype e-commerce scenario to demonstrate the use of OpenXML, FOR XML, XPath, and Updategrams. All of these technologies may be used independently or together with others; however, a natural pairing is OpenXML with FOR XML, and XPath with Updategrams. We will present a scenario and two solutions, one for each pair of technologies. The solutions presented demonstrate the strengths and weaknesses of these technologies.

We begin by describing the requirements for this project, and then outlining solutions to some of the problems presented. Next, we explore a solution using OPENXML and FOR XML, and then consider a different solution using XML Views, XPath, and Updategrams.

The Internet Lemonade Stand – Project Requirements

Let's suppose that you've decided to open your storefront online, and you've identified your target market: thirsty web surfers. Recalling a classic computer game, you are suddenly inspired: Yes, that's right, this will be the Internet lemonade stand.

Based on years of experience and substantial research in the lemonade stand business, you quickly determine the requirements for your project. Of course, you're selling online, so weather is no longer an issue - it's always sunny somewhere! There are, however, other issues to consider:

❑ You need lemons, and lots of them. You need a way to track your supplies of lemons and sugar.

❑ Of course, you need to track sales and shipping information.

❑ You need to keep a sharp eye on market trends, so you will need to track various news feeds for bulletins that could impact your online lemonade retail business.

❑ Customer loyalty is the key to your success, so you decide to allow users to create profiles to customize the web site layout (and maybe someday track buying patterns over time, to provide targeted advertising).

You're going to develop this web site entirely on your own using the super-cool XML features of SQL Server 2000, so your development budget will be smaller than usual. In fact, it will be negligible in this example, because we're going to do all the work for you. All you need to do is follow the preparatory steps below, using the sample code provided with this book.

The sample code assumes that you have created a SQL virtual directory named `lemonade` with a virtual name `template` to execute template queries. Replace all instances of `http://localhost/lemonade/template` in this example with your actual server location and virtual directory names.

Database Design

In this example, we've chosen a design that allows us to highlight various features of XML support in SQL Server 2000, but one that also shares many characteristics with real-world scenarios. We will not go into all the details of setting up the database, but will instead highlight some relevant points, such as the table structure.

Let's suppose that with the exception of news feeds that allow you to track market trends, you supply all the data yourself (supply costs, advertising costs, sales and revenues). After examining your requirements in detail, you decide to store the data in the database in five tables:

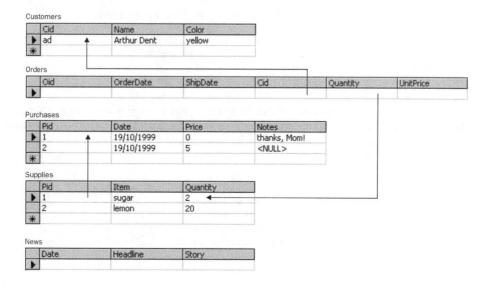

This database, and the tables within it can be created using the following script (ch20_ex22.sql):

```
CREATE DATABASE LEMONADE
GO
USE LEMONADE
GO
-- The NEWS table stores all the news bulletins you collect
CREATE TABLE NEWS
(Date    datetime      not null,    -- publication date
    Headline nvarchar(100)  not null,    -- news headline
    Story    ntext         not null)    -- news content

-- The PURCHASES table stores all the expenditures you make
CREATE TABLE PURCHASES
(Pid    int       identity primary key, -- purchase id
   Date   datetime      not null,    -- date purchased
   Price  money         not null,    -- total cost in dollars
   Notes  nvarchar(100))             -- description or other comments

-- The SUPPLIES table tracks lemon and sugar supplies
CREATE TABLE SUPPLIES
(Pid    int           foreign key references Purchases (Pid),
                      -- corresponding purchase
   Item   nvarchar(10)   not null,   -- lemon, sugar
   Quantity smallint     not null)   -- number of lemons, kilograms sugar

-- The CUSTOMERS table keeps customer-specific information
CREATE TABLE CUSTOMERS
(Cid    nvarchar(12)   primary key,  -- customer id
   Name   nvarchar(50),             -- customer name
   Color  nvarchar(20))             -- favorite color

-- The ORDERS table stores all orders placed through the Internet Lemonade Stand
CREATE TABLE ORDERS
(Oid    int       identity primary key, -- order id
   OrderDate datetime     not null,    -- time order was placed
   ShipDate datetime,                  -- time order was fulfilled
   Cid    nvarchar(12)  foreign key references Customers (cid),
                      -- customer who placed order
   Quantity smallint     not null,    -- liters of lemonade
   UnitPrice money       not null)    -- dollars per liter
```

I'd suggest creating these tables in a new database to keep your examples separate and thus more logically distributed. (I've called mine lemonade), Let's also prepare the database with a customer and initial inventory (Mom kindly supplied sugar for free), by running the following (ch20_ex23.sql) against our lemonade database:

```
INSERT INTO PURCHASES VALUES ('1999-10-19', 0.00, 'thanks, Mom!')
INSERT INTO SUPPLIES VALUES (@@identity, 'sugar', 2)
INSERT INTO PURCHASES VALUES ('1999-10-19', 5.00, NULL)
INSERT INTO SUPPLIES VALUES (@@identity, 'lemon', 20)
INSERT INTO CUSTOMERS VALUES ('ad', 'Arthur Dent', 'yellow')
```

External XML Sources

One major goal of this study is to investigate ways of importing data from external XML sources into a database table (specifically, our NEWS table, in the case of the example below). Let's suppose the news feeds are available from one or more Internet sources in XML form. External sources of XML information can be handled in many ways. In the two different solutions, we will see some of these ways, but for now, let's just look at an example XML source – we'll be using a static XML document, but in practice live, dynamic data works just as well:

```
<NewsStream>
   <Story>
      <Title>Lemon Prices Sour</Title>
      <Date>1999-09-23</Date>
      <Author>Ford Prefect</Author>
      <Text>Today, lemon prices reach a new 52-week low as ...</Text>
   </Story>
   <Story>
      <Title>The Internet Lemonade Stand Opens For Business</Title>
      <Date>1999-10-19</Date>
      <Author>Argle Fargle</Author>
      <Text>In a shrewd move, the Internet Lemonade Stand opened ...</Text>
   </Story>
   <!-- additional news items -->
</NewsStream>
```

The important point is that this XML comes in a form that you do not control, so you have to take whatever you have and map it to your database. This situation presents different problems than having total control over the XML structure. We'll consider different ways to insert this XML into our NEWS table, in the following sections.

The Two Different Solutions

Now it is time to look our two different solutions – one using OpenXML and FOR XML to implement a solution through SQL, and the other being entirely XML-based, using XML Views, XPath and Updategrams.

Each prototype consists of pages to display an internal report of the latest news and expenses, as well as pages that allow customers to create new accounts, edit their profile information, and place and track orders.

Prototyping with OpenXML and FOR XML

Sometimes, a completely SQL-based solution is required. This can be true, for example, if you already have an extensive network of stored procedures and other database logic and want only to extend this system to produce XML output. Sometimes, system constraints can require a SQL solution.

One drawback to this approach is that there is no way to perform server-side XSL transformations in SQL Server. These transformations can be performed using XML templates (as we will see in the next section), ASP, or some other mechanism. Alternatively, the transformation can be effected through the query itself; for example, a query can return HTML directly.

Displaying News and Expenses

Inserting XML into the database can be done using OpenXML. Commonly, you have some external XML source that you must match up with your database structure. To solve this problem effectively, you need to identify the top-most element in the XML that you will map to a row, and then determine how to extract the column values from the XML (relative to the element you chose).

In the case of the news feed above, each <Story> corresponds to one row of the News table, and the <Date>, <Title>, and <Text> elements under it correspond to the date, headline, and story columns, respectively.

So, we can insert the news into the database using an OpenXML statement like this (ch20_ex24.sql):

```
DECLARE @idoc int
EXEC sp_xml_preparedocument @idoc OUTPUT,
'<NewsStream>

</NewsStream>'
INSERT INTO NEWS
SELECT * FROM OpenXML(@idoc,    '/NewsStream/Story', 2)
WITH (Date       datetime    './Date',
      Headline   nvarchar(100) './Title',
      Story      ntext         './Text')
```

Each XPath in the WITH clause selects some XML node relative to the row pattern used in the OpenXML statement. Verifying the insert and displaying the news can then be done in any number of ways; perhaps the simplest is this:

```
SELECT * FROM News ORDER BY [date] FOR XML AUTO, ELEMENTS
```

We use an element-centric mapping because the story text is potentially large, and therefore better placed inside an element than in an attribute.

If this query is placed into an XML template, then the results from this query can then be post-processed using XSL to produce nicely formatted HTML. Let's combine the news with an expense report, reverse ordered by date, using the following template (ch20_ex24.xml):

```
<report sql:xsl="ch20_ex24.xsl" xmlns:sql="urn:schemas-microsoft-com:xml-sql">
   <sql:query>
      SELECT * FROM News ORDER BY Date DESC FOR XML AUTO, ELEMENTS;
      SELECT * FROM Purchases ORDER BY Date DESC FOR XML AUTO;
   </sql:query>
</report>
```

where ch20_ex24.xsl is:

```
<xsl:stylesheet version="1.0" xmlns:xsl="http://www.w3.org/1999/XSL/Transform">
<xsl:output method="html" indent="yes" media-type="text/html" />
   <xsl:template match="/">
      <xsl:apply-templates/>
   </xsl:template>
```

```
    <xsl:template match="report">
    <html>
    <head>
        <title>The Internet Lemonade Stand News And Expense Report</title>
    </head>
    <body>
        <h1>Top News</h1>
        <dl>
        <xsl:apply-templates select="News"/>
        </dl>

        <h1>Inventory Purchases</h1>
        <TABLE BORDER="2">
            <tr>
                <th>date</th>
                <th>total cost</th>
                <th>notes</th>
            </tr>
            <xsl:apply-templates select="Purchases"/>
        </TABLE>
    </body>
    </html>
    </xsl:template>

    <xsl:template match="News">
        <dt>[<xsl:value-of select="Date"/>]
        <b><xsl:value-of select="Headline"/></b></dt>
        <dd><xsl:value-of select="Story"/></dd>
    </xsl:template>

    <xsl:template match="Purchases">
    <tr>
        <td><xsl:value-of select="@Date"/></td>
        <td><xsl:value-of select="@Price" /></td>
        <td><xsl:value-of select="@Notes"/></td>
    </tr>
    </xsl:template>
</xsl:stylesheet>
```

Place Orders and Create Customer Accounts

Data may also be manipulated using plain SQL, without any XML at all. For example, suppose you already have created stored procedures for order placement and customer account manager. A query like:

```
DECLARE @cid nvarchar(12), @quantity smallint, @unit_price money
-- obtain the parameter values, and then
INSERT INTO Orders VALUES (today(), NULL, @cid, @quantity, @unit_price)
```

will create a new order, or a query like:

```
DECLARE @cid nvarchar(12), @name nvarchar(50), @color nvarchar(20)
-- obtain the parameter values, and then
INSERT INTO Customers VALUES (@cid, @name, @color)
```

791

will create a new row in the Customers table.

This technique allows you to combine ordinary relational operations with XML-based inserts using OpenXML. In this way, you can leverage any existing infrastructure to bootstrap an XML implementation (for example, you can continue to use already existing SQL statements by wrapping them in a template).

The following XML template (ch20_ex25.xml) demonstrates creating a customer account using a SQL query; presumably an HTML form supplies the parameter values:

```
<create>
  <sql:header xmlns:sql="urn:schemas-microsoft-com:xml-sql" >
    <sql:param name="color">white</sql:param>
    <sql:param name="id"/>
    <sql:param name="name"/>
  </sql:header>
  <sql:query xmlns:sql="urn:schemas-microsoft-com:xml-sql" >
    INSERT INTO Customers VALUES (@id, @name, @color)
  </sql:query>
</create>
```

Now that you've created a Customer, you might like to view the customer data. Using FOR XML, it is easy to create XML representing the customer data:

```
SELECT * FROM Customers FOR XML AUTO
```

or customers with their purchases:

```
SELECT * FROM Customers JOIN Orders ON Customers.Cid=Orders.Cid FOR XML AUTO
```

For most simple applications, this approach works well. When additional control over the XML shape beyond that provided by FOR XML AUTO is required, EXPLICIT mode can be used to obtain whatever XML shape is needed. See Chapter 14 for details on FOR XML EXPLICIT.

However, FOR XML EXPLICIT can be quite complex, both to develop and to maintain as your XML requirements change. An alternative approach is to use XML Views with XPath and updategram queries. We explore this solution next.

Prototyping with XPath and Updategrams

Using an end-to-end XML-based solution has many advantages over an ad-hoc one. For one thing, XML can be more easily interoperable among platforms and products than other, code-based solutions. For another, real-world data is often most naturally viewed as semi-structured data, not relational data. Finally, changes in the XML shape or content are more readily dealt with when you're already working at the XML level.

To improve maintainability it is also important to have a solution that allows you to work with your data as you naturally think of it. Data is often semi-structured, so XML is a natural representation. XML is also very nicely interoperable with other systems. Consequently, although XPath and Updategrams usually require a little more setup than raw SQL, the benefits pay off in the long term.

Annotate a Schema

In order to use XPath and Updategrams, you must know both the relational design and the XML shape. In our case, we have no XML schema, so we must create one. There are tools available, such as the XML View Mapper, that facilitate creating schemas from existing databases. The XML View Mapper is available from Microsoft's XML Developer Center at http://msdn.microsoft.com/xml. For this example, we'll just write a schema from scratch.

Let's begin with a very simple schema (ch20_ex26.xdr) that exposes all of our tables in the natural way, mapping rows to elements and columns to attributes:

```xml
<Schema xmlns="urn:schemas-microsoft-com:xml-data"
    xmlns:dt="urn:schemas-microsoft-com:datatypes"
    xmlns:sql="urn:schemas-microsoft-com:xml-sql">

    <ElementType name="News" sql:relation="News" sql:field="Story">
        <AttributeType name="date" />
        <AttributeType name="headline"/>
        <attribute type="date"/>
        <attribute type="headline"/>
    </ElementType>

    <ElementType name="Expense" sql:relation="Purchases">
        <AttributeType name="id"/>
        <AttributeType name="date"/>
        <AttributeType name="price"/>
        <AttributeType name="notes"/>
        <attribute type="id" sql:field="Pid"/>
        <attribute type="date"/>
        <attribute type="price"/>
        <attribute type="notes"/>
    </ElementType>

    <AttributeType name="quantity"/>

    <ElementType name="Inventory" sql:relation="Supplies">
        <AttributeType name="id"/>
        <AttributeType name="type"/>
        <attribute type="id" sql:field="Pid"/>
        <attribute type="type" />
        <attribute type="quantity"/>
    </ElementType>

    <ElementType name="Order" sql:relation="Orders">
        <AttributeType name="id"/>
        <AttributeType name="ordered" />
        <AttributeType name="shipped" />
        <AttributeType name="customer"/>
        <AttributeType name="unit-price"/>
        <attribute type="id" sql:field="Oid"/>
        <attribute type="ordered" sql:field="OrderDate"/>
        <attribute type="shipped" sql:field="ShipDate"/>
        <attribute type="customer" sql:field="Cid"/>
        <attribute type="quantity"/>
        <attribute type="unit-price" sql:field="UnitPrice"/>
    </ElementType>
```

```
    <ElementType name="Name" content="textOnly"/>
    <ElementType name="Customer" sql:relation="Customers">
        <AttributeType name="id"/>
        <AttributeType name="color"/>
        <attribute type="id" sql:field="Cid"/>
        <attribute type="color"/>
        <element type="Name"/>
    </ElementType>
</Schema>
```

This schema maps the relational data to XML fairly directly. For illustrative purposes, we have included two elements with text content. Otherwise, this schema is unremarkable, using only the `sql:relation` and `sql:field` annotations.

We can already use this schema to extract data as XML using XPath, for example, in the following template (`ch20_ex26.xml`):

```
<Example xmlns:sql="urn:schemas-microsoft-com:xml-sql">
    <Customers>
        <sql:xpath-query mapping-schema="ch20_ex26.xdr">Customer</sql:xpath-query>
    </Customers>
    <Sales>
        <sql:xpath-query mapping-schema="ch20_ex26.xdr">Order</sql:xpath-query>
    </Sales>
</Example>
```

lists all customers and all sales, using two separate XPath queries (which result in two separate database queries). If we've done everything right, the resulting XML from this query should be as follows:

```
<Example xmlns:sql="urn:schemas-microsoft-com:xml-sql">
    <Customers>
        <Customer id="ad" color="yellow">
            <Name>Arthur Dent</Name>
        </Customer>
    </Customers>
    <Sales/>
</Example>
```

Improve the Schema

However, the schema `ch20_ex26.xdr` does not really represent the shape of our data. None of the elements are connected, even though several of the tables we have in the database are normally joined together.

There are several different XML Views that could make sense for our data, but a customer-centric view is especially relevant. In this view, we list all our customers ordered by name, and the purchases made for each customer. In creating this view, we will also specify additional information about the database, such as key-fields and data types (both XDR and SQL types). We change `Customer`, `Name`, `Order` and `quantity` as follows (only the `Order` `ElementType` is shown):

```
    <AttributeType name="quantity" dt:type="i2" sql:datatype="smallint"/>
      <ElementType name="Order" sql:relation="Orders"
                   sql:key-fields="Oid">
    <AttributeType name="id" dt:type="id" sql:datatype="int"/>
    <AttributeType name="ordered"
        dt:type="dateTime" sql:datatype="datetime"/>
    <AttributeType name="shipped"
        dt:type="dateTime" sql:datatype="datetime"/>
    <AttributeType name="unit-price"
                dt:type="fixed.14.4" sql:datatype="money"/>
    <attribute type="id" sql:field="Oid" sql:id-prefix="O"/>
    <attribute type="ordered" sql:field="OrderDate"/>
    <attribute type="shipped" sql:field="ShipDate"/>
    <attribute type="quantity"/>
    <attribute type="unit-price" sql:field="UnitPrice"/>
    </ElementType>
    <ElementType name="Name" content="textOnly"
                dt:type="string" sql:datatype="nvarchar"/>
    <ElementType name="Customer" sql:relation="Customers"
                   sql:key-fields="Name Cid">
    <AttributeType name="id" dt:type="id" sql:datatype="nvarchar"/>
    <AttributeType name="color" dt:type="string" sql:datatype="nvarchar"/>
    <attribute type="id" sql:field="Cid"/>
    <attribute type="color"/>
    <element type="Name"/>
    <element type="Order">
       <sql:relationship key-relation="Customers" key="Cid"
                         foreign-relation="Orders" foreign-key="Cid"/>
    </element>
    </ElementType>
```

We generally specify the key-fields for elements as a matter of habit, and recommend you do the same (see Chapter 15 for details). In this case, we've also listed Name for Customers (even though it is not really a key of that table) to sort the <Customer> elements by name. Although this is not the recommended way to sort XML results (use XSL instead), it works well enough for this example.

Providing specific XDR types and SQL types can help eliminate unnecessary conversions in XPath. For some queries, this can result in significant performance increases (a factor of ten, or more). For Updategrams, specific SQL types are required for column types such as ntext. So while we're at it, we'll also add explicit types to the other schema components.

But first, let's also change <Inventory> and <Expense> so that they are grouped together. We can do this using <sql:relationship>, and we can also use sql:limit-field to separate the supplies by type. In this way, we replace <Inventory> with two attributes, lemons and sugar:

```
    <ElementType name="Expense" sql:relation="Purchases" sql:key-fields="Pid">
    <AttributeType name="id" dt:type="id" sql:datatype="int"/>
    <AttributeType name="date" dt:type="date" sql:datatype="datetime"/>
    <AttributeType name="price" dt:type="fixed.14.4" sql:datatype="money"/>
    <AttributeType name="notes" dt:type="string" sql:datatype="nvarchar"/>
    <AttributeType name="lemons" dt:type="i2" sql:datatype="smallint"/>
    <AttributeType name="sugar" dt:type="i2" sql:datatype="smallint"/>
    <attribute type="id" sql:field="Pid" sql:id-prefix="P"/>
    <attribute type="date"/>
    <attribute type="price"/>
```

```
        <attribute type="notes"/>
        <attribute type="lemons" sql:relation="Supplies" sql:field="quantity"
                sql:limit-field="Item" sql:limit-value="lemon">
          <sql:relationship key-relation="Purchases" key="Pid"
                        foreign-relation="Supplies" foreign-key="Pid"/>
        </attribute>
        <attribute type="sugar" sql:relation="Supplies" sql:field="quantity"
                sql:limit-field="Item" sql:limit-value="sugar">
          <sql:relationship key-relation="Purchases" key="Pid"
                        foreign-relation="Supplies" foreign-key="Pid"/>
        </attribute>
    </ElementType>
```

For reasons that will be made clear later, we'll also add a constant element that groups together expense information and news items. Putting it all together, we have the schema ch20_ex27.xdr:

```
<Schema xmlns="urn:schemas-microsoft-com:xml-data"
    xmlns:dt="urn:schemas-microsoft-com:datatypes"
    xmlns:sql="urn:schemas-microsoft-com:xml-sql">

    <ElementType name="News" sql:relation="News" sql:field="Story"
            dt:type="string" sql:datatype="ntext" >
    <AttributeType name="date" dt:type="date" sql:datatype="datetime"/>
    <AttributeType name="headline"
        dt:type="string" sql:datatype="nvarchar"/>
    <attribute type="date"/>
    <attribute type="headline"/>
    </ElementType>
    <ElementType name="Expense" sql:relation="Purchases" sql:key-fields="Pid">
    <AttributeType name="id" dt:type="id" sql:datatype="int"/>
    <AttributeType name="date" dt:type="date" sql:datatype="datetime"/>
    <AttributeType name="price" dt:type="fixed.14.4" sql:datatype="money"/>
    <AttributeType name="notes" dt:type="string" sql:datatype="nvarchar"/>
    <AttributeType name="lemons" dt:type="i2" sql:datatype="smallint"/>
    <AttributeType name="sugar" dt:type="i2" sql:datatype="smallint"/>
    <attribute type="id" sql:field="Pid" sql:id-prefix="P"/>
    <attribute type="date"/>
    <attribute type="price"/>
    <attribute type="notes"/>
    <attribute type="lemons" sql:relation="Supplies" sql:field="Quantity"
                sql:limit-field="Item" sql:limit-value="lemon">
      <sql:relationship key-relation="Purchases" key="Pid"
                    foreign-relation="Supplies" foreign-key="Pid"/>
    </attribute>
    <attribute type="sugar" sql:relation="Supplies" sql:field="Quantity"
                sql:limit-field="Item" sql:limit-value="sugar">
      <sql:relationship key-relation="Purchases" key="Pid"
                    foreign-relation="Supplies" foreign-key="Pid"/>
    </attribute>
    </ElementType>
    <ElementType name="NewsAndExpenses" sql:is-constant="1">
    <element type="News"/>
    <element type="Expense"/>
    </ElementType>
```

```
        <ElementType name="Order" sql:relation="Orders"
                    sql:key-fields="Oid">
        <AttributeType name="id" dt:type="id" sql:datatype="int"/>
        <AttributeType name="ordered"
            dt:type="dateTime" sql:datatype="datetime"/>
        <AttributeType name="shipped"
            dt:type="dateTime" sql:datatype="datetime"/>
        <AttributeType name="quantity" dt:type="i2" sql:datatype="smallint"/>
        <AttributeType name="unit-price"
                dt:type="fixed.14.4" sql:datatype="money"/>
        <attribute type="id" sql:field="Oid" sql:id-prefix="O"/>
        <attribute type="ordered" sql:field="OrderDate"/>
        <attribute type="shipped" sql:field="ShipDate"/>
        <attribute type="quantity"/>
        <attribute type="unit-price" sql:field="UnitPrice"/>
        </ElementType>
        <ElementType name="Name" content="textOnly"
                dt:type="string" sql:datatype="nvarchar"/>
        <ElementType name="Customer" sql:relation="Customers"
                    sql:key-fields="Name Cid">
        <AttributeType name="id" dt:type="id" sql:datatype="nvarchar"/>
        <AttributeType name="color" dt:type="string" sql:datatype="nvarchar"/>
        <attribute type="id" sql:field="Cid"/>
        <attribute type="color"/>
        <element type="Name"/>
        <element type="Order">
            <sql:relationship key-relation="Customers" key="Cid"
                            foreign-relation="Orders" foreign-key="Cid"/>
        </element>
        </ElementType>
    </Schema>
```

We can now use a simple template (`ch20_ex27.xml`) with this schema to return customer information:

```
<Example xmlns:sql="urn:schemas-microsoft-com:xml-sql">
<Customers>
    <sql:xpath-query xmlns:sql="urn:schemas-microsoft-com:xml-sql"
    mapping-schema="ch20_ex27.xdr">Customer</sql:xpath-query>
</Customers>
</Example>
```

returns XML data like this:

```
<Customers xmlns:sql="urn:schemas-microsoft-com:xml-sql">
    <Customer id="ad" color="yellow">
        <Name>Arthur Dent</Name>
    </Customer>
</Customers>
```

Obviously, this example is not particularly interesting until we have some more data. To create the data, we'll build several web pages. One page for internal use only displays an expense sheet and relevant news stories. Another two pages will create new customer accounts or edit existing ones, where customers can enter their own names and favorite colors. Finally, one page is personalized to each customer, displaying the list of orders that customer has placed.

Display News and Expenses

The news feed must first be connected to the database. However, it is provided in a different format than our schema describes, so we must first map the news to our pre-existing News table with another annotated schema. Then we can wrap the news in the `<after>` part of an updategram, and submit it to the database for insertion.

Here is a reminder of the XML news feed format:

```
<NewsStream>
   <Story>
      <Title>Lemon Prices Sour</Title>
      <Date>1999-09-23</Date>
      <Author>Ford Prefect</Author>
      <Text>Today, lemon prices reach a new 52-week low as ...</Text>
   </Story>
   <Story>
      <Title>The Internet Lemonade Stand Opens For Business</Title>
      <Date>1999-10-19</Date>
      <Author>Argle Fargle</Author>
      <Text>In a shrewd move, the Internet Lemonade Stand opened ...</Text>
   </Story>
   <!-- additional news items -->
</NewsStream>
```

This can be modeled using the following schema `ch20_ex28.xdr`:

```
<Schema xmlns="urn:schemas-microsoft-com:xml-data"
    xmlns:dt="urn:schemas-microsoft-com:datatypes"
    xmlns:sql="urn:schemas-microsoft-com:xml-sql">
   <ElementType name="Title" sql:field="Headline" sql:datatype="nvarchar"/>
   <ElementType name="Text" sql:field="Story" sql:datatype="ntext"/>
   <ElementType name="Date" sql:field="Date"
        dt:type="date" sql:datatype="datetime"/>
   <ElementType name="Author" content="textOnly"/>
   <ElementType name="Story" sql:relation="News">
   <element type="Title"/>
   <element type="Date" />
   <element type="Author" sql:map-field="0"/>
   <element type="Text"/>
   </ElementType>
   <ElementType name="NewsStream" sql:is-constant="1">
   <element type="Story"/>
   </ElementType>
</Schema>
```

which maps `<NewsStream>` as a constant element and `<Author>` to nothing. This is necessary because neither element corresponds to anything in the database (but `<NewsStream>` appears in the XML). The news can then be inserted into the database with the following template containing an updategram (`ch20_ex28.xml`):

```
<insert-news>
    <u:sync xmlns:u="urn:schemas-microsoft-com:xml-updategram"
mapping-schema="ch20_ex28.xdr">
    <u:after>
       <NewsStream>
       <!-- all the news here -->
       </NewsStream>
    </u:after>
    </u:sync>
</insert-news>
```

At this point, we are ready to create the third, internal web page by using a template to extract the data and a server-side XSL post-processing step to render the data as HTML. If `<News>` and `<Inventory>` elements were completely unrelated, we would require two separate XPath queries (and hence, two roundtrips to the database). However, by using the constant `<NewsAndExpense>` element, we can perform this query in a single XPath (`ch20_ex29.xml`):

```
<internal sql:xsl="ch20_ex29.xsl" xmlns:sql="urn:schemas-microsoft-com:xml-sql">
   <sql:xpath-query mapping-schema="ch20_ex27.xdr">
   NewsAndExpenses
   </sql:xpath-query>
</internal>
```

where `ch20_ex29.xsl` is

```
<xsl:stylesheet version="1.0"
    xmlns:xsl="http://www.w3.org/1999/XSL/Transform">
<xsl:output method="html" indent="yes" media-type="text/html" />

   <xsl:template match="/">
      <xsl:apply-templates/>
   </xsl:template>
   <xsl:template match="internal">
      <html>
      <head>
      <title>The Internet Lemonade Stand News And Expense Report</title>
      </head>
      <body>
      <h1>Top News</h1>
      <dl>
      <xsl:apply-templates select="NewsAndExpenses/News"/>
      </dl>
      <h1>Expense Sheet</h1>
      <table border="1">
      <tr>
        <th>date</th>
        <th>purchase</th>
        <th>total cost</th>
        <th>notes</th>
      </tr>
      <xsl:apply-templates select="NewsAndExpenses/Expense"/>
      </table>
      </body>
      </html>
   </xsl:template>

   <xsl:template match="News">
      <dt>[<xsl:value-of select="@date"/>]
      <b><xsl:value-of select="@headline"/></b></dt>
      <dd><xsl:value-of select="."/></dd>
   </xsl:template>

   <xsl:template match="Expense">
      <tr>
         <td><xsl:value-of select="@date"/></td>
         <td><xsl:choose><xsl:when test="@sugar">
         <xsl:value-of select="@sugar"/> kg. sugar
         </xsl:when><xsl:otherwise><xsl:value-of select="@lemons"/>
         lemon<xsl:if test="@lemons&gt;1">s</xsl:if>
         </xsl:otherwise></xsl:choose></td>
         <td><xsl:value-of select="@price"/></td>
        <td><xsl:value-of select="@notes"/></td>
      </tr>
   </xsl:template>
</xsl:stylesheet>
```

This stylesheet takes the following XML output from the template:

```
<internal xmlns:sql="urn:schemas-microsoft-com:xml-sql">
  <NewsAndExpenses>
    <News date="1999-09-23" headline="Lemon Prices Sour">
      Today, lemon prices reach a new 52-week low as ...
    </News>
    <News date="1999-10-19" headline="The Internet Lemonade Stand Opens For
Business">
      In a shrewd move, the Internet Lemonade Stand opened ...
    </News>
    <Expense id="P1" date="1999-10-19" price="0" notes="thanks, Mom!" sugar="2" />
    <Expense id="P2" date="1999-10-19" price="5" lemons="20" />
  </NewsAndExpenses>
</internal>
```

and reformats it into user-friendly HTML tables.

Create and Edit Customer Accounts

Previously, we demonstrated how to post a template through an HTML form. This method is straightforward but presents all sorts of security risks. A better approach is to pass parameters to a server-side template that is completely under your control. Although we are only storing each Customer's name and favorite color, this technique obviously generalizes to larger sets of parameters.

We first need a login/new account page (ch20_ex30.html):

```
<HTML>
<HEAD>
    <TITLE>Welcome to the Internet Lemonade Stand</TITLE>
</HEAD>
<BODY>
    <P>Please log in to your account</P>
    <FORM ACTION="http://localhost/virtualname/template/ch20_ex31.xml">
        <B>Username</B> <input type="text" name="cid" value=""/>
    <input type="submit"/>
    </FORM>

    <P>or create a new account</P>
    <FORM ACTION="http://localhost/virtualname/template/ch20_ex30.xml">
        <B>Username</B> <input type="text" name="id" value=""/><br>
        <B>Full Name</B> <input type="text" name="name" value=""/><br>
        <B>Favorite Color</B> <input type="text" name="color" value=""/><br>
        <input type="submit"/>
    </FORM>
</BODY>
</HTML>
```

Logging in takes the user to personalized page (see next section); otherwise, we attempt to create a new account. Using a template to create a new account can be as simple as a parameterized updategram insert, as seen in the following example, ch20_ex30.xml:

```
<create>
   <u:header xmlns:u="urn:schemas-microsoft-com:xml-updategram" >
      <u:param name="color">white</u:param>
      <u:param name="id"/>
      <u:param name="name"/>
   </u:header>
   <u:sync xmlns:u="urn:schemas-microsoft-com:xml-updategram"
      u:nullvalue="" mapping-schema="ch20_ex27.xdr">
      <u:after>
         <Customer id="$id" color="$color">
         <Name>$name</Name>
         </Customer>
      </u:after>
   </u:sync>
</create>
```

When the user successfully created a new account, they will be presented with this screen:

Of course, when the `id` collides with an existing customer's `id`, the updategram will return an error. So, we must be prepared to capture this error and display it to the user in a friendly way. We will do this using XSL by modifying the template above to use a style sheet:

```
<create sql:xsl="ch20_ex31.xsl" xmlns:sql="urn:schemas-microsoft-com:xml-sql">
```

where `ch20_ex31.xsl` is:

```
<xsl:stylesheet version="1.0" xmlns:xsl='http://www.w3.org/1999/XSL/Transform'>
<xsl:output method="html" indent="yes" media-type="text/html" />
    <xsl:template match="/">
        <html>
        <head><title>Customer Login</title></head><body>
            <xsl:apply-templates/>
            </body>
        </html>
    </xsl:template>
    <xsl:template match="create">
    <xsl:choose>
        <!-- if the template returns an error, display it
        otherwise, the new account succeeded -->
        <xsl:when test="processing-instruction('MSSQLError')">
            <p>A customer with that username already exists. Please
            try a different username.</p>
          <form action="http://localhost/lemonade/template/ch20_ex30.xml">
            <b>Username</b>
            <input type="text" name="id" value=""/>
            <b>Full Name</b>
            <input type="text" name="name" value=""/>
            <b>Favorite Color</b>
            <input type="text" name="color" value=""/>
            <input type="submit"/>
            </form>
        </xsl:when>
        <xsl:otherwise>
            Congratulations on your new account.
        </xsl:otherwise>
        </xsl:choose>
    </xsl:template>
</xsl:stylesheet>
```

When the user does error in this fashion, they are presented with this screen:

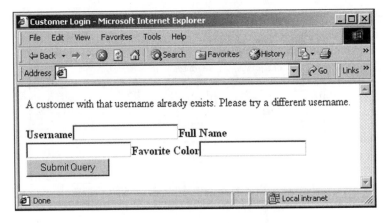

Of course, in practice, we would also want to pass the parameters through to the XSL, so that the customer does not have to enter all his or her personal data again.

Personalized Customer Page

Displaying a customer's orders is a straightforward application of the same XPath and XSL technique we used earlier for the internal page. To accomplish this task, we use the parameterized template `ch20_ex31.xml`:

```
<personal sql:xsl="ch20_ex32.xsl" xmlns:sql="urn:schemas-microsoft-com:xml-sql">
   <sql:header>
      <sql:param name="cid"/>
   </sql:header>
   <sql:xpath-query mapping-schema="ch20_ex27.xdr">
      Customer[@id=$cid]
   </sql:xpath-query>
</personal>
```

This template returns the customer data together with all the orders the customer has ever placed. We can use XSL to display these orders to the user (dividing them among orders fulfilled and orders still pending). First, prepare the database with some orders, using the following code (`ch20_ex31.sql`):

```
INSERT INTO Orders VALUES('1999-10-04', '1999-10-04', 'ad', 2, 1.75)
INSERT INTO Orders VALUES('1999-10-19', '1999-10-23', 'ad', 5, 1.50)
INSERT INTO Orders VALUES('1999-10-25', '1999-10-26', 'ad', 15, 1.00)
```

And then execute the template with this XSL named `ch20_ex32.xsl`:

```
<xsl:stylesheet version="1.0" xmlns:xsl="http://www.w3.org/1999/XSL/Transform">
<xsl:output method="html" indent="yes" media-type="text/html" />
   <xsl:template match="/">
      <xsl:apply-templates/>
   </xsl:template>
   <xsl:template match="personal">
      <xsl:apply-templates/>
   </xsl:template>
   <xsl:template match="Customer">
      <html>
      <head><title>Welcome <xsl:value-of select="Name"/>!</title></head>
      <body>
         <xsl:attribute name="BGCOLOR">
            <xsl:value-of select="@color"/>
         </xsl:attribute>
         <p>Welcome back to the Internet Lemonade Stand,
      <xsl:value-of select="Name"/>!</p>
         <p>Let us quench your thirst with our excellent lemonade!</p>

      <h2>Pending Orders</h2>
      <ul>
      <xsl:for-each select="Order[not(@shipped)]">
         <xsl:sort select="@shipped" order="descending"/>
         <li>Ship Date: <b><xsl:value-of select="@shipped"/></b>
         Order Date: <b><xsl:value-of select="@ordered"/></b><br/>
         Amount: <b><xsl:value-of select="@quantity"/> liters</b>
         Cost: <b><xsl:value-of
         select="format-number(@quantity * @unit-price, '$#.00')"/></b>
         </li>
         </xsl:for-each>
      </ul>
```

```
    <h2>Past Orders</h2>
    <ul>
    <xsl:for-each select="Order[@shipped]">
        <xsl:sort select="@shipped" order="descending"/>
        <li>Ship Date: <b><xsl:value-of select="@shipped"/></b>
        Order Date: <b><xsl:value-of select="@ordered"/></b><br/>
        Amount: <b><xsl:value-of select="@quantity"/> liters</b>
        Cost: <b><xsl:value-of
        select="format-number(@quantity * @unit-price, '$#.00')"/></b>
        </li>
    </xsl:for-each>
    </ul>
    </body>
    </html>
    </xsl:template>
</xsl:stylesheet>
```

So, from the main page, if we now log in as Arthur Dent using his Customer ID (ad), we are presented with the following report:

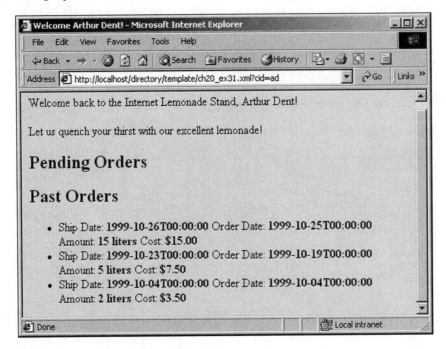

Placing new orders is a straightforward extension of the examples presented above, so we leave that as an exercise for you, the reader.

Summary

SQL Server 2000 provides feature-rich XML capabilities. This added functionality makes developing web applications much simpler. These features allow you to create powerful web applications with great ease.

With the middle-tier features – such as annotated XDR schemas and Updategrams – you can write end-to-end XML applications, and query and modify relational data as though it were XML. The support for annotated XDR schema reduces the amount of programming required to produce XML from the relational data.

On the server side, features such as OPENXML and FOR XML allow you to leverage your existing SQL knowledge and applications. Turning your relational data into XML can be as simple as adding FOR XML AUTO to an existing SQL query, or using the more complex FOR XML EXPLICIT for full control over the XML output. OPENXML, on the other hand, is rowset provider that can be used to a shred an XML document and generate a rowset view of the XML and use it along with INSERT, UPDATE and DELETE statements.

With all these features, writing web applications in this Internet world has become a lot simpler.

Helpful Web Sites

❑ You can obtain an evaluation copy of SQL Server 2000 from
http://www.microsoft.com/sql/productinfo/default.htm

❑ The MSDN website (http://msdn.microsoft.com/downloads/default.asp in particular) is the place to download the web releases of SQL Server 2000. The web releases provide you with new SQL Server XML functionality (the XML updategram and XML Bulk Load) as well as enhancements to the features that were shipped with SQL Server 2000.

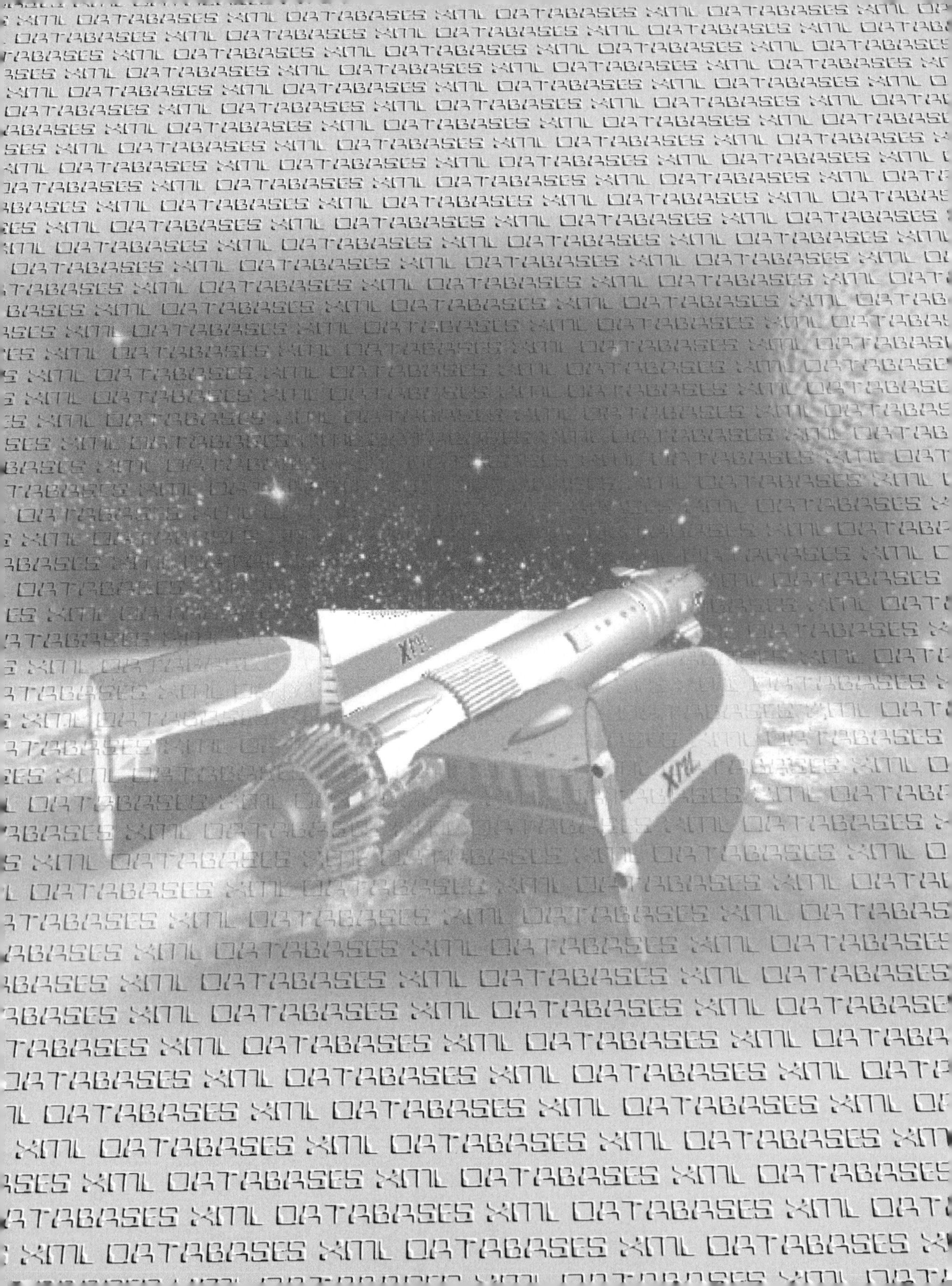
XML DATABASES
XML

21

DB Prism: A Framework to Generate Dynamic XML from a Database

In this case study, we will be looking at DB Prism, an open source framework to generate dynamic XML from a database. Unlike other technologies, such as Apache XSP or Oracle XSQL servlet, DB Prism generates the dynamic XML inside the database, transforming it into an active database. An active database means that you use the database engine not only to execute SQL statements, but to directly return a complex XML representation of the data stored inside as well.

DB Prism is a servlet engine that works in two different modes: as a standalone servlet, or plugged into the Cocoon publishing framework. In the first mode, DB Prism works like the PLSQL Cartridge of Oracle Web Server. Plugged into the Cocoon framework, DB Prism works as a DB Producer, generating dynamic XML from a database.

The main motivation to work like the PLSQL Cartridge of Oracle Web Server is to allow old technologies to coexist with new ones, helping in the migration path. Using DB Prism it is possible to run applications made to work with **O**racle **W**eb **S**erver (OWS) in the same box or the latest Oracle **I**nternet **A**pplication **S**erver (IAS) without any modifications.

This kind of application includes applications designed with Oracle Designer, Web Server Generator or Oracle Web DB, and standalone applications made using the PLSQL **HTP** toolkit (**H**tml **T**oolkit **P**rocedures is group of related procedures or functions written in PLSQL to make application for the Oracle Web Server architecture). We will not describe in detail how these applications are constructed and executed because that is not within the scope of this case study. For further information on how these applications work, refer to the developer's manuals of these products.

DB Prism plugged into the Apache Cocoon framework is a new way for making Internet applications with technologies as XML and XSLT, which is the focus of the second part of the case study. Cocoon is a presentation framework based on servlet technology, so it can run in any web server supporting servlet technology. As a presentation framework it has the responsibility for serving pages requested by the user, applying first styles as the page needs and transforming static or dynamic XML content into HTML. Cocoon is also able to perform more sophisticated formatting, such as **XSL:FO** (XSL Formatting Objects) rendering on PDF, WML formatting for WAP-enabled devices, or direct XML serving to XML and XSL aware clients. The Cocoon project aims to change the way web information is created, rendered, and served by completely separating document content, style, and logic.

DB Prism is plugged into the Cocoon framework for the XML creation step. It then moves the logic to the database, closely allied to the data itself. The most important characteristic of DB Prism is that, unlike in other technologies, the logic of the application resides in the database as a stored procedure. This approach provides several benefits such as scalability, better separation of code, security, maintainability, and re-use of developer skills (these benefits shall be discussed later in the study). The stored procedure could be written in the proprietary language or in Java. Writing stored procedure in Java with a JDBC or SQLJ call guarantees portability across different database vandors because there is a standard defined for this purpose.

DB Prism already includes support for Oracle databases, but its design allows developers to write adapters to plug into many other kinds of databases. In this case study, we will introduce a new adapter and so develop an example from it.

This case study is focused on two main topics. First, we will look at DB Prism internals – giving background information and internal information about how DB Prism works to help developers write new DB Prism adapters for new databases. The second part will look at how you can develop XML applications with DB Prism, and the presentation framework Cocoon. The examples or the installation step are based on a UNIX server environment, but there aren't restrictions for doing it in a Windows platform, you only need change the directory paths and the scripts from .sh shell scripts to .bat batch files.

Here is a more detailed outline of the contents of this case study:

- ❏ Cocoon architecture
- ❏ DB Prism architecture
    - ❏ DB Prism class diagram
    - ❏ DB Prism: Benefits provided to the Cocoon Framework

Part I. **DB Prism Internals**; focusing on "How to write a new Adapter":

- ❏ Who is who?
- ❏ Code to be taken into account
    - ❏ DB Prism
    - ❏ DBConnection
    - ❏ DBFactory
    - ❏ SPProc
- ❏ Common issues on writing a new Adapter

Part II. **Putting DB Prism at work**.

❑   Cocoon Setup on Oracle Internet Application Server (IAS)

❑   DB Prism Setup on IAS

❑   Loading DB Prism examples

❑   Making a Content Management System (CMS)

   ❑   Brief introduction to a CMS

   ❑   Design of the meta model

   ❑   Writing the Java Code

   ❑   Loading the Content

   ❑   Making two different stylesheets

❑   Conclusion and beyond

To run the examples in this case study you will need an Oracle IAS web server, an Oracle Database (8.1+), Oracle XML SQL Utility version 12 (XSU12), Oracle XML parser 2.1, the Cocoon framework from http//xml.apache.org, and the DB Prism servlet engine from http//www.plenix.com.

This case study assumes some knowledge of Java (servlet programming especially!), JDBC, SQLj, and servlet configuration on an Oracle IAS.

Cocoon Architecture

The Cocoon project aims to change the way web information is created, rendered and served. This new paradigm is based on fact that different individuals or groups often create document content, style, and logic. Cocoon aims to allow a complete separation of the three layers so that they can be independently designed, created and managed, reducing management overhead, increasing work reuse and reducing time to market.

The Cocoon design divides the creation process of an application in three different levels:

❑   **XML Creation**:

   In this level, the content owners make an XML static file with a regular XML editor. This level is a content level.

❑   **XML Processing**:

   If the XML content includes logic, this logic is processed. Cocoon XSP technology is processed here, this technology is to XML as JSP is to HTML.

❑   **XSL Rendering**:

   In this level, the XML coming from the previous level is processed by applying a stylesheet for formatting the content to several targets of devices.

Cocoon is shown in the following diagram (picture adapted from one at the Apache web site (http://xml.apache.org/cocoon/):

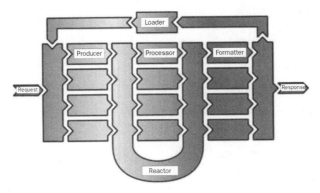

The main components in this architecture are:

❑ **Request**
A client request, normally coming from a servlet request – Cocoon also has an offline operation mode when the request is internally managed.

❑ **Producer**
Handles the request and produces an XML output (content). Cocoon has several producers, like a file producer, which takes a request and interprets it as an XML file to be uploaded from the file system. DB Prism adds a **DB producer** to Cocoon, which takes a request and interprets it as a stored procedure call on the database side. The stored procedure's return value contains the XML document generated in the database and feeds it into the processing reactor.

❑ **Processing Reactor**
Processes the processing instructions contained in the XML document. The processing instructions are delivered here from the previous step in the Cocoon 1.x architecture (the Producer). With the site map implementation of the Cocoon 2.0 architecture, these processing instructions are not necessary, making the development step clearer, without presentation responsibility. The reactor forwards the XML document to the corresponding formatter.

❑ **Formatter**
Transforms the internal representation of an XML document into a stream that may be interpreted by the client. The formatter assigns the corresponding MIME type to the output response.

❑ **Response**
This encapsulates the response information sent back to the client. This information includes the MIME type, character set, and the rest of the HTTP headers and content.

In this architecture, producers are based on static content. They do not evaluate or process anything about the request to produce the XML output. XSP Technology is included in Cocoon as the default implementation to make the content dynamically, from an originally static XML file. The file producer loads this file, and then the processing instructions included in the document are passed to the reactor to tell it to begin compilation of the page. When the page compilation is completed, compiled pages are then inserted into the Cocoon pipeline as a new producer.

With this functionality, the logic of the application runs in the middle tier. When this application interacts with a database, there are common problems and pitfalls. One is related to the performance – if the page needs to process complex logic based on a large amount of data the round trip of JDBC calls to the database will hinder the final performance of the application. Other pitfalls are related to the benefits of DB Prism shown at the beginning of the text and explained in the next section. Remember also that Cocoon is a presentation framework, not an application framework; the intention is to produce a variety of presentation styles once the content has been processed.

DB Prism Architecture

DB Prism adds a new producer to Cocoon framework – this producer makes the XML inside the database by executing a stored procedure. To deal with the portability problems of the stored procedure, the design of the DB Prism permits extension of the original framework to any database that supports stored procedures by adding a new adapter.

This design is explained in the following section, to provide internal documentation for developers who decide to write a new adapter.

The DB Prism architecture looks like this:

Wrappers	Engine		Adapters
Cocoon	DBPrism		Oracle 7x
			Oracle 8i
Servlet	Resource Manager	DAD Information	Java 8i
			Java Lite

The three different main sections are as follows:

❑ **Wrappers**:
Wrappers handle the incoming request from a Cocoon framework or a servlet engine and adapt them to the DB Prism request. They also return the generated XML or HTML page to clients.

❑ **Engine**:
The Engine processes the request calling to the specific stored procedure, analyzing the request and choosing the target database according to the information given. The Engine doesn't deal with database specific problems as the stored procedures deal with those. The Engine takes the connection from the Resource Manager, which implements a configurable pool of database connections and transactions supported by a URL demarcation. The information attached to the connection is stored in a **DAD** dictionary. DAD stands for Database Access Descriptor and is a piece of configurable information stored in the DB Prism configuration file. This file contains, for example, user name and password to connect to the database, type of the database to be connected to, and all other necessary connection information.

❑ **Adapters**:
Making the actual call to the specific stored procedure in a target database, each adapter deals with the database specific problems such as "How are stored procedures stored in the database dictionary?" and "How do I get the generated page from the database side?". Each adapter includes three classes – a Factory to handle the creation process, a Database Connection which implements the real stored procedure call (JDBC callable statement), and Stored Procedure objects that encapsulate the name and arguments of a stored procedure in the database.

In the following sections, these components are described in detail.

DB Prism Class Diagram

On the next facing pages is an overall picture of the classes of DB Prism:

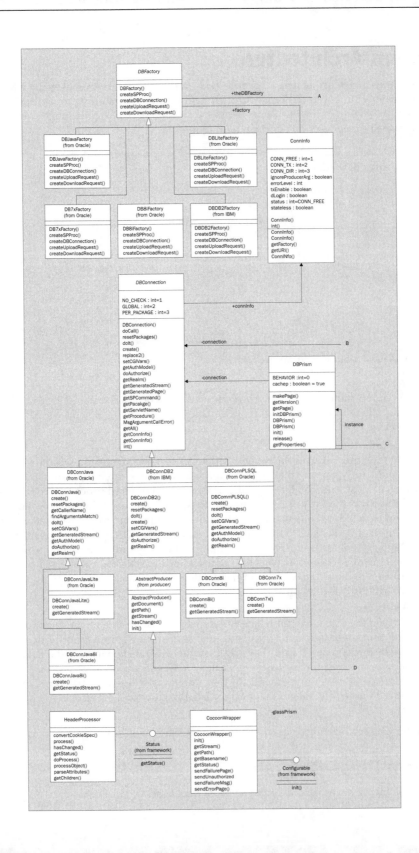

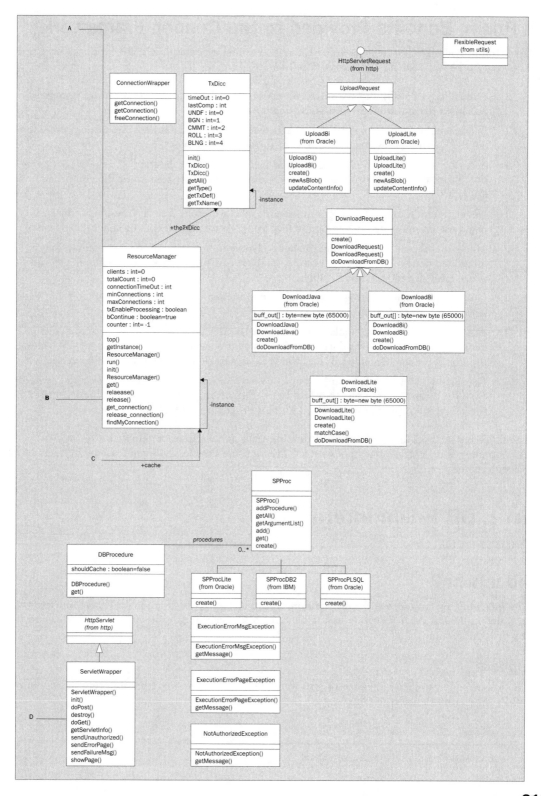

DB Prism: Benefits Provided to the Cocoon Framework

DB Prism provides several benefits to the Cocoon architecture by adding a DB Producer for Cocoon. The most important benefits are discussed below:

- ❏ Scalability: a PLSQL or Java stored procedure is scalable up to 1000 or more concurrent sessions without problems of memory leaks or concurrency.

- ❏ Better separation of concerns: the logic is handled on the database side, while presentation is left to a separate presentation tier (for example, a web server).

- ❏ Security: when the user executes a stored procedure, she or he moves to the security level of the database. The security assets are declarative and not programmatically controlled and so are safer.

- ❏ Development tools: if the programmer writes, for example, a Java stored procedure, she or he could use an integrated development tool to debug the application online.

- ❏ Maintainability: if a programmer makes a change in any table of the application, the integrated dependency manager of the database can automatically invalidate the stored procedures dependent on this table.

- ❏ Quick deployment: in a big application, a deployment stage tends to be difficult, but with stored procedures, it is very easy.

- ❏ Automated development tools: with a little work, it is possible to make an automated generator that takes logic information from a central repository and automatically generates the stored procedures, in a similar fashion to an Oracle Designer/Web Server generator.

- ❏ Reuse of developer skills: many companies have developers with a lot of experience in Oracle PLSQL. With little training, they will be able to develop an application using DB Prism and the XTP toolkit (similar to the Html Toolkit Procedures of Oracle Web Server).

The following sections first describe DB Prism internals and Adapter creation, and secondly development of an XML Application with DB Prism, using Oracle as the database and Oracle IAS as the web server.

Part I. DB Prism Internals

In this part of the case study, we will introduce DB Prism internals.

Who is who?

The following section looks at the distribution of responsibilities between the different sources included in the DB Prism distribution (the src directory), according to the architecture discussed in the previous section.

Wrappers

The following three classes have the responsibility of adapting requests from different sources into DB Prism internals representations:

```
src/com/prism/CocoonWrapper.java
src/com/prism/ConnectionWrapper.java
src/com/prism/ServletWrapper.java
```

- ❏ `CocoonWrapper` is a class that takes Cocoon requests and adapts them to a DB Prism request

- ❏ `ServletWrapper` is a class that adapts servlet requests to a DB Prism request

- ❏ `ConnectionWrapper` is a class that takes requests for connection from the Cocoon XSP pages and adapts them to a `ResourceManager` request

Engine

```
src/com/prism/DBPrism.java
src/com/prism/CgiVars.java
src/com/prism/ExecutionErrorMsgException.java
src/com/prism/ExecutionErrorPageException.java
src/com/prism/NotAuthorizedException.java
```

- ❏ `DBPrism` is the main class of the framework. It takes a request (from Cocoon or a servlet engine), gets one connection from a resource manager, and divides the process of generating a page into two steps: one for making the stored procedure calls, and another for getting the generated page from the database.

- ❏ `CgiVars` is a class that stores the CGI environment variables that will be sent to the database in the stored procedure call.

- ❏ `ExecutionErrorMsgException`, `ExecutionErrorPageException`, and `NotAuthorizedException` are exception handlers, which encapsulate the information when an error is caught.

Engine Framework Related Classes

```
src/com/prism/DBFactory.java
src/com/prism/DBConnection.java
src/com/prism/SPProc.java
src/com/prism/UploadRequest.java
src/com/prism/DownloadRequest.java
```

These classes are abstract classes that encapsulate database dependent stuff:

- ❏ `DBFactory` is a class that has methods for the creation process. It defines methods for creating connections to a particular database, stored procedures and so on.

- ❏ `DBConnection` is a class that defines the operation to be implemented for a particular database; this operation is database dependent and must be implemented by the concrete classes (adapters).

- ❏ `SPProc` is a class that stores the information about a database's stored procedure – the stored procedure can be defined with different arguments (overloading) and this class is a container for the entire version of a particular stored procedure.

- ❏ `UploadRequest` is a class that encapsulates a request of multipart form data MIME type. This type of request is not handled by the stored procedures directly; when an upload operation occurs, first the multipart form data is uploaded into the database table, and second the result of this operation is passed to the stored procedure.

- ❏ `DownloadRequest` defines the operation for downloading multimedia content from the database store to the clients.

Engine Resource Manager and DAD Information Classes

```
src/com/prism/ResourceManager.java
src/com/prism/TxDicc.java
src/com/prism/ConnInfo.java
src/com/prism/DBProcedure.java
```

❑ ResourceManager is a class that manages the connection pooling and transaction support – this class implements a list of free and busy connections and a simple algorithm to allocate and de-allocate connections.

❑ TxDicc is a dictionary of DAD information – this dictionary has the information defined for every connection in the DB Prism configuration file.

❑ ConnInfo is a class that stores the information of a particular connection at run time.

❑ DBProcedure is a dictionary for storing stored procedure information; it works like a cache of the stored procedures found in the database dictionary, which helps to improve performance.

Engine (Others)

```
src/com/prism/HeaderProcessor.java
```

❑ HeaderProcessor is an accessory class, which handles the header process of the response object. This class permits modification of the response object in the Cocoon pipeline directly through XML tags. This utilizes the XML processing instruction <?http ....?>.

Adapters (Oracle Common)

```
src/com/prism/oracle/SPProcPLSQL.java
src/com/prism/oracle/DBConnPLSQL.java
src/com/prism/oracle/DBConnJava.java
```

These three classes are common to different adapters on Oracle databases:

❑ SPProcPLSQL is a class that encapsulates the information of a stored procedure in version 7 or 8 of the Oracle database. Independent from the language of the stored procedure, Oracle stores the same information for each stored procedure.

❑ DBConnPLSQL is a class that handles the process of making a stored procedure call independent from the version of the database, but dependent on PLSQL as language of the stored procedure.

❑ DBConnJava is a similar class to the previous one but handles calls to stored procedures written in the Java language.

Adapters (Oracle 8i)

```
src/com/prism/oracle/DB8iFactory.java
src/com/prism/oracle/DBConn8i.java
```

❑ DB8iFactory is a class that returns Oracle 8i PLSQL support objects

❑ DBConn8i is a class, which implements DB Prism functionality for Oracle 8i databases, and stored procedures written in the PLSQL language

Adapters (Oracle 7x)

```
src/com/prism/oracle/DB7xFactory.java
src/com/prism/oracle/DBConn7x.java
```

`DB7xFactory` is a class that returns Oracle 7.x PLSQL support objects. `DBConn7x` is a class, which implements DB Prism functionality for Oracle 7x databases, and stored procedures written in the PLSQL language.

Adapters (Oracle 8i Java Support)

```
src/com/prism/oracle/DBJavaFactory.java
src/com/prism/oracle/DBConnJava8i.java
```

`DBJavaFactory` is a class that returns Oracle 8i Java support objects. `DBConnJava8i` is a class, which implements DB Prism functionality for Oracle 8i databases and stored procedures written in Java.

Adapters (Oracle Lite Java Support)

```
src/com/prism/oracle/DBLiteFactory.java
src/com/prism/oracle/DBConnJavaLite.java
```

❑ `DBLiteFactory` is a class that returns Oracle Lite Java support objects

❑ `DBConnJavaLite` is a class that implements DB Prism functionality for Oracle Lite databases and stored procedures written in Java

Adapters (Oracle Upload/Download functionality)

```
src/com/prism/oracle/Download8i.java
src/com/prism/oracle/DownloadJava.java
src/com/prism/oracle/DownloadLite.java
src/com/prism/oracle/Upload8i.java
src/com/prism/oracle/UploadLite.java
```

❑ `Download8i` is a class that implements the functionality of downloaded multimedia objects from version 8i of the database and stored procedures written in PLSQL.

❑ `DownloadJava` is a class that implements the functionality of downloaded multimedia objects from version 8i of the database and stored procedures written in Java.

❑ `DownloadLite` is a class that implements the functionality of downloaded multimedia objects from Oracle Lite databases and stored procedures written in Java.

❑ `Upload8i` is a class that handles uploading multipart data from a data request to version 8i databases; the uploading process does not depend on the language of the stored procedures, it only inserts rows in the content table. Then, `DB8iFactory` and `DBJavaFactory` reuse this class.

❑ `UploadLite` handles uploading multipart form data requests to Oracle Lite databases.

Adapters (DB2 skeletons)

```
src/com/prism/ibm/DBDB2Factory.java
src/com/prism/ibm/DBConnDB2.java
src/com/prism/ibm/SPProcDB2.java
```

These three classes implement the skeleton of a suggested DB2 adapter for the Java stored procedures support discussed in the next sections, these classes are only examples of a new possible adapter for any kind of database which has stored procedures support.

Common Issues with Writing a New Adapter

When considering making a new adapter for a database not supported by DB Prism (for example, IBM DB2), you need to first answer these questions:

1. Is there a JDBC driver for this database?
If not, then it is not possible to make an adapter.

2. Are stored procedures supported by this database?
Again, if not, making an adapter will be impossible.

3. Are packages supported by this database?
If not, this database probably supports the syntax of schema objects for referencing the stored procedure, and then if possible makes an adapter using user schemas as package names.

4. Are `array` types sending or receiving by the JDBC driver?
The easy way to implement an adapter for a new database is with Java stored procedures. In this way, you can use classes from existing adapters such as `DBConnJava` or `CgiVars` to facilitate the implementation of the new adapter. With these codes, you only need to check for the option of passing `byte array` data types (`byte []`) and verify how to upload the Java toolkit (`Jxtp`) in the target database. Then you only need to implement `SPProc`, `DBConnection`, and `DBFactory` subclasses. The `Jxtp` toolkit was designed to be portable. Only two classes are dependent on database-specific information, `JxtpBuff` and `JwpgDocLoad`. `JxtpBuff` implements the buffer for storing the generated page, normally in a **CLOB** (Character Large Object, as opposed to a BLOB for images) data type, and `JwpgDocLoad` implements the download functionality.

5. Does the JDBC driver support large objects?
If the answer is yes, the new adapter could use this data type for storing the generated page by the application. If not, you could download the page in smaller chunks of the usual data types. The Oracle 7x adapter uses this technique for downloading the generated page, in chunks of 32 KB.

If the questions are all answered, then you are ready to make a new adapter. Now it is time to see how a new adapter is actually written.

Writing the New Adapter

When writing a new adapter, there are several pieces of code to take into account, which will be looked at in the next section with general comments, in order to show how they work. Some of them are part of the DB Prism framework itself, and are abstract classes that define the interface or responsibility of the adapters with the DB Prism engine.

This section includes the DBPrism class, which is the main class of the framework; DBConnection, which defines the interface or responsibility of an adapter; the factory class, DBFactory, which defines the operation for the creation process; and SPProc, which defines how to represent stored procedures of any kind of databases.

DBPrism.java

There are two crucial methods in the DB Prism class – `makePage()` defines the steps to make an XML page through a stored procedure (including, for example, authorization of the request, and getting the connection to the concrete database), and `getPage()` which gets the generated page of the previous step from the database.

Before introducing the code of them, here is a UML sequence diagram of the complete process of generating a page with a request from Cocoon and the adapter for Oracle 8i databases.

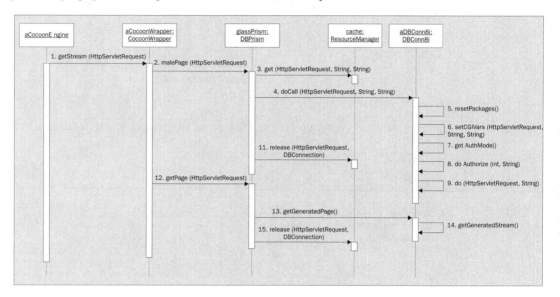

Making the Stored Procedure Call

The `makePage()` method handles the process of getting the connection from the resource manager, and makes the stored procedure call to the correct adapter. Previous to this step `makePage()` checks for the authorization requirements. The `makePage()` code is shown below:

```java
public void makePage(HttpServletRequest req) throws Exception
{
    ConnInfo cc_tmp = new ConnInfo(req);
    String name;
    String password;
    try
    {
        int i;
        String str;
        try
        {
            str = new String
                (B64.decodeBuffer(req.getHeader("Authorization").substring(6)),
                cc_tmp.clientCharset);
        }
        catch (Exception e)
        {
            str = ":";
        }
```

```
        i = str.indexOf(':');
        name = str.substring(0,i);
        password = str.substring(i+1);
        boolean dLogin = (cc_tmp.usr.equals("") || cc_tmp.pass.equals(""));
        if (!dLogin)
        {
            connection = cache.get(req,cc_tmp.usr,cc_tmp.pass);
        }
        else if (name.equals("") || password.equals(""))
        {
                throw new NotAuthorizedException(cc_tmp.dynamicLoginRealm);
            }
            else
            {
                try
                {
                    connection = cache.get(req,name,password);
                }
                catch (SQLException e)
                {
                    throw new NotAuthorizedException(cc_tmp.dynamicLoginRealm);
                }
                connection.doCall(req,name,password);
            }
        }
        catch (Exception e)
        {
            if (connection != null)
                cache.release(req,connection);
            // throw the exception as is
            throw e;
        }
    }
}
```

We will now go through some of the most important parts of the code, and discuss their role in the overall operation:

```
public void makePage(HttpServletRequest req) throws Exception
    { ConnInfo cc_tmp = new ConnInfo(req);
```

When a request is coming from a servlet, or from Cocoon, it has information about the URL, header, and so on. When the constructor of ConnInfo is called with a request as parameter, it finds the connection information by analyzing the syntax of the URL and extracts from them the **D**atabase **A**ccess **D**escriptor key. This key is used to localize the rest of information needed to connect to a desired database, this key is the last part of the value returned by method getServletPath of the HttpServletRequest class, for example, in this URL:
http://myserver.com/servlets/**demo**/pkg.startup, **demo** is used as the DAD information.

This DAD information is stored in the prism.properties file and includes the user name and password to connect to the database, and the compatibility mode set for this connection. The compatibility mode is the kind of database used. The compatibility modes are classified according to how many adapters they have, DB Prism by default includes 7x, 8i, Java, and Lite adapters.

Note: The servlet engine normally configures the servlet part of the URL to localize the servlets, and *demo* is one zone configured in the servlet repository.

```
password = str.substring(i+1);
```

A request coming from the client (browser) has header information about the user name and password; this information is used with dynamic logins. Dynamic logins mean that if there isn't a user name and password in the DAD information, DB Prism will ask them the first time that user tries to execute the application.

```
connection = cache.get(req,cc_tmp.usr,cc_tmp.pass);
```

After getting the connection information, DB Prism tries to get a connection from the **Resource Manager**. The Resource Manager makes a JDBC connection to the target database and returns a concrete object representing this connection (DBConnection). If there are problems, such as if you are denied access, it throws a NotAuthorizedException.

```
connection.doCall(req,name,password);
```

If the Resource Manager returns a valid connection in this line, DB Prism makes the stored procedure call. DBConnection is an abstract class, at run-time the calls are made to a specific class like DBConn8i or DBConnJavaLite, and then this specific class implements the real call, taking into account the database dependent code.

Getting the Page from a Database Buffer

The getPage() method handles the process of retrieving the generated page from the database buffer.

```
public Reader getPage(HttpServletRequest req) throws Exception
{
    ConnInfo cc_tmp = new ConnInfo(req);
    try
    {
        return connection.getGeneratedPage();
    }
    finally
    {
        if (connection!=null)
        {
            cache.release(req,connection);
        }
    }
}
```

Again, here is an explanation of the most important areas of this code:

```
return connection.getGeneratedPage();
```

The getPage() method returns an XML page as a java.io.reader object. This page is obtained from the database buffer by executing the getGeneratedPage() method of the DBConnection object. The connection instance variable has the connection object stored in the previous step (makePage) and then has the same connection to the target database.

```
cache.release(req,connection);
```

If getGeneratedPage() works, the connection has returned it to the Resource Manager. The Resource Manager needs the ConnInfo object to check if this connection is part of a transaction.

Note: DB Prism supports transactions by URL demarcation. You could set transaction support defining begin, commit, rollback, and belong to URLs (web pages), for example:

❑ /servlets/xml/pkg.startup (begin, the connection is taken here)

❑ /servlets/xml/pkg.commit (commits modifications, then frees the connection)

❑ /servlets/xml/pkg.rollback (rollback modifications, then frees the connection)

❑ /servlets/xml/pkg.* (any other pages that use the connection taken in the first step)

DBConnection.java

Firstly, this class declares an interface to create a connection to every database supported. The create method has to be implemented by the adapters to return the connection to the database; for example, DBConn8i class implements this method returning an instance of the DBConn8i class. In addition, it is an abstract class that defines abstract "primitive operations", which concrete subclasses define to implement steps in an algorithm (doCall and getGeneratedStream).

What Happens When a Call is Made to the Stored Procedure

The doCall() method handles the creation of a stored procedure call.:

```java
public void doCall(HttpServletRequest req, String usr, String pass)
    throws SQLException,NotAuthorizedException,ExecutionErrorPageException,
    ExecutionErrorMsgException,UnsupportedEncodingException,IOException
{
    String ppackage = getPackage(req);
    String pprocedure = getProcedure(req);
    if (!connInfo.txEnable && !connInfo.stateLess)
    {
        resetPackages();
    }
    setCGIVars(req,usr,pass);
    int authStatus = doAuthorize(connInfo.customAuthentication,ppackage);
    if (authStatus!=1)
    {
        String realms = getRealm();
        throw new NotAuthorizedException(realms);
    }

    if (type != null &&
        type.toLowerCase().startsWith("multipart/form-data"))
    {
        UploadRequest multi = connInfo.factory.createUploadRequest(req,this);
        doIt(multi,getSPCommand(multi));
    }
    else if (getSPCommand(req).startsWith("!"))
        doIt(new FlexibleRequest(req),getSPCommand(req).substring(1));
    else
        doIt(req,getSPCommand(req));
}
```

This code is explained below:

```java
String ppackage = getPackage(req);
String pprocedure = getProcedure(req);
```

Before calling the stored procedure, the request is analyzed to get the package name and the stored procedure name to be executed. A URL like http://myserver.com/servlets/xml/DEMOj.startup returns DEMOj as the package name and startup as the procedure name.

```
resetPackages();
```

According to the parameter stateLess in the DAD information, the operation resetPackages() will be called. Stateless packages are applications that don't use global states as global package variables. To guarantee a clear session in every request this operation must reset all the global information. Not all databases support this operation – Oracle Lite, for example, doesn't have this behavior but it could be implemented in the class DBMS_Session.java.

```
setCGIVars(req,usr,pass);
```

This operation sends all the HTTP CGI variables to the database environment. There are almost 30 CGI variables like PATH_INFO; these variables are used by the applications in order to get important information about the caller state. An adapter that implements Java support could use the CgiVars.java class to get this information in a concrete object.

```
int authStatus = doAuthorize(connInfo.customAuthentication,ppackage);
if (authStatus!=1)
{
    String realms = getRealm();
    throw new NotAuthorizedException(realms);
```

The doAuthorize() method is called in order to implement application authorization schemes. There are four modes of application schemes - none, global, perPackage, and custom. This value is in the DAD information and the concrete class (adapter) must implement this responsibility. If the authorization fails, the getRealm() method is called in order to get the application string from the database, to be sent back to the browser with the authorization response.

```
if (type != null &&
    type.toLowerCase().startsWith("multipart/form-data"))
{
    UploadRequest multi = connInfo.factory.createUploadRequest(req,this);
    doIt(multi,getSPCommand(multi));
```

If the request sent by the user is of multipart form data type (upload), DBConnection creates a new instance of the UploadRequest class – this class stores the information sent by the user in the content repository and returns a new request with the arguments sent in the client request plus the file(s) uploaded in the repository. UploadRequest only needs to implement two methods – newAsBlob() and updateContentInfo(). The stored procedure is then called with this new request object.

If the caller URL has the syntax: http://myserver.com/servlets/xml/!pkg.prc?a=1&b=2&a=3 it means there is functionality of flexible parameters – this functionality doesn't call a stored procedure of the form pkg.prc(a,b,a), instead the call looks like this:

```
pkg.prc(num_entries,name_array,values_array,reserved)
```

Where num_entries is 3, name_array is an array of {a,b,a}, values_array is an array of {1,2,3}, and reserved is "none".

If the URL doesn't have flexible parameter passing syntax, the stored procedure is called by calling the abstract method doIt(), with the request of the client and the stored procedure command as arguments. The second argument has the syntax [[schema.]package.]procedure, where schema is the database user name owner of the stored procedure, such as scott, package is the package name (for example, my_pkg) and procedure is the procedure name to be called. Only the last part is mandatory, and many databases don't have the concept of the package for grouping related procedures and functions; in these cases the adapter could use the syntax [schema.]procedure. Oracle Lite adapter uses the concept of table name as package name; in this database the classes uploaded to the system are attached to a particular table, and the syntax is interpreted like this –
[schema.]table_name.procedure.

Returning the Page

```
public StringReader getGeneratedPage() throws Exception
{
    StringReader pg = getGeneratedStream();
    if (!connInfo.txEnable)
    {
        sqlconn.commit();
    }
    return pg;
}
```

This code functions as follows:

```
public StringReader getGeneratedPage() throws Exception
{
    StringReader pg = getGeneratedStream();
```

GetGeneratedPage() does not need to do different things according to the database, it only needs to invoke the abstract method getGeneratedStream which has to be implemented in each subclass. Each subclass represents a different database and implements the corresponding mechanism according to the database dependent stuff. For example, in the UML sequence diagram the database used is Oracle 8i, so the subclass is DBConn8i and it codifies the corresponding getGeneratedStream.

The getGeneratedStream abstract method, generally, gets the page from a database buffer; this database buffer is filled by the application with the page to be returned to the client. According to the versatility of the database for handling large amounts of text, this buffer could be a simple data type or complex one; for example, a CLOB type is used in Oracle 8i's Java support for storing the generated page.

```
    if (!connInfo.txEnable)
    {
        sqlconn.commit();
```

If the URL is not part of a transaction, then the changes are committed, otherwise the resource manager applies this commit automatically when the connection is returned, and the URL is recognized as a commit URL.

```
    return pg;
```

Finally, the page is returned to the Wrapper.

Abstract Methods

These methods of DBConnection define the contract with the Adapters, and these methods are implemented by the sub-classes according to the functionality shown in the previous code.

```
public abstract int doAuthorize(String authMode, String ppackage) throws
    SQLException;
public abstract String getRealm() throws SQLException;
public abstract StringReader getGeneratedStream() throws Exception;
public abstract void resetPackages() throws SQLException;
public abstract void doIt(HttpServletRequest req, String servletname) throws
    SQLException,UnsupportedEncodingException;
public abstract void setCGIVars(HttpServletRequest req, String name,
    String pass) throws SQLException;
```

DBFactory.java

It has as many sub-classes as databases to be supported. If a new database that needs support appears, new subclasses must be incorporated. DBFactory declares an interface for operations to create SPProc, DBConnection, UploadRequest and DownLoadRequest objects.

```
public abstract SPProc createSPProc(ConnInfo conn, String procname, Connection
    sqlconn)  throws SQLException;
public abstract DBConnection createDBConnection(ConnInfo connInfo);
public abstract UploadRequest createUploadRequest(HttpServletRequest request,
    DBConnection repositoryConnection) throws IOException, SQLException;
public abstract DownloadRequest createDownloadRequest(HttpServletRequest
    request, HttpServletResponse response, DBConnection repositoryConnection)
    throws IOException, SQLException ;
```

❏   createSPProc must return an object of type SPProc, which represents a stored procedure in the target database. This method is mandatory.

❏   createDBConnection must return an object of type DBConnection that represents a specific connection to the target database. This method is also mandatory.

❏   createUploadRequest returns a new request after uploading the multimedia content in the database repository. If the database doesn't have support for multimedia objects such as the BLOB (Binary Large OBject) data type, a SQLException is returned.

❏   createDownloadRequest returns a DownloadRequest object to be used by the engine to return a multimedia content to the client.

SPProc.java

This class represents a stored procedure for an abstract database – it has common methods such as getAll() and addProcedure(). The sub-classes must implement this last method to represent a concrete stored procedure in the target database. SPProc has a hash table for storing the argument names and their types and a vector to store the argument list of every definition of an overload procedure.

Stored procedures in many languages have multiple definitions according to the types of arguments, and these multiple definitions are stored by an overload index starting at one. For example, in PLSQL, two stored procedures having the definition like pkg.proc(a integer, b varchar2) and pkg.proc(a integer), have two entries in the hash table, one with index 1 and the other with index 2. The vector of the argument lists has {a,b} for the first occurrence and {a} for the second occurrence.

> **Note: The concrete instance of this class must load the definition of the stored procedure from the database dictionary views – if the target database doesn't have dictionary views for stored procedures, there are two possible solutions. First, you could make your own dictionary view (this is the strategy used by the Oracle Lite Adapter) and populate the content of this view with the public procedures and their arguments. Secondly, you could use the reflection mechanism of the target language (for example: Java) to find the procedure that matches with this call.**

Part II: Putting DB Prism to Work

DB Prism and Cocoon could be installed on any web server that runs servlets; I chose Oracle Internet Application Server because it has a graphical installer, a pre-configured Apache web server 1.3.x and a servlet runner Jserv 1.1. The instructions shown below could be applied to any version of Apache web server and Jserv, and with minor changes they could be used to configure Apache web server with the newest Tomcat servlet runner.

Before Start

Before installing Cocoon and DB Prism under Oracle Internet Application Server (IAS) you have to check the correct installation of the product. For more information about this product, refer to the Oracle Technology Network web site (http://technet.oracle.com/) or the Apache web site (http://www.apache.org/).

To start the IAS web server, log into the system as the web server owner, and run this command:

```
# cd $ORACLE_HOME/Apache/Apache/bin
# ./httpdsctl start
```

These commands start the Apache IAS on port 7777. Next, open a web browser on the server machine and navigate to the following URLs: http://localhost:7777/ and http://localhost:7777/jserv/. This process helps to test the Apache listener. The last URL is only public from a localhost connection for security reasons.

These pages look like this:

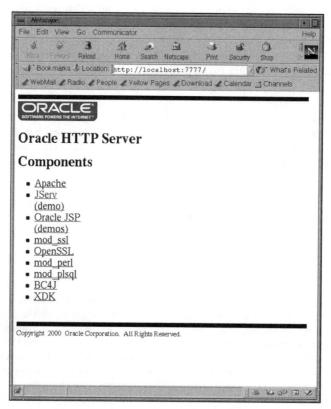

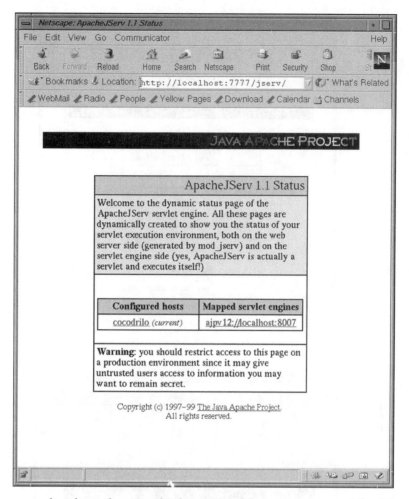

The following screenshot shows the general information of the mod_jserv module of Apache web server; mod_jserv is the Apache module that runs the servlets.

Selecting the URL of the previous screen, you have to go to the internal configuration of the servlet runtime engine.

Here are some screens about the status page of mod_jserv.

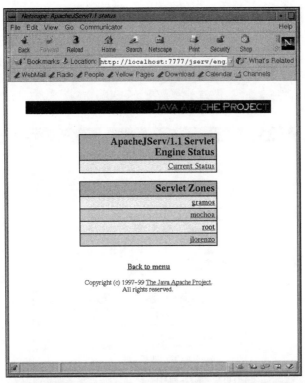

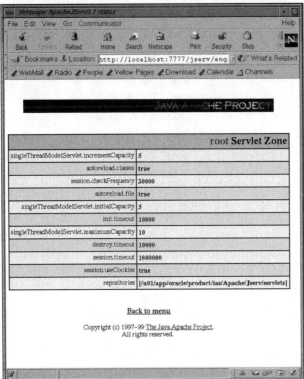

These screens show the `mod_jserv` configuration; if you don't see similar pages then refer to the IAS documentation in order to check the installation instruction of Apache/Jserv IAS.

Cocoon Setup

Downloading Cocoon

Cocoon can be downloaded from http://xml.apache.org/cocoon/dist/. At the time of writing, Cocoon version 1.8 is the latest. After downloading, it needs to be uncompressed into a suitable directory on the web server – a good location for this (I would suggest) is the directory, /usr/local. It will expand into a `cocoon-x.x` subdirectory (depending on the version you use). Create a symbolic link off `/usr/local` called `Cocoon` to point at it (`ln -s /usr/local/cocoon-x.x /usr/local/Cocoon`).

Create a Write-enabled Directory

Next, go to the `conf` directory under the Cocoon main distribution (`/usr/local/Cocoon`) and edit the `cocoon.properties` file, changing the line:

```
processor.xsp.repository = /repository
```

For the line:

```
processor.xsp.repository = /tmp/repository
```

This change is necessary in order to give a directory to Cocoon with write permissions for storing compiled XSP pages.

File Modifications

1. Edit the Apache configuration file (`$ORACLE_HOME/Apache/Apache/conf/httpds.conf`), adding a directory alias for cocoon examples, like this:

```
Alias /samples/ "/usr/local/Cocoon/samples/"
```

2. Edit the `jserv.conf` file (`$ORACLE_HOME/Apache/Jserv/etc/jserv.conf`) with these changes:

❑ Add an extension handler for files that have a `.xml` extension by un-commenting this line:

```
ApJServAction .xml /servlets/org.apache.cocoon.Cocoon
```

❑ Check for the mount point for servlet zones – it should look like this:

```
ApJServMount /servlets /root
ApJServMount /servlet /root
```

3. Edit the Apache `jserv.properties` file (`$ORACLE_HOME/Apache/Jserv/etc/jserv.properties`, adding the Cocoon libraries to the CLASSPATH environment by inserting these lines after the system CLASSPATH:

```
# Version 1.8.0
wrapper.classpath=/usr/local/Cocoon/bin/cocoon.jar
wrapper.classpath=/usr/local/Cocoon/lib/fop_0_13_0.jar
wrapper.classpath=/usr/local/Cocoon/lib/xalan_1_2_D02.jar
wrapper.classpath=/usr/local/Cocoon/lib/xerces_1_2.jar
wrapper.classpath=/usr/local/Cocoon/lib/turbine-pool.jar
```

4. Edit the zone configuration file
($ORACLE_HOME/Apache/Jserv/etc/zone.properties), and add the parameter passed
to the Cocoon engine with the configuration file for it.

```
servlet.org.apache.cocoon.Cocoon.initArgs=properties=/usr/local/Cocoon/conf/
    cocoon.properties
```

Testing Your Installation

Restart Apache IAS by running the following commands:

```
# cd $ORACLE_HOME/Apache/Apache/bin
# ./httpdsctl restart
```

Now it is time to test the Cocoon installation and samples. Go to the Cocoon status page
(http://localhost:7777/Cocoon.xml) – the page should look like this if the installation was successful:

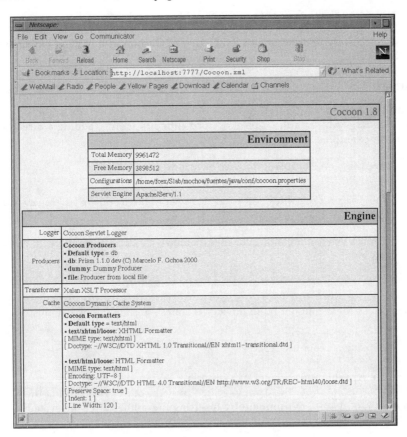

Test the examples by going to http://localhost:7777/samples/index.xml, as shown below:

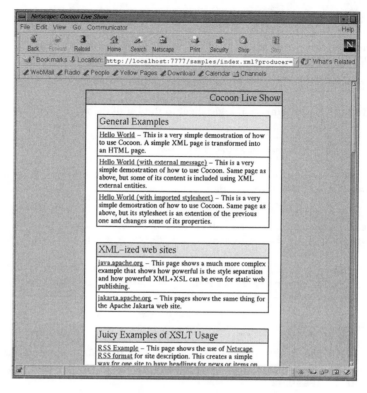

This page provides a simple menu of examples for you to test on your installation. When all of this has been completed successfully, it's time to move on to the DB Prism configuration.

DB Prism Setup

Downloading DB Prism

DB Prism can be downloaded from http://www.plenix.com/dbprism/. DB Prism version 1.1 is the latest version at time of writing; it should be downloaded and uncompressed into the same directory as Cocoon.

File Modifications

1. Go to the conf directory under the Cocoon main distribution (/usr/local/Cocoon); make the following changes to the cocoon.properties file:

❑ Add the DB Prism producer for Cocoon:

```
producer.type.db = com.prism.CocoonWrapper
producer.db.properties = /usr/local/prism/conf/prism.properties
```

❑ Make sure the default producer is set to db, rather than file (this should be okay, as the producer was added with the previous two lines); find the line:

```
producer.default = file
```

Replace this with:

```
producer.default = db
```

❑ Add the `HeaderProcessor` of DB Prism to the list of processors of Cocoon by adding this line:

```
processor.type.http = com.prism.HeaderProcessor
```

❑ Add the XSP Connection logic sheet to the list of them (all one line):

```
processor.xsp.logicsheet.connection.java =
    resource://com/prism/xsp/connection.xsl
```

❑ Finally, add the formatter lines for an Excel output example, (again, the first two lines shown are all one line of code):

```
formatter.type.application/vnd.ms-excel =
    org.apache.cocoon.formatter.TextFormatter
formatter.application/vnd.ms-excel.MIME-type = application/vnd.ms-excel
```

2. Edit the Apache configuration file, making the following change – add a directory alias for the Cocoon examples. This directory contains the stylesheet for the examples of DB Prism. This is done by adding the following line:

```
Alias /xsl/ "/usr/local/prism/xsl/"
```

3. Edit the Apache `jserv.properties` file (found in $ORACLE_HOME/Apache/Jserv/etc/) add the DB Prism library to the `classpath` environment by inserting this line, following the system `classpath`:

```
wrapper.classpath=/usr/local/prism/bin/Prism.jar
```

4. Edit the zone configuration ($ORACLE_HOME/Apache/Jserv/etc/`zone.properties`) file, firstly adding an alias for each DB Prism DAD:

```
servlet.plsql.code=com.prism.ServletWrapper
servlet.java.code=com.prism.ServletWrapper
servlet.demo.code=com.prism.ServletWrapper
servlet.xml.code=org.apache.cocoon.Cocoon
servlet.xmld.code=org.apache.cocoon.Cocoon
servlet.xmlj.code=org.apache.cocoon.Cocoon
servlet.doc.code=org.apache.cocoon.Cocoon
servlet.print.code=org.apache.cocoon.Cocoon
```

Now add the initialization parameters for the alias of the previous configuration:

```
servlet.plsql.initArgs=properties=/usr/local/prism/conf/prism.properties
servlet.java.initArgs=properties=/usr/local/prism/conf/prism.properties
servlet.xml.initArgs=properties=/usr/local/Cocoon/conf/cocoon.properties
servlet.xmld.initArgs=properties=/usr/local/Cocoon/conf/cocoon.properties
servlet.xmlj.initArgs=properties=/usr/local/Cocoon/conf/cocoon.properties
servlet.doc.initArgs=properties=/usr/local/Cocoon/conf/cocoon.properties
servlet.print.initArgs=properties=/usr/local/Cocoon/conf/cocoon.properties
```

Testing Your Installation

Restart Apache IAS by entering the following commands:

```
# cd $ORACLE_HOME/Apache/Apache/bin
# ./httpdsctl restart
```

Test the DB Prism installation by going to the Cocoon status page (http://localhost:7777/Cocoon.xml).
If the installation was successful, the page should now look like this:

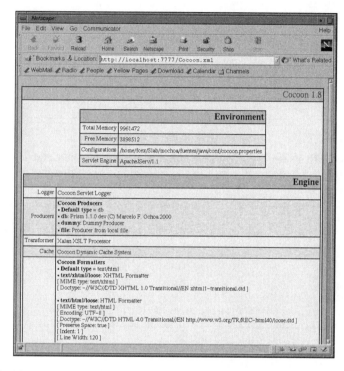

If your screen looks like the above, then this proves that Cocoon is now recognizing DB Prism as a new
producer. However, DB Prism is still not ready to connect to the database – the next section details how
to complete this set-up; how to set up the examples of DB Prism in the database.

Database Setup

We will use Oracle 8.1.6 for this study – this is fine for installation of the DB Prism examples. The
following section details a set of steps to follow to achieve this.

> **Note: remember to check for the availability of the database and log with the Oracle
> owner (normally the user ORACLE)**

1. Install the Oracle XML Utility for Java. Uncompress it and run the installation script. It
assumes a default installation on the user scott/tiger. If this has completed
successfully, you should see the following display on your screen:

```
# cd /usr/local
# jar xvf /tmp/XSU12_ver1_2_1.zip
created: OracleXSU12/
 extracted: OracleXSU12/README.html
    created: OracleXSU12/doc/
 extracted: OracleXSU12/doc/OracleXML.html
...
 extracted: OracleXSU12/env.csh
 extracted: OracleXSU12/env.bat
# cd OracleXSU12/lib
# sh oraclexmlsqlload.csh
-------------------------------------------------------------------

Loading jar files...
...
Testing..
...
Done..
#
```

2. Install the DB Prism Java Toolkit – this script assumes the database user scott/tiger. A successful installation will result in the following screen display:

```
# cd /usr/local/prism/oi
# sh install-toolkit.sh
SQL*Plus: Release 8.1.6.0.0 - Production on Mon Oct 9 15:56:33 2000

(c) Copyright 1999 Oracle Corporation.  All rights reserved.


Connected to:
Oracle8i Enterprise Edition Release 8.1.6.1.0 - Production
With the Partitioning option
JServer Release 8.1.6.1.0 - Production


Java altered.
...
Package created.

No errors.
...
Disconnected from Oracle8i Enterprise Edition Release 8.1.6.1.0 - Production
With the Partitioning option
JServer Release 8.1.6.1.0 - Production
#
```

3. Now you have to install the examples included with DB Prism:

```
# cd /usr/local/prism/oi
# sh install-demo.sh
SQL*Plus: Release 8.1.6.0.0 - Production on Mon Oct 9 15:59:20 2000
```

```
(c) Copyright 1999 Oracle Corporation.   All rights reserved.


Connected to:
Oracle8i Enterprise Edition Release 8.1.6.1.0 - Production
With the Partitioning option
JServer Release 8.1.6.1.0 - Production


Java altered.
...
Package created.

No errors.
...
Disconnected from Oracle8i Enterprise Edition Release 8.1.6.1.0 - Production
With the Partitioning option
JServer Release 8.1.6.1.0 - Production
#
```

Configuring DB Prism to Access the Database

The previous step installs the toolkit and the demo code in the database. The last step is to set it to access the database:

1. Configure the DAD information – go to the `prism.properties` file, found in the directory at `/usr/local/prism/conf/prism.properties`, and add the DAD `xmlj`, to the list of DADs:

```
global.alias=plsql xml demo servlet xmld lite org.apache.cocoon.Cocoon java
xmlj   doc print
```

> Note: Every entry in this line must be configured in the `zone.properties` as servlet alias.

2. Set the database parameter for the DAD, `xmlj`:

```
xmlj.dbusername=scott
xmlj.dbpassword=tiger
xmlj.connectString=jdbc:oracle:thin:@localhost:1521:ORCL
xmlj.errorLevel=2
xmlj.errorPage=http://localhost/error.html
xmlj.compat=java
xmlj.producerarg=ignore
```

3. Restart Apache IAS and test the DB Prism installation by issuing the following commands:

```
# cd $ORACLE_HOME/Apache/Apache/bin
# ./httpdsctl restart
```

4. Go to the DB Prism examples main page,
http://localhost:7777/servlets/xmlj/DEMOj.startup, which should look like this:

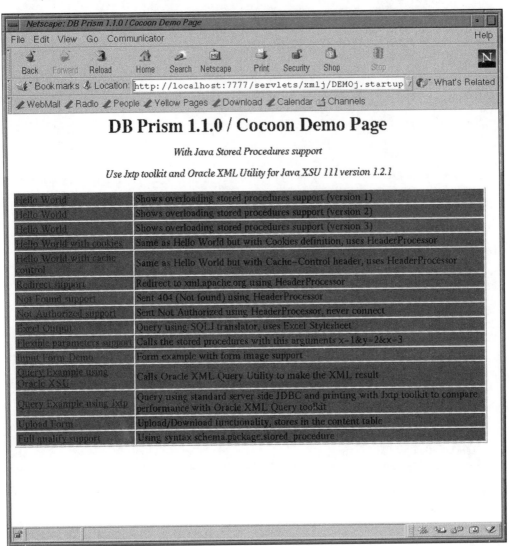

Making the Hello World Example

Now we will see how to make a simple Hello World sample application, in the context of DB Prism and Cocoon.

A quick way to install a Java stored procedure into Oracle version 8i is to make a simple file with the .sqlj extension and load it with the command loadjava. This simple example uses the Jxtp toolkit (**J**ava **X**ML **T**oolkit **P**rocedure), which provides simple procedures and functions to generate XML tags in a serialized way. The toolkit also accepts objects of type org.w3c.dom.Document, which means that it is even possible to generate the XML pages in an object-oriented way with the standard DOM API.

The code for the Hello World example is shown and discussed below:

```
package demo;
import com.prism.toolkit.*;

class Hello
{
   public static void World()
   {
      Jxtp.prolog("1.0","http://localhost/xsl/hello.xsl");
      Jxtp.process();
      Jxtp.tagOpen("page");
      Jxtp.tag("title","Hello World");
      Jxtp.tagOpen("content");
      Jxtp.tag("paragraph",
      "This is my first Prism-Cocoon code, written in Java Stored Procedures!");
      Jxtp.tagClose("content");
      Jxtp.tagClose("page");
      Jxtp.epilog();
   }
}
```

The function of the various parts of this code is as follows:

```
import com.prism.toolkit.*;
```

This package needs to use the Jxtp procedures and functions:

```
Jxtp.prolog("1.0","http://localhost/xsl/hello.xsl");
```

Jxtp.prolog creates the following XML tags:

```
<?xml version="1.0"?>
<?xml-stylesheet href="http://localhost/xsl/hello.xsl" type="text/xsl"?>
```

```
Jxtp.process();
```

The above procedure sets up the processing instruction to the Cocoon framework, as shown below:

```
<?cocoon-process type="xslt"?>
```

```
Jxtp.tagOpen("page");
```

This line generates the XML tag, <page>

```
Jxtp.tag("title","Hello World");
```

This line generates the XML element <title>Hello World</title>

```
Jxtp.epilog();
```

This line generates a comment and is not required.

Loading this code into the database executes the following command:

```
# loadjava -user scott/tiger Hello.sqlj
```

This command loads and compiles the code inside the database and is ready to be called for DB Prism. To make the Java code public, Oracle 8i requires call specs for the Java class. To make the call specs for this demo execute the following SQL code with the `sqlplus` program:

```
# sqlplus scott/tiger
SQL*Plus: Release 8.1.6.0.0 - Production on Mon Oct 9 15:59:20 2000

(c) Copyright 1999 Oracle Corporation.  All rights reserved.


Connected to:
Oracle8i Enterprise Edition Release 8.1.6.1.0 - Production
With the Partitioning option
JServer Release 8.1.6.1.0 - Production

SQL> CREATE OR REPLACE PACKAGE Hello AS
        PROCEDURE World;
     END Hello;
SQL>/
SQL> CREATE OR REPLACE PACKAGE BODY Hello AS
        PROCEDURE World
        AS LANGUAGE JAVA
        NAME 'demo.Hello.World()';
     END Hello;
SQL>/
SQL>EXIT
```

After this has been run successfully, DB Prism can execute the Hello World application. Navigate to http://localhost:7777/servlets/xmlj/Hello.World – executing the stored procedure should display a page like this:

Making a Content Management System

Brief Introduction to a CMS

When the information or the size of the web site grows, several problems appear related to deployment or maintainability of the big sites.

For example:

❑ How to make a change in the look and feel of the pages, which affects all the pages in the site

❏ How to access the assets concurrently by many content owners at the same time

- ❏ How to store the version history of the documents
- ❏ How to automatically store a link to different documents based on related information
- ❏ How to make a site search engine

These problems are solved with a database-backed CMS system. This system, at development time, stores the assets inside the database and provides online viewing directly rendering the content when a user request came. On the other hand, at the deployment time, the system provides an off-line generation of the entire site or part of it on a web server disk for improving performance.

Unlike the HTML CMS system, an XML CMS has other additional benefits. These benefits are related to XML technologies, here is a brief list of them:

- ❏ Can be used with several presentation formats, a XML content that defines a document must be independent from the presentation format
- ❏ Validation of the document format through a given DTD at import time, this validation guarantees that the imported asset is a valid document for the presentation system
- ❏ Can use search engines based on XML technologies, such as Oracle 8i *inter*Media which interprets XML documents and provides a search text with queries like this, `"find all documents containing 'CMS' within <note>"`.

Based on these points, we will show a CMS made with Java stored procedures and SQLj as an extended example of how to make an application with DB Prism / Cocoon. A DB Prism CMS divides the page content in five visible parts, the content owner defines one (content body), and the others are generated by the system automatically analyzing the information stored in the Meta model.

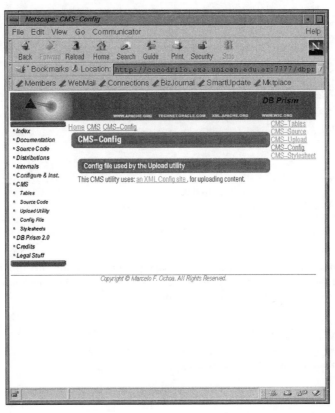

Below, we shall go through the different highlighted parts of the page, looking at the source code for each. The code is passed from the CMS as XML, and is transformed to HTML by the Cocoon framework through a modified version of the `document2html.xsl` stylesheet.

Page Header

Provides general information for the current page.

This information is taken from the meta data of the current page and the top parent page (`Category`). This information is used, for example, by the stylesheet `document2html.xsl` to show a banner image for the current category in the upper right section of the page; it also could be used by a stylesheet for a WebCrawler or Spider to give keywords for this page.

```
<document name='CMS'>
   <header>
      <name>CMS-Tables</name>
      <title>CMS</title>
      <subtitle>Tables of CMS</subtitle>
      <authors><person name='SCOTT' /></authors>
   </header>
```

Map Information

Provides information to build the left side menu bar.

This information is built using the directory-like structure of the pages (parent column of the table pages); in this code, the first level pages and the children of the current category are selected:

```
<map>
   <option>
      <linkmap id='Home' longname='Top entry'
         href='/Home'>Home</linkmap>
   </option>
   <option>
      <linkmap id='Docs' longname='Documentation'
         href='/Docs'>Docs</linkmap>
   </option>
   <option>
      <linkmap id='Source' longname='Source Code'
         href='/Source'>Source</linkmap>
   </option>
   <option>
      <linkmap id='Dist' longname='Distribution available for DB Prism'
         href='/Dist'>Dist</linkmap>
   </option>
</map>
```

Path Information

Provides information about the ancestor of this page (parents) to build the upper left links in the content area. With this information, the `document2print.xsl` stylesheet creates a navigation bar, which permits the user to go back to the previous position:

```
<path>
   <option>
      <linktopic id='10' longname='DB Prism Servlet Engine'
         href='/Home'>Home</linktopic>
   </option>
```

```
        <option>
           <linktopic id='70' longname='Content Management System'
              href='/CMS'>CMS</linktopic>
        </option>
        <option>
           <linktopic id='200' longname='Tables of CMS'
              href='/cms/CMS-Tables'>CMS-Tables</linktopic>
        </option>
     </path>
```

Related Topics

Documents related to the current page, shown by the `document2html` stylesheet in the upper right side of content area. This information provides the user with a menu bar with links to related documents off this page stored in the RELATED table:

```
<topics>
   <option>
      <linktopic href='/cms/CMS-Tables'>CMS-Tables</linktopic>
      <linktopic href='/cms/CMS-Source'>CMS-Source</linktopic>
      <linktopic href='/cms/CMS-Upload'>CMS-Upload</linktopic>
      <linktopic href='/cms/CMS-Config'>CMS-Config</linktopic>
      <linktopic href='/cms/CMS-Stylesheet'>CMS-Stylesheet</linktopic>
   </option>
</topics>
```

Content (Body)

The asset uploaded by the content owner for this page:

```
<body>
   <s1 title='Tables of CMS' level='0'>
      <!-- Content Management System Table Definition -->
   </s1>
   <s2>
      <p>
           The CMS stores page elements in the following tables:
      </p>
   </s2>
</body>
```

DB Prism queries the database for every document to be loaded, and Cocoon builds each page by combining these five elements into an HTML file, using the stylesheet associated with the top-level entry. Five elements are used because the designers of CMS identified five areas of the page that they wished to treat separately. For different page architectures, you might choose a different number of elements.

Of these five elements, the Content element is unique for each page – it is what makes a page unique. The other elements contain data that is reused by many pages to give the site consistency. Because elements are stored in the database, one change updates the entire site. For example, if you change the stylesheet code that defines the HTML Header, every page will reflect that change the next time that CMS generates files for the site.

When a browser requests a page, the Java code is executed on the server. For example, the Map Information element includes a SQL query, which builds the top navigation bar at runtime, by searching parent, neighbor, and child topics of the current page.

Design of the Meta Model

CMS Tables

The CMS stores page elements in the following tables:

❑ The PAGES table stores one row of structural information and other meta data for each page. Each page is identified by a unique number stored in the ID_PAGE column (which references the CN_ID_PAGE column of the CONTENT table). Pages have a PARENT foreign key to self, which permits a directory-like structure.

❑ The CONTENT table stores each version of a page's content in a unique row identified by CN_ID_PAGE number and VERSION number, with the actual content residing in a CLOB column. The CMS stores multiple versions of a content block and uses a specified version to build a page. The CONTENT table is linked to the PAGES table by ID number.

❑ The TEMPLATES/STYLESHEETS tables store the stylesheet(s) associated with this page.

❑ The RELATED table stores information on which pages are a related topic from other pages. RELATED has from/to information which permits a mesh structure of the related pages.

Each page in the CMS belongs to another page (analogous to a file system directory), except the top-level page(s). This page defines the stylesheet for its children. The CMS stores content, page data, and template items in separate tables. Here's a complete definition of CMS tables in SQL:

The PAGES table stores the meta-data information for a given page:

```
TABLE PAGES
(
    id_page              NUMBER(10) NOT NULL,
    parent               NUMBER(10),
    name                 VARCHAR2(255),
    longname             VARCHAR2(4000),
    owner                VARCHAR2(255),
    created              DATE,
    modified             DATE,
    comments             VARCHAR2(4000),
    meta                 VARCHAR2(4000),
    path                 VARCHAR2(4000),
    language             VARCHAR2(32),
    deleted              VARCHAR2(1),
    created_by           VARCHAR2(255),
    modified_by          VARCHAR2(255),
    status               VARCHAR2(255),
    file_size            NUMBER(10),
    current_version      NUMBER(6),
    CONSTRAINT pg_pk PRIMARY KEY (id_page),
    CONSTRAINT pg_pg_fk FOREIGN KEY (parent)
        REFERENCES PAGES(id_page)
)
```

The CONTENT table stores the asset (XML document) for a given page:

```
TABLE CONTENT
(
    cn_id_page                  NUMBER(10) NOT NULL,
    version                     NUMBER(6)NOT NULL,
    owner                       VARCHAR2(255),
    status                      VARCHAR2(255),
    source_file                 VARCHAR2(4000),
    file_size                   NUMBER(10),
    content                     CLOB,
    created                     DATE,
    modified                    DATE,
    created_by                  VARCHAR2(255),
    modified_by                 VARCHAR2(255),
    CONSTRAINT cn_pk PRIMARY KEY (cn_id_page,version),
    CONSTRAINT cn_pg_fk FOREIGN KEY (cn_id_page)
        REFERENCES PAGES(id_page)
)
```

The RELATED table defines a relation between two documents:

```
TABLE RELATED
(
    rl_id_page_from             NUMBER(10) NOT NULL,
    rl_id_page_to               NUMBER(10) NOT NULL,
    CONSTRAINT rl_pk PRIMARY KEY (rl_id_page_from , rl_id_page_to),
    CONSTRAINT rl_pg_fk1 FOREIGN KEY (rl_id_page_from)
        REFERENCES PAGES(id_page),
    CONSTRAINT rl_pg_fk2 FOREIGN KEY (rl_id_page_to)
        REFERENCES PAGES(id_page)
)
```

The TEMPLATES table defines the template (stylesheet) for a given page:

```
CREATE TABLE TEMPLATES
(
    tpl_id_page                 NUMBER(10) NOT NULL,
    tpl_id_stylesheet           NUMBER(10) NOT NULL,
    CONSTRAINT tpl_pk PRIMARY KEY (tpl_id_page , tpl_id_stylesheet),
    CONSTRAINT tpl_pg_fk FOREIGN KEY (tpl_id_page)
        REFERENCES PAGES(id_page),
    CONSTRAINT tpl_st_fk FOREIGN KEY (tpl_id_stylesheet)
        REFERENCES STYLESHEETS(id_stylesheet)
)
```

The STYLESHEETS table defines the stylesheets available on the system:

```
TABLE STYLESHEETS
(
    id_stylesheet               NUMBER(10) NOT NULL,
    owner                       VARCHAR2(255),
    status                      VARCHAR2(255),
    url                         VARCHAR2(4000),
    type                        VARCHAR2(255),
    media                       VARCHAR2(255),
    ext                         VARCHAR2(15),
    attributes                  VARCHAR2(4000),
    created                     DATE,
    modified                    DATE,
    created_by                  VARCHAR2(255),
    modified_by                 VARCHAR2(255),
    CONSTRAINT st_pk PRIMARY KEY (id_stylesheet)
)
```

Writing the Java Code

Building Pages

DB Prism CMS defines a tree-structured hierarchy by using the parent foreign key in the table pages. The site's home page is defined by the page that has no parent (Null value in the parent column of the table pages), beneath it are several pages, which define content branches such as Documentation, Source Code and so on. These content branches called categories define the layout or look and feel for your children.

Page elements are all stored in the database, so the CMS executes queries to get them out, as shown in the following Java code.

```java
public void GET(int p_id, int p_level, int p_top, int p_version) throws
    SQLException
{
    ChildIterator cIter=null;
    int topParent;
    if (p_level>1)
        topParent=p_id;
    else
        topParent = findTopParent(p_id,p_top);
    String topName,topLongName,topOwner,
        thisPageName,thisPageLongName,
        thisPageComments,thisPagePath;
    Jxtp.prolog();
    Jxtp.process("http"); // Do not cache this page
    Jxtp.header("Cache-Control","False");
    try
    {
        Integer thisPageParent;
        chooseStylesheet(topParent);
        // Gets information about the top page and the current page
        #sql {SELECT name,longname,owner INTO
            :topName,:topLongName,:topOwner
            FROM pages WHERE id_page=:topParent};
        #sql {SELECT name,longname,comments,parent,path INTO
            :thisPageName,:thisPageLongName,:thisPageComments,
            :thisPageParent,:thisPagePath
            FROM pages WHERE id_page=:p_id };
        Jxtp.tagOpen("document","name='"+topName+"'");
        Jxtp.tagOpen("header");
        Jxtp.tag("name",thisPageName);
        Jxtp.tag("title",topName);
        Jxtp.tag("subtitle",thisPageLongName);
        Jxtp.tagOpen("authors");
        Jxtp.tagOpen("person","name='"+topOwner+"'");
        Jxtp.tagClose("person");
        Jxtp.tagClose("authors");
        Jxtp.tagClose("header");
        showMapInfo(p_id,thisPageName,p_top);
        showPath(p_id,p_top);
        relatedTopics(p_id,thisPageParent,p_top);
        Jxtp.tagOpen("body");
        Jxtp.tagOpen("s1","title='"+thisPageLongName+"' level='0'");
        Jxtp.p("<!-- "+thisPageComments+" -->");
        Jxtp.tagClose("s1");
```

```
          // show Main Content
          showContent(p_id,p_version);
          // Print child up to indicated level, 1-no-child, 2-first-level-child
          #sql cIter = {SELECT id_page,current_version,
              longname,comments,level FROM pages WHERE level<:p_level
              START WITH parent=:p_id CONNECT BY prior id_page=parent};
          while(cIter.next())
          {
              Jxtp.tagOpen("s1","title='"+cIter.longname()+"'
              level='"+cIter.level()+"'");
              Jxtp.p("<!-- "+cIter.comments()+" -->");
              Jxtp.tagClose("s1");
              try
              {
                  showContent(cIter.id_page().intValue(),
                      cIter.current_version().intValue());
              }
              catch (Exception e)
              {
                  Jxtp.tag("s2",e.getMessage());
              }
          }
          Jxtp.tagClose("body");
          Jxtp.tagClose("document");
      }
      catch (Exception e)
      {
          Jxtp.tag("s1",e.getMessage());
          Jxtp.tagClose("document");
      }
      finally
      {
          if (cIter != null)
              cIter.close();
      }
  }
```

Here a brief outline of the overall process:

1. The process begins with a SELECT statement that pulls top page information and current page information for the specific arguments from the database (p_id and topParent). The topParent page was selected by the method findTopParent().

2. Next, the procedure calls the method chooseStylesheet(), which finds a correct stylesheet for the top-parent page (category). This method executes a SELECT from the tables TEMPLATES and STYLESHEETS in order to get the XSL stylesheets that Cocoon uses to format the output.

3. Then, the procedure begins with the XML page information, which is divided into five parts:

    a. **Header information (meta data)** – such as Author, and last modified date.

    b. **Map Information** – that is used by the document2html stylesheet to make the left side bar menu (showMapInfo function).

    c. **Path Information** – contains the complete path from the top level entry to the current page; this information, is used by the document2html stylesheet to make links in the content area in order to tell users how to go back. This information is generated by the stylesheet and inserted into the left upper side of the content area (showPath procedure).

    d.   **Related Information** – contains related topics extracted from the table related to the current page and the neighbors of it (relatedTopics function). These topics are generated by the stylesheet for the right upper side of the content area.

    e.   **Content Data** – the content area is acquired from the CONTENT table according to the current page and the current version (showContent function). If the p_version parameter is not null, it is used instead of the current version; p_level dictates to the procedure how many child levels are expanded from this current page. Normally the level is 0, meaning only get this page, but for other devices such as WAP or for a printable version, it is useful to get 1 or more child levels.

The function of the code is as follows:

```
if (p_level>1)
     topParent=p_id;
else
     topParent = findTopParent(p_id,p_top);
```

If p_level is greater than 1, it means that the user requires a printable version of this page; it then uses a p_id instead of top parent id for choosing the category of the page.

```
Jxtp.prolog();
Jxtp.process("http"); // Do not cache this page
Jxtp.header("Cache-Control","False");
```

These lines of code give directives about cache control to Cocoon; at development time these directives direct the proxy or browser never to cache this page because the content is dynamically generated.

```
try
   {
     Integer thisPageParent;
     chooseStylesheet(topParent);
     // Gets information about the top page and the current page
     #sql {SELECT name,longname,owner INTO
         :topName,:topLongName,:topOwner
         FROM pages WHERE id_page=:topParent};
     #sql {SELECT name,longname,comments,parent,path INTO
         :thisPageName,:thisPageLongName,:thisPageComments,
         :thisPageParent,:thisPagePath
         FROM pages WHERE id_page=:p_id };
     Jxtp.tagOpen("document","name='"+topName+"'");
     Jxtp.tagOpen("header");
     Jxtp.tag("name",thisPageName);
     Jxtp.tag("title",topName);
     Jxtp.tag("subtitle",thisPageLongName);
     Jxtp.tagOpen("authors");
     Jxtp.tagOpen("person","name='"+topOwner+"'");
     Jxtp.tagClose("person");
     Jxtp.tagClose("authors");
     Jxtp.tagClose("header");
```

This chooses the stylesheet for this category and selects the meta-data information of the top parent page (category) and the current page. With this information it creates the XML section, "Header Information", as was shown in the previous section. The `chooseStylesheet` method is explained in more detail below.

```
showMapInfo(p_id,thisPageName,p_top);
showPath(p_id,p_top);
relatedTopics(p_id,thisPageParent,p_top);
```

These lines of code make the XML sections Map Information, Path Information and Related Topics, which are explained in more detail in the next section.

```
Jxtp.tagOpen("body");
Jxtp.tagOpen("s1","title='"+thisPageLongName+"' level='0'");
Jxtp.p("<!-- "+thisPageComments+" -->");
Jxtp.tagClose("s1");
// show Main Content
showContent(p_id,p_version);
```

Makes the XML Content Body section. The content section has an `s1` tag with the `longname` column of the `PAGES` table, and as XML comments in the `comments` column. Then the `showContent` method prints the assets stored by the content owner for this current page in the `CONTENT` table.

```
#sql cIter = {SELECT id_page,current_version,
    longname,comments,level FROM pages WHERE level<:p_level
    START WITH parent=:p_id CONNECT BY prior id_page=parent};
while(cIter.next())
{
    Jxtp.tagOpen("s1","title='"+cIter.longname()+"'
    level='"+cIter.level()+"'");
    Jxtp.p("<!-- "+cIter.comments()+" -->");
    Jxtp.tagClose("s1");
    try
    {
        showContent(cIter.id_page().intValue(),
            cIter.current_version().intValue());
    }
    catch (Exception e)
    {
        Jxtp.tag("s2",e.getMessage());
    }
}
```

The above makes a hierarchical SQL query for retrieving the children of the current page. If `p_level` is 0, this query doesn't take effect. If `p_level` is greater than 1 it takes the `p_level` children of this page and shows the assets of them. For debugging purpose the "`try catch`" statement prints an s2 tag with the error, but normally this error never occurs.

```
    Jxtp.tagClose("body");
    Jxtp.tagClose("document");
}
catch (Exception e)
```

```
        {
            Jxtp.tag("s1",e.getMessage());
            Jxtp.tagClose("document");
        }
        finally
        {
            if (cIter != null)
                cIter.close();
        }
    }
```

This closes the XML tag document. For debugging purposes, it shows the error as the XML s1 tag and closes the XML tag document; again normally the error never happens. Finally as a good SQLj practice, it provides a finally section which closes all the SQLj iterators opened in this method.

Related Procedures for Making The Page

chooseStylesheet

This procedure makes the Pi tags for the stylesheets associated to this page; these Pi tags tell Cocoon to apply a selected stylesheet for formatting the output. For example, for the printable version, this procedure tells Cocoon to use the document2print.xsl stylesheet, otherwise, it tells Cocoon to use document2html.xsl.

```
public void chooseStylesheet(int p_id) throws SQLException
{
    StylesheetIterator stlsIter=null;
    try
    {
        Integer thisPageParent;
        #sql stlsIter = {SELECT tpl_id_stylesheet,st.url,st.type,
            st.media,st.ext FROM templates tpl,
            stylesheets st WHERE tpl_id_page=:p_id
            AND tpl_id_stylesheet=id_stylesheet
            AND st.ext=:ext};
        while(stlsIter.next())
            if (stlsIter.media()!=null)
                Jxtp.stylesheet(stlsIter.url(),
                    stlsIter.type(),
                    "media='"+stlsIter.media()+"'");
            else
                Jxtp.stylesheet(stlsIter.url(),stlsIter.type());
        Jxtp.process();
    }
    catch (SQLException e)
    {
        throw e;
    }
    finally
    {
        if (stlsIter != null)
            stlsIter.close();
    }
}
```

showMapInfo

This procedure creates the XML tags shown in the previous section (*Map Information*). This information is made in two steps, first a SELECT that pulls the pages of which the parent is the top page (categories), and secondly the first level children of the current category. The effect of this map information is a list of categories of the site (always shown) and an expanded list of the current categories. Finally the method closes all the SQLj iterators for this function, this `finally` section guarantees that all the SQLj cursors are closed properly, because if there are errors in any part of the code this section is always executed and so can close those cursors too.

```
private void showMapInfo(int p_id, String p_name, int p_top) throws SQLException
{
    PagesIterator pIterFirstLevel=null;
    PagesIterator pIterDownLevel=null;
    Jxtp.tagOpen("map");
    try
    {
        int topParent = findTopParent(p_id,p_top);
        Jxtp.tagOpen("option");
        Jxtp.tag("linkmap","Home",
            "id='Home' longname='Top entry'  href='/Home'");
        Jxtp.tagClose("option");
        #sql pIterFirstLevel = {SELECT * FROM pages
            WHERE parent=:p_top AND name IS NOT Null AND deleted<>'Y'
            ORDER BY id_page};
        while(pIterFirstLevel.next())
        {
            // top level path
            String name = pIterFirstLevel.name();
            Jxtp.tagOpen("option");
            Jxtp.tag("linkmap",name,"id='"+name+
                "' longname='"+pIterFirstLevel.longname()+
                "'href='"+pIterFirstLevel.path()+
                pIterFirstLevel.name()+"'");
            Jxtp.tagClose("option");
            if (pIterFirstLevel.id_page().intValue()==topParent)
            {
                // show down path (childrens) if there are
                #sql pIterDownLevel = {SELECT * FROM pages WHERE parent=:topParent
                    AND name IS NOT null AND deleted<>'Y'
                    ORDER BY id_page};
                while(pIterDownLevel.next())
                {
                    name = pIterDownLevel.name();
                    Jxtp.tagOpen("option");
                    Jxtp.tag("linkmap",name,"id='"+name+
                        "'longname='"+pIterDownLevel.longname()+
                        "' href='"+pIterDownLevel.path()+
                        pIterDownLevel.name()+"'");
                    Jxtp.tagClose("option");
                }
            }
        }
    }
    catch (SQLException e)
    {
        throw e;
    }
    finally
    {
        if (pIterDownLevel != null)
            pIterDownLevel.close();
        if (pIterFirstLevel != null)
            pIterFirstLevel.close();
        Jxtp.tagClose("map");
    }
}
```

showPath

This procedure creates the XML tags shown in the previous section (*Path Information*). This information is made by a hierarchical query that begins from the top page to the current page. This SELECT is ordered by the SQL pseudo column level in inverted form given a correct path from the home page of the site to the current page passing for all the parents.

```
private void showPath(int p_id, int p_top) throws SQLException
{
    PagesIterator pIter=null;
    Jxtp.tagOpen("path");
    try
    {
        if (p_id!=p_top)
        {
            int level = 1;
            #sql pIter = {SELECT * FROM pages START WITH id_page=:p_id
                CONNECT BY prior parent=id_page AND deleted<>'Y'
                ORDER BY level desc};
            while(pIter.next())
            {
                String name = pIter.name();
                Jxtp.tagOpen("option");
                Jxtp.tag("linktopic",name,
                    "id='"+pIter.id_page().intValue()+
                    "' longname='"+pIter.longname()+
                    "' href='"+pIter.path()+pIter.name()+"'");
                Jxtp.tagClose("option");
                level++;
            }
        }
    }
    catch (SQLException e) {
        throw e;
    }
    finally
    {
        if (pIter != null)
            pIter.close();
        Jxtp.tagClose("path");
    }
}
```

relatedTopics

This procedure creates the XML tags shown in a previous section (*Related Topics*). This function has two main branches, first if the page is a home page (p_parent == null), it selects the related pages from the RELATED table. Secondly, if is not a home page, it makes a union of the related pages with the neighbors of the current page; the neighbors are the pages which are from the same parent. Finally it closes the opened SQLj iterators.

This method also gives information about the templates associated to the current page. Every stylesheet in the system has an extension on the CMS; this means, for example, that the extension "html" is used with the document2print.xsl stylesheet and the extension "phtml" is associated to the stylesheet document2print.xsl. Then, this information is used by the document2html.xsl stylesheet to activate or deactivate the "Printable Version" link according to the existence of the "phtml" extension.

```
private void relatedTopics(int p_id, Integer p_parent, int p_top)
   throws SQLException
{
   String path,name;
   RelatedIterator rIter=null;
   StylesheetIterator stlsIter=null;
   Jxtp.tagOpen("topics");
   try
   {
      if (p_parent == null)
         #sql rIter = {SELECT rl_id_page_to id_page
            FROM related WHERE rl_id_page_from=:p_id};
      else
         #sql rIter = {SELECT rl_id_page_to id_page
            FROM related WHERE rl_id_page_from=:p_id
            UNION (SELECT id_page FROM pages WHERE
               :p_parent<>:p_top and parent=:p_parent)};
      Jxtp.tagOpen("option");
      while(rIter.next())
      {
         Integer idPageTo = rIter.id_page();
         #sql {SELECT name,path INTO :name,:path
            FROM pages WHERE id_page=:idPageTo};
         Jxtp.tag("linktopic",name,"href='"+path+name+"'");
      }
      #sql stlsIter = {SELECT tpl_id_stylesheet,st.url,st.type, st.media,st.ext
         FROM templates tpl, stylesheets st
         WHERE tpl_id_page=:p_id and tpl_id_stylesheet=id_stylesheet};
      while(stlsIter.next())
         Jxtp.tag("linktemplate",
            stlsIter.tpl_id_stylesheet().toString(),
            "ext='"+stlsIter.ext()+"'");
      Jxtp.tagClose("option");
   }
   catch (SQLException e)
   {
      throw e;
   }
   finally
   {
      if (rIter!=null)
         rIter.close();
      if (stlsIter != null)
         stlsIter.close();
   }
   Jxtp.tagClose("topics");
}
```

Importing Documents

The DB Prism CMS includes a client tool, which imports the assets from the file system to the database. This client tool has these features:

❑ It runs in the client machine facilitating the importing process by the content owner.

❑ It validates the XML document before loading it into the database, parsing and applying a given DTD.

❑ It applies a stylesheet (optional) that converts the original document to another, according to structure of the CMS. This functionality permits, for example, converting an XHTML page generated by an editor tool to the CMS model.

This application takes an input file in XML format that has information about the username and password of the repository, pages, stylesheet, templates and document to be imported. Here is the DTD of this XML file:

```
<!ELEMENT CMS:site-config (CMS:user, CMS:password, CMS:ConnectString,
    CMS:JdbcDriver, CMS:LoadPath, CMS:parserClass)>
<!ATTLIST CMS:site-config xmlns:CMS CDATA #REQUIRED>
<!ATTLIST CMS:site-config AutoCommitVersion (true|false) "true"
    LoadPath CDATA #REQUIRED>
<!ELEMENT CMS:user (#PCDATA)>
<!ELEMENT CMS:password (#PCDATA)>
<!ELEMENT CMS:ConnectString (#PCDATA)>
<!ELEMENT CMS:JdbcDriver (#PCDATA)>
<!ELEMENT CMS:xmlcms-site (CMS:pages,CMS:relateds,CMS:templates,CMS:documents)>
<!ELEMENT CMS:pages (CMS:page)*>
<!ELEMENT CMS:page (CMS:longname, CMS:comments, CMS:language)>
<!ATTLIST CMS:page id CDATA #REQUIRED parent CDATA #IMPLIED src CDATA #REQUIRED>
<!ELEMENT CMS:stylesheets (CMS:stylesheet)*>
<!ATTLIST CMS:stylesheet href CDATA #REQUIRED type CDATA #REQUIRED
    media CDATA #IMPLIED ext CDATA #IMPLIED attributes CDATA #IMPLIED>
<!ELEMENT CMS:relateds (CMS:related)*>
<!ATTLIST CMS:related from CDATA #REQUIRED to CDATA #REQUIRED>
<!ELEMENT CMS:templates (CMS:template)*>
<!ATTLIST CMS:template path CDATA #REQUIRED name CDATA #REQUIRED
    stylesheet CDATA #REQUIRED>
<!ELEMENT CMS:documents (CMS:document)+>
<!ATTLIST CMS:document src CDATA #REQUIRED parent (yes|no) "yes"
    stylesheet CDATA #IMPLIED>
<!ELEMENT CMS:path (#PCDATA)>
<!ELEMENT CMS:name (#PCDATA)>
<!ELEMENT CMS:longname (#PCDATA)>
<!ELEMENT CMS:comments (#PCDATA)>
<!ELEMENT CMS:language (#PCDATA)>
<!ELEMENT CMS:href (#PCDATA)>
<!ELEMENT CMS:type (#PCDATA)>
<!ELEMENT CMS:media (#PCDATA)>
<!ELEMENT CMS:ext (#PCDATA)>
<!ELEMENT CMS:attributes (#PCDATA)>
```

Here's an example of a site configuration file:

```
<?xml version="1.0"?>
<!DOCTYPE CMS:site-config SYSTEM "CmsConfig.dtd">
<CMS:site-config xmlns:CMS="http://www.plenix.com/dbprism/CMS/"
    AutoCommitVersion="true" LoadPath="file:///JDev/myprojects/prism/xdocs">
    <!-- Information About the server -->
    <CMS:user>scott</CMS:user>
    <CMS:password>tiger</CMS:password>
    <CMS:ConnectString>
        jdbc:oracle:thin:@cocodrilo.exa.unicen.edu.ar:1521:DUNDEE
    </CMS:ConnectString>
    <CMS:JdbcDriver>
        oracle.jdbc.driver.OracleDriver
    </CMS:JdbcDriver>
```

```xml
<!-- Site Specific Configuration Information -->
<CMS:xmlcms-site>
   <!-- List of stylesheets -->
   <CMS:stylesheets>
      <CMS:stylesheet href="http://localhost/xsl/document2html.xsl"
         type="text/xsl" ext="html" />
      <CMS:stylesheet href="http://localhost/xsl/document2print.xsl"
         type="text/xsl" ext="phtml" />
   </CMS:stylesheets>
   <!-- List of pages -->
   <CMS:pages>
      <CMS:page id="10" src="/Home.xml">
         <CMS:longname>DB Prism Servlet Engine</CMS:longname>
         <CMS:language>en</CMS:language>
      </CMS:page>
      <CMS:page id="11" src="/NotFound.xml">
         <CMS:longname>Sorry, this page not found</CMS:longname>
         <CMS:language>en</CMS:language>
      </CMS:page>
      <CMS:page id="20" parent="10" src="/Docs.xml">
         <CMS:longname>Documentation</CMS:longname>
         <CMS:comments>Documentation available for DB Prism</CMS:comments>
         <CMS:language>en</CMS:language>
      </CMS:page>
      <CMS:page id="30" parent="10" src="/Source.xml">
         <CMS:longname>Source Code</CMS:longname>
         <CMS:comments>Source Code of DB Prism</CMS:comments>
         <CMS:language>en</CMS:language>
      </CMS:page>
      <CMS:page id="40" parent="10" src="/Dist.xml">
         <CMS:longname>Distribution available for DB Prism</CMS:longname>
         <CMS:comments>Distribution available for DB Prism</CMS:comments>
         <CMS:language>en</CMS:language>
      </CMS:page>
      <CMS:page id="50" parent="10" src="/Internals.xml">
         <CMS:longname>DB Prism Internals</CMS:longname>
         <CMS:comments>DB Prism Internals</CMS:comments>
         <CMS:language>en</CMS:language>
      </CMS:page>
      <CMS:page id="60" parent="10" src="/OnNT.xml">
         <CMS:longname>
            DB Prism Installation and Configuration On NT
         </CMS:longname>
         <CMS:comments>Readme Config on NT</CMS:comments>
         <CMS:language>en</CMS:language>
      </CMS:page>
      <CMS:page id="70" parent="10" src="/CMS.xml">
         <CMS:longname>Content Management System</CMS:longname>
         <CMS:comments>
            DB Prism / Cocoon - Content Management System
         </CMS:comments>
         <CMS:language>en</CMS:language>
      </CMS:page>
      <CMS:page id="80" parent="10" src="/2.0.xml">
         <CMS:longname>Future Plan for 2.0 release</CMS:longname>
```

```
            <CMS:comments>2.0 - Next Release of DB Prism</CMS:comments>
            <CMS:language>en</CMS:language>
        </CMS:page>
        <CMS:page id="90" parent="10" src="/Credits.xml">
            <CMS:longname>Credits and Stuff</CMS:longname>
            <CMS:comments>DB Prism Project Credits and Stuff</CMS:comments>
            <CMS:language>en</CMS:language>
        </CMS:page>
        <CMS:page id="100" parent="10" src="/Legal.xml">
            <CMS:longname>Legal Stuff</CMS:longname>
            <CMS:comments>Legal Stuff and Trademarks</CMS:comments>
            <CMS:language>en</CMS:language>
        </CMS:page>
    </CMS:pages>
    <!-- List of documents to be uploaded -->
    <CMS:documents>
        <CMS:document src="/Home.xml" />
        <CMS:document src="/NotFound.xml" />
        <CMS:document src="/Docs.xml" />
        <CMS:document src="/Internals.xml" />
        <CMS:document src="/OnNT.xml" />
        <CMS:document src="/Source.xml" />
        <CMS:document src="/2.0.xml" />
        <CMS:document src="/Credits.xml" />
        <CMS:document src="/Dist.xml" />
        <CMS:document src="/CMS.xml" />
        <CMS:document src="/Legal.xml" stylesheet="/doc2document-v10.xsl" />
    </CMS:documents>
    <!-- List of templates -->
    <CMS:templates>
        <CMS:template path="/" name="Home"
            stylesheet="http://localhost/xsl/document2html.xsl" />
        <CMS:template path="/" name="NotFound"
            stylesheet="http://localhost/xsl/document2html.xsl" />
        <CMS:template path="/" name="Docs"
            stylesheet="http://localhost/xsl/document2html.xsl" />
        <CMS:template path="/" name="Source"
            stylesheet="http://localhost/xsl/document2html.xsl" />
        <CMS:template path="/" name="Dist"
            stylesheet="http://localhost/xsl/document2html.xsl" />
        <CMS:template path="/" name="Internals"
            stylesheet="http://localhost/xsl/document2html.xsl" />
        <CMS:template path="/" name="OnNT"
            stylesheet="http://localhost/xsl/document2html.xsl" />
        <CMS:template path="/" name="CMS"
            stylesheet="http://localhost/xsl/document2html.xsl" />
        <CMS:template path="/" name="2.0"
            stylesheet="http://localhost/xsl/document2html.xsl" />
        <CMS:template path="/" name="Credits"
            stylesheet="http://localhost/xsl/document2html.xsl" />
        <CMS:template path="/" name="Legal"
            stylesheet="http://localhost/xsl/document2html.xsl" />
        <CMS:template path="/" name="CMS"
            stylesheet="http://localhost/xsl/document2print.xsl" />
        <CMS:template path="/" name="OnNT"
            stylesheet="http://localhost/xsl/document2print.xsl" />
```

```
      </CMS:templates>
      <!-- List of related pages -->
      <CMS:relateds>
         <CMS:related from="Home" to="Changes" />
         <CMS:related from="Dist" to="Readme" />
         <CMS:related from="Dist" to="FAQ" />
         <CMS:related from="Dist" to="Changes" />
         <CMS:related from="Source" to="Readme" />
      </CMS:relateds>
   </CMS:xmlcms-site>
</CMS:site-config>
```

The CMS import utility has a principal method called `importPage()`, which takes the following steps:

❑   Finds the parent for this page, if the page has an entry in the table PAGES, gets the parent from this entry; otherwise, tries to get the parent from another page entry in the same directory and makes a new entry for this page in the table PAGES

❑   Makes a new entry in the table CONTENT and gets the CLOB locator for the new page to be uploaded

❑   Opens a specified URL

❑   Parses and stores the XML content; if the content has a stylesheet associated, it uses it for converting the original XML document to the new document to be uploaded

❑   Writes meta data to the PAGES table

This technique works with XML files from any source. Here is the corresponding code:

```
public boolean importPage(String src, String findParent, String xsl)
    throws SQLException, IOException
{
    Integer p_id, p_parent, newVersion;
    String p_path, p_name, p_ext;
    p_path = wwwIndex.getPath(src);
    p_name = wwwIndex.getName(src);
    p_ext = wwwIndex.getExt(src);
    CLOB tmpClob; long clobSize;
    try
    {
        #sql {SELECT id_page INTO :p_id FROM pages
           WHERE path=:p_path AND name=:p_name };
    }
    catch (SQLException e)
    {
        // This page not found, creates one
        #sql {SELECT NVL(MAX(id_page),0)+10 INTO :p_id FROM pages};
        if (findParent.equalsIgnoreCase("yes"))
           // Finds a logical parent
           try
           {
               #sql {SELECT parent INTO :p_parent FROM pages
               WHERE path=:p_path AND ROWNUM=1};
           }
```

```
            catch (SQLException se)
            {
                p_parent=null;
            }
        else
            p_parent = null;
        // creates a page belonging to p_parent
        #sql {INSERT INTO pages
            VALUES (:p_id,:p_parent,:p_name,:p_name,
            USER,SYSDATE,SYSDATE,NULL,NULL,
            :p_path,NULL,'N',USER,USER,'Not Loaded',0,1)};
    }
    Writer out = null;
    InputStream in = null;
    try
    {
        #sql {SELECT NVL(MAX(version),0)+1 INTO :newVersion
            FROM content WHERE cn_id_page = :p_id };
        #sql {INSERT INTO Content( cn_id_page, version, owner,
            status, source_file, content,created,modified,
            created_by,modified_by)
            VALUES ( :p_id, :newVersion, USER, 'Created', :p_name,
            EMPTY_CLOB(), SYSDATE, SYSDATE, USER, USER)};
        try
        {
            #sql { SELECT content INTO :tmpClob FROM content
                WHERE cn_id_page = :p_id AND version = :newVersion };
            #sql {CALL DBMS_LOB.TRIM( :inout tmpClob, 0 )};
            out = tmpClob.getCharacterOutputStream();
            URL inUrl = new URL(loadPath+p_path+p_name+"."+p_ext);
            in = inUrl.openStream();
            parseAndStore(in,out,xsl);
            in.close();
            out.close();
            #sql clobSize = {VALUE(DBMS_LOB.GETLENGTH( :tmpClob ))};
            #sql {UPDATE content SET content = :tmpClob,
                status = 'Loaded', file_size = :clobSize, modified=SYSDATE,
                modified_by=USER WHERE cn_id_page = :p_id
                AND version = :newVersion };
            if (autoCommitVersion)
                #sql { UPDATE pages SET current_version = :newVersion,
                    status = 'Loaded', file_size = :clobSize
                    WHERE id_page = :p_id };
            else
                #sql {UPDATE pages SET status = 'Loaded',
                    file_size = :clobSize WHERE id_page = :p_id };
        }
        catch (Exception e1)
        {
            if (in != null)
                in.close();
            if (out != null)
                out.close();
            String msg = "Error at importing time: "+e1.getMessage();
            System.out.println(msg);
            #sql { UPDATE content SET status = :msg
                WHERE cn_id_page = :p_id AND version = :newVersion };
            #sql { UPDATE pages SET status = :msg WHERE id_page = :p_id };
            return false;
        }
```

```
        return true;
    }
    catch (SQLException e)
    {
        System.out.println(e.getMessage());
        return false;
    }
  }
}
```

The `parseAndStore` function is below:

```
private void parseAndStore(InputStream in, Writer out, String stylesheet)
    throws IOException,SAXException,XSLException
{
    XMLDocument theXMLDoc = null;
    XSLStylesheet theXSLStylesheet = null;

    // Parse the document from the Stream
    theParser.parse( in );

    // Get the parsed XML Document from the parser
    theXMLDoc = theParser.getDocument();
    if (stylesheet != null)
    {
        URL inUrl = new URL(loadPath+stylesheet);
        InputStream XSLStream = inUrl.openStream();
        // Create the Stylesheet from the stream
        theXSLStylesheet = new XSLStylesheet(XSLStream,null);

    }
    else
        theXSLStylesheet = new XSLStylesheet(new StringReader(idenXSL),null);

    // Create an instance of XSLProcessor to perform the transformation
    XSLProcessor  processor = new XSLProcessor();

    // display any warnings that may occur
    processor.showWarnings(true);
    processor.setErrorStream(System.err);

    // Transform theXMLDoc by theXSLStylesheet and write result out to argument
    processor.processXSL(theXSLStylesheet, theXMLDoc, new PrintWriter(out));
}
```

This method executes the following tasks:

❑   It parses the XML document.

❑   It opens and executes the stylesheet if the argument stylesheet is not null. If the argument stylesheet is null, it uses an `idenXSL` stylesheet; this stylesheet copies the XML document as is, without modifications.

❑   It processes the original document with the respective stylesheet defined in the previous step.

❑   It outputs the processed document to the output stream received as a parameter.

To use this client tool, add the `CMS-Java.jar` file (located in the bin directory of DB Prism distribution) to the `CLASSPATH` environment variable and run the application with your Java virtual machine giving the XML configuration file as a parameter, for example:

```
# java com.prism.cms.Cms file:///Jdev/myprojects/prism/cms/setupcms.xml
```

> Note: Remember to add to the `CLASSPATH` environment variable the JDBC 2.0 classes (`classes111.zip` and `classes12.zip`), SQLj runtime (`runtime.zip`), and the XML parser 2.1 (`xmlparserv2.jar`) classes.

Making Two Different Stylesheets

By default, the DB Prism CMS includes two stylesheet, one for online viewing and another for printable versions. The `document2html.xsl` stylesheet uses all of the XML information generated by the CMS to make the menu bar, hyperlinks and other interactive navigational items. The `document2print.xsl` stylesheet uses a few XML elements and has a simple design optimized for printing.

At deployment time, the CMS pre-generates the online view as described previously. A user who displays the online view in a browser can click a button to request the print view; at this point, code is executed to retrieve the main topic and its children. The CMS could pre-generate a print view for each page, but CMS developers have found that print-view requests are relatively rare, so it is more efficient to treat them as exceptions and handle them on demand.

The figure below shows two views of a page: one for online viewing and one for printing.

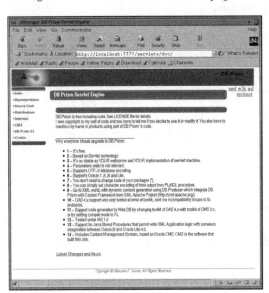
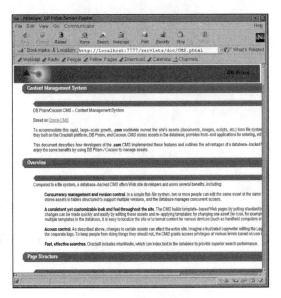

It is also easy to customize presentation for various devices (for example, you could use Cocoon to deliver content to cellular phones through a WML formatter) and even localize content by using different template items. For WML presentation, CMS includes the content block and the first level children; this information could be used by the `document2wml.xsl` stylesheet to make the elements cards of the WML page.

Installing the CMS

With the DB Prism distribution, you will find an install script called `install.sh`, in the CMS directory of the install. Its purpose is to install the DB Prism/Cocoon CMS, and it uses `scott/tiger` as the username and password.

Execute this script, and then edit `prism.properties` according to your database specific parameters (see earlier). CMS makes use of a new functionality of DB Prism version 1.1.0 – this functionality can redirect every page request to the default page stored procedure. With this functionality, the user sees the URL to a dynamic CMS page like a static page in the web server, for example: http://server:port/servlets/doc/cms/CMS.html).

Here is an example of these parameters in the DAD section of the `prism.properties` files.

```
#DAD doc, use with Content Management System
doc.dbusername=scott
doc.dbpassword=tiger
doc.connectString=jdbc:oracle:thin:@reptil:1521:ORCL
doc.errorLevel=1
doc.errorPage=http://localhost/error.html
doc.case=lower
doc.compat=java
doc.producerarg=ignore
doc.defaultPage=CMSj.get
doc.alwaysCallDefaultPage=true
doc.docAccessPath=download

#DAD print, use with Content Management System, printable version
print.dbusername=scott
print.dbpassword=tiger
print.connectString=jdbc:oracle:thin:@reptil:1521:ORCL
print.errorLevel=1
print.errorPage=http://localhost/error.html
print.case=lower
print.compat=java
print.producerarg=ignore
print.defaultPage=CMSj.get
print.alwaysCallDefaultPage=true
print.docAccessPath=download
```

Deployment

At deployment time, you could make a mirror of the entire web site or part of it with any application tool designed for downloading web sites like UNIX `wget` or Windows `OffLineExplorer`; for example, with a few simple UNIX commands you could deploy the CMS pages in a specific directory, for instance `/tmp/my_site`:

```
# cd /tmp
# mkdir my_site
# cd my_site
# wget -np --recursive --level=200 -nH --proxy=off \
  http://cocodrilo.exa.unicen.edu.ar:7777/dbprism/doc/Home.html
```

This command stores all the pages of the CMS from `Home.html`, and your children up to level 200 in the directory `/tmp/my_site/dbprism/doc`.

Conclusions and Beyond

Cocoon is an open source presentation framework, which promises to solve many of the problems concerned with the development of web applications. DB Prism is integrated with Cocoon to provide a better separation of content, leaving the application logic and the presentation logic in different tiers, transforming the database into an active XML database and the middle tier into the presentation tier.

DB Prism 2.0 is the next major release for this framework. This release is designed for the Cocoon 2.0 architecture, at this moment in alpha state. Here is a planned list of changes for DB Prism 2.0:

❑ CocoonWrapper will be rewritten as Cocoon Generator. This generator follows the new API of Cocoon 2.0; it will include the proposed technology for the compiled XML pages. Compiled XML pages promise to increase the performance of XML parsing by 200% for medium-size XML pages (45 KB) and by 45% for large-size XML pages (600 KB). Unlike serialized XML pages stored in a text string, compiled XML pages store a sequence of SAX events in a binary stream decreasing the time of parsing XML document.

❑ The file prism.properties will be re-written as prism.xml – with this new configuration file the user can use a traditional XML editor (for example a text editor) for customizing the DB Prism functionality.

❑ The sitemap functionality of Cocoon 2.0 could be used on DB Prism, avoiding the problem of hard-coding the stylesheet in the application logic. This functionality would mean that the STYLESHEETS and TEMPLATES tables of the CMS system would no longer be needed, so they can be removed.

❑ The content aggregation of the sitemap component of Cocoon 2.0 will permit removal of some of the procedures of the CMS, like showMapInfo, for example, as the site map will provide this functionality. This change will make the code of the CMS system more clear – after all, this part of the code is the responsibility of the web designers, not of the developer of the CMS.

❑ DB Prism's resource manager will be redesigned to support JDBC drivers with Java Transaction Support, providing better support for a transactional DAD.

❑ A new web server generator will automatically generate Java Stored Procedures for DB Prism/Cocoon permitting two main benefits, one to migrate actual application made by Oracle Designer Web Server Generator and the other to use actual graphical designer tools to make web application without coding. Oracle Designer Web Server Generator is a graphical tool which permits design of the application graphically using information stored in the Designer repository (table columns, types, relations, and so on). This graphical tool stores the user designed application in the repository and generates PLSQL stored procedures for the web application, then the DB Prism Web Server Generator will take this information to automatically generate the stored procedure for the same application but using XML technology.

Summary

In this case study we have looked at:

❑   Cocoon and DB Prism architecture

❑   Background information about DB Prism internals

❑   Developing applications with DB Prism/Cocoon using Java Stored Procedures

For the third point, we looked at the complete code of a CMS. This code demonstrates the benefits of XML technologies for making web applications – this CMS only needs 400 lines of Java code to provide the same functionality as any traditional CMS system.

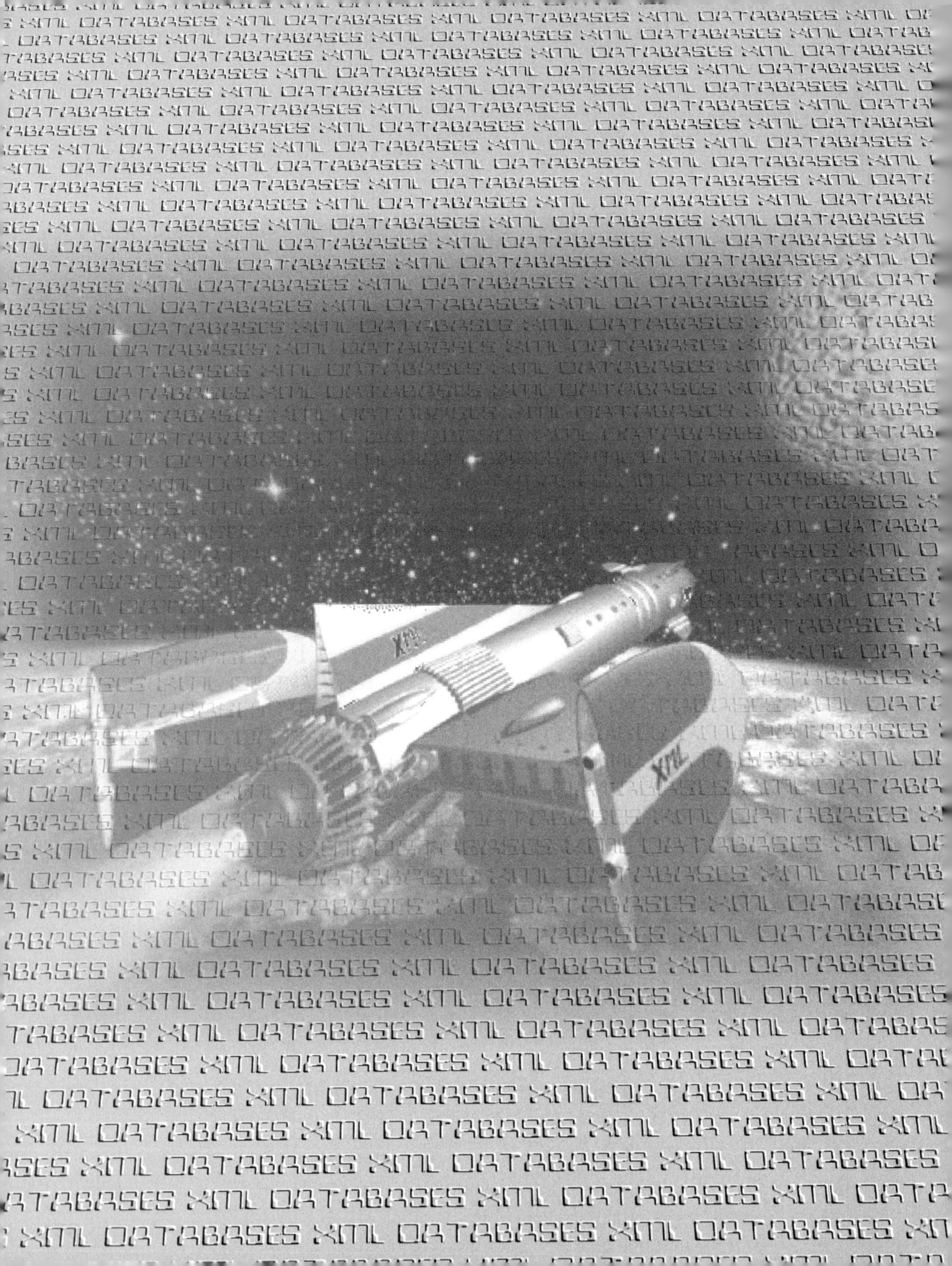
XML DATABASES
XML

XML Primer

In this Appendix, we're going to take a quick look at the basics of XML. If you use XML on a daily basis already, you can skip this. For those of you who are coming from a pure relational database background, or if you can't remember the difference between an element and an attribute, read on.

We will be looking at:

❑ Basics of XML Markup

❑ Well-formed and valid documents

❑ Related technologies and how they fit in

Of course, there are whole books devoted to teaching XML, such as **Beginning XML by David Hunter et al**, *published by Wrox Press (ISBN 1861003412)*, and this is just intended to get you up to speed with what you need to know for this book.

The first thing to make clear is that, assuming you are familiar with HTML, XML offers a new way of tagging (or marking up) your data that is so straight forward, you will wonder why it is making such big waves. Yet, while HTML and XML may look very similar, they are in fact quite different.

Before we dive into using XML and showing you how it can be used, it would be helpful to have a quick look at markup languages in general and what markup is.

What is a Markup Language?

While you may not realize it, we come across markup every day. Quite simply, markup refers to anything put on a document that adds special meaning or provides extra information. For example, highlighted or bolded text in a word-processor is a form of markup.

But unless others understand our markup it is of little use, so we need a set of rules encompassing the following points for it to be understood:

❑   To declare what constitutes markup

❑   To declare exactly what our markup means

A **markup language** is such a set of rules. A familiar example is HTML – which is a markup language that enables you to write a document for display on the Web.

Tags and Elements

Even those of us who are familiar with HTML still often get the meaning of tags and elements mixed up. Just to clarify, tags are the angled brackets (known as delimiters), and the *tag name* between them. Here are some examples of tags used in HTML:

`<P>` is a tag that marks the beginning of a new paragraph
`<I>` is a tag indicating that the following text should be rendered in italic type
`</I>` is a tag that indicates the end of a section of text to be rendered in italic type

Elements, however, refer to the tags *plus* their content. So the following is an example of an element:

```
<B>Here is some bold text</B>
```

In general terms, tags are labels that tell a user-agent (such as a browser or parser) to do something to whatever is encased in the tags.

> *A user-agent is anything that acts on your behalf. You are a user agent working for your boss, your computer is a user agent working for you, your browser is a user agent working for you and your computer, and so it goes on.*

Empty elements which don't have closing tags, such as the `<IMG>` element in HTML, have to be treated differently in XML to make up for them not having a closing tag, but don't worry about that for now, we will come back to them later.

The following diagram illustrates the parts of an element:

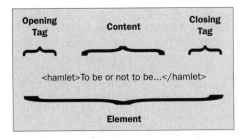

Attributes

Any tag can have an attribute as long as it is defined. They take the form of **name/value pairs** (also referred to as attribute/value pairs), in that the element can be given an attribute (with a name), and the attribute must carry a text value surrounded in quotation marks. They take the form:

```
<tagname attribute="value">
```

For example, in HTML 4.0 the <BODY> tag can take the following attributes:

```
CLASS ID      DIR       LANG      STYLE     TITLE
BACKGROUND    BGCOLOR   ALINK     LINK      VLINK     TEXT
```

So, a typical HTML BODY element might look like this:

```
<BODY BGCOLOR="#000000" ALINK="#999999" LINK="#990099" VLINK="#888888"
TEXT="#999999">
```

As we shall see shortly there are other types of markup, but these are the two most used parts.

What is XML?

XML, or **Extensible Markup Language** to give its full name, is an example of a markup language, and just like HTML, it makes extensive use of tags and attributes.

With HTML you have a fixed set of markup you can use – there is a prescribed set of tags and attributes with which you can write web pages.

XML, however, is a lot more flexible. You can make up your own tags and attributes, and its uses go beyond displaying information in a web browser. Because you can create your own tags and attributes in XML you can use markup that actually describes the content of the element, rather than just using tags that tell you how to present the data on a web page.

Because you can use tags that describe the content of an element, XML has become a general format for marking up all kinds of data – not just data that will be presented on the web. Let's dive straight in and look at an example so that we get a feel for it.

At its simplest level XML is just a way of marking up data so that it is **self-describing**. What do we mean by this? Well, imagine that you were running an e-commerce system, and that part of this system generates invoices. If a customer wanted to check their invoice over the web, it may be displayed to them marked up in HTML, and the HTML could look something like this:

```
<DOCTYPE HTML PUBLIC "-//W3C//DTD HTML 4.0 //EN">
<HTML>
   <HEAD><TITLE>Invoice</TITLE></HEAD>

<BODY>
   <H3>Invoice: Kevin Williams</H3>

<TABLE>
   <TR>
      <TD valign="top">
         <H4>Billing Address</H4>
            <UL>
               <LI>Kevin Williams</LI>
               <LI>742 Evergreen Terrace</LI>
               <LI>Springfield</LI>
               <LI>KY</LI>
               <LI>12345</LI>
            </UL>
      </TD>
```

```
            <TD valign="top">
               <H4>Shipping Address</H4>
                  <UL>
                     <LI>742 Evergreen Terrace</LI>
                     <LI>Springfield</LI>
                     <LI>KY</LI>
                     <LI>12345</LI>
                     <LI><B>Shipping Company</B> Fed Ex</LI>
                  </UL>
            </TD>
      </TR>
</TABLE>

Item
   <UL>
      <LI><B>Item Description </B>Widget (3 inch)</LI>
      <LI><B>Item Code </B>1A2A3AB</LI>
      <LI><B>Quantity </B>17</LI>
      <LI><B>Price </B> 0.10</LI>
   </UL>

Item
   <UL>
      <LI><B>Item Description </B>Grommet (0.5 inch)</LI>
      <LI><B>ItemCode </B>1A2A3AB</LI>
      <LI><B>Quantity </B>22</LI>
      <LI><B>Price </B>0.05</LI>
   </UL>

</BODY>
</HTML>
```

While this may be fine for display on a web page, and we will see the result in the next screenshot, tags like <LI> don't tell you that here they are containing information about a product you just ordered. There is nothing in the HTML markup to tell you that this is an invoice.

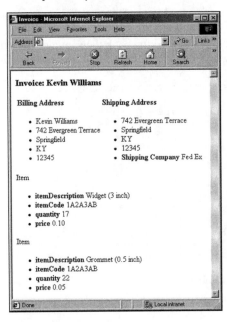

This is all very good for display on the web, but remember that we are running an e-commerce system here. Now, imagine that this e-commerce system is written in PHP, and that once it has generated the invoice information other parts of the company may need the same data:

❑ The packing department might need a copy to send the items out – but they run a UNIX-based system written in C

❑ The customer support team who can track the package may need it if there is a problem with delivery – but their system is written in Visual Basic

❑ The service department may need to check it if the product is returned because it is faulty – and they run an application written in Java

The potential number of uses for the data goes on, accounts, marketing, etc.; all of these users may need a copy of it. This means that there are a lot of uses for the same data, but the different departments that need the data use software written in different programming languages, and run on different operating systems. Wouldn't it be great if we could have a platform independent way of passing this data between programs, and of telling the programs the function of each piece of marked up data?

Well, let's change the markup language and use XML instead of HTML. As I said, we can create our own tags with XML, so how about we use tags that describe what we are trying to say about the document – that it represents an invoice, and what the invoice contains... Let's make up some of our own tags and we can re-create this information with tags that describe the data we are marking up:

```xml
<?xml version="1.0" ?>

<Invoice
    customerName="Kevin Williams"
    billingAddress="742 Evergreen Terrace"
    billingCity="Springfield"
    billingState="KY"
    billingPostalCode="12345"
    shippingAddress="742 Evergreen Terrace"
    shippingCity="Springfield"
    shippingState="KY"
    shippingPostalCode="12345"
    shippingCompany="FedEx">
    <LineItem
        itemCode="1A2A3AB"
        itemDescription="Widget (3 inch)"
        quantity="17"
        price="0.10" />
    <LineItem
        itemCode="2BC3DCB"
        itemDescription="Grommet (0.5 inch)"
        quantity="22"
        price="0.05" />
</Invoice>
```

OK, if you opened this up in a browser, it would not look like a web page, it would look like this:

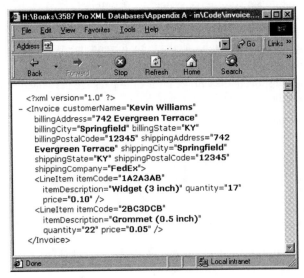

But, we do know that in the `Invoice` element, we will find an invoice, and that in the `customerName` attribute, we will find out the customer whose invoice it is.

Furthermore, this XML file is just plain text, so the data in an XML file would be available for any programming language, and it would be available on any platform, and it can easily be passed over HTTP. So, we could actually use this data we had marked up in XML in a lot more ways that we could the HTML version. Because it is just text, and because we know that every time there is a `invoice` element there will be details about an invoice inside, the data becomes a lot more flexible.

Now you have to move your thoughts away from just displaying data in a web browser... think about anywhere that you need to exchange information, or you need to store information, and there *may* be a use for XML...

Let's just look at one last example so that you can really see why this is important. Pick a programming language, any programming language in which you may write an object. If you had to represent the invoice we have just seen in an object as part of the e-commerce system, we could pass the state into and out of the object as XML. Take a look at this:

```
<? xml version="1.0" ?>
 <ObjectData id="customer125" classname="Invoice.Customer">
        <string name="sCustomerName">Kevin Williams</string>
        <string name="sAddress">744 Evergreen Terrace</string>
        <string name="sCity">Springfield</string>
        <string name="sState">KY</string>
        <string name="sPostalCode">12345</string>
    </Object>

    <Object id="order9876" classname="Invoice.Order">
        ...
    </Object>
</ObjectData>
```

Again, we are using markup that describes its content, it is simple text, it will be available to any programming language and any platform, and we can easily pass it accross a network in this form across a network. (In fact, we could even translate this into the invoice we saw earlier using a language called extensible stylesheet language.)

This set of tags and attributes that we have written to markup the invoice data are collectively known as an XML **vocabulary**. Vocabularies have already been created for a number of purposes, and it is always worth checking whether one has already been created for the task that you need to perform. But if one does not exist, you can always create your own and share it with others.

As you are able to create you own tags and attributes in XML, we obviously need some way to define a vocabulary in order for us to be able to share it with others, and get them using the same syntax. The XML 1.0 specification uses **Document Type Definitions** (**DTD**s) to do this. The DTD defines what markup can be used in a document that is supposed to conform to that vocabulary. For example, it can set out which elements a document can contain, how many instances of an element can occur, and in which order they should appear. It can set out which attributes an element can take, whether they must appear on a given element, if there is a default value should none be specified, and so on. So, in our invoice example we might have defined our markup in a way that says that every `invoice` element must contain a `customerName` attribute, a `billingAddress` attribute, and so on.

There is an interesting distinction to note here. When an XML document, using any vocabulary, conforms to the rules laid down in the XML 1.0 specification, it is said to be a **well-formed** document. When a well-formed document correctly corresponds to the rules laid out in a DTD describing that vocabulary, it is also said to be **valid**.

How XML Documents are Processed

XML documents are processed by a piece of software called a **parser**, which reads the XML document as plain text. Furthermore, they implement one or more **Application Programming Interface**(s) (or **API**s), such as the **Document Object Model** (**DOM**), or the **Simple API for XML** (**SAX**) – either of which you may or may not have heard of – if not, don't worry; we will introduce them later. The API offers programmers a set of functionality that they can call from a program to request information from the parser as it processes the document. For example, a program can ask the parser for the first child of the root element, and the text in it. Of course, there is a lot more you can do with an API implemented by a parser, but this gives you the idea of how the XML documents are actually made use of by processing applications.

Some parsers are able to check an instance of an XML document against the DTD that is used to describe the vocabulary, to check whether the markup used conforms to the intended markup. Parsers that have this functionality are known as **validating** parsers (although most validation parsers allow you to specify that they validate as an option, because validation takes up extra processing time and resources).

We now know that you can use XML to create your own markup language, and you can tell others how to use it. So, let's take a closer look at how we really structure an XML file, and then at how we declare the language we create.

The Basic Building Blocks of XML

We have seen that we can create tags and attributes that describe their content – and these usually constitute the majority of our markup – but there are also some other forms of markup available in our XML toolbox. In all we have:

- ❑ The XML Declaration
- ❑ Elements
- ❑ Attributes

- ❑ Character Data (CDATA)
- ❑ Processing Instructions
- ❑ Comments
- ❑ Entity References

Let's look at each of these in turn.

The XML Declaration

You might have noticed this at the start of the earlier examples. The **XML declaration** is actually optional, although you are strongly advised to use it so that the receiving application knows that it is an XML document and also the version used (although there is only one version of XML at the moment, it does future-proof your documents as well as indicate their format).

```
<?xml version="1.0"?>
```

If you use the XML declaration, also known as the **XML prolog**, it must be right at the start of the document (there should be nothing before it, not even white space), and the xml should be in lowercase

In this declaration, you can also define the language in which you have written your XML data. This is particularly important if your data contains characters that aren't part of the English ASCII character set. You can specify the language encoding using the optional encoding attribute:

```
<?xml version="1.0" encoding="iso-8859-1"?>
```

The most common ones are shown in the following table:

Language	Character set
Unicode (8 bit)	UTF-8
Latin 1 (Western Europe, Latin America)	ISO-8859-1
Latin 2 (Central/Eastern Europe)	ISO-8859-2
Latin 3 (SE Europe)	ISO-8859-3
Latin 4 (Scandinavia/Baltic)	ISO-8859-4
Latin/Cyrillic	ISO-8859-5
Latin/Arabic	ISO-8859-6
Latin/Greek	ISO-8859-7
Latin/Hebrew	ISO-8859-8
Latin/Turkish	ISO-8859-9
Latin/Lappish/Nordic/Eskimo	ISO-8859-10
Japanese	EUC-JP or Shift_JIS

Elements

The most important components of XML documents are elements. Every XML document must have at least one in which all other markup is nested. In the following document there is just one element `SampleDoc`:

```
<?xml version="1.0"?>
<SampleDoc>
   This is a simple, sample XML document.
</SampleDoc>
```

The highest-level element is termed the **document element** (although you may also see it referred to as the **root element**).

Elements may be used in one of two ways:

❑ As shown in this example with an opening tag and a closing tag where the element has three parts:

   ❑ A start-tag (`<SampleDoc>`)

   ❑ followed by some content (the string `"This is a simple XML document."`)

   ❑ followed by an end-tag (`</SampleDoc>`). End-tags always start with a forward slash, followed by the name of the start-tag to which they correspond.

or

❑ as an **empty element**. These are used where there is no content between a start and end tag, instead a single tag is used with a forward slash before the closing bracket, for example:

```
<?xml version="1.0"?>
<SampleDoc />
```

At first, this seems pretty silly - what's the point of having an element without any content? However, it could be that in your document the presence of the element is all that's significant – think about how the `<BR />` element is used in HTML. Also, additional information can be attached to the empty element by using attributes, which we'll talk about next.

> **Note that XML is case-sensitive, so apart from the forward slash, the elements must be exactly the same; `<SampleDoc>` and `<sampledoc>` are different tags.**

Tag names can start with a letter, an underscore (_) , or a colon character (:) , followed by any combination of letter, digits, hyphens, underscores, colons, or periods. The only exception is that you cannot start a tag with the letters XML in any combination of upper or lowercase letters. You are also advised not to start a tag with a colon, in case it gets treated as a namespace (something we shall meet later on).

All tags must nest properly; this means that there must be no **overlapping elements**. For example, this is correct:

```
<SampleDoc>
   <SomeData>Some character data</SomeData>
</SampleDoc>
```

while this would be incorrect:

```
<SampleDoc>
     <SomeData>
          Some character data
</SampleDoc>
     </SomeData>
```

This is because the closing `</SomeData>` tag is after the closing `</SampleDoc>` tag.

Attributes

You've probably used **attributes** before in HTML – for example, when using the HREF attribute on the `<A>` element to define a hyperlink:

```
<A HREF="http://www.wrox.com">Go to Wrox's web site</A>
```

They work exactly the same way in XML. Attributes are included in an element's start-tag, and are expressed as **name-value pairs**. The value must always be wrapped in single or double quotes (it doesn't matter which ones, as long as you use the same quote before and after the value). For example:

```
<?xml version="1.0"?>
<SampleDoc Author="Ron Obvious">
   This is a simple XML document.
</SampleDoc>
```

In this sample document, the SampleDoc element has one attribute associated with it. The attribute **name** is Author, and the **value** is Ron Obvious.

Also, each attribute name may only appear once for a particular start-tag. So, the following is not allowed in XML:

```
<?xml version="1.0"?>
<SampleDoc Author="Ron Obvious" Author="Ken Shabby">
   This is a simple XML document.
</SampleDoc>
```

However, the following is perfectly acceptable:

```
<?xml version="1.0"?>
<SampleDoc>
   <Sentence Author="Ron Obvious">
      This is a simple XML document.
   </Sentence>
   <Sentence Author="Ken Shabby">
      This is the second sentence of the document.
   </Sentence>
</SampleDoc>
```

It should go without saying that attributes are always associated with elements (since they appear only in start-tags or empty-element-tags, which are always part of elements). Also, attributes may not contain the characters <, &, ' or ".

Finally, it does not matter in which order you put your attributes in an element – so the following two documents are semantically identical:

```
<?xml version="1.0"?>
<SampleDoc Author="Ron Obvious" CreateDate="7/23/2000">
    This is a simple XML document.
</SampleDoc>
```

and

```
<?xml version="1.0"?>
<SampleDoc CreateDate="7/23/2000" Author="Ron Obvious">
    This is a simple XML document.
</SampleDoc>
```

Character Data

In the examples we have been looking at so far, the element `SampleDoc` contains the text `This is a simple XML document`. It is the **element content**, although it has a special name in XML – it is called **character data**. If you remember back to the section on how XML documents are processed, we said that they are processed by an application called a parser; the parser can read the content of the elements and pass it to applications that request it. We make this distinction now, because, as you will see soon, it is also possible to have data that is not parsed by the parser in this way.

As you'll see when looking further into XML technologies, contiguous blocks of text within an element are treated as one unit when being parsed or manipulated. Let's take a look at a slightly more complex example.

```
<?xml version="1.0"?>
<AlarmProcedure>
    This is a <alarmtype>test</alarmtype> of the Emergency Broadcast System.
</AlarmProcedure>
```

In this example, the element `AlarmProcedure` contains three pieces of data:

❑ the text block `"This is a"`

❑ the `alarmtype` element

❑ the text block `"of the Emergency Broadcast System."`

In turn, the `alarmtype` element contains one piece of data:

❑ the text block `test`.

This character data can appear anywhere inside elements, or as values of attributes. However, there are some special characters that are not allowed in text blocks: the ampersand symbol (&) and the less-than symbol (<). This is because these symbols are interpreted by XML parsers as the start of markup; specifically, as the start of an entity instance, and as the start of every well-formed tag. If you need to include these characters in your XML document (either in attribute values or in text blocks), you need to either use a CDATA section or entities (which we will deal with next).

CDATA Section

If you want to embed markup in your XML document, one way to do so is by wrapping the markup in a **CDATA section**. XML parsers ignore any characters wrapped in a CDATA section declaration when they are attempting to determine whether markup is present. For example, the following document will not produce the desired result:

```
<?xml version="1.0"?>
<MarkupSample>
    To start an element, use a start-element tag: <myTag>
</MarkupSample>
```

When a parser attempts to process this document, it will identify the string <myTag> as the beginning of a new element, and then complain when it doesn't find the matching end-tag </myTag>. One solution would be to embed the relevant text in a CDATA section:

```
<?xml version="1.0"?>
<MarkupSample>
    <![CDATA[To declare an element, use a start-element tag: <myTag>]]>
</MarkupSample>
```

As you can see, CDATA sections start with the CDATA start marker:

```
<![CDATA[
```

and end with the CDATA end marker

```
]]>
```

When the parser encounters the CDATA start marker, it turns off all scanning for markup except for the detection of the CDATA end marker. In the above document, the MarkupSample element contains one CDATA section item with the value "To declare an element, use a start-element tag: <myTag>."

It's important to remember that CDATA section items and text items are treated as two separate beasts by XML parsers. For example, the following two documents would seem to contain the same information:

```
<?xml version="1.0"?>
<MarkupSample>
    <![CDATA[To declare an element, use a start-element tag: <myTag>]]>
</MarkupSample>
```

```
<?xml version="1.0"?>
<MarkupSample>
    To declare an element, use a start-element tag: <![CDATA[<myTag>]]>
</MarkupSample>
```

In the second document, the parser will report the MarkupSample element as containing two items: the text string "To declare an element, use a start-element tag:" and the CDATA section item <myTag>. This can throw off a parser that is specifically looking for one item contained in the MarkupSample element.

This approach is good if you want to escape a number of characters that a parser might treat as markup; however, if you only want to escape occasional characters, you may be better off using an entity reference.

Entity References

As we mentioned before, CDATA sections are only one way to include characters like < and & in your XML documents. The other way is by using an **entity reference**. Before we dive into how entities work, let's take a look at an example.

```
<?xml version="1.0"?>
<MarkupSample>
    To declare an element, use a start-element tag: &lt;Foo>
</MarkupSample>
```

In this example, the string `&lt;` is an entity reference; specifically, it's an instance of the entity called `lt`. Entity references in XML documents (as opposed to in document type definitions) always begin with an ampersand and end with a semicolon. When a parser encounters an entity reference, it goes to the symbol table created when the document type declaration was parsed (we'll take a look at document type declarations later) and extracts the relevant string, if it's present (it might not be, as we'll see a little later). It then substitutes that string in place of the entity instance. Entities that are treated this way are known as **parsed entities**. It is also possible to declare **unparsed entities** in an XML document - we'll see how this is done a little later.

There are two types of parsed entities that may be instanced in an XML document:

❑ internal entities, which actually have their replacement content embedded in the document type declaration for the document

❑ external entities, which point to some external resource (via a URI) that contains the replacement text

A non-validating processor is not necessarily obligated to resolve external parsed entity references to their replacement content (although most do), and this can lead to the non-substituted value for an entity reference alluded to above.

There are some standard entities that are defined for XML documents:

Entity	Character
<	<
>	>
&	&
'	'
"	"

Any conformant XML parser will automatically recognize these entities and expand them to their proper values.

Additionally, you may include character references in your documents – they look almost like entities, but they are treated differently by the processor (that is, they are immediately resolved without resorting to an entity lookup). Any decimal code, preceded by `&#` and followed by `;`, is treated as a character reference; the Unicode character with the stated decimal character code is substituted for the reference. Similarly, any hex code preceded by `&#x` and followed by `;` is treated as a character reference stated in hex. So the following two character references:

```
&#38;
&#x26;
```

both correspond to the ampersand character.

Another frequently needed character in XML documents is the non-breaking space – in HTML, this is represented by the entity reference . You can specify this in your XML document by using the numeric equivalent:

```
 
```

You could also declare an entity called nbsp to have the value   and then reference that entity in your document using the name rather than the number. We'll see how this is done a little later in this appendix.

Processing Instructions

If you want a processing application to take some action when it reaches a certain point in a document, you can embed a processing instruction to indicate that some action needs to take place where it was reported. The parser indicates this – either by showing a processing instruction node at the appropriate place in the node tree (in the case of DOM parsers), or by firing a processing instruction event (in the case of SAX parsers). The code that is driving the processor may then take some action on the document based on the type and value of the processing instruction. Processing instructions start with the processing instruction markup start string <?, and end with the string ?>.

```
<?xml version="1.0"?>
<Book>
    <Author>
        <?archive 17?>
        <Name>Kevin Williams</Name>
        <Address>742 Evergreen Terrace</Address>
        <City>Springfield</City>
        <State>KY</State>
        <PostalCode>12345</PostalCode>
    </Author>
</Book>
```

In this example, the string <?archive 17?> is a processing instruction declaration. For example, this processing instruction might indicate that the author information presented is the authoritative copy of that information, and older versions of the data should be stored to an archive for the author whose primary key is 17. Processing instruction declarations always come in two parts: the processing instruction **target** (in this case, the string archive) and the string to be operated upon (in this case, 17). Everything in the processing instruction declaration before the first whitespace is considered to be the processing instruction target, and everything after that whitespace is the string used to govern the processor's behavior. So, in the following example:

```
<?xml-stylesheet type="text/xml" href="#style1"?>
```

the target would be xml:stylesheet, and the additional information string would be the rest of the text up to, but not including, the question mark at the end of the tag declaration – in other words, the entire string type="text/xml" href="#style1". Note that if you want to access the contents of this string, you'll need to parse it manually – it's not returned as name-value pairs.

The processing instruction target may not begin with the string XML, in upper, lower, or mixed cases – these targets are reserved by the W3C for future extensions to the XML specification.

Comments

Comments may be added to an XML document, using exactly the same syntax as comments in HTML. They always begin with the comment markup start string < ! - - and end with the comment markup end string: - ->:

```
<?xml version="1.0"?>
<!-- Created on 8/8/2000 -->
<DocumentElement/>
```

Note that you can't embed the string "--" in a comment – the parser will think you are indicating the end of the comment and become confused. It's important to note that comments may or may not be retained by an XML parser. When developing processing strategies, make sure to avoid processing based on statements like "the text I want is always the first item in the Foo element" – because it might not always be, unless you exclusively control the source of the XML documents. For example, say you had the following document fragment:

```
<Book>
  <!-- This is an updated book element -->
  <Author>Kevin Williams</Author>
</Book>
```

Some processors will return two child nodes of the Book node – one for the comment, and one for the Author element. Other processors will only return one node – the Author element. Thus, if you were relying on the Author element to be the second child node of the Book element, you may or may not see it where you were expecting it. It's a good practice to always use the actual node name when navigating your XML structures in this fashion.

Namespaces

If you wanted to use more than one XML vocabulary in the same document, you can do so using **Namespaces**. Namespaces are not part of the XML 1.0 specification, but the specification can be found at http://www.w3.org/TR/REC-xml-names/. They are also key to the ability to provide functionality of related specifications – such as XLink which provides linking support for XML. There is no defined markup in the XML 1.0 specification to facilitate linking, as this would go against the point of the markup describing the data. However, you can use the XLink vocabulary to indicate to an XLink aware processor that the XLink vocabulary is being used within the main vocabulary of the document to create links. The XLink-aware processor will act on XLink elements or attributes found in any document as long as they are declared as being in the XLink namespace.

To use a namespace, first it must be declared:

```
<?xml version="1.0"?>
<Foo xmlns:xlink="http://www.w3.org/1999/xlink">
  <MyLink xlink:type="simple" xlink:href="bar.xml" />
</Foo>
```

Namespaces are declared by including an attribute on an element with the `xmlns:` prefix. A namespace-aware parser interprets any attribute with this prefix as the definition of a namespace. The string following the colon in the attribute name is the **prefix** that will be used to declare attributes and elements conforming to the defined namespace (in this example it is `xlink`). The attribute value then contains the namespace name – a Uniform Resource Identifier (URI) that identifies the namespace. This URI should be unique and persistent over time. Note that the URI doesn't actually have to point to anything – although sometimes navigating to the URI using a web browser will bring you to a specification describing that namespace, nothing is obligated to be found at the URI for the namespace. In our example, then, the `xlink:` namespace prefix is declared to map to the namespace `http://www.w3.org/1999/xlink`. An XLink-aware processor will then recognize that the `MyLink` element represents a simple XLink pointing to the file `bar.xml`, and take whatever action is appropriate to indicate the simple link's presence to the user or agent.

Namespaces are only valid for the element where they are declared. For example, a parser reading the following document will correctly identify the presence of the simple link:

```
<?xml version="1.0"?>
<Foo>
    <MyLink xmlns:xlink="http://www.w3.org/1999/xlink"
            xlink:type="simple" xlink:href="bar.xml" />
</Foo>
```

However, the processor will not recognize the link in the following element (because the link declaration is outside the scope of the namespace declaration):

```
<?xml version="1.0"?>
<Foo>
    <LinkText xmlns:xlink="http://www.w3.org/1999/xlink">
        This is the text of the linkage
    </LinkText>
    <MyLink xlink:type="simple" xlink:href="bar.xml" />
</Foo>
```

Except in very unusual circumstances, you should declare all of the namespaces for your document as attributes of the root element to ensure that they are in scope for the entire document. It is also worth noting that an XML document can contain many namespaces. In XSLT transforms, the namespaces are very important – XSLT matches both the local name and the namespace, so you need to declare the namespaces properly in your XSLT stylesheet to have it recognize the corresponding elements in your documents.

Document Type Definitions

In the XML 1.0 specification, a mechanism is provided for (loosely) constraining the content that may appear in an XML document. This is done by means of a document type definition, or DTD, which is basically a set of rules that any XML document it is applied to should follow. Some XML parsers are able to validate an XML document against its respective DTD, and if it doesn't follow the rules imposed on it by the DTD, it will throw up an error. These kinds of parsers are referred to as validating parsers. If the XML is found to conform to the rules of a DTD, then it can be referred to as **valid** XML, rather than merely well-formed.

The Document Type Definition can either be an external file or it can be included in the XML document. If the DTD is in an external file it is referred to in the XML document using a **Document Type Declaration** which is written using the syntax <!DOCTYPE... >:

```
<!DOCTYPE MyXMLDoc SYSTEM "http://www.yoursite.com/xml/MyXMLDoc.dtd">
```

Here we are pointing to a DTD called MyXMLDoc; note that the name of your DTD must correspond to the root element of the XML document, so the root element of XML documents written according to this DTD must be <MyXMLDoc>. The use of the SYSTEM keyword indicates that the DTD is in an external file, whose location is referenced in the quotation marks. This type of DTD is known as an **external** DTD, because it resides in an external file. It is also possible to declare a DTD with the PUBLIC keyword – this allows you to specify the location of the DTD in some way that is understood by many different processors, eliminating the need for an always-on connection to the Internet to validate the documents. However, there isn't one well-defined way to resolve DTDs declared as PUBLIC, so you're better off using the system identifiers to point to your DTDs.

The DTD can also be written inside the document type declaration, in which case it is known as an **internal** document type definition, like:

```
<!DOCTYPE MyXMLDoc [
    <!ELEMENT MyXMLDoc (#PCDATA)>
]>
```

Here, all the constraints on the content of the document are provided as declarations inside the square brackets [...]. (Don't worry too much about the element declaration just yet – we'll be getting to that soon enough)

When a validating parser encounters an external document type definition, it accesses the resource indicated in the URI and pulls the document constraints from it; it then behaves as if these constraints were declared in-line.

If you have a situation where you can benefit from it, you can also mix the two declaration modes:

```
<!DOCTYPE MyXMLDoc SYSTEM "MyXMLDoc.dtd" [
    <!ELEMENT MyXMLDoc (#PCDATA)>
]>
```

For example, this technique would allow you to customize the allowable content of the MyXMLDoc element. Note that in the above example only the file name is included, rather than the whole path as well. This would only be suitable if the external file is in the same location as this one.

It's usually more helpful to have the document type definition be external to the document itself – this allows multiple documents to use the same rules without having to repeat the same set of constraints in each document that you wish to follow the same set of rules.

> Note that it is easy to get confused between the terms document type declaration and document type definition. To clarify, the document type definition constrains the markup and this is either contained in, or referenced to using, a document type declaration.

The Standalone Declaration

There is an attribute on the XML declaration that indicates whether a document type definition is stand-alone or not; that is, whether all of the declarations for the XML document are stated in the !DOCTYPE declaration, or whether some external URI needs to be accessed to obtain all the declarations (either through an external parameter entity, which we'll talk about later, or an external DTD). This attribute should also be used when your document declares namespaces. You don't have to explicitly declare this, but it might be useful to help streamline workflow and the transmission of XML documents.

To declare that a document stands alone, use this XML declaration:

```
<?xml version="1.0" standalone="yes"?>
```

If the declaration is omitted, the assumed default is that the document is not stand-alone.

Next, let's take a look at the various declarations you can use within a DTD to constrain the types of content an XML document conforming to that DTD may contain.

Element Declarations

The most important type of declaration in a DTD is the element declaration. Each DTD will have at least one of these (the declaration of the root element).

We saw how to simply declare an element in the previous example, but we did not explain what it was doing there:

```
<!ELEMENT MyXMLDoc (#PCDATA)>
```

We declare an element using the syntax:

```
<!ELEMENT elementName (contentModel)>
```

where *elementName* is the name of the element, and the *contentModel* is what that element can contain. This is the basic declaration that we need to start, so in our example we were declaring an element called MyXMLDoc. This element contains text only content – defined using the syntax #PCDATA.

There are five different types of element content that may be declared with an element declaration:

- ❏ Element content
- ❏ Mixed content
- ❏ Text-only content
- ❏ The EMPTY content model
- ❏ The ANY content model

Let's take a look at each, in turn.

Element Content

In the first type of element declaration, the element is defined as only containing other elements. The declaration specifies the order and cardinality with which each contained element may appear. For example, the declaration:

```
<!ELEMENT Foo (A, B, C)>
```

states that, within the Foo element, the elements A, B, and C must each appear exactly once, in that order. So for the following DTD:

```
<!ELEMENT Foo (A, B, C)>
<!ELEMENT A (#PCDATA)>
<!ELEMENT B (#PCDATA)>
<!ELEMENT C (#PCDATA)>
```

this example XML document conforms to the DTD:

```
<?xml version="1.0" standalone="no"?>
<!DOCTYPE Foo SYSTEM "Foo.DTD">
<Foo>
    <A> Some content <A />
    <B> Some more content <B />
    <C> Even more content <C />
</Foo>
```

but the following three examples do not.

```
<?xml version="1.0" standalone="no"?>
<!DOCTYPE Foo SYSTEM "Foo.DTD">
<Foo>
    <A> Some content <A />
    <B> some more content <B />
</Foo> <!-- the C element is missing -->
```

```
<?xml version="1.0" standalone="no"?>
<!DOCTYPE Foo SYSTEM "Foo.DTD">
<Foo>
    <B> Some more content <B />
    <A> Some content<A />
    <C> Even more content <C />
</Foo> <!-- the elements are not in the right order -->
```

```
<?xml version="1.0" standalone="no"?>
<!DOCTYPE Foo SYSTEM "Foo.DTD">
<Foo>
    <A> Some content <A />
    <A> Some content <A />
    <B> Some more content <B />
    <C> Even more content <C />
</Foo> <!-- too many A elements -->
```

It is also possible to define a set of elements, only one of which may be present. This is indicated by separating the possibilities with the pipe character |. So the declaration

```
<!ELEMENT Foo (A | B | C)>
```

states that the Foo element should contain either an A element, a B element, or a C element – but only one of the above.

Child elements declared in the element declaration may also take cardinality suffixes. These suffixes indicate how many of each element (or element group, which we'll talk about later) may occur at that location in the element content. The following four cardinality operators exist:

Operator	Meaning
?	Optional (may occur 0 or 1 times)
*	Optional multiple (may occur 0 or more times)
(no suffix)	Required (must occur exactly once)
+	Required multiple (must occur 1 or more times)

Additionally, child elements may be grouped together in the element declaration. They may be grouped in either a sequence or a choice list. These groupings may also have the cardinality operators specified in the previous table applied to them. At this point, some examples are probably in order.

Example 1:

This states that zero or more A elements may appear as child elements of the Foo element, followed by one or more B elements; the B element or elements may then be followed by no more than one C element.

```
<!ELEMENT Foo (A*, B+, C?)>
```

The following XML fragments for the Foo element are all valid:

```
<Foo>
   <A> Some content <A />
   <B> Some more content <B />
</Foo>
```

```
<Foo>
   <B> Some more content <B />
   <B> Some more content<B />
   <B> Some more content<B />
</Foo>
```

```
<Foo>
   <A> Some content <A />
   <A> Some content <A />
   <B> Some more content <B />
   <C> even more content <C />
</Foo>
```

Example 2:

This states that either an A element or a B element comes first in the Foo element; that element must then be followed by a C element.

```
<!ELEMENT Foo ((A | B), C)>
```

So the following two examples are the only possible examples of valid content for Foo:

```
<Foo>
   <A> Some content <A />
   <C> Even more content <C />
</Foo>
```

```
<Foo>
   <B> Some more content <B />
   <C> Even more content <C />
</Foo>
```

Example 3:

In this example, `Foo` must contain either one or more `A` elements followed optionally by a `B` element, or this group can all be replaced by zero or more `C` elements.

```
<!ELEMENT Foo ((A+, B?) | C*)>
```

Again, the following are all valid:

```
<Foo>
    <A> Some content <A />
    <A> Some content <A />
    <A> Some content <A />
</Foo>
```

```
<Foo>
    <A> Some content <A />
    <B> Some more content <B />
</Foo>
```

```
<Foo>
    <C> Even more content <C />
    <C> Even more content <C />
    <C> Even more content <C />
</Foo>
```

```
<Foo />
```

For the purposes of the XML structures we'll be creating and using in this book, for elements that have all element content we'll avoid the choice operator and stick to sequences with cardinality:

```
<!ELEMENT Foo (A?, B*, C?, D, E+)>
```

Mixed Content

Elements may also be declared as having **mixed content**. Elements declared this way may contain any of the elements included in the content list, in any order, with text interspersed anywhere in between. A mixed-content element declaration looks like this:

```
<!ELEMENT Foo (#PCDATA | A | B | C)*>
<!ELEMENT A (#PCDATA)>
<!ELEMENT B (#PCDATA)>
```

The `#PCDATA` is required to be the first thing in the pipe-delimited list – it indicates that text may be present in the element. The other listed elements may or may not appear. Note that no constraint is imposed on the order in which the elements may appear, or how many times. This is the only allowable declaration for mixed content – you are not allowed to constrain the location or number of the various subelements in a mixed-content element. Thus, the following fragments are all valid:

```
<Foo>
    Here is some <A>text</A> with interspersed <B>elements</B>
</Foo>
```

```
<Foo>
   <C /><C /><C />Why so many C elements?
</Foo>
```

```
<Foo>
   There are no child elements in this element at all.
</Foo>
```

```
<Foo />
```

If you're familiar with relational databases, you're probably wincing right now, and you have a right to be – representing mixed content in a relational database is a real headache. Some methods for doing so are looked at in Chapter 3, but for the purposes of this appendix suffice it to say that you should always avoid the mixed content model for elements whenever possible when designing XML structures for data.

Text-only Content

A special case of the mixed content model, however, may prove quite useful – that case where an element may contain only text. Elements that are defined to contain only text look like this:

```
<!ELEMENT Foo (#PCDATA)>
```

This is one of the two major ways that a data point (a value) should be represented in XML for data:

```
<!ELEMENT Author (Name, Address, City, State, PostalCode)>
<!ELEMENT Name (#PCDATA)>
<!ELEMENT Address (#PCDATA)>
<!ELEMENT City (#PCDATA)>
<!ELEMENT State (#PCDATA)>
<!ELEMENT PostalCode (#PCDATA)>
```

```
<Author>
   <Name>Kevin Williams</Name>
   <Address>742 Evergreen Terrace</Address>
   <City>Springfield</City>
   <State>KY</State>
   <PostalCode>12345</PostalCode>
</Author>
```

The EMPTY Content Model

The EMPTY content model for elements states that an element may not contain anything. Empty elements are declared as follows:

```
<!ELEMENT Foo EMPTY>
```

Elements declared this way must take one of the two following forms:

```
<Foo />
```

```
<Foo></Foo>
```

However, it is strongly advised that you stick to the first form, as the second can easily get confused with an empty PCDATA element.

We talked about the reasons you might want to define an element that has no allowable content earlier in the chapter. For our purposes, however, we will only be defining elements this way if they have attributes associated with them. We'll see how attributes are declared for elements a little later on.

The ANY Content Model

If an element is declared to have a content model of ANY, that's just what it may contain – any well-formed XML whatsoever as long as any child elements validate against their own content models as defined elsewhere, in the DTD. Elements of this type are declared like this:

```
<!ELEMENT Foo ANY>
```

The following examples are valid for this declaration:

```
<Foo>
    Here's some random thing.
</Foo>
```

```
<Foo>
    <A><B><C><D><E></E></D></C></B></A>
</Foo>
```

```
<Foo>
    <A>This</A><B>is</B><C>marked</C><D>up</D>
</Foo>
```

Note that the subelements do not inherit the "free content properties" of the Foo element – they must still conform to their own declarations. So in our second example above, a single B element must be acceptable content for the A element, a single C element acceptable for B, and so on.

For the representation of data, this syntax is perilous. Allowing users to simply include whatever elements or text they feel like in an element is another relational database nightmare, worse than that caused by mixed element content declarations because you can't even narrow down the list of elements that might occur. You should avoid using the ANY content model for elements when designing XML structures for data.

Attribute Declarations

The next most common type of declaration in DTDs is the **attribute declaration**. This allows you to define what attributes may or must appear for a given element. The general syntax for an attribute declaration looks like this:

```
<!ATTLIST element-name attribute-definition*>
```

where an attribute definition looks like this:

```
attribute-name attribute-type default-declaration
```

So, let's say we have this pair of definitions in our DTD:

```
<!ELEMENT Foo EMPTY>
<!ATTLIST Foo
    Texture CDATA #REQUIRED>
```

This says that the `Foo` element, which must be empty, has one required attribute called `Texture` that may take any string value. So the following document fragment is valid:

```
<Foo Texture="bumpy" />
```

Next, let's take a look at the various attribute types that may be defined in a DTD.

The CDATA Attribute Type

The most commonly-encountered attribute type in a DTD is `CDATA`. Attributes that take this type may take any string value. Remember that in all attribute values, the markup characters <, &, >, ", and ' should always be escaped to prevent parser confusion. So in this example:

```
<!ELEMENT Foo EMPTY>
<!ATTLIST Foo
    Texture CDATA #REQUIRED
    Color CDATA #REQUIRED
    Shape CDATA #REQUIRED>
```

the following document fragment follows the rules of the above DTD:

```
<Foo Texture="bumpy" Color="red&amp;blue" Shape="sphere" />
```

The ID Attribute Type

DTDs provide a way to assign unique identifiers to elements. This can be very useful when expressing more complex relationships in XML documents than can be shown by simple nesting, as we'll see later. In order for a document to be valid, every element that has an `ID` attribute associated with it in a single document must have a unique ID value. Also, the values for `ID` attributes must be valid XML names – in other words, they must begin with a letter (as defined by the Unicode standard) or an underscore (colons are also allowed, but their use is discouraged because of namespaces) – so simply using an identity or autoincrement value from a relational database is not sufficient. One strategy that works is to prefix that relational value with a string (unique across all elements in your document) that corresponds to the entity – this approach is looked at in Chapter 3.

Let's see some examples. For this document declaration fragment:

```
<!ELEMENT Foo EMPTY>
<!ATTLIST Foo
    FooID ID #REQUIRED>

<!ELEMENT Bar EMPTY>
<!ATTLIST Bar
    BarID ID #REQUIRED>
```

the following would be valid:

```
<Foo FooID="foo1" />
<Bar BarID="bar1" />
```

but the following examples would not:

```
<Foo FooID="17" /> <!-- ID value is not a proper XML name -->
```

```
<Foo FooID="foo1" />
<Foo FooID="foo1" /> <!-- no two elements may have the same ID value -->


<Foo FooID="foo1" />
<Bar BarID="foo1" /> <!-- no two elements may have the same ID value -->
```

It is illegal to define more than one ID attribute on the same element.

The IDREF Attribute Type

The IDREF attribute type provides a way to "point" one element to another – in effect, expressing a one-to-one relationship between the two attributes. Values for attributes that are defined as IDREF attributes must match an ID attribute found somewhere in the XML document. So for the following DTD fragment:

```
<!ELEMENT Author EMPTY>
<!ATTLIST Author
    AuthorID ID #REQUIRED>
<!ELEMENT Book EMPTY>
<!ATTLIST Book
    BookID ID #REQUIRED
    AuthorIDREF IDREF #REQUIRED>
```

the following would be valid:

```
<Author AuthorID="author1" />
<Book BookID="book1" AuthorIDREF="author1" />


<Author AuthorID="author1" />
<Book BookID="book1" AuthorIDREF="book1" />
```

The second example makes an important point. IDREF attributes do not define the type of element their value points to, so it's equally valid to have an attribute called AuthorIDREF match an ID value for a Book element. If you want to strictly enforce the types of elements that may be matched by an IDREF attribute, you'll need to do so in your processing code.

The following example, of course, is not valid, and a validating processor will throw an error:

```
<Author AuthorID="author1" />
<Book BookID="book1" AuthorIDREF="author2" /> <!-- ID does not exist -->
```

The IDREFS Attribute Type

You can think of the IDREFS attribute as a way to include multiple IDREF values in one attribute. The value for an IDREFS attribute must be a whitespace-separated list of XML names that correspond to one or more ID attribute values defined in the document. Just as IDREF can be used to express a one-to-one relationship, so can IDREFS be used to express a one-to-many relationship. Here's an example:

```
<!ELEMENT Foo EMPTY>
<!ATTLIST Foo
    FooID ID #REQUIRED>
<!ELEMENT Bar EMPTY>
<!ATTLIST Bar
    BarID ID #REQUIRED
    FooIDREF IDREFS #REQUIRED>
```

For this DTD fragment, the following document fragments are valid:

```
<Foo FooID="foo1" />
<Foo FooID="foo2" />
<Bar BarID="bar1" FooIDREF="foo1" />
```

```
<Foo FooID="foo1" />
<Foo FooID="foo2" />
<Bar BarID="bar1" FooIDREF="foo1 foo2" />
```

```
<Foo FooID="foo1" />
<Foo FooID="foo2" />
<Bar BarID="bar1" FooIDREF="foo1 foo1" />
<!-- uniqueness is not enforced -->
```

but the following examples are not valid:

```
<Foo FooID="foo1" />
<Foo FooID="foo2" />
<Bar BarID="bar1" FooIDREF="" />
<!-- there must be at least one ID value -->
```

```
<Foo FooID="foo1" />
<Foo FooID="foo2" />
<Bar BarID="bar1" FooIDREF="foo1+foo2" />
<!-- not a space-separated list -->
```

The ENTITY Attribute Type

Attributes defined with the ENTITY attribute type must match the name of an unparsed entity declared elsewhere in the DTD. Typically, you'd use this to insert non-text content into your XML document, like an image or a sound file. Here's an example (don't worry too much about the entity and notation declarations – we'll take a look at those later in this appendix):

```
<!NOTATION gif PUBLIC "GIF">
<!ENTITY BlueLine SYSTEM "blueline.gif" NDATA gif>
<!ELEMENT Separator EMPTY>
<!ATTLIST Separator
    img ENTITY #REQUIRED>
```

A valid document would then be:

```
<Separator img="BlueLine" />
```

We won't spend much time talking about this type of attribute in this book, but you might find it useful if you want to build XML documents with embedded non-XML entities.

The ENTITIES Attribute Type

Briefly, ENTITIES is to ENTITY as IDREFS is to IDREF – it's a way to include multiple unparsed entity references in the same attribute by using a space-separated list of entity names. So, for example:

```
<!NOTATION gif PUBLIC "GIF">
<!ENTITY BlueLine SYSTEM "blueline.gif" NDATA gif>
<!ENTITY RedLine SYSTEM "redline.gif" NDATA gif>
<!ELEMENT Separator EMPTY>
<!ATTLIST Separator
    img ENTITIES #REQUIRED>
```

A valid document would then be:

```
<Separator img="BlueLine RedLine" />
```

The NMTOKEN Attribute Type

Attributes with a type of NMTOKEN must have a value that contains only letters, digits, underscores, hyphens, colons, periods, and other Unicode characters that are acceptable in XML names. So for the following declaration:

```
<!ELEMENT Foo EMPTY>
<!ATTLIST Foo
    FooToken NMTOKEN #REQUIRED>
```

the following document fragments are valid:

```
<Foo
    FooToken="17" /> <!-- no leading letter or underscore is required -->
```

```
<Foo
    FooToken="____" /> <!-- underscores are fine -->
```

but the following are not:

```
<Foo
    FooToken="red&amp;blue" /> <!-- ampersands are not allowed -->
```

```
<Foo
    FooToken="bad token" /> <!-- whitespace is not allowed -->
```

Attributes with the type NMTOKEN (or NMTOKENS) give you a little more control over the allowable data in an attribute, by making the value (or each value, in the case of NMTOKENS) abide by the rules for proper XML names.

The NMTOKENS Attribute Type

Like IDREFS and ENTITIES, the NMTOKENS attribute type allows one attribute to contain a list of whitespace-separated NMTOKEN values. For this example:

```
<!ELEMENT Foo EMPTY>
<!ATTLIST Foo
    FooToken NMTOKENS #REQUIRED>
```

the following fragments are valid:

```
<Foo
    FooToken="17 19 23" />
```

```
<Foo
    FooToken="_ _ - - ." />
```

Enumerated Value Sets

Another great feature of attribute declarations in DTDs is the ability to constrain the possible values that may appear for an attribute. This is very helpful if you have data points that correspond to a well-defined set of values. Let's see how this is done.

```
<!ELEMENT Foo EMPTY>
<!ATTLIST Foo
   Color (Red | Green | Blue) #REQUIRED>
```

As you can see, in an enumerated value set declaration the possible values for an attribute are listed, separated by pipe characters. As with anything else in XML, these values are case-sensitive. For this DTD fragment, the following document fragment is valid:

```
<Foo Color="Red" />
```

but this one is not:

```
<Foo Color="Orange" />
```

This is one of the few ways to strongly constrain the allowable values for a data point in a DTD – some good uses of this are explored in Chapters 2 and 3.

Notation Attribute Declaration

Using this declaration, you can associate a particular notation (or one of a set of notations) with an element. This is useful if the element content, which for all other intents and purposes looks like text, actually needs to be processed another way – say, if it happens to be PostScript or a base-64 encoded block.

```
<!NOTATION ps PUBLIC "PostScript level 3">
<!NOTATION base64 PUBLIC "Base-64 encoded">
<!ELEMENT Foo (#PCDATA)>
<!ATTLIST Foo
   Datatype NOTATION (ps | base64) #REQUIRED>
```

Note that each possible value for the notation attribute must match the name of a notation defined elsewhere in the DTD.

A valid example of a document:

```
<Foo Datatype="ps">gsave 112 75 moveto 112 300 lineto showpage grestore</Foo>
```

Next, we need to look at the various ways in which cardinality and default values may be specified for attributes.

#REQUIRED

You've probably noticed that we've been using the #REQUIRED default declaration for all of our examples. This means what you'd expect – that the attribute value must be supplied in the XML document in order for it to be valid. So for this declaration:

```
<!ELEMENT Foo EMPTY>
<!ATTLIST Foo
   Color (Red | Green | Blue) #REQUIRED>
```

this is a valid XML fragment:

```
<Foo Color="Red" />
```

but this is not:

```
<Foo /> <!-- the Color attribute is required! -->
```

#IMPLIED

The #IMPLIED default declaration for an attribute means that the attribute may or may not be supplied. If the attribute is not supplied, then no value is available to the XML parser for that attribute when parsing that document. So in this case, with the declaration:

```
<!ELEMENT Foo EMPTY>
<!ATTLIST Foo
    Color (Red | Green | Blue) #IMPLIED>
```

both of the following are valid document fragments:

```
<Foo Color="Red" />
```

```
<Foo /> <!-- the Color attribute does not have to be supplied -->
```

Default Value Declarations

There is a third default declaration that is available when declaring an attribute. In this declaration, a value is provided for the attribute; if the attribute value is not supplied in the XML document, the default value is substituted and available to the XML parser as if it were explicitly stated in the XML document. An example is in order. For the declaration:

```
<!ELEMENT Foo EMPTY>
<!ATTLIST Foo
    Color (Red | Green | Blue) "Red">
```

when the document fragment

```
<Foo Color="Green" />
```

is parsed by the XML processor, the value Green will be returned for the Color attribute of this Foo element. Now, suppose that we have this document fragment:

```
<Foo />
```

In this case, since the Color attribute is missing from the XML fragment, the processor will automatically substitute and return the value Red for the attribute.

#FIXED Value Declarations

Finally, you may use the #FIXED declaration to indicate that the value of the attribute is always taken from the value specified in the attribute declaration. For example, you could have these declarations:

```
<!ELEMENT Foo EMPTY>
<!ATTLIST Foo
    Color CDATA "Red" #FIXED>
```

When an XML parser reads a document created using this set of declarations, the value Red will *always* be provided for the attribute Color on *all* Foo elements – even though the Color attribute is never mentioned in the XML document itself. In fact, it's an error to provide any other value – a document that looks like this will not validate against the declarations above:

```
<Foo Color="Orange" />
```

Instead, you must omit the attribute altogether, or provide the exact value in the attribute declaration:

```
<Foo />
<Foo Color="Red" />
```

One very good use for this technique is to pass version information about the DTD to the XML parser so that it can make intelligent guesses as to the available content in the XML document. You might declare a Version attribute that has a #FIXED value of 1.0, for example, and this would be available as if the XML document itself contained this value.

Notation Declarations

If you are going to use notations in your XML document (for unparsed entities, to specify a URI for the target of a processing instruction, or to annotate an element, for example), you need to declare them in the DTD. A notation declaration looks like this:

```
<!NOTATION gif PUBLIC "GIF">
```

It includes the name of the notation, as well as a system and/or public identifier that a processor can use to determine the application or information type to which the notation pertains. For the purposes of this book, we won't be spending much time on notations, but if you come across a notation declaration in an existing DTD you'll be able to figure out what it means. Several of the subsequent sections of this appendix detail various uses of these declarations.

Entity Declarations

There are two types of entities that may be declared: internal entities and external entities.

Internal Entities

Internal entities contain their replacement value in their declaration; when a parser encounters a reference to the specified internal entity, it subsitutes the replacement value found in that entity's declaration.

For example:

```
<!ENTITY DocumentStatus "Draft">
<!ELEMENT About (#PCDATA)>

<About>
    This document is currently in &DocumentStatus; status.
</About>
```

When the parser reads this document, it substitutes the string provided in the entity declaration for the entity reference string "&DocumentStatus;". To a processor, the document looks like this:

```
<About>
    This document is currently in Draft status.
</About>
```

External Entities

By contrast, external entities refer to resources outside the context of the XML document. A system identification containing a URI where the external entity content may be found is provided; additionally, some sort of public identifier may be provided so that a processor can attempt to generate an alternative URI. Here are two examples of external entity declarations:

```
<!ENTITY SalesData SYSTEM "sales/summary.xml">
```

```
<!ENTITY SiteMap SYSTEM "http://www.yoursite.com/sitemap.xml"
                 PUBLIC "//yoursite//sitemap.xml">
```

When entities are declared this way, their content is retrieved and substituted in place where they are referenced. They are known as parsed entities because they must conform to the rules of XML. It's also possible to declare external unparsed entities, as we mentioned earlier in this appendix – we'll see how that's done a little later.

Say we have the following DTD, called `invoice.dtd`:

```
<!ENTITY InvoiceLineItems SYSTEM "lineitems.xml">
<!ELEMENT Invoice (CustomerName, LineItem+)>
<!ELEMENT CustomerName (#PCDATA)>
<!ELEMENT LineItem (Item, Quantity, Price)>
<!ELEMENT Item (#PCDATA)>
<!ELEMENT Quantity (#PCDATA)>
<!ELEMENT Price (#PCDATA)>
```

and the following document, called `invoice.xml`:

```
<?xml version="1.0"?>
<!DOCTYPE Invoice SYSTEM "invoice.dtd">
<Invoice>
  <CustomerName>Kevin Williams</CustomerName>
  &InvoiceLineItems;
</Invoice>
```

If the document `lineitems.xml` contains the following:

```
<LineItem>
  <Item>Widget</Item>
  <Quantity>50</Quantity>
  <Price>75.00</Price>
</LineItem>
<LineItem>
  <Item>Sprocket</Item>
  <Quantity>25</Quantity>
  <Price>100.00</Price>
</LineItem>
```

then the document, after substitution, will be:

```
<?xml version="1.0"?>
<!DOCTYPE Invoice SYSTEM "invoice.dtd">
```

```
<Invoice>
  <CustomerName>Kevin Williams</CustomerName>
  <LineItem>
    <Item>Widget</Item>
    <Quantity>50</Quantity>
    <Price>75.00</Price>
  </LineItem>
  <LineItem>
    <Item>Sprocket</Item>
    <Quantity>25</Quantity>
    <Price>100.00</Price>
  </LineItem>
</Invoice>
```

Note that we still had to declare the substructure of the external parsed entity in our DTD. Parsed entities (whether internal or external) must conform to any document type definition provided for the document that references them. So if your lineitems.xml was instead formed like this:

```
<LineItem>
  <Item>Widget</Item>
  <Quantity>50</Quantity>
</LineItem>
```

a validating parser would complain because the Price subelement is missing from the LineItem element.

Parameter Entities

It's also possible to declare entities that are substituted into the DTD itself, rather than into the XML document. These are called **parameter entities**, and here's an example declaration:

```
<!ENTITY % ThirdColorChoice "Blue">
<!ELEMENT Foo EMPTY>
<!ATTLIST Foo (Red | Green | %ThirdColorChoice;)>
```

As you might imagine, substitution works just like it does for other entity references. To the validating parser, the DTD looks like this:

```
<!ELEMENT Foo EMPTY>
<!ATTLIST Foo (Red | Green | Blue)>
```

External parameter entities may also be declared:

```
<!ENTITY % ColorChoiceList SYSTEM "colorchoices.txt">
<!ELEMENT Foo EMPTY>
<!ATTLIST Foo (%ColorChoiceList;)>
```

colorchoices.txt could contain the following:

```
Red | Green | Blue
```

leading to the substituted DTD looking like this:

```
<!ELEMENT Foo EMPTY>
<!ATTLIST Foo (Red | Green | Blue)>
```

Unparsed Entities

Unparsed entities (entities that do not have their values extracted) may also be declared. These are the entity types we discussed when talking about attribute declarations. They may only appear as the values of attributes that are declared as having the ENTITY or ENTITIES type. To declare an unparsed entity, you use the same declaration as for an external parse entity but add a notation declaration to the end of it:

```
<!NOTATION gif PUBLIC "GIF">
<!ENTITY PropertyImage SYSTEM "image.gif" NDATA gif>
```

```
<!NOTATION midi PUBLIC "MIDI 1.0">
<!ENTITY BackgroundMusic SYSTEM "http://www.yoursite.com/music.mid"
                         NDATA midi>
```

The notation name at the end of the unparsed entity declaration must also be declared, in a notation declaration elsewhere in the document type definition, as seen in the above examples.

Conditional Sections

In a DTD, you can choose to include or ignore sections of the DTD by enclosing them in **conditional sections**. External entities may be used to control the inclusion or exclusion of document type declarations in much the same way that #define and #ifdef/#ifndef macros may be used to control the compilation of C++ source code. Let's see how this works.

If you want to include a section of declarations, you wrap them in the conditional section include markers - <![INCLUDE[at the beginning and]]> at the end. Similarly, to exclude a section of declarations, start the section with <![IGNORE[and end it with]]>. For example, the first set of declarations in the following DTD will be included (used for validating XML), and the second set will be ignored:

```
<![INCLUDE[
<!ELEMENT Foo (#PCDATA)>
]]>

<![IGNORE[
<!ELEMENT Foo EMPTY>
]]>
```

To the validating parser, this will look like

```
<!ELEMENT Foo (#PCDATA)>
```

If we add parameter entities to the mix, we can turn on or off sections at will by changing the values of the parameter entities:

```
<!ENTITY % TextContent "INCLUDE">
<!ENTITY % AttributesOnly "IGNORE">

<![&TextContent;[
<!ELEMENT Foo (#PCDATA)>
]]>

<![&AttributesOnly;[
<!ELEMENT Foo EMPTY>
]]>
```

Using parameter entities this way allows us to easily control the structure of our DTD.

Thinking in Trees

Now that we've taken a look at the building blocks that go together to make up XML documents, we need to talk about how these building blocks fit together. To do this, we're going to need to stop thinking about XML documents as serial files and start thinking about them as node trees.

Take this sample XML document:

```
<Invoice>
  <CustomerName>Kevin Williams</CustomerName>
  <ShipTo>
    <Address>742 Evergreen Terrace</Address>
    <City>Springfield</City>
    <State>KY</State>
    <PostalCode>12345</PostalCode>
  </ShipTo>
  <LineItem>
    <Item>Widget</Item>
    <Quantity>15</Quantity>
    <Price>25.00</Price>
  </LineItem>
  <LineItem>
    <Item>Sprocket</Item>
    <Quantity>22</Quantity>
    <Price>44.00</Price>
  </LineItem>
</Invoice>
```

If you're used to working with flat files, such as comma-delimited files, you are probably thinking about this file serially: there's the invoice start tag, then the customer name start tag, then the customer name, and so on. However, most of the XML technologies we'll be using in this book don't model the information this way. Instead, the information is modelled as a tree:

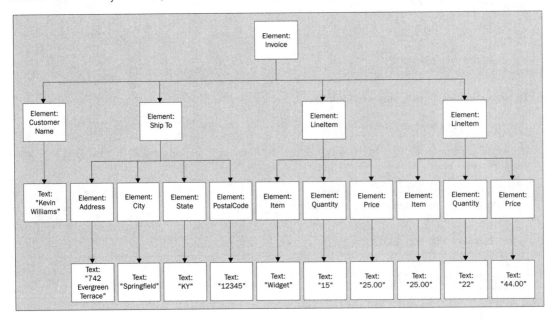

When you're working with XML documents through the DOM, or using XPath to specify a particular location in an XML document, everything is expressed in terms of child lists and branch traversals. For example, if you had to apply the following XPath expression:

```
/Invoice/LineItem[position()=2]/Quantity
```

to the serialized document, it's not immediately apparent what's being referenced. However, once you understand that this expression describes a navigation through the node tree in our diagram – "go to the Invoice element, then to the second LineItem child of that element, then to the Quantity child of that element" (which gives us 22) it's obvious what's being requested.

Learning to think of XML documents in terms of node trees, rather than in terms of serialized text, will help you to more easily query and manipulate those documents from code.

Technology Overview

Let's take a quick look at the XML technologies covered in this book. We will see how each of these technologies may be used to facilitate our access to, and manipulation of, data stored in XML documents.

XML Schemas

XML Schemas are a new mechanism that the W3C is working on to define XML Vocabularies, as a replacement for DTDs. As of this time, XML Schemas are in working draft last call status. This means that they are fairly stable, but may still change somewhat before they reach recommendation status. We cover XML Schemas in Chapter 5, along with discussion of why they're so much better than DTDs, and some techniques for their use.

The Document Object Model (DOM)

The Document Object Model, or DOM, is the mechanism specified by the W3C for the access and manipulation of XML documents. It works by reading the entire document into memory and constructing a tree from its contents, making the DOM an excellent choice for the manipulation of existing documents (to insert elements, for example, or modify the values of elements, or create new ones). However, the DOM is very memory-hungry, and may not be suitable for all applications – especially those where documents are only being read and parsed. The DOM is discussed in more detail in Chapter 6.

The Simple API for XML (SAX)

The Simple API for XML, or SAX, is the development community's response to the DOM. It also parses XML documents, but is event-driven; that is, it streams the document through the parse window and issues events to the caller when parts of the document are found (an element starts, an element ends, a processing instruction is read, and so on). Compared to the DOM, SAX has a very small memory footprint. Unfortunately, if the XML document is complexly connected (perhaps through the use of ID to IDREF relationships), using SAX can necessitate either multiple parses of a document or sophisticated buffering to retrieve needed information that has already passed through the parse window. The SAX library is covered in Chapter 7.

XSLT/XPath

XSLT is the W3C's styling language for XML. It allows XML in one form to be transformed into another form of XML, into HTML, or even into other text-based formats like a comma-delimited file. As more and more documents on the Web begin to be stored in XML as their native format, XSLT will likely be the method used to transform these documents from data-centric XML representations into presentation-friendly XHTML or WML representations, and into other XML vocabularies required by other applications. Within XSLT, the node selection language used is XPath – this language allows specific nodes or values to be selected from the source XML document for manipulation and presentation. Chapter 8 describes the XSLT and XPath languages and gives some examples of their use.

XML Query

XML Query is a language defined by the W3C to access the contents of an XML document programmatically. This specification is still in working draft status, so it will likely change somewhat before it reaches recommendation status. Chapter 9 will bring you up to speed on the current status of XML Query and prepare you to implement it as soon as it becomes widely available, as well as introduce some other query mechanisms that may be of use to you in the mean time.

XLink

XLink is a linking mechanism, similar to HTML hyperlinks, defined by the W3C to link XML documents together. Unlike HTML hyperlinks, it allows you to create bidirectional linkages or to link many documents together with one link. This specification is currently in candidate recommendation status, so you can expect to see it appearing in mainstream XML libraries soon. Chapter 10 covers XLink in detail.

XPointer

XPointer is the mechanism defined by the W3C to point to subsets of XML documents. This works something like anchors in HTML, but XPointer allows much greater flexibility – allowing specific nodes or sets of nodes to be selected from the target document using XPath. XPointer is also a candidate recommendation, so it will be available soon as well. Chapter 11 covers XPointer.

XBase

XBase is similar to HTML BASE; it allows the document to specify a root location from which all relative URIs in the XML document are assumed to start. This specification is currently a working draft in last call status, so it should be implemented before too much longer. Chapter 11 covers XBase.

XForms

XForms are the W3C's intended replacement for HTML forms. They will provide strong datatyping, masking, and other constraints not found in HTML forms, making for a richer UI experience for an end user. XForms are still in the early stages – a working draft of the data model has been prepared, but the companion grammar document has not yet been released to the public. By architecting your data with XForms in mind, however, you'll save yourself some trouble when XForms do become available. Chapter 11 covers XForms.

XML Fragment Interchange

XML Fragment Interchange is the method provided by the W3C for the transmission of fragments – part of an XML document - while still retaining enough contextual information for the fragments to be meaningful. This specification is currently in a strange state – it's been through the working draft last call process, but has been temporarily put back into working draft status rather than being promoted to a proposed recommendation as would normally be the case. However, it's been accessible to the public long enough now that it probably won't be changing much before its release. Chapter 11 covers XML Fragment Interchange.

XInclude

XInclude is a mechanism being designed by the W3C to allow the inclusion of one XML document inside another. This document was just recently made available for public review, so it will be a while before it reaches recommendation status. XInclude is discussed in Chapter 11.

Summary

In this appendix, we've spent some time bringing you up to speed (or back up to speed) on the building blocks of XML and how they fit together. We've also taken a quick look at some of the technologies we'll be using to access and manipulate XML documents throughout the remainder of the book. If you found this appendix a little overwhelming, you might find a book like *Beginning XML* (mentioned at the start) helpful to flesh out some of the details of the subjects we've discussed. In some of the chapters, we'll be building on this information as we cover strategies for using XML to represent data.

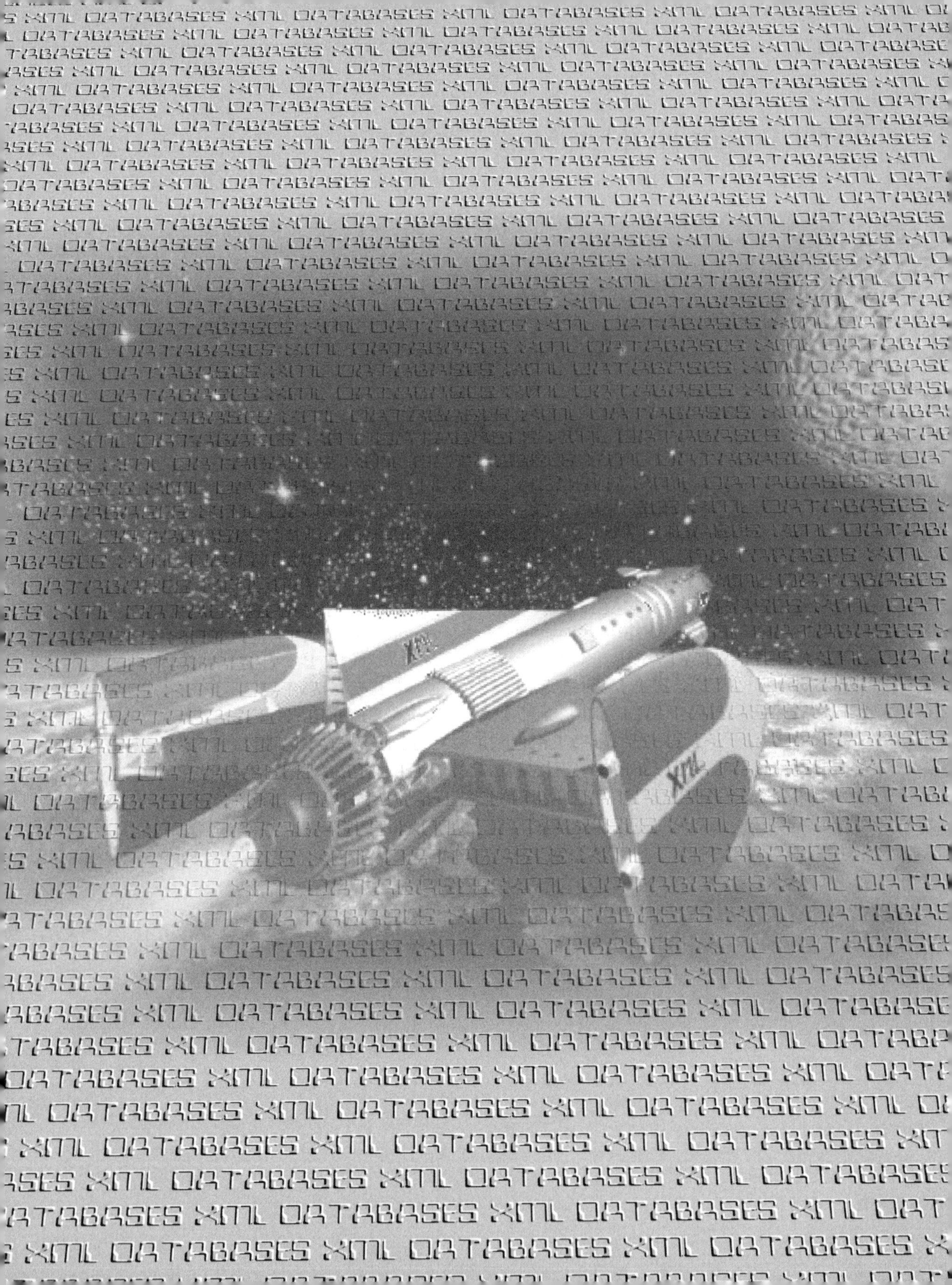
XML DATABASES XML DATABASES XML DATABASES
XML
XML

B

Relational Database Primer

This appendix is intended to give the XML developer who may be unfamiliar with relational databases a quick tutorial on the concepts of such databases. The concepts we will discuss are as follows:

- ❑ **Database Introduction** – we will have a look at the different types of Database available, and why Relational databases seem to lead the field.

- ❑ **SQL** – we will have a look at Structured Query Language (**SQL**), the language used by Microsoft SQL Server (and other database servers) to control relational databases.

- ❑ **Relational Databases, the Specifics** – we will discuss the various components and concepts that go together to create a relational database, and see how they compare with similar XML constructs.

- ❑ **A Working Example** – lastly, we will look at building up a working relational database example. All the code samples we will create are for Microsoft SQL Server; however, the general concepts should apply to any relational database platform. You can run our examples using the command-line version of the query analyzer (isql) or through SQL Server Enterprise Manager.

Most of these concepts will be skipped over fairly briefly, to give you enough information about relational databases to progress smoothly through this book. If you require more detail on any of these sections, please refer to the references section at the end.

Types of Database

Relational databases are by far the most commonly used type of database these days. In the past, many different database systems have come and gone, from old paper based systems (which, of course, still exist today, but lose out massively to computer databases in just about every way!), through Legacy mainframe (or **V**irtual **S**torage **A**ccess **M**ethod (**VSAM**)) systems, which are all about host connectivity, and dBase, and other file-based systems (including **I**nline **S**equential **A**ccess **M**ethod (**ISAM**) databases), with separate files for each table.

However, they are all overwhelmed by relational databases, such as SQL Server and Oracle. This is because relational databases can provide data for the masses (on a much larger scale than ISAM databases), while retaining much better data integrity than is possible with an old VSAM system – your data is much quicker to access, and much safer, with the database itself taking over some of the responsibility of its own integrity.

Before we exit this quick tour of database flavors, a quick mention must first be given, of Object-oriented databases. These have also been around for a while now, but are only just beginning to have any real use made of them. It is a very different way of storing data, in which each document is stored separately in an object (whose state would be maintained), instead of in several different tables. These systems allow for such concepts as inheritance and encapsulation.

SQL

The SQL language provides an easy way to query and alter databases, by means of a simple language of statements such as SELECT, INSERT and DELETE. Below are a couple of examples to give you the idea:

```
Select * From Customer Where CustomerName='John'

Delete from Customer where CustomerName='Bill'
```

The first query, when run against a database containing a customer table, will query the database to display all records that have the CustomerName "John". The second query, on the other hand, will delete all records from the customer table that have the CustomerName "Bill".

To use these queries on your databases, you need a **R**elational **D**atabase **M**anagement **S**ystem (**RDBMS**) that supports the SQL language. These come in many different flavors, from open source efforts such as MYSQL and PostGreSQL, to more commercial packages such as Microsoft's SQL Server. These typically feature a high-level database manager, which allows you to create new databases, delete entire tables in the blink of an eye, and administer security options, and a query execution program, which allows SQL queries to be run against your databases. These components are provided for in SQL Server, for example, by the Enterprise Manager and Query Analyzer tools that come with the database.

Designing Relational Databases

There are two main concepts to look at when designing a relational database:

- ❑ **logical data design**, which is concerned with theoretically modeling the actual data that the database will contain, independent of the platform it will be running on, exact table structure, relationships between the information in the tables, and other such factors (this is also referred to as **data modeling**)

❑ **physical data design,**which involves the more "real" aspects of the database design, such as choosing a platform on which to seat our information, writing the code to create the tables, defining the columns in those tables, etc.

Logical Data Design

When creating a relational database, the first step is to model the data that it will contain. As we will see, this process is very similar to the process used when modeling an XML structure to hold data. A cautionary note though: much of the jargon used in relational database design is the same as that used in XML design, but with different meanings. For the purposes of this appendix, unless we explicitly state that we are using any term in its XML context, assume that we are referring to the relational database term.

Entities

In a logical data design, the first step is to identify the **entities** that are being modeled – entities can define any person, place, thing, or concept. In a typical data modeling effort, entities correspond roughly to the nouns in the system being modeled. For example, consider the following business problem:

> *"Design an invoice tracking system. Invoices consist of a customer, invoice information, and line item information for each part ordered."*

In this business problem statement, the obvious nouns that jump out are **Customer**, **Part**, **Invoice**, and **LineItem**. These would be the starting entities in our logical data design. If we were to diagram the database design thus far, it would look like this, with each box representing a table:

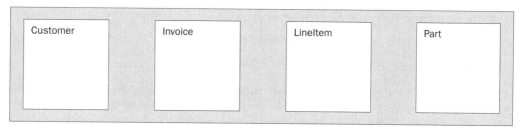

Entities are roughly analogous to structural elements in an XML database – they are aggregations of other information that correspond to a particular noun. If you are familiar with object-oriented design, you may think of these entities as roughly analogous to classes in your object-oriented system.

Attributes

The next thing to identify in the logical data design is the **attributes**. Attributes are individual data points that are used to describe the entities we defined earlier. You can think of the attributes as the adjectives that modify the nouns you decided on earlier in the logical data design process.

Digging into the business problem, we determine that:

❑ Customers have names and addresses

❑ Invoices have order dates, ship dates, and ship methods

❑ Line items have a quantity and a price

❑ Parts have a name, a size, and a color

Using this information, we define attributes for each of the entities we created earlier. These attributes should correspond to basic data types: "one value". If an attribute appears to be made up of more than one value, you should break the attribute up into more atomic attributes (for example, break an address field up into House, Street, City...etc) or create a new entity to hold the information instead. Note that you're not allowed to store substructure in attributes, as you would be able to using subelements in XML.

With this information included, our diagram now looks like this:

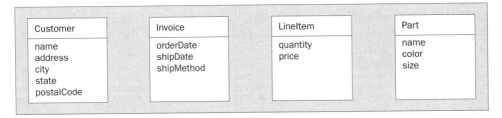

Attributes in a logical data design correspond roughly to text-only elements or attributes in an XML document (depending on your preference). They are specific values that serve to describe the entity with which they are associated.

Relationships

In the final step of logical design, we need to identify the relationships between the entities we have defined. These can be thought of as verbs that relate the defined entities. On examining the business problem further, we determine that:

- ❑ A customer may have none, or more invoices
- ❑ An invoice may contain one or more line items
- ❑ A part may appear on one or more line items

These relationships serve to constrain the information that may appear in the database. From the business rules, we know that an invoice must have a customer associated with it, or a line item must have a part associated with it. Adding this information to our diagram, we now have the following:

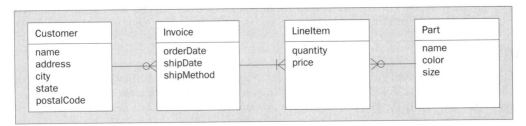

In this diagram, the circle and the crow's-foot means "zero-or-more", while the crossbar and the crow's-foot means "one-or-more". The single line means "one". Thus, the diagram states that a customer may have zero or more invoices, and each invoice may have one or more line items, and so on. These relationships serve to show how the various entities are interrelated and what information may appear in the final database tables.

To summarize, the various line ends on a diagram like this represent the following:

Symbol	Meaning
Single cross line	Exactly one
Circle and cross line	Zero or one
Circle and crows-foot	Zero or more
Cross line and crows-foot	One or more

Other notations exist that can be used to show the relationships between our elements – for more information about logical data design, check out some of the references at the end of this appendix.

Relationships may be expressed in two different ways in XML. The most obvious way is through structural containment – if element A may contain one or more structure B, then there is a "one-to-one-or-more" relationship between A and B, as shown below:

```
<Customer>
    <Order> Bananas </Order>
    <Order> Peas </Order>
    <Order> Potatoes </Order>
    <Order> Sprouts </Order>
</Customer>
```

The other way relationships may be expressed in XML is through IDREF(S) to ID pointers – if element C has an IDREF attribute that points to the ID attribute of element D, then there is a one-to-one relationship between C and D. An example of this kind of XML relationship is as follows:

```
<Customer name="Bill" nameID="1" />
<Customer name="John" nameID="2" />
<Order customerIDREF="1"> Bananas </Order>
```

This shows that the single order has been placed by Bill – there is a one-to-one relationship between Bill and his order.

At this point, we have completed our logical design for our relational database. Next, we need to transform that logical design into a physical design.

Physical Data Design

Logical data design is just that – logical. It is independent of any particular relational database platform or implementation – it simply describes how the data that makes up the relational database interacts. Before we can start using our database, we have to create a physical data design that corresponds to our target database platform.

Tables

Tables are analogous to entities (well, more specifically, tables are analogous to the relationship between entities and their attributes. There will be one table created in our physical database for every entity we created in our logical data design. Therefore, based on the four entities we created in our logical analysis, we need to create the following table definition script. Note that this script is provided here for illustrative purposes only – it will not run until we add lines that will serve to create the columns of the tables:

```
CREATE TABLE Customer (
   ...)
CREATE TABLE Invoice (
   ...)
CREATE TABLE LineItem (
   ...)
CREATE TABLE Part (
   ...)
```

Also note that we will be building up this code throughout the rest of the chapter – the code provided on the download site will be the completed code, seen at the end of this example.

Once we have defined our tables, we need to create the columns that will appear in those tables.

Columns

Columns in our database correspond directly to attributes in our logical model. Each attribute in our logical model will be represented by a column in our physical model. Before we can create those columns, however, we need to assign data types to each of the columns we will create. Let's quickly look at the available datatypes for columns, and then add the columns to our table definition script.

Integer

The integer data type corresponds to an integral value. Most database platforms offer a number of different types of integers. For SQL Server 2000, four integer types are offered:

Data type	Size	Allowable values
tinyint	1 byte	0 to 255
smallint	2 bytes	-32,768 to 32,767
int	4 bytes	-2,147,483,648 to 2,146,483,647
bigint	8 bytes	-9,223,372,036,854,775,808 to 9,223,372,036,854,775,807

Bit

The bit data type corresponds to a single bit that may take the value 0 or 1.

Decimal

These fields are fixed-precision decimal numbers. In SQL Server, the precision (number of significant figures) and scale (number of figures to the right of the decimal point) may be specified. The amount of storage taken up by decimal columns varies, depending on the precision specified:

Precision	Size
1 to 9	5 bytes
10 to 19	9 bytes
20 to 29	13 bytes
30 to 39	17 bytes

Money

Some platforms (such as SQL Server) provide a money datatype. In SQL Server, this datatype is stored in the database as an integer with an implied scale of 4 places beyond the decimal point. There are two money datatypes available in SQL Server:

Data type	Size	Allowable values
smallmoney	4 bytes	-214,748.3648 to 214,648.3647
bigmoney	8 bytes	-922,337,203,685,477.5808 to 922,337,203,685,477.5807

Real Numbers

Real numbers are numbers that are represented as a mantissa and an exponent. The mantissa is a number, between 1 and 9.999999999999, and the exponent is an integer. The value of the number is the mantissa times 2 to the value of the exponent. Since the exponent is binary, the number often can't be exactly represented as a decimal, and thus these data types are often known as the **approximate** data types. In SQL Server, this data type is called **real** or **float**, and it consumes different amounts of data depending on the number of digits of precision required:

Data type	Mantissa digits	Size	Allowable values
real	1-24	4 bytes	-3.40 E+38 to 3.40 E+38
float	25-53	8 bytes	-1.79 E+308 to 1.79 E+308

Dates and Times

Columns with this data type are used to represent date and/or time values. In SQL Server, two datatypes may be used for this purpose.

Data type	Size	Allowable values
Datetime	4 bytes	January 1, 1753 to December 31, 9999, accurate to 3.33 milliseconds
Smalldatetime	2 bytes	January 1, 1900 to June 6, 2079, accurate to one minute

Character Strings

This data type is used to hold single-byte (non-Unicode) character strings. There are three different types of character string declarations in SQL Server:

Declaration	Size	Description
char	8000 chars	Defines a fixed-length string – columns of this type always consume the max number of bytes possible (unless null)
varchar	8000 chars	Defines a variable-length string, consuming a few extra bytes per column. If the strings are shorter than the max length declared for them, the extra space is not consumed

Table continued on following page

Declaration	Size	Description
text	2Mb max size	Defines a variable-length string – they consume the database one page at a time and require special handling in SQL Server, so should only be used for strings expected to be very large. They can also be used to hold bitmaps, and other large **BLOB**s (**B**inary **L**arge **OB**jects)

Unicode Strings

Probably the least portable data type currently, this data type is used to hold double-byte (Unicode) character strings. There are three different types of Unicode string declarations in SQL Server.

Declaration	Size	Description
nchar	4000 chars	Defines a fixed-length string – columns of this type always consume the max number of bytes possible (unless null)
nvarchar	4000 chars	Defines a variable-length string, consuming a few extra bytes per column. If the strings are shorter than the max length declared for them, the extra space is not consumed
ntext	1Mb max size	Defines a variable-length string – they consume the database one page at a time and require special handling in SQL Server, so should only be used for strings expected to be very large.

Binary Strings

This data type is used to hold binary (byte) strings – that is, sequences of bytes (as opposed to character strings, which are sequences of ASCII or Unicode characters). There are three different types of binary string declarations in SQL Server.

Declaration	Size	Description
binary	8000 chars	Defines a fixed-length binary string – columns of this type always consume the max number of bytes possible (unless null)
varbinary	8000 chars	Defines a variable-length binary string, consuming a few extra bytes per column. If the strings are shorter than the max length declared for them, the extra space is not consumed
image	2Mb max size	Defines a variable-length string – they consume the database one page at a time and require special handling in SQL Server, so should only be used for strings expected to be very large.

Creating Our Tables

Now that we have discussed the various data types that are available to us, we can create our columns and assign data types to them. Each column is then added to the table where it appears (to add to our earlier example), to give us the following SQL script:

```
CREATE TABLE Customer (
    CustomerName varchar(30),
    Address varchar(50),
    City varchar(20),
    State char(2),
    PostalCode varchar(10))
CREATE TABLE Invoice (
    OrderDate datetime,
    ShipDate datetime,
    shipMethod tinyint)
CREATE TABLE LineItem (
    Quantity smallint,
    Price smallmoney)
CREATE TABLE Part (
    PartName varchar(30),
    Color varchar(10),
    PartSize varchar(10))
```

This gives us the following database tables:

CustomerName	Address	City	State	PostalCode
▶				

OrderDate	ShipDate	shipMethod
▶		

Quantity	Price
▶	

PartName	Color	PartSize
▶		

Note that we chose the type `tinyint` for the ship method; that's because we know the ship method may take one of a finite set of possible values. Using a single-byte integer rather than a string value saves space and improves processing speed in the database, as well as being the most "relational" way to enforce integrity of allowable values, this is why this is the chosen way of dealing with a column that only has a few different possible values. Typically, the list of allowable values for a column like this will be stored in a lookup table that contains the allowable column values and their string descriptions.

Primary Keys

Primary keys are used in our relational database to uniquely identify records in each table (meaning that, in a column defined as a primary key, all values **must** be unique). This can be thought of as similar to XML ID attributes, although unlike an XML document two different tables in a relational database may take the same primary key values. In most relational databases, automatically incremented integers should be used for the primary keys in all tables to keep join speeds as fast as possible – this is the purpose of the IDENTITY keyword. Joins are used when retrieving data from more than one table – for example, we might want to retrieve all the authors for all the books that start with the letter P. When we use an automatically-incremented integer for the primary key, the primary key will automatically increment when a new record is started. Let's add the primary keys to our tables now – see over:

```
CREATE TABLE Customer (
    CustomerKey integer IDENTITY PRIMARY KEY,
    CustomerName varchar(30),
    Address varchar(50),
    City varchar(20),
    State char(2),
    PostalCode varchar(10))
CREATE TABLE Invoice (
    InvoiceKey integer IDENTITY PRIMARY KEY,
    OrderDate datetime,
    ShipDate datetime,
    shipMethod tinyint)
CREATE TABLE LineItem (
    LineItemKey integer IDENTITY PRIMARY KEY,
    Quantity smallint,
    Price smallmoney)
CREATE TABLE Part (
    PartKey integer IDENTITY PRIMARY KEY,
    PartName varchar(30),
    Color varchar(10),
    PartSize varchar(10))
```

This gives us the same tables as before, it's just that now `CustomerKey`, `InvoiceKey`, `LineItemKey`, and `PartKey` have been set as primary keys.

Foreign Keys

In a relational database, foreign keys are used to express the relationships between various tables. For each relationship we identified in our logical model, we should add a foreign key relationship in our database. The foreign key references the primary key of another table to indicate how they are related – this is similar to the way `IDREF(S)-ID` pointers work in XML. Adding the foreign key relationships to our database, we now have the following table creation script:

```
CREATE TABLE Customer (
    CustomerKey integer IDENTITY PRIMARY KEY,
    CustomerName varchar(30),
    Address varchar(50),
    City varchar(20),
    State char(2),
    PostalCode varchar(10))
CREATE TABLE Invoice (
    InvoiceKey integer IDENTITY PRIMARY KEY,
    OrderDate datetime,
    ShipDate datetime,
    shipMethod tinyint,
    CustomerKey integer
    CONSTRAINT FK_Customer FOREIGN KEY (CustomerKey)
        REFERENCES Customer (CustomerKey))
CREATE TABLE Part (
    PartKey integer IDENTITY PRIMARY KEY,
    PartName varchar(30),
    Color varchar(10),
    PartSize varchar(10))
```

```
CREATE TABLE LineItem (
    LineItemKey integer IDENTITY PRIMARY KEY,
    Quantity smallint,
    Price smallmoney,
    PartKey integer
    CONSTRAINT FK_Part FOREIGN KEY (PartKey)
        REFERENCES Part (PartKey),
    InvoiceKey integer
    CONSTRAINT FK_Invoice FOREIGN KEY (InvoiceKey)
        REFERENCES Invoice (InvoiceKey))
```

For each constraint, we define which fields in our table constitute the foreign key, and which fields in the target table (the table specified in the REFERENCES clause) are on the other side of the relationship. This script produces the following table structure – the lines show the joins between tables designated by the primary and foreign keys:

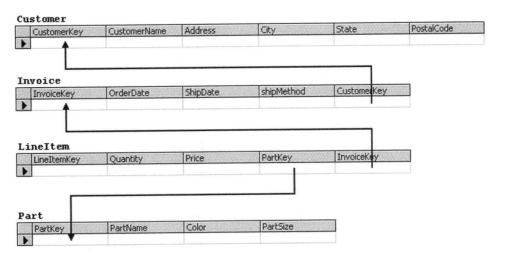

Note that we juggled the order of the table creation around, since a foreign key can't be created until the table it references has been created. Note that this doesn't however mean that the foreign key column has to have the same name as the primary key column to which it points.

Now that the constraints have been added, the relational database will not allow records to be added to the database that do not obey those constraints. For example, you can't add a record to the Invoice table unless the integer value you supply for the CustomerKey corresponds to a record that already exists in the CustomerKey table. This is similar to the way that an IDREF value is not validated in an XML document unless it refers to an ID found somewhere in the document, with the addition that foreign keys additionally require that the key value they reference appears in a particular table.

Indexes

Indexes are used by relational databases to speed access to information. Creating an index on a column or group of columns ensures that it may be sorted as fast as possible, at the expense of extra disk space consumption, and limited performance degradation of UPDATEs, INSERTs, and DELETEs. As a general rule of thumb, every foreign key should have an index created on it. In addition, any non-key field that will be the subject of searching should have an index created on it. For our sample, we'll add indexes on customer name, part name, and invoice ship date (in addition to the foreign key indexes) – to give us our completed script (AppB_01.sql), seen over:

```
CREATE TABLE Customer (
    CustomerKey integer IDENTITY PRIMARY KEY,
    CustomerName varchar(30),
    Address varchar(50),
    City varchar(20),
    State char(2),
    PostalCode varchar(10))
CREATE TABLE Invoice (
    InvoiceKey integer IDENTITY PRIMARY KEY,
    OrderDate datetime,
    ShipDate datetime,
    shipMethod tinyint,
    CustomerKey integer
    CONSTRAINT FK_Customer FOREIGN KEY (CustomerKey)
        REFERENCES Customer (CustomerKey))
CREATE TABLE Part (
    PartKey integer IDENTITY PRIMARY KEY,
    PartName varchar(30),
    Color varchar(10),
    PartSize varchar(10))
CREATE TABLE LineItem (
    LineItemKey integer IDENTITY PRIMARY KEY,
    Quantity smallint,
    Price smallmoney,
    PartKey integer
    CONSTRAINT FK_Part FOREIGN KEY (PartKey)
        REFERENCES Part (PartKey),
    InvoiceKey integer
    CONSTRAINT FK_Invoice FOREIGN KEY (InvoiceKey)
        REFERENCES Invoice (InvoiceKey))
```

```
CREATE INDEX IX_CustomerName ON Customer (CustomerName)
CREATE INDEX IX_InvoiceShipDate ON Invoice (ShipDate)
CREATE INDEX IX_InvoiceCustomerKey ON Invoice (CustomerKey)
CREATE INDEX IX_PartName ON Part (PartName)
CREATE INDEX IX_LineItemPartKey ON LineItem (PartKey)
CREATE INDEX IX_LineItemInvoiceKey ON LineItem (InvoiceKey)
```

Triggers

Triggers may be used in a relational database to take some action when a record is inserted into, updated in, or deleted from a table. These may be used to enforce business rules (such as summarizing data as it is received) or referential integrity rules (such as choice constraints or other more complex rules).

For example, we may say that one of the rules we want enforced by a trigger is that the price specified for a particular line item may not be negative. We can enforce this by creating an insert trigger on the LineItem table, using the script below (AppB_02.sql):

```
CREATE TRIGGER InsertLineItem
ON LineItem
AFTER INSERT
AS
BEGIN
    DECLARE @inserted_price smallmoney
    SELECT @inserted_price = price
        FROM inserted
    IF (@inserted_price < 0)
    BEGIN
        RAISERROR ('Line item price for a part may not be negative.', 16, 1)
        ROLLBACK TRANSACTION
    END
END
```

Triggers may be used to enforce more complex referential integrity rules on a database than may be described using foreign keys. For example, say you had the following content model in your XML structures and you were trying to replicate the behavior in your relational database:

```
<!ELEMENT a (b | c)>
```

Here, the element a may contain a b element, or a c element, but not both. You could mimic this constraint in your relational database by adding a trigger to the b-containing table, forbidding an insert if a record already exists in the c-containing table that is associated with your a record, and doing the same for the c-containing table forbidding an insert when a record from b is already present for the same a record. Of course, the preceding discussion assumes that you have access to triggers in your particular RDBMS – if you need to create tables for a platform that does not provide triggers, you will need to find another way of implementing this functionality (such as checking it in your middle layer before attempting to insert the record).

Stored Procedures

Stored procedures are used in a relational database to encapsulate business functionality in a precompiled function. They are similar to triggers, except that stored procedures may be executed on demand by a programmer (rather than being executed automatically in response to some database action, such as a table insert). Many systems perform a great deal of their business logic in stored procedures.

Some advantages of stored procedures include:

❑ Better execution speed, as the procedures are precompiled and execution plans may be cached

❑ The ability to pass parameters to sets of commands, with fewer resultant round trips to the middle layer

❑ Good encapsulation of business logic or other atomic operations

While they are outside the scope of this appendix, most databases you are likely to encounter will use stored procedures to provide a great deal of their functionality.

Summary

In this appendix, we've touched on the high level concepts of relational database design and terminology. Even if you're a relational database neophyte, the information contained in this appendix will allow you to better understand the examples presented in the body of this book.

References

What Not How: The Business Rules Approach to Application Development, by CJ Date
Published by Addison-Wesley (ISBN – 0201708507)

An Introduction to Database Systems (Introduction to Database Systems, 7th Ed), by CJ Date
Published by Addison-Wesley (ISBN – 0201385902)

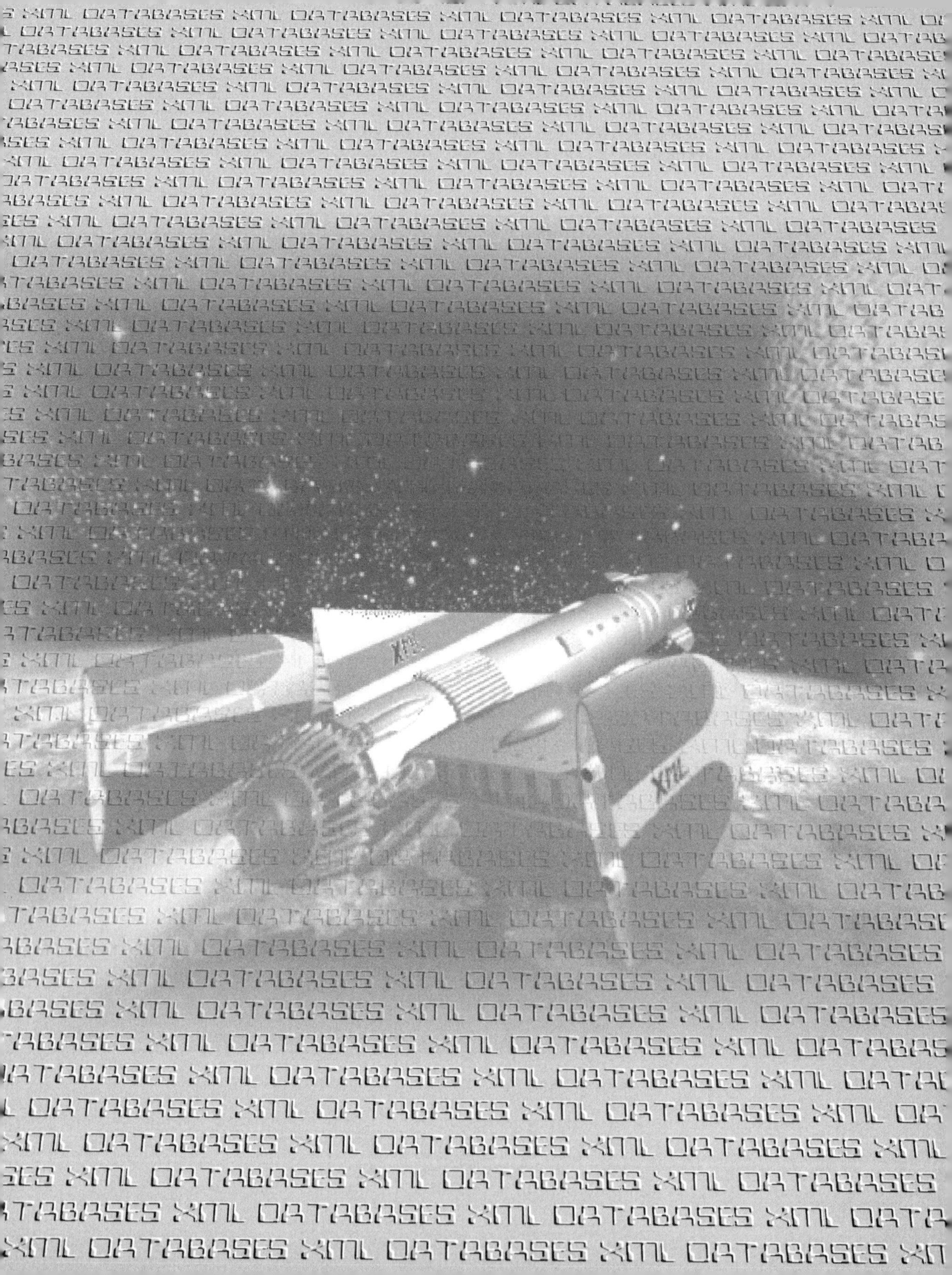
XML DATABASES

C

XML Schema Datatypes

In this appendix, we'll go through the details about XML Schema datatypes. XML Schemas provide two basic kinds of datatypes:

❑ **primitive datatypes** – those that are not defined in terms of other types

❑ **derived datatypes** – types that are defined in terms of existing types

There are three W3C documents of interest: XML Schema Part 0: Primer, XML Schema Part 1: Structures, and XML Schema Part 2: Datatypes [all 7 April 2000], at http://www.w3.org/TR/xmlschema-0, http://www.w3.org/TR/xmlschema-1, and http://www.w3.org/TR/xmlschema-2, respectively. Together, these comprise the W3C candidate recommendation of XML Schema, as of the 24th October 2000.

XML Schema is based on XML 1.0, but also requires the use of Namespaces in XML [14 January 1999], available at http://www.w3.org/TR/REC-xml-names.html.

Primitive Types

The following are the primitive datatypes that are built-in to XML Schema:

❑ string – a finite-length sequence of UCS characters

❑ boolean – a two-state "true" or "false" flag

❑ float – a 32-bit single-precision floating-point number

- ❑ double – a 64-bit double-precision floating-point number
- ❑ decimal – a decimal number of arbitrary precision
- ❑ timeDuration – a duration of time
- ❑ recurringDuration – a recurring duration of time
- ❑ binary – text-encoded binary data
- ❑ uriReference – a standard Internet URI
- ❑ ID – equivalent to the XML 1.0 ID attribute type
- ❑ IDREF – equivalent to the XML 1.0 IDREF attribute type
- ❑ ENTITY – equivalent to the XML 1.0 ENTITY attribute type
- ❑ NOTATION – equivalent to the XML 1.0 NOTATION attribute type
- ❑ QName – a legal QName string (name with qualifier), as defined in *Namespaces in XML*

Let's take a closer look at these.

string

A set of finite-length sequences of UCS characters, as defined in ISO 10646 and Unicode. Value and lexical spaces are identical. This datatype is ordered by UCS code points (integer character values). For example:

```
<an_element>This sentence is a legal string literal with élan.</an_element>
```

Built-in derived types: CDATA.

boolean

A binary value. True may be represented as "true" or "1" (one), and false may be either "false" or "0" (zero).

```
<an_element flag1="true" flag2="1" />    <!-- two flags, equivalent values -->
<an_element flag3="false" flag4="0" />   <!-- ditto -->
```

This datatype is not ordered, and there are no built-in derived types.

decimal

An arbitrary precision decimal number, with values in the range $i \times 10^n$, where **i** and **n** are integers (with **n** being the scale of the value space). This datatype is ordered by numeric value.

It's represented by a finite-length sequence of decimal digits separated by a period (.) as a decimal indicator, and an optional leading sign (+ or -). If the sign is omitted, it's assumed to be a plus. The representation is further constrained by the scale and precision facets. Leading and/or trailing zeroes are optional. For example, each of the following is a valid decimal:

```
<an_element num1="-1.23" num2="3.1416" num3="+042" num4="100.00" />
```

Built-in derived type: integer.

float

An IEEE single-precision 32-bit floating-point number as specified in IEEE 754-1985.

> *The IEEE Standard for Binary Floating-Point Arithmetic (IEEE 754-1985) is available at http://standards.ieee.org/reading/ieee/std_public/description/busarch/754-1985_desc.html. (Someone needs to talk to these people about using simpler and more reasonable URLs!)*

The value space includes all values $m \times 2^e$, where m is an integer whose absolute value is less than 2^{24}, and e is an integer between **-149** and **104**, inclusive. There are also five special values in a float's value space: positive and negative zero (represented as "**0**" and "**-0**"), positive and negative infinity ("**INF**" and "**-INF**"), and not-a-number ("**NAN**"). This datatype is ordered by numeric value.

The lexical representation is a mantissa (which must be a decimal number) optionally followed by the character **E** or **e**, followed by an exponent (which must be an integer). If the **E/e** and exponent are omitted, an exponent value of 0 (zero) is assumed. For example:

```
<an_element num1="-1E4" num2="3.1416" num3="12.78e-1" num4="NAN" />
```

There are no built-in derived types.

double

An IEEE double-precision 64-bit floating-point number as specified in IEEE 754-1985.

The value space includes all values $m \times 2^e$, where m is an integer whose absolute value is less than 2^{53}, and e is an integer between **-1075** and **970**, inclusive. There are also the same five special values as defined for the `float` type. This datatype is ordered by numeric value.

The lexical representation is the same as the `float` type. For example:

```
<an_element num1="-1E666" num2="3.1416" num3="12.78e-1040" num4="INF" />
```

There are no built-in derived types.

timeDuration

A duration of time, with a countably infinite value space, as specified in ISO 8601.

> **ISO 8601:Representations of dates and times, 1988-06-15** *is one of the few ISO standards that is available on the WWW (at http://www.iso.ch/markete/8601.pdf). Ordering information for the new draft and its corrections are at http://www.iso.ch/cate/d15903.html and http://www.iso.ch/cate/d15905.html.*

The lexical representation is the ISO 8601 extended format: P*n*Y*n*M*n*DT*n*H*n*M*n*S. The upper-case letters P, Y, M, D, T, H, M, and S in this format are called designators. The "P" stands for "period" (as in a duration of time) and is required to be the first character of any `timeDuration` string. The recurring "*n*" represents number, so *n*Y is the number of years, *n*M the number of months, *n*D of days, T is the date/time separator, *n*H is hours, the second *n*M is minutes, and *n*S is seconds. Seconds may be any decimal number of arbitrary precision.

For example:

```
<an_element duration="P12Y10M2DT0H40M27.87S" />
```

This represents a `timeDuration` of 12 years, 10 months, 2 days, 0 hours, 40 minutes, and 27.875 seconds.

Truncated lexical representations of this format are allowed provided they conform to the following:

❑ Lowest order items may be omitted. If so, their value is assumed to be zero.

❑ The lowest order item may have a decimal fraction of arbitrary precision.

❑ If any of the number values equals zero, the number and its corresponding designator may be omitted. However, at least one number and its designator must always be present.

❑ The designator **T** must be absent if all time items are omitted.

❑ The leading designator **P** must always be present.

For example:

```
<an_element duration="P12Y10M2DT40M27.87S" />
```

represents the same `timeDuration` as the previous example – except here we're using one of the truncated forms (hours have been omitted).

An optional preceding minus sign (-) is also allowed, to indicate a negative duration; if the sign is omitted, a positive duration is assumed

One more example: the durations in the first line below are all legal (meaning 500 years, 42 months, 1 year + 6 months + 2 hours, and 42 days + 1 hour + 57 minutes, respectively), whilst the subsequent two lines are both *illegal*:

```
<an_element d1="P500Y" d2="P42M" d3="P1Y6MT2H" d4="P42DT1H57M" />
<an_element d="P-1347M" />      <!-- minus sign must precede the P -->
<an_element d="P1Y2MT" />       <!-- T must be omitted in this case -->
```

There are no built-in types derived from `timeDuration`.

recurringDuration

A `timeDuration` that recurs with a specific `timeDuration` starting from a specific origin. The value space is countably infinite. (See also §5.5.3.2 of ISO 8601.)

The lexical representation is the ISO 8601 extended format `CCYY-MM-DDThh:mm:ss.sss`. The `CC` represents the century, `YY` the year, `MM` the month and `DD` the day. The `T` is the date/time separator. The `hh`, `mm`, and `ss.sss` represent hours, minutes and seconds respectively. Additional digits may be used to increase the precision of the fractional seconds, and additional digits can be added to `CC` to accommodate year values greater than 9999. An optional preceding minus sign (–) is allowed to indicate a negative duration; if the sign is omitted, a positive duration is assumed.

The basic string may be immediately followed by a Z to indicate Coordinated Universal Time (UTZ).

> *UTZ is the internationally-accepted apolitical term for the world's base time zone on the Zero Meridian, commonly-known in Anglo-countries as Greenwich Mean Time.*

A local time zone offset (the difference between the local time zone and UTZ) may also be indicated by adding another string with the format: ±hh.mm, where hh and mm are defined as above, and the sign may be either plus or minus. The two time zone options (UTZ and local) are mutually exclusive

The primary purpose, and only legal use, of recurringDuration is as a base type for some derived date/time type. This derived type must specify both the duration and period constraining facets. This primitive datatype *may not be used directly in a schema* – though it may be used indirectly via a derived type.

Built-in derived types: recurringDate, recurringDay, time, timeInstant, and timePeriod (all of these, except the first, use truncated versions of the above lexical representation).

The two required facets are specified using the same lexical format as timeDuration. These facets specify the length of the duration (duration) and after what duration it recurs (period). If duration's value is zero, it means that the duration is a single instant of time. If the period is zero, the duration doesn't recur, in other words there's only a single occurrence.

binary

Some arbitrary binary data, which is a set of finite-length sequences of binary octets (8-bit bytes). This datatype is not ordered.

The lexical representation of this datatype depends upon the choice of encoding facet (see its description in the previous section). For example:

```
<an_element encoding="hex">312D322D33</an_element>
```

This example shows the hex encoding of the ASCII string "1-2-3".

There are no built-in derived types.

This type *may not be used directly in a schema* – it may only be used indirectly via a derived type.

uriReference

An absolute or relative Uniform Resource Identifier (URI) Reference that may have an optional fragment identifier. This datatype is not ordered.

The lexical representation of this datatype is the set of strings that match the URI-reference production in Section 4 of RFC 2396. For example:

```
<an_element link="http://www.w3.org" />                      <!-- HTTP -->
<an_element link="ftp://ftp.is.co.za/rfc/rfc2396.txt" />     <!-- FTP -->
<an_element link="mailto://sales@wrox.com" />                <!-- email -->
<an_element link="telnet://melvyl.ucop.edu" />               <!-- Telnet -->
```

ID

A datatype that is equivalent to the ID attribute type as defined in the XML 1.0 recommendation (see also Chapter 11). This datatype is not ordered, and the following validity constraints apply:

❑ The value of the ID string must uniquely identify its associated element

❑ It must be used once, and only once, in a document instance

The lexical representation of this datatype is any NCName string (name without colon), as defined in *Namespaces in XML*. For example:

```
<an_element its_id="AGENT_ID_007" />
```

There are no built-in derived types.

IDREF

A datatype that is equivalent to the IDREF attribute type as defined in the XML 1.0 recommendation (see also Chapter 9). The value of the IDREF string must match the value of an element or attribute of type ID, somewhere within the same document instance. This datatype is not ordered.

The lexical representation of this datatype is any NCName string (name without colon), as defined in *Namespaces in XML*. For example:

```
<an_element codename="AGENT_ID_007" />
```

Built-in derived type is: IDREFS.

For compatibility with XML 1.0 DTDs, this datatype should only be used for attributes.

ENTITY

A datatype that's equivalent to the ENTITY attribute type as defined in the XML 1.0 recommendation (see also Chapter 11), with a value space that's scoped to a specific document instance. The ENTITY value must match an unparsed entity name that's declared in the schema. This datatype is not ordered.

The lexical representation of this datatype is any NCName string (name without colon), as defined in *Namespaces in XML*.

Built-in derived type: ENTITIES.

For compatibility with XML 1.0 DTDs, this datatype should only be used for attributes.

NOTATION

A datatype that's equivalent to the NOTATION attribute type as defined in the XML 1.0 recommendation (see also Chapter 11), with a value space that is scoped to a specific document instance. The NOTATION value must match a notation name that is declared in the schema. This datatype is not ordered.

The lexical representation of this datatype is any NCName string (name without colon), as defined in *Namespaces in XML*.

There are no built-in derived types.

For compatibility with XML 1.0 DTDs, this datatype should only be used for attributes.

QName

A qualified name, as defined in **Namespaces in XML**. Each qualified name is comprised of a pair of names, separated by the namespace delimiter (:) character, the namespace name (which is a uriReference), and the local name (which is an NCName). This datatype is not ordered.

The lexical representation of this datatype is any legal QName string (name with qualifier). For example:

```
<a_ns_name:an_element_name> .. </a_ns_name:an_element_name>
```

There are no built-in derived types.

Constraining Facets for Primitive Types

The usable constraining facets for each of the 14 primitive datatypes are:

	length	min Length /max Length	pattern	enumeration	min/max Exclusive/ Inclusive	scale, precision	encoding	duration, period
string	X	X	X	X	X			
boolean				X				
float			X	X	X			
double			X	X	X			
decimal			X	X	X	X		
timeDuration			X	X	X			
recurringDuration			X	X	X			**X** (*req*)
binary	X	X	X	X			**X** (*req*)	
uriReference	X	X	X	X				
ID	X	X	X	X	X			
IDREF	X	X	X	X	X			
ENTITY	X	X	X	X	X			
NOTATION	X	X	X	X	X			
QName	X	X	X	X	X			

Those facets labeled "(req)" are always required for any derived types based on this base datatype.

Built-in Derived Types

The following are the derived datatypes that are built-in to XML Schema:

- ❑ CDATA - representing white space normalized strings
- ❑ Token - represents tokenized strings
- ❑ language – a natural language identifier, as defined by RFC 1766
- ❑ NMTOKEN, NMTOKENS - represent NMTOKEN and NMTOKENS from the XML 1.0 recommendation (2nd ed)
- ❑ ENTITIES - represent the ENTITIES attribute type from the XML 1.0 recommendation (2nd ed)
- ❑ IDREFS - represent the IDREFS attribute type from the XML 1.0 recommendation (2nd ed)
- ❑ Name – a legal XML 1.0 name
- ❑ NCName – a legal XML 1.0 "non-colonized" name, as defined in *Namespaces in XML*
- ❑ integer – an integer number
- ❑ negativeInteger – an integer number with a value < 0
- ❑ positiveInteger – an integer number with a value > 0
- ❑ nonNegativeInteger – an integer number with a value 0
- ❑ nonPositiveInteger – an integer number with a value 0
- ❑ byte – an integer number with a value in the range -128 to +127 (inclusive)
- ❑ short – an integer number with a value in the range -32,768 to +32,767 (inclusive)
- ❑ int – an integer number with a value in the range -2,147,483,648 to +2,147,483,647 (inclusive)
- ❑ long – an integer number with a value in the range -9,223,372,036,854,775,808 to +9,223,372,036,854,775,807 (inclusive)
- ❑ unsignedByte – a non-negative integer number with a value in the range 0 to +255 (inclusive)
- ❑ unsignedShort – a non-negative integer number with a value in the range 0 to +65,535 (inclusive)
- ❑ unsignedInt – a non-negative integer number with a value in the range: 0 to +4,294,967,295 (inclusive)
- ❑ unsignedLong – a non-negative integer number with a value in the range 0 to +18,446,744,073,709,551,615 (inclusive)
- ❑ year – a Gregorian calendar year
- ❑ month – a Gregorian calendar month
- ❑ century – a Gregorian calendar century (a year without the two rightmost digits)
- ❑ date – a Gregorian calendar date (a single day)
- ❑ recurringDate – a Gregorian calendar date that recurs once every year
- ❑ recurringDay – a Gregorian calendar date that recurs once every month
- ❑ time – an instant of time that recurs every day
- ❑ timeInstant – a specific instant in time
- ❑ timePeriod – a specific period of time with a given start and end

Let's look at examples of some of these datatypes:

CDATA

CDATA represents white space normalized strings. CDATA value space is the set of strings that do not contain the characters:

- ❑ carriage-return (#xD)
- ❑ line-feed (#xA)
- ❑ tab (#x9)

CDATA lexical space is the set of strings that do not contain the characters:

- ❑ newline (#xD)
- ❑ tab (#x9)

The base type of CDATA is string, and the only datatype derived from it is TOKEN

token

token represents tokenized strings.

The value space is the string-set that do not contain the characters:

- ❑ line-feed (#xA)
- ❑ tab (#x9)
- ❑ leading or trailing spaces (#x20)

Also, they must not have any internal sequences of two or more spaces. The lexical space is the string-set that doesn't contain the characters:

- ❑ line-feed
- ❑ tab
- ❑ leading or trailing spaces

Also, they must not have any internal sequences of two or more spaces.

language, NMTOKEN and Name can be derived from this datatype

language

A natural language identifier, as defined by RFC 1766.

```
<LanguageOfOrigin>en-GB</LanguageOfOrigin>
<an_element xml:lang="en-US" > ... </an_element>
```

The first of these two examples shows an element that has its content constrained to be the language datatype. The second exploits a little-known attribute defined in the XML 1.0 REC, which uses the same type of values.

NMTOKEN, NMTOKENS

NMTOKEN represents the NMTOKEN attribute type from XML 1.0 (2nd ed). The value space and lexical space of NMTOKEN are the set of tokens, and set of strings (respectively) that match the NMTOKEN production in the above XML version. The base type of NMTOKEN is token.

The only datatype derived from NMTOKEN is NMTOKENS.

NMTOKENS represents the NMTOKENS attribute type from the above XML version The value space of NMTOKENS is the set of finite-length sequences of NMTOKENs. The lexical space of NMTOKENS is the set of white space separated tokens, each of which is in the lexical space of NMTOKEN.

The Itemtype of NMTOKENS is NMTOKEN.

For compatibility, NMTOKEN and NMTOKENS should be used only on attributes (as per terminology (§1.4)

ENTITIES

ENTITIES represents the ENTITIES from XML 1.0 (2nd ed), value space equal to the set of finite-length sequences declared as unparsed in a DTD (and is scoped to a specific instance document), and lexical space equal to the set of white space separated tokens in the lexical space of NMTOKEN.

The Itemtypeof ENTITIES is ENTITY.

For compatibility, ENTITIES should be used only on attributes, as per Terminology (§1.4)

IDREFS

IDREFS represents the IDREFS attribute type from XML 1.0 (2nd ed), with value space equal to the set of finite-length sequences of IDREFs that have been used in an XML document (and scoped to a specific instance document), and lexical space equal to the set of whitespace separated tokens, each of which is in the lexical space of IDREF.

The Itemtype of IDREFS is IDREF.

For compatibility, IDREFS should be used only on attributes, as per Terminology (§1.4)

name, NCName

Respectively a legal XML 1.0 name and a legal XML 1.0 "non-colonized" name, as defined in **Namespaces in XML.**

```
<somens:an_element_name> ... </somens:an_element_name>
<an_element_name> ... </an_element_name>
```

Both of the above examples are legal XML names that conform to the name datatype. The first is also a QName, i.e. a namespace-qualified name. The latter is a non-qualified ("non-colonized") name that conforms to the NCName datatype, a more restrictive version of name.

integer, negativeInteger, positiveInteger, nonNegativeInteger, nonPositiveInteger

These five datatypes are all integers, but negativeInteger, positiveInteger, nonNegativeInteger, nonPositiveInteger are constrained to specific (but open-ended) ranges of values. The difference between a negativeInteger and a nonPositiveInteger (or positiveInteger and nonNegativeInteger) is that the latter also includes zero in its value space.

byte, short, int, long

These four datatypes are all integer types, and are all constrained to finite ranges of values.

unsignedByte, unsignedShort, unsignedInt, unsignedLong

These four datatypes are all nonNegativeInteger types, and are also constrained to finite ranges of values (as shown in the above table).

century, year, month, date

These four datatypes are all derived from another derived datatype, the timePeriod type. They represent Gregorian calendar dates based upon the formats defined in §5.2.1 of ISO 8601, as shown in the following examples:

```
<Century>19</Century>
<Year>2525</Year>
<Month>08</Month>
<Date>31</Date>
```

Note that the names of the elements are also just examples – the correlation between these names and the datatype names is strictly illustrative. Dates in XML are always represented using numbers, in the form "YYYY-MM-DD", where "YYYY" is the year, "MM" is the month, and "DD" is the day of the month. This minimizes any confusion based upon language or cultural differences.

The century datatype is used to represent the leftmost digits of the year (underlined in the preceding format example). It is important to note that this is not the commonly used ordinal century (e.g. the 1900s were known as the "20th century" – strictly speaking this century was the years 1901-2000, since there is no year 0 in the Gregorian calendar). Rather, a century is the two (or more) leftmost digits of a year, up to and including the hundreds digits ("19" is the century of the year "1999").

A year or century may be preceded by a minus sign (-) to indicate years BCE (Before Common Era). Additional digits may be added to the left of these to represent years before -9999 BCE and after 9999 CE.

recurringDate, recurringDay

These two datatypes are derived from the recurringDuration primitive type. The former must always be represented in the truncated date form of "--MM-DD", the latter as "---DD".

```
<AnnualAppointment>--04-15</AnnualAppointment>
<MonthlyAppointment>---10</MonthlyAppointment>
```

The above examples show the date/day of two different appointments: the first on the 15th of April, the second on the 10th of every month.

time, timeInstant, timePeriod

These three datatypes are derived from the `recurringDuration` primitive type. The first two use similar formats. A `time` always uses the 24-hour clock in the form "HH:MM:SS.SSS HH:MM", where "HH" is hours (0-24), "MM" is minutes, "SS.SSS" is seconds. The fractional seconds and the decimal point are optional, as is the " HH:MM", which is used to show the difference between local time zone and UTZ (also known as GMT). Data of the `timeInstant` type must always include the full date, as well as the time-of-day.

```
<TheTimeNowIs>20:14:57+07:00</TheTimeNowIs>
<ThisInstantIs>2000-05-28T20:14:57+07:00</ThisInstantIs>
<Duration>P12Y10M2DT0H40M27.87S</Duration>
```

The `timePeriod` type uses same representation as its base type, `recurringDuration`. See its definition in the **Primitive Types** section above (the above example uses the same value as the examples in that section, only this time it's shown as the content of an element rather than the value of an attribute).

Constraining Facets for Derived Types

The usable constraining facets for each of the built-in derived datatypes are:

	length	min Length /max Length	pattern	enumeration	min/max Exclusive/ Inclusive	scale, precision	duration, period
CDATA	X	X	X	X			
token	X	X	X	X			
language	X	X	X	X	X		
Name	X	X	X	X	X		
NCName	X	X	X	X	X		
integer			X	X	X	X	
negativeInteger			X	X	X	X	
positiveInteger			X	X	X	X	
nonNegativeInteger			X	X	X	X	
nonPositiveInteger			X	X	X	X	
byte			X	X	X	X	
short			X	X	X	X	

	length	min Length /max Length	pattern	enumeration	min/max Exclusive/ Inclusive	scale, precision	duration, period
long			X	X	X	X	
int			X	X	X	X	
unsignedByte			X	X	X	X	
unsignedShort			X	X	X	X	
unsignedLong			X	X	X	X	
unsignedInt			X	X	X	X	
year			X	X	X		X
month			X	X	X		X
century			X	X	X		X
date			X	X	X		X
recurringDate			X	X	X		X
recurringDay			X	X	X		X
time			X	X	X		X
timeInstant			X	X	X		X
timePeriod			X	X	X		X
IDREFS	X	X		X			
NMTOKEN	X	X	X	X	X		
NMTOKENS	X	X		X			
ENTITIES	X	X		X			

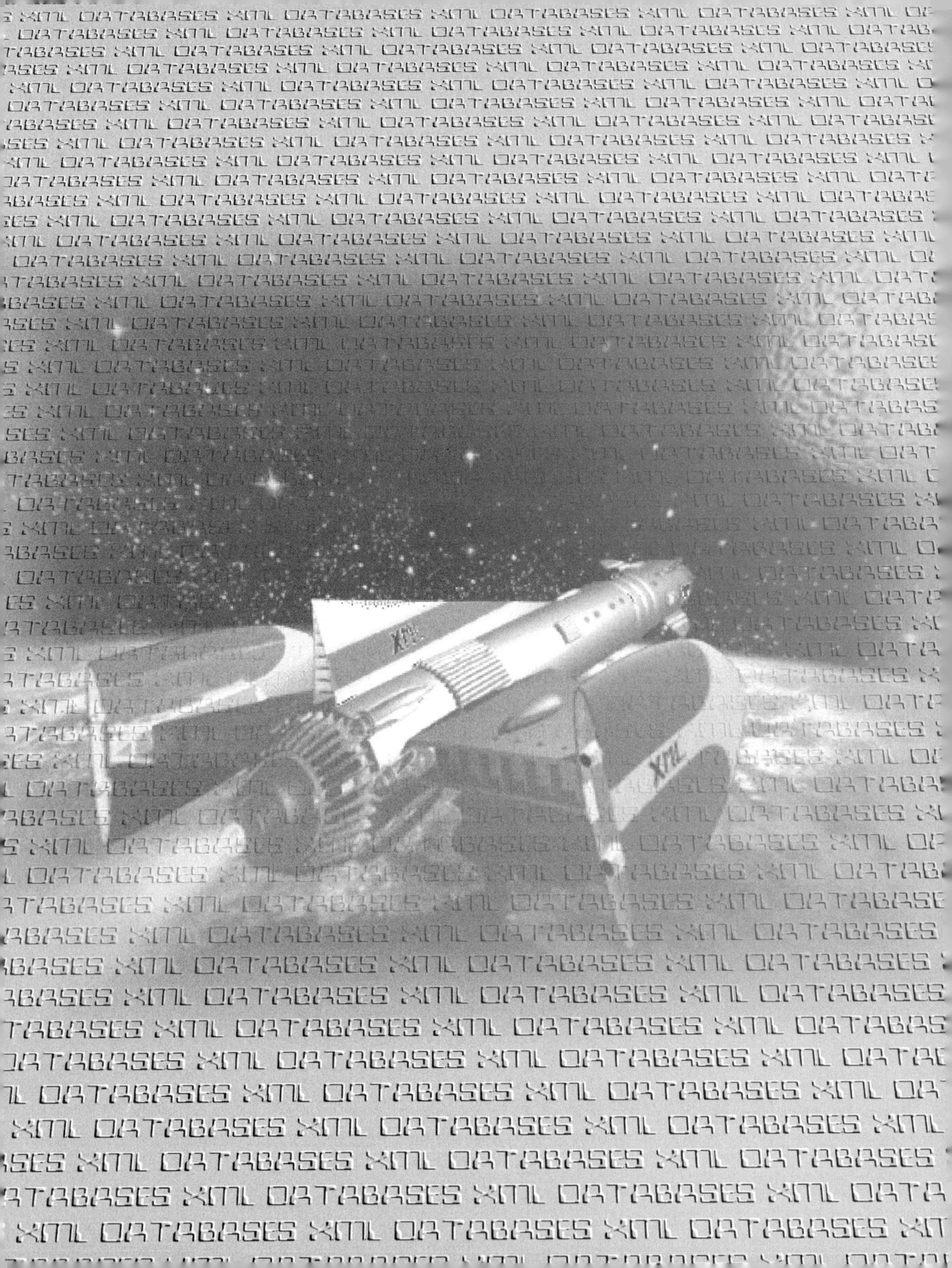
XML DATABASES

D

SAX 2.0: The Simple API for XML

This appendix contains the specification of the SAX interface, version 2.0, much of which is explained in Chapter 7. It is taken largely verbatim from the definitive specification to be found on `http://www.megginson.com/SAX/index.html`, with editorial comments added in italics.

The classes and interfaces are described in alphabetical order. Within each class, the methods are also listed alphabetically.

The SAX specification is in the public domain: see the web site quoted above for a statement of policy on copyright. Essentially the policy is: do what you like with it, copy it as you wish, but no-one accepts any liability for errors or omissions.

The SAX distribution also includes two other "helper classes":

- ❏ `LocatorImpl` is an implementation of the `Locator` interface
- ❏ `ParserFactory` is a class that enables you to load a parser identified by a parameter at run-time

The documentation of these helper classes is not included here. For this, and for SAX sample applications, see the SAX distribution available from `http://www.megginson.com`.

SAX2 contains complete Namespace support, which is available by default from any XMLReader. An XML reader can also optionally supply raw XML 1.0 names.

An XML reader is fully configurable: it is possible to attempt to query or change the current value of any feature or property. Features and properties are identified by fully-qualified URIs, and parties are free to invent their own names for new extensions.

The ContentHandler and Attributes interfaces are similar to the deprecated DocumentHandler and AttributeList interfaces, but they add support for Namespace-related information. ContentHandler also adds a callback for skipped entities, and Attributes adds the ability to look up an attribute's index by name.

The following interfaces have been deprecated:

❑   org.xml.sax.Parser

❑   org.xml.sax.DocumentHandler

❑   org.xml.sax.AttributeList

❑   org.xml.sax.HandlerBase

The following interfaces and classes have been added to SAX2:

❑   org.xml.sax.XMLReader (replaces Parser)

❑   org.xml.sax.XMLFilter

❑   org.xml.sax.ContentHandler (replaces DocumentHandler)

❑   org.xml.sax.Attributes (replaces AttributeList)

❑   org.xml.sax.SAXNotSupportedException

❑   org.xml.sax.SAXNotRecognizedException

Class Hierarchy

```
class java.lang.Object
     class org.xml.sax.HandlerBase
          (implements org.xml.sax.DocumentHandler,
                      org.xml.sax.DTDHandler,
                      org.xml.sax.EntityResolver,
                      org.xml.sax.ErrorHandler)
     class org.xml.sax.InputSource
     class java.lang.Throwable
          (implements java.io.Serializable)
     class java.lang.Exception
          class org.xml.sax.SAXException
               class org.xml.sax.SAXNotRecognizedException
               class org.xml.sax.SAXNotSupportedException
               class org.xml.sax.SAXParseException
```

Interface Hierarchy

```
class java.lang.Object
        interface org.xml.sax.AttributeList
        class org.xml.sax.helpers.AttributeListImpl
                (implements org.xml.sax.AttributeList)
        interface org.xml.sax.DTDHandler
        interface org.xml.sax.DocumentHandler
        interface org.xml.sax.EntityResolver
        interface org.xml.sax.ErrorHandler
        class org.xml.sax.HandlerBase
                (implements org.xml.EntityResolver,
                            org.xml.sax.DTDHandler,
                            org.xml.sax.DocumentHandler,
                            org.xml.sax.ErrorHandler)
        class org.xml.sax.InputSource
        interface org.xml.sax.Locator
        class org.xml.sax.helpers.LocatorsImp
                (implements org.xml.sax.Locator)
        interface org.xml.sax.Parser
        class org.xml.sax.helpers.ParserFactory
        class java.lang.Throwable
                (implements java.io.Serializable)
        class java.lang.Exception
                class org.xml.sax.SAXExeception
                        class org.xml.sax.SAXParseException
```

The diagram above shows the class hierarchy of SAX 1.0. We covered many of these classes in Chapter 7, although some were left out as they are outside of the scope of what you will most likely need to know. However, this appendix covers them all, and further details can be found at the SAX web site.

org.xml.sax.Attributes (SAX 2 Replaces AttributeList)

Interface for a list of XML attributes - This interface allows access to a list of attributes in three different ways:

- ❏ By attribute index
- ❏ By Namespace-qualified name
- ❏ By qualified (prefixed) name.

The list will not contain attributes that were declared #IMPLIED but not specified in the start tag. It will also not contain attributes used as Namespace declarations (xmlns*) unless the `http://xml.org/sax/features/namespace-prefixes` feature is set to *true* (it is *false* by default).

If the namespace-prefixes feature (see above) is *false*, access by qualified name may not be available; if the `http://xml.org/sax/features/namespaces` feature is *false*, access by Namespace-qualified names may not be available.

This interface replaces the now-deprecated SAX1 AttributeList interface, which does not contain Namespace support. In addition to Namespace support, it adds the *getIndex* methods (below).

The order of attributes in the list is unspecified, and will vary from implementation to implementation.

getLength	Return the number of attributes in the list.
public int getLength()	Once you know the number of attributes, you can iterate through the list. **Returns:** The number of attributes in the list.
getURI	Look up an attribute's Namespace URI by index.
public String getURI(int index)	**Parameters** index - The attribute index (zero-based). **Returns:** The Namespace URI, or the empty string if none is available, or null if the index is out of range.
getLocalName	Look up an attribute's local name by index.

public String
    getLocalName(
    int index)
	Parameters
	index - The attribute index (zero-based).
	
	Returns:
	The local name, or the empty string if Namespace processing is not being performed, or null if the index is out of range.

getQName	Look up an attribute's XML 1.0 qualified name by index.
public String getQName(int index)	**Parameters** index - The attribute index (zero-based). **Returns:** The XML 1.0 qualified name, or the empty string if none is available, or null if the index is out of range.
getType	Look up an attribute's type by index.
public String getType(int index)	The attribute type is one of the strings "CDATA", "ID", "IDREF", "IDREFS", "NMTOKEN", "NMTOKENS", "ENTITY", "ENTITIES", or "NOTATION" (always in upper case). If the parser has not read a declaration for the attribute, or if the parser does not report attribute types, then it must return the value "CDATA" as stated in the XML 1.0 Recommmention (clause 3.3.3, "Attribute-Value Normalization"). For an enumerated attribute that is not a notation, the parser will report the type as "NMTOKEN". **Parameters** index - The attribute index (zero-based). **Returns:** The attribute's type as a string, or null if the index is out of range.

getValue public String getValue(int index)	Look up an attribute's value by index. If the attribute value is a list of tokens (IDREFS, ENTITIES, or NMTOKENS), the tokens will be concatenated into a single string with each token separated by a single space. **Parameters** index - The attribute index (zero-based). **Returns:** The attribute's value as a string, or null if the index is out of range.

getIndex
 	
public int getIndex(
    String uri,
    String localPart)
	Look up the index of an attribute by Namespace name.
	
	Parameters
	uri - The Namespace URI, or the empty string if the name has no Namespace URI.
	localName - The attribute's local name.
	
	Returns:
	The index of the attribute, or -1 if it does not appear in the list.

getIndex public int getIndex(String qName)	Look up the index of an attribute by XML 1.0 qualified name. **Parameters** qName - The qualified (prefixed) name. **Returns:** The index of the attribute, or -1 if it does not appear in the list.

getType
 	
public String getType(
    String uri,
    String localName)
	Look up an attribute's type by Namespace name.
	
	See getType(int) for a description of the possible types.
	
	Parameters
	uri - The Namespace URI, or the empty String if the name has no Namespace URI.
	localName - The local name of the attribute.
	
	Returns:
	The attribute type as a string, or null if the attribute is not in the list or if Namespace processing is not being performed.

getType public String getType(String qName)	Look up an attribute's type by XML 1.0 qualified name. See getType(int) for a description of the possible types. **Parameters** qName - The XML 1.0 qualified name. **Returns:** The attribute type as a string, or null if the attribute is not in the list or if qualified names are not available.

Table continued on following page

getValue	Look up an attribute's value by Namespace name.

public String getValue(
    String uri,
    String localName)
	See getValue(int) for a description of the possible values.
	
	Parameters
	uri - The Namespace URI, or the empty String if the name has no Namespace URI.
	localName - The local name of the attribute.
	
	Returns:
	The attribute value as a string, or null if the attribute is not in the list.

getValue	Look up an attribute's value by XML 1.0 qualified name.
public String getValue(String qName)	See getValue(int) for a description of the possible values. **Parameters** qName - The XML 1.0 qualified name. **Returns:** The attribute value as a string, or null if the attribute is not in the list or if qualified names are not available.

Interface org.xml.sax.AttributeList – Deprecated

An AttributeList is a collection of attributes appearing on a particular start tag. The Parser supplies the DocumentHandler with an AttributeList as part of the information available on the startElement event. The AttributeList is essentially a set of name-value pairs for the supplied attributes; if the parser has analyzed the DTD it may also provide information about the type of each attribute.

Interface for an element's attribute specifications

The SAX parser implements this interface and passes an instance to the SAX application as the second argument of each startElement event.

The instance provided will return valid results only during the scope of the startElement invocation (to save it for future use, the application must make a copy: the AttributeListImpl helper class provides a convenient constructor for doing so).

An AttributeList includes only attributes that have been specified or defaulted: #IMPLIED attributes will not be included.

There are two ways for the SAX application to obtain information from the AttributeList. First, it can iterate through the entire list:

```
public void startElement (String name, AttributeList atts) {
  for (int i = 0; i < atts.getLength(); i++) {
    String name = atts.getName(i);
    String type = atts.getType(i);
    String value = atts.getValue(i);
    [...]
  }
}
```

(Note that the result of getLength() will be zero if there are no attributes.)

As an alternative, the application can request the value or type of specific attributes:

```
public void startElement (String name, AttributeList atts) {
   String identifier = atts.getValue("id");
   String label = atts.getValue("label");
   [...]
}
```

The `AttributeListImpl` helper class provides a convenience implementation for use by parser or application writers.

getLength public int getLength()	Return the number of attributes in this list. The SAX parser may provide attributes in any arbitrary order, regardless of the order in which they were declared or specified. The number of attributes may be zero. **Returns:** The number of attributes in the list.
getName public String getName(int index)	Return the name of an attribute in this list (by position). The names must be unique: the SAX parser shall not include the same attribute twice. Attributes without values (those declared #IMPLIED without a value specified in the start tag) will be omitted from the list. If the attribute name has a namespace prefix, the prefix will still be attached. **Parameters:** index - The index of the attribute in the list (starting at 0). **Returns:** The name of the indexed attribute, or null if the index is out of range.
getType public String getType(int index)	Return the type of an attribute in the list (by position). The attribute type is one of the strings "CDATA", "ID", "IDREF", "IDREFS", "NMTOKEN", "NMTOKENS", "ENTITY", "ENTITIES", or "NOTATION" (always in upper case). If the parser has not read a declaration for the attribute, or if the parser does not report attribute types, then it must return the value "CDATA" as stated in the XML 1.0 Recommendation (clause 3.3.3, "Attribute-Value Normalization"). For an enumerated attribute that is not a notation, the parser will report the type as "NMTOKEN". **Parameters:** index - The index of the attribute in the list (starting at 0). **Returns:** The attribute type as a string, or null if the index is out of range.

Table continued on following page

getType public String getType(String name)	Return the type of an attribute in the list (by name). The return value is the same as the return value for `getType(int)`. If the attribute name has a namespace prefix in the document, the application must include the prefix here. **Parameters:** name - The name of the attribute. **Returns:** The attribute type as a string, or null if no such attribute exists.

getValue public String getValue(int index)	Return the value of an attribute in the list (by position). If the attribute value is a list of tokens (IDREFS, ENTITIES, or NMTOKENS), the tokens will be concatenated into a single string separated by whitespace. **Parameters:** index - The index of the attribute in the list (starting at 0). **Returns:** The attribute value as a string, or null if the index is out of range.
getValue public String getValue(String name)	Return the value of an attribute in the list (by name). The return value is the same as the return value for `getValue(int)`. If the attribute name has a namespace prefix in the document, the application must include the prefix here. **Parameters:** name - The name of the attribute. **Returns:** The attribute value as a string, or null if no such attribute exists.

Interface org.xml.sax.ContentHandler (SAX 2 Replaces DocumentHandler)

Every SAX application is likely to include a class that implements this interface, either directly or by subclassing the supplied class `HandlerBase`.

Receive notification of general document events.

Receive notification of the logical content of a document - this is the main interface that most SAX applications implement: if the application needs to be informed of basic parsing events, it implements this interface and registers an instance with the SAX parser using the `setContentHandler` method. The parser uses the instance to report basic document-related events like the start and end of elements and character data.

The order of events in this interface is very important, and mirrors the order of information in the document itself. For example, all of an element's content (character data, processing instructions, and/or subelements) will appear, in order, between the `startElement` event and the corresponding `endElement` event.

This interface is similar to the now-deprecated SAX 1.0 `DocumentHandler` interface, but it adds support for Namespaces and for reporting skipped entities (in non-validating XML processors).

Implementors should note that there is also a Java class `ContentHandler` in the java.net package; that means that it's probably a bad idea to do the following (more like a feature than a bug anyway, as `import … *` is a sign of bad programming):

```
import java.net.*; import org.xml.sax.*;
```

| **setDocumentLocator**

public void
setDocumentLocator (
    Locator locator) | Receive an object for locating the origin of SAX document events.

SAX parsers are strongly encouraged (though not absolutely required) to supply a locator: if it does so, it must supply the locator to the application by invoking this method before invoking any of the other methods in the ContentHandler interface.

The locator allows the application to determine the end position of any document-related event, even if the parser is not reporting an error. Typically, the application will use this information for reporting its own errors (such as character content that does not match an application's business rules). The information returned by the locator is probably not sufficient for use with a search engine.

Note that the locator will return correct information only during the invocation of the events in this interface. The application should not attempt to use it at any other time.

Parameters
`locator` - An object that can return the location of any SAX document event. |

Table Continued on Following Page

startDocument public void startDocument()	Receive notification of the beginning of a document. The SAX parser will invoke this method only once, before any other methods in this interface or in DTDHandler (except for setDocumentLocator). **Throws:** SAXException- Any SAX exception, possibly wrapping another exception.
endDocument public void endDocument()	Receive notification of the end of a document. The SAX parser will invoke this method only once, and it will be the last method invoked during the parse. The parser shall not invoke this method until it has either abandoned parsing (because of an unrecoverable error) or reached the end of input. **Throws:** SAXException - Any SAX exception, possibly wrapping another exception.

startPrefixMapping
 	
public void
startPrefixMapping (
    String prefix,
    String uri)
	Begin the scope of a prefix-URI Namespace mapping.
	
	The information from this event is not necessary for normal Namespace processing: the SAX XML reader will automatically replace prefixes for element and attribute names when the http://xml.org/sax/features/namespaces feature is *true* (the default).
	
	There are cases, however, when applications need to use prefixes in character data or in attribute values, where they cannot safely be expanded automatically; the start/endPrefixMapping event supplies the information to the application to expand prefixes in those contexts itself, if necessary.
	
	Note that start/endPrefixMapping events are not guaranteed to be properly nested relative to each-other: all startPrefixMapping events will occur before the corresponding startElement event, and all endPrefixMapping events will occur after the corresponding endElement event, but their order is not otherwise guaranteed.
	
	There should never be start/endPrefixMapping events for the "xml" prefix, since it is predeclared and immutable.
	
	Parameters
	prefix - The Namespace prefix being declared.
	uri - The Namespace URI the prefix is mapped to.
	
	Throws:
	SAXException - The client may throw an exception during processing.

endPrefixMapping public void endPrefixMapping (String prefix)	End the scope of a prefix-URI mapping. See startPrefixMapping for details. This event will always occur after the corresponding endElement event, but the order of endPrefixMapping events is not otherwise guaranteed. **Parameters** prefix - The prefix that was being mapping. **Throws:** SAXException - The client may throw an exception during processing.

startElement
 	
public void startElement(
    String namespaceURI,
    String localName,
    String qName,
    Attributes atts)
	Receive notification of the beginning of an element.
	
	The Parser will invoke this method at the beginning of every element in the XML document; there will be a corresponding endElement event for every startElement event (even when the element is empty). All of the element's content will be reported, in order, before the corresponding endElement event.
	
	This event allows up to three name components for each element:
	
	    the Namespace URI;
	    the local name; and
	    the qualified (prefixed) name.
	
	Any or all of these may be provided, depending on the values of the *http://xml.org/sax/features/namespaces* and the *http://xml.org/sax/features/namespace-prefixes* properties:
	
	    The Namespace URI and local name are required when the namespaces property is *true* (the default), and are optional when the namespaces property is *false* (if one is specified, both must be)
	
	    The qualified name is required when the namespace-prefixes property is *true*, and is optional when the namespace-prefixes property is *false* (the default).
	
	Note that the attribute list provided will contain only attributes with explicit values (specified or defaulted): #IMPLIED attributes will be omitted. The attribute list will contain attributes used for Namespace declarations (xmlns* attributes) only if the http://xml.org/sax/features/namespace-prefixes property is true (it is false by default, and support for a true value is optional).

Table continued on following page

startElement (continued)	**Parameters** uri - The Namespace URI, or the empty string if the element has no Namespace URI or if Namespace processing is not being performed. localName - The local name (without prefix), or the empty string if Namespace processing is not being performed. qName - The qualified name (with prefix), or the empty string if qualified names are not available. atts - The attributes attached to the element. If there are no attributes, it shall be an empty Attributes object. **Throws:** SAXException- Any SAX exception, possibly wrapping another exception.
endElement	Receive notification of the end of an element.

public void endElement(
    String namespaceURI,
    String localName,
    String qName)
	The SAX parser will invoke this method at the end of every element in the XML document; there will be a corresponding startElement event for every endElement event (even when the element is empty).
	
	For information on the names, see startElement.
	
	Parameters
	uri - The Namespace URI, or the empty string if the element has no Namespace URI or if Namespace processing is not being performed.
	localName - The local name (without prefix), or the empty string if Namespace processing is not being performed.
	qName - The qualified XML 1.0 name (with prefix), or the empty string if qualified names are not available.
	
	Throws:
	SAXException - Any SAX exception, possibly wrapping another exception.

characters	Receive notification of character data.
public void characters (char[] ch, int start, int length)	The Parser will call this method to report each chunk of character data. SAX parsers may return all contiguous character data in a single chunk, or they may split it into several chunks; however, all of the characters in any single event must come from the same external entity so that the Locator provides useful information. The application must not attempt to read from the array outside of the specified range. Note that some parsers will report whitespace in element content using the ignorableWhitespace method rather than this one (validating parsers *must* do so).

characters (continued)	**Parameters** ch - The characters from the XML document. start - The start position in the array. length - The number of characters to read from the array. **Throws:** SAXException - Any SAX exception, possibly wrapping another exception.

ignorableWhitespace
 	
public void
ignorableWhitespace (
    char[] ch, int start,
    int length)
	Receive notification of ignorable whitespace in element content.
	
	Validating Parsers must use this method to report each chunk of whitespace in element content (see the W3C XML 1.0 recommendation, section 2.10): non-validating parsers may also use this method if they are capable of parsing and using content models.
	
	SAX parsers may return all contiguous whitespace in a single chunk, or they may split it into several chunks; however, all of the characters in any single event must come from the same external entity, so that the Locator provides useful information.
	
	The application must not attempt to read from the array outside of the specified range.
	
	Parameters
	ch - The characters from the XML document.
	start - The start position in the array.
	length - The number of characters to read from the array.
	
	Throws:
	SAXException - Any SAX exception, possibly wrapping another exception.

processingInstruction
 	
public void
processingInstruction (
    String target,
    String data)
	Receive notification of a processing instruction.
	
	The Parser will invoke this method once for each processing instruction found: note that processing instructions may occur before or after the main document element.
	
	A SAX parser must never report an XML declaration (XML 1.0, section 2.8) or a text declaration (XML 1.0, section 4.3.1) using this method.
	
	Parameters
	target - The processing instruction target.
	data - The processing instruction data, or null if none was supplied. The data does not include any whitespace separating it from the target.
	
	Throws:
	SAXException - Any SAX exception, possibly wrapping another exception.

skippedEntity	Receive notification of a skipped entity.
public void skippedEntity (String name)	The Parser will invoke this method once for each entity skipped. Non-validating processors may skip entities if they have not seen the declarations (because, for example, the entity was declared in an external DTD subset). All processors may skip external entities, depending on the values of the `http://xml.org/sax/features/external-general-entities` and the `http://xml.org/sax/features/external-parameter-entities` properties.
	Parameters name - The name of the skipped entity. If it is a parameter entity, the name will begin with '%', and if it is the external DTD subset, it will be the string "[dtd]".
	Throws: SAXException - Any SAX exception, possibly wrapping another exception.

Interface org.xml.sax.DocumentHandler – Deprecated

Every SAX application is likely to include a class that implements this interface, either directly or by subclassing the supplied class `HandlerBase`. See Chapter 6 for a full discussion of the various methods.

Receive notification of general document events

This is the main interface that most SAX applications implement: if the application needs to be informed of basic parsing events, it implements this interface and registers an instance with the SAX parser using the setDocumentHandler method. The parser uses the instance to report basic document-related events like the start and end of elements and character data.

The order of events in this interface is very important, and mirrors the order of information in the document itself. For example, all of an element's content (character data, processing instructions, and/or subelements) will appear, in order, between the startElement event and the corresponding endElement event.

Application writers who do not want to implement the entire interface can derive a class from HandlerBase, which implements the default functionality; parser writers can instantiate HandlerBase to obtain a default handler. The application can find the location of any document event using the Locator interface supplied by the Parser through the setDocumentLocator method.

characters	Receive notification of character data.
public void characters(char ch[], int start, int length) throws SAXException	The Parser will call this method to report each chunk of character data. SAX parsers may return all contiguous character data in a single chunk, or they may split it into several chunks; however, all of the characters in any single event must come from the same external entity, so that the Locator provides useful information.
	The application must not attempt to read from the array outside of the specified range *and must not attempt to write to the array*.
	Note that some parsers will report whitespace using the ignorableWhitespace() method rather than this one (validating parsers must do so).
	Parameters:
	ch - The characters from the XML document.
	start - The start position in the array.
	length - The number of characters to read from the array.
	Throws: SAXException
	Any SAX exception, possibly wrapping another exception.
endDocument	Receive notification of the end of a document.
public void endDocument() throws SAXException	The SAX parser will invoke this method only once *for each document*, and it will be the last method invoked during the parse. The parser shall not invoke this method until it has either abandoned parsing (because of an unrecoverable error) or reached the end of input.
	Throws: SAXException
	Any SAX exception, possibly wrapping another exception.

Table continued on following page

endElement

public void endElement(

String name)

throws SAXException

Receive notification of the end of an element.

The SAX parser will invoke this method at the end of every element in the XML document; there will be a corresponding startElement() event for every endElement() event (even when the element is empty).

If the element name has a namespace prefix, the prefix will still be attached to the name.

Parameters:

name - The element type name.

Throws: SAXException

Any SAX exception, possibly wrapping another exception.

ignorableWhitespace

public void
ignorableWhitespace (

char ch[],
int start,
int length)

throws SAXException

Receive notification of ignorable whitespace in element content.

Validating parsers must use this method to report each chunk of ignorable whitespace (see the W3C XML 1.0 recommendation, section 2.10): non-validating parsers may also use this method if they are capable of parsing and using content models.

SAX parsers may return all contiguous whitespace in a single chunk, or they may split it into several chunks; however, all of the characters in any single event must come from the same external entity, so that the Locator provides useful information.

The application must not attempt to read from the array outside of the specified range.

Parameters:

ch - The characters from the XML document.

start - The start position in the array.

length - The number of characters to read from the array.

Throws: SAXException

Any SAX exception, possibly wrapping another exception.

processingInstruction	Receive notification of a processing instruction.
public void processingInstruction(String target, String data) throws SAXException	The parser will invoke this method once for each processing instruction found: note that processing instructions may occur before or after the main document element.
	A SAX parser should never report an XML declaration (XML 1.0, section 2.8) or a text declaration (XML 1.0, section 4.3.1) using this method.
	Parameters:
	target - The processing instruction target.
	data - The processing instruction data, or null if none was supplied.
	Throws: SAXException
	Any SAX exception, possibly wrapping another exception.
setDocumentLocator	Receive an object for locating the origin of SAX document events.
public void setDocumentLocator (Locator locator)	A SAX parser is strongly encouraged (though not absolutely required) to supply a Locator: if it does so, it must supply the Locator to the application by invoking this method before invoking any of the other methods in the `DocumentHandler` interface.
	The Locator allows the application to determine the end position of any document-related event, even if the parser is not reporting an error. Typically, the application will use this information for reporting its own errors (such as character content that does not match an application's business rules). The information returned by the locator is probably not sufficient for use with a search engine.
	Note that the locator will return correct information only during the invocation of the events in this interface. The application should not attempt to use it at any other time.
	Parameters:
	locator - An object that can return the location of any SAX document event.

Table continued on following page

startDocument	Receive notification of the beginning of a document.
public void startDocument() throws SAXException	The SAX parser will invoke this method only once *for each document*, before any other methods in this interface or in `DTDHandler` (except for `setDocumentLocator`). **Throws**: SAXException Any SAX exception, possibly wrapping another exception.
startElement	Receive notification of the beginning of an element.
public void startElement (String name, AttributeList atts) throws SAXException	The parser will invoke this method at the beginning of every element in the XML document; there will be a corresponding `endElement()` event for every `startElement()` event (even when the element is empty). All of the element's content will be reported, in order, before the corresponding `endElement()` event. If the element name has a namespace prefix, the prefix will still be attached. Note that the attribute list provided will contain only attributes with explicit values (specified or defaulted): #IMPLIED attributes will be omitted. **Parameters:** name - The element type name. atts - The attributes attached to the element, if any. **Throws:** SAXException Any SAX exception, possibly wrapping another exception.

Interface org.xml.sax.DTDHandler

This interface should be implemented by the application, if it wants to receive notification of events related to the DTD. SAX does not provide full details of the DTD, but this interface is available because without it, it would be impossible to access notations and unparsed entities referenced in the body of the document.

Notations and unparsed entities are rather specialized facilities in XML, so most SAX applications will not need to use this interface.

Receive notification of basic DTD-related events

If a SAX application needs information about notations and unparsed entities, then the application implements this interface and registers an instance with the SAX parser using the parser's setDTDHandler method. The parser uses the instance to report notation and unparsed entity declarations to the application.

The SAX parser may report these events in any order, regardless of the order in which the notations and unparsed entities were declared; however, all DTD events must be reported after the document handler's startDocument event, and before the first startElement event.

It is up to the application to store the information for future use (perhaps in a hash table or object tree). If the application encounters attributes of type "NOTATION", "ENTITY", or "ENTITIES", it can use the information that it obtained through this interface to find the entity and/or notation corresponding with the attribute value.

The HandlerBase class provides a default implementation of this interface, which simply ignores the events.

notationDecl	Receive notification of a notation declaration event.
public void notationDecl (	
String name, String publicId, String systemId)	It is up to the application to record the notation for later reference, if necessary.
throws SAXException	
	If a system identifier is present, and it is a URL, the SAX parser must resolve it fully before passing it to the application.
	Parameters:
	name - The notation name.
	publicId - The notation's public identifier, or null if none was given.
	systemId - The notation's system identifier, or null if none was given.
	Throws: SAXException
	Any SAX exception, possibly wrapping another exception.

Table continued on following page

unparsedEntityDecl
 	
public void unparsedEntityDecl (
    String name,
 	
    String publicId,
 	
    String systemId,
 	
    String notationName)
 	
throws SAXException
	Receive notification of an unparsed entity declaration event.
	
	Note that the notation name corresponds to a notation reported by the `notationDecl()` event. It is up to the application to record the entity for later reference, if necessary.
	
	If the system identifier is a URL, the parser must resolve it fully before passing it to the application.
	
	Parameters:
	
	name - The unparsed entity's name.
	
	publicId - The entity's public identifier, or null if none was given.
	
	systemId - The entity's system identifier (it must always have one).
	
	notationName - The name of the associated notation.
	
	Throws: SAXException
	
	Any SAX exception, possibly wrapping another exception.

Interface org.xml.sax.EntityResolver

When the XML document contains references to external entities, the URL will normally be analyzed automatically by the parser: the relevant file will be located and parsed where appropriate. This interface allows an application to override this behavior. This might be needed, for example, if you want to retrieve a different version of the entity from a local server, or if the entities are cached in memory or stored in a database, or if the entity is really a reference to variable information such as the current date.

When the parser needs to obtain an entity, it calls this interface, which can respond by supplying any `InputSource` *object.*

Basic interface for resolving entities

If a SAX application needs to implement customized handling for external entities, it must implement this interface and register an instance with the SAX parser using the parser's `setEntityResolver` method.

The parser will then allow the application to intercept any external entities (including the external DTD subset and external parameter entities, if any) before including them.

Many SAX applications will not need to implement this interface, but it will be especially useful for applications that build XML documents from databases or other specialized input sources, or for applications that use URI types other than URLs.

The following resolver would provide the application with a special character stream for the entity with the system identifier "http://www.myhost.com/today":

```java
import org.xml.sax.EntityResolver;
import org.xml.sax.InputSource;

public class MyResolver implements EntityResolver {
  public InputSource resolveEntity (String publicId, String systemId)
  {
    if (systemId.equals("http://www.myhost.com/today")) {
                              // return a special input source
      MyReader reader = new MyReader();
      return new InputSource(reader);
    } else {
                              // use the default behaviour
      return null;
    }
  }
}
```

The application can also use this interface to redirect system identifiers to local URIs or to look up replacements in a catalog (possibly by using the public identifier).

The HandlerBase class implements the default behavior for this interface, which is simply always to return null (to request that the parser use the default system identifier).

resolveEntity	Allow the application to resolve external entities.
public InputSource resolveEntity(	
String publicId,	The parser will call this method before opening any external entity except the top-level document entity (including the external DTD subset, external entities referenced within the DTD, and external entities referenced within the document element): the application may request that the parser resolve the entity itself, that it use an alternative URI, or that it use an entirely different input source.
String systemId)	
throws SAXException, IOException	
	Application writers can use this method to redirect external system identifiers to secure and/or local URIs, to look up public identifiers in a catalogue, or to read an entity from a database or other input source (including, for example, a dialog box).
	If the system identifier is a URL, the SAX parser must resolve it fully before reporting it to the application.
	Parameters:
	publicId - The public identifier of the external entity being referenced, or null if none was supplied.
	systemId - The system identifier of the external entity being referenced.
	Returns:
	An InputSource object describing the new input source, or null to request that the parser open a regular URI connection to the system identifier.
	Throws: SAXException
	Any SAX exception, possibly wrapping another exception.
	Throws: IOException
	A Java-specific IO exception, possibly the result of creating a new InputStream or Reader for the InputSource.

Interface org.xml.sax.ErrorHandler

You may implement this interface in your application if you want to take special action to handle errors. There is a default implementation provided within the HandlerBase *class.*

Basic interface for SAX error handlers

If a SAX application needs to implement customized error handling, it must implement this interface and then register an instance with the SAX parser using the parser's setErrorHandler method. The parser will then report all errors and warnings through this interface.

The parser shall use this interface instead of throwing an exception: it is up to the application whether to throw an exception for different types of errors and warnings. Note, however, that there is no requirement that the parser continue to provide useful information after a call to fatalError (in other words, a SAX driver class could catch an exception and report a fatalError).

The HandlerBase class provides a default implementation of this interface, ignoring warnings and recoverable errors and throwing a SAXParseException for fatal errors. An application may extend that class rather than implementing the complete interface itself.

error public void error(SAXParseException exception) throws SAXException	Receive notification of a recoverable error. This corresponds to the definition of "error" in section 1.2 of the W3C XML 1.0 Recommendation. For example, a validating parser would use this callback to report the violation of a validity constraint. The default behavior is to take no action. The SAX parser must continue to provide normal parsing events after invoking this method: it should still be possible for the application to process the document through to the end. If the application cannot do so, then the parser should report a fatal error even if the XML 1.0 recommendation does not require it to do so. **Parameters:** exception - The error information encapsulated in a SAX parse exception. **Throws:** SAXException Any SAX exception, possibly wrapping another exception.

Table continued on following page

fatalError

public void fatalError(

SAXParseException exception)

throws SAXException

Receive notification of a non-recoverable error.

This corresponds to the definition of "fatal error" in section 1.2 of the W3C XML 1.0 Recommendation. For example, a parser would use this callback to report the violation of a well-formedness constraint.

The application must assume that the document is unusable after the parser has invoked this method, and should continue (if at all) only for the sake of collecting additional error messages: in fact, SAX parsers are free to stop reporting any other events once this method has been invoked.

Parameters:

exception - The error information encapsulated in a SAX parse exception.

Throws: SAXException

Any SAX exception, possibly wrapping another exception.

warning

public void warning (

SAXParseException exception)

throws SAXException

Receive notification of a warning.

SAX parsers will use this method to report conditions that are not errors or fatal errors as defined by the XML 1.0 recommendation. The default behavior is to take no action.

The SAX parser must continue to provide normal parsing events after invoking this method: it should still be possible for the application to process the document through to the end.

Parameters:

exception - The warning information encapsulated in a SAX parse exception.

Throws: SAXException

Any SAX exception, possibly wrapping another exception.

Class org.xml.sax.HandlerBase – Deprecated

This class is supplied with SAX itself: it provides default implementations of most of the methods that would otherwise need to be implemented by the application. If you write classes in your application as subclasses of HandlerBase, *you need only code those methods where you want something other than the default behavior.*

Default base class for handlers

This class implements the default behavior for four SAX interfaces: EntityResolver, DTDHandler, DocumentHandler, and ErrorHandler.

Application writers can extend this class when they need to implement only part of an interface; parser writers can instantiate this class to provide default handlers when the application has not supplied its own.

Note that the use of this class is optional.

In the description below, only the behavior of each method is described. For the parameters and return values, see the corresponding interface definition.

characters
 	
public void characters(
 	
    char ch[],
 	
    int start,
 	
    int length)
 	
throws SAXException
	By default, do nothing. Application writers may override this method to take specific actions for each chunk of character data (such as adding the data to a node or buffer, or printing it to a file).

endDocument public void endDocument() throws SAXException	Receive notification of the end of the document. By default, do nothing. Application writers may override this method in a subclass to take specific actions at the beginning of a document (such as finalizing a tree or closing an output file).
endElement public void endElement(String name) throws SAXException	By default, do nothing. Application writers may override this method in a subclass to take specific actions at the end of each element (such as finalizing a tree node or writing output to a file).

Table continued on following page

error public void error(SAXParseException e) throws SAXException	The default implementation does nothing. Application writers may override this method in a subclass to take specific actions for each error, such as inserting the message in a log file or printing it to the console.
fatalError public void fatalError(SAXParseException e) throws SAXException	The default implementation throws a SAXParseException. Application writers may override this method in a subclass if they need to take specific actions for each fatal error (such as collecting all of the errors into a single report): in any case, the application must stop all regular processing when this method is invoked, since the document is no longer reliable, and the parser may no longer report parsing events.

ignorableWhitespace
 	
public void ignorableWhitespace(
 	
    char ch[],
 	
    int start,
 	
    int length)
 	
throws SAXException
	By default, do nothing. Application writers may override this method to take specific actions for each chunk of ignorable whitespace (such as adding data to a node or buffer, or printing it to a file).

notationDecl
 	
public void notationDecl(
 	
    String name,
 	
    String publicId,
 	
    String systemId)
	By default, do nothing. Application writers may override this method in a subclass if they wish to keep track of the notations declared in a document.

processingInstruction
 	
public void processingInstruction(
 	
    String target,
 	
    String data)
 	
throws SAXException
	By default, do nothing. Application writers may override this method in a subclass to take specific actions for each processing instruction, such as setting status variables or invoking other methods.

resolveEntity
 	
public InputSource resolveEntity(
 	
      String publicId,
 	
      String systemId)
 	
throws SAXException
	Always return null, so that the parser will use the system identifier provided in the XML document.
	
	This method implements the SAX default behavior: application writers can override it in a subclass to do special translations such as catalog lookups or URI redirection.

setDocumentLocator public void setDocumentLocator(Locator locator)	By default, do nothing. Application writers may override this method in a subclass if they wish to store the locator for use with other document events.
startDocument public void startDocument() throws SAXException	By default, do nothing. Application writers may override this method in a subclass to take specific actions at the beginning of a document (such as allocating the root node of a tree or creating an output file).

startElement
 	
public void startElement(
 	
      String name,
 	
      AttributeList attributes)
 	
throws SAXException
	By default, do nothing. Application writers may override this method in a subclass to take specific actions at the start of each element (such as allocating a new tree node or writing output to a file).

unparsedEntityDecl
 	
public void unparsedEntityDecl(
 	
      String name,
 	
      String publicId,
 	
      String systemId,
 	
      String notationName)
	By default, do nothing. Application writers may override this method in a subclass to keep track of the unparsed entities declared in a document.

warning public void warning(SAXParseException e) throws SAXException	The default implementation does nothing. Application writers may override this method in a subclass to take specific actions for each warning, such as inserting the message in a log file or printing it to the console.

Class org.xml.sax.InputSource

An InputSource *object represents a container for the XML document or any of the external entities it references (technically, the main document is itself an entity). The* InputSource *class is supplied with SAX: generally the application instantiates an* InputSource *and updates it to say where the input is coming from, and the parser interrogates it to find out where to read the input from.*

The InputSource *object provides three ways of supplying input to the parser: a System Identifier (or URL), a* Reader *(which delivers a stream of Unicode characters), or an* InputStream *(which delivers a stream of uninterpreted bytes).*

A single input source for an XML entity

This class allows a SAX application to encapsulate information about an input source in a single object, which may include a public identifier, a system identifier, a byte stream (possibly with a specified encoding), and/or a character stream.

There are two places that the application will deliver this input source to the parser: as the argument to the Parser.parse method, or as the return value of the EntityResolver.resolveEntity method.

The SAX parser will use the InputSource object to determine how to read XML input. If there is a character stream available, the parser will read that stream directly; if not, the parser will use a byte stream, if available; if neither a character stream nor a byte stream is available, the parser will attempt to open a URI connection to the resource identified by the system identifier.

An InputSource object belongs to the application: the SAX parser shall never modify it in any way (it may modify a copy if necessary).

If you supply input in the form of a Reader *or* InputStream, *it may be useful to supply a system identifier as well. If you do this, the URI will not be used to obtain the actual XML input, but it will be used in diagnostics, and more importantly to resolve any relative URIs within the document, for example entity references.*

InputSource public InputSource()	Zero-argument default constructor.
InputSource public InputSource(String systemId)	Create a new input source with a system identifier. Applications may use setPublicId to include a public identifier as well, or setEncoding to specify the character encoding, if known. If the system identifier is a URL, it must be fully resolved. **Parameters:** systemId - The system identifier (URI).

InputSource public InputSource(InputStream byteStream)	Create a new input source with a byte stream. Application writers may use setSystemId to provide a base for resolving relative URIs, setPublicId to include a public identifier, and/or setEncoding to specify the object's character encoding. **Parameters:** byteStream - The raw byte stream containing the document.
InputSource public InputSource(Reader characterStream)	Create a new input source with a character stream. Application writers may use setSystemId() to provide a base for resolving relative URIs, and setPublicId to include a public identifier. The character stream shall not include a byte order mark.
setPublicId public void setPublicId (String publicId)	Set the public identifier for this input source. The public identifier is always optional: if the application writer includes one, it will be provided as part of the location information. **Parameters:** publicId - The public identifier as a string.
getPublicId public String getPublicId ()	Get the public identifier for this input source. **Returns:** The public identifier, or null if none was supplied.

Table continued on following page

setSystemId public void setSystemId (String systemId)	Set the system identifier for this input source. The system identifier is optional if there is a byte stream or a character stream, but it is still useful to provide one, since the application can use it to resolve relative URIs and can include it in error messages and warnings (the parser will attempt to open a connection to the URI only if there is no byte stream or character stream specified). If the application knows the character encoding of the object pointed to by the system identifier, it can register the encoding using the setEncoding method. If the system ID is a URL, it must be fully resolved. **Parameters:** systemId - The system identifier as a string.
getSystemId public String getSystemId ()	Get the system identifier for this input source. The getEncoding method will return the character encoding of the object pointed to, or null if unknown. If the system ID is a URL, it will be fully resolved. **Returns:** The system identifier.
setByteStream public void setByteStream (InputStream byteStream)	Set the byte stream for this input source. The SAX parser will ignore this if there is also a character stream specified, but it will use a byte stream in preference to opening a URI connection itself. If the application knows the character encoding of the byte stream, it should set it with the setEncoding method. **Parameters:** byteStream - A byte stream containing an XML document or other entity.

getByteStream

public InputStream getByteStream()

Get the byte stream for this input source.

The getEncoding method will return the character encoding for this byte stream, or null if unknown.

Returns:

The byte stream, or null if none was supplied.

setEncoding

public void setEncoding(

        String encoding)

Set the character encoding, if known.

The encoding must be a string acceptable for an XML encoding declaration (see section 4.3.3 of the XML 1.0 recommendation).

This method has no effect when the application provides a character stream.

Parameters:

encoding - A string describing the character encoding.

getEncoding

public String getEncoding()

Get the character encoding for a byte stream or URI.

Returns:

The encoding, or null if none was supplied.

setCharacterStream

public void setCharacterStream(

        Reader characterStream)

Set the character stream for this input source.

If there is a character stream specified, the SAX parser will ignore any byte stream and will not attempt to open a URI connection to the system identifier.

Parameters:

characterStream - The character stream containing the XML document or other entity.

getCharacterStream

public Reader getCharacterStream()

Get the character stream for this input source.

Returns:

The character stream, or null if none was supplied.

Interface org.xml.sax.Locator

This interface provides methods that the application can use to determine the current position in the source XML document.

Interface for associating a SAX event with a document location

If a SAX parser provides location information to the SAX application, it does so by implementing this interface and then passing an instance to the application using the document handler's `setDocumentLocator` method. The application can use the object to obtain the location of any other document handler event in the XML source document.

Note that the results returned by the object will be valid only during the scope of each document handler method: the application will receive unpredictable results if it attempts to use the locator at any other time.

SAX parsers are not required to supply a locator, but they are very strongly encouraged to do so. If the parser supplies a locator, it must do so before reporting any other document events. If no locator has been set by the time the application receives the `startDocument` event, the application should assume that a locator is not available.

getPublicId public String getPublicId()	Return the public identifier for the current document event. **Returns:** A string containing the public identifier, or null if none is available.
getSystemId public String getSystemId()	Return the system identifier for the current document event. If the system identifier is a URL, the parser must resolve it fully before passing it to the application. **Returns:** A string containing the system identifier, or null if none is available.
getLineNumber public int getLineNumber()	Return the line number where the current document event ends. Note that this is the line position of the first character after the text associated with the document event. In practice some parsers report the line number and column number where the event starts. **Returns:** The line number, or -1 if none is available.
getColumnNumber public int getColumnNumber()	Return the column number where the current document event ends. Note that this is the column number of the first character after the text associated with the document event. The first column in a line is position 1. **Returns:** The column number, or -1 if none is available.

Interface org.xml.sax.Parser – Deprecated

Every SAX 1.0 parser must implement this interface. An application parses an XML document by creating an instance of a parser (that is, a class that implements this interface) and calling one of its parse() *methods.*

Basic interface for SAX (Simple API for XML) parsers

All SAX parsers must implement this basic interface: it allows applications to register handlers for different types of events and to initiate a parse from a URI, or a character stream.

All SAX parsers must also implement a zero-argument constructor (though other constructors are also allowed).

SAX parsers are reusable but not re-entrant: the application may reuse a parser object (possibly with a different input source) once the first parse has completed successfully, but it may not invoke the parse() methods recursively within a parse.

parse	Parse an XML document.
public void parse(InputSource source) throws SAXException, IOException	The application can use this method to instruct the SAX parser to begin parsing an XML document from any valid input source (a character stream, a byte stream, or a URI). Applications may not invoke this method while a parse is in progress (they should create a new Parser instead for each additional XML document). Once a parse is complete, an application may reuse the same Parser object, possibly with a different input source. **Parameters:** source - The input source for the top-level of the XML document. **Throws:** SAXException Any SAX exception, possibly wrapping another exception. **Throws:** IOException An IO exception from the parser, possibly from a byte stream or character stream supplied by the application.

Table continued on following page

parse	Parse an XML document from a system identifier (URI).
public void parse(	
String systemId)	This method is a shortcut for the common case of reading a document from a system identifier. It is the exact equivalent of the following:
throws SAXException, IOException	`parse(new InputSource(systemId));`
	If the system identifier is a URL, it must be fully resolved by the application before it is passed to the parser.
	Parameters:
	systemId - The system identifier (URI).
	Throws: SAXException
	Any SAX exception, possibly wrapping another exception.
	Throws: IOException
	An IO exception from the parser, possibly from a byte stream or character stream supplied by the application.
setDocumentHandler	Allow an application to register a document event handler.
public void setDocumentHandler(	
DocumentHandler handler)	If the application does not register a document handler, all document events reported by the SAX parser will be silently ignored (this is the default behavior implemented by `HandlerBase`).
	Applications may register a new or different handler in the middle of a parse, and the SAX parser must begin using the new handler immediately.
	Parameters:
	handler - The document handler.

setDTDHandler public void setDTDHandler(DTDHandler handler)	Allow an application to register a DTD event handler. If the application does not register a DTD handler, all DTD events reported by the SAX parser will be silently ignored (this is the default behavior implemented by `HandlerBase`). Applications may register a new or different handler in the middle of a parse, and the SAX parser must begin using the new handler immediately. **Parameters:** handler - The DTD handler.
setEntityResolver public void setEntityResolver(EntityResolver resolver)	Allow an application to register a custom entity resolver. If the application does not register an entity resolver, the SAX parser will resolve system identifiers and open connections to entities itself (this is the default behavior implemented in `HandlerBase`). Applications may register a new or different entity resolver in the middle of a parse, and the SAX parser must begin using the new resolver immediately. **Parameters:** resolver - The object for resolving entities.
setErrorHandler public void setErrorHandler(ErrorHandler handler)	Allow an application to register an error event handler. If the application does not register an error event handler, all error events reported by the SAX parser will be silently ignored, except for `fatalError`, which will throw a `SAXException` (this is the default behavior implemented by `HandlerBase`). Applications may register a new or different handler in the middle of a parse, and the SAX parser must begin using the new handler immediately. **Parameters:** handler - The error handler.

Table continued on following page

setLocale	Allow an application to request a locale for errors and warnings.
public void setLocale(	
Locale locale)	SAX parsers are not required to provide localization for errors and warnings; if they cannot support the requested locale, however, they must throw a SAX exception. Applications may not request a locale change in the middle of a parse.
throws SAXException	
	Parameters:
	locale - A Java Locale object.
	Throws: SAXException
	Throws an exception (using the previous or default locale) if the requested locale is not supported.

Class org.xml.sax.SAXException

This class is used to represent an error detected during processing either by the parser or by the application.

Encapsulate a general SAX error or warning

This class can contain basic error or warning information from either the XML parser or the application: a parser writer or application writer can subclass it to provide additional functionality. SAX handlers may throw this exception or any exception subclassed from it.

If the application needs to pass through other types of exceptions, it must wrap those exceptions in a SAXException or an exception derived from a SAXException.

If the parser or application needs to include information about a specific location in an XML document, it should use the SAXParseException subclass.

getMessage	Return a detail message for this exception.
public String getMessage()	
	If there is a embedded exception, and if the SAXException has no detail message of its own, this method will return the detail message from the embedded exception.
	Returns:
	The error or warning message.

getException	Return the embedded exception, if any.
public Exception getException()	
	Returns:
	The embedded exception, or null if there is none.
toString	Convert this exception to a string.
public String toString()	
	Returns:
	A string version of this exception.

Class org.xml.sax.SAXParseException

Extends SAXException.

This exception class represents an error or warning condition detected by the parser or by the application. In addition to the basic capability of SAXException, a SAXParseException allows information to be retained about the location in the source document where the error occurred. For an application-detected error, this information might be obtained from the Locator object.

Encapsulate an XML parse error or warning

This exception will include information for locating the error in the original XML document. Note that although the application will receive a SAXParseException as the argument to the handlers in the ErrorHandler interface, the application is not actually required to throw the exception; instead, it can simply read the information in it and take a different action.

Since this exception is a subclass of SAXException, it inherits the ability to wrap another exception.

SAXParseException	Create a new SAXParseException from a message and a Locator.
public SAXParseException(	
String message,	
Locator locator)	This constructor is especially useful when an application is creating its own exception from within a DocumentHandler callback.
	Parameters:
	message - The error or warning message.
	locator - The locator object for the error or warning.

Table continued on following page

SAXParseException
 	
public SAXParseException(
      String message,
      Locator locator,
      Exception e)
	Wrap an existing exception in a `SAXParseException`.
	
	This constructor is especially useful when an application is creating its own exception from within a `DocumentHandler` callback, and needs to wrap an existing exception that is not a subclass of `SAXException`.
	
	Parameters:
	message - The error or warning message, or null to use the message from the embedded exception.
	locator - The locator object for the error or warning.
	e - Any exception

SAXParseException
 	
public SAXParseException(
      String message,
      String publicId,
      String systemId,
      int lineNumber,
      int columnNumber)
	Create a new `SAXParseException`.
	
	This constructor is most useful for parser writers. If the system identifier is a URL, the parser must resolve it fully before creating the exception.
	
	Parameters:
	message - The error or warning message.
	publicId - The public identifier of the entity that generated the error or warning.
	systemId - The system identifier of the entity that generated the error or warning.
	lineNumber - The line number of the end of the text that caused the error or warning.
	columnNumber - The column number of the end of the text that caused the error or warning.

SAXParseException
 	
public SAXParseException(
      String message,
      String publicId,
      String systemId,
      int lineNumber,
      int columnNumber,
      Exception e)
	Create a new `SAXParseException` with an embedded exception.
	
	This constructor is most useful for parser writers who need to wrap an exception that is not a subclass of `SAXException`.
	
	If the system identifier is a URL, the parser must resolve it fully before creating the exception.
	
	Parameters:
	message - The error or warning message, or null to use the message from the embedded exception.
	publicId - The public identifier of the entity that generated the error or warning.
	systemId - The system identifier of the entity that generated the error or warning.
	lineNumber - The line number of the end of the text that caused the error or warning.
	columnNumber - The column number of the end of the text that caused the error or warning.
	e - Another exception to embed in this one.

getPublicId public String getPublicId()	Get the public identifier of the entity where the exception occurred. **Returns:** A string containing the public identifier, or null if none is available.
getSystemId public String getSystemId()	Get the system identifier of the entity where the exception occurred. *Note that the term "entity" includes the top-level XML document.* If the system identifier is a URL, it will be resolved fully. **Returns:** A string containing the system identifier, or null if none is available.
getLineNumber public int getLineNumber()	The line number of the end of the text where the exception occurred. **Returns:** An integer representing the line number, or -1 if none is available.
getColumnNumber public int getColumnNumber()	The column number of the end of the text where the exception occurred. The first column in a line is position 1. **Returns:** An integer representing the column number, or -1 if none is available.

Class org.xml.sax.SAXNotRecognizedException (SAX 2)

Exception class for an unrecognized identifier - an XMLReader will throw this exception when it finds an unrecognized feature or property identifier; SAX applications and extensions may use this class for other, similar purposes.

SAXNotRecognizedException public SAXNotRecognizedException(String message)	Construct a new exception with the given message. **Parameters** message - The text message of the exception.

This class has also inherited a lot of methods from other classes. These are summarized below:

Methods inherited from class `org.xml.sax.SAXException`:

- [ ] `getException`
- [ ] `getMessage`
- [ ] `toString`

Methods inherited from class `java.lang.Throwable`:

- [ ] `fillInStackTrace`
- [ ] `getLocalizedMessage`
- [ ] `printStackTrace`
- [ ] `printStackTrace`
- [ ] `printStackTrace`

Methods inherited from class `java.lang.Object`:

- [ ] `equals`
- [ ] `getClass`
- [ ] `hashCode`
- [ ] `notify`
- [ ] `notifyAll`
- [ ] `wait`
- [ ] `wait`
- [ ] `wait`

Class org.xml.sax.SAXNotSupportedException (SAX 2)

Exception class for an unsupported operation - an `XMLReader` will throw this exception when it recognizes a feature or property identifier, but cannot perform the requested operation (setting a state or value). Other SAX2 applications and extensions may use this class for similar purposes.

SAXNotSupportedException	Construct a new exception with the given message.
public SAXNotSupportedException(String message)	**Parameters** `message` - The text message of the exception.

This class has also inherited a lot of methods from other classes. These are summarized below:

Methods inherited from class `org.xml.sax.SAXException`:

- [ ] `getException`
- [ ] `getMessage`
- [ ] `toString`

Methods inherited from class `java.lang.Throwable`:

- ❑ fillInStackTrace
- ❑ getLocalizedMessage
- ❑ printStackTrace
- ❑ printStackTrace
- ❑ printStackTrace

Methods inherited from class `java.lang.Object`:

- ❑ equals
- ❑ getClass
- ❑ hashCode
- ❑ notify
- ❑ notifyAll
- ❑ wait
- ❑ wait
- ❑ wait

Interface org.xml.sax.XMLFilter (SAX 2)

This interface is like the reader, except it is used to read documents from a source other than a document or database. it can also modify events on the way to an application (extends XMLReader).

Interface for an XML filter - an XML filter is like an XML reader, except that it obtains its events from another XML reader rather than a primary source like an XML document or database. Filters can modify a stream of events as they pass on to the final application.

The XMLFilterImpl helper class provides a convenient base for creating SAX2 filters, by passing on all `EntityResolver`, `DTDHandler`, `ContentHandler` and `ErrorHandler` events automatically.

setParent	Set the parent reader.
public void setParent(XMLReader parent)	This method allows the application to link the filter to a parent reader (which may be another filter). The argument may not be null. **Parameters** parent - The parent reader.
getParent	Get the parent reader.
public XMLReader **getParent**	This method allows the application to query the parent reader (which may be another filter). It is generally a bad idea to perform any operations on the parent reader directly: they should all pass through this filter. **Returns:** The parent filter, or null if none has been set.

Interface org.xml.sax.XMLReader (SAX 2 – Replaces Parser)

Every SAX 2.0 parser must implement this interface for reading documents using callbacks. An application parses an XML document by creating an instance of a parser (that is, a class that implements this interface) and calling one of its parse() methods.

Interface for reading an XML document using callbacks. XMLReader is the interface that an XML parser's SAX2 driver must implement. This interface allows an application to set and query features and properties in the parser, to register event handlers for document processing, and to initiate a document parse.

All SAX interfaces are assumed to be synchronous: the parse methods must not return until parsing is complete, and readers must wait for an event-handler callback to return before reporting the next event. This interface replaces the (now deprecated) SAX 1.0 parser interface. The XMLReader interface contains two important enhancements over the old Parser interface:

❑ it adds a standard way to query and set features and properties; and

❑ it adds Namespace support, which is required for many higher-level XML standards.

There are adapters available to convert a SAX1 Parser to a SAX2 XMLReader and vice-versa.

getFeature	Look up the value of a feature
public boolean **getFeature**(String name)	The feature name is any fully-qualified URI. It is possible for an XMLReader to recognize a feature name but to be unable to return its value; this is especially true in the case of an adapter for a SAX1 Parser, which has no way of knowing whether the underlying parser is performing validation or expanding external entities.
	Parameters name - The feature name, which is a fully-qualified URI **Returns:** The current state of the feature (true or false) **Throws:** SAXNotRecognizedException SAXNotSupportedException For more on getFeature, usage, see the explanation below this table
setFeature	Set the state of a feature.
public void **setFeature**(String name, boolean value)	The feature name is any fully-qualified URI. It is possible for an XMLReader to recognize a feature name but to be unable to set its value; this is especially true in the case of an adapter for a SAX1 parser, which has no way of affecting whether the underlying parser is validating, for example. **Parameters** name - The feature name, which is a fully-qualified URI state - The requested state of the feature (true or false) **Throws:** SAXNotRecognizedException SAXNotSupportedException

getProperty
 	
public Object
getProperty(
    String name)
	Look up the value of a property.
	
	The property name is any fully-qualified URI. It is possible for an XMLReader to recognize a property name but to be unable to return its state; this is especially true in the case of an adapter for a SAX1 `parser`.
	
	Parameters
	name - The feature name, which is a fully-qualified URI
	Returns:
	The current value of the property
	Throws:
	`SAXNotRecognizedException`
	`SAXNotSupportedException`

setProperty
 	
public void
setProperty(
    String name,
    Object value)
	Set the value of a property.
	
	The property name is any fully-qualified URI. It is possible for an XMLReader to recognize a property name but to be unable to set its value; this is especially true in the case of an adapter for a SAX1 `parser`.
	
	Parameters
	name - The feature name, which is a fully-qualified URI
	`state` - The requested value for the property
	
	Throws:
	`SAXNotRecognizedException`
	`SAXNotSupportedException`

setEntityResolver
 	
public void
setEntityResolver(
    EntityResolver
    resolver)
	Allow an application to register an entity resolver.
	
	If the application does not register an entity resolver, the XMLReader will perform its own default resolution.
	
	Applications may register a new or different resolver in the middle of a parse, and the SAX parser must begin using the new resolver immediately.
	
	Parameters
	`resolver` - The entity resolver.
	
	Throws:
	`java.lang.NullPointerException` - If the resolver argument is null.

getEntityResolver public **getEntityResolver**()	Return the current entity resolver. **Returns:** The current entity resolver, or null if none has been registered.

Table continued on following page

setDTDHandler	Allow an application to register a DTD event handler.

public void
setDTDHandler(
    DTDHandler
    handler)
	If the application does not register a DTD handler, all DTD events reported by the SAX parser will be silently ignored.
	Applications may register a new or different handler in the middle of a parse, and the SAX parser must begin using the new handler immediately.
	Parameters
	`handler` - The DTD handler.
	
	Throws:
	`java.lang.NullPointerException` - If the handler argument is null.

getDTDHandler	Return the current DTD handler.
public **getDTDHandler**	**Returns:** The current DTD handler, or null if none has been registered.
setContentHandler	Allow an application to register a content event handler.

public void
setContentHandler
    (ContentHandler
    handler)
	If the application does not register a content handler, all content events reported by the SAX parser will be silently ignored.
	Applications may register a new or different handler in the middle of a parse, and the SAX parser must begin using the new handler immediately.
	
	Parameters
	`handler` - The content handler.
	
	Throws:
	java.lang.NullPointerException - If the handler argument is null.

getContentHandler	Return the current content handler.
public **getContentHandler**	**Returns:** The current content handler, or null if none has been registered.
setErrorHandler	Allow an application to register an error event handler.

public void
setErrorHandler(
    ErrorHandler
    handler)
	If the application does not register an error handler, all error events reported by the SAX parser will be silently ignored; however, normal processing may not continue. It is highly recommended that all SAX applications implement an error handler to avoid unexpected bugs.
	
	Applications may register a new or different handler in the middle of a parse, and the SAX parser must begin using the new handler immediately.
	
	Parameters
	`handler` - The error handler.
	
	Throws:
	`java.lang.NullPointerException` - If the handler argument is null.

getErrorHandler	Return the current error handler.
public ErrorHandler **getErrorHandler**	**Returns:** The current error handler, or null if none has been registered.
parse	Parse an XML document.
public void parse(InputSource input)	The application can use this method to instruct the XML reader to begin parsing an XML document from any valid input source (a character stream, a byte stream, or a URI). Applications may not invoke this method while a parse is in progress (they should create a new XMLReader instead for each nested XML document). Once a parse is complete, an application may reuse the same XMLReader object, possibly with a different input source. During the parse, the XMLReader will provide information about the XML document through the registered event handlers. This method is synchronous: it will not return until parsing has ended. If a client application wants to terminate parsing early, it should throw an exception. **Parameters** `source` - The input source for the top-level of the XML document. **Throws:** `SAXExeception` - Any SAX exception, possibly wrapping another exception. `java.io.IOException` - An IO exception from the parser, possibly from a byte stream or character stream supplied by the application.
parse	Parse an XML document from a system identifier (URI).
public void **parse**(String systemId)	If the system identifier is a URL, it must be fully resolved by the application before it is passed to the parser. **Parameters** `systemId` - The system identifier (URI). **Throws:** `SAXExeception`- Any SAX exception, possibly wrapping another exception. `java.io.IOException` - An IO exception from the parser, possibly from a byte stream or character stream supplied by the application.

All XMLReaders are required to recognize the `http://xml.org/sax/features/namespaces` and the `http://xml.org/sax/features/namespace-prefixes` feature names.

Some feature values may be available only in specific contexts, such as before, during, or after a parse.

Implementors are free (and encouraged) to invent their own features, using names built on their own URIs.

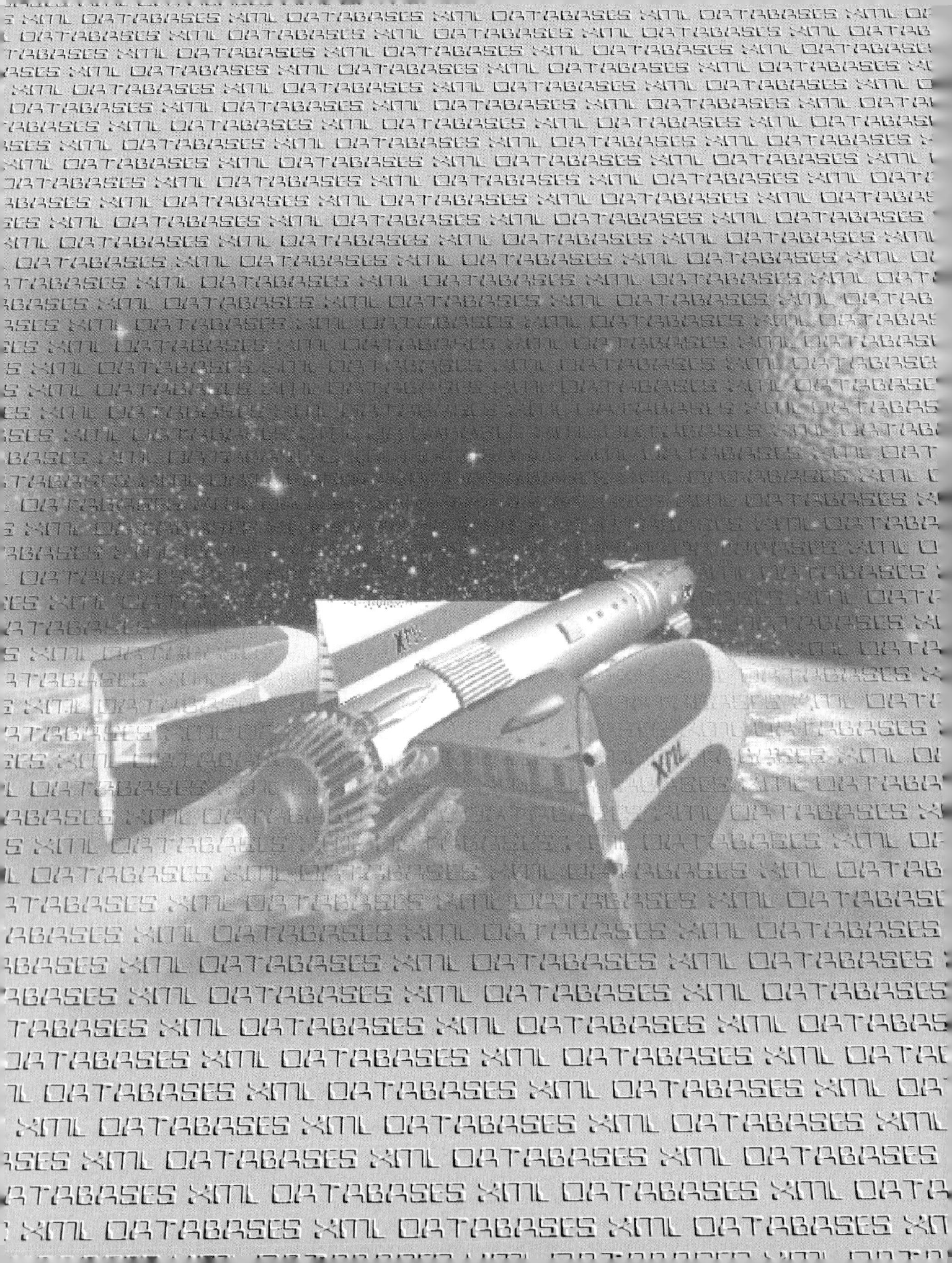
XML DATABASES XML DATABASES XML DATABASES
XML

Setting Up a Virtual Directory for SQL Server 2000

Introduction

This appendix goes through the basics of how to set up a SQL Server 2000 virtual directory, required to run examples in some of the chapters of this book. A virtual directory is a server with which to run your SQL XML examples (XPath queries, template queries, etc), just like a web server is needed to run ASP code.

Setting up Your Virtual Directory

Follow these steps to set up your SQL virtual directory:

1. Under the SQL Server 2000 start menu entry, there should be a menu option "Configure SQL XML support in IIS". Open up this option to be presented with the following management console:

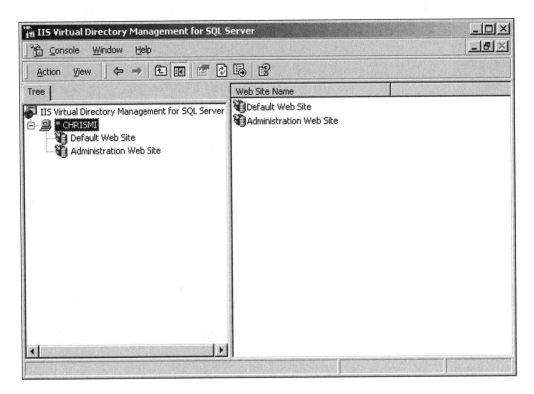

2. Now you need to right click on the Default Web Site icon, and select "New", then "Virtual Directory" from the resulting menu and sub-menu. This will bring up the New Virtual Directory Properties screen. Next, we will go through each tab of the screen (6 in total) telling you what needs to be done in each case:

The General Tab

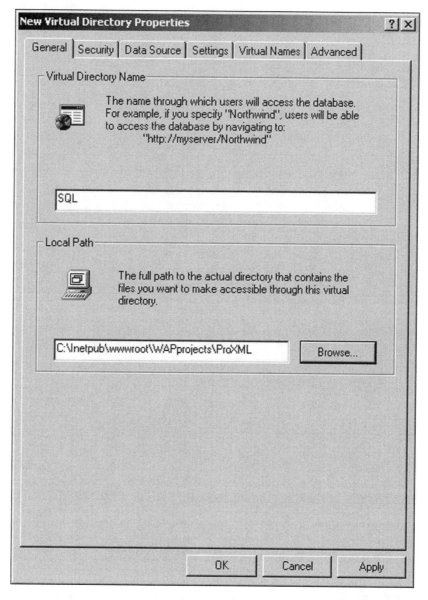

Here you need to specify a name for your virtual directory (I have chosen "SQL" as mine), then you need to specify the path that points to where the directory actually is on your hard disk. This directory is the physical location where you will need to store the code (for example, templates and schemas) that will act upon your database(s).

The Security Tab

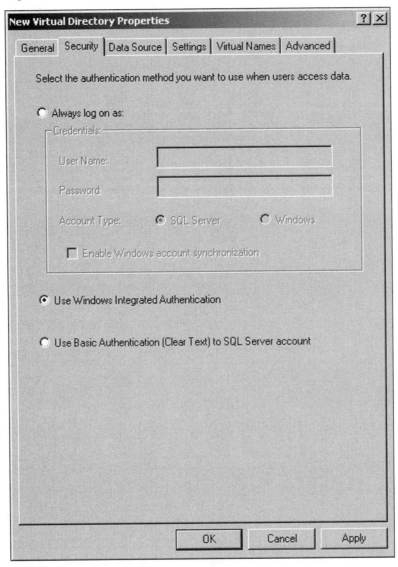

This is where you select security options for your virtual directory - note I have selected Windows Integrated Authentication - the simplest method that merely uses your Windows log on for security, and the one that I would recommend for running the examples in this book. The other options are as follows:

Always log on as allows you to set a separate password for this directory, either of account type SQL or Windows.
Use Basic Authentication enables a basic text clearing password system.

The Data Source tab

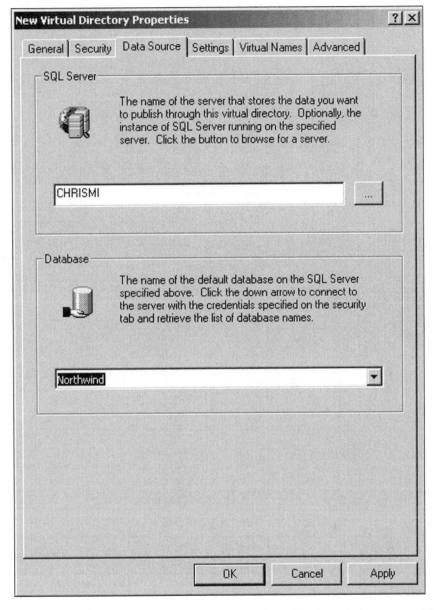

Here you need to specify firstly the SQL server that stores the information that you are publishing through your virtual directory, then the database that your schemas will be pulling data out of to display. I have chosen the Northwind database, as a lot of the examples in this book act upon it.

The Settings Tab:

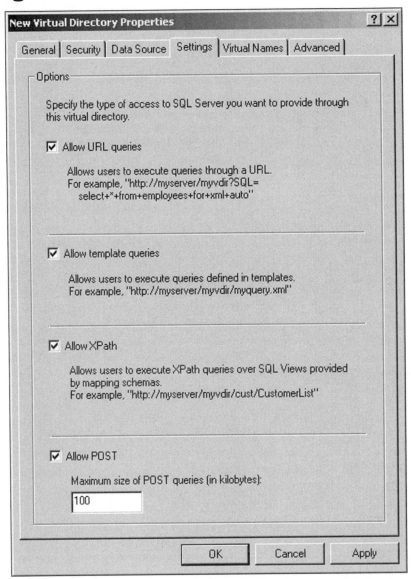

As you can see, this allows you to set what type of access to the chosen database you want to provide through your virtual directory - another security measure, as well as another way to "idiot proof" your system. I have chosen to allow all types of access, as I am using it for testing examples.

The Virtual Names Tab:

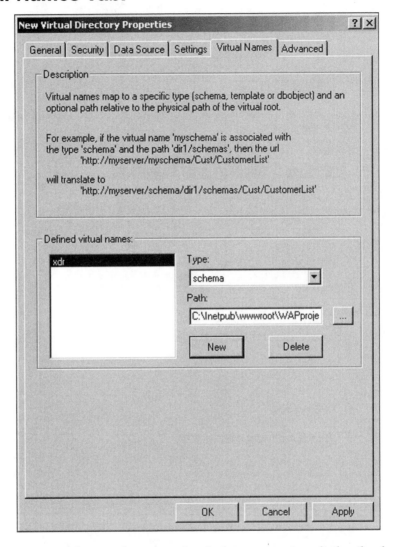

This is where you must set the virtual names and paths for your queries, whether they be schemas, dbobjects or templates. The virtual name is the name you must include in the URLs that you use to run these queries against your database, and the path is the location on your hard drive where these queries will be stored. For example, take the following URL:

```
http://localhost/sql/xdr/ch19_ex01.xdr/Customers
```

If we assume my setup is being used, this URL would run the schema ch19_ex01.xdr against the Northwind database Customers table (see chapter 15 for more on XDR schemas).

I have set my xdr schema virtual name as merely xdr, and the path for this virtual name type to the same path as that of my virtual directory, as this is where I will store examples of this type.

981

The Advanced Tab

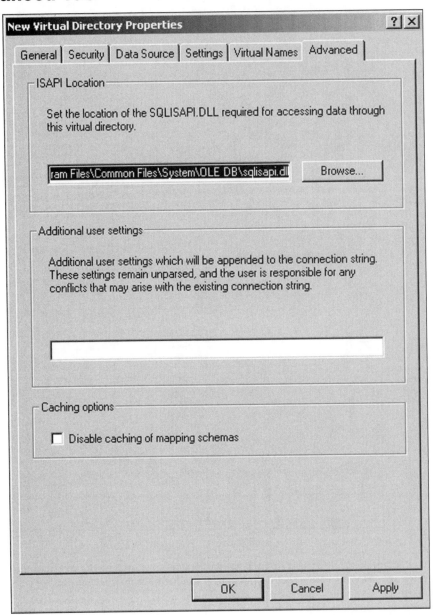

It is unlikely that you will need to change anything here at this stage. It includes setting the path to the main DLL that data access through this virtual directory needs, and additional user settings.

When you have done all this, you should now be ready to run any of the examples in the chapters that require this virtual directory.

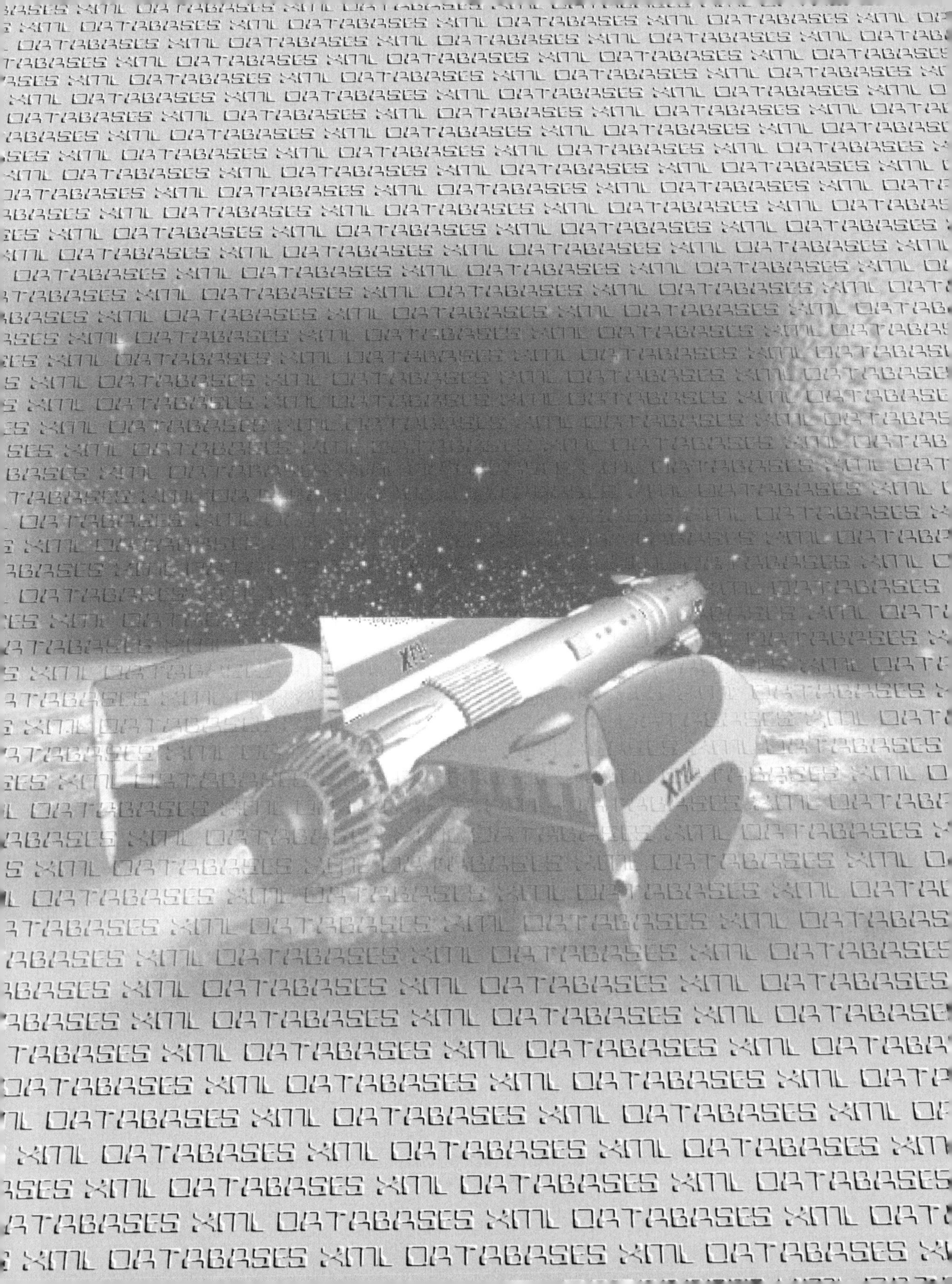
XML DATABASES

Support, Errata and P2P.Wrox.Com

One of the most irritating things about any programming book is when you find that bit of code you've just spent an hour typing simply doesn't work. You check it a hundred times to see if you've set it up correctly and then you notice the spelling mistake in the variable name on the book page. Of course, you can blame the authors for not taking enough care and testing the code, the editors for not doing their job properly, or the proofreaders for not being eagle-eyed enough, but this doesn't get around the fact that mistakes do happen.

We try hard to ensure no mistakes sneak out into the real world, but we can't promise that this book is 100% error free. What we can do is offer the next best thing by providing you with immediate support and feedback from experts who have worked on the book and try to ensure that future editions eliminate these gremlins. We also now commit to supporting you not just while you read the book, but once you start developing applications as well through our online forums where you can put your questions to the authors, reviewers, and fellow industry professionals.

In this appendix we'll look at how to:

- ❏ Enroll in the peer to peer forums at p2p.wrox.com
- ❏ Post and check for errata on our main site, www.wrox.com
- ❏ E-mail technical support a query or feedback on our books in general

Between all three support procedures, you should get an answer to your problem in no time flat.

The Online Forums at P2P.Wrox.Com

Join the JavaScript mailing list for author and peer support. Our system provides **programmer to programmer™ support** on mailing lists, forums and newsgroups all in addition to our one-to-one email system, which we'll look at in a minute. Be confident that your query is not just being examined by a support professional, but by the many Wrox authors and other industry experts present on our mailing lists.

How To Enroll For Support

Just follow this six-step system:

1. Go to p2p.wrox.com in your favorite browser.
Here you'll find any current announcements concerning P2P – new lists created, any removed and so on.

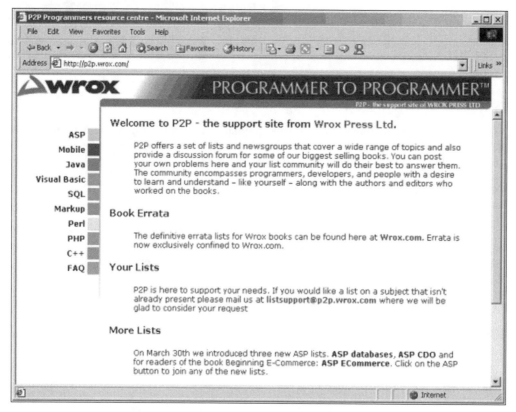

2. Click on the Markup button in the left hand column.

3. Choose to access the xml_databases list.

4. If you are not a member of the list, you can choose to either view the list without joining it or create an account in the list, by hitting the relevant buttons.

5. If you wish to join, you'll be presented with a form in which you'll need to fill in your email address, name and a password (of at least 4 digits). Choose how you would like to receive the messages from the list and then hit **Save**.

6. Congratulations. You're now a member of the XML databases mailing list.

Why this system offers the best support

You can choose to join the mailing lists or you can receive them as a weekly digest. If you don't have the time or facility to receive the mailing list, then you can search our online archives. You'll find the ability to search on specific subject areas or keywords. As these lists are moderated, you can be confident of finding good, accurate information quickly. Mails can be edited or moved by the moderator into the correct place, making this a most efficient resource. Junk and spam mail are deleted, and your own email address is protected by the unique Lyris system from web-bots that can automatically hoover up newsgroup mailing list addresses. Any queries about joining, leaving lists or any query about the list should be sent to: `listsupport@p2p.wrox.com`.

Checking The Errata Online at www.wrox.com

The following section will take you step by step through the process of posting and viewing errata on our web site to get help. The sections that follow, therefore, are:

- ❏ Finding a list of existing errata on the web site
- ❏ Adding your own errata to the existing list
- ❏ What happens to your errata once you've posted it (why doesn't it appear immediately)?

There is also a section covering how to e-mail a question for technical support. This comprises:

- ❏ What your e-mail should include
- ❏ What happens to your e-mail once it has been received by us

Finding an Errata on the Web Site

Before you send in a query, you might be able to save time by finding the answer to your problem on our web site – `http:\\www.wrox.com`.

Each book we publish has its own page and its own errata sheet. You can get to any book's page by clicking on it's category from the selection at the top of the page, in this case, click on **XML**.

This will bring up a list of all the books in that category. You then need to click on the tile of the book to bring up its details, as shown below:

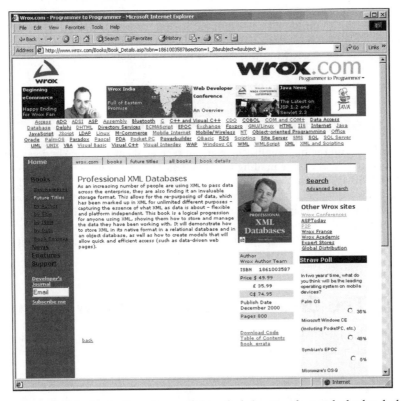

If there are any errata for the book, then there will be a link for it underneath the book details. Click on this link to brink up a list of the errata, as shown below:

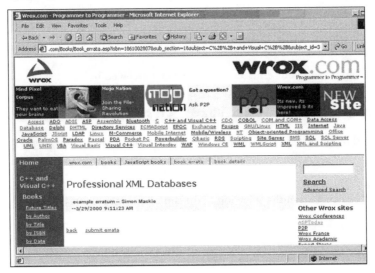

Clicking on the erratum itself will bring up the details.

Add an Erratum: E-mail Support

If you wish to point out an errata to put up on the website or directly query a problem in the book with an expert who knows the book in detail, then e-mail support@wrox.com with the title of the book and the last four numbers of the ISBN in the subject field of the e-mail. A typical email should include the following things:

- ❑ The **name**, **last four digits of the ISBN** and **page number** of the problem in the Subject field.
- ❑ Your **name**, **contact info** and the **problem** in the body of the message.

We won't send you junk mail. We need the details to save your time and ours. When you send an e-mail it will go through the following chain of support:

Customer Support

Your message is delivered to one of our customer support staff, who are the first people to read it. They have files on most frequently asked questions and will answer anything general immediately. They answer general questions about the book and the web site.

Editorial

Deeper queries are forwarded to the technical editor responsible for that book. They have experience with the programming language or particular product and are able to answer detailed technical questions on the subject. Once an issue has been resolved, the editor can post the errata to the web site.

The Authors

Finally, in the unlikely event that the editor can't answer your problem, s/he will forward the request to the author. We try to protect the author from any distractions from writing. However, we are quite happy to forward specific requests to them. All Wrox authors help with the support on their books. They'll mail the customer and the editor with their response, and again all readers should benefit.

What We Can't Answer

Obviously with an ever-growing range of books and an ever-changing technology base, there is an increasing volume of data requiring support. While we endeavor to answer all questions about the book, we can't answer bugs in your own programs that you've adapted from our code. So, while you might have loved the chapters on file handling, don't expect too much sympathy if you cripple your company with a routine which deletes the contents of your hard drive. But do tell us if you're especially pleased with the routine you developed with our help.

How to Tell Us Exactly What You Think

We understand that errors can destroy the enjoyment of a book and can cause many wasted and frustrated hours, so we seek to minimize the distress that they can cause.

You might just wish to tell us how much you liked or loathed the book in question. Or you might have ideas about how this whole process could be improved. In which case, you should e-mail feedback@wrox.com. You'll always find a sympathetic ear, no matter what the problem is. Above all you should remember that we do care about what you have to say and we will do our utmost to act upon it.

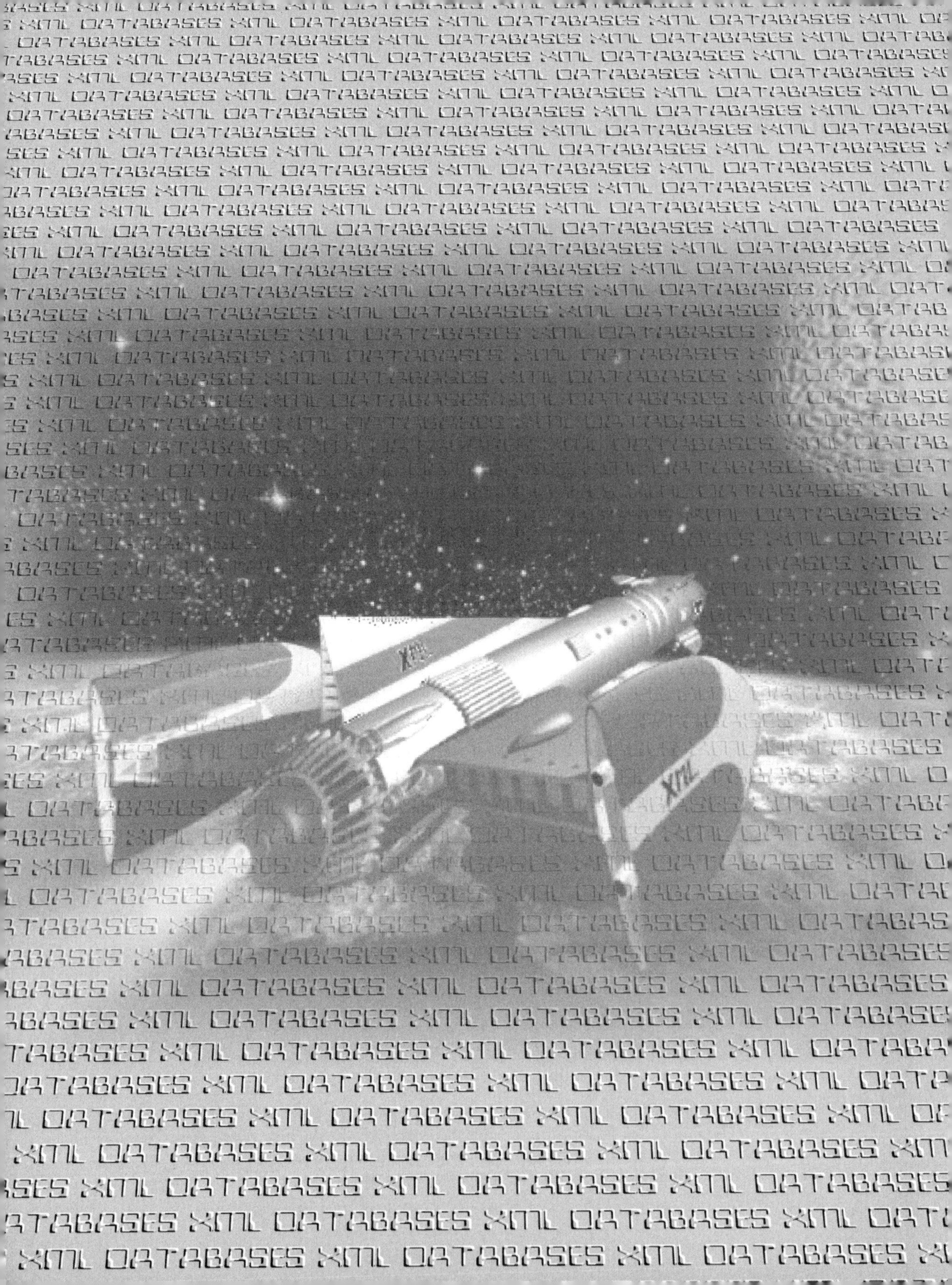
XML DATABASES
XML

Index

A Guide to the Index

The index is arranged hierarchically, in alphabetical order, with symbols preceding the letter A. Most second-level entries and many third-level entries also occur as first-level entries. This is to ensure that users will find the information they require however they choose to search for it.

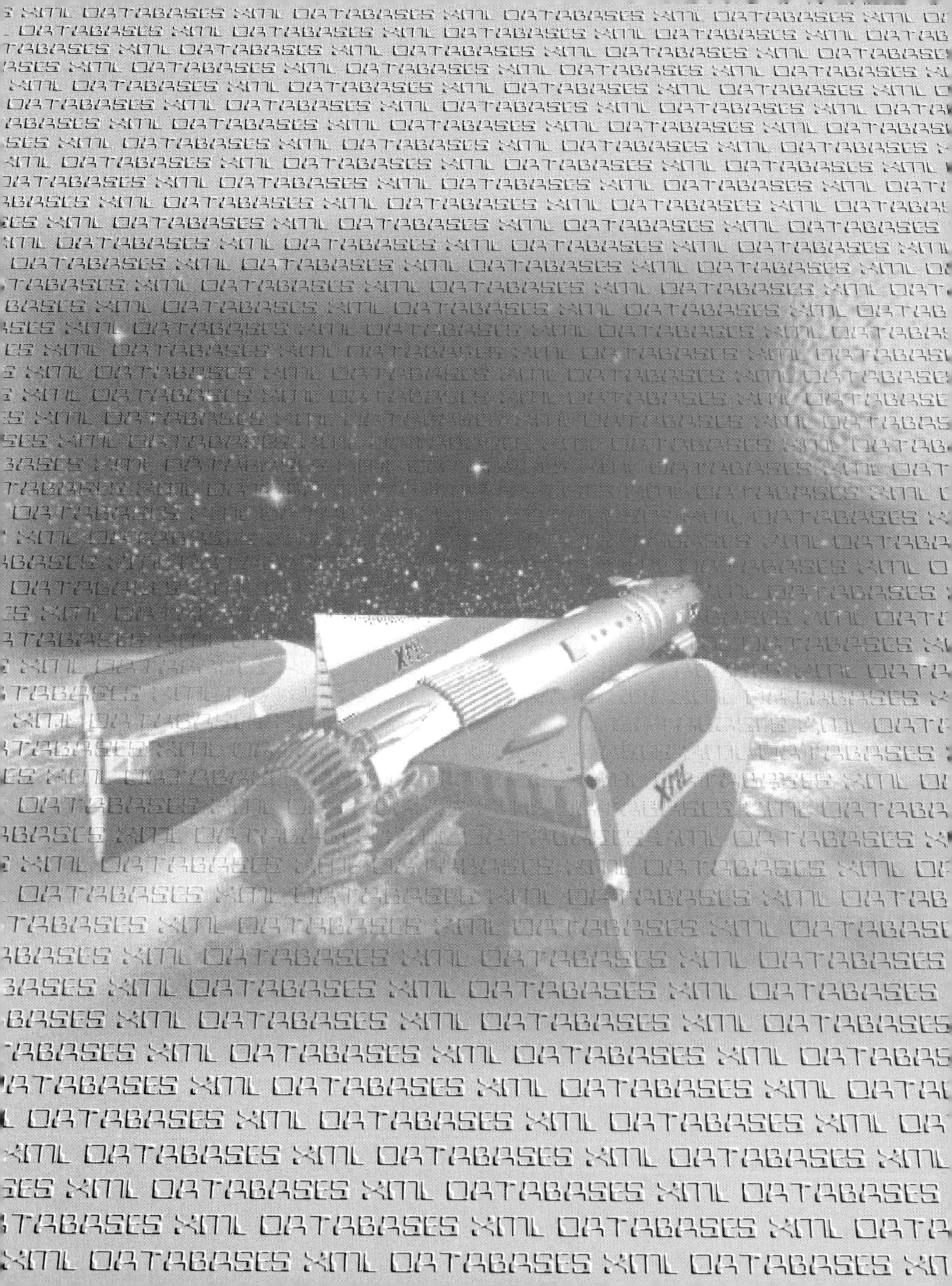
XML DATABASES
XML